THE
Norton Anthology of Poetry

REVISED

THE
Norton Anthology
of Poetry

REVISED

>>>->>>->>>->>>-<<<-<<<-<<<-<<<-<<<-<<<-<<<-<<<-<<<-<<<-<<<-<<<-<<<-<<<-<<<-<<<-<<<-<<<-<<<-<<<-<<<-<<<-<<<-<<<

ALEXANDER W. ALLISON
LATE OF THE UNIVERSITY OF MICHIGAN

HERBERT BARROWS
UNIVERSITY OF MICHIGAN

CAESAR R. BLAKE
UNIVERSITY OF TORONTO

ARTHUR J. CARR
WILLIAMS COLLEGE

ARTHUR M. EASTMAN
VIRGINIA POLYTECHNIC INSTITUTE AND STATE UNIVERSITY

HUBERT M. ENGLISH, JR.
UNIVERSITY OF MICHIGAN

W · W · NORTON & COMPANY
New York · London

William Blake: From *The Prose and Poetry of William Blake*, edited by David V. Erdman and Harold Bloom. Copyright © 1965 by David V. Erdman and Harold Bloom. Reprinted by permission of Doubleday & Co., Inc.

Robert Bly: "Walking from Sleep" reprinted from *Silence in the Snowy Fields*, Wesleyan University Press, 1962, copyright © 1962 by Robert Bly, reprinted with his permission. Other selections from *The Light Around the body*, copyright © 1967 by Robert Bly. By permission of Harper & Row, Publishers, Inc.

Gwendolyn Brooks: From *The World of Gwendolyn Brooks*: "kitchenette building" and "my dreams, my work must wait till after hell" copyright, 1945 by Gwendolyn Brooks Blakely; "The Bean Eaters" and "We Real Cool," copyright © 1959 by Gwendolyn Brooks; "Medgar Evers," copyright © 1964 by Gwendolyn Brooks Blakely; "Boy Breaking Glass," copyright © 1967 by Gwendolyn Brooks Blakely. By permission of Harper & Row, Publishers, Inc.

Basil Bunting: Reprinted by permission of the author and the Fulcrum Press.

Geoffrey Chaucer: From *Chaucer's Poetry: An Anthology for the Modern Reader*, selected and edited by E. T. Donaldson. Copyright © 1958 by The Ronald Press Company, New York. Selections reprinted by permission of the publisher. E. Talbot Donaldson's notes to *The Pardoner's Prologue and Tale* and *The Nun's Priest's Tale* reprinted from *The Norton Anthology of English Literature*, Vol. 1, Third Edition, by M. H. Abrams, General Editor. Copyright © 1968, 1962 by W. W. Norton & Company, Inc. Reprinted by permission of the publishers.

John Clare: Lord, Hear My Prayer" from *Poems of John Clare's Madness*, edited by Geoffrey Grigson, published by Routledge and Kegan Paul Ltd., 1949; "Gypsies," "Farewell," and "Badger" reprinted by permission of The Bodley Head Limited; "Love Lives Beyond the Tomb," "First Love," and "I Am" reprinted from *The Poems of John Clare*, edited by Tibble and Tibble, with the permission of J. M. Dent & Sons Ltd.

Gregory Corso: From *The Happy Birthday of Death*. Copyright © 1960 by New Directions Publishing Corporation. Reprinted by permission of New Directions Publishing Corporation.

Hart Crane: From *The Collected Poems and Selected Letters and Prose of Hart Crane*. Permission of Liveright, Publishing, New York. Copyright © 1933, 1958, 1966 by Liveright Publishing Corp.

Stephen Crane: From *The Poems of Stephen Crane*, published by Alfred A. Knopf, Inc.

Robert Creeley: "Ballad of the Despairing Husband" (copyright © 1959 Robert Creeley), "Heroes" (copyright © 1959 Robert Creeley), and "Song: What I took in My Hand" (copyright © 1962 Robert Creeley) from *For Love* by Robert Creeley are reprinted by permission of Charles Seribner's Sons. "The World" (copyright © 1965 Robert Creeley) is reprinted by permission of Charles Scribner's Sons from *Words* by Robert Creeley.

Countee Cullen: From *On These I Stand*. Copyright, 1925 by Harper & Row, Publishers, Inc.; renewed, 1953 by Ida M. Cullen. By permission of the publisher.

E. E. Cummings: "All in green went my love riding," "In Just-spring," "O sweet spontaneous," and "the Cambridge ladies who live in furnished souls" copyright 1923, 1951 by E. E. Cummings; "Spring is like a perhaps hand" copyright 1925 by E. E. Cummings; who's most afraid of death? thou" copyright 1925, 1953 by E. E. Cummings; " 'next to of course god america i," "along the brittle treacherous bright streets," and "since feeling is first" copyright 1926 by Horace Liveright; renewed 1954 by E. E. Cummings; "somewhere I have never travelled, gladly beyond" and "i sing of Olaf," copyright 1931, 1959 by E. E. Cummings; "anyone lived in a pretty how town," "my father moved through dooms of love" and "these children singing in stone a" copyright 1940 by E. E. Cummings; renewed 1968 by Marion Morehouse Cummings; "what if a much of a which of a wind" copyright 1944 by E. E. Cummings. Reprinted from his volume, *Complete Poems 1913–1962*, by permission of Harcourt, Brace, Jovanovich, Inc.

Walter de la Mare: From *Collected Poems*, 1942. Selections reprinted by permission of The Literary Trustees of Walter de la Mare and The Society of Authors as their representative.

James Dickey: Copyright © 1961, 1962, 1965 by James Dickey. Reprinted from *Poems 1957–1967* by James Dickey, by permission of Wesleyan University Press. These poems first appeared in *The New Yorker*.

Emily Dickinson: "The Bible is an antique Volume" from *Life and Letters of Emily Dickinson*, edited by Martha Dickinson Bianchi, reprinted by permission of the Houghton Mifflin Company. "The difference between Despair," copyright 1914, 1942 by Martha Dickinson Bianchi, "After great pain, a formal feeling comes" and "She dealt her pretty words like Blades" copyright 1929, © 1957 by Mary L. Hampson, "My Triumph lasted till the Drums" copyright 1935 by Martha Bianchi, © 1963 by Mary L. Hampson, from *The Poems of Emily Dickinson*, edited by Thomas H. Johnson, Reprinted by permission of Little, Brown and Company. All other selections reprinted by permission of the publishers and the Trustees of Amherst College from Thomas H. Johnson, Editor, *The Poems of Emily Dickinson*, Cambridge, Mass.: The Belknap Press of Harvard University Press, copyright, 1951, 1955 by The President and Fellows of Harvard College.

H. D. (Hilda Doolittle): From *Selected Poems*. Copyright 1925, 1953, © 1957 by Norman Holmes Pearson. From *Hermetic Definition*. Copyright © 1972 by Norman Holmes Pearson. Reprinted by printed by permission of New Directions Publishing Corporation, Agents for Norman Holmes Pearson. From *Hermetic Definition*. Copyright © 1972 by Norman Holmes Pearson. Reprinted by permission of New Directions Publishing Corporation and Norman Holmes Pearson.

Charles d'Orléans: From Early English Text Society Original Series 215, *English Poems of Charles of Orleans*, edited by R. Steele, 1941. Selections reprinted by permission of the Early English Text Society, Oxford.

Ernest Dowson: From *The Poetical Works of Ernest Dowson*, edited by Desmond Flower. Published by Fairleigh Dickinson University Press. Selections reprinted by permission of Associated University Presses, Incorporated.

Paul Laurence Dunbar: From *The Complete Poems of Paul Laurence Dunbar*. Selections reprinted by permission of Dodd, Mead & Company.

Early English carols and lyrics: From *Religions Lyrics of the XIVth Century*, edited by Carleton Brown, 2nd edition revised G. V. Smithers, 1952; *Religious Lyrics of the XVth Century*, 1939, edited by Carleton Brown; *Early English Carols*, 1935, edited by Richard

Contents

>>>->>>->>>-<<<-<<<-<<<-<<<-<<<-<<<-<<<-<<<-<<<-<<<-<<<-<<<-<<<-<<<-<<<-<<<-<<<-<<<-<<<-<<<-<<<-<<<-<<<-<<<-<<<-<<<

Preface

❦❦❦❦❦❦❦❦❦❦❦❦❦❦❦❦❦❦❦❦❦❦❦❦❦❦❦❦❦❦❦❦❦

This new edition of *The Norton Anthology of Poetry* is intended to broaden, and at the same time refine, the selection of poems through which it represents the grand sweep of poetry in English. Our efforts have been crucially helped by the practical criticism and informed suggestions provided us by many teachers who have used the *Anthology* in their classes. In a real sense, then, this work has been collaborative.

Special attention has been given to the poetry of this century. There are thirty-four new modern poets, most of them still active. We have doubled the selections from Wallace Stevens and W. H. Auden, with their publisher's permission, and have added such major poems as Yeats's "The Circus Animals' Desertion" and the first part of Pound's *Mauberley* sequence. We have included several Canadian poets— as we should have done in the first edition. Four new black poets amplify the presentation of that tradition. In the earlier pages we have made similar, though less striking, augmentations. There are now twice as many women poets as before, among them such important earlier writers as Anne Bradstreet, Emily Brontë, and Elizabeth Barrett Browning. The selection of Elizabethan lyrics has been enlarged, and we have added several major poems, including Browning's "Childe Roland to the Dark Tower Came" and the second part of Pope's "Essay on Criticism."

As before, this book presents British and American poetry from before Chaucer to the present decade. At both ends of the chronological spectrum it is particularly ample, for the medieval is lyrically richer than is sometimes recognized, and the contemporary, denied the endorsement of tradition, merits a generous if tentative acceptance. All along, the book gives rather more of the poets it contains than is usual, the goal being to allow choice and the chance to return for fuller or more varied readings. Long-familiar selections have been re-examined, though without animus, and have sometimes been displaced by works far less familiar. There are many long poems, since these fit properly into a collection representative not merely of the lyric and epigrammatic, but of the whole range of verse in English; and though it is manifestly impossible to include the unexcerpted totalities of *The Faerie Queene, Paradise Lost, The Dunciad, Don Juan, The Prelude, In Memoriam, Song of Myself,* or *The Dream Songs,* whole and self-contained segments from each of these are here.

The order is chronological, poets appearing according to the dates of their births (American poets conflated with the British), and their poems according to the dates of their publication in volume form. These dates follow the poems on the right; when two appear together, they point to significantly different published versions. Dates toward the left, when given, are those of composition.

Texts derive from authoritative editions but have been normalized in spelling and capitalization according to modern American usage—except in the many instances in which changes would significantly obscure meter or meaning. The works of Spenser and the Scottish poets, contrivedly archaic or dialectic in spelling, have been left untouched, as have the oldest of the medieval poems, which would remain to modern eyes almost as opaque after normalizing and modernizing as before. The metrically idiosyncratic Hopkins also remains unchanged. For the normalized text of Chaucer selections (except for "Lack of Steadfastness" and "Against Women Unconstant"), as well as for the notes to them, the editors particularly wish to thank Professor E. T. Donaldson.

Notes, as Dr. Johnson observed, are necessary, but necessary evils. They have been provided for information, not criticism; they gloss words and allusions but refrain, as much as possible, from interpretive comment. A terminal glossary, with prefatory commentary, identifies the technical terms of prosody.

Among the many teachers whose suggestions have aided us in preparing this revision, we particularly wish to thank Professors Daniel Mark Fogel of Cornell University, James McCord of the University of California at Santa Barbara, Paul Magnuson of the University of Pennsylvania, and W. H. New of the University of British Columbia. For their critical assistance with the first edition, we again thank Professors John E. Booty of The Episcopal Theological School, David Brewster of the University of Washington, Robert Dana of Cornell College, Lawrence Dembo of The University of Wisconsin, Donald Finkel of Bennington College, Charles Fuqua of Williams College, Cecil M. McCulley of the College of William and Mary, Robert Pack of Middlebury College, Richard Poirier of Rutgers University, and William C. Pratt of Miami University. And, most especially, we again wish to recognize the saving sanity with which M. H. Abrams guided us at certain perilous junctures, and the sharp eyes, tolerance, and immense helpfulness on which we came regularly to rely from John Francis and John Benedict, and their co-worker at W. W. Norton, Susan Bourla.

It only remains to record the untimely and lamentable death of our friend and colleague, Alexander W. Allison, whose work on the Neo-classics and on the note on prosody add so much to this book.

Note on the Modernizing of Medieval Texts

Changes that have taken place in pronunciation obscure for the modern reader the regular metrical character of some Middle English verse. The most important of these changes is the loss of an unstressed syllable in many word endings. We still pronounce some endings as separate syllables (*roses, wedded*), but for Chaucer the full syllabic value of an ending was available generally, even though its pronunciation was not always mandatory. Moreover, a great many final —*e*'s, vestiges of fuller endings at an earlier stage of the language, were still often pronounced (ə) in the ordinary speech of the day, so that the poet could treat them as syllables or not, according to the requirements of his meter, as *boughte* (pronounced either *bought* or *boughtë*) and *ofte* (pronounced either *oft* or *oftë*).

In modernizing, the editors have tried wherever possible to preserve or devise spellings that do not cut the reader off from the possibility of recovering the original rhythms. A non-modern spelling, especially at the end of a word, means that in the original text there is warrant for supposing that an "extra" syllable might have been pronounced at this point to justify metrical expectation. At the same time the editors have tried to avoid imposing a non-modern reading in those cases where a clear metrical pattern is not manifest.

THE
Norton Anthology of Poetry

REVISED

ANONYMOUS LYRICS OF THE THIRTEENTH AND FOURTEENTH CENTURIES

Now Go'th Sun Under Wood[1]

Nou goth sonne under wode[2]—
Me reweth, Marie, thi faire rode.
Nou goth sonne under tre—
Me reweth, Marie, thi sone and the.

The Cuckoo Song[3]

Sing, cuccu, nu. Sing, cuccu.
Sing, cuccu. Sing, cuccu, nu.

Sumer is i-cumen in—
Lhude sing, cuccu!
5 Groweth sed and bloweth med
And springth the wude nu.
Sing, cuccu!

Awe bleteth after lomb,
Lhouth after calve cu,
10 Bulluc sterteth, bucke verteth—
Murie sing, cuccu!
Cuccu, cuccu.
Wel singes thu, cuccu.
Ne swik thu naver nu!

Ubi Sunt Qui Ante Nos Fuerunt?

Were beth they biforen us weren,[4]
Houndes ladden and haueekes beren

1. *Translation:* Now goes the sun under the wood— / I pity, Mary, thy fair face. / Now goes the sun under the tree— / I pity, Mary, thy son and thee.
2. *Wood* and *tree* not only had their modern meanings but also meant *the cross.*
3. *Translation:* Sing, cuckoo, now. Sing, cuckoo. / Sing, cuckoo. Sing, cuckoo, now.
Spring is come in— / Sing loud, cuckoo! / The seed grows, the meadow blooms / And the wood now comes into leaf / Sing, cuckoo!
The ewe bleats after the lamb, / The cow lows after the calf, / The bullock leaps, the buck breaks wind— / Sing merrily, cuckoo! / Cuckoo, cuckoo. / Well singest thou, cuckoo. / Cease thou never now!
4. The poem's first line translates the title. *Translation:* Where be they who before us were, / Who led hounds and bore hawks / And owned fields and woods? / The rich ladies in their bowers, / That wore gold in their coiffures, / and had fair faces,
[That] ate and drank and rejoiced; / Their life was all a game; / Men knelt before them; / They bore themselves exceeding high— / And in the twinkling of an eye / Their souls were lost.
Where is that laughing and that song, / That trailing [of garments] and that proud gait, / Those hawks and those hounds? / All that joy is gone away; / That well has come to wellaway, / To many hard times.
Their paradise they took here, / And now they lie in hell together— / The fire it burns ever. / Long is their "ay" and long their "oh," / Long their "alas" and long their "woe"— / Thence shall they come never.
Suffer here, man, then if thou wilt, / The little pain thou art asked to bear. / Withdraw thine eyes oft [from the things of this world]. / Though thy pain be severe, / If thou think on thy reward, / It shall seem soft to thee.
If that fiend, that foul thing, / Through wicked counsel, through false tempting, / Has cast thee down, / Up and be a good champion! / Stand, and fall no more / For a little blast [for a mere puff of wind].
Take thou the cross for thy staff / And think on him that thereon gave / His life that was so dear. / He gave it for thee; repay him for it / Against his foe. Take thou that staff / And avenge him on that thief.
Of right belief [true faith] take thou the shield / While thou art in the field. / Seek to strengthen thy hand / And keep thy foe at staff's end / And make that traitor say the word [of surrender]. Gain that merry land
Wherein is day without night, / Without end strength and might, / And vengeance on every foe, / With God himself eternal life, / And peace and rest without strife, / Weal without woe.
Maiden mother, heaven's queen, / Thou might and can and ought to be / Our shield against the fiend. / Help us to flee from sins / That we may see thy son / In joy without end. / Amen.

And hadden feld and wode?
  The riche levedies in hoere bour,
5   That wereden gold in hoere tressour,
  With hoere brightte rode,

Eten and drounken and maden hem glad;
Hoere lif was al with gamen i-lad;
  Men keneleden hem biforen;
10   They beren hem wel swithe heye—
    And in a twincling of an eye
  Hoere soules weren forloren.

Were is that lawing and that song,
That trayling and that proude yong,
15 Tho hauekes and tho houndes?
    Al that joye is went away;
    That wele is comen to welaway,
  To manie harde stoundes.

Hoere paradis hy nomen here,
20 And nou they lien in helle i-fere—
  The fuir hit brennes hevere.
    Long is ay and long is ho,
    Long is wy and long is wo—
  Thennes ne cometh they nevere.

25 Dreghy here, man, thenne if thou wilt,
A luitel pine, that me the bit.
  Withdrau thine eyses ofte.
    They thi pine be ounrede,
    And thou thenke on thi mede,
30 Hit sal the thinken softe.

If that fend, that foule thing,
Thorou wikke roun, thorou fals egging,
  Nethere the haveth i-cast,
    Oup, and be god chaunpioun!
35   Stond, ne fal namore adoun
  For a luytel blast.

Thou tak the rode to thi staf
And thenk on him that thereonne yaf
  His lif that wes so lef.
40   He hit yaf for the; thou yelde hit him
    Ayein his fo. That staf thou nim
  And wrek him of that thef.

Of rightte bileve thou nim that sheld
The wiles that thou best in that feld.
45 Thin hond to strenkthen fonde
    And kep thy fo with staves ord
    And do that traytre seien that word.
  Biget that murie londe

Thereinne is day withouten night,
50 Withouten ende strenkthe and might,
  And wreche of everich fo,
    Mid god himselwen eche lif

And pes and rest withoute strif,
Wele withouten wo.

5   Mayden moder, hevene quene,
Thou might and const and owest to bene
Oure sheld ayein the fende.
Help ous sunne for to flen
That we moten thi sone i-seen
50 In joye withouten hende.
                        Amen.

Alison[5]

Bytuene Mersh and Averil,
When spray biginneth to springe,
The lutel foul hath hire wyl
On hyre lud to synge.
5   Ich libbe in love-longinge
For semlokest of alle thinge—
He may me blisse bringe;
Icham in hire baundoun
10 An hendy hap ichabbe yhent—
Ichot from hevene it is me sent:
From alle wymmen mi love is lent
And lyht on Alysoun.

On heu hire her is fayr ynoh,
Hire browe broune, hire eye blake—
15 With lossum chere he on me loh—
With middel smal and wel ymake.
Bote he me wolle to hire take,
Forte buen hire owen make,
Longe to lyven ichulle forsake
20 And feye fallen adoun
An hendy hap . . .

Nightes when I wende and wake—
Forthi myn wonges waxeth won—
Levedi, al for thine sake
25 Longinge is ylent me on.
In world nis non so wyter mon
That al hire bounte telle con.
Hire swyre is whittore then the swon,
And feyrest may in toune.
30 An hendy hap . . .

---

5. *Translation:* Between March and April, /
When the twigs begin to leaf, / The little bird
is free / To sing her song. / I live in love-
longing / For the seemliest of all things— /
She may bring me bliss; / I am in her power.
/ A fair chance I have got— / I know from
heaven it is sent me: / From all women my
love is turned / And lights on Alison.

In hue her hair is fair enough, / Her brow
brown, her eye black— / With a lovely face
she laughed upon me— / Her waist small and
well-made. / Unless she will take me to her, /
To be her own mate, / [The hope] to live long
I shall forsake / And, doomed, fall down [to
die]. / A fair chance . . .

Nights when I turn and wake— / For which
my cheeks wax pale— / Lady, all for thy sake
/ Longing has lighted on me. / In the world
there is no man so wise / That he all her
bounty can tell. / Her neck is whiter than the
swan, / And [she is] the fairest maid in town.
/ A fair chance . . .

I am from wooing all worn out [exhausted
from staying awake], / Weary as water on the
beach, / [For fear] lest any seize from me my
mate / [For whom] I have yearned long. / It
is better to suffer awhile sorely / Than to
mourn evermore. / Kindest of ladies [literally,
under gown], / Harken to my song. / A fair
chance . . .

Icham for wowyng al forwake,
　Wery so water in wore,
Lest eny reve me my make
　Ichabbe y-yerned yore.
35　Betere is tholien whyle sore
　Then mournen evermore.
　Geynest under gore,
Herkne to my roun.
　An hendy hap . . .

Steadfast Cross

Stedefast crosse, among all other
　Thou art a tree mickle of price;[6]
In branch and flower swilk° another   *such*
　I ne wot° none in wood no rys,°   *know / nor thicket*
5　Sweete be the nailes and sweete be the tree,
And sweeter be the burden that hanges upon thee.

Bishop Loreless

Bishop loreless,°   *without learning*
King redeless,°   *without counsel*
Young men reckless,°   *heedless*
Old man witless,
5　Woman shameless—
　I swear by heaven's king,
　Those be five lither thing!°   *evil things*

All Night by the Rose

All night by the rose, rose—
　All night by the rose I lay;
Dared I not the rose steal,
　And yet I bore the flower away.

At a Spring-Well

At a spring-well° under a thorn   *spring*
There was bote of bale[7] a little here a-forn;°   *before*
　There beside stands a maid
Full of love i-bound.°   *bound*
5　Whoso will seek true love,
In her it shall be found.

GEOFFREY CHAUCER
(ca. 1343–1400)

From THE CANTERBURY TALES

The General Prologue

Whan that April with his° showres soote°   *its / sweet*
The droughte of March hath perced to the roote,

6. Great of worth.　　　　　　　　　　7. Remedy for evil.

And bathed every veine[1] in swich° licour,°   *such / liquid*
Of which vertu[2] engendred is the flowr;
5   Whan Zephyrus[3] eek° with his sweete breeth   *also*
Inspired hath in every holt° and heeth°   *grove / field*
The tendre croppes,° and the yonge sonne[4]   *shoots*
Hath in the Ram his halve cours yronne,
And smale fowles maken melodye
10   That sleepen al the night with open yë°—   *eye*
So priketh hem° Nature in hir corages[5]—   *them*
Thanne longen folk to goon° on pilgrimages,   *go*
And palmeres[6] for to seeken straunge strondes
To ferne halwes, couthe° in sondry londes;   *known*
15   And specially from every shires ende
Of Engelond to Canterbury they wende,
The holy blisful martyr[7] for to seeke
That hem hath holpen° whan that they were seke.°   *helped / sick*
    Bifel that in that seson on a day,
20   In Southwerk[8] at the Tabard as I lay,
Redy to wenden on my pilgrimage
To Canterbury with ful° devout corage,   *very*
At night was come into that hostelrye
Wel nine and twenty in a compaignye
25   Of sondry folk, by aventure° yfalle   *chance*
In felaweshipe, and pilgrimes were they alle
That toward Canterbury wolden° ride.   *would*
The chambres and the stables weren wide,
And wel we weren esed° at the beste.[9]   *accommodated*
30   And shortly, whan the sonne was to reste,[1]
So hadde I spoken with hem everichoon°   *every one*
That I was of hir felaweshipe anoon,°   *at once*
And made forward[2] erly for to rise,
To take oure way ther as[3] I you devise.°   *describe*
35   But nathelees,° whil I have time and space,[4]   *nevertheless*
Er° that I ferther in this tale pace,°   *before / pass*
Me thinketh it accordant to resoun[5]
To telle you al the condicioun
Of eech of hem, so as it seemed me,
40   And whiche they were, and of what degree,
And eek in what array that they were inne:
And at a knight thanne° wol I first biginne.   *then*
    A Knight ther was, and that a worthy man,
That fro the time that he first bigan
45   To riden out, he loved chivalrye,
Trouthe[6] and honour, freedom and curteisye.
Ful worthy was he in his lordes werre,°   *war*
And therto hadde he riden, no man ferre,°   *further*
As wel in Cristendom as hethenesse,°   *heathen lands*
50   And[7] evere honoured for his worthinesse.

1. I.e., in plants.
2. By the power of which.
3. The west wind.
4. The sun is young because it has run only halfway through its course in Aries, the Ram —the first sign of the zodiac in the solar year.
5. Their hearts.
6. Palmers, wide-ranging pilgrims—especially those who sought out the "straunge strondes" (foreign shores) of the Holy Land. "Ferne halwes": far-off shrines.
7. St. Thomas à Becket, murdered in Canterbury Cathedral in 1170.

8. Southwark, site of the Tabard Inn, was then a suburb of London, south of the Thames River.
9. In the best possible way.
1. Had set.
2. I.e., (we) made an agreement.
3. "Ther as": where.
4. I.e., opportunity.
5. It seems to me according to reason.
6. Integrity. "Freedom" is here generosity of spirit, while "curteisye" is courtesy.
7. I.e., and he was.

At Alisandre[8] he was whan it was wonne;
Ful ofte time he hadde the boord bigonne[9]
Aboven alle nacions in Pruce;
In Lettou had he reised,° and in Ruce,   *campaigned*
55 No Cristen man so ofte of his degree;
In Gernade at the sege eek hadde he be
Of Algezir, and riden in Belmarye;
At Lyeis was he, and at Satalye,
Whan they were wonne; and in the Grete See[1]
60 At many a noble armee° hadde he be.   *assembly of forces*
    At mortal batailes[2] hadde he been fifteene,
And foughten for oure faith at Tramissene
In listes[3] thries,° and ay° slain his fo.   *thrice / always*
    This ilke° worthy Knight hadde been also   *same*
65 Somtime with the lord of Palatye[4]
Again° another hethen in Turkye;   *against*
And everemore he hadde a soverein pris.°   *reputation*
And though that he were worthy,[5] he was wis,
And of his port° as meeke as is a maide.   *demeanor*
70 He nevere yit no vilainye° ne saide   *rudeness*
In al his lif unto no manere wight:[6]
He was a verray,° parfit,° gentil knight.   *true / perfect*
But for to tellen you of his array,
His hors° were goode, but he was nat gay.   *horses*
75 Of fustian° he wered° a gipoun[7]   *thick cloth / wore*
Al bismotered with his haubergeoun,[8]
For he was late come from his viage,°   *expedition*
And wente for to doon his pilgrimage.
    With him ther was his sone, a yong Squier,[9]
80 A lovere and a lusty bacheler,
With lokkes crulle° as they were laid in presse.   *curly*
Of twenty yeer of age he was, I gesse.
Of his stature he was of evene° lengthe,   *moderate*
And wonderly delivere,° and of greet° strengthe.   *agile / great*
85 And he hadde been som time in chivachye[1]
In Flandres, in Artois, and Picardye,
And born him wel as of so litel space,[2]
In hope to stonden in his lady° grace.   *lady's*
    Embrouded° was he as it were a mede,[3]   *embroidered*
90 Al ful of fresshe flowres, white and rede;°   *red*
Singing he was, or floiting,° al the day: *whistling*
He was as fressh as is the month of May.
Short was his gowne, with sleeves longe and wide.
Wel coude he sitte on hors, and faire ride;

8. The Knight has taken part in campaigns fought against all three groups of pagans who threatened Europe during the 14th century: the Moslems in the Near East, from whom Alexandria was seized after a famous siege; the northern barbarians in Prussia, Lithuania, and Russia; and the Moors in North Africa. The place names in the following lines refer to battlegrounds in these continuing wars.
9. Sat in the seat of honor at military feasts.
1. The Mediterranean.
2. Tournaments fought to the death.
3. Lists, tournament grounds.
4. "The lord of Palatye" was a pagan: alliances of convenience were often made during the Crusades between Christians and pagans.
5. I.e., a valiant knight.
6. "No manere wight": any sort of person. In

Middle English, negatives are multiplied for emphasis, as in these two lines: "nevere," "no," "ne," "no."
7. Tunic worn underneath the coat of mail.
8. All rust-stained from his hauberk (coat of mail).
9. The vague term "Squier" (Squire) here seems to be the equivalent of "bacheler," a young knight still in the service of an older one.
1. On cavalry expeditions. The places in the next line are sites of skirmishes in the constant warfare between the English and the French.
2. I.e., considering the little time he had been in service.
3. Mead, meadow.

95　He coude songes make, and wel endite,°　　　　　　　*compose verse*
　　Juste[4] and eek daunce, and wel portraye° and write.　*sketch*
　　So hote° he loved that by nightertale[5]　　　　　　*hotly*
　　He slepte namore than dooth a nightingale.
　　Curteis he was, lowely,° and servisable,　　　　　　*humble*
100　And carf biforn his fader at the table.[6]
　　　　A Yeman[7] hadde he and servants namo°　　　　*no more*
　　At that time, for him liste[8] ride so;
　　And he[9] was clad in cote and hood of greene.
　　A sheef of pecok arwes,° bright and keene,　　　　*arrows*
105　Under his belt he bar° ful thriftily;°　　　　　　*bore / properly*
　　Wel coude he dresse° his takel° yemanly:[1]　　　*tend to / gear*
　　His arwes drouped nought with fetheres lowe.
　　And in his hand he bar a mighty bowe.
　　A not-heed° hadde he with a brown visage.　　　*close-cut head*
110　Of wodecraft wel coude° he al the usage.　　　　*knew*
　　Upon his arm he bar a gay bracer,[2]
　　And by his side a swerd° and a bokeler,[3]　　　*sword*
　　And on that other side a gay daggere,
　　Harneised° wel and sharp as point of spere;　　*mounted*
115　A Cristophre[4] on his brest of silver sheene;°　*bright*
　　An horn he bar, the baudrik[5] was of greene.
　　A forster° was he soothly,° as I gesse.　　　　*forester / truly*
　　　　Ther was also a Nonne, a Prioresse,[6]
　　That of hir smiling was ful simple° and coy.°　*sincere / mild*
120　Hir gretteste ooth was but by sainte Loy!°　　*Eloi*
　　And she was cleped° Madame Eglantine.　　　　*named*
　　Ful wel she soong° the service divine,　　　　*sang*
　　Entuned° in hir nose ful semely;[7]　　　　　*chanted*
　　And Frenssh she spak ful faire and fetisly,°　*elegantly*
125　After the scole° of Stratford at the Bowe[8]—　*school*
　　For Frenssh of Paris was to hire unknowe.
　　At mete° wel ytaught was she withalle:°　　　*meals / besides*
　　She leet° no morsel from hir lippes falle,　　*let*
　　Ne wette hir fingres in hir sauce deepe;
130　Wel coude she carye a morsel, and wel keepe°　*take care*
　　That no drope ne fille° upon hir brest.　　　*should fall*
　　In curteisye was set ful muchel hir lest.[9]
　　Hir over-lippe wiped she so clene
　　That in hir coppe° ther was no ferthing° seene　*cup / bit*
135　Of grece,° whan she dronken hadde hir draughte;　*grease*
　　Ful semely after hir mete she raughte.°　　　*reached*
　　And sikerly° she was of greet disport,[1]　　*certainly*
　　And ful plesant, and amiable of port,°　　　*mien*
　　And pained hire to countrefete cheere[2]
140　Of court, and to been statlich° of manere,　　*dignified*
　　And to been holden digne[3] of reverence.
　　But, for to speken of hir conscience,

---

4. Joust, fight in a tournament.
5. At night.
6. It was a squire's duty to carve his lord's meat.
7. The "Yeman" (Yeoman) is an independent commoner who acts as the Knight's military servant; "he" is the Knight.
8. "Him liste": it pleased him to.
9. I.e., the Yeoman.
1. In a workmanlike way.
2. Wristguard for archers.
3. Buckler (a small shield).

4. St. Christopher medal.
5. Baldric (a supporting strap).
6. The Prioress is the mother superior of her nunnery.
7. In a seemly manner.
8. The French learned in a convent school in Stratford-at-the-Bow, a suburb of London, was evidently not up to the Parisian standard.
9. I.e., her chief delight lay in good manners.
1. Of great good cheer.
2. And took pains to imitate the behavior.
3. And to be considered worthy.

She was so charitable and so pitous° *merciful*
She wolde weepe if that she saw a mous
145 Caught in a trappe, if it were deed° or bledde. *dead*
Of[4] smale houndes hadde she that she fedde
With rosted flessh, or milk and wastelbreed;° *fine white bread*
But sore wepte she if oon of hem were deed,
Or if men smoot it with a yerde smerte;[5]
150 And al was conscience and tendre herte.
Ful semely hir wimpel° pinched° was, *headdress / pleated*
Hir nose tretis,° hir yën° greye as glas, *well-formed / eyes*
Hir mouth ful smal, and therto° softe and reed,° *moreover / red*
But sikerly° she hadde a fair forheed: *certainly*
155 It was almost a spanne brood,[6] I trowe,° *believe*
For hardily,° she was nat undergrowe. *assuredly*
Ful fetis° was hir cloke, as I was war;° *becoming / aware*
Of smal° coral aboute hir arm she bar *dainty*
A paire[7] of bedes, gauded al with greene,
160 And theron heeng° a brooch of gold ful sheene,° *hung / bright*
On which ther was first writen a crowned A,[8]
And after, *Amor vincit omnia.*[9]
 Another Nonne with hire hadde she
That was hir chapelaine,° and preestes three.[1] *secretary*
165 A Monk ther was, a fair for the maistrye,[2]
An outridere[3] that loved venerye,° *hunting*
A manly man, to been an abbot able.° *worthy*
Ful many a daintee° hors hadde he in stable, *fine*
And whan he rood,° men mighte his bridel heere *rode*
170 Ginglen° in a whistling wind as clere *jingle*
And eek as loude as dooth the chapel belle
Ther as this lord was kepere of the celle.[4]
The rule of Saint Maure or of Saint Beneit,[5]
By cause that it was old and somdeel strait—
175 This ilke Monk leet olde thinges pace,° *pass away*
And heeld° after the newe world the space.[6] *held*
He yaf nought of that text a pulled hen[7]
That saith that hunteres been° nought holy men, *are*
Ne that a monk, whan he is recchelees,[8]
180 Is likned til° a fissh that is waterlees— *to*
This is to sayn, a monk out of his cloistre;
But thilke° text heeld he nat worth an oystre. *that same*
And I saide his opinion was good:
What° sholde he studye and make himselven wood° *why / crazy*
185 Upon a book in cloistre alway to poure,
Or swinke° with his handes and laboure, *work*
As Austin bit?[9] How shal the world be served?
Lat Austin have his swink to him reserved!
Therfore he was a prikasour° aright. *hard rider*
190 Grehoundes he hadde as swift as fowl in flight.

---

4. I.e., some.
5. If someone struck it with a rod sharply.
6. A handsbreadth wide.
7. String (i.e., a rosary); "gauded al with greene": provided with green beads to mark certain prayers.
8. An *A* with an ornamental crown on it.
9. A Latin motto meaning "Love conquers all."
1. Although he here awards this charming lady three priests, Chaucer later reduces the number to one.
2. I.e., a superlatively fine one.

3. A monk charged with supervising property distant from the monastery.
4. Keeper of an outlying cell (branch) of the monastery.
5. St. Maurus and St. Benedict, authors of monastic rules. "Somdeel strait": somewhat strict.
6. I.e., in his own lifetime (?).
7. He didn't give a plucked hen for that text.
8. Reckless, careless of rule.
9. I.e., as St. Augustine bids. St. Augustine had written that monks should perform manual labor.

Of priking° and of hunting for the hare   *riding*
Was al his lust,° for no cost wolde he spare.   *pleasure*
I sawgh his sleeves purfiled° at the hand   *fur-lined*
With gris,° and that the fineste of a land;   *gray fur*
95 And for to festne his hood under his chin
He hadde of gold wrought a ful curious[1] pin:
A love-knotte in the grettere° ende ther was.   *greater*
His heed was balled,° that shoon as any glas,   *bald*
And eek his face, as he hadde been anoint:
00 He was a lord ful fat and in good point;[2]
His yën steepe,° and rolling in his heed,   *protruding*
That stemed as a furnais of a leed,[3]
His bootes souple,° his hors in greet estat°—   *supple / condition*
Now certainly he was a fair prelat.[4]
05 He was nat pale as a forpined° gost: *wasted away*
A fat swan loved he best of any rost.
His palfrey° was as brown as is a berye.   *saddle horse*
   A Frere[5] ther was, a wantoune and a merye,
A limitour, a ful solempne° man.   *pompous*
10 In alle the ordres foure is noon that can°   *knows*
So muche of daliaunce° and fair langage: *flirtation*
He hadde maad ful many a mariage
Of yonge wommen at his owene cost;
Unto his ordre he was a noble post.[6]
15 Ful wel biloved and familier was he
With frankelains over al[7] in his contree,
And with worthy wommen of the town—
For he hadde power of confessioun,
As saide himself, more than a curat,°   *parish priest*
20 For of° his ordre he was licenciat.[8]   *by*
Ful swetely herde he confessioun,
And plesant was his absolucioun.
He was an esy man to yive penaunce
Ther as he wiste to have[9] a good pitaunce;°   *donation*
25 For unto a poore ordre for to yive
Is signe that a man is wel yshrive;[1]
For if he yaf, he dorste make avaunt°   *boast*
He wiste that a man was repentaunt;
For many a man so hard is of his herte
30 He may nat weepe though him sore smerte:[2]
Therfore, in stede of weeping and prayeres,
Men mote° yive silver to the poore freres.[3]   *may*
   His tipet° was ay farsed° ful of knives   *scarf / packed*
And pinnes, for to yiven faire wives;
35 And certainly he hadde a merye note;
Wel coude he singe and playen on a rote;°   *fiddle*
Of yeddinges he bar outrely the pris.[4]
His nekke whit was as the flowr-de-lis;°   *lily*

1. Of careful workmanship.
2. In good shape, plump.
3. That glowed like a furnace with a pot in it.
4. Prelate (an important churchman).
5. The "Frere" (Friar) is a member of one of the four religious orders whose members live by begging; as a "limitour" (line 209) he has been granted exclusive begging rights within a certain limited area.
6. I.e., pillar.
7. I.e., with franklins everywhere. Franklins were well-to-do country men.

8. I.e., licensed to hear confessions.
9. Where he knew he would have.
1. Shriven, absolved.
2. Though he is sorely grieved.
3. Before granting absolution, the confessor must be sure the sinner is contrite; moreover, the absolution is contingent upon the sinner's performance of an act of satisfaction. In the case of Chaucer's Friar, a liberal contribution served both as proof of contrition and as satisfaction.
4. He absolutely took the prize for ballads.

Therto he strong was as a champioun.
²⁴⁰ He knew the tavernes wel in every town,
And every hostiler° and tappestere,°   *innkeeper / barmaid*
Bet° than a lazar⁵ or a beggestere.   *better*
For unto swich a worthy man as he
Accorded nat, as by his facultee,⁶
²⁴⁵ To have with sike° lazars aquaintaunce: *sick*
It is nat honeste,° it may nought avaunce,°   *dignified / profit*
For to delen with no swich poraile,⁷
But al with riche, and selleres of vitaile;°   *foodstuffs*
And over al ther as profit sholde arise,
²⁵⁰ Curteis he was, and lowely of servise.
Ther was no man nowher so vertuous:°   *efficient*
He was the beste beggere in his hous.°   *friary*
And yaf a certain ferme for the graunt:⁸
Noon of his bretheren cam ther in his haunt.°   *assigned territory*
²⁵⁵ For though a widwe° hadde nought a sho,°   *widow / shoe*
So plesant was his *In principio*⁹
Yit wolde he have a ferthing° er he wente;   *small coin*
His purchas was wel bettre than his rente.¹
And rage he coude as it were right a whelpe,²
²⁶⁰ In love-dayes³ ther coude he muchel° helpe,   *much*
For ther he was nat lik a cloisterer,
With a thredbare cope, as is a poore scoler,
But he was lik a maister⁴ or a pope.
Of double worstede was his semicope,°   *short robe*
²⁶⁵ And rounded as a belle out of the presse.°   *bell-mold*
Somwhat he lipsed° for his wantounesse°   *lisped / affectation*
To make his Englissh sweete upon his tonge;
And in his harping, whan he hadde songe,°   *sung*
His yën twinkled in his heed aright
²⁷⁰ As doon the sterres° in the frosty night.   *stars*
This worthy limitour was cleped Huberd.
    A Marchant was ther with a forked beerd,
In motelee,⁵ and hye on hors he sat,
Upon his heed a Flandrissh° bevere hat,   *Flemish*
²⁷⁵ His bootes clasped faire and fetisly.°   *elegantly*
His resons° he spak ful solempnely,   *opinions*
Souning° alway th'encrees of his winning.   *sounding*
He wolde the see were kept for any thing⁶
Bitwixen Middelburgh and Orewelle.
²⁸⁰ Wel coude he in eschaunge sheeldes⁷ selle.
This worthy man ful wel his wit bisette:°   *employed*
Ther wiste° no wight that he was in dette,   *knew*
So statly° was he of his governaunce,⁸   *dignified*
With his bargaines,° and with his chevissaunce.°   *bargainings / borrowing*
²⁸⁵ Forsoothe he was a worthy man withalle;

---

5. Leper; "beggestere": female beggar.
6. It was not suitable because of his position.
7. I.e., poor people. The oldest order of friars had been founded by St. Francis to administer to the spiritual needs of precisely those classes the Friar avoids.
8. And he paid a certain rent for the privilege of begging.
9. A friar's usual salutation (John i.1): "In the beginning (was the Word)."
1. I.e., the money he got through such activity was more than his regular income.
2. And he could flirt wantonly, as if he were a puppy.

3. Days appointed for the settlement of lawsuits out of court.
4. A man of recognized learning.
5. Motley, a cloth of mixed color.
6. I.e., he wished the sea to be guarded at all costs. The sea route between Middleburgh (in the Netherlands) and Orwell (in Suffolk) was vital to the Merchant's export and import of wool—the basis of England's chief trade at the time.
7. Shields, *écus* (French coins): he could speculate profitably (if illegally) in foreign exchange.
8. The management of his affairs.

But, sooth to sayn, I noot° how men him calle.   *don't know*
　　A Clerk[9] ther was of Oxenforde also
That unto logik hadde longe ygo.[1]
As lene was his hors as is a rake,
90　And he was nought right fat, I undertake,
But looked holwe,° and therto sobrely.   *hollow*
Ful thredbare was his overeste courtepy,[2]
For he hadde geten him yit no benefice,
Ne was so worldly for to have office.°   *secular employment*
95　For him was levere[3] have at his beddes heed
Twenty bookes, clad in blak or reed,
Of Aristotle and his philosophye,
Than robes riche, or fithele,° or gay sautrye.[4]   *fiddle*
But al be that he was a philosophre[5]
00　Yit hadde he but litel gold in cofre;°   *coffer*
But al that he mighte of his freendes hente,°   *take*
On bookes and on lerning he it spente,
And bisily gan for the soules praye
Of hem that yaf him wherwith to scoleye.°   *study*
05　Of studye took he most cure° and most heede.   *care*
Nought oo° word spak he more than was neede,   *one*
And that was said in forme[6] and reverence,
And short and quik,° and ful of heigh sentence:[7]   *lively*
Souning° in moral vertu was his speeche,   *resounding*
10　And gladly wolde he lerne, and gladly teche.
　　A Sergeant of the Lawe,[8] war and wis,
That often hadde been at the Parvis[9]
Ther was also, ful riche of excellence.
Discreet he was, and of greet reverence—
15　He seemed swich, his wordes weren so wise.
Justice he was ful often in assise°   *circuit courts*
By patente° and by plein° commissioun.   *royal warrant / full*
For his science° and for his heigh renown   *knowledge*
Of fees and robes hadde he many oon.
20　So greet a purchasour° was nowher noon;   *speculator in land*
Al was fee simple[1] to him in effect—
His purchasing mighte nat been infect.[2]
Nowher so bisy a man as he ther nas;°   *was not*
And yit he seemed bisier than he was.
25　In termes[3] hadde he caas and doomes alle
That from the time of King William[4] were falle.
Therto he coude endite and make a thing,[5]
Ther coude no wight pinchen° at his writing;   *cavil*
And every statut coude° he plein° by rote.[6]   *knew / entire*
30　He rood but hoomly° in a medlee cote,[7]   *unpretentiously*
Girt with a ceint of silk, with barres smale.

9. The Clerk is a student at Oxford; in order to become a student, he would have had to signify his intention of becoming a cleric, but he was not bound to proceed to a positon of responsibility in the church.
1. Who had long since matriculated in philosophy.
2. Outer cloak. "Benefice": ecclesiastical living.
3. He would rather.
4. Psaltery (a kind of harp).
5. The word may also mean "alchemist."
6. With decorum.
7. Elevated thought.
8. The Sergeant is not only a practicing law-
yer, but one of the high justices of the nation. "War and wis": wary and wise.
9. The "Paradise," a meeting place for lawyers and their clients.
1. "Fee simple": owned outright without legal impediments.
2. Invalidated on a legal technicality.
3. I.e., by heart. "Caas and doomes": lawcases and decisions.
4. I.e., the Conqueror (reigned 1066–87).
5. Compose and draw up a deed.
6. By heart.
7. A coat of mixed color. "Ceint": belt; "barres": transverse stripes.

Of his array telle I no lenger tale.
　A Frankelain[8] was in his compaignye:
Whit was his beerd as is the dayesye;°　　　　　　　　　*daisy*
335　Of his complexion he was sanguin.[9]
Wel loved he by the morwe a sop in win.[1]
To liven in delit° was evere his wone,°　　*sensual delight / wont*
For he was Epicurus[2] owene sone,
That heeld opinion that plein° delit　　　　　　　　　*full*
340　Was verray felicitee parfit.
An housholdere and that a greet was he:
Saint Julian[3] he was in his contree.
His breed, his ale, was always after oon;[4]
A bettre envined° man was nevere noon.　　　*wine-stocked*
345　Withouten bake mete was nevere his hous,
Of fissh and flessh, and that so plentevous°　　　*plenteous*
It snewed° in his hous of mete and drinke,　　　*snowed*
Of alle daintees that men coude thinke.
After° the sondry sesons of the yeer　　　　*according to*
350　So chaunged he his mete[5] and his soper.
Ful many a fat partrich hadde he in mewe,°　　　　*cage*
And many a breem,° and many a luce° in stewe.[6]　　*carp / pike*
Wo was his cook but if his sauce were
Poinant° and sharp, and redy all his gere.　　　*pungent*
355　His table dormant in his halle alway
Stood redy covered all the longe day.[7]
At sessions[8] ther was he lord and sire.
Ful ofte time he was Knight of the Shire.
An anlaas° and a gipser° al of silk　　　　　*dagger / purse*
360　Heeng at his girdel,[9] whit as morne° milk.　　　*morning*
A shirreve° hadde he been, and countour.[1]　　　　*sheriff*
Was nowher swich a worthy vavasour.[2]
　An Haberdasshere and a Carpenter,
A Webbe,° a Dyere, and a Tapicer°—　　*weaver / tapestry-maker*
365　And they were clothed alle in oo liveree[3]
Of a solempne and greet fraternitee.
Ful fresshe and newe hir gere apiked° was;　　　*polished*
Hir knives were chaped° nought with bras,　　　*mounted*
But al with silver; wrought ful clene and weel
370　Hir girdles and hir pouches everydeel.°　　　*altogether*
Wel seemed eech of hem a fair burgeis°　　　　*burgher*
To sitten in a yeldehalle° on a dais.　　　　*guildhall*
Everich, for the wisdom that he can,[4]
Was shaply° for to been an alderman.　　　　*suitable*
375　For catel° hadde they ynough and rente,°　*property / income*
And eek hir wives wolde it wel assente—
And elles certain were they to blame:
It is ful fair to been ycleped "Madame,"

---

8. The "Frankelain" (Franklin) is a prosper-
ous country man, whose lower-class ancestry is
no impediment to the importance he has at-
tained in his county.
9. A reference to the fact that the Franklin's
temperament is dominated by blood as well as
to his red face.
1. I.e., in the morning he was very fond of a
piece of bread soaked in wine.
2. The Greek philosopher whose teaching is
popularly believed to make pleasure the chief
goal of life.
3. The patron saint of hospitality.
4. Always of the same high quality.
5. Dinner; "soper": supper.

6. Fishpond.
7. Tables were usually dismounted when not
in use, but the Franklin kept his mounted and
set ("covered"), hence "dormant."
8. I.e., sessions of the justices of the peace.
"Knight of the Shire": county representative
in Parliament.
9. Hung at his belt.
1. Auditor of county finances.
2. Member of an upper, but not an aristo-
cratic, feudal class.
3. In one livery, i.e., the uniform of their
"fraternitee" or guild, a partly religious,
partly social organization.
4. Was capable of.

And goon to vigilies[5] all bifore,
80 And have a mantel royalliche ybore.[6]
    A Cook they hadde with hem for the nones,[7]
To boile the chiknes with the marybones,°   *marrowbones*
And powdre-marchant tart and galingale.[8]
Wel coude he knowe° a draughte of London ale.   *recognize*
85 He coude roste, and seethe,° and broile, and frye,   *boil*
Maken mortreux,° and wel bake a pie.   *stews*
But greet harm was it thoughte° me,   *seemed to*
That on his shine a mormal° hadde he.   *ulcer*
For blankmanger,[9] that made he with the beste.
90   A Shipman was ther, woning° fer by weste—   *dwelling*
For ought I woot,° he was of Dertemouthe.[1]   *know*
He rood upon a rouncy° as he couthe,[2]   *large nag*
In a gowne of falding° to the knee.   *heavy wool*
A daggere hanging on a laas° hadde he   *strap*
95 Aboute his nekke, under his arm adown.
The hote somer hadde maad his hewe° al brown;   *color*
And certainly he was a good felawe.
Ful many a draughte of win hadde he drawe[3]
Fro Burdeuxward,[4] whil that the chapman sleep:
00 Of nice° conscience took he no keep;°   *fastidious / heed*
If that he faught and hadde the hyer hand,
By water he sente hem hoom to every land.
But of his craft, to rekene wel his tides,
His stremes° and his daungers° him bisides,[5]   *currents / hazards*
05 His herberwe° and his moone, his lodemenage,°   *anchorage / pilotage*
There was noon swich from Hulle to Cartage.[6]
Hardy he was and wis to undertake;
With many a tempest hadde his beerd been shake;
He knew alle the havenes° as they were   *harbors*
10 Fro Gotlond to the Cape of Finistere,[7]
And every crike° in Britaine° and in Spaine.   *inlet / Brittany*
His barge ycleped was the Maudelaine.°   *Magdalene*
    With us ther was a Doctour of Physik:°   *medicine*
In al this world ne was ther noon him lik
15 To speken of physik and of surgerye.
For° he was grounded in astronomye,°   *because / astrology*
He kepte° his pacient a ful greet deel[8]   *tended to*
In houres[9] by his magik naturel.
Wel coude he fortunen the ascendent
20 Of his images[1] for his pacient.
He knew the cause of every maladye,
Were it of hoot or cold or moiste or drye,
And where engendred and of what humour:[2]

5. Feasts held on the eve of saints' days. "Al bifore": i.e., at the head of the procession.
6. Royally carried.
7. For the occasion.
8. "Powdre-marchant" and "galingale" are flavoring materials.
9. An elaborate stew.
1. Dartmouth, a port in the southwest of England.
2. As best he could.
3. Drawn, i.e., stolen.
4. From Bordeaux; i.e., while carrying wine from Bordeaux (the wine center of France). "Chapman sleep": merchant slept.
5. Around him.
6. From Hull (in northern England) to Cartagena (in Spain).
7. From Gotland (an island in the Baltic) to Finisterre (the westernmost point in Spain).
8. "A ful greet deel": closely.

9. I.e., the astrologically important hours (when conjunctions of the planets might help his recovery). "Magik naturel": natural—as opposed to black—magic.
1. Assign the propitious time, according to the position of stars, for using talismanic images. Such images, representing either the patient himself or points in the zodiac, were thought to be influential on the course of the disease.
2. Diseases were thought to be caused by a disturbance of one or another of the four bodily "humors," each of which, like the four elements, was a compound of two of the elementary qualities mentioned in line 422: the melancholy humor, seated in the black bile, was cold and dry (like earth); the sanguine, seated in the blood, hot and moist (like air); the choleric, seated in the yellow bile, hot and dry (like fire); the phlegmatic, seated in the phlegm, cold and moist (like water).

He was a verray parfit praktisour.[3]
425 The cause yknowe,° and of his harm the roote,   *known*
      Anoon he yaf the sike man his boote.°   *remedy*
        Ful redy hadde he his apothecaries
      To senden him drogges° and his letuaries,°   *drugs / medicines*
      For eech of hem made other for to winne:
430 Hir frendshipe was nought newe to biginne.
      Wel knew he the olde Esculapius,[4]
      And Deiscorides and eek Rufus,
      Olde Ipocras, Hali, and Galien,
      Serapion, Razis, and Avicen,
435 Averrois, Damascien, and Constantin,
      Bernard, and Gatesden, and Gilbertin.
      Of his diete mesurable° was he,   *moderate*
      For it was of no superfluitee,
      But of greet norissing° and digestible.   *nourishment*
440 His studye was but litel on the Bible.
      In sanguin° and in pers° he clad was al,   *blood-red / blue*
      Lined with taffata and with sendal;°   *silk*
      And yit he was but esy of dispence;°   *expenditure*
      He kepte that he wan in pestilence.[5]
445 For° gold in physik is a cordial,[6]   *because*
      Therfore he loved gold in special.
        A good Wif was ther of biside Bathe,
      But she was somdeel deef, and that was scathe.°   *a pity*
      Of cloth-making she hadde swich an haunt,°   *practice*
450 She passed° hem of Ypres and of Gaunt.[7]   *surpassed*
      In al the parissh wif ne was ther noon
      That to the offring[8] bifore hire sholde goon,
      And if ther dide, certain so wroth° was she   *angry*
      That she was out of alle charitee.
455 Hir coverchiefs ful fine were of ground°—   *texture*
      I dorste° swere they weyeden° ten pound   *dare / weighed*
      That on a Sonday weren° upon hir heed.   *were*
      Hir hosen weren of fin scarlet reed,°   *red*
      Ful straite yteyd,[9] and shoes ful moiste° and newe.   *unworn*
460 Bold was hir face and fair and reed of hewe.
      She was a worthy womman al hir live:
      Housbondes at chirche dore[1] she hadde five,
      Withouten other compaigny in youthe—
      But therof needeth nought to speke as nouthe.°   *now*
465 And thries hadde she been at Jerusalem;
      She hadde passed many a straunge° streem;   *foreign*
      At Rome she hadde been, and at Boloigne,
      In Galice at Saint Jame, and at Coloigne:[2]
      She coude° muchel of wandring by the waye.   *knew*
470 Gat-toothed° was she, soothly for to saye.   *gap-toothed*

3. True perfect practitioner.
4. The Doctor is familiar with the treatises that the Middle Ages attributed to the "great names" of medical history, whom Chaucer names in lines 431–36: the purely legendary Greek demigod Aesculapius; the Greeks Dioscorides, Rufus, Hippocrates, Galen, and Serapion; the Persians Hali and Rhazes; the Arabians Avicenna and Averroës; the early Christians John (?) of Damascus and Constantine Afer; the Scotsman Bernard Gordon; the Englishmen John of Gatesden and Gilbert, the former an early contemporary of Chaucer.
5. He saved the money he made during the plague time.
6. A stimulant. Gold was thought to have some medicinal properties.
7. Ypres and Ghent ("Gaunt") were Flemish cloth-making centers.
8. The offering in church, when the congregation brought its gifts forward.
9. Tightly laced.
1. In medieval times, weddings were performed at the church door.
2. Rome; Boulogne (in France); St. James (of Compostella) in Galicia (Spain); Cologne (in Germany): all sites of shrines much visited by pilgrims.

Upon an amblere[3] esily she sat,
Ywimpled° wel, and on hir heed an hat   *veiled*
As brood as is a bokeler or a targe,[4]
A foot-mantel° aboute hir hipes large,   *riding skirt*
75 And on hir feet a paire of spores° sharpe.   *spurs*
In felaweshipe wel coude she laughe and carpe:°   *talk*
Of remedies of love she knew parchaunce,°   *as it happened*
For she coude of that art the olde daunce.[5]
    A good man was ther of religioun,
80 And was a poore Person° of a town,   *parson*
But riche he was of holy thought and werk.
He was also a lerned man, a clerk,
That Cristes gospel trewely° wolde preche;   *faithfully*
His parisshens° devoutly wolde he teche.   *parishioners*
85 Benigne he was, and wonder° diligent,   *wonderfully*
And in adversitee ful pacient,
And swich he was preved° ofte sithes.°   *proved / times*
Ful loth were him to cursen for his tithes,[6]
But rather wolde he yiven, out of doute,[7]
90 Unto his poore parisshens aboute
Of his offring[8] and eek of his substaunce:°   *property*
He coude in litel thing have suffisaunce.°   *sufficiency*
Wid was his parissh, and houses fer asonder,
But he ne lafte° nought for rain ne thonder,   *neglected*
95 In siknesse nor in meschief,° to visite   *misfortune*
The ferreste° in his parissh, muche and lite,[9]   *farthest*
Upon his feet, and in his hand a staf.
This noble ensample° to his sheep he yaf   *example*
That first he wroughte,[1] and afterward he taughte.
100 Out of the Gospel he tho° wordes caughte,°   *those / took*
And this figure he added eek therto:
That if gold ruste, what shal iren do?
For if a preest be foul, on whom we truste,
105 No wonder is a lewed° man to ruste.   *uneducated*
And shame it is, if a preest take keep,°   *heed*
A shiten° shepherde and a clene sheep.   *befouled*
Wel oughte a preest ensample for to yive
By his clennesse how that his sheep sholde live.
510 He sette nought his benefice[2] to hire
And leet his sheep encombred in the mire
And ran to London, unto Sainte Poules,[3]
To seeken him a chaunterye[4] for soules,
Or with a bretherhede to been withholde,[5]
515 But dwelte at hoom and kepte wel his folde,
So that the wolf ne made it nought miscarye:
He was a shepherde and nought a mercenarye.
And though he holy were and vertuous,
He was to sinful men nought despitous,°   *scornful*
Ne of his speeche daungerous° ne digne,°   *disdainful / haughty*

---

3. Horse with an easy gait.
4. "Bokeler" and "targe": small shields.
5. I.e., she knew all the tricks of that trade.
6. He would be most reluctant to invoke excommunication in order to collect his tithes.
7. Without doubt.
8. The offering made by the congregation of his church was at the Parson's disposal.
9. I.e., great and small.
1. I.e., he practiced what he preached.
2. I.e., his parish. A priest might rent his

parish to another and take a more profitable position. "Leet": i.e., he did not leave.
3. St. Paul's Cathedral.
4. Chantry, i.e., a foundation that employed priests for the sole duty of saying masses for the souls of certain persons. St. Paul's had many of them.
5. Or to be employed by a brotherhood; i.e., to take a lucrative and fairly easy position as chaplain with a parish guild.

520 But in his teching discreet and benigne,	
To drawen folk to hevene by fairnesse	
By good ensample—this was his bisinesse.	
But it° were any persone obstinat,	*if there*
What so he were, of heigh or lowe estat,	
525 Him wolde he snibben° sharply for the nones:[6]	*scold*
A bettre preest I trowe° ther nowher noon is.	*believe*
He waited after[7] no pompe and reverence,	
Ne maked him a spiced conscience,[8]	
But Cristes lore° and his Apostles twelve	*teaching*
530 He taughte, but first he folwed it himselve.	
With him ther was a Plowman, was his brother,	
That hadde ylad° of dong° ful many a fother.°	*carried / dung / load*
A trewe swinkere° and a good was he,	*worker*
Living in pees° and parfit charitee.	*peace*
535 God loved he best with al his hoole° herte	*whole*
At alle times, though him gamed or smerte,[9]	
And thanne his neighebor right as himselve.	
He wolde thresshe, and therto dike° and delve,	*dig ditches*
For Cristes sake, for every poore wight,	
540 Withouten hire, if it laye in his might.	
His tithes payed he ful faire and wel,	
Bothe of his propre swink[1] and his catel.°	*property*
In a tabard° he rood upon a mere.°	*short coat / mare*
Ther was also a Reeve° and a Millere,	*estate manager*
545 A Somnour, and a Pardoner[2] also,	
A Manciple,° and myself—ther were namo.	*steward*
The Millere was a stout carl° for the nones.	*fellow*
Ful big he was of brawn° and eek of bones—	*muscle*
That preved[3] wel, for overal ther he cam	
550 At wrastling he wolde have alway the ram.[4]	
He was short-shuldred, brood,° a thikke knarre.°	*broad / bully*
Ther was no dore that he nolde heve of harre,[5]	
Or breke it at a renning° with his heed.°	*running / head*
His beerd as any sowe or fox was reed,°	*red*
555 And therto brood, as though it were a spade;	
Upon the cop° right of his nose he hade	*ridge*
A werte,° and theron stood a tuft of heres,	*wart*
Rede as the bristles of a sowes eres;	
His nosethirles° blake were and wide.	*nostrils*
560 A swerd and a bokeler° bar° he by his side.	*shield / bore*
His mouth as greet was as a greet furnais.°	*furnace*
He was a janglere° and a Goliardais,[6]	*chatterer*
And that was most of sinne and harlotries.°	*obscenities*
Wel coude he stelen corn and tollen thries[7]—	
565 And yit he hadde a thombe[8] of gold, pardee.°	*by heaven*
A whit cote and a blew hood wered° he.	*wore*
A baggepipe wel coude he blowe and soune,°	*sound*
And therwithal° he broughte us out of towne.	*therewith*
A gentil Manciple[9] was ther of a temple,	

6. On any occasion.
7. I.e., expected.
8. Nor did he assume an overfastidious conscience.
9. Whether he was pleased or grieved.
1. His own work.
2. "Somnour" (Summoner): server of summonses to the ecclesiastical court; Pardoner: dispenser of papal pardons. See lines 625 and 671, and notes, below.
3. Proved, i.e., was evident.

4. A ram was frequently offered as the prize in wrestling.
5. He would not heave off (its) hinge.
6. Goliard, teller of tall stories.
7. Take toll thrice—i.e., deduct from the grain far more than the lawful percentage.
8. Thumb. The narrator seems to be questioning the validity of the adage that (only) an honest miller has a golden thumb.
9. The Manciple is the steward of a community of lawyers in London (a "temple").

70 Of which achatours° mighte take exemple   *buyers of food*
   For to been wise in bying of vitaile;°   *victuals*
   For wheither that he paide or took by taile,[1]
   Algate he waited so in his achat[2]
   That he was ay biforn[3] and in good stat.
75   Now is nat that of God a ful fair grace
   That swich a lewed° mannes wit shal pace°   *ignorant / surpass*
   The wisdom of an heep of lerned men?
   Of maistres° hadde he mo than thries ten   *masters*
   That weren of lawe expert and curious,°   *cunning*
80 Of whiche ther were a dozeine in that hous
   Worthy to been stiwardes of rente° and lond   *income*
   Of any lord that is in Engelond,
   To make him live by his propre good[4]
   In honour dettelees but if[5] he were wood,°   *insane*
85 Or live as scarsly° as him list° desire,   *sparely / it pleases*
   And able for to helpen al a shire
   In any caas° that mighte falle° or happe,   *event / befall*
   And yit this Manciple sette hir aller cappe![6]
   The Reeve[7] was a sclendre° colerik man;   *slender*
90 His beerd was shave as neigh° as evere he can;   *close*
   His heer was by his eres ful round yshorn;
   His top was dokked[8] lik a preest biforn;
   Ful longe were his legges and ful lene,
   Ylik a staf, ther was no calf yseene.°   *visible*
95 Wel coude he keepe° a gerner° and a binne—   *guard / granary*
   Ther was noon auditour coude on him winne.[9]
   Wel wiste° he by the droughte and by the rain   *knew*
   The yeelding of his seed and of his grain.
   His lordes sheep, his neet,° his dayerye,   *cattle*
100 His swin, his hors, his stoor,° and his pultrye   *stock*
   Was hoolly° in this Reeves governinge,   *wholly*
   And by his covenant yaf[1] the rekeninge,
   Sin° that his lord was twenty yeer of age.   *since*
   There coude no man bringe him in arrerage.[2]
105 Ther nas baillif, hierde, nor other hine,
   That he ne knew his sleighte and his covine[3]—
   They were adrad° of him as of the deeth.°   *afraid / plague*
   His woning° was ful faire upon an heeth;°   *dwelling / meadow*
   With greene trees shadwed was his place.
110 He coude bettre than his lord purchace.°   *acquire goods*
   Ful riche he was astored° prively.°   *stocked / secretly*
   His lord wel coude he plesen subtilly,
   To yive and lene° him of his owene good,°   *lend / property*
   And have a thank, and yit a cote and hood.
115 In youthe he hadde lerned a good mister:°   *occupation*
   He was a wel good wrighte, a carpenter.
   This Reeve sat upon a ful good stot°   *stallion*
   That was a pomely° grey and highte° Scot.   *dapple / was named*

---

1. By talley, i.e., on credit.
2. Always he was on the watch in his purchasing.
3. I.e., ahead of the game. "Stat": financial condition.
4. His own money.
5. Out of debt unless.
6. This Manciple made fools of them all.
7. The Reeve is the superintendent of a large farming estate; "colerik" (choleric) describes a man whose dominant humor is yellow bile (choler)—i.e., a hot-tempered man.
8. Cut short: the clergy wore the head partially shaved.
9. I.e., find him in default.
1. And according to his contract he gave.
2. Convict him of being in arrears financially.
3. There was no bailiff (i.e., foreman), shepherd, nor other farm laborer whose craftiness and plots he didn't know.

A long surcote° of pers° upon he hade,[4]	overcoat / blue
620 And by his side he bar° a rusty blade. | bore |
Of Northfolk was this Reeve of which I telle, | |
Biside a town men clepen Baldeswelle.° | Bawdswell |
Tukked[5] he was as is a frere aboute, | |
And evere he rood the hindreste of oure route.[6] | |
625   A Somnour[7] was ther with us in that place | |
That hadde a fir-reed° cherubinnes[8] face, | fire-red |
For saucefleem° he was, with yën narwe, | pimply |
And hoot° he was, and lecherous as a sparwe,° | hot / sparrow |
With scaled° browes blake and piled[9] beerd: | scabby |
630 Of his visage children were aferd.° | afraid |
Ther nas quiksilver, litarge, ne brimstoon, | |
Boras, ceruce, ne oile of tartre noon,[1] | |
Ne oinement that wolde clense and bite, | |
That him mighte helpen of his whelkes° white, | blotches |
635 Nor of the knobbes° sitting on his cheekes. | lumps |
Wel loved he garlek, oinons, and eek leekes, | |
And for to drinke strong win reed as blood. | |
Thanne wolde he speke and crye as he were wood;° | mad |
And whan that he wel dronken hadde the win, | |
640 Thanne wolde he speke no word but Latin: | |
A fewe termes hadde he, two or three, | |
That he hadde lerned out of som decree; | |
No wonder is—he herde it al the day, | |
And eek ye knowe wel how that a jay° | parrot |
645 Can clepen "Watte"[2] as wel as can the Pope— | |
But whoso coude in other thing him grope,° | examine |
Thanne hadde he spent all his philosophye;[3] | |
Ay *Questio quid juris*[4] wolde he crye. | |
He was a gentil harlot° and a kinde; | rascal |
650 A bettre felawe sholde men nought finde: | |
He wolde suffre,° for a quart of win, | permit |
A good felawe to have his concubin | |
A twelfmonth, and excusen him at the fulle;[5] | |
Ful prively a finch eek coude he pulle.[6] | |
655 And if he foond° owher° a good felawe | found / anywhere |
He wolde techen him to have noon awe | |
In swich caas of the Ercedekenes curs,[7] | |
But if[8] a mannes soule were in his purs, | |
For in his purs he sholde ypunisshed be. | |
660 "Purs is the Ercedekenes helle," saide he. | |
But wel I woot he lied right in deede: | |
Of cursing° oughte eech gilty man drede, | excommunication |
For curs wol slee° right as assoiling° savith— | slay / absolution |

4. "Upon he hade": he had on.
5. With clothing tucked up.
6. Hindmost of our group.
7. The "Somnour" (Summoner) is an employee of the ecclesiastical court, whose defined duty is to bring to court persons whom the archdeacon—the justice of the court—suspects of offenses against canon law. By this time, however, summoners had generally transformed themselves into corrupt detectives who spied out offenders and blackmailed them by threats of summonses.
8. Cherub's, often depicted in art with a red face.
9. Uneven, partly hairless.
1. These are all ointments for diseases affecting the skin, probably diseases of venereal origin.
2. Call out: "Walter"—like modern parrots' "Polly."
3. I.e., learning.
4. "What point of law does this investigation involve?": a phrase frequently used in ecclesiastical courts.
5. "At the fulle": fully. Ecclesiastical courts had jurisdiction over many offenses which today would come under civil law, including sexual offenses.
6. "To pull a finch" is to have carnal dealings with a woman.
7. Archdeacon's sentence of excommunication.
8. "But if": unless.

And also war him of a *significavit*.[9]
565 In daunger[1] hadde he at his owene gise°   *disposal*
The yonge girles of the diocise,
And knew hir conseil,° and was al hir reed.[2]   *secrets*
A gerland hadde he set upon his heed
As greet as it were for an ale-stake;[3]
570 A bokeler hadde he maad him of a cake.
With him ther rood a gentil Pardoner[4]
Of Rouncival, his freend and his compeer,°   *comrade*
That straight was comen fro the Court of Rome.
Ful loude he soong,° "Com hider, love, to me."   *sang*
575 This Somnour bar to him a stif burdoun:[5]
Was nevere trompe° of half so greet a soun.   *trumpet*
This Pardoner hadde heer as yelow as wex,
But smoothe it heeng° as dooth a strike° of flex;°   *hung / hank / flax*
By ounces[6] heenge his lokkes that he hadde,
580 And therwith he his shuldres overspradde;°   *overspread*
But thinne it lay, by colpons,° oon by oon;   *strands*
But hood for jolitee° wered° he noon,   *nonchalance / wore*
For it was trussed up in his walet:°   *pack*
Him thoughte he rood al of the newe jet.°   *fashion*
585 Dischevelee° save his cappe he rood al bare.   *with hair down*
Swiche glaring yën hadde he as an hare.
A vernicle[7] hadde he sowed upon his cappe,
His walet biforn him in his lappe,
Bretful° of pardon, comen from Rome al hoot.°   *brimful / hot*
590 A vois he hadde as smal° as hath a goot;°   *fine / goat*
No beerd hadde he, ne nevere sholde have;
As smoothe it was as it were late yshave:
I trowe° he were a gelding or a mare.   *believe*
But of his craft, fro Berwik into Ware,[8]
595 Ne was ther swich another pardoner;
For in his male° he hadde a pilwe-beer°   *bag / pillowcase*
Which that he saide was Oure Lady veil;
He saide he hadde a gobet° of the sail   *piece*
That Sainte Peter hadde whan that he wente
700 Upon the see, til Jesu Crist him hente.°   *seized*
He hadde a crois° of laton,° ful of stones,   *cross / brassy metal*
And in a glas he hadde pigges bones,
But with thise relikes[9] whan that he foond°   *found*
A poore person° dwelling upon lond,[1]   *parson*
705 Upon° a day he gat° him more moneye   *in / got*
Than that the person gat in monthes twaye;
And thus with feined° flaterye and japes°   *false / tricks*
He made the person and the peple his apes.°   *dupes*
But trewely to tellen at the laste,
710 He was in chirche a noble ecclesiaste;

9. And also one should be careful of a *significavit* (the writ which transferred the guilty offender from the ecclesiastical to the civil arm for punishment).
1. Under his domination.
2. Was their chief source of advice.
3. A tavern was signalized by a pole ("ale-stake"), rather like a modern flagpole, projecting from its front wall; on this hung a garland, or "bush."
4. A Pardoner dispensed papal pardon for sins to those who contributed to the charitable institution that he was licensed to represent; this Pardoner purported to be collecting

for the hospital of Roncesvalles ("Rouncival") in Spain, which had a London branch.
5. I.e., provided him with a strong vocal accompaniment.
6. I.e., thin strands.
7. Portrait of Christ's face as it was said to have been impressed on St. Veronica's handkerchief.
8. Probably towns south and north of London.
9. Relics—i.e., the pigs' bones which the Pardoner represented as saints' bones.
1. "Upon lond": upcountry.

Wel coude he rede a lesson and a storye,°   *liturgical narrative*
But alderbest° he soong an offertorye,   *best of all*
For wel he wiste° whan that song was songe,   *knew*
He moste° preche and wel affile° his tonge   *must / sharpen*
715 To winne silver, as he ful wel coude—
Therfore he soong the merierly° and loude.   *more merrily*
   Now have I told you soothly in a clause[2]
Th'estaat, th'array, the nombre, and eek the cause
Why that assembled was this compaignye
720 In Southwerk at this gentil hostelrye
That highte the Tabard, faste° by the Belle;[3]   *close*
But now is time to you for to telle
How that we baren us[4] that ilke° night   *same*
Whan we were in that hostelrye alight;
725 And after wol I telle of oure viage,°   *trip*
And al the remenant of oure pilgrimage.
But first I praye you of youre curteisye
That ye n'arette it nought my vilainye[5]
Though that I plainly speke in this matere
730 To telle you hir wordes and hir cheere,°   *behavior*
Ne though I speke hir wordes proprely;°   *accurately*
For this ye knowen also wel as I:
Who so shal telle a tale after a man
He moot° reherce,° as neigh as evere he can,   *must / repeat*
735 Everich a word, if it be in his charge,°   *responsibility*
Al speke he[6] nevere so rudeliche and large,°   *broadly*
Or elles he moot telle his tale untrewe,
Or feine° thing, or finde° wordes newe;   *falsify / devise*
He may nought spare[7] although he were his brother:
740 He moot as wel saye oo word as another.
Crist spake himself ful brode° in Holy Writ,   *broadly*
And wel ye woot no vilainye is it;
Eek Plato saith, who so can him rede,
The wordes mote be cosin to the deede.
745   Also I praye you to foryive it me
Al° have I nat set folk in hir degree   *although*
Here in this tale as that they sholde stonde:
My wit is short, ye may wel understonde.
   Greet cheere made oure Host[8] us everichoon,
750 And to the soper sette he us anoon.°   *at once*
He served us with vitaile° at the beste.   *food*
Strong was the win, and wel to drinke us leste.°   *it pleased*
A semely man oure Hoste was withalle
For to been a marchal[9] in an halle;
755 A large man he was, with yën steepe,°   *prominent*
A fairer burgeis° was ther noon in Chepe[1]—   *burgher*
Bold of his speeche, and wis, and wel ytaught,
And of manhood him lakkede right naught.
Eek therto he was right a merye man,
760 And after soper playen he bigan,
And spak of mirthe amonges othere thinges—
Whan that we hadde maad oure rekeninges[2]—

---

2. I.e., in a short space.
3. Another tavern in Southwark.
4. Bore ourselves.
5. That you do not charge it to my lack of decorum.
6. Although he speak.

7. I.e., spare anyone.
8. The Host is the landlord of the Tabard Inn.
9. Marshal, one who was in charge of feasts.
1. Cheapside, bourgeois center of London.
2. Had paid our bills.

And saide thus, "Now, lordinges, trewely,
Ye been to me right welcome, hertely.°   *heartily*
65 For by my trouthe, if that I shal nat lie,
I sawgh nat this yeer so merye a compaignye
At ones in this herberwe° as is now.   *inn*
Fain° wolde I doon you mirthe, wiste I³ how.   *gladly*
And of a mirthe I am right now bithought,
70 To doon you ese, and it shal coste nought.
    "Ye goon to Canterbury—God you speede;
The blisful martyr quite you youre meede.⁴
And wel I woot as ye goon by the waye
Ye shapen you⁵ to talen° and to playe,   *converse*
75 For trewely, confort ne mirthe is noon
To ride by the waye domb as stoon;°   *stone*
And therfore wol I maken you disport
As I saide erst,° and doon you som confort;   *before*
And if you liketh alle, by oon assent,
80 For to stonden at⁶ my juggement,
And for to werken as I shal you saye,
Tomorwe whan ye riden by the waye—
Now by my fader° soule that is deed,   *father's*
But° ye be merye I wol yive you myn heed!°   *unless / head*
85 Holde up youre handes withouten more speeche."
    Oure counseil was nat longe for to seeche;°   *seek*
Us thoughte it was nat worth to make it wis,⁷
And graunted him withouten more avis,°   *deliberation*
And bade him saye his voirdit° as him leste.⁸   *verdict*
90 "Lordinges," quod he, "now herkneth for the beste;
But taketh it nought, I praye you, in desdain.
This is the point, to speken short and plain,
That eech of you, to shorte with oure waye
In this viage, shal tellen tales twaye°—   *two*
95 To Canterburyward, I mene it so,
And hoomward he shal tellen othere two,
Of aventures that whilom° have bifalle;   *once upon a time*
And which of you that bereth him best of alle—
That is to sayn, that telleth in this cas
100 Tales of best sentence° and most solas°—   *purport / delight*
Shal have a soper at oure aller cost,⁹
Here in this place, sitting by this post,
Whan that we come again fro Canterbury.
And for to make you the more mury°   *merry*
105 I wol myself goodly° with you ride—   *kindly*
Right at myn owene cost—and be youre gide.
And who so wol my juggement withsaye°   *contradict*
Shal paye al that we spende by the waye.
And if ye vouche sauf that it be so,
110 Telle me anoon, withouten wordes mo,°   *more*
And I wol erly shape me¹ therfore."
    This thing was graunted and oure othes swore
With ful glad herte, and prayden² him also
That he wolde vouche sauf for to do so,
115 And that he wolde been oure governour,

3. If I knew.
4. Pay you your reward.
5. "Shapen you": intend.
6. Abide by.
7. We didn't think it worthwhile to make an

issue of it.
8. It pleased.
9. At the cost of us all.
1. Prepare myself.
2. I.e., we prayed.

And of oure tales juge and reportour,°	accountant
And sette a soper at a certain pris,°	price
And we wol ruled been at his devis,°	disposal
In heigh and lowe; and thus by oon assent	
820 We been accorded to his juggement.	
And therupon the win was fet° anoon;	fetched
We dronken and to reste wente eechoon	
Withouten any lenger° taryinge.	longer
Amorwe° whan that day bigan to springe	in the morning
825 Up roos oure Host and was oure aller cok,³	
And gadred us togidres in a flok,	
And forth we riden, a litel more than pas,°	a step
Unto the watering of Saint Thomas;⁴	
And ther oure Host bigan his hors arreste,°	halt
830 And saide, "Lordes, herkneth if you leste:°	it please
Ye woot youre forward° and it you recorde:⁵	agreement
If evensong and morwesong° accorde,°	morningsong / agree
Lat see now who shal telle the firste tale.	
As evere mote I drinken win or ale,	
835 Who so be rebel to my juggement	
Shal paye for al that by the way is spent.	
Now draweth cut⁶ er that we ferre twinne:	
He which that hath the shorteste shal biginne.	
"Sire Knight," quod he, "my maister and my lord,	
840 Now draweth cut, for that is myn accord.°	will
Cometh neer," quod he, "my lady Prioresse,	
And ye, sire Clerk, lat be youre shamefastnesse°—	modesty
Ne studieth nought. Lay hand to, every man!"	
Anoon to drawen every wight bigan,	
845 And shortly for to tellen as it was,	
Were it by aventure, or sort, or cas,⁷	
The soothe° is this, the cut fil° to the Knight;	truth / fell
Of which ful blithe and glad was every wight,	
And telle he moste° his tale, as was resoun,	must
850 By forward and by composicioun,⁸	
As ye han herd. What needeth wordes mo?	
And whan this goode man sawgh that it was so,	
As he that wis was and obedient	
To keepe his forward by his free assent,	
855 He saide, "Sin I shal biginne the game,	
What, welcome be the cut, in Goddes name!	
Now lat us ride, and herkneth what I saye."	
And with that word we riden forth oure waye,	
And he bigan with right a merye cheere°	countenance
860 His tale anoon, and saide as ye may heere.	

The Pardoner's Prologue and Tale

The Introduction

Oure Hoste gan to swere as he were wood;°	insane
"Harrow,"° quod he, "by nailes⁹ and by blood,	help
This was a fals cherl and a fals justice.¹	

---

3. Was rooster for us all.
4. A watering place near Southwark.
5. You recall it.
6. I.e., draw lots; "ferre twinne": go farther.
7. Whether it was luck, fate, or chance.
8. By agreement and compact.
9. I.e., God's nails.

1. The Host has been affected by the Physician's sad tale of the Roman maiden Virginia, whose great beauty caused a judge to attempt to obtain her person by means of a trumped-up lawsuit in which he connived with a "churl" who claimed her as his slave; in order to preserve her chastity, her father killed her.

As shameful deeth as herte may devise
5 Come to thise juges and hir advocats.
Algate° this sely° maide is slain, allas!   *at any rate / innocent*
Allas, too dere boughte she beautee!
Wherfore I saye alday° that men may see   *always*
The yiftes of Fortune and of Nature
10 Been cause of deeth to many a creature.
As bothe yiftes that I speke of now,
Men han ful ofte more for harm than prow.°   *benefit*
    "But trewely, myn owene maister dere,
This is a pitous tale for to heere.
15 But nathelees, passe over, is no fors:[2]
I praye to God so save thy gentil cors,°   *body*
And eek thine urinals and thy jurdones,[3]
Thyn ipocras[4] and eek thy galiones,
And every boiste° ful of thy letuarye°—   *box / medicine*
20 God blesse hem, and oure lady Sainte Marye.
So mote I theen,[5] thou art a propre man,
And lik a prelat, by Saint Ronian![6]
Saide I nat wel? I can nat speke in terme.[7]
But wel I woot, thou doost° myn herte to erme°   *make / grieve*
25 That I almost have caught a cardinacle.[8]
By corpus bones,[9] but if I have triacle.°   *medicine*
Or elles a draughte of moiste° and corny° ale,   *fresh / malty*
Or but I heere anoon° a merye tale,   *at once*
Myn herte is lost for pitee of this maide.
30   "Thou bel ami,[1] thou Pardoner," he saide,
"Tel us som mirthe or japes° right anoon."   *joke*
    "It shal be doon," quod he, "by Saint Ronion.
But first," quod he, "here at this ale-stake[2]
I wol bothe drinke and eten of a cake."
35   And right anoon thise gentils gan to crye,
"Nay, lat him telle us of no ribaudye.°   *ribaldry*
Tel us som moral thing that we may lere,°   *learn*
Som wit,[3] and thanne wol we gladly heere."
    "I graunte, ywis," quod he, "but I moot thinke
40 Upon som honeste° thing whil that I drinke.   *decent*

The Prologue

    Lordinges—quod he—in chirches whan I preche,
I paine me[4] to han an hautein° speeche,   *loud*
And ringe it out as round as gooth a belle,
For I can al by rote[5] that I telle.
45 My theme is alway oon,[6] and evere was:
Radix malorum est cupiditas.[7]
First I pronounce whennes° that I come,   *whence*
And thanne my bulles[8] shewe I alle and some:
Oure lige lordes seel on my patente,[9]

---

2. I.e., never mind.
3. Jordans (chamber pots): the Host is somewhat confused in his endeavor to use technical medical terms.
4. A medicinal drink named after Hippocrates; "galiones": a medicine, probably invented on the spot by the Host, named after Galen.
5. So might I thrive.
6. St. Ronan or St. Ninian, with a possible play on "runnion" (sexual organ).
7. Speak in technical idiom.
8. Apparently a cardiac condition, confused in the Host's mind with a cardinal.

9. An illiterate oath, mixing "God's bones" with *corpus dei*. "But if": unless.
1. Fair friend.
2. Sign of a tavern.
3. I.e., something with significance.
4. Take pains.
5. I know all by heart.
6. I.e., the same.
7. Avarice is the root of evil (I Timothy vi.10).
8. Episcopal mandates; "alle and some": each and every one.
9. I.e., the Pope's seal on my papal license.

50 That shewe I first, my body to warente,°　　　　　*keep safe*
　That no man be so bold, ne preest ne clerk,
　Me to destourbe of Cristes holy werk.
　And after that thanne telle I forth my tales[1]—
　Bulles of popes and of cardinales,
55 Of patriarkes and bisshopes I shewe,
　And in Latin I speke a wordes fewe,
　To saffron with[2] my predicacioun,°　　　　　*preaching*
　And for to stire hem to devocioun.
　　Thanne shewe I forth my longe crystal stones,°　　*jars*
60 Ycrammed ful of cloutes° and of bones—　　　　*rags*
　Relikes been they, as weenen° they eechoon.　　*suppose*
　Thanne have I in laton° a shulder-boon　　　　*zinc*
　Which that was of an holy Jewes sheep.
　"Goode men," I saye, "take of my wordes keep:°　　*notice*
65 If that this boon be wasshe in any welle,
　If cow, or calf, or sheep, or oxe swelle,
　That any worm hath ete or worm ystonge,[3]
　Take water of that welle and wassh his tonge,
　And it is hool° anoon. And ferthermoor,　　　　*sound*
70 Of pokkes° and of scabbe and every soor°　　*pox / sore*
　Shal every sheep be hool that of this welle
　Drinketh a draughte. Take keep eek° that I telle:　*also*
　If that the goode man that the beestes oweth°　　*owns*
　Wol every wike,° er that the cok him croweth,　　*week*
75 Fasting drinken of this welle a draughte—
　As thilke° holy Jew oure eldres taughte—　　*that same*
　His beestes and his stoor° shal multiplye.　　*stock*
　　"And sire, also it heleth jalousye:
　For though a man be falle in jalous rage,
80 Lat maken with this water his potage,°　　　　*soup*
　And nevere shal he more his wif mistriste,°　　*mistrust*
　Though he the soothe of hir defaute wiste,[4]
　Al hadde she[5] taken preestes two or three.
　　"Here is a mitein° eek that ye may see:　　*mitten*
85 He that his hand wol putte in this mitein
　He shal have multiplying of his grain,
　Whan he hath sowen, be it whete or otes—
　So that he offre pens or elles grotes.[6]
　　"Goode men and wommen, oo thing warne I you:
90 If any wight be in this chirche now
　That hath doon sinne horrible, that he
　Dar nat for shame of it yshriven° be,　　　　*absolved*
　Or any womman, be she yong or old,
　That hath ymaked hir housbonde cokewold,°　　*cuckold*
95 Swich folk shal have no power ne no grace
　To offren to[7] my relikes in this place;
　And whoso findeth him out of swich blame,
　He wol come up and offre in Goddes name,
　And I assoile° him by the auctoritee　　　　*absolve*
100 Which that by bulle ygraunted was to me."
　　By this gaude° have I wonne, yeer by yeer,　　*trick*
　An hundred mark[8] sith° I was pardoner.　　*since*
　I stonde lik a clerk in my pulpit,

1. I go on with my yarn.
2. To add spice to.
3. That has eaten or been bitten by any worm.
4. Knew the truth of her infidelity.
5. Even if she had.
6. Pennies, groats, coins.
7. To make gifts in reverence of.
8. Marks (pecuniary units).

And whan the lewed° peple is down yset,   *ignorant*
₅ I preche so as ye han herd bifore,
And telle an hundred false japes° more.   *tricks*
Thanne paine I me⁹ to strecche forth the nekke,
And eest and west upon the peple I bekke¹
As dooth a douve,° sitting on a berne;°   *dove / barn*
₁₀ Mine handes and my tonge goon so yerne°   *fast*
That it is joye to see my bisinesse.
Of avarice and of swich cursednesse°   *sin*
Is al my preching, for to make hem free°   *generous*
To yiven hir pens, and namely° unto me,   *especially*
₁₅ For myn entente is nat but for to winne,²
And no thing for correccion of sinne:
I rekke° nevere whan that they been beried°   *care / buried*
Though that hir soules goon a-blakeberied.³
For certes, many a predicacioun°   *sermon*
₂₀ Comth ofte time of yvel entencioun:
Som for plesance of folk and flaterye,
To been avaunced° by ypocrisye,   *promoted*
And som for vaine glorye, and som for hate;
For whan I dar noon otherways debate,°   *fight*
₂₅ Thanne wol I stinge him with my tonge smerte
In preching, so that he shal nat asterte°   *escape*
To been defamed falsly, if that he
Hath trespassed to⁴ my bretheren or to me.
For though I telle nought his propre name,
₃₀ Men shal wel knowe that it is the same
By signes and by othere circumstaunces.
Thus quite° I folk that doon us displesaunces;⁵   *pay back*
Thus spete° I out my venim under hewe°   *spit / color*
Of holinesse, to seeme holy and trewe.
₃₅ But shortly myn entente I wol devise:°   *describe*
I preche of no thing but for coveitise;
Therfore my theme is yit and evere was
Radix malorum est cupiditas.
     Thus can I preche again that same vice
₄₀ Which that I use, and that is avarice.
But though myself be gilty in that sinne,
Yit can I make other folk to twinne°   *separate*
From avarice, and sore to repente—
But that is nat my principal entente:
₄₅ I preche no thing but for coveitise.
Of this matere it oughte ynough suffise.
     Thanne telle I hem ensamples⁶ many oon
Of olde stories longe time agoon,
For lewed° peple loven tales olde—   *ignorant*
₅₀ Swiche thinges can they wel reporte and holde.⁷
What, trowe° ye that whiles I may preche,   *believe*
And winne gold and silver for° I teche,   *because*
That I wol live in poverte wilfully?
Nay, nay, I thoughte° it nevere, trewely,   *intended*
₅₅ For I wol preche and begge in sondry landes;
I wol nat do no labour with mine handes,

---

9. I take pains.   5. Do us discourtesies.
1. I.e., I shake my head.   6. *Exempla* (stories illustrating moral princi-
2. Only to gain.   ples).
3. Go blackberrying, i.e., go to hell.   7. Repeat and remember.
4. Injured.

Ne make baskettes and live therby,
By cause I wol nat beggen idelly.[8]
I wol none of the Apostles countrefete:°   *imitate*
160   I wol have moneye, wolle,° cheese, and whete,   *wool*
Al were it[9] yiven of the pooreste page,
Or of the pooreste widwe in a village—
Al sholde hir children sterve[1] for famine.
Nay, I wol drinke licour of the vine
165   And have a joly wenche in every town.
But herkneth, lordinges, in conclusioun,
Youre liking° is that I shal telle a tale: *pleasure*
Now have I dronke a draughte of corny ale,
By God, I hope I shal you telle a thing
170   That shal by reson been at youre liking;
For though myself be a ful vicious man,
A moral tale yit I you telle can,
Which I am wont to preche for to winne.
Now holde youre pees, my tale I wol biginne.

The Tale

175   In Flandres whilom° was a compaignye   *once*
Of yonge folk that haunteden° folye—   *practiced*
As riot, hasard, stewes,[2] and tavernes,
Wher as with harpes, lutes, and giternes°   *guitars*
They daunce and playen at dees° bothe day and night,   *dice*
180   And ete also and drinke over hir might,[3]
Thurgh which they doon the devel sacrifise
Within that develes temple in cursed wise
By superfluitee° abhominable.   *overindulgence*
Hir othes been so grete and so dampnable
185   That it is grisly for to heere hem swere:
Oure blessed Lordes body they totere[4]—
Hem thoughte that Jewes rente° him nought ynough.   *tore*
And eech of hem at otheres sinne lough.°   *laughed*
And right anoon thanne comen tombesteres,°   *dancing girls*
190   Fetis° and smale,° and yonge frutesteres,[5]   *shapely / neat*
Singeres with harpes, bawdes,° wafereres[6]—   *pimps*
Whiche been the verray develes officeres,
To kindle and blowe the fir of lecherye
That is annexed unto glotonye:[7]
195   The Holy Writ take I to my witnesse
That luxure° is in win and dronkenesse.   *lechery*
Lo, how that dronken Lot[8] unkindely°   *unnaturally*
Lay by his doughtres two unwitingly:
So dronke he was he niste° what he wroughte.   *didn't know*
200   Herodes, who so wel the stories soughte,[9]
Whan he of win was repleet at his feeste,
Right at his owene table he yaf his heeste°   *command*
To sleen° the Baptist John, ful giltelees.   *slay*
Senek[1] saith a good word doutelees:
205   He saith he can no difference finde

8. I.e., without profit.
9. Even though it were.
1. Even though her children should die.
2. Wild parties, gambling, brothels.
3. Beyond their capacity.
4. Tear apart (a reference to oaths sworn by parts of His body, such as "God's bones!" or "God's teeth!").
5. Fruit-selling girls.

6. Girl cake-vendors.
7. I.e., closely related to gluttony.
8. For Lot, see Genesis xix.30–36.
9. For the story of Herod and St. John the Baptist, see Mark vi.17–29. "Who so * * * soughte": i.e., whoever looked it up in the Gospel would find.
1. Seneca, the Roman Stoic philosopher.

Bitwixe a man that is out of his minde
And a man which that is dronkelewe,°   *drunken*
But that woodnesse, yfallen in a shrewe,[2]
Persevereth lenger than dooth dronkenesse.
210 O glotonye, ful of cursednesse!°   *wickedness*
O cause first of oure confusioun!°   *downfall*
O original of oure dampnacioun,°   *damnation*
Til Crist hadde bought° us with his blood again!   *redeemed*
Lo, how dere, shortly for to sayn,
215 Abought° was thilke° cursed vilainye;   *paid for / that same*
Corrupt was al this world for glotonye:
Adam oure fader and his wif also
Fro Paradis to labour and to wo
Were driven for that vice, it is no drede.°   *doubt*
220 For whil that Adam fasted, as I rede,
He was in Paradis; and whan that he
Eet° of the fruit defended° on a tree,   *ate / forbidden*
Anoon he was out cast to wo and paine.
O glotonye, on thee wel oughte us plaine!°   *complain*
225   O, wiste a man[3] how manye maladies
Folwen of excesse and of glotonies,
He wolde been the more mesurable°   *moderate*
Of his diete, sitting at his table.
230 Allas, the shorte throte, the tendre mouth,
Maketh that eest and west and north and south,
In erthe, in air, in water, men to swinke,°   *work*
To gete a gloton daintee mete and drinke.
Of this matere, O Paul, wel canstou trete:
"Mete unto wombe,° and wombe eek unto mete,   *belly*
235 Shal God destroyen bothe," as Paulus saith.[4]
Allas, a foul thing is it, by my faith,
To saye this word, and fouler is the deede
Whan man so drinketh of the white and rede[5]
That of his throte he maketh his privee°   *privy*
240 Thurgh thilke cursed superfluitee.°   *overindulgence*
     The Apostle[6] weeping saith ful pitously,
"Ther walken manye of which you told have I—
I saye it now weeping with pitous vois—
They been enemies of Cristes crois,°   *cross*
245 Of whiche the ende is deeth—wombe is hir god!"[7]
O wombe, O bely, O stinking cod,°   *bag*
Fulfilled° of dong° and of corrupcioun!   *filled full / dung*
At either ende of thee foul is the soun.°   *sound*
How greet labour and cost is thee to finde!°   *provide for*
250 Thise cookes, how they stampe° and straine and grinde, *pound*
And turnen substance into accident[8]
To fulfillen al thy likerous° talent!°   *dainty / appetite*
Out of the harde bones knokke they
The mary,° for they caste nought away   *marrow*
255 That may go thurgh the golet[9] softe and soote.°   *sweetly*
Of spicerye° of leef and bark and roote   *spices*
Shal been his sauce ymaked by delit,
To make him yit a newer appetit.

2. But that madness, occurring in a wicked
man.
3. If a man knew.
4. See I Corinthians vi.13.
5. I.e., white and red wines.
6. I.e., St. Paul.

7. See Philippians iii.18.
8. A philosophic joke, depending on the dis-
tinction between inner reality (substance) and
outward appearance (accident).
9. Through the gullet.

But certes, he that haunteth swiche delices°   *pleasures*
260 Is deed° whil that he liveth in tho° vices.   *dead / those*
A lecherous thing is win, and dronkenesse
Is ful of striving° and of wrecchednesse.   *quarreling*
O dronke man, disfigured is thy face!
Sour is thy breeth, foul artou to embrace!
265 And thurgh thy dronke nose seemeth the soun
As though thou saidest ay,° "Sampsoun, Sampsoun."   *always*
And yit, God woot,° Sampson drank nevere win.[1]   *knows*
Thou fallest as it were a stiked swin;[2]
Thy tonge is lost, and al thyn honeste cure,
270 For dronkenesse is verray sepulture°   *burial*
Of mannes wit° and his discrecioun.   *intelligence*
In whom that drinke hath dominacioun
He can no conseil° keepe, it is no drede.°   *secrets / doubt*
Now keepe you fro the white and fro the rede—
275 And namely° fro the white win of Lepe[3]   *pariticularly*
That is to selle in Fisshstreete or in Chepe:[4]
The win of Spaine creepeth subtilly
In othere wines growing faste° by,   *close*
Of which ther riseth swich fumositee°   *heady fumes*
280 That whan a man hath dronken draughtes three
And weeneth° that he be at hoom in Chepe,   *supposes*
He is in Spaine, right at the town of Lepe,
Nat at The Rochele ne at Burdeux town,[5]
And thanne wol he sayn, "Sampsoun, Sampsoun."
285 But herkneth, lordinges, oo° word I you praye,   *one*
That alle the soverein actes,[6] dar I saye,
Of victories in the Olde Testament,
Thurgh verray God that is omnipotent,
Were doon in abstinence and in prayere:
290 Looketh° the Bible and ther ye may it lere.°   *behold / learn*
Looke Attila, the grete conquerour,[7]
Deide° in his sleep with shame and dishonour,   *died*
Bleeding at his nose in dronkenesse:
A capitain sholde live in sobrenesse.
295 And overal this, aviseth° you right wel   *consider*
What was comanded unto Lamuel[8]—
Nat Samuel, but Lamuel, saye I—
Redeth the Bible and finde it expresly,
Of win-yiving° to hem that han[9] justise: *wine-serving*
300 Namore of this, for it may wel suffise.
And now that I have spoken of glotonye,
Now wol I you defende° hasardrye:°   *prohibit / gambling*
Hasard is verray moder° of lesinges,°   *mother / lies*
And of deceite and cursed forsweringes,
305 Blaspheme of Crist, manslaughtre, and wast° also   *waste*
Of catel° and of time; and ferthermo,   *property*
It is repreve° and contrarye of honour   *disgrace*
For to been holden a commune hasardour,°   *gambler*
And evere the hyer he is of estat

---

1. Before Samson's birth an angel told his
mother that he would be a Nazarite through-
out his life; members of this sect took no
strong drink.
2. Stuck pig. "Honeste cure": care for self-
respect.
3. A town in Spain.
4. Fishstreet and Cheapside in the London
market district.

5. The Pardoner is joking about the illegal
custom of adulterating fine wines of Bordeaux
and La Rochelle with strong Spanish wine.
6. Distinguished deeds.
7. Attila was the leader of the Huns who cap-
tured Rome in the 5th century.
8. Lemuel's mother told him that kings should
not drink (Proverbs xxxi.4–5).
9. I.e., administer.

10 The more is he holden desolat.[1]
If that a prince useth hasardrye,
In alle governance and policye
He is, as by commune opinioun,
Yholde the lasse° in reputacioun. — *less*

15   Stilbon, that was a wis embassadour,
Was sent to Corinthe in ful greet honour
Fro Lacedomye° to make hir alliaunce, — *Sparta*
And whan he cam him happede° parchaunce — *it happened*
That alle the gretteste° that were of that lond — *greatest*
20 Playing at the hasard he hem foond,° — *found*
For which as soone as it mighte be
He stal him[2] hoom again to his contree,
And saide, "Ther wol I nat lese° my name, — *lose*
N'I wol nat take on me so greet defame° — *dishonor*
25 You to allye unto none hasardours:
Sendeth othere wise embassadours,
For by my trouthe, me were levere[3] die
Than I you sholde to hasardours allye.
For ye that been so glorious in honours
30 Shal nat allye you with hasardours
As by my wil, ne as by my tretee."° — *treaty*
This wise philosophre, thus saide he.
    Looke eek that to the king Demetrius
The King of Parthes,° as the book[4] saith us, — *Parthians*
35 Sente him a paire of dees° of gold in scorn, — *dice*
For he hadde used hasard therbiforn,
For which he heeld his glorye or his renown
At no value or reputacioun.
Lordes may finden other manere play
40 Honeste° ynough to drive the day away; — *honorable*
    Now wol I speke of othes false and grete
A word or two, as olde bookes trete:
    Greet swering is a thing abhominable,
And fals swering is yit more reprevable.° — *reprehensible*
45 The hye God forbad swering at al—
Witnesse on Mathew.[5] But in special
Of swering saith the holy Jeremie,[6]
"Thou shalt swere sooth thine othes and nat lie,
And swere in doom[7] and eek in rightwisnesse,
50 But idel swering is a cursedness."° — *wickedness*
    Biholde and see that in the firste Table[8]
Of hye Goddes heestes° honorable — *commandments*
How that the seconde heeste of him is this:
"Take nat my name in idel or amis."
55 Lo, rather° he forbedeth swich swering — *sooner*
Than homicide, or many a cursed thing.
I saye that as by ordre thus it stondeth—
This knoweth that[9] his heestes understondeth
How that the seconde heeste of God is that.
60 And fertherover,° I wol thee telle al plat° — *moreover / flat*
That vengeance shal nat parten° from his hous — *depart*

---

1. I.e., dissolute.
2. He stole away.
3. I had rather.
4. The book that relates this and the previous incident is the *Policraticus* of the 12th-century Latin writer, John of Salisbury.
5. "But I say unto you, Swear not at all"
(Matthew v.34).
6. Jeremiah (iv.2).
7. Equity; "rightwisnesse": righteousness.
8. I.e., the first four of the Ten Commandments.
9. I.e., he that.

That of his othes is too outrageous.
"By Goddes precious herte!" and "By his nailes!"°   *fingernails*
And "By the blood of Crist that is in Hailes,[1]
365 Sevene is my chaunce, and thyn is cink and traye!"[2]
"By Goddes armes, if thou falsly playe
This daggere shal thurghout thyn herte go!"
This fruit cometh of the bicche bones[3] two—
Forswering, ire, falsnesse, homicide.
370 Now for the love of Crist that for us dyde,
Lete° youre othes bothe grete and smale.   *leave*
But sires, now wol I telle forth my tale.
        Thise riotoures° three of whiche I telle,   *revelers*
Longe erst er prime[4] ronge of any belle,
375 Were set hem in a taverne to drinke,
And as they sat they herde a belle clinke
Biforn a cors° was caried to his grave.   *corpse*
That oon of hem gan callen to his knave:°   *servant*
"Go bet,"[5] quod he, "and axe° redily°   *ask / promptly*
380 What cors is this that passeth heer forby,
And looke° that thou reporte his name weel."°   *be sure / well*
        "Sire," quod this boy, "it needeth neveradeel:[6]
It was me told er ye cam heer two houres.
He was, pardee, an old felawe of youres,
385 And sodeinly he was yslain tonight,°   *last night*
Fordronke° as he sat on his bench upright;   *very drunk*
Ther cam a privee° thief men clepeth° Deeth,   *stealthy / call*
That in this contree al the peple sleeth,°   *slays*
And with his spere he smoot his herte atwo,
390 And he wente his way withouten wordes mo.
He hath a thousand slain this° pestilence.   *during this*
And maister, er ye come in his presence,
Me thinketh that it were necessarye
For to be war of swich an adversarye;
395 Beeth redy for to meete him everemore:
Thus taughte me my dame.° I saye namore."   *mother*
        "By Sainte Marye," saide this taverner,
"The child saith sooth, for he hath slain this yeer,
Henne° over a mile, within a greet village,   *hence*
400 Bothe man and womman, child and hine° and page.   *farm laborer*
I trowe° his habitacion be there.   *believe*
To been avised° greet wisdom it were   *wary*
Er that he dide a man a dishonour."
        "Ye, Goddes armes," quod this riotour,
405 "Is it swich peril with him for to meete?
I shal him seeke by way and eek by streete,[7]
I make avow to Goddes digne° bones.   *worthy*
Herkneth, felawes, we three been alle ones:°   *of one mind*
Lat eech of us holde up his hand to other
410 And eech of us bicome otheres brother,
And we wol sleen this false traitour Deeth.
He shal be slain, he that so manye sleeth,
By Goddes dignitee, er it be night."
        Togidres han thise three hir trouthes plight[8]

---

1. An abbey in Gloucestershire supposed to possess some of Christ's blood.
2. Five and three.
3. I.e., damned dice.
4. Long before 9 A.M.
5. Better, i.e., quick.
6. It isn't a bit necessary.
7. By highway and byway.
8. Pledged their words of honor.

415 To live and dien eech of hem with other,	
As though he were his owene ybore° brother.	*born*
And up they sterte,° al dronken in this rage,	*started*
And forth they goon towardes that village	
Of which the taverner hadde spoke biforn.	
420 And many a grisly ooth thanne han they sworn,	
And Cristes blessed body they torente:°	*tore apart*
Deeth shal be deed° if that they may him hente.°	*dead / catch*
Whan they han goon nat fully half a mile,	
Right as they wolde han treden° over a stile,	*stepped*
425 An old man and a poore with hem mette;	
This olde man ful mekely hem grette,°	*greeted*
And saide thus, "Now lordes, God you see."[9]	
The pruddeste° of thise riotoures three	*proudest*
Answerde again, "What, carl° with sory grace,	*churl*
430 Why artou al forwrapped save thy face?	
Why livestou so longe in so greet age?"	
This olde man gan looke in his visage,	
And saide thus, "For° I ne can nat finde	*because*
A man, though that I walked into Inde,	
435 Neither in citee ne in no village,	
That wolde chaunge his youthe for myn age;	
And therfore moot I han myn age stille,	
As longe time as it is Goddes wille.	
"Ne Deeth, allas, ne wol nat have my lif.	
440 Thus walke I lik a resteless caitif,°	*captive*
And on the ground which is my modres° gate	*mother's*
I knokke with my staf both erly and late,	
And saye, 'Leve° moder, leet me in:	*dear*
Lo, how I vanisshe, flessh and blood and skin.	
445 Allas, whan shal my bones been at reste?	
Moder, with you wolde I chaunge° my cheste[1]	*exchange*
That in my chambre longe time hath be,	
Ye, for an haire-clout[2] to wrappe me.'	
But yit to me she wol nat do that grace,	
450 For which ful pale and welked° is my face.	*withered*
But sires, to you it is no curteisye	
To speken to an old man vilainye,°	*rudeness*
But° he trespasse° in word or elles in deede.	*unless / offend*
In Holy Writ ye may yourself wel rede,	
455 'Agains[3] an old man, hoor° upon his heed,	*hoar*
Ye shal arise.'[4] Wherfore I yive you reed,°	*advice*
Ne dooth unto an old man noon harm now,	
Namore than that ye wolde men dide to you	
In age, if that ye so longe abide.	
460 And God be with you wher ye go° or ride:	*walk*
I moot go thider as I have to go."	
"Nay, olde cherl, by God thou shalt nat so,"	
Saide this other hasardour anoon.	
"Thou partest nat so lightly,° by Saint John!	*easily*
465 Thou speke° right now of thilke traitour Deeth,	*spoke*
That in this contree alle oure freendes sleeth:	
Have here my trouthe, as thou art his espye,	
Tel wher he is, or thou shalt it abye,°	*pay for*
By God and by the holy sacrament!	

9. May God protect you.
1. Chest for one's belongings, used here as the symbol for life—or perhaps a coffin.
2. Haircloth, for a winding sheet.
3. In the presence of.
4. Cf. Leviticus xix.32.

470 For soothly thou art oon of his assent[5]
To sleen us yonge folk, thou false thief."
"Now sires," quod he, "if that ye be so lief°   *anxious*
To finde Deeth, turne up this crooked way,
For in that grove I lafte° him, by my fay,°   *left / faith*
475 Under a tree, and ther he wol abide:
Nat for youre boost° he wol him no thing hide.   *boast*
See ye that ook?° Right ther ye shal him finde.   *oak*
God save you, that boughte again[6] mankinde,
And you amende." Thus saide this olde man.
480   And everich of thise riotoures ran
Til he cam to that tree, and ther they founde
Of florins° fine of gold ycoined rounde   *coins*
Wel neigh an eighte busshels as hem thoughte—
Ne lenger thanne after Deeth they soughte,
485 But eech of hem so glad was of the sighte,
For that the florins been so faire and brighte,
That down they sette hem by this precious hoord.
The worste of hem he spak the firste word:
"Bretheren," quod he, "take keep° what that I saye: *heed*
490 My wit is greet though that I bourde° and playe.   *joke*
This tresor hath Fortune unto us yiven
In mirthe and jolitee oure lif to liven,
And lightly° as it cometh so wol we spende.   *easily*
Ey, Goddes precious dignitee, who wende[7]
495 Today that we sholde han so fair a grace?
But mighte this gold be caried fro this place
Hoom to myn hous—or elles unto youres—
For wel ye woot that al this gold is oures—
Thanne were we in heigh felicitee.
500 But trewely, by daye it mighte nat be:
Men wolde sayn that we were theves stronge,°   *flagrant*
And for oure owene tresor doon us honge.[8]
This tresor moste ycaried be by nighte,
As wisely and as slyly as it mighte.
505 Therfore I rede° that cut° amonges us alle   *advise / lots*
Be drawe, and lat see wher the cut wol falle;
And he that hath the cut with herte blithe
Shal renne° to the town, and that ful swithe,°   *run / quickly*
And bringe us breed and win ful prively;
510 And two of us shal keepen° subtilly   *guard*
This tresor wel, and if he wol nat tarye,
Whan it is night we wol this tresor carye
By oon assent wher as us thinketh best."
That oon of hem the cut broughte in his fest°   *fist*
515 And bad hem drawe and looke wher it wol falle;
And it fil° on the yongeste of hem alle,   *fell*
And forth toward the town he wente anoon.
And also° soone as that he was agoon,°   *as / gone away*
That oon of hem spak thus unto that other:
520 "Thou knowest wel thou art my sworen brother;
Thy profit wol I telle thee anoon:
Thou woost wel that oure felawe is agoon,
And here is gold, and that ful greet plentee,
That shal departed° been among us three.   *divided*

5. I.e., one of his party.
6. Redeemed.
7. Who would have supposed.
8. Have us hanged.

525 But nathelees, if I can shape° it so   *arrange*
That it departed were among us two,
Hadde I nat doon a freendes turn to thee?"
   That other answerde, "I noot[9] how that may be:
He woot that the gold is with us twaye.
530 What shal we doon? What shal we to him saye?"
"Shal it be conseil?"[1] saide the firste shrewe.°   *villain*
"And I shal telle in a wordes fewe
What we shul doon, and bringe it wel aboute."
   "I graunte," quod that other, "out of doute,
535 That by my trouthe I wol thee nat biwraye."°   *expose*
   "Now," quod the firste, "thou woost wel we be twaye,
And two of us shal strenger° be than oon: *stronger*
Looke whan that he is set that right anoon
Aris as though thou woldest with him playe,
540 And I shal rive° him thurgh the sides twaye,   *pierce*
Whil that thou strugelest with him as in game,
And with thy daggere looke thou do the same;
And thanne shal al this gold departed be,
My dere freend, bitwixe thee and me.
545 Thanne we may bothe oure lustes° al fulfille,   *desires*
And playe at dees° right at oure owene wille."   *dice*
And thus accorded been thise shrewes twaye
To sleen the thridde, as ye han herd me saye.
   This yongeste, which that wente to the town,
550 Ful ofte in herte he rolleth up and down
The beautee of thise florins newe and brighte.
"O Lord," quod he, "if so were that I mighte
Have al this tresor to myself allone,
Ther is no man that liveth under the trone°   *throne*
555 Of God that sholde live so merye as I."
And at the laste the feend oure enemy
Putte in his thought that he sholde poison beye,°   *buy*
With which he mighte sleen his felawes twaye—
Forwhy° the feend foond him in swich livinge   *because*
560 That he hadde leve° him to sorwe bringe:[2]   *permission*
For this was outrely° his fulle entente,   *plainly*
To sleen hem bothe, and nevere to repente.
   And forth he gooth—no lenger wolde he tarye—
Into the town unto a pothecarye,°   *apothecary*
565 And prayed him that he him wolde selle
Som poison that he mighte his rattes quelle,°   *kill*
And eek ther was a polcat[3] in his hawe°   *yard*
That, as he saide, his capons hadde yslawe,°   *slain*
And fain he wolde wreke him[4] if he mighte
570 On vermin that destroyed him[5] by nighte.
   The pothecarye answerde, "And thou shalt have
A thing that, also° God my soule save,   *as*
In al this world there is no creature
That ete or dronke hath of this confiture°—   *mixture*
575 Nat but the mountance° of a corn° of whete—   *amount / grain*
That he ne shal his lif anoon forlete.°   *lose*
Ye, sterve° he shal, and that in lasse° while   *die / less*

---

9. Don't know.
1. A secret.
2. Christian doctrine teaches that the devil may not tempt men except with God's permission.
3. A weasel-like animal.
4. He would gladly avenge himself.
5. I.e., were ruining his farming.

Than thou wolt goon a paas[6] nat but a mile,
The poison is so strong and violent."
580 This cursed man hath in his hand yhent°   *taken*
This poison in a box and sith° he ran   *then*
Into the nexte streete unto a man
And borwed of him large botels three,
And in the two his poison poured he—
585 The thridde he kepte clene for his drinke,
For al the night he shoop him[7] for to swinke°.   *work*
In carying of the gold out of that place.
And whan this riotour with sory grace
Hadde filled with win his grete botels three,
590 To his felawes again repaireth he.
    What needeth it to sermone of it more?
For right as they had cast° his deeth bifore,   *plotted*
Right so they han him slain, and that anoon.
And whan that this was doon, thus spak that oon:
595 "Now lat us sitte and drinke and make us merye,
And afterward we wol his body berye."°   *bury*
And with that word it happed him par cas[8]
To take the botel ther the poison was,
And drank, and yaf his felawe drinke also,
600 For which anoon they storven° bothe two.   *died*
    But certes I suppose that Avicen
Wroot nevere in no canon ne in no *fen*[9]
Mo wonder signes[1] of empoisoning
Than hadde thise wrecches two er hir ending:
605 Thus ended been thise homicides two,
And eek the false empoisonere also.
    O cursed sinne of alle cursednesse!
O traitours homicide, O wikkednesse!
O glotonye, luxure,° and hasardrye!   *lechery*
610 Thou blasphemour of Crist with vilainye
And othes grete of usage° and of pride!   *habit*
Allas, mankinde, how may it bitide
That to thy Creatour which that thee wroughte,
And with his precious herte blood thee boughte,°   *redeemed*
615 Thou art so fals and so unkinde,° allas?   *unnatural*
    Now goode men, God foryive you youre trespas,
And ware° you fro the sinne of avarice: *guard*
Myn holy pardon may you alle warice°—   *save*
So that ye offre nobles or sterlinges,[2]
620 Or elles silver brooches, spoones, ringes.
Boweth your heed under this holy bulle!
Cometh up, ye wives, offreth of youre wolle!°   *wool*
Youre name I entre here in my rolle: anoon
Into the blisse of hevene shul ye goon.
625 I you assoile° by myn heigh power—   *absolve*
Ye that wol offre—as clene and eek as cleer
As ye were born.—And lo, sires, thus I preche.
And Jesu Crist that is oure soules leeche°   *physician*
So graunte you his pardon to receive,
630 For that is best—I wol you nat deceive.

6. Take a walk.
7. He was preparing.
8. By chance.
9. The *Canon of Medicine*, by Avicenna, an
11th-century Arabic philosopher, was divided

into sections called *"fens."*
1. More wonderful symptoms.
2. "Nobles" and "sterlinges" were valuable
coins.

The Epilogue

"But sires, oo word forgat I in my tale:
I have relikes and pardon in my male°   bag
As faire as any man in Engelond,
Whiche were me yiven by the Popes hond.
635 If any of you wol of devocioun
Offren and han myn absolucioun,
Come forth anoon, and kneeleth here adown,
And mekely receiveth my pardoun,
Or elles taketh pardon as ye wende,
640 Al newe and fressh at every miles ende—
So that ye offre alway newe and newe³
Nobles or pens whiche that be goode and trewe.
It is an honour to everich that is heer
That ye have a suffisant° pardoner   competent
645 T'assoile you in contrees as ye ride,
For aventures whiche that may bitide:
Paraventure ther may falle oon or two
Down of his hors and breke his nekke atwo;
Looke which a suretee° is it to you alle   safeguard
650 That I am in youre felaweshipe yfalle
That may·assoile you, bothe more and lasse,⁴
Whan that the soule shal fro the body passe.
I rede° that oure Hoste shal biginne,   advise
For he is most envoluped° in sinne.   involved
655 Com forth, sire Host, and offre first anoon,
And thou shalt kisse the relikes everichoon,°   each one
Ye, for a grote: unbokele° anoon thy purs."   unbuckle
    "Nay, nay," quod he, "thanne have I Cristes curs!
Lat be," quod he, "it shal nat be, so theech!°   may I thrive
660 Thou woldest make me kisse thyn olde breech°   breeches
And swere it were a relik of a saint,
Though it were with thy fundament depeint.°   stained
But, by the crois which that Sainte Elaine foond,⁵
I wolde I hadde thy coilons° in myn hond,   testicles
665 In stede of relikes or of saintuarye.°   relic-box
Lat cutte hem of: I wol thee helpe hem carye.
They shal be shrined in an hogges tord."°   turd
    This Pardoner answerde nat a word:
So wroth he was no word ne wolde he saye.
670 "Now," quod oure Host, "I wol no lenger playe
With thee, ne with noon other angry man."
    But right anoon the worthy Knight bigan,
Whan that he sawgh that al the peple lough,°   laughed
"Namore of this, for it is right ynough.
675 Sire Pardoner, be glad and merye of cheere,
And ye, sire Host that been to me so dere,
I praye you that ye kisse the Pardoner,
And Pardoner, I praye thee, draw thee neer,
And as we diden lat us laughe and playe."
680 Anoon they kiste and riden forth hir waye.

---

3. Over and over.
4. Both high and low (i.e., everybody).
5. I.e., by the cross that St. Helena found.

Helena, mother of Constantine the Great, was
reputed to have found the True Cross.

The Nun's Priest's Tale

A poore widwe somdeel stape° in age	*advanced*
Was whilom° dwelling in a narwe° cotage,	*once upon a time / small*
Biside a grove, stonding in a dale:	
This widwe of which I telle you my tale,	
5 Sin thilke° day that she was last a wif,	*that same*
In pacience ladde° a ful simple lif.	*led*
For litel was hir catel° and hir rente,°	*property / income*
By housbondrye° of swich as God hire sente	*economy*
She foond° hirself and eek hir doughtren two.	*provided for*
10 Three large sowes hadde she and namo,	
Three kin,° and eek a sheep that highte Malle.	*cows*
Ful sooty was hir bowr° and eek hir halle,	*bedroom*
In which she eet ful many a sclendre° meel;	*scanty*
Of poinant° sauce hire needed neveradeel:	*pungent*
15 No daintee morsel passed thurgh hir throte—	
Hir diete was accordant to hir cote.°	*cottage*
Repleccioun° ne made hire nevere sik:	*overeating*
Attempre° diete was al hir physik,°	*moderate / medicine*
And exercise and hertes suffisaunce.°	*contentment*
20 The goute lette hire nothing for to daunce,[6]	
N'apoplexye shente° nat hir heed.°	*hurt / head*
No win ne drank she, neither whit ne reed:°	*red*
Hir boord° was served most with whit and blak,[7]	*table*
Milk and brown breed, in which she foond no lak;[8]	
25 Seind bacon, and somtime an ey° or twaye,	*egg*
For she was as it were a manere daye.[9]	
A yeerd° she hadde, enclosed al withoute	*yard*
With stikkes, and a drye dich aboute,	
In which she hadde a cok heet° Chauntecleer:	*named*
30 In al the land of crowing nas° his peer.	*was not*
His vois was merier than the merye orgon	
On massedayes that in the chirche goon;[1]	
Wel sikerer[2] was his crowing in his logge°	*dwelling*
Than is a clok or an abbeye orlogge;°	*timepiece*
35 By nature he knew eech ascensioun	
Of th'equinoxial[3] in thilke town:	
For whan degrees fifteene were ascended,	
Thanne crew° he that it mighte nat been amended.°	*crowed / improved*
His comb was redder than the fin coral,	
40 And batailed° as it were a castel wal;	*battlemented*
His bile° was blak, and as the jeet° it shoon;	*bill / jet*
Like asure° were his legges and his toon;°	*lapis lazuli / toes*
His nailes whitter° than the lilye flowr,	*whiter*
And lik the burned° gold was his colour.	*burnished*
45 This gentil cok hadde in his governaunce	
Sevene hennes for to doon al his plesaunce,°	*pleasure*
Whiche were his sustres and his paramours,[4]	
And wonder like to him as of colours;	

---

6. **The gout didn't hinder her at all from dancing.**
7. I.e., milk and bread.
8. Found no fault. "Seind": scorched (i.e., broiled).
9. I.e., a kind of dairymaid.
1. I.e., is played.
2. More reliable.

3. I.e., he knew by instinct each step in the progression of the celestial equator. The celestial equator was thought to make a 360-degree rotation around the earth every 24 hours; therefore a progression of 15 degrees would be equal to the passage of an hour (line 37).
4. His sisters and his mistresses.

Of whiche the faireste hewed° on hir throte   *colored*
50 Was cleped faire damoisele Pertelote:
Curteis she was, discreet, and debonaire,°   *meek*
And compaignable,° and bar° hirself so faire,   *companionable / bore*
Sin thilke day that she was seven night old,
That trewely she hath the herte in hold
55 Of Chauntecleer, loken° in every lith.°   *locked / limb*
He loved hire so that wel was him therwith.[5]
But swich a joye was it to heere hem singe,
Whan that the brighte sonne gan to springe,
In sweete accord *My Lief is Faren in Londe*[6]—
60 For thilke time, as I have understonde,
Beestes and briddes couden speke and singe.
     And so bifel that in a daweninge,
As Chauntecleer among his wives alle
Sat on his perche that was in the halle,
65 And next him sat this faire Pertelote,
This Chauntecleer gan gronen in his throte,
As man that in his dreem is drecched° sore.   *troubled*
     And whan that Pertelote thus herde him rore,
She was agast, and saide, "Herte dere,
70 What aileth you to grone in this manere?
Ye been a verray slepere,[7] fy, for shame!"
     And he answerde and said thus, "Madame,
I praye you that ye take it nat agrief.°   *amiss*
By God, me mette I was in swich meschief[8]
75 Right now, that yit myn herte is sore afright.
Now God," quod he, "my swevene recche aright.[9]
And keepe my body out of foul prisoun!
Me mette how that I romed up and down
Within oure yeerd, wher as I sawgh a beest,
80 Was lik an hound and wolde han maad arrest[1]
Upon my body, and han had me deed.[2]
His colour was bitwixe yelow and reed,
And tipped was his tail and bothe his eres
With blak, unlik the remenant° of his heres;°   *rest / hairs*
85 His snoute smal, with glowing yën twaye.
Yit of his look for fere almost I deye:°   *die*
This caused me my groning, doutelees."
     "Avoi,"° quod she, "fy on you, hertelees!°   *fie / coward*
Allas," quod she, "for by that God above,
90 Now han ye lost myn herte and al my love!
I can nat love a coward, by my faith.
For certes, what so any womman saith,
We alle desiren, if it mighte be,
To han housbondes hardy, wise, and free,°   *generous*
95 And secree,° and no nigard, ne no fool,   *discreet*
Ne him that is agast of every tool,°   *weapon*
Ne noon avauntour.° By that God above,   *boaster*
How dorste ye sayn for shame unto youre love
That any thing mighte make you aferd?
100 Have ye no mannes herte and han a beerd?
Allas, and conne° ye been agast of swevenes?°   *can / dreams*

5. That he was well contented.
6. A popular song of the time.
7. I.e., sound sleeper.
8. I dreamed that I was in such misfortune.

9. Interpret my dream correctly (i.e., in an auspicious manner).
1. Would have laid hold.
2. I.e., killed me.

No thing, God woot, but vanitee³ in swevene is!
Swevenes engendren of replexiouns,⁴
And ofte of fume° and of complexiouns,°   *gas / bodily humors*
105 Whan humours been too habundant in a wight.⁵
Certes, this dreem which ye han met° tonight   *dreamed*
Comth of the grete superfluitee
Of youre rede colera,⁶ pardee,
Which causeth folk to dreden° in hir dremes   *fear*
110 Of arwes,° and of fir with rede lemes,°   *arrows / flames*
Of rede beestes, that they wol hem bite,
Of contek,° and of whelpes grete and lite⁷—   *strife*
Right° as the humour of malencolye⁸   *just*
Causeth ful many a man in sleep to crye
115 For fere of blake beres° or boles° blake,   *bears / bulls*
Or elles blake develes wol hem take.
Of othere humours coude I tell also
That werken many a man in sleep ful wo,
But I wol passe as lightly° as I can.   *quickly*
120 Lo, Caton,⁹ which that was so wis a man,
Saide he nat thus? 'Ne do no fors of¹ dremes.'
Now, sire," quod she, "whan we flee fro the bemes,²
For Goddes love, as take som laxatif.
Up° peril of my soule and of my lif,   *upon*
125 I conseile you the beste, I wol nat lie,
That bothe of colere and of malencolye
Ye purge you; and for° ye shal nat tarye,   *in order that*
Though in this town is noon apothecarye,
I shal myself to herbes techen you,
130 That shal been for youre hele³ and for youre prow,
And in oure yeerd tho herbes shal I finde,
The whiche han of hir propretee by kinde°   *nature*
To purge you binethe and eek above;
Foryet° nat this, for Goddes owene love.   *forget*
135 Ye been ful colerik° of complexioun;   *bilious*
Ware° the sonne in his ascencioun   *beware that*
Ne finde you nat repleet° of humours hote;°   *filled / hot*
And if it do, I dar wel laye° a grote   *bet*
That ye shul have a fevere terciane,⁴
140 Or an agu that may be youre bane.°   *death*
A day or two ye shul han digestives
Of wormes, er ye take youre laxatives
Of lauriol, centaure, and fumetere,⁵
Or elles of ellebor° that groweth there,   *hellebore*
145 Of catapuce,° or of gaitres beries,°   *caper berry / gaiter berry*
Of herbe-ive° growing in oure yeerd ther merye is.⁶   *herb ivy*
Pekke hem right up as they growe and ete hem in.
Be merye, housbonde, for youre fader kin!
Dredeth no dreem: I can saye you namore."
150 "Madame," quod he, "graunt mercy of youre lore.⁷

---

3. I.e., empty illusion.
4. Dreams have their origin in overeating.
5. I.e., when humors are too abundant in a person. Pertelote's diagnosis is based on the familiar concept that an overabundance of one of the bodily humors in a person affected his temperament.
6. Red bile.
7. And of big and little dogs.
8. I.e., black bile.
9. Dionysius Cato, supposed author of a book

of maxims used in elementary education.
1. Pay no attention to.
2. Fly down from the rafters.
3. Health; "prow": benefit.
4. Tertian (recurring every other day).
5. Of laureole, centaury, and fumitory. These, and the herbs mentioned in the next lines, were all common medieval medicines used as cathartics.
6. Where it is pleasant.
7. Many thanks for your instruction.

But nathelees, as touching daun° Catoun,   *master*
That hath of wisdom swich a greet renown,
Though that he bad no dremes for to drede,
By God, men may in olde bookes rede
155 Of many a man more of auctoritee°   *authority*
Than evere Caton was, so mote I thee,°   *thrive*
That al the revers sayn of his sentence,°   *opinion*
And han wel founden by experience
That dremes been significaciouns
160 As wel of joye as tribulaciouns
That folk enduren in this lif present.
Ther needeth make of this noon argument:
The verray preve[8] sheweth it in deede.
    "Oon of the gretteste auctour[9] that men rede
165 Saith thus, that whilom two felawes wente
On pilgrimage in a ful good entente,
And happed so they comen in a town,
Wher as ther was swich congregacioun
Of peple, and eek so strait of herbergage,[1]
170 That they ne founde as muche as oo cotage
In which they bothe mighte ylogged° be;   *lodged*
Wherfore they mosten° of necessitee   *must*
As for that night departe° compaignye.   *part*
And eech of hem gooth to his hostelrye,
175 And took his logging as it wolde falle.°   *befall*
That oon of hem was logged in a stalle,
Fer° in a yeerd, with oxen of the plough;   *far away*
That other man was logged wel ynough,
As was his aventure° or his fortune,   *lot*
180 That us governeth alle as in commune.
And so bifel that longe er it were day,
This man mette° in his bed, ther as he lay,   *dreamed*
How that his felawe gan upon him calle,
And saide, 'Allas, for in an oxes stalle
185 This night I shal be mordred° ther I lie!   *murdered*
Now help me, dere brother, or I die!
In alle haste com to me,' he saide.
    "This man out of his sleep for fere abraide,°   *started up*
But whan that he was wakened of his sleep,
190 He turned him and took of this no keep:°   *heed*
Him thoughte his dreem nas but a vanitee.
Thus twies in his sleeping dremed he,
And atte thridde time yit his felawe
Cam, as him thoughte, and saide, 'I am now slawe:°   *slain*
195 Bihold my bloody woundes deepe and wide.
Aris up erly in the morwe tide[2]
And atte west gate of the town,' quod he,
'A carte ful of dong° ther shaltou see,   *dung*
In which my body is hid ful prively:
200 Do thilke carte arresten boldely.[3]
My gold caused my mordre, sooth to sayn'—
And tolde him every point how he was slain,
With a ful pitous face, pale of hewe.
And truste wel, his dreem he foond° ful trewe,   *found*

8. Actual experience.
9. I.e., one of the greatest authors (perhaps
Cicero).

1. And also such a shortage of lodging.
2. In the morning.
3. Boldly have this same cart stopped.

205 For on the morwe° as soone as it was day,   *morning*
    To his felawes in° he took the way,   *lodging*
    And whan that he cam to this oxes stalle,
    After his felawe he bigan to calle.
    "The hostiler° answerde him anoon,   *innkeeper*
210 And saide, 'Sire, youre felawe is agoon:°   *gone away*
    As soone as day he wente out of the town.'
        "This man gan fallen in suspecioun,
    Remembring on his dremes that he mette;°   *dreamed*
    And forth he gooth, no lenger wolde he lette,°   *tarry*
215 Unto the west gate of the town, and foond
    A dong carte, wente as it were to donge° lond,   *put manure on*
    That was arrayed in that same wise
    As ye han herd the dede° man devise;   *dead*
    And with an hardy herte he gan to crye,
220 'Vengeance and justice of this felonye!
    My felawe mordred is this same night,
    And in this carte he lith° gaping upright!°   *lies / supine*
    I crye out on the ministres,' quod he,
    'That sholde keepe and rulen this citee.
225 Harrow,° allas, here lith my felawe slain!'   *help*
    What sholde I more unto this tale sayn?
    The peple up sterte° and caste the carte to grounde,   *started*
    And in the middel of the dong they founde
    The dede man that mordred was al newe.[4]
230   "O blisful God that art so just and trewe,
    Lo, how that thou biwrayest° mordre alway!   *disclose*
    Mordre wol out, that see we day by day:
    Mordre is so wlatsom° and abhominable   *loathsome*
    To God that is so just and resonable,
235 That he ne wol nat suffre it heled° be,   *concealed*
    Though it abide a yeer or two or three.
    Mordre wol out: this my conclusioun.
    And right anoon ministres of that town
    Han hent° the cartere and so sore him pined,°   *seized / tortured*
240 And eek the hostiler so sore engined,°   *racked*
    That they biknewe° hir wikkednesse anoon,   *confessed*
    And were anhanged° by the nekke boon.   *hanged*
    Here may men seen that dremes been to drede.[5]
        "And certes, in the same book I rede—
245 Right in the nexte chapitre after this—
    I gabbe° nat, so have I joye or blis—   *lie*
    Two men that wolde han passed over see
    For certain cause into a fer contree,
    If that the wind ne hadde been contrarye
250 That made hem in a citee for to tarye,
    That stood ful merye upon an haven° side—   *harbor's*
    But on a day again° the even tide   *toward*
    The wind gan chaunge, and blewe right as hem leste:[6]
    Jolif° and glad they wenten unto reste,   *merry*
255 And casten hem[7] ful erly for to saile.
        "But to that oo man fil° a greet mervaile;   *befell*
    That oon of hem, in sleeping as he lay,
    Him mette[8] a wonder dreem again the day:

4. Recently.
5. Worthy of being feared.
6. Just as they wished.

7. Determined.
8. He dreamed.

Him thoughte a man stood by his beddes side,
260 And him comanded that he sholde abide,
And saide him thus, 'If thou tomorwe wende,
Thou shalt be dreint:° my tale is at an ende.'   *drowned*
    "He wook and tolde his felawe what he mette,
And prayed him his viage° to lette;°   *voyage / delay*
265 As for that day he prayed him to bide.
    "His felawe that lay by his beddes side
Gan for to laughe, and scorned him ful faste.°   *hard*
'No dreem,' quod he, 'may so myn herte agaste°   *terrify*
That I wol lette° for to do my thinges.°   *delay / business*
270 I sette nat a straw by thy dreminges,[9]
For swevenes been but vanitees and japes:[1]
Men dreme alday° of owles or of apes,[2]   *constantly*
And of many a maze° therwithal—   *delusion*
Men dreme of thing that nevere was ne shal.[3]
275 But sith I see that thou wolt here abide,
And thus forsleuthen° wilfully thy tide,°   *waste / time*
Good woot, it reweth me;[4] and have good day.'
And thus he took his leve and wente his way.
But er that he hadde half his cours ysailed—
280 Noot I nat why ne what meschaunce it ailed—
But casuelly the shippes botme rente,[5]
And ship and man under the water wente,
In sighte of othere shippes it biside,
That with hem sailed at the same tide.
285 And therfore, faire Pertelote so dere,
By swiche ensamples olde maistou lere°   *learn*
That no man sholde been too recchelees°   *careless*
Of dremes, for I saye thee doutelees
That many a dreem ful sore is for to drede.
290   "Lo, in the lif of Saint Kenelm[6] I rede—
That was Kenulphus sone, the noble king
Of Mercenrike°—how Kenelm mette a thing   *Mercia*
A lite° er he was mordred on a day.   *little*
His mordre in his avision° he sey.°   *dream / saw*
295 His norice° him expounded everydeel°   *nurse / entirely*
His swevene, and bad him for to keepe him[7] weel
For traison, but he nas but seven yeer old,
And therfore litel tale hath he told
Of any dreem,[8] so holy was his herte.
300 By God, I hadde levere than my sherte[9]
That ye hadde rad° his legende as have I.   *read*
    "Dame Pertelote, I saye you trewely,
Macrobeus,[1] that writ the *Avisioun*
In Affrike of the worthy Scipioun,
305 Affermeth° dremes, and saith that they been   *confirms*
Warning of thinges that men after seen.
    "And fertheremore, I praye you looketh wel
In the Olde Testament of Daniel,

9. I don't care a straw for your dreamings.
1. Dreams are but illusions and frauds.
2. I.e., of absurdities.
3. I.e., shall be.
4. I'm sorry.
5. I don't know why nor what was the trouble with it—but accidentally the ship's bottom split.
6. Kenelm succeeded his father as king of Mercia at the age of 7 but was slain by his aunt (in 821).
7. Guard himself.
8. Therefore he has set little store by any dream.
9. I.e., I'd give my shirt.
1. Macrobius wrote a famous commentary on Cicero's account in *De Republica* of the dream of Scipio Africanus Minor; the commentary came to be regarded as a standard authority on dream lore.

If he heeld° dremes any vanitee;[2]   *considered*
310 "Rede eek of Joseph[3] and ther shul ye see
Wher° dremes be sometime—I saye nat alle—   *whether*
Warning of thinges that shul after falle.
"Looke of Egypte the king daun Pharao,
His bakere and his botelere° also,   *butler*
315 Wher they ne felte noon effect in dremes.[4]
Whoso wol seeke actes of sondry remes°   *realms*
May rede of dremes many a wonder thing.
"Lo Cresus, which that was of Lyde° king,   *Lydia*
Mette° he nat that he sat upon a tree,   *dreamed*
320 Which signified he sholde anhanged° be?   *hanged*
"Lo here Andromacha, Ectores° wif,   *Hector's*
That day that Ector sholde lese° his lif,   *lose*
She dremed on the same night biforn
How that the lif of Ector sholde be lorn,°   *lost*
325 If thilke° day he wente into bataile;   *that same*
She warned him, but it mighte nat availe:°   *do any good*
He wente for to fighte nathelees,
But he was slain anoon° of Achilles.   *right away*
But thilke tale is al too long to telle,
330 And eek it is neigh day, I may nat dwelle.
Shortly I saye, as for conclusioun,
That I shal han of this avisioun[5]
Adversitee, and I saye ferthermoor
That I ne telle of[6] laxatives no stoor,
335 For they been venimes,° I woot it weel: *poisons*
I hem defye, I love hem neveradeel.°   *not a bit*
"Now lat us speke of mirthe and stinte° al this.   *stop*
Madame Pertelote, so have I blis,
Of oo thing God hath sente me large grace:
340 For whan I see the beautee of youre face—
Ye been so scarlet reed° aboute youre yën—   *red*
It maketh al my drede for to dien.
For also siker° as *In principio*,[7]   *certain*
Mulier est hominis confusio.[8]
345 Madame, the sentence° of this Latin is,   *meaning*
'Womman is mannes joye and al his blis.'
For whan I feele anight youre softe side—
Al be it that I may nat on you ride,
For that oure perche is maad so narwe, allas—
350 I am so ful of joye and of solas°   *delight*
That I defye bothe swevene and dreem."
And with that word he fleigh° down fro the beem,   *flew*
For it was day, and eek his hennes alle,
And with a "chuk" he gan hem for to calle,
355 For he hadde founde a corn lay in the yeerd.
Real° he was, he was namore aferd:°   *regal / afraid*
He fethered[9] Pertelote twenty time,
And trad[1] hire as ofte er it was prime.
He looketh as it were a grim leoun,
360 And on his toes he rometh up and doun:

2. See Daniel vii.
3. See Genesis xxxvii.
4. See Genesis xxxix–xli.
5. Divinely inspired dream (as opposed to the
more ordinary "swevene" or "dreem").
6. Set by.

7. A tag from the Gospel of St. John which
gives the essential premises of Christianity:
"In the beginning was the Word."
8. Woman is man's ruination.
9. I.e., embraced.
1. Trod, copulated with; "prime": 9 A.M.

Him deined[2] nat to sette his foot to grounde.
He chukketh whan he hath a corn yfounde,
And to him rennen° thanne his wives alle.   *run*
Thus royal, as a prince is in his halle,
365 Leve I this Chauntecleer in his pasture,
And after wol I telle his aventure.
    Whan that the month in which the world bigan,
That highte March, whan God first maked man,
Was compleet, and passed were also,
370 Sin March bigan, thritty days and two,[3]
Bifel that Chauntecleer in al his pride,
His sevene wives walking him biside,
Caste up his yën to the brighte sonne,
That in the signe of Taurus hadde yronne
375 Twenty degrees and oon and somwhat more,
And knew by kinde,° and by noon other lore,   *nature*
That it was prime, and crew with blisful stevene.°   *voice*
"The sonne," he saide, "is clomben[4] up on hevene
Fourty degrees and oon and more, ywis.
380 Madame Pertelote, my worldes blis,
Herkneth thise blisful briddes° how they singe,   *birds*
And see the fresshe flowres how they springe:
Ful is myn herte of revel and solas."
But sodeinly him fil° a sorweful cas,°   *befell / chance*
385 For evere the latter ende of joye is wo—
God woot that worldly joye is soone ago,
And if a rethor° coude faire endite,   *rhetorician*
He in a cronicle saufly° mighte it write,   *safely*
As for a soverein notabilitee.[5]
390 Now every wis man lat him herkne me:
This storye is also° trewe, I undertake,   *as*
As is the book of *Launcelot de Lake*,[6]
That wommen holde in ful greet reverence.
Now wol I turne again to my sentence.°   *main point*
395 A colfox[7] ful of sly iniquitee,
That in the grove hadde woned° yeres three,   *dwelled*
By heigh imaginacion forncast,[8]
The same night thurghout the hegges° brast°   *hedges / burst*
Into the yeerd ther Chauntecleer the faire
400 Was wont, and eek his wives, to repaire;
And in a bed of wortes° stille he lay   *cabbages*
Til it was passed undren° of the day,   *midmorning*
Waiting his time on Chauntecleer to falle,
As gladly doon thise homicides alle,
405 That in await liggen to mordre[9] men.
O false mordrour, lurking in thy den!
O newe Scariot![1] Newe Geniloun!
False dissimilour!° O Greek Sinoun,[2]   *dissembler*

2. He deigned.
3. The rhetorical time-telling is perhaps burlesque; it can be read as yielding the date April 3, though May 3 seems intended from lines 374–75: on May 3 the sun would have passed some twenty degrees through Taurus (the Bull), the second sign of the zodiac; the sun would be forty degrees from the horizon at 9 o'clock in the morning.
4. Has climbed.
5. Indisputable fact.
6. Romances of the courteous knight Lancelot

of the Lake were very popular.
7. Fox with black markings.
8. Predestined by divine planning.
9. That lie in ambush to murder.
1. Judas Iscariot. "Geniloun" is Ganelon, who betrayed Roland to the Saracens (in the medieval French epic *The Song of Roland*).
2. Sinon, who persuaded the Trojans to take the Greeks' wooden horse into their city—with, of course, the result that the city was destroyed.

That broughtest Troye al outrely° to sorwe!   *utterly*
410   O Chauntecleer, accursed be that morwe°   *morning*
That thou into the yeerd flaugh° fro the bemes!   *flew*
Thou were ful wel ywarned by thy dremes
That thilke day was perilous to thee;
But what that God forwoot° moot° needes be,   *foreknows / must*
415   After° the opinion of certain clerkes: *according to*
Witnesse on him that any parfit° clerk is   *perfect*
That in scole is greet altercacioun
In this matere, and greet disputisoun,°   *disputation*
And hath been of an hundred thousand men.
420   But I ne can nat bulte° it to the bren,°   *sift / husks*
As can the holy doctour Augustin,
Or Boece, or the bisshop Bradwardin[3]—
Wheither that Goddes worthy forwiting°   *foreknowledge*
Straineth me nedely[4] for to doon a thing
425   ("Nedely" clepe I simple necessitee),
Or elles if free chois be graunted me
To do that same thing or do it nought,
Though God forwoot° it er that I was wrought;   *foreknew*
Or if his witing° straineth neveradeel,   *knowledge*
430   But by necessitee condicionel[5]—
I wol nat han to do of swich matere:
My tale is of a cok, as ye may heere,
That took his conseil of his wif with sorwe,
To walken in the yeerd upon that morwe
435   That he hadde met° the dreem that I you tolde.   *dreamed*
Wommenes conseils been ful ofte colde,[6]
Wommanes conseil broughte us first to wo,
And made Adam fro Paradis to go,
Ther as he was ful merye and wel at ese.
440   But for I noot° to whom it mighte displese   *don't know*
If I conseil of wommen wolde blame,
Passe over, for I saide it in my game°—   *sport*
Rede auctours where they trete of swich matere,
And what they sayn of wommen ye may heere—
445   Thise been the cokkes wordes and nat mine:
I can noon harm of no womman divine.°   *guess*
    Faire in the sond° to bathe hire merily   *sand*
Lith° Pertelote, and alle hir sustres by,   *lies*
Again° the sonne, and Chauntecleer so free°   *in / noble*
450   Soong° merier than the mermaide in the see—   *sang*
For Physiologus[7] saith sikerly
How that they singen wel and merily.
    And so bifel that as he caste his yë
Among the wortes on a boterflye,°   *butterfly*
455   He was war of this fox that lay ful lowe.
No thing ne liste him[8] thanne for to crowe,
But cride anoon "Cok cok!" and up he sterte,°   *started*
As man that[9] was affrayed in his herte—
For naturelly a beest desireth flee

3. St. Augustine, Boethius (6th-century Roman philosopher, whose *Consolation of Philosophy* was translated by Chaucer), and Thomas Bradwardine (Archbishop of Canterbury, died 1349) were all concerned with the interrelationship between man's free will and God's foreknowledge.
4. Constrains me necessarily.
5. Boethius' "conditional necessity" permitted a large measure of free will.
6. I.e., baneful.
7. Supposed author of a bestiary, a book of moralized zoology describing both natural and supernatural animals (including mermaids).
8. He wished.
9. Like one who.

460 Fro his contrarye[1] if he may it see,
Though he nevere erst° hadde seen it with his yë. — *before*
This Chauntecleer, whan he gan him espye,
He wolde han fled, but that the fox anoon
Saide, "Gentil sire, allas, wher wol ye goon?
465 Be ye afraid of me that am youre freend?
Now certes, I were worse than a feend
If I to you wolde° harm or vilainye. — *meant*
I am nat come youre conseil° for t'espye, — *secrets*
But trewely the cause of my cominge
470 Was only for to herkne how that ye singe:
For trewely, ye han as merye a stevene° — *voice*
As any angel hath that is in hevene.
Therwith ye han in musik more feelinge
Than hadde Boece,[2] or any that can singe.
475 My lord your fader—God his soule blesse!—
And eek youre moder, of hir gentilesse,° — *gentility*
Han in myn hous ybeen, to my grete ese.
And certes sire, ful fain° wolde I you plese. — *gladly*
   "But for men speke of singing, I wol saye,
480 So mote I brouke[3] wel mine yën twaye,
Save ye, I herde nevere man so singe
As dide youre fader in the morweninge.
Certes, it was of herte[4] al that he soong.° — *sang*
And for to make his vois the more strong,
485 He wolde so paine him[5] that with bothe his yën
He moste winke,[6] so loude wolde he cryen;
And stonden on his tiptoon therwithal,
And strecche forth his nekke long and smal;
And eek he was of swich discrecioun
490 That ther nas no man in no regioun
That him in song or wisdom mighte passe.
I have wel rad° in *Daun Burnel the Asse*[7] — *read*
Among his vers how that ther was a cok,
For a preestes sone yaf him a knok[8]
495 Upon his leg whil he was yong and nice,° — *foolish*
He made him for to lese° his benefice.[9] — *lose*
But certain, ther nis no comparisoun
Bitwixe the wisdom and discrecioun
Of youre fader and of his subtiltee.
500 Now singeth, sire, for sainte° charitee! — *holy*
Lat see, conne° ye youre fader countrefete?"° — *can / imitate*
   This Chauntecleer his winges gan to bete,
As man that coude his traison nat espye,
So was he ravisshed with his flaterye.
505   Allas, ye lordes, many a fals flatour° — *flatterer*
Is in youre court, and many a losengeour,° — *deceiver*
That plesen you wel more, by my faith,
Than he that soothfastnesse° unto you saith! — *truth*
Redeth Ecclesiaste[1] of flaterye.
510 Beeth war, ye lordes, of hir trecherye.

---

1. I.e., his natural enemy.
2. Boethius also wrote a treatise on music.
3. So might I enjoy the use of.
4. Heartfelt.
5. Take pains.
6. He had to shut his eyes.
7. Master Brunellus, a discontented donkey, was the hero of a 12th-century satirical poem by Nigel Wireker.
8. Because a priest's son gave him a knock.
9. The offended cock neglected to crow so that his master, now grown to manhood, overslept, missing his ordination and losing his benefice.
1. The Book of Ecclesiasticus, in the Apocrypha.

This Chauntecleer stood hye upon his toos,
Strecching his nekke, and heeld his yën cloos,
And gan to crowe loude for the nones;°   *occasion*
And daun Russel the fox sterte° up atones,   *jumped*
515 And by the gargat° hente° Chauntecleer,   *throat / seized*
And on his bak toward the wode him beer,°   *bore*
For yit ne was ther no man that him sued.°   *followed*
  O destinee that maist nat been eschued!°   *eschewed*
Allas that Chauntecleer fleigh° fro the bemes!   *flew*
520 Allas his wif ne roughte nat of² dremes!
And on a Friday fil° al this meschaunce!   *befell*
  O Venus that art goddesse of plesaunce,
Sin that thy servant was this Chauntecleer,
And in thy service dide al his power—
525 More for delit than world³ to multiplye—
Why woldestou suffre him on thy day⁴ to die?
  O Gaufred,⁵ dere maister soverein,
That, whan thy worthy king Richard was slain
With shot,⁶ complainedest his deeth so sore,
530 Why ne hadde I now thy sentence and thy lore,⁷
The Friday for to chide as diden ye?
For on a Friday soothly slain was he.
Thanne wolde I shewe you how that I coulde plaine°   *lament*
For Chauntecleres drede and for his paine.
535   Certes, swich cry ne lamentacioun
Was nevere of ladies maad whan Ilioun°   *Ilium, Troy*
Was wonne, and Pyrrus⁸ with his straite swerd,
Whan he hadde hent° King Priam by the beerd   *seized*
And slain him, as saith us *Eneidos*,⁹
540 As maden alle the hennes in the cloos,°   *yard*
Whan they hadde seen of Chauntecleer the sighte.
But sovereinly° Dame Pertelote shrighte°   *splendidly / shrieked*
Ful louder than dide Hasdrubales¹ wif
Whan that hir housbonde hadde lost his lif,
545 And that the Romains hadden brend° Cartage: *burned*
She was so ful of torment and of rage°   *madness*
That wilfully unto the fir she sterte,°   *jumped*
And brende hirselven with a stedefast herte.
  O woful hennes, right so criden ye
550 As, whan that Nero brende the citee
Of Rome, criden senatoures wives
For that hir housbondes losten alle hir lives:²
Withouten gilt this Nero hath hem slain.
Now wol I turne to my tale again.
555   The sely° widwe and eek hir doughtres two   *innocent*
Herden thise hennes crye and maken wo,
And out at dores sterten° they anoon,   *leaped*
And sien° the fox toward the grove goon,   *saw*
And bar upon his bak the cok away,
560 And criden, "Out, harrow,° and wailaway,   *help*

2. Didn't care for.
3. I.e., population.
4. Friday is Venus' day.
5. Geoffrey of Vinsauf, a famous medieval rhetorician, who wrote a lament on the death of Richard I in which he scolded Friday, the day on which the king died.
6. I.e., a missile.
7. Thy wisdom and thy learning.

8. Pyrrhus was the Greek who slew Priam, king of Troy. "Straite": rigorous, unsparing.
9. As the *Aeneid* tells us.
1. Hasdrubal was king of Carthage when it was destroyed by the Romans.
2. According to the legend, Nero not only set fire to Rome (in A.D. 64) but also put many senators to death.

Ha, ha, the fox," and after him they ran,
And eek with staves many another man;
Ran Colle oure dogge, and Talbot and Gerland,[3]
And Malkin with a distaf in hir hand,

565 Ran cow and calf, and eek the verray hogges,
Sore aferd° for berking of the dogges   *frightened*
And shouting of the men and wommen eke.
They ronne° so hem thoughte hir herte breke;[4]   *ran*
They yelleden as feendes doon in helle;

570 The dokes° criden as men wolde hem quelle;°   *ducks / kill*
The gees for fere flowen° over the trees;   *flew*
Out of the hive cam the swarm of bees;
So hidous was the noise, a, benedicite,°   *bless me*
Certes, he Jakke Straw[5] and him meinee°   *company*

575 Ne made nevere shoutes half so shrille
Whan that they wolden any Fleming kille,
As thilke day was maad upon the fox:
Of bras they broughten bemes° and of box,°   *trumpets / boxwood*
Of horn, of boon,° in whiche they blewe and pouped,[6]   *bone*

580 And therwithal they skriked° and they houped°—   *shrieked / whooped*
It seemed as that hevene sholde falle.
     Now goode men, I praye you herkneth alle:
Lo, how Fortune turneth° sodeinly   *reverses, overturns*
The hope and pride eek of hir enemy.

585 This cok that lay upon the foxes bak,
In al his drede unto the fox he spak,
And saide, "Sire, if that I were as ye,
Yit sholde I sayn, as wis° God helpe me,   *surely*
'Turneth ayain, ye proude cherles alle!

590 A verray pestilence upon you falle!
Now am I come unto this wodes side,
Maugree your heed,[7] the cok shal here abide.
I wol him ete, in faith, and that anoon.'"
     The fox answerde, "In faith, it shal be doon."

595 And as he spak that word, al sodeinly
The cok brak from his mouth deliverly,°   *nimbly*
And hye upon a tree he fleigh° anoon.   *flew*
     And whan the fox sawgh that he was agoon,
"Allas," quod he, "O Chauntecleer, allas!

600 I have to you," quod he, "ydoon trespas,
In as muche as I maked you aferd
Whan I you hente° and broughte out of the yeerd.   *seized*
But sire, I dide it in no wikke° entente: *wicked*
Come down, and I shal telle you what I mente.

605 I shal saye sooth to you, God help me so."
     "Nay thanne," quod he, "I shrewe° us bothe two: *curse*
But first I shrewe myself, bothe blood and bones,
If thou bigile me ofter than ones;
Thou shalt namore thurgh thy flaterye

610 Do° me to singe and winken with myn yë.   *cause*
For he that winketh whan he sholde see,
Al wilfully, God lat him nevere thee."°   *thrive*
     "Nay," quod the fox, "but God yive him meschaunce
That is so undiscreet of governaunce°   *self-control*

---

3. Two other dogs.
4. Would break.
5. One of the leaders of the Peasant's Revolt in 1381, which was partially directed against the Flemings living in London.
6. Tooted.
7. Despite your head—i.e., despite anything you can do.

615	That jangleth° whan he sholde holde his pees."	*chatters*
	Lo, swich it is for to be recchelees°	*careless*
	And necligent and truste on flaterye.	
	But ye that holden this tale a folye	
	As of a fox, or of a cok and hen,	
620	Taketh the moralitee, goode men.	
	For Saint Paul saith that al that writen is	
	To oure doctrine it is ywrit, ywis:[8]	
	Taketh the fruit, and lat the chaf be stille.	
	Now goode God, if that it be thy wille,	
625	As saith my lord, so make us alle goode men,	
	And bringe us to his hye blisse. Amen.	

LYRICS AND OCCASIONAL VERSE

To Rosamond

	Madame, ye been of alle beautee shrine	
	As fer as cercled is the mapemounde:[9]	
	For as the crystal glorious ye shine,	
	And like ruby been youre cheekes rounde.	
5	Therwith ye been so merye and so jocounde	
	That at a revel whan that I see you daunce	
	It is an oinement unto my wounde,	
	Though ye to me ne do no daliaunce.[1]	
	For though I weepe of teres ful a tine,°	*tub*
10	Yit may that wo myn herte nat confounde;	
	Youre semy° vois, that ye so smale outtwine,[2]	*small*
	Maketh my thought in joye and blis habounde:°	*abound*
	So curteisly I go with love bounde	
	That to myself I saye in my penaunce,[3]	
15	"Suffiseth me to love you, Rosemounde,	
	Though ye to me ne do no daliaunce."	
	Was nevere pik walwed in galauntine[4]	
	As I in love am walwed and ywounde,	
	For which ful ofte I of myself divine	
20	That I am trewe Tristam[5] the secounde;	
	My love may not refreide nor affounde;[6]	
	I brenne° ay in amorous plesaunce:	*burn*
	Do what you list, I wol youre thral° be founde,	*slave*
	Though ye to me ne do no daliaunce.	

Truth

	Flee fro the prees° and dwelle with soothfastnesse;	*crowd*
	Suffise° thyn owene thing, though it be smal;	*let suffice*
	For hoord hath[7] hate, and climbing tikelnesse;°	*insecurity*
	Prees hath envye, and wele° blent° overal.	*prosperity / blinds*

8. See Romans xv.4.
9. I.e., to the farthest circumference of the map of the world.
1. I.e., show me no encouragement.
2. That you so delicately spin out.
3. I.e., pangs of unrequited love.

4. Pike rolled in galantine sauce.
5. The famous lover of Isolt (Iseult, Isolde) in medieval legend, renowned for his constancy.
6. Cool nor chill.
7. Hoarding causes.

5   Savoure° no more than thee bihoove shal;   *relish*
      Rule wel thyself that other folk canst rede:°   *advise*
      And Trouthe shal delivere,[8] it is no drede.°   *doubt*

      Tempest thee nought al crooked to redresse[9]
      In trust of hire[1] that turneth as a bal;
10   Muche wele stant in litel bisinesse;[2]
      Be war therfore to spurne ayains an al.[3]
      Strive nat as dooth the crokke° with the wal.   *pot*
      Daunte° thyself that dauntest otheres deede: *master*
      And Trouthe shal delivere, it is no drede.

15   That thee is sent, receive in buxomnesse;°   *obedience*
      The wrastling for the world axeth° a fal;   *asks for*
      Here is noon hoom, here nis but wildernesse:
      Forth, pilgrim, forth! Forth, beest, out of thy stal!
      Know thy countree, looke up, thank God of al.
20   Hold the heigh way and lat thy gost° thee lede: *spirit*
      And Trouthe shal delivere, it is no drede.

      Therfore, thou Vache,[4] leve thyn olde wrecchednesse
      Unto the world; leve[5] now to be thral.
      Crye him mercy that of his heigh goodnesse
25   Made thee of nought, and in especial
      Draw unto him, and pray in general,
      For thee and eek for othere, hevenelich meede:°   *reward*
      And Trouthe shal delivere, it is no drede.

Lack of Steadfastness

      Somtime° the world was so stedefast and stable   *once*
      That mannes word was obligacioun;
      And now it is so fals and deceivable°   *deceitful*
      That word and deed, as in conclusioun,
5   Been nothing like, for turned up-so-down
      Is al this world for meed° and wilfulnesse,   *bribery*
      That al is lost for lak of stedefastnesse.

      What maketh this world to be so variable
      But lust° that folk have in dissensioun?   *pleasure*
10   For among us now a man is holde unable,°   *incompetent*
      But if° he can, by som collusioun,   *unless*
      Doon his neighbour wrong or oppressioun.
      What causeth this but wilful wrecchednesse,
      That al is lost for lak of stedefastnesse?

15   Trouthe is put down, resoun is holden fable;
      Vertu hath now no dominacioun;
      Pitee exiled, no man is merciable;°   *merciful*
      Through coveitise is blent° discrecioun.   *blinded*
      The world hath mad a permutacioun
20   Fro right to wrong, fro trouthe to fikelnesse,
      That al is lost for lak of stedefastnesse.

8. I.e., truth shall make you free.
9. Do not disturb yourself to straighten all that's crooked.
1. Fortune, who turns like a ball in that she is always presenting a different aspect to men.
2. Peace of mind stands in little anxiety.
3. I.e., to kick against the pricks.
4. Probably Sir Philip de la Vache, with a pun on the French for "cow."
5. I.e., cease.

Envoy to King Richard

O prince, desire to be honourable,
Cherish thy folk and hate extorcioun.
Suffre nothing that may be reprevable°   shameful
25   To thyn estaat° doon in thy regioun.   status
Shew forth thy swerd of castigacioun,
Drede God, do⁸ law, love trouthe and worthinesse,
And wed thy folk again to stedefastnesse.

Complaint to His Purse

To you, my purs, and to noon other wight,
Complaine I, for ye be my lady dere.
I am so sory, now that ye be light,
For certes, but if⁹ ye make me hevy cheere,
5   Me were as lief¹ be laid upon my beere;°   bier
For which unto youre mercy thus I crye:
Beeth hevy again, or elles moot° I die.   must

Now voucheth sauf this day er it be night
That I of you the blisful soun may heere,
10   Or see youre colour, lik the sonne bright,
That of yelownesse hadde nevere peere.
Ye be my life, ye be myn hertes steere,°   rudder, guide
Queene of confort and of good compaignye:
Beeth hevy again, or elles moot I die.

15   Ye purs, that been to me my lives light
And saviour, as in this world down here,
Out of this tonne² helpe me thurgh your might,
Sith that ye wol nat be my tresorere;°   disburser
For I am shave as neigh° as any frere.°   close / friar
20   But yit I praye unto youre curteisye:
Beeth hevy again, or elles moot I die.

Envoy to Henry IV

O conquerour of Brutus Albioun,³
Which that by line and free eleccioun
Been verray king, this song to you I sende:
25   And ye, that mowen° alle oure harmes amende,   may
Have minde upon my supplicacioun.

Against Women Unconstant

Madame, for youre newefangelnesse,⁴
Many a servant have ye put out of grace.
I take my leve of your unstedefastnesse,
For wel I woot,° whil ye have lives space,   know
5   Ye can not love ful half yeer in a place,
To newe thing youre lust° is ay° so keene;   appetite / always
In stede of blew, thus may ye were al greene.⁵

---

8. *Do* means both "bring into being" and
"enforce."
9. Unless.
1. I'd just as soon.
2. Tun, meaning "predicament."
3. Britain (Albion) was supposed to have

been founded by Brutus, the grandson of
Aeneas, the founder of Rome.
4. Fondness for novelty.
5. Blue stands for constancy, green for
change.

Right as a mirour nothing may enpresse,
But, lightly as it cometh, so mote° it pace,°   *must / pass*
10 So fareth youre love, youre werkes bereth witnesse.
Ther is no faith that may your herte enbrace;
But, as a wedercok, that turneth his face
With every wind, ye fare, and this is seene;
In stede of blew, thus may ye were al greene.

15 Ye might be shrined, for youre brotelnesse,[6]
Bet than Dalida, Criseide or Candace;[7]
For ever in chaunging stant youre sikernesse;°   *constancy*
That tache° may no wight fro your herte arace.°   *blemish / uproot*
If ye lese oon, ye can wel twain purchace;
20 Al light for somer,[8] ye woot wel what I mene,
In stede of blew, thus may ye were al greene.

Merciless Beauty

1

Youre yën two wol slee° me sodeinly: *slay*
I may the beautee of hem nat sustene,°   *withstand*
So woundeth it thurghout myn herte keene.°   *keenly*

And but° youre word wol helen hastily   *unless*
5   Myn hertes wounde, whil that it is greene,[9]
Youre yën two wol slee me sodeinly:
I may the beautee of hem nat sustene.

Upon my trouthe, I saye you faithfully
That ye been of my lif and deeth the queene,
10 For with my deeth the trouthe shal be seene.
Youre yën two wol slee me sodeinly:
I may the beautee of hem nat sustene,
So woundeth it thurghout myn herte keene.

2

So hath youre beautee fro youre herte chaced
15 Pitee, that me ne availeth nought to plaine:°   *complain*
For Daunger halt[1] youre mercy in his chaine.

Giltelees my deeth thus han ye me purchased;°   *procured*
I saye you sooth, me needeth nought to feine:°   *dissemble*
So hath youre beautee fro youre herte chaced
20 Pitee, that me ne availeth nought to plaine.

Allas, that nature hath in you compaced°   *enclosed*
So greet beautee that no man may attaine
To mercy, though he sterve° for the paine.   *die*
So hath youre beautee fro youre herte chaced
25 Pitee, that me ne availeth nought to plaine:
For Daunger halt youre mercy in his chaine.

---

6. Brittleness, fickleness.
7. Respectively, Samson's betrayer (Delilah), Troilus's faithless mistress, and Alexander's temptress to sloth.
8. To travel "light for summer" as opposed to heavy for winter suggests ease of movement, readiness for change.
9. I.e., fresh.
1. Haughtiness holds.

3

Sin I fro Love escaped am so fat,
I nevere thenke° to been in his prison lene: *intend*
Sin I am free, I counte him nat a bene.[2]

30 He may answere and saye right this and that;
  I do no fors,[3] I speke right as I mene:
    Sin I fro Love escaped am so fat,
    I nevere thenke to been in his prison lene.

  Love hath my name ystrike° out of his sclat,°   *struck / slate*
35 And he is strike out of my bookes clene
  For everemo; ther is noon other mene.°   *solution*
    Sin I fro Love escaped am so fat,
    I nevere thenke to been in his prison lene:
    Sin I am free, I counte him nat a bene.

CHARLES D'ORLÉANS
(1391–1465)

My Ghostly Father

My ghostly° father, I me confess,   *spiritual*
  First to God and then to you,
    That at a window (wot° ye how)   *know*
I stole a kiss of great sweetness,
5 Which done was out° advisedness,   *without*
  But it is done, not undone, now,
My ghostly father, I me confess,
  First to God and then to you.
But I restore it shall doubtless
10   Again, if so be that I mow,°   *may*
  And that, God, I make a vow,
And else I ask forgiveness—
My ghostly father, I me confess,
  First to God and then to you.

The Smiling Mouth

The smiling mouth and laughing eyen gray,
The breastes round and long small armes twain,
  The handes smooth, the sides straight and plain,
Your feetes lit°—what should I further say?   *little*
5 It is my craft° when ye are far away   *practice*
  To muse thereon in stinting° of my pain— *soothing*
The smiling mouth and laughing eyen gray,
  The breastes round and long small armes twain.
So would I pray you, if I durst or may,
10   The sight to see as I have seen,
  Forwhy° that craft me is most fain,° *because / pleasing*
And will be to the hour in which I day°—   *die*
The smiling mouth and laughing eyen gray,
  The breastes round and long small armes twain.

---

2. I don't consider him worth a bean.   3. I don't care.

So Fair, So Fresh

So fair, so fresh, so goodly unto° see,   **to**
    So well demeaned in all your governance,°   **conduct**
    That to my heart it is a great pleasance
Of your goodness when I remember me;
5 And trusteth fully where that ever I be,
    I will abide under your obeisance°—   **dominion**
So fair, so fresh, so goodly unto see,
    So well demeaned in all your governance;
For in my thought there is no more but ye
10   Whom I have served without repentance,
    Wherefore I pray you see to my grievance
And put aside all mine adversity—
So fair, so fresh, so goodly unto see,
    So well demeaned in all your governance.

Oft in My Thought

Oft in my thought full busily have I sought,
    Against the beginning of this fresh new year,
What pretty thing that I best given ought
    To her that was mine hearte's lady dear;
5   But all that thought bitane° is fro° me clear   **taken / from**
    Since death, alas, hath closed her under clay
    And hath this world fornaked° with her here—   **stripped bare**
    God have her soul, I can no better say.

But for to keep in custom, lo, my thought,
10   And of my seely° service the manere,   **simple**
In showing als° that I forget her not   **also**
    Unto each wight I shall to my powere
    This dead[1] her serve with masses and prayere;
    For all too foul a shame were me, mafay,°   **by my faith**
15   Her to forget this time that nigheth near—
    God have her soul, I can no better say.

To her profit now nis° there to be bought   **is not**
    None other thing all° will I buy it dear;   **although**
Wherefore, thou Lord that lordest all aloft,
20   My deedes take, such as goodness steer,
    And crown her, Lord, within thine heavenly sphere
    As for most truest lady, may I say,
    Most good, most fair, and most benign of cheer°—   **countenance**
    God have her soul, I can no better say.

25 When I her praise, or praising of her hear,
    Although it whilom° were to me pleasere,   **formerly**
    It fill enough it doth mine heart today,
    And doth° me wish I clothed had my bier—   **makes**
    God have her soul, I can no better say.

---

1. Dead person, the deceased. *Her* is redundant, as is one of the *its* in line 27.

Honor, Joy

Honoure, joy, healthe, and pleasaunce,
    Virtue,° riches abundant with good ure,°   *excellence / fortune*
The Lord grant you, which hath most pruïssaunce,°   *might*
    And many a gladsome year for to endure
5   With love and praise of every creäture;
      And for my love all prevail it shall,[2]
    I give it you, as be ye very sure,
      With heart, body, my little good, and all.

And so you not displease with my desire,
10   This would I you beseech, that of your grace
It like you, lo, to grant me all this year
    As[3] in your heart to have a dwelling place
Albeit never of so lit° a space,   *little*
      For which as this the rent receive ye shall:[4]
15   My love and service as in every case,
      With heart, body, my little good, and all.

And since it is to you no prejudice,
    Some little, pretty corner seekes me
Within your heart, for pardie,[5] lo, justice,
20   If I offend, it must yourselven be
    To punish, like as ye the offences see;
      For I as name nor have no thing at all
But it is sole your own in each degree,
      With heart, body, my little good, and all.

25   What so ye will, I will it to obey,
    For pain or smart how so that me befall;
So am I yours and shall till that I dey,°   *die*
    With heart, body, my little good, and all.

ANONYMOUS LYRICS OF THE FIFTEENTH CENTURY

Adam Lay I-bounden

Adam lay i-bounden, bounden in a bond;
Foure thousand winter thought he not too long.
And all was for an apple, an apple that he took,
As clerkes finden written in theire book.

5   Ne hadde the apple take been,[1] the apple taken been,
Ne hadde never our Lady aye been Heaven's queen.
Blessed be the time that apple taken was,
Therefore we may singen, *"Deo gracias!"*[2]

---

2. I.e., and so that ("for") my love shall prevail.
3. *As* here (and in lines 15 and 22) is without meaning; it is an expletive or filler.

4. I.e. for which ye shall receive this as rent.
5. Lord! (literally, *by God*); a mild oath.
1. I.e., if the apple had not been taken.
2. Thanks be to God.

I Sing of a Maiden

I sing of a maiden
    That is makeless:°   *mateless, matchless*
King of alle kinges
    To° her son she ches.°   *for / chose*

5   He came also° stille   *as*
    Where his mother was
As dew in Aprille
    That falleth on the grass.

He came also stille
10   To his mother's bower
As dew in Aprille
    That falleth on the flower.

He came also stille
    Where his mother lay
15 As dew in Aprille
    That falleth on the spray.

Mother and maiden
    Was never none but she—
Well may such a lady
20   Godes mother be.

Out of Your Sleep Arise and Wake

Noel, noel, noel,
Noel, noel, noel!

Out of your sleep arise and wake,
For God mankind° now hath i-take,°   *human nature / taken*
5 All of° a maid without any make:°   *from / match, mate*
    Of all women she beareth the bell.[3]
    Noel!

And through a maide fair and wise
Now man is made of full great price;°   *worth*
10 Now angels kneel to man's service,
    And at this time all this befell.
    Noel!

Now man is brighter than the sun;
Now man in heaven on high shall wone;°   *dwell*
15 Blessed be God this game is begun,
    And his mother empress of hell.
    Noel!

That° ever was thrall,° now is he free;   *who / captive*
That ever was small, now great is she;
20 Now shall God deem° both thee and me   *judge*
    Unto his bliss if we do well.
    Noel!

3. "Beareth the bell": takes the prize.

Now man may to heaven wend;
Now heaven and earth to him they bend;
25 He that was foe now is our friend.
   This is no nay that I you tell.
   Noel!

Now, blesséd brother, grant us grace
At doomesday to see thy face
30 And in thy court to have a place,
   That we may there sing noel.
   Noel!

This Endris Night

This endris[4] night
I saw a sight,
   A star as bright as day,
And ever among[5]
5 A maiden sung,
   "Lullay, by, by, lullay."

That lovely lady sat and sung,
   And to her child said,
"My Son, my Brother, my Father dear,
10 Why liest thou thus in hay?
   My sweete brid,°   *bird*
   Thus it is betid,°   *happened*
      Though thou be king verray;° *in truth*
   But nevertheless
15 I will not cesse°   *cease*
      To sing 'By, by, lullay.' "

The child then spake in his talking,
   And to his mother said,
"I am kenned° for Heaven's King   *known*
20 In crib though I be laid,
   For angels bright
   Done° to me light,   *gave*
      Thou knowest it is no nay;
   And of[6] that sight
25 Thou mayst be light[7]
      To sing 'By, by, lullay.' "

"Now, sweet Son, since thou art king,
   Why art thou laid in stall?
Why ne thou ordained thy bedding
30 In some great kinge's hall?
   Methinketh it is right
   That king or knight
      Should lie in good array,
   And then among°   *in that circumstance*
35 It were no wrong
      To sing 'By, by, lullay.' "

---

4. "This endris": the other.
5. "Ever among": every now and then.

6. I.e., because of.
7. "Thou mayst be light": feel free.

"Mary mother, I am thy child,
   Though I be laid in stall;
Lords and dukes shall worship me,
40   And so shall kinges all.
         Ye shall well see
         That kinges three
            Shall come the Twelfth Day.
      For this behest°   *promise*
45   Give me thy breast
            And sing 'By, by, lullay.' "

"Now tell me, sweet Son, I thee pray,   *beloved*
   Thou are me lief° and dear,   *liking*
How should I keep thee to thy pay°   *face*
50   And make thee glad of cheer?°
         For all thy will
         I would fulfill,
            Thou wottest full well in fay,°   *faith*
      And for all this
55   I will thee kiss
            And sing 'By, by, lullay.' "

"My dear mother, when time it be,
   Thou take me up on loft,
And set me upon thy knee,
60   And handle me full soft,
         And in thy arm
         Thou hill° me warm,   *cover*
            And keepe night and day;
      If I weep
65   And may not sleep,
            Then sing 'By, by, lullay.' "

"Now, sweet Son, since it is so,
   That all thing is at thy will,
I pray thee, grante me a boon,
70   If it be both right and skill:°   *reason*
         That child or man
         That will or can
            Be merry upon my day,
      To bliss them bring,
75   And I shall sing
            'Lullay, by, by, lullay.' "

A Baby Is Born

A baby is born us bliss to bring;
A maiden I heard lullay sing:
"Dear son, now leave thy weeping,
Thy father is the king of bliss."

5 "Nay, dear mother, for you weep I not,
But for thinges that shall be wrought
Or° that I have mankind i-bought: *before*
Was there never pain like it iwis."°   *certainly*

"Peace, dear son, say thou me not so.
10 Thou art my child, I have no mo.°   *more*
Alas! that I should see this woe:
It were to me great heaviness."

"My handes, mother, that ye now see,
They shall be nailéd on a tree;
15 My feet, also, fastened shall be:
Full many shall weep that it shall see."

"Alas! dear son, sorrow now is my hap;°   *lot*
To see my child that sucks my pap°   *breast*
So ruthfully° taken out of my lap: *pitifully*
20 It were to me great heaviness."

"Also, mother, there shall a spear
My tendere heart all to-tear;°   *tear apart*
The blood shall cover my body there:
Great ruthe° it shall be to see."   *pity*

25 "Ah! dear son, that is a heavy case.
When Gabriel kneeled before my face
And said, 'Hail! Lady, full of grace,'
He never told me nothing of this."

"Dear mother, peace, now I you pray,
30 And take no sorrow for that I say,
But sing this song, 'By, by, lullay,'
To drive away all heaviness."

O! Mankind

O! Mankind,
Have in thy mind
My passion° smart,°   *suffering / bitter*
And thou shalt find
5   Me full kind—
Lo! here my heart.

I Have Labored Sore

I have labored sore and suffered death,
And now I rest and draw my breath;
But I shall come and call right soon
Heaven and earth and hell to doom;°   *judgment*
5   And then shall know both devil and man
What I was and what I am.

Quia Amore Langueo[8]

In the vale of restless mind
I sought in mountain and in mead,°   *meadow*

8. "For I am sick with love." The refrain
comes from the Song of Solomon where it is
twice uttered: ii.5, v.8. Other echoes appear at
line 18 (Song iv.9) where the beloved is called
sister; at line 82 (Song iv.16) with its fruitful
garden; at line 84 (Song v.1) with its milk,
honey, and wine; at line 103 (Song ii.9) where
the beloved stands at the windows; at line 113
(Song ii.7, viii.4) with its charge to be quiet.

Trusting a true-love for to find.
  Upon a hill then took I heed;
5 A voice I heard (and near I yede)°   *went*
  In great dolour complaining tho,°   *then*
"See, deare soul, my sides bleed
  Quia amore langueo."

Upon this mount I found a tree,
10 Under this tree a man sitting—
From head to foot wounded was he,
  His hearte blood I saw bleeding—
A seemly man to be a king,
  A gracious face to look unto.
15 I asked him why he had paining.
  He said, "*Quia amore langueo.*

"I am true-love that false was never;
  My sister, man's soul, I loved her thus:
Because I would in no wise dissever,°   *separate*
20 I left my kingdom glorious;
I purveyed° her a place full precious.   *provided*
  She fled, I followed, I loved her so
That I suffered these pains piteous,
  Quia amore langueo.

25 "My fair love and my spouse bright,
  I saved her from beating and she hath me bett;° *beat*
I clothed her in grace and heavenly light—
  This bloody shirt she hath on me set.
For longing love I will not let°—   *cease*
30 Sweete strokes be these, lo!
I have loved ever as I het,°   *promised*
  Quia amore langueo.

"I crowned her with bliss and she me with thorn;
  I led her to chamber and she me to die;
35 I brought her to worship and she me to scorn;
  I did her reverence and she me villainy.°   *indignity*
To love that loveth is no mastery:
  Her hate made never my love her foe.
Ask then no more questions why,
40 But *quia amore langueo.*

"Look unto mine handes, man!
  These gloves were given me when I her sought;
They be not white but red and wan,°   *dark*
  Embroidered with blood my spouse them bought.
45 They will not off; I leave them not;
  I woo her with them wherever she go.
These hands full friendly for her fought,
  Quia amore langueo.

"Marvel not, man, though I sit still—
50 My love hath shod me wonder° strait:°   *very / tightly*
She buckled my feet as was her will
  With sharp nailes—well thou mayest wait.°   *look*
In my love was never deceit,

For all my members I have opened her to;
55   My body I made her hearte's bait,
       Quia amore langueo.

"In my side I have made her nest.
   Look in, how wide a wound is here!
This is her chamber, here shall she rest,
60   That she and I may sleep in fere.°   together
   Here may she wash, if any filth were;
       Here is succour for all her woe.
   Come if she will, she shall have cheer,
       Quia amore langueo.

65   "I will abide till she be ready,
       I will her sue if she say nay.
   If she be reckless,° I will be ready;   uninterested
       If she be daungerous,° I will her pray;   hard to please
       If she do weep, then bid I nay.
70   Mine arms be spread to clip° her to.   clasp
   Cry once, 'I come!' now, soul, assay,
       Quia amore langueo.

"I sit on a hill for to see far;
   I look to the vale: my spouse I see.
75 Now runs she awayward, now cometh she near,
   Yet from mine eyesight she may not be.
   Some wait their prey to make her flee;⁹
       I run before to fleme° her foe.   put to flight
   Return, my soul, again to me,
80   *Quia amore langueo.*

"My sweete spouse, let us go play—
   Apples be ripe in my gardine;°   garden
I shall thee clothe in new array;
   Thy meat shall be milk, honey, and wine.
85   Now, deare soul, let us go dine—
       Thy sustenance is in my scrip,° lo!   bag
   Tarry not now, fair spouse mine,
       Quia amore langueo.

"If thou be foul, I shall make thee clean;
90   If thou be sick, I shall thee heal;
If thou aught mourn, I shall bemean.°   bemoan
   Spouse, why wilt thou not with me deal?
   Thou foundest never love so leal.°   loyal
       What wilt thou, soul, that I shall do?
95   I may of unkindness thee appeal,°   accuse
       Quia amore langueo.

"What shall I do now with my spouse?
   Abide I will her gentleness.
Would she look once out of her house
100   Of fleshly affections and uncleanness,
   Her bed is made, her bolster is in bliss,°   heaven
       Her chamber is chosen—such are no mo.°   more

---

9. I.e., some lie in wait for their prey—as does Satan for man's soul, to seize it and thus
draw it away or make it flee from Christ.

Look out at the windows of kindness,
 Quia amore langueo.

05 "My spouse is in chamber—hold your peace!
 Make no noise, but let her sleep.
My babe shall suffer no dis-ease;
 I may not hear my dear child weep,
 For with my pap° I shall her keep.   breast
110 No wonder though I tend her to,
This hole in my side had never been so deep
 But *quia amore langueo.*

"Long and love thou never so high,
 Yet is my love more than thine may be.
115 Thou gladdest, thou weepest, I sit thee by—
 Yet might thou, spouse, look once at me!
Spouse, should I always feede thee
 With childe's meat? Nay, love, not so!   test
 I will prove thy love with adversity,°
120 *Quia amore langueo.*

"Wax not weary, mine own dear wife.
 What meed° is aye to live in comfort?   reward
For in tribulation I reign more rife°   fully
 Oftertimes than in disport.
125 In weal, in woe, ever I support—
 Then, deare soul, go never me fro.°   from
Thy meed is marked, when thou art mort,°   dead
 In bliss, *quia amore langueo.*"

Jesus' Wounds So Wide

Jesus' wounds so wide
Be wells of life to the good,
Namely° the stround° of° his side   *particularly / stream / from*
That ran full breme° on the rood.°   *fiercely / cross*

5 If thee list to drink,
To flee from the fiends of hell,
Bow thou down to the brink
And meekly taste of the well.

I Have a Young Sister

I have a young sister
 Far beyond the sea;
Many be the drowries°   tokens
 That she sente me.

5 She sente me the cherry
 Withouten any stone,
And so she did the dove
 Withouten any bone.

She sente me the briar
10 Withouten any rind;°   bark
She bade me love my leman°   beloved
 Without longing.

How should any cherry
　　Be withoute stone?
15　And how should any dove
　　Be withoute bone?

How should any briar
　　Be withoute rind?
How should I love my leman
20　　Without longing?

When the cherry was a flower,
　　Then hadde it no stone.
When the dove was an egg,
　　Then hadde it no bone.

25　When the briar was unbred,[1]
　　Then hadde it no rind.
When the maiden hath that she loveth,
　　She is without longing.

I Have a Gentle Cock

I have a gentle° cock,　　　　　　　　　　　　　　　*noble*
　　Croweth me day;
He doth me risen[2] early
　　My matins for to say.

5　I have a gentle cock,
　　Comen he is of great;°　　　　　　　　　　　*lofty lineage*
His comb is of red coral,
　　His tail is of jet.

I have a gentle cock,
10　　Comen he is of kind;°　　　　　　　　　　　*good stock*
His comb is of red coral,
　　His tail is of inde.°　　　　　　　　　　　　　*indigo*

His legges be of azure,
　　So gentle and so small;
15　His spurres are of silver white
　　Into the wortewale.[3]

His eyen are of crystal,
　　Locked° all in amber;　　　　　　　　　　　　*set*
And every night he percheth him
20　　In my lady's chamber.

Jolly Jankin

"Kyrie, so kyrie,"
Jankin singeth murie,°　　　　　　　　　　　　　*merrily*
　　With "Aleison."[4]

1. I.e., still in the seed.
2. "Doth me risen": makes me rise.
3. Up to the root.
4. *Kyrie eleison,* a prayer, "Lord have mercy"; the Epistle (line 14), a reading from Paul or one of the Prophets; the *Sanctus* (line 19), a prayer of rejoicing, "Holy, Holy, Holy"; and the *Agnus* (line 29), an invocation of the Lamb of God, are early, middle, and late parts of the divine office (line 9) or Mass.

As I went on Yule Day
5 In our procession,
Knew I jolly Jankin
By his merry tone.
    Kyrieleison.

Jankin began the office
10 On the Yule Day,
And yet methinketh it does me good,
So merry gan he say,
    "Kyrieleison."

Jankin read the 'Pistle
15 Full fair and full well,
And yet methinketh it does me good,
As ever have I sel.[5]
    Kyrieleison.

Jankin at the Sanctus
20 Cracketh a merry note,
And yet methinketh it does me good—
I payed for his coat.
    Kyrieleison.

Jankin cracketh notes
25 An hundred on a knot,°   *at a time*
And yet he hacketh° them smaller   *chops up*
Than wortes° to the pot.   *herbs*
    Kyrieleison.

Jankin at the Agnus
30 Beareth the pax-bred;[6]
He twinkled but said nought,
And on my foot he tread.
    Kyrieleison.

Benedicamus Domino,[7]
35 Christ from shame me shield;
Deo gracias thereto—[8]
Alas! I go with child.
    Kyrieleison.

God, That Madest All Things

God, that madest all things of nought[6]
And with thy precious blood us bought,
    Mercy, help, and grace.
As thou art very god and man,
5 And of thy side thy blood ran,
    Forgive us our trespass.
The world, our flesh, the fiend our foe
Maketh us mis-think, mis-speak, mis-do—
    All thus we fall in blame.

---

5. I.e., as ever I (hope to) have good luck.
6. A tablet ("bred": board) bearing a representation of the Crucifixion, kissed by the priests celebrating the Mass, then by the congregation. "Pax": (the kiss of) peace.
7. Let us bless the Lord.
8. Thanks be to God, as well.
6. I.e., from nothing.

10   Of all our sinnes, less and more,
  Sweete Jesu, us rueth sore.
      Mercy, for thine holy name.

I Wend to Death

  I wend to death, knight stith in stour;[7]
  Through fight in field I won the flower;
  No fights me taught the death to quell—
  I wend to death, sooth I you tell.

5 I wend to death, a king iwis;°   *indeed*
  What helpes honor or worlde's bliss?
  Death is to man the kinde° way—   *natural*
  I wende to be clad in clay.

  I wend to death, clerk full of skill,
10 That could with words men mar and dill.[8]
  Soon has me made the death an end.
  Be ware with[9] me! To death I wend.

Timor Mortis

  In what estate° so ever I be   *condition*
  Timor mortis conturbat me.[1]

  As I went on a merry morning,
  I heard a bird both weep and sing.
5 This was the tenor of her talking:
  "Timor mortis conturbat me."

  I asked that bird what she meant.
  "I am a musket° both fair and gent;°   *male sparrowhawk / gentle*
  For dread of death I am all shent.:°   *ruined*
10 *Timor mortis conturbat me.*

  "When I shall die, I know no day;
  What country or place I cannot say;
  Wherefore this song sing I may:
  Timor mortis conturbat me.

15 "Jesu Christ, when he should die,
  To his Father he gan say,
  'Father,' he said, 'in Trinity,
  Timor mortis conturbat me.'

  "All Christian people, behold and see:
20 This world is but a vanity
  And replete with necessity.
  Timor mortis conturbat me.

  "Wake I or sleep, eate or drink,
  When I on my last end do think,

---

7. "Stith in stour": stout in battle.
8. Mar and keep secret; i.e., expose or conceal.
9. "Be ware with": take warning from.
1. The title phrase comes from the Office of the Dead: *"Peccantem me quotidie et non poenitentem timor mortis conturbat me. Quia in inferno nulla est redemptio misere mei Deus et salva me."* (Since I have been sinning daily and repenting not, *the fear of death distresses me.* Since in hell there is no redemption, have pity on me, God, and save me.)

25 For greate fear my soul do shrink:
   Timor mortis conturbat me.

"God grant us grace him for to serve,
And be at our end when we sterve,°   *die*
And from the fiend he us preserve.
30   *Timor mortis conturbat me.*

A God and Yet a Man?

A god and yet a man?
  A maid and yet a mother?
Wit wonders what wit can
  Conceive this or the other.

5 A god and can he die?
  A dead man, can he live?
What wit can well reply?
  What reason reason give?

God, truth itself, doth teach it.
10   Man's wit sinks too far under
By reason's power to reach it.
  Believe and leave° to wonder.   *cease*

The Corpus Christi[5] Carol

Lully, lullay, lully, lullay,
  The falcon hath born my make° away.   *mate*

He bore him up, he bore him down,
He bore him into an orchard brown.

5 In that orchard there was a hall
That was hanged with purple and pall.°   *rich fabric*

And in that hall there was a bed,
It was hanged with gold so red.

And in that bed there lieth a knight,
10 His woundes bleeding day and night.

By that bed's side there kneeleth a may°   *maiden*
And she weepeth both night and day.

And by that bed's side there standeth a stone,
Corpus Christi written thereon.

The Jolly Juggler

Draw me near, draw me near,
  Draw me near, the jolly juggler.

Here beside° dwelleth a rich baron's daughter: *hard by*
She would have no man that for love had sought her—
5   So nice[6] she was.

---

5. "Corpus Christi": the body of Christ.   6. Excessively fastidious, hard to please.

She would have no man that was made of mold°   *earth*
But if⁷ he had a mouth of gold to kiss her when she would—
    So daungerous° she was.   *hard to please*

Thereof heard a jolly juggler that laid was on the green,
10 And at this lady's word, iwis° he had great tene°—   *indeed / vexation*
    An-angered he was.

He juggled to him a well good steed of° an old horse bone,   *out of*
A saddle and a bridle both, and set himself thereon—
    A juggler he was.

15 He pricked° and pranced both, before that lady's gate: *spurred*
She weened° he had been an angel, was come for her sake—   *thought*
    A pricker he was.

He pricked and pranced before that lady's bower:
She weened he had been an angel come from Heaven's tower—
20   A prancer he was.

Four and twenty knightes led him into the hall,
And as many squires his horse to the stall,
    And gave him meat.

They gave him oats, and also hay;
25 He was an old shrew and held his head away—
    He would not eat.⁸

The day began to pass, the night began to come,
To bed was brought the fair gentlewoman,
    And the juggler also.

30 The night began to pass, the day began to spring;
All the birds of her bower they began to sing—
    And the cuckoo also.

"Where be ye, my merry maidens, that ye come not me to?
The jolly windows of my bower look that you undo,
35   That I may see.

"For I have in mine arms a duke or else an earl."
But when she looked him upon, he was a blear-eyed churl—
    "Alas!" she said.

She led him to an hill, and hanged should he be.
40 He juggled° himself to° a meal poke,° the dust fell in her eye—   *turned /*
    Beguiled she was.   *into / sack*

God and our Lady, and sweet Saint Johan,
Send every giglot° of this town such another leman,°   *wanton / lover*
    Even as he was!

7. "But if": unless.
8. Because he was a magic horse, not an actual or natural one.

Western Wind

Western wind, when will thou blow,
  The small rain down can rain?
Christ, if my love were in my arms
  And I in my bed again!

A Lyke-Wake[9] Dirge

This ae° night, this ae night,   *one*
  Every night and all,
Fire and sleet[1] and candle-light,
  And Christ receive thy saul.°   *soul*

5 When thou from hence away are past,
  To Whinny-muir[2] thou comest at last:

If ever thou gavest hosen and shoon,
  Sit thee down and put them on:

If hosen and shoon thou ne'er gavest nane,
10 The whins shall prick thee to the bare bane:

From Whinny-muir when thou mayst pass,
  To Brig° o' Dread thou comest at last: *bridge*

From Brig o' Dread when thou mayst pass,
  To purgatory fire thou comest at last:

15 If ever thou gavest meat or drink,
  The fire shall never make thee shrink:

If meat or drink thou ne'er gavest nane,
  The fire will burn thee to the bare bane:

This ae night, this ae night,
20 Fire and sleet and candle-light,

Jolly Good Ale and Old

  Back and side go bare, go bare,
    Both foot and hand go cold;
  But, belly, God send thee good ale enough,
    Whether it be new or old.

5 I cannot eat but little meat,
    My stomach is not good;
  But sure I think that I can drink
    With him that wears a hood.[3]
  Though I go bare, take ye no care,
10   I am nothing a-cold;
  I stuff my skin so full within
    Of jolly good ale and old.

9. The night watch (*wake*) kept over a corpse (*lyke*).
1. Salt, sometimes placed with earth on the breast of the dead as emblematic of soul and body.

2. Prickly-moor. *Whin* is a name given to various prickly shrubs: furze, heather, buckthorn.
3. I.e., as much as any friar.

I love no roast but a nut-brown toast,[4]
   And a crab° laid in the fire;   *crab apple*
15 A little bread shall do me stead,°   *service*
   Much bread I not desire.
No frost nor snow, no wind, I trow,°   *trust*
   Can hurt me if it would,
I am so wrapped and throughly° lapped°   *thoroughly / swathed*
20 Of° jolly good ale and old.   *in*

And Tib, my wife, that as her life
   Loveth well good ale to seek,
Full oft drinks she till ye may see
   The tears run down her cheek.
25 Then doth she troll° to me the bowl,   *pass*
   Even as a maltworm° should,   *toper*
And saith, "Sweetheart, I took my part
   Of this jolly good ale and old."

Now let them drink till they nod and wink,
30 Even as good fellows should do;
They shall not miss to have the bliss
   Good ale doth bring men to.
And all poor souls that have scoured bowls
   Or have them lustily trolled—
35 God save the lives of them and their wives,
   Whether they be young or old.

ROBERT HENRYSON
(ca. 1430–ca. 1506)

The Three Deid Pollis°   *skulls*

O sinful man into this mortal sea
Whilk° is the vale of murning and of care,   *which*
With ghastly sicht, behold our heidis three,
Our holkit ene,° our peilit° pollis bare: *hollowed eyes/hairless*
5 As ye are now, into this warld we were,
As fresh, as fair, as lusty to behold;
When thou lookis on this sooth examplair
Of thyself, man, thou may be richt unbold.

For sooth° it is, that every man mortale   *true*
10 Mon° suffer deid,° and dee, that life has tane;°   *must/death/taken*
Na erdly state againis deid may prevail;
The hour of death and place is uncertaine,
Whilk is referrit to the hie God alane;
Herefore have mind of death, that thou mon die;
15 This sair° example to see quotidiane,°   *sore/daily*
Suld cause all men fra wicked vicis flee.

O wanton youth as fresh as lusty May,
Fairest of flowris renewit white and reid,
Behald our heidis: O lusty gallandis gay,

4. Used as a sop with ale or wine.

20 Full laichly° thus sall lie thy lusty heid,   *lowly*
    Holkit and how,° and wallowit° as the weed,   *hollow/withered*
    Thy crampand° hair and eik° thy crystal ene;   *curling/also*
    Full carefully conclude sall duleful deid;
    Example here be° us it may be seen.   *by*

25 O ladies white, in claithis° corruscant,°   *garments/glittering*
    Polist° with pearl, and money precious stane;   *decorated*
    With pappis° white, and hals° so elegant,   *breasts/throat*
    Circlit with gold and sapphiris mony ane;
    Your fingaris small, white as the whalis bane,
30 Arrayit with ringis, and mony ruby reid:
    As we lie thus, so sall ye lie ilk ane,°   *every one*
    With peilit pollis, and holkit thus your heid.

    O woeful pride, the root of all distress,
    With humill hairt upon our pollis pense:°   *think*
35 Man, for thy miss° ask mercy with meekness;   *sin*
    Aganis deid may na man mak defence.
    The emperour, for all his excellence,
    King and queen and eik all erdly state,
    Poor and rich, sall be but° difference,   *without*
40 Turnit in ash, and thus in erthe translait.

    This question wha can absolve,° lat see,   *answer*
    What phisnymour,° or perfect palmystar:°   *physiognomer/palmist*
    Wha was fairest, or foulest, of us three?
    Or whilk of us of kin was gentillar?°   *nobler*
45 Or maist expert in science,° or in lare,   *learning*
    In art, music or in astronomy?
    Here suld be your study and repair,
    And think as thus all your heidis mon be.

    O feeble age, aye drawand near thy date
50 Of doolie° deid, that has thy dayis complete,   *mournful*
    Behold our heidis with murning and regrate:°   *lament*
    Fall on thy knees; ask grace at God, and greet
    With orisonis° and haly psalmis sweet,   *prayers*
    Beseikand Him on thee to have mercy;
55 And of our saulis bidand° the decreet°   *awaiting/judgment*
    Of His godheid, when He sall call and cry.

    Als we exhort that every man mortal,
    For His sake that made of nocht all thing,
    For our sawlis to pray in general,
60 To Jesus Christ of heaven and erd the king;
    That throuch His blood we may aye live and reign
    With the High Father, be eternity,
    The Son alswa,° the Holy Ghaist condigne,°   *also/worthy*
    Three knit in ane be perfyt unit.

                                        ca. 1480   1865

WILLIAM DUNBAR
(ca. 1460–ca. 1525)

Lament for the Makaris°   *poets*

I that in heill° was and gladness,   *health*
Am troublit now with great seikness,
And feeblit with infirmity:
    Timor Mortis conturbat me.[1]

5 Our plesance here is all vain-glory
This false warld is bot transitory,
The flesh is brukill,° the Fiend is sle;°   *frail/sly*
    Timor Mortis conturbat me.

The state of man dois change and vary,
10 Now sound, now seik, now blyth, now sary,
Now dansand merry, now like to die;
    Timor Mortis conturbat me.

No state in erd here standis siccar;°   *securely*
As with the wind wavis the wicker,°   *willow*
15 Wavis this warldis vanitie;
    Timor Mortis conturbat me.

Unto the deid gois all Estatis,
Princes, Prelatis, and Potestatis,°   *potentates*
Baith rich and puir of all degree;
20   *Timor Mortis conturbat me.*

He takis the knichtis into the field,
Enarmit under helm and shield;
Victor he is at all mêlée;
    Timor Mortis conturbat me.

25 That strang unmerciful tyrand
Takis on the moderis breist soukand°   *sucking*
The babe, full of benignite;
    Timor Mortis conturbat me.

He takis the champion in the stour,°   *battle*
30 The capitane closit in the tour,
The lady in bour full of beautie;
    Timor Mortis conturbat me.

He sparis no lord for his puissance,
Na clerk° for his intelligence;   *scholar*
35 His awful straik may no man flee;
    Timor Mortis conturbat me.

Art magicianis, and astrologis,°   *astrologers*
Rethoris,° logicianis, and theologis,   *rhetoricians*
Them helpis no conclusionis sle;
40   *Timor Mortis conturbat me.*

1. "The fear of death confounds me," a line from the Office for the Dead. Cf. the anonymous 15th-century poem with the same refrain on p. 66.

In medicine the most° practicianis,
Leechis,° surigianis, and phisicianis,
Them-self fra deid° may not supple;°
Timor Mortis conturbat me.

greatest
doctors
death/help

45   I see that makaris amang the lave°
Playis here their pageant, syne° gois to grave;
Sparit is nocht their facultie;
Timor Mortis conturbat me.

remainder
then

He has done piteously devour
50   The noble Chaucer, of makaris flour,
The Monk of Bery, and Gower, all three;
Timor Mortis conturbat me.

The gude Sir Hew of Eglintoun,
And eik° Heriot, and Wintoun,
55   He has ta'en out of this countrie;
Timor Mortis conturbat me.

also

That scorpion fell has done infec'
Maister John Clerk and James Affleck,
Fra ballad-making and tragedie;
60   *Timor Mortis conturbat me.*

Holland and Barbour he has bereavit;
Alas! that he nought with us leavit
Sir Mungo Lockhart of the Lea;
Timor Mortis conturbat me.

65   Clerk of Tranent eke he has ta'en,
That made the Aunteris° of Gawain;[2]
Sir Gilbert Hay endit has he;
Timor Mortis conturbat me.

adventures

He has Blind Harry, and Sandy Traill
70   Slain with his shour of mortal hail,
Whilk° Patrick Johnstoun micht nocht flee;
Timor Mortis conturbat me.

which

He has reft° Merser endite,°
That did in luve so lively write,
75   So short, so quick, of sentence hie;
Timor Mortis conturbat me.

taken from/talent

He has ta'en Roull of Aberdeen,
And gentle Roull of Corstorphin;
Two better fellowis did no man see;
80   *Timor Mortis conturbat me.*

In Dunfermline he has done roune°
With Maister Robert Henryson;
Sir John the Ross embraced has he;
Timor Mortis conturbat me.

whisper

2. A hero of Arthurian romance.

85   And he has now ta'en, last of a',
     Gude gentle Stobo and Quintin Shaw,
     Of wham all wichtis° has pitie: *creatures*
          Timor Mortis conturbat me.

     Gude Maister Walter Kennedy
90   In point of deid lies verily,
     Great ruth° it were that so suld be;   *pity*
          Timor Mortis conturbat me.

     Sen he has all my brether ta'en,
     He will nocht lat me live alane,
95   On force I maun° his next prey be;   *must*
          Timor Mortis conturbat me.

     Sen for the deid remead° is none,   *remedy*
     Best is that we for deid dispone,°   *prepare*
     Eftir our deid that live may we;
100   *Timor Mortis conturbat me.*

                                                                 1508

Done Is a Battle

     Done is a battle on the dragon black,
     Our campion Christ confoundit has his force;
     The yettis° of hell are broken with a crack,   *gates*
     The sign triumphal raisit is of the cross,
5   The devillis trymmillis° with hiddous voce,   *tremble*
     The saulis are borrowit° and to the bliss can go,   *ransomed*
     Christ with his blood our ransonis dois indoce:°   *endorse*
     Surrexit Dominus de sepulchro.[1]

     Dungen° is the deidly dragon Lucifer,   *beaten*
10   The cruel serpent with the mortal stang;
     The auld keen tiger, with his teeth on char,°   *ajar*
     Whilk° in a wait has lyen for us so lang,   *which*
     Thinking to grip us in his clawis strang;
     The merciful Lord wald° nocht that it were so,   *would*
15   He made him for to failye of that fang:°   *prey*
     Surrexit Dominus de sepulchro.

     He for our sake that sufferit to be slain,
     And like a lamb in sacrifice was dicht,°   *prepared*
     Is like a lion risen up again,
20   And as a gyane° raxit° him on hicht;°   *giant/stretched/high*
     Sprungen is Aurora[2] radious° and bricht,   *radiant*
     On loft is gone the glorious Apollo,[3]
     The blissful day departit° fro the nicht: *separated*
     Surrexit Dominus de sepulchro.

25   The great victour again is risen on hicht,
     That for our quarrel to the death was woundit;
     The sun that wox° all pale now shinis bricht,   *waxed*
     And, darkness clearit, our faith is now refoundit;
     The knell of mercy fra the heaven is soundit,

1. "The Lord is risen from the grave."   3. God of the sun.
2. Goddess of the dawn.

30 The Christian are deliverit of their woe,
    The Jewis and their error are confoundit:
    Surrexit Dominus de sepulchro.

    The foe is chasit, the battle is done cease,
    The prison broken, the jevellouris° fleit° and flemit;°   *jailers/fled/banished*
35 The weir° is gone, confermit is the peace,   *war*
    The fetteris lowsit° and the dungeon temit,°   *loosed/emptied*
    The ranson made, the prisoneris redeemit;
    The field is won, owrecomen is the foe,
    Despoilit of the treasure that he yemit:°   *kept*
    Surrexit Dominus de sepulchro.

                                ca. 1510

JOHN SKELTON
(1460–1529)

My Darling Dear, My Daisy Flower

    With lullay, lullay, like a child,
    Thou sleepest too long, thou art beguiled.

  My darling dear, my daisy flower,
    Let me, quod° he, lie in your lap.   *quoth*
5 Lie still, quod she, my paramour,
    Lie still hardely,° and take a nap.   *indeed*
    His head was heavy, such was his hap,°   *luck*
  All drowsy dreaming, drowned in sleep,
  That of his love he took no keep.

10 With ba, ba, ba!¹ and bas,° bas, bas!   *kiss*
    She cherished him both cheek and chin,
  That he wist° never where he was: *knew*
    He had forgotten all deadly sin.
    He wanted wit her love to win:
15 He trusted her payment and lost all his pay;
  She left him sleeping and stole away.

  The rivers rough, the waters wan,
    She spARéd not to wet her feet;
  She waded over, she found a man
20   That halséd° her heartily and kissed her sweet: *embraced*
    Thus after her cold she caught a heat.
  My love, she said, routeth° in his bed;   *roots*
  Ywis° he hath an heavy head.   *for certain*

  What dreamest thou, drunkard, drowsy pate?
25   Thy lust° and liking is from thee gone;   *desire*
  Thou blinkard blowbowl,² thou wakest too late,
    Behold thou liest, luggard,° alone.   *sluggard*
    Well may thou sigh, well may thou groan,
    To deal with her so cowardly:
30 Ywis, pole hatchet,° she bleared thine eye.   *blockhead*

---

1. The "by" of *lullaby.*   2. Blinking sot.

Mannerly Margery Milk and Ale[3]

Ay, beshrew° you! by my fay,°   *curse / faith*
These wanton clerks be nice[4] alway!
Avaunt, avaunt, my popinjay!
What, will ye do nothing but play?
5   Tilly vally, straw,[5] let be I say!
    Gup,[6] Christian Clout, gup, Jack of the Vale!
    With Mannerly Margery Milk and Ale.

By God, ye be a pretty pode,°   *toad*
And I love you an whole cart-load.
10 Straw, James Foder, ye play the fode,°   *deceiver*
I am no hackney[7] for your rod:°   *riding*
Go watch a bull, your back is broad!
    Gup, Christian Clout, gup, Jack of the Vale!
    With Mannerly Margery Milk and Ale.

15 Ywis° ye deal uncourteously;   *for certain*
What, would ye frumple[8] me? now fy!
What, and ye shall be my pigesnye?°   *pet*
By Christ, ye shall not, no hardely:°   *indeed*
I will not be japéd° bodily!   *fooled with*
20   Gup, Christian Clout, gup, Jack of the Vale!
    With Mannerly Margery Milk and Ale.

Walk forth your way, ye cost me nought;
Now have I found that I have sought:
The best cheap flesh that ever I bought.
25 Yet, for His love that all hath wrought,
Wed me, or else I die for thought.
    Gup, Christian Clout, your breath is stale!
    Go, Mannerly Margery Milk and Ale!
    Gup, Christian Clout, gup, Jack of the Vale!
30   With Mannerly Margery Milk and Ale.

To Mistress Margaret Hussey

Merry Margaret,
   As midsummer flower,
Gentle as falcon
Or hawk of the tower:[9]
5 With solace and gladness,
Much mirth and no madness,
All good and no badness;
   So joyously,
   So maidenly,
10   So womanly
   Her demeaning
   In every thing,

3. On the somewhat uncertain basis of the original musical setting for three voices (and internal evidence), this lyric is sometimes printed as a dialogue between the title character and James Foder (named in line 10), to whom are given lines 4, 8–9, 17, 22–24, and sometimes the refrain lines.
4. "Nice" variously meant foolish, finicky, lascivious.
5. Expressions of contemptuous rejection: fiddlesticks, poppycock, nonsense.
6. Contracted (?) from *go up;* sometimes an exclamation of derision, remonstrance, or surprise, sometimes a command: get along, get out; get up.
7. I.e., an ordinary riding horse (as distinct from a warhorse or a plowhorse).
8. Wrinkle; rumple; muss up.
9. Hawk trained to fly high (*tower*).

Far, far passing
That I can indite,
15   Or suffice to write
Of Merry Margaret
   As midsummer flower,
Gentle as falcon
Or hawk of the tower.
20   As patient and still
And as full of good will
As fair Isaphill,[1]
Coriander,[2]
Sweet pomander,[3]
25 Good Cassander,[4]
Steadfast of thought,
Well made, well wrought,
Far may be sought
Ere that ye can find
30 So courteous, so kind
As Merry Margaret,
   This midsummer flower,
Gentle as falcon
Or hawk of the tower.

KING HENRY VIII
(1491–1547)

Green Groweth the Holly

Green groweth the holly,
So doth the ivy.
Though winter blasts blow never so high,
Green groweth the holly.

5 As the holly groweth green,
   And never changeth hue,
So I am, ever hath been,
   Unto my lady true.

As the holly groweth green
10   With ivy all alone
When flowers cannot be seen
   And greenwood leaves be gone,

Now unto my lady,
   Promise to her I make
15 From all other only
   To her I me betake.

Adieu, mine owne lady,
   Adieu, my speciall,
Who hath my heart truely,
20   Be sure, and ever shall.

1. Hypsipyle, princess of Lemnos, savior of her father's life, comforter of the Argives, mother of twins by Jason.
2. An aromatic herb.
3. A mixture of perfumed or aromatic substances made into a ball.
4. Cassandra, daughter of Priam and Hecuba; according to myth her beauty bedazzled Apollo himself, who conferred on her the gift of prophecy.

POPULAR BALLADS

Riddles Wisely Expounded[1]

1

There was a knicht riding frae° the east,   *from*
   Sing the cather banks, the bonnie brume[2]
Wha had been wooing at monie a place.
   And ye may beguile a young thing soon.

2

5 He came unto a widow's door,
And speird° where her three dochters were.   *asked*

3

"The auldest ane's to a washing gane,
The second's to a baking gane.

4

The youngest ane's to a wedding gane,
10 And it will be nicht or° she be hame."   *ere*

5

He sat him doun upon a stane,
Till thir° three lasses came tripping hame.   *these*

6

The auldest ane's to the bed making,
And the second ane's to the sheet spreading.

7

15 The youngest ane was bauld and bricht,
And she was to lie wi' this unco° knicht.   *stranger*

8

"Gin° ye will answer me questions ten,   *if*
The morn ye sall° be made my ain.   *shall*

9

"O what is higher nor the tree?
20 And what is deeper nor the sea?

10

"Or what is heavier nor the lead?
And what is better nor the bread?

11

"O what is whiter nor the milk?
Or what is safter nor the silk?

12

25 "Or what is sharper nor a thorn?
Or what is louder nor a horn?

13

"Or what is greener nor the grass?
Or what is waur° nor a woman was?"   *worse*

14

"O heaven is higher nor the tree,
30 And hell is deeper nor the sea.

15

"O sin is heavier nor the lead,
The blessing's better nor the bread.

1. Ballad versions are conventionally identified by the number and letter assigned them in the monumental collection, *The English and Scottish Popular Ballads*, 1892–98, edited by Francis James Child. "Riddles Wisely Expounded" is No. 1.C.
2. Hemp (cather) and broom are wildflowers to which folklore attributed properties pertinent to young love. Hempseed, sown on Hallowe'en, permitted a sight, over the left shoulder, of one's true love; broom, associated with witchcraft, provided oracular revelation in matters of the heart.

16

"The snaw is whiter nor the milk,
And the down is safter nor the silk.

17

35 "Hunger is sharper nor a thorn,
And shame is louder nor a horn.

18

"The pies[3] are greener nor the grass,
And Clootie's[4] waur nor a woman was."

19

As soon as she the fiend did name,
40 He flew awa' in a blazing flame.

The Douglas Tragedy[5]

1

"Rise up, rise up, now, Lord Douglas," she says,
  "And put on your armor so bright;
Let it never be said that a daughter of thine
  Was married to a lord under night.

2

5 "Rise up, rise up, my seven bold sons,
  And put on your armor so bright,
And take better care of your youngest sister,
  For your eldest's awa' the last night."

3

He's mounted her on a milk-white steed,
10 And himself on a dapple gray,
With a bugelet horn hung down by his side,
  And lightly they rode away.

4

Lord William looked o'er his left shoulder,
  To see what he could see,
15 And there he spied her seven brethren bold,
  Come riding over the lea.

5

"Light down, light down, Lady Margret," he said,
  "And hold my steed in your hand,
Until that against your seven brethren bold,
20 And your father, I mak a stand."

6

She held his steed in her milk-white hand,
  And never shed one tear,
Until that she saw her seven brethren fa',
  And her father hard fighting, who loved her so dear.

7

25 "O hold your hand, Lord William!" she said,
  "For your strokes they are wondrous sair;°   *sore*
True lovers I can get many a ane,
  But a father I can never get mair."

8

O she's ta'en out her handkerchief,
30 It was o' the holland° sae° fine,   *linen / so*
And aye she dighted° her father's bloody wounds,   *dressed*
  That were redder than the wine.

3. A name given to various species of wood-pecker.
4. Like "Hornie" and "Old Nick," a familiar name for the devil.
5. Child, No. 7.B.

9

"O choose, O choose, Lady Margret," he said,
   "O whether will ye gang° or bide?"   go
35 "I'll gang, I'll gang, Lord William," she said,
   "For ye have left me no other guide."

10

He's lifted her on a milk-white steed,
   And himself on a dapple gray,
With a bugelet horn hung down by his side,
40   And slowly they baith rade away.

11

O they rade on, and on they rade,
   And a' by the light of the moon,
Until they came to yon wan water,
   And there they lighted down.

12

45 They lighted down to tak a drink
   Of the spring that ran sae clear,
And down the stream ran his good heart's blood,
   And sair she 'gan to fear.

13

"Hold up, hold up, Lord William," she says,
50   "For I fear that you are slain."
" 'Tis naething but the shadow of my scarlet cloak,
   That shines in the water sae plain."

14

O they rade on, and on they rade,
   And a' by the light of the moon,
55 Until they cam to his mother's ha' door,
   And there they lighted down.

15

"Get up, get up, lady mother," he says,
   "Get up, and let me in!
Get up, get up, lady mother," he says,
60   "For this night my fair lady I've win.

16

"O mak my bed, lady mother," he says,
   "O mak it braid and deep,
And lay Lady Margret close at my back,
   And the sounder I will sleep."

17

65 Lord William was dead lang ere midnight,
   Lady Margret lang ere day,
And all true lovers that go thegither,
   May they have mair luck than they!

18

Lord William was buried in St. Mary's kirk,
70   Lady Margret in Mary's choir;
Out o' the lady's grave grew a bonny red rose,
   And out o' the knight's a briar.

19

And they twa met, and they twa plat,°   plaited
   And fain they wad° be near;   would
75 And a' the warld might ken° right weel   know
   They were twa lovers dear.

20
But by and rade the Black Douglas,
   And wow but he was rough!
For he pulled up the bonny briar,
80   And flang 't in St. Mary's Loch.

The Twa Sisters[6]

1
There was twa sisters in a bower,
   Edinburgh, Edinburgh
There was twa sisters in a bower,
   Stirling for ay
5 There was twa sisters in a bower,
There came a knight to be their wooer.
   Bonny Saint Johnston stands upon Tay.[7]

2
He courted the eldest wi' glove and ring,
But he loved the youngest above a' thing.

3
10 He courted the eldest wi' brotch° and knife,   *brooch*
But loved the youngest as his life.

4
The eldest she was vexed sair,°   *sore*
And much envied her sister fair.

5
Into her bower she could not rest,
15 Wi' grief and spite she almos' brast.°   *burst*

6
Upon a morning fair and clear,
She cried upon her sister dear:

7
"O sister, come to yon sea stran',
And see our father's ships come to lan'."

8
20 She's ta'en her by the milk-white han',
And led her down to yon sea stran'.

9
The youngest stood upon a stane,
The eldest came and threw her in.

10
She took her by the middle sma',
25 And dashed her bonny back to the jaw.°   *wave*

11
"O sister, sister, tak my han',
And I s'° mak you heir to a' my lan'.   *I shall*

12
"O sister, sister, tak my middle,
And ye s'° get my goud° and my gouden girdle.   *ye shall / gold*

13
30 "O sister, sister, save my life,
And I swear I's never be nae man's wife."

6. Child, No. 10.B.
7. Edinburgh, Stirling, and Perth (formerly St. John's Town, at the mouth of the river Tay) were ancient and rival Scottish cities, each in its day a capital; but it is not clear what relevance their cheers or slogans have to the story of the two sisters.

14

"Foul fa' the han' that I should tak,
It twin'd° me and my warlde's make.⁸   *parted*

15

"Your cherry cheeks and yellow hair
35   Gars° me gae° maiden for evermair."   *makes / go*

16

Sometimes she sank, and sometimes she swam,
Till she came down yon bonny mill-dam.

17

O out it came the miller's son,
And saw the fair maid swimmin' in.

18

40   "O father, father, draw your dam,
Here's either a mermaid or a swan."

19

The miller quickly drew the dam,
And there he found a drowned woman.

20

You coudna see her yellow hair
45   For goud° and pearl that were so rare.   *gold*

21

You coudna see her middle sma'
For gouden girdle that was sae° braw.°   *so / fine*

22

You coudna see her fingers white,
For gouden rings that was sae gryte.°   *great, large*

23

50   And by there came a harper fine,
That harped to the king at dine.

24

When he did look that lady upon,
He sighed and made a heavy moan.

25

He's ta'en three locks o' her yellow hair,
55   And wi' them strung his harp sae fair.

26

The first tune he did play and sing,
Was, "Farewell to my father, the king."

27

The nextin tune that he played syne,°   *then*
Was, "Farewell to my mother, the queen."

28

60   The lasten tune that he played then,
Was, "Wae° to my sister, fair Ellen."   *woe*

Lord Randal⁹

1

"O where ha' you been, Lord Randal, my son?
And where ha' you been, my handsome young man?"
"I ha' been at the greenwood; mother, mak my bed soon,
For I'm wearied wi' huntin', and fain wad° lie down."   *would*

---

8. "Warlde's make": earthly mate.   9. Child, No. 12.A.

2

"And wha met ye there, Lord Randal, my son?
And wha met you there, my handsome young man?"
"O I met wi' my true-love; mother, mak my bed soon,
For I'm wearied wi' huntin', and fain wad lie down."

3

"And what did she give you, Lord Randal, my son?
And what did she give you, my handsome young man?"
"Eels fried in a pan; mother, mak my bed soon,
For I'm wearied wi' huntin', and fain wad lie down."

4

"And wha gat your leavin's, Lord Randal, my son?
And wha gat your leavin's, my handsome young man?"
"My hawks and my hounds; mother, mak my bed soon,
For I'm wearied wi' huntin', and fain wad lie down."

5

"And what becam of them, Lord Randal, my son?
And what becam of them, my handsome young man?"
"They stretched their legs out and died; mother, mak my bed soon,
For I'm wearied wi' huntin', and fain wad lie down."

6

"O I fear you are poisoned, Lord Randal, my son!
I fear you are poisoned, my handsome young man!"
"O yes, I am poisoned; mother, mak my bed soon,
For I'm sick at the heart, and I fain wad lie down."

7

"What d' ye leave to your mother, Lord Randal, my son?
What d'ye leave to your mother, my handsome young man?"
"Four and twenty milk kye°; mother, mak my bed soon,   *kine, cattle*
For I'm sick at the heart, and I fain wad lie down."

8

"What d' ye leave to your sister, Lord Randal, my son?
What d' ye leave to your sister, my handsome young man?"
"My gold and my silver; mother, mak my bed soon,
For I'm sick at the heart, and I fain wad lie down."

9

"What d' ye leave to your brother, Lord Randal, my son?
What d' ye leave to your brother, my handsome young man?"
"My houses and my lands; mother, mak my bed soon,
For I'm sick at the heart, and I fain wad lie down."

10

"What d' ye leave to your true-love, Lord Randal, my son?
What d' ye leave to your true-love, my handsome young man?"
"I leave her hell and fire; mother, mak my bed soon,
For I'm sick at the heart, and I fain wad lie down."

Edward[1]

1

"Why does your brand° sae° drap wi' bluid,   *sword / so*
        Edward, Edward,
Why does your brand sae drap wi' bluid,
        And why sae sad gang° ye, O?"   *go*
"O I ha'e killed my hawk sae guid,
        Mither, mither,

1. Child, No. 13.B.

O I ha'e killed my hawk sae guid,
  And I had nae mair but he, O."
        2
"Your hawke's bluid was never sae reid,°   *red*
10   Edward, Edward,
Your hawke's bluid was never sae reid,
  My dear son I tell thee, O."
"O I ha'e killed my reid-roan steed,
    Mither, mither,
15 O I ha'e killed my reid-roan steed,
    That erst was sae fair and free, O."
        3
"Your steed was auld, and ye ha'e gat mair,
      Edward, Edward,
Your steed was auld, and ye ha'e gat mair,
20   Some other dule° ye drie,° O."   *grief / suffer*
"O I ha'e killed my fader dear,
    Mither, mither,
O I ha'e killed my fader dear,
    Alas, and wae° is me, O!"   *woe*
        4
25 "And whatten° penance wul ye drie for that,   *what sort of*
      Edward, Edward?
And whatten penance wul ye dree for that,
    My dear son, now tell me O?"
"I'll set my feet in yonder boat,
30   Mither, mither,
I'll set my feet in yonder boat,
    And I'll fare over the sea, O."
        5
"And what wul ye do wi' your towers and your ha',
      Edward, Edward?
35 And what wul ye do wi' your towers and your ha',
    That were sae fair to see, O?"
"I'll let them stand tul they down fa',
      Mither, mither,
I'll let them stand tul they down fa',
40   For here never mair maun° I be, O."   *must*
        6
"And what wul ye leave to your bairns° and your wife,   *children*
      Edward, Edward?
And what wul ye leave to your bairns and your wife,
    Whan ye gang over the sea, O?"
45 "The warlde's room,² let them beg thrae° life,   *through*
      Mither, mither,
The warlde's room, let them beg thrae life,
    For them never mair wul I see, O."
        7
"And what wul ye leave to your ain mither dear,
50   Edward, Edward?
And what wul ye leave to your ain mither dear,
    My dear son, now tell me, O?"
"The curse of hell frae° me sall° ye bear,   *from / shall*
      Mither, mither,
55 The curse of hell frae me sall ye bear,
    Sic° counsels ye gave to me, O."   *such*

2. I.e., the wide world.

Hind Horn[3]

1

In Scotland there was a baby born,
  Lill lal, etc.
And his name it was called young Hind Horn.
  With a fal lal, etc.

2

5 He sent a letter to our king.
That he was in love with his daughter Jean.

3

He's gi'en to her a silver wand,
With seven living lavrocks° sitting thereon.   *larks*

4

She's gi'en to him a diamond ring,
10 With seven bright diamonds set therein.

5

"When this ring grows pale and wan,
You may know by it my love is gane."

6

One day as he looked his ring upon,
He saw the diamonds pale and wan.

7

15 He left the sea and came to land,
And the first that he met was an old beggar man.

8

"What news, what news?" said young Hind Horn;
"No news, no news," said the old beggar man.

9

"No news," said the beggar, "no news at a',
20 But there is a wedding in the king's ha'.

10

"But there is a wedding in the king's ha',
That has halden these forty days and twa."

11

"Will ye lend me your begging coat?
And I'll lend you my scarlet cloak.

12

25 "Will you lend me your beggar's rung?°   *staff*
And I'll gi'e you my steed to ride upon.

13

"Will you lend me your wig o' hair,
To cover mine, because it is fair?"

14

The auld beggar man was bound for the mill,
30 But young Hind Horn for the king's hall.

15

The auld beggar man was bound for to ride,
But young Hind Horn was bound for the bride.

16

When he came to the king's gate,
He sought a drink for Hind Horn's sake.

17

35 The bride came down with a glass of wine,
When he drank out the glass, and dropped in the ring.

3. Child, No. 17.A.

18

"O got ye this by sea or land?
Or got ye it off a dead man's hand?"

19

I got not it by sea, I got it by land,
40 And I got it, madam, out of your own hand."

20

"O I'll cast off my gowns of brown,
And beg wi' you frae° town to town.   *from*

21

"O I'll cast off my gowns of red,
And I'll beg wi' you to win my bread."

22

45 "Ye needna cast off your gowns of brown,
For I'll make you lady o' many a town.

23

"Ye needna cast off your gowns of red,
It's only a sham, the begging o' my bread."

24

The bridegroom he had wedded the bride,
50 But young Hind Horn he took her to bed.

St. Stephen and Herod[7]

1

Saint Stephene was a clerk
    In King Herodes' hall,
And served him of° bread and cloth   *for*
    As every king befall.[8]

2

5 Stephen out of kitchen came
    With boare's head in hand;
He saw a star was fair and bright
    Over Bedlem° stand.   *Bethlehem*

3

He cast adown the boare's head
10   And went into the hall:
"I forsake thee, King Herodes,
    And thy workes all.

4

"I forsake thee, King Herodes,
    And thy workes all:
15 There is a child in Bedlem born
    Is better than we all."

5

"What aileth thee, Stephene?
    What is thee befall?
Lacketh thee either meat or drink
20   In King Herodes' hall?"

6

"Lacketh me neither meat ne drink
    In King Herodes' hall:
There is a child in Bedlem born
    Is better than we all."

7. Child, No. 22.
8. "As is appropriate to every king" [Donaldson's note].

7

²⁵ "What aileth thee, Stephen? Art thou wode,°   *mad*
Or thou 'ginnest to breed?⁹
Lacketh thee either gold or fee°   *property*
Or any riche weed?"°   *clothing*

8

"Lacketh me neither gold ne fee
³⁰ Ne none riche weed:
There is a child in Bedlem born
Shall help us at our need."

9

"That is also sooth,¹ Stephen,
Also sooth, iwis,°   *certainly*
³⁵ As this capon crowe shall
That li'th° here in my dish."

10

That word was not so soone said,
That word in that hall,
The capon crew *Christus natus est*²
⁴⁰ Among the lordes all.

11

"Riseth up, my tormentors,
By two and all be one,
And leadeth Stephen out of this town,
And stoneth him with stone."

12

⁴⁵ Tooken they Stephene,
And stoned him in the way;°   *road*
And therefore is his even° on   *eve*
Christe's owen day.

The Three Ravens³

1

There were three ravens sat on a tree,
   Down a down, hay down, hay down
There were three ravens sat on a tree,
   With a down
⁵ There were three ravens sat on a tree,
They were as black as they might be.
   With a down derry, derry, derry, down, down.

2

The one of them said to his mate,
"Where shall we our breakfast take?"

3

¹⁰ "Down in yonder greene field,
There lies a knight slain under his shield.

4

"His hounds they lie down at his feet,
So well they can their master keep.

5

"His hawks they fly so eagerly,°   *fiercely*
¹⁵ There's no fowl dare him come nigh."

9. I.e., getting strange notions as pregnant women do.
1. "Also sooth": as true.
2. Christ is born.
3. Child, No. 26.

6

Down there comes a fallow[4] doe,
As great with young as she might go.

7

She lift up his bloody head
And kissed his wounds that were so red.

8

20 She got him up upon her back
And carried him to earthen lake.°   *pit*

9

She buried him before the prime;[5]
She was dead herself ere even-song time.

10

God send every gentleman
25 Such hawks, such hounds, and such a leman.°   *lover, sweetheart*

The Twa Corbies[6]

1

As I was walking all alane,
I heard twa corbies making a mane;°   *moan*
The tane° unto the t'other say,   *one*
"Where sall° we gang° and dine to-day?"   *shall / go*

2

5 "In behint you auld fail° dike,   *turf*
I wot there lies a new slain knight;
And naebody kens° that he lies there,   *knows*
But his hawk, his hound, and lady fair.

3

"His hound is to the hunting gane,
10 His hawk to fetch the wild-fowl hame,
His lady's ta'en another mate,
So we may mak our dinner sweet.

4

"Ye'll sit on his white hause-bane,°   *neck-bone*
And I'll pike° out his bonny blue een;°   *pick / eyes*
15 Wi' ae° lock o' his gowden° hair   *one / golden*
We'll theek° our nest when it grows bare.   *thatch*

5

"Mony a one for him makes mane,
But nane sall ken where he is gane;
O'er his white banes, when they are bare,
20 The wind sall blaw for evermair."

Dives and Lazarus[2]

1

As it fell out upon a day,
    Rich Dives he made a feast,
And he invited all his friends,
    And gentry of the best.

---

4. A species of deer distinguished by color
(fallow: pale brownish or reddish yellow)
from the red deer.

5. The first hour of the day, sunrise.
6. Child, No. 26. "Corbies" are ravens.
2. Child, No. 56.A. See Luke xvi.19–31.

2

5 Then Lazarus laid him down and down,
       And down at Dives' door:
    "Some meat, some drink, brother Dives,
       Bestow upon the poor."
                    3
    "Thou art none of my brother, Lazarus,
10   That lies begging at my door;
    No meat nor drink will I give thee,
       Nor bestow upon the poor."
                    4
    Then Lazarus laid him down and down,
       And down at Dives' wall:
15 "Some meat, some drink, brother Dives,
       Or with hunger starve I shall."
                    5
    "Thou art none of my brother, Lazarus,
       That lies begging at my wall;
    No meat nor drink will I give thee,
20   But with hunger starve you shall."
                    6
    Then Lazarus laid him down and down,
       And down at Dives' gate:
    "Some meat, some drink, brother Dives,
       For Jesus Christ his sake."
                    7
25 "Thou art none of my brother, Lazarus,
       That lies begging at my gate;
    No meat nor drink will I give thee,
       For Jesus Christ his sake."
                    8
    Then Dives sent out his merry men,
30   To whip poor Lazarus away;
    They had no power to strike a stroke,
       But flung their whips away.
                    9
    Then Dives sent out his hungry dogs,
       To bite him as he lay;
35 They had no power to bite at all,
       But licked his sores away.
                    10
    As it fell out upon a day,
       Poor Lazarus sickened and died;
    Then came two angels out of heaven
40   His soul therein to guide.
                    11
    "Rise up, rise up, brother Lazarus,
       And go along with me;
    For you've a place prepared in heaven,
       To sit on an angel's knee."
                    12
45 As it fell out upon a day,
       Rich Dives sickened and died;
    Then came two serpents out of hell,
       His soul therein to guide.

13

"Rise up, rise up, brother Dives,
50   And go with us to see
A dismal place, prepared in hell,
    From which thou canst not flee."

14

Then Dives looked up with his eyes,
    And saw poor Lazarus blest:
55   "Give me one drop of water, brother Lazarus,
    To quench my flaming thirst.

15

"Oh had I as many years to abide
    As there are blades of grass,
Then there would be an end, but now
60   Hell's pains will ne'er be past.

16

"Oh was I now but álive again,
    The space of one half hour!
Oh that I had my peace secure!
    Then the devil should have no power."

Sir Patrick Spens[3]

1

The king sits in Dumferling town,
    Drinking the blude-reid° wine: *blood-red*
"O whar will I get guid sailor,
    To sail this ship of mine?"

2

5   Up and spak an eldern knicht,
    Sat at the king's richt knee:
"Sir Patrick Spens is the best sailor
    That sails upon the sea."

3

The king has written a braid° letter   *broad*
10   And signed it wi' his hand,
And sent it to Sir Patrick Spens,
    Was walking on the sand.

4

The first line that Sir Patrick read,
    A loud lauch° lauched he;   *laugh*
15   The next line that Sir Patrick read,
    The tear blinded his ee.°   *eye*

5

"O wha is this has done this deed,
    This ill deed done to me,
To send me out this time o' the year,
20   To sail upon the sea?

6

"Mak haste, mak haste, my mirry men all,
    Our guid ship sails the morn."
"O say na sae,° my master dear,   *so*
    For I fear a deadly storm.

3. Child, No. 58.A.

7

"Late, late yestre'en I saw the new moon
  Wi' the auld moon in hir arm,
And I fear, I fear, my dear master,
  That we will come to harm."

8

O our Scots nobles were richt laith°   *loath*
  To weet° their cork-heeled shoon,°   *wet / shoes*
But lang or° a' the play were played   *before*
  Their hats they swam aboon.[4]

9

O lang, lang may their ladies sit,
  Wi' their fans into their hand,
Or ere they see Sir Patrick Spens
  Come sailing to the land.

10

O lang, lang may the ladies stand
  Wi' their gold kems° in their hair,   *combs*
Waiting for their ain dear lords,
  For they'll see them na mair.

11

Half o'er, half o'er to Aberdour
  It's fifty fadom deep,
And there lies guid Sir Patrick Spens
  Wi' the Scots lords at his feet.

Lord Thomas and Fair Annet[1]

1

Lord Thomas and Fair Annet
  Sat a' day on a hill;
Whan night was come and sun was set,
  They had not talked their fill.

2

Lord Thomas said a word in jest,
  Fair Annet took it ill:
"A,° I will never wed a wife   *ah*
  Against my ain friends' will."

3

"Gif° ye wull never wed a wife,   *if*
  A wife wull ne'er wed ye:"
Sae° he is hame to tell his mither,   *so*
  And knelt upon his knee.

4

"O rede,° O rede, mither," he says,   *counsel*
  "A gude rede gi'e to me;
O sall° I tak the nut-brown bride,   *shall*
  And let Fair Annet be?"

5

"The nut-brown bride has gowd° and gear,° *gold / property*
  Fair Annet she has gat nane;
And the little beauty Fair Annet has
  O it wull soon be gane."

---

4. I.e., their hats swam above (them).   1. Child, No. 73.A.

6

And he has till° his brother gane: *to*
"Now, brother, rede ye me;
A, sall I marry the nut-brown bride,
And let Fair Annet be?"

7

25   "The nut-brown bride has oxen, brother,
The nut-brown bride has kye;°   *kine, cattle*
I wad° ha'e ye marry the nut-brown bride,   *would*
And cast Fair Annet by."

8

"Her oxen may die i' the house, billie,°   *brother*
30   And her kye into the byre,°   *barn*
And I sall ha'e nothing to mysell
But a fat fadge° by the fire."   *baggage*

9

And he has till his sister gane:
"Now, sister, rede ye me;
35   O sall I marry the nut-brown bride,
And set Fair Annet free?"

10

I s'° rede ye tak Fair Annet, Thomas,   *shall*
And let the brown bride alane;
Lest ye should sigh, and say, 'Alas,
40   What is this we brought hame!' "

11

"No, I will tak my mither's counsel,
And marry me out o' hand;[2]
And I will tak the nut-brown bride,
Fair Annet may leave the land."

12

45   Up then rose Fair Annet's father,
Twa hours or° it were day,   *before*
And he is gane into the bower
Wherein Fair Annet lay.

13

"Rise up, rise up, Fair Annet," he says,
50   "Put on your silken sheen;°   *shoes*
Let us gae° to St Marie's kirk,   *go*
And see that rich weddeen."

14

"My maids, gae to my dressing-room,
And dress to° me my hair;   *for*
55   Where'er ye laid a plait before,
See ye lay ten times mair.

15

"My maids, gae to my dressing-room,
And dress to me my smock;
The one half is o' the holland° fine,   *linen*
60   The other o' needle-work."

16

The horse Fair Annet rade upon,
He ambled like the wind;
Wi' siller° he was shod before,   *silver*
Wi' burning gowd° behind.   *gold*

2. "Out o' hand": at once.

17

65 Four and twenty siller bells
    Were a' tied till his mane,
And yae tift[3] o' the norland wind,
    They tinkled ane by ane.

18

Four and twenty gay gude knichts
70   Rade by Fair Annet's side,
And four and twenty fair ladies,
    As gin° she had bin a bride.   *if*

19

And when she cam to Marie's kirk,
    She sat on Marie's stean:[4]
75 The cleading° that Fair Annet had on   *clothing*
    It skinkled° in their een.°   *sparkled / eyes*

20

And whan she cam into the kirk,
    She shimmered like the sun;
The belt that was about her waist
80   Was a' wi' pearls bedone.°   *worked*

21

She sat her by the nut-brown bride,
    And her een they were sae clear,
Lord Thomas he clean forgat the bride,
    Whan Fair Annet drew near.

22

85 He had a rose into his hand,
    He ga'e it kisses three,
And reaching by the nut-brown bride,
    Laid it on Fair Annet's knee.

23

Up than spak the nut-brown bride,
90   She spak wi' meikle° spite: *great*
"And where gat ye that rose-water,
    That does mak ye sae white?"

24

"O I did get the rose-water
    Where ye wull ne'er get nane,
95 For I did get that very rose-water
    Into my mither's wame."°   *womb*

25

The bride she drew a long bodkin
    Frae° out her gay head-gear,   *from*
And strake Fair Annet unto the heart,
100   That word spak never mair.

26

Lord Thomas he saw Fair Annet wex pale,
    And marveled what mote° be;   *might*
But whan he saw her dear heart's blude,
    A' wood-wroth° wexed he.   *furious*

27

105 He drew his dagger, that was sae sharp,
    That was sae sharp and meet,°   *fit*
And drave it into the nut-brown bride,
    That fell dead at his feet.

---

3. "Yae tift": every puff.
4. "A stone seat at the door of St. Mary's Church" [Child's note].

28

"Now stay for me, dear Annet," he said,
110   "Now stay, my dear," he cried;
Then strake the dagger untill° his heart,   *into*
    And fell dead by her side.

29

Lord Thomas was buried without kirk-wa',
    Fair Annet within the choir,
115 And o' the tane° there grew a birk,°   *one / birch*
    The other a bonny briar.

30

And ay they grew, and ay they threw,°   *intertwined*
    As they wad fain be near;
And by this ye may ken° right weil   *know*
120   They were twa lovers dear.

The Unquiet Grave[9]

1

"The wind doth blow today, my love,
    And a few small drops of rain;
I never had but one true-love,
    In cold grave she was lain.

2

5 "I'll do as much for my true-love
    As any young man may;
I'll sit and mourn all at her grave
    For a twelvemonth and a day."

3

The twelvemonth and a day being up,
10   The dead began to speak:
"Oh who sits weeping on my grave,
    And will not let me sleep?"

4

" 'T is I, my love, sits on your grave,
    And will not let you sleep;
15 For I crave one kiss of your clay-cold lips,
    And that is all I seek."

5

"You crave one kiss of my clay-cold lips,
    But my breath smells earthy strong;
If you have one kiss of my clay-cold lips,
20   Your time will not be long.

6

" 'T is down in yonder garden green,
    Love, where we used to walk,
The finest flower that e'er was seen
    Is withered to a stalk.

7

25 "The stalk is withered dry, my love,
    So will our hearts decay;
So make yourself content, my love,
    Till God calls you away."

9. Child, No. 78.A.

The Wife of Usher's Well[1]

1

There lived a wife at Usher's Well,
And a wealthy wife was she;
She had three stout and stalwart sons,
And sent them o'er the sea.

2

5 They hadna been a week from her,
A week but barely ane,
When word came to the carlin° wife   *peasant*
That her three sons were gane.

3

They hadna been a week from her,
10 A week but barely three,
When word came to the carlin wife
That her sons she'd never see.

4

"I wish the wind may never cease,
Nor fashes° in the flood,   *troubles*
15 Till my three sons come hame to me,
In earthly flesh and blood."

5

It fell about the Martinmass,[2]
When nights are lang and mirk,
The carlin wife's three sons came hame,
20 And their hats were o' the birk.°   *birch*

6

It neither grew in syke° nor ditch,   *trench*
Nor yet in any sheugh;°   *furrow*
But at the gates o' Paradise,
That birk grew fair eneugh.

7

25 "Blow up the fire, my maidens,
Bring water from the well;
For a' my house shall feast this night,
Since my three sons are well."

8

And she has made to them a bed,
30 She's made it large and wide,
And she's ta'en her mantle her about,
Sat down at the bed-side.

9

Up then crew the red, red cock,
And up and crew the gray;
35 The eldest to the youngest said,
" 'T is time we were away."

10

The cock he hadna crawed but once,
And clapped his wings at a',
When the youngest to the eldest said,
40 "Brother, we must awa'.

---

1. Child, No. 79.A.
2. The feast of St. Martin (the martyred Pope Martin I, died 655), November 11.

11

"The cock doth craw, the day doth daw,
  The channerin'° worm doth chide;   *fretting*
Gin° we be missed out o' our place,   *if*
  A sair° pain we maun° bide.   *sore / must*

12

45 "Fare ye weel, my mother dear!
  Fareweel to barn and byre!°   *cowhouse*
And fare ye weel, the bonny lass,
  That kindles my mother's fire!"

Little Musgrave and Lady Barnard[3]

1

As it fell one holy-day, *Hay down*
  As many be in the year,
When young men and maids together did go,
  Their matins and mass to hear,

2

5 Little Musgrave came to the church-door;
  The priest was at private mass;
But he had more mind of the fair women
  Then he had of our lady's grace.

3

The one of them was clad in green,
10 Another was clad in pall,°   *velvet*
And then came in my Lord Barnard's wife,
  The fairest amongst them all.

4

She cast an eye on Little Musgrave,
  As bright as the summer sun;
15 And then bethought this Little Musgrave,
  This lady's heart have I won.

5

Quoth she, "I have loved thee, Little Musgrave,
  Full long and many a day";
"So have I loved you, fair lady,
20 Yet never word durst I say."

6

"I have a bower at Bucklesfordbery,
  Full daintily it is dight;°   *fitted out*
If thou wilt wend thither, thou Little Musgrave,
  Thou s' lig[4] in mine arms all night."

7

25 Quoth he, "I thank ye, fair lady,
  This kindness thou showest to me;
But whether it be to my weal or woe,
  This night I will lig with thee."

8

With that he heard, a little tiny page,
30 By his lady's coach as he ran:
"Although I am my lady's foot-page,
  Yet I am Lord Barnard's man.

---

3. Child, No. 81.A.   4. Thou shalt lie.

9

"My Lord Barnard shall know of this,
   Whether I sink or swim";
35 And ever where the bridges were broke
   He laid him down to swim.

10

"A sleep or wake,[5] thou Lord Barnard,
   As thou art a man of life,
For Little Musgrave is at Bucklesfordbery,
40   Abed with thine own wedded wife."

11

"If this be true, thou little tiny page,
   This thing thou tellest to me,
Then all the land in Bucklesfordbery
   I freely will give to thee.

12

45 "But if it be a lie, thou little tiny page,
   This thing thou tellest to me,
On the highest tree in Bucklesfordbery
   Then hanged shalt thou be."

13

He called up his merry men all:
50   "Come saddle me my steed;
This night must I to Bucklesfordbery,
   For I never had greater need."

14

And some of them whistled, and some of them sung,
   And some these words did say,
55 And ever when my Lord Barnard's horn blew,
   "Away, Musgrave, away!"

15

"Methinks I hear the threstle-cock,°   *thrush*
   Methinks I hear the jay,
Methinks I hear my Lord Barnard,
60   And I would I were away."

16

"Lie still, lie still, thou Little Musgrave,
   And huggle me from the cold;[6]
'T is nothing but a shepherd's boy,
   A driving his sheep to the fold.

17

65 "Is not thy hawk upon a perch?
   Thy steed eats oats and hay;
And thou a fair lady in thine arms,
   And wouldst thou be away?"

18

With that my Lord Barnard came to the door,
70   And lit a stone upon;
He plucked out three silver keys,
   And he opened the doors each one.

19

He lifted up the coverlet,
   He lifted up the sheet:
75 "How now, how now, thou Little Musgrave,
   Dost thou find my lady sweet?"

5. Forever (*A*: aye) sleep or awake (at once).   6. Hug (*huggle*) me (to keep me) from the cold.

20

"I find her sweet," quoth Little Musgrave,
    "The more 'tis to my pain;
80 I would gladly give three hundred pounds
    That I were on yonder plain."

21

"Arise, arise, thou Little Musgrave,
    And put thy clothés on;
It shall ne'er be said in my country
    I have killed a naked man.

22

85 "I have two swords in one scabberd,
    Full dear they cost my purse;
And thou shalt have the best of them,
    And I will have the worse."

23

The first stroke that Little Musgrave stroke,
90   He hurt Lord Barnard sore;
The next stroke that Lord Barnard stroke,
    Little Musgrave ne'er struck more.

24

With that bespake this fair lady,
    In bed whereas° she lay: *where*
95 "Although thou'rt dead, thou Little Musgrave,
    Yet I for thee will pray.

25

"And wish well to thy soul will I,
    So long as I have life;
So will I not for thee, Barnard,
100   Although I am thy wedded wife."

26

He cut her paps from off her breast;
    Great pity it was to see
That some drops of this lady's heart's blood
    Ran trickling down her knee.

27

105 "Woe worth° you, woe worth, my merry men all,   *become*
    You were ne'er born for my good;
Why did you not offer to stay my hand,
    When you see me wax so wood?°   *furious*

28

"For I have slain the bravest sir knight
110   That ever rode on steed;
So have I done the fairest lady
    That ever did woman's deed.

29

"A grave, a grave," Lord Barnard cried,
    "To put these lovers in;
115 But lay my lady on the upper hand,
    For she came of the better kin."

Bonny Barbara Allan[7]

1

It was in and about the Martinmas[8] time,
    When the green leaves were a falling,

7. Child, No. 84.A.
8. The feast of St. Martin (the martyred Pope Martin I, died 655), November 11.

That Sir John Græme, in the West Country,
    Fell in love with Barbara Allan.

2

5 He sent his man down through the town,
    To the place where she was dwelling:
"O haste and come to my master dear,
    Gin° ye be Barbara Allan."   *if*

3

O hooly,° hooly rose she up,   *slowly, gently*
10   To the place where he was lying,
And when she drew the curtain by:
    "Young man, I think you're dying."

4

"O it's I'm sick, and very, very sick,
    And 'tis a' for Barbara Allan."
15 "O the better for me ye s'° never be,   *ye shall*
    Though your heart's blood were a-spilling.

5

"O dinna° ye mind, young man," said she,   *don't*
    "When ye was in the tavern a drinking,
That ye made the healths gae° round and round,   *go*
20   And slighted Barbara Allan?"

6

He turned his face unto the wall,
    And death was with him dealing:
"Adieu, adieu, my dear friends all,
    And be kind to Barbara Allan."

7

25 And slowly, slowly raise she up,
    And slowly, slowly left him,
And sighing said, she could not stay,
    Since death of life had reft him.

8

She had not gane a mile but twa,
30   When she heard the dead-bell ringing,
And every jow° that the dead-bell geid,°   *stroke / gave*
    It cried, "Woe to Barbara Allan!"

9

"O mother, mother, make my bed!
    O make it saft and narrow!
35 Since my love died for me to-day,
    I'll die for him to-morrow."

The Bailiff's Daughter of Islington[9]

1

There was a youth, and a well beloved youth,
    And he was a esquire's son,
He loved the bailiff's daughter dear,
    That lived in Islington.

2

5 She was coy, and she would not believe
    That he did love her so,
No, nor at any time she would
    Any countenance to him show.

9. Child, No. 105.

3

But when his friends did understand
   His fond and foolish mind,
10 They sent him up to fair London,
   An apprentice for to bind.

4

And when he had been seven long years,
   And his love he had not seen:
15 "Many a tear have I shed for her sake
   When she little thought of me."

5

All the maids of Islington
   Went forth to sport and play;
All but the bailiff's daughter dear;
20   She secretly stole away.

6

She put off her gown of gray,
   And put on her puggish° attire;   *trampish*
She's up to fair London gone,
   Her true love to require.°   *inquire after*

7

25 As she went along the road,
   The weather being hot and dry,
There was she aware of her true love,
   At length came riding by.

8

She stepped to him, as red as any rose,
30   And took him by the bridle-ring:
"I pray you, kind sir, give me one penny,
   To ease my weary limb."

9

"I prithee, sweetheart, canst thou tell me
   Where that thou wast born?"
35 "At Islington, kind sir," said she,
   "Where I have had many a scorn."

10

"I prithee, sweetheart, canst thou tell me
   Whether thou dost know
The bailiff's daughter of Islington?"
40   "She's dead, sir, long ago."

11

"Then will I sell my goodly steed,
   My saddle and my bow;
I will into some far country,
   Where no man doth me know."

12

45 "O stay, O stay, thou goodly youth!
   She's alive, she is not dead;
Here she standeth by thy side,
   And is ready to be thy bride."

13

"O farewell grief, and welcome joy,
50   Ten thousand times and more!
For now I have seen my own true love,
   That I thought I should have seen no more."

The Baffled Knight[1]

1

There was a knight, and he was young,
  A-riding along the way, sir,
And there he met a lady fair,
  Among the cocks of hay, sir.

2

5 Quoth he, "Shall you and I, lady,
  Among the grass lie down a?
And I will have a special care
  Of rumpling of your gown a."

3

"If you will go along with me
10 Unto my father's hall, sir,
You shall enjoy my maidenhead,
  And my estate and all, sir."

4

So he mounted her on a milk-white steed,
  Himself upon another,
15 And then they rid upon the road,
  Like sister and like brother.

5

And when she came to her father's house,
  Which was moated round about, sir,
She stepped straight within the gate,
20 And shut this young knight out, sir.

6

"Here is a purse of gold," she said,
  "Take it for your pains, sir;
And I will send my father's man
  To go home with you again, sir.

7

25 "And if you meet a lady fair,
  As you go through the next town, sir,
You must not fear the dew of the grass,
  Nor the rumpling of her gown, sir.

8

"And if you meet a lady gay,
30 As you go by the hill, sir,
If you will not when you may,
  You shall not when you will, sir."

Johnie Armstrong[2]

1

There dwelt a man in fair Westmoreland,
  Johnie Armstrong men did him call,
He had neither lands nor rents coming in,
  Yet he kept eight score men in his hall.

2

5 He had horse and harness for them all,
  Goodly steeds were all milk-white;
O the golden bands an about their necks,
  And their weapons, they were all alike.

1. Child, No. 112.B.   2. Child, No. 169.A.

3

News then was brought unto the king
10   That there was sic° a one as he,   *such*
That livéd lyke a bold outlaw,
    And robbéd all the north country.

4

The king he writ an a letter then,
    A letter which was large and long;
15 He signéd it with his owne hand,
    And he promised to do him no wrong.

5

When this letter came Johnie untill,
    His heart it was as blythe as birds on the tree:
"Never was I sent for before any king,
20   My father, my grandfather, nor none but me.

6

"And if we go the king before,
    I would we went most orderly;
Every man of you shall have his scarlet cloak,
    Laced with silver laces three.

7

25 "Every one of you shall have his velvet coat,
    Laced with silver lace so white;
O the golden bands an about your necks,
    Black hats, white feathers, all alike."

8

By the morrow morning at ten of the clock,
30   Towards Edinburgh gone was he,
And with him all his eight score men;
    Good Lord, it was a goodly sight for to see!

9

When Johnie came before the king,
    He fell down on his knee;
35 "O pardon, my sovereign leige," he said,
    "O pardon my eight score men and me!"

10

"Thou shalt have no pardon, thou traitor strong,
    For thy eight score men nor thee;
For tomorrow morning by ten of the clock,
40   Both thou and them shall hang on the gallow-tree."

11

But Johnie looked over his left shoulder,
    Good Lord, what a grevious look looked he!
Saying, "Asking grace of a graceless face—
    Why there is none for you nor me."

12

45 But Johnie had a bright sword by his side,
    And it was made of the metal so free,[3]
That had not the king stepped his foot aside,
    He had smitten his head from his fair body.

13

Saying, "Fight on, my merry men all,
50   And see that none of you be ta'en;
For rather than men shall say we were hanged,
    Let them report how we were slain."

---

3. "Free" has a range of meanings: noble, ready, workable.

14

Then, God wot, fair Edinburgh rose,
    And so beset poor Johnie round,
55 That fourscore and ten of Johnie's best men
    Lay gasping all upon the ground.

15

Then like a mad man Johnie laid about,
    And like a mad man then fought he,
Until a false Scot came Johnie behind,
60   And run him through the fair body.

16

Saying, "Fight on, my merry men all,
    And see that none of you be ta'en;
For I will stand by and bleed but awhile,
    And then will I come and fight again."

17

65 News then was brought to young Johnie Armstrong,
    As he stood by his nurse's knee,
Who vowed if e'er he lived for to be a man,
    O' the treacherous Scots revenged he'd be.

Mary Hamilton[4]

1

Word's gane to the kitchen,
    And word's gane to the ha',
That Marie Hamilton gangs° wi' bairn°   *goes / child*
    To the hichest° Stewart of a'.   *highest*

2

5 He's courted her in the kitchen,
    He's courted her in the ha',
He's courted her in the laigh cellar,[5]
    And that was warst of a'.

3

She's tied it in her apron
10   And she's thrown it in the sea;
Says, "Sink ye, swim ye, bonny wee babe!
    You'll ne'er get mair o' me."

4

Down then cam the auld queen,   *gold*
    Goud° tassels tying her hair:
15 "O Marie, where's the bonny wee babe
    That I heard greet sae sair?"[6]

5

"There was never a babe intill° my room,   *in*
    As little designs to be;
It was but a touch o' my sair side,
20   Come o'er my fair body."

6

"O Marie, put on your robes o' black,
    Or else your robes o' brown,
For ye maun° gang wi' me the night,   *must*
    To see fair Edinbro' town."

4. Child, No. 173.A.
5. "Laigh cellar": low cellar, basement.

6. "Greet sae sair": cry so sorely.

7

25 "I winna° put on my robes o' black,   *won't*
 Nor yet my robes o' brown;
But I'll put on my robes o' white,
 To shine through Edinbro' town."

8

When she gaed° up the Cannogate,[7]   *went*
30 She laughed loud laughters three;
But when she cam down the Cannogate
 The tear blinded her ee.°   *eye*

9

When she gaed up the Parliament stair,
 The heel cam aff her shee;
35 And lang or° she cam down again   *before*
 She was condemned to dee.

10

When she cam down the Cannogate,
 The Cannogate sae free,
Many a lady looked o'er her window,
40 Weeping for this lady.

11

"Ye need nae weep for me," she says,
 "Ye need nae weep for me;
For had I not slain mine own sweet babe,
 This death I wadna dee.

12

45 "Bring me a bottle of wine," she says,
 "The best that e'er ye ha'e,
That I may drink to my weil-wishers,
 And they may drink to me.

13

"Here's a health to the jolly sailors,
50 That sail upon the main;
Let them never let on to my father and mother
 But what I'm coming hame.

14

"Here's a health to the jolly sailors,
 That sail upon the sea;
55 Let them never let on to my father and mother
 That I cam here to dee.

15

"Oh little did my mother think,
 The day she cradled me,
What lands I was to travel through,
60 What death I was to dee.

16

"Oh little did my father think,
 The day he held up me,
What lands I was to travel through,
 What death I was to dee.

17

65 "Last night I washed the queen's feet,
 And gently laid her down;

7. The Canongate is the Edinburgh street leading uphill from Holyrood House (where the queen and the "four Maries" of line 69 lived) to the Tolbooth, which was both jail and judicial chamber and, on occasion, the place where Parliament (line 33) sat.

And a' the thanks I've gotten the night[8]
  To be hanged in Edinbro' town!
      18
"Last night there was four Maries,
  The night there'll be but three;
There was Marie Seton, and Marie Beton,
  And Marie Carmichael, and me."

Bonnie George Campbell[9]

     1
High upon Highlands,
  And laigh° upon Tay,[1]   *low*
Bonnie George Campbell
  Rode out on a day.
     2
He saddled, he bridled,
  And gallant rode he,
And hame cam his guid horse,
  But never cam he.

     3
Out cam his mother dear,
  Greeting° fu' sair,°   *weeping / sore[ly]*
And out cam his bonnie bride,
  Riving° her hair.   *tearing*

     4
"The meadow lies green,
  The corn is unshorn,
But bonnie George Campbell
  Will never return."

     5
Saddled and bridled
  And booted rode he,
A plume in his helmet,
  A sword at his knee.
     6
But toom° cam his saddle,   *empty*
  All bloody to see,
Oh, hame cam his guid horse,
  But never cam he!

Get Up and Bar the Door[2]

     1
It fell about the Martinmas[3] time,
  And a gay time it was then,
When our goodwife got puddings to make,
  And she's boiled them in the pan.

     2
The wind sae° cauld blew south and north,   *so*
  And blew into the floor;
Quoth our goodman to our goodwife,
  "Gae° out and bar the door."   *go*

8. I.e., tonight.
9. Child, No. 210.C.
1. The longest river in Sotland, coming down from the Highlands into the Lowlands and entering the North Sea at Perth.
2. Child, No. 275.A.
3. The feast of St. Martin (the martyred Pope Martin I, died 655), November 11.

3

"My hand is in my hussyfskap.°   *housewifery*
    Goodman, as ye may see;
An° it should nae be barred this hundred year,   *if*
    It s'° no be barred for me."   *shall*

4

They made a paction 'tween them twa,
    They made it firm and sure,
That the first word whae'er should speak,
    Should rise and bar the door.

5

Then by there came two gentlemen,
    At twelve o'clock at night,
And they could neither see house nor hall,
    Nor coal nor candle-light.

6

"Now whether is this a rich man's house,
    Or whether is it a poor?"
But ne'er a word wad° ane o' them speak,   *would*
    For barring of the door.

7

And first they ate the white puddings,
    And then they ate the black;
Though muckle° thought the goodwife to hersel,   *much, a lot*
    Yet ne'er a word she spak.

8

Then said the one unto the other,
    "Here, man, tak ye my knife;
Do ye tak aff° the auld man's beard,   *off*
    And I'll kiss the goodwife."

9

"But there's nae water in the house,
    And what shall we do then?"
"What ails ye at⁴ the pudding-broo,°   *-broth*
    That boils into the pan?"

10

O up then started our goodman,
    An angry man was he:
"Will ye kiss my wife before my een,°   *eyes*
    And scad° me wi' pudding-bree?"°   *scald / -broth*

11

Then up and started our goodwife,
    Gied° three skips on the floor: *gave*
"Goodman, you've spoken the foremost word,
    Get up and bar the door."

The Bitter Withy

1

As it fell out on a holy day,
    The drops of rain did fall, did fall,
Our Saviour asked leave of his mother Mary
    If he might go play at ball.

2

"To play at ball, my own dear son,
    It's time you was going or gone,

4. I.e., what's the matter with.

But be sure let me hear no complain of you,
   At night when you do come home."

      3
It was upling scorn and downling scorn,[5]
   Oh, there he met three jolly jerdins;°   *boys?*
Oh, there he asked the jolly jerdins
   If they would go play at ball.

      4
"Oh, we are lords' and ladies' sons,
   Born in bower or in hall,
And you are some poor maid's child
   Borned in an ox's stall."

      5
"If you are lords' and ladies' sons,
   Borned in bower or in hall,
Then at last I'll make it appear
   That I am above you all."

      6
Our Saviour built a bridge with the beams of the sun,
   And over it he gone, he gone he.
And after followed the three jolly jerdins,
   And drownded they were all three.

      7
It was upling scorn and downling scorn,
   The mothers of them did whoop and call,
Crying out, "Mary mild, call home your child,
   For ours are drownded all."

      8
Mary mild, Mary mild, called home her child,
   And laid our Saviour across her knee,
And with a whole handful of bitter withy°   *willow*
   She gave him slashes three.

      9
Then he says to his mother, "Oh! the withy, oh! the withy,
   The bitter withy that causes me to smart, to smart,
Oh! the withy, it shall be the very first tree
   That perishes at the heart."

ANONYMOUS ELIZABETHAN AND JACOBEAN POEMS

When Flora Had Ourfret the Firth

When Flora [1] had ourfret° the firth,°   *adorned/forest*
   In May of every moneth queen;
When merle° and mavis° singis with mirth,   *blackbird/thrush*
   Sweet melling° in the shawis° sheen;° *blending/woods/shining*
   When all luvaris rejoicit been,
And most desirous of their prey;
   I heard a lusty luvar maen:°   *moan*
   "I luve, bot I dar nocht assay.°   *attempt*

---

5. There was scorn everywhere (*upling, downling*).   1. Goddess of springtime.

"Strang are the painis I daily prove°   *experience*
10   Bot yit with patience I sustene,
I am so fetterit with the luve
        Only of my lady sheen,
        Whilk° for her beauty micht be queen;   *who*
Nature sa craftily alway
15   Has done depaint that sweet serene;
Whom I luve I dar nocht assay.

"She is so bricht of hide and hue,
        I luve bot her alone, I ween;°   *believe*
Is none her luve that may eschew,
20   That blenkis° of that dulce° amene.°   *catches a glimpse/sweet/agreeable*
        So comely clear are her twa een,°   *eyes*
That she ma° luvaris does effray,°   *more/frighten*
        Than ever of Greece did fair Helene,[2]
Whom I luve I dar nocht assay."

before 1568

Love Me Little, Love Me Long

Love me little, love me long,
Is the burden of my song.
Love that is too hot and strong
        Burneth soon to waste.
5   Still, I would not have thee cold,
Not too backward, nor too bold;
Love that lasteth till 'tis old
        Fadeth not in haste.
        Love me little, love me long,
10   *Is the burden of my song.*

If thou lovest me too much,
It will not prove as true as touch;[1]
Love me little, more than such,
        For I fear the end.
15 I am with little well content,
And a little from thee sent
Is enough, with true intent
        To be steadfast friend.

Say thou lov'st me while thou live;
20 I to thee my love will give,
Never dreaming to deceive
        Whiles that life endures.
Nay, and after death, in sooth,
I to thee will keep my truth,
25 As now, when in my May of youth;
        This my love assures.

Constant love is moderate ever,
And it will through life persever;
Give me that, with true endeavor
30   I will it restore.

2. Helen of Troy, renowned as the most beauti-
ful woman in the world.
1. Touchstone or basanite; gold or silver

rubbed on touchstone produces a streak, the
appearance of which was formerly used as a
test for the purity of the metal.

A suit of durance° let it be,   *durability*
For all weathers that for me,
For the land or for the sea,
    Lasting evermore.

35 Winter's cold, or summer's heat,
Autumn's tempests on it beat,
It can never know defeat,
    Never can rebel.
Such the love that I would gain,
40 Such the love, I tell thee plain,
Thou must give, or woo in vain;
    So to thee, farewell!

                                                  ca. 1570

As You Came from the Holy Land of Walsingham[2]

As you came from the holy land
    Of Walsingham,
Met you not with my true love,
    By the way as you came?

5 "How should I know your true love
    That have met many a one
As I came from the holy land,
    That have come, that have gone?"

She is neither white nor brown,
10   But as the heavens fair;
There is none hath her form so divine,
    On the earth, in the air.

"Such a one did I meet, good sir,
    With angel-like face,
15 Who like a nymph, like a queen did appear
    In her gait, in her grace."

She hath left me here alone,
    All alone unknown,
Who sometime loved me as her life,
20   And called me her own.

"What is the cause she hath left thee alone,
    And a new way doth take,
That sometime did thee love as herself,
    And her joy did thee make?"

25 I have loved her all my youth,
    But now am old as you see;
Love liketh not the falling fruit,
    Nor the withered tree.

For love is a careless child,
30   And forgets promise past;
He is blind, he is deaf, when he list,°   *pleases*
    And in faith never fast.

2. A shrine in Norfolk, famous as a place of pilgrimage.

His desire is fickle found,
  And a trustless joy;
35 He is won with a world of despair,
  And is lost with a toy.

Such is the love of womenkind,
  Or the word, love, abused,
Under which many childish desires
40   And conceits are excused.

But love, it is a durable fire
  In the mind ever burning,
Never sick, never dead, never cold,
  From itself never turning.

                              ca. 1593   1678

Sweet Violets

Sweet violets, Love's paradise, that spread
  Your gracious odors, which you couchéd bear
      Within your paly faces,
Upon the gentle wing of some calm breathing wind
5   That plays amidst the plain,
  If by the favor of propitious stars you gain
Such grace as in my lady's bosom place to find,
      Be proud to touch those places;
  And when her warmth your moisture forth doth wear,
10 Whereby her dainty parts are sweetly fed,
    Your honors of the flowery meads, I pray,
      You pretty daughters of the earth and sun,
  With mild and seemly breathing straight display
      My bitter sighs, that have my heart undone.

15 Vermilion roses, that with new day's rise
    Display your crimson folds, fresh-looking, fair,
        Whose radiant bright disgraces
  The rich adorned rays of roseate rising morn;
      Ah! if her virgin's hand
20 Do pluck your pure, ere Phoebus view the land [5]
  And veil your gracious pomp in lovely Nature's scorn;
      If chance my mistress traces
    Fast by your flowers to take the summer's air,
  Then, woeful blushing, tempt her glorious eyes
25   To spread their tears, Adonis' death reporting, [6]
      And tell Love's torments, sorrowing for her friend,
    Whose drops of blood within your leaves consorting,
      Report fair Venus moans withouten end.

  Then may remorse, in pitying of my smart,
30 Dry up my tears, and dwell within her heart.

                                          1593

5. Phoebus Apollo was god of the sun; here, the sun itself. The sense and the meter of this line both suggest that a word has been lost; note that the corresponding line in the first stanza (line 6) contains two more syllables.

6. Adonis, a beautiful youth beloved of Venus, goddess of love, died from a wound inflicted by a boar. Where his blood (or, in another version, Venus' tears) fell to the ground, roses sprang up.

A Nymph's Disdain of Love

Hey down, a down, did Dian⁷ sing,
   Amongst her virgins sitting,
Than love there is no vainer thing,
   For maidens most unfitting.
5 And so think I, with a down, down, derry.

When women knew no woe,
   But lived themselves to please,
Men's feigning guiles they did not know,
   The ground of their disease.
10 Unborn was false suspect,°   *suspicion*
   No thought of jealousy;
From wanton toys° and fond affect°   *pastimes/disposition*
   The virgin's life was free.

15 At length men uséd charms;
   To which what maids gave ear,
Embracing gladly endless harms,
   Anon° enthralléd were.   *promptly*
Thus women welcomed woe
20   Disguised in name of love;
A jealous hell, a painted show,
   So shall they find that prove.°   *experience*
                                   1600

Fine Knacks for Ladies

Fine knacks for ladies, cheap, choice, brave and new!
Good pennyworths—but money cannot move:
I keep a fair but for the fair to view;
A beggar may be liberal of love.
5 Though all my wares be trash, the heart is true,
        The heart is true.

Great gifts are guiles and look for gifts again;
My trifles come as treasures from my mind.
It is a precious jewel to be plain;
10 Sometimes in shell the orient'st° pearls we find.   *most lustrous*
Of others take a sheaf, of me a grain!
        Of me a grain!

Within this pack pins, points,⁴ laces, and gloves,
And divers toys fitting a country fair;
15 But in my heart, where duty serves and loves,
Turtles° and twins, court's brood, a heavenly pair.   *turtledoves*
Happy the heart that thinks of no removes!
        Of no removes!

                                   1600

---

7. Diana, goddess of chastity.
4. A lace (such as a shoelace) with the ends tagged or pointed for convenience in lacing.

Jerusalem, My Happy Home

Jerusalem, my happy home,
When shall I come to thee?
When shall my sorrows have an end,
Thy joys when shall I see?

5 O happy harbor of the saints,
O sweet and pleasant soil,
In thee no sorrow may be found,
No grief, no care, no toil.

There lust and lucre cannot dwell,
10 There envy bears no sway;
There is no hunger, heat, nor cold,
But pleasure every way.

Thy walls are made of precious stones,
Thy bulwarks diamonds square;
15 Thy gates are of right orient pearl,
Exceeding rich and rare.

Thy turrets and thy pinnacles
With carbuncles° do shine;   precious stones
Thy very streets are paved with gold,
20 Surpassing clear and fine.

Ah, my sweet home, Jerusalem,
Would God I were in thee!
Would God my woes were at an end,
Thy joys that I might see!

25 Thy gardens and thy gallant walks
Continually are green;
There grows such sweet and pleasant flowers
As nowhere else are seen.

Quite through the streets, with silver sound,
30 The flood of life doth flow;
Upon whose banks on every side
The wood of life doth grow.

There trees forevermore bear fruit,
And evermore do spring;
35 There evermore the angels sit,
And evermore do sing.

Our Lady sings *Magnificat*[3]
With tune surpassing sweet;
And all the virgins bear their part,
40 Sitting about her feet.

3. The first word of the canticle of the Virgin Mary beginning "My soul doth magnify the Lord"
(Luke i.46–55).

Jerusalem, my happy home,
Would God I were in thee!
Would God my woes were at an end,
Thy joys that I might see!

1601

My Love in Her Attire

My love in her attire doth show her wit,
  It doth so well become her:
For every season she hath dressings fit,
  For winter, spring, and summer.
5 No beauty she doth miss,
  When all her robes are on;
But Beauty's self she is,
  When all her robes are gone.

1602

Weep You No More, Sad Fountains

Weep you no more, sad fountains;
    What need you flow so fast?
  Look how the snowy mountains
    Heaven's sun doth gently waste.
5   But my sun's heavenly eyes
      View not your weeping,
      That now lie sleeping
  Softly, now softly lies
      Sleeping.

10 Sleep is a reconciling,
      A rest that peace begets.
  Doth not the sun rise smiling
      When fair at even he sets?
  Rest you then, rest, sad eyes,
15   Melt not in weeping
      While she lies sleeping
  Softly, now softly lies
      Sleeping.

1603

There Is a Lady Sweet and Kind

  There is a lady sweet and kind,
  Was never face so pleased my mind;
  I did but see her passing by,
  And yet I love her till I die.

5 Her gesture, motion and her smiles,
  Her wit, her voice, my heart beguiles,
  Beguiles my heart, I know not why,
  And yet I love her till I die.

  Her free behavior, winning looks,
10 Will make a lawyer burn his books.
  I touched her not, alas, not I,
  And yet I love her till I die.

Had I her fast betwixt mine arms,
Judge you that think such sports were harms,
Were't any harm? No, no, fie, fie!
For I will love her till I die.

Should I remain confinéd there,
So long as Phoebus[5] in his sphere,
I to request, she to deny,
Yet would I love her till I die.

Cupid is wingéd and doth range;
Her country so my love doth change,
But change she earth, or change she sky,
Yet will I love her till I die.

1607

The Silver Swan

The silver swan, who living had no note,
When death approached, unlocked her silent throat;
Leaning her breast against the reedy shore,
Thus sung her first and last, and sung no more:
"Farewell, all joys; Oh death, come close mine eyes;
More geese than swans now live, more fools than wise."

1612

Yet If His Majesty, Our Sovereign Lord

Yet if his majesty, our sovereign lord,
Should of his own accord
Friendly himself invite,
And say, "I'll be your guest tomorrow night,"
How should we stir ourselves, call and command
All hands to work! "Let no man idle stand.
Set me fine Spanish tables in the hall,
See they be fitted all;
Let there be room to eat,
And order taken that there want no meat.
See every sconce and candlestick made bright,
That without tapers they may give a light.
Look to the presence:[6] are the carpets spread,
The dais° o'er the head,   canopy
The cushions in the chair,
And all the candles lighted on the stair?
Perfume the chambers, and in any case
Let each man give attendance in his place."
Thus if the king were coming would we do,
And 'twere good reason too;
For 'tis a duteous thing
To show all honor to an earthly king,
And, after all our travail and our cost,
So he be pleased, to think no labor cost.
But at the coming of the King of Heaven
All's set at six and seven:[7]
We wallow in our sin;

5. Apollo, god of the sun.
6. The area around the place where the king   will sit.
7. In disorder.

Christ cannot find a chamber in the inn.
We entertain him always like a stranger,
30 And, as at first, still lodge him in the manger.

THOMAS WYATT
(1503–1542)

The Long Love That in My Thought Doth Harbor[1]

The long love that in my thought doth harbor,
And in my heart doth keep his residence,
Into my face presseth with bold pretense
And there encampeth, spreading his banner.
5 She that me learns° to love and suffer   *teaches*
And wills that my trust and lust's negligence
Be reined by reason, shame, and reverence
With his hardiness takes displeasure.
Wherewithal unto the heart's forest he fleeth,
10 Leaving his enterprise with pain and cry,
And there him hideth, and not appeareth.
What may I do, when my master feareth,
But in the field with him to live and die?
For good is the life ending faithfully.

1557

Whoso List To Hunt[2]

Whoso list to hunt, I know where is an hind,
But as for me, alas, I may no more;
The vain travail hath wearied me so sore,
I am of them that furthest come behind.
5 Yet may I by no means my wearied mind
Draw from the deer, but as she fleeth afore
Fainting I follow; I leave off therefore,
Since in a net I seek to hold the wind.
Who list her hunt, I put him out of doubt,
10 As well as I, may spend his time in vain.
And graven with diamonds in letters plain,
There is written her fair neck round about,
"*Noli me tangere,*[3] for Caesar's I am,
And wild for to hold, though I seem tame."

Egerton Ms.

My Galley Charged with Forgetfulness

My galley charged[4] with forgetfulness
Thorough sharp seas in winter nights doth pass
'Tween rock and rock; and eke° mine enemy, alas,   *also*

1. Translated from Petrarch. Compare the translation by the Earl of Surrey, *Love That Doth Reign and Live Within My Thought.*
2. This poem, like many of Wyatt's, existed only in manuscript form until comparatively recently. In place of a date of publication, the manuscript source is given for all such poems in this selection.
3. Touch me not.
4. Wyatt's meter is so often irregular that it is difficult to say with certainty when he intended an *-ed* ending to be pronounced as a second syllable and when not. Hence no attempt has been made to mark syllabic endings with an accent in any of Wyatt's poems, although in this particular poem such endings appear to be intended in lines 1, 8, 11, and 13.

That is my lord, steereth with cruelness;
5   And every oar a thought in readiness,
       As though that death were light in such a case.
       An endless wind doth tear the sail apace
       Of forced sighs, and trusty fearfulness.
       A rain of tears, a cloud of dark disdain,
10   Hath done the wearied cords great hinderance;
       Wreathed with error and eke with ignorance,
       The stars be hid that led me to this pain;
          Drowned is reason that should me consort,
       And I remain despairing of the port.

1557

Madam, Withouten Many Words

Madam, withouten many words,
   Once, I am sure ye will, or no;
And if ye will, then leave your bords,°   *jests*
   And use your wit, and show it so.

5   And with a beck ye shall me call,
       And if of one that burneth alway,
     Ye have any pity at all,
       Answer him fair with yea or nay.

     If it be yea, I shall be fain;
10   If it be nay, friends as before;
     Ye shall another man obtain,
       And I mine own, and yours no more.

1557

They Flee from Me

They flee from me, that sometime did me seek,
With naked foot stalking in my chamber.
I have seen them, gentle, tame, and meek,
That now are wild, and do not remember
5   That sometime they put themselves in danger
To take bread at my hand; and now they range,
Busily seeking with a continual change.

Thanked be Fortune it hath been otherwise,
Twenty times better; but once in special,
10   In thin array, after a pleasant guise,
When her loose gown from her shoulders did fall,
And she me caught in her arms long and small,°   *slender*
And therewith all sweetly did me kiss
And softly said, "Dear heart, how like you this?"
15   It was no dream, I lay broad waking.
But all is turned, thorough my gentleness,
Into a strange fashion of forsaking;
And I have leave to go, of her goodness,
And she also to use newfangleness.
20   But since that I so kindely[5] am served,
I fain would know what she hath deserved.

1557

5. I.e., in the normal way of womankind, an older meaning that does not exclude the modern
meaning of "kindly."

Patience, Though I Have Not

Patience, though I have not
    The thing that I require,
I must of force, God wot,°   *knows*
    Forbear my most desire;
5 For no ways can I find
To sail against the wind.

    Patience, do what they will
        To work me woe or spite,
    I shall content me still
10   To think both day and night;
To think and hold my peace,
Since there is no redress.

    Patience, withouten blame,
        For I offended nought,
15   I know they know the same,
        Though they have changed their thought.
Was ever thought so moved
To hate that it hath loved?

    Patience of all my harm,
20   For fortune is my foe;
    Patience must be the charm
        To heal me of my woe.
Patience without offence
Is a painful patience.

                                Egerton Ms.

My Lute, Awake!

My lute, awake! Perform the last
Labor that thou and I shall waste,
And end that I have now begun;
For when this song is sung and past,
5 My lute, be still, for I have done.

As to be heard where ear is none,
As lead to grave° in marble stone,   *engrave*
My song may pierce her heart as soon.
Should we then sigh or sing or moan?
10 No, no, my lute, for I have done.

The rocks do not so cruelly
Repulse the waves continually
As she my suit and affection.
So that I am past remedy,
15 Whereby my lute and I have done.

Proud of the spoil that thou hast got
Of simple hearts, thorough love's shot;
By whom, unkind, thou hast them won,
Think not he hath his bow forgot,
20 Although my lute and I have done.

Vengeance shall fall on thy disdain
That makest but game on earnest pain.
Think not alone under the sun
Unquit° to cause thy lovers plain,   *unrequited*
25   Although my lute and I have done.

Perchance thee lie withered and old
The winter nights that are so cold,
Plaining in vain unto the moon.
Thy wishes then dare not be told.
30   Care then who list,° for I have done.   *likes*

And then may chance thee to repent
The time that thou hast lost and spent
To cause thy lovers sigh and swoon.
Then shalt thou know beauty but lent,
35   And wish and want as I have done.

Now cease, my lute. This is the last
Labor that thou and I shall waste,
And ended is that we begun.
Now is this song both sung and past;
40   My lute, be still, for I have done.

1557

Is It Possible

Is it possible
    That so high debate,
So sharp, so sore, and of such rate,
Should end so soon and was begun so late?
5   Is it possible?

Is it possible
    So cruel intent,
So hasty heat, and so soon spent,
From love to hate, and thence for to relent?
10   Is it possible?

Is it possible
    That any may find
Within one heart so diverse mind,
To change or turn as weather and wind?
15   Is it possible?

Is it possible
    To spy it in an eye
That turns as oft as chance on die?
The truth whereof can any try?
20   Is it possible?

It is possible
    For to turn so oft,
To bring that lowest that was most aloft,
And to fall highest, yet to light soft?
25   It is possible.

All is possible.
   Whoso list° believe,   *cares to*
Trust therefore first, and after preve;[6]
As men wed ladies by license and leave,
30   All is possible.

                                            Devonshire Ms.

So Unwarely Was Never No Man Caught

So unwarely was never no man caught
   With steadfast look upon a goodly face
As I of late; for suddenly, methought,
   My heart was torn out of his° place.   *its*

5 Thorough mine eye the stroke from hers did slide,
   Directly down unto my heart it ran;
In help whereof the blood thereto did glide,
   And left my face both pale and wan.

Then was I like a man for woe amazed,
10   Or like the bird that flieth into the fire;
For while that I on her beauty gazed,
   The more I burned in my desire.

Anon° the blood start[7] in my face again,   *immediately*
   Inflamed with heat that it had at my heart,
15 And brought therewith throughout in every vein
   A quaking heat with pleasant smart.

Then was I like the straw, when that the flame
   Is driven therein by force and rage of wind;
I cannot tell, alas, what I shall blame,
20   Nor what to seek, nor what to find.

But well I wot° the grief holds me so sore   *know*
   In heat and cold, betwixt hope and dread,
That, but her help to health doth me restore,
   This restless life I may not lead.   1557

Forget Not Yet

Forget not yet the tried intent
Of such a truth as I have meant;
My great travail so gladly spent
     Forget not yet.

5 Forget not yet when first began
The weary life ye know, since whan°   *when*
The suit, the service none tell can;
     Forget not yet.

Forget not yet the great assays,°   *trials*
10 The cruel wrong, the scornful ways,
The painful patience in denays,°   *denials*
     Forget not yet.

---

6. Prove, i.e., learn by (bitter) experience.   7. I.e., started.

Forget not yet, forget not this,
How long ago hath been and is
15 The mind that never meant amiss;
          Forget not yet.

Forget not then thine own approved,
The which so long hath thee so loved,
Whose steadfast faith yet never moved;
20   Forget not this.

Devonshire Ms.

What Should I Say

What should I say,
  Since faith is dead,
And truth away
  From you is fled?
5 Should I be led
  With doubleness?
  Nay, nay, Mistress!

I promised you,
  And you promised me,
10 To be as true
  As I would be;
But since I see
  Your double heart,
  Farewell my part!

15 Though for to take
  It is not my mind,
But to forsake,
  I am not blind,
And as I find,
20   So will I trust.
  Farewell, unjust!

Can ye say nay
  But you said
That I always
25   Should be obeyed?
  And thus betrayed
  Or° that I wist°
  Farewell, unkist!

ere / knew·

Devonshire Ms.

Lux, My Fair Falcon

Lux, my fair falcon, and your fellows all,
  How well pleasant it were your liberty!
Ye not forsake me that fair might ye befall.
  But they that sometime liked my company,
5 Like lice away from dead bodies they crawl;
  Lo, what a proof in light adversity!
But ye, my birds, I swear by all your bells,
Ye be my friends, and so be but few else.

Stand Whoso List

Stand whoso list° upon the slipper° top   *likes / slippery*
   Of court's estate, and let me here rejoice,
And use me quiet without let or stop,°   *hindrance*
   Unknown in court, that hath such brackish joys.
5   In hidden places so let my days forth pass,
   That when my years be done, withouten noise,
I may die aged after the common trace°:   *way*
   For him death gripeth right hard by the crop
That is much known of other, and of himself, alas,
10 Doth die unknown, dazed with dreadful face.

                                                         1557

Mine Own John Poins

Mine own John Poins, since ye delight to know
The cause why that homeward I me draw,
And flee the press of courts, whereso they go,
Rather than to live thrall, under the awe
5 Of lordly looks, wrapped within my cloak,
To will and lust° learning to set a law;   *pleasure*
It is not for because I scorn and mock
The power of them to whom Fortune hath lent
Charge over us, of right to strike the stroke.
10 But true it is that I have always meant
Less to esteem them than the common sort,
Of outward things that judge in their intent
Without regard what doth inward resort.
I grant sometime that of glory the fire
15 Doth touch my heart; me list not[8] to report
Blame by honor, and honor to desire.
But how may I this honor now attain
That cannot dye the color black a liar?
My Poins, I cannot frame me tune to feign,
20 To cloak the truth, for praise without desert,
Of them that list all vice for to retain.
I cannot honor them that sets their part
With Venus and Bacchus[9] all their life long;
Nor hold my peace of them, although I smart.
25 I cannot crouch nor kneel to do so great a wrong,
To worship them like God on earth alone,
That are as wolves these sely° lambs among.   *innocent*
I cannot with my words complain and moan
Nor suffer naught, nor smart without complaint,
30 Nor turn the word that from my mouth is gone;
I cannot speak and look like a saint,
Use wiles for wit, or make deceit a pleasure;
And call craft counsel, for profit still to paint;
I cannot wrest the law to fill the coffer,
35 With innocent blood to feed myself fat,
And do most hurt where most help I offer.
I am not he that can allow the state

8. "Me list not": I care not.
9. Venus was the goddess of love and Bacchus the god of wine.

Of high Caesar, and damn Cato[1] to die,
That with his death did 'scape out of the gate
40 From Caesar's hands, if Livy do not lie,
And would not live where liberty was lost,
So did his heart the common weal apply.[2]
I am not he, such eloquence to boast
To make the crow in singing as the swan,
45 Nor call the lion of coward beasts the most,
That cannot take a mouse as the cat can;
And he that dieth of hunger of the gold,
Call him Alexander,[3] and say that Pan
Passeth Apollo in music manifold;[4]
50 Praise Sir Thopas for a noble tale,
And scorn the story that the Knight told,[5]
Praise him for counsel that is drunk of ale;
Grin when he laugheth that beareth all the sway,
Frown when he frowneth, and groan when he is pale;
55 On others' lust to hang both night and day—
None of these points would ever frame in me;
My wit is naught: I cannot learn the way;
And much the less of things that greater be
That asken help of colors of device[6]
60 To join the mean with each extremity.
With nearest virtue to cloak alway the vice,
And as to purpose, likewise it shall fall
To press the virtue that it may not rise;
As drunkenness good fellowship to call;
65 The friendly foe, with his double face,
Say he is gentle and courteous therewithal;
And say that favel° hath a goodly grace   *flattery*
In eloquence; and cruelty to name
Zeal of justice, and change in time and place;
70 And he that suff'reth offense without blame,
Call him pitiful, and him true and plain
That raileth reckless to every man's shame,
Say he is rude that cannot lie and feign,
The lecher a lover, and tyranny
75 To be the right of a prince's reign.
I cannot, I: no, no, it will not be.
This is the cause that I could never yet
Hang on their sleeves, that weigh, as thou mayst see,
A chip of chance more than a pound of wit.
80 This maketh me at home to hunt and hawk,
And in foul weather at my book to sit,
In frost and snow then with my bow to stalk.
No man doth mark whereso I ride or go.
In lusty leas° at liberty I walk,   *pleasant meadows*
85 And of these news I feel nor weal nor woe,
Save that a clog doth hang yet at my heel.
No force° for that, for it is ordered so   *no matter*
That I may leap both hedge and dike full well;

1. The Roman historian Livy recounts the death of Cato the Younger, who chose suicide in preference to tyranny.
2. I.e., so did his heart practice the common good.
3. Alexander the Great, conqueror of the entire known world, lamented that there was nothing left for him to conquer.

4. The god Pan played simple ditties on his syrinx; Apollo, divine melodies on his lyre.
5. Chaucer's tale of *Sir Thopas* (in *The Canterbury Tales*) is a deliberately dull parody that is cut off after a few stanzas by the Host. The *Knight's Tale* is perhaps the most impressive of all the tales.
6. Artful language that "colors" or falsifies.

I am not now in France, to judge the wine,
90 With sav'ry sauce those delicates to feel;
Nor yet in Spain, where one must him incline,
Rather than to be, outwardly to seem.
I meddle not with wits that be so fine;
Nor Flanders' cheer[7] letteth° not my sight to deem   *hinders*
95 Of black and white, nor taketh my wit away
With beastliness, they beasts do so esteem.
Nor am I not where Christ is given in prey
For money, poison, and treason—at Rome
A common practice, used night and day.
00 But here I am in Kent and Christendom,
Among the Muses, where I read and rhyme;
Where, if thou list, my Poins, for to come,
Thou shalt be judge how I do spend my time.

           1536   1557

HENRY HOWARD, EARL OF SURREY
(ca. 1517–1547)

My Friend, the Things That Do Attain

My friend, the things that do attain
The happy life be these, I find:
The riches left, not got with pain;
The fruitful ground; the quiet mind;

5 The equal friend; no grudge, no strife;
No charge of rule, nor governance;
Without disease, the healthy life;
The household of continuance;

The mean diet, no dainty fare;
10 Wisdom joined with simpleness;
The night dischargéd of all care,
Where wine the wit may not oppress;

The faithful wife, without debate;
Such sleeps as may beguile the night;
15 Content thyself with thine estate,
Neither wish death, nor fear his might.

           1547

The Soote Season

The soote° season, that bud and bloom forth brings,   *sweet*
With green hath clad the hill and eke° the vale;   *also*
The nightingale with feathers new she sings;
The turtle° to her make° hath told her tale.   *turtledove / mate*
5 Summer is come, for every spray now springs;
The hart hath hung his old head on the pale;
The buck in brake his winter coat he flings,
The fishes float with new repairéd scale;

7. Flemings were reputed to be heavy drinkers.

The adder all her slough away she slings,
10   The swift swallow pursueth the flies small;
The busy bee her honey now she mings.°   *remembers*
Winter is worn, that was the flowers' bale.°   *harm*
And thus I see among these pleasant things,
Each care decays, and yet my sorrow springs.

1557

Love, That Doth Reign and Live Within My Thought[1]

Love, that doth reign and live within my thought,
And built his seat within my captive breast,
Clad in the arms wherein with me he fought,
Oft in my face he doth his banner rest.
5   But she that taught me love and suffer pain,
My doubtful hope and eke my hot desire
With shamefast° look to shadow and refrain,   *shamefaced*
Her smiling grace converteth straight to ire.
And coward Love, then, to the heart apace
10   Taketh his flight, where he doth lurk and plain,°   *complain*
His purpose lost, and dare not show his face.
For my lord's guilt thus faultless bide I pain,
Yet from my lord shall not my foot remove:
Sweet is the death that taketh end by love.

1557

Wyatt Resteth Here

Wyatt resteth here, that quick° could never rest;   *living*
Whose heavenly gifts increaséd by disdain,
And virtue sank the deeper in his breast;
Such profit he of envy could obtain.
5   A head where wisdom mysteries did frame,
Whose hammers beat still in that lively brain
As on a stithy,° where some work of fame   *anvil*
Was daily wrought, to turn to Britain's gain.
A visage stern and mild, where both did grow,
10   Vice to contemn, in virtues to rejoice,
Amid great storms, whom grace assuréd so,
To live upright, and smile at fortune's choice.
A hand that taught what might be said in rhyme;
That reft Chaucer the glory of his wit;
15   A mark, the which—unperfited,° for time—   *uncompleted*
Some may approach, but never none shall hit.
A tongue that served in foreign realms his king;
Whose courteous talk to virtue did enflame
Each noble heart; a worthy guide to bring
20   Our English youth, by travail, unto fame.
An eye whose judgment no affect° could blind,   *passion*
Friends to allure, and foes to reconcile;
Whose piercing look did represent a mind
With virtue fraught, reposéd, void of guile.
25   A heart where dread yet never so impressed
To hide the thought that might the truth advance;
In neither fortune lost, nor so repressed,

1. Translated from Petrarch. Compare the   *Love That in My Thought Doth Harbor.*
translation by Sir Thomas Wyatt, *The Long*

To swell in wealth, nor yield unto mischance.
A valiant corps,° where force and beauty met,　　　　　　*body*
30　Happy, alas! too happy, but for foes,
Livéd, and ran the race that nature set;
Of manhood's shape, where she the mold did lose.
But to the heavens that simple soul is fled,
Which left with such as covet Christ to know
35　Witness of faith that never shall be dead,
Sent for our health, but not receivéd so.
Thus, for our guilt, this jewel have we lost;
The earth his bones, the heavens possess his ghost.

　　　　　　1557

So Cruel Prison²

So cruel prison how could betide, alas,
As proud Windsor? Where I in lust° and joy　　　　　*pleasure*
With a king's son my childish years did pass
In greater feast than Priam's sons of Troy;
5　Where each sweet place returns a taste full sour:
The large green courts where we were wont to hove°　　*linger*
With eyes cast up unto the maidens' tower,
And easy sighs, such as folk draw in love;
The stately sales,° the ladies bright of hue,　　　　　*halls*
10　The dances short, long tales of great delight;
With words and looks that tigers could but rue,
Where each of us did plead the other's right;
The palm play,° where, despoiléd° for the game,　　*handball / disrobed*
With dazéd eyes oft we by gleams of love
15　Have missed the ball and got sight of our dame,
To bait³ her eyes, which kept the leads above;
The graveled ground, with sleeves tied on the helm,
On foaming horse, with swords and friendly hearts,
With cheer, as though the one should overwhelm;
20　Where we have fought, and chaséd oft with darts,
With silver drops the meads° yet spread for ruth,°　　*meadows / pity*
In active games of nimbleness and strength,
Where we did strain, trailed by swarms of youth,
Our tender limbs that yet shot up in length;
25　The secret groves which oft we made resound
Of pleasant plaint and of our ladies' praise,
Recording soft what grace each one had found,
What hope of speed, what dread of long delays;
The wild forest, the clothéd holt° with green,　　　*small wood*
30　With reins avaled,° and swift ybreathéd horse,　　*slackened*
With cry of hounds and merry blasts between,
Where we did chase the fearful hart aforce;°　　　*strenuously*
The void walls eke that harbored us each night,
Wherewith, alas, revive within my breast
35　The sweet accord; such sleeps as yet delight,
The pleasant dreams, the quiet bed of rest;
The secret thoughts imparted with such trust,
The wanton talk, the divers change of play,

2. As a boy and young man, Surrey had enjoyed the life at Windsor Palace as the close friend of Henry Fitzroy, an illegitimate son of Henry VIII. In 1537, a year after the death of his friend, Surrey was imprisoned temporarily at Windsor for striking another courtier.
3. To feed, as a fire with fuel. The "leads" from which the lady watches may be either a leaded window or a flat, leaded roof.

The friendship sworn, each promise kept so just,
40 Wherewith we passed the winter nights away.
And with this thought the blood forsakes my face,
The tears berain my cheeks of deadly hue,
The which as soon as sobbing sighs, alas,
Upsuppéd have, thus I my plaint renew:
45 O place of bliss, renewer of my woes,
Give me accompt—where is my noble fere?°   companion
Whom in thy walls thou didst each night enclose,
To other lief,° but unto me most dear!   beloved
Echo, alas, that doth my sorrow rue,
50 Returns thereto a hollow sound of plaint.
Thus I, alone, where all my freedom grew,
In prison pine with bondage and restraint;
And with remembrance of the greater grief
To banish the less, I find my chief relief.

1557

Although I Had a Check

Although I had a check,
    To give the mate is hard;
For I have found a neck,°   nook
    To keep my men in guard.
5 And you that hardy are
    To give so great assay°   assault
Unto a man of war
    To drive his men away,

I rede° you take good heed,   advise
10   And mark this foolish verse;
For I will so provide
    That I will have your fers.°   queen
And when your fers is had
    And all your war is done,
15 Then shall yourself be glad
    To end that you begun.

For if by chance I win
    Your person in the field,
Too late then come you in,
20   Yourself to me to yield.
For I will use my power
    As captain full of might,
And such I will devour
    As use to show me spite.

25 And for because you gave
    Me check in such degree
This vantage, lo, I have:
    Now check, and guard to thee.
Defend it if thou may,
30   Stand stiff in thine estate;
For sure I will assay,°   try
    If I can give thee mate.

1557

ALEXANDER SCOTT
(ca. 1524–1584)

Lo! What It Is to Luve

Lo! what it is to luve,
Learn ye, that list to pruve,
Be° me, I say, that no wayis may   *by*
The grund of grief remuve,
5   Bot still decay, both nicht and day:
Lo! what it is to luve.

Luve is ane fervent fire,
Kendillit without desire:
Short plesour, lang displesour,
10   Repentance is the hire;°   *reward*
Ane puir tressour without mesour:
Luve is ane fervent fire.

To luve and to be wise,
To rege° with gud advice,   *quarrel*
15 Now thus, now than,° so goes the game,   *otherwise*
Incertain is the dice:
There is no man, I say, that can
Both luve and to be wise.

Flee alwayis from the snare;
20   Learn at me to be ware;
It is ane pain and double trane°   *snare*
Of endless woe and care;
For to refrain that danger plain,
Flee alwayis from the snare.

before 1568

QUEEN ELIZABETH I
(1533–1603)

When I Was Fair and Young

When I was fair and young, and favor gracéd me,
Of many was I sought, their mistress for to be;
But I did scorn them all, and answered them therefore,
    "Go, go, go seek some otherwhere!
5   Importune me no more!"

How many weeping eyes I made to pine with woe,
How many sighing hearts, I have no skill to show;
Yet I the prouder grew, and answered them therefore,
    "Go, go, go seek some otherwhere!
10   Importune me no more!"

Then spake fair Venus' son, that proud victorious boy,
And said, "Fine dame, since that you be so coy,
I will so pluck your plumes that you shall say no more,
   'Go, go, go seek some otherwhere!
15   Importune me no more!' "

When he had spake these words, such change grew in my breast
That neither night nor day since that, I could take any rest.
Then lo! I did repent that I had said before,
   "Go, go, go seek some otherwhere!
20   Importune me no more!"

GEORGE GASCOIGNE
(ca. 1535–1577)

And If I Did What Then?

"And if I did what then?
Are you aggrieved therefore?
The sea hath fish for every man,
And what would you have more?"

5   Thus did my mistress once
Amaze my mind with doubt,
And popped a question for the nonce
To beat my brains about.

Whereto I thus replied:
10 "Each fisherman can wish
That all the sea at every tide
Were his alone to fish.

And so did I, in vain;
But since it may not be,
15 Let such fish there as find the gain,
And leave the loss for me.

And with such luck and loss
I will content myself,
Till tides of turning time may toss
20 Such fishers on the shelf.

And when they stick on sands,
That every man may see,
Then will I laugh and clap my hands,
As they do now at me."

1573

For That He Looked Not upon Her

You must not wonder, though you think it strange,
To see me hold my louring° head so low,   *sullen*
And that mine eyes take no delight to range
About the gleams which on your face do grow.

5 The mouse which once hath broken out of trap
  Is seldom 'ticéd° with the trustless bait,   *enticed*
  But lies aloof for fear of more mishap,
  And feedeth still in doubt° of deep deceit.   *suspicion*
  The scorchéd fly, which once hath 'scaped the flame,
10 Will hardly come to play again with fire,
  Whereby I learn that grievous is the game
  Which follows fancy dazzled by desire:
    So that I wink or else hold down my head,
    Because your blazing eyes my bale° have bred.   *misery*
                                              1573

Gascoigne's Lullaby

Sing lullaby, as women do,
  Wherewith they bring their babes to rest,
And lullaby can I sing too,
  As womanly as can the best.
5 With lullaby they still the child,
  And if I be not much beguiled,
  Full many wanton babes have I,
  Which must be stilled with lullaby.

First, lullaby, my youthful years,
10 It is now time to go to bed,
For crooked age and hoary hairs
  Have won the haven within my head.
  With lullaby then, youth, be still,
  With lullaby content they will,
15 Since courage quails and comes behind,
  Go sleep, and so beguile thy mind.

Next, lullaby, my gazing eyes,
  Which wonted were to glance apace.
For every glass may now suffice
20 To show the furrows in my face.
  With lullaby then wink awhile,
  With lullaby your looks beguile.
  Let no fair face nor beauty bright
  Entice you eft° with vain delight.   *after*

25 And lullaby, my wanton will,
  Let reason's rule now rein thy thought,
Since all too late I find by skill
  How dear I have thy fancies bought.
  With lullaby now take thine ease,
30 With lullaby thy doubts appease.
  For trust to this, if thou be still,
  My body shall obey thy will.

Eke° lullaby, my loving boy,   *also*
  My little Robin, take thy rest.
Since age is cold and nothing coy,°   *lascivious*
  Keep close thy coin, for so is best.
  With lullaby be thou content,
  With lullaby thy lusts relent.
  Let others pay which° hath mo° pence;   *who/more*
40 Thou art too poor for such expense.

Thus, lullaby, my youth, mine eyes,
My will, my ware, and all that was.
I can no mo delays devise,
But welcome pain, let pleasure pass.
45 With lullaby now take your leave,
With lullaby your dreams deceive,
And when you rise with waking eye,
Remember Gascoigne's lullaby.

1573

BARNABE GOOGE
(1540–1594)

To Alexander Neville

The little fish that in the stream doth fleet,
With broad forth-stretchéd fins for his disport,
Whenas he spies the fish's bait so sweet,
In haste he hies, fearing to come too short.
5 But all too soon (alas!) his greedy mind
By rash attempt doth bring him to his bane,°   destruction
For where he thought a great relief to find,
By hidden hook the simple fool is tane.°   taken
So fareth man, that wanders here and there,
10 Thinking no hurt to happen him thereby,
He runs amain to gaze on Beauty's cheer,
Takes all for gold that glisters in the eye,
And never leaves to feed by looking long
On Beauty's bait, where bondage lies enwrapped;
15 Bondage that makes him to sing another song,
And makes him curse the bait that him entrapped.
Neville, to thee, that lovest their wanton looks,
Feed on the bait, but yet beware the hooks.

1563

Once Musing as I Sat

Once musing as I sat,
  and candle burning by,
When all were hushed, I might discern
  a simple silly° fly,   innocent
5 That flew before mine eyes
  with free rejoicing heart,
And here and there with wings did play,
  as void of pain and smart.
Sometime by me she sat,
10 when she had played her fill,
And ever when she rested had,
  about she flittered still.
When I perceived her well,
  rejoicing in her place,
15 "O happy fly," quoth I, "and eke°   also
  O worm in happy case,
Which two of us is best?
  I that have reason? No;
But thou that reason art without
20 and therewith void of woe.

I live, and so dost thou,
 but I live all in pain,
And subject am to her, alas,
 that makes my grief her gain.
25 Thou liv'st, but feel'st no grief,
 no love doth thee torment;
A happy thing for me it were,
 if God were so content,
That thou with pen wert placéd here
30 and I sat in thy place,
Then I should joy, as thou dost now,
 and thou shouldst wail thy case."

           1563

Out of Sight, Out of Mind

The oftener seen, the more I lust,
 The more I lust, the more I smart,
The more I smart, the more I trust,
 The more I trust, the heavier heart,
5 The heavy heart breeds mine unrest,
Thy absence, therefore, like I best.

The rarer seen, the less in mind,
 The less in mind, the lesser pain,
The lesser pain, less grief I find,
10 The lesser grief, the greater gain,
The greater gain, the merrier I,
Therefore I wish thy sight to fly.

The further off, the more I joy,
 The more I joy, the happier life,
15 The happier life, less hurts annoy,
 The lesser hurts, pleasure most rife:
Such pleasures rife shall I obtain
When distance doth depart° us twain.   *separate*

           1563

A Refusal

Sith° Fortune favors not and all things backward go,   *since*
And sith your mind hath so decreed to make an end of woe,
Sith now is no redress, but hence I must away,
Farewell, I waste no vainer words. I hope for better day.

           1563

Of Money

Give money me, take friendship whoso list,°   *pleases*
For friends are gone come once adversity.
When money yet remaineth safe in chest,
That quickly can thee bring from misery.
5 Fair face show friends when riches do abound;
Come time of proof, farewell, they must away.
Believe me well, they are not to be found,
If God but send thee once a lowering day.
Gold never starts aside, but in distress
10 Finds ways enough to ease thine heaviness.

           1563

GEORGE TURBERVILLE
(ca. 1540–ca. 1610)

The Lover to the Thames of London to Favor His Lady Passing Thereon

Thou stately stream that with the swelling tide
'Gainst London walls incessantly dost beat,
Thou Thames, I say, where barge and boat doth ride,
And snow-white swans do fish for needful meat:

5 When so my love, of force or pleasure, shall
Flit on thy flood as custom is to do,
Seek not with dread her courage to appall,
But calm thy tide, and smoothly let it go,
As she may joy, arrived to siker° shore,   *secure*
10 To pass the pleasant stream she did before.

To welter up and surge in wrathful wise,
As did the flood where Helle [1] drenchéd° was,   *drowned*
Would but procure defame° of thee to rise;   *disgrace*
Wherefore let all such ruthless rigor pass.
15 So wish I that thou may'st with bending side
Have power for aye in wonted gulf to glide.

1567

Of Drunkenness

At night when ale is in,
  Like friends we part to bed;
In morrow gray, when ale is out,
  Then hatred is in head.

1567

CHIDIOCK TICHBORNE
(d. 1586)

Tichborne's Elegy

WRITTEN WITH HIS OWN HAND
IN THE TOWER BEFORE HIS EXECUTION

My prime of youth is but a frost of cares,
My feast of joy is but a dish of pain,
My crop of corn is but a field of tares,°   *weeds*
And all my good is but vain hope of gain;
5 The day is past, and yet I saw no sun,
And now I live, and now my life is done.

1. Maiden in Greek legend who, to escape the plotting of her jealous stepmother, fled with her brother on the back of a flying golden ram. Growing tired, she fell into the strait subsequently named the Hellespont in her memory (now the Dardanelles).

My tale was heard and yet it was not told,
My fruit is fallen and yet my leaves are green,
My youth is spent and yet I am not old,
10   I saw the world and yet I was not seen;
My thread is cut and yet it is not spun,[2]
And now I live, and now my life is done.

I sought my death and found it in my womb,
I looked for life and saw it was a shade,
15   I trod the earth and knew it was my tomb,
And now I die, and now I was but made;
My glass° is full, and now my glass is run,   *hourglass*
And now I live, and now my life is done.

1586

SIR WALTER RALEGH
(ca. 1552–1618)

The Nymph's Reply to the Shepherd[1]

If all the world and love were young,
And truth in every shepherd's tongue,
These pretty pleasures might me move
To live with thee and be thy love.

5   Time drives the flocks from field to fold
When rivers rage and rocks grow cold,
And Philomel° becometh dumb;   *the nightingale*
The rest complains of cares to come.

The flowers do fade, and wanton fields
10   To wayward winter reckoning yields;
A honey tongue, a heart of gall,
Is fancy's spring, but sorrow's fall.

Thy gowns, thy shoes, thy beds of roses,
Thy cap, thy kirtle,[2] and thy posies
15   Soon break, soon wither, soon forgotten—
In folly ripe, in reason rotten.

Thy belt of straw and ivy buds,
Thy coral clasps and amber studs,
All these in me no means can move
20   To come to thee and be thy love.

But could youth last and love still breed,
Had joys no date[3] nor age no need,
Then these delights my mind might move
To live with thee and be thy love.

1600

2. An allusion to the three Fates, who spun
the thread that determined the length of man's
life and cut it when he was destined to die.
1. Written in reply to Christopher Marlowe's

The Passionate Shepherd to His Love.
2. A long dress, often worn under an outer
garment.
3. I.e., terminal date.

The Passionate Man's Pilgrimage

Give me my scallop-shell[4] of quiet,
My staff of faith to walk upon,
My scrip[5] of joy, immortal diet,
My bottle of salvation,
5   My gown of glory, hope's true gage,°   *pledge*
And thus I'll take my pilgrimage.

Blood must be my body's balmer,
No other balm will there be given,
Whilst my soul like a white palmer[6]
10   Travels to the land of heaven,
Over the silver mountains,
Where spring the nectar fountains;
And there I'll kiss
The bowl of bliss,
15   And drink my eternal fill
On every milken hill.
My soul will be a-dry before,
But after it will ne'er thirst more;
And by the happy blissful way
20   More peaceful pilgrims I shall see
That have shook off their gowns of clay
And go appareled fresh like me.
I'll bring them first
To slake their thirst,
25   And then to taste those nectar suckets,°   *confections*
At the clear wells
Where sweetness dwells,
Drawn up by saints in crystal buckets.

And when our bottles and all we
30   Are filled with immortality,
Then the holy paths we'll travel,
Strewed with rubies thick as gravel,
Ceilings of diamonds, sapphire floors,
High walls of coral, and pearl bowers,
35   From thence to heaven's bribeless hall
Where no corrupted voices brawl,
No conscience molten into gold,
Nor forged accusers bought and sold,
No cause deferred, nor vain-spent journey,
40   For there Christ is the king's attorney,
Who pleads for all, without degrees,
And he hath angels,[7] but no fees.
When the grand twelve million jury
Of our sins and sinful fury,
45   'Gainst our souls black verdicts give,
Christ pleads his death, and then we live.
Be thou my speaker, taintless pleader,
Unblotted lawyer, true proceeder;
Thou movest salvation even for alms,

4. A scallop shell or something resembling it
was worn as the sign of a pilgrim.
5. Pilgrim's knapsack or bag.
6. A person wearing a palm leaf as a sign that
he had made a pilgrimage to the Holy Land.
7. A punning reference to the gold coin of that
name, ten shillings in value.

0   Not with a bribed lawyer's palms.
And this is my eternal plea
To him that made heaven, earth, and sea,
Seeing my flesh must die so soon,
And want a head to dine next noon,
5   Just at the stroke when my veins start and spread,
Set on my soul an everlasting head.
Then am I ready, like a palmer fit,
To tread those blest paths which before I writ.

1604

The Lie

Go, soul, the body's guest,
Upon a thankless errand;
Fear not to touch the best;
The truth shall be thy warrant.
5   Go, since I needs must die,
And give the world the lie.

Say to the court, it glows
And shines like rotten wood;
Say to the church, it shows
10   What's good, and doth no good.
If church and court reply,
Then give them both the lie.

Tell potentates, they live
Acting by others' action;
15   Not loved unless they give,
Not strong but by a faction.
If potentates reply,
Give potentates the lie.

Tell men of high condition,
20   That manage the estate,
Their purpose is ambition,
Their practice only hate.
And if they once reply,
Then give them all the lie.

25   Tell them that brave it most,
They beg for more by spending,
Who, in their greatest cost,
Seek nothing but commending.
And if they make reply,
30   Then give them all the lie.

Tell zeal it wants devotion;
Tell love it is but lust;
Tell time it is but motion;
Tell flesh it is but dust.
35   And wish them not reply,
For thou must give the lie.

Tell age it daily wasteth;
Tell honor how it alters;

Tell beauty how she blasteth;
40   Tell favor how it falters.
And as they shall reply,
Give every one the lie.

Tell wit how much it wrangles
In tickle° points of niceness;   *delicate*
45   Tell wisdom she entangles
Herself in overwiseness.
And when they do reply,
Straight give them both the lie.

Tell physic of her boldness;
50   Tell skill it is pretension;
Tell charity of coldness;
Tell law it is contention.
And as they do reply,
So give them still the lie.

55   Tell fortune of her blindness;
Tell nature of decay;
Tell friendship of unkindness;
Tell justice of delay.
And if they will reply,
60   Then give them all the lie.

Tell arts they have no soundness,
But vary by esteeming;
Tell schools they want profoundness,
And stand too much on seeming.
65   If arts and schools reply,
Give arts and schools the lie.

Tell faith it's fled the city;
Tell how the country erreth;
Tell manhood shakes off pity;
70   Tell virtue least preferreth.
And if they do reply,
Spare not to give the lie.

So when thou hast, as I
Commanded thee, done blabbing—
75   Although to give the lie
Deserves no less than stabbing—
Stab at thee he that will,
No stab the soul can kill.

                                                            1608

Nature, That Washed Her Hands in Milk

Nature, that washed her hands in milk,
And had forgot to dry them,
Instead of earth took snow and silk,
At love's request to try them,
5   If she a mistress could compose
To please love's fancy out of those.

Her eyes he would should be of light,
A violet breath, and lips of jelly;
Her hair not black, nor overbright,
10   And of the softest down her belly;
As for her inside he'd have it
Only of wantonness and wit.

At love's entreaty such a one
Nature made, but with her beauty
15   She hath framed a heart of stone;
So as love, by ill destiny,
Must die for her whom nature gave him,
Because her darling would not save him.

But time (which nature doth despise,
20   And rudely gives her love the lie,
Makes hope a fool, and sorrow wise)
His hands do neither wash nor dry;
But being made of steel and rust,
Turns snow and silk and milk to dust.

25   The light, the belly, lips, and breath,
He dims, discolors, and destroys;
With those he feeds but fills not death,
Which sometimes were the food of joys.
Yea, time doth dull each lively wit,
30   And dries all wantonness with it.

Oh, cruel time! which takes in trust
Our youth, our joys, and all we have,
And pays us but with age and dust;
Who in the dark and silent grave
35   When we have wandered all our ways
Shuts up the story of our days.[8]

ca. 1610

Three Things There Be

Three things there be that prosper up apace
And flourish, whilst they grow asunder far,
But on a day, they meet all in one place,
And when they meet, they one another mar;
5   And they be these: the wood, the weed, the wag.
The wood is that which makes the gallow tree,
The weed is that which strings the hangman's bag,
The wag, my pretty knave, betokeneth thee.
Mark well, dear boy, whilst these assemble not,
10   Green springs the tree, hemp grows, the wag is wild;
But when they meet, it makes the timber rot,
It frets° the halter, and it chokes the child.   *frays*
Then bless thee, and beware, and let us pray
We part not with thee at this meeting day.

ca. 1610

8. Another version of this stanza, traditionally supposed to have been written by Ralegh on the night before his execution, was published in 1628. In it the first three words are changed to "Even such is time," and the following couplet is added: "And from which earth, and grave, and dust/The Lord shall raise me up, I trust." The poem as a whole existed only in manuscript form until 1902.

EDMUND SPENSER
(ca. 1552–1599)

From THE FAERIE QUEENE

Book III, Canto IX

Malbecco will no straunge knights host,
  For peevish gealosie:
Paridell giusts° with Britomart: jousts
Both shew their auncestrie.

                              1
Redoubted knights, and honorable Dames,
  To whom I levell all my labours end,
  Right sore I feare, least° with unworthy blames   lest
  This odious argument my rimes should shend,°   shame
5 Or ought your goodly patience offend,
  Whiles of a wanton Lady I do write,
  Which with her loose incontinence doth blend°   blind, obscure
  The shyning glory of your soveraigne light,
And knighthood fowle defacéd by a faithlesse knight.

                              2
10 But never let th' ensample of the bad
  Offend the good: for good by paragone°   comparison
  Of evill, may more notably be rad,°   read, discerned
  As white seemes fairer, macht° with blacke attone;°   matched / together
  Ne° all are shaméd by the fault of one: nor
15 For lo in heaven, whereas° all goodnesse is,   where
  Emongst the Angels, a whole legione
  Of wicked Sprights did fall from happy blis;
What wonder then, if one of women all did mis?°   go astray

                              3
Then listen Lordings, if ye list to weet°   know
20 The cause, why Satyrane and Paridell[1]
  Mote° not be entertaynd, as seeméd meet,   may
  Into that Castle (as that Squire does tell).
  "Therein a cancred crabbéd Carle° does dwell,   churl
  That has no skill of Court nor courtesie,
25 Ne cares, what men say of him ill or well;
  For all his dayes he drownes in privitie,°   seclusion
Yet has full large to live,[2] and spend at libertie.

                              4
  "But all his mind is set on mucky pelfe,°   money
  To hoord up heapes of evill gotten masse,
30 For which he others wrongs, and wreckes himselfe;
  Yet is he linckéd to a lovely lasse,
  Whose beauty doth her bounty° far surpasse,   goodness
  The which to him both far unequall yeares,
  And also far unlike conditions has;
35 For she does joy to play emongst her peares,[3]
And to be free from hard restraint and gealous feares.

---

1. These two traveling knights, with the Squire of Dames, have just sought shelter for the night at a nearby castle but have been turned away, a serious breach of courtesy. The Squire, who knows something of the castle's owner, now offers an explanation.
2. I.e., yet has enough to live very well.
3. I.e., participate in social life.

5

"But he is old, and witheréd like hay,
    Unfit faire Ladies service to supply;
    The privie guilt whereof makes him alway
40 Suspect her truth, and keepe continuall spy
    Upon her with his other blinckéd⁴ eye;
    Ne suffreth° he resort° of living wight   *permits / visiting*
    Approch to her, ne keepe her company,
    But in close bowre her mewes° from all men's sight,   *shuts up*
45 Deprived of kindly joy and naturall delight.

6

"Malbecco he, and Hellenore she hight,°   *is called*
    Unfitly yokt together in one teeme,
    That is the cause, why never any knight
    Is suffred here to enter, but he seeme
50 Such, as no doubt of him he neede misdeeme."°   *suspect*
    Thereat Sir Satyrane gan smile, and say;
    "Extremely mad the man I surely deeme,
    That weenes° with watch and hard restraint to stay   *expects*
A woman's will, which is disposd to go astray.

7

55 "In vaine he feares that, which he cannot shonne:
    For who wotes° not, that woman's subtiltyes   *knows*
    Can guilen° Argus,⁵ when she list misdonne?°   *beguile / misdo*
    It is not yron bandes, nor hundred eyes,
    Nor brasen walls, nor many wakefull spyes,
60 That can withhold her wilfull wandring feet;
    But fast good will with gentle courtesyes,
    And timely service to her pleasures meet
May her perhaps containe, that else would algates° fleet."°   *wholly / fly away*

8

"Then is he not more mad," said Paridell,
65 That hath himselfe unto such service sold,
    In dolefull thraldome all his dayes to dwell?
    For sure a foole I do him firmely hold,
    That loves his fetters, though they were of gold.
    But why do we devise° of others ill,   *converse*
70 Whiles thus we suffer this same dotard old
    To keepe us out, in scorne of his owne will,
And rather do not ransack all, and him selfe kill?"

9

"Nay let us first," said Satyrane, "entreat
    The man by gentle meanes, to let us in,
75 And afterwardes affray° with cruell threat,   *frighten*
    Ere that we to efforce it do begin:
    Then if all fayle, we will by force it win,
    And eke° reward the wretch for his mesprise,°   *also / scorn*
    As may be worthy of his haynous sin."
80 That counsell pleasd: then Paridell did rise,
And to the Castle gate approcht in quiet wise.

10

Whereat soft knocking, entrance he desyrd.
    The good man⁶ selfe, which then the Porter playd,
    Him answeréd, that all were now retyrd
85 Unto their rest, and all the keyes convayd

---

4. Half-shut or winking, with poor vision. His
other eye is blind (see line 240).
5. Whose hundred eyes never closed more
than two at a time.
6. Goodman, head of the household.

Unto their maister, who in bed was layd,
That none him durst awake out of his dreme;
And therefore them of patience gently prayd.
Then Paridell began to chaunge his theme,
90   And threatned him with force and punishment extreme.

11

But all in vaine; for nought mote him relent,°   *soften*
And now so long before the wicket° fast   *gate*
They wayted, that the night was forward spent,
And the faire welkin° fowly overcast,   *sky*
95   Gan blowen up a bitter stormy blast,
With shoure and hayle so horrible and dred,
That this faire many° were compeld at last,   *company*
To fly for succour to a little shed,
The which beside the gate for swine was orderéd.°   *prepared*

12

100   It fortunéd, soone after they were gone,
Another knight, whom tempest thither brought,
Came to that Castle, and with earnest mone,°   *plea*
Like as the rest, late entrance deare besought;
But like so as the rest he prayd for nought,
105   For flatly he of entrance was refusd,
Sorely thereat he was displeasd, and thought
How to avenge himselfe so sore abusd,
And evermore the Carle of curtesie⁷ accusd.

13

But to avoyde th'intollerable stowre,°   *storm*
110   He was compeld to seeke some refuge neare,
And to that shed, to shrowd him from the showre,
He came, which full of guests he found whyleare,°   *already*
So as he was not let to enter there:
Whereat he gan to wex exceeding wroth,
115   And swore, that he would lodge with them yfere,°   *together*
Or them dislodge, all were they liefe or loth;
And so defide them each, and so defide them both.

14

Both were full loth to leave that needfull tent,°   *shelter*
And both full loth in darkenesse to debate;°   *do battle*
120   Yet both full liefe him lodging to have lent,
And both full liefe his boasting to abate;
But chiefly Paridell his hart did grate,
To heare him threaten so despightfully,
As if he did a dogge to kenell rate,⁸
125   That durst not barke; and rather had he dy,
Then° when he was defide, in coward corner ly.   *than*

15

Tho° hastily remounting to his steed,   *then*
He forth issewed; like as a boistrous wind,
Which in th'earthes hollow caves hath long bin hid,
130   And shut up fast within her prisons blind,
Makes the huge element° against her kind°   *earth / nature*
To move, and tremble as it were agast,
Untill that it an issew forth may find;
Then forth it breakes, and with his° furious blast   *its*
135   Confounds both land and seas, and skyes doth overcast.

---

7. I.e., of a lack of courtesy.   8. Drive by scolding.

16

Their steel-hed speares they strongly coucht, and met
  Together with impetuous rage and forse,
  That with the terrour of their fierce affret,°   *onslaught*
  They rudely drove to ground both man and horse,
40 That each awhile lay like a sencelesse corse.
  But Paridell sore bruséd with the blow,
  Could not arise, the counterchaunge to scorse,°   *trade*
  Till that young Squire him rearéd from below;
Then drew he his bright sword, and gan about him throw.° *thrust*

17

45 But Satyrane forth stepping, did them stay
  And with faire treatie pacifide their ire,
  Then when they were accorded from the fray,
  Against that Castles Lord they gan conspire,
  To heape on him dew vengeaunce for his hire.°   *payment*
50 They bene° agreed, and to the gates they goe   *are*
  To burne the same with unquenchable fire,
  And that uncurteous Carle their commune foe
To do fowle death to dye, or wrap in grievous woe.

18

Malbecco seeing them resolved in deed
55 To flame the gates, and hearing them to call
  For fire in earnest, ran with fearfull speed,
  And to them calling from the castle wall,
  Besought them humbly, him to beare with all,
  As ignoraunt of servants bad abuse,
60 And slacke attendaunce unto straungers call.
  The knights were willing all things to excuse,
Though nought beleved, and entraunce late did not refuse.

19

They bene ybrought into a comely bowre,°   *room*
  And served of all things that mote needfull bee;
65 Yet secretly their hoste did on them lowre,°   *glower*
  And welcomde more for feare, then charitee;
  But they dissembled, what they did not see,
  And welcoméd themselves. Each gan undight°   *take off*
  Their garments wet, and weary armour free,
70 To dry them selves by Vulcanes flaming light,[9]
And eke their lately bruzéd parts to bring in plight.° *good condition*

20

And eke that straunger knight emongst the rest
  Was for like need enforst to disaray:[1]
  Tho whenas vailéd° was her loftie crest,°   *lowered / helmet*
75 Her golden locks, that were in tramels° gay   *nets*
  Upbounden, did them selves adowne display,
  And raught° unto her heeles; like sunny beames, *reached*
  That in a cloud their light did long time stay,
  Their vapour vaded,° shew their golden gleames, *vanished*
80 And through the persant° aire shoote forth their azure streames. *pierced*

21

She also dofte her heavy habergeon,°   *coat of mail*
  Which the faire feature of her limbs did hyde,
  And her well plighted° frock, which she did won° *pleated / was accustomed*

---

9. I.e., the fire.
1. The ensuing description makes it clear to the reader who knows the story up to this point that the stranger knight is Britomart, who is the passionate and virtuous heroine of Book III, the Book of Chastity.

To tucke about her short, when she did ryde,
185   She low let fall, that flowd from her lanck° syde   *slender*
  Downe to her foot, with carelesse° modestee.   *unconscious*
  Then of them all she plainly was espyde,
    To be a woman wight,° unwist° to bee,   *human being / unknown*
The fairest woman wight, that ever eye did see.

          22
190 Like as Minerva, being late returnd
  From slaughter of the Giaunts conqueréd;
  Where proud Encelade, whose wide nosethrils° burnd   *nostrils*
  With breathéd flames, like to a furnace red,
  Transfixéd with the speare, downe tombled ded
195   From top of Hemus, by him heapéd hye;
  Hath loosd her helmet from her lofty hed,
  And her Gorgonian shield gins to untye
From her left arme, to rest in glorious victorye.

          23
Which whenas they beheld, they smitten were
200   With great amazement of so wondrous sight,
  And each on other, and they all on her
  Stood gazing, as if suddein great affright
  Had them surprised. At last avizing° right,   *perceiving*
  Her goodly personage and glorious hew,°   *form*
205   Which they so much mistooke, they tooke delight
  In their first errour, and yet still anew
With wonder of her beauty fed their hungry vew.

          24
Yet note° their hungry vew be sa·isfide,   *could not*
  But seeing still the more desired to see,
210   And ever firmely fixéd did abide
  In contemplation of divinitie:
  But most they mervaild at her chevalree,
  And noble prowesse, which they had approved,°   *tested*
  That much they faynd° to know, who she mote bee;   *desired*
215   Yet none of all them her thereof amoved,[2]
Yet every one her likte, and every one her loved.

          25
And Paridell though partly discontent
  With his late fall, and fowle indignity,
  Yet was soone wonne his malice to relent,°   *soften*
220   Through gracïous regard of her faire eye,
  And knightly worth, which he too late did try,
  Yet triéd did adore. Supper was dight;°   *prepared*
  Then they Malbecco prayd of curtesy,
  That of his Lady they might have the sight,
225 And company at meat, to do them more delight.

          26
But he to shift their curious request,
  Gan causen,° why she could not come in place;   *give reasons*
  Her craséd° health, her late recourse to rest,   *impaired*
  And humid evening, ill for sicke folkes cace:
230   But none of those excuses could take place;
  Ne would they eate, till she in presence came.
  She came in presence with right comely grace,
  And fairely them saluted,° as became,   *greeted*
And shewd her selfe in all a gentle curteous Dame.

2. I.e., moved her to tell them who she was.

27

They sate to meat, and Satyrane his chaunce
  Was her before,[3] and Paridell besyde;
  But he him selfe sate looking still askaunce,
  Gainst° Britomart, and ever closely eyde   *opposite*
  Sir Satyrane, that glaunces might not glyde:
  But his blind eye, that syded Paridell,
  All his demeasnure° from his sight did hyde: *demeanor*
  On her faire face so did he feede his fill,
And sent close messages of love to her at will.

28

And ever and anone, when none was ware,
  With speaking lookes, that close embassage° bore,   *hidden message*
  He roved[4] at her, and told his secret care:
  For all that art he learnéd had of yore.
  Ne was she ignoraunt of that lewd lore,
  But in his eye his meaning wisely red,
  And with the like him answerd evermore:
  She sent at him one firie dart, whose hed
Empoisned was with privy° lust, and gealous dred.   *secret*

29

He from that deadly throw made no defence,
  But to the wound his weake hart opened wyde;
  The wicked engine[5] through false influence,°   *treacherous inflow*
  Past through his eyes, and secretly did glyde
  Into his hart, which it did sorely gryde.°   *pierce*
  But nothing new to him was that same paine,
  Ne paine at all; for he so oft had tryde
  The powre thereof, and loved so oft in vaine,
That thing of course[6] he counted, love to entertaine.

30

Thenceforth to her he sought to intimate
  His inward griefe, by meanes to him well knowne,
  Now Bacchus fruit[7] out of the silver plate
  He on the table dasht, as overthrowne,
  Or of the fruitfull liquor overflowne,
  And by the dauncing bubbles did divine,[8]
  Or therein write to let his love be showne;
  Which well she red out of the learnéd line,
A sacrament prophane in mistery of wine.

31

And when so of his hand the pledge[9] she raught,
  The guilty cup she fainéd to mistake,
  And in her lap did shed her idle draught,
  Shewing desire her inward flame to slake:
  By such close signes they secret way did make
  Unto their wils, and one eyes watch escape;
  Two eyes him needeth, for to watch and wake,
  Who lovers will deceive. Thus was the ape,
By their faire handling, put into Malbeccoes cape.[1]

32

Now when of meats and drinks they had their fill,
  Purpose was movéd by that gentle Dame,
  Unto those knights adventurous, to tell

---

3. I.e., was to sit across from her.
4. Shot (a term from archery).
5. The "dart" of line 251.
6. I.e., as a matter of course.
7. Grapes; i.e., the wine.

8. Give a sign. Paridell is employing a clandestine lovers' code, well understood by Hellenore, to communicate his passion.
9. Wine offered as a toast. "Raught": reached.
1. I.e., thus they made a fool of Malbecco.

Of deeds of armes, which unto them became,°   *happened*
And every one his kindred, and his name.
285 Then Paridell, in whom a kindly° pryde   *natural*
Of gracious speach, and skill his words to frame
Abounded, being glad of so fit tyde°   *opportunity*
Him to commend to her, thus spake, of all well eyde.

33

"Troy, that art now nought, but an idle name,
290 And in thine ashes buried low dost lie,
Though whilome° far much greater then thy fame,   *formerly*
Before that angry Gods, and cruell skye
Upon thee heapt a direfull destinie,
What boots it boast thy glorious descent,
295 And fetch from heaven thy great Genealogie,
Sith° all thy worthy prayses being blent,°   *since / added together*
Their of-spring hath embaste,[2] and later glory shent.°   *disgraced*

34

"Most famous Worthy of the world, by whome
That warre was kindled, which did Troy inflame,
300 And stately towres of Ilion whilome
Brought unto balefull ruine, was by name
Sir Paris far renowmd through noble fame,
Who through great prowesse and bold hardinesse,
From Lacedaemon fetcht the fairest Dame,
305 That ever Greece did boast, or knight possesse,
Whom Venus to him gave for meed[3] of worthinesse.

35

"Faire Helene, flowre of beautie excellent,
And girlond of the mighty Conquerours,
That madest many Ladies deare lament
310 The heavie losse of their brave Paramours,
Which they far off beheld from Trojan toures,
And saw the fieldes of faire Scamander strowne
With carcases of noble warrioures,
Whose fruitlesse lives were under furrow sowne,
315 And Xanthus sandy bankes with bloud all overflowne.

36

"From him my linage I derive aright,
Who long before the ten yeares siege of Troy,
Whiles yet on Ida he a shepheard hight,
On faire Oenone got a lovely boy,
320 Whom for remembraunce of her passéd joy,
She of his Father Parius did name;
Who, after Greekes did Priams realme destroy,
Gathred the Trojan reliques saved from flame,
And with them sayling thence, to th'Isle of Paros came.

37

325 "That was by him cald Paros, which before
Hight Nausa, there he many yeares did raine,
And built Nausicle by the Pontick shore,
The which he dying left next in remaine
To Paridas his sonne.[4]
330 From whom I Paridell by kin descend;

2. Debased, i.e., surpassed.
3. Reward. In fact, Venus bribed Paris to declare her the winner in a beauty contest by promising Helen to him. Paridell's account is biased in favor of his ancestor Paris, who was actually something of a dandy and not especially courageous.
4. A metrically deficient line.

But for faire Ladies love, and glories gaine,
My native soile have left, my dayes to spend
In sewing° deeds of armes, my lives and labours end."   *pursuing*

38

Whenas the noble Britomart heard tell
Of Trojan warres, and Priams Citie sackt,
The ruefull story of Sir Paridell,
She was empassiond at that piteous act,
With zelous envy° of Greekes cruell fact,°   *anger / deed*
Against that nation, from whose race of old
She heard, that she was lineally extract:°   *descended*
For noble Britons sprong from Trojans bold,
And Troynovant⁵ was built of old Troyes ashes cold.

39

Then sighing soft awhile, at last she thus:
"O lamentable fall of famous towne,
Which raignd so many yeares victorious,
And of all Asie bore the soveraigne crowne,
In one sad night consumd, and throwen downe:
What stony hart, that heares thy haplesse fate,
Is not empierst with deepe compassiowne,
And makes ensample of mans wretched state,
That floures so fresh at morne, and fades at evening late?

40

"Behold, Sir, how your pitifull complaint°   *lament*
Hath found another partner of your payne:
For nothing may impresse so deare constraint,°   *distress*
As countries cause, and commune foes disdayne.
But if it should not grieve you, backe agayne
To turne your course, I would to heare desyre,
What to Aeneas fell; sith that men sayne
He was not in the Cities wofull fyre
Consumed, but did him selfe to safétie retyre."

41

"Anchyses sonne begot of Venus faire,"
Said he, "out of the flames for safegard fled,
And with a remnant did to sea repaire,
Where he through fatall errour° long was led   *fated wandering*
Full many yeares, and weetlesse° wanderéd   *unknowing*
From shore to shore, emongst the Lybicke sands,
Ere rest he found. Much there he sufferéd,
And many perils past in forreine lands,
To save his people sad from victours vengefull hands.

42

"At last in Latium he did arrive,
Where he with cruell warre was entertaind
Of th'inland folke, which sought him backe to drive,
Till he with old Latinus was constraind,
To contract wedlock:⁶ (so the fates ordaind.)
Wedlock contract in bloud, and eke in blood
Accomplishéd, that many deare complaind:
The rivall slaine, the victour through the flood
Escapéd hardly, hardly praisd his wedlock good.

---

5. "New Troy"; i.e., London.   6. I.e., with Latinus' daughter Lavinia.

43

"Yet after all, he victour did survive,
380   And with Latinus did the kingdome part.°   *divide*
But after, when both nations gan to strive,
Into their names the title to convart,[7]
His sonne Iülus did from thence depart,
With all the warlike youth of Trojans bloud,
385   And in long Alba plast his throne apart,
Where faire it florishéd, and long time stoud,
Till Romulus renewing it, to Rome removd."

44

"There there," said Britomart, "a fresh appeard
The glory of the later world to spring,
390   And Troy againe out of her dust was reard,
To sit in second seat of soveraigne king,
Of all the world under her governing.
But a third kingdome yet is to arise,
Out of the Trojans scatteréd of-spring,
395   That in all glory and great enterprise,
Both first and second Troy shall dare to equalise.°   *equal*

45

"It Troynovant is hight, that with the waves
Of wealthy Thamis[8] washéd is along,
Upon whose stubborne neck, wherat he raves
400   With roring rage, and sore him selfe does throng,°   *press*
That all men feare to tempt his billowes strong,
She fastned hath her foot, which standes so hy,
That it a wonder of the world is song
In forreine landes, and all which passen by,
405 Beholding it from far, do thinke it threates the skye.

46

"The Trojan Brute did first that Citie found,
And Hygate made the meare° thereof by West,   *boundary*
And Overt gate by North: that is the bound
Toward the land; two rivers bound the rest.
410   So huge a scope at first him seeméd best,
To be the compasse of his kingdomes seat:
So huge a mind could not in lesser rest,
Ne in small meares containe his glory great,
That Albion° had conquered first by warlike feat."   *Britain*

47

415 "Ah fairest Lady knight," said Paridell,
"Pardon I pray my heedlesse oversight,
Who had forgot, that° whilome I heard tell   *what*
From aged Mnemon;[9] for my wits bene light.
Indeed he said (if I remember right,)
420   That of the antique Trojan stocke, there grew
Another plant, that raught to wondrous hight,
And far abroad his mighty branches threw,
Into the utmost Angle of the world he knew.

48

"For that same Brute, whom much he did advaunce
425   In all his speach, was Sylvius his[1] sonne,
Whom having slaine, through luckles arrowes glaunce
He fled for feare of that he had misdonne,

7. I.e., each nation attempted to gain control   9. Greek for *memory*.
over the other.   1. I.e., Sylvius'.
8. The Thames.

Or else for shame, so fowle reproch to shonne,
And with him led to sea an youthly trayne,°   *band*
Where wearie wandring they long time did wonne,°   *abide*
And many fortunes proved° in th'Ocean mayne,   *experienced*
And great adventures found, that now were long to sayne.

49

"At last by fatall course they driven were
Into an Island spatious and brode,
The furthest North, that did to them appeare:
Which after rest they seeking far abrode,
Found it the fittest soyle for their abode,
Fruitfull of all things fit for living foode,
But wholy wast, and void of peoples trode,°   *footstep*
Save an huge nation of the Geaunts broode,
That fed on living flesh, and druncke mens vitall blood.

50

"Whom he through wearie wars and labours long,
Subdewd with losse of many Britons bold:
In which the great Goemagot of strong
Corineus, and Coulin of Debon old
Were overthrowne, and layd on th'earth full cold,
Which quakéd under their so hideous masse,
A famous history to be enrold
In everlasting moniments of brasse,
That all the antique Worthies merits far did passe.

51

"His worke great Troynovant, his worke is eke
Faire Lincolne, both renowméd far away,
That who from East to West will endlong² seeke,
Cannot two fairer Cities find this day,
Except Cleopolis:³ so heard I say
Old Mnemon. Therefore Sir, I greet you well
Your countrey kin, and you entirely pray
Of pardon for the strife, which late befell
Betwixt us both unknowne." So ended Paridell.

52

But all the while, that he these speaches spent,
Upon his lips hong faire Dame Hellenore,
With vigilant regard, and dew attent,°   *attention*
Fashioning worlds of fancies evermore
In her fraile wit, that now her quite forlore:°   *deserted*
The whiles unwares away her wondring eye,
And greedy eares her weake hart from her bore:
Which he perceiving, ever privily
In speaking, many false belgardes° at her let fly.   *loving looks*

53

So long these knights discourséd diversly,
Of straunge affaires, and noble hardiment,
Which they had past with mickle° jeopardy,   *great*
That now the humid night was farforth spent,
And heavenly lampes were halfendeale ybrent:⁴
Which th'old man seeing well, who too long thought
Every discourse and every argument,
Which by the houres he measuréd, besought
Them go to rest. So all unto their bowres were brought.

2. From end to end.   4. Half burnt out.
3. The city of the Fairy Queen.

Book III, Canto X

Paridell rapeth Hellenore:
Malbecco her pursewes:
Findes emongst Satyres, whence with him
To turne she doth refuse.

1

The morow next, so soone as Phoebus Lamp
  Bewrayéd° had the world with early light,   *revealed*
  And fresh Aurora had the shady damp
  Out of the goodly heaven amovéd quight,
5 Faire Britomart and that same Faerie knight[5]
  Uprose, forth on their journey for to wend:
  But Paridell complaynd, that his late fight
  With Britomart, so sore did him offend,°   *trouble*
That ryde he could not, till his hurts he did amend.

2

10 So forth they fared, but he behind them stayd,
  Maulgre° his host, who grudgéd grievously,   *in spite of*
  To house a guest, that would be needes obayd,
  And of his owne him left not liberty:
  Might wanting measure moveth surquedry.[6]
15 Two things he fearéd, but the third was death;
  That fierce youngmans unruly maistery;
  His money, which he loved as living breath;
And his faire wife, whom honest long he kept uneath.°   *with difficulty*

3

But patience perforce he must abie,°   *endure*
20 What fortune and his fate on him will lay,
  Fond° is the feare, that findes no remedie;   *found*
  Yet warily he watcheth every way,
  By which he feareth evill happen may:
  So th' evill thinkes by watching to prevent;
25 Ne doth he suffer her, nor night, nor day,
  Out of his sight her selfe once to absent.
So doth he punish her and eke himselfe torment.

4

But Paridell kept better watch, then hee,
  A fit occasion° for his turne to find: *opportunity*
30 False love, why do men say, thou canst not see,
  And in their foolish fancy feigne thee blind,
  That with thy charmes the sharpest sight doest bind,
  And to thy will abuse? Thou walkest free,
  And seest every secret of the mind;
35 Thou seest all, yet none at all sees thee;
All that is by the working of thy Deitee.

5

So perfect in that art was Paridell,
  That he Malbeccoes halfen eye did wyle,°   *beguile*
  His halfen eye he wiléd wondrous well,
40 And Hellenors both eyes did eke beguyle,
  Both eyes and hart attonce, during the whyle
  That he there sojournéd his wounds to heale;
  That Cupid selfe it seeing, close did smyle,

5. I.e., Satyrane.
6. I.e., the absence of restraint on power promotes arrogance.

To weet how he her love away did steale,
45 And bad, that none their joyous treason should reveale.

6

The learnéd lover lost no time nor tyde,
   That least avantage mote to him afford,
   Yet bore so faire a saile, that none espyde
   His secret drift, till he her layd abord.[7]
50 When so in open place, and commune bord,°   *table*
   He fortuned her to meet, with commune speach
   He courted her, yet bayted° every word,   *moderated*
   That his ungentle hoste n'ote° him appeach°   *might not / accuse*
Of vile ungentlenesse, or hospitages° breach.   *hospitality's*

7

55 But when apart (if ever her apart)
   He found, then his false engins° fast he plyde,   *techniques*
   And all the sleights unbosomd in his hart;
   He sighed, he sobd, he swownd,° he perdy° dyde, *swooned / indeed*
   And cast himselfe on ground her fast besyde:
60 Tho when againe he him bethought to live,
   He wept, and wayld, and false laments belyde,° *counterfeited*
   Saying, but if° she Mercie would him give,   *unless*
That he mote algates° dye, yet did his death forgive. *must necessarily*

8

And otherwhiles with amorous delights,
65 And pleasing toyes he would her entertaine,
   Now singing sweetly, to surprise her sprights,
   Now making layes of love and lovers paine,
   Bransles,° ballads, virelayes,° and verses vaine; *dances / songs*
   Oft purposes,° oft riddles he devysd,   *games*
70 And thousands like, which flowéd in his braine,
   With which he fed her fancie, and entysd
To take to his new love, and leave her old despysd.

9

And every where he might, and every while
   He did her service dewtifull, and sewed°   *followed*
75 At hand with humble pride, and pleasing guile,
   So closely yet, that none but she it vewed,
   Who well perceivéd all, and all indewed.°   *took in*
   Thus finely did he his false nets dispred,
   With which he many weake harts had subdewd
80 Of yore, and many had ylike misled:
What wonder then, if she were likewise carriéd?

10

No fort so fensible,° no wals so strong,   *defensible*
   But that continuall battery will rive,
   Or daily siege through dispurvayance° long, *want of provisions*
85 And lacke of reskewes will to parley drive;
   And Peace, that unto parley eare will give,
   Will shortly yeeld it selfe, and will be made
   The vassall of the victors will bylive:°   *immediately*
   That strategeme had oftentimes assayd°   *tried*
90 This crafty paramoure, and now it plaine displayd.

11

For through his traines° he her intrapped hath, *snares*
   That she her love and hart hath wholy sold
   To him, without regard of gaine, or scath,°   *harm*

---

7. "Layd abord" (a nautical term): placed his ship alongside hers preparatory to boarding.

Or care of credite, or of husband old,
95 Whom she hath vowed to dub a faire cucquold.
Nought wants but time and place, which shortly shee
Devizéd hath, and to her lover told.
It pleaséd well. So well they both agree;
So readie rype to ill, ill wemens counsels bee.

12

100 Darke was the evening, fit for lovers stealth,
When chaunst Malbecco busie be elsewhere,
She to his closet° went, where all his wealth   *private room*
Lay hid: thereof she countlesse summes did reare,°   *take*
The which she meant away with her to beare;
105 The rest she fyred for sport, or for despite;
As Hellene, when she saw aloft appeare
The Trojane flames, and reach to heavens hight,
Did clap her hands, and joyéd at that dolefull sight.

13

This second Hellene, faire Dame Hellenore,
110 The whiles her husband ran with sory haste,
To quench the flames which she had tyned° before,   *kindled*
Laught at his foolish labour spent in waste;
And ran into her lovers armes right fast;
Where streight embracéd, she to him did cry
115 And call aloud for helpe, ere helpe were past;
For loe that guest would beare her forcibly,
And meant to ravish her, that rather had to dy.

14

The wretched man hearing her call for ayd,
And readie seeing him with her to fly,
120 In his disquiet mind was much dismayd:
But when againe he backward cast his eye,
And saw the wicked fire so furiously
Consume his hart, and scorch his Idoles face,
He was therewith distresséd diversly,
125 Ne wist he how to turne, nor to what place;
Was never wretched man in such a wofull cace.

15

Ay° when to him she cryde, to her he turnd,   *ever*
And left the fire; love money overcame:
But when he markéd, how his money burnd,
130 He left his wife; money did love disclame:°   *renounce*
Both was he loth to loose his lovéd Dame,
And loth to leave his liefest pelfe° behind,   *dearest money*
Yet sith he n'ote° save both, he saved that same,   *might not*
Which was the dearest to his donghill mind,
135 The God of his desire, the joy of misers blind.

16

Thus whilest all things in troublous uprore were,
And all men busie to suppresse the flame,
The loving couple neede no reskew feare,
But leasure had, and libertie to frame
140 Their purpost flight, free from all mens reclame;°   *recall*
And Night, the patronesse of love-stealth faire,
Gave them safe conduct, till to end they came:
So bene they gone yfeare,° a wanton paire   *together*
Of lovers loosely knit, where list them to repaire.

17

45 Soone as the cruell flames yslakéd were,
    Malbecco seeing, how his losse did lye,
    Out of the flames, which he had quencht whylere°   *just now*
    Into huge waves of griefe and gealosye
    Full deepe emplongéd was, and drownéd nye,°   *nigh, nearly*
50   Twixt inward doole° and felonous despight;°   *grief / wrath*
    He raved, he wept, he stampt, he lowd did cry,
    And all the passions, that in man may light,
Did him attonce oppresse, and vex his caytive spright.

18

Long thus he chawd the cud of inward griefe,
55   And did consume his gall with anguish sore,
    Still when he muséd on his late mischiefe,
    Then still the smart thereof increaséd more,
    And seemed more grievous, then it was before:
    At last when sorrow he saw booted nought,
60   Ne griefe might not his love to him restore,
    He gan devise, how her he reskew mought,°   *might*
Ten thousand wayes he cast in his confuséd thought.

19

At last resolving, like a pilgrim pore,
    To search her forth, where so she might be fond,
65   And bearing with him treasure in close store,
    The rest he leaves in ground: So takes in hond
    To seeke her endlong, both by sea and lond.
    Long he her sought, he sought her farre and nere,
    And every where that he mote understond,
70   Of knights and ladies any meetings were,
And of eachone he met, he tydings did inquere.

20

But all in vaine, his woman was too wise,
    Ever to come into his clouch againe,
    And he too simple ever to surprise
75   The jolly Paridell, for all his paine.
    One day, as he forpasséd° by the plaine   *passed over*
    With weary pace, he farre away espide
    A couple, seeming well to be his twaine,
    Which hovéd° close under a forrest side,   *lingered*
80 As if they lay in wait, or else themselves did hide.

21

Well weenéd he, that those the same mote bee,
    And as he better did their shape avize,°   *perceive*
    Him seeméd more their manner did agree;
    For th' one was arméd all in warlike wize,
85   Whom, to be Paridell he did devize;°   *surmise*
    And th' other all yclad in garments light,
    Discolour'd° like to womanish disguise,   *varicolored*
    He did resemble° to his Ladie bright;   *find similar*
And ever his faint hart much earnéd° at the sight.   *yearned*

22

90 And ever faine° he towards them would goe,   *eagerly*
    But yet durst not for dread approchen nie,
    But stood aloofe, unweeting what to doe;
    Till that prickt forth with loves extremitie,
    That is the father of foule gealosy,

195 He closely nearer crept, the truth to weet:
But, as he nigher drew, he easily
Might scerne,° that it was not his sweetest sweet,   *discern*
Ne yet her belamour,° the partner of his sheet.   *lover*

23

But it was scornefull Braggadochio,
200 That with his servant Trompart hoverd there,
Sith late he fled from his too earnest foe:[8]
Whom such when as Malbecco spyéd clere,
He turnéd backe, and would have fled arere;
Till Trompart ronning hastily, him did stay,
205 And bad before his soveraine Lord appere:
That was him loth, yet durst he not gainesay,
And comming him before, low louted on the lay.[9]

24

The Boaster at him sternely bent his browe,
As if he could have kild him with his looke,
210 That to the ground him meekely made to bowe,
And awfull terror deepe into him strooke,
That every member of his bodie quooke.°   *quaked*
Said he, "Thou man of nought, what doest thou here,
Unfitly furnisht with thy bag and booke,
215 Where I expected one with shield and spere,
To prove some deedes of armes upon an equall pere."

25

The wretched man at his imperious speach,
Was all abasht, and low prostrating, said;
"Good Sir, let not my rudenesse be no breach
220 Unto your patience, ne be ill ypaid;°   *appeased*
For I unwares this way by fortune straid,
A silly Pilgrim driven to distresse,
That seeke a Lady," There he suddein staid,
And did the rest with grievous sighes suppresse,
225 While teares stood in his eies, few drops of bitternesse.

26

"What Ladie, man?" said Trompart, "take good hart,
And tell thy griefe, if any hidden lye;
Was never better time to shew thy smart,
Then now, that noble succor is thee by,
230 That is the whole worlds commune remedy."
That chearefull word his weake hart much did cheare,
And with vaine hope his spirits faint supply,
That bold he said; "O most redoubted Pere,°   *champion*
Vouchsafe with mild regard a wretches cace to heare."

27

235 Then sighing sore, "It is not long," said hee,
"Sith I enjoyd the gentlest Dame alive;
Of whom a knight, no knight at all perdee,
But shame of all, that doe for honor strive,
By treacherous deceipt did me deprive;
240 Through open outrage he her bore away,
And with fowle force unto his will did drive,
Which all good knights, that armes do beare this day,
Are bound for to revenge, and punish if they may.

---

8. The beautiful virgin huntress Belphoebe,   embrace her.
who in Book II had frightened Braggadochio   9. Bowed low on the ground.
with her javelin when he lustfully tried to

28

"And you most noble Lord, that can and dare
  Redresse the wrong of miserable wight,
  Cannot employ your most victorious speare
  In better quarrell, then defence of right,
  And for a Ladie gainst a faithlesse knight;
  So shall your glory be advauncéd much,
  And all faire Ladies magnifie your might,
  And eke my selfe, albe I simple such,[1]
Your worthy paine shall well reward with guerdon° rich."   *reward*

29

With that out of his bouget° forth he drew   *bag*
  Great store of treasure, therewith him to tempt;
  But he on it lookt scornefully askew,
  As much disdeigning to be so misdempt,
  Or a war-monger° to be basely nempt;°   *mercenary soldier / named*
  And said; "Thy offers base I greatly loth,
  And eke thy words uncourteous and unkempt;
  I tread in dust thee and thy money both,
That, were it not for shame," So turnéd from him wroth.

30

But Trompart, that his maisters humor knew,
  In lofty looks to hide an humble mind,
  Was inly tickled with that golden vew,
  And in his eare him rounded° close behind: *whispered*
  Yet stoupt[2] he not, but lay still in the wind,
  Waiting advauntage on the pray to sease;
  Till Trompart lowly to the ground inclind,
  Besought him his great courage° to appease,   *anger*
And pardon simple man, that rash did him displease.

31

Bigge looking like a doughtie Doucepere,[3]
  At last he thus; "Thou clod of vilest clay,
  I pardon yield, and with thy rudenesse beare;
  But weete henceforth, that all that golden pray,°   *booty*
  And all that else the vaine world vaunten° may,   *boast*
  I loath as doung, ne deeme my dew reward:
  Fame is my meed,° and glory vertues pray.   *reward*
  But minds of mortall men are muchell mard,
And moved amisse with massie mucks unmeet regard.

32

"And more, I graunt to thy great miserie
  Gratious respect, thy wife shall backe be sent,
  And that vile knight, who ever that he bee,
  Which hath thy Lady reft,° and knighthood shent,°   *seized / dishonored*
  By Sanglamort[4] my sword, whose deadly dent°   *blow*
  The bloud hath of so many thousands shed,
  I sweare: ere long shall dearely it repent;
  Ne he twixt heaven and earth shall hide his hed,
But soone he shall be found, and shortly doen° be ded."   *caused to*

33

The foolish man thereat woxe wondrous blith,
  As if the word so spoken, were halfe donne,
  And humbly thankéd him a thousand sith,°   *times*

---

1. Although I am a plain man, such as you see.
2. A hawking term: swooped down.
3. One of the twelve champions of Charlemagne.
4. "Bloody Death."

That had from death to life him newly wonne.
Tho° forth the Boaster marching, brave begonne   *then*
His stolen steed⁵ to thunder° furiously,   *thunder at*
295   As if he heaven and hell would overronne,
And all the world confound with cruelty,
That much Malbecco joyéd in his jollity.°   *bravery*

                    34
Thus long they three together traveiléd,
Through many a wood, and many an uncouth° way,   *unknown*
300   To seeke his wife, that was farre wanderéd:
But those two sought nought, but the present pray,
To weete the treasure, which he did bewray,°   *reveal*
On which their eies and harts were wholly set,
With purpose, how they might it best betray,°   *steal*
305   For sith the houre, that first he did them let
The same behold, therewith their keene desires were whet.

                    35
It fortunéd as they together fared,
They spide, where Paridell came pricking° fast   *spurring*
Upon the plaine, the which himselfe prepared
310   To giust° with that brave straunger knight a cast,   *joust*
As on adventure by the way he past:
Alone he rode without his Paragone;°   *companion*
For having filcht her bels,⁶ her up he cast
To the wide world, and let her fly alone,
315   He nould° be clogd. So had he servéd many one.   *would not*

                    36
The gentle Lady, loose at randon left,
The greene-wood long did walke, and wander wide
At wilde adventure, like a forlorne weft,°   *waif*
Till on a day the Satyres her espide
320   Straying alone withouten groome or guide;
Her up they tooke, and with them home her led,
With them as housewife ever to abide,
To milk their gotes, and make them cheese and bred,
And every one as commune good° her handeléd.   *goods, property*

                    37
325   That shortly she Malbecco has forgot,
And eke Sir Paridell, all° were he deare;   *although*
Who from her went to seeke another lot,
And now by fortune was arrivéd here,
Where those two guilers with Malbecco were:
330   Soone as the oldman saw Sir Paridell,
He fainted, and was almost dead with feare,
Ne word he had to speake, his griefe to tell,
But to him louted° low, and greeted goodly well.   *bowed*

                    38
And after askéd him for Hellenore:
335   "I take no keepe of her," said Paridell,
"She wonneth° in the forrest there before."   *dwells*
So forth he rode, as his adventure fell;
The whiles the Boaster from his loftie sell°   *saddle*
Faynd to alight, something amisse to mend;
340   But the fresh Swayne would not his leasure dwell,°   *wait on*

---

5. Braggadochio had acquired horse and arms   6. Hunting hawks often had bells fastened to
by stealing them from Sir Guyon, the hero of   their legs.
the Book of Temperance (Book II).

But went his way; whom when he passéd kend,°   *perceived*
He up remounted light, and after faind to wend.

39

"Perdy nay," said Malbecco, "shall ye not:
But let him passe as lightly, as he came:
For litle good of him is to be got,
And mickle perill to be put to shame.
But let us go to seeke my dearest Dame,
Whom he hath left in yonder forrest wyld:
For of her safety in great doubt I am,
Least salvage° beastes her person have despoyld: *savage*
Then all the world is lost, and we in vaine have toyld."

40

They all agree, and forward them addrest:
"Ah but," said craftie Trompart, "weete ye well,
That yonder in that wastefull wildernesse
Huge monsters haunt, and many dangers dwell;
Dragons, and Minotaures, and feendes of hell,
And many wilde woodmen, which robbe and rend
All travellers; therefore advise ye well,
Before ye enterprise that way to wend:
One may his journey bring too soone to evill end."

41

Malbecco stopt in great astonishment,
And with pale eyes fast fixéd on the rest,
Their counsell craved, in daunger imminent.
Said Trompart, "You that are the most opprest
With burden of great treasure, I thinke best
Here for to stay in safetie behind;
My Lord and I will search the wide forrest."
That counsell pleaséd not Malbeccoes mind;
For he was much affraid, himselfe alone to find.

42

"Then is it best," said he, "that ye doe leave
Your treasure here in some securitie,
Either fast closéd in some hollow greave,°   *grove*
Or buried in the ground from jeopardie,
Till we returne againe in safetie:
As for us two, least doubt of us ye have,
Hence farre away we will blindfolded lie,
Ne privie be unto your treasures grave."
It pleaséd: so he did. Then they march forward brave.

43

Now when amid the thickest woods they were,
They heard a noyse of many bagpipes shrill,
And shrieking Hububs them approching nere,
Which all the forrest did with horror fill:
That dreadfull sound the boasters hart did thrill,°   *pierce*
With such amazement, that in haste he fled,
Ne ever lookéd backe for good or ill,
And after him eke fearefull Trompart sped;
The old man could not fly, but fell to ground halfe ded.

44

Yet afterwards close creeping, as he might,
He in a bush did hide his fearefull hed,
The jolly Satyres full of fresh delight,
Came dauncing forth, and with them nimbly led
Faire Hellenore, with girlonds all bespred,

Whom their May-lady they had newly made:
She proud of that new honour, which they red,°   *declared*
395   And of their lovely fellowship full glade,
Daunst lively, and her face did with a lawrell shade.

45

The silly° man that in the thicket lay   *simple*
Saw all this goodly sport, and grievéd sore,
Yet durst he not against it doe or say,
400   But did his hart with bitter thoughts engore,
To see th' unkindnesse° of his Hellenore.   *unnatural behavior*
All day they dauncéd with great lustihed,
And with their hornéd feet the greene grasse wore,
The whiles their gotes upon the brouzes° fed,   *twigs*
405   Till drouping Phoebus gan to hide his golden hed.

46

Tho° up they gan their merry pypes to trusse,   *then*
And all their goodly heards did gather round,
But every Satyre first did give a busse°   *kiss*
To Hellenore: so busses did abound.
410   Now gan the humid vapour shed the ground
With perly deaw, and th' Earthés gloomy shade
Did dim the brightnesse of the welkin° round,   *sky*
That every bird and beast awarnéd made,
To shrowd themselves, whiles sleepe their senses did invade.

47

415   Which when Malbecco saw, out of his bush
Upon his hands and feete he crept full light,
And like a gote emongst the gotes did rush,
That through the helpe of his faire hornes on hight,[7]
And misty dampe of misconceiving° night,   *misleading*
420   And eke through likenesse of his gotish beard,
He did the better counterfeite aright:
So home he marcht emongst the hornéd heard,
That none of all the Satyres him espyde or heard.

48

At night, when all they went to sleepe, he vewd,
425   Whereas his lovely wife emongst them lay,
Embracéd of a Satyre rough and rude,
Who all the night did minde his joyous play:
Nine times he heard him come aloft ere day,
That all his hart with gealosie did swell;
430   But yet that nights ensample did bewray,°   *reveal*
That not for nought his wife them loved so well,
When one so oft a night did ring his matins bell.

49

So closely as he could, he to them crept,
When wearie of their sport to sleepe they fell,
435   And to his wife, that now full soundly slept,
He whispered in her eare, and did her tell,
That it was he, which by her side did dwell,
And therefore prayd her wake, to heare him plaine.
As one out of a dreame not wakéd well,
440   She turned her, and returnéd backe againe:
Yet her for to awake he did the more constraine.

---

7. Horns on his forehead, the sign of a cuckold.

50

At last with irkesome trouble she abrayd;°   *aroused*
  And then perceiving, that it was indeed
  Her old Malbecco, which did her upbrayd,
445 With loosenesse of her love, and loathly deed,
  She was astonisht with exceeding dreed,
  And would have wakt the Satyre by her syde;
  But he her prayd, for mercy, or for meed,°   *reward*
  To save his life, ne let him be descryde,
450 But hearken to his lore, and all his counsell hyde.

51

Tho gan he her perswade, to leave that lewd
  And loathsome life, of God and man abhord,
  And home returne, where all should be renewd
  With perfect peace, and bandes° of fresh accord,   *bonds*
455 And she received againe to bed and bord,
  As if no trespasse ever had bene donne:
  But she it all refuséd at one word,
  And by no meanes would to his will be wonne,
But chose emongst the jolly Satyres still to wonne.

52

460 He wooéd her, till day spring he espyde;
  But all in vaine: and then turnd to the heard,
  Who butted him with hornes on every syde,
  And trode downe in the durt, where his hore° beard   *hoary*
  Was fowly dight,° and he of death afeard.   *adorned*
465 Early before the heavens fairest light
  Out of the ruddy East was fully reard,
  The heardes out of their foldes were looséd quight,
And he emongst the rest crept forth in sory plight.

53

So soone as he the Prison dore did pas,
470 He ran as fast, as both his feete could beare,
  And never lookéd, who behind him was,
  Ne scarsely who before: like as a beare
  That creeping close, amongst the hives to reare°   *take*
  An hony combe, the wakefull dogs espy,
475 And him assayling, sore his carkasse teare,
  That hardly he with life away does fly,
Ne stayes, till safe himselfe he see from jeopardy.

54

Ne stayd he, till he came unto the place,
480 Where late his treasure he entombéd had,
  Where when he found it not (for Trompart bace
  Had it purloynéd for his maister bad):
  With éxtreme fury he became quite mad,
  And ran away, ran with himselfe away:
  That who so straungely had him seene bestad,°   *hard pressed*
485 With upstart haire, and staring eyes dismay,
From Limbo[8] lake him late escapéd sure would say.

55

High over hilles and over dales he fled,
  As if the wind him on his winges had borne,
  Ne banck nor bush could stay him, when he sped

8. A region believed to exist on the border of hell.

His nimble feet, as treading still on thorne:
Griefe, and despight, and gealosie, and scorne
Did all the way him follow hard behind,
And he himselfe himselfe loathed so forlorne,°   *ruined*
So shamefully forlorne of womankind;
That as a snake, still lurkéd in his wounded mind.

56

Still fled he forward, looking backward still,
Ne stayd his flight, nor fearefull agony,
Till that he came unto a rockie hill,
Over the sea, suspended dreadfully,
That living creature it would terrify,
To looke adowne, or upward to the hight:
From thence he threw himselfe dispiteously,
All desperate of his fore-damnéd spright,
That seemed no helpe for him was left in living sight.

57

But through long anguish, and selfe-murdring thought
He was so wasted and forpinéd quight,
That all his substance was consumed to nought,
And nothing left, but like an aery Spright,
That on the rockes he fell so flit° and light,   *weightless*
That he thereby received no hurt at all;
But chauncéd on a craggy cliff to light;
Whence he with crooked clawes so long did crall,
That at the last he found a cave with entrance small.

58

Into the same he creepes, and thenceforth there
Resolved to build his balefull mansion,
In drery darkenesse, and continuall feare
Of that rockes fall, which ever and anon
Threates with huge ruine him to fall upon,
That he dare never sleepe, but that one eye
Still ope he keepes for that occasion;
Ne ever rests he in tranquillity,
The roring billowes beat his bowre so boystrously.

59

Ne ever is he wont on ought to feed,
But toades and frogs, his pasture° poysonous,   *diet*
Which in his cold complexion° do breed   *character*
A filthy bloud, or humour[9] rancorous,
Matter of doubt and dread suspitious,
That doth with curelesse care consume the hart,
Corrupts the stomacke with gall vitious,
Croscuts the liver with internall smart,
And doth transfixe the soule with deathes eternall dart.

60

Yet can he never dye, but dying lives,
And doth himselfe with sorrow new sustaine,
That death and life attonce unto him gives,
And painefull pleasure turnes to pleasing paine.
There dwels he ever, miserable swaine,
Hatefull both to him selfe and every wight;
Where he through privy griefe, and horrour vaine,
Is woxen so deformed, that he has quight
Forgot he was a man, and Gealosie is hight.°   *called*

1590

9. A bodily fluid believed to control a person's disposition.

From Amoretti

Sonnet 8

More then° most faire, full of the living fire,   *than*
Kindled above unto the maker neere:
No eyes but joyes, in which al powers conspire,
That to the world naught else be counted deare.
5 Thrugh your bright beams doth not the blinded guest,[1]
Shoot out his darts to base affections wound:
But Angels come to lead fraile mindes to rest
In chast desires on heavenly beauty bound.
You frame my thoughts and fashion me within,
10 You stop my toung, and teach my hart to speake,
You calme the storme that passion did begin,
Strong thrugh your cause, but by your vertue weak.
Dark is the world, where your light shined never;
Well is he borne, that may behold you ever.

Sonnet 10

Unrighteous Lord of love, what law is this,
That me thou makest thus tormented be:
The whiles she lordeth in licentious blisse
Of her freewill, scorning both thee and me.
5 See how the Tyrannesse doth joy to see
The huge massácres which her eyes do make:
And humbled harts brings captives unto thee,
That thou of them mayst mightie vengeance take.
But her proud hart doe thou a little shake
10 And that high look, with which she doth comptroll
All this worlds pride, bow to a baser make,°   *lowlier manner*
And al her faults in thy black booke enroll.
That I may laugh at her in equall sort,
As she doth laugh at me and makes my pain her sport.

Sonnet 37

What guyle is this, that those her golden tresses,
She doth attyre under a net of gold:
And with sly skill so cunningly them dresses,
That which is gold or heare, may scarse be told?
5 Is it that mens frayle eyes, which gaze too bold,
She may entangle in that golden snare:
And being caught may craftily enfold,
Theyr weaker harts, which are not wel aware?
Take heed therefore, myne eyes, how ye doe stare
10 Henceforth too rashly on that guilefull net,
In which if ever ye entrapped are,
Out of her bands ye by no meanes shall get.
Fondnesse° it were for any being free,   *folly*
To covet fetters, though they golden bee.

Sonnet 54

Of this worlds Theatre in which we stay,
My love lyke the Spectátor ydly sits
Beholding me that all the pageants° play,   *roles*
Disguysing diversly my troubled wits.

1. I.e., Cupid.

⁵ Sometimes I joy when glad occasion fits,
And mask in myrth lyke to a Comedy:
Soone after when my joy to sorrow flits,
I waile and make my woes a Tragedy.
¹⁰ Yet she beholding me with constant eye,
Delights not in my merth nor rues° my smart: pities
But when I laugh she mocks, and when I cry
She laughes, and hardens evermore her hart.
What then can move her? if nor merth nor mone,
She is no woman, but a sencelesse stone.

Sonnet 56

Fayre ye be sure, but cruell and unkind,
As is a Tygre that with greedinesse
Hunts after bloud, when he by chance doth find
A feeble beast, doth felly him oppresse.
⁵ Fayre be ye sure, but proud and pittilesse,
As is a storme, that all things doth prostrate:
Finding a tree alone all comfortlesse,
Beats on it strongly it to ruinate.
Fayre be ye sure, but hard and obstinate,
¹⁰ As is a rocke amidst the raging floods:
Gaynst which a ship of succour desolate,
Doth suffer wreck both of her selfe and goods.
That ship, that tree, and that same beast am I,
Whom ye doe wreck, doe ruine, and destroy.

Sonnet 67

Lyke as a huntsman after weary chace,
Seeing the game from him escapt away,
Sits downe to rest him in some shady place,
With panting hounds beguiléd of their pray:
⁵ So after long pursuit and vaine assay,
When I all weary had the chace forsooke,
The gentle deare returnd the selfe-same way,
Thinking to quench her thirst at the next brooke.
There she beholding me with mylder looke,
¹⁰ Sought not to fly, but fearelesse still did bide:
Till I in hand her yet halfe trembling tooke,
And with her owne goodwill hir fyrmely tyde.
Strange thing me seemd to see a beast so wyld,
So goodly wonne with her owne will beguyld.

Sonnet 68

Most glorious Lord of lyfe, that on this day,[2]
Didst make thy triumph over death and sin:
And having harrowd hell,[3] didst bring away
Captivity thence captive us to win:[4]
⁵ This joyous day, deare Lord, with joy begin,
And grant that we for whom thou diddest dye
Being with thy deare blood clene washt from sin,
May live for ever in felicity.
And that thy love we weighing worthily,
¹⁰ May likewise love thee for the same againe:

2. Easter.
3. A reference to the apocryphal account of Christ's descent into hell, after his crucifixion, in order to rescue the captive souls of the just.
4. "When he ascended up on high, he led captivity captive" (Ephesians iv.8).

And for thy sake that all lyke deare didst buy,
With love may one another entertayne.
So let us love, deare love, lyke as we ought,
Love is the lesson which the Lord us taught.[5]

Sonnet 70

Fresh spring the herald of loves mighty king,
In whose cote armour° richly are displayd   *coat of arms*
All sorts of flowers the which on earth do spring
In goodly colours gloriously arrayd.
5   Goe to my love, where she is carelesse layd,
Yet in her winters bowre not well awake:
Tell her the joyous time wil not be staid
Unless she doe him by the forelock take.[6]
Bid her therefore her selfe soone ready make,
10   To wayt on love amongst his lovely crew:
Where every one that misseth then her make,°   *mate*
Shall be by him amearst° with penance dew.   *punished*
Make hast therefore sweet love, whilest it is prime,°   *spring*
For none can call againe the passéd time.

Sonnet 75

One day I wrote her name upon the strand,
But came the waves and washéd it away:
Agayne I wrote it with a second hand,°   *a second time*
But came the tyde, and made my paynes his pray.
5   "Vayne man," sayd she, "that doest in vaine assay,
A mortall thing so to immortalize,
For I my selve shall lyke to this decay,
And eek° my name bee wypéd out lykewize."   *also*
"Not so," quod° I, "let baser things devize°   *quoth / plan*
10   To dy in dust, but you shall live by fame:
My verse your vertues rare shall eternize,
And in the hevens wryte your glorious name.
Where whenas death shall all the world subdew,
Our love shall live, and later life renew."

Sonnet 81

Fayre is my love, when her fayre golden heares,
With the loose wynd ye waving chance to marke:
Fayre when the rose in her red cheekes appeares,
Or in her eyes the fyre of love does sparke.
5   Fayre when her brest lyke a rich laden barke,
With pretious merchandize she forth doth lay:
Fayre when that cloud of pryde, which oft doth dark
Her goodly light with smiles she drives away.
But fayrest she, when so she doth display,
10   The gate with pearles and rubyes richly dight:°   *adorned*
Throgh which her words so wise do make their way
To beare the message of her gentle spright.
The rest be works of natures wonderment,
But this the worke of harts astonishment.

1595

---

5. "This is my commandment, That ye love one another, as I have loved you" (John xv.12).

6. "To take time by the forelock" is to act promptly.

Epithalamion[7]

Ye learned sisters[8] which have oftentimes
Beene to me ayding, others to adorne:
Whom ye thought worthy of your gracefull rymes,
That even the greatest did not greatly scorne
5 To heare theyr names sung in your simple layes,
But joyéd in theyr prayse.
And when ye list your owne mishaps to mourne,
Which death, or love, or fortunes wreck did rayse,
Your string could soone to sadder tenor° turne,   *strain*
10 And teach the woods and waters to lament
Your dolefull dreriment.
Now lay those sorrowfull complaints aside,
And having all your heads with girland crownd,
Helpe me mine owne loves prayses to resound,
15 Ne let the same of any be envíde:
So Orpheus[9] did for his owne bride,
So I unto my selfe alone will sing,
The woods shall to me answer and my Eccho ring.

Early before the worlds light giving lampe,
20 His golden beame upon the hils doth spred,
Having disperst the nights unchearefull dampe,
Doe ye awake, and with fresh lustyhed
Go to the bowre° of my belovéd love,   *bedchamber*
My truest turtle dove,
25 Bid her awake; for Hymen[1] is awake,
And long since ready forth his maske to move,
With his bright Tead that flames with many a flake,°   *spark*
And many a bachelor to waite on him,
In theyr fresh garments trim.
30 Bid her awake therefore and soone her dight,°   *dress*
For lo the wishéd day is come at last,
That shall for al the paynes and sorrowes past,
Pay to her usury of long delight:
And whylest she doth her dight,
35 Doe ye to her of joy and solace° sing,   *pleasure*
That all the woods may answer and your eccho ring.

Bring with you all the Nymphes that you can heare[2]
Both of the rivers and the forrests greene:
And of the sea that neighbours to her neare,
40 Al with gay girlands goodly wel beseene.
And let them also with them bring in hand,
Another gay girland
For my fayre love of lillyes and of roses,
Bound truelove wize with a blew silke riband.
45 And let them make great store of bridale poses,°   *posies*
And let them eeke bring store of other flowers
To deck the bridale bowers.
And let the ground whereas her foot shall tread,

For feare the stones her tender foot should wrong
50   Be strewed with fragrant flowers all along,
And diapred lyke the discolored mead.³
Which done, doe at her chamber dore awayt,
For she will waken strayt,°   *straightway*
The whiles doe ye this song unto her sing,
55   The woods shall to you answer and your Eccho ring.

Ye Nymphes of Mulla⁴ which with carefull heed,
The silver scaly trouts doe tend full well,
And greedy pikes which use therein to feed,
(Those trouts and pikes all others doo excell)
60   And ye likewise which keepe the rushy lake,
Where none doo fishes take,
Bynd up the locks the which hang scatterd light,
And in his waters which your mirror make,
Behold your faces as the christall bright,
65   That when you come whereas my love doth lie,
No blemish she may spie.
And eke ye lightfoot mayds which keepe the deere,
That on the hoary mountayne use to towre,⁵
And the wylde wolves which doo seeke them to devoure,
70   With your steele darts doo chace from comming neer
Be also present heere,
To helpe to decke her and to help to sing,
That all the woods may answer and your eccho ring.

Wake, now my love, awake; for it is time,
75   The Rosy Morne long since left Tithones bed,⁶
All ready to her silver coche to clyme,
And Phoebus gins to shew his glorious hed.
Hark how the cheerefull birds do chaunt theyr laies
And carroll of loves praise.
80   The merry Larke hir mattins sings aloft.
The thrush replyes, the Mavis descant⁷ playes,
The Ouzell shrills, the Ruddock warbles soft,
So goodly all agree with sweet consent,
To this dayes merriment.
85   Ah my deere love why doe ye sleepe thus long,
When meeter were that ye should now awake,
T' awayt the comming of your joyous make,°   *mate*
And hearken to the birds lovelearnéd song,
The deawy leaves among.
90   For they of joy and pleasance to you sing,
That all the woods them answer and theyr eccho ring.

My love is now awake out of her dreame,
And her fayre eyes like stars that dimméd were
With darksome cloud, now shew theyr goodly beams
95   More bright then Hesperus° his head doth rere.   *evening star*
Come now ye damzels, daughters of delight,
Helpe quickly her to dight,
But first come ye fayre houres which were begot

3. And variegated like the many-colored
meadow.
4. The Awbeg River in Ireland, near
Spenser's home.
5. A hawking term meaning "to climb high."
6. The dawn, personified in mythology as the
goddess Eos or Aurora, was the wife of
Tithonus.
7. Melodic counterpart. The mavis, ouzell (or
European blackbird), and ruddock (or robin)
are all varieties of thrush.

In Joves sweet paradice, of Day and Night,
100 Which doe the seasons of the yeare allot,
And al that ever in this world is fayre
Doe make and still° repayre.   *continually*
And ye three handmayds of the Cyprian Queene,[8]
The which doe still adorne her beauties pride,
105 Helpe to addorne my beautifullest bride:
And as ye her array, still throw betweene°   *at intervals*
Some graces to be seene,
And as ye use to Venus, to her sing,
The whiles the woods shal answer and your eccho ring.

110 Now is my love all ready forth to come,
Let all the virgins therefore well awayt,
And ye fresh boyes that tend upon her groome
Prepare your selves; for he is comming strayt.
Set all your things in seemely good aray
115 Fit for so joyfull day,
The joyfulst day that ever sunne did see.
Faire Sun, shew forth thy favourable ray,
And let thy lifull° heat not fervent be   *lifegiving*
For feare of burning her sunshyny face,
120 Her beauty to disgrace.°   *spoil*
O fayrest Phoebus, father of the Muse,
If ever I did honour thee aright,
Or sing the thing, that mote° thy mind delight,   *might*
Doe not thy servants simple boone° refuse,   *request*
125 But let this day let this one day be myne,
Let all the rest be thine.
Then I thy soverayne prayses loud wil sing,
That all the woods shal answer and theyr eccho ring.

Harke how the Minstrels gin to shrill aloud
130 Their merry Musick that resounds from far
The pipe, the tabor,° and the trembling Croud,°   *drum / viol*
That well agree withouten breach or jar.°   *discord*
But most of all the Damzels doe delite,
When they their tymbrels° smyte,   *tambourines*
135 And thereunto doe daunce and carrol sweet,
That all the sences they doe ravish quite,
The whyles the boyes run up and downe the street,
Crying aloud with strong confuséd noyce,
As if it were one voyce.
140 *Hymen iô*[9] *Hymen, Hymen* they do shout,
That even to the heavens theyr shouting shrill
Doth reach, and all the firmament doth fill,
To which the people standing all about,
As in approvance doe thereto applaud
145 And loud advaunce her laud,
And evermore they *Hymen Hymen* sing,
That al the woods them answer and theyr eccho ring.

Loe where she comes along with portly° pace   *stately*
Lyke Phoebe[1] from her chamber of the East,

8. Venus, whose handmaids were the three
Graces: Aglaia, Thalia, and Euphrosyne. Their
names mean "the brilliant one," "she who
brings flowers," and "she who rejoices the
heart."
9. A shout of joy or triumph (Greek).
1. Another name for the moon goddess
Diana.

0   Arysing forth to run her mighty race,
    Clad all in white, that seemes° a virgin best.   *befits*
    So well it her beseemes that ye would weene
    Some angell she had beene.
    Her long loose yellow locks lyke golden wyre,
55   Sprinckled with perle, and perling° flowres a tweene,   *intermingling*
    Doe lyke a golden mantle her attyre,
    And being crownéd with a girland greene,
    Seeme lyke some mayden Queene.
    Her modest eyes abashéd to behold
60   So many gazers, as on her do stare,
    Upon the lowly ground affixéd are.
    Ne dare lift up her countenance too bold,
    But blush to heare her prayses sung so loud,
    So farre from being proud.
65   Nathlesse° doe ye still loud her prayses sing.   *nevertheless*
    That all the woods may answer and your eccho ring.

    Tell me ye merchants daughters did ye see
    So fayre a creature in your towne before,
    So sweet, so lovely, and so mild as she,
70   Adornd with beautyes grace and vertues store,°   *wealth*
    Her goodly eyes lyke Saphyres shining bright,
    Her forehead yvory white,
    Her cheekes lyke apples which the sun hath rudded,
    Her lips lyke cherryes charming men to byte,
75   Her brest like to a bowle of creame uncrudded,°   *uncurdled*
    Her paps lyke lyllies budded,
    Her snowie necke lyke to a marble towre,
    And all her body lyke a pallace fayre,
    Ascending uppe with many a stately stayre,
80   To honors seat and chastities sweet bowre.
    Why stand ye still ye virgins in amaze,
    Upon her so to gaze,
    Whiles ye forget your former lay to sing,
    To which the woods did answer and your eccho ring.

85   But if ye saw that which no eyes can see,
    The inward beauty of her lively spright,°   *spirit*
    Garnisht with heavenly guifts of high degree,
    Much more then would ye wonder at that sight,
    And stand astonisht lyke to those which red°   *saw*
190   Medusaes mazeful hed.[2]
    There dwels sweet love and constant chastity,
    Unspotted fayth and comely womanhood,
    Regard of honour and mild modesty,
    There vertue raynes as Queene in royal throne,
195   And giveth lawes alone.
    The which the base affections° doe obay,   *lowly emotions*
    And yeeld theyr services unto her will,
    Ne thought of thing uncomely ever may
    Thereto approch to tempt her mind to ill.
200   Had ye once seene these her celestial threasures,
    And unrevealéd pleasures,
    Then would ye wonder and her prayses sing,
    That al the woods should answer and your eccho ring.

2. The Gorgon Medusa had serpents for hair; whoever looked upon her was turned to stone.

Open the temple gates unto my love,
205 Open them wide that she may enter in,
And all the postes adorne as doth behove,[3]
And all the pillours deck with girlands trim,
For to recyve this Saynt with honour dew,
That commeth in to you.
210 With trembling steps and humble reverence,
She commeth in, before th' almighties vew,
Of her ye virgins learne obedience,
When so ye come into those holy places,
To humble your proud faces:
215 Bring her up to th' high altar, that she may
The sacred ceremonies there partake,
The which do endlesse matrimony make,
And let the roring Organs loudly play
The praises of the Lord in lively notes,
220 The whiles with hollow throates
The Choristers the joyous Antheme sing,
That al the woods may answere and their eccho ring.

Behold whiles she before the altar stands
Hearing the holy priest that to her speakes
225 And blesseth her with his two happy hands,
How the red roses flush up in her cheekes,
And the pure snow with goodly vermill° stayne,   *vermilion*
Like crimsin dyde in grayne,[4]
That even th' Angels which continually,
230 About the sacred Altare doe remaine,
Forget their service and about her fly,
Ofte peeping in her face that seemes more fayre,
The more they on it stare.
But her sad° eyes still fastened on the ground,   *sober*
235 Are governéd with goodly modesty,
That suffers not one looke to glaunce awry,
Which may let in a little thought unsownd.
Why·blush ye love to give to me your hand,
The pledge of all our band?°   *bond*
240 Sing ye sweet Angels, Alleluya sing,
That all the woods may answere and your eccho ring.

Now al is done; bring home the bride againe,
Bring home the triumph of our victory,
Bring home with you the glory of her gaine,[5]
245 With joyance bring her and with jollity.
Never had man more joyfull day then this,
Whom heaven would heape with blis.
Make feast therefore now all this live long day,
This day for ever to me holy is,
250 Poure out the wine without restraint or stay,
Poure not by cups, but by the belly full,
Poure out to all that wull,°   *will*
And sprinkle all the postes and wals with wine,
That they may sweat, and drunken be withall.
255 Crowne ye God Bacchus with a coronall,°   *garland*
And Hymen also crowne with wreathes of vine,
And let the Graces daunce unto the rest;

3. I.e., as is fitting.   5. I.e., of gaining her.
4. I.e., dyed with colorfast dye.

For they can doo it best:
The whiles the maydens doe theyr carroll sing,
60   To which the woods shal answer and theyr eccho ring.

Ring ye the bels, ye yong men of the towne,
And leave your wonted labors for this day:
This day is holy; doe ye write it downe,
That ye for ever it remember may.
65   This day the sunne is in his chiefest hight,
With Barnaby the bright,[6]
From whence declining daily by degrees,
He somewhat loseth of his heat and light,
When once the Crab[7] behind his back he sees.
70   But for this time it ill ordainéd was,
To chose the longest day in all the yeare,
And shortest night, when longest fitter weare:
Yet never day so long, but late° would passe.   *finally*
Ring ye the bels, to make it weare away,
75   And bonefiers make all day,
And daunce about them, and about them sing:
That all the woods may answer, and your eccho ring.

Ah when will this long weary day have end,
And lende me leave to come unto my love?
80   How slowly do the houres theyr numbers spend?
How slowly does sad Time his feathers move?
Hast thee O fayrest Planet to thy home[8]
Within the Westerne fome:
Thy tyred steedes long since have need of rest.
85   Long though it be, at last I see it gloome,
And the bright evening star with golden creast
Appeare out of the East.
Fayre childe of beauty, glorious lampe of love
That all the host of heaven in rankes doost lead,
90   And guydest lovers through the nightés dread,
How chearefully thou lookest from above,
And seemst to laugh atweene thy twinkling light
As joying in the sight
Of these glad many which for joy doe sing,
95   That all the woods them answer and their eccho ring.

Now ceasse ye damsels your delights forepast;
Enough is it, that all the day was youres:
Now day is doen, and night is nighing fast:
Now bring the Bryde into the brydall boures.
300   Now night is come, now soone her disaray,
And in her bed her lay;
Lay her in lillies and in violets,
And silken courteins over her display,
And odourd sheetes, and Arras° coverlets.   *tapestry*
305   Behold how goodly my faire love does ly
In proud humility;
Like unto Maia,[9] when as Jove her tooke,

6. St. Barnabas's day (July 11) was also the day of the summer solstice in the calendar in use during Spenser's time.
7. Cancer the Crab, the fourth constellation in the zodiac, through which the sun passes in July.

8. In Ptolemaic astronomy, still often accepted in Spenser's time, the sun was one of the planets, which revolved about the earth.
9. The most beautiful of the Pleiades, who by Jove became the mother of the god Hermes.

In Tempe, lying on the flowry gras,
Twixt sleepe and wake, after she weary was,
310   With bathing in the Acidalian brooke.
Now it is night, ye damsels may be gon,
And leave my love alone,
And leave likewise your former lay to sing:
The woods no more shal answere, nor your eccho ring.

315   Now welcome night, thou night so long expected,°   *awaited*
That long daies labour doest at last defray,°   *requite*
And all my cares, which cruell love collected,
Hast sumd in one, and cancelléd for aye:
Spread thy broad wing over my love and me,
320   That no man may us see,
And in thy sable mantle us enwrap,
From feare of perill and foule horror free.
Let no false treason seeke us to entrap,
Nor any dread disquiet once annoy
325   The safety of our joy:
But let the night be calme and quietsome,
Without tempestuous storms or sad afray:°   *dark terror*
Lyke as when Jove with fayre Alcmena¹ lay,
When he begot the great Tirynthian groome:
330   Or lyke as when he with thy selfe did lie,
And begot Majesty.
And let the mayds and yongmen cease to sing:
Ne let the woods them answer, nor theyr eccho ring.

Let no lamenting cryes, nor dolefull teares,
335   Be heard all night within nor yet without:
Ne let false whispers, breeding hidden feares,
Breake gentle sleepe with misconceivéd dout.°   *fear*
Let no deluding dreames, nor dreadful sights
Make sudden sad affrights;
340   Ne let housefyres, nor lightnings helpelesse harmes,
Ne let the Pouke,² nor other evill sprights,
Ne let mischívous witches with theyr charmes,
Ne let hob Goblins, names whose sence we see not,
Fray us with things that be not.
345   Let not the shriech Oule, nor the Storke be heard:
Nor the night Raven that still° deadly yels,   *continually*
Nor damnéd ghosts cald up with mighty spels,
Nor griesly vultures make us once affeard:
Ne let th' unpleasant Quyre of Frogs still croking
350   Make us to wish theyr choking.
Let none of these theyr drery accents sing;
Ne let the woods them answer, nor theyr eccho ring.

But let stil Silence trew night watches keepe,
That sacred peace may in assurance rayne,
355   And tymely sleep, when it is tyme to sleepe,
May poure his limbs forth on your pleasant playne,
The whiles an hundred little wingéd loves,°   *cupids*
Like divers fethered doves,
Shall fly and flutter round about your bed,

---

1. The mother of Hercules, who as groom or servant to the king of Tiryns performed twelve prodigious labors.

2. Puck, also called Hobgoblin. The same Puck appears as the merely mischievous Robin Goodfellow in Shakespeare's *A Midsummer Night's Dream.*

60 And in the secret darke, that none reproves,
   Their prety stealthes shal worke, and snares shal spread
   To filch away sweet snatches of delight,
   Conceald through covert night.
   Ye sonnes of Venus, play your sports at will,
65 For greedy pleasure, carelesse of your toyes,°   *amorous sports*
   Thinks more upon her paradise of joyes,
   Then what ye do, albe it good or ill.
   All night therefore attend your merry play,
   For it will soone be day:
70 Now none doth hinder you, that say or sing,
   Ne will the woods now answer, nor your Eccho ring.

   Who is the same, which at my window peepes?
   Or whose is that faire face, that shines so bright,
   Is it not Cinthia,³ she that never sleepes,
75 But walkes about high heaven al the night?
   O fayrest goddesse, do thou not envý
   My love with me to spy:
   For thou likewise didst love, though now unthought,⁴
   And for a fleece of woll,° which privily,   *wool*
80 The Latmian shephard once unto thee brought,
   His pleasures with thee wrought.
   Therefore to us be favorable now;
   And sith of wemens labours thou hast charge,⁵
   And generation goodly dost enlarge,
85 Encline thy will t' effect our wishfull vow,
   And the chast wombe informe with timely seed,
   That may our comfort breed:
   Till which we cease our hopefull hap to sing,
   Ne let the woods us answere, nor our Eccho ring.

90 And thou great Juno, which with awful° might   *awe-inspiring*
   The lawes of wedlock still dost patronize,
   And the religion° of the faith first plight   *sanctity*
   With sacred rites hast taught to solemnize:
   And eeke for comfort often calléd art
95 Of women in their smart,°   *pains of childbirth*
   Eternally bind thou this lovely band,
   And all thy blessings unto us impart.
   And thou glad Genius,⁶ in whose gentle hand,
   The bridale bowre and geniall° bed remaine,   *marriage*
400 Without blemish or staine,
   And the sweet pleasures of theyr loves delight
   With secret ayde doest succour and supply,
   Till they bring forth the fruitfull progeny,
   Send us the timely fruit of this same night.
405 And thou fayre Hebe,⁷ and thou Hymen free,
   Grant that it may so be.
   Til which we cease your further prayse to sing,
   Ne any woods shal answer, nor your Eccho ring.

---

3. Yet another name for the moon goddess
Diana.
4. The moon was often regarded as a symbol
of virginity, in spite of several myths recount-
ing her amours. In the next three lines
Spenser, perhaps mistakenly, blends the story
about Pan, who loved Diana disguised in
the fleece of a white ram, with the story of
Endymion ("The Latmian shephard"), whom
Diana visited nightly in his sleep.

5. Lucina, the goddess of childbirth, is often
identified with both Diana and Juno (see
lines 394–95).
6. The universal god of generation. By in-
voking both Juno and Genius as patrons of
the marriage bed, Spenser draws also on the
belief that each individual is watched over
from birth by a tutelary spirit called "a
Genius" (for boys) or "a Juno" (for girls).
7. Daughter of Juno and goddess of youth.

And ye high heavens, the temple of the gods,
410 In which a thousand torches flaming bright
Doe burne, that to us wretched earthly clods,
In dreadful darknesse lend desiréd light;
And all ye powers which in the same remayne,
More then we men can fayne,°   *imagine*
415 Poure out your blessing on us plentiously,
And happy influence upon us raine,
That we may raise a large posterity,
Which from the earth, which they may long possesse,
With lasting happinesse,
420 Up to your haughty pallaces may mount,
And for the guerdon° of theyr glorious merit   *reward*
May heavenly tabernacles there inherit,
Of blessed Saints for to increase the count.
So let us rest, sweet love, in hope of this,
425 And cease till then our tymely joyes to sing,
The woods no more us answer, nor our eccho ring.

Song made in lieu of many ornaments,
With which my love should duly have bene dect,
Which cutting off through hasty accidents,
430 Ye would not stay your dew time to expect,
But promist both to recompens,
Be unto her a goodly ornament,
And for short time an endlesse moniment.

1595

FULKE GREVILLE, LORD BROOKE
(1554–1628)

You Little Stars

You little stars that live in skies
And glory in Apollo's [1] glory,
In whose aspécts conjoinéd lies
The heaven's will and nature's story,[2]
5 Joy to be likened to those eyes,
Which eyes make all eyes glad or sorry;
    For when you force thoughts from above,
    These overrule your force by love.

And thou, O Love, which in these eyes
10 Hast married Reason with Affection,
And made them saints of Beauty's skies,
Where joys are shadows of perfection,
Lend me thy wings that I may rise
Up, not by worth, but thy election; [3]
15   For I have vowed in strangest fashion
    To love and never seek compassion.

ca. 1580   1633

1. Apollo was god of the sun; here, the sun itself.
2. As in astrology. The "aspect" of a star or planet was its position in the sky from an observation point on earth. When two heavenly bodies occupied approximately the same position, their aspects were said to be "conjoined" or "in conjunction," a circumstance thought to exert a powerful influence ("the heaven's will") on mundane affairs ("nature's story").
3. Calvinist theology held that salvation depended not on human merit but on "election" by God.

Of His Cynthia

Away with these self-loving lads,
Whom Cupid's arrow never glads.
Away, poor souls that sigh and weep,
In love of them that lie and sleep;
5   For Cupid is a meadow god,
    And forceth none to kiss the rod.

God Cupid's shaft, like destiny,
Doth either good or ill decree;
Desert is born out of his bow,
10   Reward upon his feet doth go.
    What fools are they that have not known
    That Love likes no laws but his own?

My songs they be of Cynthia's praise,
I wear her rings on holy-days,
15   On every tree I write her name,
And every day I read the same.
    Where Honor Cupid's rival is,
    There miracles are seen of his.

If Cynthia crave her ring of me,
20   I blot her name out of the tree.
If doubt do darken things held dear,
Then well fare nothing once a year.
    For many run, but one must win;
    Fools only hedge the cuckoo in.

25   The worth that worthiness should move
Is love, which is the due of love.
And love as well the shepherd can
As can the mighty nobleman.
    Sweet nymph, 'tis true you worthy be,
30   Yet without love, nought worth to me.

1600

Sion Lies Waste

Sion[9] lies waste, and thy Jerusalem,
O Lord, is fallen to utter desolation.
Against thy prophets and thy holy men
The sin hath wrought a fatal combination:
5   Profaned thy name, thy worship overthrown,
   And made thee, living Lord, a God unknown.

Thy powerful laws, thy wonders of creation,
Thy word incarnate, glorious heaven, dark hell,
Lie shadowed under man's degeneration,
10   Thy Christ still crucified for doing well.
   Impiety, O Lord, sits on thy throne,
   Which makes thee, living light, a God unknown.

Man's superstition hath thy truths entombed,
His atheism again her pomps defaceth;

9. A hill near Jerusalem, site of the Temple.

15 That sensual unsatiable vast womb
Of thy seen church thy unseen church disgraceth.
    There lives no truth with them that seem thine own,
    Which makes thee, living Lord, a God unknown.

    Yet unto thee, Lord, mirror of transgression,
20 We who for earthly idols have forsaken
Thy heavenly image, sinless, pure impression,
And so in nets of vanity lie taken,
    All desolate implore that to thine own,
    Lord, thou no longer live a God unknown.

25 Yet, Lord, let Israel's plagues not be eternal,
Nor sin forever cloud thy sacred mountains,
Nor with false flames, spiritual but infernal,
Dry up thy mercy's ever springing fountains.
    Rather, sweet Jesus, fill up time and come
30   To yield the sin her everlasting doom.

1633

JOHN LYLY
(1554–1606)

Cupid and My Campaspe

Cupid and my Campaspe played
At cards for kisses; Cupid paid.
He stakes his quiver, bow, and arrows,
His mother's[1] doves and team of sparrows,
5   Loses them too; then down he throws
The coral of his lip, the rose
Growing on 's cheek (but none knows how),
With these the crystal of his brow,
And then the dimple of his chin:
10 All these did my Campaspe win.
At last he set her both his eyes;
She won, and Cupid blind did rise.
    Oh Love! has she done this to thee?
    What shall, alas, become of me?

1632

Oh, For a Bowl of Fat Canary

Oh, for a bowl of fat Canary,
Rich Palermo, sparkling Sherry,
Some nectar else, from Juno's dairy;[2]
Oh, these draughts would make us merry!

5   Oh, for a wench (I deal in faces,
And in other daintier things);
Tickled am I with her embraces,
Fine dancing in such fairy rings.

---

1. I.e., Venus'.
2. Nectar, the drink of the gods, was some-
times thought to resemble mead, a drink made
from milk and honey; hence it might be re-
garded figuratively as coming from the
"dairy" of Juno, the queen of the gods.

Oh, for a plump fat leg of mutton,
10 Veal, lamb, capon, pig, and coney;°   *rabbit*
None is happy but a glutton,
None an ass but who wants money.

Wines indeed and girls are good,
15 But brave victuals feast the blood;
For wenches, wine, and lusty cheer,
Jove would leap down to surfeit here.

1640

SIR PHILIP SIDNEY
(1554–1586)

Ye Goatherd Gods[1]

STREPHON.[2] Ye goatherd gods, that love the grassy mountains,
          Ye nymphs which haunt the springs in pleasant valleys,
          Ye satyrs joyed with free and quiet forests,
          Vouchsafe your silent ears to plaining music,
5   Which to my woes gives still an early morning,
          And draws the dolor on till weary evening.

KLAIUS.   O Mercury,[3] foregoer to the evening,
          O heavenly huntress of the savage mountains,
          O lovely star, entitled of the morning,
10   While that my voice doth fill these woeful valleys,
          Vouchsafe your silent ears to plaining music,
          Which oft hath Echo tired in secret forests.

STREPHON. I, that was once free burgess° of the forests,   *citizen*
          Where shade from sun, and sport I sought in evening,
15   I, that was once esteemed for pleasant music,
          Am banished now among the monstrous mountains
          Of huge despair, and foul affliction's valleys,
          Am grown a screech owl to myself each morning.

KLAIUS.   I, that was once delighted every morning,
20   Hunting the wild inhabiters of forests,
          I, that was once the music of these valleys,
          So darkened am that all my day is evening,
          Heartbroken so, that molehills seem high mountains
          And fill the vales with cries instead of music.

25 STREPHON. Long since, alas, my deadly swannish[4] music
          Hath made itself a crier of the morning,
          And hath with wailing strength climbed highest mountains;
          Long since my thoughts more desert be than forests,

1. The poem is in the form of a double sestina, two sets of six six-line stanzas, with a triplet concluding the whole. The same six key words end the lines of each stanza; their order is always a permutation of the order in the stanza just preceding: the pattern is 6 1 5 2 4 3, i.e., the last word of line 1 of any stanza is always the same as the last word of line 6 in the preceding stanza. Line 2 always ends like the preceding stanza's line 1; line 3 like line 5; line 4 like line 2; line 5 like line 4; and line 6 like line 3. All six key words appear in the triplet in the same order as that of the first and seventh stanzas.
2. Strephon and Klaius are shepherds in Sidney's heroic romance *Arcadia*, in which this poem appears.
3. The evening star. The "heavenly huntress" is the goddess Diana, the moon.
4. The swan was supposed to sing only just before it died.

30   Long since I see my joys come to their evening,
      And state° thrown down to overtrodden valleys.   *high position*

KLAIUS.   Long since the happy dwellers of these valleys
           Have prayed me leave my strange exclaiming music,
           Which troubles their day's work and joys of evening;
           Long since I hate the night, more hate the morning;
35   Long since my thoughts chase me like beasts in forests
           And make me wish myself laid under mountains.

STREPHON.   Meseems° I see the high and stately mountains   *it seems to me*
             Transform themselves to low dejected valleys;
             Meseems I hear in these ill-changéd forests
40   The nightingales do learn of owls their music;
             Meseems I feel the comfort of the morning
             Turned to the mortal serene[5] of an evening.

KLAIUS.   Meseems I see a filthy cloudy evening
           As soon as sun begins to climb the mountains;
45   Meseems I feel a noisome° scent, the morning   *offensive*
           When I do smell the flowers of these valleys;
           Meseems I hear, when I do hear sweet music,
           The dreadful cries of murdered men in forests.

STREPHON.   I wish to fire the trees of all these forests;
50   I give the sun a last farewell each evening;
             I curse the fiddling finders-out of music;
             With envy I do hate the lofty mountains
             And with despite despise the humble valleys;
             I do detest night, evening, day, and morning.

55 KLAIUS.   Curse to myself my prayer is, the morning;
               My fire is more than can be made with forests,
               My state more base than are the basest valleys.
               I wish no evenings more to see, each evening;
               Shaméd, I hate myself in sight of mountains
60   And stop mine ears, lest I grow mad with music.

STREPHON.   For she whose parts maintained a perfect music,
             Whose beauties shined more than the blushing morning,
             Who much did pass° in state the stately mountains,   *surpass*
             In straightness passed the cedars of the forests,
65   Hath cast me, wretch, into eternal evening
             By taking her two suns from these dark valleys.

KLAIUS.   For she, with whom compared, the Alps are valleys,
           She, whose least word brings from the spheres their music,
           At whose approach the sun rose in the evening,
70   Who where she went bare° in her forehead morning,   *bore*
           Is gone, is gone, from these our spoiléd forests,
           Turning to deserts our best pastured mountains.

STREPHON.   These mountains witness shall, so shall these valleys,
KLAIUS.   These forests eke,° made wretched by our music,   *also*
75   Our morning hymn this is, and song at evening.
                                              1577–80   1593

5. Damp evening air, thought to produce sickness ("mortal": deadly). The stress is on the first syllable.

The Nightingale

The nightingale, as soon as April bringeth
Unto her rested sense a perfect waking,
While late bare earth, proud of new clothing, springeth,
Sings out her woes, a thorn her song-book making,
5   And mournfully bewailing,
Her throat in tunes expresseth
What grief her breast oppresseth
For Tereus' force on her chaste will prevailing.[6]
Oh Philomela fair, Oh take some gladness,
10   That here is juster cause of plaintful sadness:
Thine earth now springs, mine fadeth;
Thy thorn without, my thorn my heart invadeth.

Alas, she hath no other cause of anguish
But Tereus' love, on her by strong hand wroken,[7]
15   Wherein she suffering, all her spirits languish;
Full womanlike complains her will was broken.
But I, who daily craving,
Cannot have to content me,
Have more cause to lament me,
20   Since wanting is more woe than too much having.
O Philomela fair, O take some gladness,
That here is juster cause of plaintful sadness:
Thine earth now springs, mine fadeth;
Thy thorn without, my thorn my heart invadeth.

1581   1598

Ring Out Your Bells

Ring out your bells, let mourning shows be spread,
For Love is dead.
All Love is dead, infected
With plague of deep disdain;
5   Worth as naught worth rejected,
And Faith fair scorn[8] doth gain.
From so ungrateful fancy,
From such a female franzy,°   *frenzy*
From them that use men thus,
10   Good Lord, deliver us!

Weep, neighbors, weep; do you not hear it said
That Love is dead?
His deathbed peacock's folly,
His winding sheet is shame,
15   His will false-seeming holy,
His sole exec'tor blame.
From so ungrateful . . .

Let dirge be sung and trentals[9] rightly read,
For Love is dead.
20   Sir Wrong his tomb ordaineth
My mistress, marble heart,

6. Tereus, the ravisher of Philomela, cut out her tongue to keep her from accusing him. Transformed into a nightingale, she expressed her grief in song.

7. Old past participle of *wreak*, "to urge or force upon."
8. Scorn from the fair.
9. A series of thirty masses for the dead.

Which epitaph containeth,
"Her eyes were once his dart."
From so ungrateful . . .

25 Alas, I lie, rage hath this error bred;
Love is not dead.
Love is not dead, but sleepeth
In her unmatchéd mind,
Where she his counsel keepeth,
30 Till due desert she find.
Therefore from so vile fancy,
To call such wit a franzy,
Who Love can temper thus,
Good Lord, deliver us!

1581   1598

From Astrophel and Stella

1

Loving in truth, and fain° in verse my love to show,   *eager*
That the dear she might take some pleasure of my pain,
Pleasure might cause her read, reading might make her know,
Knowledge might pity win, and pity grace obtain,
5 I sought fit words to paint the blackest face of woe:
Studying inventions fine, her wits to entertain,
Oft turning others' leaves, to see if thence would flow
Some fresh and fruitful showers upon my sunburned brain.
But words came halting forth, wanting Invention's stay;
10 Invention, Nature's child, fled stepdame Study's blows;
And others' feet still seemed but strangers in my way.
Thus, great with child to speak, and helpless in my throes,
Biting my truant pen, beating myself for spite:
"Fool," said my Muse to me, "look in thy heart, and write."

14

Alas, have I not pain enough, my friend,
Upon whose breast a fiercer gripe° doth tire°   *vulture / rend*
Than did on him who first stale down the fire,[2]
While Love on me doth all his quiver spend,
5 But with your rhubarb words you must contend
To grieve me worse, in saying that Desire
Doth plunge my well-formed soul even in the mire
Of sinful thoughts, which do in ruin end?
If that be sin which doth the manners frame,[3]
10 Well stayed with truth in word and faith of deed,
Ready of wit, and fearing naught but shame;
If that be sin which in fixed hearts doth breed
A loathing of all loose unchastity,
Then love is sin, and let me sinful be.

25

The wisest scholar of the wight most wise
By Phoebus' doom,[4] with sugared sentence says
That Virtue, if it once met with our eyes,
Strange flames of love it in our souls would raise;

2. Prometheus, for having stolen fire for man's benefit, was chained to a rock and preyed upon daily by a vulture that tore at his vitals.
3. "Doth the manners frame": builds character.

4. Judgment. The "wight most wise" was Socrates, so called by the oracle of Apollo (Phoebus) at Delphi. His "wisest scholar," or pupil, was Plato, who (in *Phaedrus* 250D) provides the basis for lines 3–8.

5   But, for that° man with pain this truth descries,   *because*
      While he each thing in sense's balance weighs,
      And so nor will nor can behold those skies
      Which inward sun to heroic mind displays,
10   Virtue of late, with virtuous care to stir
      Love of herself, takes Stella's shape, that she
      To mortal eyes might sweetly shine in her.
      It is most true, for since I her did see,
      Virtue's great beauty in that face I prove,°   *experience*
      And find th'effect, for I do burn in love.

31

With how sad steps, Oh Moon, thou climb'st the skies,
How silently, and with how wan a face!
What, may it be that even in heav'nly place
That busy archer[5] his sharp arrows tries?
5   Sure, if that long-with-love-acquainted eyes
      Can judge of love, thou feel'st a lover's case;
      I read it in thy looks: thy languished grace,
      To me that feel the like, thy state descries.
      Then even of fellowship, Oh Moon, tell me,
10   Is constant love deemed there but want of wit?
      Are beauties there as proud as here they be?
      Do they above love to be loved, and yet
      Those lovers scorn whom that love doth possess?
      Do they call virtue there ungratefulness?

39

Come sleep, Oh sleep, the certain knot of peace,
The baiting place[6] of wit, the balm of woe,
The poor man's wealth, the prisoner's release,
Th'indifferent° judge between the high and low;   *impartial*
5   With shield of proof[7] shield me from out the prease°   *press, multitude*
      Of those fierce darts Despair at me doth throw;
      Oh make in me those civil wars to cease;
      I will good tribute pay, if thou do so.
      Take thou of me smooth pillows, sweetest bed,
10   A chamber deaf to noise and blind to light,
      A rosy garland and a weary head;
      And if these things, as being thine by right,
      Move not thy heavy grace, thou shalt in me,
      Livelier than elsewhere, Stella's image see.

48

Soul's joy, bend not those morning stars from me,
Where virtue is made strong by beauty's might,
Where love is chasteness, pain doth learn delight,
And humbleness grows one with majesty.
5   Whatever may ensue, O let me be
      Co-partner of the riches of that sight;
      Let not mine eyes be hell-driv'n from that light;
      O look, O shine, O let me die and see.
      For though I oft my self of them bemoan,
10   That through my heart their beamy darts be gone,
      Whose cureless wounds even now most freshly bleed,
      Yet since my death wound is already got,
      Dear killer, spare not thy sweet cruel shot;
      A kind of grace it is to slay with speed.

---

5. I.e., Cupid.
6. A place where a traveler might stop for
rest and refreshment.
7. Of proven strength.

49

I on my horse, and Love on me, doth try
Our horsemanships, while by strange work I prove
A horseman to my horse, a horse to Love,
And now man's wrongs in me, poor beast, descry.
5 The reins wherewith my rider doth me tie
Are humbled thoughts, which bit of reverence move,
Curbed[8] in with fear, but with gilt boss above
Of hope, which makes it seem fair to the eye.
The wand is will; thou, fancy, saddle art,
10 Girt fast by memory; and while I spur
My horse, he spurs with sharp desire my heart;
He sits me fast, however I do stir;
And now hath made me to his hand so right
That in the manage[9] myself takes delight.

71

Who will in fairest book of Nature know
How virtue may best lodged in beauty be,
Let him but learn of love to read in thee,
Stella, those fair lines which true goodness show.
5 There shall he find all vices' overthrow,
Not by rude force, but sweetest sovereignty
Of reason, from whose light those night birds fly,
That inward sun in thine eyes shineth so.
And, not content to be perfection's heir
10 Thyself, dost strive all minds that way to move,
Who mark in thee what is in thee most fair.
So while thy beauty draws the heart to love,
As fast thy virtue bends that love to good.
"But ah," Desire still cries, "give me some food."

Eighth Song [1]

In a grove most rich of shade,
Where birds wanton music made,
May, then young, his pied weeds° showing,   *garments*
New-perfumed with flowers fresh growing,

5 Astrophel with Stella sweet
Did for mutual comfort meet,
Both within themselves oppresséd,
But each in the other blesséd.

Him great harms had taught much care,
10 Her fair neck a foul yoke bare;°   *bore*
But her sight his cares did banish,
In his sight her yoke did vanish.

Wept they had, alas the while,
But now tears themselves did smile,
15 While their eyes, by love directed,
Interchangeably reflected.

Sigh they did, but now betwixt
Sighs of woe were glad sighs mixed,

---

8. The curb is a short chain or strap connecting the upper branches of the bit and ornamented, in this case, with a metal *boss* or decorative stud.

9. The schooling or handling of a horse.
1. This is one of a group of 11 songs, loosely related to the sonnet sequence, that begin to appear irregularly after sonnet 63.

With arms crossed, yet testifying
20 Restless rest and living dying.

Their ears hungry of each word
Which the dear tongue would afford,
But their tongues restrained from walking
Till their hearts had ended talking.

25 But, when their tongues could not speak,
Love itself did silence break;
Love did set his lips asunder,
Thus to speak in love and wonder:

"Stella, sovereign of my joy,
30 Fair triumpher of annoy,°   *grief*
Stella, star of heavenly fire,
Stella, lodestar of desire,

"Stella, in whose shining eyes
Are the lights of Cupid's skies,
35 Whose beams, where they once are darted,
Love therewith is straight imparted,

"Stella whose voice, when it speaks,
Senses all asunder breaks,
Stella whose voice, when it singeth,
40 Angels to acquaintance bringeth,

"Stella, in whose body is
Writ each character of bliss,
Whose face all, all beauty passeth,
Save thy mind, which yet surpasseth,

45 "Grant, O grant—but speech, alas,
Fails me, fearing on to pass!—
Grant, O me! what am I saying?
But no fault there is in praying.

"Grant, O dear, on knees I pray,"
50 (Knees on ground he then did stay)
"That, not I, but, since I love you,
Time and place for me may move you.

"Never season was more fit,
Never room more apt for it;
55 Smiling air allows my reason;
These birds sing, 'Now use the season.'

"This small wind, which so sweet is,
See how it the leaves doth kiss;
Each tree in his best attiring
60 Sense of love to love inspiring.

"Love makes earth the water drink,
Love to earth makes water sink;
And, if dumb things be so witty,°   *wise*
Shall a heavenly grace want pity?"

⁶⁵ There his hands, in their speech, fain
Would have made tongue's language plain;
But her hands, his hands repelling,
Gave repulse all grace excelling.

Then she spake; her speech was such,
⁷⁰ As not ears but heart did touch,
While suchwise she loved deniéd,
As yet love she signifiéd.

"Astrophel," said she, "my love,
Cease in these effects to prove;
⁷⁵ Now be still, yet still believe me,
Thy grief more than death would grieve me.

"If that any thought in me
Can taste comfort but of thee,
Let me, fed with hellish anguish,
⁸⁰ Joyless, hopeless, endless languish.

"If those eyes you praiséd be
Half so dear as you to me,
Let me home return, stark blinded
Of those eyes, and blinder minded.

⁸⁵ "If to secret of my heart
I do any wish impart
Where thou art not foremost placéd,
Be both wish and I defacéd.°   destroyed

"If more may be said, I say
⁹⁰ All my bliss in thee I lay;
If thou love, my love, content thee,
For all love, all faith, is meant thee.

"Trust me, while I thee deny,
In myself the smart I try;
⁹⁵ Tyrant honor doth thus use thee:
Stella's self might not refuse thee.

"Therefore, dear, this no more move,
Lest, though I leave not thy love,
Which too deep in me is framéd,
¹⁰⁰ I should blush when thou art naméd."

Therewithal away she went,
Leaving him to passion, rent
With what she had done and spoken,
That therewith my song is broken.

107

Stella, since thou so right a princess art
Of all the powers which life bestows on me,
That ere by them aught undertaken be
They first resort unto that sovereign part;
⁵ Sweet, for a while give respite to my heart,
Which pants as though it still should leap to thee,
And on my thoughts give thy lieutenancy

To this great cause, which needs both use° and art,   *experience*
And as a queen, who from her presence sends
o   Whom she employs, dismiss from thee my wit,
Till it have wrought what thy own will attends.°   *is concerned about*
On servants' shame oft master's blame doth sit.
Oh let not fools in me thy works reprove,
And scorning say, "See what it is to love."

108

When Sorrow, using mine own fire's might,
Melts down his lead into my boiling breast,
Through that dark furnace to my heart oppressed
There shines a joy from thee my only light;
5   But soon as thought of thee breeds my delight,
And my young soul flutters to thee his nest,
Most rude despair, my daily unbidden guest,
Clips straight my wings, straight wraps me in his night,
And makes me then bow down my head and say:
10   "Ah, what doth Phoebus' gold [2] that wretch avail
Whom iron doors do keep from use of day?"
So strangely, alas, thy works in me prevail,
    That in my woes for thee thou art my joy,
    And in my joys for thee my only annoy.°   *grief*

1582   1591

ALEXANDER MONTGOMERIE
(1556?–1610?)

The Solsequium°   *marigold*

Like as the dumb solsequium, with care ourcome
    Dois° sorrow, when the sun goes out of sicht,   *does*
Hings doun his head, and droops as dead, nor will not spread,
    Bot locks his leavis through langour all the nicht,
5   Till foolish Phaeton [1] rise
            With whip in hand,
        To purge the crystal skyis
        And licht the land.
Birds in their bour waitis for that hour
10   And to their prince ane glaid good-morrow givis;
Fra then, that flour list not till lour,°   *to hide*
    Bot laughis on Phoebus loosing out his leavis.

So standis with me except° I be where I may see   *unless*
    My lamp of licht, my lady and my luve;
15   Fra [2] she depairts, ane thousand dairts, in sundry airts,°   *directions*
    Thirlis° through my heavy hairt but° rest or rove;°   *pierces/without/ peace*
        My countenance declares
            My inward grief,
        And hope almaist despairs
20   To find relief.
I die, I dwine,° play dois me° pyne,   *fade away/causes me to°*

2. I.e., the sun's gold. Phoebus Apollo was god of the sun.
1. Son of Phoebus Apollo, god of the sun (see line 12); "foolish" because he presumed, with disastrous results, to drive the unruly horses that drew the chariot of the sun. Both Phaeton and Apollo are frequently taken, as here, to represent the sun itself.
2. From the time when.

    I loathe on every thing I look, alace!
Till Titan [3] mine upon me shine
    That I revive through favor of her face.

25 Fra she appear into her sphere begins to clear
    The dawing of my long desirit day:
Then Courage cryis on Hope to rise, when he espyis
    My noysome° nicht of absence went away.   *harmful*
         No woe, fra I awauk,
30   May me empesh;°   *injure*
        Bot on my stately stalk
         I flourish fresh.
I spring, I sprout, my leavis lie out,
    My color changes in ane heartsome hue.
No more I lout,° bot stand up stout,   *hang down*
    As glad of her for whom I only grew.

O happy day! go not away, Apollo! stay
    Thy chair° from going doun into the west: *chariot*
Of me thou mak thy zodiac, that I may tak
40   My pleasure to behold whom I luve best.
        Thy presence me restores
          To life from death;
        Thy absence likewayis schores°   *threatens*
          To cut my breath.
45 I wish, in vain, thee to remain,
    Sen *primum mobile* [4] sayis me alwayis nay;
At least, thy wain° turn soon again,   *chariot*
    Fareweill, with patience perforce till day.

GEORGE PEELE
(1557–1596)

His Golden Locks Time Hath to Silver Turned[3]

His golden locks time hath to silver turned;
    Oh, time too swift, oh, swiftness never ceasing!
His youth 'gainst time and age hath ever spurned,°   *kicked*
    But spurned in vain; youth waneth by increasing.
5 Beauty, strength, youth, are flowers but fading seen;
Duty, faith, love, are roots, and ever green.

His helmet now shall make a hive for bees,
    And lover's sonnets turned to holy psalms,
A man-at-arms must now serve on his knees,
10   And feed on prayers, which are age his[4] alms;
But though from court to cottage he depart,
His saint is sure of his unspotted heart.

---

3. Another personification of the sun in Greek mythology.
4. The outermost of the nine celestial spheres in the old astronomy; it imparts motion to all the inner spheres, including the sphere of the sun.
3. This poem refers to Sir Henry Lee, for years Queen Elizabeth's champion in courtly jousts or contests of arms. At the age of sixty, too old to take part in the queen's birthday tournament of 1590, he retired in favor of a younger man.
4. "Age his": age's.

And when he saddest sits in homely cell,
   He'll teach his swains this carol for a song:
15 Blest be the hearts that wish my sovereign well,
   Cursed be the souls that think her any wrong!
Goddess, allow this aged man his right,
To be your beadsman⁵ now, that was your knight.

                         1590

When As the Rye Reach to the Chin

When as the rye reach to the chin,
And chopcherry, chopcherry ripe within,
Strawberries swimming in the cream,
And schoolboys playing in the stream;
5 Then O, then O, then O my truelove said,
Till that time come again
She could not live a maid.

                         1595

Hot Sun, Cool Fire

Hot sun, cool fire, tempered with sweet air,
Black shade, fair nurse, shadow my white hair.
Shine, sun; burn, fire; breathe, air, and ease me;
Black shade, fair nurse, shroud me and please me.
5 Shadow, my sweet nurse, keep me from burning;
Make not my glad cause cause of mourning.
   Let not my beauty's fire
   Inflame unstaid desire,
   Nor pierce any bright eye
10   That wandereth lightly.

                         1599

THOMAS LODGE
(1558–1625)

Rosalind's Madrigal

Love in my bosom like a bee
   Doth suck his sweet;
Now with his wings he plays with me,
   Now with his feet.
Within mine eyes he makes his nest,
His bed amidst my tender breast;
My kisses are his daily feast,
And yet he robs me of my rest.
   Ah, wanton, will ye?

And if I sleep, then percheth he
   With pretty flight,
And makes his pillow of my knee
   The livelong night.
Strike I my lute, he tunes the string;

5. One who offers prayers for the soul of another.

He music plays if so I sing;
He lends me every lovely thing;
Yet cruel he my heart doth sting.
    Whist,° wanton, still ye!   *be silent*

Else I with roses every day
    Will whip you hence,
And bind you, when you long to play,
    For your offense.
I'll shut mine eyes to keep you in,
I'll make you fast it for your sin,
I'll count your power not worth a pin.
Alas! what hereby shall I win
    If he gainsay me?

What if I beat the wanton boy
    With many a rod?
He will repay me with annoy,
    Because a god.
Then sit thou safely on my knee,
And let thy bower my bosom be;
Lurk in mine eyes, I like of thee.
O Cupid, so thou pity me,
    Spare not, but play thee!

                    1590

ROBERT GREENE
(1560–1592)

Sweet Adon[6]

Sweet Adon, darest not glance thine eye
  N'oserez vous, mon bel ami?[7]
Upon thy Venus that must die?
  Je vous en prie,[8] pity me.
5 *N'oserez vous, mon bel, mon bel,*
  N'oserez vous, mon bel ami?

See how sad thy Venus lies,
  N'oserez vous, mon bel ami?
Love in heart and tears in eyes,
10 *Je vous en prie . . .*

Thy face as fair as Paphos brooks,
  N'oserez vous, mon bel ami?
Wherein fancy baits her hooks,
  Je vous en prie . . .

15 Thy cheeks like cherries that do grow,
  N'oserez vous, mon bel ami?
Amongst the western mounts of snow,
  Je vous en prie . . .

---

6. Adonis, a mortal youth loved by Venus. He is often represented as indifferent to her charms.

7. Will you not dare, my handsome friend?
8. I beg of you.

Thy lips vermilion, full of love,
20   *N'oserez vous, mon bel ami?*
Thy neck as silver-white as dove,
Je vous en prie . . .

Thine eyes like flames of holy fires,
N'oserez vous, mon bel ami?
25   Burn all my thoughts with sweet desires,
Je vous en prie . . .

All thy beauties sting my heart,
N'oserez vous, mon bel ami?
I must die through Cupid's dart,
30   *Je vous en prie* . . .

Wilt thou let thy Venus die?
N'oserez vous, mon bel ami?
Adon were unkind, say I,
Je vous en prie . . .

35   To let fair Venus die for woe,
N'oserez vous, mon bel ami?
That doth love sweet Adon so,
Je vous en prie . . .

1590

Sitting by a River's Side

Sitting by a river's side,
Where a silent stream did glide,
Muse I did of many things
That the mind in quiet brings.
5   I 'gan think how some men deem°   consider
Gold their god, and some esteem
Honor is the chief content
That to man in life is lent;
And some others do contend
10   Quiet none like to a friend;
Others hold there is no wealth
Compared to a perfect health;
Some man's mind in quiet stands
When he is lord of many lands.
15   But I did sigh, and said all this
Was but a shade of perfect bliss,
And in my thoughts I did approve
Nought so sweet as is true love.
Love 'twixt lovers passeth these,
20   When mouth kisseth and heart 'grees,
With folded arms and lips meeting,
Each soul another sweetly greeting;
For by the breath the soul fleeteth,
And soul with soul in kissing meeteth.
25   If love be so sweet a thing,
That such happy bliss doth bring,
Happy is love's sugared thrall,
But unhappy maidens all
Who esteem your virgin blisses

30   Sweeter than a wife's sweet kisses.
      No such quiet to the mind
      As true love with kisses kind;
      But if a kiss prove unchaste,
      Then is true love quite disgraced.
35   Though love be sweet, learn this of me:
      No love sweet but honesty.

1592

ROBERT SOUTHWELL
(ca. 1561–1595)

The Burning Babe

As I in hoary winter's night stood shivering in the snow,
Surprised I was with sudden heat which made my heart to glow;
And lifting up a fearful eye to view what fire was near,
A pretty babe all burning bright did in the air appear;
5   Who, scorchéd with excessive heat, such floods of tears did shed
As though his floods should quench his flames which with his tears were fed.
"Alas," quoth he, "but newly born in fiery heats I fry,
Yet none approach to warm their hearts or feel my fire but I!
My faultless breast the furnace is, the fuel wounding thorns,
10   Love is the fire, and sighs the smoke, the ashes shame and scorns;
The fuel justice layeth on, and mercy blows the coals,
The metal in this furnace wrought are men's defiléd souls,
For which, as now on fire I am to work them to their good,
So will I melt into a bath to wash them in my blood."
15   With this he vanished out of sight and swiftly shrunk away,
And straight I calléd unto mind that it was Christmas day.

1602

New Heaven, New War

Come to your heaven, you heavenly choirs,
Earth hath the heaven of your desires.
Remove your dwelling to your God;
A stall is now his best abode.
5   Sith° men their homage do deny,   *since*
Come, angels, all their fault supply.

His chilling cold doth heat require;
Come, seraphins,° in lieu of fire.   *angels*
This little ark no cover hath;
10   Let cherubs' wings his body swathe.
Come, Raphael,[1] this babe must eat;
Provide our little Toby meat.

Let Gabriel be now his groom,
That first took up his earthly room.
15   Let Michael stand in his defense,
Whom love hath linked to feeble sense.
Let graces rock when he doth cry,
And angels sing his lullaby.

1. One of the seven archangels, the companion and protector of Tobias in the book of Tobit (one of the apocryphal books of the Old Testament). Gabriel (line 13) and Michael (line 15) are also archangels.

The same you saw in heavenly seat
20 Is he that now sucks Mary's teat;
Agnize° your king a mortal wight,   *acknowledge*
His borrowed weed° lets° not your sight.   *clothing / hinders*
Come, kiss the manger where he lies,
That is your bliss above the skies.

25 This little babe, so few days old,
Is come to rifle Satan's fold;
All hell doth at his presence quake,
Though he himself for cold do shake,
For in this weak unarmèd wise°   *manner*
30 The gates of hell he will surprise.

With tears he fights and wins the field;
His naked breast stands for a shield;
His battering shot are babish cries,
His arrows looks of weeping eyes,
35 His martial ensigns cold and need,
And feeble flesh his warrior's steed.

His camp is pitchèd in a stall,
His bulwark but a broken wall,
The crib his trench, hay stalks his stakes,
40 Of shepherds he his muster makes;
And thus, as sure his foe to wound,
The angels' trumps alarum sound.

My soul, with Christ join thou in fight;
Stick to the tents that he hath pight;°   *pitched*
45 Within his crib is surest ward,°   *protection*
This little babe will be thy guard.
If thou wilt foil thy foes with joy,
Then flit not from this heavenly boy.

                                                      1602

SAMUEL DANIEL
(ca. 1562–1619)

From Delia

6

Fair is my love, and cruel as she's fair:
Her brow shades frowns, although her eyes are sunny,
Her smiles are lightning, though her pride despair,
And her disdains are gall, her favors honey.
5 A modest maid, decked with a blush of honor,
Whose feet do tread green paths of youth and love;
The wonder of all eyes that look upon her,
Sacred on earth, designed a saint above.
Chastity and Beauty, which were deadly foes,
10 Live reconcilèd friends within her brow;
And had she pity to conjoin with those,
Then who had heard the plaints I utter now?
Oh had she not been fair and thus unkind,
My muse had slept, and none had known my mind.

31

Look, Delia, how we 'steem the half-blown rose,
The image of thy blush and summer's honor,
Whilst in her tender green she doth inclose
That pure sweet beauty time bestows upon her.
5   No sooner spreads her glory in the air
But straight her full-blown pride is in declining.
She then is scorned that late adorned the fair;
So clouds thy beauty after fairest shining.
No April can revive thy withered flowers,
10   Whose blooming grace adorns thy glory now;
Swift speedy time, feathered with flying hours,
Dissolves the beauty of the fairest brow.
Oh let not then such riches waste in vain,
But love whilst that thou mayst be loved again.

32

But love whilst that thou mayst be loved again,
Now whilst thy May hath filled thy lap with flowers,
Now whilst thy beauty bears without a stain,
Now use the summer smiles, ere winter lowers.
5   And whilst thou spread'st unto the rising sun
The fairest flower that ever saw the light,
Now joy thy time before thy sweet be done,
And, Delia, think thy morning must have night,
And that thy brightness sets at length to west,
10   When thou wilt close up that which now thou shew'st;
And think the same becomes thy fading best
Which then shall most inveil and shadow most.
    Men do not weigh the stalk for what it was,
    When once they find her flower, her glory, pass.

33

When men shall find thy flower, thy glory pass,
And thou, with careful brow sitting alone,
Receivéd hast this message from thy glass,
That tells thee truth, and says that all is gone,
5   Fresh shalt thou see in me the wounds thou madest,
Though spent thy flame, in me the heat remaining,
I that have loved thee thus before thou fadest,
My faith shall wax, when thou art in thy waning.
The world shall find this miracle in me,
10   That fire can burn when all the matter's spent;
Then what my faith hath been thyself shall see,
And that thou wast unkind thou mayst repent.
Thou mayst repent that thou hast scorned my tears,
When winter snows upon thy golden hairs.

45

Care-charmer Sleep, son of the sable Night,
Brother to Death, in silent darkness born.
Relieve my languish and restore the light;
With dark forgetting of my cares, return.
5   And let the day be time enough to mourn
The shipwreck of my ill-adventured youth;
Let waking eyes suffice to wail their scorn
Without the torment of the night's untruth.
Cease, dreams, th' imagery of our day desires,
10   To model forth the passions of the morrow;
Never let rising sun approve you liars,

To add more grief to aggravate my sorrow.
Still let me sleep, embracing clouds in vain,
And never wake to feel the day's disdain.
46
Let others sing of knights and paladins
In aged accents of untimely° words,   outdated
Paint shadows in imaginary lines
Which well the reach of their high wits records;
5 But I must sing of thee and those fair eyes.
Authentic shall my verse in time to come,
When yet th' unborn shall say, "Lo where she lies,
Whose beauty made him speak that else was dumb."
These are the arks, the trophies I erect,
10 That fortify thy name against old age;
And these thy sacred virtues must protect
Against the dark and time's consuming rage.
Though th' error of my youth they shall discover,
Suffice, they show I lived and was thy lover.

1592

Ulysses and the Siren

SIREN. Come, worthy Greek, Ulysses, come,
Possess these shores with me;
The winds and seas are troublesome,
And here we may be free.
5 Here may we sit and view their toil
That travail in the deep,
And joy the day in mirth the while,
And spend the night in sleep.

ULYSSES. Fair nymph, if fame or honor were
10 To be attained with ease,
Then would I come and rest me there,
And leave such toils as these.
But here it dwells, and here must I
With danger seek it forth;
15 To spend the time luxuriously
Becomes not men of worth.

SIREN. Ulysses, Oh be not deceived
With that unreal name;
This honor is a thing conceived,
20 And rests on others' fame.
Begotten only to molest
Our peace, and to beguile
The best thing of our life, our rest,
And give us up to toil.

25 ULYSSES. Delicious nymph, suppose there were
Nor honor nor report,
Yet manliness would scorn to wear
The time in idle sport.
For toil doth give a better touch,
30 To make us feel our joy;
And ease finds tediousness, as much
As labor yields annoy.

SIREN. Then pleasure likewise seems the shore
Whereto tends all your toil,
35 Which you forgo to make it more,
And perish oft the while.
Who may disport them diversly,
Find never tedious day,
And ease may have variety
40 As well as action may.

ULYSSES. But natures of the noblest frame
These toils and dangers please,
And they take comfort in the same
As much as you in ease,
45 And with the thoughts of actions past
Are recreated still;
When pleasure leaves a touch at last
To show that it was ill.

SIREN. That doth opinion only cause
50 That's out of custom bred,
Which makes us many other laws
Than ever nature did.
No widows wail for our delights,
Our sports are without blood;
55 The world, we see, by warlike wights
Receives more hurt than good.

ULYSSES. But yet the state of things require
These motions of unrest,
And these great spirits of high desire
60 Seem born to turn them best,
To purge the mischiefs that increase
And all good order mar;
For oft we see a wicked peace
To be well changed for war.

65 SIREN. Well, well, Ulysses, then I see
I shall not have thee here,
And therefore I will come to thee,
And take my fortunes there.
I must be won that cannot win,
70 Yet lost were I not won;
For beauty hath created been
T' undo, or be undone.

1605

Are They Shadows

Are they shadows that we see?
And can shadows pleasure give?
Pleasures only shadows be
Cast by bodies we conceive
5 And are made the things we deem
In those figures which they seem.

But these pleasures vanish fast
Which by shadows are expressed;

10 Pleasures are not, if they last;
In their passing is their best.
Glory is most bright and gay
In a flash, and so away.

Feed apace then, greedy eyes,
On the wonder you behold;
15 Take it sudden as it flies,
Though you take it not to hold.
When your eyes have done their part,
Thought must length it in the heart.

1610

Love Is a Sickness

Love is a sickness full of woes,
   All remedies refusing,
A plant that with most cutting grows,
   Most barren with best using.
5   Why so?
More we enjoy it, more it dies,
If not enjoyed it sighing cries,
      Hey ho.

Love is a torment of the mind,
10   A tempest everlasting,
And Jove hath made it of a kind
   Not well, nor full, nor fasting.
      Why so?
More we enjoy it, more it dies,
15 If not enjoyed it sighing cries,
      Hey ho.

1623

MARK ALEXANDER BOYD
(1563–1601)

Fra Bank to Bank

Fra bank to bank, fra wood to wood I rin,
   Ourhailit° with my feeble fantasie;   *overwhelmed*
   Like til a leaf that fallis from a tree,
Or til a reed ourblawin with the win'.

5 Twa gods¹ guidis me; the ane of them is blin',
   Yea and a bairn° brocht up in vanitie;   *child*
   The next a wife° ingenrit of the sea,   *woman*
And lichter° nor° a dauphin with her fin.   *more wanton/than*

Unhappy is the man for evermair
10   That tills the sand and sawis° in the air;   *sows*
   But twice unhappier is he, I lairn,
That feedis in his hairt a mad desire,
And follows on a woman throw the fire,
   Led by a blind and teachit by a bairn.

1. Venus, goddess of love, supposedly born from the sea, and Cupid, her blind son.

MICHAEL DRAYTON
(1563–1631)

His Ballad of Agincourt[4]

Fair stood the wind for France,
When we our sails advance,
Nor now to prove our chance,
    Longer will tarry;
5 But putting to the main
At Kaux, the mouth of Seine,
With all his martial train,
    Landed King Harry.

And taking many a fort,
10 Furnished in warlike sort,
Marcheth towards Agincourt,
    In happy hour;
Skirmishing day by day
With those that stopped his way,
15 Where the French gen'ral lay
    With all his power.

Which in his height of pride,
King Henry to deride,
His ransom to provide
20   To the King sending;
Which he neglects the while
As from a nation vile,
Yet with an angry smile
    Their fall portending.

25 And turning to his men,
Quoth our brave Henry then:
Though they to one be ten,
    Be not amazed.
Yet have we well begun,
30 Battles so bravely won
Have ever to the sun
    By fame been raised.

And for myself, quoth he,
This my full rest shall be,
35 England ne'er mourn for me,
    Nor more esteem me;
Victor I will remain,
Or on this earth lie slain,
Never shall she sustain
40   Loss to redeem me.

Poitiers and Crecy[5] tell,
When most their pride did swell,

---

4. Site of a battle in the Hundred Years' War, October 25, 1415. The English army under King Henry V decisively defeated a numerically superior French force.
5. Sites of two earlier English victories in the Hundred Years' War (Crécy, 1346; Poitiers, 1356). At Crécy the English army was led by King Edward III, great-grandfather of Henry V.

Under our swords they fell;
  No less our skill is
45 Than when our grandsire great,
  Claiming the regal seat
  By many a warlike feat,
    Lopped the French lilies.

The Duke of York so dread
50 The eager vaward° led;   *vanguard*
  With the main Henry sped
    Amongst his henchmen.
  Excester° had the rear,   *Exeter*
  A braver man not there,
55 Oh Lord, how hot they were
    On the false Frenchmen!

They now to fight are gone,
Armor on armor shone,
Drum now to drum did groan,
60   To hear was wonder,
  That with cries they make
  The very earth did shake,
  Trumpet to trumpet spake,
    Thunder to thunder.

65 Well it thine age became,
  Oh noble Erpingham,
  Which didst the signal aim
    To our hid forces;
  When from a meadow by,
70 Like a storm suddenly,
  The English archery
    Struck the French horses.

With Spanish yew so strong,
Arrows a cloth-yard long,
75 That like to serpents stung,
    Piercing the weather;
  None from his fellow starts,
  But playing manly parts,
  And like true English hearts,
80   Stuck close together.

When down their bows they threw,
And forth their bilboes° drew,   *swords*
And on the French they flew,
  Not one was tardy;
85 Arms were from shoulders sent,
Scalps to the teeth were rent,
Down the French peasants went;
  Our men were hardy.

This while our noble King,
90 His broad sword brandishing,
Down the French host did ding,
  As to o'erwhelm it;
And many a deep wound lent,

His arms with blood besprent,
95   And many a cruel dent
    Bruiséd his helmet.

Gloster, that Duke so good,
Next of the royal blood,
For famous England stood
100   With his brave brother;
Clarence, in steel so bright,
Though but a maiden knight,
Yet in that furious fight,
    Scarce such another.

105   Warwick in blood did wade,
Oxford the foe invade,
And cruel slaughter made,
    Still as they ran up;
Suffolk his ax did ply,
110   Beaumont and Willoughby
Bare them right doughtily,
    Ferrers and Fanhope.

Upon Saint Crispin's day
Fought was this noble fray,
115   Which fame did not delay
    To England to carry;
Oh, when shall English men
With such acts fill a pen,
Or England breed again
120   Such a King Harry?

1619

From Idea

To the Reader of these Sonnets

Into these loves who but for passion looks,
At this first sight here let him lay them by
And seek elsewhere, in turning other books,
Which better may his labor satisfy.
5   No far-fetched sigh shall ever wound my breast,
Love from mine eye a tear shall never wring,
Nor in *Ah me*'s my whining sonnets dressed,
A libertine, fantastically I sing.
My verse is the true image of my mind,
10   Ever in motion, still desiring change;
And as thus to variety inclined,
So in all humors sportively I range:
    My muse is rightly of the English strain,
    That cannot long one fashion entertain.

6

How many paltry, foolish, painted things,
That now in coaches trouble every street,
Shall be forgotten, whom no poet sings,
Ere they be well wrapped in their winding-sheet?
5   Where I to thee eternity shall give,
When nothing else remaineth of these days,
And queens hereafter shall be glad to live

Upon the alms of thy superfluous praise.
Virgins and matrons reading these my rhymes
Shall be so much delighted with thy story
That they shall grieve they lived not in these times,
To have seen thee, their sex's only glory.
   So shalt thou fly above the vulgar throng,
   Still to survive in my immortal song.

14

If he from heaven that filched that living fire[6]
Condemned by Jove to endless torment be,
I greatly marvel how you still go free,
That far beyond Prometheus did aspire.
The fire he stole, although of heavenly kind,
Which from above he craftily did take,
Of liveless clods, us living men to make,
He did bestow in temper of the mind.
But you broke into heaven's immortal store,
Where virtue, honor, wit, and beauty lay;
Which taking thence you have escaped away,
Yet stand as free as ere you did before;
   Yet old Prometheus punished for his rape.
   Thus poor thieves suffer when the greater 'scape.

61

Since there's no help, come let us kiss and part;
Nay, I have done, you get no more of me,
And I am glad, yea glad with all my heart
That thus so cleanly I myself can free;
Shake hands forever, cancel all our vows,
And when we meet at any time again,
Be it not seen in either of our brows
That we one jot of former love retain.
Now at the last gasp of love's latest breath,
When, his pulse failing, passion speechless lies,
When faith is kneeling by his bed of death,
And innocence is closing up his eyes,
   Now if thou wouldst, when all have given him over,
   From death to life thou mightst him yet recover.

63

Truce, gentle love, a parley now I crave,
Methinks 'tis long since first these wars begun;
Nor thou nor I the better yet can have;
Bad is the match where neither party won.
I offer free conditions of fair peace,
My heart for hostage that it shall remain;
Discharge our forces, here let malice cease,
So for my pledge thou give me pledge again.
Or if no thing but death will serve thy turn,
Still thirsting for subversion of my state,
Do what thou canst, raze, massacre, and burn,
Let the world see the utmost of thy hate:
   I send defiance, since if overthrown,
   Thou vanquishing, the conquest is mine own.

1619

6. Prometheus, having stolen fire for mankind, was chained to a rock and preyed upon daily by a vulture that tore at his vitals. The gift of fire is sometimes interpreted to mean that Prometheus created mankind.

CHRISTOPHER MARLOWE
(1564–1593)

Hero and Leander

First Sestiad[1]

On Hellespont,[2] guilty of true love's blood,
In view and opposite, two cities stood,
Sea-borderers, disjoined by Neptune's might;
The one Abydos, the other Sestos hight.°   called
5   At Sestos Hero dwelt; Hero the fair,
Whom young Apollo courted for her hair,
And offered as a dower his burning throne,
Where she should sit for men to gaze upon.[3]
The outside of her garments were of lawn,[4]
10 The lining purple silk, with gilt stars drawn;
Her wide sleeves green, and bordered with a grove
Where Venus in her naked glory strove
To please the careless and disdainful eyes
Of proud Adonis, that before her lies;
15 Her kirtle° blue, whereon was many a stain,   gown
Made with the blood of wretched lovers slain.
Upon her head she ware a myrtle wreath,
From whence her veil reached to the ground beneath.
Her veil was artificial flowers and leaves,
20 Whose workmanship both man and beast deceives;
Many would praise the sweet smell as she passed,
When 'twas the odor which her breath forth cast;
And there for honey, bees have sought in vain,
And, beat from thence, have lighted there again.
25 About her neck hung chains of pebble-stone,
Which, lightened by her neck, like diamonds shone.
She ware no gloves, for neither sun nor wind
Would burn or parch her hands, but to her mind[5]
Or warm or cool them, for they took delight
30 To play upon those hands, they were so white.
Buskins[6] of shells all silvered, uséd she,
And branched with blushing coral to the knee,
Where sparrows perched, of hollow pearl and gold,
Such as the world would wonder to behold;
35 Those with sweet water oft her handmaid fills,
Which, as she went, would chirrup through the bills.
Some say, for her the fairest Cupid pined,
And looking in her face, was strooken blind.
But this is true: so like was one the other,
40 As he imagined Hero was his mother;[7]
And oftentimes into her bosom flew,
About her naked neck his bare arms threw,
And laid his childish head upon her breast,

---

1. A term for a book or canto (from Hero's
city Sestos).
2. The modern Dardanelles, a strait between
the Aegean Sea and the Sea of Marmora, one
mile wide at its narrowest point.
3. Apollo was the god of the sun.

4. A sheer cotton or linen fabric.
5. "To her mind": as she wished.
6. Laced foot coverings reaching halfway or
more to the knees.
7. I.e., Venus.

And with still panting rocked, there took his rest.
45 So lovely fair was Hero, Venus' nun,
As Nature wept, thinking she was undone,
Because she took more from her than she left
And of such wondrous beauty her bereft;
Therefore, in sign her treasure suffered wrack,
50 Since Hero's time hath half the world been black.
Amorous Leander, beautiful and young,
(Whose tragedy divine Musaeus[8] sung)
Dwelt at Abydos; since him dwelt there none
For whom succeeding times make greater moan.
55 His dangling tresses that were never shorn,
Had they been cut and unto Colchos[9] borne,
Would have allured the vent'rous youth of Greece
To hazard more than for the Golden Fleece.
Fair Cynthia[1] wished his arms might be her sphere;°   orbit
60 Grief makes her pale, because she moves not there.
His body was as straight as Circe's wand;[2]
Jove might have sipped out nectar from his hand.
Even as delicious meat is to the taste,
So was his neck in touching, and surpassed
65 The white of Pelops' shoulder.[3] I could tell ye
How smooth his breast was, and how white his belly,
And whose immortal fingers did imprint
That heavenly path, with many a curious° dint,   exquisite
That runs along his back; but my rude pen
70 Can hardly blazon forth the loves of men,
Much less of powerful gods; let it suffice
That my slack° muse sings of Leander's eyes,   feeble
Those orient[4] cheeks and lips, exceeding his
That leapt into the water for a kiss
75 Of his own shadow,[5] and despising many,
Died ere he could enjoy the love of any.
Had wild Hippolytus[6] Leander seen,
Enamored of his beauty had he been;
His presence made the rudest peasant melt,
80 That in the vast uplandish country dwelt;
The barbarous Thracian soldier, moved with naught,
Was moved with him, and for his favor sought.
Some swore he was a maid in man's attire,
For in his looks were all that men desire:
85 A pleasant smiling cheek, a speaking° eye,   expressive
A brow for love to banquet royally;
And such as knew he was a man, would say,
"Leander, thou art made for amorous play;
Why art thou not in love, and loved of all?
90 Though thou be fair, yet be not thine own thrall."
    The men of wealthy Sestos every year,
For his sake whom their goddess held so dear,
Rose-cheeked Adonis, kept a solemn feast.
Thither resorted many a wandering guest

8. A fifth-century Alexandrian whose poem on Hero and Leander served Marlowe as a source. Marlowe's term "divine" suggests that he may have identified him with an earlier, legendary Musaeus.
9. The country in Asia where Jason and his Argonauts found the Golden Fleece.
1. The moon.
2. The enchantress Circe, in the *Odyssey*, possessed a magical wand capable of turning men into beasts.
3. Pelops' shoulder was made of ivory.
4. Glowing, like eastern skies or gems.
5. I.e., Narcissus.
6. A great hunter, contemptuous of love.

95   To meet their loves; such as had none at all
Came lovers home from this great festival;
For every street, like to a firmament,
Glistered with breathing stars, who, where they went,
Frighted the melancholy earth, which deemed
100   Eternal heaven to burn, for so it seemed
As if another Phaeton[7] had got
The guidance of the sun's rich chariot.
But, far above the loveliest, Hero shined,
And stole away the enchanted gazer's mind;
105   For like sea nymphs' inveigling harmony,
So was her beauty to the standers by.
Nor that night-wandering pale and watery star[8]
(When yawning dragons draw her thirling[9] car
From Latmus' mount up to the gloomy sky,
110   Where, crowned with blazing light and majesty,
She proudly sits) more over-rules° the flood,   *rules over*
Than she the hearts of those that near her stood.
Even as when gaudy nymphs pursue the chase,
Wretched Ixion's shaggy-footed race,[1]
115   Incensed with savage heat, gallop amain
From steep pine-bearing mountains to the plain,
So ran the people forth to gaze upon her,
And all that viewed her were enamored on her.
And as in fury of a dreadful fight,
120   Their fellows being slain or put to flight,
Poor soldiers stand with fear of death dead-strooken,
So at her presence all, surprised and tooken,
Await the sentence of her scornful eyes;
He whom she favors lives, the other dies.
125   There might you see one sigh, another rage,
And some, their violent passions to assuage,
Compile sharp satires; but alas, too late,
For faithful love will never turn to hate.
And many, seeing great princes were denied,
130   Pined as they went, and thinking on her, died.
On this feast day, oh, cursed day and hour!
Went Hero thorough° Sestos, from her tower   *through*
To Venus' temple, where unhappily,
As after chanced, they did each other spy.
135   So fair a church as this had Venus none;
The walls were of discolored° jasper stone,   *varicolored*
Wherein was Proteus carvéd, and o'erhead
A lively° vine of green sea-agate spread,   *lifelike*
Where, by one hand, light-headed Bacchus hung,
140   And with the other, wine from grapes out-wrung.
Of crystal shining fair the pavement was;
The town of Sestos called it Venus' glass;
There might you see the gods in sundry shapes,
Committing heady° riots, incest, rapes;   *violent, impetuous*
145   For know that underneath this radiant floor

7. Son of Apollo, the sun god, who reluctantly allowed him to drive the chariot of the sun across the sky for one day. When the plunging horses drew the sun below its normal path, the earth was set on fire and Phaeton was destroyed.
8. The moon.
9. Piercing, like a flying arrow. Latmus was the home of the shepherd Endymion, loved by Diana the moon goddess.
1. The centaurs, offspring of Ixion and a cloud. For loving Juno, Ixion was made "wretched" by being chained to a ceaselessly rolling wheel.

Was Danae's statue in a brazen tower;[2]
Jove slyly stealing from his sister's bed
To dally with Idalian Ganymed,
And for his love Europa bellowing loud,
150 And tumbling with the rainbow in a cloud;
Blood-quaffing Mars heaving the iron net[3]
Which limping Vulcan and his Cyclops set;
Love kindling fire to burn such towns as Troy;
Silvanus weeping for the lovely boy
155 That now is turned into a cypress tree,[4]
Under whose shade the wood gods love to be.
And in the midst a silver altar stood;
There Hero sacrificing turtles'° blood,   *turtledoves'*
Veiled to the ground, veiling her eyelids close,
160 And modestly they opened as she rose;
Thence flew love's arrow with the golden head,[5]
And thus Leander was enamoréd.
Stone still he stood, and evermore he gazed,
Till with the fire that from his countenance blazed,
165 Relenting Hero's gentle heart was strook;
Such force and virtue hath an amorous look.
     It lies not in our power to love or hate,
For will in us is over-ruled by fate.
When two are stripped, long ere the course begin
170 We wish that one should lose, the other win;
And one especially do we affect
Of two gold ingots, like in each respect.
The reason no man knows, let it suffice,
What we behold is censured by our eyes.
175 Where both deliberate, the love is slight;
Who ever loved, that loved not at first sight?
     He kneeled, but unto her devoutly prayed;
Chaste Hero to herself thus softly said:
"Were I the saint he worships, I would hear him";
180 And as she spake these words, came somewhat near him.
He started up; she blushed as one ashamed;
Wherewith Leander much more was inflamed.
He touched her hand; in touching it she trembled;
Love deeply grounded hardly is dissembled.
185 These lovers parled° by the touch of hands;   *spoke*
True love is mute, and oft amazed stands.
Thus while dumb signs their yielding hearts entangled,
The air with sparks of living fire was spangled,
And night, deep drenched in misty Acheron,[6]
190 Heaved up her head, and half the world upon
Breathed darkness forth (dark night is Cupid's day).
And now begins Leander to display
Love's holy fire with words, with sighs, and tears,
Which like sweet music entered Hero's ears;
195 And yet at every word she turned aside,

2. Jove frequently left his sister (and wife) Juno to pursue other loves. He visited Danae in a shower of gold, had the Trojan prince Ganymede abducted from Mount Ida, and seduced Europa in the form of a bull. The goddess of the rainbow (line 150) was his messenger Iris.
3. Vulcan with his helpers the Cyclopes trapped his wife Venus in bed with Mars and exposed them to the laughter of the other gods.
4. Cyparissus, changed by Apollo into a cypress tree, was mourned by the forest god Sylvanus.
5. Cupid's arrows were tipped with gold or lead, the one producing love and the other loathing.
6. The river of woe in the underworld.

And always cut him off as he replied.
At last, like to a bold sharp sophister,[7]
With cheerful hope thus he accosted her:
"Fair creature, let me speak without offense;
200   I would my rude words had the influence
To lead thy thoughts as thy fair looks do mine!
Then shouldst thou be his prisoner who is thine.
Be not unkind and fair; misshapen stuff°   *persons*
Are of behavior boisterous and rough.
205   Oh, shun me not, but hear me ere you go,
God knows I cannot force love, as you do.
My words shall be as spotless as my youth,
Full of simplicity and naked truth.
This sacrifice, whose sweet perfume descending
210   From Venus' altar to your footsteps bending,
Doth testify that you exceed her far,
To whom you offer, and whose nun you are.
Why should you worship her? her you surpass
As much as sparkling diamonds flaring glass.
215   A diamond set in lead his worth retains;
A heavenly nymph, beloved of human swains,
Receives no blemish, but ofttimes more grace;
Which makes me hope, although I am but base,
Base in respect of thee, divine and pure,
220   Dutiful service may thy love procure,
And I in duty will excel all other,
As thou in beauty dost exceed Love's mother.[8]
Nor heaven, nor thou, were made to gaze upon;
As heaven preserves all things, so save thou one.
225   A stately builded ship, well rigged and tall,
The ocean maketh more majestical;
Why vowest thou then to live in Sestos here,
Who on love's seas more glorious wouldst appear?
Like untuned golden strings all women are,
230   Which long time lie untouched,[9] will harshly jar.
Vessels of brass, oft handled, brightly shine;
What difference betwixt the richest mine
And basest mold, but use? for both, not used,
Are of like worth. Then treasure is abused,
235   When misers keep it; being put to loan,
In time it will return us two for one.
Rich robes themselves and others do adorn;
Neither themselves nor others, if not worn.
Who builds a palace, and rams up the gate,
240   Shall see it ruinous and desolate.
Ah, simple Hero, learn thyself to cherish!
Lone women, like to empty houses, perish.
Less sins the poor rich man that starves himself
In heaping up a mass of drossy pelf,°   *base riches*
245   Than such as you; his golden earth remains,
Which, after his decease, some other gains;
But this fair gem, sweet in the loss alone,
When you fleet hence, can be bequeathed to none.
Or if it could, down from th' enameled sky
250   All heaven would come to claim this legacy,

---

7. One who reasons adroitly rather than
soundly; also, a university student in his
junior or senior year.

8. I.e., Venus, mother of Cupid.
9. I.e., "Which, if they lie untouched for a
long time."

And with intestine° broils the world destroy,   *civil*
And quite confound nature's sweet harmony.
Well therefore by the gods decreed it is
We human creatures should enjoy that bliss.

55   One is no number; maids are nothing, then,
Without the sweet society of men.
Wilt thou live single still? one shalt thou be
Though never-singling Hymen[1] couple thee.
Wild savages, that drink of running springs,

60   Think water far excels all earthly things,
But they that daily taste neat wine, despise it;
Virginity, albeit some highly prize it,
Compared with marriage, had you tried them both,
Differs as much as wine and water doth.

65   Base bullion for the stamp's[2] sake we allow;
Even so for men's impression do we you,
By which alone, our reverend fathers say,
Women receive perfection every way.
This idol which you term virginity

70   Is neither essence[3] subject to the eye,
No, nor to any one exterior sense,
Nor hath it any place of residence,
Nor is 't of earth or mold celestial,
Or capable of any form at all.

75   Of that which hath no being, do not boast;
Things that are not at all, are never lost.
Men foolishly do call it virtuous;
What virtue is it, that is born with us?
Much less can honor be ascribed thereto;

80   Honor is purchased by the deeds we do.
Believe me, Hero, honor is not won
Until some honorable deed be done.
Seek you, for chastity, immortal fame,
And know that some have wronged Diana's[4] name?

85   Whose name is it, if she be false or not,
So she be fair, but some vile tongues will blot?
But you are fair, ay me, so wondrous fair,
So young, so gentle, and so debonair,
As Greece will think, if thus you live alone,

90   Some one or other keeps you as his own.
Then, Hero, hate me not, nor from me fly
To follow swiftly blasting infamy.
Perhaps thy sacred priesthood makes thee loath;
Tell me, to whom mad'st thou that heedless oath?"

95   "To Venus," answered she, and as she spake,
Forth from those two tralucent° cisterns brake   *translucent*
A stream of liquid pearl, which down her face
Made milk-white paths, whereon the gods might trace°   *go*
To Jove's high court. He thus replied: "The rites

300   In which love's beauteous empress most delights
Are banquets, Doric music,[5] midnight revel,
Plays, masques, and all that stern age counteth evil.
Thee as a holy idiot° doth she scorn,   *untutored person*

---

1. The god of marriage.
2. I.e., the impression that turns a mere piece of metal into a coin.
3. An existing thing.
4. Goddess of chastity, to whom, nevertheless,
some stories attribute amorous relationships.
5. Leander apparently confuses Doric music, which was stirring and martial, with Lydian music, which was soft and voluptuous.

For thou, in vowing chastity, hast sworn
305 To rob her name and honor, and thereby
Commit'st a sin far worse than perjury,
Even sacrilege against her deity,
Through regular and formal purity.
To expiate which sin, kiss and shake hands;
310 Such sacrifice as this Venus demands."
    Thereat she smiled, and did deny him so
As, put° thereby, yet might he hope for mo.°   *put off / more*
Which makes him quickly reinforce his speech,
And her in humble manner thus beseech:
315   "Though neither gods nor men may thee deserve,
Yet for her sake whom you have vowed to serve,
Abandon fruitless cold virginity,
The gentle queen of love's sole enemy.
Then shall you most resemble Venus' nun,
320 When Venus' sweet rites are performed and done.
Flint-breasted Pallas[6] joys in single life,
But Pallas and your mistress are at strife.
Love, Hero, then, and be not tyrannous,
But heal the heart that thou hast wounded thus;
325 Nor stain thy youthful years with avarice;
Fair fools delight to be accounted nice.°   *reticent*
The richest corn dies if it be not reaped;
Beauty alone is lost, too warily kept."
    These arguments he used, and many more,
330 Wherewith she yielded, that was won before.
Hero's looks yielded, but her words made war;
Women are won when they begin to jar.°   *argue*
Thus having swallowed Cupid's golden hook,
The more she strived, the deeper was she strook;
335 Yet, evilly feigning anger, strove she still,
And would be thought to grant against her will.
So having paused awhile, at last she said:
"Who taught thee rhetoric to deceive a maid?
Ay me! such words as these should I abhor,
340 And yet I like them for the orator."
    With that Leander stooped to have embraced her,
But from his spreading arms away she cast her,
And thus bespake him: "Gentle youth, forbear
To touch the sacred garments which I wear.
345 Upon a rock, and underneath a hill,
Far from the town, where all is whist° and still   *silent*
Save that the sea playing on yellow sand
Sends forth a rattling murmur to the land,
Whose sound allures the golden Morpheus°   *god of sleep*
350 In silence of the night to visit us,
My turret stands; and there, God knows, I play
With Venus' swans and sparrows all the day.
A dwarfish beldame° bears me company,   *old woman*
That hops about the chamber where I lie,
355 And spends the night, that might be better spent,
In vain discourse and apish merriment,
Come thither." As she spake this, her tongue tripped,
For unawares, "Come thither," from her slipped;
And suddenly her former color changed,

---

6. **Pallas Athena**, the virgin goddess of wisdom.

360 And here and there her eyes, through anger, ranged.
And like a planet moving several ways
At one self instant, she, poor soul, assays,
Loving, not to love at all, and every part
Strove to resist the motions of her heart;
365 And hands so pure, so innocent, nay such
As might have made heaven stoop to have a touch,
Did she uphold to Venus, and again
Vowed spotless chastity, but all in vain.
Cupid beats down her prayers with his wings;
370 Her vows above the empty air he flings;
All deep enraged, his sinewy bow he bent,
And shot a shaft that burning from him went;
Wherewith she, strooken, looked so dolefully,
As made Love sigh to see his tyranny.
375 And as she wept, her tears to pearl he turned,
And wound them on his arm, and for her mourned.
Then towards the palace of the Destinies,
Laden with languishment and grief, he flies,
And to those stern nymphs humbly made request,
380 Both might enjoy each other, and be blest.
But with a ghastly dreadful countenance,
Threatening a thousand deaths at every glance,
They answered Love, nor would vouchsafe so much
As one poor word, their hate to him was such.
385 Hearken awhile, and I will tell you why:
Heaven's winged herald, Jove-born Mercury,
The selfsame day that he asleep had laid
Enchanted Argus,[7] spied a country maid,
Whose careless hair, instead of pearl t' adorn it,
390 Glistered with dew, as one that seemed to scorn it;
Her breath as fragrant as the morning rose,
Her mind pure, and her tongue untaught to gloze;°   *flatter*
Yet proud she was, for lofty pride that dwells
In towered courts is oft in shepherds' cells,
395 And too too well the fair vermilion knew,
And silver tincture of her cheeks, that drew
The love of every swain. On her this god
Enamored was, and with his snaky rod[8]
Did charm her nimble feet, and made her stay,
400 The while upon a hillock down he lay,
And sweetly on his pipe began to play,
And with smooth speech her fancy to assay;°   *try*
Till in his twining arms he locked her fast,
And then he wooed with kisses, and at last,
405 As shepherds do, her on the ground he laid,
And tumbling in the grass, he often strayed
Beyond the bounds of shame, in being bold
To eye those parts which no eye should behold.
And like an insolent commanding lover,
410 Boasting his parentage, would needs discover
The way to new Elysium; but she,
Whose only dower was her chastity,
Having striv'n in vain, was now about to cry,
And crave the help of shepherds that were nigh.

7. The watchman with a hundred eyes set by Juno to guard Io, beloved of Jupiter. Mercury lulled Argus asleep with his music, then killed him.
8. The caduceus, Mercury's magic staff.

415 Herewith he stayed his fury, and began
      To give her leave to rise; away she ran;
      After went Mercury, who used such cunning,
      As she, to hear his tale, left off her running;
      Maids are not won by brutish force and might,
420 But speeches full of pleasure and delight;
      And knowing Hermes[9] courted her, was glad
      That she such loveliness and beauty had
      As could provoke his liking, yet was mute,
      And neither would deny nor grant his suit.
425 Still vowed he love, she wanting no excuse
      To feed him with delays, as women use,
      Or thirsting after immortality—
      All women are ambitious naturally—
      Imposed upon her lover such a task
430 As he ought not perform, nor yet she ask.
      A draught of flowing nectar she requested,
      Wherewith the king of gods and men is feasted.
      He, ready to accomplish what she willed,
      Stole some from Hebe (Hebe Jove's cup filled)
435 And gave it to his simple rustic love;
      Which being known (as° what is hid from Jove?)   *for*
      He inly stormed, and waxed more furious
      Than for the fire filched by Prometheus,[1]
      And thrusts him down from heaven; he wandering here
440 In mournful terms, with sad and heavy cheer,
      Complained to Cupid. Cupid, for his sake,
      To be revenged on Jove did undertake;
      And those on whom heaven, earth, and hell relies,
      I mean the adamantine Destinies,
445 He wounds with love, and forced them equally
      To dote upon deceitful Mercury.
      They offered him the deadly fatal knife
      That shears the slender threads of human life;
      At his fair-feathered feet the engines laid
450 Which th' earth from ugly Chaos' den upweighed;
      These he regarded not, but did entreat
      That Jove, usurper of his[2] father's seat,
      Might presently be banished into hell,
      And aged Saturn in Olympus dwell;
455 They granted what he craved, and once again
      Saturn and Ops began their golden reign.
      Murder, rape, war, lust, and treachery
      Were with Jove closed in Stygian[3] empery.
      But long this blessed time continued not;
460 As soon as he his wishéd purpose got,
      He, reckless of his promise, did despise
      The love of th' everlasting Destinies.
      They seeing it, both Love and him abhorred,
      And Jupiter unto his place restored.
465 And but that Learning,[4] in despite of Fate,
      Will mount aloft, and enter heaven gate,
      And to the seat of Jove itself advance,
      Hermes had slept in hell with Ignorance;

9. Another name for Mercury.
1. Prometheus angered Jove by stealing fire from the gods for the benefit of mankind.
2. I.e., Jove's father, Saturn, whose peaceful and happy reign in Italy, after Jove had de-
throned him, was known as the Golden Age.
3. Pertaining to the river Styx in Hades. "Empery": dominion.
4. Represented by Mercury.

Yet as a punishment they added this,
470 That he and Poverty should always kiss.
And to this day is every scholar poor;
Gross gold from them runs headlong to the boor.
Likewise, the angry sisters thus deluded,
To venge themselves on Hermes, have concluded
475 That Midas'⁵ brood shall sit in Honor's chair,
To which the Muses' sons are only heir;
And fruitful wits that inaspiring are
Shall, discontent, run into regions far;
And few great lords in virtuous deeds shall joy,
480 But be surprised with every garish toy;⁶
And still enrich the lofty servile clown,
Who with encroaching guile keeps learning down.
Then muse not Cupid's suit no better sped,
Seeing in their loves the Fates were injuréd.

Second Sestiad

By this, sad Hero, with love unacquainted,
Viewing Leander's face, fell down and fainted.
He kissed her and breathed life into her lips,
Wherewith, as one displeased, away she trips.
5 Yet as she went, full often looked behind,
And many poor excuses did she find
To linger by the way, and once she stayed
And would have turned again, but was afraid,
In offering parley, to be counted light.°   *wanton*
10 So on she goes, and in her idle flight,
Her painted fan of curléd plumes let fall,
Thinking to train° Leander therewithal.   *draw along*
He, being a novice, knew not what she meant,
But stayed, and after her a letter sent,
15 Which joyful Hero answered in such sort
As he had hoped to scale the beauteous fort
Wherein the liberal graces locked their wealth,
And therefore to her tower he got by stealth.
Wide open stood the door, he need not climb;
20 And she herself, before the 'pointed time,
Had spread the board, with roses strewed the room,
And oft looked out, and mused he did not come.
At last he came; Oh, who can tell the greeting
These greedy lovers had at their first meeting?
25 He asked, she gave, and nothing was denied;
Both to each other quickly were affied.°   *affianced*
Look how their hands, so were their hearts united,
And what he did she willing requited.
Sweet are the kisses, the embracements sweet,
30 When like desires and affections meet;
For from the earth to heaven is Cupid raised,
Where fancy is in equal balance peised.°   *weighed*
Yet she this rashness suddenly repented,
And turned aside, and to herself lamented,
35 As if her name and honor had been wronged
By being possessed of him for whom she longed;
Aye, and she wished, albeit not from her heart,
That he would leave her turret and depart.

5. The king whose touch turned objects to   6. I.e., be delighted with trivial things.
gold.

The mirthful god of amorous pleasure smiled
40 To see how he this captive nymph beguiled;
For hitherto he did but fan the fire,
And kept it down that it might mount the higher.
Now waxed she jealous lest his love abated,
Fearing her own thoughts made her to be hated.
45 Therefore unto him hastily she goes,
And like light Salmacis,[7] her body throws
Upon his bosom, where with yielding eyes
She offers up herself, a sacrifice
To slake his anger if he were displeased.
50 Oh, what god would not therewith be appeased?
Like Aesop's cock,[8] this jewel he enjoyed,
And as a brother with his sister toyed,
Supposing nothing else was to be done,
Now he her favor and good will had won.
55 But know you not that creatures wanting sense[9]
By nature have a mutual appetence,
And wanting organs to advance a step,
Moved by love's force, unto each other leap?
Much more in subjects having intellect,
60 Some hidden influence breeds like effect.
Albeit Leander, rude° in love and raw,   *untutored*
Long dallying with Hero, nothing saw
That might delight him more, yet he suspected
Some amorous rites or other were neglected.
65 Therefore unto his body hers he clung;
She, fearing on the rushes to be flung,
Strived with redoubled strength; the more she strived,
The more a gentle pleasing heat revived,
Which taught him all that elder lovers know;
70 And now the same gan so to scorch and glow,
As in plain terms, yet cunningly, he craved it;
Love always makes those eloquent that have it.
She, with a kind of granting, put him by it,[1]
And ever as he thought himself most nigh it,
75 Like to the tree of Tantalus[2] she fled,
And, seeming lavish, saved her maidenhead.
Ne'er king more sought to keep his diadem,
Than Hero this inestimable gem.
Above our life we love a steadfast friend,
80 Yet when a token of great worth we send,
We often kiss it, often look thereon,
And stay the messenger that would be gone;
No marvel then though Hero would not yield
So soon to part from that she dearly held;
85 Jewels being lost are found again, this never;
'Tis lost but once, and once lost, lost forever.
    Now had the morn espied her lover's steeds,
Whereat she starts, puts on her purple weeds,
And, red for anger that he stayed so long,

7. A nymph who became enamored of Her-
maphroditus when she saw him bathing in her
lake. Throwing herself upon him in spite of
his resistance, she called upon the gods to keep
them forever together. In answer to her prayer
their two bodies united and became one, both
male and female.
8. Finding a jewel in a dung heap, the cock
had no notion of its value and was willing to
trade it for a grain of corn.
9. Inanimate objects "Appetence": attraction
(i.e., magnetism).
1. Denied it to him.
2. Tantalus was punished by being placed in a
pool in Hades. Whenever he bent to drink, the
water receded from his lips; when he reached
for the fruit which dangled above his head, it
rose up out of his grasp.

90   All headlong throws herself the clouds among.
And now Leander, fearing to be missed,
Embraced her suddenly, took leave, and kissed.
Long was he taking leave, and loath to go,
And kissed again, as lovers use to do.
95   Sad Hero wrung him by the hand and wept,
Saying, "Let your vows and promises be kept."
Then, standing at the door, she turned about,
As loath to see Leander going out.
And now the sun that through th' horizon peeps,
100   As pitying these lovers, downward creeps,
So that in silence of the cloudy night,
Though it was morning, did he take his flight.
But what the secret trusty night concealed,
Leander's amorous habit° soon revealed;   *clothing*
105   With Cupid's myrtle was his bonnet crowned,
About his arms the purple riband wound
Wherewith she wreathed her largely spreading hair;
Nor could the youth abstain, but he must wear
The sacred ring wherewith she was endowed,
110   When first religious chastity she vowed,
Which made his love through Sestos to be known,
And thence unto Abydos sooner blown
Than he could sail; for incorporeal Fame,
Whose weight consists in nothing but her name,
115   Is swifter than the wind, whose tardy plumes
Are reeking³ water and dull earthly fumes.
Home, when he came, he seemed not to be there,
But like exiléd heir thrust from his sphere,
Set in a foreign place; and straight from thence,
120   Alcides° like, by mighty violence   *Hercules*
He would have chased away the swelling main
That him from her unjustly did detain.
Like as the sun in a diameter⁴
Fires and inflames objects removéd far,
125   And heateth kindly, shining laterally,
So beauty sweetly quickens when 'tis nigh,
But being separated and removed,
Burns where it cherished, murders where it loved.
Therefore even as an index to a book,
130   So to his mind was young Leander's look.
Oh, none but gods have power their love to hide;
Affection by the countenance is descried.
The light of hidden fire itself discovers,
And love that is concealed betrays poor lovers.
135   His secret flame apparently⁵ was seen;
Leander's father knew where he had been,
And for the same mildly rebuked his son,
Thinking to quench the sparkles new begun.
But love, resisted once, grows passionate,
140   And nothing more than counsel lovers hate;
For as a hot proud horse highly disdains
To have his head controlled, but breaks the reins,
Spits forth the ringled° bit, and with his hooves   *ringed*
Checks° the submissive ground, so he that loves,   *stamps*

3. Producing fog and mist.   farther off than when low in the sky.
4. Directly overhead, where it appears to be   5. I.e., it was apparent.

145 The more he is restrained, the worse he fares.
 What is it now but mad Leander dares?
 "Oh Hero, Hero!" thus he cried full oft,
 And then he got him to a rock aloft,
 Where having spied her tower, long stared he on 't,
150 And prayed the narrow toiling Hellespont
 To part in twain, that he might come and go;
 But still the rising billows answered "No."
 With that he stripped him to the ivory skin,
 And crying, "Love, I come!" leaped lively in.
155 Whereat the sapphire-visaged god[6] grew proud,
 And made his capering Triton sound aloud,
 Imagining that Ganymede,[7] displeased,
 Had left the heavens; therefore on him he seized.
 Leander strived; the waves about him wound,
160 And pulled him to the bottom, where the ground
 Was strewed with pearl, and in low coral groves
 Sweet singing mermaids sported with their loves
 On heaps of heavy gold, and took great pleasure
 To spurn in careless sort the shipwreck treasure.
165 For here the stately azure palace stood,
 Where kingly Neptune and his train abode.
 The lusty god embraced him, called him love,
 And swore he never should return to Jove.
 But when he knew it was not Ganymede,
170 For under water he was almost dead,
 He heaved him up, and looking on his face,
 Beat down the bold waves with his triple mace,
 Which mounted up, intending to have kissed him,
 And fell in drops like tears, because they missed him.
175 Leander, being up, began to swim,
 And looking back, saw Neptune follow him;
 Whereat aghast, the poor soul gan to cry:
 "Oh, let me visit Hero ere I die!"
 The god put Helle's[8] bracelet on his arm,
180 And swore the sea should never do him harm.
 He clapped his plump cheeks, with his tresses played,
 And smiling wantonly, his love bewrayed.°   *revealed*
 He watched his arms, and as they opened wide,
 At every stroke betwixt them would he slide,
185 And steal a kiss, and then run out and dance,
 And as he turned, cast many a lustful glance,
 And threw him gaudy toys to please his eye,
 And dive into the water, and there pry
 Upon his breast, his thighs, and every limb,
190 And up again, and close beside him swim,
 And talk of love. Leander made reply:
 "You are deceived, I am no woman, I."
 Thereat smiled Neptune, and then told a tale
 How that a shepherd, sitting in a vale,
195 Played with a boy so lovely, fair, and kind,
 As for his love both earth and heaven pined;
 That of the cooling river durst not drink

---

6. Neptune, god of the sea. "Triton": his son
and trumpeter.
7. A very handsome young Trojan prince ab-
ducted by Zeus.
8. Fleeing from her stepmother with her

brother Phrixus on the back of a wonderful
golden ram which bore them through the air,
Helle fell into the strait which separates Europe
and Asia, whence the name Hellespont.

Lest water nymphs should pull him from the brink;
And when he sported in the fragrant lawns,
₀₀ Goat-footed satyrs and up-staring fauns
Would steal him thence. Ere half this tale was done,
"Ay me," Leander cried, "th' enamored sun,
That now should shine on Thetis' glassy bower,[9]
Descends upon my radiant Hero's tower.
₀₅ Oh, that these tardy arms of mine were wings!"
And as he spake, upon the waves he springs.
Neptune was angry that he gave no ear,
And in his heart revenging malice bare;
He flung at him his mace, but as it went
₁₀ He called it in, for love made him repent.
The mace returning back, his own hand hit,
As meaning to be venged for darting it.
When this fresh bleeding wound Leander viewed,
His color went and came, as if he rued
₁₅ The grief which Neptune felt. In gentle breasts
Relenting thoughts, remorse, and pity rests;
And who have hard hearts and obdurate minds
But vicious, harebrained, and illiterate hinds?
The god, seeing him with pity to be moved,
₂₀ Thereon concluded that he was beloved.
(Love is too full of faith, too credulous,
With folly and false hope deluding us.)
Wherefore, Leander's fancy to surprise,
To the rich ocean for gifts he flies.
₂₅ 'Tis wisdom to give much; a gift prevails
When deep persuading oratory fails.
  By this, Leander, being near the land,
Cast down his weary feet and felt the sand.
Breathless albeit he were, he rested not
₃₀ Till to the solitary tower he got,
And knocked and called, at which celestial noise
The longing heart of Hero much more joys
Than nymphs or shepherds when the timbrel° rings,   *tambourine*
Or crooked dolphin when the sailor sings;
₃₅ She stayed not for her robes, but straight arose,
And drunk with gladness, to the door she goes;
Where seeing a naked man, she screeched for fear,
(Such sights as this to tender maids are rare)
And ran into the dark herself to hide.
₄₀ Rich jewels in the dark are soonest spied;
Unto her was he led, or rather drawn,
By those white limbs which sparkled through the lawn.
The nearer that he came, the more she fled,
And seeking refuge, slipped into her bed.
₄₅ Whereon Leander sitting, thus began,
Through numbing cold all feeble, faint, and wan:
  "If not for love, yet, love, for pity sake,
Me in thy bed and maiden bosom take;
At least vouchsafe these arms some little room,
₅₀ Who, hoping to embrace thee, cheerly° swum;   *gladly*
This head was beat with many a churlish billow,
And therefore let it rest upon thy pillow."

---

9. I.e., the sea. Thetis was a daughter of the sea-god Nereus.

Herewith affrighted Hero shrunk away,
And in her lukewarm place Leander lay,
255 Whose lively heat like fire from heaven fet,°   *fetched*
Would animate gross clay, and higher set
The drooping thoughts of base declining souls,
Than dreary° Mars carousing nectar bowls.   *cruel, bloody*
His hands he cast upon her like a snare;
260 She, overcome with shame and sallow fear,
Like chaste Diana, when Actaeon spied her,[1]
Being suddenly betrayed, dived down to hide her;
And as her silver body downward went,
With both her hands she made the bed a tent,
265 And in her own mind thought herself secure,
O'ercast with dim and darksome coverture.
And now she lets him whisper in her ear,
Flatter, entreat, promise, protest, and swear;
Yet ever as he greedily assayed
270 To touch those dainties, she the harpy played,
And every limb did, as a soldier stout,
Defend the fort and keep the foeman out;
For though the rising ivory mount he scaled,
Which is with azure circling lines empaled,
275 Much like a globe (a globe may I term this,
By which love sails to regions full of bliss)
Yet there with Sisyphus[2] he toiled in vain,
Till gentle parley did the truce obtain.
Wherein Leander on her quivering breast,
280 Breathless spoke something, and sighed out the rest;
Which so prevailed, as he with small ado
Enclosed her in his arms and kissed her too.
And every kiss to her was as a charm,
And to Leander as a fresh alarm,°   *summons to action*
285 So that the truce was broke, and she, alas,
Poor silly maiden, at his mercy was.
Love is not full of pity, as men say,
But deaf and cruel where he means to prey.
Even as a bird, which in our hands we wring,
290 Forth plungeth and oft flutters with her wing,
She trembling strove; this strife of hers, like that
Which made the world, another world begat
Of unknown joy. Treason was in her thought,
And cunningly to yield herself she sought.
295 Seeming not won, yet won she was at length;
In such wars women use but half their strength.
Leander now, like Theban Hercules,
Entered the orchard of th' Hesperides,[3]
Whose fruit none rightly can describe but he
300 That pulls or shakes it from the golden tree.
And now she wished this night were never done,
And sighed to think upon th' approaching sun;
For much it grieved her that the bright daylight
Should know the pleasure of this blessed night,
305 And them like Mars and Erycine[4] display,
Both in each other's arms chained as they lay.

1. Actaeon came accidentally upon the naked
Diana, about to bathe in her favorite pool.
2. Sisyphus was condemned to Hades and
made to roll a stone uphill forever.

3. Daughters of Atlas and custodians of a
wonderful tree that bore golden apples.
4. Venus; see note to Sestiad I, line 151.

Again she knew not how to frame her look,
Or speak to him who in a moment took
That which so long, so charily she kept;
10 And fain by stealth away she would have crept,
And to some corner secretly have gone,
Leaving Leander in the bed alone.
But as her naked feet were whipping out,
He on the sudden clinged her so about,
15 That mermaid-like unto the floor she slid,
One half appeared, the other half was hid.
Thus near the bed she blushing stood upright,
And from her countenance behold ye might
A kind of twilight break, which through the hair,
20 As from an orient cloud, glimpse here and there;
And round about the chamber this false morn
Brought forth the day before the day was born.
So Hero's ruddy cheek Hero betrayed,
And her all naked to his sight displayed;
25 Whence his admiring eyes more pleasure took
Than Dis[5] on heaps of gold fixing his look.
By this, Apollo's golden harp began
To sound forth music to the ocean;[6]
Which watchful Hesperus no sooner heard,
30 But he the day-bright-bearing car prepared,
And ran before, as harbinger of light,
And with his flaring beams mocked ugly night
Till she, o'ercome with anguish, shame, and rage,
Danged° down to hell her loathsome carriage.   *drove violently*

  Desunt nonnulla.[7]

                1598

The Passionate Shepherd to His Love[8]

Come live with me and be my love,
And we will all the pleasures prove°   *try*
That valleys, groves, hills, and fields,
Woods, or steepy mountain yields.

5 And we will sit upon the rocks,
Seeing the shepherds feed their flocks,
By shallow rivers to whose falls
Melodious birds sing madrigals.

And I will make thee beds of roses
10 And a thousand fragrant posies,
A cap of flowers, and a kirtle
Embroidered all with leaves of myrtle;

A gown made of the finest wool
Which from our pretty lambs we pull;
15 Fair lined slippers for the cold,
With buckles of the purest gold;

---

5. Pluto, god of the underworld and god of wealth.
6. Presaging the rising of the sun. Hesperus is normally the evening star; Marlowe here applies the name to the morning star, usually called Phosphorus.

7. "Something is lacking." Four more sestiads were later added by George Chapman (1559?–1634?).
8. See the response by Sir Walter Ralegh, *The Nymph's Reply to the Shepherd.*

A belt of straw and ivy buds,
With coral clasps and amber studs:
And if these pleasures may thee move,
20   Come live with me, and be my love.

The shepherds' swains shall dance and sing
For thy delight each May morning:
If these delights thy mind may move,
Then live with me and be my love.

1599, 1600

WILLIAM SHAKESPEARE
(1564–1616)

From Sonnets

12

When I do count the clock that tells the time,
And see the brave day sunk in hideous night;
When I behold the violet past prime,
And sable curls, all silvered o'er with white;
5   When lofty trees I see barren of leaves,
Which erst° from heat did canopy the herd,   *formerly*
And summer's green all girded up in sheaves,
Borne on the bier with white and bristly beard,
Then of thy beauty do I question make,
10   That thou among the wastes of time must go,
Since sweets and beauties do themselves forsake
And die as fast as they see others grow;
And nothing 'gainst time's scythe can make defense
Save breed,° to brave him when he takes thee hence.   *progeny*

18

Shall I compare thee to a summer's day?
Thou art more lovely and more temperate:
Rough winds do shake the darling buds of May,
And summer's lease hath all too short a date:
5   Sometimes too hot the eye of heaven shines,
And often is his gold complexion dimmed;
And every fair from fair sometimes declines,
By chance or nature's changing course untrimmed;[1]
But thy eternal summer shall not fade,
10   Nor lose possession of that fair thou ow'st;°   *ownest*
Nor shall death brag thou wander'st in his shade,
When in eternal lines to time thou grow'st:
So long as men can breathe, or eyes can see,
So long lives this, and this gives life to thee.

29

When, in disgrace with fortune and men's eyes,
I all alone beweep my outcast state,
And trouble deaf heaven with my bootless° cries,   *futile*
And look upon myself, and curse my fate,
5   Wishing me like to one more rich in hope,
Featured like him, like him with friends possessed,
Desiring this man's art and that man's scope,

1. Divested of its beauty.

With what I most enjoy contented least;
Yet in these thoughts myself almost despising,
Haply I think on thee—and then my state,
Like to the lark at break of day arising
From sullen earth, sings hymns at heaven's gate;
For thy sweet love remembered such wealth brings
That then I scorn to change my state with kings.

30

When to the sessions² of sweet silent thought
I summon up remembrance of things past,
I sigh the lack of many a thing I sought,
And with old woes new wail my dear time's waste:
Then can I drown an eye, unused to flow,
For precious friends hid in death's dateless° night,   *endless*
And weep afresh love's long since canceled woe,
And moan the expense° of many a vanished sight: *loss*
Then can I grieve at grievances foregone,
And heavily from woe to woe tell o'er
The sad account of fore-bemoanéd moan,
Which I new pay as if not paid before.
But if the while I think on thee, dear friend,
All losses are restored and sorrows end.

33

Full many a glorious morning have I seen
Flatter the mountain-tops with sovereign eye,
Kissing with golden face the meadows green,
Gilding pale streams with heavenly alchemy;
Anon permit the basest clouds to ride
With ugly rack³ on his celestial face,
And from the forlorn world his visage hide,
Stealing unseen to west with this disgrace:
Even so my sun one early morn did shine
With all-triumphant splendor on my brow;
But, out, alack! he was but one hour mine,
The region cloud⁴ hath masked him from me now.
Yet him for this my love no whit disdaineth;
Suns of the world may stain⁵ when heaven's sun staineth.

35

No more be grieved at that which thou hast done:
Roses have thorns, and silver fountains mud;
Clouds and eclipses stain both moon and sun,
And loathsome canker lives in sweetest bud.
All men make faults, and even I in this,
Authorizing thy trespass with compare,°   *comparison*
Myself corrupting, salving thy amiss,°   *wrongdoing*
Excusing thy sins more than thy sins are;
For to thy sensual fault I bring in sense—
Thy adverse party is thy advocate—
And 'gainst myself a lawful plea commence.
Such civil war is in my love and hate
That I an áccessary needs must be
To that sweet thief which sourly robs from me.

55

Not marble, nor the gilded monuments
Of princes, shall outlive this powerful rhyme;
But you shall shine more bright in these conténts

---

2. Sittings of a court.   4. I.e., the clouds in the vicinity.
3. A wind-driven mass of high, broken clouds.   5. I.e., be stained.

Than unswept stone, besmeared with sluttish time.
5 When wasteful war shall statues overturn,
And broils root out the work of masonry,
Nor Mars his[6] sword nor war's quick fire shall burn
The living record of your memory.
'Gainst death and all-oblivious enmity
10 Shall you pace forth; your praise shall still find room
Even in the eyes of all posterity
That wear this world out to the ending doom.°   *Judgment Day*
So, till the judgment that yourself arise,
You live in this, and dwell in lovers' eyes.

64

When I have seen by time's fell° hand defaced   *destroying*
The rich-proud cost of outworn buried age;
When sometime° lofty towers I see down-razed,   *formerly*
And brass eternal slave to mortal rage;
5 When I have seen the hungry ocean gain
Advantage on the kingdom of the shore,
And the firm soil win of the watery main,
Increasing store with loss, and loss with store;
When I have seen such interchange of state,
10 Or state itself confounded to decay,
Ruin hath taught me thus to ruminate,
That time will come and take my love away.
This thought is as a death, which cannot choose
But weep to have that which it fears to lose.

65

Since brass, nor[7] stone, nor earth, nor boundless sea
But sad mortality o'er-sways their power,
How with this rage shall beauty hold a plea,
Whose action is no stronger than a flower?
5 O, how shall summer's honey breath hold out
Against the wreckful siege of battering days,
When rocks impregnable are not so stout,
Nor gates of steel so strong, but Time decays?
O fearful meditation! where, alack,
10 Shall Time's best jewel from Time's chest lie hid?
Or what strong hand can hold his swift foot back?
Or who his spoil of beauty can forbid?
O, none, unless this miracle have might,
That in black ink my love may still shine bright.

71

No longer mourn for me when I am dead
Than you shall hear the surly sullen bell
Give warning to the world that I am fled
From this vile world, with vilest worms to dwell:
5 Nay, if you read this line, remember not
The hand that writ it; for I love you so,
That I in your sweet thoughts would be forgot,
If thinking on me then should make you woe.
Oh, if, I say, you look upon this verse
10 When I perhaps compounded am with clay,
Do not so much as my poor name rehearse,
But let your love even with my life decay;
Lest the wise world should look into your moan,
And mock you with me after I am gone.

---

6. I.e., Mars'.   7. I.e., since there is neither brass nor.

73

That time of year thou mayst in me behold
When yellow leaves, or none, or few, do hang
Upon those boughs which shake against the cold,
Bare ruined choirs, where late the sweet birds sang.
5 In me thou see'st the twilight of such day
As after sunset fadeth in the west;
Which by and by black night doth take away,
Death's second self, that seals up all in rest.
In me thou see'st the glowing of such fire,
10 That on the ashes of his youth doth lie,
As the deathbed whereon it must expire,
Consumed with that which it was nourished by.
This thou perceiv'st, which makes thy love more strong,
To love that well which thou must leave ere long.

94

They that have power to hurt and will do none,
That do not do the thing they most do show,
Who, moving others, are themselves as stone,
Unmovéd, cold, and to temptation slow;
5 They rightly do inherit heaven's graces
And husband nature's riches from expense;°   *expenditure*
They are the lords and owners of their faces,
Others but stewards of their excellence.
The summer's flower is to the summer sweet,
10 Though to itself it only live and die,
But if that flower with base infection meet,
The basest weed outbraves° his dignity: *excels*
For sweetest things turn sourest by their deeds;
Lilies that fester smell far worse than weeds.

106

When in the chronicle of wasted° time   *past*
I see descriptions of the fairest wights,
And beauty making beautiful old rhyme
In praise of ladies dead and lovely knights,
5 Then, in the blazon⁹ of sweet beauty's best,
Of hand, of foot, of lip, of eye, of brow,
I see their antique pen would have expressed
Even such a beauty as you master now.
So all their praises are but prophecies
10 Of this our time, all you prefiguring;
And, for° they looked but with divining eyes,   *because*
They had not skill enough your worth to sing:
For we, which now behold these present days,
Have eyes to wonder, but lack tongues to praise.

107

Not mine own fears, nor the prophetic soul
Of the wide world dreaming on things to come,
Can yet the lease of my true love control,
Supposed as forfeit to a cónfined doom.
5 The mortal moon¹ hath her eclipse endured,
And the sad augurs mock their own presage;
Incertainties now crown themselves assured,
And peace proclaims olives of endless age.
Now with the drops of this most balmy time

9. A catalogue of a lady's charms.
1. Queen Elizabeth, whose sixty-third year had been anticipated by astrologers ("augurs") as a time of disaster.

10 My love looks fresh, and death to me subscribes,°   **submits**
Since, spite of him, I'll live in this poor rhyme,
While he insults o'er dull and speechless tribes:
And thou in this shalt find thy monument,
When tyrants' crests and tombs of brass are spent.

116

Let me not to the marriage of true minds
Admit impediments. Love is not love
Which alters when it alteration finds,
Or bends with the remover to remove:
5 Oh, no! it is an ever-fixéd mark,
That looks on tempests and is never shaken;
It is the star to every wandering bark,
Whose worth's unknown, although his height be taken.[2]
Love's not Time's fool, though rosy lips and cheeks
10 Within his bending sickle's compass come;
Love alters not with his brief hours and weeks,
But bears it out even to the edge of doom.[3]
If this be error and upon me proved,
I never writ, nor no man ever loved.

129

Th' expense of spirit in a waste of shame
Is lust in action; and till action, lust
Is perjured, murderous, bloody, full of blame,
Savage, extreme, rude, cruel, not to trust;
5 Enjoyed no sooner but despiséd straight:
Past reason hunted; and no sooner had,
Past reason hated, as a swallowed bait,
On purpose laid to make the taker mad:
Mad in pursuit, and in possession so;
10 Had, having, and in quest to have, extreme;
A bliss in proof,[4] and proved, a very woe;
Before, a joy proposed; behind, a dream.
All this the world well knows; yet none knows well
To shun the heaven that leads men to this hell.

130

My mistress' eyes are nothing like the sun;
Coral is far more red than her lips' red;
If snow be white, why then her breasts are dun;
If hairs be wires, black wires grow on her head.
5 I have seen roses damasked,° red and white,   **variegated**
But no such roses see I in her cheeks;
And in some perfumes is there more delight
Than in the breath that from my mistress reeks.
I love to hear her speak, yet well I know
10 That music hath a far more pleasing sound;
I grant I never saw a goddess go;°   **walk**
My mistress, when she walks, treads on the ground.
And yet, by heaven, I think my love as rare
As any she belied with false compare.

138

When my love swears that she is made of truth,
I do believe her, though I know she lies,
That she might think me some untutored youth,
Unlearnéd in the world's false subtleties.
5 Thus vainly thinking that she thinks me young,

---

2. I.e., although its elevation may be meas-
ured.

3. Judgment Day, the end of the world.
4. I.e., in the experience.

Although she knows my days are past the best,
Simply I credit her false-speaking tongue:
On both sides thus is simple truth suppressed.
But wherefore says she not she is unjust?
And wherefore say not I that I am old?
Oh, love's best habit is in seeming trust,
And age in love loves not to have years told.
Therefore I lie with her and she with me,
And in our faults by lies we flattered be.

146

Poor soul, the center of my sinful earth,
Lord of[5] these rebel powers that thee array,°   *dress, deck out*
Why dost thou pine within and suffer dearth,
Painting thy outward walls so costly gay?
Why so large cost, having so short a lease,
Dost thou upon thy fading mansion spend?
Shall worms, inheritors of this excess,
Eat up thy charge? Is this thy body's end?
Then, soul, live thou upon thy servant's loss,
And let that pine to aggravate° thy store;   *increase*
Buy terms divine in selling hours of dross;
Within be fed, without be rich no more.
So shalt thou feed on death, that feeds on men,
And death once dead, there's no more dying then.

1609

The Phoenix and the Turtle[7]

Let the bird of loudest lay,
On the sole Arabian tree,
Herald sad and trumpet be,
To whose sound chaste wings obey.

But thou shrieking harbinger,
Foul precurrer° of the fiend,   *forerunner*
Augur of the fever's end,
To this troop come thou not near!

From this session interdict
Every fowl of tyrant wing,
Save the eagle, feathered king:
Keep the obsequy so strict.

Let the priest in surplice white,
That defunctive° music can,°   *funereal / knows*
Be the death-divining swan,[8]
Lest the requiem lack his right.

And thou treble-dated crow,[9]
That thy sable gender mak'st
With the breath thou giv'st and tak'st,
'Mongst our mourners shalt thou go.

5. The original text repeats "My sinful earth," apparently a mistake, in place of "Lord of" at the beginning of this line. Other possibilities have been suggested, e.g., "Rebuke," "Thrall to," "Pressed by."
7. Turtledove, famous for steadfastness in love. The phoenix is a legendary bird, the only one of its kind, represented as living five hundred years in the Arabian desert, being consumed in fire, then rising anew from its own ashes.
8. The swan was supposed to sing only as its death drew near.
9. The crow was supposed to live three lives and to conceive its young ("sable gender") through its beak.

Here the anthem doth commence:
Love and constancy is dead,
Phoenix and the turtle fled
In a mutual flame from hence.

25 So they loved as love in twain
Had the essence but in one;
Two distincts, division none:
Number there in love was slain.

Hearts remote, yet not asunder;
30 Distance, and no space was seen
'Twixt this turtle and his queen;
But° in them it were a wonder.   *except*

So between them love did shine
That the turtle saw his right
35 Flaming in the phoenix' sight:
Either was the other's mine.

Property was thus appalled,
That the self was not the same;
Single nature's double name
40 Neither two nor one was called.

Reason, in itself confounded,
Saw division grow together,
To themselves yet either neither,
Simple were so well compounded;

45 That it cried, "How true a twain
Seemeth this concordant one!
Love hath reason, reason none,
If what parts can so remain."

Whereupon it made this threne[1]
50 To the phoenix and the dove,
Co-supremes and stars of love,
As chorus to their tragic scene.

Threnos

Beauty, truth, and rarity,
Grace in all simplicity,
55 Here enclosed in cinders lie.

Death is now the phoenix' nest;
And the turtle's loyal breast
To eternity doth rest,

Leaving no posterity:
60 'Twas not their infirmity,
It was married chastity.

Truth may seem, but cannot be;
Beauty brag, but 'tis not she:
Truth and Beauty buried be.

1. Threnos or threnody, a lyrical lament over the dead.

65 To this urn let those repair
    That are either true or fair;
    For these dead birds sigh a prayer.

                                                    1601

When Daisies Pied[3]

Spring

When daisies pied and violets blue
    And ladysmocks all silver-white
And cuckoobuds of yellow hue
    Do paint the meadows with delight,
5 The cuckoo then, on every tree,
Mocks married men;[4] for thus sings he,
                Cuckoo;
Cuckoo, cuckoo: Oh word of fear,
Unpleasing to a married ear!

10 When shepherds pipe on oaten straws,
    And merry larks are plowmen's clocks,
When turtles tread,[5] and rooks, and daws,
    And maidens bleach their summer smocks,
The cuckoo then, on every tree,
15 Mocks married men; for thus sings he,
                Cuckoo;
Cuckoo, cuckoo: Oh word of fear,
Unpleasing to a married ear!

Winter

When icicles hang by the wall
20 And Dick the shepherd blows his nail[6]
And Tom bears logs into the hall,
    And milk comes frozen home in pail.
When blood is nipped and ways be foul,
Then nightly sings the staring owl,
25   Tu-who;
Tu-whit, tu-who: a merry note,
While greasy Joan doth keel[7] the pot.

When all aloud the wind doth blow,
    And coughing drowns the parson's saw,°   *wise saying*
30 And birds sit brooding in the snow,
    And Marian's nose looks red and raw,
When roasted crabs° hiss in the bowl,   *crab apples*
Then nightly sings the staring owl,
                Tu-who;
35 Tu-whit, tu-who: a merry note
While greasy Joan doth keel the pot.

                              1595?   1598

---

3. From *Love's Labour's Lost.*
4. The cuckoo's song was often taken fancifully as "Cuckold!"
5. I.e., when turtledoves mate.
6. I.e., breathes on his fingers to warm them.
7. Keep from boiling over by stirring.

Under the Greenwood Tree[9]

Under the greenwood tree
Who loves to lie with me,
And turn his merry note
Unto the sweet bird's throat,
5   Come hither, come hither, come hither:
        Here shall he see
        No enemy
But winter and rough weather.

Who doth ambition shun
10   And loves to live i' the sun,
Seeking the food he eats,
And pleased with what he gets,
Come hither, come hither, come hither:
        Here shall he see
        No enemy
But winter and rough weather.

                                        1599?   1623

Blow, Blow, Thou Winter Wind[1]

Blow, blow, thou winter wind,
Thou art not so unkind
        As man's ingratitude;
Thy tooth is not so keen,
5   Because thou art not seen,
        Although thy breath be rude.
Heigh-ho! sing, heigh-ho! unto the green holly:
Most friendship is feigning, most loving mere folly:
        Then, heigh-ho, the holly!
10   This life is most jolly.

Freeze, freeze, thou bitter sky,
That dost not bite so nigh
        As benefits forgot:
Though thou the waters warp,
15   Thy sting is not so sharp
        As friend remembered not.
Heigh-ho! sing, . . .

                                        1599?   1623

It Was a Lover and His Lass[2]

It was a lover and his lass,
        With a hey, and a ho, and a hey nonino,
That o'er the green corn field did pass
        In springtime, the only pretty ring time,
5   When birds do sing, hey ding a ding, ding:
Sweet lovers love the spring.

Between the acres of the rye,
        With a hey, and a ho, and a hey nonino,
These pretty country folks would lie,
10   In springtime, . . .

9. From *As You Like It.*   2. From *As You Like It.*
1. From *As You Like It.*

This carol they began that hour,
  With a hey, and a ho, and a hey nonino,
How that a life was but a flower
  In springtime, . . .

15 And therefore take the present time,
  With a hey, and a ho, and a hey nonino;
For love is crownéd with the prime
  In springtime, . . .

                                    1599?   1623

Oh Mistress Mine[3]

Oh mistress mine! where are you roaming?
Oh! stay and hear; your true love's coming,
  That can sing both high and low.
Trip no further, pretty sweeting;
5 Journeys end in lovers meeting,
  Every wise man's son doth know.

What is love? 'tis not hereafter;
Present mirth hath present laughter;
  What's to come is still unsure:
10 In delay there lies no plenty;
Then come kiss me, sweet and twenty,
  Youth's a stuff will not endure.

                                    1602   1623

Come Away, Come Away, Death[4]

Come away, come away, death,
  And in sad cypress let me be laid.
Fly away, fly away, breath;
  I am slain by a fair cruel maid.
5 My shroud of white, stuck all with yew,
      O, prepare it!
My part of death, no one so true
      Did share it.

Not a flower, not a flower sweet,
10 On my black coffin let there be strown.
Not a friend, not a friend greet
  My poor corpse, where my bones shall be thrown.
A thousand thousand sighs to save,
      Lay me, O, where
15 Sad true lover never find my grave,
      To weep there!

                                    1602   1623

When That I Was and a Little Tiny Boy[5]

When that I was and a little tiny boy,
  With hey, ho, the wind and the rain,
A foolish thing was but a toy,°   *trifle*
  For the rain it raineth every day.

3. From *Twelfth Night*.
4. From *Twelfth Night*.

5. From *Twelfth Night;* sung by the clown to
conclude the play.

5 But when I came to man's estate,
       With hey, ho, . . .
   'Gainst knaves and thieves men shut their gate,
       For the rain, . . .

   But when I came, alas! to wive,
10   With hey, ho, . . .
   By swaggering could I never thrive,
       For the rain, . . .

   But when I came unto my beds,
       With hey, ho, . . .
15 With toss-pots still had drunken heads,
       For the rain, . . .

   A great while ago the world begun,
       With hey, ho, . . .
   But that's all one, our play is done,
20   And we'll strive to please you every day.

                                    1602   1623

Hark! Hark! the Lark[6]

Hark, hark! the lark at heaven's gate sings,
    And Phoebus[7] 'gins arise,
His steeds to water at those springs
    On chaliced[8] flowers that lies;
5 And winking Mary-buds begin
    To ope their golden eyes:
With every thing that pretty is,
    My lady sweet, arise:
    Arise, arise!

                                    1610?   1623

Fear No More the Heat o' the Sun[9]

Fear no more the heat o' the sun,
    Nor the furious winter's rages;
Thou thy worldly task hast done,
    Home art gone, and ta'en thy wages:
5 Golden lads and girls all must,
As chimney-sweepers, come to dust.

Fear no more the frown o' the great;
    Thou art past the tyrant's stroke;
Care no more to clothe and eat;
10   To thee the reed is as the oak:
The scepter, learning, physic, must
All follow this, and come to dust.

Fear no more the lightning flash,
    Nor the all-dreaded thunder stone;[1]
15 Fear not slander, censure rash;
    Thou hast finished joy and moan:
All lovers young, all lovers must
Consign to thee, and come to dust.

6. From *Cymbeline*.
7. Apollo, god of the sun.
8. Having a cup-shaped blossom.

9. From *Cymbeline*.
1. Thunder was thought to be caused by meteorites falling from the sky.

No exorciser harm thee!
20 Nor no witchcraft charm thee!
Ghost unlaid forbear thee!
Nothing ill come near thee!
Quiet consummation have;
And renownéd be thy grave!

1610?   1623

When Daffodils Begin to Peer[2]

When daffodils begin to peer,
  With heigh! the doxy° over the dale,   *trollop, mistress*
Why, then comes in the sweet o' the year;
  For the red blood reigns in the winter's pale.[3]

5 The white sheet bleaching on the hedge,
  With heigh! the sweet birds, Oh, how they sing!
Doth set my pugging° tooth on edge;   *thieving*
  For a quart of ale is a dish for a king.

The lark, that tirra-lirra chants,
10 With heigh! with heigh! the thrush and the jay,
Are summer songs for me and my aunts,°   *sweethearts*
  While we lie tumbling in the hay.

1611   1623

Come Unto These Yellow Sands[4]

Come unto these yellow sands,
  And then take hands.
Curtsied when you have, and kissed
  The wild waves whist,°   *quiet*
5 Foot it featly° here and there,   *nimbly*
And, sweet sprites, the burden bear.
    Hark, hark!
      Bow-wow.
The watch-dogs bark!
10   Bow-wow.
Hark, hark! I hear
The strain of strutting chanticleer[5]
Cry, "Cock-a-diddle-dow."

1611   1623

Full Fathom Five[6]

Full fathom five thy father lies;
  Of his bones are coral made;
Those are pearls that were his eyes:
  Nothing of him that doth fade,
5 But doth suffer a sea change
Into something rich and strange.
Sea nymphs hourly ring his knell:
  Ding-dong.
Hark! now I hear them—Ding-dong, bell.

1611   1623

---

2. From *The Winter's Tale.*
3. Territory, as well as lack of color.
4. From *The Tempest.*

5. The name of a cock in several old beast fables.
6. From *The Tempest.*

Where the Bee Sucks, There Suck I[7]

Where the bee sucks, there suck I:
In a cowslip's bell I lie;
There I couch when owls do cry.
On the bat's back I do fly
5   After summer merrily.
Merrily, merrily shall I live now
Under the blossom that hangs on the bough.

1611   1623

Roses, Their Sharp Spines Being Gone[8]

Roses, their sharp spines being gone,
Not royal in their smells alone,
    But in their hue;
Maiden pinks, of odor faint,
5   Daisies smell-less, yet most quaint,
    And sweet thyme true;
Primrose, firstborn child of Ver,°   *spring*
Merry springtime's harbinger,
    With her bells dim;
10 Oxlips in their cradles growing,
Marigolds on death-beds blowing,
    Larks'-heels trim;
All dear Nature's children sweet
Lie 'fore bride and bridegroom's feet
15   Blessing their sense.
Not an angel of the air,
Bird melodious, or bird fair,
    Is absent hence.
The crow, the slanderous cuckoo, nor
20 The boding raven, nor chough° hoar,   *jay*
    Nor chattering pie°   *magpie*
May on our bride-house perch or sing,
Or with them any discord bring,
    But from it fly.

1612?   1634

THOMAS CAMPION
(1567–1620)

My Sweetest Lesbia[1]

My sweetest Lesbia, let us live and love,
And though the sager sort our deeds reprove,
Let us not weigh them. Heaven's great lamps do dive
Into their west, and straight again revive,
5   But soon as once set is our little light,
Then must we sleep one ever-during night.

---

7. From *The Tempest*.
8. From *The Two Noble Kinsmen*, by Shakespeare and John Fletcher.
1. The Roman poet Catullus sang the praises
of his Lesbia in a poem here imitated and
partly translated by Campion.

If all would lead their lives in love like me,
Then bloody swords and armor should not be;
No drum nor trumpet peaceful sleeps should move,
10 Unless alarm came from the camp of love.
But fools do live, and waste their little light,
And seek with pain their ever-during night.

When timely death my life and fortune ends,
Let not my hearse be vexed with mourning friends,
15 But let all lovers, rich in triumph, come
And with sweet pastimes grace my happy tomb;
And Lesbia, close up thou my little light,
And crown with love my ever-during night.

1601

I Care Not for These Ladies

I care not for these ladies,
That must be wooed and prayed:
Give me kind Amaryllis,
The wanton country maid.
5 Nature art disdaineth,
Her beauty is her own.
  Her when we court and kiss,
  She cries, "Forsooth, let go!"
  But when we come where comfort is,
10 She never will say no.

If I love Amaryllis,
She gives me fruit and flowers:
But if we love these ladies,
We must give golden showers.
15 Give them gold, that sell love,
Give me the nut-brown lass,
  Who, when we court and kiss,
  She cries, "Forsooth, let go!"
  But when we come where comfort is,
20 She never will say no.

These ladies must have pillows,
And beds by strangers wrought;
Give me a bower of willows,
Of moss and leaves unbought,
25 And fresh Amaryllis,
With milk and honey fed;
  Who, when we court and kiss,
  She cries, "Forsooth, let go!"
  But when we come where comfort is,
30 She never will say no.

1601

Follow Thy Fair Sun

Follow thy fair sun, unhappy shadow;
Though thou be black as night,
And she made all of light,
Yet follow thy fair sun, unhappy shadow.

5   Follow her whose light thy light depriveth;
     Though here thou liv'st disgraced,
     And she in heaven is placed,
     Yet follow her whose light the world reviveth!

     Follow those pure beams whose beauty burneth,
10   That so have scorched thee,
     As thou still black must be,
     Till her kind beams thy black to brightness turneth.

     Follow her while yet her glory shineth;
     There comes a luckless night,
15   That will dim all her light;
     And this the black unhappy shade divineth.

     Follow still since so thy fates ordained;
     The sun must have his shade,
     Till both at once do fade;
20   The sun still proved,° the shadow still disdained.

approved
1601

When to Her Lute Corinna Sings

     When to her lute Corinna sings,
     Her voice revives the leaden strings,
     And doth in highest notes appear
     As any challenged echo clear;
5   But when she doth of mourning speak,
     Ev'n with her sighs the strings do break.

     And as her lute doth live or die,
     Led by her passion, so must I:
     For when of pleasure she doth sing,
10   My thoughts enjoy a sudden spring,
     But if she doth of sorrow speak,
     Ev'n from my heart the strings do break.

1601

Follow Your Saint

     Follow your saint, follow with accents sweet;
     Haste you, sad notes, fall at her flying feet.
     There, wrapped in cloud of sorrow, pity move,
     And tell the ravisher of my soul I perish for her love.
5   But if she scorns my never-ceasing pain,
     Then burst with sighing in her sight and ne'er return again.

     All that I sung still to her praise did tend;
     Still she was first, still she my songs did end.
     Yet she my love and music both doth fly,
10   The music that her echo is and beauty's sympathy.
     Then let my notes pursue her scornful flight:
     It shall suffice that they were breathed and died for her delight.

1601

When Thou Must Home

When thou must home to shades of underground,
And there arrived, a new admiréd guest,
The beauteous spirits do engirt thee round,
White Iope, blithe Helen,[2] and the rest,
5   To hear the stories of thy finished love
From that smooth tongue whose music hell can move,

Then wilt thou speak of banqueting delights,
Of masques and revels which sweet youth did make,
Of tourneys and great challenges of knights,
10   And all these triumphs for thy beauty's sake;
When thou hast told these honors done to thee,
Then tell, Oh tell, how thou didst murther me.

1601

Rose-cheeked Laura

Rose-cheeked Laura, come,
Sing thou smoothly with thy beauty's
Silent music, either other
    Sweetly gracing.

5   Lovely forms do flow
From concent° divinely framed;   *sounds in harmony*
Heav'n is music, and thy beauty's
    Birth is heavenly.

These dull notes we sing
10   Discords need for helps to grace them;
Only beauty purely loving
    Knows no discord,

But still moves delight,
Like clear springs renewed by flowing,
15   Ever perfect, ever in them-
    Selves eternal.

1602

What If a Day

What if a day, or a month, or a year
Crown thy delights with a thousand sweet contentings?
Cannot a chance of a night or an hour
Cross thy desires with as many sad tormentings?
5   Fortune, honor, beauty, youth
        Are but blossoms dying;
        Wanton pleasure, doting love
        Are but shadows flying.
        All our joys are but toys,
10   Idle thoughts deceiving;
        None have power of an hour
        In their lives' bereaving.

2. Iope or Cassiopeia and Helen of Troy, the first renowned for beauty and vanity, the second for beauty and fickleness.

Earth's but a point to the world, and a man
Is but a point to the world's compared centure;°   center
15   Shall then a point of a point be so vain
As to triumph[3] in a sely° point's adventure?   insignificant
          All is hazard that we have,
          There is nothing biding;
          Days of pleasure are like streams
20   Through fair meadows gliding.
          Weal and woe, time doth go,
          Time is never turning;
          Secret fates guide our states,
          Both in mirth and mourning.

                                                              1606

Now Winter Nights Enlarge

Now winter nights enlarge
     The number of their hours;
And clouds their storms discharge
     Upon the airy towers.
5   Let now the chimneys blaze
     And cups o'erflow with wine,
Let well-tuned words amaze
     With harmony divine.
Now yellow waxen lights
10   Shall wait on honey love
While youthful revels, masques, and courtly sights
     Sleep's leaden spells remove.

This time doth well dispense
     With[5] lovers' long discourse;
15 Much speech hath some defense,
     Though beauty no remorse.
All do not all things well;
     Some measures comely tread,
Some knotted riddles tell,
20   Some poems smoothly read.
The summer hath his joys,
     And winter his delights;
Though love and all his pleasures are but toys,
     They shorten tedious nights.

                                                              1617

Thrice Toss These Oaken Ashes

Thrice toss these oaken ashes in the air,
Thrice sit thou mute in this enchanted chair;
Then thrice three times tie up this truelove's knot,
And murmur soft "She will, or she will not."

5   Go burn these poisonous weeds in yon blue fire,
These screech-owl's feathers and this prickling briar,
This cypress gathered at a dead man's grave,
That all thy fears and cares an end may have.

---

3. Often stressed on second syllable.   5. Put up with, deal indulgently with.

10   Then come, you fairies, dance with me a round;
   Melt her hard heart with your melodious sound.
   In vain are all the charms I can devise:
   She hath an art to break them with her eyes.

                                                                    1617

There Is a Garden in Her Face

   There is a garden in her face,
   Where roses and white lilies grow,
   A heavenly paradise is that place,
   Wherein all pleasant fruits do flow.
5   There cherries grow, which none may buy
   Till "Cherry ripe!"[6] themselves do cry.

   Those cherries fairly do enclose
   Of orient pearl a double row,
   Which when her lovely laughter shows,
10   They look like rosebuds filled with snow.
   Yet them nor peer nor prince can buy,
   Till "Cherry ripe!" themselves do cry.

   Her eyes like angels watch them still;
   Her brows like bended bows do stand,
15   Threatening with piercing frowns to kill
   All that attempt with eye or hand
   Those sacred cherries to come nigh,
   Till "Cherry ripe!" themselves do cry.

                                                                    1617

Think'st Thou To Seduce Me Then

   Think'st thou to seduce me then with words that have no meaning?
   Parrots so can learn to prate, our speech by pieces gleaning;
   Nurses teach their children so about the time of weaning.

   Learn to speak first, then to woo; to wooing much pertaineth;
5   He that courts us, wanting art, soon falters when he feigneth,
   Looks asquint on his discourse,[7] and smiles when he complaineth.

   Skilful anglers hide their hooks, fit baits for every season;
   But with crooked pins fish thou, as babes do that want reason:
   Gudgeons only can be caught with such poor tricks of treason.

10   Ruth° forgive me, if I erred from human heart's compassion,   *sympathy*
   When I laughed sometimes too much to see thy foolish fashion;
   But, alas, who less could do that found so good occasion?

                                                                    1617

---

6. A London street vendor's cry.   7. I.e., steals a glance at previously prepared
                                           notes.

THOMAS NASHE
(1567–1601)

Spring, the Sweet Spring

Spring, the sweet spring, is the year's pleasant king,
Then blooms each thing, then maids dance in a ring,
Cold doth not sting, the pretty birds do sing:
    Cuckoo, jug-jug, pu-we, to-witta-woo!⁹

5   The palm and may make country houses gay,
Lambs frisk and play, the shepherds pipe all day,
And we hear aye birds tune this merry lay:
    Cuckoo, jug-jug, pu-we, to-witta-woo!

The fields breathe sweet, the daisies kiss our feet,
10   Young lovers meet, old wives a-sunning sit,
In every street these tunes our ears do greet:
    Cuckoo, jug-jug, pu-we, to-witta-woo!
    Spring, the sweet spring!

1600

A Litany in Time of Plague

Adieu, farewell, earth's bliss;
This world uncertain is;
Fond° are life's lustful joys;   *foolish*
Death proves them all but toys;°   *trifles*
5   None from his darts can fly;
I am sick, I must die.
    Lord, have mercy on us!

Rich men, trust not in wealth,
Gold cannot buy you health;
10   Physic himself must fade.
All things to end are made,
The plague full swift goes by;
I am sick, I must die
    Lord, have mercy on us!

15   Beauty is but a flower
Which wrinkles will devour;
Brightness falls from the air;.
Queens have died young and fair;
Dust hath closed Helen's eye.
20   I am sick, I must die.
    Lord, have mercy on us!

Strength stoops unto the grave,
Worms feed on Hector brave;
Swords may not fight with fate,
25   Earth still holds ope her gate.
"Come, come!" the bells do cry.
I am sick, I must die.
    Lord, have mercy on us.

9. Bird songs of the cuckoo, nightingale, lapwing, owl.

Wit with his wantonness
30 Tasteth death's bitterness;
Hell's executioner
Hath no ears for to hear
What vain art can reply.
I am sick, I must die.
35   Lord, have mercy on us.

Haste, therefore, each degree,
To welcome destiny;
Heaven is our heritage,
Earth but a player's stage;
40 Mount we unto the sky.
I am sick, I must die.
    Lord, have mercy on us.

1592   1600

ROBERT HAYMAN
(d. 1631?)

Of the Great and Famous
Ever-to-be-honored Knight, Sir Francis Drake,
and of My Little-Little Self

The Dragon that our seas did raise his crest
And brought back heaps of gold unto his nest,
Unto his foes more terrible than thunder,
Glory of his age, after-ages' wonder,
5 Excelling all those that excelled before—
It's feared we shall have none such any more—
Effecting all, he sole did undertake,
Valiant, just, wise, mild, honest, godly Drake.
This man when I was little I did meet
10 As he was walking up Totnes' long street.
He asked me whose I was. I answered him.
He asked me if his good friend were within.
A fair red orange in his hand he had;
He gave it me, whereof I was right glad,
15 Takes and kissed me, and prays, "God bless my boy,"
Which I record with comfort to this day.
Could he on me have breathéd with his breath
His gifts, Elias-like,[1] after his death,
Then had I been enabled for to do
20 Many brave things I have a heart unto.
I have as great desire as e'er had he
To joy, annoy, friends, foes; but 'twill not be.

1628

---

1. The prophet Elijah, who departed from earth in a chariot of fire, leaving his sacred mantle and a share of his spirit to his disciple Elisha (II Kings ii.9–14).

JOHN DONNE
(1572–1631)

Song

Go and catch a falling star,
  Get with child a mandrake root,[1]
Tell me where all past years are,
  Or who cleft the Devil's foot,
5 Teach me to hear mermaids singing,
Or to keep off envy's stinging,
      And find
      What wind
Serves to advance an honest mind.

10 If thou beest born to strange sights,
  Things invisible to see,
Ride ten thousand days and nights,
  Till age snow white hairs on thee.
Thou, when thou return'st, wilt tell me
15 All strange wonders that befell thee,
      And swear
      Nowhere
Lives a woman true, and fair.

If thou find'st one, let me know,
20 Such a pilgrimage were sweet;
Yet do not, I would not go,
  Though at next door we might meet;
Though she were true when you met her,
And last till you write your letter,
25   Yet she
      Will be
False, ere I come, to two, or three.

                                    1633

Woman's Constancy

Now thou hast loved me one whole day,
Tomorrow when thou leav'st, what wilt thou say?
Wilt thou then antedate some new-made vow?
      Or say that now
5 We are not just those persons which we were?
Or, that oaths made in reverential fear
Of love, and his wrath, any may forswear?
Or, as true deaths true marriages untie,
So lovers' contracts, images of those,
10 Bind but till sleep, death's image, them unloose?
      Or, your own end to justify,
For having purposed change, and falsehood, you
Can have no way but falsehood to be true?
Vain lunatic,[2] against these 'scapes I could

---

1. The large, forked root of the mandrake, roughly resembling a human body, was often credited with human attributes. As a medicine, it was supposed to promote conception.

2. The word has for Donne the additional meaning of *inconstant* or *fickle*, since lunacy (from *luna*, moon) was supposed to be affected by the changing phases of the moon.

15   Dispute, and conquer, if I would,
       Which I abstain to do,
   For by tomorrow, I may think so too.

1633

The Sun Rising

       Busy old fool, unruly sun,
         Why dost thou thus,
   Through windows and through curtains call on us?
   Must to thy motions lovers' seasons run?
5   Saucy pedantic wretch, go chide
           Late school boys and sour prentices,
         Go tell court huntsmen that the king will ride,
         Call country ants to harvest offices;
       Love, all alike, no season knows nor clime,
10   Nor hours, days, months, which are the rags of time.

       Thy beams, so reverend and strong
         Why shouldst thou think?
   I could eclipse and cloud them with a wink,
   But that I would not lose her sight so long;
15   If her eyes have not blinded thine,
           Look, and tomorrow late tell me,
         Whether both th' Indias[3] of spice and mine
         Be where thou leftst them, or lie here with me.
       Ask for those kings whom thou saw'st yesterday,
20   And thou shalt hear, All here in one bed lay.

       She's all states, and all princes, I,
         Nothing else is.
   Princes do but play us; compared to this,
   All honor's mimic, all wealth alchemy.[4]
25   Thou, sun, art half as happy as we,
           In that the world's contracted thus;
         Thine age asks ease, and since thy duties be
         To warm the world, that's done in warming us.
       Shine here to us, and thou art everywhere;
30   This bed thy center is, these walls, thy sphere.

1633

The Canonization

   For God's sake hold your tongue, and let me love,
       Or chide my palsy, or my gout,
   My five gray hairs, or ruined fortune, flout,
   With wealth your state, your mind with arts improve,
5   Take you a course, get you a place,
         Observe His Honor, or His Grace,
   Or the King's real, or his stampéd face[7]
       Contémplate; what you will, approve,°   *try*
       So you will let me love.

10   Alas, alas, who's injured by my love?
       What merchant's ships have my sighs drowned?
     Who says my tears have overflowed his ground?

---

3. India and the West Indies, whence came   4. I.e., a fraud.
spices and gold, respectively.   7. I.e., on coins.

When did my colds a forward spring remove?
  When did the heats which my veins fill
15   Add one more to the plaguy bill?[8]
Soldiers find wars, and lawyers find out still
  Litigious men, which quarrels move,
  Though she and I do love.

Call us what you will, we're made such by love;
20 Call her one, me another fly,
We're tapers too, and at our own cost die,[9]
  And we in us find th' eagle and the dove.[1]
    The phoenix[2] riddle hath more wit°   *sense*
    By us: we two being one, are it.
25 So, to one neutral thing both sexes fit.
  We die and rise the same, and prove
  Mysterious by this love.

We can die by it, if not live by love,
  And if unfit for tombs and hearse
30 Our legend be, it will be fit for verse;
    And if no piece of chronicle we prove,
    We'll build in sonnets pretty rooms;
    As well a well-wrought urn becomes
The greatest ashes, as half-acre tombs;
35 And by these hymns, all shall approve
  Us canonized for love:

And thus invoke us: You whom reverend love
  Made one another's hermitage;
You, to whom love was peace, that now is rage;
40 Who did the whole world's soul contract, and drove
    Into the glasses of your eyes
    (So made such mirrors, and such spies,
That they did all to you epitomize)
  Countries, towns, courts: Beg from above
45 A pattern of your love!

1633

Song

Sweetest love, I do not go
  For weariness of thee,
Nor in hope the world can show
  A fitter love for me;
5   But since that I
Must die at last, 'tis best
To use myself in jest,
  Thus by feigned deaths to die.

Yesternight the sun went hence,
10 And yet is here today;
He hath no desire nor sense,
  Nor half so short a way:

8. Weekly list of plague victims.
9. Death was a popular metaphor for sexual intercourse in the 17th century. "At our own cost" reflects the common superstition that each act of lovemaking shortened one's life by a day.

1. Common symbols of strength and peace.
2. A legendary bird, the only one of its kind, represented as living five hundred years in the Arabian desert, being consumed in fire, then rising anew from its own ashes.

Then fear not me,
But believe that I shall make
15 Speedier journeys, since I take
More wings and spurs than he.

O how feeble is man's power,
That if good fortune fall,
Cannot add another hour,
20 Nor a lost hour recall!
But come bad chance,
And we join to'it[3] our strength,
And we teach it art and length,
Itself o'er us to'advance.

25 When thou sigh'st, thou sigh'st not wind,
But sigh'st my soul away;
When thou weep'st, unkindly kind,
My life's blood doth decay.
It cannot be
30 That thou lov'st me, as thou say'st,
If in thine my life thou waste;
Thou art the best of me.

Let not thy divining heart
Forethink me any ill;
35 Destiny may take thy part
And may thy fears fulfill;
But think that we
Are but turned aside to sleep;
They who one another keep
40 Alive, ne'er parted be.

1633

Air and Angels

Twice or thrice had I loved thee,
Before I knew thy face or name;
So in a voice, so in a shapeless flame,
Angels affect us oft, and worshiped be;
5 Still when, to where thou wert, I came,
Some lovely glorious nothing I did see.
But since my soul, whose child love is,
Takes limbs of flesh, and else could nothing do,
More subtle than the parent is
10 Love must not be, but take a body too;
And therefore what thou wert, and who,
I bid love ask, and now
That it assume thy body I allow,
And fix itself in thy lip, eye, and brow.

15 Whilst thus to ballast love I thought,
And so more steadily to have gone,

3. Donne frequently uses an apostrophe be-
tween words to indicate that the neighboring
syllables are fused in pronunciation and
counted as one metrically. Such contractions
occur only under certain phonetic conditions
(e.g., when one word ends, and the next be-
gins, with a vowel). They continue to be
common in modern speech, although in writ-
ing we now limit use of the apostrophe to
those contractions which omit letters from the
usual spelling of the words (*you're, don't*).

With wares which would sink admiration,
   I saw I had love's pinnace° overfraught;   *a light ship*
      Every thy hair[3] for love to work upon
20 Is much too much, some fitter must be sought;
      For, nor in nothing, nor in things
Extreme and scatt'ring bright, can love inhere.
      Then as an angel, face and wings
Of air, not pure as it, yet pure doth wear,
25   So thy love may be my love's sphere.[4]
         Just such disparity
As is 'twixt air and angels' purity,
'Twixt women's love and men's will ever be.

                                                    1633

The Anniversary

      All kings, and all their favorites,
      All glory'of honors, beauties, wits,
The sun itself, which makes times, as they pass,
Is elder by a year, now, than it was
5 When thou and I first one another saw:
All other things to their destruction draw,
      Only our love hath no decay;
This, no tomorrow hath, nor yesterday;
Running it never runs from us away,
10 But truly keeps his first, last, everlasting day.

      Two graves must hide thine and my corse;
If one might, death were no divorce:
Alas, as well as other princes, we
   (Who prince enough in one another be)
15 Must leave at last in death, these eyes, and ears,
Oft fed with true oaths, and with sweet salt tears;
      But souls where nothing dwells but love
(All other thoughts being inmates°) then shall prove°   *lodgers / experience*
This, or a love increaséd there above,
20 When bodies to their graves, souls from their graves remove.

      And then we shall be throughly° blest,   *thoroughly*
      But we no more than all the rest;
Here upon earth, we're kings, and none but we
Can be such kings, nor of such subjects be;
25 Who is so safe as we, where none can do
Treason to us, except one of us two?
      True and false fears let us refrain,
Let us love nobly,'and live, and add again
Years and years unto years, till we attain
30 To write threescore, this is the second of our reign.

                                                    1633

Love's Growth

I scarce believe my love to be so pure
      As I had thought it was,
      Because it doth endure

---

3. I.e., every hair of thine.
4. I.e., embodiment. An angel or "intelligence" was thought to inhabit each of the nine celestial spheres of Ptolemaic astronomy.

Vicissitude, and season, as the grass;
5   Methinks I lied all winter, when I swore
My love was infinite, if spring make' it more.

But if this medicine, love, which cures all sorrow
With more, not only be no quíntessence,[1]
But mixed of all stuffs paining soul or sense,
10   And of the sun his working vigor borrow,
Love's not so pure, and abstract, as they use
To say, which have no mistress but their muse,
But as all else, being elemented [2] too,
Love sometimes would contémplate, sometimes do.

15   And yet no greater, but more eminent,
Love by the spring is grown;
As, in the firmament,
Stars by the sun are not enlarged, but shown,
Gentle love deeds, as blossoms on a bough,
20   From love's awakened root do bud out now.

If, as in water stirred more circles be
Produced by one, love such additions take,
Those, like so many spheres, but one heaven make,
For they are all concentric unto thee;[3]
25   And though each spring do add to love new heat,
As princes do in times of action get
New taxes, and remit them not in peace,
No winter shall abate the spring's increase.

                                                    1633

A Valediction: Of Weeping

Let me pour forth
My tears before thy face whilst I stay here,
For thy face coins them, and thy stamp they bear,
And by this mintage they are something worth,
5   For thus they be
Pregnant of thee;
Fruits of much grief they are, emblems of more;
When a tear falls, that Thou falls which it bore,
So thou and I are nothing then, when on a diverse shore.

10   On a round ball
A workman that hath copies by, can lay
An Europe, Afric, and an Asïa,
And quickly make that, which was nothing, all,
So doth each tear
15   Which thee doth wear,[5]
A globe, yea world, by that impression grow,
Till thy tears mixed with mine do overflow
This world; by waters sent from thee, my heaven dissolvéd so.

O more than moon,
20   Draw not up seas to drown me in thy sphere;

1. In alchemy, the perfectly pure substance of which the heavenly bodies were supposedly made.
2. Made up of various elements.
3. Astronomy up to Donne's time conceived of nine concentric spheres, each of transparent crystal, turning around the earth. The various heavenly bodies were thought to be fixed in the surfaces of these spheres.
5. I.e., doth wear thee.

Weep me not dead, in thine arms, but forbear
To teach the sea what it may do too soon.
      Let not the wind
      Example find
25 To do me more harm than it purposeth;
Since thou and I sigh one another's breath,
Whoe'er sighs most is cruelest, and hastes the other's death.

                                                  1633

Love's Alchemy

Some that have deeper digged love's mine than I,
Say where his centric happiness doth lie;
    I've loved, and got, and told,
But should I love, get, tell, till I were old,
5 I should not find that hidden mystery;
      O, 'tis imposture all:
And as no chemic yet th' elixir[6] got,
    But glorifies his pregnant pot,
    If by the way to him befall
10 Some odoriferous thing, or médicinal;
    So lovers dream a rich and long delight,
    But get a winter-seeming summer's night.

Our ease, our thrift, our honor, and our day,
Shall we for this vain bubble's shadow pay?
15   Ends love in this, that my man°   *servant*
Can be as happy'as I can if he can
Endure the short scorn of a bridegroom's play?
    That loving wretch that swears,
'Tis not the bodies marry, but the minds,
20   Which he in her angelic finds,
    Would swear as justly that he hears,
In that day's rude hoarse minstrelsy, the spheres.[7]
    Hope not for mind in women; at their best
Sweetness and wit they're but mummy,[8] possessed.

                                                1633

A Nocturnal upon St. Lucy's Day, Being the Shortest Day[9]

'Tis the year's midnight, and it is the day's,
Lucy's, who scarce seven hours herself unmasks;
    The sun is spent, and now his flasks[1]
Send forth light squibs, no constant rays;
5   The world's whole sap is sunk;
The general balm th' hydroptic° earth hath drunk,   *thirsty*
Whither, as to the bed's-feet, life is shrunk,
Dead and interred; yet all these seem to laugh,
Compared with me, who am their epitaph.

---

6. A hypothetical substance, the goal of the alchemists' endeavors, supposedly capable of transmuting base metals into gold, curing all illnesses, and prolonging life indefinitely.
7. I.e., the music of the spheres, concentric transparent shells containing the heavenly bodies in Ptolemaic astronomy; they were thought to produce angelic music as they turned.

8. Lifeless flesh; also, a medication prepared from mummified remains.
9. In Donne's time the winter solstice or shortest day of the year fell on December 12, the eve of St. Lucy's Day.
1. I.e., powder flasks. The "squibs" of the next line are small fireworks that spurt and fizzle as they burn.

10 Study me then, you who shall lovers be
    At the next world, that is, at the next spring:
        For I am every dead thing,
        In whom love wrought new alchemy.
            For his art did express°   *squeeze out*
15 A quintessence² even from nothingness,
    From dull privations, and lean emptiness;
    He ruined me, and I am re-begot
    Of absence, darkness, death; things which are not.

    All others, from all things, draw all that's good,
20 Life, soul, form, spirit, whence they being have;
        I, by love's limbeck,° am the grave   *retort*
    Of all that's nothing. Oft a flood
        Have we two wept, and so
    Drowned the whole world, us two; oft did we grow
25 To be two chaoses, when we did show
    Care to aught else; and often absences
    Withdrew our souls, and made us carcasses.

    But I am by her death (which word wrongs her)
    Of the first nothing the elixir³ grown;
30   Were I a man, that I were one
        I needs must know; I should prefer,
            If I were any beast,
    Some ends, some means; yea plants, yea stones detest,
    And love; all, all some properties invest;
35 If I an ordinary nothing were,
    As shadow,'a light and body must be here.

    But I am none; nor will my Sun renew.
    You lovers, for whose sake the lesser sun
        At this time to the Goat⁴ is run
40   To fetch new lust, and give it you,
            Enjoy your summer all;
    Since she enjoys her long night's festival,
    Let me prepare towards her, and let me call
    This hour her Vigil, and her Eve, since this
45 Both the year's, and the day's deep midnight is.

                                                              1633

A Valediction: Forbidding Mourning

    As virtuous men pass mildly'away,
        And whisper to their souls to go,
    Whilst some of their sad friends do say
        The breath goes now, and some say, No;

5   So let us melt, and make no noise,
        No tear-floods, nor sigh-tempests move,
    'Twere profanation of our joys
        To tell the laity our love.

---

2. A highly concentrated essence or extract.
3. I.e., the quintessence of the nothing that preceded creation of the world.

4. The sun is in the constellation of Capricorn ("the Goat") during the month of December. Goats were proverbial for their lustfulness.

10
Moving of th' earth brings harms and fears,
      Men reckon what it did and meant;
But trepidation of the spheres,[5]
      Though greater far, is innocent.

Dull sublunary[6] lovers' love
      (Whose soul is sense) cannot admit
15
Absence, because it doth remove
      Those things which elemented it.

But we by'a love so much refined
      That our selves know not what it is,
Inter-assuréd of the mind,
20
      Care less, eyes, lips, and hands to miss.

Our two souls therefore, which are one,
      Though I must go, endure not yet
A breach, but an expansion,
      Like gold to airy thinness beat.

25
If they be two, they are two so
      As stiff twin compasses are two;
Thy soul, the fixed foot, makes no show
      To move, but doth, if th' other do.

And though it in the center sit,
30
      Yet when the other far doth roam,
It leans and hearkens after it,
      And grows erect, as that comes home.

Such wilt thou be to me, who must
      Like th' other foot, obliquely run;
35
Thy firmness makes my circle[7] just,
      And makes me end where I begun.

1633

The Ecstasy[8]

Where, like a pillow on a bed,
      A pregnant bank swelled up to rest
The violet's reclining head,
      Sat we two, one another's best.
5
Our hands were firmly cémented
      With a fast balm, which thence did spring.
Our eye-beams twisted, and did thread
      Our eyes upon one double string;
So to'intergraft our hands, as yet
10
      Was all the means to make us one;
And pictures in our eyes to get°   *beget*
      Was all our propagation.
As 'twixt two equal armies, Fate
      Suspends uncertain victory,

5. A trembling of the celestial spheres, hypothesized by Ptolemaic astronomers to account for unpredicted variations in the paths of the heavenly bodies.
6. Beneath the moon; earthly—hence, changeable.
7. The circle was a symbol of perfection; with a dot in the middle, it was also the alchemist's symbol for gold.
8. Literally, "a standing out." The term was used by religious mystics to describe the experience in which the soul seemed to leave the body and rise superior to it in a state of heightened awareness.

15 Our souls (which to advance their state,
    Were gone out) hung 'twixt her and me.
And whilst our souls negotiate there,
    We like sepulchral statues lay;
All day the same our postures were,
20   And we said nothing all the day.
If any, so by love refined
    That he soul's language understood,
And by good love were grown all mind,
    Within convenient distance stood,
25 He (though he knew not which soul spake,
    Because both meant, both spake the same)
Might thence a new concoction[9] take,
    And part far purer than he came.
This ecstasy doth unperplex,
30   We said, and tell us what we love;
We see by this it was not sex;
    We see we saw not what did move;
But as all several° souls contain   *separate*
    Mixture of things, they know not what,
35 Love these mixed souls doth mix again,
    And makes both one, each this and that.
A single violet transplant,
    The strength, the colour, and the size
    (All which before was poor, and scant)
40   Redoubles still, and multiplies.
When love, with one another so
    Interinanimates two souls,
That abler soul, which thence doth flow,
    Defects of loneliness controls.
45 We then, who are this new soul, know,
    Of what we are composed, and made,
For, th' atomies° of which we grow,   *atoms*
    Are souls, whom no change can invade.
But O alas, so long, so far
50   Our bodies why do we forbear?
They're ours, though they're not we; we are
    Th' intelligences, they the spheres.[1]
We owe them thanks because they thus,
    Did us to us at first convey,
55 Yielded their forces, sense, to us,
    Nor are dross to us, but allay.°   *alloy*
On man heaven's influence works not so
    But that it first imprints the air,[2]
So soul into the soul may flow,
60   Though it to body first repair.
As our blood labors to beget
    Spirits as like souls as it can,[3]
Because such fingers need to knit
    That subtle knot which makes us man:
65 So must pure lovers' souls descend
    To' affections, and to faculties

---

9. Mixture of diverse elements refined by heat (alchemical term).
1. The nine orders of angels ("intelligences") were believed to govern the nine spheres of Ptolemaic astronomy.
2. Influences from the heavenly bodies were conceived of as being transmitted through the medium of the air; also, angels were thought to assume bodies of air in their dealings with men.
3. "Spirits" were vapors believed to permeate the blood and to mediate between the body and the soul.

Which sense may reach and apprehend;
    Else a great Prince in prison lies.
To'our bodies turn we then, that so
70   Weak men on love revealed may look;
Love's mysteries in souls do grow,
    But yet the body is his book.
And if some lover, such as we,
    Have heard this dialogue of one,
75 Let him still mark us; he shall see
    Small change when we're to bodies gone.

1633

The Funeral

Whoever comes to shroud me, do not harm
    Nor question much
That subtle wreath of hair which crowns my arm;
The mystery, the sign you must not touch,
5   For 'tis my outward soul,
Viceroy to that, which then to heaven being gone,
    Will leave this to control,
And keep these limbs, her provinces, from dissolution.

For if the sinewy thread my brain lets fall
10   Through every part
Can tie those parts and make me one of all;
These hairs, which upward grew, and strength and art
    Have from a better brain,
Can better do'it; except she meant that I
15   By this should know my pain,
As prisoners then are manacled, when they're condemned to die.

Whate'er she meant by 'it, bury it with me,
    For since I am
Love's martyr, it might breed idolatry,
20 If into other's hands these relics came;
    As 'twas humility
To'afford to it all that a soul can do,
    So 'tis some bravery,
That since you would save none of me, I bury some of you.

1633

The Relic

When my grave is broke up again
Some second guest to entertain[4]
    (For graves have learned that woman-head°   *womanhood*
    To be to more than one a bed),
5   And he that digs it, spies
A bracelet of bright hair about the bone,
    Will he not let'us alone,
And think that there a loving couple lies,
Who thought that this device might be some way
10 To make their souls, at the last busy day,[5]
Meet at this grave, and make a little stay?

---

4. Re-use of a grave, after an interval of years, was a common 17th-century practice. 5. Judgment Day, when all parts of the body would be reassembled and reunited with the soul in the resurrection.

If this fall in a time, or land,
　Where mis-devotion doth command,
　Then he that digs us up, will bring
15　Us to the Bishop and the King,
　　To make us relics; then
Thou shalt be'a Mary Magdalen,[6] and I
　A something else thereby;
All women shall adore us, and some men;
20 And since at such time, miracles are sought,
I would have that age by this paper taught
What miracles we harmless lovers wrought.

　First, we loved well and faithfully,
　Yet knew not what we loved, nor why,
25　Difference of sex no more we knew,
　　Than our guardian angels do;
　　　Coming and going, we
Perchance might kiss, but not between those meals;
　Our hands ne'er touched the seals,
Which nature, injured by late law, sets free:
30 These miracles we did; but now, alas,
All measure and all language I should pass,
Should I tell what a miracle she was.

1633

Elegy IX. The Autumnal[7]

No spring, nor summer beauty hath such grace,
　As I have seen in one autumnal face.
Young beauties force our love, and that's a rape,
　This doth but counsel, yet you cannot 'scape.
5 If 'twere a shame to love, here 'twere no shame,
　Affection here takes reverence's name.
Were her first years the Golden Age?[8] That's true,
　But now she's gold oft tried, and ever new.
That was her torrid and inflaming time,
10　This is her tolerable tropic clime.
Fair eyes, who asks more heat than comes from hence,
　He in a fever wishes pestilence.
Call not these wrinkles, graves;° if graves they were,   *engraved lines*
　They were Love's graves; for else he is no where.
15 Yet lies not Love dead here, but here doth sit
　Vowed to this trench, like an anachorit.°   *anchorite, religious recluse*
And here, till hers, which must be his death, come,
　He doth not dig a grave, but build a tomb.
Here dwells he, though he sojourn ev'rywhere,
20　In progress,[9] yet his standing house° is here.   *permanent residence*
Here, where still evening is; not noon, nor night;
　Where no voluptuousness, yet all delight.
In all her words, unto all hearers fit,
　You may at revels, you at council, sit.
25 This is love's timber, youth his underwood;

6. The woman out of whom Christ had cast seven devils (Luke viii.2), traditionally identified with the repentant prostitute of Luke vii.37–50.
7. The term *elegy*, referring to an expression of sorrow in couplet verse, had become detached from its usual subject matter even in classical times. In the 17th century it was used loosely to describe a poem in couplets on almost any subject.
8. The first and best age of the world, when mankind lived in innocence and happiness.
9. An official journey in stages undertaken by a king or other dignitary.

There he, as wine in June, enrages blood,
Which then comes seasonabliest, when our taste
   And appetite to other things is past.
Xerxes' strange Lydian love, the platane tree,[1]
30   Was loved for age, none being so large as she,
Or else because, being young, nature did bless
   Her youth with age's glory, barrenness.
If we love things long sought, age is a thing
   Which we are fifty years in compassing;
35 If transitory things, which soon decay,
   Age must be loveliest at the latest day.
But name not winter-faces, whose skin's slack,
   Lank, as an unthrift's purse, but a soul's sack;
Whose eyes seek light within, for all here's shade;
40   Whose mouths are holes, rather worn out, than made;
Whose every tooth to'a several place is gone,
   To vex their souls at Resurrection;[2]
Name not these living death's-heads unto me,
   For these not ancient, but antique be.
45 I hate extremes; yet I had rather stay
   With tombs than cradles, to wear out a day.
Since such love's natural lation° is, may still   *motion*
   My love descend and journey down the hill,
Not panting after growing beauties, so,
50   I shall ebb on with them who homeward go.

                                       1633

Elegy XIX. To His Mistress Going to Bed

Come, madam, come, all rest my powers defy,
Until I labor, I in labor lie.
The foe oft-times having the foe in sight,
Is tired with standing though he never fight.
5 Off with that girdle, like heaven's zone glistering,
But a far fairer world encompassing.
Unpin that spangled breastplate which you wear,
That th' eyes of busy fools may be stopped there.
Unlace yourself, for that harmonious chime
10 Tells me from you that now it is bed time.
Off with that happy busk,° which I envy,   *corset*
That still can be, and still can stand so nigh.
Your gown, going off, such beauteous state reveals,
As when from flowry meads th' hill's shadow steals.
15 Off with that wiry coronet and show
The hairy diadem which on you doth grow:
Now off with those shoes, and then safely tread
In this love's hallowed temple, this soft bed.
In such white robes, heaven's angels used to be
20 Received by men; thou, Angel, bring'st with thee
A heaven like Mahomet's Paradise; and though
Ill spirits walk in white, we easily know
By this these angels from an evil sprite:
Those set our hairs, but these our flesh upright.
25   License my roving hands, and let them go
Before, behind, between, above, below.

1. The Persian king Xerxes had a platane, or plane, tree decorated with gold.
2. On Judgment Day all parts of the bodies of the dead were to be reassembled and reunited with their souls in resurrection.

O my America! my new-found-land,
My kingdom, safeliest when with one man manned,
My mine of precious stones, my empery,°   *empire*
30 How blest am I in this discovering thee!
To enter in these bonds is to be free;
Then where my hand is set, my seal shall be.
     Full nakedness! All joys are due to thee,
As souls unbodied, bodies unclothed must be
35 To taste whole joys. Gems which you women use
Are like Atlanta's balls,[3] cast in men's views,
That when a fool's eye lighteth on a gem,
His earthly soul may covet theirs, not them.
Like pictures, or like books' gay coverings made
40 For lay-men, are all women thus arrayed;
Themselves are mystic books, which only we
(Whom their imputed grace will dignify)
Must see revealed. Then, since that I may know,
As liberally as to a midwife, show
45 Thyself: cast all, yea, this white linen hence,
There is no penance due to innocence.
     To teach thee, I am naked first; why than,°   *then*
What needst thou have more covering than a man?

                                                 1669

Satire III. Religion

Kind pity chokes my spleen; brave scorn forbids
Those tears to issue which swell my eyelids;
I must not laugh, nor weep sins, and be wise,
Can railing then cure these worn maladies?
5 Is not our mistress, fair Religion,
As worthy'of all our souls' devotion,
As virtue was to the first blinded age?[4]
Are not heaven's joys as valiant to assuage
Lusts, as earth's honor was to them? Alas,
10 As we do them in means, shall they surpass
Us in the end, and shall thy father's spirit
Meet blind philosophers in heaven, whose merit
Of strict life may be'imputed faith, and hear
Thee, whom he taught so easy ways and near
15 To follow, damned? O, if thou dar'st, fear this;
This fear great courage and high valor is.
Dar'st thou aid mutinous Dutch,[5] and dar'st thou lay
Thee in ships, wooden sepulchers, a prey
To leaders' rage, to storms, to shot, to dearth?
20 Dar'st thou dive seas and dungeons of the earth?
Hast thou courageous fire to thaw the ice
Of frozen North discoveries? and thrice
Colder than salamanders,[6] like divine
Children in the oven, fires of Spain, and the line,°   *equator*
25 Whose countries limbecks° to our bodies be,   *retorts*

---

3. Atalanta agreed to marry Hippomenes if he could defeat her in a foot race. As she was about to overtake him, he cast in her path three golden apples given to him by Venus. Distracted by their beauty, Atalanta stopped to retrieve them, and Hippomenes won the race.
4. I.e., before the Christian revelation.

5. In 1582 the English had aided the Dutch in their revolt against rule by Spain.
6. Salamanders were thought to be able to endure fire. The "divine children" were Shadrach, Meshach, and Abednego, who survived the fiery furnace unharmed (Daniel iii.20–30). "Fires of Spain" refers to the Inquisition, in which heretics were burned at the stake.

Canst thou for gain bear? And must every he
Which cries not, "Goddess!" to thy mistress, draw,
Or eat thy poisonous words? Courage of straw!
O desperate coward, wilt thou seem bold, and
30   To thy foes and his (who made thee to stand
Sentinel in his world's garrison) thus yield,
And for forbidden wars, leave th' appointed field?
Know thy foes: The foul Devil he'is, whom thou
Strivest to please: for hate, not love, would allow
35   Thee fain his whole realm to be quit;[7] and as
The world's all parts wither away and pass,
So the world's self, thy other loved foe, is
In her decrepit wane, and thou, loving this,
Dost love a withered and worn strumpet; last,
40   Flesh (itself's death) and joys which flesh can taste,
Thou lovest; and thy fair goodly soul, which doth
Give this flesh power to taste joy, thou dost loathe.
Seek true religion. O, where? Mirreus,
Thinking her unhoused here, and fled from us,
45   Seeks her at Rome; there, because he doth know
That she was there a thousand years ago.
He loves her rags so, as we here obey
The statecloth where the Prince sat yesterday.
Crantz to such brave loves will not be enthralled,
50   But loves her only, who'at Geneva'[8] is called
Religion—plain, simple, sullen, young,
Contemptuous, yet unhandsome; as among
Lecherous humors,° there is one that judges   *dispositions*
No wenches wholesome but coarse country drudges.
55   Graius stays still at home here, and because
Some preachers, vile ambitious bawds, and laws
Still new, like fashions, bid him think that she
Which dwells with us, is only perfect, he
Embraceth her whom his Godfathers will
60   Tender to him, being tender, as wards still
Take such wives as their guardians offer, or
Pay values.° Careless Phrygius doth abhor   *fines*
All, because all cannot be good, as one
Knowing some women whores, dares marry none.
65   Graccus loves all as one, and thinks that so
As women do in divers countries go
In divers habits, yet are still one kind,
'So doth, so is religion; and this blind-
ness too much light breeds; but unmovéd thou
70   Of force must one, and forced but one allow;
And the right, ask thy father which is she,
Let him ask his; though truth and falsehood be
Near twins, yet truth a little elder is;
Be busy to seek her, believe me this,
75   He's not of none, nor worst, that seeks the best.
To'adore, or scorn an image, or protest,
May all be bad; doubt wisely; in strange way
To stand inquiring right, is not to stray;
To sleep, or run wrong, is. On a huge hill,
80   Craggéd and steep, Truth stands, and he that will
Reach her, about must, and about must go,

---

7. To have concluded a bargain.   8. The center of Calvinism.

And what th' hill's suddenness resists, win so;
Yet strive so, that before age, death's twilight,
Thy soul rest, for none can work in that night.
85 To will implies delay, therefore now do.
Hard deeds, the body's pains; hard knowledge too
The mind's endeavors reach, and mysteries
Are like the sun, dazzling, yet plain to'all eyes.
Keep th' truth which thou hast found; men do not stand
90 In so ill case that God hath with his hand
Signed kings' blank charters[9] to kill whom they hate,
Nor are they vicars, but hangmen to fate.
Fool and wretch, wilt thou let thy soul be tied
To man's laws, by which she shall not be tried
95 At the last day? O, will it then boot° thee   *profit*
To say a Philip, or a Gregory,
A Harry, or a Martin[1] taught thee this?
Is not this excuse for mere contraries
Equally strong? Cannot both sides say so?
100 That thou mayest rightly'obey power, her bounds know;
Those passed, her nature'and name is changed; to be
Then humble to her is idolatry.
As streams are, power is; those blest flowers that dwell
At the rough stream's calm head, thrive and do well,
105 But having left their roots, and themselves given
To the stream's tyrannous rage, alas, are driven
Through mills, and rocks, and woods, and at last, almost
Consumed in going, in the sea are lost.
So perish souls, which more choose men's unjust
110 Power from God claimed, than God himself to trust.

                                              1633

Good Friday, 1613. Riding Westward

Let man's soul be a sphere, and then, in this,
Th' intelligence that moves,[2] devotion is,
And as the other spheres, by being grown
Subject to foreign motions, lose their own,
5 And being by others hurried every day,
Scarce in a year their natural form obey;
Pleasure or business, so, our souls admit
For their first mover, and are whirled by it.
Hence is 't, that I am carried towards the West
10 This day, when my soul's form bends towards the East.
There I should see a Sun, by rising, set,
And by that setting endless day beget:
But that Christ on this cross did rise and fall,
Sin had eternally benighted all.
15 Yet dare I'almost be glad I do not see
That spectacle, of too much weight for me.
Who sees God's face, that is self-life, must die;
What a death were it then to see God die?
It made his own lieutenant, Nature, shrink;

9. *Carte blanche,* i.e., unconditional authority.
1. Philip II of Spain, Pope Gregory XIII, Henry VIII of England, and Martin Luther.
2. An angel was believed to govern the movements of each of the nine celestial spheres in Ptolemaic astronomy. Each sphere, in addition to its own motion, was influenced by the motions of those outside it ("foreign motions," line 4), the outermost being known as the *primum mobile,* "first mover" (line 8).

20   It made his footstool crack, and the sun wink.[3]
     Could I behold those hands which span the poles,
     And tune all spheres at once, pierced with those holes?
     Could I behold that endless height which is
     Zenith to us, and to'our antipodes,[4]
25   Humbled below us? Or that blood which is
     The seat of all our souls, if not of His,
     Make dirt of dust, or that flesh which was worn
     By God, for his apparel, ragg'd and torn?
     If on these things I durst not look, durst I
30   Upon his miserable mother cast mine eye,
     Who was God's partner here, and furnished thus
     Half of that sacrifice which ransomed us?
     Though these things, as I ride, be from mine eye,
     They're present yet unto my memory,
35   For that looks towards them; and Thou look'st towards me,
     O Saviour, as Thou hang'st upon the tree.
     I turn my back to Thee but to receive
     Corrections, till Thy mercies bid Thee leave.
     O think me worth Thine anger; punish me;
40   Burn off my rusts and my deformity;
     Restore Thine image so much, by Thy grace,
     That Thou may'st know me, and I'll turn my face.

1633

From Holy Sonnets

1

   Thou hast made me, and shall Thy work decay?
   Repair me now, for now mine end doth haste;
   I run to death, and death meets me as fast,
   And all my pleasures are like yesterday.
5 I dare not move my dim eyes any way,
   Despair behind, and death before doth cast
   Such terror, and my feeble flesh doth waste
   By sin in it, which it towards hell doth weigh.
   Only Thou art above, and when towards Thee
10 By Thy leave I can look, I rise again;
   But our old subtle foe so tempteth me
   That not one hour myself I can sustain.
   Thy grace may wing me to prevent his art,
   And Thou like adamant° draw mine iron heart.   *loadstone*

1635

5

   I am a little world made cunningly
   Of elements, and an angelic sprite;
   But black sin hath betrayed to endless night
   My world's both parts, and O, both parts must die.
5 You which beyond that heaven which was most high
   Have found new spheres, and of new lands can write,[5]
   Pour new seas in mine eyes, that so I might

---

3. "Thus saith the Lord * * * the earth is my footstool" (Isaiah lxvi.1). An earthquake and an eclipse accompanied the crucifixion of Jesus (Matthew xxvii.45, 51).
4. The zenith is that part of the heavens directly above any point on earth; the antipodes are that part of the earth diametrically oppo-

site such a point.
5. Copernican astronomy (which placed the sun at the center of our system and not the earth, as in Ptolemaic astronomy) had enlarged men's ideas about the extent of the universe, just as recent terrestrial exploration had changed their idea of the world.

Drown my world with my weeping earnestly,
Or wash it if it must be drowned no more.[6]
10 But O, it must be burnt! Alas, the fire
Of lust and envy'have burnt it heretofore,
And made it fouler; let their flames retire,
And burn me, O Lord, with a fiery zeal
Of Thee'and Thy house, which doth in eating heal.[7]

1635

7

At the round earth's imagined corners, blow
Your trumpets, angels;[8] and arise, arise
From death, you numberless infinities
Of souls, and to your scattered bodies go;
5 All whom the flood did, and fire shall,[9] o'erthrow,
All whom war, dearth, age, agues, tyrannies,
Despair, law, chance hath slain, and you whose eyes
Shall behold God, and never taste death's woe.[1]
But let them sleep, Lord, and me mourn a space;
10 For, if above all these, my sins abound,
'Tis late to ask abundance of Thy grace
When we are there. Here on this lowly ground,
Teach me how to repent; for that's as good
As if Thou'hadst sealed my pardon with Thy blood.

1633

8

If faithful souls be alike glorified
As angels, then my father's soul doth see,
And adds this even to full felicity,
That valiantly I hell's wide mouth o'erstride.
5 But if our minds to these souls be descried
By circumstances, and by signs that be
Apparent in us, not immediately,
How shall my mind's white truth by them be tried?
They see idolatrous lovers weep and mourn,
10 And vile blasphemous conjurers to call
On Jesus' name, and Pharisaical
Dissemblers feign devotion. Then turn,
O pensive soul, to God, for He knows best
Thy grief, for He put it into my breast.

1635

9

If poisonous minerals, and if that tree
Whose fruit threw death on else immortal us,
If lecherous goats, if serpents envious
Cannot be damned, alas, why should I be?
5 Why should intent or reason, born in me,
Make sins, else equal, in me more heinous?
And mercy being easy and glorious
To God, in his stern wrath why threatens he?
But who am I, that dare dispute with thee,
10 O God? Oh! of thine only worthy blood,

---

6. God promised Noah that he would never
again cover the earth with a flood (Genesis
ix.11).
7. "* * * the zeal of thine house hath eaten
me up" (Psalms lxix.9).
8. "* * * I saw four angels standing on the
four corners of the earth, holding the four
winds of the earth * * *" (Revelation vii.1).

9. At the end of the world, "* * * the ele-
ments shall melt with fervent heat, the earth
also and the works that are therein shall be
burned up" (II Peter iii.10).
1. "But I tell you of a truth, there be some
standing here, which shall not taste of death,
till they see the kingdom of God" (Christ's
words to his disciples, Luke ix.27).

And my tears, make a heavenly Lethean[2] flood,
And drown in it my sins' black memory.
That thou remember them, some claim as debt;
I think it mercy if thou wilt forget.

1633

10

Death, be not proud, though some have callèd thee
Mighty and dreadful, for thou are not so;
For those whom thou think'st thou dost overthrow
Die not, poor Death, nor yet canst thou kill me.
5   From rest and sleep, which but thy pictures be,
Much pleasure; then from thee much more must flow,
And soonest our best men with thee do go,
Rest of their bones, and soul's delivery.
Thou'art slave to fate, chance, kings, and desperate men,
10   And dost with poison, war, and sickness dwell,
And poppy'or charms can make us sleep as well
And better than thy stroke; why swell'st thou then?
One short sleep past, we wake eternally
And death shall be no more; Death, thou shalt die.

1633

14

Batter my heart, three-personed God; for You
As yet but knock, breathe, shine, and seek to mend;
That I may rise and stand, o'erthrow me,'and bend
Your force to break, blow, burn, and make me new.
5   I, like an usurped town, to'another due,
Labor to'admit You, but O, to no end;
Reason, Your viceroy'in me, me should defend,
But is captíved, and proves weak or untrue.
Yet dearly'I love You,'and would be lovèd fain,
10   But am betrothed unto Your enemy.
Divorce me,'untie or break that knot again;
Take me to You, imprison me, for I,
Except You'enthrall me, never shall be free,
Nor ever chaste, except You ravish me.

1633.

18

Show me, dear Christ, Thy spouse[3] so bright and clear.
What! is it she which on the other shore
Goes richly painted? or which, robbed and tore,
Laments and mourns in Germany and here?
5   Sleeps she a thousand, then peeps up one year?
Is she self-truth, and errs? now new, now'outwore?
Doth she,'and did she, and shall she evermore
On one, on seven, or on no hill[4] appear?
Dwells she with us, or like adventuring knights
10   First travel[5] we to seek, and then make love?
Betray,° kind husband, Thy spouse to our sights,   *reveal*
And let mine amorous soul court Thy mild dove,
Who is most true and pleasing to Thee then
When she's embraced and open to most men.

after 1615

---

2. Lethe was a river in the classical under-
world; drinking of its waters caused one to
forget the past.
3. The true church, "the bride of Christ."
Lines 2–4 ask if it is the Roman Catholic or
the Protestant church.

4. Probably Mt. Moriah (site of Solomon's
temple), the seven hills of Rome, and Geneva
or Canterbury (centers of Calvinism and An-
glicanism, respectively).
5. Formerly, "labor" as well as "journey."

Hymn to God My God, in My Sickness

Since I am coming to that holy room
  Where, with Thy choir of saints for evermore,
I shall be made Thy music; as I come
  I tune the instrument here at the door,
5 And what I must do then, think here before.

Whilst my physicians by their love are grown
  Cosmographers, and I their map, who lie
Flat on this bed, that by them may be shown
  That this is my southwest discovery[7]
10 *Per fretum febris,* by these straits to die,

I joy, that in these straits, I see my West;[8]
  For, though their currents yield return to none,
What shall my West hurt me? As West and East
  In all flat maps (and I am one) are one,
15 So death doth touch the resurrection.

Is the Pacific Sea my home? Or are
  The Eastern riches? Is Jerusalem?
Anyan,° and Mágellan, and Gíbraltar,   *Bering Straits*
  All straits, and none but straits, are ways to them,
20 Whether where Japhet dwelt, or Cham, or Shem.[9]

We think that Paradise and Calvary,
  Christ's cross, and Adam's tree, stood in one place;
Look, Lord, and find both Adams met in me;
  As the first Adam's sweat surrounds my face,
25 May the last Adam's blood my soul embrace.

So, in his purple wrapped, receive me, Lord;
  By these his thorns give me his other crown;
And, as to others' souls I preached Thy word,
  Be this my text, my sermon to mine own:
30 Therefore that he may raise the Lord throws down.[10]

                             1635

BEN JONSON
(1573–1637)

To the Reader

Pray thee, take care, that tak'st my book in hand,
To read it well: that is, to understand.

                             1616

7. Magellan had discovered the straits which bear his name in 1520. They lie at the southern tip of South America and are hence southwest from England. *"Per fretum febris"*: through the straits of fever.
8. "* * * strait is the gate, and narrow is the way, which leadeth unto life * * *" (Matthew vii.14). "West": i.e., death.
9. The three sons of Noah, who settled in Europe, Africa, and Asia respectively after the Flood.
10. Adapted from Psalms cxlvi.8: "* * * the Lord raiseth them that are bowed down."

To Doctor Empirick

When men a dangerous disease did 'scape
Of old, they gave a cock to Aesculape;[1]
Let me give two, that doubly am got free
From my disease's danger, and from thee.

1616

On My First Daughter

Here lies, to each her parents' ruth,°   *sorrow*
Mary, the daughter of their youth;
Yet all heaven's gifts being heaven's due,
It makes the father less to rue.
5 At six months' end she parted hence
With safety of her innocence;
Whose soul heaven's queen, whose name she bears,
In comfort of her mother's tears,
Hath placed amongst her virgin-train:
10 Where, while that severed doth remain,
This grave partakes the fleshly birth;
Which cover lightly, gentle earth!

1616

On My First Son

Farewell, thou child of my right hand,[2] and joy;
My sin was too much hope of thee, loved boy:
Seven years thou'wert lent to me, and I thee pay,
Exacted by thy fate, on the just day.[3]
5 O could I lose all father now! for why
Will man lament the state he should envý,
To have so soon 'scaped world's and flesh's rage,
And, if no other misery, yet age?
Rest in soft peace, and asked, say, "Here doth lie
10 Ben Jonson his best piece of poetry."
For whose sake henceforth all his vows be such
As what he loves may never like too much.

1616

On Spies

Spies, you are lights in state, but of base stuff,
Who, when you've burnt yourselves down to the snuff,°   *candle end*
Stink and are thrown away. End fair enough.

1616

To Fool or Knave

Thy praise or dispraise is to me alike:
One doth not stroke me, nor the other strike.

1616

1. Aesculapius, the Roman god of medicine and healing.
2. A literal translation of the Hebrew *Ben-*
jamin, the boy's name.
3. Jonson's son died on his seventh birthday in 1603.

To Fine Lady Would-Be

Fine Madam Would-Be, wherefore should you fear,
That love to make so well, a child to bear?
The world reputes you barren; but I know
Your 'pothecary, and his drug says no.
Is it the pain affrights? That's soon forgot.
Or your complexion's loss? You have a pot
That can restore that. Will it hurt your feature?
To make amends, you're thought a wholesome creature.
What should the cause be? Oh, you live at court,
And there's both loss of time and loss of sport
In a great belly. Write, then, on thy womb,
Of the not born, yet buried, here's the tomb.

1616

To Sir Henry Cary

That neither fame nor love might wanting be
To greatness, Cary, I sing that and thee;
Whose house, if it no other honor had,
In only thee might be both great and glad;
Who, to upbraid the sloth of this our time,
Durst valor make almost, but not, a crime;
Which deed I know not, whether were more high,
Or thou more happy, it to justify
Against thy fortune: when no foe, that day,
Could conquer thee but chance, who did betray.
Love thy great loss, which a renown hath won,
To live when Broick not stands, nor Ruhr doth run.[4]
Love honors, which of best example be
When they cost dearest and are done most free;
Though every fortitude deserves applause,
It may be much or little in the cause.
He's valiant'st that dares fight, and not for pay;
That virtuous is, when the reward's away.

1616

On Playwright

Playwright, convict° of public wrongs to men,   *convicted*
Takes private beatings and begins again.
Two kinds of valor he doth show at once:
Active in 's brain, and passive in his bones.

1616

To Elizabeth, Countess of Rutland

That poets are far rarer births than kings
Your noblest father[5] proved; like whom before,
Or then, or since, about our Muses springs,
Came not that soul exhausted so their store.
Hence was it that the destinies decreed
(Save that most masculine issue of his brain)

---

4. "The castle and river near where he was   5. Sir Philip Sidney.
taken" [Jonson's note].

No male unto him; who could so exceed
Nature, they thought, in all that he would fain.
At which she, happily displeased, made you,
10 On whom, if he were living now to look,
He should those rare and absolute numbers° view,   *verses*
As he would burn or better far his book.

1616

To Sir Henry Goodyear

Goodyear, I'm glad and grateful to report
Myself a witness of thy few days' sport,
Where I both learned why wise men hawking follow,
And why that bird was sacred to Apollo.
5 She doth instruct men by her gallant flight
That they to knowledge so should tower⁶ upright,
And never stoop but to strike ignorance;
Which, if they miss, they yet should re-advance
To former height, and there in circle tarry,
10 Till they be sure to make the fool their quarry.
Now, in whose pleasures I have this discerned,
What would his serious actions me have learned?°   *taught*

1616

On English Monsieur

Would you believe, when you this mónsieur⁷ see,
That his whole body should speak French, not he?
That so much scarf of France, and hat, and feather,
And shoe, and tie, and garter should come hether,°   *hither*
5 And land on one whose face durst never be
Toward the sea farther than Half-Way Tree?⁸
That he, untraveled, should be French so much
As Frenchmen in his company should seem Dutch?
Or had his father, when he did him get,
10 The French disease,⁹ with which he labors yet?
Or hung some mónsieur's picture on the wall,
By which his dam conceived him, clothes and all?
Or is it some French statue? No: 'T doth move,
And stoop, and cringe. O then, it needs must prove
15 The new French tailor's motion,° monthly made,   *puppet*
Daily to turn in Paul's,¹ and help the trade.

1616

To John Donne

Who shall doubt, Donne, where° I a poet be,   *whether*
When I dare send my epigrams to thee?
That so alone canst judge, so'alone dost make;
And, in thy censures, evenly dost take
5 As free simplicity to disavow
As thou hast best authority t' allow.

6. To fly high before diving ("stooping") on
the prey (a falconry term).
7. Stress on first syllable; often spelled *monser*
in Jonson's time, suggesting an Anglicized
pronunciation.
8. Perhaps a landmark between London and
Dover, where a traveler would embark for
France.
9. I.e., syphilis.
1. St. Paul's Cathedral in London. In the 17th
century St. Paul's was a popular gathering
place; merchants hired men to walk up and
down in the yard advertising their wares.

Read all I send, and if I find but one
Marked by thy hand, and with the better stone,[2]
My title's sealed. Those that for claps° do write,   *applause*
Let pui'nies',[3] porters', players' praise delight,
And, till they burst, their backs like asses load:
A man should seek great glory, and not broad.

Inviting a Friend to Supper

Tonight, grave sir, both my poor house, and I
Do equally desire your company;
Not that we think us worthy such a guest,
But that your worth will dignify our feast
5   With those that come, whose grace may make that seem
Something, which else could hope for no esteem.
It is the fair acceptance, sir, creates
The entertainment perfect, not the cates.°   *food*
Yet shall you have, to rectify your palate,
10   An olive, capers, or some better salad
Ushering the mutton; with a short-legged hen,
If we can get her, full of eggs, and then
Lemons, and wine for sauce; to these a cony°   *rabbit*
Is not to be despaired, for our money;
15   And, though fowl now be scarce, yet there are clerks,
The sky not falling, think we may have larks.[4]
I'll tell you of more, and lie, so you will come:
Of partridge, pheasant, woodcock, of which some
May yet be there, and godwit,[5] if we can;
20   Knot, rail, and ruff too. Howsoe'er, my man
Shall read a piece of Virgil, Tacitus,
Livy, or of some better book to us,
Of which we'll speak our minds, amidst our meat;
And I'll profess no verses to repeat.
25   To this, if aught appear which I not know of,
That will the pastry, not my paper, show of.
Digestive[6] cheese and fruit there sure will be;
But that which most doth take my Muse and me,
Is a pure cup of rich Canary wine,
30   Which is the Mermaid's[7] now, but shall be mine;
Of which had Horace, or Anacreon tasted,
Their lives, as do their lines, till now had lasted.
Tobacco,[8] nectar, or the Thespian spring,
Are all but Luther's beer[9] to this I sing.
35   Of this we will sup free, but moderately,
And we will have no Pooley, or Parrot[1] by,
Nor shall our cups make any guilty men;
But, at our parting we will be as when
We innocently met. No simple word

2. The allusion may be to the Thracian custom of recording the good or evil fortunes of each day by placing a stone counter of corresponding color in an urn. Jonson refers elsewhere to Pliny's description of this custom in his *Natural History*, VII, 40.
3. Puisnies (pronounced like *punies*), insignificant persons.
4. According to an old proverb, "When the sky falls we shall have larks."
5. The godwit, knot, rail, and ruff are all wading birds related to the curlew or sandpiper. They were formerly regarded as delicacies.
6. Promoting or aiding digestion.
7. A famous tavern—a favorite haunt of Jonson's.
8. Smoking was often called "drinking tobacco."
9. German beer, considered inferior.
1. Notorious government informers.

40 That shall be uttered at our mirthful board,
Shall make us sad next morning or affright
The liberty that we'll enjoy tonight.

1616

On Gut

Gut eats all day and lechers all the night;
So all his meat he tasteth over twice;
And, striving so to double his delight,
He makes himself a thoroughfare of vice.
5 Thus in his belly can he change a sin:
Lust it comes out, that gluttony went in.

1616

Epitaph on Salomon Pavy, a Child of Queen Elizabeth's Chapel[2]

Weep with me, all you that read
This little story,
And know, for whom a tear you shed,
Death's self is sorry.
5 'Twas a child, that so did thrive
In grace and feature,
As Heaven and Nature seemed to strive
Which owned the creature.
Years he numbered scarce thirteen
10   When Fates turned cruel,
Yet three filled zodiacs[3] had he been
The stage's jewel,
And did act, what now we moan,
Old men so duly,
15 As, sooth, the Parcae[4] thought him one,
He played so truly.
So, by error, to his fate
They all consented;
But viewing him since (alas, too late)
20   They have repented.
And have sought, to give new birth,
In baths to steep him;[5]
But, being so much too good for earth,
Heaven vows to keep him.

1616

Epitaph on Elizabeth, L. H.

Woudst thou hear what man can say
In a little? Reader, stay.
Underneath this stone doth lie
As much beauty as could die;
5 Which in life did harbor give
To more virtue than doth live.
If at all she had a fault,

2. The Children of Queen Elizabeth's Chapel
were a company of boy actors. Salomon Pavy
had acted in Jonson's plays.
3. I.e., three years.
4. The three Fates, who determined men's

destinies.
5. Aeson, the father of Jason, was made
young again by a magic bath prepared by
Jason's wife Medea.

Leave it buried in this vault.
One name was Elizabeth;
Th' other, let it sleep with death:
Fitter, where it died, to tell,
Than that it lived at all. Farewell.

1616

To Penshurst[6]

Thou art not, Penshurst, built to envious show,
Of touch° or marble; nor canst boast a row   touchstone, basanite
Of polished pillars, or a roof of gold;
Thou hast no lantern,[7] whereof tales are told,
5 Or stair, or courts; but stand'st an ancient pile,
And, these grudged at, art reverenced the while.
Thou joy'st in better marks, of soil, of air,
Of wood, of water; therein thou art fair.
Thou hast thy walks for health, as well as sport;
10 Thy mount, to which the dryads° do resort,   wood nymphs
Where Pan and Bacchus their high feasts have made,
Beneath the broad beech and the chestnut shade;
That taller tree, which of a nut was set
At his great birth[8] where all the Muses met.
15 There in the writhéd bark are cut the names
Of many a sylvan,° taken with his flames;   forest dweller
And thence the ruddy satyrs oft provoke
The lighter fauns to reach thy Lady's Oak.
Thy copse too, named of Gamage,[9] thou hast there,
20 That never fails to serve thee seasoned deer
When thou wouldst feast or exercise thy friends.
The lower land, that to the river bends,
Thy sheep, thy bullocks, kine, and calves do feed;
The middle grounds thy mares and horses breed.
25 Each bank doth yield thee conies;° and the tops,   rabbits
Fertile of wood, Ashore and Sidney's copse,
To crown thy open table, doth provide
The purpled pheasant with the speckled side;
The painted partridge lies in every field,
30 And for thy mess is willing to be killed.
And if the high-swollen Medway[1] fail thy dish,
Thou hast thy ponds, that pay thee tribute fish,
Fat aged carps that run into thy net,
And pikes, now weary their own kind to eat,
35 As loath the second draught or cast to stay,°   await
Officiously° at first themselves betray;   dutifully
Bright eels that emulate them, and leap on land
Before the fisher, or into his hand.
Then hath thy orchard fruit, thy garden flowers,
40 Fresh as the air, and new as are the hours.
The early cherry, with the later plum,
Fig, grape, and quince, each in his time doth come;
The blushing apricot and woolly peach
Hang on thy walls, that every child may reach.

6. The country estate of the Sidney family, in
Kent.
7. A glassed or open structure raised above
the roof of a house.
8. Sir Philip Sidney's, November 30, 1554.

9. Barbara Gamage, wife of Sir Robert Sid-
ney, Philip's younger brother and the current
owner of Penshurst.
1. The local river.

45 And though thy walls be of the country stone,
   They're reared with no man's ruin, no man's groan;
   There's none that dwell about them wish them down;
   But all come in, the farmer and the clown,°   *countryman*
   And no one empty-handed, to salute
50 Thy lord and lady, though they have no suit.
   Some bring a capon, some a rural cake,
   Some nuts, some apples; some that think they make
   The better cheeses bring them, or else send
   By their ripe daughters, whom they would commend
55 This way to husbands, and whose baskets bear
   An emblem of themselves in plum or pear.
   But what can this (more than express their love)
   Add to thy free provisions, far above
   The need of such? whose liberal board doth flow
60 With all that hospitality doth know;
   Where comes no guest but is allowed to eat,
   Without his fear, and of thy lord's own meat;
   Where the same beer and bread, and selfsame wine,
   That is his lordship's shall be also mine,
65 And I not fain° to sit (as some this day   *obliged*
   At great men's tables), and yet dine away.
   Here no man tells° my cups; nor, standing by,   *counts*
   A waiter doth my gluttony envý,
   But gives me what I call, and lets me eat;
70 He knows below he shall find plenty of meat.
   Thy tables hoard not up for the next day;
   Nor, when I take my lodging, need I pray
   For fire, or lights, or livery;° all is there,   *provisions*
   As if thou then wert mine, or I reigned here:
75 There's nothing I can wish, for which I stay.
   That found King James when, hunting late this way
   With his brave son, the prince, they saw thy fires
   Shine bright on every hearth, as the desires
   Of thy Penates[2] had been set on flame
80 To entertain them; or the country came
   With all their zeal to warm their welcome here.
   What (great I will not say, but) sudden cheer
   Didst thou then make 'em! and what praise was heaped
   On thy good lady then, who therein reaped
85 The just reward of her high housewifery;
   To have her linen, plate, and all things nigh,
   When she was far; and not a room but dressed
   As if it had expected such a guest!
   These, Penshurst, are thy praise, and yet not all.
90 Thy lady's noble, friutful, chaste withal.
   His children thy great lord may call his own,
   A fortune in this age but rarely known.
   They are, and have been, taught religion; thence
   Their gentler spirits have sucked innocence.
95 Each morn and even they are taught to pray,
   With the whole household, and may, every day,
   Read in their virtuous parents' noble parts
   The mysteries of manners, arms, and arts.
   Now, Penshurst, they that will proportion° thee   *compare*

2. Roman household gods.

00 With other edifices, when they see
    Those proud, ambitious heaps, and nothing else,
    May say their lords have built, but thy lord dwells.

1616

Song: To Celia

    Drink to me only with thine eyes,
    And I will pledge with mine;
    Or leave a kiss but in the cup,
    And I'll not look for wine.
5   The thirst that from the soul doth rise,
    Doth ask a drink divine:
    But might I of Jove's nectar sup,
    I would not change for thine.

    I sent thee late a rosy wreath,
10 Not so much honoring thee,
    As giving it a hope, that there
    It could not withered be.
    But thou thereon did'st only breathe,
    And sent'st it back to me;
15 Since when it grows and smells, I swear,
    Not of itself, but thee.

1616

A Hymn to God the Father

    Hear me, O God!
    A broken heart,
    Is my best part;
    Use still thy rod,
5   That I may prove°   *experience*
    Therein thy love.

    If thou hadst not
    Been stern to me,
    But left me free,
10 I had forgot
    Myself and thee.

    For sin's so sweet,
    As minds ill bent
    Rarely repent,
15 Until they meet
    Their punishment.

    Who more can crave
    Than thou hast done,
    That gav'st a Son,
20 To free a slave?
    First made of naught,
    With all since bought.

    Sin, Death, and Hell,
    His glorious Name
25 Quite overcame,
    Yet I rebel,
    And slight the same.

But I'll come in
Before my loss
30   Me farther toss,
As sure to win
Under his Cross.

1640

The Triumph of Charis

See the chariot at hand here of Love,
    Wherein my lady rideth!
Each that draws is a swan or a dove,
    And well the care Love guideth.
5   As she goes, all hearts do duty
        Unto her beauty;
And, enamored, do wish, so they might
        But enjoy such a sight,
That they still were to run by her side,
10   Through[3] swords, through seas, whither she would ride.

    Do but look on her eyes; they do light
        All that Love's world compriseth!
    Do but look on her hair; it is bright
        As Love's star when it riseth!
15   Do but mark, her forehead's smoother
        Than words that soothe her!
And from her arched brows, such a grace
        Sheds itself through the face,
As alone there triumphs to the life
20   All the gain, all the good, of the elements' strife.
    Have you seen but a bright lily grow,
        Before rude hands have touched it?
    Ha' you marked but the fall o' the snow
        Before the soil hath smutched it?
25   Ha' you felt the wool o' the beaver?
        Or swan's down ever?
    Or have smelt o' the bud o' the brier?
        Or the nard[4] in the fire?
    Or have tasted the bag o' the bee?
30   O so white, O so soft, O so sweet is she!

1640

Song

Oh, do not wanton with those eyes,
    Lest I be sick with seeing;
Nor cast them down, but let them rise,
    Lest shame destroy their being.
5   Oh be not angry with those fires,
    For then their threats will kill me;
Nor look too kind on my desires,
    For then my hopes will spill° me.
Oh do not steep them in thy tears,

destroy

---

3. Here pronounced as two syllables (often spelled *thorough*).
4. Spikenard, an aromatic plant.

10 For so will sorrow slay me;
Nor spread them as distract with fears,
Mine own enough betray me.

1640

An Elegy

Though beauty be the mark of praise,
   And yours of whom I sing be such
   As not the world can praise too much,
Yet is 't your virtue now I raise.

5 A virtue, like allay,° so gone   *alloy*
   Throughout your form as, though that move
   And draw and conquer all men's love,
This súbjects you to love of one.

   Wherein you triumph yet; because
10   'Tis of yourself, and that you use
   The noblest freedom, not to choose
Against or faith or honor's laws.

But who should less expect from you,
   In whom alone Love lives again?
15   By whom he is restored to men,
And kept, and bred, and brought up true.
His falling temples you have reared,
   The withered garlands ta'en away;
   His altars kept from the decay
20 That envy wished, and nature feared;

And on them burn so chaste a flame,
   With so much loyalties' expense,
   As Love, t' acquit such excellence,
Is gone himself into your name.[5]

25 And you are he; the deity
   To whom all lovers are designed
   That would their better objects find;
Among which faithful troop am I.

Who, as an offspring[6] at your shrine,
30   Have sung this hymn, and here entreat
   One spark of your diviner heat
To light upon a love of mine.

Which, if it kindle not, but scant
   Appear, and that to shortest view,
35   Yet give me leave t' adore in you
What I in her am grieved to want.

1640

An Ode to Himself

Where dost thou careless lie
   Buried in ease and sloth?

5. I.e., the lady's name includes the letters of   6. Possibly a misprint for *offering.*
love.

Knowledge that sleeps doth die;
And this security,°   *overconfidence*
5   It is the common moth
That eats on wits and arts, and oft destroys them both.

Are all th' Aonian springs
    Dried up?[7] Lies Thespia waste?
Doth Clarius' harp[8] want strings,
10   That not a nymph now sings;
    Or droop they as disgraced,
To see their seats and bowers by chattering pies[9] defaced?

If hence thy silence be,
    As 'tis too just a cause,
15   Let this thought quicken thee:
    Minds that are great and free
        Should not on fortune pause;
'Tis crown enough to virtue still, her own applause.

What though the greedy fry
20   Be taken with false baits
Of worded balladry,
    And think it poesy?
        They die with their conceits,
And only piteous scorn upon their folly waits.
25   Then take in hand thy lyre,
        Strike in thy proper strain,
    With Japhet's line,[1] aspire
    Sol's chariot for new fire
        To give the world again;
30 Who aided him will thee, the issue of Jove's brain.[2]

And since our dainty age
    Cannot endure reproof,
Make not thyself a page
To that strumpet the stage,
35   But sing high and aloof,
Safe from the wolve's black jaw, and the dull ass's hoof.

1640

To the Immortal Memory and Friendship of That Noble Pair, Sir Lucius Cary and Sir Henry Morrison

The Turn[8]

Brave infant of Saguntum,[9] clear
Thy coming forth in that great year,
When the prodigious Hannibal did crown

His rage with razing your immortal town.
5   Thou, looking then about,
Ere thou wert half got out,
Wise child, didst hastily return,
And mad'st thy mother's womb thine urn.
How summed a circle didst thou leave mankind
10   Of deepest lore, could we the center find!

The Counterturn

Did wiser Nature draw thee back
From out the horror of that sack,
Where shame, faith, honor, and regard of right
Lay trampled on; the deeds of death and night
15   Urged, hurried forth, and hurled
Upon th' affrighted world;
Sword, fire, and famine, with fell fury met,
And all on utmost ruin set,
As, could they but life's miseries foresee,
20   No doubt all infants would return like thee?

The Stand

For what is life, if measured by the space,
Not by the act?
Or maskéd man, if valued by his face
Above his fact?
25   Here's one outlived his peers
And told forth fourscore years;
He vexéd time and busied the whole state,
Troubled both foes and friends;
But ever to no ends:
30   What did this stirrer but die late?
How well at twenty had he fall'n or stood!
For three of his fourscore he did no good.

The Turn

He entered well, by virtuous parts,
Got up and thrived with honest arts;
35   He purchased friends, and fame, and honors then,
And had his noble name advanced with men;
But weary of that flight
He stooped in all men's sight
To sordid flatteries, acts of strife,
40   And sunk in that dead sea of life
So deep, as he did then death's waters sup,
But that the cork of title buoyed him up.

The Counterturn

Alas, but Morrison fell young;
He never fell, thou fall'st, my tongue.
45   He stood, a soldier to the last right end,
A perfect patriot, and a noble friend,
But most a virtuous son.
All offices were done
By him so ample, full, and round,
50   In weight, in measure, number, sound,
As, though his age imperfect° might appear,
His life was of humanity the sphere.

incomplete

The Stand

Go now, and tell out days summed up with fears,
    And make them years;
55 Produce thy mass of miseries on the stage
    To swell thine age;
Repeat of things a throng,
To show thou hast been long,
Not lived; for life doth her great actions spell
60 By what was done and wrought
    In season, and so brought
To light: her measures are, how well
Each syllabe° answered, and was formed how fair;   **syllable**
These make the lines of life, and that's her air.

The Turn

65 It is not growing like a tree
    In bulk doth make man better be;
Or standing long an oak, three hundred year,
To fall a log at last, dry, bald, and sere:
A lily of a day
70 Is fairer far in May;
Although it fall and die that night,
It was the plant and flower of light.
In small proportions we just beauties see,
And in short measures life may perfect be.

The Counterturn

75 Call, noble Lucius, then for wine,
    And let thy looks with gladness shine;
Accept this garland, plant it on thy head,
And think, nay know, thy Morrison's not dead.
He leaped the present age,
80 Possessed with holy rage,
To see that bright eternal day;
Of which we priests and poets say
Such truths as we expect for happy men,
And there he lives with memory, and Ben

The Stand

85 Jonson! who sung this of him, ere he went
    Himself to rest,
Or taste a part of that full joy he meant
To have expressed
In this bright asterism;°   **constellation**
90 Where it were friendship's schism
(Were not his Lucius long with us to tarry)
To separate these twi-
Lights, the Dioscuri,[1]
And keep the one half from his Harry.
95 But fate doth so altérnate the design,
Whilst that in heaven, this light on earth must shine.

---

1. Castor and Pollux, twin sons of Zeus, famous for brotherly devotion. When Castor was killed, Zeus granted Pollux' prayer that he be allowed to share his life with his brother; henceforward each lived half the time on earth and half in heaven. Their constellation is Gemini, the Twins.

The Turn

And shine as you exalted are,
Two names of friendship, but one star:
Of hearts the union. And those not by chance
Made, or indenture, or leased out t'advance

The profits for a time.
No pleasures vain did chime
Of rimes, or riots, at your feasts,
Orgies of drink, or feigned protests,°   protestations
But simple love of greatness and of good;
That knits brave minds and manners more than blood.

The Counterturn

This made you first to know the why
You liked, then after to apply
That liking, and approach so one the tother,°   other
Till either grew a portion of the other:

Each styled by his end
The copy of his friend.
You lived to be the great surnames
And titles by which all made claims
Unto the virtue. Nothing perfect done,
But as a Cary, or a Morrison.

The Stand

And such a force the fair example had,
As they that saw
The good, and durst not practice it, were glad
That such a law

Was left yet to mankind;
Where they might read and find
Friendship, indeed, was written, not in words;
And with the heart, not pen,
Of two so early men,
Whose lines her rolls were, and recórds,
Who, ere the first down blooméd on the chin,
Had sowed these fruits, and got the harvest in.

1640

Fragmentum Petronius Arbiter,[2] Translated

Doing a filthy pleasure is and short;
And done we straight repent us of the sport:
Let us not then rush blindly on unto it,
Like lustful beasts, that only know to do it,

For lust will languish and that heat decay;
But thus, thus, keeping endless holiday,
Let us together closely lie and kiss;
There is no labor, nor no shame in this.
This hath pleased, doth please, and long will please; never
Can this decay, but is beginning ever.

1640

---

2. A Roman author of the first century A.D. and companion to the emperor Nero, who be- stowed on him the title "Arbiter of Elegance."

Slow, Slow, Fresh Fount[3]

Slow, slow, fresh fount, keep time with my salt tears;
Yet slower, yet, O faintly, gentle springs!
List to the heavy part the music bears,
Woe weeps out her division,[4] when she sings.
     Droop herbs and flowers;
     Fall grief in showers;
Our beauties are not ours. O, I could still,
Like melting snow upon some craggy hill,
     Drop, drop, drop, drop,
Since nature's pride is now a withered daffodil.

                                  1600

Queen and Huntress[5]

Queen and huntress, chaste and fair,
Now the sun is laid to sleep,
Seated in thy silver chair,
State in wonted manner keep;
Hesperus entreats thy light,
Goddess excellently bright.

Earth, let not thy envious shade
Dare itself to interpose;
Cynthia's shining orb was made
Heaven to clear, when day did close.
Bless us then with wishèd sight,
Goddess excellently bright.

Lay thy bow of pearl apart,
And thy crystal-shining quiver;
Give unto the flying hart
Space to breathe, how short soever.
Thou that mak'st a day of night,
Goddess excellently bright.

                                  1600

Come, My Celia[6]

Come, my Celia, let us prove,°   *experience*
While we can, the sports of love;
Time will not be ours forever;
He at length our good will sever.
Spend not then his gifts in vain.
Suns that set may rise again;
But if once we lose this light,
'Tis with us perpetual night.
Why should we defer our joys?

3. From *Cynthia's Revels,* sung by Echo for Narcissus, who fell in love with his own reflection and was changed into the flower that bears his name. The daffodil (line 11) is a species of narcissus.
4. Part in a song.
5. From *Cynthia's Revels,* sung by Hesperus to Cynthia (Diana, goddess of the moon and of the hunt).
6. From *Volpone.* The lecherous Volpone is attempting to seduce Celia, the virtuous wife of Corvino, whom Volpone has gotten out of the way by a stratagem (line 14).

o   Fame and rumor are but toys.
    Cannot we delude the eyes
    Of a few poor household spies,
    Or his easier ears beguile,
    So removéd by our wile?
5   'Tis no sin love's fruit to steal;
    But the sweet thefts to reveal,
    To be taken, to be seen,
    These have crimes accounted been.

                                          1606

Still to Be Neat[7]

Still to be neat, still to be dressed,
As you were going to a feast;
Still to be powdered, still perfumed;
Lady, it is to be presumed,
5 Though art's hid causes are not found,
All is not sweet, all is not sound.

Give me a look, give me a face
That makes simplicity a grace;
Robes loosely flowing, hair as free;
10 Such sweet neglect more taketh me
Then all th' adulteries of art.
They strike mine eyes, but not my heart.

                                          1609

Gypsy Songs[8]

1

The faery beam upon you,
The stars to glister on you;
    A moon of light
    In the noon of night,
5 Till the fire-drake[9] hath o'ergone you!
The wheel of fortune guide you,
The boy with the bow[1] beside you;
    Run ay in the way
    Till the bird of day,
10 And the luckier lot betide you!

2

To the old, long life and treasure!
To the young, all health and pleasure!
    To the fair, their face
    With eternal grace
5 And the soul to be loved at leisure!
To the witty, all clear mirrors;
To the foolish, their dark errors;
    To the loving sprite,
    A secure delight;
10 To the jealous, his own false terrors!

                                          1621

7. From *The Silent Woman.*
8. From *The Gypsies Metamorphosed.*
9. "Firedragon," a term for the will-o'-the-

wisp or *ignis fatuus*, a nocturnal light caused by the combustion of marsh gas.
1. I.e., Cupid.

Though I Am Young and Cannot Tell[2]

Though I am young, and cannot tell
  Either what Death or Love is well,
Yet I have heard they both bear darts,
And both do aim at human hearts.
5 And then again, I have been told
  Love wounds with heat, as Death with cold;
So that I fear they do but bring
  Extremes to touch, and mean one thing.

As in a ruin we it call
10 One thing to be blown up, or fall;
Or to our end like way may have
  By a flash of lightning, or a wave;
So Love's inflaméd shaft or brand
  May kill as soon as Death's cold hand;
15 Except Love's fires the virtue have
  To fright the frost out of the grave.

1641

To the Memory of My Beloved, the Author
Mr. William Shakespeare

AND WHAT HE HATH LEFT US[3]

To draw no envy, Shakespeare, on thy name,
Am I thus ample to thy book and fame,
While I confess thy writings to be such
As neither man nor Muse can praise too much.
5 'Tis true, and all men's suffrage.° But these ways   *consent*
Were not the paths I meant unto thy praise:
For silliest ignorance on these may light,
Which, when it sounds at best, but echoes right;
Or blind affection,° which doth ne'er advance   *feeling*
10 The truth, but gropes, and urgeth all by chance;
Or crafty malice might pretend this praise,
And think to ruin where it seemed to raise.
These are as some infamous bawd or whore
Should praise a matron. What could hurt her more?
15 But thou art proof against them, and, indeed,
Above th' ill fortune of them, or the need.
I therefore will begin. Soul of the age!
The applause! delight! the wonder of our stage!
My Shakespeare, rise; I will not lodge thee by
20 Chaucer or Spenser, or bid Beaumont lie
A little further to make thee a room:[4]
Thou art a monument without a tomb,
And art alive still while thy book doth live,
And we have wits to read and praise to give.
25 That I not mix thee so, my brain excuses,
I mean with great, but disproportioned° Muses;   *not comparable*
For, if I thought my judgment were of years,
I should commit thee surely with thy peers,

---

2. From *The Sad Shepherd.*
3. Prefixed to the first folio edition of Shakespeare's works, 1623.
4. Chaucer, Spenser, and Beaumont are all buried in Westminster Abbey.

And tell how far thou didst our Lyly outshine,
30 Or sporting Kyd, or Marlowe's mighty line.[5]
And though thou hadst small Latin and less Greek,
From thence to honor thee I would not seek
For names, but call forth thund'ring Aeschylus,
Euripides, and Sophocles to us,
35 Pacuvius, Accius, him of Cordova dead,[6]
To life again, to hear thy buskin[7] tread
And shake a stage; or, when thy socks were on,
Leave thee alone for the comparison
Of all that insolent Greece or haughty Rome
40 Sent forth, or since did from their ashes come.
Triumph, my Britain; thou hast one to show
To whom all scenes° of Europe homage owe.   *stages*
He was not of an age, but for all time!
And all the Muses still were in their prime
45 When like Apollo he came forth to warm
Our ears, or like a Mercury to charm.
Nature herself was proud of his designs,
And joyed to wear the dressing of his lines,
Which were so richly spun, and woven so fit,
50 As, since, she will vouchsafe no other wit:
The merry Greek, tart Aristophanes,
Neat Terence, witty Plautus[8] now not please,
But antiquated and deserted lie,
As they were not of Nature's family.
55 Yet must I not give Nature all; thy Art,
My gentle Shakespeare, must enjoy a part.
For though the poet's matter Nature be,
His Art doth give the fashion; and that he
Who casts to write a living line must sweat
60 (Such as thine are) and strike the second heat
Upon the muses' anvil; turn the same,
And himself with it, that he thinks to frame,
Or for the laurel he may gain a scorn;
For a good poet's made as well as born.
65 And such wert thou! Look how the father's face
Lives in his issue, even so the race
Of Shakespeare's mind and manners brightly shines
In his well-turnéd and true-filéd lines,
In each of which he seems to shake a lance,
70 As brandished at the eyes of ignorance.
Sweet swan of Avon, what a sight it were
To see thee in our waters yet appear,
And make those flights upon the banks of Thames
That so did take Eliza and our James![9]
75 But stay; I see thee in the hemisphere
Advanced and made a constellation there!
Shine forth, thou star of poets, and with rage
Or influence[10] chide or cheer the drooping stage,
Which, since thy flight from hence, hath mourned like night,
80 And despairs day, but for thy volume's light.

1623

5. John Lyly, Thomas Kyd, and Christopher Marlowe, all Elizabethan dramatists.
6. Marcus Pacuvius and Lucius Accius were Roman tragedians of the second century B.C.; "him of Cordova" is the Roman tragedian Seneca of the first century A.D.
7. The high-heeled boot worn by Greek tragic actors; the "sock" or light shoe was worn in comedies.
8. Aristophanes (Greek) and Terence and Plautus (Roman) were comic writers of the fourth to second centuries B.C.
9. Queen Elizabeth and King James.
10. A supposed emanation of power from stars.

EDMUND BOLTON
(ca. 1575–ca. 1633)

A Palinode [1]

As withereth the primrose by the river,
As fadeth summer's sun from gliding fountains,
As vanisheth the light-blown bubble ever,
As melteth snow upon the mossy mountains:
5 So melts, so vanisheth, so fades, so withers
The rose, the shine, the bubble, and the snow,
Of praise, pomp, glory, joy, which short life gathers,
Fair praise, vain pomp, sweet glory, brittle joy.
The withered primrose by the mourning river,
10 The faded summer's sun from weeping fountains,
The light-blown bubble, vanishéd for ever,
The molten snow upon the naked mountains,
    Are emblems that the treasures we uplay
    Soon wither, vanish, fade, and melt away.

15 For as the snow, whose lawn did overspread
Th' ambitious hills which giant-like did threat
To pierce the heaven with their aspiring head,
Naked and bare doth leave their craggy seat;
Whenas the bubble, which did empty fly
20 The dalliance of the undiscernéd wind
On whose calm rolling waves it did rely,
Hath shipwreck made where it did dalliance find;
And when the sunshine which dissolved the snow,
Colored the bubble with a pleasant vary,°   *variation*
25 And made the rathe° and timely primrose grow,   *early*
Swarth° clouds withdrawn, which longer time do tarry: *swarthy*
    Oh, what is praise, pomp, glory, joy, but so
    As shine by fountains, bubbles, flowers, or snow?

1600

FRANCIS DAVISON
(ca. 1575–ca. 1619)

My Only Star

    My only star,
Why, why are your dear eyes,
Where all my life's peace lies,
    With me at war?
5 Why, to my ruin tending,
    Do they still lighten woe
    On him that loves you so,
That all his thoughts in you have birth and ending?

    Hope of my heart,
10 Oh, wherefore° do the words,   *why*
    Which your sweet tongue affords,

---

1. Literally, "sing back again." The term originally referred to a repetitive stanza structure in ancient Greek odes, but Bolton has here applied it to a unique form of his own devising.

           No hope impart?
But, cruel without measure,
      To my eternal pain
      Still thunder forth disdain
On him whose life depends upon your pleasure?

           Sunshine of joy,
Why do your gestures, which
All eyes and hearts bewitch,
      My bliss destroy?
And pity's sky o'erclouding,
      Of hate an endless shower
      On that poor heart still pour,
Which in your bosom seeks his only shrouding?

           Balm of my wound,
Why are your lines, whose sight
Should cure me with delight,
      My poison found?
Which through my veins dispersing
      Doth make my heart and mind
      And all my senses find
A living death in torments past rehearsing.°   *telling*

           Alas, my fate
Hath of your eyes deprived me,
Which both killed and revived me
      And sweetened hate;
Your sweet voice and sweet graces,
      Which clothed in lovely weeds°   *garments*
      Your cruel words and deeds,
Are intercepted° by far distant places.   *kept from (me)*

           But O the anguish,
Which presence still pretended,°   *presented*
Absence hath not absented,
      Nor made to languish.
No, no, t'increase my paining,
      The cause being, ah, removed
      For which th'effect I loved,
Th'effect is still in greatest force remaining.

           O cruel tiger,
If to your hard heart's center
Tears, vows, and prayers may enter,
      Desist your rigor;
And let kind lines assure me
      (Since to my deadly wound
      No slave else can be found)
That you that kill me, yet at length will cure me.

                     1602

Upon His Timorous Silence in Her Presence

Are lovers full of fire?
How comes it then my verses are so cold?
    And how, when I am nigh her,

And fit occasion wills me to be bold,
5 The more I burn, the more I do desire,
    The less I dare require?
Ah, love, this is thy wondrous art,
To freeze the tongue, and fire the heart.

1602

JOHN FLETCHER
(1579–1625)

Take, Oh, Take Those Lips Away[1]

Take, oh, take those lips away
That so sweetly were forsworn
And those eyes, like break of day,
Lights that do mislead the morn;
5 But my kisses bring again,
Seals of love, though sealed in vain.

Hide, oh, hide those hills of snow,
Which thy frozen bosom bears,
On whose tops the pinks that grow
10 Are of those that April wears;
But first set my poor heart free,
Bound in those icy chains by thee.

1639

JOHN WEBSTER
(1580–1625)

Call for the Robin Redbreast and the Wren

Call for the robin redbreast and the wren,
Since o'er shady groves they hover,
And with leaves and flowers do cover
The friendless bodies of unburied men.
5 Call unto his funeral dole°   *sorrow*
The ant, the field mouse, and the mole,
To rear him hillocks that shall keep him warm,
And, when gay tombs are robbed, sustain no harm;
But keep the wolf far thence, that's foe to men,
10 For with his nails he'll dig them up again.

1612

Hark, Now Everything Is Still

Hark, now everything is still;
The screech owl and the whistler shrill
Call upon our dame aloud,
And bid her quickly don her shroud.
5 Much you had of land and rent;
Your length in clay's now competent.
A long war disturbed your mind;

1. The first stanza of this song appears as a complete poem in Shakespeare's play *Measure for Measure*. It is likely that Fletcher simply appropriated it.

Here your perfect peace is signed.
Of what is 't fools make such vain keeping?
10 Sin their conception, their birth weeping,
Their life a general mist of error,
Their death a hideous storm of terror.
Strew your hair with powders sweet,
Don clean linen, bathe your feet,
15 And, the foul fiend more to check,
A crucifix let bless your neck.
'Tis now full tide, 'tween night and day,
End your groan and come away.

1623

ROBERT HERRICK
(1591–1674)

The Argument[1] of His Book

I sing of brooks, of blossoms, birds, and bowers,
Of April, May, of June, and July flowers.
I sing of Maypoles, hock carts, wassails, wakes,[2]
Of bridegrooms, brides, and of their bridal cakes.
5 I write of youth, of love, and have access
By these to sing of cleanly wantonness.
I sing of dews, of rains, and, piece by piece,
Of balm, of oil, of spice, and ambergris.
I sing of times trans-shifting, and I write
10 How roses first came red and lilies white.
I write of groves, of twilights, and I sing
The court of Mab[3] and of the fairy king.
I write of hell; I sing (and ever shall)
Of heaven, and hope to have it after all.

1648

To the Sour Reader

If thou dislik'st the piece thou light'st on first,
Think that of all that I have writ the worst;
But if thou read'st my book unto the end,
And still dost this and that verse reprehend,
5 O perverse man! If all disgustful be,
The extreme scab[1] take thee and thine, for me.

1648

To Perilla

Ah, my Perilla! dost thou grieve to see
Me, day by day, to steal away from thee?
Age calls me hence, and my gray hairs bid come
And haste away to mine eternal home;

1. I.e., subject matter.
2. The hock cart brought in the last load of the harvest. "Wakes": parish festivals as well as watches over the dead.
3. Queen of the fairies.
1. The mange. "The extreme scab" is a borrowing from Horace's *Art of Poetry* (416–18), where an unpracticed dabbler in poetry is represented as saying, "*Ego mira poemata pango:/*

Occupet extremum scabies, mihi turpe relinqui/ Et quod non didici sane nescire fateri." In the translation of Herrick's admired master, Ben Jonson, these lines are: "I make/An admirable verse: the great scab take/Him that is last, I scorn to come behind/Or, of the things that ne'er came in my mind,/Once say I'm ignorant. . . ."

5   'Twill not be long, Perilla, after this,
   That I must give thee the supremest° kiss: *last*
   Dead when I am, first cast in salt,[4] and bring
   Part of the cream from that religious spring,
   With which, Perilla, wash my hands and feet;
10 That done, then wind me in that very sheet
   Which wrapped thy smooth limbs, when thou didst implore
   The gods' protection but the night before;
   Follow me weeping to my turf, and there
   Let fall a primrose, and with it a tear;
15 Then lastly, let some weekly strewings be
   Devoted to the memory of me:
   Then shall my ghost not walk about, but keep
   Still in the cool and silent shades of sleep.

                                    1648

The Scare-Fire [1]

Water, water I desire,
Here's a house of flesh on fire;
Ope' the fountains and the springs,
And come all to bucketings.
What ye cannot quench, pull down,
Spoil a house to save a town:
Better 'tis that one should fall,
Than by one to hazard all.

                                    1648

Delight in Disorder

A sweet disorder in the dress
Kindles in clothes a wantonness.
A lawn about the shoulders thrown
Into a fine distractiön;
5   An erring lace, which here and there
Enthralls the crimson stomacher;[5]
A cuff neglectful, and thereby
Ribbons to flow confusedly;
A winning wave, deserving note,
10 In the tempestuous petticoat;
A careless shoestring, in whose tie
I see a wild civility;
Do more bewitch me than when art
Is too precise in every part.

                                    1648

Upon Scobble

Scobble for whoredom whips his wife and cries
He'll slit her nose; but blubbering she replies,
"Good sir, make no more cuts i' th' outward skin,
One slit's enough to let adultery in."

                                    1648

---

4. Salt in classical times was sometimes re-
garded as an emblem of the soul. Here and in
the following lines, as often in his poetry,
Herrick describes rituals that bear some re-
semblance to historical practice but seem to
be largely of his own invention.
1. A sudden conflagration.
5. An ornamental piece worn under the open
(and often laced) front of a bodice.

Corinna's Going A-Maying

Get up! get up for shame! the blooming morn
Upon her wings presents the god unshorn.[6]
   See how Aurora[7] throws her fair
   Fresh-quilted colors through the air:
5   Get up, sweet slug-a-bed, and see
   The dew bespangling herb and tree.
Each flower has wept and bowéd toward the east
Above an hour since, yet you not dressed;
   Nay, not so much as out of bed?
10   When all the birds have matins said,
   And sung their thankful hymns, 'tis sin,
   Nay, profanation to keep in,
Whenas a thousand virgins on this day
Spring, sooner than the lark, to fetch in May.[8]

15 Rise, and put on your foliage, and be seen
To come forth, like the springtime, fresh and green,
   And sweet as Flora.[9] Take no care
   For jewels for your gown or hair;
   Fear not; the leaves will strew
20   Gems in abundance upon you;
Besides, the childhood of the day has kept,
Against[1] you come, some orient pearls unwept;
   Come and receive them while the light
   Hangs on the dew-locks of the night,
25   And Titan[2] on the eastern hill
   Retires himself, or else stands still
Till you come forth. Wash, dress, be brief in praying:
Few beads[3] are best when once we go a-Maying.

Come, my Corinna, come; and, coming mark
30 How each field turns a street, each street a park
   Made green and trimmed with trees; see how
   Devotion gives each house a bough
   Or branch: each porch, each door ere this,
   An ark, a tabernacle is,
35 Made up of whitethorn neatly interwove,
As if here were those cooler shades of love.
   Can such delights be in the street
   And open fields, and we not see 't?
   Come, we'll abroad; and let's obey
40   The proclamation made for May,
And sin no more, as we have done, by staying;
But, my Corinna, come, let's go a-Maying.

There's not a budding boy or girl this day
But is got up and gone to bring in May;
45   A deal of youth, ere this, is come
   Back, and with whitethorn laden home.
   Some have dispatched their cakes and cream
   Before that we have left to dream;

6. I.e., Apollo, god of the sun.
7. Goddess of the dawn.
8. Boughs of white hawthorn, traditionally gathered to decorate streets and houses on May Day.
9. Goddess of flowers.
1. I.e., in readiness for the time when. "Orient": lustrous, glowing.
2. The sun.
3. I.e., prayers.

And some have wept, and wooed, and plighted troth,
50   And chose their priest, ere we can cast off sloth.
 Many a green-gown has been given,
 Many a kiss, both odd and even,
 Many a glance, too, has been sent
 From out the eye, love's firmament;
55   Many a jest told of the keys betraying
This night, and locks picked; yet we're not a-Maying.

Come, let us go while we are in our prime,
And take the harmless folly of the time.
 We shall grow old apace, and die
60   Before we know our liberty.
 Our life is short, and our days run
 As fast away as does the sun;
And, as a vapor or a drop of rain
Once lost, can ne'er be found again;
65   So when or you or I are made
 A fable, song, or fleeting shade,
 All love, all liking, all delight
 Lies drowned with us in endless night.
Then while time serves, and we are but decaying,
70   Come, my Corinna, come, let's go a-Maying.

             1648

To the Virgins, to Make Much of Time

Gather ye rosebuds while ye may,
 Old time is still a-flying;
And this same flower that smiles today
 Tomorrow will be dying.

5   The glorious lamp of heaven, the sun,
 The higher he's a-getting,
The sooner will his race be run,
 And nearer he's to setting.

That age is best which is the first,
10   When youth and blood are warmer;
But being spent, the worse, and worst
 Times still succeed the former.

Then be not coy, but use your time,
 And, while ye may, go marry;
15   For, having lost but once your prime,
 You may forever tarry.

             1648

Upon Julia's Breasts

Display thy breasts, my Julia, there let me
Behold that circummortal [1] purity;
Between whose glories, there my lips I'll lay,
Ravished in that fair *Via Lactea*. [2]

             1648

---

1. A coinage by Herrick, literally "around or encompassing what is mortal"; therefore, per- haps, beyond or more than mortal.
2. Milky Way.

Upon a Child That Died

Here she lies, a pretty bud,
Lately made of flesh and blood,
Who as soon fell fast asleep
As her little eyes did peep.
5 Give her strewings, but not stir
The earth that lightly covers her.

1648

To Daffodils

Fair daffodils, we weep to see
    You haste away so soon:
As yet the early-rising sun
    Has not attained his noon.
5   Stay, stay,
    Until the hasting day
        Has run
    But to the evensong;
And, having prayed together, we
10   Will go with you along.

We have short time to stay as you;
    We have as short a spring;
As quick a growth to meet decay,
    As you or anything.
15   We die,
    As your hours do, and dry
        Away
    Like to the summer's rain;
Or as the pearls of morning's dew,
20   Ne'er to be found again.

1648

Upon Urles

Urles had the gout so, that he could not stand;
Then from his feet it shifted to his hand.
When 'twas in's feet, his charity was small;
Now 'tis in's hand, he gives no alms at all.

1648

His Prayer to Ben Jonson

When I a verse shall make,
    Know I have prayed thee,
For old religion's sake,
    Saint Ben, to aid me.

5 Make the way smooth for me,
    When I, thy Herrick,
Honoring thee, on my knee
    Offer my lyric.

Candles I'll give to thee,
10   And a new altar;
And thou, Saint Ben, shalt be
    Writ in my psalter.

1648

The Night Piece, to Julia

Her eyes the glowworm lend thee;
The shooting stars attend thee;
    And the elves also,
    Whose little eyes glow
5 Like the sparks of fire, befriend thee.

No will-o'-the-wisp[8] mislight thee;
Nor snake or slowworm° bite thee;   *adder*
    But on, on thy way,
    Not making a stay,
10 Since ghost there's none to affright thee.

Let not the dark thee cumber;°   *trouble*
What though the moon does slumber?
    The stars of the night
    Will lend thee their light,
15 Like tapers clear without number.

Then, Julia, let me woo thee,
Thus, thus to come unto me;
    And when I shall meet
    Thy silvery feet,
20 My soul I'll pour into thee.

                                  1648

Upon a Child

Here a pretty baby lies
Sung asleep with lullabies:
Pray be silent, and not stir
Th' easy earth that covers her.

                                  1648

Up Tails All

  Begin with a kiss,
    Go on too with this,
And thus, thus, thus let us smother
    Our lips for a while,
5   But let's not beguile°   *cheat*
Our hope of one for the other.

  This play, be assured,
    Long enough has endured,
Since more and more is exacted;
10   For love he doth call
    For his up tails all,
And that's the part to be acted.

                                  1648

Upon Julia's Clothes

Whenas in silks my Julia goes,
Then, then, methinks, how sweetly flows
That liquefaction of her clothes.

---

8. *Ignis fatuus,* a nocturnal light caused by the combustion of marsh gas.

Next, when I cast mine eyes, and see
5   That brave vibration, each way free,
O, how that glittering taketh me!

         1648

Upon Prue, His Maid

In this little urn is laid
Prudence Baldwin, once my maid,
From whose happy spark here let
Spring the purple violet.

         1648

Upon Ben Jonson

Here lies Jonson with the rest
Of the poets; but the best.
Reader, would'st thou more have known?
Ask his story, not this stone.
5   That will speak what this can't tell
Of his glory. So farewell.

         1648

An Ode for Him

         Ah, Ben!
       Say how or when
       Shall we, thy guests,
    Meet at those lyric feasts
5   Made at the Sun,
   The Dog, the Triple Tun,[2]
  Where we such clusters had
As made us nobly wild, not mad;
   And yet each verse of thine
10   Outdid the meat, outdid the frolic wine.

         My Ben!
       Or come again,
       Or send to us
    Thy wit's great overplus;
15   But teach us yet
   Wisely to husband it,
  Lest we that talent spend,
And having once brought to an end
   That precious stock, the store
20   Of such a wit the world should have no more.

         1648

A Thanksgiving to God for His House

Lord, Thou hast given me a cell
       Wherein to dwell,
A little house, whose humble roof
       Is weather-proof;
5   Under the spars of which I lie
       Both soft and dry;

2. The names of taverns.

Where Thou, my chamber for to ward,
    Hast set a guard
Of harmless thoughts, to watch and keep
10   Me while I sleep.
Low is my porch, as is my fate,
    Both void of state;
And yet the threshold of my door
    Is worn by' the poor,
15 Who thither come and freely get
    Good words, or meat.
Like as my parlor, so my hall
    And kitchen's small;
A little buttery and therein
20   A little bin,
Which keeps my little loaf of bread
    Unchipped, unflead;°   *intact*
Some brittle sticks of thorn or brier
    Make me a fire,
25 Close by whose living coal I sit,
    And glow like it.
Lord, I confess too, when I dine,
    The pulse is Thine,
And all those other bits that be
30   There placed by Thee;
The worts,° the purslane,[5] and the mess   *cabbages*
    Of watercress,
Which of Thy kindness Thou hast sent;
    And my content
35 Makes those, and my belovéd beet,
    To be more sweet.
'Tis Thou that crown'st my glittering hearth
    With guiltless mirth,
And giv'st me wassail bowls to drink,
40   Spiced to the brink.
Lord, 'tis Thy plenty-dropping hand
    That soils my land,
And giv'st me, for my bushel sown,
    Twice ten for one;
45 Thou mak'st my teeming hen to lay
    Her egg each day;
Besides my healthful ewes to bear
    Me twins each year;
The while the conduits of my kine
50   Run cream for wine.
All these, and better, Thou dost send
    Me, to this end,
That I should render, for my part,
    A thankful heart;
55 Which, fired with incense, I resign
    As wholly Thine;
But the acceptance, that must be,
    My Christ, by Thee.

                                   1648

5. A salad green.

Neutrality Loathsome

God will have all or none; serve Him, or fall
Down before Baal, Bel, or Belial.[1]
Either be hot or cold: God doth despise,
Abhor, and spew out all neutralities.[2]

                                                    1648

To His Conscience

Can I not sin, but thou wilt be
My private protonotary?[1]
Can I not woo thee to pass by
A short and sweet iniquity?
5 I'll cast a mist and cloud upon
My delicate transgression,
So utter dark, as that no eye
Shall see the hugged impiety.
Gifts blind the wise,[2] and bribes do please,
10 And wind° all other witnesses;   *pervert*
And wilt not thou, with gold, be tied
To lay thy pen and ink aside?
That in the murk° and tongueless night,   *murky*
Wanton I may, and thou not write?
15 It will not be; and therefore now,
For times to come, I'll make this vow:
From aberrations to live free;
So I'll not fear the judge or thee.

                                                    1648

The White Island, or Place of the Blest

In this world, the isle of dreams,
While we sit by sorrow's streams,
Tears and terrors are our themes
    Reciting:

5 But when once from hence we fly,
More and more approaching nigh
Unto young eternity,
    Uniting:

In that whiter island, where
10 Things are evermore sincere;
Candor° here and luster there   *whiteness*
    Delighting:

There no monstrous fancies shall
Out of hell an horror call,
15 To create, or cause at all,
    Affrighting.

---

1. Baal (or Bel) and Belial were pagan divinities; hence, false gods in general.
2. See Revelation iii.16: ". . . because thou art lukewarm, and neither cold nor hot, I will spew thee out of my mouth."

1. Chief recorder in a law court.
2. Deuteronomy xvi.19: ". . . a gift doth blind the eyes of the wise, and pervert the words of the righteous."

There, in calm and cooling sleep
We our eyes shall never steep,
But eternal watch shall keep,
20   Attending

Pleasures, such as shall pursue
Me immortalized, and you;
And fresh joys, as never too
        Have ending.

                                        1648

HENRY KING
(1592–1669)

The Exequy

Accept, thou shrine of my dead saint,
Instead of dirges, this complaint;
And for sweet flowers to crown thy hearse,
Receive a strew of weeping verse
5   From thy grieved friend, whom thou might'st see
Quite melted into tears for thee.

Dear loss! since thy untimely fate
My task hath been to meditate
On thee, on thee; thou art the book,
10 The library whereon I look,
Though almost blind. For thee, loved clay,
I languish out, not live, the day,
Using no other exercise
But what I practice with mine eyes;
15 By which wet glasses I find out
How lazily time creeps about
To one that mourns: this, only this,
My exercise and business is.
So I compute the weary hours
20 With sighs dissolvéd into showers.

Nor wonder if my time go thus
Backward and most preposterous;
Thou hast benighted me, thy set
This eve of blackness did beget,
25 Who wast my day, though overcast
Before thou hadst thy noontide passed;
And I remember must in tears,
Thou scarce hadst seen so many years
As day tells hours. By thy clear sun
30 My love and fortune first did run;
But thou wilt never more appear
Folded within my hemisphere,
Since both thy light and motïon
Like a fled star is fallen and gone;
35 And 'twixt me and my soul's dear wish
An earth now interposéd is,
Which such a strange eclipse doth make
As ne'er was read in almanac.

I could allow thee for a time
40 To darken me and my sad clime;
Were it a month, a year, or ten,
I would thy exile live till then,
And all that space my mirth adjourn,
So thou wouldst promise to return;
45 And putting off thy ashy shroud,
At length disperse this sorrow's cloud.

But woe is me! the longest date
Too narrow is to calculate
These empty hopes; never shall I
50 Be so much blest as to descry
A glimpse of thee, till that day come
Which shall the earth to cinders doom,
And a fierce fever must calcine[1]
The body of this world—like thine,
55 My little world! That fit of fire
Once off, our bodies shall aspire
To our souls' bliss; then we shall rise
And view ourselves with clearer eyes
In that calm region where no night
60 Can hide us from each other's sight.

Meantime, thou hast her, earth: much good
May my harm do thee. Since it stood
With heaven's will I might not call
Her longer mine, I give thee all
65 My short-lived right and interest
In her whom living I loved best;
With a most free and bounteous grief
I give thee what I could not keep.
Be kind to her, and prithee look
70 Thou write into thy doomsday book
Each parcel of this rarity
Which in thy casket shrined doth lie.
See that thou make thy reckoning straight,
And yield her back again by weight;
75 For thou must audit on thy trust
Each grain and atom of this dust,
As thou wilt answer Him that lent,
Not gave thee, my dear monument.

So close the ground, and 'bout her shade
80 Black curtains draw; my bride is laid.

Sleep on, my love, in thy cold bed,
Never to be disquieted!
My last good-night! Thou wilt not wake
Till I thy fate shall overtake;
85 Till age, or grief, or sickness must
Marry my body to that dust
It so much loves; and fill the room
My heart keeps empty in thy tomb.
Stay for me there; I will not fail
90 To meet thee in that hollow vale.
And think not much of my delay;

1. Reduce to dust by heat.

I am already on the way,
And follow thee with all the speed
Desire can make, or sorrows breed.
95   Each minute is a short degree,
And every hour a step towards thee.
At night when I betake to rest,
Next morn I rise nearer my west
Of life, almost by eight hours' sail,
100   Than when sleep breathed his drowsy gale.

Thus from the sun my bottom° steers,   **vessel**
And my day's compass downward bears;
Nor labor I to stem the tide
Through which to thee I swiftly glide.

105   'Tis true, with shame and grief I yield,
Thou like the van° first took'st the field,   **vanguard**
And gotten hast the victory
In thus adventuring to die
Before me, whose more years might crave
110   A just precédence in the grave.
But hark! my pulse like a soft drum
Beats my approach, tells thee I come;
And slow howe'er my marches be,
I shall at last sit down by thee.

115   The thought of this bids me go on,
And wait my dissolutïon
With hope and comfort. Dear (forgive
The crime), I am content to live
Divided, with but half a heart,
120   Till we shall meet and never part.

                                                              1657

A Contemplation Upon Flowers

Brave flowers, that I could gallant it like you,
And be as little vain;
You come abroad and make a harmless show,
And to your beds of earth again;
5   You are not proud, you know your birth,
For your embroidered garments are from earth.

You do obey your months and times, but I
Would have it ever spring;
My fate would know no winter, never die,
10   Nor think of such a thing;
Oh that I could my bed of earth but view,
And smile and look as cheerfully as you.

Oh teach me to see death and not to fear,
But rather to take truce;
15   How often have I seen you at a bier,
And there look fresh and spruce;
You fragrant flowers then teach me that my breath
Like yours may sweeten and perfume my death.

                                                              ca. 1660

GEORGE HERBERT
(1593–1633)

Redemption

Having been tenant long to a rich lord,
   Not thriving, I resolvéd to be bold,
   And make a suit unto him, to afford°   *grant*
A new small-rented lease, and cancel the old.

5   In heaven at his manor I him sought;
   They told me there that he was lately gone
   About some land, which he had dearly bought
Long since on earth, to take possessïon.

   I straight returned, and knowing his great birth,
10   Sought him accordingly in great resorts;
   In cities, theaters, gardens, parks, and courts;
At length I heard a ragged noise and mirth
   Of thieves and murderers; there I him espied,
   Who straight, *Your suit is granted,* said, and died.

1633

Easter Wings

Lord, who createdst man in wealth and store,°   *abundance*
   Though foolishly he lost the same,
      Decaying more and more
         Till he became
5   Most poor:
            With thee
         O let me rise
      As larks, harmoniously,
   And sing this day thy victories:
10 Then shall the fall further the flight in me.

My tender age in sorrow did begin;
   And still with sicknesses and shame
      Thou didst so punish sin,
         That I became
15   Most thin.
            With thee
         Let me combine,
      And feel this day[1] thy victory;
   For, if I imp[2] my wing on thine,
20 Affliction shall advance the flight in me.

1633

---

1. The words "this day," which are superflu-
ous in the metrical scheme of the poem, were
perhaps included in the early editions to
emphasize the occasion, Easter. They are
omitted, however, in the only surviving manu-
script book of Herbert's poems.
2. A term from falconry: additional feathers
were "imped" or grafted onto the wing of a
hawk to improve its powers of flight.

Affliction (I)

When first thou didst entice to thee my heart,
      I thought the service brave°:   *splendid*
So many joys I writ down for my part,
      Besides what I might have
5 Out of my stock of natural delights,
Augmented with thy gracious benefits.

I lookéd on thy furniture so fine,
      And made it fine to me;
Thy glorious household stuff did me entwine,
10   And 'tice me unto thee.
Such stars I counted mine: both heaven and earth
Paid me my wages in a world of mirth.

What pleasures could I want, whose king I served,
      Where joys my fellows were?
15 Thus argued into hopes, my thoughts reserved
      No place for grief or fear;
Therefore my sudden soul caught at the place,
And made her youth and fierceness seek thy face:

At first thou gav'st me milk and sweetnesses;
20   I had my wish and way:
My days were strawed° with flowers and happiness;   *strewed*
      There was no month but May.
But with my years sorrow did twist and grow.
And made a party unawares for woe.

25 My flesh began unto my soul in pain,
      "Sicknesses cleave my bones;
Consuming agues dwell in every vein,
      And tune my breath to groans."
Sorrow was all my soul; I scarce believed,
30 Till grief did tell me roundly,° that I lived.   *bluntly*

When I got health, thou took'st away my life,
      And more; for my friends die:
My mirth and edge was lost: a blunted knife
      Was of more use than I.
35 Thus thin and lean without a fence or friend,
I was blown through with every storm and wind.

Whereas my birth and spirit rather took
      The way that takes the town,
Thou didst betray me to a lingering book,
40   And wrap me in a gown.
I was entangled in the world of strife,
Before I had the power to change my life.

Yet, for I threatened oft the siege to raise,
      Not simpering all mine age,
45 Thou often didst with academic praise
      Melt and dissolve my rage.
I took thy sweetened pill, till I came where
I could not go away, nor persevere.

Yet lest perchance I should too happy be
          In my unhappiness,
50 Turning my purge to food, thou throwest me
          Into more sicknesses.
Thus doth thy power cross-bias[3] me, not making
Thine own gift good, yet me from my ways taking.

55 Now I am here, what thou wilt do with me
          None of my books will show:
I read, and sigh, and wish I were a tree,
          For sure then I should grow
To fruit or shade; at least, some bird would trust
60 Her household to me, and I should be just.

Yet, though thou troublest me, I must be meek;
          In weakness must be stout:
Well, I will change the service, and go seek
          Some other master out.
65 Ah, my dear God! though I am clean forgot,
Let me not love thee, if I love thee not.

                          1633

Prayer (I)

Prayer, the church's banquet, angels' age,
   God's breath in man returning to his birth,
   The soul in paraphrase, heart in pilgrimage,
The Christian plummet sounding heaven and earth;

5 Engine against th' Almighty, sinner's tower,
   Reverséd thunder, Christ-side-piercing spear,
   The six-days' world[4] transposing in an hour,
A kind of tune, which all things hear and fear;

Softness, and peace, and joy, and love, and bliss,
10   Exalted manna, gladness of the best,
   Heaven in ordinary,[5] man well dressed,
The Milky Way, the bird of Paradise,

Church bells beyond the stars heard, the soul's blood,
The land of spices; something understood.

                          1633

Jordan (I)[6]

Who says that fictions only and false hair
Become a verse? Is there in truth no beauty?
Is all good structure in a winding stair?
May no lines pass, except they do their duty
5   Not to a true, but painted chair?[7]

3. A term from the game of bowls: to cause the natural path of the ball to be altered.
4. God created the world in six days (Genesis i). Also, of course, the six weekdays might be thought of as a "world" distinct from that of the Sabbath.
5. In the everyday course of things. More specifically, *ordinary* also meant a daily allowance of food or an established order or form, as of the divine service.
6. A river in the Holy Land, the cleansing waters of which cured leprosy (II Kings v.10).
7. It was customary to bow or "do one's duty" to the king's chair of state even when unoccupied.

Is it no verse, except enchanted groves
And sudden arbors[8] shadow coarse-spun lines?
Must purling streams refresh a lover's loves?
Must all be veiled while he that reads, divines,
10   Catching the sense at two removes?

Shepherds are honest people; let them sing:
Riddle who list, for me, and pull for prime:[9]
I envy no man's nightingale or spring;
Nor let them punish me with loss of rhyme,
15   Who plainly say, *My God, My King.*

1633

Church Monuments

While that my soul repairs to her devotion,
Here I intomb my flesh, that it betimes
May take acquaintance of this heap of dust;
To which the blast of death's incessant motion,
5   Fed with the exhalation of our crimes,
Drives all at last. Therefore I gladly trust

My body to this school, that it may learn
To spell his elements, and find his birth
Written in dusty heraldry and lines;
10   Which dissolution sure doth best discern,
Comparing dust with dust, and earth with earth.
These laugh at jet, and marble put for signs,

To sever the good fellowship of dust,
And spoil the meeting. What shall point out them,
15   When they shall bow, and kneel, and fall down flat
To kiss those heaps, which now they have in trust?
Dear flesh, while I do pray, learn here thy stem
And true descent, that when thou shalt grow fat

And wanton in thy cravings, thou mayst know
20   That flesh is but the glass which holds the dust
That measures all our time; which also shall
Be crumbled into dust. Mark, here below
How tame these ashes are, how free from lust,
That thou mayst fit thyself against thy fall.

1633

The Windows

Lord, how can man preach thy eternal word?
      He is a brittle crazy° glass;   *flawed*
Yet in thy temple thou dost him afford
      This glorious and transcendent place,
5   To be a window, through thy grace.

But when thou dost anneal in glass thy story,
      Making thy life to shine within

---

8. One aim of garden design was to incorporate attractive features in such a way that they would be revealed unexpectedly in the course of a walk.
9. Draw for a winning card.

The holy preachers, then the light and glory
    More reverend grows, and more doth win;
10   Which else shows waterish, bleak, and thin.

Doctrine and life, colors and light, in one
    When they combine and mingle, bring
A strong regard and awe; but speech alone
    Doth vanish like a flaring thing,
15   And in the ear, not conscience, ring.

                                      1633

Denial

When my devotions could not pierce
        Thy silent ears,
Then was my heart broken, as was my verse;
        My breast was full of fears
5   And disorder.

My bent thoughts, like a brittle bow,
        Did fly asunder:
Each took his way; some would to pleasures go,
        Some to the wars and thunder
10   Of alarms.

"As good go anywhere," they say,
        "As to benumb
Both knees and heart, in crying night and day,
        Come, come, my God, O come!
15   But no hearing."

O that thou shouldst give dust a tongue
        To cry to thee,
And then not hear it crying! All day long
        My heart was in my knee,
20   But no hearing.

Therefore my soul lay out of sight,
        Untuned, unstrung:
My feeble spirit, unable to look right,
        Like a nipped blossom, hung
25   Discontented.

O cheer and tune my heartless breast,
        Defer no time;
That so thy favors granting my request,
        They and my mind may chime,
30   And mend my rhyme.

                                      1633

The Temper (I)

How should I praise thee, Lord! how should my rhymes
    Gladly engrave thy love in steel,
If what my soul doth feel sometimes,
    My soul might ever feel!

5   Although there were some forty heavens, or more,
           Sometimes I peer above them all;
           Sometimes I hardly reach a score;
               Sometimes to hell I fall.

       O rack me not to such a vast extent;
10   Those distances belong to thee:
           The world's too little for thy tent,
               A grave too big for me.

       Wilt thou meet arms with man, that thou dost stretch
           A crumb of dust from heaven to hell?
15   Will great God measure with a wretch?
               Shall he thy stature spell?

       O let me, when thy roof my soul hath hid,
           O let me roost and nestle there;
           Then of a sinner thou art rid,
20   And I of hope and fear.

       Yet take thy way; for, sure, thy way is best:
           Stretch or contract me, thy poor debtor:
           This is but tuning of my breast,
               To make the music better.

25   Whether I fly with angels, fall with dust,
           Thy hands made both, and I am there.
           Thy power and love, my love and trust,
               Make one place everywhere.

                                                            1633

Vanity (I)

       The fleet astronomer can bore
   And thread the spheres with his quick-piercing mind:
   He views their stations, walks from door to door,
           Surveys, as if he had designed
5 To make a purchase there; he sees their dances,
               And knoweth long before
   Both their full-eyed aspécts, and secret glances.

       The nimble diver with his side
   Cuts through the working waves, that he may fetch
10 His dearly-earnéd pearl, which God did hide
           On purpose from the venturous wretch;
   That he might save his life, and also hers
               Who with excessive pride
   Her own destruction and his danger wears.

15   The subtle chymic° can divest   *chemist*
   And strip the creature naked, till he find
   The callow principles within their nest:
           There he imparts to them his mind,
   Admitted to their bed-chamber, before
20   They appear trim and dressed
   To ordinary suitors at the door.

What hath not man sought out and found,
But his dear God? who yet his glorious law
Embosoms in us, mellowing the ground
    With showers and frosts, with love and awe,
5 So that we need not say, "Where's this command?"
        Poor man, thou searchest round
To find out death, but missest life at hand.

1633

Virtue

Sweet day, so cool, so calm, so bright,
    The bridal of the earth and sky:
The dew shall weep thy fall tonight;
    For thou must die.

5 Sweet rose, whose hue, angry and brave,
    Bids the rash gazer wipe his eye:
Thy root is ever in its grave,
    And thou must die.

Sweet spring, full of sweet days and roses,
10   A box where sweets° compacted lie;   *perfumes*
My music shows ye have your closes,[1]
    And all must die.

Only a sweet and virtuous soul,
    Like seasoned timber, never gives;
15 But though the whole world turn to coal,[2]
    Then chiefly lives.

1633

Man

    My God, I heard this day
That none doth build a stately habitation,
    But he that means to dwell therein.
    What house more stately hath there been,
5 Or can be, than is Man? to[3] whose creation
    All things are in decay.

    For Man is every thing,
And more: he is a tree, yet bears more fruit;
    A beast, yet is or should be more:
10   Reason and speech we only bring.
Parrots may thank us, if they are not mute,
    They go upon the score.[4]

    Man is all symmetry,
Full of proportions, one limb to another,
15   And all to all the world besides:
    Each part may call the furthest, brother;
For head with foot hath private amity,
    And both with moons and tides.

1. A close is a cadence, the conclusion of a musical strain.
2. An allusion to Judgment Day, when the world will end in a general conflagration.
3. I.e., compared to.
4. I.e., they are in our debt.

Nothing hath got so far,
20 But man hath caught and kept it, as his prey.
His eyes dismount the highest star:
He is in little all the sphere.
Herbs gladly cure our flesh, because that they
Find their acquaintance there.

25   For us the winds do blow,
The earth doth rest, heaven move, and fountains flow.
Nothing we see but means our good,
As our delight or as our treasure:
The whole is either our cupboard of food,
30   Or cabinet of pleasure.

The stars have us to bed;
Night draws the curtain, which the sun withdraws;
Music and light attend our head.
All things unto our flesh are kind°   kin
35 In their descent and being; to our mind
In their ascent and cause.

Each thing is full of duty:
Waters united are our navigation;
Distinguishéd, our habitation;
40 Below, our drink; above, our meat;
Both are our cleanliness. Hath one such beauty?
Then how are all things neat?

More servants wait on Man
Than he'll take notice of: in every path
45 He treads down that which doth befriend him
When sickness makes him pale and wan.
O mighty love! Man is one world, and hath
Another to attend him.

Since then, my God, thou hast
50 So brave a palace built, O dwell in it,
That it may dwell with thee at last!
Till then, afford us so much wit,
That, as the world serves us, we may serve thee,
And both thy servants be.

1633

Life

I made a posy, while the day ran by:
"Here will I smell my remnant out, and tie
My life within this band."
But Time did beckon to the flowers, and they
5 By noon must cunningly did steal away,
And withered in my hand.

My hand was next to them, and then my heart;
I took, without more thinking, in good part
Time's gentle admonition;
10 Who did so sweetly death's sad taste convey,
Making my mind to smell my fatal day,
Yet sugaring the suspicion.

Farewell dear flowers, sweetly your time ye spent,
Fit, while ye lived, for smell or ornament,
                    And after death for cures.[5]
I follow straight without complaints or grief,
Since, if my scent be good, I care not if
                    It be as short as yours.

1633

Artillery

As I one evening sat before my cell,
Methought[6] a star did shoot into my lap.
I rose and shook my clothes, as knowing well
That from small fires comes oft no small mishap;
     When suddenly I heard one say,
     "Do as thou usest, disobey,
     Expel good motions from thy breast,
Which have the face of fire, but end in rest."

I, who had heard of music in the spheres,
But not of speech in stars, began to muse;
But turning to my God, whose ministers
The stars and all things are: "If I refuse,
     Dread Lord," said I, "so oft my good,
     Then I refuse not ev'n with blood
     To wash away my stubborn thought;
For I will do or suffer what I ought.

"But I have also stars and shooters too,
Born where thy servants both artilleries use.
My tears and prayers night and day do woo
And work up to thee; yet thou dost refuse.
     Not but I am (I must say still)
     Much more obliged to do thy will
     Than thou to grant mine; but because
Thy promise now hath ev'n set thee thy laws.

"Then we are shooters both, and thou dost deign
To enter combat with us, and contest
With thine own clay. But I would parley fain:
Shun not my arrows, and behold my breast.
     Yet if thou shunnest, I am thine:
     I must be so, if I am mine.
     There is no articling° with thee: *negotiating*
I am but finite, yet thine infinitely."

1633

The Bag

Away despair! my gracious Lord doth hear;
     Though winds and waves assault my keel,
     He doth preserve it: he doth steer,
     Ev'n when the boat seems most to reel.
          Storms are the triumph of his art:
Well may he close his eyes, but not his heart.

---

5. Roses were sometimes used as an ingredient   6. It seemed to me.
in medicines.

Hast thou not heard, that my Lord Jesus died?
　　Then let me tell thee a strange story.
　　The God of power, as he did ride
10　　In his majestic robes of glory,
　　Resolved to light; and so one day
He did descend, undressing all the way.

The stars his tire° of light and rings obtained,　　*attire*
　　The cloud his bow, the fire° his spear,　　*lightning*
15　　The sky his azure mantle gained.
　　And when they asked what he would wear,
　　He smiled and said as he did go,
He had new clothes a making here below.

When he was come, as travelers are wont,
20　　He did repair unto an inn.
　　Both then, and after, many'a brunt
　　He did endure to cancel sin:
　　And having giv'n the rest before,
Here he gave up his life to pay our score.

25　But as he was returning, there came one
　　That ran upon him with a spear.
　　He, who came hither all alone,
　　Bringing nor man, nor arms, nor fear,
　　Received the blow upon his side,
30　And straight he turned, and to his brethren cried,

"If ye have any thing to send or write,
　　I have no bag, but here is room:
　　Unto my Father's hands and sight,
　　Believe me, it shall safely come.
35　　That I shall mind what you impart,
Look, you may put it very near my heart.

"Or if hereafter any of my friends
　　Will use me in this kind,° the door　　*way*
　　Shall still be open; what he sends
40　　I will present, and somewhat more,
　　Not to this hurt. Sighs will convey
Any thing to me." Hark, Despair away.

　　　　　　　　　　　　　　　　　1633

The Collar

I struck the board° and cried, "No more;　　*table*
　　I will abroad!
What? shall I ever sigh and pine?
My lines and life are free, free as the road,
5　　Loose as the wind, as large as store.°　　*abundance*
　　　　Shall I be still in suit?
Have I no harvest but a thorn
To let me blood, and not restore
What I have lost with cordial° fruit?　　*life-giving*
10　　　Sure there was wine
Before my sighs did dry it; there was corn

Before my tears did drown it.
Is the year only lost to me?
Have I no bays[7] to crown it,
15 No flowers, no garlands gay? All blasted?
All wasted?
Not so, my heart; but there is fruit,
And thou hast hands.
Recover all thy sigh-blown age
20 On double pleasures: leave thy cold dispute
Of what is fit and not. Forsake thy cage,
Thy rope of sands,
Which petty thoughts have made, and made to thee
Good cable, to enforce and draw,
25 And be thy law,
While thou didst wink and wouldst not see.
Away! take heed;
I will abroad.
Call in thy death's-head[8] there; tie up thy fears.
30 He that forbears
To suit and serve his need,
Deserves his load."
But as I raved and grew more fierce and wild
At every word,
35 Methought I heard one calling, *Child!*
And I replied, *My Lord.*

1633

The Pulley

When God at first made man,
Having a glass of blessings standing by,
"Let us," said he, "pour on him all we can.
Let the world's riches, which dispersèd lie,
5   Contract into a span."

So strength first made a way;
Then beauty flowed, then wisdom, honor, pleasure.
When almost all was out, God made a stay,
Perceiving that, alone of all his treasure,
10   Rest in the bottom lay.

"For if I should," said he,
"Bestow this jewel also on my creature,
He would adore my gifts instead of me,
And rest in Nature, not the God of Nature;
15   So both should losers be.

"Yet let him keep the rest,
But keep them with repining restlessness.
Let him be rich and weary, that at least,
If goodness lead him not, yet weariness
20   May toss him to my breast."

1633

7. A laurel garland symbolizing honor or renown.
8. A representation of a human skull intended to serve as a *memento mori*, a reminder that all men must die.

The Flower

How fresh, oh Lord, how sweet and clean
Are thy returns! even as the flowers in spring;
   To which, besides their own demean,[9]
The late-past frosts tributes of pleasure bring.
5   Grief melts away
        Like snow in May,
   As if there were no such cold thing.

   Who would have thought my shriveled heart
Could have have recovered greenness? It was gone
10   Quite underground; as flowers depart
To see their mother-root, when they have blown,°   *bloomed*
       Where they together
       All the hard weather,
Dead to the world, keep house unknown.

15   These are thy wonders, Lord of power,
Killing and quickening, bringing down to hell
   And up to heaven in an hour;
Making a chiming of a passing-bell[1]
       We say amiss
20   This or that is:
   Thy word is all, if we could spell.

   Oh that I once past changing were,
Fast in thy Paradise, where no flower can wither!
   Many a spring I shoot up fair,
25 Offering° at heaven, growing and groaning thither;   *aiming*
       Nor doth my flower
       Want a spring shower,
   My sins and I joining together.

   But while I grow in a straight line,
30 Still upwards bent, as if heaven were mine own,
   Thy anger comes, and I decline:
What frost to that? what pole is not the zone
       Where all things burn,
       When thou dost turn,
35   And the least frown of thine is shown?

   And now in age I bud again,
After so many deaths I live and write;
   I once more smell the dew and rain,
And relish versing. Oh, my only light,
40   It cannot be
       That I am he
On whom thy tempests fell all night.

   These are thy wonders, Lord of love,
To make us see we are but flowers that glide;
45   Which when we once can find and prove,
Thou hast a garden for us where to bide;

---

9. Demeanor; possibly also *demesne*, "estate."   **1.** A single bell tolled to announce a death.

Who would be more,
Swelling through store,°   *possessions*
Forfeit their Paradise by their pride.

                                                              1633

Bitter-Sweet

Ah, my dear angry Lord,
Since thou dost love, yet strike;
Cast down, yet help afford;
Sure I will do the like.

5   I will complain, yet praise;
I will bewail, approve;
And all my sour-sweet days
I will lament and love.

                                                              1633

The Forerunners

The harbingers² are come. See, see their mark:
White is their color, and behold my head.
But must they have my brain? Must they dispark³
Those sparkling notions, which therein were bred?
5   Must dullness turn me to a clod?
Yet have they left me, *Thou art still my God.*

Good men ye be, to leave me my best room,
Ev'n all my heart, and what is lodgéd there:
I pass not,° I, what of the rest become,   *I care not*
10 So *Thou art still my God* be out of fear.
        He will be pleaséd with that ditty;
And if I please him, I write fine and witty.

Farewell sweet phrases, lovely metaphors.
But will ye leave me thus? When ye before
15 Of stews and brothels only knew the doors,
Then did I wash you with my tears, and more,
        Brought you to church well dressed and clad:
My God must have my best, ev'n all I had.

Lovely enchanting language, sugar-cane,
20 Honey of roses, wither wilt thou fly?
Hath some fond lover 'ticed thee to thy bane?
And wilt thou leave the church and love a sty?
        Fie, thou wilt soil thy broidered coat,
And hurt thyself, and him that sings the note.

25 Let foolish lovers, if they will love dung,
With canvas, not with arras, clothe their shame:
Let folly speak in her own native tongue.
True beauty dwells on high: ours is a flame
        But borrowed thence to light us thither.
30 Beauty and beauteous words should go together.

---

2. The advance agents of the king and his
party on a royal progress or tour. They
marked with chalk the doors of those dwellings
where the court would be accommodated.

3. I.e., *dis-park*, to turn out, as of a park;
there may also be a play on *dis-spark* (from
"sparkling notions" in the next line).

Yet if you go, I pass not; take your way:
For *Thou art still my God* is all that ye
Perhaps with more embellishment can say.
Go, birds of spring: let winter have his fee;
35   Let a bleak paleness chalk the door,
So all within be livelier than before.

1633

Discipline

Throw away thy rod,
Throw away thy wrath:
          O my God,
Take the gentle path.

5   For my heart's desire
Unto thine is bent:
          I aspire
To a full consent.

Not a word or look
10 I affect to own,
          But by book,
And thy book alone.

Though I fail, I weep:
Though I halt in pace,
15   Yet I creep
To the throne of grace.

Then let wrath remove;
Love will do the deed:
          For with love
20 Stony hearts will bleed.

Love is swift of foot;
Love's a man of war,[4]
          And can shoot,
And can hit from far.

25 Who can 'scape his bow?
That which wrought on thee,
          Brought thee low,
Needs must work on me.

Throw away thy rod;
30 Though man frailties hath,
          Thou art God:
Throw away thy wrath.

1633

The Elixir

Teach me, my God and King,
In all things thee to see,
And what I do in anything,
To do it as for thee.

4. "The Lord is a man of war" (Exodus xv.3).

5 Not rudely, as a beast,
   To run into an action;
But still to make thee prepossest,
   And give it his° perfection.   *its*

   A man that looks on glass,
10   On it may stay his eye,
Or, if he pleaseth, through it pass,
   And then the heaven espy.

   All may of thee partake:
   Nothing can be so mean
15 Which with this tincture[5] (*for thy sake*)
   Will not grow bright and clean.

   A servant with this clause
   Makes drudgery divine:
Who sweeps a room as for thy laws,
20   Makes that and th' action fine.

   This is the famous stone[6]
   That turneth all to gold;
For that which God doth touch[7] and own
   Cannot for less be told.

                                    1633

Death

Death, thou wast once an uncouth hideous thing,
        Nothing but bones,
   The sad effect of sadder groans:
Thy mouth was open, but thou couldst not sing.

5 For we considered thee as at some six
        Or ten years hence,
   After the loss of life and sense,
Flesh being turned to dust, and bones to sticks.

We looked on this side of thee, shooting short;
10   Where we did find
   The shells of fledge souls left behind,
Dry dust, which sheds no tears, but may extort.

But since our Savior's death did put some blood
        Into thy face,
15   Thou art grown fair and full of grace,
Much in request, much sought for as a good.

For we do now behold thee gay and glad,
        As at Doomsday;
   When souls shall wear their new array,
20 And all thy bones with beauty shall be clad.

---

5. An alchemical term: an immaterial principle capable of imbuing and altering the character of a material substance.

6. The "philosopher's stone," the elixir of the alchemists.
7. To test (gold) for purity by rubbing it with a touchstone.

Therefore we can go die as sleep, and trust
    Half that we have
  Unto an honest faithful grave;
Making our pillows either down, or dust.

1633

Love (III)

Love bade me welcome: yet my soul drew back,
    Guilty of dust and sin.
But quick-eyed Love, observing me grow slack
    From my first entrance in,
5 Drew nearer to me, sweetly questioning
    If I lacked anything.

"A guest," I answered, "worthy to be here":
    Love said, "You shall be he."
"I, the unkind, ungrateful? Ah, my dear,
10   I cannot look on thee."
Love took my hand, and smiling did reply,
    "Who made the eyes but I?"

"Truth, Lord; but I have marred them; let my shame
    Go where it doth deserve."
15 "And know you not," says Love, "who bore the blame?"
    "My dear, then I will serve."
"You must sit down," says Love, "and taste my meat."
    So I did sit and eat.

1633

JAMES SHIRLEY
(1596–1666)

The Glories of Our Blood and State

The glories of our blood and state
Are shadows, not substantial things;
There is no armor against fate;
Death lays his icy hand on kings.
5   Scepter and crown
    Must tumble down
And in the dust be equal made
With the poor crooked scythe and spade.

Some men with swords may reap the field
10 And plant fresh laurels where they kill,
But their strong nerves at last must yield;
They tame but one another still.
    Early or late
    They stoop to fate
15 And must give up their murmuring breath,
When they, pale captives, creep to death.

The garlands wither on your brow,
Then boast no more your mighty deeds;

Upon death's purple altar now
20 See where the victor-victim bleeds.
   Your heads must come
    To the cold tomb;
Only the actions of the just
Smell sweet and blossom in their dust.

1659

THOMAS CAREW
(1598?–1639?)

A Song

Ask me no more where Jove bestows,
When June is past, the fading rose;
For in your beauty's orient deep,
These flowers, as in their causes,[1] sleep.

5 Ask me no more whither do stray
The golden atoms of the day;
For in pure love heaven did prepare
Those powders to enrich your hair.

Ask me no more whither doth haste
10 The nightingale when May is past;
For in your sweet dividing[2] throat
She winters, and keeps warm her note.

Ask me no more where those stars light,
That downwards fall in dead of night;
15 For in your eyes they sit, and there
Fixéd become, as in their sphere.

Ask me no more if east or west
The phoenix[3] builds her spicy nest;
For unto you at last she flies,
20 And in your fragrant bosom dies.

1640

Mediocrity in Love Rejected

Give me more love, or more disdain;
   The torrid or the frozen zone
Bring equal ease unto my pain;
   The temperate affords me none:
5 Either extreme, of love or hate,
Is sweeter than a calm estate.

Give me a storm; if it be love,
   Like Danaë in that golden shower,[4]
I swim in pleasure; if it prove

---

1. Aristotelian philosophy regarded that from which a thing is made or comes into being as the "material cause" of the thing.
2. Executing a "division," an embellished musical phrase.
3. A legendary bird, the only one of its kind, represented as living five hundred years in the Arabian desert, being consumed in fire, then rising anew from its own ashes.
4. Danaë, imprisoned by her father in a house of bronze, was visited by Zeus in a shower of gold. The result of their union was the hero Perseus.

10   Disdain, that torrent will devour
My vulture hopes; and he's possessed
Of heaven that's but from hell released.
    Then crown my joys, or cure my pain;
    Give me more love or more disdain.

                                        1640

An Elegy upon the Death of the Dean of Paul's, Dr. John Donne

    Can we not force from widowed poetry,
Now thou art dead, great Donne, one elegy
To crown thy hearse? Why yet did we not trust,
Though with unkneaded dough-baked prose, thy dust,
5   Such as the unscissored[5] lect'rer from the flower
Of fading rhetoric, short-lived as his hour,
Dry as the sand that measures it,[6] should lay
Upon the ashes on the funeral day?
Have we nor tune, nor voice? Didst thou dispense
10 Through all our language both the words and sense?
'Tis a sad truth. The pulpit may her plain
And sober Christian precepts still retain;
Doctrines it may, and wholesome uses, frame,
Grave homilies and lectures; but the flame
15 Of thy brave soul, that shot such heat and light
As burnt our earth and made our darkness bright,
Committed holy rapes upon our will,
Did through the eye the melting heart distil,
And the deep knowledge of dark truths so teach
20 As sense might judge what fancy could not reach,
Must be desired forever. So the fire
That fills with spirit and heat the Delphic choir,[7]
Which, kindled first by thy Promethean[8] breath,
Glowed here a while, lies quenched now in thy death.
25 The Muses' garden, with pedantic weeds
O'erspread, was purged by thee; the lazy seeds
Of servile imitation thrown away,
And fresh invention planted; thou didst pay
The debts of our penurious bankrupt age;
30 Licentious thefts, that make poetic rage
A mimic fury, when our souls must be
Possessed, or with Anacreon's ecstasy,
Or Pindar's,[9] not their own; the subtle cheat
Of sly exchanges, and the juggling feat
35 Of two-edged words, or whatsoever wrong
By ours was done the Greek or Latin tongue,
Thou hast redeemed, and opened us a mine
Of rich and pregnant fancy, drawn a line
Of masculine expression, which had good
40 Old Orpheus[1] seen, or all the ancient brood
Our superstitious fools admire, and hold
Their lead more precious than thy burnished gold,

5. I.e., with uncut hair.
6. I.e., the sand in an hourglass.
7. Ie., the choir of poets. Delphi was the site of an oracle of Apollo, the god of poetry.
8. The fire which Prometheus stole from the gods for the benefit of mankind was some-
times interpreted as man's vital spirit.
9. Anacreon and Pindar were famous Greek poets.
1. In Greek mythology, the son of one of the Muses and the greatest of poets and musicians.

Thou hadst been their exchequer, and no more
They in each other's dung had searched for ore.
45 Thou shalt yield no precédence, but of time
And the blind fate of language, whose tuned chime
More charms the outward sense; yet thou mayest claim
From so great disadvantage greater fame,
Since to the awe of thy imperious wit
50 Our troublesome language bends, made only fit
With her tough thick-ribbed hoops, to gird about
Thy giant fancy, which had proved too stout
For their soft melting phrases. As in time
They had the start, so did they cull the prime
55 Buds of invention many a hundred year,
And left the rifled fields, besides the fear
To touch their harvest; yet from those bare lands
Of what is only thine, thy only hands
(And that their smallest work) have gleanéd more
60 Than all those times and tongues could reap before.
    But thou art gone, and thy strict laws will be
Too hard for libertines in poetry.
They will recall the goodly exiled train
Of gods and goddesses, which in thy just reign
65 Were banished nobler poems; now with these
The silenced tales i' th' *Metamorphoses*[2]
Shall stuff their lines and swell the windy page,
Till verse, refined by thee in this last age,
Turn ballad-rhyme, or those old idols be
70 Adored again with new apostasy.
    O pardon me, that break with untuned verse
The reverend silence that attends thy hearse,
Whose solemn awful murmurs were to thee,
More than these faint lines, a loud elegy,
75 That did proclaim in a dumb eloquence
The death of all the arts, whose influence,
Grown feeble, in these panting numbers lies
Gasping short-winded accents, and so dies:
So doth the swiftly turning wheel not stand
80 In th' instant we withdraw the moving hand,
But some small time retain a faint weak course
By virtue of the first impulsive force;
And so whilst I cast on thy funeral pile
Thy crown of bays,[3] oh, let it crack awhile
85 And spit disdain, till the devouring flashes
Suck all the moisture up; then turn to ashes.
    I will not draw thee envy to engross
All thy perfections, or weep all the loss;
Those are too numerous for one elegy,
90 And this too great to be expressed by me.
Let others carve the rest; it shall suffice
I on thy grave this epitaph incise:

   Here lies a king, that ruled as he thought fit
   The universal monarchy of wit;
95 *Here lie two flamens,° and both those the best:*   priests
   Apollo's first, at last the true God's priest.

1633, 1640

2. Earlier poets had drawn heavily on the stories in Ovid's *Metamorphoses* for the materials of their poetry.

3. In classical times a crown of bays or laurel was the reward of the victor in a poetic competition.

EDMUND WALLER
(1607–1687)

At Penshurst[5]

Had Sacharissa,[6] lived when mortals made
Choice of their deities, this sacred shade
Had held an altar to her power, that gave
The peace and glory which these alleys have;
5　Embroidered so with flowers where she stood,
That it became a garden of a wood.
Her presence has such more than human grace
That it can civilize the rudest place;
And beauty too, and order, can impart,
10　Where nature ne'er intended it, nor art.
The plants acknowledge this, and her admire°   wonder at
No less than those of old did Orpheus' lyre;[7]
If she sit down, with tops all towards her bowed,
They round about her into arbors crowd;
15　Or if she walk, in even ranks they stand,
Like some well-marshaled and obsequious band.
Amphion so made stones and timber leap
Into fair figures from a cónfused heap;[8]
And in the symmetry of her parts is found
20　A power like that of harmony in sound.
　Ye lofty beeches, tell this matchless dame
That if together ye fed all one flame,
It could not equalize the hundredth part
Of what her eyes have kindled in my heart!
25　Go, boy, and carve this passion on the bark
Of yonder tree,[9] which stands the sacred mark
Of noble Sidney's birth; when such benign,
Such more than mortal making[1] stars did shine,
That there they cannot but forever prove
30　The monument and pledge of humble love;
His humble love whose hopes shall ne'er rise higher
Than for a pardon that he dares admire.

1638?　　　　1645

To Phyllis

Phyllis! why should we delay
Pleasures shorter than the day?
Could we (which we never can)
Stretch our lives beyond their span,
5　Beauty like a shadow flies,
And our youth before us dies;

5. The estate of the Sidneys, the family of which the poet and statesman Sir Philip Sidney (1554–86) was the most eminent member.
6. "The sweet one," Waller's poetic designation for Lady Dorothy Sidney.
7. The playing and singing of the legendary Greek poet Orpheus induced even trees to follow him.
8. Amphion, by playing his lyre, caused stones to leap spontaneously into place to form the wall of Thebes.
9. A beech tree, planted at the birth of Dorothy's great-uncle, Sir Philip. It was lavishly inscribed (see Ben Jonson's *Penshurst*, lines 13–16).
1. This compounding of words ("more-than-mortal-making") recalls a poetic technique of Sir Philip Sidney's.

Or would youth and beauty stay,
Love hath wings, and will away.
Love hath swifter wings than Time,
10 Change in love to heaven does climb;
Gods, that never change their state,
Vary oft their love and hate.
Phyllis! to this truth we owe
All the love betwixt us two:
15 Let not you and I require[2]
What has been our past desire;
On what shepherds you have smiled,
Or what nymphs I have beguiled;
Leave it to the planets too,[3]
20 What we shall hereafter do;
For the joys we now may prove,
Take advice of present love.

                                                    1645

On a Girdle

That which her slender waist confined,
Shall now my joyful temples bind;
No monarch but would give his crown,
His arms might do what this has done.

5   It was my heaven's extremest sphere,[4]
The pale° which held that lovely dear;   *enclosure*
My joy, my grief, my·hope, my love
Did all within this circle move!

A narrow compass! and yet there
10 Dwelt all that's good, and all that's fair;
Give me but what this ribbon bound,
Take all the rest the sun goes round!

                                                    1645

Song

Go, lovely rose!
Tell her that wastes her time and me
That now she knows,
When I resemble° her to thee,   *liken*
5 How sweet and fair she seems to be.

Tell her that's young,
And shuns to have her graces spied,
That hadst thou sprung
In deserts, where no men abide,
10 Thou must have uncommended died.

Small is the worth
Of beauty from the light retired;
Bid her come forth,
Suffer herself to be desired,
15 And not blush so to be admired.

2. I.e., demand to know.
3. Planets, unlike the fixed stars, are change-
able in their courses.

4. The outermost sphere of the Ptolemaic
universe; a supposed source of cosmic har-
monies.

Then die! that she
The common fate of all things rare
    May read in thee;
How small a part of time they share
20 That are so wondrous sweet and fair!

1645

Of the Last Verses in the Book

When we for age could neither read nor write,
The subject made us able to indite;
The soul, with nobler resolutions decked,
The body stooping, does herself erect.
5 No mortal parts are requisite to raise
Her that, unbodied, can her Maker praise.
    The seas are quiet when the winds give o'er;
So calm are we when passions are no more!
For then we know how vain it was to boast
10 Of fleeting things, so certain to be lost.
Clouds of affection° from our younger eyes   *emotion*
Conceal that emptiness which age descries.
    The soul's dark cottage, battered and decayed,
Lets in new light through chinks that time has made;
15 Stronger by weakness, wiser men become,
As they draw near to their eternal home.
Leaving the old, both worlds at once they view,
That stand upon the threshold of the new.

1686

JOHN MILTON
(1608–1674)

Lycidas

IN THIS MONODY[1] THE AUTHOR BEWAILS A LEARNED FRIEND, UNFORTU-
NATELY DROWNED IN HIS PASSAGE FROM CHESTER ON THE IRISH SEAS,
1637. AND BY OCCASION FORETELLS THE RUIN OF OUR CORRUPTED
CLERGY, THEN IN THEIR HEIGHT.

Yet once more, O ye laurels[2] and once more
Ye myrtles brown,° with ivy never sere,°   *dark / withered*
I come to pluck your berries harsh and crude,°   *unripe*
And with forced fingers rude,
5 Shatter your leaves before the mellowing year.
Bitter constraint, and sad occasion dear,°   *severe*
Compels me to disturb your season due;
For Lycidas is dead, dead ere his prime,
Young Lycidas, and hath not left his peer.
10 Who would not sing for Lycidas? He knew
Himself to sing, and build the lofty rhyme.
He must not float upon his watery bier
Unwept, and welter° to the parching wind,   *roll about*

---

1. An elegy or dirge sung by a single voice.
The "learned friend" was Edward King, Mil-
ton's fellow student at Cambridge.

2. The laurel, myrtle, and ivy were all tra-
ditional materials for poetic garlands.

Without the meed° of some melodious tear.   *tribute*
15   Begin then, sisters of the sacred well[3]
That from beneath the seat of Jove doth spring,
Begin, and somewhat loudly sweep the string.
Hence with denial vain, and coy excuse;
So may some gentle Muse°   *poet*
20   With lucky words favor my destined urn,
And as he passes turn,
And bid fair peace be to my sable shroud.
For we were nursed upon the selfsame hill,
Fed the same flock, by fountain, shade, and rill.
25   Together both, ere the high lawns° appeared   *pastures*
Under the opening eyelids of the morn,
We drove afield, and both together heard
What time the grayfly winds her sultry horn,
Battening° our flocks with the fresh dews of night,   *fattening*
30   Oft till the star that rose at evening bright
Toward Heaven's descent had sloped his westering wheel.
Meanwhile the rural ditties were not mute,
Tempered to th' oaten flute,
Rough satyrs danced, and fauns with cloven heel
35   From the glad sound would not be absent long,
And old Damoetas[4] loved to hear our song.
    But O the heavy change, now thou art gone,
Now thou art gone, and never must return!
Thee, shepherd, thee the woods and desert caves,
40   With wild thyme and the gadding° vine o'ergrown,   *wandering*
And all their echoes mourn.
The willows and the hazel copses green
Shall now no more be seen,
Fanning their joyous leaves to thy soft lays.
45   As killing as the canker to the rose,
Or taint-worm to the weanling herds that graze,
Or frost to flowers that their gay wardrobe wear,
When first the white thorn blows;°   *blooms*
Such, Lycidas, thy loss to shepherd's ear.
50   Where were ye, nymphs, when the remorseless deep
Closed o'er the head of your loved Lycidas?
For neither were ye playing on the steep,
Where your old Bards, the famous Druids lie,
Nor on the shaggy top of Mona high,
55   Nor yet where Deva spreads her wizard stream:[5]
Ay me! I fondly° dream—   *foolishly*
Had ye been there—for what could that have done?
What could the Muse[6] herself that Orpheus bore,
The Muse herself, for her inchanting son
60   Whom universal Nature did lament,
When by the rout that made the hideous roar,
His gory visage down the stream was sent,
Down the swift Hebrus to the Lesbian shore?

3. The Muses. The well sacred to them was
Aganippe, at the foot of Mt. Helicon, where
they danced about the altar of Jove.
4. A conventional pastoral name, here perhaps
referring to one of the tutors at Cambridge.
5. The "steep" is probably the mountain
Kerig-y-Druidion in northern Wales, a Druid
burial ground. Mona is the Isle of Anglesey,
Deva the River Dee, called "wizard" because
its changes of course were supposed to foretell
the country's fortune. All three places are just
south of that part of the Irish Sea where King
was drowned.
6. Calliope, the Muse of epic poetry. Her son
Orpheus, the greatest of all poets and musi-
cians, was torn limb from limb by a band of
Thracian Maenads, who flung his head into
the River Hebrus, whence it drifted across
the Aegean to the island of Lesbos.

65 Alas! What boots° it with uncessant care   profits
    To tend the homely slighted shepherd's trade,
    And strictly meditate the thankless Muse?
    Were it not better done as others use,
    To sport with Amaryllis[7] in the shade,
    Or with the tangles of Neaera's hair?
70 Fame is the spur that the clear spirit doth raise
    (That last infirmity of noble mind)
    To scorn delights, and live laborious days;
    But the fair guerdon° when we hope to find,   reward
    And think to burst out into sudden blaze,
75 Comes the blind Fury[8] with th' abhorréd shears,
    And slits the thin spun life. "But not the praise,"
    Phoebus[9] replied, and touched my trembling ears;
    "Fame is no plant that grows on mortal soil,
    Nor in the glistering foil[1]
80 Set off to th' world, nor in broad rumor lies,
    But lives and spreads aloft by those pure eyes,
    And perfect witness of all-judging Jove;
    As he pronounces lastly on each deed,
    Of so much fame in Heaven expect thy meed."
85   O fountain Arethuse,[2] and thou honored flood,
    Smooth-sliding Mincius, crowned with vocal reeds,
    That strain I heard was of a higher mood.
    But now my oat[3] proceeds,
    And listens to the herald of the sea[4]
90 That came in Neptune's plea.
    He asked the waves, and asked the felon winds,
    "What hard mishap hath doomed this gentle swain?"
    And questioned every gust of rugged wings
    That blows from off each beakéd promontory;
95 They knew not of his story,
    And sage Hippotades[5] their answer brings,
    That not a blast was from his dungeon strayed,
    The air was calm, and on the level brine,
    Sleek Panope[6] with all her sisters played.
100 It was that fatal and perfidious bark
    Built in th' eclipse, and rigged with curses dark,
    That sunk so low that sacred head of thine.
      Next Camus,[7] reverend sire, went footing slow,
    His mantle hairy, and his bonnet sedge,
105 Inwrought with figures dim, and on the edge
    Like to that sanguine flower inscribed with woe.[8]
    "Ah! who hath reft," quoth he, "my dearest pledge?"
    Last came and last did go
    The pilot of the Galilean lake,[9]

7. A conventional pastoral name, like Neaera in the next line.
8. Atropos, the third of the three Fates, who cut the thread of a man's life after it had been spun and measured by her sisters.
9. Apollo, god of poetic inspiration.
1. The setting for a gem, especially one that enhances the appearance of an inferior or false stone.
2. A fountain in Sicily, associated with the pastoral poems of Theocritus. The Mincius is a river in Italy described in one of Virgil's pastorals.
3. Oaten pipe, song.
4. The merman Triton, who came to plead his master Neptune's innocence of Lycidas' death.

5. Aeolus, son of Hippotas and god of the winds.
6. One of the Nereids, daughters of Nereus, the Old Man of the Sea.
7. The god of the river Cam, representing Cambridge University.
8. The hyacinth, created by Apollo from the blood of the youth Hyacinthus, whom he had killed by accident with a discus. Certain markings on the flower are supposed to be the letters AIAI ("Alas, alas!"), inscribed there by Apollo.
9. St. Peter, the Galilean fisherman, to whom Christ promised the keys of the kingdom of heaven (Matthew xvi.19). He wears the bishop's miter (line 112) as the first head of Christ's church.

110 Two massy keys he bore of metals twain
      (The golden opes, the iron shuts amain).
      He shook his mitered locks, and stern bespake:
      "How well could I have spared for thee, young swain,
      Enow° of such as for their bellies' sake,   *enough*
115 Creep and intrude, and climb into the fold!
      Of other care they little reckoning make,
      Than how to scramble at the shearers' feast,
      And shove away the worthy bidden guest.
      Blind mouths! That scarce themselves know how to hold
120 A sheep-hook, or have learned aught else the least
      That to the faithful herdsman's art belongs!
      What recks it them?[1] What need they? They are sped;
      And when they list, their lean and flashy° songs   *insipid*
      Grate on their scrannel° pipes of wretched straw.   *meager*
125 The hungry sheep look up, and are not fed,
      But swoln with wind, and the rank mist they draw,
      Rot inwardly, and foul contagion spread,
      Besides what the grim wolf with privy paw[2]
      Daily devours apace, and nothing said.
130 But that two-handed engine at the door
      Stands ready to smite once, and smite no more."[3]
        Return, Alpheus,[4] the dread voice is past,
      That shrunk thy streams; return, Sicilian muse,
      And call the vales, and bid them hither cast
135 Their bells and flowerets of a thousand hues.
      Ye valleys low where the mild whispers use,°   *frequent*
      Of shades and wanton winds, and gushing brooks,
      On whose fresh lap the swart star[5] sparely looks,
      Throw hither all your quaint enameled eyes,
140 That on the green turf suck the honeyed showers,
      And purple all the ground with vernal flowers.
      Bring the rathe° primrose that forsaken dies,   *early*
      The tufted crow-toe, and pale jessamine,
      The white pink, and the pansy freaked° with jet,   *mottled*
145 The glowing violet,
      The musk-rose, and the well attired woodbine.
      With cowslips wan that hang the pensive head,
      And every flower that sad embroidery wears:
      Bid amaranthus[6] all his beauty shed,
150 And daffadillies fill their cups with tears,
      To strew the laureate hearse° where Lycid lies.   *bier*
      For so to interpose a little ease,
      Let our frail thoughts dally with false surmise.
      Ay me! Whilst thee the shores and sounding seas
155 Wash far away, where'er thy bones are hurled,
      Whether beyond the stormy Hebrides,
      Where thou perhaps under the whelming tide
      Visit'st the bottom of the monstrous world;
      Or whether thou, to our moist vows denied,

---

1. What does it matter to them?
2. I.e., anti-Protestant forces, either Roman Catholic or Anglican.
3. A satisfactory explanation of these two lines has yet to be made, although many have been attempted. Most have taken the "two-handed engine" as an instrument of retribution against those clergy who neglect their responsibilities (such as the ax of reformation; the two-handed sword of the archangel Mi-

chael; the two houses of Parliament; death and damnation).
4. A river god who fell in love with the nymph Arethusa. When she fled to Sicily he pursued her by diving under the sea and coming up in the island. There she was turned into a fountain (see line 85) and their waters mingled.
5. Sirius, the Dog Star, thought to have a swart or malignant influence.
6. A legendary flower, supposed never to fade.

160 Sleep'st by the fable of Bellerus old,[7]
Where the great vision of the guarded mount
Looks toward Namancos and Bayona's hold;
Look homeward angel now, and melt with ruth:°   *pity*
And, O ye dolphins, waft the hapless youth.
165   Weep no more, woeful shepherds, weep no more,
For Lycidas your sorrow is not dead,
Sunk though he be beneath the watery floor,
So sinks the day-star° in the ocean bed,   *sun*
And yet anon repairs his drooping head,
170 And tricks° his beams, and with new-spangled ore,°   *dresses / gold*
Flames in the forehead of the morning sky:
So Lycidas sunk low, but mounted high,
Through the dear might of him that walked the waves,
Where other groves, and other streams along,
175 With nectar pure his oozy locks he laves,
And hears the unexpressive° nuptial song,[8]   *inexpressible*
In the blest kingdoms meek of joy and love.
There entertain him all the saints above,
In solemn troops and sweet societies
180 That sing, and singing in their glory move,
And wipe the tears forever from his eyes.
Now, Lycidas, the shepherds weep no more;
Henceforth thou art the genius° of the shore,   *local divinity*
In thy large recompense, and shalt be good
185 To all that wander in that perilous flood.
        Thus sang the uncouth° swain to th' oaks and rills,   *unlettered*
While the still morn went out with sandals gray;
He touched the tender stops of various quills,[9]
With eager thought warbling his Doric[1] lay:
190 And now the sun had stretched out all the hills,
And now was dropped into the western bay;
At last he rose, and twitched his mantle blue:
Tomorrow to fresh woods, and pastures new.

1637

On the Morning of Christ's Nativity

1

This is the month, and this the happy morn,
Wherein the Son of Heaven's Eternal King,
Of wedded maid and virgin mother born,
Our great redemption from above did bring;
5 For so the holy sages[2] once did sing,
    That he our deadly forfeit[3] should release,
And with his Father work us a perpetual peace.

2

That glorious form, that light unsufferable,
And that far-beaming blaze of majesty,
10 Wherewith he wont at Heaven's high council-table
To sit the midst of Trinal Unity,

7. A legendary figure supposedly buried at Land's End in Cornwall. The "mount" of the next line is St. Michael's Mount at the tip of Land's End, "guarded" by the archangel Michael, who gazes southward toward Nemancos and the stronghold of Bayona in northwestern Spain.
8. Milton may have been thinking of the "marriage supper of the Lamb" mentioned in Revelation xix.9.
9. The individual reeds in a set of Panpipes.
1. Pastoral, because Doric was the dialect of the Greek pastoral writers Theocritus, Bion, and Moschus.
2. I.e., the Hebrew prophets.
3. The penalty of death, occasioned by the sin of Adam.

He laid aside, and, here with us to be,
    Forsook the courts of everlasting day,
And chose with us a darksome house of mortal clay.

           3
15 Say, Heavenly Muse,[4] shall not thy sacred vein
Afford a present to the Infant God?
Hast thou no verse, no hymn, or solemn strain,
To welcome him to this his new abode,
Now while the heaven, by the Sun's team untrod,
20   Hath took no print of the approaching light,
And all the spangled host keep watch in squadrons
      bright?

           4
See how from far upon the eastern road
The star-led wizards[5] haste with odors sweet!
Oh run, prevent° them with thy humble ode,   *go before*
25 And lay it lowly at his blessed feet;
Have thou the honor first thy Lord to greet,
    And join thy voice unto the angel choir
From out his secret altar touched with hallowed fire.

    The Hymn

          1
    It was the winter wild,
30   While the heaven-born child
All meanly wrapt in the rude manger lies;
    Nature, in awe to him,
    Had doffed her gaudy trim,
With her great Master so to sympathize:
35 It was no season then for her
To wanton with the Sun, her lusty paramour.

          2
    Only with speeches fair
    She woos the gentle air
To hide her guilty front with innocent snow,
40   And on her naked shame,
    Pollute with sinful blame,
The saintly veil of maiden white to throw;
Confounded, that her Maker's eyes
Should look so near upon her foul deformities.

          3
45   But he, her fears to cease,
    Sent down the meek-eyed Peace:
She, crowned with olive green, came softly sliding
    Down through the turning sphere,[6]
    His ready harbinger,
50   With turtle° wing the amorous clouds dividing;   *dove*
And, waving wide her myrtle wand,
She strikes a universal peace through sea and land.

          4
    No war, or battle's sound,
    Was heard the world around;
55   The idle spear and shield were high uphung;

4. Urania, the Muse of Astronomy, later
identified with divine wisdom and treated by
Milton as the source of creative inspiration.
5. The "wise men from the east" (Matthew
ii.1).

6. The heavens as a whole, which "turn"
once daily about the earth because of the
earth's rotation.

The hookéd chariot[7] stood,
Unstained with hostile blood;
The trumpet spake not to the arméd throng;
And kings sat still with awful eye,
60 As if they surely knew their sovran Lord was by.

5

But peaceful was the night
Wherein the Prince of Light
His reign of peace upon the earth began.
The winds, with wonder whist,°   *hushed*
65 Smoothly the waters kissed,
Whispering new joys to the mild Ocean,
Who now hath quite forgot to rave,
While birds of calm[8] sit brooding on the charméd wave.

6

The stars, with deep amaze,
70 Stand fixed in steadfast gaze,
Bending one way their precious influence,[9]
And will not take their flight,
For all the morning light,
Or Lucifer[1] that often warned them thence;
75 But in their glimmering orbs[2] did glow,
Until their Lord himself bespake, and bid them go.

7

And, though the shady gloom
Had given day her room,
The Sun himself withheld his wonted speed,
80 And hid his head for shame,
As his inferior flame
The new-enlightened world no more should need:
He saw a greater Sun appear
Than his bright throne or burning axletree could bear.

8

85 The shepherds on the lawn,°   *meadow*
Or ere the point of dawn,
Sat simply chatting in a rustic row;
Full little thought they than°   *then*
That the mighty Pan[3]
90 Was kindly come to live with them below:
Perhaps their loves, or else their sheep,
Was all that did their silly° thoughts so busy keep.   *simple*

9

When such music sweet
Their hearts and ears did greet
95 As never was by mortal finger strook,°   *struck*
Divinely-warbled voice
Answering the stringéd noise,
As all their souls in blissful rapture took:

7. War chariots were sometimes armed with sickle-like hooks projecting from the hubs of the wheels.
8. Halcyons or kingfishers, which in ancient times were believed to build floating nests at sea about the time of the winter solstice, and to calm the waves during the incubation of their young.
9. Medieval astrologers believed that stars emitted an ethereal liquid ("influence") that had the power to nourish or otherwise affect all things on earth.
1. Probably the morning star, although Milton sometimes uses the word for the sun.
2. The concentric crystalline spheres of Ptolemaic astronomy. Each sphere was supposed to contain one or more of the heavenly bodies in its surface and to revolve about the earth.
3. The Greek shepherd god Pan (whose name means "all") was often associated with Christ.

The air, such pleasure loth to lose,
With thousand echoes still prolongs each heavenly close.°   *cadence*

10

Nature, that heard such sound
Beneath the hollow round
Of Cynthia's seat[4] the airy region thrilling,
Now was almost won
To think her part was done,
And that her reign had here its last fulfilling:
She knew such harmony alone
Could hold all Heaven and Earth in happier union.

11

At last surrounds their sight
A globe of circular light,
That with long beams the shamefaced Night arrayed;
The helméd cherubim
And sworded seraphim[5]
Are seen in glittering ranks with wings displayed,
Harping loud and solemn quire,
With unexpressive° notes, to Heaven's new-born Heir.   *inexpressible*

12

Such music (as 'tis said)
Before was never made,
But when of old the sons of morning sung,[6]
While the Creator great
His constellations set,
And the well-balanced world on hinges hung,
And cast the dark foundations deep,
And bid the weltering waves their oozy channel keep.

13

Ring out, ye crystal spheres,
Once bless our human ears,
If ye have power to touch our senses so;
And let your silver chime
Move in melodious time;
And let the bass of heaven's deep organ blow;
And with your ninefold harmony
Make up full consort to th' angelic symphony.

14

For, if such holy song
Enwrap our fancy long,
Time will run back and fetch the age of gold;[7]
And speckled vanity
Will sicken soon and die;
And leprous sin will melt from earthly mold;
And Hell itself will pass away,
And leave her dolorous mansions to the peering day.

15

Yea, Truth and Justice then
Will down return to men,
Orbed in a rainbow; and, like glories wearing,
Mercy will sit between,

---

4. I.e., beneath the sphere of the moon.
5. Seraphim and cherubim (both are plural forms) are the two highest of the nine orders of angels in the medieval classification.
6. Job speaks of the creation of the universe as the time "when the morning stars sang together, and all the sons of God shouted for joy" (Job xxxviii.7).
7. The Romans believed that Saturn, after his dethronement by Jupiter, fled to Italy and there brought in the Golden Age, a time of perfect peace and happiness.

145   Throned in celestial sheen,
With radiant feet the tissued clouds down steering;
And Heaven, as at some festival,
Will open wide the gates of her high palace-hall.
        16
        But wisest Fate says no,
150   This must not yet be so;
    The Babe lies yet in smiling infancy
        That on the bitter cross
        Must redeem our loss,
    So both himself and us to glorify:
155 Yet first, to those ychained[8] in sleep,
    The wakeful° trump of doom must thunder through the   *awakening*
        deep,
        17
        With such a horrid clang
        As on Mount Sinai rang,[9]
    While the red fire and smoldering clouds outbrake:
160   The aged Earth, aghast,
        With terror of that blast,
    Shall from the surface to the center shake,
    When, at the world's last sessïon,
    The dreadful Judge in middle air shall spread his throne.
        18
165   And then at last our bliss
        Full and perfect is,
    But now begins; for from this happy day
        Th' old Dragon° under ground,   *Satan*
        In straiter limits bound,
170   Not half so far casts his usurpéd sway,
    And, wroth to see his kingdom fail,
    Swinges° the scaly horror of his folded tail.   *lashes*
        19
        The Oracles are dumb;
        No voice or hideous hum
175 Runs through the archéd roof in words deceiving.
        Apollo from his shrine
        Can no more divine,
    With hollow shriek the steep of Delphos leaving.
    No nightly trance, or breathéd spell,
180 Inspires the pale-eyed priest from the prophetic cell.
        20
        The lonely mountains o'er,
        And the resounding shore,
    A voice of weeping heard and loud lament;
        From haunted spring, and dale
185   Edged with poplar pale,
    The parting genius° is with sighing sent;   *local spirit*
    With flower-inwoven tresses torn
    The Nymphs in twilight shade of tangled thickets mourn.
        21
        In consecrated earth,
190   And on the holy hearth,

8. Milton uses the archaic form of the past participle, common in Chaucer and imitated by Spenser, in which *y-* represents a reduced form of the Old English prefix *ge-*.

9. Moses received the Ten Commandments on Mount Sinai: "* * * there were thunders and lightnings * * * and the voice of the trumpet exceeding loud" (Exodus xix.16).

The Lars[1] and Lemures moan with midnight plaint;
  In urns and altars round,
  A drear and dying sound
Affrights the flamens° at their service quaint;°   *priests / elaborate*
95 And the chill marble seems to sweat,
While each peculiar power forgoes his wonted seat.

    22
  Peor[2] and Baälim
  Forsake their temples dim,
With that twice-battered God of Palestine;[3]
00   And moonéd Ashtaroth,[4]
  Heaven's queen and mother both,
Now sits not girt with tapers' holy shine:
  The Libyc Hammon[5] shrinks his horn;
In vain the Tyrian maids their wounded Thammuz mourn.[6]

    23
05 And sullen Moloch,[7] fled,
  Hath left in shadows dread
His burning idol all of blackest hue;
  In vain with cymbals' ring
  They call the grisly king,
210 In dismal dance about the furnace blue;
  The brutish gods of Nile as fast,
Isis, and Orus, and the dog Anubis,[8] haste.

    24
  Nor is Osiris seen
  In Memphian grove or green,
215 Trampling the unshowered grass with lowings loud;
  Nor can he be at rest
  Within his sacred chest;
Nought but profoundest Hell can be his shroud;
  In vain, with timbreled anthems dark,
220 The sable-stoléd sorcerers bear his worshiped ark.

    25
  He feels from Juda's land
  The dreaded Infant's hand;
The rays of Bethlehem blind his dusky eyn;°   *eyes*
  Nor all the gods beside
225   Longer dare abide,
Not Typhon[9] huge ending in snaky twine:
  Our Babe, to show his Godhead true,
Can in his swaddling bands control the damnéd crew.

    26
  So, when the sun in bed,
230   Curtained with cloudy red,
Pillows his chin upon an orient° wave,   *eastern*
  The flocking shadows pale

1. Tutelary gods or spirits of the ancient Romans associated with particular places. Lemures were hostile spirits of the unburied dead.
2. Baal or Baal-Peor, the highest Canaanite god, whose shrine was at Mount Peor. Baalim (the plural form) are lesser gods related to him.
3. Dagon, god of the Philistines, whose statue twice fell to the ground before the ark of the Lord (I Samuel v.1–4).
4. Astarte, a Phoenician goddess identified with the moon.
5. The Egyptian god Ammon, represented as a horned ram. He had a famous temple and oracle at an oasis in the Libyan desert.
6. The death of the god Thammuz, Ashtaroth's lover, symbolized the coming of winter. The Tyrian (Phoenician) women mourned for him in an annual ceremony.
7. A pagan god to whom children were sacrificed. Their cries were drowned out by the clang of cymbals.
8. The Egyptian goddess Isis was represented as a cow, the gods Orus and Anubis as a hawk and a dog (hence "brutish"). Osiris (line 213) the creator, who had a shrine at Memphis, was represented as a bull.
9. A hundred-headed monster destroyed by Zeus.

Troop to th' infernal jail;
Each fettered ghost slips to his several grave,
235 And the yellow-skirted fays
Fly after the night-steeds, leaving their moon-loved maze.
                27
    But see! the Virgin blest
    Hath laid her Babe to rest.
    Time is our tedious song should here have ending:
240   Heaven's youngest-teeméd star[1]
        Hath fixed her polished car,
    Her sleeping Lord with handmaid lamp attending;
    And all about the courtly stable
    Bright-harnessed angels sit in order serviceable.

                                            1629   1645

L'Allegro[2]

Hence loathéd Melancholy
    Of Cerberus[3] and blackest midnight born,
In Stygian[4] cave forlorn
    'Mongst horrid shapes, and shrieks, and sights unholy,
5   Find out some uncouth° cell,   *unknown*
    Where brooding Darkness spreads his jealous wings,
    And the night-raven sings;
    There under ebon shades, and low-browed rocks,
    As ragged as thy locks,
10   In dark Cimmerian[5] desert ever dwell.
    But come thou goddess fair and free,
    In Heaven yclept° Euphrosyne,[6]   *called*
    And by men, heart-easing Mirth,
    Whom lovely Venus at a birth
15 With two sister Graces more
    To ivy-crownéd Bacchus[7] bore;
    Or whether (as some sager sing)[8]
    The frolic wind that breathes the spring,
    Zephyr with Aurora playing,
20 As he met her once a-Maying,
    There on beds of violets blue,
    And fresh-blown° roses washed in dew,   *newly bloomed*
    Filled her with thee a daughter fair,
    So buxom,° blithe, and debonair.°   *merry / pleasant*
25 Haste thee nymph, and bring with thee
    Jest and youthful Jollity,
    Quips and Cranks,° and wanton Wiles,   *jests*
    Nods, and Becks,° and wreathéd Smiles,   *curtseys*
    Such as hang on Hebe's[9] cheek,
30 And love to live in dimple sleek;
    Sport that wrinkled Care derides,
    And Laughter, holding both his sides.

1. I.e., newest-born star, the star that guided the wise men, now imagined as having halted its "car" or chariot over the manger.
2. The cheerful man.
3. The three-headed dog that guarded the gates of hell.
4. Pertaining to the Styx, one of the rivers of the classical underworld.
5. In classical mythology the Cimmerians lived in a mysterious land somewhere across the ocean, where the sun never shone.

6. One of the three Graces, who were believed to bring joy into men's lives. Her name means "mirth."
7. The god of wine.
8. It is generally believed that the following mythical account of the birth of Euphrosyne is Milton's own invention. Zephyr is the west wind; Aurora, the dawn.
9. The cupbearer of Zeus, a goddess who personified youth.

Come, and trip it as ye go
On the light fantastic toe,
35 And in thy right hand lead with thee,
The mountain nymph, sweet Liberty;
And if I give thee honor due,
Mirth, admit me of thy crew
To live with her and live with thee,
40 In unreprovéd pleasures free;
To hear the lark begin his flight,
And, singing, startle the dull night,
From his watch-tower in the skies,
Till the dappled dawn doth rise;
45 Then to come in spite°of sorrow,   *contempt*
And at my window bid good morrow,
Through the sweetbriar, or the vine,
Or the twisted eglantine.
While the cock with lively din,
50 Scatters the rear of darkness thin,
And to the stack, or the barn door,
Stoutly struts his dames before;
Oft listening how the hounds and horn
Cheerly rouse the slumbering morn,
55 From the side of some hoar hill,
Through the high wood echoing shrill.
Sometime walking not unseen
By hedgerow elms, on hillocks green,
Right against the eastern gate,
60 Where the great sun begins his state,°   *progress*
Robed in flames, and amber light,
The clouds in thousand liveries dight;°   *dressed*
While the plowman near at hand,
Whistles o'er the furrowed land,
65 And the milkmaid singeth blithe,
And the mower whets his scythe,
And every shepherd tells his tale,
Under the hawthorn in the dale.
Straight mine eye hath caught new pleasures
70 Whilst the landscape round it measures,
Russet lawns and fallows gray,
Where the nibbling flocks do stray,
Mountains on whose barren breast
The laboring clouds do often rest;
75 Meadows trim with daisies pied,°   *variegated*
Shallow brooks, and rivers wide.
Towers and battlements it sees
Bosomed high in tufted trees,
Where perhaps some beauty lies,
80 The cynosure° of neighboring eyes.   *North Star*
Hard by, a cottage chimney smokes,
From betwixt two aged oaks,
Where Corydon and Thyrsis[1] met,
Are at their savory dinner set
85 Of herbs, and other country messes,
Which the neat-handed Phyllis dresses;
And then in haste her bower she leaves,

---

1. Conventional names in pastoral poetry, like Phyllis (line 86) and Thestylis (line 88).

With Thestylis to bind the sheaves;
Or if the earlier season lead
90 To the tanned haycock in the mead.
Sometimes with secure° delight   *carefree*
The upland hamlets will invite,
When the merry bells ring round
And the jocund rebecks[2] sound
95 To many a youth and many a maid,
Dancing in the checkered shade;
And young and old come forth to play
On a sunshine holiday,
Till the livelong daylight fail;
100 Then to the spicy nut-brown ale,
With stories told of many a feat,
How fairy Mab[3] the junkets eat;°   *ate*
She was pinched and pulled, she said,
And he, by Friar's lantern° led,   *will-o'-the-wisp*
105 Tells how the drudging goblin[4] sweat
To earn his cream-bowl, duly set,
When in one night, ere glimpse of morn,
His shadowy flail hath threshed the corn
That ten day-laborers could not end;
110 Then lies him down the lubber° fiend,   *loutish*
And, stretched out all the chimney's° length,   *fireplace's*
Basks at the fire his hairy strength;
And crop-full out of doors he flings
Ere the first cock his matin rings.
115 Thus done the tales, to bed they creep,
By whispering winds soon lulled asleep.
Towered cities please us then,
And the busy hum of men,
Where throngs of knights and barons bold,
120 In weeds° of peace high triumphs hold,   *garments*
With store of ladies, whose bright eyes
Rain influence,[5] and judge the prize
Of wit, or arms, while both contend
To win her grace, whom all commend.
125 There let Hymen[6] oft appear
In saffron robe, with taper clear,
And pomp, and feast, and revelry,
With masque, and antique pageantry;
Such sights as youthful poets dream
130 On summer eves by haunted stream.
Then to the well-trod stage anon,
If Jonson's learned sock[7] be on,
Or sweetest Shakespeare, fancy's child,
Warble his native wood-notes wild.
135 And ever against eating cares
Lap me in soft Lydian airs[8]
Married to immortal verse
Such as the meeting soul may pierce
In notes, with many a winding bout°   *turn*

2. A rebeck is a kind of three-stringed fiddle.
3. Queen of the fairies. The behavior attributed to fairies in this and the following lines reflects traditional rustic lore.
4. Hobgoblin or Robin Goodfellow.
5. Medieval astrologers believed that the stars emitted an ethereal liquid ("influence") that could powerfully affect the lives of men.
6. God of marriage.
7. The light shoe worn by Greek comic actors, here standing for the comedies of Ben Jonson.
8. Lydian music was noted for its voluptuous sweetness.

40   Of linkéd sweetness long drawn out,
    With wanton heed, and giddy cunning,
    The melting voice through mazes running;
    Untwisting all the chains that tie
    The hidden soul of harmony;
45   That Orpheus' self[9] may heave his head
    From golden slumber on a bed
    Of heaped Elysian flowers, and hear
    Such strains as would have won the ear
    Of Pluto, to have quite set free
50   His half-regained Eurydice.
    These delights if thou canst give,
    Mirth, with thee I mean to live.

                ca. 1631   1645

Il Penseroso[1]

    Hence vain deluding Joys,
      The brood of Folly without father bred.
    How little you bestead,°   *profit*
      Or fill the fixéd mind with all your toys;°   *trifles*
5   Dwell in some idle brain,
      And fancies fond° with gaudy shapes possess,   *foolish*
    As thick and numberless
      As the gay motes that people the sunbeams,
    Or likest hovering dreams,
10   The fickle pensioners° of Morpheus'[2] train.   *retainers*
    But hail thou Goddess, sage and holy,
    Hail, divinest Melancholy,
    Whose saintly visage is too bright
    To hit° the sense of human sight;   *affect*
15   And therefore to our weaker view,
    O'erlaid with black, staid Wisdom's hue.
    Black, but such as in esteem,
    Prince Memnon's sister[3] might beseem,
    Or that starred Ethiope queen[4] that strove
20   To set her beauty's praise above
    The sea nymphs, and their powers offended.
    Yet thou art higher far descended;
    Thee bright-haired Vesta long of yore
    To solitary Saturn bore;[5]
25   His daughter she (in Saturn's reign
    Such mixture was not held a stain).
    Oft in glimmering bowers and glades
    He met her, and in secret shades
    Of woody Ida's inmost grove,
30   While yet there was no fear of Jove.
    Come pensive nun, devout and pure,

---

9. The great musician of classical mythology, whose wife Eurydice died on their wedding day. He won permission from Pluto, god of the underworld, to lead her back to the land of the living, but only on the condition that he not look to see if she was following him. Unable to resist a backward glance, he lost her forever.
1. The pensive man.
2. God of sleep.
3. Memnon, an Ethiopian prince, was called the handsomest of men. His sister was Hemera, whose name means "day."

4. Cassiopeia, who boasted that her beauty (or her daughter's, in some accounts) surpassed that of the daughters of the sea-god Nereus. "Starred" refers to the fact that a constellation bears her name.
5. The parentage here attributed to Melancholy is Milton's invention. Saturn, who ruled on Mt. Ida before being overthrown by his son Jove, was associated with melancholy because of the supposedly "saturnine" influence of the planet which bears his name. His daughter Vesta was the goddess of purity.

Sober, steadfast, and demure,
All in a robe òf darkest grain,°   *color*
Flowing with majestic train,
35 And sable stole of cypress lawn[6]
Over thy decent shoulders drawn.
Come, but keep thy wonted state,
With even step and musing gait,
And looks commercing with the skies,
40 Thy rapt soul sitting in thine eyes:
There held in holy passion still,
Forget thyself to marble, till
With a sad° leaden downward cast,   *serious*
Thou fix them on the earth as fast.
45 And join with thee calm Peace and Quiet,
Spare Fast, that oft with gods doth diet,
And hears the Muses in a ring
Aye round about Jove's altar sing.
And add to these retired Leisure,
50 That in trim gardens takes his pleasure;
But first, and chiefest, with thee bring,
Him that yon soars on golden wing,
Guiding the fiery-wheeléd throne,
The cherub Contemplation;[7]
55 And the mute Silence hist° along   *beckon*
'Less Philomel[8] will deign a song,
In her sweetest, saddest plight,
Smoothing the rugged brow of night,
While Cynthia[9] checks her dragon yoke
60 Gently o'er th' accustomed oak;
Sweet bird that shunn'st the noise of folly,
Most musical, most melancholy!
Thee chantress oft the woods among,
I woo to hear thy evensong;
65 And missing thee, I walk unseen
On the dry smooth-shaven green,
To behold the wandering moon,
Riding near her highest noon,
Like one that had been led astray
70 Through the Heaven's wide pathless way;
And oft as if her head she bowed,
Stooping through a fleecy cloud.
Oft on a plat° of rising ground,   *plot*
I hear the far-off curfew sound,
75 Over some wide-watered shore,
Swinging slow with sullen roar;
Or if the air will not permit,
Some still removéd place will fit,
Where glowing embers through the room
80 Teach light to counterfeit a gloom
Far from all resort of mirth,
Save the cricket on the hearth,
Or the bellman's° drowsy charm,   *night-watchman's*
To bless the doors from nightly harm;

6. A gauzy, crepe-like material, usually dyed black and used for mourning garments. Cypress: Cyprus, where the material was originally made.
7. Milton is thinking of the vision of the four cherubim (a high order of angels) stationed beside four wheels of fire under the throne of the Lord (Ezekiel i and x).
8. The nightingale, often associated with a sad or contemplative mood.
9. Goddess of the moon, sometimes represented as driving a team of dragons.

85 Or let my lamp at midnight hour
Be seen in some high lonely tower,
Where I may oft outwatch the Bear,[1]
With thrice great Hermes,[2] or unsphere
The spirit of Plato to unfold
90 What worlds, or what vast regions hold
The immortal mind that hath forsook
Her mansion in this fleshly nook;
And of those demons[3] that are found
In fire, air, flood, or underground,
95 Whose power hath a true consent°   correspondence
With planet, or with element.
Some time let gorgeous Tragedy
In sceptered pall° come sweeping by,   robe
Presenting Thebes, or Pelops' line,
00 Or the tale of Troy divine.[4]
Or what (though rare) of later age
Ennobled hath the buskined[5] stage.
But, O sad virgin, that thy power
Might raise Musaeus[6] from his bower,
105 Or bid the soul of Orpheus sing
Such notes as, warbled to the string,
Drew iron tears down Pluto's cheek,
And made Hell grant what Love did seek.
Or call up him[7] that left half told
110 The story of Cambuscan bold,
Of Camball, and of Algarsife,
And who had Canacee to wife,
That owned the virtuous° ring and glass,   potent
And of the wondrous horse of brass,
115 On which the Tartar king did ride;
And if aught else great bards beside
In sage and solemn tunes have sung,
Of tourneys and of trophies hung,
Of forests and enchantments drear,
120 Where more is meant than meets the ear.
Thus, Night, oft see me in thy pale career,
Till civil-suited morn[8] appear,
Not tricked and frounced° as she was wont,   curled
With the Attic boy to hunt,
125 But kerchiefed in a comely cloud,
While rocking winds are piping loud,
Or ushered with a shower still,
When the gust hath blown his fill,
Ending on the rustling leaves,
130 With minute-drops from off the eaves.
And when the sun begins to fling
His flaring beams, me, Goddess, bring

1. The Great Bear or Big Dipper, which in northern latitudes never sets.
2. Hermes Trismegistus ("thrice-great"), a name given by Neo-Platonists to the Egyptian god Thoth, who was sometimes identified with the Greek Hermes. He was thought to be the actual author of some forty books embodying mystical, theosophical, astrological, and alchemical doctrines. "Unsphere": call back from his present sphere.
3. Supernatural beings inhabiting each of the four "elements": fire, air, water, and earth.
4. The city of Thebes, the descendants of Pelops, and the Trojan War afforded the subjects of most Greek tragedies.
5. The buskin was the high boot worn by Greek tragic actors.
6. A legendary Greek poet, contemporary of Orpheus (line 105), for whose story see the note to *L'Allegro*, line 145.
7. Chaucer, whose *Squire's Tale* leaves unfinished the story of Cambuscan and his three children, Cambala, Algarsyf, and Canacee.
8. Aurora, goddess of the dawn, who loved Cephalus ("the Attic boy," line 124).

To archéd walks of twilight groves,
And shadows brown that Sylvan[9] loves
135 Of pine or monumental oak,
Where the rude ax with heavéd stroke,
Was never heard the nymphs to daunt,
Or fright them from their hallowed haunt.
There in close covert by some brook,
140 Where no profaner eye may look,
Hide me from day's garish eye,
While the bee with honeyed thigh,
That at her flowery work doth sing,
And the waters murmuring
145 With such consort° as they keep,   *harmony*
Entice the dewy-feathered sleep;
And let some strange mysterious dream,
Wave at his wings in airy stream,
Of lively portraiture displayed,
150 Softly on my eyelids laid.
And as I wake, sweet music breathe
Above, about, or underneath,
Sent by some spirit to mortals good,
Or th' unseen genius° of the wood.   *indwelling spirit*
155 But let my due feet never fail
To walk the studious cloister's pale,°   *enclosure*
And love the high embowéd roof,
With antic[1] pillars massy proof,
And storied windows richly dight,°   *dressed*
160 Casting a dim religious light.
There let the pealing organ blow,
To the full-voicéd choir below,
In service high, and anthems clear,
As may with sweetness, through mine ear,
165 Dissolve me into ectasies,
And bring all heaven before mine eyes.
And may at last my weary age
Find out the peaceful hermitage,
The hairy gown and mossy cell,
170 Where I may sit and rightly spell°   *speculate*
Of every star that Heaven doth show,
And every herb that sips the dew
Till old experience do attain
To something like prophetic strain.
175 These pleasures, Melancholy, give,
And I with thee will choose to live.

ca.1631   1645

On Shakespeare

What needs my Shakespeare for his honored bones
The labor of an age in piléd stones?
Or that his hallowed reliques should be hid
Under a star-ypointing[2] pyramid?
5   Dear son of Memory,[3] great heir of Fame,

9. Sylvanus, god of forests.
1. Fancifully decorated. "Massy proof": massive solidity. "Storied windows" (line 159): windows with representations of Biblical stories in stained glass.
2. Milton uses the archaic form of the past participle, common in Chaucer and imitated by Spenser, in which y- represents a reduced form of the Old English prefix *ge-*.
3. Memory (Mneymosyne) was the mother of the Muses.

What need'st thou such weak witness of thy name?
Thou in our wonder and astonishment
Hast built thyself a livelong monument.
For whilst, to th' shame of slow-endeavoring art,
10 Thy easy numbers° flow, and that each heart   *verses*
Hath from the leaves of thy unvalued° book   *invaluable*
Those Delphic[4] lines with deep impression took,
Then thou, our fancy of itself bereaving,
Dost make us marble with too much conceiving,
15 And so sepúlchred in such pomp dost lie
That kings for such a tomb would wish to die.

                                        1630   1645

How Soon Hath Time

How soon hath Time, the subtle thief of youth,
  Stoln on his wing my three and twentieth year!
  My hasting days fly on with full career,
  But my late spring no bud or blossom shew'th.°   *showeth*
5 Perhaps my semblance might deceive the truth,
  That I to manhood am arrived so near,
  And inward ripeness doth much less appear,
  That some more timely-happy spirits endu'th.°   *endoweth*
Yet be it less or more, or soon or slow,
10   It shall be still in strictest measure even°   *equal*
  To that same lot, however mean or high,
Toward which Time leads me, and the will of Heaven;
  All is, if I have grace to use it so,
  As ever in my great Taskmaster's eye.

                                        1631   1645

When the Assault Was Intended to the City[5]

Captain or colonel,[6] or knight in arms,
  Whose chance on these defenseless doors may seize,
  If deed of honor did thee ever please,
  Guard them, and him within protect from harms.
5 He can requite thee; for he knows the charms
  That call fame on such gentle acts as these,
  And he can spread thy name o'er lands and seas,
  Whatever clime the sun's bright circle warms.
Lift not thy spear against the Muses' bower:
10   The great Emathian conqueror[7] bid spare
  The house of Pindarus, when temple and tower
Went to the ground; and the repeated air
  Of sad Electra's poet[8] had the power
  To save the Athenian walls from ruin bare.

                                        1642   1645

4. Pertaining to Apollo, god of poetry, who had an oracle at Delphi.
5. In November 1642, a Royalist army advanced on London with the hope of capturing it but turned back without a battle when it discovered that it faced a well-trained militia of 20,000 men.
6. Three syllables.
7. Alexander the Great, who in destroying Thebes for its revolt against him is reported by Pliny to have spared the house of the poet Pindar.
8. Euripides. According to Plutarch, Athens was saved from destruction when one of its Spartan conquerors urged clemency on his fellows by quoting from the first chorus of Euripides' *Electra*.

Lady That in the Prime

Lady, that in the prime of earliest youth
    Wisely hast shunned the broad way and the green,
    And with those few art eminently seen
    That labor up the hill of heavenly truth,
5   The better part with Mary[9] and with Ruth
    Chosen thou hast; and they that overween,
    And at thy growing virtues fret their spleen,
    No anger find in thee, but pity and ruth.
Thy care is fixed, and zealously attends
10   To fill thy odorous lamp with deeds of light,[1]
    And hope that reaps not shame. Therefore be sure
Thou, when the bridegroom with his feastful friends
    Passes to bliss at the mid-hour of night,
    Hast gained thy entrance, virgin wise and pure.

                           1644   1645

To Mr. H. Lawes,[2] On His Airs

Harry, whose tuneful and well-measured song
    First taught our English music how to span
    Words with just note and accent, not to scan
    With Midas' ears,[3] committing° short and long,   *misjoining*
5   Thy worth and skill exempts thee from the throng,
    With praise enough for Envy to look wan;
    To after-age thou shalt be writ the man
    That with smooth air couldst humor best our tongue.
Thou honor'st Verse, and Verse must lend her wing
10   To honor thee, the priest of Phœbus' choir,[4]
    That tun'st their happiest lines in hymn or story.
Dante shall give Fame leave to set thee higher
    Than his Casella,[5] whom he wooed to sing,
    Met in the milder shades of Purgatory.

                           1645   1648

I Did But Prompt the Age

I did but prompt the age to quit their clogs
    By the known rules of ancient liberty,
    When straight a barbarous noise environs me
    Of owls and cuckoos, asses, apes, and dogs;[6]
5   As when those hinds that were transformed to frogs
    Railed at Latona's twin-born progeny,[7]

9. Commended by Jesus for having "chosen that good part, which shall not be taken away," when she listened to his words instead of helping her sister Martha (Luke x.38–42). Ruth, steadfastly devoted to her mother-in-law Naomi after both their husbands had died, chose to give up her home in Moab in order to follow Naomi when she returned to her native Judah (Ruth i.16).
1. The allusion is to the parable of the ten virgins. When they went forth to meet the bridegroom, only five took extra oil for their lamps. Hence, when the bridegroom came after a delay, only they were admitted to the marriage feast, the other five having gone to seek more oil for their spent lamps (Matthew xxv.1–13).
2. The composer Henry Lawes, who had writ-

ten the music for Milton's mask *Comus*.
3. Midas was given ass's ears for having preferred Pan's music to Apollo's.
4. Phoebus Apollo was god of music and poetry.
5. In the *Divine Comedy* Dante represents himself, on the threshold of Purgatory, as meeting the shade of his musician friend Casella, who sings a ballad to him.
6. Milton had been attacked for advocating liberalized divorce laws. "Ancient liberty" (line 2) refers to the law of divorce set forth in Deuteronomy xxiv.1.
7. Apollo and Diana, afterwards deities of the sun and moon respectively. Their mother Latona was refused a drink by Lycian peasants, who were thereupon transformed to frogs by the twins' father Jove.

Which after held the sun and moon in fee.°   *possession*
  But this is got by casting pearl to hogs,
That bawl for freedom in their senseless mood,
10   And still revolt when truth would set them free.
  License they mean when they cry liberty;
For who loves that must first be wise and good:
  But from that mark how far they rove we see,
For all this waste of wealth and loss of blood.

                      1645   1673

When I Consider How My Light Is Spent[8]

When I consider how my light is spent
  Ere half my days, in this dark world and wide,
  And that one talent which is death to hide[9]
  Lodged with me useless, though my soul more bent
5 To serve therewith my Maker, and present
  My true account, lest he returning chide;
  "Doth God exact day-labor, light denied?"
I fondly° ask; but Patience to prevent   *foolishly*
That murmur, soon replies, "God doth not need
10   Either man's work or his own gifts; who best
  Bear his mild yoke, they serve him best. His state
Is kingly. Thousands at his bidding speed
  And post o'er land and ocean without rest:
  They also serve who only stand and wait."

                  ca. 1652   1673

On the Late Massacre in Piedmont[1]

Avenge, O Lord, thy slaughtered saints, whose bones
  Lie scattered on the Alpine mountains cold,
  Even them who kept thy truth so pure of old
  When all our fathers worshiped stocks° and stones,[2]   *idols*
5 Forget not: in thy book record their groans
  Who were thy sheep and in their ancient fold
  Slain by the bloody Piedmontese that rolled
Mother with infant down the rocks. Their moans
The vales redoubled to the hills, and they
10   To Heaven. Their martyred blood and ashes sow
  O'er all th' Italian fields where still doth sway
The triple tyrant:[3] that from these may grow
  A hundredfold, who having learnt thy way
  Early may fly the Babylonian woe.[4]

                  1655   1673

---

8. Milton had become totally blind in 1651.
9. An allusion to the parable of the talents, in which the servant who buried the single talent his lord had given him, instead of investing it, was deprived of all he had and cast "into outer darkness" at the lord's return (Matthew xxv.14–30).
1. Some 1700 members of the Protestant Waldensian sect in the Piedmont in northwestern Italy died as a result of a treacherous attack by the Duke of Savoy's forces on Easter Day, 1655.

2. The Waldenses had existed as a sect, first within the Catholic Church and then as heretics, since the 12th century. They were particularly critical of materialistic tendencies in the Church.
3. The Pope, whose tiara has three crowns.
4. Babylon, as a city of luxury and vice, was often linked with the Papal Court by Protestants, who took the destruction of the city described in Revelation xviii as an allegory of the fate in store for the Roman Church.

Lawrence[5] of Virtuous Father

Lawrence, of virtuous father virtuous son,
 Now that the fields are dank, and ways are mire,
 Where shall we sometimes meet, and by the fire
 Help waste a sullen day, what may be won
5 From the hard season gaining? Time will run
 On smoother, till Favonius[6] reinspire
 The frozen earth, and clothe in fresh attire
 The lily and rose, that neither sowed nor spun.[7]
What neat repast shall feast us, light and choice,
10 Of Attic[8] taste, with wine, whence we may rise
 To hear the lute well touched, or artful voice
Warble immortal notes and Tuscan air?
 He who of those delights can judge, and spare
 To interpose them oft, is not unwise.

          ca. 1655   1673

Cyriack,[9] Whose Grandsire

Cyriack, whose grandsire on the royal bench
 Of British Themis,[1] with no mean applause,
 Pronounced, and in his volumes taught, our laws,
 Which others at their bar so often wrench,
5 Today deep thoughts resolve with me to drench
 In mirth that after no repenting draws;
 Let Euclid rest, and Archimedes pause,
 And what the Swede intend, and what the French.
To measure life learn thou betimes,° and know   *early*
10 Toward solid good what leads the nearest way;
 For other things mild Heaven a time ordains,
And disapproves that care, though wise in show,
 That with superfluous burden loads the day,
 And, when God sends a cheerful hour, refrains.

          ca. 1655   1673

Methought I Saw

Methought I saw my late espousèd saint[2]
 Brought to me like Alcestis[3] from the grave,
 Whom Jove's great son to her glad husband gave,
 Rescued from Death by force, though pale and faint.
5 Mine, as whom washed from spot of child-bed taint
 Purification in the Old Law did save,[4]
 And such, as yet once more I trust to have
 Full sight of her in heaven without restraint,

5. Edward Lawrence, a friend of Milton's though twenty-five years his junior, was the son of Henry Lawrence, Lord President of the Council of State at the time this sonnet was written.
6. The Latin name of the west wind.
7. "Consider the lilies of the field, how they grow; they toil not, neither do they spin" (Matthew vi.28).
8. Athenian; i.e., delicate, discriminating.
9. Cyriack Skinner, a pupil of Milton's and grandson of Sir Edward Coke, the great jurist who had been Chief Justice of the King's Bench under James I.

1. The Greek goddess of justice.
2. The "saint," or soul in heaven, is Milton's second wife, Katherine Woodcock, to whom he had been married less than two years (hence "late espousèd") when she died in 1658. Since Milton had become blind in 1651, it is almost certain that he had never seen his wife.
3. The wife who is brought back from the dead to her husband Admetus by Hercules ("Jove's great son") in Euripides' *Alcestis.*
4. Hebrew law (Leviticus xii) prescribed certain sacrificial rituals for the purification of women after childbirth.

Came vested all in white, pure as her mind.
10   Her face was veiled; yet to my fancied sight
Love, sweetness, goodness, in her person shined
So clear as in no face with more delight.
But O, as to embrace me she inclined,
I waked, she fled, and day brought back my night.

                                         ca. 1658   1673

To the Lord General Cromwell[8]

Cromwell, our chief of men, who through a cloud,
    Not of war only, but detractions rude,
    Guided by faith and matchless fortitude,
    To peace and truth thy glorious way hast ploughed,
5 And on the neck of crownéd Fortune[9] proud
    Hast reared God's trophies, and His work pursued,
    While Darwen stream,[1] with blood of Scots imbrued,
    And Dunbar field, resounds thy praises loud,
And Worcester's laureate wreath: yet much remains
10   To conquer still; peace hath her victories
    No less renowned than war: new foes arise,
Threatening to bind our souls with secular chains.
    Help us to save free conscience from the paw
    Of hireling wolves, whose gospel is their maw.

                                         1652   1694

From PARADISE LOST

Book IX

The Argument

Satan, having compassed the Earth, with meditated guile returns as a mist by
night into Paradise; enters into the Serpent sleeping. Adam and Eve in the morn-
ing go forth to their labors, which Eve proposes to divide in several places, each
laboring apart: Adam consents not, alleging the danger lest that enemy of whom
they were forewarned should attempt her found alone. Eve, loth to be thought
not circumspect or firm enough, urges her going apart, the rather desirous to
make trial of her strength; Adam at last yields. The Serpent finds her alone: his
subtle approach, first gazing, then speaking, with much flattery extolling Eve
above all other creatures. Eve, wondering to hear the Serpent speak, asks how
he attained to human speech and such understanding not till now; the Serpent
answers that by tasting of a certain tree in the Garden he attained both to speech
and reason, till then void of both. Eve requires him to bring her to that tree,
and finds it to be the Tree of Knowledge forbidden; the Serpent, now grown
bolder, with many wiles and arguments induces her at length to eat. She, pleased
with the taste, deliberates a while whether to impart thereof to Adam or not;
at last brings him of the fruit; relates what persuaded her to eat thereof. Adam,
at first amazed, but perceiving her lost, resolves, through vehemence of love,
to perish with her, and, extenuating the trespass, eats also of the fruit. The ef-
fects thereof in them both; they seek to cover their nakedness; then fall to
variance and accusation of one another.

---

8. Oliver Cromwell, successor to Sir Thomas
Fairfax as commander-in-chief of the Parlia-
mentary armies.
9. Charles I had been executed in 1649.

1. A river near Preston, where Cromwell had
won a victory in 1648. Dunbar (line 8) and
Worcester (line 9) were the sites of victories
in 1650 and 1651.

No more of talk where God or angel guest[2]
With man, as with his friend, familiar used
To sit indulgent, and with him partake
Rural repast, permitting him the while
5   Venial° discourse unblamed. I now must change   *allowable*
Those notes to tragic—foul distrust, and breach
Disloyal, on the part of man, revolt
And disobedience; on the part of Heaven,
Now alienated, distance and distaste,
10   Anger and just rebuke, and judgment given,
That brought into this world a world of woe,
Sin and her shadow Death, and Misery,
Death's harbinger. Sad task, yet argument
Not less but more heroic than the wrath
15   Of stern Achilles on his foe pursued
Thrice fugitive about Troy wall; or rage
Of Turnus for Lavinia disespoused;
Or Neptune's ire, or Juno's, that so long
Perplexed the Greek, and Cytherea's son:[3]
20   If answerable style I can obtain
Of my celestial Patroness,[4] who deigns
Her nightly visitation unimplored,
And dictates to me slumbering, or inspires
Easy my unpremeditated verse,
25   Since first this subject for heroic song
Pleased me, long choosing and beginning late,
Not sedulous by nature to indite°   *write about*
Wars, hitherto the only argument
Heroic deemed, chief mastery to dissect
30   With long and tedious havoc fabled knights
In battles feigned (the better fortitude
Of patience and heroic martyrdom
Unsung), or to describe races and games,
Or tilting furniture,[5] emblazoned shields,
35   Impresses quaint, caparisons and steeds,
Bases and tinsel trappings, gorgeous knights
At joust and tournament; then marshaled feast
Served up in hall with sewers and seneschals:[6]
The skill of artifice or office mean;
40   Not that which justly gives heroic name
To person or to poem. Me, of these
Nor skilled nor studious, higher argument
Remains, sufficient of itself to raise
That name, unless an age too late, or cold
45   Climate, or years, damp my intended wing
Depressed; and much they may if all be mine,
Not hers who brings it nightly to my ear.
     The sun was sunk, and after him the star
Of Hesperus, whose office is to bring

---

2. Adam has just concluded a conversation with the angel Raphael at the end of Book VIII.
3. Important moments in important epics. Achilles, whose "wrath" is the epic subject announced in the first line of the *Iliad*, pursued Hector three times around the walls of Troy before slaying him. Turnus (in the *Aeneid*) fought with Aeneas for the hand of Lavinia. Neptune hindered Odysseus ("the Greek") in his attempts to return home after the Trojan War, and Juno, hostile to Venus ("Cytherea"), made difficulties for Venus' son Aeneas.
4. Urania, the "Heavenly Muse" whose aid Milton had invoked at the beginning of Book I.
5. The equipment used in a "tilt" or tournament, examples of which follow. Impresses were heraldic emblems displayed on shields. Bases were skirt-like coverings, sometimes of mail, intended to decorate and protect warhorses.
6. High-ranking household servants.

50 Twilight upon the Earth, short arbiter
'Twixt day and night, and now from end to end
Night's hemisphere had veiled the horizon round,
When Satan, who late fled before the threats
Of Gabriel out of Eden, now improved
55 In meditated fraud and malice, bent
On man's destruction, maugre° what might hap   *despite*
Of heavier on himself, fearless returned.
By night he fled, and at midnight returned
From compassing the Earth—cautious of day
60 Since Uriel,[7] regent of the sun, descried
His entrance, and forewarned the Cherubim
That kept their watch. Thence, full of anguish, driven,
The space of seven continued nights he rode
With darkness; thrice the equinoctial line
65 He circled, four times crossed the car of Night
From pole to pole, traversing each colure;[8]
On the eighth returned, and on the coast averse°   *side opposite*
From entrance or cherubic watch by stealth
Found unsuspected way. There was a place
70 (Now not, though Sin, not Time, first wrought the change)
Where Tigris, at the foot of Paradise,
Into a gulf shot under ground, till part
Rose up a fountain by the Tree of Life.
In with the river sunk and with it rose
75 Satan, involved in rising mist; then sought
Where to lie hid. Sea he had searched and land,
From Eden over Pontus,[9] and the pool
Maeotis, up beyond the river Ob;
Downward as far antarctic; and, in length,
80 West from Orontes to the ocean barred
At Darien, thence to the land where flows
Ganges and Indus. Thus the orb he roamed
With narrow search, and with inspection deep
Considered every creature, which of all
85 Most opportune might serve his wiles, and found
The serpent subtlest beast of all the field.
Him, after long debate, irresolute
Of thoughts revolved, his final sentence chose
Fit vessel, fittest imp° of fraud, in whom   *graft*
90 To enter, and his dark suggestions hide
From sharpest sight; for in the wily snake
Whatever sleights none would suspicious mark,
As from his wit and native subtlety
Proceeding, which, in other beasts observed,
95 Doubt° might beget of diabolic power   *suspicion*
Active within beyond the sense of brute.
Thus he resolved, but first from inward grief
His bursting passion into plaints thus poured:
    "O Earth, how like to Heaven, if not preferred

---

7. In medieval astronomy, each of the concentric crystalline spheres containing one of the heavenly bodies was supposed to be inhabited by an angel, its "intelligence," who governed its motion.
8. The *equinoctial line* is the equator. The colures (line 66) are two of the great circles that pass through the celestial poles, one intersecting the ecliptic at the equinoxes, the other at the solstices. Satan circles the earth for the space of seven days, first along the equator and then over the poles, always timing his flight so as to remain hidden on the dark side.
9. Satan's search had extended from the Black Sea (Pontus) to the connecting Sea of Azov (the pool Maeotis) and northward beyond the river Ob in Siberia: southward to the antarctic; and westward from the Orontes River in Syria to the isthmus of Panama (Darien) and on around the world to India.

100 More justly, seat worthier of Gods, as built
With second thoughts, reforming what was old!
For what God, after better, worse would build?
Terrestrial Heaven, danced round by other Heavens,
That shine, yet bear their bright officious° lamps,   *obliging*
105 Light above light, for thee alone, as seems,
In thee concentring all their precious beams
Of sacred influence! As God in Heaven
Is center, yet extends to all, so thou
Centring receiv'st from all those orbs; in thee,
110 Not in themselves, all their known virtue appears,
Productive in herb, plant, and nobler birth
Of creatures animate with gradual life
Of growth, sense, reason, all summed up in man.
With what delight could I have walked thee round,
115 If I could joy in aught; sweet interchange
Of hill and valley, rivers, woods, and plains,
Now land, now sea, and shores with forest crowned,
Rocks, dens, and caves! But I in none of these
Find place or refuge; and, the more I see
120 Pleasures about me, so much more I feel
Torment within me, as from the hateful siege
Of contraries; all good to me becomes
Bane, and in Heaven much worse would be my state.
But neither here seek I, no, nor in Heaven,
125 To dwell, unless by mastering Heaven's Supreme;
Nor hope to be myself less miserable
By what I seek, but others to make such
As I, though thereby worse to me redound.
For only in destroying I find ease
130 To my relentless thoughts; and him destroyed,
Or won to what may work his utter loss,
For whom all this was made, all this will soon
Follow, as to him linked in weal or woe:
In woe then, that destruction wide may range!
135 To me shall be the glory sole among
The infernal Powers, in one day to have marred
What he, Almighty styled, six nights and days
Continued making, and who knows how long
Before had been contriving; though perhaps
140 Not longer than since I in one night freed
From servitude inglorious well nigh half
The angelic name,[1] and thinner left the throng
Of his adorers. He, to be avenged,
And to repair his numbers thus impaired—
145 Whether such virtue, spent of old, now failed
More angels to create (if they at least
Are his created), or to spite us more—
Determined to advance into our room
A creature formed of earth, and him endow,
150 Exalted from so base original,
With Heavenly spoils, our spoils. What he decreed
He effected; Man he made, and for him built
Magnificent this World, and Earth his seat,

---

1. I.e., half the angels. Satan alludes to the revolt he led against God, the consequence of which was that he and his supporters (whose number he exaggerates here) were cast out of heaven into hell.

Him Lord pronounced, and, O indignity!
55 Subjected to his service angel-wings
And flaming ministers, to watch and tend
Their earthy charge. Of these the vigilance
I dread, and to elude, thus wrapped in mist
Of midnight vapor, glide obscure, and pry
60 In every bush and brake, where hap may find
The serpent sleeping, in whose mazy folds
To hide me, and the dark intent I bring.
O foul descent! that I, who erst contended
With Gods to sit the highest, am now constrained
65 Into a beast, and, mixed with bestial slime,
This essence to incarnate and imbrute,
That to the height of deity aspired!
But what will not ambition and revenge
Descend to? Who aspires must down as low
70 As high he soared, obnoxious,° first or last,   *subject*
To basest things. Revenge, at first though sweet,
Bitter ere long back on itself recoils.
Let it; I reck not, so it light well aimed,
Since higher I fall short, on him who next
75 Provokes my envy, this new favorite
Of Heaven, this man of clay, son of despite,
Whom, us the more to spite, his Maker raised
From dust: spite then with spite is best repaid."
        So saying, through each thicket, dank or dry,
80 Like a black mist low-creeping, he held on
His midnight search, where soonest he might find
The serpent. Him fast sleeping soon he found,
In labyrinth of many a round self-rolled,
His head the midst, well stored with subtle wiles:
185 Not yet in horrid shade or dismal den,
Nor nocent° yet, but on the grassy herb,   *harmful*
Fearless, unfeared, he slept. In at his mouth
The Devil entered, and his brutal sense,
In heart or head, possessing soon inspired
190 With act intelligential; but his sleep
Disturbed not, waiting close the approach of morn.
        Now, whenas sacred light began to dawn
In Eden on the humid flowers, that breathed
Their morning incense, when all things that breathe
195 From th' Earth's great altar send up silent praise
To the Creator, and his nostrils fill
With grateful smell, forth came the human pair,
And joined their vocal worship to the choir
Of creatures wanting voice; that done, partake
200 The season, prime for sweetest scents and airs;
Then cómmune how that day they best may ply
Their growing work; for much their work outgrew
The hands' dispatch of two gardening so wide:
And Eve first to her husband thus began:
205 "Adam, well may we labor still° to dress   *constantly*
This garden, still to tend plant, herb, and flower,
Our pleasant task enjoined; but, till more hands
Aid us, the work under our labor grows,
Luxurious by restraint: what we by day
210 Lop overgrown, or prune, or prop, or bind,

One night or two with wanton growth derides,
Tending to wild. Thou, therefore, now advise,
Or hear what to my mind first thoughts present.
Let us divide our labors; thou where choice
215 Leads thee, or where most needs, whether to wind
The woodbine round this arbor, or direct
The clasping ivy where to climb; while I
In yonder spring of roses intermixed
With myrtle find what to redress till noon.
220 For, while so near each other thus all day
Our task we choose, what wonder if so near
Looks intervene and smiles, or object new
Casual discourse draw on, which intermits
Our day's work, brought to little, though begun
225 Early, and the hour of supper comes unearned!"
      To whom mild answer Adam thus returned:
"Sole Eve, associate sole, to me beyond
Compare above all living creatures dear!
Well hast thou motioned,° well thy thoughts employed   suggested
230 How we might best fulfil the work which here
God hath assigned us, nor of me shalt pass
Unpraised; for nothing lovelier can be found
In woman than to study household good,
And good works in her husband to promote.
235 Yet not so strictly hath our Lord imposed
Labor as to debar us when we need
Refreshment, whether food, or talk between,
Food of the mind, or this sweet intercourse
Of looks and smiles; for smiles from reason flow,
240 To brute denied, and are of love the food;
Love, not the lowest end of human life.
For not to irksome toil, but to delight,
He made us, and delight to reason joined.
These paths and bowers doubt not but our joint hands
245 Will keep from wilderness with ease, as wide
As we need walk, till younger hands ere long
Assist us. But, if much converse perhaps
Thee satiate, to short absence I could yield;
For solitude sometimes is best society,
250 And short retirement urges sweet return.
But other doubt possesses me, lest harm
Befall thee, severed from me; for thou know'st
What hath been warned us—what malicious foe,
Envying our happiness, and of his own
255 Despairing, seeks to work us woe and shame
By sly assault, and somewhere nigh at hand
Watches, no doubt, with greedy hope to find
His wish and best advantage, us asunder,
Hopeless to circumvent us joined, where each
260 To other speedy aid might lend at need.
Whether his first design be to withdraw
Our fealty from God, or to disturb
Conjugal love—than which perhaps no bliss
Enjoyed by us excites his envy more—
265 Or this, or worse, leave not the faithful side
That gave thee being, still shades thee and protects.
The wife, where danger or dishonor lurks,

Safest and seemliest by her husband stays,
Who guards her, or with her the worst endures."
270   To whom the virgin° majesty of Eve,   *innocent*
As one who loves, and some unkindness meets,
With sweet austere composure thus replied:
"Offspring of Heaven and Earth, and all Earth's lord!
That such an enemy we have, who seeks
275 Our ruin, both by thee informed I learn,
And from the parting angel overheard,
As in a shady nook I stood behind,
Just then returned at shut of evening flowers.
But that thou shouldst my firmness therefore doubt
280 To God or thee, because we have a foe
May tempt it, I expected not to hear.
His violence thou fear'st not, being such
As we, not capable of death or pain,
Can either not receive, or can repel.
285 His fraud is, then, thy fear; which plain infers
Thy equal fear that my firm faith and love
Can by his fraud be shaken or seduced:
Thoughts, which how found they harbor in thy breast,
Adam, misthought of her to thee so dear?"
290   To whom, with healing words, Adam replied:
"Daughter of God and Man, immortal Eve!
For such thou art, from sin and blame entire°   *wholly free*
Not diffident° of thee do I dissuade   *mistrustful*
Thy absence from my sight, but to avoid
295 Th' attempt itself, intended by our foe.
For he who tempts, though in vain, at least asperses[2]
The tempted with dishonor foul, supposed
Not incorruptible of faith, not proof
Against temptation. Thou thyself with scorn
300 And anger wouldst resent the offered wrong,
Though ineffectual found; misdeem not, then,
If such affront I labor to avert
From thee alone, which on us both at once
The enemy, though bold, will hardly dare;
305 Or, daring, first on me th' assault shall light.
Nor thou his malice and false guile contemn—
Subtle he needs must be who could seduce
Angels—nor think superfluous others' aid.
I from the influence of thy looks receive
310 Access° in every virtue—in thy sight   *increase*
More wise, more watchful, stronger, if need were
Of outward strength; while shame, thou looking on,
Shame to be overcome or overreached,
Would utmost vigor raise, and raised unite.
315 Why shouldst not thou like sense within thee feel
When I am present, and thy trial choose
With me, best witness of thy virtue tried?"
     So spake domestic Adam in his care
And matrimonial love; but Eve, who thought
320 Less áttributed to her faith sincere,
Thus her reply with accent sweet renewed:
"If this be our condition, thus to dwell

2. Maligns (literally, "sprinkles").

In narrow circuit straitened by a foe,
Subtle or violent, we not endued°   *endowed*
325 Single with like defense wherever met,
How are we happy, still in fear of harm?
But harm precedes not sin: only our foe
Tempting affronts us with his foul esteem
Of our integrity: his foul esteem
330 Sticks no dishonor on our front,° but turns   *brow*
Foul on himself; then wherefore shunned or feared
By us, who rather double honor gain
From his surmise proved false, find peace within,
Favor from Heaven, our witness, from the event?
335 And what is faith, love, virtue, unassayed
Alone, without exterior help sustained?
Let us not then suspect our happy state
Left so imperfect by the Maker wise
As not secure to single or combined.
340 Frail is our happiness, if this be so;
And Eden were no Eden, thus exposed."
     To whom thus Adam fervently replied:
"O woman, best are all things as the will
Of God ordained them; his creating hand
345 Nothing imperfect or deficient left
Of all that he created, much less man,
Or aught that might his happy state secure,
Secure from outward force. Within himself
The danger lies, yet lies within his power;
350 Against his will he can receive no harm.
But God left free the will; for what obeys
Reason is free; and reason he made right,
But bid her well beware, and still erect,°   *alert*
Lest, by some fair appearing good surprised,
355 She dictate false, and misinform the will
To do what God expressly hath forbid.
Not then mistrust, but tender love, enjoins
That I should mind° thee oft; and mind thou me.   *remind*
Firm we subsist, yet possible to swerve,
360 Since reason not impossibly may meet
Some specious object by the foe suborned,
And fall into deception unaware,
Not keeping strictest watch, as she was warned.
Seek not temptation, then, which to avoid
365 Were better, and most likely if from me
Thou sever not: trial will come unsought.
Wouldst thou approve° thy constancy, approve   *prove*
First thy obedience; the other who can know,
Not seeing thee attempted, who attest?
370 But, if thou think trial unsought may find
Us both securer° than thus warned thou seem'st,   *more careless*
Go; for thy stay, not free, absents thee more.
Go in thy native innocence; rely
On what thou hast of virtue; summon all;
375 For God towards thee hath done his part: do thine."
     So spake the patriarch of mankind; but Eve
Persisted; yet submiss, though last, replied:
     "With thy permission, then, and thus forewarned,
Chiefly by what thy own last reasoning words

Touched only, that our trial, when least sought,
May find us both perhaps far less prepared,
The willinger I go, nor much expect
A foe so proud will first the weaker seek;
So bent, the more shall shame him his repulse."
Thus saying, from her husband's hand her hand
Soft she withdrew, and like a wood nymph light,
Oread or dryad,[3] or of Delia's train,
Betook her to the groves, but Delia's self
In gait surpassed and goddesslike deport,
Though not as she with bow and quiver armed,
But with such gardening tools as art yet rude,
Guiltless of fire had formed, or angels brought.
To Pales, or Pomona, thus adorned,
Likest she seemed, Pomona when she fled
Vertumnus, or to Ceres in her prime,
Yet virgin of Proserpina from Jove[4]
Her long with ardent look his eye pursued
Delighted, but desiring more her stay.
Oft he to her his charge of quick return
Repeated; she to him as oft engaged
To be returned by noon amid the bower,
And all things in best order to invite
Noontide repast, or afternoon's repose.
O much deceived, much failing, hapless Eve,
Of thy presumed return! Event perverse!
Thou never from that hour in Paradise
Found'st either sweet repast, or sound repose;
Such ambush hid among sweet flowers and shades
Waited with hellish rancor imminent
To intercept thy way, or send thee back
Despoiled of innocence, of faith, of bliss.
For now, and since first break of dawn, the fiend,
Mere serpent in appearance, forth was come,
And on his quest, where likeliest he might find
The only two of mankind, but in them
The whole included race, his purposed prey.
In bower and field he sought, where any tuft
Of grove or garden-plot more pleasant lay,
Their tendance° or plantation for delight;   *object of care*
By fountain or by shady rivulet
He sought them both, but wished his hap might find
Eve separate; he wished, but not with hope
Of what so seldom chanced; when to his wish,
Beyond his hope, Eve separate he spies,
Veiled in a cloud of fragrance, where she stood,
Half spied, so thick the roses bushing round
About her glowed, oft stooping to support
Each flower of slender stalk, whose head though gay
Carnation, purple, azure, or specked with gold,
Hung drooping unsustained, them she upstays
Gently with myrtle band, mindless the while
Herself, though fairest unsupported flower,

3. Mountain or wood nymph. Delia is Diana, goddess of the hunt, so called from her birthplace at Delos.
4. Roman goddesses, the first of flocks, the second of fruits. Pomona's suitor, Vertumnus, won her only after long wooing. Ceres, the supreme agricultural goddess, bore Proserpina to Jove.

From her best prop so far, and storm so nigh.
Nearer he drew, and many a walk traversed
435   Of stateliest covert, cedar, pine, or palm;
Then voluble° and bold, now hid, now seen   *twining*
Among thick-woven arborets and flowers
Embordered on each bank, the hand° of Eve: *handiwork*
Spot more delicious than those gardens feigned[5]
440   Or of revived Adonis, or renowned
Alcinous, host of old Laertes' son,
Or that, not mystic, where the sapient king
Held dalliance with his fair Egyptian spouse.
Much he the place admired, the person more.
445   As one who long in populous city pent,
Where houses thick and sewers annoy° the air,   *pollute*
Forth issuing on a summer's morn to breathe
Among the pleasant villages and farms
Adjoined, from each thing met conceives delight,
450   The smell of grain, or tedded[6] grass, or kine,
Or dairy, each rural sight, each rural sound:
If chance with nymphlike step fair virgin pass,
What pleasing seemed, for her now pleases more,
She most, and in her look sums all delight.
455   Such pleasure took the serpent to behold
This flowery plat,° the sweet recess of Eve   *plot*
Thus early, thus alone; her heavenly form
Angelic, but more soft, and feminine,
Her graceful innocence, her every air
460   Of gesture or least action overawed
His malice, and with rapine° sweet bereaved   *robbery*
His fierceness of the fierce intent it brought:
That space the evil one abstracted stood
From his own evil, and for the time remained
465   Stupidly good, of enmity disarmed,
Of guile, of hate, of envy, of revenge.
But the hot Hell that always in him burns,
Though in mid Heaven, soon ended his delight,
And tortures him now more, the more he sees
470   Of pleasure not for him ordained: then soon
Fierce hate he recollects, and all his thoughts
Of mischief, gratulating,° thus excites: *exulting*
"Thoughts, whither have ye led me? with what sweet
Compulsion thus transported to forget
475   What hither brought us? hate, not love, nor hope
Of Paradise for Hell, hope here to taste
Of pleasure, but all pleasure to destroy,
Save what is in destroying; other joy
To me is lost. Then let me not let pass
480   Occasion which now smiles; behold alone
The woman, opportune to all attempts,
Her husband, for I view far round, not nigh,
Whose higher intellectual° more I shun,   *intellect*
And strength, of courage haughty, and of limb
485   Heroic built, though of terrestrial mold;

5. Mythical or legendary gardens. In the first
Adonis was nursed by Venus after having been
wounded by a boar; the second was visited
by Odysseus ("Laertes' son"), who found
spring time and harvest time both continuous

there. The third garden mentioned Milton re-
gards as historical, not "mystic" or mythical;
it is the garden of Solomon ("the sapient
king") and his bride, the Pharaoh's daughter.
6. Spread out to dry to make hay.

Foe not informidable, exempt from wound,
I not; so much hath Hell debased, and pain
Enfeebled me, to what I was in Heaven.
She fair, divinely fair, fit love for gods,
Not terrible, though terror be in love
And beauty, not approached by stronger hate,
Hate stronger, under show of love well feigned,
The way which to her ruin now I tend."
   So spake the enemy of mankind, enclosed
In serpent, inmate bad, and toward Eve
Addressed his way, not with indented wave,
Prone on the ground, as since, but on his rear,
Circular base of rising folds, that towered
Fold above fold a surging maze; his head
Crested aloft, and carbuncle° his eyes;   *ruby-colored*
With burnished neck of verdant gold, erect
Amidst his circling spires,° that on the grass   *coils*
Floated redundant. Pleasing was his shape,
And lovely; never since of serpent kind
Lovelier, not those that in Illyria changed
Hermione and Cadmus, or the god
In Epidaurus; nor to which transformed
Ammonian Jove, or Capitoline was seen,
He with Olympias, this with her who bore
Scipio, the height of Rome.[7] With tract oblique
At first, as one who sought access, but feared
To interrupt, sidelong he works his way.
As when a ship by skillful steersman wrought
Nigh river's mouth or foreland, where the wind
Veers oft, as oft so steers, and shifts her sail:
So varied he, and of his tortuous train
Curled many a wanton wreath in sight of Eve,
To lure her eye: she busied heard the sound
Of rustling leaves, but minded not, as used
To such disport before her through the field,
From every beast, more duteous at her call,
Than at Circean call the herd disguised.[8]
He bolder now, uncalled before her stood:
But as in gaze admiring; oft he bowed
His turret crest, and sleek enameled neck,
Fawning, and licked the ground whereon she trod.
His gentle dumb expression turned at length
The eye of Eve to mark his play: he, glad
Of her attention gained, with serpent tongue
Organic, or impulse of vocal air,
His fraudulent temptation thus began.
   "Wonder not, sovereign mistress, if perhaps
Thou canst, who art sole wonder; much less arm
Thy looks, the heaven of mildness, with disdain,
Displeased that I approach thee thus, and gaze
Insatiate, I thus single, nor have feared

7. Cadmus king of Thebes and his wife Harmonia ("Hermione") were transformed to serpents after their retirement to Illyria. The "god in Epidaurus" is Aesculapius, god of healing, whose art included the use of serpents and who sometimes appeared in the form of a serpent at his temple in Epidaurus. Jove (here called Ammonian and Capitoline after temples associated with him) was reputed to have visited Olympias and Sempronia in the form of a serpent and to have fathered upon the first Alexander the Great and upon the second the Roman leader Scipio Africanus.
8. In the *Odyssey* the enchantress Circe changed men into swine, who then dutifully followed her about.

Thy awful brow, more awful thus retired.
Fairest resemblance of thy Maker fair,
Thee all things living gaze on, all things thine
540 By gift, and thy celestial beauty adore
With ravishment beheld, there best beheld
Where universally admired: but here
In this enclosure wild, these beasts among,
Beholders rude, and shallow to discern
545 Half what in thee is fair, one man except,
Who sees thee? (and what is one?) who shouldst be seen
A goddess among gods, adored and served
By angels numberless, thy daily train."
        So glozed° the tempter, and his proem tuned;   *flattered*
550 Into the heart of Eve his words made way,
Though at the voice much marveling: at length,
Not unamazed, she thus in answer spake.
"What may this mean? Language of man pronounced
By tongue of brute, and human sense expressed?
555 The first at least of these I thought denied
To beasts, whom God on their creation-day
Created mute to all articulate sound;
The latter I demur,° for in their looks   *hesitate about*
Much reason, and in their actions oft appears.
560 Thee, serpent, subtlest beast of all the field
I knew, but not with human voice endued:
Redouble then this miracle, and say,
How cam'st thou speakable of mute, and how
To me so friendly grown above the rest
565 Of brutal kind, that daily are in sight?
Say, for such wonder claims attention due."
        To whom the guileful tempter thus replied:
"Empress of this fair world, resplendent Eve!
Easy to me it is to tell thee all
570 What thou command'st and right thou shouldst be obeyed:
I was at first as other beasts that graze
The trodden herb, of abject thoughts and low,
As was my food, nor aught but food discerned
Or sex, and apprehended nothing high:
575 Till on a day, roving the field, I chanced
A goodly tree far distant to behold
Loaden with fruit of fairest colors mixed,
Ruddy and gold; I nearer drew to gaze;
When from the boughs a savory odor blown,
580 Grateful to appetite, more pleased my sense
Than smell of sweetest fennel,[9] or the teats
Of ewe or goat dropping with milk at even,
Unsucked of lamb or kid, that tend their play.
To satisfy the sharp desire I had
585 Of tasting those fair apples, I resolved
Not to defer: hunger and thirst at once,
Powerful persuaders, quickened at the scent
Of that alluring fruit, urged me so keen.
About the mossy trunk I wound me soon,
590 For, high from ground, the branches would require
Thy utmost reach, or Adam's: round the tree

---

9. It was popularly believed that snakes were especially fond of fennel and that they stole milk
from sheep and goats.

All other beasts that saw, with like desire
Longing and envying stood, but could not reach.
Amid the tree now got, where plenty hung
Tempting so nigh, to pluck and eat my fill
I spared not; for such pleasure till that hour
At feed or fountain never had I found.
Sated at length, ere long I might perceive
Strange alteration in me, to degree
Of reason in my inward powers, and speech
Wanted not long, though to this shape retained.
Thenceforth to speculations high or deep
I turned my thoughts, and with capacious mind
Considered all things visible in Heaven,
Or Earth, or middle, all things fair and good:
But all that fair and good in thy divine
Semblance, and in thy beauty's heavenly ray
United I beheld: no fair to° thine   compared to
Equivalent or second, which compelled
Me thus, though importune perhaps, to come
And gaze, and worship thee of right declared
Sovereign of creatures, universal dame."
   So talked the spirited° sly snake: and Eve   spirit-possessed
Yet more amazed, unwary thus replied:
   "Serpent, thy overpraising leaves in doubt
The virtue of that fruit, in thee first proved.
But say, where grows the tree, from hence how far?
For many are the trees of God that grow
In Paradise, and various, yet unknown
To us; in such abundance lies our choice,
As leaves a greater store of fruit untouched,
Still hanging incorruptible, till men
Grow up to their provision, and more hands
Help to disburden Nature of her birth."[1]
   To whom the wily adder, blithe and glad:
"Empress, the way is ready, and not long,
Beyond a row of myrtles, on a flat,
Fast by a fountain, one small thicket past
Of blowing myrrh and balm: if thou accept
My conduct, I can bring thee thither soon."
   "Lead then," said Eve. He leading swiftly rolled
In tangles, and made intricate seem straight,
To mischief swift. Hope elevates, and joy
Brightens his crest; as when a wandering fire
Compact of unctuous vapor,[2] which the night
Condenses, and the cold environs round,
Kindled through agitation to a flame
(Which oft, they say, some evil spirit attends),
Hovering and blazing with delusive light,
Misleads th' amazed night-wanderer from his way
To bogs and mires, and oft through pond or pool,
There swallowed up and lost, from succor far:
So glistered the dire snake, and into fraud
Led Eve our credulous mother, to the tree
Of prohibition,[3] root of all our woe:
Which when she saw, thus to her guide she spake:

---

1. I.e., what Nature bears.
2. Made up of oily vapor. The allusion is to *ignis fatuus,* or will-o'-the-wisp.
3. I.e., the prohibited tree.

"Serpent, we might have spared our coming hither,
Fruitless to me, though fruit be here to excess,
The credit of whose virtue rest with thee;[4]
650 Wondrous indeed, if cause of such effects!
But of this tree we may not taste nor touch:
God so commanded, and left that command
Sole daughter of his voice; the rest, we live
Law to ourselves; our reason is our law."
655   To whom the Tempter guilefully replied:
"Indeed? Hath God then said that of the fruit
Of all these garden trees ye shall not eat,
Yet lords declared of all in Earth or air?"
To whom thus Eve, yet sinless: "Of the fruit
660 Of each tree in the garden we may eat,
But of the fruit of this fair tree amidst
The garden, God hath said, 'Ye shall not eat
Thereof, nor shall ye touch it, lest ye die.'"
She scarce had said, though brief, when now more bold,
665 The tempter, but with show of zeal and love
To man, and indignation at his wrong,
New part puts on, and as to passion moved,
Fluctuates disturbed, yet comely, and in act
Raised, as of some great matter to begin.
670 As when of old some orator renowned
In Athens or free Rome, where eloquence
Flourished, since mute, to some great cause addressed,
Stood in himself collected, while each part,
Motion, each act, won audience ere the tongue,
675 Sometimes in height began, as no delay
Of preface brooking, through his zeal of right.
So standing, moving, or to height upgrown
The tempter all impassioned thus began:
"O sacred, wise, and wisdom-giving plant,
680 Mother of science!° now I feel thy power   *knowledge*
Within me clear, not only to discern
Things in their causes, but to trace the ways
Of highest agents, deemed however wise.
Queen of this universe! do not believe
685 Those rigid threats of death. Ye shall not die;
How should ye? By the fruit? it gives you life
To° knowledge; by the Threatener? look on me,   *in addition to*
Me who have touched and tasted, yet both live,
And life more perfect have attained than Fate
690 Meant me, by venturing higher than my lot.
Shall that be shut to man, which to the beast
Is open? Or will God incense his ire
For such a petty trespass, and not praise
Rather your dauntless virtue, whom the pain
695 Of death denounced, whatever thing death be,
Deterred not from achieving what might lead
To happier life, knowledge of good and evil?
Of good, how just! Of evil, if what is evil
Be real, why not known, since easier shunned?
700 God therefore cannot hurt ye, and be just;
Not just, not God; not feared then, nor obeyed:
Your fear itself of death removes the fear.

4. I.e., my belief in the effects of the fruit must continue to depend solely on your testimony.

Why then was this forbid? Why but to awe,
Why but to keep ye low and ignorant,
His worshippers? He knows that in the day
Ye eat thereof, your eyes that seem so clear,
Yet are but dim, shall perfectly be then
Opened and cleared, and ye shall be as gods,
Knowing both good and evil, as they know.
That ye should be as gods, since I as man,
Internal man,[5] is but proportion meet,
I, of brute, human; ye, of human, gods.
So ye shall die perhaps, by putting off
Human, to put on gods: death to be wished,
Though threatened, which no worse than this can bring.
And what are gods that man may not become
As they, participating° godlike food?   *sharing*
The gods are first, and that advantage use
On our belief, that all from them proceeds.
I question it; for this fair Earth I see,
Warmed by the sun, producing every kind,
Them nothing: If they all things, who enclosed
Knowledge of good and evil in this tree,
That whoso eats thereof forthwith attains
Wisdom without their leave? And wherein lies
Th' offense, that man should thus attain to know?
What can your knowledge hurt him, or this tree
Impart against his will if all be his?
Or is it envy, and can envy dwell
In heavenly breasts? These, these, and many more
Causes import your need of this fair fruit.
Goddess humane, reach then, and freely taste!"
    He ended, and his words, replete with guile,
Into her heart too easy entrance won:
Fixed on the fruit she gazed, which to behold
Might tempt alone, and in her ears the sound
Yet rung of his persuasive words, impregned°   *impregnated*
With reason, to her seeming, and with truth;
Meanwhile the hour of noon drew on, and waked
An eager appetite, raised by the smell
So savory of that fruit, which with desire,
Inclinable now grown to touch or taste,
Solicited her longing eye; yet first
Pausing a while, thus to herself she mused:
    "Great are thy virtues, doubtless, best of fruits,
Though kept from man, and worthy to be admired,
Whose taste, too long forborn, at first essay
Gave elocution to the mute, and taught
The tongue not made for speech to speak thy praise:
Thy praise he also who forbids thy use,
Conceals not from us, naming thee the Tree
Of Knowledge, knowledge both of good and evil;
Forbids us then to taste; but his forbidding
Commends thee more, while it infers the good
By thee communicated, and our want:
For good unknown, sure is not had, or had
And yet unknown, is as not had at all.
In plain[6] then, what forbids he but to know?

5. I.e., internally man.   6. In plain language.

Forbids us good, forbids us to be wise!
760 Such prohibitions bind not. But if Death
Bind us with after-bands, what profits then
Our inward freedom? In the day we eat
Of this fair fruit, our doom is, we shall die.
How dies the serpent? He hath eaten and lives,
765 And knows, and speaks, and reasons, and discerns,
Irrational till then. For us alone
Was death invented? Or to us denied
This intellectual food, for beasts reserved?
For beasts it seems: yet that one beast which first
770 Hath tasted, envies not, but brings with joy
The good befallen him, author unsuspect,[7]
Friendly to man, far from deceit or guile.
What fear I then, rather what know to fear
Under this ignorance of good and evil,
775 Of God or death, of law or penalty?
Here grows the cure of all, this fruit divine,
Fair to the eye, inviting to the taste,
Of virtue° to make wise: what hinders then   power
To reach, and feed at once both body and mind?"
780   So saying, her rash hand in evil hour,
Forth reaching to the fruit, she plucked, she eat.°   ate
Earth felt the wound, and Nature from her seat
Sighing through all her works gave signs of woe,
That all was lost. Back to the thicket slunk
785 The guilty serpent, and well might, for Eve
Intent now wholly on her taste, naught else
Regarded; such delight till then, as seemed,
In fruit she never tasted, whether true
Or fancied so, through expectation high
790 Of knowledge; nor was godhead from her thought.
Greedily she engorged without restraint,
And knew not eating death: satiate at length,
And heightened as with wine, jocund and boon,°   jovial
Thus to herself she pleasingly began:
795   "O sovereign, virtuous, precious of all trees
In Paradise! of operation blest
To sapience, hitherto obscured, infamed,°   defamed
And thy fair fruit let hang, as to no end
Created; but henceforth my early care,
800 Not without song each morning, and due praise
Shall tend thee, and the fertile burden ease
Of thy full branches offered free to all;
Till dieted by thee I grow mature
In knowledge, as the gods who all things know;
805 Though others envy what they cannot give:
For had the gift been theirs, it had not here
Thus grown. Experience, next to thee I owe,
Best guide; not following thee I had remained
In ignorance; thou open'st Wisdom's way,
810 And giv'st access, though secret she retire.
And I perhaps am secret; Heaven is high,
High and remote to see from thence distinct
Each thing on Earth; and other care perhaps

---

7. I.e., authority whose testimony does **not** arouse suspicion.

May have diverted from continual watch
15 Our great Forbidder, safe with all his spies
About him. But to Adam in what sort
Shall I appear? Shall I to him make known
As yet my change, and give him to partake
Full happiness with me, or rather not,
20 But keep the odds of knowledge in my power
Without copartner? so to add what wants
In female sex, the more to draw his love,
And render me more equal, and perhaps,
A thing not undesirable, sometime
25 Superior: for, inferior, who is free?
This may be well: but what if God have seen
And death ensue? Then I shall be no more,
And Adam, wedded to another Eve,
Shall live with her enjoying, I extinct;
30 A death to think. Confirmed then I resolve,
Adam shall share with me in bliss or woe:
So dear I love him, that with him all deaths
I could endure, without him live no life."
   So saying, from the tree her step she turned,
35 But first low reverence done, as to the power
That dwelt within, whose presence had infused
Into the plant sciental° sap, derived   *knowledge-giving*
From nectar, drink of gods. Adam the while
Waiting desirous her return, had wove
40 Of choicest flowers a garland to adorn
Her tresses, and her rural labors crown,
As reapers oft are wont their harvest queen.
Great joy he promised to his thoughts, and new
Solace in her return, so long delayed:
45 Yet oft his heart, divine° of something ill,   *apprehensive*
Misgave him; he the faltering measure felt;
And forth to meet her went, the way she took
That morn when first they parted. By the Tree
Of Knowledge he must pass; there he her met,
50 Scarce from the tree returning; in her hand
A bough of fairest fruit that downy smiled,
New gathered, and ambrosial smell diffused.
To him she hastened, in her face excuse
Came prologue, and apology to prompt,
55 Which with bland words at will she thus addressed:
   "Hast thou not wondered, Adam, at my stay?
Thee I have missed, and thought it long, deprived
Thy presence, agony of love till now
Not felt, nor shall be twice; for never more
360 Mean I to try, what rash untried I sought,
The pain of absence from thy sight. But strange
Hath been the cause, and wonderful to hear:
This tree is not as we are told, a tree
Of danger tasted, nor to evil unknown
365 Opening the way, but of divine effect
To open eyes, and make them gods who taste;
And hath been tasted such. The serpent wise,
Or not restrained as we, or not obeying,
Hath eaten of the fruit, and is become,
370 Not dead, as we are threatened, but thenceforth

Endued with human voice and human sense,
Reasoning to admiration,[8] and with me
Persuasively hath so prevailed, that I
Have also tasted, and have also found
875   Th' effects to correspond—opener mine eyes
Dim erst, dilated spirits, ampler heart,
And growing up to godhead; which for thee
Chiefly I sought, without thee can despise.
For bliss, as thou hast part, to me is bliss,
880   Tedious, unshared with thee, and odious soon.
Thou therefore also taste, that equal lot
May join us, equal joy, as equal love;
Lest, thou not tasting, different degree
Disjoin us, and I then too late renounce
885   Deity for thee, when Fate will not permit."
    Thus Eve with countenance blithe her story told;
But in her cheek distemper flushing glowed.
On th' other side, Adam, soon as he heard
The fatal trespass done by Eve, amazed,
890   Astonied° stood and blank, while horror chill   *stunned*
Ran through his veins, and all his joints relaxed;
From his slack hand the garland wreathed for Eve
Down dropped, and all the faded roses shed.
Speechless he stood and pale, till thus at length
895   First to himself he inward silence broke:
    "O fairest of creation, last and best
Of all God's works, creature in whom excelled
Whatever can to sight or thought be formed,
Holy, divine, good, amiable, or sweet!
900   How art thou lost, how on a sudden lost,
Defaced, deflowered, and now to death devote?°   *doomed*
Rather how hast thou yielded to transgress
The strict forbiddance, how to violate
The sacred fruit forbidden! Some cursèd fraud
905   Of enemy hath beguiled thee, yet unknown,
And me with thee hath ruined, for with thee
Certain my resolution is to die.
How can I live without thee, how forgo
Thy sweet converse and love so dearly joined,
910   To live again in these wild woods forlorn?
Should God create another Eve, and I
Another rib afford, yet loss of thee
Would never from my heart; no, no! I feel
The link of nature draw me: flesh of flesh,
915   Bone of my bone thou art, and from thy state
Mine never shall be parted, bliss or woe."
    So having said, as one from sad dismay
Recomforted, and after thoughts disturbed
Submitting to what seemed remediless,
920   Thus in calm mood his words to Eve he turned:
    "Bold deed thou hast presumed, adventurous Eve
And peril great provoked, who thus hast dared
Had it been only coveting to eye
That sacred fruit, sacred° to abstinence,   *dedicated*
925   Much more to taste it, under ban to touch.

8. So as to produce admiration.

But past who can recall, or done undo?
Not God omnipotent, nor Fate! Yet so
Perhaps thou shalt not die, perhaps the fact
Is not so heinous now, foretasted fruit,
930 Profaned first by the serpent, by him first
Made common and unhallowed ere our taste,
Nor yet on him found deadly; he yet lives,
Lives, as thou saidst, and gains to live as man
Higher degree of life: inducement strong
935 To us, as likely, tasting, to attain
Proportional ascent, which cannot be
But to be gods, or angels, demigods.
Nor can I think that God, Creator wise,
Though threatening, will in earnest so destroy
940 Us his prime creatures, dignified so high,
Set over all his works, which in our fall,
For us created, needs with us must fail,
Dependent made; so God shall uncreate,
Be frustrate, do, undo, and labor lose;
945 Not well conceived of God, who, though his power
Creation could repeat, yet would be loath
Us to abolish, lest the adversary
Triumph and say: 'Fickle their state whom God
Most favors; who can please him long? Me first
950 He ruined, now mankind; whom will he next?'
Matter of scorn, not to be given the foe.
However, I with thee have fixed my lot,
Certain° to undergo like doom: if death   *resolved*
Consort with thee, death is to me as life;
955 So forcible within my heart I feel
The bond of nature draw me to my own,
My own in thee, for what thou art is mine;
Our state cannot be severed; we are one,
One flesh; to lose thee were to lose myself."
960   So Adam, and thus Eve to him replied:
"O glorious trial of exceeding love,
Illustrious evidence, example high!
Engaging me to emulate; but short
Of thy perfection, how shall I attain,
965 Adam? from whose dear side I boast me sprung,
And gladly of our union hear thee speak,
One heart, one soul in both; whereof good proof
This day affords, declaring thee resolved,
Rather than death or aught than death more dread
970 Shall separate us, linked in love so dear,
To undergo with me one guilt, one crime,
If any be, of tasting this fair fruit;
Whose virtue (for of good still good proceeds,
Direct, or by occasion) hath presented
975 This happy trial of thy love, which else
So eminently never had been known.
Were it I thought death menaced would ensue
This my attempt, I would sustain alone
The worst, and not persuade thee, rather die
980 Deserted, than oblige° thee with a fact   *involve in guilt*
Pernicious to thy peace, chiefly assured

Remarkably so late of thy so true,
So faithful love unequaled; but I feel
Far otherwise th' event°—not death, but life   *outcome*
985 Augmented, opened eyes, new hopes, new joys,
Taste so divine, that what of sweet before
Hath touched my sense, flat seems to this, and harsh.
On my experience, Adam, freely taste,
And fear of death deliver to the winds."
990   So saying, she embraced him, and for joy
Tenderly wept, much won that he his love
Had so ennobled, as of choice to incur
Divine displeasure for her sake, or death.
In recompense (for such compliance bad
995 Such recompense best merits), from the bough
She gave him of that fair enticing fruit
With liberal hand; he scrupled not to eat,
Against his better knowledge, not deceived,
But fondly overcome with female charm.
1000 Earth trembled from her entrails, as again
In pangs, and Nature gave a second groan,
Sky lowered, and muttering thunder, some sad drops
Wept at completing of the mortal sin
Original; while Adam took no thought,
1005 Eating his fill, nor Eve to iterate
Her former trespass feared, the more to soothe
Him with her loved society; that now
As with new wine intoxicated both,
They swim in mirth, and fancy that they feel
1010 Divinity within them breeding wings
Wherewith to scorn the Earth. But that false fruit
Far other operation first displayed,
Carnal desire inflaming; he on Eve
Began to cast lacivous eyes, she him
1015 As wantonly repaid; in lust they burn,
Till Adam thus 'gan Eve to dalliance move:
"Eve, now I see thou art exact° of taste,   *discriminating*
And elegant, of sapience no small part,
Since to each meaning savor we apply,
1020 And palate call judicious. I the praise
Yield thee, so well this day thou hast purveyed.
Much pleasure we have lost, while we abstained
From this delightful fruit, nor known till now
True relish, tasting; if such pleasure be
1025 In things to us forbidden, it might be wished,
For this one tree had been forbidden ten.
But come; so well refreshed, now let us play,
As meet is, after such delicious fare;
For never did thy beauty, since the day
1030 I saw thee first and wedded thee, adorned
With all perfections, so enflame my sense
With ardor to enjoy thee, fairer now
Than ever, bounty of this virtuous tree."
So said he, and forbore not glance or toy°   *caress*
1035 Of amorous intent, well understood
Of° Eve, whose eye darted contagious fire.   *by*
Her hand he seized, and to a shady bank,

Thick overhead with verdant roof embowered
He led her, nothing loath; flowers were the couch,
⁴⁰ Pansies, and violets, and asphodel,
And hyacinth—Earth's freshest, softest lap.
There they their fill of love and love's disport
Took largely, of their mutual guilt the seal,
The solace of their sin, till dewy sleep
⁴⁵ Oppressed them, wearied with their amorous play.
 Soon as the force of that fallacious fruit,
That with exhilarating vapor bland
About their spirits had played, and inmost powers
Made err, was now exhaled, and grosser sleep
⁵⁰ Bred of unkindly° fumes, with conscious dreams   *unnatural*
Encumbered, now had left them, up they rose
As from unrest, and each the other viewing,
Soon found their eyes how opened, and their minds
How darkened. Innocence, that as a veil
⁵⁵ Had shadowed them from knowing ill, was gone;
Just confidence, and native righteousness,
And honor from about them, naked left
To guilty Shame; he covered, but his robe
Uncovered more. So rose the Danite strong,
⁶⁰ Herculean Samson, from the harlot-lap
Of Philstean Dalilah, and waked
Shorn of his strength;⁹ they destitute and bare
Of all their virtue. Silent, and in face
Confounded, long they sat, as strucken mute;
⁶⁵ Till Adam, though not less than Eve abashed,
At length gave utterance to these words constrained:
 "O Eve, in evil hour thou didst give ear
To that false worm,° of whomsoever taught   *serpent*
To counterfeit man's voice, true in our fall,
⁷⁰ False in our promised rising; since our eyes
Opened we find indeed, and find we know
Both good and evil, good lost, and evil got:
Bad fruit of knowledge, if this be to know,
Which leaves us naked thus, of honor void,
⁷⁵ Of innocence, of faith, of purity,
Our wonted ornaments now soiled and stained,
And in our faces evident the signs
Of foul concupiscence; whence evil store,
Even shame, the last of evils; of the first
⁸⁰ Be sure then. How shall I behold the face
Henceforth of God or angel, erst with joy
And rapture so oft beheld? Those heavenly shapes
Will dazzle now this earthly with their blaze
Insufferably bright. O might I here
⁸⁵ In solitude live savage, in some glade
Obscured, where highest woods, impenetrable
To star or sunlight, spread their umbrage broad,
And brown as evening! Cover me, ye pines,
Ye cedars, with innumerable boughs
⁹⁰ Hide me, where I may never see them more!
But let us now, as in bad plight, devise
What best may for the present serve to hide

9. As told in Judges xvi.4–20.

The parts of each from other, that seem most
To shame obnoxious,° and unseemliest seen;   *liable*
1095 Some tree whose broad smooth leaves together sewed,
And girded on our loins, may cover round
Those middle parts, that this newcomer, Shame,
There sit not, and reproach us as unclean."
      So counseled he, and both together went
1100 Into the thickest wood; there soon they chose
The figtree, not that kind for fruit renowned,
But such as at this day, to Indians known,
In Malabar or Deccan spreads her arms
Branching so broad and long, that in the ground
1105 The bended twigs take root, and daughters grow
About the mother tree, a pillared shade
High overarched, and echoing walks between;
There oft the Indian herdsman, shunning heat,
Shelters in cool, and tends his pasturing herds
1110 At loopholes cut through thickest shade. Those leaves
They gathered, broad as Amazonian targe,°   *shield*
And with what skill they had, together sewed,
To gird their waist; vain covering, if to hide
Their guilt and dreaded shame! O how unlike
1115 To that first naked glory! Such of late
Columbus found th' American, so girt
With feathered cincture,° naked else and wild   *belt*
Among the trees on isles and woody shores.
Thus fenced, and, as they thought, their shame in part
1120 Covered, but not at rest or ease of mind,
They sat them down to weep; nor only tears
Rained at their eyes, but high winds worse within
Began to rise, high passions, anger, hate,
Mistrust, suspicion, discord, and shook sore
1125 Their inward state of mind, calm region once
And full of peace, now tossed and turbulent:
For Understanding ruled not, and the Will
Heard not her lore, both in subjection now
To sensual Appetite, who, from beneath
1130 Usurping over sovereign Reason, claimed
Superior sway. From thus distempered breast,
Adam, estranged in look and altered style,
Speech intermitted thus to Eve renewed:
      "Would thou hadst hearkened to my words, and stayed
1135 With me, as I besought thee, when that strange
Desire of wandering, this unhappy morn,
I know not whence possessed thee! we had then
Remained still happy, not as now, despoiled
Of all our good, shamed, naked, miserable.
1140 Let none henceforth seek needless cause to approve°   *prove*
The faith they owe;° when earnestly they seek   *own*
Such proof, conclude, they then begin to fail."
      To whom, soon moved with touch of blame, thus Eve:
"What words have passed thy lips, Adam severe?
1145 Imput'st thou that to my default, or will
Of wandering, as thou call'st it, which who knows
But might as ill have happened, thou being by,
Or to thyself perhaps? Hadst thou been there,

Or here th' attempt, thou couldst not have discerned
50 Fraud in the serpent, speaking as he spake;
No ground of enmity between us known,
Why he should mean me ill, or seek to harm?
Was I to have never parted from thy side?
As good have grown there still a lifeless rib.
55 Being as I am, why didst not thou, the head,
Command me absolutely not to go,
Going into such danger, as thou saidst?
Too facile then, thou didst not much gainsay,
Nay, didst permit, approve, and fair dismiss.
60 Hadst thou been firm and fixed in thy dissent,
Neither had I transgressed, nor thou with me."
    To whom, then first incensed, Adam replied:
"Is this the love, is this the recompense
Of mine to thee, ingrateful Eve, expressed
65 Immutable when thou were lost, not I,
Who might have lived and joyed immortal bliss,
Yet willingly chose rather death with thee?
And am I now upbraided as the cause
Of thy transgressing? not enough severe,
70 It seems, in thy restraint! What could I more?
I warned thee, I admonished thee, foretold
The danger, and the lurking enemy
That lay in wait: beyond this had been force,
And force upon free will hath here no place.
75 But confidence then bore thee on, secure
Either to meet no danger, or to find
Matter of glorious trial; and perhaps
I also erred in overmuch admiring
What seemed in thee so perfect, that I thought
80 No evil durst attempt thee! but I rue
That error now, which is become my crime,
And thou th' accuser. Thus it shall befall
Him who, to worth in women overtrusting,
Lets her will rule; restraint she will not brook,
85 And, left to herself, if evil thence ensue,
She first his weak indulgence will accuse."
    Thus they in mutual accusation spent
The fruitless hours, but neither self-condemning;
And of their vain contést appeared no end.

1667

SIR JOHN SUCKLING
(1609–1642)

Song

Why so pale and wan, fond lover?
    Prithee, why so pale?
Will, when looking well can't move her,
    Looking ill prevail?
5   Prithee, why so pale?

Why so dull and mute, young sinner?
   Prithee, why so mute?
Will, when speaking well can't win her,
   Saying nothing do 't?
10   Prithee, why so mute?

Quit, quit, for shame; this will not move,
   This cannot take her.
If of herself she will not love,
   Nothing can make her:
15   The devil take her!

                                                1638

Sonnet II[1]

Of thee, kind boy,[2] I ask no red and white,
   To make up my delight;
   No odd becoming graces,
Black eyes, or little know-not-whats in faces;
5 Make me but mad enough, give me good store
   Of love for her I count;
     I ask no more,
'Tis love in love that makes the sport.

There's no such thing as that we beauty call,
10   It is mere cozenage° all;   *fraud*
   For though some, long ago,
Liked certain colors mingled so and so,
That doth not tie me now from choosing new;
If I a fancy take
15   To black and blue,
That fancy doth it beauty make.

'Tis not the meat, but 'tis the appetite
   Makes eating a delight;
   And if I like one dish
20 More than another, that a pheasant is;
What in our watches, that in us is found:
So to the height and nick°   *critical point*
   We up be wound,
No matter by what hand or trick.

                                                1646

Song

No, no, fair heretic, it needs must be
   But an ill love in me,
   And worse for thee.
For were it in my power
5 To love thee now this hour
   More than I did the last,
   'Twould then so fall
   I might not love at all.
Love that can flow, and can admit increase,
10 Admits as well an ebb, and may grow less.

1. The term "sonnet" was formerly applied to   2. Cupid, as god of love.
any short love lyric.

True love is still the same; the torrid zones
  And those more frigid ones,
    It must not know;
For love, grown cold or hot,
5 Is lust or friendship, not
    The thing we have;
For that's a flame would die,
  Held down or up too high.
Then think I love more than I can express,
20 And would love more, could I but love thee less.

1646

A Ballad upon a Wedding

I tell thee, Dick, where I have been,
Where I the rarest things have seen,
    Oh, things without compare!
Such sights again cannot be found
5 In any place on English ground,
    Be it at wake° or fair.   *festival*

At Charing Cross, hard by the way
Where we (thou know'st) do sell our hay,
    There is a house with stairs;
10 And there did I see coming down
Such folk as are not in our town,
    Forty, at least, in pairs.

Amongst the rest, one pest'lent fine
(His beard no bigger, though, than thine)
15   Walked on before the rest.
Our landlord looks like nothing to him;
The king (God bless him!), 'twould undo him
    Should he go still° so dressed.   *always*

At course-a-park,[1] without all doubt,
20 He should have first been taken out
    By all the maids i' th' town,
Though lusty Roger there had been,
Or little George upon the Green,
    Or Vincent of the Crown.

25 But wot° you what? the youth was going   *know*
To make an end of all his wooing;
    The parson for him stayed.
Yet by his leave, for all his haste,
He did not so much wish all past,
30   Perchance, as did the maid.

The maid (and thereby hangs a tale),
For such a maid no Whitsun-ale[2]
    Could ever yet produce;
No grape, that's kindly[3] ripe, could be
35 So round, so plump, so soft as she,
    Nor half so full of juice.

1. A rural game in which a girl chooses a boy to chase her.
2. A church festival held at Whitsuntide.
3. Naturally; i.e., vine-ripened.

Her finger was so small the ring
Would not stay on, which they did bring;
   It was too wide a peck:
40 And to say truth (for out it must),
It looked like the great collar (just)
   About our young colt's neck.

Her feet beneath her petticoat,
Like little mice, stole in and out,
45   As if they feared the light;
But oh, she dances such a way,
No sun upon an Easter day
   Is half so fine a sight!

He would have kissed her once or twice,
50 But she would not, she was so nice,°   *delicate*
   She would not do 't in sight;
And then she looked as who should say,
"I will do what I list today;
   And you shall do 't at night."

55 Her cheeks so rare a white was on,
No daisy makes comparison
   (Who sees them is undone),
For streaks of red were mingled there,
Such as are on a Catherine pear
60   (The side that's next the sun).

Her lips were red, and one was thin
Compared to that was next her chin
   (Some bee had stung it newly);
But, Dick, her eyes so guard her face
65 I durst no more upon them gaze
   Than on the sun in July.

Her mouth so small, when she does speak,
Thou 'dst swear her teeth her words did break,
   That they might passage get;
But she so handled still the matter,
70 They came as good as ours, or better,
   And are not spent a whit.

If wishing should be any sin,
The parson himself had guilty been
75   (She looked that day so purely);
And did the youth so oft the feat
At night, as some did in conceit,°   *imagination*
   It would have spoiled him, surely.

Passion o' me, how I run on![4]
80 There's that that would be thought upon,
   I trow,° besides the bride.   *suppose*
The business of the kitchen's great,
For it is fit that man should eat,
   Nor was it there denied.

---

4. In the 1646 edition this stanza, with the first three lines following the last three, appears after line 96. The order preferred here is that of the 1648 and subsequent editions.

85 Just in the nick the cook knocked thrice,
And all the waiters in a trice
    His summons did obey;
Each serving-man, with dish in hand,
Marched boldly up, like our trained band,°   *militia*
90   Presented, and away.

When all the meat was on the table,
What man of knife or teeth was able
    To stay to be entreated?
And this the very reason was,
95 Before the parson could say grace,
    The company was seated.

Now hats fly off, and youths carouse;
Healths first go round, and then the house;
    The bride's came thick and thick:
100 And when 'twas named another's health,
Perhaps he made it hers by stealth;
    And who could help it, Dick?

O' th' sudden up they rise and dance;
Then sit again and sigh and glance;
105   Then dance again and kiss.
Thus several ways the time did pass,
Till every woman wished her place,
    And every man wished his!

By this time all were stolen aside
110 To counsel and undress the bride,
    But that he must not know;
But yet 'twas thought he guessed her mind,
And did not mean to stay behind
    Above an hour or so.

115 When in he came, Dick, there she lay
Like new-fallen snow melting away
    ('Twas time, I trow, to part);
Kisses were now the only stay,
Which soon she gave, as who would say,
120   "God b' w' ye,[5] with all my heart."

But just as heaven would have, to cross it,
In came the bridesmaids with the posset.[6]
    The bridegroom ate in spite,
For had he left the women to 't,
125 It would have cost two hours to do 't,
    Which were too much that night.

At length the candle's out, and now
All that they had not done, they do.
    What that is, who can tell?
130 But I believe it was no more
Than thou and I have done before
    With Bridget and with Nell.

                           ca. 1641   1646

5. A contraction for "God be with ye," pronounced in two syllables.

6. A hot drink of spiced milk curdled with ale or wine.

Out upon It!

Out upon it! I have loved
  Three whole days together;
And am like to love three more,
  If it prove fair weather.

5 Time shall molt away his wings,
  Ere he shall discover
In the whole wide world again
  Such a constant lover.

But the spite on 't is, no praise
10 Is due at all to me:
Love with me had made no stays
  Had it any been but she.

Had it any been but she,
  And that very face,
There had been at least ere this
  A dozen dozen in her place.

1659

ANNE BRADSTREET
(ca. 1612–1672)

The Vanity of All Worldly Things

As he[1] said vanity, so vain say I,
Oh! vanity, O vain all under sky;
Where is the man can say, "Lo, I have found
On brittle earth a consolation sound"?
5 What is't in honor to be set on high?
No, they like beasts and sons of men shall die,
And whilst they live, how oft doth turn their fate;
He's now a captive that was king of late.
What is't in wealth great treasures to obtain?
10 No, that's but labor, anxious care, and pain.
He heaps up riches, and he heaps up sorrow,
It's his today, but who's his heir tomorrow?
What then? Content in pleasures canst thou find?
More vain than all, that's but to grasp the wind.
15 The sensual senses for a time they please,
Meanwhile the conscience rage, who shall appease?
What is't in beauty? No that's but a snare,
They're foul enough today, that once were fair.
What is't in flow'ring youth, or manly age?
20 The first is prone to vice, the last to rage.
Where is it then, in wisdom, learning, arts?
Sure if on earth, it must be in those parts;
Yet these the wisest man of men did find
But vanity, vexation of mind.

---

1. The preacher of Ecclesiastes i.2: "Vanity of vanity, saith the Preacher, vanity of vanities; all is vanity."

And he that knows the most doth still bemoan
He knows not all that here is to be known.
What is it then? to do as stoics tell,
Nor laugh, nor weep, let things go ill or well?
Such stoics are but stocks, such teaching vain,
While man is man, he shall have ease or pain.
If not in honor, beauty, age, nor treasure,
Nor yet in learning, wisdom, youth, nor pleasure,
Where shall I climb, sound, seek, search, or find
That *summum bonum* [2] which may stay my mind?
There is a path no vulture's eye hath seen,
Where lion fierce, nor lion's whelps have been,
Which leads unto that living crystal fount,
Who drinks thereof, the world doth nought account.
The depth and sea have said "'tis not in me,"
With pearl and gold it shall not valued be.
For sapphire, onyx, topaz who would change;
It's hid from eyes of men, they count it strange.
Death and destruction the fame hath heard,
But where and what it is, from heaven's declared;
It brings to honor which shall ne'er decay,
It stores with wealth which time can't wear away.
It yieldeth pleasures far beyond conceit,
And truly beautifies without deceit.
Nor strength, nor wisdom, nor fresh youth shall fade,
Nor death shall see, but are immortal made.
This pearl of price, this tree of life, this spring,
Who is possessed of shall reign a king.
Nor change of state nor cares shall ever see,
But wear his crown unto eternity.
This satiates the soul, this stays the mind,
And all the rest, but vanity we find.

1650

A Letter to Her Husband, Absent upon Public Employment

My head, my heart, mine eyes, my life, nay, more,
My joy, my magazine of earthly store,
If two be one, as surely thou and I,
How stayest thou there, whilst I at Ipswich lie?
So many steps, head from the heart to sever,
If but a neck, soon should we be together.
I, like the Earth this season, mourn in black,
My Sun is gone so far in's zodiac,
Whom whilst I' joyed, nor storms, nor frost I felt,
His warmth such frigid colds did cause to melt.
My chilled limbs now numbed lie forlorn;
Return, return, sweet Sol, from Capricorn; [3]
In this dead time, alas, what can I more
Than view those fruits which through thy heat I bore?
Which sweet contentment yield me for a space,
True living pictures of their father's face.
O strange effect! now thou art southward gone,
I weary grow the tedious day so long;

2. The highest good (Latin).
3. When the sun "enters" the constellation Capricorn, it is at its furthest south. This occurs at the winter solstice, the shortest day and longest night of the year in the northern hemisphere.

But when thou northward to me shalt return,
20 I wish my Sun may never set, but burn
Within the Cancer [4] of my glowing breast,
The welcome house of him my dearest guest.
Where ever, ever stay, and go not thence,
Till nature's sad decree shall call thee hence;
25 Flesh of thy flesh, bone of thy bone,
I here, thou there, yet both but one.

1678

RICHARD CRASHAW
(1613–1649)

On the Baptized Ethiopian[1]

Let it no longer be a forlorn hope
          To wash an Ethiope;
He's washed, his gloomy skin a peaceful shade
          For his white soul is made,
And now, I doubt not, the Eternal Dove
          A black-faced house will love.

1646

To the Infant Martyrs[2]

Go, smiling souls, your new-built cages break,
In heaven you'll learn to sing, ere here to speak,
Nor let the milky fonts that bathe your thirst
          Be your delay;
The place that calls you hence is, at the worst,
          Milk all the way.

1646

Upon the Infant Martyrs

To see both blended in one flood,
The mothers' milk, the children's blood,
Make me doubt° if heaven will gather   *wonder*
Roses hence, or lilies rather.

1646

4. The sun is in Cancer at the summer
solstice.
1. Acts viii.26–39 tells how an Ethiopian
eunuch of great authority under Queen
Candace was converted and baptized by Philip
the Evangelist.

2. The Holy Innocents, all the children of
Bethlehem of two years and under, who were
slain by Herod in an effort to destroy the one
who, according to prophecy, would become the
ruler of Israel (Matthew ii.16).

A Hymn to the Name and Honor of the Admirable Saint Teresa[3]

FOUNDRESS OF THE REFORMATION OF THE DISCALCED[4] CARMELITES, BOTH MEN AND WOMEN. A WOMAN FOR ANGELICAL HEIGHT OF SPECULATION, FOR MASCULINE COURAGE OF PERFORMANCE, MORE THAN A WOMAN; WHO YET A CHILD OUTRAN MATURITY, AND DURST PLOT A MARTYRDOM.

Love, thou art absolute sole lord
Of life and death. To prove the word,
We'll now appeal to none of all
Those thy old soldiers, great and tall,
5 Ripe men of martyrdom, that could reach down
With strong arms their triumphant crown;
Such as could with lusty breath
Speak loud into the face of death
Their great Lord's glorious name; to none
10 Of those whose spacious bosoms spread a throne
For Love at large to fill. Spare blood and sweat,
And see Him take a private seat;
Making His mansion in the mild
And milky soul of a soft child.
15   Scarce has she learnt to lisp the name
Of Martyr, yet she thinks it shame
Life should so long play with that breath
Which spent can buy so brave a death.
She never undertook to know
20 What death with love should have to do;
Nor has she e'er yet understood
Why to show love she should shed blood;
Yet though she cannot tell you why,
She can love and she can die.
25   Scarce has she blood enough to make
A guilty sword blush for her sake;
Yet has she a heart dares hope to prove
How much less strong is death than love.
    Be love but there, let poor six years
30 Be posed with the maturest fears
Man trembles at, you straight shall find
Love knows no nonage, nor the mind.
'Tis love, not years or limbs, that can
Make the martyr or the man.
35   Love touched her heart, and lo it beats
High, and burns with such brave heats,
Such thirsts to die, as dares drink up
A thousand cold deaths in one cup.
Good reason, for she breathes all fire;
40 Her weak breast heaves with strong desire

---

3. The remarkable Spanish mystic (1515–82), canonized in 1622. Her autobiography records how, at the age of six, she ran away from home to convert the Moors. In later visions she saw a seraph with a fire-tipped golden dart who pierced her heart repeatedly, causing simultaneously intense pain and joy. It is these "wounds of love" that constitute the "death more mystical and high" referred to in line 76.
4. Barefoot.

Of what she may with fruitless wishes
Seek for amongst her mother's kisses.
   Since 'tis not to be had at home,
   She'll travel to a martyrdom.
45 No home for hers confesses she
But where she may a martyr be.
   She'll to the Moors and trade with them
   For this unvalued° diadem.   *invaluable*
She'll offer them her dearest breath,
50 With Christ's name in 't, in change for death.
She'll bargain with them, and will give
   Them God, teach them how to live
   In Him; or, if they this deny,
   For Him she'll teach them how to die.
55 So shall she leave amongst them sown
   Her Lord's blood, or at least her own.
     Farewell then, all the world, adieu!
   Teresa is no more for you.
Farewell, all pleasures, sports, and joys,
60 Never till now esteeméd toys;
Farewell, whatever dear may be,
   Mother's arms, or father's knee;
Farewell house and farewell home,
   She's for the Moors and martyrdom!
65   Sweet, not so fast! lo, thy fair Spouse
Whom thou seek'st with so swift vows
   Calls thee back, and bids thee come
   T' embrace a milder martyrdom.
     Blest powers forbid thy tender life
70 Should bleed upon a barbarous knife;
Or some base hand have power to rase°   *cut*
Thy breast's chaste cabinet, and uncase
A soul kept there so sweet; oh no,
   Wise Heav'n will never have it so.
75 Thou art Love's victim, and must die
   A death more mystical and high;
Into Love's arms thou shalt let fall
   A still surviving funeral.
   His is the dart must make the death
80 Whose stroke shall taste thy hallowed breath;
A dart thrice dipped in that rich flame
Which writes thy Spouse's radiant name
Upon the roof of heaven, where aye
   It shines, and with a sovereign ray
85 Beats bright upon the burning faces
Of souls which in that name's sweet graces
Find everlasting smiles. So rare,
   So spiritual, pure, and fair
Must be th' immortal instrument
90 Upon whose choice point shall be sent
A life so loved; and that there be
   Fit executioners for thee,
The fair'st and first-born sons of fire,
Blest seraphim, shall leave their choir
95 And turn Love's soldiers, upon thee
   To exercise their archery.

Oh, how oft shalt thou complain
Of a sweet and subtle pain,
Of intolerable joys,
Of a death, in which who dies
Loves his death and dies again,
And would for ever so be slain,
And lives and dies, and knows not why
To live, but that he thus may never leave to die!
    How kindly will thy gentle heart
Kiss the sweetly killing dart!
And close in his embraces keep
Those delicious wounds, that weep
Balsam to heal themselves with. Thus
When these thy deaths, so numerous,
Shall all at last die into one,
And melt thy soul's sweet mansion;
Like a soft lump of incense, hasted
By too hot a fire, and wasted
Into perfuming clouds, so fast
Shalt thou exhale to heaven at last
In a resolving sigh; and then,
Oh, what? Ask not the tongues of men;
Angels cannot tell; suffice,
Thyself shall feel thine own full joys
And hold them fast for ever. There,
So soon as thou shalt first appear,
The moon of maiden stars, thy white
Mistress, attended by such bright
Souls as thy shining self, shall come
And in her first ranks make thee room;
Where 'mongst her snowy family
Immortal welcomes wait for thee.
Oh, what delight when revealed life shall stand
And teach thy lips heaven with his hand,
On which thou now mayst to thy wishes
Heap up thy consecrated kisses.
What joys shall seize thy soul when she,
Bending her blessed eyes on thee,
Those second smiles of heaven, shall dart
Her mild rays through thy melting heart!
    Angels, thy old friends, there shall greet thee,
Glad at their own home now to meet thee.
    All thy good works which went before
And waited for thee at the door
Shall own thee there, and all in one
Weave a constellatïon
Of crowns, with which the King, thy Spouse,
Shall build up thy triumphant brows.
    All thy old woes shall now smile on thee,
And thy pains sit bright upon thee;
All thy sorrows here shall shine,
All thy sufferings be divine;
Tears shall take comfort and turn gems,
And wrongs repent to diadems.
Even thy deaths shall live, and new
Dress the soul that erst they slew;

Thy wounds shall blush to such bright scars
As keep account of the Lamb's wars.
155   Those rare works where thou shalt leave writ
Love's noble history, with wit
Taught thee by none but Him, while here
They feed our souls, shall clothe thine there.
Each heavenly word by whose hid flame
160   Our hard hearts shall strike fire, the same
Shall flourish on thy brows, and be
Both fire to us and flame to thee,
Whose light shall live bright in thy face
By glory, in our hearts by grace.
165   Thou shalt look round about and see
Thousands of crowned souls throng to be
Themselves thy crown; sons of thy vows,
The virgin-births with which thy sovereign Spouse
Made fruitful thy fair soul, go now
170   And with them all about thee, bow
To Him. "Put on," He'll say, "put on,
My rosy love, that, thy rich zone
Sparkling with the sacred flames
Of thousand souls whose happy names
175   Heav'n keeps upon thy score. Thy bright
Life brought them first to kiss the light
That kindled them to stars." And so
Thou with the Lamb, thy Lord, shalt go,
And whereso'er He sets His white
180   Steps, walk with Him those ways of light
Which who in death would live to see
Must learn in life to die like thee.

1652

ABRAHAM COWLEY
(1618–1667)

The Wish

Well then; I now do plainly see,
This busy world and I shall ne'er agree;
The very honey of all earthly joy
Does of all meats the soonest cloy;
5   And they, methinks, deserve my pity
Who for it can endure the stings,
The crowd, and buzz, and murmurings
Of this great hive, the city.

Ah, yet, ere I descend to the grave
10   May I a small house and large garden have!
And a few friends, and many books, both true,
Both wise, and both delightful too!
And since love ne'er will from me flee,
A mistress moderately fair,
15   And good as guardian angels are,
Only beloved, and loving me!

O fountains, when in you shall I
Myself, eased of unpeaceful thoughts, espy?
O fields! O woods! when, when shall I be made
20   The happy tenant of your shade?
Here's the spring-head of pleasure's flood,
Here's wealthy Nature's treasury,
Where all the riches lie that she
      Has coined and stamped for good.

25   Pride and ambition here
Only in farfetched metaphors appear;
Here naught but winds can hurtful murmurs scatter,
      And naught but Echo flatter.
The gods, when they descended, hither
30 From heaven did always choose their way;
And therefore we may boldly say
      That 'tis the way, too, thither.

How happy here should I
And one dear she live and, embracing, die!
35 She who is all the world, and can exclude
      In deserts, solitude.
I should have then this only fear,
Lest men, when they my pleasures see,
Should hither throng to live like me,
40   And so make a city here.
                                1647

From Anacreontics

OR SOME COPIES OF VERSES TRANSLATED
PARAPHRASTICALLY OUT OF ANACREON [1]

Drinking

The thirsty earth soaks up the rain,
And drinks, and gapes for drink again.
The plants suck in the earth, and are
With constant drinking fresh and fair.
5   The sea itself, which one would think
Should have but little need of drink,
Drinks ten thousand rivers up,
So filled that they o'erflow the cup.
The busy sun—and one would guess
10 By's drunken, fiery face no less—
Drinks up the sea, and when he's done,
The moon and stars drink up the sun.
They drink and dance by their own light;
They drink and revel all the night.
15 Nothing in nature's sober found,
But an eternal health goes round.
Fill up the bowl, then, fill it high,
Fill all the glasses there, for why
Should every creature drink but I?
20 Why, man of morals, tell me why?

                                1656

1. (572?–488? B.C.), Greek lyric poet, famous for his verse praising love and wine, called "Anacreontics."

RICHARD LOVELACE
(1618–1658)

To Althea, from Prison

When Love with unconfinéd wings
Hovers within my gates,
And my divine Althea brings
To whisper at the grates;
5 When I lie tangled in her hair
And fettered to her eye,
The gods[1] that wanton in the air
Know no such liberty.

When flowing cups run swiftly round,
10 With no allaying Thames,[2]
Our careless heads with roses bound,
Our hearts with loyal flames;
When thirsty grief in wine we steep,
When healths and draughts go free,
15 Fishes, that tipple in the deep,
Know no such liberty.

When, like committed° linnets, I   *caged*
With shriller throat shall sing
The sweetness, mercy, majesty,
20 And glories of my King;
When I shall voice aloud how good
He is, how great should be,
Enlargéd winds, that curl the flood,
Know no such liberty.

25 Stone walls do not a prison make,
Nor iron bars a cage;
Minds innocent and quiet take
That for an hermitage.
If I have freedom in my love,
30 And in my soul am free,
Angels alone, that soar above,
Enjoy such liberty.

1649

The Scrutiny

Why should you swear I am forsworn,
    Since thine I vowed to be?
Lady, it is already morn,
    And 'twas last night I swore to thee
5 That fond° impossibility.   *foolish*

Have I not loved thee much and long,
    A tedious twelve hours' space?

---

1. Most 17th-century versions read "birds"   2. I.e., without dilution (the Thames River
for "gods."   flows through London).

I must all other beauties wrong,
   And rob thee of a new embrace,
Could I still dote upon thy face.

Not but [1a] all joy in thy brown hair
   By others may be found;
But I must search the black and fair,
   Like skillful mineralists that sound
For treasure in unplowed-up ground.

Then, if when I have loved my round,
   Thou prov'st the pleasant she,
With spoils of meaner beauties crowned
   I laden will return to thee,
Ev'n sated with variety.

1649

To Lucasta, Going to the Wars

Tell me not, sweet, I am unkind
   That from the nunnery
Of thy chaste breast and quiet mind,
   To war and arms I fly.

True, a new mistress now I chase,
   The first foe in the field;
And with a stronger faith embrace
   A sword, a horse, a shield.

Yet this inconstancy is such
   As you too shall adore;
I could not love thee, dear, so much,
   Loved I not honor more.

1649

To Amarantha, That She Would Dishevel Her Hair

   Amarantha sweet and fair,
Ah, braid no more that shining hair!
   As my curious hand or eye,
Hovering round thee, let it fly.

   Let it fly as unconfined
As its calm ravisher, the wind,
   Who hath left his darling, th' East,
To wanton o'er that spicy nest.

   Every tress must be confessed
But neatly tangled at the best,
   Like a clue° of golden thread,   ***ball***
Most excellently raveléd.

   Do not then wind up that light
In ribands, and o'ercloud in night;
   Like the sun in's early ray,
But shake your head and scatter day.

1a. I.e., "I do not deny that . . ."

See, 'tis broke! Within this grove,
The bower and the walks of love,
  Weary lie we down and rest
20 And fan each other's panting breast.

Here we'll strip and cool our fire
In cream below, in milk-baths higher;
  And when all wells are drawn dry,
I'll drink a tear out of thine eye.

25 Which our very joys shall leave,
That sorrows thus we can deceive;
  Or our very sorrows weep,
That joys so ripe so little keep.

1649

The Grasshopper

TO MY NOBLE FRIEND, MR. CHARLES COTTON

O thou that swing'st upon the waving hair
  Of some well-filléd oaten beard,
Drunk every night with a delicious tear
  Dropped thee from heaven, where now th' art reared;

5 The joys of earth and air are thine entire,
  That with thy feet and wings dost hop and fly;
And, when thy poppy° works, thou dost retire   *sleeping potion*
  To thy carved acorn-bed to lie.

Up with the day, the sun thou welcom'st then,
10   Sport'st in the gilt plats° of his beams,   *hair braids*
And all these merry days mak'st merry men,
  Thyself, and melancholy streams.

But ah, the sickle! Golden ears are cropped;
  Ceres and Bacchus[3] bid good night;
15 Sharp, frosty fingers all your flowers have topped,
  And what scythes spared, winds shave off quite.

Poor verdant fool, and now green ice! thy joys,
  Large and as lasting as thy perch of grass,
Bid us lay in 'gainst winter rain, and poise°   *balance*
20   Their floods with an o'erflowing glass.

Thou best of men and friends! we will create
  A genuine summer in each other's breast,
And spite of this cold time and frozen fate,
  Thaw us a warm seat to our rest.

25 Our sacred hearths shall burn eternally,
  As vestal flames;[4] the North Wind, he
Shall strike his frost-stretched wings, dissolve, and fly
  This Etna[5] in epitome.

---

3. The grain and the grape, from Ceres, goddess of the harvest, and Bacchus, god of wine.
4. The vestal virgins, consecrated to the Roman goddess Vesta, kept a sacred fire burning perpetually on her altar.
5. A Sicilian volcano.

Dropping December shall come weeping in,
　　Bewail th' usurping of his reign:
But when in showers of old Greek[6] we begin,
　　Shall cry he hath his crown again!

Night, as clear Hesper,[7] shall our tapers whip
　　From the light casements where we play,
And the dark hag from her black mantle strip,
　　And stick there everlasting day.

Thus richer than untempted kings are we,
　　That, asking nothing, nothing need:
Though lord of all what seas embrace, yet he
　　That wants himself is poor indeed.

　　　　　　　　　　　　　　　　　　　1649

ANDREW MARVELL
(1621–1678)

The Coronet

When for the thorns with which I long, too long,
　　With many a piercing wound,
　　My Savior's head have crowned,
I seek with garlands to redress that wrong;
5　　Through every garden, every mead,
I gather flowers (my fruits are only flowers)
　　Dismantling all the fragrant towers°   *high headdresses*
That once adorned my shepherdess's head.
And now when I have summed up all my store,
10　　Thinking (so I myself deceive)
　　So rich a chaplet° thence to weave   *garland*
As never yet the king of glory wore;
　　Alas I find the serpent old
　　That, twining in his speckled breast,
15　　About the flowers disguised does fold,
　　With wreaths of fame and interest.
Ah, foolish man, that wouldst debase with them,
And mortal glory, heaven's diadem!
　　But Thou who only couldst the serpent tame,
20　　Either his slippery knots at once untie,
　　And disentangle all his winding snare;
Or shatter too with him my curious° frame,°   *elaborate/structure*
And let these wither, so that he may die,
Though set with skill and chosen out with care,
25　　That they, while Thou on both their spoils dost tread,
　　May crown Thy feet, that could not crown Thy head.

　　　　　　　　　　　　　　　　　　　1681

---

6. Old Greek wine.   7. The morning star.

Bermudas

Where the remote Bermudas ride,
In th' ocean's bosom unespied,
From a small boat that rowed along,
The listening winds received this song:
5   "What should we do but sing His praise,
That led us through the watery maze
Unto an isle so long unknown,
And yet far kinder than our own?
Where He the huge sea monsters wracks,°   *casts ashore*
10 That lift the deep upon their backs;
He lands us on a grassy stage,
Safe from the storms, and prelate's rage.[1]
He gave us this eternal spring
Which here enamels everything,
15 And sends the fowls to us in care,
On daily visits through the air;
He hangs in shades the orange bright,
Like golden lamps in a green night,
And does in the pomegranates close
20 Jewels more rich than Ormus[2] shows;
He makes the figs our mouths to meet,
And throws the melons at our feet;
But apples° plants of such a price,   *pineapples*
No tree could ever bear them twice;
25 With cedars, chosen by His hand,
From Lebanon, He stores the land;
And makes the hollow seas, that roar,
Proclaim the ambergris[3] on shore;
He cast (of which we rather boast)
30 The Gospel's pearl upon our coast,
And in these rocks for us did frame
A temple, where to sound His name.
O! let our voice His praise exalt,
Till it arrive at heaven's vault,
35 Which, thence (perhaps) rebounding, may
Echo beyond the Mexique Bay."[4]
    Thus sung they in the English boat,
An holy and a cheerful note;
And all the way, to guide their chime,
40 With falling oars they kept the time.

1681

A Dialogue Between the Soul and Body

Soul

Oh, who shall from this dungeon raise
A soul enslaved so many ways?
With bolts of bones that fettered stands
In feet, and manacled in hands;
5 Here blinded with an eye, and there

1. Marvell indicates Puritan sympathies by associating the wrath of prelates with storms at sea.
2. An island off Persia whence gems were exported.
3. A soapy secretion of the sperm whale, gathered on beaches and used in perfumes.
4. I.e., the Gulf of Mexico.

Deaf with the drumming of an ear;
A soul hung up, as 'twere, in chains
Of nerves and arteries and veins;
Tortured, besides each other part,
10 In a vain head and double heart.

Body

Oh, who shall me deliver whole
From bonds of this tyrannic soul?
Which stretched upright, impales me so
That mine own precipice I go,
15 And warms and moves this needless frame—
A fever could but do the same—
And, wanting where its spite to try,
Has made me live to let me die:
A body that could never rest,
20 Since this ill spirit it possessed.

Soul

What magic could me thus confine
Within another's grief to pine?
Where whatsoever it complain,
I feel, that cannot feel, the pain,
25 And all my care itself employs,
That to preserve which me destroys,
Constrained not only to endure
Diseases, but, what's worse, the cure;
And ready oft the port to gain,
30 And shipwrecked into health again.

Body

But physic° yet could never reach   *medicine*
The maladies thou me dost teach:
Whom first the cramp of hope does tear,
And then the palsy shakes of fear;
35 The pestilence of love does heat,
Or hatred's hidden ulcer eat;
Joy's cheerful madness does perplex,
Or sorrow's other madness vex;
Which knowledge forces me to know,
40 And memory will not forgo.
What but a soul could have the wit
To build me up for sin so fit?
So architects do square and hew
Green trees that in the forest grew.

1681

The Nymph Complaining for the Death of Her Fawn[5]

The wanton troopers riding by
Have shot my fawn, and it will die.
Ungentle men! they cannot thrive
To kill thee. Thou ne'er didst alive
5 Them any harm, alas! nor could

---

5. "Complaining" means "uttering a poetic lament." Marvell's original spelling "Faun" (for "Fawn") creates an ambiguous expectation, perhaps deliberately.

Thy death yet do them any good.
I'm sure I never wished them ill,
Nor do I for all this, nor will;
But if my simple prayers may yet
10   Prevail with heaven to forget
Thy murder, I will join my tears,
Rather than fail. But, O my fears!
It cannot die so. Heaven's King
Keeps register of everything,
15   And nothing may we use in vain;
Even beasts must be with justice slain,
Else men are made their deodands.[6]
Though they should wash their guilty hands
In this warm life-blood, which doth part
20   From thine, and wound me to the heart,
Yet could they not be clean, their stain
Is dyed in such a purple° grain.°   *brilliant / hue*
There is not such another in
The world to offer for their sin.
25   Unconstant Sylvio, when yet
I had not found him counterfeit,
One morning (I remember well)
Tied in this silver chain and bell,
Gave it to me: nay, and I know
30   What he said then; I'm sure I do:
Said he, "Look how your huntsman here
Hath taught a fawn to hunt his *dear*."
But Sylvio soon had me beguiled;
This waxéd tame, while he grew wild,
35   And quite regardless of my smart,
Left me his fawn, but took his heart.
        Thenceforth I set myself to play
My solitary time away
With this, and very well content,
40   Could so mine idle life have spent;
For it was full of sport, and light
Of foot and heart, and did invite
Me to its game: it seemed to bless
Itself in me; how could I less
45   Than love it? Oh, I cannot be
Unkind to a beast that loveth me.
        Had it lived long, I do not know
Whether it too might have done so
As Sylvio did; his gifts might be
50   Perhaps as false, or more, than he;
But I am sure, for aught that I
Could in so short a time espy,
Thy love was far more better than
The love of false and cruel men.
55   With sweetest milk and sugar, first
I it at mine own fingers nursed;
And as it grew, so every day
It waxed more white and sweet than they.
It had so sweet a breath! And oft
60   I blushed to see its foot more soft

6. In English law, a deodand was an animal   death, was forfeited to the crown to be applied
(or object) which, having caused a person's   to pious uses.

And white, shall I say than my hand?
Nay, any lady's of the land.
   It is a wondrous thing how fleet
'Twas on those little silver feet;
65 With what a pretty skipping grace
It oft would challenge me the race;
And when 't had left me far away,
'Twould stay, and run again, and stay;
For it was nimbler much than hinds,
70 And trod as if on the four winds.
   I have a garden of my own,
But so with roses overgrown,
And lilies, that you would it guess
To be a little wilderness;
75 And all the springtime of the year
It only loved to be there.
Among the beds of lilies I
Have sought it oft, where it should lie,
Yet could not, till itself would rise,
80 Find it, although before mine eyes;
For, in the flaxen lilies' shade,
It like a bank of lilies laid.
Upon the roses it would feed,
Until its lips e'en seemed to bleed;
85 And then to me 'twould boldly trip,
And print those roses on my lip.
But all its chief delight was still
On roses thus itself to fill,
And its pure virgin limbs to fold
90 In whitest sheets of lilies cold:
Had it lived long, it would have been
Lilies without, roses within.
   O help! O help! I see it faint
And die as calmly as a saint!
95 See how it weeps! the tears do come
Sad, slowly dropping like a gum.
So weeps the wounded balsam; so
The holy frankincense[7] doth flow;
The brotherless Heliades[8]
100 Melt in such amber tears as these.
   I in a golden vial will
Keep these two crystal tears, and fill
It till it do o'erflow with mine;
Then place it in Diana's shrine.
105   Now my sweet fawn is vanished to
Whither the swans and turtles° go,   *turtledoves*
In fair Elysium to endure,
With milk-white lambs and ermines pure.
O do not run too fast; for I
110 Will but bespeak° thy grave, and die.   *address*
   First, my unhappy statue shall
Be cut in marble, and withal,

---

7. Frankincense, called holy because it is burned in religious ceremonies, is the aromatic gum of an African tree.
8. A name denoting children of Helios, the sun god. Phaethon, the brother referred to, had ventured to drive his father's chariot (the sun) and had been struck dead by Zeus when his wild career endangered the earth. His sisters wept for him until they were turned into poplar trees and their tears into amber.

Let it be weeping too; but there
The engraver sure his art may spare;
115 For I so truly thee bemoan
That I shall weep, though I be stone,
Until my tears, still dropping, wear
My breast, themselves engraving there.
There at my feet shalt thou be laid,
120 Of purest alabaster made;
For I would have thine image be
White as I can, though not as thee.

1681

To His Coy Mistress

Had we but world enough, and time,
This coyness, lady, were no crime.
We would sit down, and think which way
To walk, and pass our long love's day.
5 Thou by the Indian Ganges' side
Shoudst rubies⁹ find; I by the tide
Of Humber¹ would complain. I would
Love you ten years before the flood,
And you should, if you please, refuse
10 Till the conversion of the Jews.²
My vegetable³ love should grow
Vaster than empires and more slow;
An hundred years should go to praise
Thine eyes, and on thy forehead gaze;
15 Two hundred to adore each breast,
But thirty thousand to the rest;
An age at least to every part,
And the last age should show your heart.
For, lady, you deserve this state,°   *dignity*
20 Nor would I love at lower rate.
    But at my back I always hear
Time's wingéd chariot hurrying near;
And yonder all before us lie
Deserts of vast eternity.
25 Thy beauty shall no more be found;
Nor, in thy marble vault, shall sound
My echoing song; then worms shall try
That long-preserved virginity,
And your quaint° honor turn to dust,   *over-subtle*
30 And into ashes all my lust:
The grave's a fine and private place,
But none, I think, do there embrace.
    Now therefore, while the youthful hue
Sits on thy skin like morning glow,⁴
35 And while thy willing soul transpires°   *breathes out*
At every pore with instant fires,
Now let us sport us while we may,

---

9. Rubies are talismans, preserving virginity.
1. The Humber flows through Marvell's native town of Hull.
2. To occur, as tradition had it, at the end of recorded history.
3. A technical term: "possessing, like plants, the power of growth but not of consciousness";
in context, "being magnified without conscious nurture."
4. In these rhyme-words (originally spelled *hew* and *glew*) the vowel sounds are probably similar and possibly identical: an *eh* gliding into an *oo*.

And now, like amorous birds of prey,
Rather at once our time devour
40   Than languish in his slow-chapped° power.   *slow-jawed*
Let us roll all our strength and all
Our sweetness up into one ball,
And tear our pleasures with rough strife
Thorough the iron gates[5] of life:
45   Thus, though we cannot make our sun
Stand still,[6] yet we will make him run.

1681

The Definition of Love[7]

My Love is of a birth as rare
As 'tis, for object, strange and high;
It was begotten by Despair
Upon Impossibility.

5   Magnanimous Despair alone
Could show me so divine a thing,
Where feeble Hope could ne'er have flown
But vainly flapped its tinsel wing.

And yet I quickly might arrive
10   Where my extended soul is fixed;
But Fate does iron wedges drive,
And always crowds itself betwixt.

For Fate with jealous eye does see
Two perfect loves, nor lets them close;°   *unite*
15   Their union would her ruin be,
And her tyrannic power depose.[8]

And therefore her decrees of steel
Us as the distant poles have placed
(Though Love's whole world on us doth wheel),[9]
20   Not by themselves to be embraced,

Unless the giddy heaven fall,
And earth some new convulsion tear,
And, us to join, the world should all
Be cramped into a planisphere.[1]

25   As lines, so loves oblique may well
Themselves in every angle greet;[2]
But ours, so truly parallel,
Though infinite, can never meet.

5. The obscurity "iron gates" suggests that the "ball" of line 42 has become a missile from a siege gun, battering its way into a citadel.
6. We lack, that is, the power of Zeus, who, to prolong his enjoyment of the mortal Alcmena, arrested the diurnal course and created a week-long night.
7. The poem plays upon a Platonic definition of love as a longing which is unfulfilled.
8. In the old chemistry, it was assumed that an even mixture of pure elements formed an altogether stable compound, proof against all vicissitudes and hence, in context, defying fate.
9. I.e., the relationship (literally, the line) between us forms the axis on which Love's world turns.
1. A sphere projected on a plane surface, perhaps here conceivable as plane projections of the northern and southern hemispheres on opposite sides of a disc.
2. I.e., may converge to form any angle up to 180 degrees.

30 Therefore the love which us doth bind,
But Fate so enviously debars,
Is the conjunction of the mind,
And opposition of the stars.[3]

The Picture of Little T. C.[4] in a Prospect of Flowers

See with what simplicity
This nymph begins her golden days!
In the green grass she loves to lie,
And there with her fair aspect tames
5 The wilder flowers, and gives them names;
But only with the roses plays,
        And them does tell
What color best becomes them, and what smell.

Who can foretell for what high cause
10 This darling of the gods was born?
Yet this is she whose chaster laws
The wanton Love shall one day fear,
And, under her command severe,
See his bow broke and ensigns torn.
15   Happy who can
Appease this virtuous enemy of man!

O then let me in time compound°   *bargain*
And parley with those conquering eyes,
Ere they have tried their force to wound;
20 Ere with their glancing wheels they drive
In triumph over hearts that strive,
And them that yield but more despise:
        Let me be laid
Where I may see thy glories from some shade.

25 Meantime, whilst every verdant thing
Itself does at thy beauty charm,[5]
Reform the errors of the spring;
Make that the tulips may have share
Of sweetness, seeing they are fair;
30 And roses of their thorns disarm;
        But most procure
That violets may a longer age endure.

But, O young beauty of the woods,
Whom nature courts with fruits and flowers,
35 Gather the flowers, but spare the buds,
Lest Flora,[6] angry at thy crime
To kill her infants in their prime,
Do quickly make the example yours;
        And ere we see,
Nip in the blossom all our hopes and thee.

3. In this astronomical image, the minds of the lovers are in accord (literally in *conjunction*, or occupying the same celestial longitude), but the stars determining their destinies are entirely hostile (literally in *opposition*, or 180 degrees apart).

4. Possibly Theophila Cornewall (says Marvell's editor), whose family infant mortality had scourged.
5. Enchants itself at thy beauty.
6. Goddess of flowers.

The Mower Against Gardens

Luxurious° man, to bring his vice in use, *lustful*
    Did after him the world seduce,
And from the fields the flowers and plants allure,
    Where Nature was most plain and pure.
5 He first enclosed within the gardens square
    A dead and standing pool of air,
And a more luscious earth for them did knead,
    Which stupefied them while it fed.
The pink grew then as double as his mind;
10   The nutriment did change the kind.
With strangé perfumes he did the roses taint;
    And flowers themselves were taught to paint.
The tulip white did for complexion seek,
    And learned to interline its cheek;
15 Its onion root they then so high did hold,
    That one was for a meadow sold: [1]
Another world was searched through oceans new,
    To find the Marvel of Peru; [2]
And yet these rarities might be allowed
20   To man, that sovereign thing and proud,
Had he not dealt between the bark and tree,
    Forbidden mixtures there to see.
No plant now knew the stock from which it came;
    He grafts upon the wild the tame,
25 That the uncertain and adulterate fruit
    Might put the palate in dispute.
His green seraglio has its eunuchs too,
    Lest any tyrant him outdo;
And in the cherry he does Nature vex,
30   To procreate without a sex.
'Tis all enforced, the fountain and the grot,
    While the sweet fields do lie forgot,
Where willing Nature does to all dispense
    A wild and fragrant innocence;
35 And fauns° and fairies do the meadows till *rural gods*
    More by their presence than their skill.
Their statues polished by some ancient hand,
    May to adorn the gardens stand;
But, howsoe'er the figures do excel,
40   The Gods themselves with us do dwell.

    1681

The Mower to the Glowworms

Ye living lamps, by whose dear light
The nightingale does sit so late,
And studying all the summer night,
Her matchless songs does meditate;

---

1. A tulip fad in the 1630's brought extremely
high prices for rare varieties.

2. A tuliplike flower from tropical America.

5   Ye country comets, that portend
     No war nor prince's funeral,[1]
     Shining unto no higher end
     Than to presage the grass's fall;

     Ye glowworms, whose officious° flame   *serviceable*
10   To wandering mowers shows the way,
     That in the night have lost their aim,
     And after foolish fires [2] do stray;

     Your courteous lights in vain you waste,
     Since Juliana here is come,
15   For she may mind hath so displaced
     That I shall never find my home.

                                                              1681

The Garden

     How vainly men themselves amaze°   *perplex*
     To win the palm, the oak, or bays,[8]
     And their incessant° labors see   *unceasing*
     Crowned from some single herb, or tree,
5   Whose short and narrow-vergéd[9] shade
     Does prudently their toils upbraid;
     While all flowers and all trees do close°   *join*
     To weave the garlands of repose!

     Fair Quiet, have I found thee here,
10   And Innocence, thy sister dear?
     Mistaken long, I sought you then
     In busy companies of men.
     Your sacred plants,° if here below,   *cuttings*
     Only among the plants will grow;
15   Society is all but rude[1]
     To this delicious solitude.

     No white nor red was ever seen
     So amorous as this lovely green.
     Fond lovers, cruel as their flame,
20   Cut in these trees their mistress' name:
     Little, alas, they know or heed
     How far these beauties hers exceed!
     Fair trees, wheresoe'er your barks I wound,
     No name shall but your own be found.

25   When we have run our passion's heat,°   *course*
     Love hither makes his best retreat.
     The gods, that mortal beauty chase,
     Still in a tree did end their race:
     Apollo hunted Daphne so,
30   Only that she might laurel grow;
     And Pan did after Syrinx speed,
     Not as a nymph, but for a reed.[2]

1. Comets were sometimes believed to be portents of approaching disasters.
2. *Ignis fatuus* ("foolish fire"): the will-o'-the-wisp.
8. The wreaths awarded, respectively, for athletic, civic, and poetic accomplishments.
9. Confined, not spreading luxuriantly like the living branch.
1. I.e., all merely barbarous.
2. In the original myths, as told by Ovid, the nymphs frustrated the pursuing gods by turning into the plants named. In Marvell's version, the gods intended the transformations.

What wondrous life is this I lead!
Ripe apples drop about my head;
35 The luscious clusters of the vine
Upon my mouth do crush their wine;
The nectarine and curious° peach   *exquisite*
Into my hands themselves do reach;
Stumbling on melons, as I pass,
40 Insnared with flowers, I fall on grass.

Meanwhile the mind, from pleasure less,
Withdraws into its happiness;³
The mind, that ocean where each kind
Does straight its own resemblance find;⁴
45 Yet it creates, transcending these,
Far other worlds and other seas,
Annihilating all that's made
To a green thought in a green shade.

Here at the fountain's sliding foot,
50 Or at some fruit tree's mossy root,
Casting the body's vest° aside,   *garment*
My soul into the boughs does glide:
There, like a bird, it sits and sings,
Then whets⁵ and combs its silver wings,
55 And, till prepared for longer flight,
Waves in its plumes the various° light.   *iridescent*

Such was that happy garden-state,
While man there walked without a mate:
After a place so pure and sweet,
60 What other help could yet be meet!⁵ᵃ
But 'twas beyond a mortal's share
To wander solitary there:
Two paradises 'twere in one
To live in paradise alone.

65 How well the skillful gardener drew
Of flowers and herbs this dial⁶ new,
Where, from above, the milder sun
Does through a fragrant zodiac run;
And as it works, th' industrious bee
70 Computes its time as well as we!
How could such sweet and wholesome hours
Be reckoned but with herbs and flowers?

1681

An Horatian Ode

UPON CROMWELL'S RETURN FROM IRELAND⁷

The forward youth that would appear
Must now forsake his Muses dear,

3. I.e., its own intellectual happiness is a greater pleasure than the taste of fruits.
4. Every land creature was thought to have its counterpart sea creature.
5. Sharpens its beak. But birds apparently whetting their beaks are actually cleaning them.
5a. God created Eve because "for Adam there was not found an help meet for him" (Genesis ii.20).
6. A plantation of flowers forming a dial face, perhaps surrounding an actual sundial.
7. Cromwell returned from a successful Irish campaign in 1650 to direct action against the Scots.

Nor in the shadows sing
His numbers° languishing:

5 'Tis time to leave the books in dust,
And oil the unuséd armor's rust,
   Removing from the wall
   The corslet of the hall.[8]

So restless Cromwell could not cease
10 In the inglorious arts of peace,
   But through adventurous war
   Urgéd his active star;

And like the three-forked lightning, first
Breaking the clouds where it was nursed,
15   Did thorough° his own side
   His fiery way divide.[9]

through

For 'tis all one to courage high,
The emulous or enemy;
   And with such to inclose
20   Is more than to oppose.[1]

Then burning through the air he went,
And palaces and temples rent;
   And Caesar's head at last
   Did through his laurels blast.[2]

25 'Tis madness to resist or blame
The force of angry heaven's flame;[3]
   And if we would speak true,
   Much to the man is due,

Who, from his private gardens, where
30 He lived reservéd and austere
   (As if his highest plot
   To plant the bergamot°),

pear tree

Could by industrious valor climb
To ruin the great work of time,
35   And cast the kingdom old
   Into another mold;

Though Justice against Fate complain,
And plead the ancient rights in vain;
   But those do hold or break,
40   As men are strong or weak.

---

8. The suit of armor belonging to the household.
9. Originally a Presbyterian, Cromwell rose to power as an Independent.
1. Possible paraphrase of stanza: It challenges high courage as much to deal with competitors as to deal with the enemy; and to make common cause with men like the sectarians of the Parliamentary party is more of an accomplishment than effectually to oppose them.

(Marvell's obscurities may be deliberate and politic.)
2. The laurel wreath of the civic leader was supposed proof against lightning, which was taken in primitive superstition to represent the jealousy of the gods. Charles I had been beheaded a year and a half before.
3. The lightning hurled by Zeus represents divine judgment.

Nature, that hateth emptiness,
Allows of penetration less,[4]
    And therefore must make room
    Where greater spirits come.

45 What field of all the civil wars,
Where his were not the deepest scars?
    And Hampton shows what part
    He had of wiser art;[5]

Where, twining subtle fears with hope,
50 He wove a net of such a scope
    That Charles himself might chase
    To Carisbrooke's narrow case,[6]

That thence the royal actor borne
The tragic scaffold might adorn;
55   While round the arméd bands
    Did clap their bloody hands.

He[7] nothing common did or mean
Upon that memorable scene,
    But with his keener eye
60   The axe's edge did try;

Nor called the gods with vulgar spite
To vindicate his helpless right;
    But bowed his comely head
    Down, as upon a bed.

65 This was that memorable hour
Which first assured the forcéd power:
    So, when they did design
    The Capitol's first line,

A bleeding head, where they begun,
70 Did fright the architects to run;
    And yet in that the state
    Foresaw its happy fate.[8]

And now the Irish are ashamed
To see themselves in one year tamed;
75   So such one man can do
    That does both act and know.

They can affirm his praises best,
And have, though overcome, confessed
    How good he is, how just,
80   And fit for highest trust.

4. I.e., Nature, which abhors a vacuum, is even less willing to let two bodies occupy the same space.
5. Cromwell purportedly let Charles escape from Hampton Court to Carisbrooke Castle on the Isle of Wight, so that Charles's irresponsibility might become evident.
6. *Case* may mean either *plight* or *prison*.

7. I.e., Charles.
8. A bloody head unearthed by workmen digging foundations for the Temple of Jupiter was interpreted to mean that Rome would be "head" of an empire. The temple and the hill on which it stood were thereafter called Capitoline or the Capitol (from *caput*, head).

Nor yet grown stiffer with command,
But still in the republic's hand—
    How fit he is to sway
    That can so well obey!

85 He to the Commons' feet presents
A kingdom for his first year's rents;
    And, what he may, forbears
    His fame to make it theirs;

And has his sword and spoils ungirt,
90 To lay them at the public's skirt:[9]
    So when the falcon high
    Falls heavy from the sky,

She, having killed, no more does search
But on the next green bough to perch;
95 Where, when he first does lure,[1]
    The falconer has her sure.

What may not, then, our isle presume,
While victory his crest[2] does plume?
    What may not others fear,
100 If thus he crown each year?

A Caesar he, ere long, to Gaul
To Italy an Hannibal,
    And to all states not free
    Shall climactéric[3] be.

105 The Pict no shelter now shall find
Within his parti-colored mind,[4]
    But from this valor sad
    Shrink underneath the plaid;

Happy if in the tufted brake
110 The English hunter him mistake,
    Nor lay his hounds in near
    The Caledonian° deer.   Scottish

But thou, the war's and fortune's son,
March indefatigably on!
115   And for the last effect,
    Still keep thy sword erect;

Besides the force it has to fright
The spirits of the shady night,[5]
    The same arts that did gain
120   A power must it maintain.

1681

9. I.e., at the feet of the Republic, conceived as a Roman senator wearing a toga.
1. I.e., when the falcon casts out his lure—a bunch of feathers attached to a cord and baited with meat.
2. Of the falcon; also the plumed helmet of the warrior.
3. I.e., ushering in a new epoch.
4. The Scots, called *Picti* ("painted men") by the Romans because they painted their bodies for battle, are stigmatized as factious (with a pun on *party* and *parti-colored*). They were in fact torn between their Calvinism and their loyalty to the Catholic or Anglo-Catholic Stuart kings.
5. The hilt of a sword held upright (line 116) made the sign of the cross, dispelling evil spirits. But Marvell seems, above and below, to be commending to Cromwell a resolute use of the sword in simple warfare.

HENRY VAUGHAN
(1622–1695)

Regeneration

A ward, and still in bonds, one day
    I stole abroad;
It was high spring, and all the way
    Primrosed and hung with shade;
5   Yet was it frost within,
      And surly winds
Blasted my infant buds, and sin
    Like clouds eclipsed my mind.

Stormed thus, I straight perceived my spring
10   Mere stage and show,
My walk a monstrous, mountained thing,
    Roughcast with rocks and snow;
    And as a pilgrim's eye,
     Far from relief,
15   Measures the melancholy sky,
    Then drops and rains for grief,

So sighed I upwards still; at last
    'Twixt steps and falls
I reached the pinnacle, where placed
20   I found a pair of scales;
    I took them up and laid
     In th' one, late pains;
The other smoke and pleasures weighed,
    But proved the heavier grains.[1]

25 With that some cried, "Away!" Straight I
    Obeyed, and led
Full east, a fair, fresh field could spy;
    Some called it Jacob's bed,[2]
    A virgin soil which no
30   Rude feet ere trod,
Where, since he stepped there, only go
    Prophets and friends of God.

Here I reposed; but scarce well set,
    A grove descried
35 Of stately height, whose branches met
    And mixed on every side;
    I entered, and once in,
     Amazed to see 't,
Found all was changed, and a new spring
40   Did all my senses greet.

The unthrift sun shot vital gold,
    A thousand pieces,

1. Units of weight.
2. Sleeping in a field, Jacob saw a ladder reaching from earth to heaven, with angels ascending and descending on it (Genesis xxviii.10–12).

And heaven its azure did unfold,
　　Checkered with snowy fleeces;
45　　　The air was all in spice,
　　　　And every bush
　A garland wore; thus fed my eyes,
　　But all the ear lay hush.

Only a little fountain lent
50　　　Some use for ears,
And on the dumb shades language spent,
　　The music of her tears;
　　　I drew her near, and found
　　　　The cistern full
55 Of divers stones, some bright and round,
　　Others ill-shaped and dull.

The first, pray mark, as quick as light
　　　Danced through the flood,
But the last, more heavy than the night,
60　　Nailed to the center stood;
　　　I wondered much, but tired
　　　　At last with thought,
My restless eye that still desired
　　As strange an object brought.

65 It was a bank of flowers, where I descried
　　　Though 'twas midday,
Some fast asleep, others broad-eyed
　　And taking in the ray;
　　　Here, musing long, I heard
70　　　A rushing wind
Which still increased, but whence it stirred
　　No where I could not find.

I turned me round, and to each shade
　　　Dispatched an eye
75 To see if any leaf had made
　　　Least motion or reply,
　　But while I listening sought
　　　My mind to ease
By knowing where 'twas, or where not,
80　　It whispered, "Where I please."[3]

"Lord," then said I, "on me one breath,
And let me die before my death!"

　　　　　　　　　　　　　　　　　1650

The Retreat

Happy those early days! when I
Shined in my angel infancy.
Before I understood this place
Appointed for my second race,
5　Or taught my soul to fancy aught

---

3. "The wind bloweth where it listeth, and   so is every one that is born of the Spirit"
thou hearest the sound thereof, but canst not   (John iii.8).
tell whence it cometh, and whither it goeth:

But a white, celestial thought;
When yet I had not walked above
A mile or two from my first love,
And looking back, at that short space,
10   Could see a glimpse of His bright face;
When on some gilded cloud or flower
My gazing soul would dwell an hour,
And in those weaker glories spy
Some shadows of eternity;
15   Before I taught my tongue to wound
My conscience with a sinful sound,
Or had the black art to dispense
A several° sin to every sense,   *separate*
But felt through all this fleshly dress
20   Bright shoots of everlastingness.
    O, how I long to travel back,
And tread again that ancient track!
That I might once more reach that plain
Where first I left my glorious train,
25   From whence th' enlightened spirit sees
That shady city of palm trees.
But, ah! my soul with too much stay
Is drunk, and staggers in the way.
Some men a forward motion love;
30   But I by backward steps would move,
And when this dust falls to the urn,
In that state I came, return.   1650

The World

I saw eternity the other night
Like a great ring of pure and endless light,
        All calm as it was bright;
And round beneath it, Time, in hours, days, years,
5   Driven by the spheres,[4]
Like a vast shadow moved, in which the world
        And all her train were hurled.
The doting lover in his quaintest° strain   *most fanciful*
        Did there complain;
10   Near him, his lute, his fancy, and his flights,
        Wit's sour delights,
With gloves and knots,[5] the silly snares of pleasure,
        Yet his dear treasure,
All scattered lay, while he his eyes did pour
15   Upon a flower.

The darksome statesman, hung with weights and woe,
Like a thick midnight fog, moved there so slow
        He did nor stay nor go;
Condemning thoughts, like sad eclipses, scowl
20   Upon his soul,
And clouds of crying witnesses without
        Pursued him with one shout.

4. In Ptolemaic cosmology, the concentric re-
volving spheres which surrounded the earth
and contained the heavenly bodies.
5. Decorative knots, used as emblems of love.

Yet digged the mole, and, lest his ways be found,
    Worked underground,
25 Where he did clutch his prey. But one did see
    That policy:°   *strategy*
Churches and altars fed him; perjuries
    Were gnats and flies;
It rained about him blood and tears; but he
30   Drank them as free.

The fearful miser on a heap of rust
Sat pining all his life there, did scarce trust
    His own hands with the dust;
Yet would not place one piece above, but lives
35   In fear of thieves.[6]
Thousands there were as frantic as himself,
    And hugged each one his pelf:
The downright epicure placed heaven in sense,
    And scorned pretense;
40 While others, slipped into a wide excess,
    Said little less;
The weaker sort, slight, trivial wares enslave,
    Who think them brave;°
And poor, despiséd Truth sat counting by°   *beautiful*
45   Their victory.   *observing*

Yet some, who all this while did weep and sing,
And sing and weep, soared up into the ring;
    But most would use no wing.
"O fools!" said I, "thus to prefer dark night
50   Before true light!
To live in grots and caves, and hate the day
    Because it shows the way,

The way which from this dead and dark abode
    Leads up to God,
55 A way where you might tread the sun and be
    More bright than he!"
But, as I did their madness so discuss,
    One whispered thus:
"This ring the bridegroom did for none provide,
60   But for His bride."[7]

                                      1650

They Are All Gone into the World of Light!

They are all gone into the world of light!
    And I alone sit lingering here;
Their very memory is fair and bright,
    And my sad thoughts doth clear.

5 It glows and glitters in my cloudy breast
    Like stars upon some gloomy grove,
Or those faint beams in which this hill is dressed
    After the sun's remove.

---

6. "But lay up for yourselves treasures in heaven, where neither moth nor rust doth corrupt, and where thieves do not break through nor steal" (Matthew vi.20).

7. The bride of Christ is his church, the communion of saints who will inhabit the New Jerusalem (see Revelation xix.7–8 and xxi.9–27).

I see them walking in an air of glory,
    Whose light doth trample on my days;
My days, which are at best but dull and hoary,
    Mere glimmering and decays.

O holy hope, and high humility,
    High as the heavens above!
These are your walks, and you have showed them me
    To kindle my cold love.

Dear, beauteous death! the jewel of the just,
    Shining nowhere but in the dark;
What mysteries do lie beyond thy dust,
    Could man outlook that mark!°   *boundary*

He that hath found some fledged bird's nest may know
    At first sight if the bird be flown;
But what fair well or grove he sings in now,
    That is to him unknown.

And yet, as angels in some brighter dreams
    Call to the soul when man doth sleep,
So some strange thoughts transcend our wonted themes,
    And into glory peep.

If a star were confined into a tomb,
    Her captive flames must needs burn there;
But when the hand that locked her up gives room,
    She'll shine through all the sphere.

O Father of eternal life, and all
    Created glories under Thee!
Resume° Thy spirit from this world of thrall   *take back*
    Into true liberty!

Either disperse these mists, which blot and fill
    My perspective° still as they pass;   *telescope*
Or else remove me hence unto that hill
    Where I shall need no glass.

                                        1655

The Timber

Sure thou didst flourish once! and many springs,
Many bright mornings, much dew, many showers
Passed o'er thy head; many light hearts and wings,
Which now are dead, lodged in thy living bowers.

And still a new succession sings and flies;
Fresh groves grow up, and their green branches shoot
Toward the old and still enduring skies,
While the low violet thrives at their root.

But thou beneath the sad and heavy line
Of death, doth waste all senseless, cold, and dark;
Where not so much as dreams of light may shine,
Nor any thought of greenness, leaf, or bark.

And yet (as if some deep hate and dissent,
Bred in thy growth betwixt high winds and thee,
15 Were still alive) thou dost great storms resent
Before they come, and know'st how near they be.[8]

Else all at rest thou liest, and the fierce breath
Of tempests can no more disturb thy ease;
But this thy strange resentment after death
20 Means° only those who broke in life thy peace.   *is directed at*

So murdered man, when lovely life is done
And his blood freezed, keeps in the center still
Some secret sense, which makes the dead blood run
At his approach, that did the body kill.

25 And is there any murderer worse than sin?
Or any storms more foul than a lewd life?
Or what resentient[9] can work more within
Than true remorse, when with past sins at strife?

He that hath left life's vain joys and vain care,
30 And truly hates to be detained on earth,
Hath got an house where many mansions are,[1]
And keeps his soul unto eternal mirth.

But though thus dead unto the world, and ceased
From sin, he walks a narrow, private way;
35 Yet grief and old wounds make him sore displeased,
And all his life a rainy, weeping day.

For though he would forsake the world, and live
As mere° a stranger, as men long since dead;   *total*
Yet joy itself will make a right soul grieve
40 To think he should be so long vainly led.

But as shades set off light, so tears and grief
(Though of themselves but a sad blubbered story)
By showing the sin great, show the relief
Far greater, and so speak my Saviour's glory.

45 If my way lies through deserts and wild woods,
Where all the land with scorching heat is curst,
Better the pools should flow with rain and floods
To fill my bottle, than I die with thirst.

Blest showers they are, and streams sent from above
50 Begetting virgins where they use to flow;
And trees of life no other water love;[2]
These upper springs, and none else make them grow.

---

8. An allusion to foxfire, the eerie phosphorescent light given off by decaying wood, especially before a storm.
9. That which causes a change of heart.
1. "In my Father's house are many mansions" (John xiv.2). "Mansions": rooms.

2. "And he shewed me a pure river of water of life, clear as crystal, proceeding out of the throne of God and of the Lamb. In the midst of the street of it, and on either side of the river, was there the tree of life * * * " (Revelation xxii.1–2).

But these chaste fountains flow not till we die;
Some drops may fall before, but a clear spring
55 And ever running, till we leave° to fling   *cease*
Dirt in her way, will keep above the sky.

                                                                1655

The Waterfall

With what deep murmurs through time's silent stealth
Doth thy transparent, cool, and watery wealth
    Here flowing fall,
    And chide, and call,
5 As if his liquid, loose retínue stayed
Lingering, and were of this steep place afraid,
    The common pass
    Where, clear as glass,
    All must descend—
10   Not to an end,
But quickened by this deep and rocky grave,
Rise to a longer course more bright and brave.°   *sparkling*

    Dear stream! dear bank, where often I
    Have sat and pleased my pensive eye,
15 Why, since each drop of thy quick° store   *living*
Runs thither whence it flowed before,
Should poor souls fear a shade or night,
Who came, sure, from a sea of light?
Or since those drops are all sent back
20 So sure to thee, that none doth lack,
Why should frail flesh doubt any more
That what God takes He'll not restore?

    O useful element and clear!
    My sacred wash and cleanser here,[3]
25 My first consignor unto those
Fountains of life where the Lamb goes![4]
What sublime truths and wholesome themes
Lodge in thy mystical deep streams!
Such as dull man can never find
30 Unless that Spirit lead his mind
Which first upon thy face did move,[5]
And hatched all with His quickening love.
As this loud brook's incessant fall
In streaming rings restagnates° all,   *becomes stagnant*
35 Which reach by course the bank, and then
Are no more seen, just so pass men.
    O my invisible estate,
    My glorious liberty,[6] still late!
    Thou art the channel my soul seeks,
40   Not this with cataracts and creeks.

                                                                1655

3. I.e., through baptism.
4. "For the Lamb which is in the midst of the throne shall feed them, and shall lead them unto living fountains of waters: and God shall wipe away all tears from their eyes" (Revelation vii.17).

5. "And the Spirit of God moved upon the face of the waters" (Genesis i.2).
6. "Because the creature itself also shall be delivered from the bondage of corruption into the glorious liberty of the children of God" (Romans viii.21).

The Night

      Through that pure virgin shrine,
That sacred veil drawn o'er Thy glorious noon,
That men might look and live, as glowworms shine,
      And face the moon,
5   Wise Nicodemus saw such light
As made him know his God by night.[7]

      Most blest believer he!
Who in that land of darkness and blind eyes
Thy long-expected healing wings[8] could see,
10   When Thou didst rise!
And, what can never more be done,
Did at midnight speak with the Sun!

      O who will tell me where
He found Thee at that dead and silent hour?
15 What hallowed solitary ground did bear
      So rare a flower,
Within whose sacred leaves did lie
The fulness of the Deity?

      No mercy-seat of gold,
20 No dead and dusty cherub,[9] nor carved stone,
But His own living works did my Lord hold
      And lodge alone;
Where trees and herbs did watch and peep
And wonder, while the Jews did sleep.

25   Dear night! this world's defeat;
The stop to busy fools; care's check and curb;
The day of spirits; my soul's calm retreat
      Which none disturb!
Christ's progress, and His prayer time;[1]
30 The hours to which high heaven doth chime;

      God's silent, searching flight;
When my Lord's head is filled with dew, and all
His locks are wet with the clear drops of night;
      His still, soft call;
35 His knocking time;[2] the soul's dumb watch,
When spirits their fair kindred catch.

      Were all my loud, evil days
Calm and unhaunted as is thy dark tent,
Whose peace but by some angel's wing or voice
40   Is seldom rent,

---

7. Nicodemus, coming to Christ at night, addressed him as "come from God"; in the same account Christ speaks of his coming as "the light" (John iii.1–21).
8. "But unto you that fear my Name shall the Sun of righteousness arise with healing in his wings * * * " (Malachi iv.2).
9. "And thou shalt make a mercy seat of pure gold * * * And thou shalt make two cherubims of gold, of beaten work shalt thou make them, in the two ends of the mercy seat" (Ex-

odus xxv.17–18).
1. "*Mark, chap.* i.35. *S. Luke, chap.* xxi.37" [Vaughan's note]. The cited passages mention Christ's praying at night.
2. "I sleep, but my heart waketh: it is the voice of my beloved that knocketh, saying, Open to me, my sister, my love, my dove, my undefiled: for my head is filled with dew, and my locks with the drops of the night" (Song of Solomon v.2).

Then I in heaven all the long year
    Would keep, and never wander here.

        But living where the sun
Doth all things wake, and where all mix and tire
45 Themselves and others, I consent and run
            To every mire,
    And by this world's ill-guiding light,
    Err more than I can do by night.

        There is in God, some say,
50 A deep but dazzling darkness, as men here
    Say it is late and dusky, because they
            See not all clear.
        O for that night! where I in Him
        Might live invisible and dim!

                                                    1655

JOHN DRYDEN
(1631–1700)

Song from *The Indian Emperor*

Ah, fading joy, how quickly art thou past!
    Yet we thy ruin haste.
As if the cares of human life were few,
    We seek out new:
5 And follow fate, which would too fast pursue.[1]

See how on every bough the birds express
    In their sweet notes their happiness.
    They all enjoy and nothing spare;
But on their mother nature lay their care:
10 Why then should man, the lord of all below,
    Such troubles choose to know
As none of all his subjects undergo?

Hark, hark, the waters fall, fall, fall,
    And with a murmuring sound
15   Dash, dash upon the ground,
        To gentle slumber's call.

                            1665   1667

Prologue to *The Tempest*[2]

OR, THE ENCHANTED ISLAND

As, when a tree's cut down, the secret root
Lives underground, and thence new branches shoot;
So from old Shakespeare's honored dust, this day
Springs up and buds a new reviving play:
5 Shakespeare, who (taught by none) did first impart

---

1. I.e., which, even if we did not conspire
with it, would hurry us too quickly to our
end.

2. Restoration adaptation of Shakespeare's
play.

To Fletcher[3] wit, to laboring Jonson art.
He, monarch-like, gave those, his subjects, law;
And is that nature which they paint and draw.
Fletcher reached that which on his heights did grow,
10   Whilst Jonson crept, and gathered all below.
This did his love, and this[4] his mirth digest:
One imitates him most, the other best.
If they have since outwrit all other men,
'Tis with the drops which fell from Shakespeare's pen.
15   The storm which vanished on the neighboring shore,
Was taught by Shakespeare's *Tempest* first to roar.
That innocence and beauty which did smile
In Fletcher, grew on this *Enchanted Isle*.
But Shakespeare's magic could not copied be;
20   Within that circle none durst walk but he.
I must confess 'twas bold nor would you now
That liberty to vulgar wits[5] allow,
Which works by magic supernatural things;
But Shakespeare's power is sacred as a king's.
25   Those legends from old priesthood were received,
And he then writ, as people then believed.
But if for Shakespeare we your grace implore,
We for our theater shall want it more:
Who by our dearth of youths are forced to employ
30   One of our women to present a boy;
And that's a transformation, you will say,
Exceeding all the magic in the play.
Let none expect in the last act to find
Her sex transformed from man to womankind.
35   Whate'er she was before the play began,
All you shall see of her is perfect man.
Or if your fancy will be farther led
To find her woman, it must be abed.

1670

Song from *Troilus and Cressida*

1

Can life be a blessing,
Or worth the possessing,
Can life be a blessing, if love were away?
Ah, no! though our love all night keep us waking,
5   And though he torment us with cares all the day,
Yet he sweetens, he sweetens our pains in the taking;
There's an hour at the last, there's an hour to repay.

2

In every possessing
The ravishing blessing,
10   In every possessing the fruit of our pain,
Poor lovers forget long ages of anguish,
Whate'er they have suffered and done to obtain;
'Tis a pleasure, a pleasure to sigh and to languish,
When we hope, when we hope to be happy again.

1679

---

3. John Fletcher (1579–1625), English play-
wright who, as Dryden would have it, learned
sprightliness from Shakespeare and went on
to write enduringly popular tragicomedies.
4. "This * * * this": Fletcher . . . Jonson.
5. I.e., ordinary poets.

Absalom and Achitophel:[6] A Poem

In pious times, ere priestcraft did begin,
Before polygamy was made a sin;
When man on many multiplied his kind,
Ere one to one was cursedly confined;
5 When nature prompted and no law denied
Promiscuous use of concubine and bride;
Then Israel's monarch after Heaven's own heart,[7]
His vigorous warmth did variously impart
To wives and slaves; and, wide as his command,
10 Scattered his Maker's image through the land.
Michal,[8] of royal blood, the crown did wear,
A soil ungrateful to the tiller's care:
Not so the rest; for several mothers bore
To godlike David several sons before.
15 But since like slaves his bed they did ascend,
No true succession could their seed attend.
Of all this numerous progeny was none
So beautiful, so brave, as Absalom:
Whether, inspired by some diviner lust,
20 His father got° him with a greater gust,°   *begot / relish*
Or that° his conscious destiny made way,   *whether*
By manly beauty, to imperial sway,
Early in foreign fields he won renown,
With kings and states allied to Israel's crown:
25 In peace the thoughts of war he could remove,
And seemed as he were only born for love.
Whate'er he did, was done with so much ease,
In him alone 'twas natural to please;
His motions all accompanied with grace;
30 And paradise was opened in his face.
With secret joy indulgent David viewed
His youthful image in his son renewed:
To all his wishes nothing he denied;
And made the charming Annabel his bride.[9]
35 What faults he had (for who from faults is free?)
His father could not, or he would not see.
Some warm excesses which the law forbore,
Were cónstrued youth that purged by boiling o'er:
And Amnon's murder,[1] by a specious name,
40 Was called a just revenge for injured fame.
Thus praised and loved the noble youth remained,
While David, undisturbed, in Sion[2] reigned.
But life can never be sincerely° blest;   *wholly*

6. The names immediately refer the reader to II Samuel xiii–xviii. Absalom there rebels against his father King David; Achitophel advises him to destroy David at once. In Dryden's poem, David stands for Charles II and Absalom for the Duke of Monmouth, Charles's illegitimate son. Achitophel is the Earl of Shaftesbury, who had urged Monmouth, against Charles's will, to seek the succession to the throne. Monmouth would have displaced Charles's brother James, the Duke of York, whose Catholicism made him repugnant to many Protestants.
7. God calls David "a man after mine own heart" in Acts xiii.22.
8. David's childless wife. She stands for Charles's childless queen, Catherine of Portugal.
9. These lines record the personal attractiveness of Monmouth, his prowess in wars against the Dutch and later the French, and his marriage (arranged by the King) to the Scottish heiress Anne Scott.
1. Absalom had killed Amnon to avenge his rape of Absalom's sister (II Samuel xiii.28–29). An obscure historical reference, but Monmouth had had a reputation for violence in his youth, and, more recently, his troopers had violently attacked an abusive Parliamentarian, Sir John Coventry.
2. London.

Heaven punishes the bad, and proves° the best.   *tries*
45   The Jews,[3] a headstrong, moody, murmuring race,
As ever tried the extent and stretch of grace;
God's pampered people, whom, debauched with ease,
No king could govern, nor no God could please
(Gods they had tried of every shape and size
50   That god-smiths could produce, or priests devise);[4]
These Adam-wits,[5] too fortunately free,
Began to dream they wanted° liberty;   *lacked*
And when no rule, no precedent was found,
Of men by laws less circumscribed and bound,
55   They led their wild desires to woods and caves,
And thought that all but savages were slaves.
They who, when Saul was dead, without a blow,
Made foolish Ishbosheth the crown forego;[6]
Who banished David did from Hebron[7] bring,
60   And with a general shout proclaimed him king:
Those very Jews, who, at their very best,
Their humor° more than loyalty expressed,   *caprice*
Now wondered why so long they had obeyed
An idol monarch, which their hands had made;
65   Thought they might ruin him they could create,
Or melt him to that golden calf, a state.[8]
But these were random bolts;° no formed design   *shots*
Nor interest made the factious crowd to join:
The sober part of Israel, free from stain,
70   Well knew the value of a peaceful reign;
And, looking backward with a wise affright,
Saw seams of wounds, dishonest° to the sight: *dishonorable*
In contemplation of whose ugly scars
They cursed the memory of civil wars.
75   The moderate sort of men, thus qualified,°   *mollified*
Inclined the balance to the better side;
And David's mildness managed it so well,
The bad found no occasion to rebel.
But when to sin our biased nature leans,
80   The careful Devil is still at hand with means;
And providently pimps for ill desires:
The Good Old Cause[9] revived, a plot requires.
Plots, true or false, are necessary things,
To raise up commonwealths and ruin kings.
85   The inhabitants of old Jerusalem
Were Jebusites;[1] the town so called from them;
And theirs the native right.
But when the chosen people[2] grew more strong,
The rightful cause at length became the wrong;
90   And every loss the men of Jebus bore,

---

3. English.
4. Dryden refers to novelties in doctrine and church practice which had issued in the disestablishment of the Anglican Church under the Commonwealth.
5. The word calls attention to the supposedly untutored quality of the dissenters from the Anglican communion, and also the biblical Adam's rebellion against the single restraint imposed on him: eating the fruit of the tree of the knowledge of good and evil (Genesis ii.16–17).
6. Saul is Oliver Cromwell; Ishbosheth, his ineffectual son Richard.
7. David was first crowned king of the tribe of Judah only, in Hebron; Charles had been crowned king of Scotland before he fled to the Continent.
8. I.e., that idol, a republic. The biblical reference is to the image of a calf, made of golden earrings melted down, which the Israelites worshiped while Moses was on Mount Sinai (Exodus xxxii.1–4).
9. The Commonwealth.
1. The Jebusites (Judges i.21) are Roman Catholics; Jerusalem is London.
2. The Protestants, some of whom claimed for England a divinely appointed destiny like that of the Hebrews.

They still were thought God's enemies the more.
Thus worn and weakened, well or ill content,
Submit they must to David's government:
Impoverished and deprived of all command,
95 Their taxes doubled as they lost their land;
And, what was harder yet to flesh and blood,
Their gods disgraced, and burnt like common wood.
This set the heathen priesthood[3] in a flame;
For priests of all religions are the same:
100 Of whatsoe'er descent their godhead be,
Stock, stone, or other homely pedigree,
In his defense his servants are as bold,
As if he had been born of beaten gold.
The Jewish rabbins,[4] though their enemies,
105 In this conclude them honest men and wise:
For 'twas their duty, all the learned think,
To espouse his cause, by whom they eat and drink.
From hence began that Plot,[5] the nation's curse,
Bad in itself, but represented worse;
110 Raised in extremes, and in extremes decried;
With oaths affirmed, with dying vows denied;
Not weighed or winnowed by the multitude;
But swallowed in the mass, unchewed and crude.
Some truth there was, but dashed° and brewed with lies,   *mixed*
115 To please the fools, and puzzle all the wise.
Succeeding times did equal folly call,
Believing nothing, or believing all.
The Egyptian[6] rites the Jebusites embraced,
Where gods were recommended by their taste.
120 Such savory deities must needs be good,
As served at once for worship and for food.
By force they could not introduce these gods,
For ten to one in former days was odds;
So fraud was used (the sacrificer's trade):
125 Fools are more hard to conquer than persuade.
Their busy teachers mingled with the Jews,
And raked for converts even the court and stews:°   *brothels*
Which Hebrew priests the more unkindly took,
Because the fleece accompanies the flock.[7]
130 Some thought they God's anointed[8] meant to slay
By guns, invented since full many a day:
Our author swears it not; but who can know
How far the Devil and Jebusites may go?
This Plot, which failed for want of common sense,
135 Had yet a deep and dangerous consequence:
For, as when raging fevers boil the blood,
The standing lake soon floats into a flood,
And every hostile humor, which before
Slept quiet in its channels, bubbles o'er;
140 So several factions from this first ferment

3. The Catholic clergy, suffering from the recent flare-up of prejudice as well as from the long history of restrictions to which Dryden has just alluded.
4. Anglican divines.
5. An inchoate Roman Catholic scheme for deposing (possibly murdering) Charles and placing his brother James on the throne. The witnesses to this plot, of whom Titus Oates was chief, were so irresponsible in their testi-mony that historians have never known how far it actually proceeded.
6. French, hence Roman Catholic. The allusion is to the Mass, incorporating the doctrine of transubstantiation.
7. The Anglican clergy ("Hebrew priests") valued the tithes paid to the established church.
8. The King.

Work up to foam, and threat the government.
Some by their friends, more by themselves thought wise,
Opposed the power to which they could not rise.
Some had in courts been great, and thrown from thence,
145 Like fiends were hardened in impenitence;
Some, by their monarch's fatal mercy, grown
From pardoned rebels kinsmen to the throne,
Were raised in power and public office high;
Strong bands, if bands ungrateful men could tie.
150   Of these the false Achitophel⁹ was first;
A name to all succeeding ages cursed:
For close designs, and crooked counsels fit;
Sagacious, bold, and turbulent of wit;°   *imagination*
Restless, unfixed in principles and place;
155 In power unpleased, impatient of disgrace:
A fiery soul, which, working out its way, ⎫
Fretted the pygmy body to decay,   ⎬
And o'er-informed the tenement of clay.¹ ⎭
A daring pilot in extremity;
160 Pleased with the danger, when the waves went high,
He sought the storms; but, for a calm unfit,
Would steer too nigh the sands, to boast his wit.
Great wits° are sure to madness near allied,   *geniuses*
And thin partitions do their bounds divide;
165 Else why should he, with wealth and honor blest,
Refuse his age the needful hours of rest?
Punish a body which he could not please,
Bankrupt of life, yet prodigal of ease?
And all to leave what with his toil he won,
170 To that unfeathered two-legged thing,² a son;
Got,° while his soul did huddled° notions try;   *begotten / confused*
And born a shapeless lump, like anarchy.
In friendship false, implacable in hate,
Resolved to ruin or to rule the state.
175 To compass this the triple bond³ he broke, ⎫
The pillars of the public safety shook,   ⎬
And fitted Israel for a foreign yoke;   ⎭
Then seized with fear, yet still affecting fame,
Usurped a patriot's all-atoning name.⁴
180 So easy still it proves in factious times,
With public zeal to cancel private crimes.
How safe is treason, and how sacred ill,
Where none can sin against the people's will!
Where crowds can wink, and no offense be known,
185 Since in another's guilt they find their own!
Yet fame deserved, no enemy can grudge;
The statesman we abhor, but praise the judge.
In Israel's courts ne'er sat an Abbethdin⁵
With more discerning eyes, or hands more clean;
190 Unbrided, unsought, the wretched to redress;
Swift of dispatch, and easy of access.

---

9. Shaftesbury had been a prime mover in the campaign to exclude James from the succession and replace him with Monmouth. He was awaiting trial for treason when this poem was written; Dryden is implicitly pressing for a conviction.
1. I.e., over-animated his body.
2. Plato's definition of cloddish man.

3. An alliance between England, Sweden, and the Dutch Republic against France; France (line 177) was thought to pose the threat of invasion.
4. The name of Patriot was affected, then and thereafter, by the party out of power.
5. A rabbinical term for a justice. Shaftesbury had ably presided over the Court of Chancery.

Oh, had he been content to serve the crown,
With virtues only proper to the gown;°   *judiciary*
Or had the rankness of the soil been freed
195 From cockle, that oppressed the noble seed;
David for him his tuneful harp had strung,
And Heaven had wanted one immortal song.[6]
But wild Ambition loves to slide, not stand,
And Fortune's ice prefers to Virtue's land.
200 Achitophel, grown weary to possess
A lawful fame, and lazy happiness,
Disdained the golden fruit to gather free,
And lent the crowd his arm to shake the tree.
Now, manifest of° crimes contrived long since,   *detected in*
205 He stood at bold defiance with his prince;
Held up the buckler of the people's cause
Against the crown, and skulked behind the laws.
The wished occasion of the Plot he takes;
Some circumstances finds, but more he makes.
210 By buzzing emissaries fills the ears
Of listening crowds with jealousies° and fears   *suspicions*
Of arbitrary counsels brought to light,
And proves the king himself a Jebusite.
Weak arguments! which yet he knew full well
215 Were strong with people easy to rebel.
For, governed by the moon, the giddy Jews
Tread the same track when she the prime renews;[7]
And once in twenty years, their scribes record,
By natural instinct they change their lord.
220 Achitophel still wants a chief, and none
Was found so fit as warlike Absalom:
Not that he wished his greatness to create
(For politicians neither love nor hate),
But, for he knew his title not allowed,
225 Would keep him still depending on the crowd,
That kingly power, thus ebbing out, might be
Drawn to the dregs of a democracy.°   *mob rule*
Him he attempts with studied arts to please,
And sheds his venom in such words as these:
230 "Auspicious prince, at whose nativity
Some royal planet ruled the southern sky;
Thy longing country's darling and desire;
Their cloudy pillar and their guardian fire:[8]
Their second Moses, whose extended wand
235 Divides the seas, and shows the promised land;
Whose dawning day in every distant age
Has exercised the sacred prophet's rage:
The people's prayer, the glad diviners' theme,
The young men's vision, and the old men's dream!
240 Thee, savior, thee, the nation's vows confess,
And, never satisfied with seeing, bless:
Swift unbespoken° pomps° thy steps proclaim,   *voluntary / celebrations*
And stammering babes are taught to lisp they name.

---

6. I.e., heaven would have lacked one Psalm
of David; probably Psalm iii, written, as tra-
dition would have it, when David fled from
Absalom.

7. The phases of the moon fall on the same
day of the calendar year at roughly twenty-
year intervals. Crises in English politics oc-

curred in 1640 (the rebellion against Charles
I), 1660 (the restoration of Charles II), and
the time of the poem.
8. Pillars of cloud by day and of fire by night
guided the Israelites out of Egypt (Exodus
xiii.21).

How long wilt thou the general joy detain,
245 Starve and defraud the people of thy reign?
Content ingloriously to pass thy days
Like one of Virtue's fools that feeds on praise;
Till thy fresh glories, which now shine so bright,
Grow stale and tarnish with our daily sight.
250 Believe me, royal youth, thy fruit must be
Or gathered ripe, or rot upon the tree.
Heaven has to all allotted, soon or late,
Some lucky revolution of their fate;
Whose motions if we watch and guide with skill
255 (For human good depends on human will),
Our Fortune rolls as from a smooth descent,
And from the first impression takes the bent;
But, if unseized, she glides away like wind,
And leaves repenting Folly far behind.
260 Now, now she meets you with a glorious prize,
And spreads her locks before her as she flies.[9]
Had thus Old David, from whose loins you spring,
Not dared, when Fortune called him, to be king,
At Gath[1] an exile he might still remain,
265 And heaven's anointing oil had been in vain.
Let his successful youth your hopes engage;
But shun the example of declining age;
Behold him setting in his western skies,
The shadows lengthening as the vapors rise.
270 He is not now, as when on Jordan's sand[2]
The joyful people thronged to see him land,
Covering the beach, and blackening all the strand;
But, like the Prince of Angels, from his height
Comes tumbling downward with diminished light,
275 Betrayed by one poor plot to public scorn
(Our only blessing since his cursed return),
Those heaps of people which one sheaf did bind,
Blown off and scattered by a puff of wind.
What strength can he to your designs oppose,
280 Naked of friends, and round beset with foes?
If Pharaoh's[3] doubtful succor he should use,
A foreign aid would more incense the Jews:
Proud Egypt would dissembled friendship bring;
Foment the war, but not support the king:
285 Nor would the royal party e'er unite
With Pharaoh's arms to assist the Jebusite;
Or if they should, their interest soon would break,
And with such odious aid make David weak.
All sorts of men by my successful arts,
290 Abhorring kings, estrange their altered hearts
From David's rule: and 'tis the general cry,
'Religion, commonwealth, and liberty.'
If you, as champion of the public good,
Add to their arms a chief of royal blood,
295 What may not Israel hope, and what applause
Might such a general gain by such a cause?
Not barren praise alone, that gaudy flower

---

9. Dryden embroiders on the proverbial im-
age of "seizing opportunity by the forelock."
1. Brussels, where Charles spent much of his
exile. David escaped Saul by fleeing to Gath

(I Samuel xxvii.1–4).
2. At Dover.
3. Louis XIV's.

Fair only to the sight, but solid power;
And nobler is a limited command,
300 Given by the love of all your native land,
Than a successive title, long and dark,
Drawn from the moldy rolls of Noah's ark."[4]
What cannot praise effect in mighty minds,
When flattery soothes, and when ambition blinds!
305 Desire of power, on earth a vicious weed,
Yet, sprung from high, is of celestial seed:
In God 'tis glory; and when men aspire,
'Tis but a spark too much of heavenly fire.
The ambitious youth, too covetous of fame,
310 Too full of angel's metal[5] in his frame,
Unwarily was led from virtue's ways,
Made drunk with honor, and debauched with praise.
Half loath, and half consenting to the ill
(For loyal blood within him struggled still),
315 He thus replied: "And what pretense have I
To take up arms for public liberty?
My father governs with unquestioned right;
The faith's defender, and mankind's delight,
Good, gracious, just, observant of the laws:
320 And heaven by wonders has espoused his cause.
Whom has he wronged in all his peaceful reign?
Who sues for justice to his throne in vain?
What millions has he pardoned of his foes,
Whom just revenge did to his wrath expose?
325 Mild, easy, humble, studious of our good,
Inclined to mercy, and averse from blood;
If mildness ill with stubborn Israel suit,
His crime is God's belovéd attribute.
What could he gain, his people to betray,
330 Or change his right for arbitrary sway?
Let haughty Pharaoh curse with such a reign
His fruitful Nile, and yoke a servile train.
If David's rule Jerusalem displease,
The Dog Star[6] heats their brains to this disease.
335 Why then should I, encouraging the bad,
Turn rebel and run popularly mad?
Were he a tyrant, who, by lawless might
Oppressed the Jews, and raised the Jebusite,
Well might I mourn; but nature's holy bands
340 Would curb my spirits and restrain my hands:
The people might assert their liberty,
But what was right in them were crime in me.
His favor leaves me nothing to require,
Prevents my wishes, and outruns desire.
345 What more can I expect while David lives?
All but his kingly diadem he gives:
And that"—But there he paused; then sighing, said—
"Is justly destined for a worthier head.
For when my father from his toils shall rest
350 And late augment the number of the blest,

4. Shaftesbury espouses constitutional mon-
archy ("a limited command") and parlia-
mentary as opposed to hereditary determina-
tion of the succession.
5. A double pun: 1) the gold of which the
coin "angel" is made; 2) the spirit ("mettle")
of the rebellious angels led by Satan.
6. Sirius, the morning and evening star of
late summer, associated with crazing heat.

His lawful issue shall the throne ascend,
Or the collateral° line, where that shall end.   **brother's**
His brother, though oppressed with vulgar spite,
Yet dauntless, and secure of native right,
355 Of every royal virtue stands possessed;
Still dear to all the bravest and the best.
His courage foes, his friends his truth proclaim;
His loyalty the king, the world his fame.
His mercy even the offending crowd will find,
360 For sure he comes of a forgiving kind.°   **family**
Why should I then repine at heaven's decree,
Which gives me no pretense to royalty?
Yet O that fate, propitiously inclined,
Had raised my birth, or had debased my mind;
365 To my large soul not all her treasure lent,
And then betrayed it to a mean descent!
I find, I find my mounting spirits bold,
And David's part disdains my mother's mold.
Why am I scanted by a niggard[7] birth?
370 My soul disclaims the kindred of her earth;
And, made for empire, whispers me within,
'Desire of greatness is a godlike sin.'"
     Him staggering so when hell's dire agent found,
While fainting Virtue scarce maintained her ground,
375 He pours fresh forces in, and thus replies:
     "The eternal God, supremely good and wise,
Imparts not these prodigious gifts in vain:
What wonders are reserved to bless your reign!
Against your will, your arguments have shown,
380 Such virtue's only given to guide a throne.
Not that your father's mildness I contemn,
But manly force becomes the diadem.
'Tis true he grants the people all they crave;
And more, perhaps, than subjects ought to have:
385 For lavish grants suppose a monarch tame,
And more his goodness than his wit° proclaim.   **intelligence**
But when should people strive their bonds to break,
If not when kings are negligent or weak?
Let him give on till he can give no more,
390 The thrifty Sanhedrin[8] shall keep him poor;
And every shekel which he can receive,
Shall cost a limb of his prerogative.
To ply him with new plots shall be my care;
Or plunge him deep in some expensive war;
395 Which when his treasure can no more supply,
He must, with the remains of kingship, buy.
His faithful friends our jealousies and fears
Call Jebusites, and Pharaoh's pensioners;
Whom when our fury from his aid has torn,
400 He shall be naked left to public scorn.
The next successor, whom I fear and hate,
My arts have made obnoxious to the state;
Turned all his virtues to his overthrow,
And gained our elders[9] to pronounce a foe.

7. Ungenerous; the birth of a king's son
should confer succession to the throne.
8. The high council of the Jews; here the
English Parliament, which provided the crown
with its monies.
9. In the Bible, the Jewish magistrates; in the
poem, the Parliamentarians who voted to ex-
clude James from the succession.

405 His right, for sums of necessary gold,
     Shall first be pawned, and afterward be sold;
     Till time shall ever-wanting David draw,
     To pass your doubtful title into law:
     If not, the people have a right supreme
410 To make their kings; for kings are made for them.
     All empire is no more than power in trust,
     Which, when resumed, can be no longer just.
     Succession, for the general good designed,
     In its own wrong a nation cannot bind;
415 If altering that the people can relieve,
     Better one suffer than a nation grieve.
     The Jews well know their power: ere Saul they chose,
     God was their king, and God they durst depose.[1]
     Urge now your piety,° your filial name,   *dutifulness*
420 A father's right, and fear of future fame;
     The public good, that universal call,
     To which even heaven submitted, answers all.
     Nor let his love enchant your generous mind;
     'Tis Nature's trick to propagate her kind.
425 Our fond begetters, who would never die,
     Love but themselves in their posterity.
     Or let his kindness by the effects be tried,
     Or let him lay his vain pretense aside.
     God said he loved your father; could he bring
430 A better proof than to anoint him king?
     It surely showed he loved the shepherd well,
     Who gave so fair a flock as Israel.
     Would David have you thought his darling son?
     What means he then, to alienate[2] the crown?
435 The name of godly he may blush to bear:
     'Tis after God's own heart to cheat his heir.
     He to his brother gives supreme command;
     To you a legacy of barren land,[3]
     Perhaps the old harp, on which he thrums his lays,
440 Or some dull Hebrew ballad in your praise.
     Then the next heir, a prince severe and wise,
     Already looks on you with jealous eyes;
     Sees through the thin disguises of your arts,
     And marks your progress in the people's hearts.
445 Though now his mighty soul its grief contains,
     He meditates revenge who least complains;
     And, like a lion, slumbering in the way,
     Or sleep dissembling, while he waits his prey,
     His fearless foes within his distance draws,
450 Constrains his roaring, and contracts his paws;
     Till at the last, his time for fury found,
     He shoots with sudden vengeance from the ground;
     The prostrate vulgar° passes o'er and spares,   *populace*
     But with a lordly rage his hunters tears.
455 Your case no tame expedients will afford:
     Resolve on death, or conquest by the sword,
     Which for no less a stake than life you draw;

---

1. The Israelites' demand that a secular king
(Saul, as it eventuated) replace the theocratic
Judges was condemned as impious: "And the
Lord said * * * , they have rejected me, that
I should not reign over them"(I Samuel
viii.7). As Saul replaced the Judges, so, in the
poem, Oliver Cromwell took over authority
from the theocrats of the Commonwealth.
2. I.e., transfer title to another (a legal term).
3. James had been titled generalissimo in
1678; Monmouth had been exiled in the fol-
lowing year.

And self-defense is nature's eldest law.
Leave the warm people no considering time;
460 For then rebellion may be thought a crime.
Prevail yourself of what occasion gives,
But try your title while your father lives;
And that your arms may have a fair pretense,°   *pretext*
Proclaim you take them in the king's defense;
465 Whose sacred life each minute would expose
To plots, from seeming friends, and secret foes.
And who can sound the depth of David's soul?
Perhaps his fear his kindness may control.
He fears his brother, though he loves his son,
470 For plighted vows too late to be undone.
If so, by force he wishes to be gained,
Like women's lechery, to seem constrained.
Doubt not; but when he most affects the frown,
Commit a pleasing rape upon the crown.
475 Secure his person to secure your cause:
They who possess the prince, possess the laws."
      He said, and this advice above the rest
With Absalom's mild nature suited best:
Unblamed of life (ambition set aside),
480 Not stained with cruelty, nor puffed with pride,
How happy had he been, if destiny
Had higher placed his birth, or not so high!
His kingly virtues might have claimed a throne,
And blest all other countries but his own.
485 But charming greatness since so few refuse,
'Tis juster to lament him than accuse.
Strong were his hopes a rival to remove,
With blandishments to gain the public love;
To head the faction while their zeal was hot,
490 And popularly prosecute the Plot.
To further this, Achitophel unites
The malcontents of all the Israelites;
Whose differing parties he could wisely join,
For several ends, to serve the same design:
495 The best (and of the princes some were such),
Who thought the power of monarchy too much;
Mistaken men, and patriots in their hearts;
Not wicked, but seduced by impious arts.
By these the springs of property were bent,
500 And wound so high, they cracked the government.
The next for interest sought to embroil the state,
To sell their duty at a dearer rate;
And make their Jewish markets of the throne,
Pretending public good, to serve their own.
505 Others thought kings an useless heavy load,
Who cost too much, and did too little good.
These were for laying honest David by,
On principles of pure good husbandry.°   *economy*
With them joined all the haranguers of the throng,
510 That thought to get preferment by the tongue.
Who follow next, a double danger bring,
Not only hating David, but the king:
The Solymaean rout,[4] well-versed of old

___
4. The London populace. Solyma was a name for Jerusalem.

In godly faction, and in treason bold;
515 Cowering and quaking at a conqueror's sword,
But lofty to a lawful prince restored;
Saw with disdain an ethnic[5] plot begun,
And scorned by Jebusites to be outdone.
Hot Levites[6] headed these; who, pulled before
520 From the ark, which in the Judges' days they bore,
Resumed their cant, and with a zealous cry
Pursued their old beloved theocracy:
Where Sanhedrin and priest enslaved the nation,
And justified their spoils by inspiration:
525 For who so fit for reign as Aaron's race,[7]
If once dominion they could found in grace?
These led the pack; though not of surest scent,
Yet deepest-mouthed° against the government.   *baying loudest*
A numerous host of dreaming saints° succeed,   *sectarians*
530 Of the true old enthusiastic° breed: *fanatic*
'Gainst form and order they their power employ,
Nothing to build, and all things to destroy.
But far more numerous was the herd of such,
Who think too little, and who talk too much.
535 These out of mere instinct, they knew not why,
Adored their fathers' God and property;
And, by the same blind benefit of fate,
The Devil and the Jebusite did hate:
Born to be saved, even in their own despite,
540 Because they could not help believing right.[8]
Such were the tools; but a whole Hydra[9] more
Remains, of sprouting heads too long to score.
Some of their chiefs were princes of the land:
In the first rank of these did Zimri[1] stand;
545 A man so various, that he seemed to be
Not one, but all mankind's epitome:
Stiff in opinions, always in the wrong;
Was everything by starts, and nothing long;
But, in the course of one revolving moon,
550 Was chemist, fiddler, statesman, and buffoon:
Then all for women, painting, rhyming, drinking,
Besides ten thousand freaks° that died in thinking.   *whims*
Blest madman, who could every hour employ,
With something new to wish, or to enjoy!
555 Railing and praising were his usual themes;
And both (to show his judgment) in extremes:
So over-violent, or over-civil,
That every man, with him, was God or Devil.
In squandering wealth with his peculiar art:
560 Nothing went unrewarded but desert.
Beggared by fools, whom still° he found too late,   *always*
He had his jest, and they had his estate.

---

5. In the bibilical context, gentile; in the historical, Catholic.
6. Men of the tribe of Levi conveyed the Ark of the Covenant when Israel moved camp (Numbers iv.15); the Presbyterian clergy administered the state religion under the Commonwealth ("in the Judges' days").
7. The priestly family; (derisively) the theocratically disposed dissenters.
8. Dryden calls attention to the Calvinist doctrines of predestination and election, and (in line 536) to the commercial origins of many dissenters.
9. Mythical beast with nine heads, each of which was replaced by two heads when it was cut off.
1. An Israelite executed for whoredom (Numbers xxv); also a traitor and regicide (I Kings xvi.8–20). Dryden gives the name to the gifted wastrel George Villiers, Duke of Buckingham, a late-comer to Monmouth's cause.

He laughed himself from court; then sought relief
By forming parties, but could ne'er be chief;
565 For, spite of him, the weight of business fell
On Absalom and wise Achitophel:
Thus, wicked but in will, of means bereft,
He left not faction, but of that was left.
Titles and names 'twere tedious to rehearse
570 Of lords, below the dignity of verse.
Wits, warriors, Commonwealth's men, were the best;
Kind husbands, and mere nobles, all the rest.
And therefore, in the name of dullness, be
The well-hung Balaam and cold Caleb,[2] free;
575 And canting Nadab[3] let oblivion damn,
Who made new porridge for the paschal lamb.
Let friendship's holy band some names assure;
Some their own worth, and some let scorn secure.
Nor shall the rascal rabble here have place,
580 Whom kings no titles gave, and God no grace:
Not bull-faced Jonas,[4] who could statutes draw
To mean rebellion, and make treason law.
But he, though bad, is followed by a worse,
The wretch who heaven's anointed dared to curse:
585 Shimei,[5] whose youth did early promise bring
Of zeal to God and hatred to his king,
Did wisely from expensive sins refrain,
And never broke the Sabbath, but for gain;
Nor ever was he known an oath to vent,
590 Or curse, unless against the government.
Thus heaping wealth, by the most ready way
Among the Jews, which was to cheat and pray,
The city, to reward his pious hate
Against his master, chose him magistrate.
595 His hand a vare° of justice did uphold;   **staff**
His neck was loaded with a chain of gold.
During his office, treason was no crime;
The sons of Belial[6] had a glorious time;
For Shimei, though not prodigal of pelf,
600 Yet loved his wicked neighbor as himself.
When two or three were gathered to declaim ⎫
Against the monarch of Jerusalem,   ⎬
Shimei was always in the midst of them; ⎭
And if they cursed the king when he was by,
605 Would rather curse than break good company.
If any durst his factious friends accuse,
He packed a jury of dissenting Jews;[7]
Whose fellow-feeling in the godly cause
Would free the suffering saint from human laws.
610 For laws are only made to punish those

2. Balaam has been identified as the Earl of
Huntingdon and Caleb as Lord Grey. Grey
purportedly allowed his wife intimacies with
the Duke of Monmouth. Balaam's epithet is
antithetical to Caleb's.
3. Nadab (who "offered strange fire before
the Lord" in Leviticus x.1) is traditionally,
though dubiously, identified with Lord How-
ard of Escrick, who devised a communion
draught of ale poured on roasted apples and
sugar. In general the Anglicans found the
communion services of the dissenters indeco-
rous. The "paschal lamb" (i.e., the offering at
the Jewish Passover) conventionally sym-
bolizes the Christian communion.

4. Sir William Jones, a former attorney gen-
eral under Charles, had subsequently joined
the opposition and drawn up bills limiting
the power of the government to act against sus-
pected traitors.
5. A member of Saul's household who cursed
David (II Samuel xvi.5–13), Shimei stands
for Slingsby Bethel, a sheriff of London.
6. Sons of Wickedness. See *Paradise Lost*
I.490–505. There may be a pun on Balliol Col-
lege, Oxford, where Whig Parliamentarians
met in 1681.
7. The sheriffs could pack London juries to
protect their partisans (like Shaftesbury) from
conviction.

Who serve the king, and to protect his foes.
If any leisure time he had from power
(Because 'tis sin to misemploy an hour),
His business was, by writing, to persuade
15 That kings were useless, and a clog to trade;[8]
And, that his noble style he might refine,
No Rechabite more shunned the fumes of wine.[9]
Chaste were his cellars, and his shrieval board[1]
The grossness of a city feast abhorred:
20 His cooks, with long disuse, their trade forgot;
Cool was his kitchen, though his brains were hot.
Such frugal virtue malice may accuse,
But sure 'twas necessary to the Jews;
For towns once burnt[2] such magistrates require
25 As dare not tempt God's providence by fire.
With spiritual food he fed his servants well,
But free from flesh that made the Jews rebel;
And Moses' laws he held in more account,
For forty days of fasting in the mount.[3]
30 To speak the rest, who better are forgot,
Would tire a well-breathed° witness of the Plot.   *long-winded*
Yet, Corah,[4] thou shalt from oblivion pass:
Erect thyself, thou monumental brass,
High as the serpent of thy metal made,[5]
35 While nations stand secure beneath thy shade.
What though his birth were base, yet comets rise
From earthy vapors, ere they shine in skies.
Prodigious actions may as well be done
By weaver's issue, as by prince's son.
40 This arch-attestor for the public good
By that one deed ennobles all his blood.
Who ever asked the witnesses' high race
Whose oath with martyrdom did Stephen grace?[6]
Ours was a Levite, and as times went then,
545 His tribe were God Almighty's gentlemen.
Sunk were his eyes, his voice was harsh and loud,
Sure signs he neither choleric° was nor proud: *irascible*
His long chin proved his wit; his saintlike grace
A church vermilion, and a Moses' face.[7]
550 His memory, miraculously great,
Could plots, exceeding man's belief, repeat;
Which therefore cannot be accounted lies,
For human wit could never such devise.
Some future truths are mingled in his book;
555 But where the witness failed, the prophet spoke:
Some things like visionary flights appear;
The spirit caught him up, the Lord knows where,
And gave him his rabbinical degree,

8. Bethel wrote republican tracts.
9. Bethel was niggardly enough of his hospitality to suggest comparison with the Rechabites, a clan of Jews who drank no wine (Jeremiah xxxv).
1. Sheriff's table.
2. In the great fire of 1666.
3. The Law was delivered to Moses during his forty-day fast on Mount Sinai.
4. Corah (a rebellious Levite, Numbers xvi) is Titus Oates. Of a dissenting family who were ribbon-weavers by trade, he became an Anglican and subsequently, at least by his own profession, a Roman Catholic. He claimed to have gained knowledge, during a stay on the Continent, of Jesuit plots to restore Catholicism in England. After his original testimony, he continued to "recall" details of the plotting.
5. Dryden plays on Horace's line ascribing to poetry the power of resisting oblivion: "I have erected an eternal monument of brass"; and on the brazen serpent lifted up in the wilderness by Moses (Numbers xxi.9).
6. The suborned witness against the martyr Stephen is described in Acts vi.11–13.
7. A ruddy, shining face (ironically called Mosaic, after Exodus xxxiv.29) is a sign of high living.

Unknown to foreign university.[8]
660 His judgment yet his memory did excel;
Which pieced his wondrous evidence so well,
And suited to the temper of the times,
Then groaning under Jebusitic crimes.
Let Israel's foes suspect his heavenly call,
665 And rashly judge his writ apocryphal;[9]
Our laws for such affronts have forfeits made:
He takes his life, who takes away his trade.
Were I myself in witness Corah's place,
The wretch who did me such a dire disgrace
670 Should whet my memory, though once forgot,
To make him an appendix of my plot.
His zeal to heaven made him his prince despise,
And load his person with indignities;
But zeal peculiar privilege affords,
675 Indulging latitude to deeds and words;
And Corah might for Agag's murder call,[1]
In terms as coarse as Samuel used to Saul.
What others in his evidence did join
(The best that could be had for love or coin),
680 In Corah's own predicament will fall;
For *witness* is a common name to all.
    Surrounded thus with friends of every sort,
Deluded Absalom forsakes the court:[2]
Impatient of high hopes, urged with renown,
685 And fired with near possession of a crown.
The admiring crowd are dazzled with surprise,
And on his goodly person feed their eyes:
His joy concealed, he sets himself to show,
On each side bowing popularly low;
690 His looks, his gestures, and his words he frames,
And with familiar ease repeats their names.
Thus formed by nature, furnished out with arts,
He glides unfelt into their secret hearts.
Then, with a kind compassionating look,
695 And sighs, bespeaking pity ere he spoke,
Few words he said; but easy those and fit,
More slow than Hybla-drops,° and far more sweet.   *honey*
    "I mourn, my countrymen, your lost estate;
Though far unable to prevent your fate:
700 Behold a banished man, for your dear cause
Exposed a prey to arbitrary laws!
Yet oh! that I alone could be undone,
Cut off from empire, and no more a son!
Now all your liberties a spoil are made;⎫
705 Egypt and Tyrus[3] intercept your trade, ⎬
And Jebusites your sacred rites invade. ⎭
My father, whom with reverence yet I name,

8. Oates claimed to have earned a degree from the University of Salamanca.
9. Not in the accepted biblical canon; with a pun on the legal term "writ" (referring to Oates's deposition) and "Holy Writ."
1. Samuel berated Saul for sparing Agag, the king of a hostile tribe, and himself "hewed Agag in pieces before the Lord" (I Samuel xv.33). Oates implicated Lord Stafford and other Catholic peers in supposed plotting, for which they were executed. It has been pro-posed also that Dryden is accusing Oates of complicity in the notorious (and still unre-solved) murder of Sir Edmund Berry God-frey, the magistrate before whom he had made his deposition.
2. Monmouth, whom Charles had sent abroad, returned without royal consent. The king, of-fended, dismissed him abroad again. Mon-mouth instead undertook to curry favor in the English provinces.
3. France and Holland.

Charmed into ease, is careless of his fame;
And, bribed with petty sums of foreign gold,
Is grown in Báthsheba's embraces old;[4]
Exalts his enemies, his friends destroys;
And all his power against himself employs.
He gives, and let him give, my right away;
But why should he his own, and yours betray?
He only, he can make the nation bleed,
And he alone from my revenge is freed.
Take then my tears (with that he wiped his eyes),
'Tis all the aid my present power supplies:
No court-informer can these arms accuse;
These arms may sons against their fathers use:
And 'tis my wish, the next successor's reign
May make no other Israelite complain."
    Youth, beauty, graceful action seldom fail;
But common interest always will prevail;
And pity never ceases to be shown
To him who makes the people's wrongs his own.
The crowd (that still believe their kings oppress),
With lifted hands their young Messiah bless:
Who now begins his progress to ordain
With chariots, horsemen, and a numerous train;
From east to west his glories he displays,
And, like the sun, the promised land surveys.
Fame runs before him as the morning star,
And shouts of joy salute him from afar:
Each house receives him as a guardian god,
And consecrates the place of his abode:
But hospitable treats did most commend
Wise Issachar,[5] his wealthy western friend.
This moving court, that caught the people's eyes,
And seemed but pomp, did other ends disguise:
Achitophel had formed it, with intent
To sound the depths, and fathom, where it went,
The people's hearts; distinguish friends from foes,
And try their strength, before they came to blows.
Yet all was colored with a smooth pretense
Of specious love, and duty to their prince.
Religion, and redress of grievances,
Two names that always cheat and always please,
Are often urged; and good King David's life
Endangered by a brother and a wife.[6]
Thus, in a pageant show, a plot is made,
And peace itself is war in masquerade.
O foolish Israel! never warned by ill,
Still the same bait, and circumvented still!
Did ever men forsake their present ease,
In midst of health imagine a disease,
Take pains contingent mischiefs to foresee,
Make heirs for monarchs, and for God decree?
What shall we think! Can people give away

4. Charles was receiving subsidies from Louis XIV and was devoted to a mistress, the Duchess of Portsmouth. Bathsheba was the consort whom David took from his warrior Uriah (II Samuel xi).
5. Thomas Thynne of Longleat, who entertained Monmouth in Wiltshire in 1680. The "wise" is ironic.
6. Oates had implicated Charles's brother James and his queen Catherine in the supposed plotting.

760 Both for themselves and sons, their native sway?
     Then they are left defenseless to the sword
     Of each unbounded, arbitrary lord:
     And laws are vain, by which we right enjoy,
     If kings unquestioned can those laws destroy.
765 Yet if the crowd be judge of fit and just,
     And kings are only officers in trust,
     Then this resuming covenant was declared
     When kings were made, or is forever barred.
     If those who gave the scepter could not tie
770 By their own deed their own posterity,
     How then could Adam bind his future race?
     How could his forfeit on mankind take place?
     Or how could heavenly justice damn us all,
     Who ne'er consented to our father's fall?
775 Then kings are slaves to those whom they command,
     And tenants to their people's pleasure stand.
     Add, that the power for property allowed
     Is mischievously seated in the crowd;
     For who can be secure of private right,
780 If sovereign sway may be dissolved by might?
     Nor is the people's judgment always true:
     The most may err as grossly as the few;
     And faultless kings run down, by common cry,
     For vice, oppression, and for tyranny.
785 What standard is there in a fickle rout,
     Which, flowing to the mark,[7] runs faster out?
     Nor only crowds, but Sanhedrins may be
     Infected with this public lunacy,
     And share the madness of rebellious times,
790 To murder monarchs for imagined crimes.
     If they may give and take whene'er they please,
     Not kings alone (the Godhead's images),
     But government itself at length must fall
     To nature's state, where all have right to all.
795 Yet, grant our lords the people kings can make,
     What prudent men a settled throne would shake?
     For whatsoe'er their sufferings were before,
     That change they covet makes them suffer more.
     All other errors but disturb a state,
800 But innovation is the blow of fate.
     If ancient fabrics nod, and threat to fall,
     To patch the flaws, and buttress up the wall,
     Thus far 'tis duty; but here fix the mark;
     For all beyond it is to touch our ark.[8]
805 To change foundations, cast the frame anew,
     Is work for rebels, who base ends pursue,
     At once divine and human laws control,
     And mend the parts by ruin of the whole.
     The tampering world is subject to this curse,
810 To physic their disease into a worse.
         Now what relief can righteous David bring?
     How fatal 'tis to be too good a king!
     Friends he has few, so high the madness grows:

---

7. I.e., like water attaining the level of a
spillway.
8. To commit sacrilege. An Israelite was
struck dead for touching the Ark (II Samuel
vi.6–7).

Who dare be such, must be the people's foes:
5 Yet some there were, even in the worst of days;
Some let me name, and naming is to praise.
    In this short file Barzillai[9] first appears;
Barzillai, crowned with honor and with years:
Long since, the rising rebels he withstood
20 In regions waste, beyond the Jordan's flood:
Unfortunately brave to buoy the State;
But sinking underneath his master's fate:
In exile with his godlike prince he mourned;
For him he suffered, and with him returned.
25 The court he practiced, not the courtier's art:
Large was his wealth, but larger was his heart:
Which well the noblest objects knew to choose,
The fighting warrior, and recording Muse.
His bed could once a fruitful issue boast;
30 Now more than half a father's name is lost.
His eldest hope,[1] with every grace adorned,
By me (so Heaven will have it) always mourned,
And always honored, snatched in manhood's prime
By unequal fates, and Providence's crime:
35 Yet not before the goal of honor won,
All parts fulfilled of subject and of son;
Swift was the race, but short the time to run.
O narrow circle, but of power divine,
Scanted in space, but perfect in thy line!
40 By sea, by land, thy matchless worth was known,
Arms thy delight, and war was all thy own:
Thy force, infused, the fainting Tyrians propped;
And haughty Pharaoh found his fortune stopped.
Oh ancient honor! Oh unconquered hand,
45 Whom foes unpunished never could withstand!
But Israel was unworthy of thy name:
Short is the date of all immoderate fame.
It looks as Heaven our ruin had designed,
And durst not trust thy fortune and thy mind.
50 Now free from earth, thy disencumbered soul
Mounts up, and leaves behind the clouds and starry pole:
From thence thy kindred legions mayst thou bring,
To aid the guardian angel of thy king.
Here stop my Muse, here cease thy painful flight;
55 No pinions can pursue immortal height:
Tell good Barzillai thou canst sing no more,
And tell thy soul she should have fled before.
Or fled she with his life, and left this verse
To hang on her departed patron's hearse?[2]
60 Now take thy steepy flight from heaven, and see
If thou canst find on earth another *he:*
Another *he* would be too hard to find;
See then whom thou canst see not far behind.
Zadoc the priest,[3] whom, shunning power and place,

9. David's venerable benefactor (II Samuel xix.31–39); in Dryden's poem, the Duke of Ormond, who had fought for Charles I when Lord Lieutenant of Ireland and had attended Charles II into exile.
1. Ormond's son Thomas, who had fought with distinction for the Dutch (the "Tyrians"), had recently died of a fever.

2. "A temple-shaped structure of wood used in * * * noble funerals. * * * It was customary for friends to pin short poems or epitaphs upon it"(OED).
3. Zadoc, David's chief priest (II Samuel viii.17), is William Sancroft, Archbishop of Canterbury.

865 His lowly mind advanced to David's grace:
With him the Sagan of Jerusalem,[4]
Of hospitable soul, and noble stem;
Him of the western dome,[5] whose weighty sense
Flows in fit words and heavenly eloquence.
870 The prophets' sons, by such example led,
To learning and to loyalty were bred:
For colleges on bounteous kings depend,
And never rebel was to arts a friend.
To these succeed the pillars of the laws,
875 Who best could plead, and best can judge a cause.
Next them a train of loyal peers ascend;
Sharp-judging Adriel,[6] the Muses' friend,
Himself a Muse—in Sanhedrin's debate
True to his prince, but not a slave of state:
880 Whom David's love with honors did adorn,
That from his disobedient son were torn.[7]
Jotham[8] of piercing wit, and pregnant thought,
Indued by nature, and by learning taught
To move assemblies, who but only tried
885 The worse a while, then chose the better side;
Nor chose alone, but turned the balance too;
So much the weight of one brave man can do.
Hushai,[9] the friend of David in distress,
In public storms, of manly steadfastness:
890 By foreign treaties he informed his youth,
And joined experience to his native truth.
His frugal care supplied the wanting throne,
Frugal for that, but bounteous of his own:
'Tis easy conduct when exchequers° flow,   *treasuries*
895 But hard the task to manage well the low;
For sovereign power is too depressed or high,
When kings are forced to sell, or crowds to buy.
Indulge one labor more, my weary Muse,
For Amiel:[1] who can Amiel's praise refuse?
900 Of ancient race by birth, but nobler yet
In his own worth, and without title great:
The Sanhedrin long time as chief he ruled,
Their reason guided, and their passion cooled:
So dextrous was he in the crown's defence,
905 So formed to speak a loyal nation's sense,
That, as their band was Israel's tribes in small,
So fit was he to represent them all.
Now rasher charioteers the seat ascend,
Whose loose careers his steady skill commend:
910 They like the unequal ruler of the day,[2]
Misguide the seasons, and mistake the way;

---

4. Henry Compton, Bishop of London. *Sagan:* Hebrew for "deputy high priest."
5. John Dolben, Dean of Westminster; hence an example to the boys of Westminster School ("the prophets' sons," line 870). Dryden had attended Westminster.
6. John Sheffield, Earl of Mulgrave; a man of letters, Dryden's patron.
7. For example, the governorship of Hull and the lord lieutenancy of Yorkshire, both taken from Monmouth.
8. Jotham, who argued persuasively against a conspiracy (see Judges ix), is George Saville, Marquis of Halifax. Himself an independent,

Halifax brought about the defeat of the Exclusion Act in the House of Lords, preserving the succession for James.
9. Hushai overturned Achitophel's counsel against David (II Samuel xvii.7 ff.); in the poem he is Lawrence, Viscount Hyde, First Lord of the Treasury.
1. Edward Seymour, Speaker of the House of Commons from 1673 to 1679.
2. The chariot of the sun as driven by Phaethon, the son of Apollo. Phaethon strayed so dangerously from his course that Zeus struck him dead with a thunderbolt.

While he withdrawn at their mad labor smiles,
And safe enjoys the sabbath of his toils.
    These were the chief, a small but faithful band ⎤
5 Of worthies, in the breach who dared to stand, ⎬
And tempt the united fury of the land. ⎦
With grief they viewed such powerful engines bent,
To batter down the lawful government:
A numerous faction, with pretended frights,
10 In Sanhedrins to plume° the regal rights;   *pluck off*
The true successor from the court removed:[3]
The Plot, by hireling witnesses, improved.
These ills they saw, and, as their duty bound,
They showed the king the danger of the wound:
15 That no concessions from the throne would please,
But lenitives° fomented the disease;   *partial cures*
That Absalom, ambitious of the crown,
Was made the lure to draw the people down;
That false Achitophel's pernicious hate
20 Had turned the Plot to ruin Church and State:
The council violent, the rabble worse;
That Shimei taught Jerusalem to curse.
    With all these loads of injuries oppressed,
And long revolving in his careful breast
25 The event of things, at last, his patience tired,
Thus from his royal throne, by Heaven inspired,
The godlike David spoke: with awful fear
His train their Maker in their master hear.
    "Thus long have I, by native mercy swayed,
40 My wrongs dissembled, my revenge delayed:
So willing to forgive the offending age,
So much the father did the king assuage.
But now so far my clemency they slight,
The offenders question my forgiving right.[4]
45 That one was made for many, they contend;
But 'tis to rule; for that's a monarch's end.
They call my tenderness of blood my fear;
Though manly tempers can the longest bear.
Yet, since they will divert my native course,
50 'Tis time to show I am not good by force.
Those heaped affronts that haughty subjects bring,
Are burdens for a camel, not a king:
Kings are the public pillars of the State,
Born to sustain and prop the nation's weight:
55 If my young Samson will pretend a call
To shake the column, let him share the fall:[5]
But, oh, that yet he would repent and live!
How easy 'tis for parents to forgive!
With how few tears a pardon might be won
60 From nature, pleading for a darling son!
Poor pitied youth, by my paternal care
Raised up to all the height his frame could bear:
Had God ordained his fate for empire born,
He would have given his soul another turn:
65 Gulled° with a patriot's name, whose modern sense   *deceived*

---

3. James had been sent expediently out of the country.
4. The right of the king to pardon, questioned by some members of the opposition.

5. Samson, pulling down the supporting columns of a Philistine temple, was destroyed in the ruin (Judges xvi.29–30).

Is one that would by law supplant his prince:
The people's brave,[6] the politician's tool;
Never was patriot yet, but was a fool.
Whence comes it that religion and the laws
970   Should more be Absalom's than David's cause?
His old instructor, ere he lost his place,[7]
Was never thought indued with so much grace.
Good heavens, how faction can a patriot paint!
My rebel ever proves my people's saint:
975   Would *they* impose an heir upon the throne?
Let Sanhedrins be taught to give their own.
A king's at least a part of government,
And mine as requisite as their consent;
Without my leave a future king to choose,
980   Infers a right the present to depose:
True, they petition me to approve their choice;
But Esau's hands suit ill with Jacob's voice.[8]
My pious subjects for my safety pray,
Which to secure, they take my power away.
985   From plots and treasons Heaven preserve my years,
But save me most from my petitioners.
Unsatiate as the barren womb or grave;
God cannot grant so much as they can crave.
What then is left but with a jealous eye
990   To guard the small remains of royalty?
The law shall still direct my peaceful sway,
And the same law teach rebels to obey:
Votes shall no more established power control—
Such votes as make a part exceed the whole:
995   No groundless clamors shall my friends remove,
Nor crowds have power to punish ere they prove:
For gods and godlike kings their care express,
Still to defend their servants in distress.
O that my power to saving were confined:
1000   Why am I forced, like Heaven, against my mind, ⎫
To make examples of another kind? ⎬
Must I at length the sword of justice draw? ⎭
O curst effects of necessary law!
How ill my fear they by my mercy scan!
1005   Beware the fury of a patient man.
Law they require, let Law then show her face;
They could not be content to look on Grace,
Her hinder parts, but with a daring eye
To tempt the terror of her front and die.[9]
1010   By their own arts, 'tis righteously decreed,
Those dire artificers of death shall bleed.
Against themselves their witnesses will swear,
Till viper-like their mother Plot they tear:
And suck for nutriment that bloody gore,
1015   Which was their principle of life before.
Their Belial with their Belzebub[1] will fight;

6. I.e., hero (derisive); show-off.
7. Shaftesbury had been dismissed as Chancellor in 1673 and as Lord President of the Council in 1679.
8. Jacob, posing as his brother Esau in order to win the inheritance due to the first-born son, deceived his old blind father by making his hands hairy (like Esau's) with animal fur; but he could not mask his voice (Genesis

xxvii).
9. Moses, on Mount Sinai, was forbidden upon pain of death to look upon the face of God, but he glimpsed Him from behind after He had passed by (Exodus xxxiii.20–23).
1. I.e., their principal leaders; in *Paradise Lost* Belial and Beelzebub are leaders of Satan's host.

Thus on my foes, my foes shall do me right:
Nor doubt the event,° for factious crowds engage,   *outcome*
In their first onset, all their brutal rage.
20 Then let 'em take an unresisted course,
Retire and traverse, and delude their force:
But when they stand all breathless, urge the fight,
And rise upon 'em with redoubled might:
For lawful power is still superior found,
25 When long driven back, at length it stands the ground."
He said. The Almighty, nodding, gave consent;
And peals of thunder shook the firmament.
Henceforth a series of new time began,
The mighty years in long procession ran:
30 Once more the godlike David was restored,
And willing nations knew their lawful lord.

1681

Mac Flecknoe

OR A SATIRE UPON THE
TRUE-BLUE-PROTESTANT POET, T. S.[2]

All human things are subject to decay,
And when fate summons, monarchs must obey.
This Flecknoe found, who, like Augustus,[3] young
Was called to empire, and had governed long;
5   In prose and verse, was owned, without dispute,
Through all the realms of Nonsense, absolute.
This aged prince, now flourishing in peace,
And blest with issue of a large increase,
Worn out with business, did at length debate
10 To settle the succession of the state;
And, pondering which of all his sons was fit
To reign, and wage immortal war with wit,[4]
Cried: " 'Tis resolved; for nature pleads that he
Should only rule, who most resembles me.
15 Sh——[5] alone my perfect image bears,
Mature in dullness from his tender years:
Sh—— alone, of all my sons, is he
Who stands confirmed in full stupidity.
The rest to some faint meaning make pretense,
20 But Sh—— never deviates into sense.
Some beams of wit on other souls may fall,
Strike through, and make a lucid interval;
But Sh——'s genuine night admits no ray,
His rising fogs prevail upon the day.
25 Besides, his goodly fabric fills the eye,
And seems designed for thoughtless majesty:

2. Thomas Shadwell (1640–92), a comic play-
wright of respectable talents, who considered
himself the dramatic heir of Ben Jonson. He
was vain, corpulent, and probably overbearing
in manner. Dryden names him *Mac* (son of)
Flecknoe, making him heir not of Jonson but
of the recently dead Irish priest Richard
Flecknoe, a poet at once tiresome and prolific.
The subtitle (presumably added when the
poem, itself non-political, was published in
1682) acknowledges a political controversy fed
by Dryden's poems *Absalom and Achitophel*
and *The Medal* (a satire on Shaftesbury's ac-
quittal) and Shadwell's rejoinder *The Medal
of John Bayes* (John Dryden). Shadwell be-
longed to the Whig party, the political haven
of dissenting Protestants.
3. Augustus became Roman emperor at thirty-
two and reigned for forty years.
4. *Wit,* here as in other poems of the time,
variously denotes the intellect, the poetic
imagination, and a general sprightliness of
mind.
5. A transparent pretense to anonymity, ad-
mitting here and there a scatological sug-
gestion.

Thoughtless as monarch oaks that shade the plain,
And, spread in solemn state, supinely reign.
Heywood and Shirley[6] were but types of thee,
30 Thou last great prophet of tautology.
Even I, a dunce of more renown than they,
Was sent before but to prepare thy way;
And, coarsely clad in Norwich drugget,[7] came
To teach the nations in thy greater name.
35 My warbling lute, the lute I whilom° strung,   *formerly*
When to King John of Portugal I sung,[8]
Was but the prelude to that glorious day,
When thou on silver Thames didst cut thy way,
With well-timed oars before the royal barge,
40 Swelled with the pride of thy celestial charge;
And big with hymn, commander of a host,
The like was ne'er in Epsom blankets tossed.[9]
Methinks I see the new Arion[1] sail,
The lute still trembling underneath thy nail.
45 At thy well-sharpened thumb from shore to shore
The treble squeaks for fear, the basses roar;
Echoes from Pissing Alley Sh—— call,
And Sh—— they resound from Aston Hall.
About thy boat the little fishes throng,
50 As at the morning toast[2] that floats along.
Sometimes, as prince of thy harmonious band,
Thou wield'st thy papers in thy threshing hand.
St. André's[3] feet ne'er kept more equal time,
Not ev'n the feet of thy own *Psyche's* rhyme;
55 Though they in number as in sense excel:
So just, so like tautology, they fell,
That, pale with envy, Singleton[4] forswore   ⎫
The lute and sword, which he in triumph bore, ⎬
And vowed he ne'er would act Villerius[5] more."⎭
60 Here stopped the good old sire, and wept for joy
In silent raptures of the hopeful boy.
All arguments, but most his plays, persuade,
That for anointed dullness he was made.
    Close to the walls which fair Augusta[6] bind
65 (The fair Augusta much to fears inclined),
An ancient fabric° raised to inform the sight,   *building*
There stood of yore, and Barbican it hight:
A watchtower once; but now, so fate ordains,
Of all the pile an empty name remains.
70 From its old ruins brothel houses rise,
Scenes of lewd loves, and of polluted joys,
Where their vast courts the mother-strumpets keep,
And, undisturbed by watch, in silence sleep.
Near these a Nursery[7] erects its head,

6. Playwrights of the time of Charles I, now out of fashion. Dryden suggests that they prefigure Shadwell as the Old-Testament prophets and (in lines 31–34) John the Baptist prefigured the ultimate revelation in Jesus Christ.
7. A coarse cloth.
8. Flecknoe claimed the king of Portugal as his patron.
9. A simultaneous reference to two of Shadwell's plays: *The Virtuoso*, in which a character is tossed in a blanket, and *Epsom Wells*.
1. When the Greek poet Arion was cast into the sea, a dolphin, charmed by his singing, bore him ashore. Shadwell was proud of his musical accomplishments.
2. A euphemism for sewage.
3. St. André, a French dancing-master, was choreographer of Shadwell's opera *Psyche*.
4. John Singleton, a musician of the Theatre Royal.
5. A role in Sir William Davenant's opera, *The Siege of Rhodes*.
6. London. (She "fears" Catholic plots.)
7. A training school for actors.

75 Where queens are formed, and future heroes bred;
   Where unfledged actors learn to laugh and cry,⎫
   Where infant punks° their tender voices try,   ⎬   *prostitutes*
   And little Maximins[8] the gods defy.   ⎭
   Great Fletcher[9] never treads in buskins here,
80 Nor greater Jonson dares in socks appear;
   But gentle Simkin[1] just reception finds
   Amidst this monument of vanished minds:
   Pure clinches° the suburban Muse affords,   *puns*
   And Panton[2] waging harmless war with words.
85 Here Flecknoe, as a place to fame well known,
   Ambitiously designed his Sh———'s throne;
   For ancient Dekker[3] prophesied long since, ⎫
   That in this pile would reign a mighty prince, ⎬
   Born for a scourge of wit, and flail of sense; ⎭
90 To whom true dullness should some *Psyches* owe,
   But worlds of *Misers* from his pen should flow;[4]
   Humorists and *Hypocrites* it should produce,
   Whole Raymond families, and tribes of Bruce.
      Now Empress Fame had published the renown
95 Of Sh———'s coronation through the town.
   Roused by report of Fame, the nations meet,
   From near Bunhill, and distant Watling Street.[5]
   No Persian carpets spread the imperial way,
   But scattered limbs of mangled poets lay;
100 From dusty shops neglected authors[6] come,
   Martyrs of pies, and relics of the bum.
   Much Heywood, Shirley, Ogilby[7] there lay,
   But loads of Sh——— almost choked the way.
   Bilked stationers[8] for yeomen stood prepared,
105 And Herringman was captain of the guard.
   The hoary prince in majesty appeared,
   High on a throne of his own labors reared.
   At his right hand our young Ascanius[9] sate,
   Rome's other hope, and pillar of the state.
110 His brows thick fogs, instead of glories, grace,
   And lambent dullness played around his face.
   As Hannibal did to the altars come,
   Sworn by his sire a mortal foe to Rome,[1]
   So Sh——— swore, nor should his vow be vain,
115 That he till death true dullness would maintain;
   And, in his father's right, and realm's defense,
   Ne'er to have peace with wit, nor truce with sense.
   The king himself the sacred unction° made,   *ointment*
   As king by office, and as priest by trade.

---

8. The bombastic emperor in Dryden's own *Tyrannic Love.*
9. Early 17th-century playwright; *buskins,* the high-soled boots worn in Athenian tragedy, are opposed to *socks,* the low shoes worn in comedy.
1. A clown.
2. A punster.
3. Elizabethan playwright satirized by Jonson.
4. In these lines Dryden names plays of (and characters in plays by) Shadwell.
5. These locations, both within a half-mile of the scene of the supposed coronation ("the Nursery"), circumscribe Shadwell's fame within an unfashionable bourgeois part of London.
6. I.e., unsold books, the paper of which, in that time of relative scarcity, found various uses.
7. John Ogilby, a translator of Virgil and Homer; the derided competitor of Dryden and (later) of Pope.
8. Booksellers, impoverished because they had stocked the works of Shadwell and others, were the guard of honor ("yoemen of the guard"). Their "captain," Henry Herringman, however, had been Dryden's publisher as well as Shadwell's.
9. Aeneas' son; hence, like Shadwell, the destined heir.
1. Hannibal, the Carthaginian general who invaded Italy, was dedicated to his hatred of Rome (it was said) at the age of nine.

120 In his sinister[2] hand, instead of ball,
He placed a mighty mug of potent ale;
Love's Kingdom[3] to his right he did convey,
At once his scepter, and his rule of sway;
Whose righteous lore the prince had practiced young,
125 And from whose loins recorded *Psyche* sprung.
His temples, last, with poppies[4] were o'erspread,
That nodding seemed to consecrate his head.
Just at that point of time, if fame not lie,
On his left hand twelve reverend owls did fly.
130 So Romulus, 'tis sung, by Tiber's brook,
Presage of sway from twice six vultures took.[5]
The admiring throng loud acclamations make,
And omens of his future empire take.
The sire then shook the honors° of his head,   locks
135 And from his brows damps° of oblivion shed   vapors
Full on the filial dullness: long he stood, ⎤
Repelling from his breast the raging god; ⎬
At length burst out in this prophetic mood: ⎦
  "Heavens bless my son, from Ireland let him reign
140 To far Barbadoes on the western main;[6]
Of his dominion may no end be known,
And greater than his father's be his throne;
Beyond *Love's Kingdom* let his stretch his pen!"
He paused, and all the people cried, "Amen."
145 Then thus continued he: "My son, advance
Still in new imprudence, new ignorance.
Success let others teach, learn thou from me
Pangs without birth, and fruitless industry.
Let *Virtuosos* in five years be writ;
150 Yet not one thought accuse thy toil of wit.
Let gentle George[7] in triumph tread the stage,
Make Dorimant betray, and Loveit rage;
Let Cully, Cockwood, Fopling, charm the pit,
And in their folly show the writer's wit.
155 Yet still thy fools shall stand in thy defense,
And justify their author's want of sense.
Let 'em be all by thy own model made
Of dullness, and desire no foreign aid;
That they to future ages may be known,
160 Not copies drawn, but issue of thy own.
Nay, let thy men of wit too be the same,
All full of thee, and differing but in name.
But let no alien S—dl—y[8] interpose,
To lard with wit thy hungry *Epsom* prose.
165 And when false flowers of rhetoric thou wouldst cull,
Trust nature, do not labor to be dull;
But write thy best, and top; and, in each line,
Sir Formal's[9] oratory will be thine:

2. In British coronations the monarch holds
in his left ("sinister") hand a globe sur-
mounted by a cross.
3. A "pastoral tragicomedy" by Flecknoe, ap-
parently visualized by Dryden as a rolled-up
manuscript held like a scepter.
4. Connoting both intellectual heaviness and
Shadwell's addiction to opiates.
5. When the site which Romulus had chosen
for Rome was visited by twelve vultures, or
twice as many as had visited the site picked
by his brother Remus, the kingship ("sway")

of Romulus was presaged.
6. I.e., a realm of empty ocean.
7. George Etherege (ca. 1635–91), playwright
who set the tone for stylish Restoration com-
edy; Dryden proceeds to name five of his
characters.
8. Sir Charles Sedley (ca. 1639–1701), Res-
toration wit who had contributed a prologue
and (Dryden suggests) a part of the text to
Shadwell's *Epsom Wells*.
9. Sir Formal Trifle was an inflated orator in
The Virtuoso.

Sir Formal, though unsought, attends thy quill,
And does thy northern dedications[1] fill.
Nor let false friends seduce thy mind to fame,
By arrogating Jonson's hostile name.
Let father Flecknoe fire thy mind with praise,
And uncle Ogilby thy envy raise.
Thou art my blood, where Jonson has no part:
What share have we in nature, or in art?
Where did his wit on learning fix a brand,
And rail at arts he did not understand?
Where made he love in Prince Nicander's vein,
Or swept the dust in *Psyche's* humble strain?[2]
Where sold he bargains,[3] 'whip-stitch, kiss my arse,'
Promised a play and dwindled to a farce?
When did his Muse from Fletcher scenes purloin,
As thou whole Eth'rege dost transfuse to thine?
But so transfused, as oil on water's flow,
His always floats above, thine sinks below.
This is thy province, this thy wondrous way,
New humors to invent for each new play:
This is that boasted bias of thy mind,
By which one way, to dullness, 'tis inclined;
Which makes thy writings lean on one side still,
And, in all changes, that way bends thy will.
Nor let thy mountain-belly make pretense
Of likeness; thine's a tympany[4] of sense.
A tun of man in thy large bulk is writ,
But sure thou'rt but a kilderkin of wit.[5]
Like mine, thy gentle numbers feebly creep;
Thy tragic Muse gives smiles, thy comic sleep.
With whate'er gall thou sett'st thyself to write,
Thy inoffensive satires never bite.
In thy felonious heart though venom lies,
It does but touch thy Irish pen, and dies.
Thy genius calls thee not to purchase fame
In keen iambics,[6] but mild anagram.
Leave writing plays, and choose for thy command
Some peaceful province in acrostic land.
There thou may'st wings display and altars raise,
And torture one poor word ten thousand ways.[7]
Or, if thou wouldst thy different talent suit,
Set thy own songs, and sing them to thy lute."
   He said: but his last words were scarcely heard⌉
For Bruce and Longville had a trap prepared, ⎬
And down they sent the yet declaiming bard.[8] ⌋
Sinking he left his drugget robe behind,
Borne upwards by a subterranean wind.
The mantle fell to the young prophet's part,[9]
With double portion of his father's art.

ca. 1679   1682

1. I.e., to Shadwell's patron the Duke of Newcastle, whose seat was in northern England.
2. Nicander pays court to the title character Psyche in Shadwell's opera.
3. A "bargain" is a gross rejoinder to an innocent question. The rest of the line, itself a kind of bargain, echoes a farcical character in *The Virtuoso*.
4. A swelling caused by air.
5. Tuns are big casks; kilderkins, little ones.
6. The meter of (Greek) satire; hence satire itself.
7. Ingenuities like those mentioned, frequent in the early century, had been put away as trivial.
8. These characters in *The Virtuoso* so trap Sir Formal Trifle.
9. Like the prophet Elijah's mantle falling on Elisha. See II Kings ii, or Cowley's elegy on Crashaw, line 66n.

To the Memory of Mr. Oldham[6]

Farewell, too little, and too lately known,
Whom I began to think and call my own:
For sure our souls were near allied, and thine
Cast in the same poetic mold with mine.
5 One common note on either lyre did strike,
And knaves·and fools we both abhorred alike.
To the same goal did both our studies° drive;   *endeavors*
The last set out the soonest did arrive.
Thus Nisus[7] fell upon the slippery place,
10 While his young friend performed° and won the race.   *completed*
O early ripe! to thy abundant store
What could advancing age have added more?
It might (what nature never gives the young)
Have taught the numbers° of thy native tongue.   *metrics*
15 But satire needs not those, and wit will shine
Through the harsh cadence of a rugged line:
A noble error, and but seldom made,
When poets are by too much force betrayed.
Thy generous fruits, though gathered ere their prime, ⎤
20 Still showed a quickness,° and maturing time   ⎬ *pungency*
But mellows what we write to the dull sweets of rhyme. ⎦
Once more, hail and farewell; farewell, thou young,
But ah too short, Marcellus[8] of our tongue;
Thy brows with ivy, and with laurels bound;
25 But fate and gloomy night encompass thee around.[9]

1684

Song from *Cleomenes*

1

No, no, poor suffering heart, no change endeavor,
Choose to sustain the smart, rather than leave her;
My ravished eyes behold such charms about her,
I can die with her, but not live without her;
5 One tender sigh of hers to see me languish,
Will more than pay the price of my past anguish:
Beware, O cruel fair, how you smile on me,
'Twas a kind look of yours that has undone me.

2

Love has in store for me one happy minute,
10 And she will end my pain, who did begin it;
Then no day void of bliss, or pleasure, leaving,
Ages shall slide away without perceiving:
Cupid shall guard the door, the more to please us,
And keep out Time and Death, when they would seize us;
15 Time and Death shall depart, and say, in flying,
Love has found out a way to live by dying.

1692

---

6. John Oldham (1653–83), author of *Satires Upon the Jesuits*, was a promising young poet, harsh (partly by calculation) in metrics and manner, but earnest and vigorous.
7. A foot racer in Virgil's *Aeneid;* his young friend Euryalus came from behind to reach the goal before him (V.315 ff.).
8. Augustus Caesar's nephew, who died at twenty after a meteoric military career.
9. The Roman elegiac phrase "Hail and farewell!" in line 22; the mention of Marcellus (line 23) and of the classical poet's wreath (line 24); and the echo of Virgil's lament for Marcellus (see *Aeneid* VI.566) conspire to Romanize Oldham.

Alexander's Feast[1]

OR THE POWER OF MUSIC;
AN ODE IN HONOR OF ST. CECILIA'S DAY

1

'Twas at the royal feast, for Persia won
    By Philip's warlike son:
    Aloft in awful state
    The godlike hero sate
5   On his imperial throne;
His valiant peers were placed around;
Their brows with roses and with myrtles[2] bound:
  (So should desert in arms be crowned).
The lovely Thaïs, by his side,
10 Sate like a blooming Eastern bride
In flower of youth and beauty's pride.
    Happy, happy, happy pair!
    None but the brave,
    None but the brave,
15   None but the brave deserves the fair.

Chorus

Happy, happy, happy pair!
None but the brave,
None but the brave,
None but the brave deserves the fair.

2

20 Timotheus, placed on high
    Amid the tuneful choir,
    With flying fingers touched the lyre:
The trembling notes ascend the sky,
    And heavenly joys inspire.
25 The song began from Jove,
Who left his blissful seats above
(Such is the power of mighty love).
A dragon's fiery form belied the god:
Sublime on radiant spires° he rode,   *coils*
30   When he to fair Olympia[3] pressed;
    And while he sought her snowy breast:
Then, round her slender waist he curled,
And stamped an image of himself, a sovereign of the world.
The listening crowd admire° the lofty sound: *wonder at*
35 "A present deity," they shout around;
"A present deity," the vaulted roofs rebound.

---

1. Alexander the Great, son of King Philip of Macedon, conquered the Persian Emperor Darius III in 331 B.C. and occupied his capital, Persopolis. During a victory feast, Alexander, at the instigation of his Athenian mistress Thaïs, set fire to the royal palace to avenge the burning of Athens by the Persians fifty years before. Dryden attributed Alexander's act to the influence of his musician Timotheus and made the episode the basis for a St. Cecilia's Day ode: namely, a poem set to music and sung at an annual concert on the saint's day of the Roman martyr Cecilia, patroness of music and supposed inventor of the organ. Settings for Dryden's poem were composed by Jeremiah Clarke (for the original performance in 1697) and later by Handel.
2. Emblems of love, like roses.
3. More accurately Olympias, Philip of Macedon's wife and Alexander's mother. According to an oracle, Jove, in characteristic disguise, had begotten the young hero upon her. Alexander hence enjoyed the status of a demigod (line 35).

> With ravished ears
> The monarch hears,
> Assumes the god,
40   Affects to nod,
> And seems to shake the spheres.[4]

Chorus

> *With ravished ears,*
> *The monarch hears,*
> *Assumes the god,*
45   *Affects to nod,*
> *And seems to shake the spheres.*

3

> The praise of Bacchus[5] then the sweet musician sung,
>   Of Bacchus ever fair and ever young:
>   The jolly god in triumph comes;
50   Sound the trumpets; beat the drums;
>   Flushed with a purple grace
>   He shows his honest face:
> Now give the hautboys° breath; he comes, he comes!   *oboes*
>   Bacchus, ever fair and young
55   Drinking joys did first ordain;
> Bacchus' blessings are a treasure,
> Drinking is a soldier's pleasure;
>   Rich the treasure,
>   Sweet the pleasure,
60   Sweet is pleasure after pain.

Chorus

> *Bacchus' blessings are a treasure,*
> *Drinking is the soldier's pleasure;*
>   *Rich the treasure,*
>   *Sweet the pleasure,*
65   *Sweet is pleasure after pain.*

4

> Soothed with the sound, the king grew vain;
>   Fought all his battles o'er again.
> And thrice he routed all his foes, and thrice he slew the slain.
> The master saw the madness rise,
70 His glowing cheeks, his ardent eyes;
> And, while he heaven and earth defied,
> Changed his hand, and checked his pride.[6]
>   He chose a mournful Muse,
>   Soft pity to infuse:
75 He sung Darius great and good,
>   By too severe a fate
> Fallen, fallen, fallen, fallen,
>   Fallen from his high estate,
>   And weltering in his blood;
80 Deserted at his utmost need
> By those his former bounty fed;[7]
> On the bare earth exposed he lies,
> With not a friend to close his eyes.

4. Like Jove, the thunderer; or Neptune, "the earth-shaker," god of the sea.
5. God of wine.
6. I.e., while Alexander defied heaven and earth, Timotheus changed his (Timotheus') hand on the lyre and checked Alexander's pride.
7. Darius, defeated, was killed by his own men.

With downcast looks the joyless victor sate,
85   Revolving° in his altered soul   *pondering*
        The various turns of chance below;
And, now and then, a sigh he stole,
        And tears began to flow.

                Chorus

        Revolving in his altered soul
90   *The various turns of chance below;*
        And, now and then, a sigh he stole,
            And tears began to flow.

                    5

The mighty master smiled to see
That love was in the next degree;
95 'Twas but a kindred sound to move,[8]
For pity melts the mind to love.
        Softly sweet, in Lydian[9] measures,
        Soon he soothed his soul to pleasures.
        "War," he sung, "is toil and trouble;
100   Honor, but an empty bubble.
            Never ending, still beginning,
        Fighting still, and still destroying:
            If the world be worth thy winning,
            Think, O think it worth enjoying.
105   Lovely Thaïs sits beside thee,
                Take the good the gods provide thee."
The many° rend the skies with loud applause;   *company*
So Love was crowned, but Music won the cause.
        The prince, unable to conceal his pain,
110   Gazed on the fair
                Who caused his care,
        And sighed and looked, sighed and looked,
        Sighed and looked, and sighed again:
At length, with love and wine at once oppressed,
115 The vanquished victor sunk upon her breast.

                Chorus

        The prince, unable to conceal his pain,
                Gazed on the fair
                Who caused his care,
            And sighed and looked, sighed and looked,
120   *Sighed and looked, and sighed again:*
        At length, with love and wine at once oppressed,
        The vanquished victor sunk upon her breast.

                    6

Now strike the golden lyre again:
A louder yet, and yet a louder strain.
125 Break his bands of sleep asunder,
And rouse him, like a rattling peal of thunder.
            Hark, hark, the horrid° sound   *bristling*
            Has raised up his head:
                As waked from the dead,
130   And amazed, he stares around.
"Revenge, revenge!" Timotheus cries,
        "See the Furies[1] arise!

---

8. I.e., he had only to actuate the next sound.   1. Avengers; dreaded **female deities with**
9. The musical mode expressing sadness.   **snakes in their hair.**

See the snakes that they rear,
How they hiss in their hair,
¹³⁵ And the sparkles that flash from their eyes!
Behold a ghastly band,
Each a torch in his hand!
Those are Grecian ghosts, that in battle were slain,
And unburied² remain
¹⁴⁰ Inglorious on the plain:
Give the vengeance due
To the valiant crew.
Behold how they toss their torches on high,
How they point to the Persian abodes,
¹⁴⁵ And glittering temples of their hostile gods!"
The princes applaud, with a furious joy;
And the king seized a flambeau° with zeal to destroy;   *torch*
Thaïs led the way,
To light him to his prey,
¹⁵⁰ And, like another Helen, fired another Troy.³

Chorus

And the king seized a flambeau with zeal to destroy;
Thaïs led the way,
To light him to his prey,
And, like another Helen, fired another Troy.

7
¹⁵⁵   Thus long ago,
Ere heaving bellows learned to blow,
While organs yet were mute;
Timotheus, to his breathing flute,
And sounding lyre,
¹⁶⁰ Could swell the soul to rage, or kindle soft desire.
At last, divine Cecilia came,
Inventress of the vocal frame;⁴
The sweet enthusiast,° from her sacred store,   *religious zealot*
Enlarged the former narrow bounds,
¹⁶⁵ And added length to solemn sounds,
With nature's mother wit, and arts unknown before.
Let old Timotheus yield the prize,
Or both divide the crown:
He raised a mortal to the skies;
¹⁷⁰ She drew an angel down.

Grand Chorus

At last, divine Cecilia came,
Inventress of the vocal frame;
The sweet enthusiast, from her sacred store,
Enlarged the former narrow bounds,
¹⁷⁵ *And added length to solemn sounds,*
With nature's mother wit, and arts unknown before.
Let old Timotheus yield the prize,
Or both divide the crown:
He raised a mortal to the skies;
¹⁸⁰ *She drew an angel down.*

1697

2. Hence, in ancient belief, unable to find rest among the shades of the dead.
3. Helen, wife of the Spartan king Menelaus, eloped to Troy with Paris and thereby brought about the Trojan War and the eventual burning of Troy.
4. "Vocal frame": organ.

THOMAS TRAHERNE
(1637–1674)

The Salutation

These little limbs,
These eyes and hands which here I find,
These rosy cheeks wherewith my life begins,
Where have ye been? behind
5 What curtain were ye from me hid so long?
Where was, in what abyss, my speaking tongue?

When silent I
So many thousand, thousand years
Beneath the dust did in a chaos lie,
10 How could I smiles or tears,
Or lips or hands or eyes or ears perceive?
Welcome ye treasures which I now receive.

I that so long
Was nothing from eternity,
15 Did little think such joys as ear or tongue
To celebrate or see:
Such sounds to hear, such hands to feel, such feet,
Beneath the skies on such a ground to meet.

New burnished joys,
20 Which yellow gold and pearls excel!
Such sacred treasures are the limbs in boys,
In which a soul doth dwell;
Their organizéd joints and azure veins
More wealth include than all the world contains.

25 From dust I rise,
And out of nothing now awake;
These brighter regions which salute mine eyes,
A gift from God I take.
The earth, the seas, the light, the day, the skies,
30 The sun and stars are mine if those I prize.

Long time before
I in my mother's womb was born,
A God, preparing, did this glorious store,
The world, for me adorn.
35 Into this Eden so divine and fair,
So wide and bright, I come His son and heir.

A stranger here
Strange things doth meet, strange glories see;
Strange treasures lodged in this fair world appear,
40 Strange all and new to me;
But that they mine should be, who nothing was,
That strangest is of all, yet brought to pass.

ca. 1665   1906

Wonder

How like an angel came I down!
  How bright are all things here!
When first among His works I did appear
  Oh, how their glory me did crown!
5 The world resembled His eternity,
  In which my soul did walk;
  And everything that I did see
    Did with me talk.

  The skies in their magnificence,
10   The lively, lovely air,
Oh, how divine, how soft, how sweet, how fair!
  The stars did entertain my sense,
And all the works of God, so bright and pure,
  So rich and great did seem,
15 As if they ever must endure
    In my esteem.

  A native health and innocence
    Within my bones did grow;
And while my God did all His glories show,
20 I felt a vigor in my sense
That was all spirit. I within did flow
  With seas of life, like wine;
  I nothing in the world did know
    But 'twas divine.

25 Harsh ragged objects were concealed;
    Oppressions, tears, and cries,
Sins, griefs, complaints, dissensions, weeping eyes
  Were hid, and only things revealed
Which heavenly spirits and the angels prize.
30   The state of innocence
  And bliss, not trades and poverties,
    Did fill my sense.

  The streets were paved with golden stones,
    The boys and girls were mine,
35 Oh, how did all their lovely faces shine!
  The sons of men were holy ones,
In joy and beauty they appeared to me,
    And everything I found,
  While like an angel I did see,
40   Adorned the ground.

  Rich diamond and pearl and gold
    In every place was seen;
Rare splendors, yellow, blue, red, white, and green,
  Mine eyes did everywhere behold.
45 Great wonders clothed with glory did appear,
    Amazement was my bliss,
  That and my wealth met everywhere;
    No joy to° this!

compared to

Cursed and devised proprieties,[1]
50   With envy, avarice,
And fraud, those fiends that spoil even paradise,
    Flew from the splendor of mine eyes;
And so did hedges, ditches, limits, bounds:
    I dreamed not aught of those,
55 But wandered over all men's grounds,
    And found repose.

Proprieties themselves were mine,
    And hedges ornaments;
Walls, boxes, coffers, and their rich contents
60   To make me rich combine.
Clothes, ribbons, jewels, laces, I esteemed
    My joys by others worn:
For me they all to wear them seemed
    When I was born.

1903

To the Same Purpose

To the same purpose: he, not long before
    Brought home from nurse, going to the door
        To do some little thing
        He must not do within,
5   With wonder cries,
          As in the skies
He saw the moon, "O yonder is the moon,
    Newly come after me to town,
That shined at Lugwardin but yesternight,
10   Where I enjoyed the self-same sight."

As if it had ev'n twenty thousand faces,
    It shines at once in many places;
        To all the earth so wide
        God doth the stars divide,
15   With so much art
          The moon impart,
They serve us all; serve wholly every one
    As if they servéd him alone.
While every single person hath such store,
20   'Tis want of sense that makes us poor.

ca. 1665   1910

Shadows in the Water

In unexperienced infancy
Many a sweet mistake doth lie:
Mistake though false, intending° true;   *directing to*
A seeming somewhat more than view;
5   That doth instruct the mind
    In things that lie behind,
And many secrets to us show
Which afterwards we come to know.

---

1. Proprietorships, devised or bequeathed in a will.

Thus did I by the water's brink
10 Another world beneath me think;
And while the lofty spacious skies
Reverséd there, abused mine eyes,
    I fancied other feet
    Came mine to touch or meet;
15 As by some puddle I did play
Another world within it lay.

Beneath the water people drowned,
Yet with another heaven crowned,
In spacious regions seemed to go
20 As freely moving to and fro:
    In bright and open space
    I saw their very face;
Eyes, hands, and feet they had like mine;
Another sun did with them shine.

25 'Twas strange that people there should walk,
And yet I could not hear them talk:
That through a little watery chink,
Which one dry ox or horse might drink,
    We other worlds should see,
30   Yet not admitted be;
And other confines there behold
Of light and darkness, heat and cold.

I called them oft, but called in vain;
No speeches we could entertain:
35 Yet did I there expect to find
Some other world, to please my mind.
    I plainly saw by these
    A new antipodes,[2]
Whom, though they were so plainly seen,
40 A film kept off that stood between.

By walking men's reverséd feet
I chanced another world to meet;
Though it did not to view exceed
A phantom, 'tis a world indeed,
45   Where skies beneath us shine,
    And earth by art divine
Another face presents below,
Where people's feet against ours go.

Within the regions of the air,
50 Compassed about with heavens fair,
Great tracts of land there may be found
Enriched with fields and fertile ground;
    Where many numerous hosts
    In those far distant coasts,
55 For other great and glorious ends
Inhabit, my yet unknown friends.

O ye that stand upon the brink,
Whom I so near me through the chink

2. People living at a diametrically opposite point on the globe (literally, "with the feet opposite").

With wonder see: what faces there,
60 Whose feet, whose bodies, do ye wear?
    I my companions see
    In you, another me.
They seeméd others, but are we;
Our second selves these shadows be.

65 Look how far off those lower skies
Extend themselves! scarce with mine eyes
I can them reach. O ye my friends,
What secret borders on those ends?
    Are lofty heavens hurled
70   'Bout your inferior world?
Are yet the representatives
Of other peoples' distant lives?

Of all the playmates which I knew
That here I do the image view
75 In other selves, what can it mean?
But that below the purling stream
    Some unknown joys there be
    Laid up in store for me;
To which I shall, when that thin skin
80 Is broken, be admitted in.

                                ca. 1665   1910

EDWARD TAYLOR
(ca. 1642–1729)

Meditation 6

Am I thy gold? Or purse, Lord, for thy wealth,
    Whether in mine or mint refined for thee?
I'm counted so, but count me o'er thyself,
    Lest gold washed face, and brass in heart I be.
5   I fear my touchstone[1] touches when I try[2]
    Me and my counted gold too overly.

Am I new minted by thy stamp indeed?
    Mine eyes are dim; I cannot clearly see.
Be thou my spectacles that I may read
10   Thine image and inscription stamped on me.
    If thy bright image do upon me stand,
    I am a golden angel[3] in thy hand.

Lord, make my soul thy plate,[4] thine image bright
    Within the circle of the same enfile.[5]
15 And on its brims in golden letters write
    Thy superscription in an holy style.
    Then I shall be thy money, thou my horde:
    Let me thy angel be, be thou my Lord.

                                                1939

---

1. A stone once believed capable of testing the quality of gold or silver when these metals were rubbed against the stone.
2. To separate or distinguish one thing from another; or, in another sense, to prove or test.
3. A pun implying both a heavenly being and an old English gold coin called an "angel."
4. Precious metal; more particularly, utensils of silver or gold, or pieces of money.
5. "Enfile," as a verb, means here to *inscribe* or *engrave;* as a noun, it suggests the *inscription* or *engraving* itself.

Meditation 8[6]

I kenning° through astronomy divine   *discerning, knowing*
   The world's bright battlement, wherein I spy
A golden path my pencil cannot line,
   From that bright throne unto my threshold lie.
5   And while my puzzled thoughts about it pore
   I find the bread of life in it at my door.

When that this bird of paradise put in
   This wicker cage (my corpse)[7] to tweedle° praise   *sing*
Had pecked the fruit forbad, and so did fling
10   Away its food, and lost its golden days,
   It fell into celestial famine sore,
   And never could attain a morsel more.

Alas! alas! Poor bird, what wilt thou do?
   The creatures' field no food for souls e'er gave.
15 And if thou knock at angels' doors they show
   An empty barrel; they no soul bread have.
   Alas! Poor bird, the world's white loaf is done,
   And cannot yield thee here the smallest crumb.

In this sad state, God's tender bowels[8] run
20   Out streams of grace; and he to end all strife
The purest wheat in heaven, his dear, dear son
   Grinds, and kneads up into this bread of life.
   Which bread of life from heaven down came and stands
   Dished on my table up by angels' hands.

25 Did God mould up this bread in heaven, and bake,
   Which from his table came, and to thine goeth?
Doth he bespeak thee thus: This soul bread take;
   Come eat thy fill of this thy God's white loaf?
   It's food too fine for angels, yet come, take
30   And eat thy fill: it's heaven's sugar cake.

What grace is this knead in this loaf? This thing
   Souls are but petty things it to admire.
Ye angels, help. This fill would to the brim
   Heaven's whelmed-down[9] crystal meal bowl, yea and higher,
35   This bread of life dropped in thy mouth, doth cry:
   Eat, eat me, soul, and thou shalt never die.

                          1684   1937

Meditation 32[1]

Thy grace, dear Lord's my golden wrack,° I find,   *ruin, downfall*
   Screwing my fancy into ragged rimes,
Tuning thy praises in my feeble mind
   Until I come to strike them on my chimes.

---

6. Based on John vi.51: "I am the living bread which came down from heaven: if any man eat of this bread, he shall live for ever: and the bread that I will give is my flesh, which I will give for the life of the world."
7. In this context, the living body.
8. I.e., God's powers of mercy and compassion.

9. Turned over upon something so as to cover it.
1. Based on I Corinthians iii.21–23: "Therefore let no man glory in man. For all things are yours; Whether Paul, or Apollos, or Cephas, or the world, or life, or death, or things present, or things to come; all are yours; And ye are Christ's; and Christ is God's."

5   Were I an angel bright, and borrow could
      King David's harp, I would them play on gold.

    But plunged I am, my mind is puzzléd,
       When I would spin my fancy thus unspun,
    In finest twine of praise I'm muzzléd;
10   My tazzled° thoughts twirled into snick-snarls° run.   *twisted / tangles*
       Thy grace, my Lord, is such a glorious thing,
       It doth confound me when I would it sing.

    Eternal love an object mean did smite,
       Which by the Prince of Darkness was beguiled,
15 That from this love it ran and swelled with spite
       And in the way with filth was all defiled;
       Yet must be reconciled, cleansed, and begraced
       Or from the fruits of God's first love displaced.

    Then grace, my Lord, wrought in thy heart a vent;
20   Thy soft, soft hand to this hard work did go,
    And to the milk-white throne of justice went
       And entered bond that grace might overflow.
       Hence did thy person to my nature tie,
       And bleed through human veins to satisfy.

25 Oh! Grace, grace, grace! This wealthy grace doth lay
       Her golden channels from thy father's throne,
    Into our earthen pitchers to convey
       Heaven's aqua vitae[2] to us for our own.
       O! Let thy golden gutters run into
30   My cup this liquor till it overflow.

    Thine ordinances, grace's wine-vats where
       Thy spirit's walks and grace's runs do lie,[3]
    And angels waiting stand with holy cheer
       From grace's conduit head, with all supply.
35   These vessels full of grace are, and the bowls
       In which their taps do run are precious souls.

    Thou to the cups dost say (that catch this wine):
       This liquor, golden pipes, and wine-vats plain,
    Whether Paul, Apollos, Cephas, all are thine.
40   Oh golden word! Lord, speak it o'er again.
       Lord, speak it home to me, say these are mine:
       My bells shall then thy praises bravely chime.

                                            1689   1954

The Glory of and Grace in the Church Set Out

    Come now behold
      Within this knot[4] what flowers do grow,
         Spangled like gold,
      Whence wreaths of all perfumes do flow.
5   Most curious° colors of all sorts you shall   *amazing*
      With all sweet spirits° scent. Yet that's not all.   *odors*

---

2. Literally, *water of life;* generally, any spiritous drink.
3. "Where * * * runs do lie" (lines 31–32): i.e., both the place where grace operates or functions ("runs"), and the flowing of grace itself.
4. Plot of ground, or planting-bed.

Oh! Look, and find
These choicest flowers most richly sweet
Are disciplined
10   With artificial angels meet.[5]
An heap of pearls is precious; but they shall,
When set by art, excel. Yet that's not all.

Christ's spirit showers
Down in his word, and sacraments
15   Upon these flowers
The clouds of grace divine contents.
Such things of wealthy blessings on them fall
As make them sweetly thrive. Yet that's not all.

Yet still behold!
20   All flourish not at once. We see
While some unfold
Their blushing leaves, some buds there be.
Here's faith, hope, charity in flower, which call
On yonders in the bud. Yet that's not all.

25   But as they stand
Like beauties reeking in° perfume   *giving off*
A divine hand
Doth hand them up to glory's room,
Where each in sweetened songs all praises shall
30   Sing all o'er heaven for aye. And that's but all.

1937

Upon Wedlock, and Death of Children

A curious knot God made in paradise,
And drew it out enameled° neatly fresh.   *variously colored*
It was the truelove knot, more sweet than spice
And set with all the flowers of grace's dress.
5   Its wedding knot, that ne'er can be untied;
No Alexander's sword[6] can it divide.

The slips here planted, gay and glorious grow,
Unless an hellish breath do singe their plumes.
Here primrose, cowslips, roses, lilies blow
10   With violets and pinks that void° perfumes: *give off, exude*
Whose beauteous leaves o'er laid with honey-dew,
And chanting birds chirp out sweet music true.

When in this knot I planted was, my stock°   *stem*
Soon knotted, and a manly flower out brake.
15   And after it my branch again did knot;
Brought out another flower its sweet breathed mate.
One knot gave one t'other the t'other's place;
Whence chuckling smiles fought in each other's face.

But oh! a glorious hand from glory came
20   Guarded with angels, soon did crop this flower

---

5. "Artificial angels meet": i.e., appropriate angel-artificers.
6. Gordius, king of Phrygia, devised a compli-cated knot to be undone only by him who was to rule Asia. Alexander the Great cut the knot with a blow of his sword.

Which almost tore the root up of the same
   At that unlooked for, dolesome, darksome hour.
In prayer to Christ perfumed it did ascend,
   And angels bright did it to heaven tend.

25 But pausing on't, this sweet perfumed my thought,
    Christ would in glory have a flower, choice, prime,
And having choice, chose this my branch forth brought.
    Lord take't. I thank thee, thou takest aught of mine,
     It is my pledge in glory; part of me
30   Is now in it, Lord, glorified with thee.

But praying o'er my branch, my branch did sprout
    And bore another manly flower, and gay;
And after that another, sweet, brake out,
    The which the former hand soon got away.
35   But oh! the tortures, vomit, screechings, groans,
    And six weeks fever would pierce hearts like stones.

Grief o'er doth flow, and nature fault would find
    Were not thy will, my spell charm, joy, and gem;
That as I said, I say, take, Lord, they're thine.
40   I piecemeal pass to glory bright in them.
     I joy, may I sweet flowers for glory breed,
    Whether thou getst them green, or let them seed.

1937

Upon a Spider Catching a Fly

Thou sorrow, venom elf:
   Is this thy play,
To spin a web out of thyself
   To catch a fly?
5   For why?

I saw a pettish° wasp   *peevish, petulant*
   Fall foul therein,
Whom yet thy whorl-pins[7] did not clasp
   Lest he should fling
10   His sting.

But as afraid, remote
   Didst stand hereat
And with thy little fingers stroke
   And gently tap
15   His back.

Thus gently him didst treat
   Lest he should pet,
And in a froppish,° waspish heat   *fretful*
   Should greatly fret
20   Thy net.

---

7. Technically, the flywheel holding the thread on the spindle of a spinning wheel; here, the spider's legs.

Whereas the silly fly,
  Caught by its leg
Thou by the throat tookst hastily
  And hind the head
25   Bite dead.

This goes to pot,[8] that not
  Nature doth call.
Strive not above what strength hath got
  Lest in the brawl
30   Thou fall.

This fray seems thus to us.
  Hell's spider gets
His entrails spun to whip-cords[9] thus,
  And wove to nets
35   And sets.

To tangle Adam's race
  In's strategems
To their destructions, spoiled, made base
  By venom things,
40   Damned sins.

But mighty, gracious Lord
  Communicate
Thy grace to break the cord, afford
  Us glory's gate
45   And state.

We'll nightingale sing like
  When perched on high
In glory's cage, thy glory, bright,
  And thankfully,
50   For joy.

1939

Housewifery

Make me, O Lord, thy spinning wheel complete.[1]
  Thy holy word my distaff make for me.
Make mine affections thy swift flyers neat,
  And make my soul thy holy spool to be.
5 My conversation make to be thy reel,
  And reel the yarn thereon spun on thy wheel.

Make me thy loom then, knit therein this twine;
  And make thy holy spirit, Lord, wind quills.[2]
Then weave the web thyself. The yarn is fine.
10 Thine ordinances make my fulling mills.[3]
Then dye the same in heavenly colors choice,
All pinked° with varnished° flowers of paradise.   *ornamented / luminous*

8. As in the modern sense, deteriorates.
9. Strong cord or binding, like that made of hemp or catgut.
1. In the first stanza, parts of the spinning wheel specified are: the *distaff*, which holds the material to be spun; *flyers*, which twist the thread as it conducts it to and winds it upon the bobbin; *spool*, on which the thread is wound as it is spun; *reel*, which receives the finished thread [S.O.E.D.].
2. *Quills* are the spools of a looming machine.
3. In the *fulling mills*, the cloth is "fulled" or milled by being pressed between rollers and cleansed with soap or fuller's earth [S.O.E.D.].

Then clothe therewith mine understanding, will,
Affections, judgment, conscience, memory,
15 My words, and actions, that their shine may fill
My ways with glory and thee glorify.
Then mine apparel shall display before ye
That I am clothed in holy robes for glory.

1939

JOHN WILMOT, EARL OF ROCHESTER
(1647–1680)

A Satire Against Mankind

Were I, who to my cost already am,
One of those strange, prodigious creatures, *Man,*
A spirit free, to choose for my own share,
What case of flesh and blood I pleased to wear,
5 I'd be a dog, a monkey, or a bear,
Or anything but that vain animal,
Who is so proud of being rational.
The senses are too gross,° and he'll contrive   *inexact*
A sixth, to contradict the other five:
10 And before certain instinct will prefer
Reason, which fifty times for one does err.
Reason, an *ignis fatuus*[1] of the mind,
Which leaves the light of Nature, sense, behind.
Pathless and dangerous, wandering ways it takes,
15 Through Error's fenny bogs, and thorny brakes:
Whilst the misguided follower climbs with pain,
Mountains of whimsies heaped in his own brain:
Stumbling from thought to thought, falls headlong down
Into Doubt's boundless sea, where like to drown
20 Books bear him up awhile, and make him try
To swim with bladders[2] of philosophy:
In hopes still to o'ertake the skipping light,
The vapor dances in his dazzled sight,
Till spent, it leaves him to eternal night.
25 Then old age, and experience, hand in hand,
Lead him to death, and make him understand,
After a search so painful, and so long,
That all his life he has been in the wrong;
Huddled in dirt, the reasoning engine lies,
30 Who was so proud, so witty, and so wise.
Pride drew him in, as cheats their bubbles° catch,   *dupes*
And made him venture to be made a wretch:
His wisdom did his happiness destroy,
Aiming to know the world he should enjoy.
35 And wit was his vain frivolous pretense,
Of pleasing others at his own expense.
For wits are treated just like common whores;
First they're enjoyed, and then kicked out of doors.
The pleasure past, a threatening doubt remains,
40 That frights the enjoyer with succeeding pains.

1. Will-o'-the wisp.   2. Inflated bladders, buoying him up.

Women, and men of wit, are dangerous tools,
And ever fatal to admiring° fools.   *wondering*
Pleasure allures, and when the fops escape,
'Tis not that they're beloved, but fortunate;
45 And therefore what they fear, at heart they hate.
    But now, methinks, some formal Band[3] and Beard
Takes me to task. Come on, sir, I'm prepared:
"Then, by your favor, anything that's writ
Against this gibing, jingling knack, called wit,
50 Likes° me abundantly; but you'll take care   *pleases*
Upon this point, not to be too severe.
Perhaps my Muse were fitter for this part,
For, I profess, I can be very smart
On wit, which I abhor with all my heart.
55 I long to lash it, in some sharp essáy,
But your grand indiscretion bids me stay,
And turns my tide of ink another way.
What rage ferments in your degenerate mind,
To make you rail at reason and Mankind?
60 Blest glorious Man! to whom alone kind heaven
An everlasting soul has freely given;
Whom his great Maker took such care to make,
That from himself he did the image take,
And this fair frame in shining reason dressed,
65 To dignify his nature above beast.
Reason, by whose aspiring influence,
We take a flight beyond material sense,
Dive into mysteries, then soaring pierce
The flaming limits of the universe,
70 Search heaven and hell, find out what's acted there,
And give the world true grounds of hope and fear."
    Hold, mighty man, I cry; all this we know,
From the pathetic pen of Ingelo,
From Patrick's *Pilgrim*, Sibbe's *Soliloquies*,[4]
75 And 'tis this very reason I despise,
This supernatural gift, that makes a mite
Think he's the image of the Infinite;
Comparing his short life, void of all rest,
To the Eternal and the ever Blest;
80 This busy, puzzling stirrer up of doubt,
That frames deep mysteries, then finds 'em out,
Filling with frantic crowds of thinking fools,
Those reverend Bedlams,° colleges and schools,   *madhouses*
Borne on whose wings, each heavy sot can pierce
85 The limits of the boundless universe:
So charming ointments[5] make an old witch fly,
And bear a crippled carcass through the sky.
'Tis this exalted power, whose business lies
In nonsense and impossibilities:
90 This made a whimsical philosopher,
Before the spacious world his tub prefer,[6]

3. A Geneva band, worn by the clergy. A Band and Beard is hence a venerable parson.
4. Nathaniel Ingello, whose pen is derisively called "pathetic" (heart-rending), wrote an allegorical romance *Bentivolio and Urania*. Simon Patrick's *The Parable of the Pilgrim* (another allegory), and Richard Sibbe's dis-
courses (none actually called *Soliloquies*) were other current instructional works.
5. The magical preparations of witches, usually (as in *Macbeth*) mixtures of outlandish things.
6. Diogenes the Cynic, who (in legend) inhabited a tub.

And we have modern cloistered coxcombs, who
Retire to think, 'cause they have nought to do.
But thoughts were given for action's government;
95 Where action ceases, thought's impertinent.°   *irrelevant*
Our sphere of action is life's happiness,
And he who thinks beyond, thinks like an ass.
Thus whilst against false reasoning I inveigh,
I own right reason, which I would obey:
00 That reason, that distinguishes by sense,
And gives us rules of good and ill from thence;
That bounds desires with a reforming will,
To keep them more in vigor, not to kill.
Your reason hinders, mine helps to enjoy;
05 Renewing appetites, yours would destroy.
My reason is my friend, yours is a cheat:
Hunger calls out, my reason bids me eat;
Perversely yours, your appetite does mock;
This asks for food, that answers, "What's o'clock?"
110 This plain distinction, sir, your doubt° secures;°   *suspicion / confirms*
'Tis not true reason I despise, but yours.
Thus, I think reason righted: but for Man,
I'll ne'er recant, defend him if you can.
For all his pride, and his philosophy, ⎤
115 'Tis evident beasts are, in their degree, ⎬
As wise at least, and better far than he. ⎦
Those creatures are the wisest, who attain,
By surest means, the ends at which they aim.
If therefore Jowler finds, and kills his hares,
120 Better than Meres supplies committee chairs;[7]
Though one's a statesman, the other but a hound,
Jowler in justice will be wiser found.
You see how far Man's wisdom here extends:
Look next if human nature makes amends;
125 Whose principles most generous are and just,
And to those whose morals you would sooner trust.
Be judge yourself, I'll bring it to the test,
Which is the basest creature, Man or beast?
Birds feed on birds, beasts on each other prey,
130 But savage Man alone does Man betray.
Pressed by necessity, *they* kill for food,
Man undoes Man to do himself no good.
With teeth and claws by Nature armed, *they* hunt
Nature's allowance, to supply their want:
135 But Man, with smiles, embraces, friendships, praise,
Unhumanly, his fellow's life betrays:
With voluntary pains works his distress;
Not through necessity, but wantonness.
For hunger, or for love, *they* bite or tear,
140 Whilst wretched Man is still in arms for fear:
For fear he arms, and is of arms afraid;
From fear to fear successively betrayed.
Base fear, the source whence his best passions came,
His boasted honor, and his dear-bought fame,
145 That lust of power, to which he's such a slave,
And for the which alone he dares be brave:

7. Sir Thomas Meres, a Whig member of Parliament.

To which his various projects are designed,
Which makes him generous, affable, and kind,
For which he takes such pains to be thought wise,
150 And screws° his actions, in a forced disguise: ***distorts***
Leading a tedious life, in misery,
Under laborious, mean Hypocrisy.
Look to the bottom of his vast design,
Wherein Man's wisdom, power, and glory join;
155 The good he acts, the ill he does endure,
'Tis all from fear, to make himself secure.
Merely for safety, after fame we thirst,
For all men would be cowards if they durst:
And honesty's against all common sense:
160 Men must be knaves; 'tis in their own defense.
Mankind's dishonest; if you think it fair,
Amongst known cheats, to play upon the square,
You'll be undone——
Nor can weak truth your reputation save;
165 The knaves will all agree to call you knave.
Wronged shall he live, insulted o'er, oppressed,
Who dares be less a villain than the rest.
Thus, sir, you see what human nature craves,
Most men are cowards, all men should be knaves.
170 The difference lies, as far as I can see,
Not in the thing itself, but the degree;
And all the subject matter of debate,
Is only who's a knave of the first rate.

1675

MATTHEW PRIOR
(1664–1721)

A Fable

In Æsop's tales an honest wretch we find,
Whose years and comforts equally declined;
He in two wives had two domestic ills,
For different age they had, and different wills;
5 One plucked his black hairs out, and one his gray,
The man for quietness did both obey,
Till all his parish saw his head quite bare,
And thought he wanted brains as well as hair.

The Moral.

The parties, henpecked William,[1] are thy wives,
10 The hairs they pluck are thy prerogatives;[2]
Tories thy person hate, the Whigs thy power,[3]
Though much thou yieldest, still they tug for more,
Till this poor man and thou alike are shown,
He without hair, and thou without a crown.

1703

---

1. King William III (1650–1702), who ruled
England from 1689 until his death.
2. The rights of the king, previously not sub-
ject to parliamentary restriction.

3. The Whigs and Tories were the two main
political parties in late 17th- and 18th-century
England.

To a Lady: She Refusing to Continue a Dispute with Me, and Leaving Me in the Argument

1

Spare, gen'rous victor, spare the slave,
    Who did unequal war pursue;
That more than triumph he might have,
    In being overcome by you.

2

5 In the dispute whate'er I said,
    My heart was by my tongue belied;
And in my looks you might have read,
    How much I argued on your side.

3

You, far from danger as from fear,
10   Might have sustained an open fight:
For seldom your opinions err;
    Your eyes are always in the right.

4

Why, fair one, would you not rely
    On reason's force with beauty's joined?
15 Could I their prevalence deny;
    I must at once be deaf and blind.

5

Alas! not hoping to subdue,
    I only to the fight aspired:
To keep the beauteous foe in view
20   Was all the glory I desired.

6

But she, howe'er of vict'ry sure,
    Contemns the wreath too long delayed;
And, armed with more immediate Pow'r,
    Calls cruel silence to her aid.

7

25 Deeper to wound, she shuns the fight:
    She drops her arms, to gain the field:
Secures her conquest by her flight;
    And triumphs, when she seems to yield.

8

So when the Parthian⁴ turned his steed,
30   And from the hostile camp withdrew;
With cruel skill the backward reed°   arrow
    He sent; and as he fled, he slew.

1718

An Ode

The merchant, to secure his treasure,
    Conveys it in a borrowed name;
Euphelia serves to grace my measure,
    But Cloe is my real flame.

---

4. A people of western Asia, whose cavalry fought in the manner Prior describes.

5   My softest verse, my darling lyre,
     Upon Euphelia's toilet° lay;   *dressing table*
  When Cloe noted her desire
     That I should sing, that I should play.

My lyre I tune, my voice I raise,
10   But with my numbers mix my sighs;
  And whilst I sing Euphelia's praise,
     I fix my soul on Cloe's eyes.

Fair Cloe blushed; Euphelia frowned;
     I sung and gazed; I played and trembled;
15 And Venus to the Loves around[5]
     Remarked how ill we all dissembled.

                                      1718

A Reasonable Affliction

On his deathbed poor Lubin lies:
     His spouse is in despair:
With frequent sobs, and mutual cries,
     They both express their care.

5   A diff'rent cause, says Parson Sly,
     The same effect may give:
Poor Lubin fears, that he shall die;
     His wife, that he may live.

                                      1718

JONATHAN SWIFT
(1667–1745)

Frances Harris's Petition

TO THEIR EXCELLENCIES THE LORDS JUSTICES OF
IRELAND,[1] WRITTEN IN THE YEAR 1701

The humble petition of Frances Harries,
Who must starve and die a maid if it miscarries;
Humbly sheweth, that I went to warm myself in Lady Betty's
    chamber, because I was cold;
And I had in a purse seven pound, four shillings, and sixpence,
    besides farthings, in money and gold;
5 So because I had been buying things for my lady last night,
I was resolved to tell° my money, to see if it was right.   *count*
Now, you must know, because my trunk has a very bad lock,
Therefore all the money I have, which, God knows, is a very
    small stock,
I keep in my pocket, tied about my middle, next my smock.
10 So when I went to put up my purse, as God would have it,
    my smock was unripped,

5. Venus is the goddess of love; her attendant "Loves" are, in mythology, the goddesses of beauty; in the social context, they are attractive young ladies.
1. The Lord Justice chiefly involved was the Earl of Berkeley, whom Swift served in the capacity of chaplain from 1699 to 1701. Berkeley's daughter ("Lady Betty"), Frances Harris's mistress, was then a girl of sixteen. The other domestics in the poem are identifiable members of Berkeley's household.

And instead of putting it into my pocket, down it slipped;
Then the bell rung, and I went down to put my lady to bed;
And, God knows, I thought my money was as safe as my
   maidenhead.
So, when I came up again, I found my pocket feel very light;
15 But when I searched, and missed my purse, Lord! I thought
   I should have sunk outright.
"Lord! madam," says Mary,[2] "how d'ye do?"—"Indeed," says I,
   "never worse:
But pray, Mary, can you tell what I have done with my purse?"
"Lord help me!" says Mary, "I never stirred out of this place!"
"Nay," said I, "I had it in Lady Betty's chamber, that's a
   plain case."
20 So Mary got me to bed, and covered me up warm:
However, she stole away my garters, that I might do myself
   no harm.
So I tumbled and tossed all night, as you may very well think,
But hardly ever set my eyes together, or slept a wink.
So I was a-dreamed, methought, that I went and searched the
   folks round,
25 And in a corner of Mrs. Dukes's[3] box, tied in a rag, the
   money was found.
So next morning we told Whittle,[4] and he fell a-swearing:
Then my dame Wadgar[5] came, and she, you know, is thick
   of hearing.
"Dame," said I, as loud as I could bawl, "do you know what
   a loss I have had?"
"Nay," says she, "my Lord Colway's[6] folks are all very sad:
30 For my Lord Dromedary[7] comes a Tuesday without fail."
"Pugh!" said I, "but that's not the business that I ail."
Says Cary,[8] says he, "I have been a servant this five and twenty
   years come spring,
And in all the places I lived I never heard of such a thing."
"Yes," says the steward,[9] "I remember when I was at my
   Lord Shrewsbury's,
35 Such a thing as this happened, just about the time of
   gooseberries."
So I went to the party suspected, and I found her full of grief:
(Now, you must know, of all things in the world I hate a thief.)
However, I was resolved to bring the discourse slily about:
"Mrs. Dukes," said I, "here's an ugly accident has happened out:
40 'Tis not that I value the money three skips of a louse;
But the thing I stand upon is the credit of the house.
'Tis true, seven pound, four shillings, and sixpence, makes a
   great hole in my wages:
Besides, as they say, service is no inheritance in these ages.
Now, Mrs. Dukes, you know, and everybody understands,
45 That though 'tis hard to judge, yet money can't go without
   hands."
"The devil take me!" said she (blessing herself), "if ever
   I saw't!"
So she roared like a bedlam,° as though I had called her   **mad person**
   all to naught.

---

2. A housemaid.
3. Wife to one of the footmen.
4. The Earl of Berkeley's valet.
5. The old housekeeper.
6. A mispronunciation of "Galway," the Lord

Justice whose term coincided with Berkeley's.
7. Drogheda, a newly appointed Lord Justice.
8. Clerk of the kitchen.
9. One Ferris, whom Swift elsewhere called "a
scoundrel dog."

So, you know, what could I say to her any more?
I e'en left her, and came away as wise as I was before.
50 Well; but then they would have had me gone to the
cunning man:°   *fortune-teller*
"No," said I, " 'tis the same thing, the Chaplain[1] will be
here anon."
So the Chaplain came in. Now the servants say he is my
sweetheart,
Because he's always in my chamber, and I always take his part.
So, as the devil would have it, before I was aware, out I blundered,
55 "Parson," said I, "can you cast a nativity[2] when a body's
plundered?"
(Now you must know, he hates to be called Parson, like the
devil!)
"Truly," says he, "Mrs. Nab, it might become you to be
more civil;
If your money be gone, as a learned Divine[3] says, d'ye see,
You are no text for my handling; so take that from me:
60 I was never taken for a conjurer before, I'd have you to know."
"Lord!" said I, "don't be angry, I am sure I never thought
you so;
You know I honor the cloth; I design to be a parson's wife;
I never took one in your coat[4] for a conjurer in all my life."
With that he twisted his girdle at me like a rope, as who
should say,
65 "Now you may go hang yourself for me," and so went away.
Well: I thought I should have swooned. "Lord!" said I, "what
shall I do?
I have lost my money, and shall lose my true love too."
Then my lord called me: "Harry," said my lord, "don't cry;
I'll give you something toward thy loss." "And," says my lady,
"so will I."
70 "Oh! but," said I, "what if, after all, the Chaplain won't
come to?"
For that, he said (an't please your Excellencies) I must
petition you.
The premises tenderly considered, I desire your Excellencies'
protection,
And that I may have a share in next Sunday's collection;
And, over and above, that I may have your Excellencies' letter,
75 With an order for the Chaplain aforesaid, or, instead of him,
a better:
And then your poor petitioner, both night and day,
Or the Chaplain (for 'tis his trade) as in duty bound, shall
ever pray.

                                        1701   1709

A Description of a City Shower

Careful observers may foretell the hour
(By sure prognostics) when to dread a shower:
While rain depends,° the pensive cat gives o'er   *impends*
Her frolics, and pursues her tail no more.
5 Returning home at night, you'll find the sink°   *sewer*

---

1. Swift himself.
2. Discover things by astrology.
3. Conjecturally, a Dr. Bolton, who had been
advanced in the Church before Swift.
4. I.e., clerical garb.

Strike your offended sense with double stink.
If you be wise, then go not far to dine;
You'll spend in coach hire more than save in wine.
A coming shower your shooting corns presage,
10 Old aches throb, your hollow tooth will rage.
Sauntering in coffeehouse is Dulman° seen;   *dull-man*
He damns the climate and complains of spleen.°   *melancholy*
  Meanwhile the South,° rising with dabbled wings,   *south wind*
A sable cloud athwart the welkin° flings,   *sky*
15 That swilled more liquor than it could contain,
And, like a drunkard, gives it up again.
Brisk Susan whips her linen from the rope,
While the first drizzling shower is borne aslope:
Such is that sprinkling which some careless quean°   *wench*
20 Flirts on you from her mop, but not so clean:
You fly, invoke the gods; then turning, stop
To rail; she singing, still whirls on her mop.
Not yet the dust had shunned the unequal strife,
But, aided by the wind, fought still for life,
25 And wafted with its foe by violent gust,
'Twas doubtful which was rain and which was dust.
Ah! where must needy poet seek for aid,
When dust and rain at once his coat invade?
Sole coat, where dust cemented by the rain
30 Erects the nap, and leaves a mingled stain.
  Now in contiguous drops the flood comes down,   *doomed*
Threatening with deluge this devoted° town.   *spattered*
To shops in crowds the daggled° females fly,   *price*
Pretend to cheapen° goods, but nothing buy.   *law student / running*
35 The Templar° spruce, while every spout's abroach,°
Stays till 'tis fair, yet seems to call a coach.
The tucked-up sempstress walks with hasty strides,
While streams run down her oiled umbrella's sides.
Here various kinds, by various fortunes led,
40 Commence acquaintance underneath a shed.
Triumphant Tories and desponding Whigs[5]
Forget their feuds, and join to save their wigs.
Boxed in a chair° the beau impatient sits,   *sedan chair*
While spouts run clattering o'er the roof by fits,
45 And ever and anon with frightful din
The leather[6] sounds; he trembles from within.
So when Troy chairmen bore the wooden steed,
Pregnant with Greeks impatient to be freed
(Those bully Greeks, who, as the moderns do,
50 Instead of paying chairmen, run them through),
Laocoön struck the outside with his spear,
And each imprisoned hero quaked for fear.[7]
  Now from all parts the swelling kennels° flow,   *gutters*
And bear their trophies with them as they go:
55 Filth of all hues and odors seem to tell
What street they sailed from, by their sight and smell.
They, as each torrent drives with rapid force,
From Smithfield or St. Pulchre's shape their course,
And in huge confluence joined at Snow Hill ridge,

---

5. The Tories (Swift's party) had recently assumed power.
6. Leather roof of the sedan chair.

7. In *Aeneid* II, Laocoön so struck the side of the Trojan horse, frightening the Greeks within.

60   Fall from the conduit prone to Holborn Bridge.[8]
    Sweepings from butchers' stalls, dung, guts, and blood, ⎤
    Drowned puppies, stinking sprats,° all drenched in mud, ⎬   *herring*
    Dead cats, and turnip tops, come tumbling down the flood. ⎦

                                                       1710

A Satirical Elegy on the Death of a Late Famous General [9]

His Grace! impossible! what dead!
Of old age too, and in his bed!
And could that mighty warrior fall?
And so inglorious, after all!
5   Well, since he's gone, no matter how,
The last loud trump [1] must wake him now:
And, trust me, as the noise grows stronger,
He'd wish to sleep a little longer.
And could he be indeed so old
10 As by the newspapers we're told?
Threescore, I think, is pretty high;
'Twas time in conscience he should die.
This world he cumbered long enough;
He burnt his candle to the snuff;
15 And that's the reason, some folks think,
He left behind so great a s - - - k.
Behold his funeral appears,
Nor widow's sighs, nor orphan's tears,
Wont at such times each heart to pierce,
20 Attend the progress of his hearse.
But what of that, his friends may say,
He had those honors in his day.
True to his profit and his pride,
He made them weep before he died.
25   Come hither, all ye empty things,
Ye bubbles raised by breath of kings;
Who float upon the tide of state,
Come hither, and behold your fate.
Let pride be taught by this rebuke,
30 How very mean a thing's a Duke;
From all his ill-got honors flung,
Turned to that dirt from whence he sprung.

                                    1722   1764

Stella's Birthday[2]

MARCH 13, 1727

    This day, whate'er the fates decree,
Shall still° be kept with joy by me: *always*
This day then, let us not be told
That you are sick, and I grown old,
5 Nor think on our approaching ills,
And talk of spectacles and pills;
Tomorrow will be time enough

---

8. The sewage system referred to is fed first by the refuse of the Smithfield cattle market and drains at last into the open Fleet Ditch at Holborn Bridge.
9. The Duke of Marlborough, who died on June 16, 1722.
1. Or trumpet, calling the souls of the dead to judgment.
2. The forty-sixth birthday of Swift's devoted companion and protégée Esther Johnson.

To hear such mortifying stuff.
Yet since from reason may be brought
10 A better and more pleasing thought,
Which can in spite of all decays
Support a few remaining days:
From not the gravest of divines,
Accept for once some serious lines.
15   Although we now can form no more
Long schemes of life, as heretofore;
Yet you, while time is running fast,
Can look with joy on what is past.
      Were future happiness and pain
20 A mere contrivance of the brain,
As atheists argue, to entice
And fit their proselytes for vice
(The only comfort they propose,
To have companions in their woes),
25 Grant this the case, yet sure 'tis hard
That virtue, styled its own reward,
And by all sages understood
To be the chief of human good,
Should acting, die, nor leave behind
30 Some lasting pleasure in the mind,
Which, by remembrance, will assuage
Grief, sickness, poverty, and age;
And strongly shoot a radiant dart,
To shine through life's declining part.
35   Say, Stella, feel you no content,
Reflecting on a life well spent?
Your skillful hand employed to save
Despairing wretches from the grave;
And then supporting from your store
40 Those whom you dragged from death before
(So Providence on mortals waits,
Preserving what it first creates);
Your generous boldness to defend
An innocent and absent friend;
45 That courage which can make you just,
To merit humbled in the dust:
The detestation you express
For vice in all its glittering dress:
That patience under torturing pain,
50 Where stubborn stoics would complain.
      Must these like empty shadows pass,
Or forms reflected from a glass?
Or mere chimeras in the mind,
That fly and leave no marks behind?
55 Does not the body thrive and grow
By food of twenty years ago?
And, had it not been still supplied,
It must a thousand times have died.
Then who with reason can maintain
60 That no effects of food remain?
And is not virtue in mankind
The nutriment that feeds the mind?
Upheld by each good action past,
And still continued by the last:

65 Then who with reason can pretend
That all effects of virtue end?
     Believe me, Stella, when you show
That true contempt for things below,
Nor prize your life for other ends
70 Than merely to oblige your friends,
Your former actions claim their part,
And join to fortify your heart.
For virtue in her daily race,
Like Janus,[1] bears a double face,
75 Looks back with joy where she has gone,
And therefore goes with courage on.
She at your sickly couch will wait,
And guide you to some better state.
     O then, whatever Heaven intends,
80 Take pity on your pitying friends;
Nor let your ills affect your mind,
To fancy they can be unkind.
Me, surely me, you ought to spare,
Who gladly would your sufferings share;
85 Or give my scrap of life to you,
And think it far beneath your due;
You, to whose care so oft I owe
That I'm alive to tell you so.

1727

The Lady's Dressing Room

Five hours, (and who can do it less in?)
By haughty Celia spent in dressing;
The goddess from her chamber issues,
Arrayed in lace, brocades and tissues.
5   Strephon, who found the room was void,
And Betty otherwise employed,
Stole in, and took a strict survey,
Of all the litter as it lay;
Whereof, to make the matter clear,
10 An inventory follows here.
     And first a dirty smock appeared,
Beneath the armpits well besmeared.
Strephon, the rogue, displayed it wide,
And turned it round on every side.
15 On such a point few words are best,
And Strephon bids us guess the rest,
But swears how damnably the men lie,
In calling Celia sweet and cleanly.
Now listen while he next produces
20 The various combs for various uses,
Filled up with dirt so closely fixt,
No brush could force a way betwixt.
A paste of composition rare,
Sweat, dandruff, powder, lead [3] and hair;
25 A forehead cloth with oil upon't
To smooth the wrinkles on her front;

---

1. The Roman god of doors, with opposed faces,
one looking forward, the other back.   3. Then used to make hair glossy.

Here alum flower to stop the steams,
Exhaled from sour unsavory streams,
There night-gloves made of Tripsy's hide,
30 Bequeathed by Tripsy when she died,
With puppy water, beauty's help
Distilled from Tripsy's darling whelp;
Here gallypots [4] and vials placed,
Some filled with washes, some with paste,
35 Some with pomatum, paints and slops,
And ointments good for scabby chops.
Hard by a filthy basin stands,
Fouled with the scouring of her hands;
The basin takes whatever comes
40 The scrapings of her teeth and gums,
A nasty compound of all hues,
For here she spits, and here she spews.
But oh! it turned poor Strephon's bowels,
When he beheld and smelled the towels,
45 Begummed, bemattered, and beslimed
With dirt, and sweat, and earwax grimed.
No object Strephon's eye escapes,
Here petticoats in frowzy heaps;
Nor be the handkerchiefs forgot
50 All varnished o'er with snuff and snot.
The stockings why should I expose,
Stained with the marks of stinking toes;
Or greasy coifs and pinners [5] reeking,
Which Celia slept at least a week in?
55 A pair of tweezers next he found
To pluck her brows in arches round,
Or hairs that sink the forehead low,
Or on her chin like bristles grow.
    The virtues we must not let pass,
60 Of Celia's magnifying glass.
When frighted Strephon cast his eye on't
It showed visage of a giant.
A glass that can to sight disclose,
The smallest worm in Celia's nose,
65 And faithfully direct her nail
To squeeze it out from head to tail;
For catch it nicely by the head,
It must come out alive or dead.
    Why Strephon will you tell the rest?
70 And must you needs describe the chest?
That careless wench! no creature warn her
To move it out from yonder corner;
But leave it standing full in sight
For you to exercise your spite.
75 In vain the workman showed his wit
With rings and hinges counterfeit
To make it seem in this disguise
A cabinet to vulgar eyes;
For Strephon ventured to look in,
80 Resolved to go through thick and thin;
He lifts the lid, there needs no more,

---

4. Small ceramic pots, often containers for medicine.   5. Types of headwear.

He smelled it all the time before.
As from within Pandora's box,
When Epimetheus [6] op'd the locks,
85 A sudden universal crew
Of human evils upwards flew;
He still was comforted to find
That Hope at last remained behind;
So Strephon lifting up the lid,
90 To view what in the chest was hid.
The vapors flew from out the vent,
But Strephon cautious never meant
The bottom of the pan to grope,
And foul his hands in search of Hope.
95 O never may such vile machine
Be once in Celia's chamber seen!
O may she better learn to keep
Those "secrets of the hoary deep!"
     As mutton cutlets, prime of meat,
100 Which though with art you salt and beat
As laws of cookery require,
And toast them at the clearest fire;
If from adown the hopeful chops
The fat upon a cinder drops,
105 To stinking smoke it turns the flame
Pois'ning the flesh from whence it came,
And up exhales a greasy stench,
For which you curse the careless wench;
So things, which must not be expressed,
110 When plumped into the reeking chest,
Send up an excremental smell
To taint the parts from whence they fell.
The petticoats and gown perfume,
Which waft a stink round every room.
115 Thus finishing his grand survey,
Disgusted Strephon stole away
Repeating in his amorous fits,
Oh! Celia, Celia, Celia shits!
     But Vengeance, goddess never sleeping
120 Soon punished Strephon for his peeping;
His foul imagination links
Each Dame he sees with all her stinks:
And, if unsavory odors fly,
Conceives a lady standing by:
125 All women his description fits,
And both ideas jump like wits:
By vicious fancy coupled fast,
And still appearing in contrast.
I pity wretched Strephon blind
130 To all the charms of female kind;
Should I the queen of love refuse,
Because she rose from stinking ooze?
To him that looks behind the scene,
Satira's but some pocky quean.°   *whore*
135 When Celia in her glory shows,
If Strephon would but stop his nose

6. Pandora, created by the Greek gods as the
first human woman, brought with her to earth
a box containing all human ills which, when
it was opened, were released into the world,
leaving only Hope behind. Epimetheus, brother
of Prometheus, was her husband.

(Who now so impiously blasphemes
Her ointments, daubs, and paints and creams,
Her washes, slops, and every clout,°   *rag*
140 With which he makes so foul a rout°)   *fuss*
He soon would learn to think like me,
And bless his ravished sight to see
Such order from confusion sprung,
Such gaudy tulips raised from dung.

                                                         1730

The Day of Judgment

With a whirl of thought oppressed,
I sink from reverie to rest.
An horrid vision seized my head,
I saw the graves give up their dead.
5 Jove, armed with terrors, burst the skies,
And thunder roars and lightning flies.
Amazed, confused, its fate unknown,
The world stands trembling at his throne.
While each pale sinner hangs his head,
10 Jove, nodding, shook the heavens and said,
"Offending race of human kind,
By nature, reason, learning, blind;
You who through frailty stepped aside,
And you who never fell—through *pride;*
15 You who in different sects have shammed,
And come to see each other damned
(So some folks told you, but they knew
No more of Jove's designs than you);
The world's mad business now is o'er,
20 And I resent these pranks no more.
I to such blockheads set my wit!
I damn such fools!—Go, go, you're bit."°   *deceived*
                              ca. 1731   1775

JOSEPH ADDISON
(1672–1719)

Ode

The spacious firmament on high,
With all the blue ethereal sky,
And spangled heavens, a shining frame,
Their great Original proclaim.
5 The unwearied sun from day to day
Does his Creator's power display,
And publishes to every land
The work of an almighty hand.

Soon as the evening shades prevail,
10 The moon takes up the wondrous tale,
And nightly to the listening earth
Repeats the story of her birth;

Whilst all the stars that round her burn,
And all the planets in their turn,
15   Confirm the tidings as they roll,
And spread the truth from pole to pole.

What though in solemn silence, all
Move round this dark terrestrial ball?
What though nor real voice nor sound
20   Amidst their radiant orbs be found?
In Reason's ear they all rejoice,
And utter forth a glorious voice,
Forever singing as they shine:
"The hand that made us is divine!"

1712

ISAAC WATTS
(1674–1748)

The Day of Judgment

AN ODE ATTEMPTED IN ENGLISH SAPPHIC[1]

When the fierce north wind with his airy forces
Rears up the Baltic to a foaming fury,
And the red lightning with a storm of hail comes
          Rushing amain down,

5   How the poor sailors stand amazed and tremble,
While the hoarse thunder, like a bloody trumpet,
Roars a loud onset to the gaping waters,
          Quick to devour them!

Such shall the noise be and the wild disorder,
10   (If things eternal may be like these earthly)
Such the dire terror, when the great Archangel
          Shakes the creation,

Tears the strong pillars of the vault of heaven,
Breaks up old marble, the repose of princes;
15   See the graves open, and the bones arising,
          Flames all around 'em!

Hark, the shrill outcries of the guilty wretches!
Lively bright horror and amazing anguish
Stare through their eyelids, while the living worm lies
20   Gnawing within them.

Thoughts like old vultures prey upon their heart-strings,
And the smart twinges, when the eye beholds the
Lofty Judge frowning, and a flood of vengeance
          Rolling afore him.

25   Hopeless immortals! how they scream and shiver,
While devils push them to the pit wide-yawning
Hideous and gloomy, to receive them headlong
          Down to the center.

1. See Glossary, entry on **Sapphic strophe**, at the end of this anthology.

Stop here, my fancy: (all away ye horrid
30 Doleful ideas); come, arise to Jesus;
   How He sits God-like! and the saints around him
         Throned, yet adoring!

   Oh may I sit there when he comes triumphant
   Dooming the nations! then ascend to glory
35 While our hosannas all along the passage
         Shout the Redeemer.

1706

A Prospect of Heaven Makes Death Easy

There is a land of pure delight
  Where saints immortal reign;
Infinite day excludes the night,
  And pleasures banish pain.

5 There everlasting spring abides,
    And never-withering flowers:
  Death like a narrow sea divides
    This heavenly land from ours.

  Sweet fields beyond the swelling flood
10   Stand dressed in living green:
  So to the Jews old Canaan stood,
    While Jordan rolled between.

  But timorous mortals start and shrink
    To cross this narrow sea,
15 And linger shivering on the brink,
    And fear to launch away.

  Oh could we make our doubts remove,
    These gloomy doubts that rise,
  And see the Canaan that we love,
20   With unbeclouded eyes;

  Could we but climb where Moses stood
    And view the landscape o'er,
  Not Jordan's stream, nor death's cold flood,
    Should fright us from the shore.

1707

A Cradle Hymn

Hush, my dear, lie still and slumber;
Holy angels guard thy bed!
Heavenly blessings without number
Gently falling on thy head.

5 Sleep, my babe; thy food and raiment,
House and home thy friends provide;
All without thy care or payment,
All thy wants are well supplied.

How much better thou'rt attended
Than the Son of God could be,
When from Heaven he descended,
And became a child like thee!

Soft and easy is thy cradle;
Coarse and hard thy Saviour lay,
When his birth-place was a stable,
And his softest bed was hay.

Blessed Babe! what glorious features,
Spotless fair, divinely bright!
Must he dwell with brutal creatures?
How could angels bear the sight?

Was there nothing but a manger
Curséd sinners could afford,
To receive the heavenly Stranger?
Did they thus affront their Lord?

Soft, my child; I did not chide thee,
Though my song might sound too hard;
'Tis thy $\begin{Bmatrix} \text{Mother[2]} \\ \text{Nurse that} \end{Bmatrix}$ sits beside thee
And her arm shall be thy guard.

Yet to read the shameful story,
How the Jews abused their King,
How they served the Lord of Glory,
Makes me angry while I sing.

See the kinder shepherds round him,
Telling wonders from the sky;
There they sought him, there they found him,
With his Virgin-Mother by.

See the lovely Babe a-dressing;
Lovely Infant, how he smiled!
When he wept, the Mother's blessing
Soothed and hushed the holy Child.

Lo, he slumbers in his manger,
Where the hornéd oxen fed;
Peace, my darling, here's no danger,
Here's no ox anear thy bed.

'Twas to save thee, child, from dying,
Save my dear from burning flame,
Bitter groans, and endless crying,
That my blest Redeemer came.

Mayst thou live to know and fear him,
Trust and love him all thy days!
Then go dwell forever near him,
See his face, and sing his praise!

---

2. "Here you may use the words *Brother, Sister, Neighbor, Friend,* &c" [Watts's note].

I could give thee thousand kisses,
Hoping what I most desire;
55 Not a mother's fondest wishes
Can to greater joys aspire.

1720

JOHN GAY
(1685–1732)

Sweet William's Farewell to Black- eyed Susan

A BALLAD

All in the Downs[1] the fleet was moored,
    The streamers waving in the wind,
When black-eyed Susan came aboard.
    "Oh! where shall I my true love find?
5 Tell me, ye jovial sailors, tell me true,
If my sweet William sails among the crew."

William, who high upon the yard
    Rocked with the billow to and fro,
Soon as her well-known voice he heard,
10   He sighed and cast his eyes below;
The cord slides swiftly through his glowing hands,
And quick as lightning on the deck he stands.

So the sweet lark, high-poised in air,
    Shuts close his pinions to his breast,
15   (If, chance, his mate's shrill call he hear)
    And drops at once into her nest.
The noblest Captain in the British fleet
Might envy William's lip those kisses sweet.

"O Susan, Susan, lovely dear,
20   My vows shall ever true remain;
Let me kiss off that falling tear;
    We only part to meet again.
Change, as ye list, ye winds! my heart shall be
The faithful compass that still points to thee.

25 "Believe not what the landmen say,
    Who tempt with doubts thy constant mind;
They'll tell thee, sailors, when away,
    In every port a mistress find.
Yes, yes, believe them when they tell thee so,
30 For thou art present wheresoe'er I go.

"If to far India's coast we sail,
    Thy eyes are seen in diamonds bright,
Thy breath is Afric's spicy gale,
    Thy skin is ivory, so white.
35 Thus every beauteous object that I view,
Wakes in my soul some charm of lovely Sue.

1. An anchorage up the English Channel from Dover.

"Though battle call me from thy arms,
　　Let not my pretty Susan mourn;
Though cannons roar, yet safe from harms.
40　　William shall to his dear return.
Love turns aside the balls that round me fly,
Lest precious tears should drop from Susan's eye."

The boatswain gave the dreadful word,
　　The sails their swelling bosom spread,
45　No longer must she stay aboard;
　　They kissed, she sighed, he hung his head;
Her lessening boat unwilling rows to land;
"Adieu!" she cries, and waved her lily hand.

　　　　　　　　　　　　　　　　　　　　　　　　1720

From The Beggar's Opera[2]

Air XVI. *Over the Hills and Far Away*

MACH.　Were I laid on Greenland's coast,
　　　　And in my arms embraced my lass:
　　　　Warm amidst eternal frost,
　　　　Too soon the half year's night would pass.
5　POLLY.　Were I sold on Indian soil,
　　　　Soon as the burning day was closed,
　　　　I could mock the sultry toil,
　　　　When on my charmer's breast reposed.
MACH.　And I would love you all the day,
10　POLLY.　Every night would kiss and play,
MACH.　If with me you'd fondly stray
POLLY.　Over the hills and far away.

Air XXI. *Would You Have a Young Virgin*

If the heart of a man is depressed with cares,
The mist is dispelled when a woman appears;
　　Like the notes of a fiddle, she sweetly, sweetly
Raises the spirits, and charms our ears.
5　Roses and lilies her cheeks disclose,
　　But her ripe lips are more sweet than those.
　　　　　　Press her,
　　　　　　Caress her
　　　　　　With blisses,
10　　　　　Her kisses
Dissolve us in pleasure, and soft repose.

Air XLIV. *Lillibullero*

The modes of the court so common are grown
　　That a true friend can hardly be met;
Friendship for interest is but a loan,
　　Which they let out for what they can get.
5　　'Tis true, you find
　　　Some friends so kind,
Who will give you good counsel themselves to defend.

---

2. The following lyrics were written to be sung to the popular tunes identified in the headings. The singers in the first lyric are the highwayman Macheath, hero of the opera, and the heroine, Polly Peachum.

In sorrowful ditty,
They promise, they pity,
10 But shift you, for money, from friend to friend.

1728

ALEXANDER POPE
(1688–1744)

Ode on Solitude

Happy the man whose wish and care
A few paternal acres bound,
Content to breathe his native air,
In his own ground.

5 Whose herds with milk, whose fields with bread,
Whose flocks supply him with attire,
Whose trees in summer yield him shade,
In winter fire.

Blest, who can unconcernedly find
10 Hours, days, and years slide soft away,
In health of body, peace of mind,
Quiet by day,

Sound sleep by night; study and ease,
Together mixed; sweet recreation;
15 And innocence, which most does please
With meditation.

Thus let me live, unseen, unknown;
Thus unlamented let me die;
Steal from the world, and not a stone
20 Tell where I lie.

1700–1709   1717, 1736

From An Essay on Criticism

Part II

Of all the causes which conspire to blind
Man's erring judgment, and misguide the mind,
What the weak head with strongest bias rules,
Is pride, the never-failing vice of fools.
205 Whatever Nature has in worth denied,
She gives in large recruits° of needful pride;   *supplies*
For as in bodies, thus in souls, we find
What wants in blood and spirits swelled with wind:
Pride, where wit fails, steps in to our defense,
210 And fills up all the mighty void of sense.
If once right reason drives that cloud away,
Truth breaks upon us with resistless day.
Trust not yourself: but your defects to know,
Make use of every friend—and every foe.

215 A little learning is a dangerous thing;
Drink deep, or taste not the Pierian spring.[1]
There shallow draughts intoxicate the brain,
And drinking largely sobers us again.
Fired at first sight with what the Muse imparts,
220 In fearless youth we tempt° the heights of arts,   *attempt*
While from the bounded level of our mind
Short views we take, nor see the lengths behind;
But more advanced, behold with strange surprise
New distant scenes of endless science rise!
225 So pleased at first the towering Alps we try,
Mount o'er the vales, and seem to tread the sky,
The eternal snows appear already past,
And the first clouds and mountains seem the last;
But, those attained, we tremble to survey
230 The growing labors of the lengthened way,
The increasing prospect tires our wandering eyes,
Hills peep o'er hills, and Alps on Alps arise!
  A perfect judge will read each work of wit
With the same spirit that its author writ:
235 Survey the whole, nor seek slight faults to find
Where Nature moves, and rapture warms the mind;
Nor lose, for that malignant dull delight,
The generous pleasure to be charmed with wit.
But in such lays as neither ebb nor flow,
240 Correctly cold, and regularly low,
That, shunning faults, one quiet tenor keep,
We cannot blame indeed—but we may sleep.
In wit, as nature, what affects our hearts
Is not the exactness of peculiar° parts;   *particular*
245 'Tis not a lip, or eye, we beauty call,
But the joint force and full result of all.
Thus when we view some well-proportioned dome
(The world's just wonder, and even thine, O Rome! [2]),
No single parts unequally surprise,
250 All comes united to the admiring eyes:
No monstrous height, or breadth, or length appear;
The whole at once is bold and regular.
  Whoever thinks a faultless piece to see,
Thinks what ne'er was, nor is, nor e'er shall be.
255 In every work regard the writer's end,
Since none can compass more than they intend;
And if the means be just, the conduct true,
Applause, in spite of trivial faults, is due.
As men of breeding, sometimes men of wit,
260 To avoid great errors must the less commit,
Neglect the rules each verbal critic lays,
For not to know some trifles is a praise.
Most critics, fond of some subservient art,
Still make the whole depend upon a part:
265 They talk of principles, but notions prize,
And all to one loved folly sacrifice.
  Once on a time La Mancha's knight,[3] they say,
A certain bard encountering on the way,

---

1. The spring in Pieria on Mount Olympus, sacred to the muses.
2. Refers to the dome of St. Peter's Cathedral in the Vatican.
3. Don Quixote, hero of Cervantes' novel; but this story comes from a sequel to it by Don Alonzo Fernandez de Avellaneda.

Discoursed in terms as just, with looks as sage,
270 As e'er could Dennis,[4] of the Grecian stage;
Concluding all were desperate sots and fools
Who durst depart from Aristotle's rules.[5]
Our author, happy in a judge so nice,°   *overrefined*
Produced his play, and begged the knight's advice;
275 Made him observe the subject and the plot,
The manners, passions, unities; what not?
All which exact to rule were brought about,
Were but a combat in the lists° left out.   *arena*
"What! leave the combat out?" exclaims the knight.
280 "Yes, or we must renounce the Stagirite." [6]
"Not so, by Heaven!" he answers in a rage,
"Knights, squires, and steeds must enter on the stage."
"So vast a throng the stage can ne'er contain."
"Then build a new, or act it in a plain."
285   Thus critics of less judgment than caprice,
Curious,° not knowing, not exact, but nice,   *laboriously careful*
Form short ideas, and offend in arts
(As most in manners), by a love to parts.
Some to conceit [7] alone their taste confine,
290 And glittering thoughts struck out at every line;
Pleased with a work where nothing's just or fit,
One glaring chaos and wild heap of wit.
Poets, like painters, thus unskilled to trace
The naked nature and the living grace,
295 With gold and jewels cover every part,
And hide with ornaments their want of art.
True wit is Nature to advantage dressed,
What oft was thought, but ne'er so well expressed;
Something worse truth convinced at sight we find,
300 That gives us back the image of our mind.
As shades more sweetly recommend the light,
So modest plainness sets off sprightly wit;
For works may have more wit than does them good,
As bodies perish through excess of blood.
305   Others for language all their care express,
And value books, as women men, for dress.
Their praise is still—the style is excellent;
The sense they humbly take upon contént.°   *mere acquiescence*
Words are like leaves; and where they most abound,
310 Much fruit of sense beneath is rarely found.
False eloquence, like the prismatic glass,
Its gaudy colors spreads on every place;
The face of Nature we no more survey,
All glares alike, without distinction gay.
315 But true expression, like the unchanging sun,   ⎫
Clears and improves whate'er it shines upon;   ⎬
It gilds all objects, but it alters none.   ⎭
Expression is the dress of thought, and still
Appears more decent as more suitable.
320 A vile conceit in pompous words expressed
Is like a clown in regal purple dressed:

---

4. John Dennis (1657–1734), an Engish critic.
5. Refers to the description of the purpose
and forms of tragic drama contained in
Aristotle's *Poetics*.
6. That is, Aristotle, who was a native of
Stagira. One of his principles was that tragic

drama should maintain unity of time and
place.
7. Pointed wit, ingenuity and extravagance,
or affectation in the use of figures, especially
similes and metaphors.

For different styles with different subjects sort,
As several garbs with country, town, and court.
Some by old words to fame have made pretense,
325 Ancients in phrase, mere moderns in their sense.
Such labored nothings, in so strange a style,
Amaze the unlearn'd, and make the learned smile;
Unlucky as Fungoso [8] in the play,
These sparks with awkward vanity display
330 What the fine gentleman wore yesterday;
And but so mimic ancient wits at best,
As apes our grandsires in their doublets [9] dressed.
In words as fashions the same rule will hold,
Alike fantastic if too new or old.
335 Be not the first by whom the new are tried,
Nor yet the last to lay the old aside.

But most by numbers° judge a poet's song,   *versification*
And smooth or rough with them is right or wrong.
In the bright Muse though thousand charms conspire,
340 Her voice is all these tuneful fools admire,
Who haunt Parnassus [1] but to please their ear,
Not mend their minds; as some to church repair,
Not for the doctrine, but the music there.
These equal syllables alone require,
345 Though oft the ear the open vowels tire,
While expletives [2] their feeble aid do join,
And ten low words oft creep in one dull line:
While they ring round the same unvaried chimes,
With sure returns of still expected rhymes;
350 Where'er you find "the cooling western breeze,"
In the next line, it "whispers through the trees";
If crystal streams "with pleasing murmurs creep,"
The reader's threatened (not in vain) with "sleep";
Then, at the last and only couplet fraught
355 With some unmeaning thing they call a thought,
A needless Alexandrine [3] ends the song
That, like a wounded snake, drags its slow length along.
Leave such to tune their own dull rhymes, and know
What's roundly smooth or languishingly slow;
360 And praise the easy vigor of a line
Where Denham's strength and Waller's sweetness join.[4]
True ease in writing comes from art, not chance,
As those move easiest who have learned to dance.
'Tis not enough no harshness gives offense,
365 The sound must seem an echo to the sense.
Soft is the strain when Zephyr [5] gently blows,
And the smooth stream in smoother numbers flows;
But when loud surges lash the sounding shore,
The hoarse, rough verse should like the torrent roar.
370 When Ajax [6] strives some rock's vast weight to throw,
The line too labors, and the words move slow;

---

8. A character in Ben Jonson's comedy *Every Man out of His Humor.*
9. A jacket in a style popular in the 16th and 17th centuries.
1. The mountain in Greece sacred to the Muses.
2. A word added to fill out a line—for example, "do" in this line.
3. A line in iambic hexameter—for example, the next line.

4. Dryden, whom Pope echoes here, considered Sir John Denham (1615–1669) and Edmund Waller (1606–1687) to have been the principal shapers of the closed pentameter couplet.
5. The west wind.
6. The strongest, though not the most intelligent, of the Greek warriors in the war with Troy. He is contrasted with Camilla, a swift-footed messenger of the moon goddess Diana.

Not so when swift Camilla scours the plain,
Flies o'er the unbending corn, and skims along the main.
Hear how Timotheus' [7] varied lays surprise,
75   And bid alternate passions fall and rise!
While at each change the son of Libyan Jove [8]
Now burns with glory, and then melts with love;
Now his fierce eyes with sparkling fury glow,
Now sighs steal out, and tears begin to flow:
380   Persians and Greeks like turns of nature [9] found
And the world's victor stood subdued by sound!
The power of music all our hearts allow,
And what Timotheus was is Dryden now.

　　Avoid extremes; and shun the fault of such
385   Who still are pleased too little or too much.
At every trifle scorn to take offense:
That always shows great pride, or little sense.
Those heads, as stomachs, are not sure the best,
Which nauseate all, and nothing can digest.
390   Yet let not each gay turn thy rapture move;
For fools admire,° but men of sense approve: [1]   *wonder*
As things seem large which we through mists descry,
Dullness is ever apt to magnify.

　　Some foreign writers, some our own despise;
395   The ancients only, or the moderns prize.
Thus wit, like faith, by each man is applied
To one small sect, and all are damned beside.
Meanly they seek the blessing to confine,
And force that sun but on a part to shine,
400   Which not alone the southern wit sublimes,
But ripens spirits in cold northern climes;
Which from the first has shone on ages past,
Enlights the present, and shall warm the last;
Though each may feel increases and decays,
405   And see now clearer and now darker days.
Regard not then if wit be old or new,
But blame the false and value still the true.

　　Some ne'er advance a judgment of their own,
But catch the spreading notion of the town;
410   They reason and conclude by precedent,
And own [2] stale nonsense which they ne'er invent.
Some judge of authors' names, not works, and then
Nor praise nor blame the writings, but the men.
Of all this servile herd the worst is he
415   That in proud dullness joins with quality,
A constant critic at the great man's board,
To fetch and carry nonsense for my lord.
What woeful stuff this madrigal would be
In some starved hackney [3] sonneteer or me!
420   But let a lord once own [4] the happy lines,
How the wit brightens! how the style refines!
Before his sacred name flies every fault,
And each exalted stanza teems with thought!

　　The vulgar thus through imitation err;
425   As oft the learn'd by being singular;°   *peculiar*

7. The musician in Dryden's *Alexander's Feast.*
8. Alexander the Great.
9. Alternations of feelings.

1. I.e., only after due deliberation.
2. Claim as their own.
3. For hire.
4. Acknowledge as his.

So much they scorn the crowd, that if the throng
By chance go right, they purposely go wrong.
So schísmatics⁵ the plain believers quit,
And are but damned for having too much wit.
430 Some praise at morning what they blame at night,
But always think the last opinion right.
A Muse by these is like a mistress used,
This hour she's idolized, the next abused;
While their weak heads like towns unfortified,
435 'Twixt sense and nonsense daily change their side.
Ask them the cause; they're wiser still, they say;
And still tomorrow's wiser than today.
We think our fathers fools, so wise we grow;
Our wiser sons, no doubt, will think us so.
440 Once school divines⁶ this zealous isle o'erspread;
Who knew most sentences⁷ was deepest read.
Faith, Gospel, all seemed made to be disputed,
And none had sense enough to be confuted.
Scotists and Thomists now in peace remain
445 Amidst their kindred cobwebs in Duck Lane.⁸
If faith itself has different dresses worn,
What wonder modes in wit should take their turn?
Oft, leaving what is natural and fit,
The current folly proves the ready wit;
450 And authors think their reputation safe,
Which lives as long as fools are pleased to laugh.
      Some valuing those of their own side or mind,
Still make themselves the measure of mankind:
Fondly° we think we honor merit then,   *foolishly*
455 When we but praise ourselves in other men.
Parties in wit attend on those of state,
And public faction doubles private hate.
Pride, Malice, Folly against Dryden rose,
In various shapes of parsons, critics, beaux;
460 But sense survived, when merry jests were past;
For rising merit will buoy up at last.
Might he return and bless once more our eyes,
New Blackmores and new Milbourns must arise.⁹
Nay, should great Homer lift his awful head,
465 Zoilus¹ again would start up from the dead.
Envy will merit, as its shade, pursue,
But like a shadow, proves the substance true;
For envied wit, like Sol° eclipsed, makes known   *the sun*
The opposing body's grossness, not its own.
470 When first that sun too powerful beams displays,
It draws up vapors which obscure its rays;
But even those clouds at last adorn its way,
Reflect new glories, and augment the day.
      Be thou the first true merit to befriend;
475 His praise is lost who stays till all commend.
Short is the date, alas! of modern rhymes,

---

5. Those who divide the church on points of theology.
6. Scholastic philosophers such as the Scotists and Thomists (followers of the medieval theologians Duns Scotus and St. Thomas Aquinas) mentioned below.
7. Alludes to Peter Lombard's *Book of Sentences,* a theological work.

8. Where second-hand and remaindered books were sold.
9. Sir Richard Blackmore, physician and poet, had attacked Dryden for the immorality of his plays; the Rev. Luke Milbourn had attacked his translation of Virgil.
1. A Greek critic of the 4th century B.C. who wrote a book of carping criticism of Homer.

And 'tis but just to let them live betimes.°   *early*
No longer now that golden age appears,
When patriarch wits survived a thousand years:
80   Now length of fame (our second life) is lost,
And bare threescore is all even that can boast;
Our sons their fathers' failing language see,
And such as Chaucer is shall Dryden be.
So when the faithful pencil has designed
85   Some bright idea of the master's mind,
Where a new world leaps out at his command,
And ready Nature waits upon his hand;
When the ripe colors soften and unite,
And sweetly melt into just shade and light;
90   When mellowing years their full perfection give,
And each bold figure just begins to live,
The treacherous colors the fair art betray,
And all the bright creation fades away!
    Unhappy wit, like most mistaken things,
495   Atones not for that envy which it brings.
In youth alone its empty praise we boast,
But soon the short-lived vanity is lost;
Like some fair flower the early spring supplies,
That gaily blooms, but even in blooming dies,
500   What is this wit, which must our cares employ?
The owner's wife, that other men enjoy;
Then most our trouble still when most admired,
And still the more we give, the more required;
Whose fame with pains we guard, but lose with ease,
505   Sure some to vex, but never all to please;
'Tis what the vicious fear, the virtuous shun,
By fools 'tis hated, and by knaves undone!
    If wit so much from ignorance undergo,
Ah, let not learning too commence its foe!
510   Of old those met rewards who could excel,
And such were praised who but endeavored well;
Though triumphs were to generals only due,
Crowns were reserved to grace the soldiers too.
Now they who reach Parnassus' lofty crown
515   Employ their pains to spurn some others down;
And while self-love each jealous writer rules,
Contending wits become the sport of fools;
But still the worst with most regret commend,
For each ill author is as bad a friend.
520   To what base ends, and by what abject ways,
Are morals urged through sacred° lust of praise!   *accursed*
Ah, ne'er so dire a thirst of glory boast,
Nor in the critic let the man be lost!
Good nature and good sense must ever join;
525   To err is human, to forgive divine.
    But if in the noble minds some dregs remain
Nor yet purged off, spleen and sour disdain,
Discharge that rage on more provoking crimes,
Nor fear a dearth in these flagitious° times.   *shameful, wicked*
530   No pardon vile obscenity should find,
Though wit and art conspire to move your mind;
But dullness with obscenity must prove
As shameful sure as impotence in love.

₅₃₅ In the fat age of pleasure, wealth, and ease
Sprung the rank weed, and thrived with large increase:
When love was all an easy monarch's [2] care,
Seldom at council, never in a war;
Jilts ruled the state, and statesmen farces writ;
Nay, wits had pensions, and young lords had wit;
₅₄₀ The fair sat panting at a courtier's play,
And not a mask [3] went unimproved away;
The modest fan was lifted up no more,
And virgins smiled at what they blushed before.
The following license of a foreign reign [4]
₅₄₅ Did all the dregs of bold Socinus [5] drain;
Then unbelieving priests reformed the nation,
And taught more pleasant methods of salvation;
Where Heaven's free subjects might their rights dispute,
Lest God himself should seem too absolute;
₅₅₀ Pulpits their sacred satire learned to spare,
And Vice admired to find a flatterer there!
Encouraged thus, wit's Titans [6] braved the skies,
And the press groaned with licensed blasphemies.
These monsters, critics! with your darts engage,
₅₅₅ Here point your thunder, and exhaust your rage!
Yet shun their fault, who, scandalously nice,
Will needs mistake an author into vice;
All seems infected that the infected spy,
As all looks yellow to the jaundiced eye.

                                                    1709   1711

The Rape of the Lock

AN HEROI-COMICAL POEM[1]

Nolueram, Belinda, tuos violare capillos;
sed juvat hoc precibus me tribuisse tuis.[2]
                    —MARTIAL

Canto I

What dire offense from amorous causes springs,
What mighty contests rise from trivial things,
I sing—This verse to Caryll, Muse! is due:
This, even Belinda may vouchsafe to view:
₅ Slight is the subject, but not so the praise,
If she inspire, and he approve my lays.
Say what strange motive, Goddess! could compel
A well-bred lord to assault a gentle belle?
Oh, say what stranger cause, yet unexplored,

---

2. Charles II, king of England from 1660 to 1685. The following lines describe the corruption of morals and letters under this recently dead monarch.
3. A woman in a mask, as at a masquerade.
4. That of William III, king of England from 1689 to 1702. He was born in Holland.
5. The name of two Italian theologians of the 16th century who denied the divinity of Jesus.
6. Primordial giants, whose rule over the earth was broken by the Greek gods.
1. Based on an actual incident. A young man, Lord Petre, had sportively cut off a lock of a Miss Arabella Fermor's hair. She and her family were angered by the prank, and Pope's friend John Caryll (line 3), a relative

of Lord Petre's, asked the poet to turn the incident into jest, so that good relations (and possibly negotiations toward a marriage between the principals) might be resumed. Pope responded by treating the incident in a mock epic or "heroi-comical poem." The epic conventions first encountered are the immediate statement of the topic, which the poet says he will "sing" as if in oral recitation, and the request to the Muse (line 7) to grant him the necessary insight.
2. "I did not want, Belinda, to violate your locks, but it pleases me to have paid this tribute to your prayers." Miss Fermor did not in fact request the poem.

10 Could make a gentle belle reject a lord?
    In tasks so bold can little men engage,
    And in soft bosoms dwells such mighty rage?
        Sol through white curtains shot a timorous ray,
    And oped those eyes that must eclipse the day.[3]
15 Now lapdogs give themselves the rousing shake,
    And sleepless lovers just at twelve awake:
    Thrice rung the bell, the slipper knocked the ground,[4]
    And the pressed watch returned a silver sound.[5]
    Belinda still her downy pillow pressed,
20 Her guardian Sylph[6] prolonged the balmy rest:
    'Twas he had summoned to her silent bed
    The morning dream that hovered o'er her head.
    A youth more glittering than a birthnight beau[7]
    (That even in slumber caused her cheek to glow)
25 Seemed to her ear his winning lips to lay,
    And thus in whispers said, or seemed to say:
        "Fairest of mortals, thou distinguished care
    Of thousand bright inhabitants of air!
    If e'er one vision touched thy infant thought,
30 Of all the nurse and all the priest have taught,
    Of airy elves by moonlight shadows seen,
    The silver token, and the circled green,[8]
    Or virgins visited by angel powers,
    With golden crowns and wreaths of heavenly flowers,
35 Hear and believe! thy own importance know,
    Nor bound thy narrow views to things below.
    Some secret truths, from learned pride concealed,
    To maids alone and children are revealed:
    What though no credit doubting wits may give?
40 The fair and innocent shall still believe.
    Know, then, unnumbered spirits round thee fly,
    The light militia of the lower sky:
    These, though unseen, are ever on the wing,
    Hang o'er the box, and hover round the Ring.[9]
45 Think what an equipage thou hast in air,
    And view with scorn two pages and a chair.°   *sedan chair*
    As now your own, our beings were of old,
    And once enclosed in woman's beauteous mold;
    Thence, by a soft transition, we repair
50 From earthly vehicles[1] to these of air.
    Think not, when woman's transient breath is fled,
    That all her vanities at once are dead:
    Succeeding vanities she still regards,
    And though she plays no more, o'erlooks the cards.
55 Her joy in gilded chariots,° when alive,   *carriages*
    And love of ombre,[2] after death survive.
    For when the Fair in all their pride expire,

---

3. The eyes of lovely young women—though Belinda herself is still asleep.
4. These are two ways of summoning servants.
5. In the darkened beds, one discovered the approximate time by a watch which chimed the hour and quarter-hour when the stem was pressed.
6. Air-spirit. He accounts for himself in the lines below.
7. Courtier dressed for a royal birthday celebration.

8. The silver token is the coin left by a fairy or elf, and the circled green is a ring of bright green grass, supposed dancing circle of fairies.
9. The box is a theater box; the Ring, the circular carriage course in Hyde Park.
1. Mediums of existence, with a side glance at the fondness of young women for riding in carriages.
2. A popular card game, pronounced *omber*.

To their first elements their souls retire:[3]
The sprites of fiery termagants in flame
60 Mount up, and take a Salamander's name.
Soft yielding minds to water glide away,
And sip, with Nymphs, their elemental tea.[4]
The graver prude sinks downward to a Gnome,
In search of mischief still on earth to roam.
65 The light coquettes in Sylphs aloft repair,
And sport and flutter in the fields of air.
    "Know further yet; whoever fair and chaste
Rejects mankind, is by some Sylph embraced:
For spirits, freed from mortal laws, with ease
70 Assume what sexes and what shapes they please.[5]
What guards the purity of melting maids,
In courtly balls, and midnight masquerades,
Safe from the treacherous friend, the daring spark,
The glance by day, the whisper in the dark,
75 When kind occasion prompts their warm desires,
When music softens, and when dancing fires?
'Tis but their Sylph, the wise Celestials know,
Though Honor is the word with men below.
    "Some nymphs there are, too conscious of their face,
80 For life predestined to the Gnomes' embrace.
These swell their prospects and exalt their pride,
When offers are disdained, and love denied:
Then gay ideas° crowd the vacant brain,   imaginings
While peers, and dukes, and all their sweeping train,
85 And garters, stars, and coronets[6] appear,
And in soft sounds, 'your Grace' salutes their ear.
'Tis these that early taint the female soul,
Instruct the eyes of young coquettes to roll,
Teach infant cheeks a bidden blush to know,
90 And little hearts to flutter at a beau.
    "Oft, when the world imagine women stray,
The Sylphs through mystic mazes guide their way,
Through all the giddy circle they pursue,
And old impertinence expel by new.
95 What tender maid but must a victim fall
To one man's treat, but for another's ball?
When Florio speaks what virgin could withstand,
If gentle Damon did not squeeze her hand?
With varying vanities, from every part,
100 They shift the moving toyshop of their heart;
Where wigs with wigs, with sword-knots sword-knots strive,[7]
Beaux banish beaux, and coaches coaches drive.
This erring mortals levity may call;
Oh, blind to truth! the Sylphs contrive it all.

3. Namely, to fire, water, earth, and air, the four elements of the old cosmology and the several habitats (in the Rosicrucian myths upon which Pope embroiders) of four different kinds of "spirit." Envisaging these spirits as the transmigrated souls of different kinds of women, Pope causes termagants (scolds) to become fire-spirits or Salamanders (line 60); irresolute women to become water-spirits or Nymphs (line 62); prudes, or women who delight in rejection and negation, to become earth-spirits or Gnomes (line 64); and coquettes to become air-spirits or Sylphs. Since "nymph" could designate either a water-spirit or (in literary usage) a young lady, Pope permits his water-spirits to claim tea as their native element (line 62) and to keep their former company at tea-parties.
4. Pronounced *tay.*
5. Like Milton's angels (*Paradise Lost* I.423 ff.).
6. Insignia of rank and court status.
7. Sword-Knots are ribbons tied to hilts. The verbal repetition and the tangled syntax recall descriptions of the throng and press of battle appearing in English translations of classical epic.

105   "Of these am I, who thy protection claim,
A watchful sprite, and Ariel is my name.
Late, as I ranged the crystal wilds of air,
In the clear mirror of thy ruling star
I saw, alas! some dread event impend,
110   Ere to the main this morning sun descend,
But Heaven reveals not what, or how, or where:
Warned by the Sylph, O pious maid, beware!
This to disclose is all thy guardian can:
Beware of all, but most beware of Man!"
115   He said; when Shock,[8] who thought she slept too long,
Leaped up, and waked his mistress with his tongue.
'Twas then, Belinda, if report say true,
Thy eyes first opened on a billet-doux;[9]
Wounds, charms, and ardors were no sooner read,
120   But all the vision vanished from thy head.
    And now, unveiled, the toilet stands displayed,
Each silver vase in mystic order laid.
First, robed in white, the nymph intent adores,
With head uncovered, the cosmetic powers.
125   A heavenly image in the glass[1] appears;
To that she bends, to that her eyes she rears.
The inferior priestess, at her altar's side,
Trembling begins the sacred rites of pride.
Unnumbered treasures ope at once, and here
130   The various offerings of the world appear;
From each she nicely culls with curious toil,
And decks the goddess with the glittering spoil.
This casket India's glowing gems unlocks,
And all Arabia[2] breathes from yonder box.
135   The tortoise here and elephant unite,
Transformed to combs, the speckled and the white.
Here files of pins extend their shining rows,
Puffs, powders, patches, Bibles, billet-doux.
Now awful Beauty put on all its arms;
140   The fair each moment rises in her charms,
Repairs her smiles, awakens every grace,
And calls forth all the wonders of her face;
Sees by degrees a purer blush arise,
And keener lightnings quicken in her eyes.
145   The busy Sylphs surround their darling care,
These set the head, and those divide the hair,
Some fold the sleeve, whilst others plait the gown;
And Betty's praised for labors not her own.

Canto II

    Not with more glories, in the ethereal plain,
The sun first rises o'er the purpled main,
Than, issuing forth, the rival of his beams[3]
Launched on the bosom of the silver Thames.
5   Fair nymphs and well-dressed youths around her shone,

---

8. A name for lapdogs (like "Poll" for parrots); they looked like little "shocks" of hair.
9. A love letter. The affected language of the fashionable love letter is exhibited in the next line.
1. The mirror. Her image is the object of veneration, the "goddess" named later. Belinda presides over the appropriate rites. Betty, her maid, is the "inferior priestess."
2. Source of perfumes.
3. I.e., Belinda. She is en route to Hampton Court, a royal palace some twelve miles up the river Thames from London.

But every eye was fixed on her alone.
On her white breast a sparkling cross she wore,
Which Jews might kiss, and infidels adore.
Her lively looks a sprightly mind disclose,
10   Quick as her eyes, and as unfixed as those:
Favors to none, to all she smiles extends;
Oft she rejects, but never once offends.
Bright as the sun, her eyes the gazers strike,
And, like the sun, they shine on all alike.
15   Yet graceful ease, and sweetness void of pride,
Might hide her faults, if belles had faults to hide:
If to her share some female errors fall,
Look on her face, and you'll forget 'em all.
     This nymph, to the destruction of mankind,
20   Nourished two locks which graceful hung behind
In equal curls, and well conspired to deck
With shining ringlets the smooth ivory neck.
Love in these labyrinths his slaves detains,
And mighty hearts are held in slender chains.
25   With hairy springes° we the birds betray,   *snares*
Slight lines of hair surprise the finny prey,
Fair tresses man's imperial race ensnare,
And beauty draws us with a single hair.
     The adventurous Baron the bright locks admired,
30   He saw, he wished, and to the prize aspired.
Resolved to win, he meditates the way,
By force to ravish, or by fraud betray;
For when success a lover's toil attends,
Few ask if fraud or force attained his ends.
35   For this, ere Phoebus rose, he had implored
Propitious Heaven, and every power adored,
But chiefly Love—to Love an altar built,
Of twelve vast French romances, neatly gilt.
There lay three garters, half a pair of gloves,
40   And all the trophies of his former loves.
With tender billet-doux he lights the pyre,
And breathes three amorous sighs to raise the fire.
Then prostrate falls, and begs with ardent eyes
Soon to obtain, and long possess the prize:
45   The powers gave ear, and granted half his prayer,
The rest the winds dispersed in empty air.
     But now secure the painted vessel glides,
The sunbeams trembling on the floating tides,
While melting music steals upon the sky,
50   And softened sounds along the waters die.
Smooth flow the waves, the zephyrs gently play,
Belinda smiled, and all the world was gay.
All but the Sylph—with careful thoughts oppressed,
The impending woe sat heavy on his breast.
55   He summons straight his denizens° of air;   *inhabitants*
The lucid squadrons round the sails repair:°   *assemble*
Soft o'er the shrouds aërial whispers breathe
That seemed but zephyrs to the train beneath.
Some to the sun their insect-wings unfold,
60   Waft on the breeze, or sink in clouds of gold.
Transparent forms too fine for mortal sight,
Their fluid bodies half dissolved in light,

Loose to the wind their airy garments flew,
Thin glittering textures of the filmy dew,[4]
65 Dipped in the richest tincture of the skies,
Where light disports in ever-mingling dyes,
While every beam new transient colors flings,
Colors that change whene'er they wave their wings.
Amid the circle, on the gilded mast,
70 Superior by the head was Ariel placed;
His purple° pinions opening to the sun,   *brilliant*
He raised his azure wand, and thus begun:
    "Ye Sylphs and Sylphids, to your chief give ear!
Fays, Fairies, Genii, Elves, and Daemons, hear!
75 Ye know the spheres and various tasks assigned
By laws eternal to the aërial kind.
Some in the fields of purest ether play,
And bask and whiten in the blaze of day.
Some guide the course of wandering orbs on high,
80 Or roll the planets through the boundless sky.
Some less refined, beneath the moon's pale light
Pursue the stars that shoot athwart the night,
Or suck the mists in grosser air below,
Or dip their pinions in the painted bow,°   *rainbow*
85 Or brew fierce tempests on the wintry main,
Or o'er the glebe° distill the kindly rain.   *farmland*
Others on earth o'er human race preside,
Watch all their ways, and all their actions guide:
Of these the chief the care of nations own,
90 And guard with arms divine the British Throne.
    "Our humbler province is to tend the Fair,
Not a less pleasing, though less glorious care:
To save the powder from too rude a gale,
Nor let the imprisoned essences exhale;
95 To draw fresh colors from the vernal flowers;
To steal from rainbows e'er they drop in showers
A brighter wash;° to curl their waving hairs,   *(cosmetic) wash*
Assist their blushes, and inspire their airs;
Nay oft, in dreams invention we bestow,
100 To change a flounce, or add a furbelow.
    "This day black omens threat the brightest fair,
That e'er deserved a watchful spirit's care;
Some dire disaster, or by force or slight,
But what, or where, the Fates have wrapped in night:
105 Whether the nymph shall break Diana's law,[5]
Or some frail china jar receive a flaw,
Or stain her honor or her new brocade,
Forget her prayers, or miss a masquerade,
Or lose her heart, or necklace, at a ball;
110 Or whether Heaven has doomed that Shock must fall.
Haste, then, ye spirits! to your charge repair:
The fluttering fan be Zephyretta's care;
The drops° to thee, Brillante, we consign;   *earrings*
And, Momentilla, let the watch be thine;
115 Do thou, Crispissa,[6] tend her favorite Lock;
Ariel himself shall be the guard of Shock.

---

4. The supposed material of spider webs.   6. To "crisp" is to curl (hair).
5. Of chastity.

"To fifty chosen Sylphs, of special note,
We trust the important charge, the petticoat;
Oft have we known that sevenfold fence to fail,
120 Though stiff with hoops, and armed with ribs of whale.
Form a strong line about the silver bound,
And guard the wide circumference around.
"Whatever spirit, careless of his charge,
His post neglects, or leaves the fair at large,
125 Shall feel sharp vengeance soon o'ertake his sins,
Be stopped in vials, or transfixed with pins,
Or plunged in lakes of bitter washes lie,
Or wedged whole ages in a bodkin's° eye;   *large needle's*
Gums and pomatums shall his flight restrain,
130 While clogged he beats his silken wings in vain,
Or alum styptics with contracting power
Shrink his thin essence like a riveled° flower: *shriveled*
Or, as Ixion[7] fixed, the wretch shall feel
The giddy motion of the whirling mill,°   *cocoa-mill*
135 In fumes of burning chocolate shall glow,
And tremble at the sea that froths below!"
    He spoke; the spirits from the sails descend;
Some, orb in orb, around the nymph extend;
Some thread the mazy ringlets of her hair;
140 Some hang upon the pendants of her ear:
With beating hearts the dire event they wait,
Anxious, and trembling for the birth of Fate.

Canto III

Close by those meads, forever crowned with flowers,
Where Thames with pride surveys his rising towers,
There stands a structure of majestic frame,[8]
Which from the neighboring Hampton takes its name.
5 Here Britain's statesmen oft the fall foredoom
Of foreign tyrants and of nymphs at home;
Here thou, great Anna! whom three realms obey,
Dost sometimes counsel take—and sometimes tea.
    Hither the heroes and the nymphs resort,
10 To taste awhile the pleasures of a court;
In various talk the instructive hours they passed,
Who gave the ball, or paid the visit last;
One speaks the glory of the British Queen,
And one describes a charming Indian screen;
15 A third interprets motions, looks, and eyes;
At every word a reputation dies.
Snuff, or the fan, supply each pause of chat,
With singing, laughing, ogling, and all that.
    Meanwhile, declining from the noon of day,
20 The sun obliquely shoots his burning ray;
The hungry judges soon the sentence sign,
And wretches hang that jurymen may dine;
The merchant from the Exchange° returns in peace,   *stock market*
And the long labors of the toilet cease.
25 Belinda now, whom thirst of fame invites,
Burns to encounter two adventurous knights,

---

7. For an affront to Juno, Ixion was bound   8. Hampton Court.
eternally to a turning wheel.

At ombre[9] singly to decide their doom,
And swells her breast with conquests yet to come.
Straight the three bands prepare in arms° to join,   *combat*
30   Each band the number of the sacred nine.
Soon as she spreads her hand, the aërial guard
Descend, and sit on each important card:
First Ariel perched upon a Matadore,
Then each according to the rank they bore;
35   For Sylphs, yet mindful of their ancient race,
Are, as when women, wondrous fond of place.
   Behold, four Kings in majesty revered,
With hoary whiskers and a forky beard;
And four fair Queens whose hands sustain a flower,
40   The expressive emblem of their softer power;
Four Knaves in garbs succinct,[1] a trusty band,
Caps on their heads, and halberts in their hand;
And parti-colored troops, a shining train,
Draw forth to combat on the velvet plain.
45   The skillful nymph reviews her force with care;
"Let Spades be trumps!" she said, and trumps they were.
   Now move to war her sable Matadores,
In show like leaders of the swarthy Moors.
Spadillio first, unconquerable lord!
50   Led off two captive trumps, and swept the board.
As many more Manillio forced to yield,
And marched a victor from the verdant field.
Him Basto followed, but his fate more hard
Gained but one trump and one plebeian card.
55   With his broad saber next, a chief in years,
The hoary Majesty of Spades appears,
Puts forth one manly leg, to sight revealed,
The rest his many-colored robe concealed.
The rebel Knave, who dares his prince engage,
60   Proves the just victim of his royal rage.
Even mighty Pam,[2] that kings and queens o'erthrew
And mowed down armies in the fights of loo,
Sad chance of war! now distitute of aid,
Falls undistinguished by the victor Spade.
65   Thus far both armies to Belinda yield;
Now to the Baron fate inclines the field.
His warlike amazon her host invades,
The imperial consort of the crown of Spades.
The Club's black tyrant first her victim died,
70   Spite of his haughty mien and barbarous pride.

---

9. This game is like three-handed bridge with some features of poker added. From a deck lacking 8's, 9's and 10's are dealt to each player (line 30) and the rest put in a central pool. A declarer called the *Ombre* (Spanish *hombre*, man) commits himself to taking more tricks than either of his opponents individually; hence Belinda would "encounter two knights *singly*." Declarer, followed by the other players, then selects discards and replenishes his hand with cards drawn sight unseen from the pool (line 45). He proceeds to name his trumps (line 46). The three principal trumps, called *Matadors* (line 47), always include the black aces. When spades are declared, the Matadors are, in order of value, the ace of spades (called *Spadille*, line 49), the deuce of spades (called *Manille*, line 51), and the ace of clubs (called *Basto*, line 53). The remaining spades fill out the trump suit. In the game here described, Belinda leads out her high trumps (lines 49–56), but the suit breaks badly (line 54); the Baron retains the queen (line 67), with which he presently trumps her king of clubs (line 69). He then leads high diamonds until she is on the verge of a set (called *Codille*, line 92). But she makes her bid at the last trick (line 94), taking his ace of hearts with her king (line 95), this being, in ombre, the highest card in the heart suit. The game is played on a green velvet cloth (line 44).
1. Hemmed up short, not flowing.
2. The jack of clubs, paramount trump in the game of loo.

What boots the regal circle on his head,
His giant limbs, in state unwieldy spread?
That long behind he trails his pompous robe,
And of all monarchs only grasps the globe?
75   The Baron now his Diamonds pours apace;
The embroidered King who shows but half his face,
And his refulgent Queen, with powers combined
Of broken troops an easy conquest find.
Clubs, Diamonds, Hearts, in wild disorder seen,
80   With throngs promiscuous strew the level green.
Thus when dispersed a routed army runs,
Of Asia's troops, and Afric's sable sons,
With like confusion different nations fly,
Of various habit,° and of various dye,°   dress / color
85   The pierced battalions disunited fall
In heaps on heaps; one fate o'erwhelms them all.
      The Knave of Diamonds tries his wily arts,
And wins (oh, shameful chance!) the Queen of Hearts.
At this, the blood the virgin's cheek forsook,
90   A livid paleness spreads o'er all her look;
She sees, and trembles at the approaching ill,
Just in the jaws of ruin, and Codille,
And now (as oft in some distempered state)
On one nice trick depends the general fate.
95   An Ace of Hearts steps forth: the King unseen
Lurked in her hand, and mourned his captive Queen.
He springs to vengeance with an eager pace,
And falls like thunder on the prostrate Ace.
The nymph exulting fills with shouts the sky,
100   The walls, the woods, and long canals[3] reply.
      O thoughtless mortals! ever blind to fate,
Too soon dejected, and too soon elate:
Sudden these honors shall be snatched away,
And cursed forever this victorious day.
105   For lo! the board with cups and spoons is crowned,
The berries crackle, and the mill turns round;[4]
On shining altars of Japan[5] they raise
The silver lamp; the fiery spirits blaze:
From silver spouts the grateful liquors glide,
110   While China's earth[6] receives the smoking tide.
At once they gratify their scent and taste,
And frequent cups prolong the rich repast.
Straight hover round the fair her airy band;
Some, as she sipped, the fuming liquor fanned,
115   Some o'er her lap their careful plumes displayed,
Trembling, and conscious of the rich brocade.
Coffee (which makes the politician wise,
And see through all things with his half-shut eyes)
Sent up in vapors to the Baron's brain
120   New stratagems, the radiant Lock to gain.
Ah, cease, rash youth! desist ere 'tis too late,
Fear the just Gods, and think of Scylla's fate![7]
Changed to a bird, and sent to flit in air,

3. Passages between avenues of trees.
4. As coffee beans are roasted and ground.
5. Lacquered tables.
6. Ceramic cups.
7. Scylla cut from the head of her father

Nisus the lock of hair on which his life de-
pended and gave it to her lover Minos of
Crete, who was Scylla's enemy. For this she
was turned into a sea-bird relentlessly pursued
by an eagle.

She dearly pays for Nisus' injured hair!
25   But when to mischief mortals bend their will,
How soon they find fit instruments of ill!
Just then, Clarissa drew with tempting grace
A two-edged weapon from her shining case:
So ladies in romance assist their knight,
30   Present the spear, and arm him for the fight.
He takes the gift with reverence, and extends
The little engine on his fingers' ends;
This just behind Belinda's neck he spread,
As o'er the fragrant steams she bends her head.
35   Swift to the Lock a thousand sprites repair,
A thousand wings, by turns, blow back the hair,
And thrice they twitched the diamond in her ear,
Thrice she looked back, and thrice the foe drew near.
Just in that instant, anxious Ariel sought
40   The close recesses of the virgin's thought;
As on the nosegay in her breast reclined,
He watched the ideas rising in her mind,
Sudden he viewed, in spite of all her art,
An earthly lover lurking at her heart,
45   Amazed, confused, he found his power expired,[8]
Resigned to fate, and with a sigh retired.
    The Peer now spreads the glittering forfex° wide,   *scissors*
To enclose the Lock; now joins it, to divide.
Even then, before the fatal engine closed,
50   A wretched Sylph too fondly interposed;
Fate urged the shears, and cut the Sylph in twain
(But airy substance soon unites again):[9]
The meeting points the sacred hair dissever
From the fair head, forever, and forever!
55   Then flashed the living lightning from her eyes,
And screams of horror rend the affrighted skies.
Not louder shrieks to pitying heaven are cast,
When husbands, or when lapdogs breathe their last;
Or when rich china vessels fallen from high,
160   In glittering dust and painted fragments lie!
"Let wreaths of triumph now my temples twine,"
The victor cried, "the glorious prize is mine!
While fish in streams, or birds delight in air,
Or in a coach and six the British Fair,
165   As long as *Atalantis*[1] shall be read,
Or the small pillow grace a lady's bed,
While visits shall be paid on solemn days,
When numerous wax-lights in bright order blaze,[2]
While nymphs take treats, or assignations give,
170   So long my honor, name, and praise shall live!
What Time would spare, from Steel receives its date,°   *termination*
And monuments, like men, submit to fate!
Steel could the labor of the Gods destroy,[3]
And strike to dust the imperial towers of Troy;
175   Steel could the works of mortal pride confound,

---

8. Belinda, being strongly attracted to the Baron (line 144), can no longer merely coquette. She hence passes beyond Ariel's control.
9. Again as with Milton's angels (*Paradise Lost* VI.329–31).

1. A set of memoirs which, under thin disguise, recounted actual scandals.
2. Attending the formal evening visits of the previous line.
3. Troy (named in the next line) was built by Apollo and Poseidon.

And hew triumphal arches to the ground.
What wonder then, fair nymph! thy hairs should feel,
The conquering force of unresisted Steel?"

Canto IV

But anxious cares the pensive nymph oppressed,
And secret passions labored in her breast.
Not youthful kings in battle seized alive,
Not scornful virgins who their charms survive,
5   Not ardent lovers robbed of all their bliss,
Not ancient ladies when refused a kiss,
Not tyrants fierce that unrepenting die,
Not Cynthia when her manteau's⁴ pinned awry,
E'er felt such rage, resentment, and despair,
10   As thou, sad virgin! for thy ravished hair.
    For, that sad moment, when the Sylphs withdrew
And Ariel weeping from Belinda flew,
Umbriel,⁵ a dusky, melancholy sprite
As ever sullied the fair face of light,
15   Down to the central earth, his proper scene,
Repaired to search the gloomy Cave of Spleen.⁶
    Swift on his sooty pinions flits the Gnome,
And in a vapor reached the dismal dome.
No cheerful breeze this sullen region knows,
20   The dreaded east is all the wind that blows.
Here in a grotto, sheltered close from air,
And screened in shades from day's detested glare,
She sighs forever on her pensive bed,
Pain at her side, and Megrim° at her head.   *migraine*
25   Two handmaids wait the throne: alike in place,
But differing far in figure and in face.
Here stood Ill-Nature like an ancient maid,
Her wrinkled form in black and white arrayed;
With store of prayers for mornings, nights, and noons,
30   Her hand is filled; her bosom with lampoons.°   *slanders*
    There Affectation, with a sickly mien,
Shows in her cheek the roses of eighteen,
Practiced to lisp, and hang the head aside,
Faints into airs, and languishes with pride,
35   On the rich quilt sinks with becoming woe,
Wrapped in a gown, for sickness and for show.
The fair ones feel such maladies as these,
When each new nightdress gives a new disease.
    A constant vapor o'er the palace flies,
40   Strange phantoms rising as the mists arise;
Dreadful as hermit's dreams in haunted shades,
Or bright as visions of expiring maids.
Now glaring fiends, and snakes on rolling spires,°   *coils*
Pale specters, gaping tombs, and purple fires;
45   Now lakes of liquid gold, Elysian scenes,
And crystal domes, and angels in machines.⁷

4. I.e., robe is.
5. Suggesting *umbra*, shadow; and *umber*, brown. The final *el* of this name is a further reminiscence of Milton's angels: Gabriel, Abdiel, Zophiel.
6. This journey is formally equivalent to Odysseus' and Aeneas' visits to the underworld. "Spleen" refers to the human organ, the supposed seat of melancholy; hence to melancholy itself. Believed to be induced by misty weather such as the east wind brings (lines 18–20), the condition was also called the "vapors." In its severer manifestations it tends toward madness; in its milder forms, it issues in peevishness and suspicion.
7. These images are both 1) the hallucinations of insane melancholy and 2) parodies of stage properties and effects.

Unnumbered throngs on every side are seen
Of bodies changed to various forms by Spleen.
Here living teapots stand, one arm held out,
50   One bent; the handle this, and that the spout:
A pipkin[8] there, like Homer's tripod, walks;
Here sighs a jar, and there a goose pie talks;
Men prove with child, as powerful fancy works,
And maids, turned bottles, call aloud for corks.
55   Safe passed the Gnome through this fantastic band,
A branch of healing spleenwort[9] in his hand.
Then thus addressed the Power: "Hail, wayward Queen!
Who rule the sex to fifty from fifteen:
Parent of vapors and of female wit,
60   Who give the hysteric or poetic fit,
On various tempers act by various ways,
Make some take physic, others scribble plays;
Who cause the proud their visits to delay,
And send the godly in a pet to pray.
65   A nymph there is that all thy power disdains,
And thousands more in equal mirth maintains.
But oh! if e'er thy Gnome could spoil a grace,
Or raise a pimple on a beauteous face,
Like citron-waters° matrons' cheeks inflame,   *orange brandy*
70   Or change complexions at a losing game;
If e'er with airy horns I planted heads,[1]
Or rumpled petticoats, or tumbled beds,
Or caused suspicion when no soul was rude,
Or discomposed the headdress of a prude,
75   Or e'er to costive lapdog gave disease,
Which not the tears of brightest eyes could ease,
Hear me, and touch Belinda with chagrin:°   *annoyance*
That single act gives half the world the spleen."
The Goddess with a discontented air
80   Seems to reject him though she grants his prayer.
A wondrous bag with both her hands she binds,
Like that where once Ulysses held the winds;[2]
There she collects the force of female lungs,
Sighs, sobs, and passions, and the war of tongues.
85   A vial next she fills with fainting fears,
Soft sorrows, melting griefs, and flowing tears.
The Gnome rejoicing bears her gifts away,
Spreads his black wings, and slowly mounts to day.
Sunk in Thalestris'[3] arms the nymph he found,
90   Her eyes dejected and her hair unbound.
Full o'er their heads the swelling bag he rent,
And all the Furies issued at the vent.
Belinda burns with more than mortal ire,
And fierce Thalestris fans the rising fire.
95   "O wretched maid!" she spreads her hands, and cried
(While Hampton's echoes, "Wretched maid!" replied),
"Was it for this you took such constant care
The bodkin,° comb, and essence to prepare?   *hairpin*

---

8. An earthen pot; it walks like the three-legged stools which Vulcan made for the gods in *Iliad* XVIII.
9. A kind of fern, purgative of spleen; suggesting the golden bough which Aeneas bore as a passport to Hades in *Aeneid* VI.
1. I.e., made men imagine they were being cuckolded.
2. Aeolus, the wind god, enabled Odysseus so to contain all adverse winds in *Odyssey* X.
3. The name of an Amazon.

For this your locks in paper durance bound,
100 For this with torturing irons wreathed around?
    For this with fillets° strained your tender head,   *bands*
    And bravely bore the double loads of lead?[4]
    Gods! shall the ravisher display your hair,
    While the fops envy, and the ladies stare!
105 Honor forbid! at whose unrivaled shrine
    Ease, pleasure, virtue, all, our sex resign.
    Methinks already I your tears survey,
    Already hear the horrid things they say,
    Already see you a degraded toast,
110 And all your honor in a whisper lost!
    How shall I, then, your helpless fame defend?
    'Twill then be infamy to seem your friend!
    And shall this prize, the inestimable prize,
    Exposed through crystal to the gazing eyes,
115 And heightened by the diamond's circling rays,
    On that rapacious hand forever blaze?
    Sooner shall grass in Hyde Park Circus[5] grow,
    And wits take lodgings in the sound of Bow;[6]
    Sooner let earth, air, sea, to chaos fall,
120 Men, monkeys, lapdogs, parrots, perish all!"
        She said; then raging to Sir Plume repairs,
    And bids her beau demand the precious hairs
    (Sir Plume of amber snuffbox justly vain,
    And the nice° conduct° of a clouded cane).   *precise / handling*
125 With earnest eyes, and round unthinking face,
    He first the snuffbox opened, then the case,
    And thus broke out—"My Lord, why, what the devil!
    Zounds! damn the lock! 'fore Gad, you must be civil!
    Plague on't! 'tis past a jest—nay prithee, pox!
130 Give her the hair"—he spoke, and rapped his box.
        "It grieves me much," replied the Peer again,
    "Who speaks so well should ever speak in vain.
    But by this Lock, this sacred Lock I swear
    (Which never more shall join its parted hair;
135 Which never more its honors shall renew,
    Clipped from the lovely head where late it grew),
    That while my nostrils draw the vital air,
    This hand, which won it, shall forever wear."
    He spoke, and speaking, in proud triumph spread
140 The long-contended honors° of her head.   *ornaments*
        But Umbriel, hateful Gnome, forbears not so;
    He breaks the vial whence the sorrows flow.
    Then see! the nymph in beauteous grief appears,
    Her eyes half languishing, half drowned in tears;
145 On her heaved bosom hung her drooping head,
    Which with a sigh she raised, and thus she said:
        "Forever cursed be this detested day,
    Which snatched my best, my favorite curl away!
    Happy! ah, ten times happy had I been,
150 If Hampton Court these eyes had never seen!
    Yet am not I the first mistaken maid,
    By love of courts to numerous ills betrayed.

4. The means by which Belinda's locks were
fashioned into a ringlet: lead strips held her
curl papers in place.
5. The fashionable carriage course (the

"Ring" of I.44).
6. I.e., the sound of the bells of Bowchurch
in the unfashionable commercial section of
London.

Oh, had I rather unadmired remained
In some lone isle, or distant northern land;
5   Where the gilt chariot never marks the way,
Where none learn ombre, none e'er taste bohea!°   *fine tea*
There kept my charms concealed from mortal eye,
Like roses that in deserts bloom and die.
What moved my mind with youthful lords to roam?
60   Oh, had I stayed, and said my prayers at home!
'Twas this the morning omens seemed to tell,
Thrice from my trembling hand the patch box⁷ fell;
The tottering china shook without a wind,
Nay, Poll sat mute, and Shock was most unkind!
65   A Sylph too warned me of the threats of fate,
In mystic visions, now believed too late!
See the poor remnants of these slighted hairs!
My hands shall rend what e'en thy rapine spares.
These in two sable ringlets taught to break,
70   Once gave new beauties to the snowy neck;
The sister lock now sits uncouth, alone,
And in its fellow's fate foresees its own;
Uncurled it hangs, the fatal shears demands,
And tempts once more thy sacrilegious hands.
75   Oh, hadst thou, cruel! been content to seize
Hairs less in sight, or any hairs but these!"

Canto V

She said: the pitying audience melt in tears.
But Fate and Jove had stopped the Baron's ears.
In vain Thalestris with reproach assails,
For who can move when fair Belinda fails?
5   Not half so fixed the Trojan could remain,
While Anna begged and Dido raged in vain.⁸
Then grave Clarissa graceful waved her fan;
Silence ensued, and thus the nymph began:
"Say why are beauties praised and honored most,
10   The wise man's passion, and the vain man's toast?
Why decked with all that land and sea afford,
Why angels called, and angel-like adored?
Why round our coaches crowd the white-gloved beaux,
Why bows the side box from its inmost rows?
15   How vain are all these glories, all our pains,
Unless good sense preserve what beauty gains;
That men may say when we the front box grace,
'Behold the first in virtue as in face!'
Oh! if to dance all night, and dress all day,
20   Charmed the smallpox, or chased old age away,
Who would not scorn what housewife's cares produce,
Or who would learn one earthly thing of use?
To patch, nay ogle, might become a saint,
Nor could it sure be such a sin to paint.
25   But since, alas! frail beauty must decay,
Curled or uncurled, since locks will turn to gray;
Since painted, or not painted, all shall fade,
And she who scorns a man must die a maid;
What then remains but well our power to use,

7. A box for ornamental patches to accent the face.
8. Aeneas was determined to leave Carthage for Italy, though the enamored queen Dido raved and her sister Anna pleaded with him to stay.

30 And keep good humor still whate'er we lose?
And trust me, dear, good humor can prevail
When airs, and flights, and screams, and scolding fail.
Beauties in vain their pretty eyes may roll;
Charms strike the sight, but merit wins the soul."[9]
35   So spoke the dame, but no applause ensued;
Belinda frowned, Thalestris called her prude.
"To arms, to arms!" the fierce virago cries,
And swift as lightning to the combat flies.
All side in parties, and begin the attack;
40 Fans clap, silks rustle, and tough whalebones crack;
Heroes' and heroines' shouts confusedly rise,
And bass and treble voices strike the skies.
No common weapons in their hands are found,
Like Gods they fight, nor dread a mortal wound.
45   So when bold Homer makes the Gods engage,
And heavenly breasts with human passions rage;
'Gainst Pallas, Mars; Latona, Hermes arms;[1]
And all Olympus rings with loud alarms:
Jove's thunder roars, heaven trembles all around,
50 Blue Neptune storms, the bellowing deeps resound:
Earth shakes her nodding towers, the ground gives way,
And the pale ghosts start at the flash of day!
Triumphant Umbriel on a sconce's height
Clapped his glad wings, and sat to view the fight:
55 Propped on the bodkin spears, the sprites survey
The growing combat, or assist the fray.
While through the press enraged Thalestris flies,
And scatters death around from both her eyes,
A beau and witling perished in the throng,
60 One died in metaphor, and one in song.
"O cruel nymph! a living death I bear,"
Cried Dapperwit, and sunk beside his chair.
A mournful glance Sir Fopling upwards cast,
"Those eyes are made so killing"—was his last.
65 Thus on Maeander's flowery margin lies
The expiring swan, and as he sings he dies.
When bold Sir Plume had drawn Clarissa down,
Chloe stepped in, and killed him with a frown;
She smiled to see the doughty hero slain,
70 But, at her smile, the beau revived again.
Now Jove suspends his golden scales in air,[2]
Weighs the men's wits against the lady's hair;
The doubtful beam long nods from side to side;
At length the wits mount up, the hairs subside.
75   See, fierce Belinda on the Baron flies,
With more than usual lightning in her eyes;
Nor feared the chief the unequal fight to try,
Who sought no more than on his foe to die.
But this bold lord with manly strength endued,
80 She with one finger and a thumb subdued:
Just where the breath of life his nostrils drew,
A charge of snuff the wily virgin threw;

9. Clarissa's address parallels a speech in
Iliad XII, wherein Sarpedon tells Glaucus
that, as leaders of the army, they must justify
their privilege by extraordinary prowess.
1. Mars arms against Pallas, and Hermes
against Latona in *Iliad* XX. The tangled syn-
tax is supposed to mirror the press of battle.
2. He so weighs the fortunes of war in classi-
cal epic.

The Gnomes direct, to every atom just,
The pungent grains of titillating dust.
85 Sudden, with starting tears each eye o'erflows,
And the high dome re-echoes to his nose.
"Now meet thy fate," incensed Belinda cried,
And drew a deadly bodkin[3] from her side.
(The same, his ancient personage to deck,
90 Her great-great-grandsire wore about his neck,
In three seal rings; which after, melted down,
Formed a vast buckle for his widow's gown:
Her infant grandame's whistle next it grew,
The bells she jingled, and the whistle blew;
95 Then in a bodkin graced her mother's hairs,
Which long she wore, and now Belinda wears.)
"Boast not my fall," he cried, "insulting foe!
Thou by some other shalt be laid as low.
Nor think to die dejects my lofty mind:
100 All that I dread is leaving you behind!
Rather than so, ah, let me still survive,
And burn in Cupid's flames—but burn alive."
"Restore the Lock!" she cries; and all around
"Restore the Lock!" the vaulted roofs rebound.
105 Not fierce Othello in so loud a strain
Roared for the handkerchief that caused his pain.[4]
But see how oft ambitious aims are crossed,
And chiefs contend till all the prize is lost!
The lock, obtained with guilt, and kept with pain,
110 In every place is sought, but sought in vain:
With such a prize no mortal must be blessed,
So Heaven decrees! with Heaven who can contest?
Some thought it mounted to the lunar sphere,
Since all things lost on earth are treasured there.
115 There heroes' wits are kept in ponderous vases,
And beaux' in snuffboxes and tweezer cases.
There broken vows and deathbed alms are found,
And lovers' hearts with ends of riband bound,
The courtier's promises, and sick man's prayers,
120 The smiles of harlots, and the tears of heirs,
Cages for gnats, and chains to yoke a flea,
Dried butterflies, and tomes of casuistry.
But trust the Muse—she saw it upward rise,
Though marked by none but quick, poetic eyes
125 (So Rome's great founder to the heavens withdrew,[5]
To Proculus alone confessed in view);
A sudden star, it shot through liquid° air,   *clear*
And drew behind a radiant trail of hair.
Not Berenice's locks first rose so bright,[6]
130 The heavens bespangling with disheveled light.
The Sylphs behold it kindling as it flies,
And pleased pursue its progress through the skies.
This the beau monde shall from the Mall[7] survey,
And hail with music its propitious ray.

---

3. Here an ornamental hairpin. Its history suggests that of Agamemnon's scepter in *Iliad* II. "Seal rings" (line 91) are for impressing seals on letters and legal documents.
4. In *Othello* III.iv.
5. Romulus was borne heavenward in a storm-cloud and later deified.
6. The locks which the Egyptian queen Berenice dedicated to her husband's safe return were turned into a constellation.
7. A fashionable walk which (like Rosamonda's Lake [line 136]) was in St. James's Park.

135   This the blest lover shall for Venus take,
     And send up vows from Rosamonda's Lake.
     This Partridge[8] soon shall view in cloudless skies,
     When next he looks through Galileo's eyes;
     And hence the egregious wizard shall foredoom
140   The fate of Louis, and the fall of Rome.
       Then cease, bright nymph! to mourn thy ravished hair,
     Which adds new glory to the shining sphere!
     Not all the tresses that fair head can boast,
     Shall draw such envy as the Lock you lost.
145   For, after all the murders of your eye,
     When, after millions slain, yourself shall die:
     When those fair suns shall set, as set they must,
     And all those tresses shall be laid in dust,
     This Lock the Muse shall consecrate to fame,
150   And 'midst the stars inscribe Belinda's name.

                                  1712   1714

Elegy to the Memory of an Unfortunate Lady

    What beckoning ghost, along the moonlight shade
    Invites my steps, and points to yonder glade?
    'Tis she!—but why that bleeding bosom gored,
    Why dimly gleams the visionary sword?
5   O ever beauteous, every friendly! tell,
    Is it, in Heaven, a crime to love too well?
    To bear too tender, or too firm a heart,
    To act a lover's or a Roman's part?[9]
    Is there no bright reversion° in the sky,   *inheritance*
10   For those who greatly think, or bravely die?
      Why bade ye else, ye Powers! her soul aspire
    Above the vulgar flight of low desire?
    Ambition first sprung from your blest abodes;
    The glorious fault of angels and of gods:
15   Thence to their images on earth it flows,
    And in the breasts of kings and heroes glows.
    Most souls, 'tis true, but peep out once an age,
    Dull sullen prisoners in the body's cage:
    Dim lights of life, that burn a length of years
20   Useless, unseen, as lamps in sepulchers;
    Like Eastern kings a lazy state° they keep,   *sedateness*
    And close confined to their own palace, sleep.
      From these perhaps (ere Nature bade her die)
    Fate snatched her early to the pitying sky.
25   As into air the purer spirits flow,
    And separate from their kindred dregs below;
    So flew the soul to its congenial place,
    Nor left one virtue to redeem her race.°   *family*
      But thou, false guardian of a charge too good,
30   Thou, mean deserter of thy brother's blood!
    See on these ruby lips the trembling breath,
    These cheeks, now fading at the blast of death;
    Cold is that breast which warmed the world before,
    And those love-darting eyes must roll no more.

---

8. A London astrologer who predicted calamities on the enemies of England and Protestantism. "Galileo's eyes": the telescope.

9. To commit suicide, as the Roman Stoics recommended to persons in irremediable distress.

35 Thus, if Eternal Justice rules the ball,
    Thus shall your wives, and thus your children fall:
    On all the line a sudden vengeance waits,
    And frequent hearses shall besiege your gates.
    There passengers shall stand, and pointing say
40 (While the long funerals blacken all the way),
    Lo these were they, whose souls the Furies steeled,
    And cursed with hearts unknowing how to yield.
    Thus unlamented pass the proud away,
    The gaze of fools, and pageant of a day!
45 So perish all, whose breast ne'er learned to glow
    For others' good, or melt at others' woe.
        What can atone (oh, ever-injured shade!)
    Thy fate unpitied, and thy rites unpaid?[1]
    No friend's complaint, no kind domestic tear
50 Pleased thy pale ghost, or graced thy mournful bier.
    By foreign hands thy dying eyes were closed,
    By foreign hands thy decent limbs composed,
    By foreign hands thy humble grave adorned,
    By strangers honored, and by strangers mourned!
55 What though no friends in sable weeds appear,
    Grieve for an hour, perhaps, then mourn a year,
    And bear about the mockery of woe
    To midnight dances, and the public show?
    What though no weeping Loves thy ashes grace,
60 Nor polished marble emulate thy face?
    What though no sacred earth allow thee room,
    Nor hallowed dirge be muttered o'er thy tomb?
    Yet shall thy grave with rising flowers be dressed,
    And the green turf lie lightly on thy breast:
65 There shall the morn her earliest tears bestow,
    There the first roses of the year shall blow;
    While angels with their silver wings o'ershade
    The ground, now sacred by thy reliques made.
        So peaceful rests, without a stone, a name,
70 What once had beauty, titles, wealth, and fame.
    How loved, how honored once, avails thee not,
    To whom related, or by whom begot;
    A heap of dust alone remains of thee,
    'Tis all thou art, and all the proud shall be!
75   Poets themselves must fall, like those they sung,
    Deaf the praised ear, and mute the tuneful tongue.
    Even he, whose soul now melts in mournful lays,
    Shall shortly want the generous tear he pays;
    Then from his closing eyes thy form shall part,
80 And the last pang shall tear thee from his heart,
    Life's idle business at one gasp be o'er,
    The Muse forgot, and thou beloved no more!

                                                1717

---

1. Suicides were denied certain rites of Christian burial.

From An Essay on Man

TO HENRY ST. JOHN, LORD BOLINGBROKE

*Epistle I. Of the Nature and State of Man,
With Respect to the Universe*

Awake, my St. John![2] leave all meaner things
To low ambition, and the pride of kings.
Let us (since life can little more supply
Than just to look about us and to die)
5 Expatiate° free° o'er all this scene of man;   *range / freely*
A mighty maze! but not without a plan;
A wild, where weeds and flowers promiscuous shoot,
Or garden, tempting with forbidden fruit.
Together let us beat this ample field,
10 Try what the open, what the covert yield;
The latent tracts, the giddy heights, explore
Of all who blindly creep, or sightless soar;
Eye Nature's walks, shoot folly as it flies,
And catch the manners living as they rise;
15 Laugh where we must, be candid° where we can;   *serious and plain*
But vindicate the ways of God to man.[3]
    1. Say first, of God above, or man below,
What can we reason, but from what we know?
Of man, what see we but his station here,
20 From which to reason, or to which refer?
Through worlds unnumbered though the God be known,
'Tis ours to trace him only in our own.
He, who through vast immensity can pierce,
See worlds on worlds compose one universe,
25 Observe how system° into system runs,   *solar system*
What other planets circle other suns,
What varied Being peoples every star,
May tell why Heaven has made us as we are.
But of this frame the bearings, and the ties,
30 The strong connections, nice dependencies,
Gradations just, has thy pervading soul
Looked through? or can a part contain the whole?
    Is the great chain, that draws all to agree,
And drawn supports, upheld by God, or thee?
35   2. Presumptuous man! the reason wouldst thou find,
Why formed so weak, so little, and so blind?
First, if thou canst, the harder reason guess,
Why formed no weaker, blinder, and no less!
Ask of thy mother earth, why oaks are made
40 Taller or stronger than the weeds they shade?
Or ask of yonder argent fields above,
Why Jove's satellites[4] are less than Jove?
    Of systems possible, if 'tis confessed
That Wisdom Infinite must form the best,
45 Where all must full or not coherent be,
And all that rises, rise in due degree;
Then, in the scale of reasoning life, 'tis plain,
There must be, somewhere, such a rank as man:

2. Pronounced *sinjin*.
3. An echo of Milton's statement of purpose, *Paradise Lost* I.26.
4. The moons of the planet Jupiter; pronounced *satéllités*.

And all the question (wrangle e'er so long)
50   Is only this, if God has placed him wrong?
      Respecting man, whatever wrong we call,
May, must be right, as relative to all.
In human works,° though labored on with pain,   *mechanical systems*
A thousand movements scarce one purpose gain;
55   In God's, one single can its end produce;
Yet serves to second too some other use.
So man, who here seems principal alone,
Perhaps acts second to some sphere unknown,
Touches some wheel, or verges to some goal;
60   'Tis but a part we see, and not a whole.
      When the proud steed shall know why man restrains
His fiery course, or drives him o'er the plains;
When the dull ox, why now he breaks the clod,
Is now a victim, and now Egypt's god:
65   Then shall man's pride and dullness comprehend
His actions', passions', being's use and end;
Why doing, suffering, checked, impelled; and why
This hour a slave, the next a deity.
      Then say not man's imperfect, Heaven in fault;
70   Say rather, man's as perfect as he ought:
His knowledge measured to his state and place,
His time a moment, and a point his space.
If to be perfect in a certain sphere,
What matter, soon or late, or here or there?
75   The blest today is as completely so,
As who began a thousand years ago.
      3. Heaven from all creatures hides the book of Fate,
All but the page prescribed, their present state:
From brutes what men, from men what spirits know:
80   Or who could suffer Being here below?
The lamb thy riot dooms to bleed today,
Had he thy reason, would he skip and play?
Pleased to the last, he crops the flowery food,
And licks the hand just raised to shed his blood.
85   O blindness to the future! kindly given,
That each may fill the circle marked by Heaven:
Who sees with equal eye, as God of all,
A hero perish, or a sparrow fall,
Atoms or systems into ruin hurled,
90   And now a bubble burst, and now a world.°   *universe*
      Hope humbly then; with trembling pinions soar;
Wait the great teacher Death, and God adore!
What future bliss, he gives not thee to know,
But gives that hope to be thy blessing now.
95   Hope springs eternal in the human breast:
Man never is, but always to be blest:
The soul, uneasy and confined from home,
Rests and expatiates in a life to come.
      Lo! the poor Indian, whose untutored mind
100   Sees God in clouds, or hears him in the wind;
His soul proud Science never taught to stray
Far as the solar walk, or milky way;
Yet simple Nature to his hope has given,
Behind the cloud-topped hill, an humbler heaven;
105   Some safer world in depth of woods embraced,
Some happier island in the watery waste,

Where slaves once more their native land behold,
No fiends torment, no Christians thirst for gold!
To Be, contents his natural desire,
110   He asks no angel's wing, no seraph's[5] fire;
But thinks, admitted to that equal° sky,   *equable*
His faithful dog shall bear him company.
      4. Go, wiser thou! and, in thy scale of sense,
Weigh thy opinion against Providence;
115   Call imperfection what thou fancy'st such,
Say, here he gives too little, there too much;
Destroy all creatures for thy sport or gust,°   *taste*
Yet cry, if man's unhappy, God's unjust;
If man alone engross not Heaven's high care,
120   Alone made perfect here, immortal there:
Snatch from his hand the balance and the rod,
Rejudge his justice, be the God of God!
In pride, in reasoning pride, our error lies;
All quit their sphere, and rush into the skies.
125   Pride still is aiming at the blest abodes,
Men would be angels, angels would be gods.
Aspiring to be gods, if angels fell,
Aspiring to be angels, men rebel:
And who but wishes to invert the laws
130   Of order, sins against the Eternal Cause.
      5. Ask for what end the heavenly bodies shine,
Earth for whose use? Pride answers, " 'Tis for mine:
For me kind Nature wakes her genial power,
Suckles each herb, and spreads out every flower;
135   Annual for me, the grape, the rose renew
The juice nectareous, and the balmy dew;
For me, the mine a thousand treasures brings;
For me, health gushes from a thousand springs;
Seas roll to waft me, suns to light me rise;
140   My footstool earth, my canopy the skies."
      But errs not Nature from this gracious end,
From burning suns when livid deaths° descend,   *plagues*
When earthquakes swallow, or when tempests sweep
Towns to one grave, whole nations to the deep?
145   "No," 'tis replied, "the first Almighty Cause
Acts not by partial, but by general laws;
The exceptions few; some change since all began,
And what created perfect?"—Why then man?
If the great end be human happiness,
150   Then Nature deviates; and can man do less?
As much that end a constant course requires
Of showers and sunshine, as of man's desires;
As much eternal springs and cloudless skies,
As men forever temperate, calm, and wise.
155   If plagues or earthquakes break not Heaven's design,
Why then a Borgia, or a Catiline?[6]
Who knows but he whose hand the lightning forms,
Who heaves old ocean, and who wings the storms,
Pours fierce ambition in a Caesar's mind,
160   Or turns young Ammon[7] loose to scourge mankind?
From pride, from pride, our very reasoning springs;

5. Seraphim are fiery through devotion—an
attribute also noted in line 278.
6. Cesare Borgia, Italian cardinal notorious

for his crimes, and Lucius Sergius Catilina,
conspirator against the Roman Republic.
7. Alexander the Great.

Account for moral, as for natural things:
Why charge we Heaven in those, in these acquit?
In both, to reason right is to submit.
55   Better for us, perhaps, it might appear,
Were there all harmony, all virtue here;
That never air or ocean felt the wind;
That never passion discomposed the mind:
But ALL subsists by elemental strife;
70 And passions are the elements of life.
The general ORDER, since the whole began,
Is kept in Nature, and is kept in man.
   6. What would this man? Now upward will he soar,
And little less than angel, would be more;
75 Now looking downwards, just as grieved appears
To want the strength of bulls, the fur of bears.
Made for his use all creatures if he call,
Say what their use, had he the powers of all?
Nature to these, without profusion, kind,
80 The proper organs, proper powers assigned;
Each seeming want compénsated of course,°   *naturally*
Here with degrees of swiftness, there of force;
All in exact proportion to the state;
Nothing to add, and nothing to abate.
85 Each beast, each insect, happy in its own;
Is Heaven unkind to man, and man alone?
Shall he alone, whom rational we call,
Be pleased with nothing, if not blessed with all?
   The bliss of man (could pride that blessing find)
90 Is not to act or think beyond mankind;
No powers of body or of soul to share,
But what his nature and his state can bear.
Why has not man a microscopic eye?
For this plain reason, man is not a fly.
195 Say what the use, were finer optics given,
To inspect a mite, not comprehend the heaven?
Or touch, if trembling alive all o'er,
To smart and agonize at every pore?
Or quick effluvia[8] darting through the brain,
200 Die of a rose in aromatic pain?
If nature thundered in his opening ears,
And stunned him with the music of the spheres,
How would he wish that Heaven had left him still
The whispering zephyr, and the purling rill?
205 Who finds not Providence all good and wise,
Alike in what it gives, and what it denies?
   7. Far as creation's ample range extends,
The scale of sensual,° mental powers ascends: *sensory*
Mark how it mounts, to man's imperial race,
210 From the green myriads in the peopled grass:
What modes of sight betwixt each wide extreme,
The mole's dim curtain, and the lynx's beam:[9]
Of smell, the headlong lioness between,
And hound sagacious on the tainted green:[1]

---

8. Streams of particles which supposedly conducted sense impressions to the brain.
9. I.e., eyesight; in older (erroneous) optics, sight depended on an emission ("beam") of particles from the eye.

1. I.e., the hound with its acute sense of smell on the trail of game in the meadow; lionesses, by contrast, have a poor sense of smell and rush upon a visible or audible quarry.

215   Of hearing, from the life that fills the flood,
      To that which warbles through the vernal wood:
      The spider's touch, how exquisitely fine!
      Feels at each thread, and lives along the line:
      In the nice° bee, what sense so subtly true   *discriminating*
220   From poisonous herbs extracts the healing dew:
      How instinct varies in the groveling swine,
      Compared, half-reasoning elephant, with thine!
      'Twixt that, and reason, what a nice barrier;[2]
      Forever separate, yet forever near!
225   Remembrance and reflection how allied;
      What thin partitions sense from thought divide:
      And middle natures, how they long to join,
      Yet never pass the insuperable line!
      Without this just gradation, could they be
230   Subjected, these to those, or all to thee?
      The powers of all subdued by thee alone,
      Is not thy reason all these powers in one?
          8. See, through this air, this ocean, and this earth,
      All matter quick,° and bursting into birth.   *alive*
235   Above, how high progressive life may go!
      Around, how wide! how deep extend below!
      Vast Chain of Being! which from God began,
      Natures ethereal, human, angel, man,
      Beast, bird, fish, insect, what no eye can see,
240   No glass can reach! from Infinite to thee,
      From thee to nothing.—On superior powers
      Were we to press, inferior might on ours:
      Or in the full creation leave a void,
      Where, one step broken, the great scale's destroyed:
245   From Nature's chain whatever link you strike,
      Tenth or ten thousandth, breaks the chain alike.
          And, if each system in gradation roll
      Alike essential to the amazing Whole,
      The least confusion but in one, not all
250   That system only, but the Whole must fall.
      Let earth unbalanced from her orbit fly,
      Planets and suns run lawless through the sky,
      Let ruling angels from their spheres[3] be hurled,
      Being on being wrecked, and world on world,
255   Heaven's whole foundations to their center nod,
      And Nature tremble to the throne of God:
      All this dread ORDER break—for whom? for thee?
      Vile worm!—oh, madness, pride, impiety!
          9. What if the foot, ordained the dust to tread,
260   Or hand, to toil, aspired to be the head?
      What if the head, the eye, or ear repined
      To serve mere engines to the ruling Mind?[4]
      Just as absurd for any part to claim
      To be another, in this general frame:
265   Just as absurd, to mourn the tasks or pains,
      The great directing MIND of ALL ordains.
          All are but parts of one stupendous whole,

2. Pronounced *bar-eér*.
3. Of the Ptolemaic universe, the images of
which were still available to poetry.

4. Pope echoes I Corinthians xii. *Engines*
means *instruments*.

Whose body Nature is, and God the soul;
That, changed through all, and yet in all the same,
270 Great in the earth, as in the ethereal frame,°   *heavens*
Warms in the sun, refreshes in the breeze,
Glows in the stars, and blossoms in the trees,
Lives through all life, extends through all extent,
Spreads undivided, operates unspent,
275 Breathes in our soul, informs our mortal part,
As full, as perfect, in a hair as heart;
As full, as perfect, in vile man that mourns,
As the rapt seraph that adores and burns;
To him no high, no low, no great, no small;
280 He fills, he bounds, connects, and equals° all.   *makes equal*
     10. Cease then, nor ORDER imperfection name:
Our proper bliss depends on what we blame.
Know thy own point: this kind, this due degree
Of blindness, weakness, Heaven bestows on thee.
285 Submit—In this, or any other sphere,
Secure to be as blest as thou canst bear:
Safe in the hand of one disposing Power,
Or in the natal, or the mortal hour.
All Nature is but art, unknown to thee;
290 All chance, direction, which thou canst not see;
All discord, harmony not understood;
All partial evil, universal good:
And, spite of pride, in erring reason's spite,
One truth is clear: Whatever IS, is RIGHT.

                                                             1733

From Epistle II. Of the Nature and State of Man
With Respect to Himself, as an Individual

Know then thyself, presume not God to scan;
The proper study of mankind is Man.
Placed on this isthmus of a middle state,
A being darkly wise, and rudely great:
5 With too much knowledge for the skeptic side,
With too much weakness for the Stoic's pride,
He hangs between; in doubt to act, or rest,
In doubt to deem himself a god, or beast;
In doubt his mind or body to prefer,
10 Born but to die, and reasoning but to err;
Alike in ignorance, his reason such,
Whether he thinks too little, or too much:
Chaos of thought and passion, all confused;
Still by himself abused, or disabused;
15 Created half to rise, and half to fall;
Great lord of all things, yet a prey to all;
Sole judge of truth, in endless error hurled:
The glory, jest, and riddle of the world!

                                                             1733

From The Dunciad

[*The Booksellers' Race*]⁵

And now the Queen,⁶ to glad her sons, proclaims,
By herald hawkers, high heroic games.
They summon all her race: an endless band
²⁰ Pours forth, and leaves unpeopled half the land.
A motley mixture! in long wigs, in bags,⁷
In silks, in crepes, in Garters, and in rags,⁸
From drawing-rooms, from colleges, from garrets,
On horse, on foot, in hacks, and gilded chariots:
²⁵ All who true dunces in her cause appeared,
And all who knew those dunces to reward.
     Amid that area wide they took their stand,
Where the tall maypole once o'er-looked the Strand.
But now (so ANNF and Piety ordain)
³⁰ A church collects the saints of Drury Lane.⁹
     With authors, stationers° obeyed the call,   booksellers
(The field of glory is a field for all).
Glory, and gain, the industrious tribe provoke;
And gentle Dullness ever loves a joke.
³⁵ A Poet's form she placed before their eyes,
And bade the nimblest racer seize the prize;
No meagre, muse-rid mope, adust° and thin,   gloomy
In a dun night-gown of his own loose skin;
But such a bulk as no twelve bards could raise,
⁴⁰ Twelve starveling bards of these degenerate days.
All as a partridge plump, full-fed, and fair,
She formed this image of well-bodied air;
With pert flat eyes she windowed well its head:
A brain of feathers, and a heart of lead;
⁴⁵ And empty words she gave, and sounding strain,
But senseless, lifeless! idol void and vain!
Never was dashed out, at one lucky hit,
A fool, so just a copy of a wit;
So like, that critics said, and courtiers swore,
⁵⁰ A wit it was, and called the phantom Moore.¹
     All gaze with ardor: some a poet's name,
Others a sword-knot° and laced suit inflame.   tassel
But lofty Lintot² in the circle rose:
"This prize is mine; who tempt it are my foes;
⁵⁵ With me began this genius, and shall end."
He spoke: and who with Lintot shall contend?
     Fear held them mute. Alone, untaught to fear,
Stood dauntless Curll;³ "Behold that rival here!

5. *Dunciad* (B) ii.17–120.
6. The Goddess of Dullness. Through street-criers, she proclaims games which are the burlesque equivalent of the funeral games in the *Iliad* and the *Aeneid*.
7. Short wigs (contained in snoods or "bags").
8. I.e., in fine clothes and in modest; wearing tokens of the highest place (the Order of the Garter) and of the lowest.
9. St. Mary le Strand, on the former site of a maypole, was one of fifty new churches built or projected under Queen Anne. The phrase "saints of Drury Lane" ironically

acknowledges the many prostitutes in the area.
1. James Moore Smyth; a plagiarist, hence without substance as a poet.
2. Barnaby Bernard Lintot (the "Bérnard" of the next paragraph) was a publisher, "a great sputtering fellow," who quarreled with Pope over Pope's translation of the *Odyssey*.
3. Edmund Curll, "an unscrupulous, persistent and adroit publisher, who realized the commercial value of scandal and impudence" (Sutherland). He pirated some of Pope's works and also published personal attacks on him.

The race by vigor, not by vaunts is won;
60 So take the hindmost, Hell," he said, and run.
Swift as a bard the bailiff° leaves behind,   *collector of debts*
He left huge Lintot, and outstripped the wind.
As when a dab-chick waddles through the copse
On feet and wings, and flies, and wades, and hops:
65 So laboring on, with shoulders, hands, and head,
Wide as a windmill all his figure spread,
With arms expanded Bérnard rows his state,
And left-legged Jacob[4] seems to emulate.
Full in the middle way there stood a lake,
70 Which Curll's Corinna[5] chanced that morn to make:
(Such was her wont, at early dawn to drop
Her evening cates° before his neighbour's shop,)   *dainties*
Here fortuned Curll to slide; loud shout the band,
And "Bérnard! Bérnard!" rings through all the Strand.
75 Obscene with filth the miscreant lies bewrayed,
Fallen in the plash his wickedness had laid:
Then first (if poets aught of truth declare)
The caitiff vaticide° conceived a prayer.   *poet-murderer*
    "Hear, Jove! whose name my bards and I adore,
80 As much at least as any God's, or more;
And him and his if more devotion warms,
Down with the Bible, up with the Pope's Arms."[6]
    A place there is, betwixt earth, air, and seas,
Where, from ambrosia,[7] Jove retires for ease,
85 There in his seat two spacious vents appear,
On this he sits, to that he leans his ear,
And hears the various vows of fond mankind;
Some beg an eastern, some a western wind:
All vain petitions, mounting to the sky,
90 With reams abundant this abode supply;
Amused he reads, and then returns the bills
Signed with that ichor which from gods distils.
    In office here fair Cloacina[8] stands,
And ministers to Jove with purest hands.
95 Forth from the heap she picked her votary's prayer,
And placed it next him, a distinction rare!
Oft had the goddess heard her servants call,
From her black grottos[9] near the Temple-wall,
Listening delighted to the jest unclean
100 Of link-boys° vile, and watermen obscene;   *torch-bearers*
Where as he fished her nether realms for wit,
She oft had favored him, and favors yet.
Renewed by ordure's sympathetic force,
As oiled with magic juices for the course,
105 Vigorous he rises; from the effluvia strong
Imbibes new life, and scours and stinks along;
Re-passes Lintot, vindicates the race,
Nor heeds the brown dishonors of his face.
    And now the victor stretched his eager hand,
110 Where the tall nothing stood, or seemed to stand;

4. Jacob Tonson, the leading publisher of the age. His gait was ungainly.
5. Elizabeth Thomas, a woman of easy virtue ("Corinna" was the Roman poet Ovid's mistress) who stole some of Pope's letters and sold them to Curll.
6. Curll's trademark and Lintot's, respectively.
7. Ambrosia is the food of the gods; ichor (below) is their ethereal "blood."
8. The Roman goddess of the common sewers.
9. I.e., the coal-wharves.

A shapeless shade, it melted from his sight,
Like forms in clouds, or visions of the night.
To seize his papers, Curll, was next thy care;
His papers light fly diverse, tost in air;
115   Songs, sonnets, epigrams the winds uplift,
And whisk 'em back to Evans, Young, and Swift.[1]
The embroidered suit at least he deemed his prey;
That suit an unpaid tailor snatched away.
No rag, no scrap, of all the beau, or wit,
120   That once so fluttered, and that once so writ.

1728   1741

[*The Triumph of Dulness*][3]

In vain, in vain,—the all-composing hour
Resistless° falls: the Muse obeys the power.   *irresistibly*
She comes! she comes![4] the sable throne behold
630   Of *Night* primeval, and of *Chaos* old![5]
Before her, *Fancy's* gilded clouds decay,
And all its varying rainbows die away.
Wit shoots in vain its momentary fires,
The meteor drops, and in a flash expires.
635   As one by one, at dread Medea's strain,
The sickening stars fade off the ethereal plain;[6]
As Argus' eyes by Hermes' wand oppressed,
Closed one by one to everlasting rest;[7]
Thus at her felt approach, and secret might,
640   *Art* after *Art* goes out, and all is night.
See skulking *Truth* to her old cavern fled,[8]
Mountains of casuistry heaped o'er her head!
Philosophy, that leaned on Heaven before,
Shrinks to her second cause,[9] and is no more.
645   *Physic*° of *Metaphysic* begs defense,   *natural science*
And *Metaphysic* calls for aid on *Sense!*
See *Mystery*[1] to *Mathematics* fly!
In vain! they gaze, turn giddy, rave, and die.
Religion blushing veils her sacred fires,
650   And unawares *Morality* expires.
Nor public flame, nor private, dares to shine;
Nor human spark is left, nor glimpse divine!
Lo! thy dread empire, Chaos is restored;
Light dies before thy uncreating word:[2]
655   Thy hand, great Anarch! lets the curtain fall;
And universal darkness buries all.

1743

---

1. Curll had owned writings of these men.
3. *Dunciad* (B) iv.627–656.
4. Dulness, the center of a mock-apocalyptic vision in which the light of the arts and sciences is extinguished.
5. Milton, in *Paradise Lost* I.543, describe the elements separating Heaven and Hell as "Chaos and old Night," or disorder and darkness, the first materials of the cosmos.
6. In Seneca's *Medea*, the stars obey the curse of Medea, a magician and avenger.
7. Hermes, the Greek gods' messenger, charmed the hundred-eyed watchman Argus to sleep and then killed him.
8. "Alluding to the saying of Democritus, that Truth lay at the bottom of a deep well" [Pope's note].
9. In classical philosophy, God is defined as the first cause of all things. Under the sway of Dulness, a materialistic explanation (or "second cause") is substituted.
1. Mystical knowledge.
2. As opposed to God's first creating words in Genesis, "Let there be light."

Epistle to Dr. Arbuthnot[1]

P. Shut, shut the door, good John![2] (fatigued, I said),
Tie up the knocker, say I'm sick, I'm dead.
The Dog Star[3] rages! nay 'tis past a doubt
All Bedlam, or Parnassus,[4] is let out:
5 Fire in each eye, and papers in each hand,
They rave, recite, and madden round the land.
    What walls can guard me, or what shades can hide?
They pierce my thickets, through my grot[5] they glide,
By land, by water, they renew the charge,
10 They stop the chariot, and they board the barge.[6]
No place is sacred, not the church is free;
Even Sunday shines no Sabbath day to me:
Then from the Mint[7] walks forth the man of rhyme,
Happy to catch me just at dinner time.
15   Is there a parson, much bemused in beer,
A maudlin poetess, a rhyming peer,
A clerk foredoomed his father's soul to cross,
Who pens a stanza when he should engross?[8]
Is there who,[9] locked from ink and paper, scrawls
20 With desperate charcoal round his darkened walls?
All fly to Twit'nam,° and in humble strain   *Twickenham*
Apply to me to keep them mad or vain.
Arthur,[1] whose giddy son neglects the laws,
Imputes to me and my damned works the cause:
25 Poor Cornus[2] sees his frantic wife elope,
And curses wit, and poetry, and Pope.
    Friend to my life (which did not you prolong,
The world had wanted many an idle song)
What drop or nostrum° can this plague remove?   *drug*
30 Or which must end me, a fool's wrath or love?
A dire dilemma! either way I'm sped,°   *ruined*
If foes, they write, if friends, they read me dead.
Seized and tied down to judge, how wretched I!
Who can't be silent, and who will not lie.
35 To laugh were want of goodness and of grace,
And to be grave exceeds all power of face.
I sit with sad° civility, I read   *sober*
With honest anguish and an aching head,
And drop at last, but in unwilling ears,
40 This saving counsel, "Keep your piece nine years."[3]
    "Nine years!" cries he, who high in Drury Lane,[4]
Lulled by soft zephyrs through the broken pane,
Rhymes ere he wakes, and prints before term° ends,   *the publishing season*

---

1. John Arbuthnot, former physician to Queen Anne, was Pope's physician, and friend and literary collaborator of Pope, Swift, and Gay. He had asked Pope to moderate his attacks on his personal and literary enemies and was hence a logical person to whom to address an apology for writing satire.
2. Pope's servant, John Serle.
3. The summer star Sirius, attendant upon crazing heat. In ancient Rome, late summer was a season for public recitations of poetry.
4. Bedlam is a hospital for the insane; Mt. Parnassus, the haunt of the Muses.
5. Pope's "grotto," one entrance to the grounds of his villa at Twickenham.

6. Pope often traveled from Twickenham to London by water.
7. A sanctuary for debtors. They emerged on Sunday, being everywhere immune from arrest on that day.
8. Prepare legal documents.
9. I.e., one who.
1. Arthur Moore, father of James Moore Smythe, a playwright who had plagiarized some lines from Pope.
2. From Latin *cornu*, horn; hence a cuckold.
3. Horace's advice (*Ars Poetica*, 386–89).
4. The theater district, where the speaker occupies a garret.

Obliged by hunger and request of friends:
45 "The piece, you think, is incorrect? why, take it,
I'm all submission, what you'd have it, make it."
   Three things another's modest wishes bound,
My friendship, and a prologue, and ten pound.
   Pitholeon[5] sends to me: "You know his Grace,
50 I want a patron; ask him for a place."
Pitholeon libeled me—"but here's a letter
Informs you, sir, 'twas when he knew no better.
Dare you refuse him? Curll[6] invites to dine,
He'll write a *Journal*, or he'll turn divine."[7]
55 Bless me! a packet.—" 'Tis a stranger sues,
A virgin tragedy, an orphan Muse."
If I dislike it, "Furies, death, and rage!"
If I approve, "Commend it to the stage."
There (thank my stars) my whole commission ends,
60 The players and I are, luckily, no friends.
Fired that the house° reject him, " 'Sdeath, I'll print it,   *playhouse*
And shame the fools—Your interest, sir, with Lintot!"[8]
Lintot, dull rogue, will think your price too much.
"Not, sir, if you revise it, and retouch."
65 All my demurs but double his attacks;
At last he whispers, "Do; and we go snacks."°   *shares*
Glad of a quarrel, straight I clap the door,
"Sir, let me see your works and you no more."
   'Tis sung, when Midas' ears began to spring
70 (Midas, a sacred person and a king),
His very minister who spied them first
(Some say his queen) was forced to speak, or burst.[9]
And is not mine, my friend, a sorer case,
When every coxcomb perks them in my face?
75   A. Good friend, forbear! you deal in dangerous things.
I'd never name queens, ministers, or kings;
Keep close to ears, and those let asses prick;
'Tis nothing—— P. Nothing? if they bite and kick?
Out with it, *Dunciad!* let the secret pass,
80 That secret to each fool, that he's an ass:
The truth once told (and wherefore should we lie?)
The queen of Midas slept, and so may I.
   You think this cruel? take it for a rule,
No creature smarts so little as a fool.
85 Let peals of laughter, Codrus![1] round thee break,
Thou unconcerned canst hear the mighty crack.
Pit, box, and gallery in convulsions hurled,
Thou stand'st unshook amidst a bursting world.
Who shames a scribbler? break one cobweb through,
90 He spins the slight, self-pleasing thread anew:
Destroy his fib or sophistry, in vain;
The creature's at his dirty work again,

5. "A foolish poet of Rhodes, who pretended much to Greek" [Pope's note]. He stands for Leonard Welsted, translator of Longinus and an enemy of Pope's.
6. Edmund Curll, an unscrupulous publisher; the bookseller principally derided in the *Dunciad* (above).
7. Referring to attacks on Pope in *The London Journal* and (perhaps) to Welsted's theological writing.
8. Bernard Lintot, an early publisher of Pope's.
9. King Midas, preferring Pan's music to Apollo's, was given ass's ears by the affronted god. His barber (in Chaucer's version of the tale, his wife) discovered the ears and, fairly bursting with the secret, whispered it into a hole in the ground. It is suggested that the prime minister (Walpole) and Queen Caroline know that George II is an ass.
1. A poet ridiculed by Virgil and Juvenal.

Throned in the center of his thin designs,
Proud of a vast extent of flimsy lines.
95 Whom have I hurt? has poet yet or peer
Lost the arched eyebrow or Parnassian sneer?
And has not Colley[2] still his lord and whore?
His butchers Henley? his freemasons Moore?[3]
Does not one table Bavius still admit?
100 Still to one bishop Philips seem a wit?
Still Sappho—— A. Hold! for God's sake—you'll offend.
No names—be calm—learn prudence of a friend.
I too could write, and I am twice as tall;
But foes like these!—— P. One flatterer's worse than all.
105 Of all mad creatures, if the learn'd are right,
It is the slaver kills, and not the bite.
A fool quite angry is quite innocent:
Alas! 'tis ten times worse when they repent.
    One dedicates in high heroic prose,
110 And ridicules beyond a hundred foes;
One from all Grub Street[4] will my fame defend,
And, more abusive, calls himself my friend.
This prints my letters,[5] that expects a bribe,
And others roar aloud, "Subscribe, subscribe!"[6]
115   There are, who to my person pay their court:
I cough like Horace, and, though lean, am short;
Ammon's great son° one shoulder had too high,   *Alexander the Great*
Such Ovid's nose, and "Sir! you have an eye—"
Go on, obliging creatures, make me see
120 All that disgraced my betters met in me.
Say for my comfort, languishing in bed,
"Just so immortal Maro° held his head":   *Virgil*
And when I die, be sure you let me know
Great Homer died three thousand years ago.
125   Why did I write? what sin to me unknown
Dipped me in ink, my parents', or my own?
As yet a child, nor yet a fool to fame,
I lisped in numbers, for the numbers came.
I left no calling for this idle trade,
130 No duty broke, no father disobeyed.
The Muse but served to ease some friend, not wife,
To help me through this long disease, my life,
To second, Arbuthnot! thy art and care,
And teach the being° you preserved, to bear.   *life*
135   A. But why then publish? P. Granville the polite,[7]
And knowing Walsh, would tell me I could write;
Well-natured Garth inflamed with early praise,
And Congreve loved, and Swift endured my lays;
The courtly Talbot, Somers, Sheffield, read;
140 Even mitered Rochester[8] would nod the head,
And St. John's[9] self (great Dryden's friends before)
With open arms received one poet more.

2. Colley Cibber, poet laureate.
3. John Henley ("Orator Henley") was an independent preacher with a mass following. James Moore Smythe was a member of the Masonic order. Bavius (line 99) is a bad poet referred to by Virgil. The Bishop of Armagh employed Ambrose Philips (line 100 [called "Namby-Pamby" by the wits]) as his secretary. "Sappho" (line 101) is Lady Mary Wortley Montagu.

4. The traditional haunt of hack writers.
5. As Curll had done without permission.
6. Pay for copies in advance of publication.
7. There follow the names of poets and men of letters, Pope's early friends. They were literary elder statesmen, chiefly, who had befriended Dryden in the preceding century.
8. The Bishop of Rochester.
9. Pronounced *sinjin*.

Happy my studies, when by these approved!
Happier their author, when by these beloved!
145 From these the world will judge of men and books,
Not from the Búrnets, Óldmixons, and Cookes.[1]
　　Soft were my numbers; who could take offense
While pure description held the place of sense?
Like gentle Fanny's[2] was my flowery theme,
150 A painted mistress, or a purling stream.
Yet then did Gildon[3] draw his venal quill;
I wished the man a dinner, and sat still.
Yet then did Dennis[4] rave in furious fret;
I never answered, I was not in debt.
155 If want provoked, or madness made them print,
I waged no war with Bedlam or the Mint.
　　Did some more sober critic come abroad?
If wrong, I smiled; if right, I kissed the rod.
Pains, reading, study are their just pretense,
160 And all they want is spirit, taste, and sense.
Commas and points they set exactly right,
And 'twere a sin to rob them of their mite.
Yet ne'er one sprig of laurel graced these ribalds,
From slashing Bentley down to piddling Tibbalds.[5]
165 Each wight who reads not, and but scans and spells,
Each word-catcher that lives on syllables,
Even such small critics some regard may claim,
Preserved in Milton's or in Shakespeare's name.
Pretty! in amber to observe the forms
170 Of hairs, or straws, or dirt, or grubs, or worms!
The things, we know, are neither rich nor rare,
But wonder how the devil they got there.
　　Were others angry? I excused them too;
Well might they rage; I gave them but their due.
175 A man's true merit 'tis not hard to find;
But each man's secret standard in his mind,
That casting weight[6] pride adds to emptiness,
This, who can gratify? for who can guess?
The bard whom pilfered pastorals renown,
180 Who turns a Persian tale for half a crown,[7]
Just writes to make his barrenness appear,
And strains from hard-bound brains eight lines a year:
He, who still wanting, though he lives on theft,
Steals much, spends little, yet has nothing left;
185 And he who now to sense, now nonsense leaning,
Means not, but blunders round about a meaning:
And he whose fustian's so sublimely bad,
It is not poetry, but prose run mad:
All these, my modest satire bade translate,
190 And owned that nine such poets made a Tate.[8]
How did they fume, and stamp, and roar, and chafe!

1. Thomas Burnet, John Oldmixon and Arthur
Cooke had all attacked Pope or his works.
2. Lord Hervey, satirized as Sporus in lines
305 ff.
3. Charles Gildon, a critic who had, as Pope
believed, written against him "venally," to
curry favor with Addison. (See line 209n.
below.)
4. John Dennis, who wrote a furious con-
demnation of Pope's *Essay on Criticism*.
5. Richard Bentley, a classical scholar, had
edited *Paradise Lost* with undue license on

the ground that Milton was blind and never
saw his text. Lewis Theobald, no wit but a
closer scholar than Pope, had exposed the
faults of Pope's edition of Shakespeare in a
subsequent edition of his own.
6. Weight tipping the scales.
7. Ambrose Philips (named in line 100), who
had competed with the youthful Pope as a
pastoral poet; author of *Persian Tales*.
8. Nahum Tate, successor to Dryden as poet
laureate.

And swear, not Addison himself was safe.
   Peace to all such! but were there one whose fires
True Genius kindles, and fair Fame inspires;
195 Blessed with each talent and each art to please,
And born to write, converse, and live with ease:
Should such a man, too fond to rule alone,
Bear, like the Turk, no brother near the throne;[9]
View him with scornful, yet with jealous eyes,
200 And hate for arts that caused himself to rise;
Damn with faint praise, assent with civil leer,
And without sneering, teach the rest to sneer;
Willing to wound, and yet afraid to strike,
Just hint a fault, and hesitate dislike;
205 Alike reserved to blame or to commend,
A timorous foe, and a suspicious friend;
Dreading even fools; by flatterers besieged,
And so obliging that he ne'er obliged;
Like Cato, give his little senate laws,[1]
210 And sit attentive to his own applause;
While wits and Templars° every sentence raise,   *law students*
And wonder with a foolish face of praise—
Who but must laugh, if such a man there be?
Who would not weep, if Atticus[2] were he?
215   What though my name stood rubric° on the walls?   *in red letters*
Or plastered posts, with claps,° in capitals?   *posters*
Or smoking forth, a hundred hawkers' load,
On wings of winds came flying all abroad?
I sought no homage from the race that write;
220 I kept, like Asian monarchs, from their sight:
Poems I heeded (now berhymed so long)
No more than thou, great George! a birthday song.
I ne'er with wits or witlings passed my days
To spread about the itch of verse and praise;
225 Nor like a puppy daggled through the town
To fetch and carry sing-song up and down;
Nor at rehearsals sweat, and mouthed, and cried,
With handkerchief and orange at my side;
But sick of fops, and poetry, and prate,
230 To Bufo left the whole Castalian state.[3]
   Proud as Apollo on his forkéd hill,[4]
Sat full-blown Bufo, puffed by every quill;
Fed with soft dedication all day long,
Horace and he went hand in hand in song.
235 His library (where busts of poets dead
And a true Pindar stood without a head)
Received of wits an undistinguished race,
Who first his judgment asked, and then a place:
Much they extolled his pictures, much his seat,°   *estate*
240 And flattered every day, and some days eat:°   *ate*
Till grown more frugal in his riper days,
He paid some bards with port, and some with praise;

9. The Ottoman Emperors, Europeans believed, regularly killed their principal kinsmen upon ascending the throne.
1. Addison (author of the immensely popular tragedy *Cato*) presided over an admiring company of political and literary partisans at Button's Coffee House.
2. A friend of Cicero's; here a pseudonym for Addison.
3. Pope leaves Bufo the whole republic of letters, named from the spring Castalia, which was sacred to Apollo and the Muses. Bufo is perhaps a composite of Lord Halifax and "Bubo," Bubb Dodington.
4. The twin peaks of Parnassus.

To some a dry° rehearsal was assigned,   *without performance*
And others (harder still) he paid in kind.[5]
245   Dryden alone (what wonder?) came not nigh;
Dryden alone escaped this judging eye:
But still the great have kindness in reserve;
He helped to bury whom he helped to starve.
      May some choice patron bless each gray goose quill!°   *quill pen*
250   May every Bavius have his Bufo still!
So when a statesman wants a day's defense,
Or Envy holds a whole week's war with Sense,
Or simple Pride for flattery makes demands,
May dunce by dunce be whistled off my hands!
255   Blessed be the great! for those they take away,
And those they left me—for they left me Gay;[6]
Left me to see neglected genius bloom,
Neglected die, and tell it on his tomb;
Of all thy blameless life the sole return
260   My verse, and Queensberry weeping o'er thy urn!
Oh, let me live my own, and die so too!
("To live and die is all I have to do")
Maintain a poet's dignity and ease,
And see what friends, and read what books I please;
265   Above a patron, though I condescend
Some times to call a minister my friend.
I was not born for courts or great affairs;
I pay my debts, believe, and say my prayers,
Can sleep without a poem in my head,
270   Nor know if Dennis be alive or dead.
      Why am I asked what next shall see the light?
Heavens! was I born for nothing but to write?
Has life no joys for me? or (to be grave)
Have I no friend to serve, no soul to save?
275   "I found him close with Swift"—"Indeed? no doubt,"
Cries prating Balbus, "something will come out."
'Tis all in vain, deny it as I will.
"No, such a genius never can lie still,"
And then for mine obligingly mistakes
280   The first lampoon Sir Will or Bubo[7] makes.
Poor guiltless I! and can I choose but smile,
When every coxcomb knows me by my style?
      Cursed be the verse, how well soe'er it flow,
That tends to make one worthy man my foe,
285   Give Virtue scandal, Innocence a fear,
Or from the soft-eyed virgin steal a tear!
But he who hurts a harmless neighbor's peace,
Insults fallen worth, or Beauty in distress,
Who loves a lie, lame Slander helps about,
290   Who writes a libel, or who copies out:
That fop whose pride affects a patron's name,
Yet absent, wounds an author's honest fame;
Who can your merit selfishly approve,
And show the sense of it without the love;
295   Who has the vanity to call you friend,
Yet wants the honor, injured, to defend;

---

5. I.e., he read them his poetry in turn.
6. John Gay, author of *The Beggar's Opera*,
associate of Pope and Swift; befriended (line
260) by the Duke and Duchess of Queens-
berry.
7. Sir William Yonge or Bubb Dodington.
Both were Pope's political adversaries as well
as, in some degree, silly men.

Who tells whate'er you think, whate'er you say,
And, if he lie not, must at least betray:
Who to the dean and silver bell can swear,
300 And sees at Cannons what was never there:[8]
Who reads but with a lust to misapply,
Make satire a lampoon, and fiction, lie:
A lash like mine no honest man shall dread,
But all such babbling blockheads in his stead.
305   Let Sporus[9] tremble—— A. What? that thing of silk,
Sporus, that mere white curd of ass's milk?
Satire or sense, alas! can Sporus feel?
Who breaks a butterfly upon a wheel?
   P. Yet let me flap this bug with gilded wings,
310 This painted child of dirt, that stinks and stings;
Whose buzz the witty and the fair annoys,
Yet wit ne'er tastes, and beauty ne'er enjoys;
So well-bred spaniels civilly delight
In mumbling of the game they dare not bite.
315 Eternal smiles his emptiness betray,
As shallow streams run dimpling all the way.
Whether in florid impotence he speaks,
And, as the prompter breathes, the puppet squeaks;
Or at the ear of Eve,[1] familiar toad,
320 Half froth, half venom, spits himself abroad,
In puns, or politics, or tales, or lies,
Or spite, or smut, or rhymes, or blasphemies.
His wit all seesaw between *that* and *this,*
Now high, now low, now master up, now miss,
325 And he himself one vile antithesis.
Amphibious thing! that acting either part,
The trifling head or the corrupted heart,
Fop at the toilet, flatterer at the board,
Now trips a lady, and now struts a lord.
330 Eve's tempter thus the rabbins° have expressed,   *Hebrew scholars*
A cherub's face, a reptile all the rest;
Beauty that shocks you, parts° that none will trust,   *talents*
Wit that can creep, and pride that licks the dust.
   Not Fortune's worshiper, nor Fashion's fool,
335 Not Lucre's° madman, nor Ambition's tool,   *Money's*
Not proud, nor servile, be one poet's praise,
That if he pleased, he pleased by manly ways:
That flattery, even to kings, he held a shame,
And thought a lie in verse or prose the same:
340 That not in fancy's maze he wandered long,
But stooped[2] to truth, and moralized his song:
That not for fame, but Virtue's better end,
He stood the furious foe, the timid friend,
The damning critic, half approving wit,
345 The coxcomb hit, or fearing to be hit;
Laughed at the loss of friends he never had,

8. In his *Epistle to Burlington,* Pope satirized "Timon's Villa," an estate where a silver bell and an obsequious dean invite worshipers to an overstuffed chapel. Mischief-makers had identified this estate with Cannons, the ostentatious home of Pope's well-wisher the Duke of Chandos.
9. Roman eunuch, victim of the Emperor Nero's perversions; in the poem, Lord Hervey, a foppish and effeminate courtier who was Pope's personal, political, and literary enemy. He attested his frailty by drinking ass's milk as a tonic.
1. Like Satan in Eden (*Paradise Lost* IV. 790 ff.). Hervey was Queen Caroline's confidant; the word *familiar* suggests a demonic ministrant.
2. Swooped down perceiving prey (a term from falconry).

The dull, the proud, the wicked, and the mad;
The distant threats of vengeance on his head,
The blow unfelt, the tear he never shed;
350   The tale revived, the lie so oft o'erthrown,
The imputed trash, and dullness not his own;
The morals blackened when the writings 'scape,
The libeled person, and the pictured shape;[3]
Abuse on all he loved, or loved him, spread,
355   A friend in exile, or a father dead;
The whisper,[4] that to greatness still too near,
Perhaps yet vibrates on his sovereign's ear—
Welcome for thee, fair Virtue! all the past!
For thee, fair Virtue! welcome even the last!
360   A. But why insult the poor, affront the great?
P. A knave's a knave to me in every state:
Alike my scorn, if he succeed or fail,
Sporus at court, or Japhet[5] in a jail,
A hireling scribbler, or a hireling peer,
365   Knight of the post[6] corrupt, or of the shire,
If on a pillory, or near a throne,
He gain his prince's ear, or lose his own.
Yet soft by nature, more a dupe than wit,
Sappho can tell you how this man was bit:°   *deceived*
370   This dreaded satirist Dennis will confess
Foe to his pride, but friend to his distress:[7]
So humble, he has knocked at Tibbald's door,
Has drunk with Cibber, nay, has rhymed for Moore.
Full ten years slandered, did he once reply?
375   Three thousand suns went down on Welsted's lie.[8]
To please a mistress one aspersed his life;
He lashed him not, but let her be his wife.
Let Budgell charge low Grub Street on his quill,
And write whate'er he pleased, except his will;[9]
380   Let the two Curlls, of town and court,[1] abuse
His father, mother, body, soul, and muse.
Yet why? that father held it for a rule,
It was a sin to call our neighbor fool;
That harmless mother thought no wife a whore:
385   Hear this, and spare his family, James Moore!
Unspotted names, and memorable long,
If there be force in virtue, or in song.
Of gentle blood (part shed in honor's cause,
While yet in Britain honor had applause)
390   Each parent sprung—— A. What fortune, pray?—— P. Their own,
And better got than Bestia's[2] from the throne.
Born to no pride, inheriting no strife,
Nor marrying discord in a noble wife,
Stranger to civil and religious rage,
395   The good man walked innoxious through his age.
No courts he saw, no suits would ever try,

3. Cartoons were drawn of Pope's hunched posture.
4. Hervey's whisper to Queen Caroline.
5. Japhet Crook, a forger; his ears were cropped for his crime (line 367).
6. "Knight of the post": professional witness.
7. Pope contributed to a benefit performance for the aging Dennis.
8. A hint that Pope had contributed to the death of the "Unfortunate Lady" celebrated in the *Elegy* above. (The lady seems actually to have been a fiction.)
9. Budgell (perhaps falsely) attributed to Pope a squib in the *Grub-Street Journal* charging that Budgell had forged a will.
1. Edmund Curll, the publisher; and Lord Hervey.
2. A Roman consul who was bribed to arrange a dishonorable peace; in the poem, probably the Duke of Marlborough.

Nor dared an oath, nor hazarded a lie.[3]
Unlearn'd, he knew no schoolman's subtle art,
No language but the language of the heart.
400 By nature honest, by experience wise,
Healthy by temperance, and by exercise;
His life, though long, to sickness passed unknown,
His death was instant, and without a groan.
Oh, grant me thus to live, and thus to die!
405 Who sprung from kings shall know less joy than I.
  O friend! may each domestic bliss be thine!
Be no unpleasing melancholy mine:
Me, let the tender office long engage,
To rock the cradle of reposing Age,
410 With lenient arts extend a mother's breath,
Make Languor smile, and smooth the bed of Death,
Explore the thought, explain the asking eye,
And keep a while one parent from the sky!
On cares like these if length of days attend,
415 May Heaven, to bless those days, preserve my friend,
Preserve him social, cheerful, and serene,
And just as rich as when he served a Queen![4]
A. Whether that blessing be denied or given,
Thus far was right—the rest belongs to Heaven.

1735

JAMES THOMSON
(1700–1748)

From The Seasons

From *Winter*

The keener tempests come: and, fuming dun
From all the livid east or piercing north,
225 Thick clouds ascend, in whose capacious womb
A vapory deluge lies, to snow congealed.
Heavy they roll their fleecy world along,
And the sky saddens with the gathered storm.
Through the hushed air the whitening shower descends,
230 At first thin-wavering; till at last the flakes
Fall broad and wide and fast, dimming the day
With a continual flow. The cherished fields
Put on their winter robe of purest white.
'Tis brightness all; save where the new snow melts
235 Along the mazy current. Low the woods
Bow their hoar head; and, ere the languid sun
Faint from the west emits his evening ray,
Earth's universal face, deep-hid and chill,
Is one wild dazzling waste that buries wide
240 The works of man. Drooping, the laborer-ox
Stands covered o'er with snow, and then demands
The fruit of all his toil. The fowls of heaven,

---

3. He did not take the special oath required
of Catholics wanting to enter public life or
the professions, nor did he evade by falsehood
the restrictions on Catholics.

4. Arbuthnot, who had sought no professional
profit as physician to Queen Anne, continued
to earn the same income after her death.

Tamed by the cruel season, crowd around
The winnowing store, and claim the little boon
245 Which Providence assigns them. One alone,
The redbreast, sacred to the household gods,
Wisely regardful of the embroiling sky,
In joyless fields and thorny thickets leaves
His shivering mates, and pays to trusted man
250 His annual visit. Half afraid, he first
Against the window beats; then brisk alights
On the warm hearth; then, hopping o'er the floor,
Eyes all the smiling family askance,
And pecks, and starts, and wonders where he is—
255 Till, more familiar grown, the table crumbs
Attract his slender feet. The foodless wilds
Pour forth their brown inhabitants. The hare,
Though timorous of heart, and hard beset
By death in various forms, dark snares, and dogs,
260 And more unpitying men, the garden seeks,
Urged on by fearless want. The bleating kind°   *race*
Eye the bleak heaven, and next the glistening earth,
With looks of dumb despair; then, sad-dispersed,
Dig for the withered herb through heaps of snow.
265   Now, shepherds, to your helpless charge be kind;
Baffle the raging year, and fill their pens
With food at will; lodge them below the storm,
And watch them strict, for, from the bellowing east,
In this dire season, oft the whirlwind's wing
270 Sweeps up the burden of whole wintry plains
In one wide weft,° and o'er the hapless flocks,   *web*
Hid in the hollow of two neighboring hills,
The billowy tempest whelms,° till, upward urged,   *engulfs*
The valley to a shining mountain swells,
275 Tipped with a wreath high-curling in the sky.
    As thus the snows arise, and, foul and fierce,
All Winter drives along the darkened air,
In his own loose-revolving° fields the swain   *freely whirling*
Disastered stands; sees other hills ascend,
280 Of unknown joyless brow, and other scenes,
Of horrid prospect, shag° the trackless plain;   *make shaggy*
Nor finds the river nor the forest, hid
Beneath the formless wild, but wanders on
From hill to dale, still more and more astray,
285 Impatient flouncing through the drifted heaps,
Stung with the thoughts of home—the thoughts of home
Rush on his nerves and call their vigor forth
In many a vain attempt. How sinks his soul!
What black despair, what horror fills his heart,
290 When, for the dusky spot which fancy feigned
His tufted cottage rising through the snow,
He meets the roughness of the middle waste,
Far from the track and blest abode of man,
While round him night resistless closes fast,
295 And every tempest, howling o'er his head,
Renders the savage wilderness more wild.
Then throng the busy shapes into his mind
Of covered pits, unfathomably deep,
A dire descent! beyond the power of frost;

300 Of faithless bogs; of precipices huge,
    Smoothed up with snow; and (what is land unknown,
    What water) of the still unfrozen spring,
    In the loose marsh or solitary lake,
    Where the fresh fountain from the bottom boils.
305 These check his fearful steps; and down he sinks
    Beneath the shelter of the shapeless drift,
    Thinking o'er all the bitterness of death,
    Mixed with the tender anguish nature shoots
    Through the wrung bosom of the dying man—
310 His wife, his children, and his friends unseen.
    In vain for him the officious° wife prepares   *dutiful*
    The fire fair-blazing and the vestment warm;
    In vain his little children, peeping out
    Into the mingling storm, demand their sire
315 With tears of artless innocence. Alas!
    Nor wife nor children more shall he behold,
    Nor friends, nor sacred home. On every nerve
    The deadly winter seizes, shuts up sense,
    And, o'er his inmost vitals creeping cold,
320 Lays him along the snows a stiffened corse,°   *corpse*
    Stretched out and bleaching in the northern blast.
        Ah! little think the gay licentious proud,
    Whom pleasure, power, and affluence surround—
    They who their thoughtless hours in giddy mirth,
325 And wanton, often cruel, riot° waste—   *revelry*
    Ah! little think they, while they dance along,
    How many feel, this very moment, death
    And all the sad variety of pain;
    How many sink in the devouring flood,
330 Or more devouring flame; how many bleed,
    By shameful variance° betwixt man and man;   *quarreling*
    How many pine in want, and dungeon glooms,
    Shut from the common air and common use
    Of their own limbs; how many drink the cup
335 Of baleful grief, or eat the bitter bread
    Of misery; sore pierced by wintry winds,
    How many shrink into the sordid hut
    Of cheerless poverty; how many shake
    With all the fiercer tortures of the mind,
340 Unbounded passion, madness, guilt, remorse—
    Whence, tumbled headlong from the height of life,
    They furnish matter for the Tragic Muse;
    Even in the vale, where wisdom loves to dwell,
    With friendship, peace, and contemplation joined,
345 How many, racked with honest passions, droop
    In deep retired distress; how many stand
    Around the death-bed of their dearest friends,
    And point° the parting anguish! Thought fond man   *accentuate*
    Of these, and all the thousand nameless ills
350 That one incessant struggle render life,[1]
    One scene of toil, of suffering, and of fate,
    Vice in his high career would stand appalled,
    And heedless rambling Impulse learn to think;

---

1. I.e., if foolish man thought of these, and of all the thousand nameless ills that render life one incessant struggle.

The conscious° heart of Charity would warm,   *sympathetic*
355 And her wide wish Benevolence dilate;°   *diffuse*
The social tear would rise, the social sigh;
And into clear perfection, gradual° bliss,   *progressive*
Refining still, the social passions work.

1726

Rule, Britannia!

When Britain first, at heaven's command,
  Arose from out the azure main,
This was the charter of the land,
  And guardian angels sung this strain—
5   "Rule, Britannia, rule the waves;
    Britons never will be slaves."

The nations, not so blest as thee,
  Must in their turns to tyrants fall;
While thou shalt flourish great and free,
10   The dread and envy of them all.
    "Rule, . . ."

Still more majestic shalt thou rise,
  More dreadful from each foreign stroke;
As the loud blast that tears the skies
15   Serves but to root thy native oak.
    "Rule, . . ."

Thee haughty tyrants ne'er shall tame;
  All their attempts to bend thee down
Will but arouse thy generous flame,
20   But work their woe and thy renown.
    "Rule, . . ."

To thee belongs the rural reign;
  Thy cities shall with commerce shine;
All thine shall be the subject main,
25   And every shore it circles thine.
    "Rule, . . ."

The Muses, still with freedom found,
  Shall to thy happy coast repair:
Blest isle! with matchless beauty crowned,
30   And manly hearts to guard the fair.
    "Rule, Britannia, rule the waves;
    Britons never will be slaves."

1740

SAMUEL JOHNSON
(1709–1784)

Prologue Spoken by Mr. Garrick[1]

AT THE OPENING OF THE THEATER ROYAL, DRURY LANE, 1747

When Learning's triumph o'er her barbarous foes
First reared the stage, immortal Shakespeare rose;
Each change of many-colored life he drew,
Exhausted worlds, and then imagined new:
5   Existence saw him spurn her bounded reign,
And panting Time toiled after him in vain.
His powerful strokes presiding Truth impressed,
And unresisted Passion stormed the breast.
   Then Jonson came, instructed from the school
10 To please in method and invent by rule;
His studious patience and laborious art
By regular approach essayed the heart;
Cold Approbation gave the lingering bays,
For those who durst not censure, scarce could praise.
15 A mortal born, he met the general doom,
But left, like Egypt's kings, a lasting tomb.
   The wits of Charles[2] found easier ways to fame,
Nor wished for Jonson's art, or Shakespeare's flame;
Themselves they studied; as they felt, they writ;
20 Intrigue was plot, obscenity was wit.
Vice always found a sympathetic friend;
They pleased their age, and did not aim to mend.°   *amend it*
Yet bards like these aspired to lasting praise,
And proudly hoped to pimp in future days.
25 Their cause was general, their supports were strong,
Their slaves were willing, and their reign was long:
Till Shame regained the post that Sense betrayed,
And Virtue called Oblivion to her aid.
   Then, crushed by rules, and weakened as refined,
30 For years the power of Tragedy declined;
From bard to bard the frigid caution crept,
Till Declamation roared while Passion slept;
Yet still did Virtue deign the stage to tread;
Philosophy remained though Nature fled;
35 But forced at length her ancient reign to quit,
She saw great Faustus[3] lay the ghost of Wit;
Exulting Folly hailed the joyous day,
And Pantomime and Song confirmed her sway.
   But who the coming changes can presage,
40 And mark the future periods of the stage?
Perhaps if skill could distant times explore,
New Behns, new Durfeys,[4] yet remain in store;
Perhaps where Lear has raved, and Hamlet died,

---

1. David Garrick, the actor and theater-manager.
2. The comic playwrights of the Restoration.
3. As treated in current farce and pantomime.

4. Aphra Behn, Restoration author noted for her salacious plays; and Thomas Durfey, playwright and poetaster at the turn of the century who was a standing joke among the wits.

On flying cars new sorcerers may ride;
45 Perhaps (for who can guess the effects of chance?)
Here Hunt may box, or Mahomet may dance.[5]
  Hard is his lot that, here by fortune placed,
Must watch the wild vicissitudes of taste;
With every meteor of caprice must play,
50 And chase the new-blown bubbles of the day.
Ah! let not censure term our fate our choice,
The stage but echoes back the public voice;
The drama's laws, the drama's patrons give,
For we that live to please, must please to live.
55   Then prompt no more the follies you decry,
As tyrants doom their tools of guilt to die;
'Tis yours this night to bid the reign commence
Of rescued Nature and reviving Sense;
To chase the charms of Sound, the pomp of Show,
60 For useful Mirth and salutary Woe;
Bid scenic Virtue form the rising age,
And Truth diffuse her radiance from the stage.

                                             1747

The Vanity of Human Wishes

IN IMITATION OF THE TENTH SATIRE OF JUVENAL

   Let Observation, with extensive view,
Survey mankind, from China to Peru;
Remark each anxious toil, each eager strife,
And watch the busy scenes of crowded life;
5 Then say how hope and fear, desire and hate
O'erspread with snares the clouded maze of fate,
Where wavering man, betrayed by venturous pride
To tread the dreary paths without a guide,
As treacherous phantoms in the mist delude,
10 Shuns fancied ills, or chases airy good;
How rarely Reason guides the stubborn choice,
Rules the bold hand, or prompts the suppliant voice;
How nations sink, by darling schemes oppressed,
When Vengeance listens to the fool's request.[6]
15 Fate wings with every wish the afflictive dart,
Each gift of nature, and each grace of art;[7]
With fatal heat impetuous courage glows,
With fatal sweetness elocution flows,
Impeachment stops the speaker's powerful breath,
20 And restless fire precipitates on death.[8]
   But scarce observed, the knowing and the bold
Fall in the general massacre of gold;
Wide-wasting pest! that rages unconfined,
And crowds with crimes the records of mankind;
25 For gold his sword the hireling ruffian draws,
For gold the hireling judge distorts the laws;
Wealth heaped on wealth, nor truth nor safety buys,
The dangers gather as the treasures rise.

---

5. A pugilist and a tightrope dancer currently popular.
6. I.e., when vengeance hangs over a nation, ready to descend on it if the proposals of political fools prevail.
7. The sense of this couplet is that men can be hurried toward misery by their desires and even by their talents and accomplishments.
8. Perhaps, that is, impetuous energy hastens men to their death.

Let History tell where rival kings command,
30 And dubious title shakes the madded land,
When statutes glean the refuse of the sword,
How much more safe the vassal than the lord,
Low skulks the hind beneath the rage of power,
And leaves the wealthy traitor in the Tower,
35 Untouched his cottage, and his slumbers sound,
Though Confiscation's vultures hover round.
    The needy traveler, serene and gay,
Walks the wild heath, and sings his toil away.
Does envy seize thee? crush the upbraiding joy,
40 Increase his riches and his peace destroy;
New fears in dire vicissitude invade,
The rustling brake° alarms, and quivering shade,   **thicket**
Nor light nor darkness bring his pain relief,
One shows the plunder, and one hides the thief.
45   Yet still one general cry the skies assails,
And gain and grandeur load the tainted gales;
Few know the toiling statesman's fear or care,
The insidious rival and the gaping heir.
    Once more, Democritus,[9] arise on earth,
50 With cheerful wisdom and instructive mirth,
See motley life in modern trappings dressed,
And feed with varied fools the eternal jest:
Thou who couldst laugh where Want enchained Caprice,
Toil crushed Conceit, and man was of a piece;
55 Where Wealth unloved without a mourner died;
And scarce a sycophant was fed by Pride;
Where ne'er was known the form of mock debate,
Or seen a new-made mayor's unwieldy state;°   **pomp**
Where change of favorites made no change of laws,
60 And senates heard before they judged a cause;
How wouldst thou shake at Britain's modish tribe,
Dart the quick taunt, and edge the piercing gibe?
Attentive truth and nature to descry,
And pierce each scene with philosophic eye,
65 To thee were solemn toys or empty show
The robes of pleasures and the veils of woe:
All aid the farce, and all thy mirth maintain,
Whose joys are causeless, or whose griefs are vain.
    Such was the scorn that filled the sage's mind,
70 Renewed at every glance on human kind;
How just that scorn ere yet thy voice declare,
Search every state, and canvass every prayer.
    Unnumbered suppliants crowd Preferment's gate,
Athirst for wealth, and burning to be great;
75 Delusive Fortune hears the incessant call,
They mount, they shine, evaporate, and fall.
On every stage the foes of peace attend,
Hate dogs their flight, and Insult mocks their end.
Love ends with hope, the sinking statesman's door
80 Pours in the morning worshiper no more;[1]
For growing names the weekly scribbler lies,
To growing wealth the dedicator flies;

---

9. Greek philosopher, a fatalist who exalted cheerfulness and derided all immoderate pretensions.

1. Important personages received petitions and official calls in the morning.

From every room descends the painted face,
That hung the bright palladium[2] of the place;
85 And smoked in kitchens, or in auctions sold,
To better features yields the frame of gold;
For now no more we trace in every line
Heroic worth, benevolence divine:
The form distorted justifies the fall,
90 And Detestation rids the indignant wall.
　　But will not Britain hear the last appeal,
Sign her foes' doom, or guard her favorites' zeal?
Through Freedom's sons no more remonstrance rings,
Degrading nobles and controlling kings;
95 Our supple tribes repress their patriot throats,
And ask no questions but the price of votes,
With weekly libels and septennial ale.[3]
Their wish is full° to riot and to rail.   *satisfied*
　　In full-blown dignity, see Wolsey[4] stand,
100 Law in his voice, and fortune in his hand:
To him the church, the realm, their powers consign,
Through him the rays of regal bounty shine;
Turned by his nod the stream of honor flows,
His smile alone security bestows:
105 Still to new heights his restless wishes tower,
Claim leads to claim, and power advances power;
Till conquest unresisted ceased to please,
And rights submitted, left him none to seize.
At length his sovereign frowns—the train of state
110 Mark the keen glance, and watch the sign to hate.
Where'er he turns, he meets a stranger's eye,
His suppliants scorn him, and his followers fly;
At once is lost the pride of awful state,
The golden canopy, the glittering plate,
115 The regal palace, the luxurious board,
The liveried army, and the menial lord.
With age, with cares, with maladies oppressed,
He seeks the refuge of monastic rest.
Grief aids disease, remembered folly stings,
120 And his last sighs reproach the faith of kings.
　　Speak thou, whose thoughts at humble peace repine,
Shall Wolsey's wealth, with Wolsey's end be thine?
Or liv'st thou now, with safer pride content,
The wisest justice on the banks of Trent?
125 For why did Wolsey, near the steeps of fate,
On weak foundations raise the enormous weight?
Why but to sink beneath misfortune's blow,
With louder ruin to the gulfs below?
What gave great Villiers[5] to the assassin's knife,
130 And fixed disease on Harley's closing life?
What murdered Wentworth, and what exiled Hyde,
By kings protected and to kings allied?

2. An image of Pallas which supposedly pre-served Troy from capture as long as it re-mained in the city; hence, a safeguard.
3. I.e., public attacks in the weekly press and ale distributed at the parliamentary elections held every seventh year.
4. Thomas, Cardinal Wolsey, Lord Chancellor under Henry VIII.
5. Duke of Buckingham, court favorite of James I and Charles I; assassinated in 1628.

Robert Harley (line 130), Earl of Oxford, a member of the Tory ministry under Queen Anne, was subsequently imprisoned and suf-fered a decline. Thomas Wentworth, Earl of Strafford, advisor to Charles I, was executed under the Long Parliament. Edward Hyde, Earl of Clarendon, who was Charles II's Lord Chancellor and whose daughter married into the royal family, was impeached and exiled in 1667.

What but their wish indulged in courts to shine,
And power too great to keep or to resign?
When first the college rolls receive his name,
The young enthusiast quits his ease for fame;
Resistless burns the fever of renown
Caught from the strong contagion of the gown:[6]
O'er Bodley's dome his future labors spread,
And Bacon's mansion trembles o'er his head.[7]
Are these thy views? proceed, illustrious youth,
And Virtue guard thee to the throne of Truth!
Yet should thy soul indulge the generous heat,
Till captive Science yields her last retreat;
Should Reason guide thee with her brightest ray,
And pour on misty Doubt resistless day;
Should no false kindness lure to loose delight,
Nor praise relax, nor difficulty fright;
Should tempting Novelty thy cell refrain,
And Sloth effuse her opiate fumes in vain;
Should Beauty blunt on fops her fatal dart,
Nor claim the triumph of a lettered heart;
Should no disease thy torpid veins invade,
Nor Melancholy's phantoms haunt thy shade;
Yet hope not life from grief or danger free,
Nor think the doom of man reversed for thee:
Deign on the passing world to turn thine eyes,
And pause a while from letters, to be wise;
There mark what ills the scholar's life assail,
Toil, envy, want, the patron, and the jail.
See nations slowly wise, and meanly just,
To buried merit raise the tardy bust.
If dreams yet flatter, once again attend,
Hear Lydiat's life, and Galileo's end.[8]
Nor deem, when Learning her last prize bestows,
The glittering eminence exempt from foes;
See when the vulgar 'scapes, despised or awed,
Rebellion's vengeful talons seize on Laud.[9]
From meaner minds though smaller fines content,
The plundered palace, or sequestered° rent;   *confiscated*
Marked out by dangerous parts he meets the shock,
And fatal Learning leads him to the block:
Around his tomb let Art and Genius weep,
But hear his death, ye blockheads, hear and sleep.[1]
The festal blazes, the triumphal show,
The ravished standard, and the captive foe,
The senate's thanks, the gazette's pompous tale,
With force resistless o'er the brave prevail.
Such bribes the rapid Greek[2] o'er Asia whirled,
For such the steady Romans shook the world;
For such in distant lands the Britons shine,
And stain with blood the Danube or the Rhine;

---

6. Academic gown, put on upon entering the university, with allusion to the shirt of Nessus, the flaming robe which clung to Hercules and drove him to his death.
7. "There is a tradition, that the study of friar Bacon, built on an arch over the bridge, will fall, when a man greater than Bacon shall pass under it" [Johnson's note]. "Bodley's dome" is the Bodleian Library at Oxford; "dome" means *domus*, house.
8. Thomas Lydiat (1572–1646), the Oxford mathematician and don, endured lifelong poverty. Galileo, the Italian astronomer, was imprisoned for heresy by the Inquisition; he died blind in 1642.
9. Archbishop of Canterbury under Charles I; executed in 1645 for his devotion to episcopacy.
1. Rest secure, that is, since you lack Laud's learning and gifts.
2. I.e., Alexander.

This power has praise that virtue scarce can warm,[3]
Till fame supplies the universal charm.
185 Yet Reason frowns on War's unequal game,
Where wasted nations raise a single name,
And mortgaged states their grandsires' wreaths regret
From age to age in everlasting debt;
Wreaths which at last the dear-bought right convey
190 To rust on medals, or on stones decay.
   On what foundation stands the warrior's pride,
How just his hopes, let Swedish Charles[4] decide;
A frame of adamant, a soul of fire,
No dangers fright him, and no labors tire;
195 O'er love, o'er fear, extends his wide domain,
Unconquered lord of pleasure and of pain;
No joys to him pacific scepters yield,
War sounds the trump, he rushes to the field;
Behold surrounding kings their powers combine,
200 And one capitulate, and one resign;[5]
Peace courts his hand, but spreads her charms in vain;
"Think nothing gained," he cries, "till naught remain,
On Moscow's walls till Gothic° standards fly,   *Teutonic*
And all be mine beneath the polar sky."
205 The march begins in military state,
And nations on his eye suspended wait;
Stern Famine guards the solitary coast,
And Winter barricades the realms of Frost;
He comes, nor want nor cold his course delay—
210 Hide, blushing Glory, hide Pultowa's day:
The vanquished hero leaves his broken bands,
And shows his miseries in distant lands;
Condemned a needy supplicant to wait,
While ladies interpose, and slaves debate.
215 But did not Chance at length her error mend?
Did no subverted empire mark his end?
Did rival monarchs give the fatal wound?
Or hostile millions press him to the ground?
His fall was destined to a barren strand,
220 A petty fortress, and a dubious hand;
He left the name at which the world grew pale,
To point a moral, or adorn a tale.
   All times their scenes of pompous woes afford,
From Persia's tyrant to Bavaria's lord.[6]
225 In gay hostility, and barbarous pride,
With half mankind embattled at his side,
Great Xerxes comes to seize the certain prey,
And starves exhausted regions in his way;
Attendant Flattery counts his myriads o'er,
230 Till counted myriads soothe his pride no more;
Fresh praise is tried till madness fires his mind,
The waves he lashes, and enchains the wind;
New powers are claimed, new powers are still bestowed,

3. I.e., praise has a power (to activate the brave) which an abstract love of virtue can scarcely begin to kindle.
4. King Charles XII. Peter the Great defeated him at Pultowa in 1709. Escaping, "a needy supplicant," he sought an alliance with the Turkish Sultan. He was killed in an attack on "a petty fortress," Fredrikshald in Norway.
5. Frederick IV of Denmark capitulated, and Augustus II of Poland resigned his throne.

6. "Persia's tyrant" is the emperor Xerxes, whose forces the Greeks defeated by sea at Salamis in 480 B.C. and later, on land, at Plataea. "Bavaria's Lord" is Charles Albert, Elector of Bavaria, who successfully aspired to the crown of the Holy Roman Empire but was deposed in a few years through the political skill of Maria Theresa ("fair Austria," line 245).

Till rude resistance lops the spreading god;
235 The daring Greeks deride the martial show,
And heap their valleys with the gaudy foe;
The insulted sea with humbler thought he gains,
A single skiff to speed his flight remains;
The encumbered oar scarce leaves the dreaded coast
240 Through purple° billows and a floating host.   *blood-stained*
    The bold Bavarian, in a luckless hour,
Tries the dread summits of Caesarean° power,   *imperial*
With unexpected legions bursts away,
And sees defenseless realms receive his sway;
245 Short sway! fair Austria spreads her mournful charms,
The queen, the beauty, sets the world in arms;
From hill to hill the beacon's rousing blaze
Spreads wide the hope of plunder and of praise;
The fierce Croatian, and the wild Hussar,[7]
250 With all the sons of ravage crowd the war;
The baffled prince, in honor's flattering bloom,
Of hasty greatness finds the fatal doom,
His foes' derision, and his subjects' blame,
And steals to death from anguish and from shame.
255   Enlarge my life with multitude of days!
In health, in sickness, thus the suppliant prays;
Hides from himself his state, and shuns to know,
That life protracted is protracted woe.
Time hovers o'er, impatient to destroy,
260 And shuts up all the passages of joy;
In vain their gifts the bounteous seasons pour,
The fruit autumnal, and the vernal flower;
With listless eyes the dotard views the store,
He views, and wonders that they please no more;
265 Now pall the tasteless meats, and joyless wines,
And Luxury with sighs her slave resigns.
Approach, ye minstrels, try the soothing strain,
Diffuse the tuneful lenitives° of pain: *softeners*
No sounds, alas! would touch the impervious ear,
270 Though dancing mountains witnessed Orpheus near;[8]
Nor lute nor lyre his feeble powers attend,
Nor sweeter music of a virtuous friend,
But everlasting dictates crowd his tongue,
Perversely grave, or positively wrong.
275 The still returning tale, and lingering jest,
Perplex the fawning niece and pampered guest,
While growing hopes scarce awe the gathering sneer,
And scarce a legacy can bribe to hear;
The watchful guests still hint the last offense;
280 The daughter's petulance, the son's expense,
Improve° his heady rage with treacherous skill,   *play upon*
And mold his passions till they make his will.
    Unnumbered maladies his joints invade,
Lay siege to life and press the dire blockade;
285 But unextinguished avarice still remains,
And dreaded losses aggravate his pains;
He turns, with anxious heart and crippled hands,
His bonds of debt, and mortgages of lands;
Or views his coffers with suspicious eyes,

---

7. Hungarian cavalryman.

8. The legendary Thracian bard whose playing could move even trees and hills.

290   Unlocks his gold, and counts it till he dies.
           But grant, the virtues of a temperate prime
       Bless with an age exempt from scorn or crime;
       An age that melts with unperceived decay,
       And glides in modest innocence away;
295   Whose peaceful day Benevolence endears,
       Whose night congratulating Conscience cheers;
       The general favorite as the general friend:
       Such age there is, and who shall wish its end?
           Yet even on this her load Misfortune flings,
300   To press the weary minutes' flagging wings;
       New sorrow rises as the day returns,
       A sister sickens, or a daughter mourns.
       Now kindred Merit fills the sable bier,
       Now lacerated Friendship claims a tear;
305   Year chases year, decay pursues decay,
       Still drops some joy from withering life away;
       New forms arise, and different views engage,
       Superfluous lags the veteran[9] on the stage,
       Till pitying Nature signs the last release,
310   And bids afflicted Worth retire to peace.
           But few there are whom hours like these await,
       Who set unclouded in the gulfs of Fate.
       From Lydia's monarch[1] should the search descend,
       By Solon cautioned to regard his end,
315   In life's last scene what prodigies surprise,
       Fears of the brave, and follies of the wise!
       From Marlborough's eyes the streams of dotage flow,
       And Swift expires a driveler and a show.[2]
           The teeming mother, anxious for her race,
320   Begs for each birth the fortune of a face:
       Yet Vane could tell what ills from beauty spring;[3]
       And Sedley cursed the form that pleased a king.
       Ye nymphs of rosy lips and radiant eyes,
       Whom Pleasure keeps too busy to be wise,
325   Whom Joys with soft varieties invite,
       By day the frolic, and the dance by night;
       Who frown with vanity, who smile with art,
       And ask the latest fashion of the heart;
       What care, what rules your heedless charms shall save,
330   Each nymph your rival, and each youth your slave?
       Against your fame with Fondness Hate combines,
       The rival batters, and the lover mines.°   *undermines*
       With distant voice neglected Virtue calls,
       Less heard and less, the faint remonstrance falls;
335   Tired with contempt, she quits the slippery reign,
       And Pride and Prudence take her seat in vain.
       In crowd at once, where none the pass defend,
       The harmless freedom, and the private friend.
       The guardians yield, by force superior plied:
340   To Interest, Prudence; and to Flattery, Pride.
       Now Beauty falls betrayed, despised, distressed,
       And hissing Infamy proclaims the rest.

9. I.e., an aged person.
1. Croesus, whom Solon advised to regard no
living man as securely happy, was later de-
posed by the Persian Cyrus.
2. Both the Duke of Marlborough (the mili-
tary hero) and Jonathan Swift declined into
senility.
3. Anne Vane, the mistress of Frederick
Prince of Wales, died in 1736 at the age of
thirty-one. Catherine Sedley was mistress to
James II.

Where then shall Hope and Fear their objects find?
Must dull Suspense corrupt the stagnant mind?
45   Must helpless man, in ignorance sedate,
Roll darkling down the torrent of his fate?
Must no dislike alarm, no wishes rise,
No cries invoke the mercies of the skies?
Inquirer, cease; petitions yet remain,
50   Which Heaven may hear, nor deem religion vain.
Still raise for good the supplicating voice,
But leave to Heaven the measure and the choice.
Safe in His power, whose eyes discern afar
The secret ambush of a specious prayer.
355   Implore His aid, in His decisions rest,
Secure, whate'er He gives, He gives the best.
Yet when the sense of sacred presence fires,
And strong devotion to the skies aspires,
Pour forth thy fervors for a healthful mind,
360   Obedient passions, and a will resigned;
For love, which scarce collective man can fill;
For patience sovereign o'er transmuted ill;[4]
For faith, that panting for a happier seat,
Counts death kind Nature's signal of retreat:
365   These goods for man the laws of Heaven ordain,
These goods He grants, who grants the power to gain;
With these celestial Wisdom calms the mind,
And makes the happiness she does not find.

1749

On the Death of Dr. Robert Levet[5]

Condemned to Hope's delusive mine,
     As on we toil from day to day,
By sudden blasts, or slow decline,
     Our social comforts drop away.

5   Well tried through many a varying year,
     See Levet to the grave descend;
Officious,° innocent, sincere,   *dutiful*
     Of every friendless name the friend.

Yet still he fills Affection's eye,
10   Obscurely wise, and coarsely kind;
Nor, lettered Arrogance, deny
     Thy praise to merit unrefined.

When fainting Nature called for aid,
     And hovering Death prepared the blow,
15   His vigorous remedy displayed
     The power of art without the show.

In Misery's darkest cavern known,
     His useful care was ever nigh,
Where hopeless Anguish poured his groan,
20   And lonely Want retired to die.

---

4. I.e., a capacity for love such that all mankind together can hardly engage it fully; and for patience which, by asserting sovereignty over ills, changes their nature.

5. An unlicensed physician practicing among the poor, who had long lived in Dr. Johnson's house. He was uncouth in appearance and stiff in manner.

No summons mocked by chill delay,
  No petty gain disdained by pride,
The modest wants of every day
  The toil of every day supplied.

25 His virtues walked their narrow round,
      Nor made a pause, nor left a void;
    And sure the Eternal Master found
      The single talent[6] well employed.

    The busy day, the peaceful night,
30   Unfelt, uncounted, glided by;
    His frame was firm, his powers were bright,
      Though now his eightieth year was nigh.

    Then with no throbbing fiery pain,
      No cold gradations of decay,
35 Death broke at once the vital chain,
      And freed his soul the nearest way.

1783

THOMAS GRAY
(1716–1771)

Sonnet

ON THE DEATH OF MR. RICHARD WEST[1]

In vain to me the smiling mornings shine,
  And reddening Phoebus° lifts his golden fire;   *the sun-god*
The birds in vain their amorous descant join,°   *harmonize*
  Or cheerful fields resume their green attire;
5 These ears, alas! for other notes repine,
    A different object do these eyes require;°   *ask for*
  My lonely anguish melts no heart but mine,
    And in my breast the imperfect joys expire.
  Yet morning smiles the busy race to cheer,
10   And newborn pleasure brings to happier men;
  The fields to all their wonted tribute bear;
    To warm their little loves the birds complain:[2]
  I fruitless mourn to him that cannot hear,
    And weep the more, because I weep in vain.

1742   1775

Ode on a Distant Prospect of Eton College

"Ἄνθρωπος· ἱκανὴ πρόφασις εἰς τὸ δυστυχεῖν.[3]
—MENANDER

Ye distant spires, ye antique towers,
  That crown the watery glade,

---

6. An allusion to the portion of wealth given in trust in the parable of the talents, Matthew xxv.14–30.
1. West, a friend of Gray's since preparatory school, had died at the age of twenty-six.
2. I.e., sing of their unfulfilled desire.
3. I am a man, and that is reason enough for being miserable.

learning

Where grateful Science° still adores
    Her Henry's holy shade;[4]
5   And ye, that from the stately brow
Of Windsor's heights the expanse below
    Of grove, of lawn, of mead survey,
Whose turf, whose shade, whose flowers among
Wanders the hoary Thames along
10   His silver-winding way.

Ah happy hills, ah pleasing shade,
    Ah fields beloved in vain,
Where once my careless childhood strayed,
    A stranger yet to pain!
15 I feel the gales, that from ye blow,
A momentary bliss bestow,
    As waving fresh their gladsome wing,
My weary soul they seem to soothe,
And, redolent of joy and youth,
20   To breathe a second spring.

Say, Father Thames, for thou hast seen
    Full many a sprightly race
Disporting on thy margent green
    The paths of pleasure trace,
25 Who foremost now delight to cleave
With pliant arm thy glassy wave?
    The captive linnet which enthrall?°   *imprison*
What idle progeny succeed[5]
To chase the rolling circle's[6] speed,
30   Or urge the flying ball?

While some on earnest business bent
    Their murmuring labors ply
'Gainst graver hours, that bring constraint
    To sweeten liberty:
35 Some bold adventurers disdain
The limits of their little reign,
    And unknown regions dare descry:°   *discover*
Still as they run they look behind,
They hear a voice in every wind,
40   And snatch a fearful joy.

Gay hope is theirs by fancy fed,
    Less pleasing when possessed;
The tear forgot as soon as shed,
    The sunshine of the breast:
45 Theirs buxom° health of rosy hue,   *vigorous*
Wild wit, invention ever new,
    And lively cheer of vigor born;
The thoughtless day, the easy night,
The spirits pure, the slumbers light,
50   That fly the approach of morn.

Alas, regardless of their doom,
    The little victims play!

---

4. Henry VI, founder of Eton.
5. Follow the example of the preceding gen-
eration.
6. "The rolling circle": the hoop.

No sense have they of ills to come,
   Nor care beyond today.
55 Yet see how all around 'em wait
   The ministers of human fate,
      And black Misfortune's baleful train!
   Ah, show them where in ambush stand
   To seize their prey the murderous band!
60   Ah, tell them they are men!

These shall the fury Passions tear,
   The vultures of the mind,
Disdainful Anger, pallid Fear,
   And Shame that skulks behind;
65 Or pining Love shall waste their youth,
   Or Jealousy with rankling tooth,
      That inly gnaws the secret heart,
   And Envy wan, and faded Care,
   Grim-visaged comfortless Despair,
70   And Sorrow's piercing dart.

Ambition this[7] shall tempt to rise,
   Then whirl the wretch from high,
To bitter Scorn a sacrifice,
   And grinning Infamy.
75 The stings of Falsehood those[8] shall try,
   And hard Unkindness' altered eye,
      That mocks the tear it forced to flow;
   And keen Remorse with blood defiled,
   And moody Madness laughing wild
80   Amid severest woe.

Lo, in the vale of years beneath
   A grisly troop are seen,
The painful family of Death,
   More hideous than their queen:
85 This racks the joints, this fires the veins,
   That every laboring sinew strains,
      Those in the deeper vitals rage:
   Lo, Poverty, to fill the band,
   That numbs the soul with icy hand,
90   And slow-consuming Age.

To each his sufferings: all are men,
   Condemned alike to groan;
The tender for another's pain,
   The unfeeling for his own.
95 Yet ah! why should they know their fate?
   Since sorrow never comes too late,
      And happiness too swiftly flies.
   Thought would destroy their paradise.
   No more; where ignorance is bliss,
100   'Tis folly to be wise.

1742   1747

---

7. I.e., one of them.   8. I.e., others.

Ode

ON THE DEATH OF A FAVORITE CAT,
DROWNED IN A TUB OF GOLDFISHES

'Twas on a lofty vase's side,
Where China's gayest art had dyed
   The azure flowers that blow;°   *bloom*
Demurest of the tabby kind,
5 The pensive Selima, reclined,
   Gazed on the lake below.

Her conscious tail her joy declared;
The fair round face, the snowy beard,
   The velvet of her paws,
10 Her coat, that with the tortoise vies,
Her ears of jet, and emerald eyes,
   She saw; and purred applause.

Still had she gazed; but 'midst the tide
Two angel forms were seen to glide,
15   The genii° of the stream: *guardian spirits*
Their scaly armor's Tyrian hue
Through richest purple to the view
   Betrayed a golden gleam.[9]

The hapless nymph with wonder saw:
20 A whisker first and then a claw,
   With many an ardent wish,
She stretched in vain to reach the prize.
What female heart can gold despise?
   What cat's averse to fish?

25 Presumptuous maid! with looks intent
Again she stretched, again she bent,
   Nor knew the gulf between.
(Malignant Fate sat by and smiled)
The slippery verge her feet beguiled,
30   She tumbled headlong in.

Eight times emerging from the flood
She mewed to every watery god,
   Some speedy aid to send.
No dolphin came, no Nereid stirred;[1]
35 Nor cruel Tom, nor Susan heard;
   A favorite has no friend!

From hence, ye beauties, undeceived,
Know, one false step is ne'er retrieved,
   And be with caution bold.
40 Not all that tempts your wandering eyes
And heedless hearts, is lawful prize;
   Nor all that glisters, gold.

1748

9. "Tyrian" and (in classical reference) "purple" cover a considerable spectrum, including crimson. The fish are seen, through red highlights, as golden.

1. A dolphin appeared to save the singer Arion when he was cast overboard. Nereids are sea-nymphs.

Elegy Written in a Country Churchyard

The curfew tolls the knell of parting day,
　　The lowing herd wind slowly o'er the lea,
The plowman homeward plods his weary way,
　　And leaves the world to darkness and to me.

5　Now fades the glimmering landscape on the sight,
　　And all the air a solemn stillness holds,
Save where the beetle wheels his droning flight,
　　And drowsy tinklings lull the distant folds;

Save that from yonder ivy-mantled tower
10　　The moping owl does to the moon complain
Of such, as wandering near her secret bower,
　　Molest her ancient solitary reign.

Beneath those rugged elms, that yew tree's shade,
　　Where heaves the turf in many a moldering heap,
15　Each in his narrow cell forever laid,
　　The rude° forefathers of the hamlet sleep.   *rustic*

The breezy call of incense-breathing morn,
　　The swallow twittering from the straw-built shed,
The cock's shrill clarion, or the echoing horn,°   *hunting horn*
20　　No more shall rouse them from their lowly bed.

For them no more the blazing hearth shall burn,
　　Or busy housewife ply her evening care;
No children run to lisp their sire's return,
　　Or climb his knees the envied kiss to share.

25　Oft did the harvest to their sickle yield,
　　Their furrow oft the stubborn glebe° has broke;   *soil*
How jocund did they drive their team afield!
　　How bowed the woods beneath their sturdy stroke!

Let not Ambition mock their useful toil,
30　　Their homely joys, and destiny obscure;
Nor Grandeur hear with a disdainful smile
　　The short and simple annals of the poor.

The boast of heraldry,[2] the pomp of power,
　　And all that beauty, all that wealth e'er gave,
35　Awaits alike the inevitable hour.
　　The paths of glory lead but to the grave.

Nor you, ye proud, impute to these the fault,
　　If Memory o'er their tomb no trophies[3] raise,
Where through the long-drawn aisle and fretted° vault   *ornamented*
40　　The pealing anthem swells the note of praise.

Can storied urn[4] or animated° bust   *lifelike*
　　Back to its mansion call the fleeting breath?

2. I.e., noble family.
3. Memorials to military heroes; typically, statuary representations of arms captured in battle.
4. Funeral urn with descriptive epitaph.

Can Honor's voice provoke° the silent dust,   *call forth*
   Or Flattery soothe the dull cold ear of Death?

45 Perhaps in this neglected spot is laid
      Some heart once pregnant with celestial fire;
   Hands that the rod of empire might have swayed,
      Or waked to ecstasy the living lyre.

   But Knowledge to their eyes her ample page
50   Rich with the spoils of time did ne'er unroll;
   Chill Penury repressed their noble rage,
      And froze the genial current of the soul.

   Full many a gem of purest ray serene,
      The dark unfathomed caves of ocean bear:
55 Full many a flower is born to blush unseen,
      And waste its sweetness on the desert air.

   Some village Hampden,[5] that with dauntless breast
      The little tyrant of his fields withstood;
   Some mute inglorious Milton here may rest,
60   Some Cromwell guiltless of his country's blood.

   The applause of listening senates to command,
      The threats of pain and ruin to despise,
   To scatter plenty o'er a smiling land,
      And read their history in a nation's eyes,

65 Their lot forbade: nor circumscribed alone
      Their growing virtues, but their crimes confined;
   Forbade to wade through slaughter to a throne,
      And shut the gates of mercy on mankind,

   The struggling pangs of conscious truth to hide,
70   To quench the blushes of ingenuous shame,
   Or heap the shrine of Luxury and Pride
      With incense kindled at the Muse's flame.

   Far from the madding° crowd's ignoble strife,   *milling*
      Their sober wishes never learned to stray;
75 Along the cool sequestered vale of life
      They kept the noiseless tenor of their way.

   Yet even these bones from insult to protect
      Some frail memorial still erected nigh,
   With uncouth rhymes and shapeless sculpture decked,
80   Implores the passing tribute of a sigh.

   Their name, their years, spelt by the unlettered Muse,
      The place of fame and elegy supply:
   And many a holy text around she strews,
      That teach the rustic moralist to die.

85 For who to dumb Forgetfulness a prey,
      This pleasing anxious being e'er resigned,

5. Leader of the opposition to Charles I in the controversy over ship money; killed in battle
in the Civil Wars.

Left the warm precincts of the cheerful day,
   Nor cast one longing lingering look behind?

90
On some fond breast the parting soul relies,
   Some pious drops the closing eye requires;
Even from the tomb the voice of Nature cries,
   Even in our ashes live their wonted fires.

For thee, who mindful of the unhonored dead
   Dost in these lines their artless tale relate;
95
If chance, by lonely contemplation led,
   Some kindred spirit shall inquire thy fate,

Haply some hoary-headed swain may say,
   "Oft have we seen him at the peep of dawn
Brushing with hasty steps the dews away
100
   To meet the sun upon the upland lawn.

"There at the foot of yonder nodding beech
   That wreathes its old fantastic roots so high,
His listless length at noontide would he stretch,
   And pore upon the brook that babbles by.

105
"Hard by yon wood, now smiling as in scorn,
   Muttering his wayward fancies he would rove,
Now drooping, woeful wan, like one forlorn,
   Or crazed with care, or crossed in hopeless love.

"One morn I missed him on the customed hill,
110
   Along the heath and near his favorite tree;
Another came; nor yet beside the rill,
   Nor up the lawn, nor at the wood was he;

"The next with dirges due in sad array
   Slow through the churchway path we saw him borne.
115
Approach and read (for thou canst read) the lay,
   Graved on the stone beneath yon aged thorn."

     The Epitaph

Here rests his head upon the lap of Earth
   A youth to Fortune and to Fame unknown.
Fair Science° frowned not on his humble birth,   Learning
120
   And Melancholy marked him for her own.

Large was his bounty, and his soul sincere,
   Heaven did a recompense as largely send:
He gave to Misery all he had, a tear,
   He gained from Heaven ('twas all he wished) a friend.

125
No farther seek his merits to disclose,
   Or draw his frailties from their dread abode
(There they alike in trembling hope repose),
   The bosom of his Father and his God.

                           ca. 1742–50   1751

Stanzas to Mr. Bentley[6]

In silent gaze the tuneful choir among,
   Half pleased, half blushing, let the Muse admire,
While Bentley leads her sister-art along,
   And bids the pencil° answer to the lyre.   *painter's brush*

5 See, in their course, each transitory thought
   Fixed by his touch a lasting essence take;
Each dream, in fancy's airy coloring wrought,
   To local symmetry and life awake!

The tardy rhymes that used to linger on,
10   To censure cold, and negligent of fame,
In swifter measures animated run,
   And catch a luster from his genuine flame.

Ah! could they catch his strength, his easy grace,
   His quick creation, his unerring line;
15 The energy of Pope they might efface,
   And Dryden's harmony submit to mine.

But not to one in this benighted age
   Is that diviner inspiration given,
That burns in Shakespeare's or in Milton's page,
20   The pomp and prodigality of Heaven.

As when, conspiring in the diamond's blaze,
   The meaner gems that singly charm the sight
Together dart their intermingled rays,
   And dazzle with a luxury of light.

25 Enough for me, if to some feeling breast,
   My lines a secret sympathy [impart;]
And as their pleasing influence [is confessed,]
   A sigh of soft reflection [stirs the heart.]

                         ca. 1752   1775

The Progress of Poesy

A PINDARIC ODE

Φωνᾶντα συνετοῖσιν· ἐς
Δὲ τὸ πᾶν ἑρμηνέων χατίζει.[7]
      —PINDAR

I—1

Awake, Aeolian[8] lyre, awake,
And give to rapture all thy trembling strings.
From Helicon's harmonious springs[9]
A thousand rills their mazy° progress take;   *winding*
5 The laughing flowers that round them blow

6. Written while Richard Bentley was preparing the designs for *Six Poems by Mr. T. Gray.* The manuscript in which this poem was preserved was torn in its lower right-hand corner. The missing words are here conjecturally supplied in brackets.
7. "Comprehensible to the intelligent; for the world at large needing interpretation." See Glossary, entry on ode, in this anthology.
8. Pindaric. "Pindar styles his poetry with its accompaniment 'Aeolian song, Aeolian strings' " [Gray's note].
9. The springs of Mount Helicon (Aganippe and Hippocrene) are haunts of the Muses and sources of inspiration and aesthetic harmony.

Drink life and fragrance as they flow.
Now the rich stream of music winds along,
Deep, majestic, smooth, and strong,
Through verdant vales and Ceres' golden reign;[1]
10 Now rolling down the steep amain,
Headlong, impetuous, see it pour;
The rocks and nodding groves rebellow to the roar.

        I—2
Oh! Sovereign of the willing soul,
Parent of sweet and solemn-breathing airs,
15 Enchanting shell![2] the sullen Cares
And frantic Passions hear thy soft control.
On Thracia's hills the Lord of War[3]
Has curbed the fury of his car,
And dropped his thirsty lance at thy command.
20 Perching on the sceptered hand
Of Jove, thy magic lulls the feathered king,°   eagle
With ruffled plumes and flagging wing;
Quenched in dark clouds of slumber lie
The terror of his beak, and lightnings of his eye.

        I—3
25 Thee the voice, the dance, obey,
Tempered to thy warbled lay.
O'er Idalia's[4] velvet-green
The rosy-crownéd Loves are seen
On Cytherea's day;
30 With antic Sports, and blue-eyed Pleasures,
Frisking light in frolic measures;
Now pursuing, now retreating,
Now in circling troops they meet,
To brisk notes in cadence beating
35 Glance their many-twinkling feet.
Slow melting strains their queen's approach declare;
Where'er she turns the Graces homage pay.
With arms sublime° that float upon the air,   upraised
In gliding state she wins her easy way;
40 O'er her warm cheek and rising bosom move
The bloom of young desire and purple light of love.

        II—1
Man's feeble race what ills await,
Labor, and penury, the racks of pain,
Disease, and sorrow's weeping train,
45 And death, sad refuge from the storms of fate!
The fond complaint, my song, disprove,
And justify the laws of Jove.[5]
Say, has he given in vain the heavenly Muse?
Night, and all her sickly dews,
50 Her specters wan, and birds of boding cry[6]
He gives° to range the dreary sky;   permits
Till down the eastern cliffs afar
Hyperion's° march they spy, and glittering shafts of war.   the sun-god's

---

1. Ripe grain fields. Ceres is the goddess of
grain.
2. The harp, as invented by Hermes, was
strung on a tortoise shell.
3. I.e., Mars.
4. Town in Cyprus where there is a temple to
Venus. "Cytherea" (below) is one of Venus'
names.
5. An echo of Milton's statement of purpose,
"To justify the ways of God to men" (*Para-
dise Lost* I.26).
6. Screech owls, whose cry traditionally bodes
death.

II—2

In climes beyond the solar road,
55 Where shaggy forms o'er ice-built mountains roam,
The Muse has broke the twilight-gloom
To cheer the shivering native's dull abode.
And oft, beneath the odorous shade
Of Chili's boundless forests laid,
60 She deigns to hear the savage youth repeat
In loose numbers wildly sweet
Their feather-cinctured chiefs and dusky loves.
Her track, where'er the goddess roves,
Glory pursue, and generous shame,
65 The unconquerable mind, and Freedom's holy flame.

II—3

Woods that wave o'er Delphi's[7] steep,
Isles that crown the Aegean deep,
Fields that cool Ilissus laves,
Or where Meander's amber waves
70 In lingering labyrinths creep,
How do your tuneful echoes languish,
Mute, but to the voice of anguish!
Where each old poetic mountain
Inspiration breathed around,
75 Every shade and hallowed fountain
Murmured deep a solemn sound;
Till the sad Nine° in Greece's evil hour   *Muses*
Left their Parnassus for the Latian° plains.   *Roman*
Alike they scorn the pomp of tyrant Power,
80 And coward Vice, that revels in her chains.
When Latium had her lofty spirit lost,
They sought, O Albion!° next, thy sea-encircled coast.   *England*

III—1

Far from the sun and summer-gale,
In thy green lap was Nature's darling[8] laid,
85 What time,° where lucid Avon strayed,   *when*
To him the mighty mother did unveil
Her awful° face; the dauntless child   *awe-inspiring*
Stretched forth his little arms, and smiled.
"This pencil° take," she said, "whose colors clear   *painter's brush*
90 Richly paint the vernal year;
Thine too these golden keys, immortal boy!
This can unlock the gates of joy;
Of horror that, and thrilling fears,
Or ope the sacred source of sympathetic tears."

III—2

95 Nor second he that rode sublime[9]
Upon the seraph-wings of ecstasy,
The secrets of the abyss to spy.°   *behold*
He passed the flaming bounds of place and time;
The living throne, the sapphire-blaze,
100 Where angels tremble while they gaze,
He saw; but blasted with excess of light,
Closed his eyes in endless night.

---

7. Delphi is the site of the oracle of Apollo.
Ilissus (line 68) is a Greek river; Meander
(line 69), a notably winding river in Asia
Minor; Parnassus (line 78), a mountain in
central Greece sacred to the Muses.
8. Shakespeare.
9. "He that rode sublime": Milton.

Behold where Dryden's less presumptuous car,
Wide o'er the fields of glory bear
105   Two coursers of ethereal race,[1]
With necks in thunder clothed, and long-resounding pace.

            III—3
Hark, his hands the lyre explore!
Bright-eyed Fancy, hovering o'er,
Scatters from her pictured urn
110   Thoughts that breathe and words that burn.
But ah! 'tis heard no more—
O lyre divine, what daring spirit
Wakes thee now? Though he inherit
Nor the pride nor ample pinion
115   That the Theban Eagle[2] bear,
Sailing with supreme dominion
Through the azure deep of air;
Yet oft before his infant eyes would run
Such forms as glitter in the Muse's ray
120   With orient hues, unborrowed of the sun;
Yet shall he mount, and keep his distant way
Beyond the limits of a vulgar° fate—   *common*
Beneath the good how far—but far above the great.

                                                1754   1757

WILLIAM COLLINS
(1721–1759)

Ode Written in the Beginning of the Year 1746[1]

How sleep the brave who sink to rest
By all their country's wishes blest!
When Spring, with dewy fingers cold,
Returns to deck their hallowed mold,
5   She there shall dress a sweeter sod
Than Fancy's feet have ever trod.

By fairy hands their knell is rung,
By forms unseen their dirge is sung;
There Honor comes, a pilgrim gray,
10   To bless the turf that wraps their clay,
And Freedom shall awhile repair,
To dwell a weeping hermit there!

                                                1746

Ode to Simplicity

O thou by Nature taught
To breathe her genuine thought,
In numbers warmly pure and sweetly strong;
Who first, on mountains wild,
5   In Fancy, loveliest child,
Thy babe or Pleasure's, nursed the powers of song!

---

1. Swift horses, paired because Dryden wrote
in couplets.
2. Representing Pindar, a Theban, who had
likened himself to an eagle.

1. The poem celebrates Englishmen who fell
resisting the pretender to the throne ("Bonnie
Prince Charlie," the grandson of James II)
in the previous year.

Thou, who with hermit heart
Disdain'st the wealth of art,
And gauds, and pageant weeds, and trailing pall;[2]
10   But com'st a decent° maid,   *decorous*
    In Attic° robe arrayed,   *Athenian*
O chaste unboastful nymph, to thee I call!

By all the honeyed store
On Hybla's thymy shore;[3]
15 By all her blooms and mingled murmurs dear;
    By her whose lovelorn woe,
    In evening musings slow,
Soothed sweetly sad Electra's poet's ear:[4]

By old Cephisus deep,[5]
20 Who spread his wavy sweep
In warbled wanderings round thy green retreat:
    On whose enameled° side,   *flower-dappled*
    When holy Freedom died,
No equal haunt allured thy future feet:

25   O sister meek of Truth,
    To my admiring youth,
Thy sober aid and native charms infuse!
    The flowers that sweetest breathe,
    Though Beauty culled the wreath,
30 Still ask thy hand to range their ordered hues.

While Rome could none esteem
But virtue's patriot theme,
You loved her hills, and led her laureate band;[6]
    But stayed to sing alone
35   To one distinguished throne,[7]
And turned thy face, and fled her altered land.

No more, in hall or bower,
The Passions own thy power;
Love, only Love her forceless numbers° mean: *verses*
40   For thou hast left her shrine;
    Nor olive more, nor vine,
Shall gain thy feet to bless the servile scene.

Though taste, though genius bless
To some divine excess,
45 Faints the cold work till thou inspire the whole;
    What each, what all supply,
    May court, may charm, our eye;
Thou, only thou, canst raise the meeting soul!

Of these let others ask,
50   To aid some mighty task;

2. I.e., and ornaments and showy clothing and trailing cloak.
3. The Sicilian shore by the city of Hybla, where the thyme flowers supported many bees.
4. The plaintive nightingale soothed the ear of the Greek playwright Sophocles, author of *Electra*. She is lovelorn because she was once the young woman Philomela, whose husband, in one version of the legend, had forsaken her for her sister.
5. The river Cephisus flows by Athens, called (line 21) the "green retreat" of Simplicity. Freedom died there when Athens was defeated by Sparta in the Peloponnesian War.
6. Under the old republic, Simplicity loved the seven hills of Rome and was cultivated by her "laureate band" of poets.
7. Under the Roman Empire, Simplicity "sang" only during the reign of Augustus, when Horace and Virgil flourished.

I only seek to find thy temperate vale,
    Where oft my reed° might sound   *shepherd's pipe*
    To maids and shepherds round,
And all thy sons, O Nature, learn my tale.

1746

Ode to Evening

If aught of oaten stop,[8] or pastoral song,
May hope, chaste Eve, to soothe thy modest ear,
    Like thy own solemn springs,
    Thy springs and dying gales,
5 O nymph reserved, while now the bright-haired sun
Sits in yon western tent, whose cloudy skirts,
    With brede° ethereal wove,   *braid*
    O'erhang his wavy bed:
Now air is hushed, save where the weak-eyed bat,
10 With short shrill shriek flits by on leathern wing,
    Or where the beetle winds
    His small but sullen horn,
As oft he rises 'midst the twilight path,
Against the pilgrim° borne in heedless hum: *wayfarer*
15   Now teach me, maid composed,
    To breathe some softened strain,
Whose numbers, stealing through thy darkening vale,
May not unseemly with its stillness suit,
    As, musing slow, I hail
20   Thy genial loved return!
For when thy folding-star[9] arising shows
His paly circlet, at his warning lamp
    The fragrant Hours, and elves
    Who slept in flowers the day,
25 And many a nymph who wreaths her brows with sedge,
And sheds the freshening dew, and, lovelier still,
    The pensive Pleasures sweet,
    Prepare thy shadowy car.
Then lead, calm votaress, where some sheety lake
30 Cheers the lone heath, or some time-hallowed pile
    Or upland fallows gray
    Reflect its last cool gleam.
But when chill blustering winds, or driving rain,
Forbid my willing feet, be mine the hut
35   That from the mountain's side
    Views wilds, and swelling floods,
And hamlets brown, and dim-discovered spires,
And hears their simple bell, and marks o'er all
    Thy dewy fingers draw
40   The gradual dusky veil.
While Spring shall pour his showers, as oft he wont,
And bathe thy breathing tresses, meekest Eve;
    While Summer loves to sport
    Beneath thy lingering light;
45 While sallow Autumn fills thy lap with leaves;
Or Winter, yelling through the troublous air,
    Affrights thy shrinking train,

8. "If any modulation of a (shepherd's) reed."

9. The evening star, which, when it becomes visible, tells the shepherd to drive his flock to the sheepfold.

And rudely rends thy robes;
So long, sure-found beneath the sylvan shed,[10]
Shall Fancy, Friendship, Science, rose-lipped Health,
Thy gentlest influence own,
And hymn thy favorite name!

1746, 1748

CHRISTOPHER SMART
(1722–1771)

From Jubilate Agno[1]

For I will consider my Cat Jeoffry.
For he is the servant of the Living God, duly and daily serving him.
For at the first glance of the glory of God in the East he worships in his way.
For is this done by wreathing his body seven times round with elegant quickness.
For then he leaps up to catch the musk,[2] which is the blessing of God upon his prayer.
For he rolls upon prank to work it in.
For having done duty and received blessing he begins to consider himself.
For this he performs in ten degrees.
For first he looks upon his forepaws to see if they are clean.
For secondly he kicks up behind to clear away there.
For thirdly he works it upon stretch with the forepaws extended.
For fourthly he sharpens his paws by wood.
For fifthly he washes himself.
For sixthly he rolls upon wash.
For seventhly he fleas himself, that he may not be interrupted upon the beat.[3]
For eighthly he rubs himself against a post.
For ninthly he looks up for his instructions.
For tenthly he goes in quest of food.
For having considered God and himself he will consider his neighbor.
For if he meets another cat he will kiss her in kindness.
For when he takes his prey he plays with it to give it a chance.
For one mouse in seven escapes by his dallying.
For when his day's work is done his business more properly begins.
For he keeps the Lord's watch in the night against the adversary.
For he counteracts the powers of darkness by his electrical skin and glaring eyes.
For he counteracts the Devil, who is death, by brisking about the life.
For in his morning orisons he loves the sun and the sun loves him.
For he is of the tribe of Tiger.
For the Cherub Cat is a term of the Angel Tiger.[4]
For he has the subtlety and hissing of a serpent, which in goodness he suppresses.
For he will not do destruction if he is well-fed, neither will he spit without provocation.
For he purrs in thankfulness when God tells him he's a good Cat.
For he is an instrument for the children to learn benevolence upon.

---

10. I.e., securely attained beneath the shelter of the forest.
1. "Rejoice in the Lamb"; i.e., in Jesus, the Lamb of God; written while Smart was confined for insanity.
2. Perhaps a scented plant, played with like catnip.
3. Upon his daily round, possibly of hunting.
4. Smart apparently thinks of Jeoffry as an immature or diminutive phase of a larger creature—cherubs being by artistic convention small and childlike.

730   For every house is incomplete without him, and a blessing is lacking in the spirit.

For the Lord commanded Moses concerning the cats at the departure of the Children of Israel from Egypt.

For every family had one cat at least in the bag.[5]

For the English Cats are the best in Europe.

For he is the cleanest in the use of his forepaws of any quadruped.

735   For the dexterity of his defense is an instance of the love of God to him exceedingly.

For he is the quickest to his mark of any creature.

For he is tenacious of his point.

For he is a mixture of gravity and waggery.

For he knows that God is his Saviour.

740   For there is nothing sweeter than his peace when at rest.

For there is nothing brisker than his life when in motion.

For he is of the Lord's poor, and so indeed is he called by benevolence perpetually—Poor Jeoffry! poor Jeoffry! the rat has bit thy throat.

For I bless the name of the Lord Jesus that Jeoffry is better.

For the divine spirit comes about his body to sustain it in complete cat.

745   For his tongue is exceeding pure so that it has in purity what it wants in music.

For he is docile and can learn certain things.

For he can sit up with gravity, which is patience upon approbation.

For he can fetch and carry, which is patience in employment.

For he can jump over a stick, which is patience upon proof positive.

750   For he can spraggle upon waggle at the word of command.

For he can jump from an eminence into his master's bosom.

For he can catch the cork and toss it again.

For he is hated by the hypocrite and miser.

For the former is afraid of detection.

755   For the latter refuses the charge.

For he camels his back to bear the first notion of business.

For he is good to think on, if a man would express himself neatly.

For he made a great figure in Egypt for his signal services.

For he killed the Icneumon rat, very pernicious by land.[6]

760   For his ears are so acute that they sting again.

For from this proceeds the passing quickness of his attention.

For by stroking of him I have found out electricity.

For I perceived God's light about him both wax and fire.

For the electrical fire is the spiritual substance which God sends from heaven to sustain the bodies both of man and beast.

765   For God has blessed him in the variety of his movements.

For, though he cannot fly, he is an excellent clamberer.

For his motions upon the face of the earth are more than any other quadruped.

For he can tread to all the measures upon the music.

For he can swim for life.

780   For he can creep.

ca. 1760   1939

5. The Israelites took with them silver and gold ornaments and raiment, as well as flocks and herds (Exodus xi.2 and xii.32,35). Smart adds the cats.

6. The rats encountered by Jeoffry may have impressed Smart as resembling mongooses (one sense of *ichneumon*); or there may be some reference to the ichneumon fly, a wasplike insect parasitic upon caterpillars.

OLIVER GOLDSMITH
(1730–1774)

When Lovely Woman Stoops to Folly

When lovely woman stoops to folly,
   And finds too late that men betray,
What charm can soothe her melancholy,
   What art can wash her guilt away?

5 The only art her guilt to cover,
   To hide her shame from every eye,
To give repentance to her lover,
   And wring his bosom—is to die.

1766

The Deserted Village

  Sweet Auburn! loveliest village of the plain,
Where health and plenty cheered the laboring swain,
Where smiling spring its earliest visit paid,
And parting summer's lingering blooms delayed:
5 Dear lovely bowers of innocence and ease,
Seats of my youth, when every sport could please,
How often have I loitered o'er thy green,
Where humble happiness endeared each scene;
How often have I paused on every charm,
10 The sheltered cot, the cultivated farm,
The never-failing brook, the busy mill,
The decent church that topped the neighboring hill,
The hawthorn bush, with seats beneath the shade,
For talking age and whispering lovers made;
15 How often have I blessed the coming day,
When toil remitting lent its turn to play,
And all the village train, from labor free,
Led up their sports beneath the spreading tree,
While many a pastime circled in the shade,
20 The young contending as the old surveyed;
And many a gambol frolicked o'er the ground,
And sleights of art and feats of strength went round;
And still as each repeated pleasure tired,
Succeeding sports the mirthful band inspired;
25 The dancing pair that simply sought renown,
By holding out to tire each other down;
The swain mistrustless of his smutted face,
While secret laughter tittered round the place;
The bashful virgin's sidelong looks of love,
30 The matron's glance that would those looks reprove:
These were thy charms, sweet village! sports like these,
With sweet succession, taught even toil to please;
These round thy bowers their cheerful influence shed,
These were thy charms—But all these charms are fled.
35   Sweet smiling village, loveliest of the lawn,
Thy sports are fled, and all thy charms withdrawn;
Amidst thy bowers the tyrant's hand is seen,
And desolation saddens all thy green:

One only master grasps the whole domain,
40   And half a tillage¹ stints thy smiling plain;
No more thy glassy brook reflects the day,
But choked with sedges, works its weedy way;
Along thy glades, a solitary guest,
The hollow-sounding bittern guards its nest;
45   Amidst thy desert walks the lapwing flies,
And tires their echoes with unvaried cries.
Sunk are thy bowers, in shapeless ruin all,
And the long grass o'ertops the moldering wall,
And, trembling, shrinking from the spoiler's hand,
50   Far, far away thy children leave the land.

Ill fares the land, to hastening ills a prey,
Where wealth accumulates, and men decay;
Princes and lords may flourish, or may fade;
A breath can make them, as a breath has made;
55   But a bold peasantry, their country's pride,
When once destroyed, can never be supplied.

A time there was, ere England's griefs began,
When every rood of ground maintained its man;
For him light labor spread her wholesome store,
60   Just gave what life required, but gave no more:
His best companions, innocence and health;
And his best riches, ignorance of wealth.

But times are altered; Trade's unfeeling train
Usurp the land and dispossess the swain;
65   Along the lawn, where scattered hamlets rose,
Unwieldy wealth, and cumbrous pomp repose;
And every want to opulence allied,
And every pang that folly pays to pride.
These gentle hours that plenty bade to bloom,
70   Those calm desires that asked but little room,
Those healthful sports that graced the peaceful scene,
Lived in each look, and brightened all the green;
These far departing seek a kinder shore,
And rural mirth and manners are no more.

75   Sweet Auburn! parent of the blissful hour,
Thy glades forlorn confess the tyrant's power.
Here, as I take my solitary rounds,
Amidst thy tangling walks, and ruined grounds,
And, many a year elapsed, return to view
80   Where once the cottage stood, the hawthorn grew,
Remembrance wakes with all her busy train,
Swells at my breast, and turns the past to pain.
In all my wanderings round this world of care,
In all my griefs—and God has given my share—
85   I still had hopes my latest hours to crown,
Amidst these humble bowers to lay me down;
To husband out life's taper at the close,
And keep the flame from wasting by repose.
I still had hopes, for pride attends us still,
90   Amidst the swains to show my book-learned skill,
Around my fire an evening group to draw,
And tell of all I felt, and all I saw;
And, as an hare whom hounds and horns pursue,

---

1. The landlord's exorbitant share of the crop. The large landowners were displacing small freeholders and at the same time appropriating grazing lands formerly held in common.

Pants to the place from whence at first she flew,
95 I still had hopes, my long vexations past,
Here to return—and die at home at last.
    O blest retirement, friend to life's decline,
Retreats from care that never must be mine,
How happy he who crowns in shades like these
100 A youth of labor with an age of ease;
Who quits a world where strong temptations try,
And, since 'tis hard to combat, learns to fly!
For him no wretches, born to work and weep,
Explore the mine, or tempt the dangerous deep;
105 No surly porter stands in guilty state
To spurn imploring famine from the gate;
But on he moves to meet his latter end,
Angels around befriending virtue's friend;
Bends to the grave with unperceived decay,
110 While Resignation gently slopes the way;
And, all his prospects brightening to the last,
His Heaven commences ere the world be passed!
    Sweet was the sound when oft at evening's close,
Up yonder hill the village murmur rose;
115 There, as I passed with careless steps and slow,
The mingling notes came softened from below;
The swain responsive as the milkmaid sung,
The sober herd that lowed to meet their young,
The noisy geese that gabbled o'er the pool,
120 The playful children just let loose from school;
The watchdog's voice that bayed the whispering wind,
And the loud laugh that spoke the vacant° mind;   *idle*
These all in sweet confusion sought the shade,
And filled each pause the nightingale had made.
125 But now the sounds of population fail,
No cheerful murmurs fluctuate in the gale,
No busy steps the grass-grown footway tread,
For all the bloomy flush of life is fled.
All but yon widowed, solitary thing
130 That feebly bends beside the plashy spring;
She, wretched matron, forced, in age, for bread,
To strip the brook with mantling cresses spread,
To pick her wintry faggot from the thorn,
To seek her nightly shed, and weep till morn;
135 She only left of all the harmless train,
The sad historian of the pensive plain.
    Near yonder copse, where once the garden smiled,
And still where many a garden flower grows wild,
There, where a few torn shrubs the place disclose,
140 The village preacher's modest mansion rose.
A man he was, to all the country dear,
And passing rich with forty pounds a year;
Remote from towns he ran his godly race,
Nor e'er had changed, nor wished to change his place;
145 Unpracticed he to fawn, or seek for power,
By doctrines fashioned to the varying hour;
Far other aims his heart had learned to prize,
More skilled to raise the wretched than to rise.
His house was known to all the vagrant train,
150 He chid their wanderings, but relieved their pain;

The long-remembered beggar was his guest,
Whose beard descending swept his aged breast;
The ruined spendthrift, now no longer proud,
Claimed kindred there, and had his claims allowed;
155 The broken soldier, kindly bade to stay,
Sate by his fire, and talked the night away;
Wept o'er his wounds, or tales of sorrow done,
Shouldered his crutch, and showed how fields were won.
Pleased with his guests, the good man learned to glow,
160 And quite forgot their vices in their woe;
Careless their merits, or their faults to scan,
His pity gave ere charity began.
　　Thus to relieve the wretched was his pride,
And even his failings leaned to Virtue's side;
165 But in his duty prompt at every call,
He watched and wept, he prayed and felt, for all.
And, as a bird each fond endearment tries,
To tempt its new-fledged offspring to the skies,
He tried each art, reproved each dull delay,
170 Allured to brighter worlds, and led the way.
　　Beside the bed where parting life was laid,
And sorrow, guilt, and pain, by turns dismayed,
The reverend champion stood. At his control,
Despair and anguish fled the struggling soul;
175 Comfort came down the trembling wretch to raise,
And his last faltering accents whispered praise.
　　At church, with meek and unaffected grace,
His looks adorned the venerable place;
Truth from his lips prevailed with double sway,
180 And fools, who came to scoff, remained to pray.
The service past, around the pious man,
With steady zeal each honest rustic ran;
Even children followed with endearing wile,
And plucked his gown, to share the good man's smile.
185 His ready smile a parent's warmth expressed,
Their welfare pleased him, and their cares distressed;
To them his heart, his love, his griefs were given,
But all his serious thoughts had rest in Heaven.
As some tall cliff that lifts its awful form,
190 Swells from the vale, and midway leaves the storm,
Though round its breast the rolling clouds are spread,
Eternal sunshine settles on its head.
　　Beside yon straggling fence that skirts the way,
With blossomed furze unprofitably gay,
195 There, in his noisy mansion, skilled to rule,
The village master taught his little school;
A man severe he was, and stern to view,
I knew him well, and every truant knew;
Well had the boding tremblers learned to trace
200 The day's disasters in his morning face;
Full well they laughed with counterfeited glee,
At all his jokes, for many a joke had he;
Full well the busy whisper circling round,
Conveyed the dismal tidings when he frowned;
205 Yet he was kind, or if severe in aught,
The love he bore to learning was in fault;[2]

2. Pronounced like *fought*.

The village all declared how much he knew;
'Twas certain he could write, and cipher too;
Lands he could measure, terms and tides presage,[3]
210   And even the story ran that he could gauge.
In arguing too, the parson owned° his skill,   *manifested*
For even though vanquished, he could argue still;
While words of learned length, and thundering sound,
Amazed the gazing rustics ranged around;
215   And still they gazed, and still the wonder grew,
That one small head could carry all he knew.
     But past is all his fame. The very spot
Where many a time he triumphed, is forgot.
Near yonder thorn, that lifts its head on high,
220   Where once the signpost caught the passing eye,
Low lies that house where nut-brown draughts inspired,
Where graybeard Mirth and smiling Toil retired,
Where village statesmen talked with looks profound,
And news much older than their ale went round.
225   Imagination fondly stoops to trace
The parlor splendors of that festive place:
The whitewashed wall, the nicely sanded floor,
The varnished clock that clicked behind the door;
The chest contrived a double debt to pay,
230   A bed by night, a chest of drawers by day;
The pictures placed for ornament and use,
The twelve good rules, the royal game of goose;[4]
The hearth, except when winter chilled the day,
With aspen boughs, and flowers, and fennel gay,
235   While broken teacups, wisely kept for show,
Ranged o'er the chimney, glistened in a row.
     Vain transitory splendors! Could not all
Reprieve the tottering mansion from its fall!
Obscure it sinks, nor shall it more impart
240   An hour's importance to the poor man's heart;
Thither no more the peasant shall repair
To sweet oblivion of his daily care;
No more the farmer's news, the barber's tale,
No more the woodman's ballad shall prevail;
245   No more the smith his dusky brow shall clear,
Relax his ponderous strength, and lean to hear;
The host himself no longer shall be found
Careful to see the mantling bliss[5] go round;
Nor the coy maid, half willing to be pressed,
250   Shall kiss the cup to pass it to the rest.
     Yes! let the rich deride, the proud disdain,
These simple blessings of the lowly train,
To me more dear, congenial to my heart,
One native charm, than all the gloss of art;
255   Spontaneous joys, where nature has its play,
The soul adopts, and owns their first-born sway;
Lightly they frolic o'er the vacant mind,
Unenvied, unmolested, unconfined.
But the long pomp, the midnight masquerade,

3. He could calculate (for example) when rents were due and the date of the next Easter. *Tides* here means *times*. To "gauge" (line 210) is to calculate the fluid content of vessels.

4. The "twelve good rules" are rules of conduct often posted in taverns; "goose" is a board game.
5. The ale covering itself with foam.

260 With all the freaks of wanton wealth arrayed,
     In these, ere triflers half their wish obtain,
     The toiling pleasure sickens into pain;
     And, even while fashion's brightest arts decoy,
     The heart distrusting asks if this be joy.
265   Ye friends to truth, ye statesmen, who survey
     The rich man's joys increase, the poor's decay,
     'Tis yours to judge how wide the limits stand
     Between a splendid and an happy land.
     Proud swells the tide with loads of freighted ore,
270 And shouting Folly hails them from her shore;
     Hoards, even beyond the miser's wish abound,
     And rich men flock from all the world around.
     Yet count our gains. This wealth is but a name
     That leaves our useful products still the same.
275 Not so the loss. The man of wealth and pride,
     Takes up a space that many poor supplied;
     Space for his lake, his park's extended bounds,
     Space for his horses, equipage, and hounds;
     The robe that wraps his limbs in silken sloth
280 Has robbed the neighboring fields of half their growth;
     His seat, where solitary sports are seen,
     Indignant spurns the cottage from the green;
     Around the world each needful product flies,
     For all the luxuries the world supplies.
285 While thus the land adorned for pleasure, all
     In barren splendor feebly waits the fall.
     As some fair female unadorned and plain,
     Secure to please while youth confirms her reign,
     Slights every borrowed charm that dress supplies,
290 Nor shares with art the triumph of her eyes:
     But when those charms are past, for charms are frail,
     When time advances, and when lovers fail,
     She then shines forth, solicitous to bless,
     In all the glaring impotence of dress.
295 Thus fares the land, by luxury betrayed;
     In nature's simplest charms at first arrayed;
     But verging to decline, its splendors rise,
     Its vistas strike, its palaces surprise;
     While scourged by famine from the smiling land,
300 The mournful peasant leads his humble band;
     And while he sinks without one arm to save,
     The country blooms—a garden, and a grave.
     Where then, ah where, shall Poverty reside,
     To 'scape the pressure of contiguous Pride?
305 If to some common's fenceless limits strayed,
     He drives his flock to pick the scanty blade,
     Those fenceless fields the sons of wealth divide,
     And even the bare-worn common is denied.
     If to the city sped—What waits him there?
310 To see profusion that he must not share;
     To see ten thousand baneful arts combined
     To pamper luxury, and thin mankind;
     To see those joys the sons of pleasure know,
     Extorted from his fellow creature's woe.
315 Here, while the courtier glitters in brocade,
     There the pale artist° plies the sickly trade;   *artisan*

Here, while the proud their long-drawn pomps display,
There the black gibbet glooms beside the way.
The dome where Pleasure holds her midnight reign,
²⁰ Here, richly decked, admits the gorgeous train;
Tumultuous grandeur crowds the blazing square,
The rattling chariots clash, the torches glare.
Sure scenes like these no troubles e'er annoy!
Sure these denote one universal joy!
²⁵ Are these thy serious thoughts?—Ah, turn thine eyes
Where the poor houseless shivering female lies.
She once, perhaps, in village plenty blest,
Has wept at tales of innocence distressed;
Her modest looks the cottage might adorn,
³⁰ Sweet as the primrose peeps beneath the thorn;
Now lost to all; her friends, her virtue fled,
Near her betrayer's door she lays her head,
And pinched with cold, and shrinking from the shower,
With heavy heart deplores that luckless hour,
³⁵ When idly first, ambitious of the town,
She left her wheel and robes of country brown.
    Do thine, sweet Auburn, thine, the loveliest train,
Do thy fair tribes participate her pain?
Even now, perhaps, by cold and hunger led,
⁴⁰ At proud men's doors they ask a little bread!
    Ah, no. To distant climes, a dreary scene,
Where half the convex world intrudes between,
Through torrid tracts with fainting steps they go,
Where wild Altama⁶ murmurs to their woe.
⁴⁵ Far different there from all that charmed before,
The various terrors of that horrid shore;
Those blazing suns that dart a downward ray,
And fiercely shed intolerable day;
Those matted woods where birds forget to sing,
⁵⁰ But silent bats in drowsy clusters cling,
Those poisonous fields with rank luxuriance crowned,
Where the dark scorpion gathers death around;
Where at each step the stranger fears to wake
The rattling terrors of the vengeful snake;
³⁵⁵ Where crouching tigers° wait their hapless prey,   *pumas*
And savage men, more murderous still than they;
While oft in whirls the mad tornado flies,
Mingling the ravaged landscape with the skies.
    Far different these from every former scene,
³⁶⁰ The cooling brook, the grassy-vested green,
The breezy covert of the warbling grove,
That only sheltered thefts of harmless love.
    Good Heaven! what sorrows gloomed that parting day,
That called them from their native walks away;
³⁶⁵ When the poor exiles, every pleasure past,
Hung round their bowers, and fondly looked their last,
And took a long farewell, and wished in vain
For seats like these beyond the western main;
And shuddering still to face the distant deep,
³⁷⁰ Returned and wept, and still returned to weep.
The good old sire, the first prepared to go

6. Altahama, a river in Georgia.

To new-found worlds, and wept for other's woe.
But for himself, in conscious virtue brave,
He only wished for worlds beyond the grave.
375 His lovely daughter, lovelier in her tears,
The fond companion of his helpless years,
Silent went next, neglectful of her charms,
And left a lover's for a father's arms.
With louder plaints the mother spoke her woes,
380 And blessed the cot where every pleasure rose;
And kissed her thoughtless babes with many a tear,
And clasped them close in sorrow doubly dear;
Whilst her fond husband strove to lend relief
In all the silent manliness of grief.
385   O luxury! Thou cursed by Heaven's decree,
How ill exchanged are things like these for thee!
How do thy potions, with insidious joy,
Diffuse their pleasures only to destroy!
Kingdoms, by thee, to sickly greatness grown,
390 Boast of a florid vigor not their own.
At every draught more large and large they grow,
A bloated mass of rank unwieldy woe;
Till sapped their strength, and every part unsound,
Down, down they sink, and spread a ruin round.
395   Even now the devastation is begun,
And half the business of destruction done;
Even now, methinks, as pondering here I stand,
I see the rural Virtues leave the land.
Down where yon anchoring vessel spreads the sail,
400 That idly waiting flaps with every gale,
Downward they move, a melancholy band,
Pass from the shore, and darken all the strand.
Contented Toil, and hospitable Care,
And kind connubial Tenderness are there;
405 And Piety, with wishes placed above,
And steady Loyalty, and faithful Love:
And thou, sweet Poetry, thou loveliest maid,
Still first to fly where sensual joys invade;
Unfit in these degenerate times of shame,
410 To catch the heart, or strike for honest fame;
Dear charming Nymph, neglected and decried,
My shame in crowds, my solitary pride;
Thou source of all my bliss, and all my woe,
That found'st me poor at first, and keep'st me so;
415 Thou guide by which the nobler arts excel,
Thou nurse of every virtue, fare thee well.
Farewell, and O! where'er thy voice be tried,
On Torno's cliffs, or Pambamarca's side,[7]
Whether where equinoctial fervors glow,
420 Or winter wraps the polar world in snow,
Still let thy voice, prevailing over time,
Redress the rigors of the inclement clime;
Aid slighted truth, with thy persuasive strain
Teach erring man to spurn the rage of gain;
425 Teach him that states of native strength possessed,
Though very poor, may still be very blest;

7. I.e., on the cliffs overlooking the river Torne in Sweden or the side of Mount Pambamarca in Ecuador.

That Trade's proud empire hastes to swift decay,
As ocean sweeps the labored mole° away;   *breakwater*
While self-dependent power can time defy,
30   As rocks resist the billows and the sky.[8]

1770

WILLIAM COWPER
(1731–1800)

Lines Written During a Period of Insanity[1]

Hatred and vengeance, my eternal portion,
Scarce can endure delay of execution,
Wait, with impatient readiness, to seize my
        Soul in a moment.

5   Damned below Judas: more abhorred than he was,
Who for a few pence sold his holy Master.
Twice betrayed Jesus me, the last delinquent,
        Deems the profanest.

Man disavows, and Deity disowns me:
10   Hell might afford my miseries a shelter;
Therefore hell keeps her ever hungry mouths all
        Bolted against me.

Hard lot! encompassed with a thousand dangers;
Weary, faint, trembling with a thousand terrors;
15   I'm called, if vanquished, to receive a sentence
        Worse than Abiram's.[2]

Him the vindictive rod of angry justice
Sent quick and howling to the center headlong;
I, fed with judgment, in a fleshly tomb, am
20   Buried above ground.

ca. 1774   1816

From Olney Hymns

Light Shining out of Darkness

God moves in a mysterious way,
   His wonders to perform;
He plants his footsteps in the sea,
   And rides upon the storm.

5   Deep in unfathomable mines
   Of never failing skill,
He treasures up his bright designs,
   And works his sovereign will.

---

8. The last four lines are by Dr. Johnson.
1. See Glossary, entry on **Sapphic strophe**, at the end of this anthology.
2. Judas (line 5) betrayed Jesus to the chief priests for money (Matthew xxvi.14–16).

Abiram, rebelling against the authority of Moses and Aaron, was swallowed up with his fellow-dissidents in a cleft of the earth. They "went down alive into the pit, and the earth closed upon them" (Numbers xvi.33).

Ye fearful saints, fresh courage take,
10   The clouds ye so much dread
Are big with mercy, and shall break
    In blessings on your head.

Judge not the Lord by feeble sense,
    But trust him for his grace;
15 Behind a frowning providence,
    He hides a smiling face.

His purposes will ripen fast,
    Unfolding every hour;
The bud may have a bitter taste,
20   But sweet will be the flower.

Blind unbelief is sure to err,
    And scan his work in vain;
God is his own interpreter,
    And he will make it plain.

1779

Epitaph on a Hare

Here lies, whom hound did ne'er pursue,
    Nor swifter greyhound follow,
Whose foot ne'er tainted° morning dew,   *left a scent on*
    Nor ear heard huntsman's hallo',

5   Old Tiney, surliest of his kind,
    Who, nursed with tender care,
And to domestic bounds confined,
    Was still a wild jack-hare.

Though duly from my hand he took
10   His pittance every night,
He did it with a jealous look,
    And, when he could, would bite.

His diet was of wheaten bread,
    And milk, and oats, and straw,
15 Thistles, or lettuces instead,
    With sand to scour his maw.

On twigs of hawthorn he regaled,°   *feasted*
    On pippins' russet peel;
And, when his juicy salads failed,
20   Sliced carrot pleased him well.

A Turkey carpet was his lawn,[5]
    Whereon he loved to bound,
To skip and gambol like a fawn,
    And swing his rump around.

25 His frisking was at evening hours,
    For then he lost his fear;

5. Cowper exercised his hares on his parlor carpet of Turkey red.

But most before approaching showers,
    Or when a storm drew near.

30 Eight years and five round-rolling moons
    He thus saw steal away,
Dozing out all his idle noons,
    And every night at play.

I kept him for his humor's sake,
    For he would oft beguile
35 My heart of thoughts that made it ache,
    And force me to a smile.

But now, beneath this walnut-shade
    He finds his long, last home,
And waits in snug concealment laid,
40   Till gentler Puss shall come.

He,[6] still more agéd, feels the shocks
    From which no care can save,
And, partner once of Tiney's box,
    Must soon partake his grave.

1783   1784

From The Task[7]

From Book VI: The Winter Walk at Noon

    The groans of nature in this nether world,
730 Which Heav'n has heard for ages, have an end.
Foretold by prophets, and by poets sung,
Whose fire was kindled at the prophets' lamp,
The time of rest, the promised Sabbath, comes.[1]
Six thousand years [2] of sorrow have well-nigh
735 Fulfilled their tardy and disastrous course
Over a sinful world; and what remains
Of this tempestuous state of human things
Is merely as the working of a sea
Before a calm, that rocks itself to rest:
740 For He, whose car° the winds are, and the clouds   *chariot*
The dust that waits upon his sultry march,
When sin hath moved him, and his wrath is hot,
Shall visit earth in mercy; shall descend,
Propitious, in his chariot paved with love;
745 And what his storms have blasted and defaced
For man's revolt shall with a smile repair.
    Sweet is the harp of prophecy; too sweet
Not to be wronged by a mere mortal touch:
Nor can the wonders it records be sung
750 To meaner music, and not suffer loss.
But, when a poet, or when one like me,

6. **Puss, the longest-lived of Cowper's three hares.**
7. So called because, when he complained of the want of a poetic topic, a friend, Lady Austen (the "fair" of line 7), set him the task of writing about the parlor sofa. The completed work ran to six books and ranged over a diversity of subjects.
1. An allusion to the end of the world and the second coming of Christ, when God will make "a new heaven and a new earth" (Revelation xxi.1). Lines 759–817 are Cowper's visionary description of this "promised Sabbath."
2. The creation of the world was traditionally believed to have taken place 4000 years before the birth of Christ.

Happy to rove among poetic flowers,
Though poor in skill to rear them, lights at last
On some fair theme, some theme divinely fair,
755 Such is the impulse and the spur he feels
To give it praise proportioned to its worth,
That not t' attempt it, arduous as he deems
The labor, were a task more arduous still.
　　Oh scenes surpassing fable, and yet true,
760 Scenes of accomplished bliss! which who can see,
Though but in distant prospect, and not feel
His soul refreshed with foretaste of the joy?
Rivers of gladness water all the earth,
And clothe all climes with beauty; the reproach
765 Of barrenness is past. The fruitful field
Laughs with abundance; and the land, once lean,
Or fertile only in its own disgrace,
Exults to see its thistly curse repealed.
The various seasons woven into one,
770 And that one season an eternal spring,
The garden fears no blight, and needs no fence,
For there is none to covet, all are full.
The lion, and the libbard,° and the bear   *leopard*
Graze with the fearless flocks; all bask at noon
775 Together, or all gambol in the shade
Of the same grove, and drink one common stream.
Antipathies are none. No foe to man
Lurks in the serpent now: the mother sees,
And smiles to see, her infant's playful hand
780 Stretched forth to dally with the crested worm,°   *serpent*
To stroke his azure neck, or to receive
The lambent homage of his arrowy tongue.
All creatures worship man, and all mankind
One Lord, one Father. Error has no place:
785 That creeping pestilence is driv'n away;
The breath of heav'n has chased it.   In the heart
No passion touches a discordant string,
But all is harmony and love. Disease
Is not: the pure and uncontam'nate blood
790 Holds its due course, nor fears the frost of age.
One song employs all nations; and all cry,
"Worthy the Lamb, for he was slain for us!"
The dwellers in the vales and on the rocks
Shout to each other, and the mountain tops
795 From distant mountains catch the flying joy;
Till, nation after nation taught the strain,
Earth rolls the rapturous hosanna round.
Behold the measure of the promise filled;
See Salem [3] built, the labor of a God!
800 Bright as a sun the sacred city shines;
All kingdoms and all princes of the earth
Flock to that light; the glory of all lands
Flows into her; unbounded is her joy,
And endless her increase.   Thy rams are there,

3. Jerusalem; not only the terrestrial city but the New Jerusalem or Holy City, God's perfect and eternal order of the future. See Revela-tion xxxi.2: "And I John saw the holy city, new Jerusalem, coming down from God out of heaven. . . ."

805 Nebaioth, and the flocks of Kedar there; [4]
The looms of Ormus, and the mines of Ind,
And Saba's spicy groves, pay tribute there. [5]
Praise is in all her gates: upon her walls,
And in her streets, and in her spacious courts,
810 Is heard salvation. Eastern Java there
Kneels with the native of the farthest west;
And Ethiopia spreads abroad the hand,
And worships. Her report has traveled forth
Into all lands. From every clime they come
815 To see thy beauty and to share thy joy,
O Sion! [6] an assembly such as earth
Saw never, such as heav'n stoops down to see.
 Thus heav'n-ward all things tend. For all were once
Perfect, and all must be at length restored.
820 So God has greatly purposed; who would else
In his dishonored works himself endure
Dishonor, and be wronged without redress.
Haste, then, and wheel away a shattered world,
Ye slow-revolving seasons! we would see
825 (A sight to which our eyes are strangers yet)
A world that does not dread and hate his laws,
And suffer for its crime; would learn how fair
The creature is that God pronounces good,
How pleasant in itself what pleases him.
830 Here every drop of honey hides a sting,
Worms wind themselves into our sweetest flowers;
And ev'n the joy that haply° some poor heart   *luckily*
Derives from heav'n, pure as the fountain is,
Is sullied in the stream, taking a taint
835 From touch of human lips, at best impure.
Oh for a world in principle as chaste
As this is gross and selfish! over which
Custom and prejudice shall bear no sway,
That govern all things here, shouldering aside
840 The meek and modest truth, and forcing her
To seek a refuge from the tongue of strife
In nooks obscure, far from the ways of men;
Where violence shall never lift the sword,
Nor cunning justify the proud man's wrong,
845 Leaving the poor no remedy but tears;
Where he that fills an office shall esteem
Th' occasion it presents of doing good
More than the perquisite; where law shall speak
Seldom, and never but as wisdom prompts
850 And equity; not jealous more to guard
A worthless form, than to decide aright;
Where fashion shall not sanctify abuse,
Nor smooth good breeding (supplemental grace)
With lean performance ape the work of love!

---

4. "Nebaioth and Kedar, the sons of Ishmael and progenitors of the Arabs, in the prophetic Scripture here alluded to may be reasonably considered as representatives of the Gentiles at large" [Cowper's note]. By "the prophetic Scripture here alluded to" Cowper means Isaiah lx.3–7, where God promises a blessed future to Jerusalem: "And the Gentiles shall come to thy light. . . . All the flocks of Keder shall be gathered together unto thee, the rams of Nebaioth shall minister unto thee."

5. Ormus (an island in the Persian Gulf), India, and Saba (Sheba, a country in Arabia) were renowned for their wealth.
6. Often, as here, equivalent to Jerusalem.

855   Come then, and, added to thy many crowns,
Receive yet one, the crown of all the earth,
Thou who alone art worthy! It was thine
By ancient covenant, ere nature's birth;
And thou hast made it thine by purchase since,
860 And overpaid its value with thy blood.
Thy saints proclaim thee king; and in their hearts
Thy title is engraven with a pen
Dipped in the fountain of eternal love.
Thy saints proclaim thee king; and thy delay
865 Gives courage to their foes, who, could they see
The dawn of thy last advent, long desired,
Would creep into the bowels of the hills,
And flee for safety to the falling rocks.
The very spirit of the world is tired
870 Of its own taunting question, asked so long,
"Where is the promise of your Lord's approach?"
The infidel has shot his bolts° away,   *arrows*
Till, his exhausted quiver yielding none,
He gleans the blunted shafts that have recoiled,
875 And aims them at the shield of truth again.
The veil is rent, rent too by priestly hands,
That hides divinity from mortal eyes; [7]
And all the mysteries to faith proposed,
Insulted and traduced, are cast aside,
880 As useless, to the moles and to the bats.
They now are deemed the faithful, and are praised,
Who, constant only in rejecting thee,
Deny thy Godhead with a martyr's zeal,
And quit their office for their error's sake.
885 Blind, and in love with darkness! yet ev'n these
Worthy, compared with sycophants, who knee
Thy name adoring, and then preach thee man!
So fares thy church. But how thy church may fare
The world takes little thought. Who will may preach,
890 And what they will. All pastors are alike
To wandering sheep, resolved to follow none.
Two gods divide them all—Pleasure and Gain:
For these they live, they sacrifice to these,
And in their service wage perpetual war
895 With conscience and with thee. Lust in their hearts,
And mischief in their hands, they roam the earth
To prey upon each other: stubborn, fierce,
High-minded, foaming out their own disgrace.
Thy prophets speak of such; and, noting down
900 The features of the last degenerate times,
Exhibit every lineament of these.
Come then, and, added to thy many crowns,
Receive yet one, as radiant as the rest,
Due to thy last and most effectual work,
905 Thy word fulfilled, the conquest of a world!
    He is the happy man, whose life ev'n now
Shows somewhat of that happier life to come;

7. The veil of the Temple in Jerusalem divided the inner sanctuary from the rest of the Temple. For Christians, rending of the veil represented gaining direct access to God, notably through Christ's death. "And Jesus cried with a loud voice, and gave up the ghost. And the veil of the temple was rent in twain from the top to the bottom" (Mark xv. 37–8).

Who, doomed to an obscure but tranquil state,
Is pleased with it, and, were he free to choose,
910   Would make his fate his choice; whom peace, the fruit
Of virtue, and whom virtue, fruit of faith,
Prepare for happiness; bespeak° him one   *signify*
Content indeed to sojourn while he must
Below the skies, but having there his home.
915   The world o'erlooks him in her busy search
Of objects, more illustrious in her view;
And, occupied as earnestly as she,
Though more sublimely, he o'erlooks the world.
She scorns his pleasures, for she knows them not;
920   He seeks not hers, for he has proved them vain.
He cannot skim the ground like summer birds
Pursuing·gilded flies; and such he deems
Her honors, her emoluments, her joys.
Therefore in contemplation is his bliss,
925   Whose power is such, that whom she lifts from earth
She makes familiar with a heav'n unseen,
And shows him glories yet to be revealed.
Not slothful he, though seeming unemployed,
And censured oft as useless.   Stillest streams
930   Oft water fairest meadows, and the bird
That flutters least is longest on the wing.
Ask him, indeed, what trophies he has raised,
Or what achievements of immortal fame
He purposes, and he shall answer—None.
935   His warfare is within. There unfatigued
His fervent spirit labors. There he fights,
And there obtains fresh triumphs o'er himself,
And never withering wreaths, compared with which
The laurels that a Caesar reaps are weeds.
940   Perhaps the self-approving haughty world,
That as she sweeps him with her whistling silks
Scarce deigns to notice him, or, if she see,
Deems him a cipher° in the works of God,   *nonentity*
Receives advantage from his noiseless hours,
945   Of which she little dreams. Perhaps she owes
Her sunshine and her rain, her blooming spring
And plenteous harvest, to the prayer he makes,
When, Isaac-like,[8] the solitary saint
Walks forth to meditate at even tide,
950   And think on her, who thinks not for herself.
Forgive him, then, thou bustler in concerns
Of little worth, an idler in the best,
If, author of no mischief and some good,
He seek his proper happiness by means
955   That may advance, but cannot hinder, thine.
Nor, though he tread the secret path of life,
Engage no notice, and enjoy much ease,
Account him an encumbrance on the state,
Receiving benefits, and rendering none.
960   His sphere though humble, if that humble sphere
Shine with his fair example, and though small
His influence, if that influence all be spent

---

8. Isaac, son of Abraham and Sarah, was as-   See Genesis xxiv.63: "And Isaac went out to
sociated with a contemplative turn of mind.   meditate in the field at the eventide. . . ."

In soothing sorrow and in quenching strife,
In aiding helpless indigence, in works
965 From which at least a grateful few derive
Some taste of comfort in a world of woe,
Then let the supercilious great confess
He serves his country, recompenses well
The state, beneath the shadow of whose vine
970 He sits secure, and in the scale of life
Holds no ignoble, though a slighted, place.
The man, whose virtues are more felt than seen,
Must drop indeed the hope of public praise;
But he may boast what few that win it can—
975 That if his country stand not by his skill,
At least his follies have not wrought her fall.
Polite refinement offers him in vain
Her golden tube, through which a sensual world
Draws gross impurity, and likes it well,
980 The neat conveyance hiding all th' offense.
Not that he peevishly rejects a mode
Because that world adopts it. If it bear
The stamp and clear impression of good sense,
And be not costly more than of true worth,
985 He puts it on, and, for decorum's sake,
Can wear it e'en as gracefully as she.
She judges of refinement by the eye,
He by the test of conscience, and a heart
Not soon deceived; aware that what is base
990 No polish can make sterling; and that vice,
Though well perfumed and elegantly dressed,
Like an unburied carcass tricked with flowers,
Is but a garnished nuisance, fitter far
For cleanly riddance than for fair attire.
995 So life glides smoothly and by stealth away,
More golden than that age of fabled gold
Renowned in ancient song; [9] not vexed with care
Or stained with guilt, beneficent, approved
Of God and man, and peaceful in its end.
1000 So glide my life away! and so at last,
My share of duties decently fulfilled,
May some disease, not tardy to perform
Its destined office, yet with gentle stroke,
Dismiss me, weary, to a safe retreat,
1005 Beneath the turf that I have often trod.

1785

The Castaway

Obscurest night involved the sky,
    The Atlantic billows roared,
When such a destined wretch as I,
    Washed headlong from on board,
5 Of friends, of hope, of all bereft,
His floating home forever left.

9. In classical mythology, the age of Saturn, a time of perfection when the world knew
neither evil nor sorrow.

No braver chief could Albion boast
    Than he with whom he went,[4]
Nor ever ship left Albion's coast,
    With warmer wishes sent.
He loved them both, but both in vain,
Nor him beheld, nor her again.

Not long beneath the whelming brine,
    Expert to swim, he lay;
Nor soon he felt his strength decline,
    Or courage die away;
But waged with death a lasting strife,
Supported by despair of life.

He shouted; nor his friends had failed
    To check the vessel's course,
But so the furious blast prevailed,
    That, pitiless perforce,
They left their outcast mate behind,
And scudded still before the wind.

Some succor yet they could afford;
    And, such as storms allow,
The cask, the coop, the floated cord,
    Delayed not to bestow.
But he (they knew) nor ship, nor shore,
Whate'er they gave, should visit more.

Nor, cruel as it seemed, could he
    Their haste himself condemn,
Aware that flight, in such a sea,
    Alone could rescue them;
Yet bitter felt it still to die
Deserted, and his friends so nigh.

He long survives, who lives an hour
    In ocean, self-upheld;
And so long he, with unspent power,
    His destiny repelled;
And ever, as the minutes flew,
Entreated help, or cried, "Adieu!"

At length, his transient respite past,
    His comrades, who before
Had heard his voice in every blast,
    Could catch the sound no more.
For then, by toil subdued, he drank
The stifling wave, and then he sank.

No poet wept him; but the page
    Of narrative sincere,
That tells his name, his worth, his age,
    Is wet with Anson's tear.
And tears by bards or heroes shed
Alike immortalize the dead.

4. Namely, George, Lord Anson, who told the castaway's story in his *Voyage Round the World* (1748).

55   I therefore purpose not, or dream,
     Descanting on his fate,
   To give the melancholy theme
     A more enduring date:
   But misery still delights to trace
60   Its semblance in another's case.

   No voice divine the storm allayed,
     No light propitious shone,
   When, snatched from all effectual aid,
     We perished, each alone;
65   But I beneath a rougher sea,
   And whelmed in deeper gulfs than he.

          1799   1803

PHILIP FRENEAU
(1752–1832)

The Indian Burying Ground

In spite of all the learned have said,
   I still my opinion keep;
The posture, that we give the dead,
   Points out the soul's eternal sleep.

5   Not so the ancients of these lands—
     The Indian, when from life released,
   Again is seated with his friends,
     And shares again the joyous feast.[1]

   His imaged birds, and painted bowl,
10   And venison, for a journey dressed,
   Bespeak the nature of the soul,
     Activity, that knows no rest.

   His bow, for action ready bent,
     And arrows, with a head of stone,
15   Can only mean that life is spent,
     And not the old ideas gone.

   Thou, stranger, that shalt come this way,
     No fraud upon the dead commit—
   Observe the swelling turf, and say
20   They do not lie, but here they sit.

   Here still a lofty rock remains,
     On which the curious eye may trace
   (Now wasted, half, by wearing rains)
     The fancies of a ruder race.

25   Here still an aged elm aspires,
     Beneath whose far-projecting shade
   (And which the shepherd still admires)
     The children of the forest played!

1. Referring to the ancient Indian custom of burying the dead in a sitting position.

There oft a restless Indian queen
30   (Pale Shebah, with her braided hair)
And many a barbarous form is seen
    To chide the man that lingers there.

By midnight moons, o'er moistening dews;
    In habit for the chase arrayed,
35 The hunter still the deer pursues,
    The hunter and the deer, a shade!

And long shall timorous fancy see
    The painted chief, and pointed spear,
And Reason's self shall bow the knee
40   To shadows and delusions here.

1787   1788

GEORGE CRABBE
(1754–1832)

From The Borough

Letter XXII, The Poor of The Borough: Peter Grimes

Old Peter Grimes made fishing his employ,⎤
His wife he cabined with him and his boy,⎬
And seemed that life laborious to enjoy;⎦
To town came quiet Peter with his fish,
5   And had of all a civil word and wish.
He left his trade upon the sabbath-day,
And took young Peter in his hand to pray;
But soon the stubborn boy from care broke loose,
At first refused, then added his abuse;
10 His father's love he scorned, his power defied,
But being drunk, wept sorely when he died.
    Yes! then he wept, and to his mind there came
Much of his conduct, and he felt the shame—
How he had oft the good old man reviled,
15 And never paid the duty of a child;
How, when the father in his Bible read,
He in contempt and anger left the shed;
"It is the word of life," the parent cried;
—"This is the life itself," the boy replied;
20 And while old Peter in amazement stood,
Gave the hot spirit to his boiling blood;
How he, with oath and furious speech, began
To prove his freedom and assert the man;
And when the parent checked his impious rage,
25 How he had cursed the tyranny of age—
Nay, once had dealt the sacrilegious blow
On his bare head, and laid his parent low;
The father groaned—"If thou art old," said he,
"And hast a son—thou wilt remember me.
30 Thy mother left me in a happy time,
Thou kill'dst not her—Heaven spares the double crime."

On an inn-settle,° in his maudlin grief,   *tavern bench*
This he revolved,° and drank for his relief.   *pondered*
   Now lived the youth in freedom, but debarred
35 From constant pleasure, and he thought it hard;
Hard that he could not every wish obey,
But must awhile relinquish ale and play;
Hard! that he could not to his cards attend,
But must acquire the money he would spend.
40   With greedy eye he looked on all he saw,
He knew not justice, and he laughed at law;
On all he marked he stretched his ready hand;
He fished by water, and he filched by land.
Oft in the night has Peter dropped his oar,
45 Fled from his boat and sought for prey on shore;
Oft up the hedgerow glided, on his back   ⎫
Bearing the orchard's produce in a sack,   ⎬
Or farmyard load, tugged fiercely from the stack; ⎭
And as these wrongs to greater numbers rose,
50 The more he looked on all men as his foes.
   He built a mud-walled hovel, where he kept
His various wealth, and there he ofttimes slept;
But no success could please his cruel soul,
He wished for one to trouble and control;
55 He wanted some obedient boy to stand
And bear the blow of his outrageous hand,
And hoped to find in some propitious hour
A feeling creature subject to his power.
   Peter had heard there were in London then—
60 Still have they being!—workhouse-clearing men,[1]
Who, undisturbed by feelings just or kind,
Would parish-boys[2] to needy tradesmen bind;
They in their want a trifling sum would take,
And toiling slaves of piteous orphans make.
65   Such Peter sought, and when a lad was found,
The sum was dealt him, and the slave was bound.°   *bound over*
Some few in town observed in Peter's trap°   *fish-trap*
A boy, with jacket blue and woollen cap;
But none inquired how Peter used the rope,
70 Or what the bruise, that made the stripling stoop;
None could the ridges on his back behold,
None sought him shivering in the winter's cold;
None put the question—"Peter, dost thou give
The boy his food?—What, man! the lad must live!
75 Consider, Peter, let the child have bread,
He'll serve thee better if he's stroked and fed."
None reasoned thus—and some, on hearing cries,
Said calmly, "Grimes is at his exercise."
   Pinned, beaten, cold, pinched, threatened, and abused—
80 His efforts punished and his food refused—
Awake tormented—soon aroused from sleep—
Struck if he wept, and yet compelled to weep,
The trembling boy dropped down and strove to pray,
Received a blow, and trembling turned away,
85 Or sobbed and hid his piteous face; while he,

---

1. Men who removed persons from the workhouses, where the indigent were kept at the public charge.

2. Boys on relief. The local ecclesiastical unit, the parish, administered poor-relief.

The savage master, grinned in horrid glee;
He'd now the power he ever loved to show,
A feeling being subject to his blow.
    Thus lived the lad, in hunger, peril, pain,
90 His tears despised, his supplications vain;
Compelled by fear to lie, by need to steal,
His bed uneasy and unblessed his meal,
For three sad years the boy his tortures bore,
And then his pains and trials were no more.
95   "How died he, Peter?" when the people said,
He growled—"I found him lifeless in his bed,"
Then tried for softer tone, and sighed, "Poor Sam is dead."
Yet murmurs were there, and some questions asked—
How he was fed, how punished, and how tasked?
100 Much they suspected, but they little proved,
And Peter passed untroubled and unmoved.
    Another boy with equal ease was found,
The money granted, and the victim bound.
And what his fate?—One night it chanced he fell
105 From the boat's mast and perished in her well,
Where fish were living kept, and where the boy
(So reasoned men) could not himself destroy.
    "Yes, so it was," said Peter, "in his play
(For he was idle both by night and day),
110 He climbed the main-mast and then fell below"—
Then showed his corpse and pointed to the blow.
What said the jury?—They were long in doubt,
But sturdy Peter faced the matter out;
So they dismissed him, saying at the time,
115 "Keep fast your hatchway when you've boys who climb."
This hit the conscience, and he colored more
Than for the closest questions put before.
    Thus all his fears the verdict set aside,
And at the slave-shop Peter still applied.
120   Then came a boy of manners soft and mild—
Our seamen's wives with grief beheld the child;
All thought (the poor themselves) that he was one
Of gentle blood, some noble sinner's son,
Who had, belike, deceived some humble maid,
125 Whom he had first seduced and then betrayed.
However this, he seemed a gracious lad,
In grief submissive and with patience sad.
    Passive he labored, till his slender frame
Bent with his loads, and he at length was lame;
130 Strange that a frame so weak could bear so long
The grossest insult and the foulest wrong!
But there were causes: in the town they gave
Fire, food, and comfort to the gentle slave,
And though stern Peter, with a cruel hand
135 And knotted rope, enforced the rude command,
Yet he considered what he'd lately felt,
And his vile blows with selfish pity dealt.
    One day such draughts° the cruel fisher made,   *catches*
He could not vend them in his borough-trade,
140 But sailed for London-mart; the boy was ill,
But ever humbled to his master's will;
And on the river, where they smoothly sailed,

He strove with terror and awhile prevailed;
But new to danger on the angry sea,
145 He clung affrightened to his master's knee.
The boat grew leaky and the wind was strong,
Rough was the passage and the time was long;
His liquor failed, and Peter's wrath arose—
No more is known—the rest we must suppose,
150 Or learn of Peter; Peter says, he "spied
The stripling's danger and for harbor tried;
Meantime the fish, and then the apprentice died."
    The pitying women raised a clamor round,
And weeping said, "Thou hast thy 'prentice drowned."
155   Now the stern man was summoned to the hall,
To tell his tale before the burghers all;
He gave the account, professed the lad he loved,
And kept his brazen features all unmoved.
    The mayor himself with tone severe replied,
160 "Henceforth with thee shall never boy abide;
Hire thee a freeman, whom thou durst not beat,
But who, in thy despite, will sleep and eat;
Free thou art now!—Again shouldst thou appear,
Thou'lt find thy sentence, like thy soul, severe."
165   Alas! for Peter, not a helping hand,
So was he hated, could he now command.
Alone he rowed his boat, alone he cast
His nets beside, or made his anchor fast;
To hold a rope or hear a curse was none—
170 He toiled and railed, he groaned and swore alone.
    Thus by himself compelled to live each day,
To wait for certain hours the tide's delay;
At the same times the same dull views to see,
The bounding marsh-bank and the blighted tree;
175 The water only, when the tides were high,
When low, the mud half-covered and half-dry;
The sun-burnt tar that blisters on the planks,
And bank-side stakes in their uneven ranks;
Heaps of entangled weeds that slowly float,
180 As the tide rolls by the impeded boat.
    When tides were neap° and, in the sultry day,   *low*
Through the tall bounding mud-banks made their way,
Which on each side rose swelling, and below
The dark warm flood ran silently and slow;
185 There anchoring, Peter chose from man to hide,
There hang his head, and view the lazy tide
In its hot slimy channel slowly glide;
Where the small eels that left the deeper way
For the warm shore within the shallows play;
190 Where gaping mussels, left upon the mud,
Slope their slow passage to the fallen flood,
Here dull and hopeless he'd lie down and trace
How sidelong crabs had scrawled their crooked race,
Or sadly listen to the tuneless cry
195 Of fishing gull or clanging golden-eye;°   *wild duck*
What time the sea-birds to the marsh would come,
And the loud bittern, from the bulrush home,
Gave from the salt-ditch side the bellowing boom.
He nursed the feelings these dull scenes produce,

200 And loved to stop beside the opening sluice;
Where the small stream, confined in narrow bound,
Ran with a dull, unvaried, saddening sound;
Where all, presented to the eye or ear,
Oppressed the soul with misery, grief, and fear.
205   Besides these objects, there were places three,
Which Peter seemed with certain dread to see;
When he drew near them he would turn from each,
And loudly whistle till he passed the reach.
   A change of scene to him brought no relief;
210 In town, 'twas plain, men took him for a thief.
The sailors' wives would stop him in the street,
And say, "Now, Peter, thou'st no boy to beat!"
Infants at play, when they perceived him, ran,
Warning each other—"That's the wicked man!"
215 He growled an oath, and in an angry tone
Cursed the whole place and wished to be alone.
   Alone he was, the same dull scenes in view,
And still more gloomy in his sight they grew;
Though man he hated, yet employed alone
220 At bootless labor, he would swear and groan,
Cursing the shoals° that glided by the spot,   *schools of fish*
And gulls that caught them when his arts could not.
   Cold nervous tremblings shook his sturdy frame,
And strange disease—he couldn't say the name;
225 Wild were his dreams, and oft he rose in fright,
Waked by his view of horrors in the night—
Horrors that would the sternest minds amaze,
Horrors that demons might be proud to raise;
And though he felt forsaken, grieved at heart   ⎫
230 To think he lived from all mankind apart,   ⎬
Yet, if a man approached, in terrors he would start. ⎭
   A winter passed since Peter saw the town,
And summer lodgers were again come down.
These, idly curious, with their glasses spied
235 The ships in bay as anchored for the tide—
The river's craft—the bustle of the quay—
And sea-port views, which landmen love to see.
   One, up the river, had a man and boat
Seen day by day, now anchored, now afloat;
240 Fisher he seemed, yet used no net nor hook,   ⎫
Of sea-fowl swimming by no heed he took,   ⎬
But on the gliding waves still fixed his lazy look. ⎭
At certain stations he would view the stream,
As if he stood bewildered in a dream,
245 Or that[3] some power had chained him for a time,
To feel a curse or meditate on crime.
   This known, some curious, some in pity went,
And others questioned—"Wretch, dost thou repent?"
He heard, he trembled, and in fear resigned
250 His boat; new terror filled his restless mind;
Furious he grew, and up on the country ran,
And there they seized him—a distempered man.
Him we received, and to a parish-bed,[4]
Followed and cursed, the groaning man was led.

---

3. I.e., or as if.   4. A bed in the charity-hospital.

255 Here when they saw him whom they used to shun,
A lost, lone man, so harassed and undone,
Our gentle females, ever prompt to feel,
Perceived compassion on their anger steal;
His crimes they could not from their memories blot,
260 But they were grieved, and trembled at his lot.
    A priest too came, to whom his words are told;
And all the signs they shuddered to behold.
"Look! look!" they cried, "his limbs with horror shake,⎫
And as he grinds his teeth, what noise they make! ⎬
265 How glare his angry eyes, and yet he's not awake. ⎭
See! what cold drops upon his forehead stand,
And how he clenches that broad bony hand."
    The priest attending, found he spoke at times
As one alluding to his fears and crimes:
270 "It was the fall," he muttered; "I can show
The manner how—I never struck a blow"—
And then aloud—"Unhand me, free my chain!
On oath, he fell—it struck him to the brain—
Why ask my father?—that old man will swear
275 Against my life; besides, he wasn't there—
What, all agreed?—Am I to die today?—
My Lord, in mercy, give me time to pray."
    Then, as they watched him, calmer he became,
And grew so weak he couldn't move his frame,
280 But murmuring spake—while they could see and hear
The start of terror and the groan of fear;
See the large dew-beads on his forehead rise,
And the cold death-drop glaze his sunken eyes;
Nor yet he died, but with unwonted force
285 Seemed with some fancied being to discourse.
He knew not us, or with accustomed art
He hid the knowledge, yet exposed his heart;
'Twas part confession and the rest defence,
A madman's tale, with gleams of waking sense.
290 "I'll tell you all," he said, "the very day
When the old man first placed them in my way,
My father's spirit—he who always tried
To give me trouble, when he lived and died—
When he was gone, he could not be content
295 To see my days in painful labor spent,
But would appoint his meetings, and he made
Me watch at these, and so neglect my trade.
    " 'Twas one hot noon, all silent, still, serene,
No living being had I lately seen;
300 I paddled up and down and dipped my net,
But (such his pleasure) I could nothing get—
A father's pleasure, when his toil was done,
To plague and torture thus an only son!
And so I sat and looked upon the stream,
305 How it ran on and felt as in a dream,
But dream it was not; no!—I fixed my eyes
On the mid stream and saw the spirits rise;
I saw my father on the water stand,
And hold a thin pale boy in either hand;
310 And there they glided ghastly on the top
Of the salt flood, and never touched a drop;
I would have struck them, but they knew the intent,

And smiled upon the oar, and down they went.
  "Now, from that day, whenever I began
To dip my net, there stood the hard old man—
He and those boys. I humbled me and prayed
They would be gone—they heeded not, but stayed;
Nor could I turn, nor would the boat go by,
But gazing on the spirits, there was I;
They bade me leap to death, but I was loth to die.
And every day, as sure as day arose,
Would these three spirits meet me ere the close;
To hear and mark them daily was my doom,
And 'Come,' they said, with weak, sad voices, 'come.'
To row away with all my strength I tried,
But there were they, hard by me in the tide,
The three unbodied forms—and 'Come,' still 'come,' they cried.
  "Fathers should pity—but this old man shook
His hoary locks, and froze me by a look.
Thrice, when I struck them, through the water came
A hollow groan, that weakened all my frame.
'Father!' said I, 'have mercy!'—He replied,
I know not what—the angry spirit lied—
'Didst thou not draw thy knife?' said he—'Twas true,
But I had pity and my arm withdrew:
He cried for mercy which I kindly gave,
But he has no compassion in his grave.
  "There were three places, where they ever rose—
The whole long river has not such as those—
Places accursed, where, if a man remain,
He'll see the things which strike him to the brain;
And there they made me on my paddle lean,
And look at them for hours—accurséd scene!
When they would glide to that smooth eddy-space,
Then bid me leap and join them in the place;
And at my groans each little villain sprite
Enjoyed my pains and vanished in delight.
  "In one fierce summer day, when my poor brain
Was burning hot and cruel was my pain,
Then came this father-foe, and there he stood
With his two boys again upon the flood;
There was more mischief in their eyes, more glee
In their pale faces when they glared at me.
Still did they force me on the oar to rest,
And when they saw me fainting and oppressed,
He, with his hand, the old man, scooped the flood,
And there came flame about him mixed with blood;
He bade me stoop and look upon the place,
Then flung the hot-red liquor in my face;
Burning it blazed, and then I roared for pain,
I thought the demons would have turned my brain.
  "Still there they stood, and forced me to behold
A place of horrors—they cannot be told—
Where the flood opened, there I heard the shriek
Of tortured guilt—no earthly tongue can speak:
'All days alike! for ever!' did they say,
'And unremitted torments every day!'—
Yes, so they said."—But here he ceased and gazed
On all around, affrightened and amazed;
And still he tried to speak, and looked in dread

Of frightened females gathering round his bed;
Then dropped exhausted and appeared at rest,
Till the strong foe the vital powers possessed;
Then with an inward, broken voice he cried,
375 "Again they come," and muttered as he died.

1810

WILLIAM BLAKE
(1757–1827)

From POETICAL SKETCHES

To the Muses[1]

Whether on Ida's[2] shady brow,
    Or in the chambers of the East,
The chambers of the sun, that now
    From antient melody have ceas'd;

5   Whether in Heav'n ye wander fair,
    Or the green corners of the earth,
Or the blue regions of the air,
    Where the melodious winds have birth;

Whether on chrystal rocks ye rove,
10   Beneath the bosom of the sea
Wand'ring in many a coral grove,
    Fair Nine, forsaking Poetry!

How have you left the antient love
    That bards of old enjoy'd in you!
15 The languid strings do scarcely move!
    The sound is forc'd, the notes are few!

1783

Song

How sweet I roam'd from field to field,
    And tasted all the summer's pride,
'Till I the prince of love beheld,
    Who in the sunny beams did glide!

5   He shew'd me lilies for my hair,
    And blushing roses for my brow;
He led me through his gardens fair,
    Where all his golden pleasures grow.

With sweet May dews my wings were wet,
10   And Phoebus fir'd my vocal rage;[3]
He caught me in his silken net,
    And shut me in his golden cage.

---

1. Nine goddesses who, in Greek myth, pre-
side over the arts and sciences, especially
poetry.
2. Mountain in Asia Minor, distant from the
mountains sacred to the Muses (Helicon and
Parnassus) in Greece.
3. Impassioned song. Phoebus is Apollo, god of
poetic inspiration.

He loves to sit and hear me sing,
    Then, laughing, sports and plays with me;
15 Then stretches out my golden wing,
    And mocks my loss of liberty.

                                1783

To the Evening Star

Thou fair-hair'd angel of the evening,
Now, while the sun rests on the mountains, light
Thy bright torch of love; thy radiant crown
Put on, and smile upon our evening bed!
5 Smile on our loves; and, while thou drawest the
Blue curtains of the sky, scatter thy silver dew
On every flower that shuts its sweet eyes
In timely sleep. Let thy west wind sleep on
The lake; speak silence with thy glimmering eyes,
10 And wash the dusk with silver. Soon, full soon,
Dost thou withdraw; then the wolf rages wide,
And the lion glares thro' the dun forest:
The fleeces of our flocks are cover'd with
Thy sacred dew: protect them with thine influence.[4]

                                1783

From SONGS OF INNOCENCE

Introduction

Piping down the valleys wild
Piping songs of pleasant glee
On a cloud I saw a child,
And he laughing said to me,

5 "Pipe a song about a Lamb";
So I piped with merry chear.
"Piper pipe that song again"—
So I piped, he wept to hear.

"Drop thy pipe thy happy pipe
10 Sing thy songs of happy chear";
So I sung the same again
While he wept with joy to hear.

"Piper sit thee down and write
In a book that all may read"—
15 So he vanish'd from my sight.
And I pluck'd a hollow reed,

And I made a rural pen,
And I stain'd the water clear,
And I wrote my happy songs
20 Every child may joy to hear.

                                1789

---

4. In astrology, the effect that heavenly bodies exert on earthly things and creatures.

The Lamb

Little Lamb, who made thee?
Dost thou know who made thee?
Gave thee life & bid thee feed,
By the stream & o'er the mead;
5   Gave thee clothing of delight,
Softest clothing wooly bright;
Gave thee such a tender voice,
Making all the vales rejoice!
Little Lamb who made thee?
10 Dost thou know who made thee?

Little Lamb I'll tell thee,
Little Lamb I'll tell thee!
He° is callèd by thy name,   *Christ*
For he calls himself a Lamb:
15 He is meek & he is mild,
He became a little child:
I a child & thou a lamb,
We are callèd by his name.
Little Lamb God bless thee.
20 Little Lamb God bless thee.

                                                              1789

Holy Thursday [I.]

'Twas on a Holy Thursday,[5] their innocent faces clean,
The children[6] walking two & two, in red & blue & green,
Grey headed beadles[7] walkd before with wands as white as snow,
Till into the high dome of Paul's they like Thames' waters flow.

5   O what a multitude they seemd, these flowers of London town!
Seated in companies they sit with radiance all their own.
The hum of multitudes was there, but multitudes of lambs,
Thousands of little boys & girls raising their innocent hands.

Now like a mighty wind they raise to heaven the voice of song,
10 Or like harmonious thunderings the seats of heaven among.
Beneath them sit the aged men, wise guardians of the poor;
Then cherish pity, lest you drive an angel from your door.

                                                              1789

The Divine Image

To Mercy, Pity, Peace, and Love,
All pray in their distress:
And to these virtues of delight
Return their thankfulness.

5   For Mercy, Pity, Peace, and Love,
Is God, our father dear:
And Mercy, Pity, Peace, and Love,
Is Man, his child and care.

---

5. Probably Ascension Day (40 days after Easter).

6. Here the children of charity schools are depicted in St. Paul's Cathedral, London.
7. Ushers charged with keeping order.

For Mercy has a human heart,
10   Pity, a human face:
And Love, the human form divine,
And Peace, the human dress.

Then every man of every clime,
That prays in his distress,
15   Prays to the human form divine,
Love, Mercy, Pity, Peace.

And all must love the human form,
In heathen, Turk, or Jew.
Where Mercy, Love, & Pity dwell,
20   There God is dwelling too.

1789

The Little Black Boy

My mother bore me in the southern wild,
And I am black, but O! my soul is white;
White as an angel is the English child:
But I am black as if bereav'd of light.

5   My mother taught me underneath a tree,
And sitting down before the heat of day,
She took me on her lap and kisséd me,
And pointing to the east, began to say:

"Look on the rising sun: there God does live,
10   And gives his light, and gives his heat away;
And flowers and trees and beasts and men receive
Comfort in morning, joy in the noon day.

"And we are put on earth a little space,
That we may learn to bear the beams of love,
15   And these black bodies and this sun-burnt face
Is but a cloud, and like a shady grove.

"For when our souls have learn'd the heat to bear,
The cloud will vanish; we shall hear his voice,
Saying: 'Come out from the grove, my love & care,
20   And round my golden tent like lambs rejoice.'"

Thus did my mother say, and kisséd me;
And thus I say to little English boy:
When I from black and he from white cloud free,
And round the tent of God like lambs we joy,

25   I'll shade him from the heat till he can bear
To lean in joy upon our father's knee;
And then I'll stand and stroke his silver hair,
And be like him, and he will then love me.

1789

The Little Boy Lost

"Father, father, where are you going?
O do not walk so fast.
Speak father, speak to your little boy
Or else I shall be lost."

5   The night was dark, no father was there,
The child was wet with dew.
The mire was deep, & the child did weep,
And away the vapour flew.

                                                                    1789

The Little Boy Found

The little boy lost in the lonely fen,
Led by the wand'ring light,[1]
Began to cry, but God ever nigh
Appeard like his father in white.

5   He kissed the child & by the hand led
And to his mother brought,
Who in sorrow pale, thro' the lonely dale,
Her little boy weeping sought.

                                                                    1789

THE BOOK OF THEL[8]

Thel's Motto

Does the Eagle know what is in the pit?
Or wilt thou go ask the Mole?
Can Wisdom be put in a silver rod?
Or Love in a golden bowl?

                    1
5   The daughters of Mne[9] Seraphim led round their sunny flocks,
All but the youngest; she in paleness sought the secret air,
To fade away like morning beauty from her mortal day;
Down by the river of Adona her soft voice is heard,
And thus her gentle lamentation falls like morning dew:

10   "O life of this our spring! why fades the lotus of the water?
Why fade these children of the spring? born but to smile & fall.
Ah! Thel is like a watry bow, and like a parting cloud,
Like a reflection in a glass, like shadows in the water,
Like dreams of infants, like a smile upon an infant's face,
15   Like the dove's voice, like transient day, like music in the air.
Ah! gentle may I lay me down, and gentle rest my head,
And gentle sleep the sleep of death and gentle hear the voice
Of him that walketh in the garden in the evening time."

1. A will-o'-the-wisp.
8. *Thel*, like the other proper names in the poem, is Blake's invention, and its meaning can only be inferred.
9. Possibly a misprint for *the*. Seraphim are angels who guard Jehovah's throne.

The Lilly of the valley, breathing in the humble grass,
20 Answer'd the lovely maid and said: "I am a watry weed,
And I am very small, and love to dwell in lowly vales;
So weak, the gilded butterfly scarce perches on my head;
Yet I am visited from heaven, and he that smiles on all
Walks in the valley and each morn over me spreads his hand,
25 Saying: 'Rejoice, thou humble grass, thou new-born lilly flower,
Thou gentle maid of silent valleys and of modest brooks;
For thou shalt be clothed in light, and fed with morning manna,
Till summer's heat melts thee beside the fountains and the springs
To flourish in eternal vales.' Then why should Thel complain?

30 Why should the mistress of the vales of Har utter a sigh?"

She ceasd & smild in tears, then sat down in her silver shrine.

Thel answerd: "O thou little virgin of the peaceful valley,
Giving to those that cannot crave, the voiceless, the o'ertired;
Thy breath doth nourish the innocent lamb, he smells thy milky garments,
35 He crops thy flowers, while thou sittest smiling in his face,
Wiping his mild and meekin[1] mouth from all contagious taints.
Thy wine doth purify the golden honey; thy perfume,
Which thou dost scatter on every little blade of grass that springs,
Revives the milkéd cow, & tames the fire-breathing steed.
40 But Thel is like a faint cloud kindled at the rising sun:
I vanish from my pearly throne, and who shall find my place?"
"Queen of the vales," the Lilly answered, "ask the tender cloud,
And it shall tell thee why it glitters in the morning sky,
And why it scatters its bright beauty thro' the humid air.
45 Descend, O little cloud, & hover before the eyes of Thel."

The Cloud descended, and the Lilly bowd her modest head,
And went to mind her numerous charge among the verdant grass.

2
"Oh little Cloud," the virgin said, "I charge thee tell to me,
Why thou complainest not when in one hour thou fade away:
50 Then we shall seek thee but not find; ah, Thel is like to Thee.
I pass away, yet I complain, and no one hears my voice."

The Cloud then shew'd his golden head & his bright form emerg'd,
Hovering and glittering on the air before the face of Thel.

"O virgin, know'st thou not our steeds drink of the golden springs
55 Where Luvah doth renew his horses? Look'st thou on my youth,
And fearest thou, because I vanish and am seen no more,
Nothing remains? O maid, I tell thee, when I pass away,
It is to tenfold life, to love, to peace, and raptures holy:
Unseen descending, weigh my light wings upon balmy flowers,
60 And court the fair eyed dew, to take me to her shining tent;
The weeping virgin trembling kneels before the risen sun,
Till we arise link'd in a golden band, and never part,
But walk united, bearing food to all our tender flowers."

"Dost thou O little Cloud? I fear that I am not like thee;
65 For I walk through the vales of Har and smell the sweetest flowers,

1. Perhaps describing a lamb's delicately wrinkling mouth.

But I feed not the little flowers; I hear the warbling birds,
But I feed not the warbling birds; they fly and seek their food;
But Thel delights in these no more, because I fade away,
And all shall say, 'Without a use this shining woman liv'd,
70 Or did she only live to be at death the food of worms?' "

The Cloud reclind upon his airy throne and answer'd thus:

"Then if thou art the food of words, O virgin of the skies,
How great thy use, how great thy blessing! Every thing that lives
Lives not alone, nor for self; fear not, and I will call
75 The weak worm from its lowly bed, and thou shalt hear its voice.
Come forth, worm of the silent valley, to thy pensive queen."

The helpless worm arose, and sat upon the Lilly's leaf,
And the bright Cloud saild on, to find his partner in the vale.

                    3
Then Thel astonish'd view'd the Worm upon its dewy bed.

80 "Art thou a Worm? Image of weakness, art thou but a Worm?
I see thee like an infant wrapped in the Lilly's leaf;
Ah, weep not, little voice, thou can'st not speak, but thou can'st weep.
Is this a Worm? I see thee lay helpless & naked, weeping,
And none to answer, none to cherish thee with mother's smiles."

85 The Clod of Clay heard the Worm's voice, & raisd her pitying head;
She bow'd over the weeping infant, and her life exhal'd
In milky fondness; then on Thel she fix'd her humble eyes.

"O beauty of the vales of Har! we live not for ourselves;
Thou seest me the meanest thing, and so I am indeed.
90 My bosom of itself is cold, and of itself is dark;

But he that loves the lowly, pours his oil upon my head,
And kisses me, and binds his nuptial bands around my breast,
And says: 'Thou mother of my children, I have lovéd thee,
And I have given thee a crown that none can take away.'
95 But how this is, sweet maid, I know not, and I cannot know;
I ponder, and I cannot ponder; yet I live and love."

The daughter of beauty wip'd her pitying tears with her white veil,
And said: "Alas! I knew not this, and therefore did I weep.
That God would love a Worm, I knew, and punish the evil foot
100 That, wilful, bruis'd its helpless form; but that he cherish'd it
With milk and oil I never knew; and therefore did I weep,
And I complain in the mild air, because I fade away,
And lay me down in thy cold bed, and leave my shining lot."

"Queen of the vales," the matron Clay answer'd, "I heard thy sighs,
105 And all thy moans flew o'er my roof, but I have call'd them down.
Wilt thou, O Queen, enter my house? 'Tis given thee to enter
And to return; fear nothing, enter thy virgin feet."

                    4
The eternal gates' terrific porter lifted the northern bar:[2]
Thel enter'd in & saw the secrets of the land unknown.

---

2. Possibly, the gate through which a soul or spirit enters the world of earthly life and death.

110 She saw the couches of the dead, & where the fibrous roots
Of every heart on earth infixes deep its restless twists:
A land of sorrows & of tears where never smile was seen.

She wanderd in the land of clouds thro' valleys dark, listning
Dolours & lamentations; waiting oft beside a dewy grave,
115 She stood in silence, listning to the voices of the ground,
Till to her own grave plot she came, & there she sat down,
And heard this voice of sorrow breathéd from the hollow pit:

"Why cannot the Ear be closed to its own destruction?
Or the glistning Eye to the poison of a smile?
120 Why are Eyelids stord with arrows ready drawn,
Where a thousand fighting men in ambush lie?
Or an Eye of gifts & graces, show'ring fruits & coinéd gold?
Why a Tongue impress'd with honey from every wind?
Why an Ear, a whirlpool fierce to draw creations in?
125 Why a Nostril wide inhaling terror, trembling, & affright?
Why a tender curb upon the youthful burning boy?
Why a little curtain of flesh on the bed of our desire?"

The Virgin started from her seat, & with a shriek
Fled back unhinderd till she came into the vales of Har.

THE END

1789–91

From Songs of Experience

Introduction

Hear the voice of the Bard!
Who Present, Past, & Future sees,
Whose ears have heard
The Holy Word
5 That walk'd among the ancient trees; [2]

Calling the lapséd Soul
And weeping in the evening dew;
That might controll
The starry pole,
10 And fallen fallen light renew!

"O Earth O Earth return!
Arise from out the dewy grass;
Night is worn,
And the morn
15 Rises from the slumberous mass.

"Turn away no more:
Why wilt thou turn away?
The starry floor
The watry shore
20 Is giv'n thee till the break of day."

1794

2. "And Adam and Eve heard the voice of the Lord God walking in the garden in the cool of the day" (Genesis iii.8).

A Divine Image

Cruelty has a Human heart
And Jealousy a Human Face,
Terror, the Human Form Divine,
And Secrecy, the Human Dress.

5   The Human Dress is forgéd Iron,
The Human Form, a fiery Forge,
The Human Face, a Furnace seal'd,
The Human Heart, its hungry Gorge.°   *throat*

                                          1790–91   1921

Holy Thursday [II.]

Is this a holy thing to see,
In a rich and fruitful land,
Babes reducd to misery,
Fed with cold and usurous hand?

5   Is that trembling cry a song?
Can it be a song of joy?
And so many children poor?
It is a land of poverty!

10   And their sun does never shine,
And their fields are bleak & bare,
And their ways are fill'd with thorns;
It is eternal winter there.

For where-e'er the sun does shine,
And where-e'er the rain does fall,
15   Babe can never hunger there,
Nor poverty the mind appall.

                                          1794

The Clod & the Pebble

"Love seeketh not Itself to please,
Nor for itself hath any care;
But for another gives its ease,
And builds a Heaven in Hells despair."

5   So sang a little Clod of Clay,
Trodden with the cattle's feet;
But a Pebble of the brook,
Warbled out these metres meet:°   *appropriate*

"Love seeketh only Self to please,
10   To bind another to its delight,
Joys in another's loss of ease,
And builds a Hell in Heaven's despite."

                                          1794

The Sick Rose

O Rose, thou art sick.
The invisible worm
That flies in the night
In the howling storm

Has found out thy bed
Of crimson joy,
And his dark secret love
Does thy life destroy.

1794

A Poison Tree

I was angry with my friend:
I told my wrath, my wrath did end.
I was angry with my foe:
I told it not, my wrath did grow.

5   And I waterd it in fears,
Night & morning with my tears;
And I sunnéd it with smiles,
And with soft deceitful wiles.

And it grew both day and night,
10   Till it bore an apple bright.
And my foe beheld it shine,
And he knew that it was mine,

And into my garden stole,
When the night had veild the pole;
15   In the morning glad I see
My foe outstretchd beneath the tree.

1794

The Tyger

Tyger! Tyger! burning bright
In the forests of the night,
What immortal hand or eye
Could frame thy fearful symmetry?

5   In what distant deeps or skies
Burnt the fire of thine eyes?
On what wings dare he aspire?
What the hand, dare seize the fire?

10   And what shoulder, & what art,
Could twist the sinews of thy heart?
And when thy heart began to beat,
What dread hand? & what dread feet?

What the hammer? what the chain?
In what furnace was thy brain?
15   What the anvil? what dread grasp
Dare its deadly terrors clasp?

When the stars threw down their spears,
And water'd heaven with their tears,
Did he smile his work to see?
20   Did he who made the Lamb make thee?

Tyger! Tyger! burning bright
In the forests of the night,
What immortal hand or eye
Dare frame thy fearful symmetry?

1794

Ah Sun-flower

Ah Sun-flower! weary of time,
Who countest the steps of the Sun,
Seeking after that sweet golden clime
Where the traveller's journey is done;

5   Where the Youth pined away with desire,
And the pale Virgin shrouded in snow,
Arise from their graves and aspire,
Where my Sun-flower wishes to go.

1794

The Garden of Love

I went to the Garden of Love,
And saw what I never had seen:
A Chapel was built in the midst,
Where I used to play on the green.

5   And the gates of this Chapel were shut,
And "Thou shalt not" writ over the door;
So I turn'd to the Garden of Love,
That so many sweet flowers bore,

And I saw it was filled with graves,
10   And tomb-stones where flowers should be:
And Priests in black gowns were walking their rounds,
And binding with briars my joys & desires.

1794

London

I wander thro' each charter'd³ street,
Near where the charter'd Thames does flow,
And mark in every face I meet
Marks of weakness, marks of woe.

3. Mapped out, legally defined, constricted.

5 In every cry of every man,
   In every Infant's cry of fear,
   In every voice, in every ban,[4]
   The mind-forg'd manacles I hear.

   How the Chimney-sweeper's cry
10 Every blackning Church appalls;
   And the hapless Soldier's sigh
   Runs in blood down Palace walls.

   But most thro' midnight streets I hear
   How the youthful Harlot's curse
15 Blasts the new-born Infant's tear,
   And blights with plagues the Marriage hearse.

                                        1794

From SONGS AND BALLADS

I Askéd a Thief

   I askéd a thief to steal me a peach,
   He turned up his eyes;
   I ask'd a lithe lady to lie her down,
   Holy & meek she cries.

5 As soon as I went
   An angel came.
   He wink'd at the thief
   And smild at the dame—

   And without one word said
10 Had a peach from the tree
   And still as a maid
   Enjoy'd the lady.

                          1796   1863

Auguries of Innocence[5]

   To see a World in a Grain of Sand
   And a Heaven in a Wild Flower
   Hold Infinity in the palm of your hand
   And Eternity in an hour
5 A Robin Red breast in a Cage
   Puts all Heaven in a Rage
   A dove house filld with doves & Pigeons
   Shudders Hell thro all its regions
   A dog starvd at his Masters Gate
10 Predicts the ruin of the State
   A Horse misusd upon the Road
   Calls to Heaven for Human blood
   Each outcry of the hunted Hare
   A fibre from the Brain does tear
15 A Skylark wounded in the wing

---

4. A law or notice commanding or forbidding;
a published penalty.

5. To assist the reader in visualizing Blake's
manuscripts, the text of this poem has not
been editorially corrected.

A Cherubim does cease to sing
The Game Cock clipd & armd for fight
Does the Rising Sun affright
Every Wolfs & Lions howl
20 Raises from Hell a Human Soul
The wild deer wandring here & there
Keeps the Human Soul from Care
The Lamb misusd breeds Public strife
And yet forgives the Butchers Knife
25   The Bat that flits at close of Eve
Has left the Brain that wont Believe
The Owl that calls upon the Night
Speaks the Unbelievers fright
He who shall hurt the little Wren
30 Shall never be belovd by Men
He who the Ox to wrath has movd
Shall never be by Woman lovd
The wanton Boy that kills the Fly
Shall feel the Spiders enmity
35 He who torments the Chafers° sprite   *beetle's*
Weaves a Bower in endless Night
The Catterpiller on the Leaf
Repeats to thee thy Mothers grief
Kill not the Moth nor Butterfly
40 For the Last Judgment draweth nigh
He who shall train the Horse to War
Shall never pass the Polar Bar
The Beggers Dog & Widows Cat
Feed them & thou wilt grow fat
45 The Gnat that sings his Summers song
Poison gets from Slanders tongue
The poison of the Snake & Newt
Is the sweat of Envys Foot
The Poison of the Honey Bee
50 Is the Artists Jealousy
The Princes Robes & Beggars Rags
Are Toadstools on the Misers Bags
A truth thats told with bad intent
55 Beats all the Lies you can invent
It is right it should be so
Man was made for Joy & Woe
And when this we rightly know
Thro the World we safely go
Joy & Woe are woven fine
60 A Clothing for the Soul divine
Under every grief & pine
Runs a joy with silken twine
The Babe is more than swadling Bands
Throughout all these Human Lands
65 Tools were made & Born were hands
Every Farmer Understands
Every Tear from Every Eye
Becomes a Babe in Eternity
This is caught by Females bright
70 And returned to its own delight
The Bleat the Bark Bellow & Roar
Are Waves that Beat on Heavens Shore

The Babe that weeps the Rod beneath
Writes Revenge in realms of death
75 The Beggars Rags fluttering in Air
Does to Rags the Heavens tear
The Soldier armd with Sword & Gun
Palsied strikes the Summers Sun
The poor Mans Farthing is worth more
80 Than all the Gold on Africs Shore
One Mite wrung from the Labrers hands
Shall buy & sell the Misers Lands
Or if protected from on high
Does that whole Nation sell & buy
85 He who mocks the Infants Faith
Shall be mock'd in Age & Death
He who shall teach the Child to Doubt
The rotting Grave shall neer get out
He who respects the Infants faith
90 Triumphs over Hell & Death
The Childs Toys & the Old Mans Reasons
Are the Fruits of the Two seasons
The Questioner who sits so sly
Shall never know how to Reply
95 He who replies to words of Doubt
Doth put the Light of Knowledge out
The Strongest Poison ever known
Came from Caesars Laurel Crown
Nought can deform the Human Race
100 Like to the Armours iron brace
When Gold & Gems adorn the Plow
To peaceful Arts shall Envy Bow
A Riddle or the Crickets Cry
Is to Doubt a fit Reply
105 The Emmets° Inch & Eagles Mile   ant's
Make Lame Philosophy to smile
He who Doubts from what he sees
Will neer Believe do what you Please
If the Sun & Moon should doubt
110 Theyd immediately Go out
To be in a Passion you Good many do
But no Good if a Passion is in you
The Whore & Gambler by the State
Licencd build that Nations Fate
115 The Harlots cry from Street to Street
Shall weave Old Englands winding Sheet
The Winners Shout the Losers Curse
Dance before dead Englands Hearse
Every Night & every Morn
120 Some to Misery are Born
Every Morn & every Night
Some are Born to sweet delight
Some are Born to sweet delight
Some are Born to Endless Night
125 We are led to Believe a Lie
When we see not Thro the Eye
Which was Born in a Night to perish in a Night
When the Soul Slept in Beams of Light
God Appears & God is Light

130   To those poor Souls who dwell in Night
      But does a Human Form Display
      To those Who Dwell in Realms of day

1800–08   1863

Mock on, Mock on, Voltaire, Rousseau

Mock on, Mock on, Voltaire, Rousseau;[6]
Mock on, Mock on, 'tis all in vain.
You throw the sand against the wind,
And the wind blows it back again.

5   And every sand becomes a Gem
     Reflected in the beams divine;
     Blown back, they blind the mocking Eye,
     But still in Israel's paths they shine.

     The Atoms of Democritus
10   And Newton's Particles of light[7]
     Are sands upon the Red sea shore,[8]
     Where Israel's tents do shine so bright.

1800–08   1863

Eternity

He who binds to himself a joy
Does the wingéd life destroy
But he who kisses the joy as it flies
Lives in eternity's sun rise.

1800–1808   1863

A Question Answered

What is it men in women do require?
The lineaments of Gratified Desire.
What is it women do in men require?
The lineaments of Gratified Desire.

1800–1808   1863

From LETTERS

With Happiness Stretchd Across the Hills[9]

With happiness stretchd across the hills
In a cloud that dewy sweetness distills
With a blue sky spread over with wings
And a mild sun that mounts & sings
5   With trees & fields full of Fairy elves

---

6. Leaders of the pre-Revolutionary French "Enlightenment"; critics of the established order, here representing thinkers who destroy without creating.
7. Democritus (Greek philosopher, fifth century B.C.) and Sir Isaac Newton (1642–1727), both represented as nonsensically reducing nature to inanimate matter.
8. Where God delivered the Israelites from the Egyptians (Exodus xiv).
9. Lines included in a letter to Blake's friend and supporter, Thomas Butts. To assist the reader in visualizing Blake's manuscripts, the text of this poem has not been editorially corrected.

And little devils who fight for themselves
Remembring the Verses that Hayley[1] sung
When my heart knockd against the root of my tongue
With Angels planted in Hawthorn bowers
10   And God himself in the passing hours
With Silver Angels across my way
And Golden Demons that none can stay
With my Father hovering upon the wind
And my Brother Robert just behind
15   And my Brother John the evil one
In a black cloud making his mone
Tho dead they appear upon my path
Notwithstanding my terrible wrath
They beg they intreat they drop their tears
20   Filld full of hopes filld full of fears
With a thousand Angels upon the Wind
Pouring disconsolate from behind
To drive them off & before my way
A frowning Thistle implores my stay
25   What to others a trifle appears
Fills me full of smiles or tears
For double the vision my Eyes do see
And a double vision is always with me
With my inward Eye 'tis an old Man grey
30   With my outward a Thistle across my way
"If thou goest back the thistle said
Thou art to endless woe betrayd
For here does Theotormon[2] lower
And here is Enitharmons bower
35   And Los the terrible thus hath sworn
Because thou backward dost return
Poverty Envy old age & fear
Shall bring thy Wife upon a bier
And Butts shall give what Fuseli[3] gave
40   A dark black Rock & a gloomy Cave."

I struck the Thistle with my foot
And broke him up from his delving root
"Must the duties of life each other cross"
"Must every joy be dung & dross"
45   "Must my dear Butts feel cold neglect"
"Because I give Hayley his due respect"
"Must Flaxman[4] look upon me as wild"
"And all my friends be with doubts beguild"
"Must my Wife live in my Sisters bane"
50   "Or my sister survive on my Loves pain"
The curses of Los the terrible shade"
"And his dismal terrors make me afraid"

So I spoke & struck in my wrath
The old man weltering upon my path
55   Then Los appeard in all his power

1. William Hayley, Blake's friend and benefactor.
2. Like Enitharmon (line 34) one of the four sons of Los (line 35), together representing human powers and instincts in Blake's allegorical system.
3. Henry Fuseli, an artist who influenced Blake deeply, but with whom he quarreled.
4. John Flaxman, a sculptor, Blake's friend.

In the Sun he appeard descending before
My face in fierce flames in my double sight
Twas outward a Sun: inward Los in his might

60   "My hands are labourd day & night"
      "And Ease comes never in my sight"
      "My Wife has no indulgence given"
      "Except what comes to her from heaven"
      "We eat little we drink less"
65   "This Earth breeds not our happiness"
      "Another Sun feeds our lifes streams"
      "We are not warmed with thy beams"
      "Thou measurest not the Time to me"
      "Nor yet the Space that I do see"
      "My Mind is not with thy light arrayd"
70   "Thy terrors shall not make me afraid"

When I had my Defiance given
The Sun stood trembling in heaven
The Moon that glowd remote below
Became leprous & white as snow
75   And every Soul of men on the Earth
Felt affliction & sorrow & sickness & dearth
Los flamd in my path & the Sun was hot
With the bows of my Mind & the Arrows of Thought
My bowstring fierce with Ardour breathes
80   My arrows glow in their golden sheaves
My brothers & father march before
The heavens drop with human gore

Now I a fourfold vision see
And a fourfold vision is given to me
85   Tis fourfold in my supreme delight
And three fold in soft Beulahs[5] night
And twofold Always. May God us keep
From Single vision & Newtons[6] sleep

                                        1802   1880

From MILTON

And Did Those Feet

And did those feet in ancient time
Walk upon England's mountains green?
And was the holy Lamb of God
On England's pleasant pastures seen?

5   And did the Countenance Divine
Shine forth upon our clouded hills?
And was Jerusalem builded here,
Among these dark Satanic Mills?[7]

5. Beulah, in Christian tradition, was a land of peace and joy; for Blake a state of poetic insight.
6. Sir Isaac Newton (1642–1727), the mathematician and physicist, regarded by Blake as an enemy of spiritual truth.
7. The primary meaning is "millstone"—two heavy cylindrical stones that grind grain into meal between them; "factory" is an extended meaning.

10 Bring me my Bow of burning gold:
Bring me my Arrows of desire:
Bring me my Spear: O clouds unfold!
Bring me my Chariot of fire!

I will not cease from Mental Fight,
Nor shall my Sword sleep in my hand,
15 Till we have built Jerusalem
In England's green & pleasant Land.

1804–10

From Jerusalem

England! Awake! Awake! Awake!

England! awake! awake! awake!
Jerusalem thy Sister calls!
Why wilt thou sleep the sleep of death?
And close her from thy ancient walls.

5 Thy hills & valleys felt her feet,
Gently upon their bosoms move:
Thy gates beheld sweet Zions ways;
Then was a time of joy and love.

And now the time returns again:
10 Our souls exult & Londons towers,
Receive the Lamb of God to dwell
In Englands green & pleasant bowers.

1804–09   1818

From For the Sexes: *The Gates of Paradise*

To The Accuser who is The God of This World[8]

Truly My Satan thou art but a Dunce,
And dost not know the Garment from the Man;
Every Harlot was a Virgin once,
Nor canst thou ever change Kate into Nan.

5 Tho thou are Worshipd by the Names Divine
Of Jesus & Jehovah: thou art still
The Son of Morn in weary Night's decline,
The lost Traveller's Dream under the Hill.

1793–1818

---

8. God conceived of as a harsh taskmaster and merciless judge; Blake rejected this concept as "Satanic."

ROBERT BURNS
(1759–1796)

To a Mouse

ON TURNING HER UP IN HER NEST WITH THE PLOUGH,
NOVEMBER, 1785

Wee, sleekit,° cow'rin, tim'rous beastie,   *sleek*
O, what a panic's in thy breastie!
Thou need na start awa sae hasty,
        Wi' bickering° brattle!°   *hurried / scamper*
5 I wad be laith to rin an' chase thee,
        Wi' murd'ring pattle!°   *plowstaff ("paddle")*

I'm truly sorry man's dominion
Has broken Nature's social union,
An' justifies that ill opinion
10   Which makes thee startle
At me, thy poor earth-born companion,
        An' fellow-mortal!

I doubt na, whiles,° but thou may thieve;   *sometimes*
What then? poor beastie, thou maun° live!   *must*
15 A daimen° icker° in a thrave°   *random / corn-ear / shock*
        'S a sma' request:
I'll get a blessin wi' the lave,°   *rest*
        And never miss't!

Thy wee bit housie, too, in ruin!
20 Its silly° wa's the win's are strewin!   *frail*
An' naething, now, to big° a new ane,   *build*
        O' foggage° green!   *mosses*
An' bleak December's winds ensuin,
        Baith snell° an' keen!   *bitter*

25 Thou saw the fields laid bare and waste,
An' weary winter comin fast,
An' cozie here, beneath the blast,
        Thou thought to dwell,
Till crash! the cruel coulter° past   *plowshare*
30   Out thro' thy cell.

That wee bit heap o' leaves an' stibble°   *stubble*
Has cost thee mony a weary nibble!
Now thou's turned out, for a' thy trouble,
        But° house or hald,°   *without / home ("hold")*
35 To thole° the winter's sleety dribble,   *endure*
        An' cranreuch° cauld!   *hoarfrost*

But, Mousie, thou art no thy lane,[1]
In proving foresight may be vain:

---

1. "No thy lane": not alone.

The best laid schemes o' mice an' men
         Gang° aft a-gley.°   *go / astray*
An' lea'e us nought but grief an' pain
         For promised joy.

Still thou art blest, compared wi' me!
The present only toucheth thee:
But och! I backward cast my e'e
         On prospects drear!
An' forward, tho' I canna see,
         I guess an' fear!

40

45

1785, 1786

Epistle to J. Lapraik,[2] an Old Scottish Bard

While briers an' woodbines budding green,
An' paitricks° scraichin'° loud at e'en,   *partridges / calling ("screeching")*
An' morning poussie° whiddin° seen,   *hare / scurrying*
         Inspire my Muse,
This freedom, in an unknown frien',
         I pray excuse.

On Fasten-een[3] we had a rockin,°   *party*
To ca' the crack[4] and weave our stockin;
And there was muckle fun and jokin,
         Ye need na doubt;
At length we had a hearty yokin°   *bout*
         At sang about.[5]

There was ae° sang, amang the rest,   *one*
Aboon° them a' it pleas'd me best,   *above*
That some kind husband had addrest
         To some sweet wife:
It thirled° the heart-strings thro' the breast,   *thrilled*
         A' to the life.

I've scarce heard ought described sae weel,
What gen'rous, manly bosoms feel;
Thought I, "Can this be Pope, or Steele,
         Or Beattie's[6] wark!"
They tauld me 'twas an odd kind chiel°   *fellow*
         About Muirkirk.

It put° me fidgin-fain° to hear' t,   *made / wriggling-happy*
And sae about him there I spier't,°   *asked*
Then a' that ken't him round declared
         He had ingine,°   *genius*
That nane excelled it, few cam near' t,
         It was sae fine.

That, set him to a pint of ale,
An' either douce° or merry tale,   *sober*

5

10

15

20

25

30

2. John Lapraik (1727–1803), a poet and farmer from Muirkirk, Ayrshire, Burns's native region. His song *When I Upon thy Bosom Lean* (the "ae sang" of line 12) was later published with Burns's aid.
3. The day before the fasting, i.e., Shrove Tuesday, a traditional day of merrymaking before Lent.
4. "Ca' the crack": have a chat.
5. "Sang about"; singing in turn.
6. James Beattie, a Scottish poet (1735–1803), author of a long poem, *The Minstrel*.

Or rhymes an' sangs he'd made himsel,
    Or witty catches,
35 'Tween Inverness and Teviotdale,[7]
    He had few matches.

Then up I gat, an' swoor an aith,
Tho' I should pawn my pleugh and graith,°   *harness*
Or die a cadger° pownie's° death,   *hawker / pony's*
40   At some dyke-back[8]
A pint an' gill° I'd gie them baith   *quarter-pint*
    To hear your crack.°   *conversation*

But, first an' foremost, I should tell,
Amaist as soon as I could spell,
45 I to the crambo-jingle° fell;   *game of rhyming*
        Tho' rude an' rough,
Yet crooning° to a body's sel,°   *humming / self*
        Does weel eneugh.

I am nae poet, in a sense,
50 But just a rhymer like by chance,
An' hae to learning nae pretence,
        Yet, what the matter?
Whene'er my Muse does on me glance,
    I jingle at her.

55 Your critic-folk may cock their nose,
And say, "How can you e'er propose,
You wha ken° hardly verse frae prose,   *know*
        To mak a sang?"
But, by your leaves, my learned foes,
60   Ye're maybe wrang.

What's a' your jargon o' your schools,
Your Latin names for horns an' stools;[9]
If honest nature made you fools,
        What sairs° your grammars?   *serves*
65 Ye'd better ta'en up spades and shools,°   *shovels*
    Or knappin'°-hammers.   *stone-breaking*

A set o' dull, conceited hashes°   *dolts*
Confuse their brains in college classes!
They gang in stirks,° and come out asses,   *bullocks*
70   Plain truth to speak;
An' syne° they think to climb Parnassus   *then*
    By dint o' Greek!

Gie me ae spark o' Nature's fire,
That's a' the learning I desire;
75 Then tho' I drudge thro' dub° an' mire   *puddle*
        At pleugh or cart,
My Muse, though hamely in attire,
        May touch the heart.

---

7. Between Inverness in northwest Scotland and the valley of the Teviot in the southeast.
8. "At some dyke-back": behind some wall.

9. Words recurring in elementary Latin grammars.

O for a spunk° o' Allan's glee,   *spark*
80 Or Fergusson's,[1] the bauld° an' slee,°   *bold / subtle ("sly")*
Or bright Lapraik's, my friend to be,
    If I can hit it!
That would be lear° eneugh for me,   *learning*
    If I could get it.

85 Now, sir, if ye hae friends enow,
Tho' real friends, I b'lieve, are few,
Yet, if your catalogue be fou,°   *full*
    I'se° no insist,   *I'll*
But gif ye want ae friend that's true,
90   I'm on your list.

I winna blaw about mysel;
As ill I like my fauts to tell;
But friends, an' folks that wish me well,
    They sometimes roose° me;   *praise*
95 Tho' I maun own, as mony still
    As far abuse me.

There's ae wee faut they whiles lay to me,
I like the lasses—Gude forgie me!
For mony a plack° they wheedle frae me,   *coin*
100   At dance or fair;
Maybe some ither thing they gie me
    They weel can spare.

But Mauchline[2] race, or Mauchline fair,
I should be proud to meet you there;
105 We'se gie ae night's discharge to care,
    If we forgather,
An' hae a swap o' rhymin'-ware
    Wi' ane anither.

The four-gill chap,° we'se gar° him clatter,   *cup / make*
110 An' kirsen° him wi' reekin° water;   *christen / steaming*
Syne we'll sit down an' tak our whitter,°   *draught*
    To cheer our heart;
An' faith, we'se be acquainted better
    Before we part.

115 Awa, ye selfish warly° race,   *worldly*
Wha think that havins,° sense, an' grace,   *manners*
Ev'n love an' friendship, should give place
    To catch-the-plack!°   *coin*
I dinna like to see your face,
120   Nor hear your crack.

But ye whom social pleasure charms,
Whose hearts the tide of kindness warms,
Who hold your being on the terms,
    "Each aid the others,"
125 Come to my bowl, come to my arms.
    My friends, my brothers!

---

1. Allan Ramsay (ca. 1685–1758) and Robert   2. A town near Burns's farm.
Fergusson (1750–74), Scottish poets.

But to conclude my lang epistle,
As my auld pen's worn to the gristle;
Twa lines frae you wad gar me fissle,°   *tingle with pleasure*
130   Who am, most fervent,
While I can either sing, or whistle,
                Your friend and servant.

                                                1785   1786

Holy Willie's³ Prayer

O Thou, wha in the heavens dost dwell,
Wha, as it pleases best thysel',
Sends ane to heaven and ten to hell,
                A' for thy glory,
5   And no for ony guid or ill
                They've done afore thee!

I bless and praise thy matchless might,
Whan thousands thou hast left in night,
That I am here afore thy sight,
10   For gifts an' grace
A burnin' an' a shinin' light,
                To a' this place.

What was I, or my generation,
That I should get sic exaltation?
15 I, wha deserve most just damnation,
                For broken laws,
Sax thousand years 'fore my creation,
                Thro' Adam's cause.

When frae my mither's womb I fell,
20 Thou might hae plungéd me in hell,
To gnash my gums, to weep and wail,
                In burnin lakes,
Where damnéd devils roar and yell,
                Chained to their stakes;

25 Yet I am here a chosen sample,
To show thy grace is great and ample;
I'm here a pillar in thy temple,
                Strong as a rock,
A guide, a buckler, an example
30   To a' thy flock.

O Lord, thou kens what zeal I bear,
When drinkers drink, and swearers swear.
And singin' there and dancin' here,
                Wi' great an' sma':
35 For I am keepit by thy fear
                Free frae them a'.

3. One William Fisher, an elder in the church at Mauchline, the seat of Burns's farm. He habitually censured other men's behavior and doctrine, but was himself rebuked for drunkenness and was suspected of stealing church funds.

But yet, O Lord! confess I must
At times I'm fashed° wi' fleshy lust;   *troubled*
An' sometimes too, wi' warldly trust,
40   Vile self gets in;
But thou remembers we are dust,
            Defiled in sin.

O Lord! yestreen,° thou kens, wi' Meg—   *last night*
Thy pardon I sincerely beg;
45 O! may't ne'er be a livin' plague
            To my dishonour,
An' I'll ne'er lift a lawless leg
            Again upon her.

Besides I farther maun allow,
50 Wi' Lizzie's lass, three times I trow—
But, Lord, that Friday I was fou,°   *full (of liquor)*
            When I cam near her,
Or else thou kens thy servant true
            Wad never steer° her.   *touch ("stir")*

55 May be thou lets this fleshly thorn
Beset thy servant e'en and morn
Lest he owre high and proud should turn,
            That he's sae gifted;
If sae, thy hand maun e'en be borne,
60   Until thou lift it.

Lord, bless thy chosen in this place,
For here thou hast a chosen race;
But God confound their stubborn face,
            And blast their name,
65 Wha bring thy elders to disgrace
            An' public shame.

Lord, mind Gawn Hamilton's[4] deserts,
He drinks, an' swears, an' plays at cartes,
Yet has sae mony takin arts
70   Wi' great an' sma',
Frae God's ain priest the people's hearts
            He steals awa'.

An' when we chastened him therefor,
Thou kens how he bred sic a splore°   *row*
75 As set the warld in a roar
            O' laughin' at us;
Curse thou his basket and his store,
            Kail° and potatoes.   *cabbage*

Lord, hear my earnest cry an' pray'r,
80 Against that presbytery o' Ayr;
Thy strong right hand, Lord, make it bare
            Upo' their heads;
Lord, weigh it down, and dinna spare,
            For their misdeeds.

4. Gavin Hamilton, a convivial lawyer friend of Burns's. Accused of Sabbath-breaking and other offenses by the elders of Mauchline church, he was cleared by the Presbytery of Ayr (line 80) with the help of his counsel Robert Aiken (line 85).

⁸⁵ O Lord my God, that glib-tongued Aiken,
My very heart and soul are quakin',
To think how we stood sweatin, shakin,
    An' pissed wi' dread,
While he, wi' hingin° lips and snakin,°   *hanging / sneering*
⁹⁰   Held up his head.

Lord in the day of vengeance try him;
Lord, visit them wha did employ him,
And pass not in thy mercy by them,
    Nor hear their pray'r:
⁹⁵ But, for thy people's sake, destroy them,
    And dinna spare.

But, Lord, remember me and mine
Wi' mercies temp'ral and divine,
That I for gear° and grace may shine   *wealth*
¹⁰⁰   Excelled by nane,
And a' the glory shall be thine,
    Amen, Amen!

                        1785   1808

Address to the Unco° Guid, or   *unbelievably*
the Rigidly Righteous

    My son, these maxims make a rule,
      And lump them ay thegither;
    The Rigid Righteous *is a fool,*
      The Rigid Wise *anither:*
    The cleanest corn that e'er was dight°   *threshed*
      May hae some pyles° o' caff° in;   *bristles/chaff*
    So ne'er a fellow-creature slight
      For random fits o' daffin.°   *frivolity*
        SOLOMON—Eccles. vii, 16 [1]

A° ye wha are sae guid yoursel,   *all*
    Sae pious and sae holy,
Ye've nought to do but mark and tell
    Your neebours' fauts and folly!
⁵ Whase life is like a weel-gaun° mill,   *well-running*
    Supply'd wi' store o' water,
The heaped happer's° ebbing still,   *hopper's*
    And still the clap plays clatter.[2]

Hear me, ye venerable core,°   *company*
¹⁰   As counsel for poor mortals,
That frequent pass douce° Wisdom's door   *sober*
    For glaikit° Folly's portals;   *thoughtless*
I, for their thoughtless, careless sakes
    Would here propone° defenses,   *propose*
¹⁵ Their donsie° tricks, their black mistakes,   *mischievous*
    Their failings and mischances.

---

1. "Be not righteous overmuch; neither make   thyself?"
thyself overwise; why shouldest thou destroy   2. The clapper makes a chattering noise.

Ye see your state wi' theirs compared,
   And shudder at the niffer,°   *difference*
But cast a moment's fair regard
20   What maks the mighty differ;
Discount what scant occasion gave,
   That purity ye pride in,
And (what's aft° mair than a' the lave°)   *often/rest*
   Your better art o' hiding.

25 Think, when your castigated pulse
   Gies now and then a wallop,
What ragings must his veins convulse,
   That still eternal gallop:
Wi' wind and tide fair i' your tails,
30   Right on ye scud your sea-way;
But, in the teeth o' baith to sail,
   It makes an unco° leeway.   *remarkable*

See Social-life and Glee sit down,
   All joyous and unthinking,
35 Till, quite transmugrify'd,° they're grown   *grotesquely changed*
   Debauchery and Drinking:
O would they stay to calculate
   Th' eternal consequences;
Or—your more dreaded hell to state—
40   Damnation of expenses!

Ye high, exalted, virtuous dames,
   Tied up in godly laces,
Before ye gie poor *Frailty* names,
   Suppose a change o' cases;
45 A dear-loved lad, convenience snug,
   A treacherous inclination——
But, let me whisper i' your lug,°   *ear*
   Ye're aiblins° nae temptation.   *possibly*

Then gently scan your brother man,
50   Still gentler sister woman;
Tho' they may gang a kennin° wrang,   *wee bit*
   To step aside is human:
One point must still be greatly dark,
   The moving *Why* they do it;
55 And just as lamely can ye mark,
   How far perhaps they rue it.

Who made the heart, 'tis He alone
   Decidedly can try us,
He knows each chord its various tone,
60   Each spring its various bias:
Then at the balance let's be mute,
   We never can adjust it;
What's *done* we partly may compute,
   But know not what's *resisted*.

                        1786   1787

Green Grow the Rashes

Chorus

Green grow the rashes,° O;   *tall grasses or rushes*
  Green grow the rashes, O;
The sweetest hours that e'er I spend,
  Are spent amang the lasses, O!

5 There's nought but care on ev'ry han',
    In ev'ry hour that passes, O:
What signifies the life o' man,
    An'° 'twere na for the lasses, O.   *if*
              (*Chorus*)

The warly° race may riches chase,   *worldly*
10   An' riches still may fly them, O;
An' though at last they catch them fast,
    Their hearts can ne'er enjoy them, O.
              (*Chorus*)

But gie me a canny° hour at e'en,   *pleasant*
  My arms about my dearie, O;
15 An' warly cares, an' warly men,
    May a' gae tapsalteerie,° O!   *topsy turvy*
              (*Chorus*)

For you sae douce,° ye sneer at this,   *prudent*
  Ye're nought but senseless asses, O:
The wisest man [1] the warl' saw,
20   He dearly loved the lasses, O.
              (*Chorus*)

Auld nature swears, the lovely dears
  Her noblest work she classes, O:
Her prentice han' she tried on man,
  An' then she made the lasses, O.
              (*Chorus*)

1784   1787

Of A' the Airts[2]

Of a' the airts° the wind can blaw,   *quarters*
  I dearly like the west,
For there the bonie lassie lives,
  The lassie I lo'e best:
5 There's wild woods grow, and rivers row,°   *flow*
  And mony a hill between;
But day and night my fancy's flight
  Is ever wi' my Jean.

I see her in the dewy flowers,
10 I see her sweet and fair;
I hear her in the tunefu' birds,
  I hear her charm the air:

---

1. King Solomon, who had many wives.
2. Written from Dumfriesshire to Burns's   wife, Jean Armour, in Ayrshire, the county to the west.

There's not a bonie flower that springs
 By fountain, shaw,° or green,   *wood*
15 There's not a bonie bird that sings,
 But minds me o' my Jean.

1788   1790

John Anderson, My Jo

John Anderson my jo,° John,   *joy*
 When we were first acquent,
Your locks were like the raven,
 Your bonie brow was brent;[3]
5 But now your brow is beld, John,
 Your locks are like the snow;
But blessings on your frosty pow,°   *head*
 John Anderson, my jo.

John Anderson my jo, John,
10 We clamb° the hill thegither;   *climbed*
And mony a canty° day, John,.   *merry*
 We've had wi' ane anither:
Now we maun totter down, John,
 And hand in hand we'll go,
15 And sleep thegither at the foot,
 John Anderson, my jo.

1789   1790

Tam O' Shanter

Of Brownyis and of Bogillis full is this Buke.[5]
 —GAWIN DOUGLAS

When chapman° billies° leave the street,   *peddler / fellows*
And drouthy° neebors neebors meet,   *thirsty*
As market-days are wearing late,
An' folk begin to tak the gate;°   *road*
5 While we sit bousing at the nappy,°   *ale*
An' getting fou° and unco happy,   *full*
We think na on the lang Scots miles,
The mosses,° waters, slaps,° and styles,   *bogs / gaps in walls*
That lie between us and our hame,
10 Where sits our sulky sullen dame,
Gathering her brows like gathering storm,
Nursing her wrath to keep it warm.
 This truth fand° honest Tam o' Shanter,   *found*
As he frae Ayr ae night did canter,
15 (Auld Ayr, wham ne'er a town surpasses
For honest men and bonnie lasses).
 O Tam! hadst thou but been sae wise,
As ta'en thy ain wife Kate's advice!
She tauld thee weel thou was a skellum,°   *good-for-nothing*
20 A bletherin',° blusterin', drunken blellum,° *babbling / windbag*
That frae November till October,
Ae market-day thou was na sober;
That ilka° melder,° wi' the miller   *every / meal-grinding*
Thou sat as lang as thou had siller;°   *silver*

3. Straight, steep; not rounding off into a bald pate.
5. From the prologue to the sixth book of the *Aeneid*, translated into Scots dialect by Gavin Douglas (1474–1522). Brownies are friendly goblins and bogles unfriendly.

25 That every naig° was ca'd° a shoe on,   *horse / driven*
The smith and thee gat roarin' fou on;
That at the Lord's house, even on Sunday,
Thou drank wi' Kirkton Jean[6] till Monday.
She prophesied that, late or soon,
30 Thou would be found deep drowned in Doon;
Or catched wi' warlocks° in the mirk,°   *wizards / dark*
By Alloway's auld haunted kirk.[7]
   Ah, gentle dames! it gars° me greet°   *makes / weep*
To think how mony counsels sweet,
35 How mony lengthened sage advices,
The husband frae the wife despises!
   But to our tale: Ae market night,
Tam had got planted unco° right;   *uncommonly*
Fast by an ingle,° bleezing° finely,   *fireplace / blazing*
40 Wi' reaming° swats,° that drank divinely;   *foaming / ale*
And at his elbow, Souter° Johnny,   *cobbler*
His ancient, trusty, drouthy crony;
Tam lo'ed him like a vera brither;
They had been fou for weeks thegither.
45 The night drave on wi' sangs and clatter;°   *talk*
And aye the ale was growing better:
The landlady and Tam grew gracious,
Wi' favours secret, sweet, and precious:
The souter tauld his queerest stories;
50 The landlord's laugh was ready chorus:
The storm without might rair° and rustle,   *roar*
Tam did na mind the storm a whistle.
   Care, mad to see a man sae happy,
E'en drowned himsel amang the nappy;
55 As bees flee hame wi' lades° o' treasure,   *loads*
The minutes winged their way wi' pleasure;
Kings may be blest, but Tam was glorious,
O'er a' the ills o' life victorious!
   But pleasures are like poppies spread,
60 You seize the flow'r, its bloom is shed;
Or like the snow falls in the river,
A moment white—then melts for ever;
Or like the borealis race,
That flit ere you can point their place;
65 Or like the rainbow's lovely form
Evanishing amid the storm—
Nae man can tether time nor tide;
The hour approaches Tam maun ride;
That hour, o' night's black arch the key-stane,
70 That dreary hour, he mounts his beast in;
And sic a night he taks the road in,
As ne'er poor sinner was abroad in.
   The wind blew as 'twad° blawn its last;   *it would have*
The rattling show'rs rose on the blast;
75 The speedy gleams the darkness swallowed;
Loud, deep, and lang, the thunder bellowed:
That night, a child might understand,
The Deil° had business on his hand.   *Devil*

6. Mistress of a tavern.   7. The ruins of a church near Burns's home,
the object of much superstitious dread.

Weel mounted on his grey mare, Meg,
80 A better never lifted leg,
Tam skelpit° on thro' dub° and mire,   hurried / puddle
Despising wind, and rain, and fire;
Whiles° holding fast his guid blue bonnet;   sometimes
Whiles crooning° o'er some auld Scots sonnet;°   humming / song
85 Whiles glow'ring° round wi' prudent cares,   staring
Lest bogles° catch him unawares.   bogies
Kirk-Alloway was drawing nigh,
Whare ghaists and houlets° nightly cry.   owls
By this time he was cross the ford,
90 Where in the snaw the chapman smoored;°   smothered
And past the birks° and meikle° stane,°   birches / great / stone
Where drunken Charlie brak's neck-bane;
And thro' the whins,° and by the cairn,   furze
Where hunters fand the murdered bairn;
95 And near the thorn, aboon° the well,   above
Where Mungo's mither hanged hersel.
Before him Doon pours all his floods;
The doubling storm roars thro' the woods;
The lightnings flash from pole to pole;
100 Near and more near the thunders roll:
When, glimmering thro' the groaning trees,
Kirk-Alloway seemed in a bleeze;°   blaze
Thro' ilka° bore° the beams were glancing;   every / chink
And loud resounded mirth and dancing.
105 Inspiring bold John Barleycorn!
What dangers thou canst make us scorn!
Wi' tippenny,° we fear nae evil;   twopenny ale
Wi' usquebae° we'll face the devil!   whisky
The swats° sae reamed° in Tammie's noddle,   ale / foamed
110 Fair play, he cared na deils a boddle.°   farthing
But Maggie stood right sair° astonished,   sorely
Till, by the heel and hand admonished,
She ventured forward on the light;
And, vow! Tam saw an unco sight!
115 Warlocks and witches in a dance;
Nae cotillon brent° new frae France,   brand
But hornpipes, jigs, strathspeys,° and reels,   Highland dances
Put life and mettle in their heels.
A winnock-bunker° in the east,   window-seat
120 There sat auld Nick, in shape o' beast;
A touzie° tyke,° black, grim, and large!   tousled / dog
To gie them music was his charge:
He screwed the pipes and gart° them skirl,°   made / shrill
Till roof and rafters a' did dirl.°   ring
125 Coffins stood round like open presses,°   closets
That shawed the dead in their last dresses;
And by some devilish cantraip° slight°   weird / trick
Each in its cauld hand held a light,
By which heroic Tam was able
130 To note upon the haly table
A murderer's banes in gibbet-airns;°   -irons
Twa span-lang, wee, unchristened bairns;
A thief new-cutted frae a rape,
Wi' his last gasp his gab° did gape;   mouth
135 Five tomahawks, wi' blude red-rusted;

Five scymitars, wi' murder crusted;
A garter, which a babe had strangled;
A knife, a father's throat had mangled,
Whom his ain son o' life bereft,
140   The gray hairs yet stack to the heft;
Wi' mair of horrible and awfu',
Which even to name wad be unlawfu'.
   As Tammie glowred,° amazed, and curious,   *stared*
The mirth and fun grew fast and furious:
145   The piper loud and louder blew;
The dancers quick and quicker flew;
They reeled, they set, they crossed, they cleekit,°   *joined hands*
Till ilka carlin° swat° and reekit,°   *witch / sweated / steamed*
And coost° her duddies° to the wark,   *cast off / dress*
150   And linkit° at it in her sark!°   *tripped nimbly / shift*
   Now Tam, O Tam! had thae been queans,°   *girls*
A' plump and strapping in their teens;
Their sarks, instead o' creeshie° flannen,°   *greasy / flannel*
Been snaw-white hunder seventeen linen!⁸
155   Thir° breeks o' mine, my only pair,   *these*
That ance were plush, o' gude blue hair,
I wad hae gi'en them off my hurdies,°   *buttocks*
For ae blink o' the bonie burdies!°   *maidens*
   But wither'd beldams, auld and droll,
160   Rigwoodie° hags wad spean° a foal,   *scrawny / wean*
Louping° and flinging on a crummock,°   *leaping / staff*
I wonder didna turn thy stomach.
   But Tam kend what was what fu' brawlie,°   *well*
There was ae winsome wench and wawlie°   *buxom*
165   That night enlisted in the core,°   *company*
Lang after kent° on Carrick shore   *known*
(For mony a beast to dead she shot,
And perished mony a bonie boat,
And shook baith meikle° corn and bear,°   *much / barley*
170   And kept the country-side in fear).
Her cutty° sark, o' Paisley harn,°   *short / coarse cloth*
That while a lassie she had worn,
In longitude tho' sorely scanty,
It was her best, and she was vauntie.
175   Ah! little kend thy reverend grannie
That sark she coft° for her wee Nannie   *bought*
Wi' twa pund Scots ('twas a' her riches)
Wad ever graced a dance of witches!
   But here my Muse her wing maun cour;°   *stoop*
180   Sic flights are far beyond her pow'r—
To sing how Nannie lap° and flang,   *leaped*
(A souple jade she was, and strang),
And how Tam stood, like ane bewitched,
And thought his very een enriched;
185   Even Satan glowr'd, and fidged° fu' fain,°   *wriggled / happy*
And hotched° and blew wi' might and main: *hitched (himself)*
Till first ae caper, syne° anither,   *then*
Tam tint° his reason a' thegither,   *lost*
And roars out, "Weel done, Cutty-sark!"
190   And in an instant all was dark!
And scarcely had he Maggie rallied,

8. Fine linen, with 1700 threads to a width.

When out the hellish, legion sallied.
  As bees bizz out wi' angry fyke,°   *fuss*
When plundering herds° assail their byke;° *shepherds / hive*
195 As open° pussie's° mortal foes,   *bay / the hare's*
When pop! she starts before their nose;
As eager runs the market-crowd,
When "Catch the thief!" resounds aloud;
So Maggie runs; the witches follow,
200 Wi' mony an eldritch° skriech and hollow. *unearthly*
  Ah, Tam! ah, Tam! thou'll get thy fairin!° *punishment*
In hell they'll roast thee like a herrin!
In vain thy Kate awaits thy comin!
Kate soon will be a woefu' woman!
205 Now do thy speedy utmost, Meg,
And win the key-stane° o' the brig;° *central stone / bridge*
There at them thou thy tail may toss,
A running stream they darena cross.
But ere the key-stane she could make,
210 The fient a° tail she had to shake! *devil-a*
For Nannie, far before the rest,
Hard upon noble Maggie prest,
And flew at Tam wi' furious ettle;° *purpose*
But little wist she Maggie's mettle.
215 Ae spring brought off her master hale,° *whole*
But left behind her ain gray tail:
The carlin claught her by the rump,
And left poor Maggie scarce a stump.
220   Now, wha this tale o' truth shall read,
Each man and mother's son, take heed:
Whene'er to drink you are inclined,
Or cutty-sarks rin in your mind,
Think! ye may buy the joys o'er dear;
225 Remember Tam o' Shanter's mare.

             1790   1791

Bonie Doon

Ye flowery banks o' bonie Doon,
  How can ye blume sae fair?
How can ye chant, ye little birds,
  And I sae fu' o' care?

5 Thou'll break my heart, thou bonie bird,
  That sings upon the bough;
Thou minds me o' the happy days,
  When my fause° luve was true. *false*

Thou'll break my heart, thou bonie bird,
10   That sings beside thy mate;
For sae I sat, and sae I sang,
  And wist° na o' my fate. *knew*

Aft hae I roved by bonie Doon
  To see the wood-bine twine,
15 And ilka° bird sang o' its luve, *every*
  And sae did I o' mine.

Wi' lightsome heart I pu'd a rose
    Frae aff its thorny tree;
And my fause luver staw° my rose   *stole*
20   But left the thorn wi' me.

                                     1791   1792

A Red, Red Rose

O my luve's like a red, red rose,
    That's newly sprung in June;
O my luve's like the melodie
    That's sweetly played in tune.

5   As fair art thou, my bonnie lass,
    So deep in luve am I;
And I will luve thee still, my dear,
    Till a' the seas gang dry.

Till a' the seas gang dry, my dear,
10   And the rocks melt wi' the sun:
O I will love thee still, my dear,
    While the sands o' life shall run.

And fare thee weel, my only luve,
    And fare thee weel awhile!
15   And I will come again, my luve,
    Though it were ten thousand mile.

                                         1796

O, Wert Thou in the Cauld Blast

O, wert thou in the cauld blast
    On yonder lea, on yonder lea,
My plaidie to the angry airt,°   *quarter (of the wind)*
    I'd shelter thee, I'd shelter thee.
5   Or did misfortune's bitter storms
    Around thee blaw, around thee blaw,
Thy bield° should be my bosom,   *shelter*
    To share it a', to share it a'.

Or were I in the wildest waste,
10   Sae black and bare, sae black and bare,
The desert were a paradise,
    If thou wert there, if thou wert there.
Or were I monarch o' the globe,
    Wi' thee to reign, wi' thee to reign,
15   The brightest jewel in my crown
    Wad be my queen, wad be my queen.

                                   1796   1800

WILLIAM WORDSWORTH
(1770–1850)

Lines

COMPOSED A FEW MILES ABOVE TINTERN ABBEY ON REVISITING THE
BANKS OF THE WYE DURING A TOUR. JULY 13, 1798[1]

Five years have passed; five summers, with the length
Of five long winters! and again I hear
These waters, rolling from their mountain-springs
With a soft inland murmur. Once again
5 Do I behold these steep and lofty cliffs,
That on a wild secluded scene impress
Thoughts of more deep seclusion; and connect
The landscape with the quiet of the sky.
The day is come when I again repose
10 Here, under this dark sycamore, and view
These plots of cottage ground, these orchard tufts,
Which at this season, with their unripe fruits,
Are clad in one green hue, and lose themselves
'Mid groves and copses. Once again I see
15 These hedgerows, hardly hedgerows, little lines
Of sportive wood run wild; these pastoral farms,
Green to the very door; and wreaths of smoke
Sent up, in silence, from among the trees!
With some uncertain notice, as might seem
20 Of vagrant dwellers in the houseless woods,
Or of some Hermit's cave, where by his fire
The Hermit sits alone.

              These beauteous forms,
Through a long absence, have not been to me
As is a landscape to a blind man's eye;
25 But oft, in lonely rooms, and 'mid the din
Of towns and cities, I have owed to them,
In hours of weariness, sensations sweet,
Felt in the blood, and felt along the heart;
And passing even into my purer mind,
30 With tranquil restoration—feelings too
Of unremembered pleasure; such, perhaps,
As have no slight or trivial influence
On that best portion of a good man's life,
His little, nameless, unremembered, acts
35 Of kindness and of love. Nor less, I trust,
To them I may have owed another gift,
Of aspect more sublime; that blessed mood,
In which the burthen of the mystery,
In which the heavy and the weary weight
40 Of all this unintelligible world,
Is lightened—that serene and blessed mood,
In which the affections gently lead us on—

1. Ruins of a medieval abbey situated in the valley of the river Wye, in Monmouthshire, noted
for its scenery.

Until, the breath of this corporeal frame
And even the motion of our human blood
45   Almost suspended, we are laid asleep
In body, and become a living soul;
While with an eye made quiet by the power
Of harmony, and the deep power of joy,
We see into the life of things.

                                    If this
50   Be but a vain belief, yet, oh! how oft—
In darkness and amid the many shapes
Of joyless daylight; when the fretful stir
Unprofitable, and the fever of the world,
Have hung upon the beatings of my heart—
55   How oft, in spirit, have I turned to thee,
O sylvan Wye! thou wanderer through the woods,
How often has my spirit turned to thee!

      And now, with gleams of half-extinguished thought,
With many recognitions dim and faint,
60   And somewhat of a sad perplexity,
The picture of the mind revives again;
While here I stand, not only with the sense
Of present pleasure, but with pleasing thoughts
That in this moment there is life and food
65   For future years. And so I dare to hope,
Though changed, no doubt, from what I was when first
I came among these hills; when like a roe
I bounded o'er the mountains, by the sides
Of the deep rivers, and the lonely streams,
70   Wherever nature led—more like a man
Flying from something that he dreads than one
Who sought the thing he loved. For nature then
(The coarser² pleasures of my boyish days,
And their glad animal movements all gone by)
75   To me was all in all.—I cannot paint
What then I was. The sounding cataract
Haunted me like a passion; the tall rock,
The mountain, and the deep and gloomy wood,
Their colors and their forms, were then to me
80   An appetite; a feeling and a love,
That had no need of a remoter charm,
By thought supplied, nor any interest
Unborrowed from the eye.—That time is past,
And all its aching joys are now no more,
85   And all its dizzy raptures. Not for this
Faint° I, nor mourn nor murmur; other gifts   *become discouraged*
Have followed; for such loss, I would believe,
Abundant recompense. For I have learned
To look on nature, not as in the hour
90   Of thoughtless youth; but hearing oftentimes
The still, sad music of humanity,
Nor harsh nor grating, though of ample power
To chasten and subdue. And I have felt
A presence that disturbs me with the joy
95   Of elevated thoughts; a sense sublime

2. I.e., primarily physical.

Of something far more deeply interfused,
Whose dwelling is the light of setting suns,
And the round ocean and the living air,
And the blue sky, and in the mind of man:
100   A motion and a spirit, that impels
All thinking things, all objects of all thought,
And rolls through all things. Therefore am I still
A lover of the meadows and the woods,
And mountains; and of all that we behold
105   From this green earth; of all the mighty world
Of eye, and ear—both what they half create,
And what perceive; well pleased to recognize
In nature and the language of the sense
The anchor of my purest thoughts, the nurse,
110   The guide, the guardian of my heart, and soul
Of all my moral being.

           Nor perchance,
If I were not thus taught, should I the more
Suffer my genial spirits° to decay: *vital energies*
For thou art with me here upon the banks
115   Of this fair river; thou my dearest Friend,[3]
My dear, dear Friend; and in thy voice I catch
The language of my former heart, and read
My former pleasures in the shooting lights
Of thy wild eyes. Oh! yet a little while
120   May I behold in thee what I was once,
My dear, dear Sister! and this prayer I make,
Knowing that Nature never did betray
The heart that loved her; 'tis her privilege,
Through all the years of this our life, to lead
125   From joy to joy: for she can so inform
The mind that is within us, so impress
With quietness and beauty, and so feed
With lofty thoughts, that neither evil tongues,
Rash judgments, nor the sneers of selfish men,
130   Nor greetings where no kindness is, nor all
The dreary intercourse of daily life,
Shall e'er prevail against us, or disturb
Our cheerful faith, that all which we behold
Is full of blessings. Therefore let the moon
135   Shine on thee in thy solitary walk;
And let the misty mountain winds be free
To blow against thee: and, in after years,
When these wild ecstasies shall be matured
Into a sober pleasure; when thy mind
140   Shall be a mansion for all lovely forms,
Thy memory be as a dwelling place
For all sweet sounds and harmonies; oh! then,
If solitude, or fear, or pain, or grief
Should be thy portion, with what healing thoughts
145   Of tender joy wilt thou remember me,
And these my exhortations! Nor, perchance—
If I should be where I no more can hear
Thy voice, nor catch from thy wild eyes these gleams
Of past existence—wilt thou then forget

---

3. Wordsworth's sister Dorothy, who accompanied him on the walking trip here commemorated.

¹⁵⁰ That on the banks of this delightful stream
We stood together; and that I, so long
A worshiper of Nature, hither came
Unwearied in that service; rather say
With warmer love—oh! with far deeper zeal
¹⁵⁵ Of holier love. Nor wilt thou then forget,
That after many wanderings, many years
Of absence, these steep woods and lofty cliffs,
And this green pastoral landscape, were to me
More dear, both for themselves and for thy sake!

                                                      1798

From The Excursion[4]

Prospectus

On Man, on Nature, and on Human Life,
Musing in solitude, I oft perceive
Fair trains of imagery before me rise,
Accompanied by feelings of delight
⁵ Pure, or with no unpleasing sadness mixed;
And I am conscious of affecting thoughts
And dear remembrances, whose presence soothes
Or elevates the Mind, intent to weigh
The good and evil of our mortal state.
¹⁰ —To these emotions, whencesoe'er they come,
Whether from breath of outward circumstance,
Or from the Soul—an impulse to herself—
I would give utterance in numerous° verse.   *metrical*
Of Truth, of Grandeur, Beauty, Love, and Hope,
¹⁵ And melancholy Fear subdued by Faith;
Of blessed consolations in distress;
Of moral strength, and intellectual Power;
Of joy in widest commonalty spread;
Of the individual Mind that keeps her own
²⁰ Inviolate retirement, subject there
To Conscience only, and the law supreme
Of that Intelligence which governs all,
I sing—"fit audience let me find though few!"[5]
    So prayed, more gaining than he asked, the Bard—
²⁵ In holiest mood. Urania,[6] I shall need
Thy guidance, or a greater Muse, if such
Descend to earth or dwell in highest heaven!
For I must tread on shadowy ground, must sink
Deep—and, aloft ascending, breathe in worlds
³⁰ To which the heaven of heavens is but a veil.
All strength—all terror, single or in bands,
That ever was put forth in personal form—
Jehovah—with his thunder, and the choir
Of shouting Angels, and the empyreal thrones—
³⁵ I pass them unalarmed. Not Chaos, not
The darkest pit of lowest Erebus,°   *hell, the underworld*
Nor aught of blinder vacancy, scooped out
By help of dreams—can breed such fear and awe

4. Part of a long philosophic poem never completed, the whole, including *The Prelude*, to have been named *The Recluse. Prospectus* introduces the entire work.

5. From Milton, *Paradise Lost*, VII.31.
6. The heavenly Muse invoked also by Milton in *Paradise Lost*.

As fall upon us often when we look
40 Into our Minds, into the Mind of Man—
My haunt, and the main region of my song.
—Beauty—a living Presence of the earth,
Surpassing the most fair ideal Forms
Which craft of delicate Spirits hath composed
45 From earth's materials—waits upon my steps;
Pitches her tents before me as I move,
An hourly neighbor. Paradise, and groves
Elysian,[7] Fortunate Fields—like those of old
Sought in the Atlantic Main[8]—why should they be
50 A history only of departed things,
Or a mere fiction of what never was?
For the discerning intellect of Man,
When wedded to this goodly universe
In love and holy passion, shall find these
55 A simple produce of the common day.
—I, long before the blissful hour arrives,
Would chant, in lonely peace, the spousal verse°   *wedding song*
Of this great consummation—and, by words
Which speak of nothing more than what we are,
60 Would I arouse the sensual from their sleep
Of Death, and win the vacant and the vain
To noble raptures; while my voice proclaims
How exquisitely the individual Mind
(And the progressive powers perhaps no less
65 Of the whole species) to the external World
Is fitted—and how exquisitely, too—
Theme this but little heard of among men—
The external World is fitted to the Mind;
And the creation (by no lower name
70 Can it be called) which they with blended might
Accomplish—this is our high argument.[9]
—Such grateful haunts foregoing, if I oft
Must turn elsewhere—to travel near the tribes
And fellowships of men, and see ill sights
75 Of madding passions mutually inflamed;
Must hear Humanity in fields and groves
Pipe solitary anguish; or must hang
Brooding above the fierce confederate storm
Of sorrow, barricadoed evermore
80 Within the walls of cities—may these sounds
Have their authentic comment; that even these
Hearing, I be not downcast or forlorn!—
Descend, prophetic Spirit! that inspir'st
The human Soul of universal earth,
85 Dreaming on things to come; and dost possess
A metropolitan[1] temple in the hearts
Of mighty Poets: upon me bestow
A gift of genuine insight; that my Song
With starlike virtue in its place may shine,
90 Shedding benignant influence, and secure,
Itself, from all malevolent effect
Of those mutations that extend their sway

---

7. In Greek myth the souls of the blest dwelt
in the Elysian Fields.
8. The islands of the happy ("fortunate")
dead were once thought to be in the Atlantic.
9. I.e., theme.
1. Pre-eminent, as of a capital city.

Throughout the nether sphere!²—And if with this
I mix more lowly matter; with the thing
95   Contemplated, describe the Mind and Man
Contemplating; and who, and what he was—
The transitory Being that beheld
The Vision; when and where, and how he lived—
Be not this labor useless. If such theme
100   May sort with highest objects, then—dread Power!
Whose gracious favor is the primal source
Of all illumination—may my Life
Express the image of a better time,
More wise desires, and simpler manners—nurse
105   My Heart in genuine freedom—all pure thoughts
Be with me—so shall thy unfailing love
Guide, and support, and cheer me to the end!

ca. 1798–1814   1814

From The Prelude

From *Book I*

Fair seedtime had my soul, and I grew up
Fostered alike by beauty and by fear:
Much favored in my birthplace,³ and no less
In that belovéd Vale⁴ to which erelong
305   We were transplanted—there were we let loose
For sports of wider range. Ere I had told
Ten birthdays, when among the mountain slopes
Frost, and the breath of frosty wind, had snapped
The last autumnal crocus, 'twas my joy
310   With store of springes° o'er my shoulder hung   *snares*
To range the open heights where woodcocks run
Along the smooth green turf. Through half the night,
Scudding away from snare to snare, I plied
That anxious visitation—moon and stars
315   Were shining o'er my head. I was alone,
And seemed to be a trouble to the peace
That dwelt among them. Sometimes it befell
In these night wanderings, that a strong desire
O'erpowered my better reason, and the bird
320   Which was the captive of another's toil
Became my prey; and when the deed was done
I heard among the solitary hills
Low breathings coming after me, and sounds
Of undistinguishable motion, steps
325   Almost as silent as the turf they trod.

Nor less, when spring had warmed the cultured° Vale,   *cultivated*
Moved we as plunderers where the mother bird
Had in high places built her lodge; though mean
Our object and inglorious, yet the end
330   Was not ignoble. Oh! when I have hung
Above the raven's nest, by knots of grass
And half-inch fissures in the slippery rock
But ill sustained, and almost (so it seemed)

2. The earth (beneath the "sphere" of the
stars above).
3. Cockermouth, in the northern part of the

English Lake District.
4. Esthwaite, also in the Lakes.

Suspended by the blast that blew amain,
35 Shouldering the naked crag, oh, at that time
While on the perilous ridge I hung alone,
With what strange utterance did the loud dry wind
Blow through my ear! the sky seemed not a sky
Of earth—and with what motion moved the clouds!

40   Dust as we are, the immortal spirit grows
Like harmony in music; there is a dark
Inscrutable workmanship that reconciles
Discordant elements, makes them cling together
In one society. How strange that all
45 The terrors, pains, and early miseries,
Regrets, vexations, lassitudes interfused
Within my mind, should e'er have borne a part,
And that a needful part, in making up
The calm existence that is mine when I
350 Am worthy of myself! Praise to the end!
Thanks to the means which Nature deigned to employ;
Whether her fearless visitings, or those
That came with soft alarm, like hurtless light
Opening the peaceful clouds; or she may use
355 Severer interventions, ministry
More palpable, as best might suit her aim.

One summer evening (led by her) I found
A little boat tied to a willow tree
Within a rocky cave, its usual home.
360 Straight I unloosed her chain, and stepping in
Pushed from the shore. It was an act of stealth
And troubled pleasure, nor without the voice
Of mountain echoes did my boat move on;
Leaving behind her still, on either side,
365 Small circles glittering idly in the moon,
Until they melted all into one track
Of sparkling light. But now, like one who rows,
Proud of his skill, to reach a chosen point
With an unswerving line, I fixed my view
370 Upon the summit of a craggy ridge,
The horizon's utmost boundary; for above
Was nothing but the stars and the gray sky.
She was an elfin pinnace; lustily
I dipped my oars into the silent lake,
375 And, as I rose upon the stroke, my boat
Went heaving through the water like a swan;
When, from behind that craggy steep till then
The horizon's bound, a huge peak, black and huge,
As if with voluntary power instinct,
380 Upreared its head. I struck and struck again,
And growing still in stature the grim shape
Towered up between me and the stars, and still,
For so it seemed, with purpose of its own
And measured motion like a living thing,
385 Strode after me. With trembling oars I turned,
And through the silent water stole my way
Back to the covert of the willow tree;
There in her mooring place I left my bark,
And through the meadows homeward went, in grave

390 And serious mood; but after I had seen
 That spectacle, for many days, my brain
 Worked with a dim and undetermined sense
 Of unknown modes of being; o'er my thoughts
 There hung a darkness, call it solitude
395 Or blank desertion. No familiar shapes
 Remained, no pleasant images of trees,
 Of sea or sky, no colors of green fields;
 But huge and mighty forms, that do not live
 Like living men, moved slowly through the mind
400 By day, and were a trouble to my dreams.

 Wisdom and Spirit of the universe!
 Thou Soul that art the eternity of thought,
 That givest to forms and images a breath
 And everlasting motion, not in vain
405 By day or starlight thus from my first dawn
 Of childhood didst thou intertwine for me
 The passions that build up our human soul;
 Not with the mean and vulgar works of man,
 But with high objects, with enduring things—
410 With life and nature—purifying thus
 The elements of feeling and of thought,
 And sanctifying, by such discipline,
 Both pain and fear, until we recognize
 A grandeur in the beating of the heart.
415 Nor was this fellowship vouchsafed to me
 With stinted kindness. In November days,
 When vapors rolling down the valley made
 A lonely scene more lonesome, among woods,
 At noon and 'mid the calm of summer nights,
420 When, by the margin of the trembling lake,
 Beneath the gloomy hills homeward I went
 In solitude, such intercourse was mine;
 Mine was it in the fields both day and night,
 And by the waters, all the summer long.

425 And in the frosty season, when the sun
 Was set, and visible for many a mile
 The cottage windows blazed through twilight gloom,
 I heeded not their summons: happy time
 It was indeed for all of us—for me
430 It was a time of rapture! Clear and loud
 The village clock tolled six—I wheeled about,
 Proud and exulting like an untired horse
 That cares not for his home. All shod with steel,
 We hissed along the polished ice in games
435 Confederate, imitative of the chase
 And woodland pleasures—the resounding horn,
 The pack loud chiming, and the hunted hare.
 So through the darkness and the cold we flew,
 And not a voice was idle; with the din
440 Smitten, the precipices rang aloud;
 The leafless trees and every icy crag
 Tinkled like iron; while far distant hills
 Into the tumult sent an alien sound
 Of melancholy not unnoticed, while the stars

45 Eastward were sparkling clear, and in the west
The orange sky of evening died away.
Not seldom from the uproar I retired
Into a silent bay, or sportively
Glanced sideway, leaving the tumultuous throng,
50 To cut across the reflex° of a star   *reflection*
That fled, and, flying still before me, gleamed
Upon the glassy plain; and oftentimes,
When we had given our bodies to the wind,
And all the shadowy banks on either side
55 Came sweeping through the darkness, spinning still
The rapid line of motion, then at once
Have I, reclining back upon my heels,
Stopped short; yet still the solitary cliffs
Wheeled by me—even as if the earth had rolled
60 With visible motion her diurnal round!
Behind me did they stretch in solemn train,
Feebler and feebler, and I stood and watched
Till all was tranquil as a dreamless sleep.

Ye Presences of Nature in the sky
465 And on the earth! Ye Visions of the hills!
And Souls of lonely places! can I think
A vulgar° hope was yours when ye employed   *lowly*
Such ministry, when ye, through many a year
Haunting me thus among my boyish sports,
470 On caves and trees, upon the woods and hills,
Impressed upon all forms the characters
Of danger or desire; and thus did make
The surface of the universal earth
With triumph and delight, with hope and fear,
Work like a sea?   Not uselessly employed,
475 Might I pursue this theme through every change
Of exercise and play, to which the year
Did summon us in his delightful round.

We were a noisy crew; the sun in heaven
480 Beheld not vales more beautiful than ours;
Nor saw a band in happiness and joy
Richer, or worthier of the ground they trod.
I could record with no reluctant voice
The woods of autumn, and their hazel bowers
485 With milk-white clusters hung; the rod and line,
True symbol of hope's foolishness, whose strong
And unreproved enchantment led us on
By rocks and pools shut out from every star,
All the green summer, to forlorn cascades
490 Among the windings hid of mountain brooks.
—Unfading recollections! at this hour
The heart is almost mine with which I felt,
From some hill-top on sunny afternoons,
The paper kite high among fleecy clouds
495 Pull at her rein like an impetuous courser;
Or, from the meadows sent on gusty days,
Beheld her breast the wind, then suddenly
Dashed headlong, and rejected by the storm.

Ye lowly cottages wherein we dwelt,
500 A ministration of your own was yours;
Can I forget you, being as you were
So beautiful among the pleasant fields
In which ye stood? or can I here forget
The plain and seemly countenance with which
505 Ye dealt out your plain comforts? Yet had ye
Delights and exultations of your own.
Eager and never weary we pursued
Our home-amusements by the warm peat-fire
At evening, when with pencil, and smooth slate
510 In square divisions parceled out and all
With crosses and with cyphers scribbled o'er,
We schemed and puzzled, head opposed to head
In strife too humble to be named in verse:
Or round the naked table, snow-white deal,°   *pine board*
515 Cherry or maple, sate in close array,
And to the combat, Loo or Whist,[5] led on
A thick-ribbed army; not, as in the world,
Neglected and ungratefully thrown by
Even for the very service they had wrought,
520 But husbanded through many a long campaign.
Uncouth assemblage was it, where no few
Had changed their functions; some, plebeian cards
Which Fate, beyond the promise of their birth,
Had dignified, and called to represent
525 The persons of departed potentates.
Oh, with what echoes on the board they fell!
Ironic diamonds,—clubs, hearts, diamonds, spades,
A congregation piteously akin!
Cheap matter offered they to boyish wit,
530 Those sooty knaves, precipitated down
With scoffs and taunts, like Vulcan[6] out of heaven:
The paramount ace, a moon in her eclipse,
Queens gleaming through their splendor's last decay,
And monarchs surly at the wrongs sustained
535 By royal visages. Meanwhile abroad
Incessant rain was falling, or the frost
Raged bitterly, with keen and silent tooth;
And, interrupting oft that eager game,
From under Esthwaite's splitting fields of ice
540 The pent-up air, struggling to free itself,
Gave out to meadow grounds and hills a loud
Protracted yelling, like the noise of wolves
Howling in troops along the Bothnic main.[7]

Nor, sedulous as I have been to trace
545 How Nature by extrinsic passion first
Peopled the mind with forms sublime or fair,
And made me love them, may I here omit
How other pleasures have been mine, and joys
Of subtler origin; how I have felt,
550 Not seldom even in that tempestuous time,
Those hallowed and pure motions of the sense

5. Card games resembling poker and bridge; the pack of cards described in lines 516–535 through long use has been damaged and repaired, with low (line 522, "plebeian") cards made into high (line 525, "potentates") and others partially defaced.
6. In Roman mythology, the god of fire, or the smith of the gods (hence "sooty," line 530); his father Jove once hurled him out of heaven.
7. Baltic Sea.

Which seem, in their simplicity, to own
An intellectual charm; that calm delight
Which, if I err not, surely must belong
555 To those first-born affinities that fit
Our new existence to existing things,
And, in our dawn of being, constitute
The bond of union between life and joy.

Yes, I remember when the changeful earth,
560 And twice five summers on my mind had stamped
The faces of the moving year, even then
I held unconscious intercourse with beauty
Old as creation, drinking in a pure
Organic pleasure from the silver wreaths
565 Of curling mist, or from the level plain
Of waters colored by impending clouds.

The sands of Westmoreland, the creeks and bays
Of Cumbria's rocky limits,[8] they can tell
How, when the Sea threw off his evening shade,
570 And to the shepherd's hut on distant hills
Sent welcome notice of the rising moon,
How I have stood, to fancies such as these
A stranger, linking with the spectacle
No conscious memory of a kindred sight,
575 And bringing with me no peculiar sense
Of quietness or peace; yet have I stood,
Even while mine eye hath moved o'er many a league
Of shining water, gathering as it seemed,
Through every hairbreadth in that field of light,
580 New pleasure like a bee among the flowers.

Thus oft amid those fits of vulgar° joy   *ordinary, unreflective*
Which, through all seasons, on a child's pursuits
Are prompt attendants, 'mid that giddy bliss
Which, like a tempest, works along the blood
585 And is forgotten; even then I felt
Gleams like the flashing of a shield—the earth
And common face of Nature spake to me
Rememberable things; sometimes, 'tis true,
By chance collisions and quaint accidents
590 (Like those ill-sorted unions, work supposed
Of evil-minded fairies), yet not vain
Nor profitless, if haply they impressed
Collateral objects and appearances,
Albeit lifeless then, and doomed to sleep
595 Until maturer seasons called them forth
To impregnate and to elevate the mind.
—And if the vulgar joy by its own weight
Wearied itself out of the memory,
The scenes which were a witness of that joy
600 Remained in their substantial lineaments
Depicted on the brain, and to the eye
Were visible, a daily sight; and thus
By the impressive discipline of fear,
By pleasure and repeated happiness,

---

8. Coastline areas of the Lake District.

605 So frequently repeated, and by force
Of obscure feelings representative
Of things forgotten, these same scenes so bright,
So beautiful, so majestic in themselves,
Though yet the day was distant, did become
610 Habitually dear, and all their forms
And changeful colors by invisible links
Were fastened to the affections.
                                        I began
My story early—not misled, I trust,
By an infirmity of love for days
615 Disowned by memory—fancying flowers where none
Not even the sweetest do or can survive
For him at least whose dawning day they cheered.
Nor will it seem to thee, O Friend![9] so prompt
In sympathy, that I have lengthened out
620 With fond and feeble tongue a tedious tale.
Meanwhile, my hope has been, that I might fetch
Invigorating thoughts from former years;
Might fix the wavering balance of my mind,
And haply meet reproaches too, whose power
625 May spur me on, in manhood now mature,
To honorable toil. Yet should these hopes
Prove vain, and thus should neither I be taught
To understand myself, nor thou to know
With better knowledge how the heart was framed
630 Of him thou lovest; need I dread from thee
Harsh judgments, if the song be loth to quit
Those recollected hours that have the charm
Of visionary things, those lovely forms
And sweet sensations that throw back our life,
635 And almost make remotest infancy
A visible scene, on which the sun is shining?

        One end at least hath been attained; my mind
Hath been revived, and if this genial mood
Desert me not, forthwith shall be brought down
640 Through later years the story of my life.
The road lies plain before me—'tis a theme
Single and of determined bounds; and hence
I choose it rather at this time, than work
Of ampler or more varied argument,
645 Where I might be discomfited and lost:
And certain hopes are with me, that to thee
This labor will be welcome, honored Friend!

                                1798–1800   1850

She Dwelt Among the Untrodden Ways

She dwelt among the untrodden ways
    Beside the springs of Dove.[1]
A Maid whom there were none to praise
    And very few to love;

9. Samuel Taylor Coleridge, the poet and
philosopher to whom *The Prelude* was ad-
dressed; Wordsworth's particular friend and
collaborator.
1. Several rivers in England are named Dove.

5   A violet by a mossy stone
      Half hidden from the eye!
  —Fair as a star, when only one
      Is shining in the sky.

    She lived unknown, and few could know
10   When Lucy ceased to be;
    But she is in her grave, and, oh,
      The difference to me!

1800

Three Years She Grew

  Three years she grew in sun and shower,
  Then Nature said, "A lovelier flower
  On earth was never sown;
  This Child I to myself will take;
5   She shall be mine, and I will make
  A Lady of my own.

  "Myself will to my darling be
  Both law and impulse: and with me
  The Girl, in rock and plain,
10   In earth and heaven, in glade and bower,
  Shall feel an overseeing power
  To kindle or restrain.

  "She shall be sportive as the fawn
  That wild with glee across the lawn
15   Or up the mountain springs;
  And hers shall be the breathing balm,
  And hers the silence and the calm
  Of mute insensate things.

  "The floating clouds their state shall lend
20   To her; for her the willow bend;
  Nor shall she fail to see
  Even in the motions of the Storm
  Grace that shall mold the Maiden's form
  By silent sympathy.

25   "The stars of midnight shall be dear
  To her; and she shall lean her ear
  In many a secret place
  Where rivulets dance their wayward round,
  And beauty born of murmuring sound
30   Shall pass into her face.

  "And vital feelings of delight
  Shall rear her form to stately height,
  Her virgin bosom swell;
  Such thoughts to Lucy I will give
35   While she and I together live
  Here in this happy dell."

  Thus Nature spake—the work was done—
  How soon my Lucy's race was run!

40 She died, and left to me
This health, this calm, and quiet scene;
The memory of what has been,
And never more will be.

1800

A Slumber Did My Spirit Seal

A slumber did my spirit seal;
I had no human fears:
She seemed a thing that could not feel
The touch of earthly years.

5   No motion has she now, no force;
She neither hears nor sees;
Rolled round in earth's diurnal course,
With rocks, and stones, and trees.

1800

Michael

A PASTORAL POEM

If from the public way you turn your steps
Up the tumultuous brook of Greenhead Ghyll,[2]
You will suppose that with an upright path
You feet must struggle; in such bold ascent
5   The pastoral mountains front you, face to face.
But, courage! for around that boisterous brook
The mountains have all opened out themselves,
And made a hidden valley of their own.
No habitation can be seen; but they
10 Who journey thither find themselves alone
With a few sheep, with rocks and stones, and kites°   *small hawks*
That overhead are sailing in the sky.
It is in truth an utter solitude;
Nor should I have made mention of this dell
15 But for one object which you might pass by,
Might see and notice not. Beside the brook
Appears a straggling heap of unhewn stones!
And to that simple object appertains
A story—unenriched with strange events,
20 Yet not unfit, I deem, for the fireside,
Or for the summer shade. It was the first
Of those domestic tales that spake to me
Of Shepherds, dwellers in the valleys, men
Whom I already loved—not verily
25 For their own sakes, but for the fields and hills
Where was their occupation and abode.
And hence this Tale, while I was yet a Boy
Careless of books, yet having felt the power
Of Nature, by the gentle agency
30 Of natural objects, led me on to feel
For passions that were not my own, and think
(At random and imperfectly indeed)
On man, the heart of man, and human life.

2. A *ghyll* is a ravine.

Therefore, although it be a history
Homely and rude, I will relate the same
For the delight of a few natural hearts;
And, with yet fonder feeling, for the sake
Of youthful Poets, who among these hills
Will be my second self when I am gone.

    Upon the forest side in Grasmere Vale
There dwelt a Shepherd, Michael was his name;
An old man, stout of heart, and strong of limb.
His bodily frame had been from youth to age
Of an unusual strength: his mind was keen,
Intense, and frugal, apt for all affairs,
And in his shepherd's calling he was prompt
And watchful more than ordinary men.
Hence had he learned the meaning of all winds,
Of blasts of every tone; and oftentimes,
When others heeded not, he heard the South
Make subterraneous music, like the noise
Of bagpipers on distant Highland hills.
The Shepherd, at such warning, of his flock
Bethought him, and he to himself would say,
"The winds are now devising work for me!"
And, truly, at all times, the storm, that drives
The traveler to a shelter, summoned him
Up to the mountains: he had been alone
Amid the heart of many thousand mists,
That came to him, and left him, on the heights.
So lived he till his eightieth year was past.
And grossly that man errs, who should suppose
That the green valleys, and the streams and rocks,
Were things indifferent to the Shepherd's thoughts.
Fields, where with cheerful spirits he had breathed
The common air; hills, which with vigorous step
He had so often climbed; which had impressed
So many incidents upon his mind
Of hardship, skill or courage, joy or fear;
Which, like a book, preserved the memory
Of the dumb animals, whom he had saved,
Had fed or sheltered, linking to such acts
The certainty of honorable gain;
Those fields, those hills—what could they less? had laid
Strong hold on his affections, were to him
A pleasurable feeling of blind love,
The pleasure which there is in life itself.
His days had not been passed in singleness.
His Helpmate was a comely matron, old—
Though younger than himself full twenty years.
She was a woman of a stirring life,
Whose heart was in her house; two wheels she had
Of antique form: this large, for spinning wool;
That small, for flax; and, if one wheel had rest,
It was because the other was at work.
The Pair had but one inmate in their house,
An only Child, who had been born to them
When Michael, telling o'er his years, began
To deem that he was old—in shepherd's phrase,
With one foot in the grave. This only Son,

With two brave sheep dogs tried in many a storm,
The one of an inestimable worth,
Made all their household. I may truly say,
That they were as a proverb in the vale
95 For endless industry. When day was gone,
And from their occupations out of doors
The Son and Father were come home, even then,
Their labor did not cease; unless when all
Turned to the cleanly supper board, and there,
100 Each with a mess of pottage° and skimmed milk,   *thick soup*
Sat round the basket piled with oaten cakes,
And their plain homemade cheese. Yet when the meal
Was ended, Luke (for so the Son was named)
And his old Father both betook themselves
105 To such convenient work as might employ
Their hands by the fireside; perhaps to card
Wool for the Housewife's spindle, or repair
Some injury done to sickle, flail, or scythe,
Or other implement of house or field.

110   Down from the ceiling, by the chimney's edge,
That in our ancient uncouth country style
With huge and black projection overbrowed
Large space beneath, as duly as the light
Of day grew dim the Housewife hung a lamp;
115 An aged utensil, which had performed
Service beyond all others of its kind.
Early at evening did it burn—and late,
Surviving comrade of uncounted hours,
Which, going by from year to year, had found,
120 And left, the couple neither gay perhaps
Nor cheerful, yet with objects and with hopes,
Living a life of eager industry.
And now, when Luke had reached his eighteenth year,
There by the light of this old lamp they sate,
125 Father and Son, while far into the night
The Housewife plied her own peculiar work,
Making the cottage through the silent hours
Murmur as with the sound of summer flies.
This light was famous in its neighborhood,
130 And was a public symbol of the life
That thrifty Pair had lived. For, as it chanced,
Their cottage on a plot of rising ground
Stood single, with large prospect, north and south,
High into Easedale, up to Dunmail Raise,
135 And westward to the village near the lake;
And from this constant light, so regular,
And so far seen, the House itself, by all
Who dwelt within the limits of the vale,
Both old and young, was named The Evening Star.

140   Thus living on through such a length of years,
The Shepherd, if he loved himself, must needs
Have loved his Helpmate; but to Michael's heart
This son of his old age was yet more dear—
Less from instinctive tenderness, the same
145 Fond spirit that blindly works in the blood of all—

Than that a child, more than all other gifts
That earth can offer to declining man,
Brings hope with it, and forward-looking thoughts,
And stirrings of inquietude, when they
50 By tendency of nature needs must fail.
Exceeding was the love he bare to him,
His heart and his heart's joy! For oftentimes
Old Michael, while he was a babe in arms,
Had done him female service, not alone
55 For pastime and delight, as is the use
Of fathers, but with patient mind enforced
To acts of tenderness; and he had rocked
His cradle, as with a woman's gentle hand.

And in a later time, ere yet the Boy
60 Had put on boy's attire, did Michael love,
Albeit of a stern unbending mind,
To have the Young one in his sight, when he
Wrought in the field, or on his shepherd's stool
Sate with a fettered sheep before him stretched
65 Under the large old oak, that near his door
Stood single, and, from matchless depth of shade,
Chosen for the Shearer's covert from the sun,
Thence in our rustic dialect was called
The Clipping Tree, a name which yet it bears.
70 There, while they two were sitting in the shade,
With others round them, earnest all and blithe,
Would Michael exercise his heart with looks
Of fond correction and reproof bestowed
Upon the Child, if he disturbed the sheep
75 By catching at their legs, or with his shouts
Scared them, while they lay still beneath the shears.

And when by Heaven's good grace the boy grew up
A healthy Lad, and carried in his cheek
Two steady roses that were five years old;
180 Then Michael from a winter coppice[3] cut
With his own hand a sapling, which he hooped
With iron, making it throughout in all
Due requisites a perfect shepherd's staff,
And gave it to the Boy; wherewith equipped
185 He as a watchman oftentimes was placed
At gate or gap, to stem or turn the flock;
And, to his office prematurely called,
There stood the urchin, as you will divine,
Something between a hindrance and a help;
190 And for this cause not always, I believe,
Receiving from his Father hire of praise;
Though nought was left undone which staff, or voice,
Or looks, or threatening gestures, could perform.

But soon as Luke, full ten years old, could stand
195 Against the mountain blasts, and to the heights,
Not fearing toil, nor length of weary ways,
He with his Father daily went, and they

3. Thicket regularly thinned for firewood.

Were as companions, why should I relate
That objects which the Shepherd loved before
200   Were dearer now? that from the Boy there came
Feelings and emanations—things which were
Light to the sun and music to the wind;
And that the old Man's heart seemed born again?

Thus in his Father's sight the Boy grew up:
205   And now, when he had reached his eighteenth year,
He was his comfort and his daily hope.

While in this sort the simple household lived
From day to day, to Michael's ear there came
Distressful tidings. Long before the time
210   Of which I speak, the Shepherd had been bound
In surety[4] for his brother's son, a man
Of an industrious life, and ample means;
But unforeseen misfortunes suddenly
Had pressed upon him; and old Michael now
215   Was summoned to discharge the forfeiture,
A grievous penalty, but little less
Than half his substance. This unlooked-for claim,
At the first hearing, for a moment took
More hope out of his life than he supposed
220   That any old man ever could have lost.
As soon as he had armed himself with strength
To look his trouble in the face, it seemed
The Shepherd's sole resource to sell at once
A portion of his patrimonial[5] fields.
225   Such was his first resolve; he thought again,
And his heart failed him. "Isabel," said he,
Two evenings after he had heard the news,
"I have been toiling more than seventy years,
And in the open sunshine of God's love
230   Have we all lived; yet, if these fields of ours
Should pass into a stranger's hand, I think
That I could not lie quiet in my grave.
Our lot is a hard lot; the sun himself
Has scarcely been more diligent than I;
235   And I have lived to be a fool at last
To my own family. An evil man
That was, and made an evil choice, if he
Were false to us; and, if he were not false,
There are ten thousand to whom loss like this
240   Had been no sorrow. I forgive him—but
'Twere better to be dumb than to talk thus.

"When I began, my purpose was to speak
Of remedies and of a cheerful hope.
Our Luke shall leave us, Isabel; the land
245   Shall not go from us, and it shall be free;
He shall possess it, free as is the wind
That passes over it. We have, thou know'st,
Another kinsman—he will be our friend
In this distress. He is a prosperous man,
250   Thriving in trade—and Luke to him shall go,

---

4. To bind in surety is to guarantee a loan.   5. Inherited through generations.

And with his kinsman's help and his own thrift
He quickly will repair this loss, and then
He may return to us. If here he stay,
What can be done? Where everyone is poor,
What can be gained?"
                              At this the old Man paused,
And Isabel sat silent, for her mind
Was busy, looking back into past times.
There's Richard Bateman, thought she to herself,
He was a parish boy—at the church door
They made a gathering for him, shillings, pence,
And halfpennies, wherewith the neighbors bought
A basket, which they filled with peddler's wares;
And, with this basket on his arm, the lad
Went up to London, found a master there,
Who, out of many, chose the trusty boy
To go and overlook his merchandise
Beyond the seas; where he grew wondrous rich,
And left estates and monies to the poor,
And, at his birthplace, built a chapel floored
With marble, which he sent from foreign lands.
These thoughts, and many others of like sort,
Passed quickly through the mind of Isabel,
And her face brightened. The old Man was glad,
And thus resumed :"Well, Isabel! this scheme
These two days has been meat and drink to me.
Far more than we have lost is left us yet.
We have enough—I wish indeed that I
Were younger—but this hope is a good hope.
Make ready Luke's best garments, of the best
Buy for him more, and let us send him forth
Tomorrow, or the next day, or tonight:
If he *could* go, the Boy should go tonight."

Here Michael ceased, and to the fields went forth
With a light heart. The Housewife for five days
Was restless morn and night, and all day long
Wrought on with her best fingers to prepare
Things needful for the journey of her son.
But Isabel was glad when Sunday came
To stop her in her work; for, when she lay
By Michael's side, she through the last two nights
Heard him, how he was troubled in his sleep;
And when they rose at morning she could see
That all his hopes were gone. That day at noon
She said to Luke, while they two by themselves
Were sitting at the door, "Thou must not go;
We have no other Child but thee to lose,
None to remember—do not go away,
For if thou leave thy Father he will die."
The Youth made answer with a jocund voice;
And Isabel, when she had told her fears,
Recovered heart. That evening her best fare
Did she bring forth, and all together sat
Like happy people round a Christmas fire.

With daylight Isabel resumed her work;
An all the ensuing week the house appeared

As cheerful as a grove in spring; at length
The expected letter from their kinsman came,
With kind assurances that he would do
His utmost for the welfare of the Boy;
310 To which requests were added that forthwith
He might be sent to him. Ten times or more
The letter was read over; Isabel
Went forth to show it to the neighbors round;
Nor was there at that time on English land
315 A prouder heart than Luke's. When Isabel
Had to her house returned, the old Man said,
"He shall depart tomorrow." To this word
The Housewife answered, talking much of things
Which, if at such short notice he should go,
320 Would surely be forgotten. But at length
She gave consent, and Michael was at ease.

Near the tumultuous brook of Greenhead Ghyll,
In that deep valley, Michael had designed
To build a Sheepfold;° and, before he heard   *pen for sheep*
325 The tidings of his melancholy loss,
For this same purpose he had gathered up
A heap of stones, which by the streamlet's edge
Lay thrown together, ready for the work.
With Luke that evening thitherward he walked;
330 And soon as they had reached the place he stopped,
And thus the old Man spake to him: "My son,
Tomorrow thou wilt leave me: with full heart
I look upon thee, for thou art the same
That wert a promise to me ere thy birth,
335 And all thy life hast been my daily joy.
I will relate to thee some little part
Of our two histories; 'twill do thee good
When thou art from me, even if I should touch
On things thou canst not know of. After thou
340 First cam'st into the world—as oft befalls
To newborn infants—thou didst sleep away
Two days, and blessings from thy Father's tongue
Then fell upon thee. Day by day passed on,
And still I loved thee with increasing love.
345 Never to living ear came sweeter sounds
Than when I heard thee by our own fireside
First uttering, without words, a natural tune;
While thou, a feeding babe, didst in thy joy
Sing at thy Mother's breast. Month followed month,
350 And in the open fields my life was passed
And on the mountains; else I think that thou
Hadst been brought up upon thy Father's knees.
But we were playmates, Luke; among these hills,
As well thou knowest, in us the old and young
355 Have played together, nor with me didst thou
Lack any pleasure which a boy can know."
Luke had a manly heart; but at these words
He sobbed aloud. The old Man grasped his hand,
And said, "Nay, do not take it so—I see
360 That these are things of which I need not speak.
Even to the utmost I have been to thee

A kind and a good Father: and herein
I but repay a gift which I myself
Received at others' hands; for, though now old
55 Beyond the common life of man, I still
Remember them who loved me in my youth.
Both of them sleep together; here they lived,
As all their Forefathers had done; and, when
At length their time was come, they were not loath
70 To give their bodies to the family mold.°   *ground*
I wished that thou shouldst live the life they lived,
But 'tis a long time to look back, my son,
And see so little gain from threescore years.
These fields were burthened° when they came to me;   *under debt*
75 Till I was forty years of age, not more
Than half of my inheritance was mine.
I toiled and toiled; God blessed me in my work,
And till these three weeks past the land was free.
It looks as if it never could endure
80 Another master. Heaven forgive me, Luke,
If I judge ill for thee, but it seems good
That thou shouldst go."
                          At this the old Man paused;
Then, pointing to the stones near which they stood,
Thus, after a short silence, he resumed:
85 "This was a work for us; and now, my Son,
It is a work for me. But, lay one stone—
Here, lay it for me, Luke, with thine own hands.
Nay, Boy, be of good hope—we both may live
To see a better day. At eighty-four
90 I still am strong and hale; do thou thy part;
I will do mine. I will begin again
With many tasks that were resigned to thee:
Up to the heights, and in among the storms,
Will I without thee go again, and do
95 All works which I was wont to do alone,
Before I knew thy face. Heaven bless thee, Boy!
Thy heart these two weeks has been beating fast
With many hopes; it should be so—yes—yes—
I knew that thou couldst never have a wish
100 To leave me, Luke; thou hast been bound to me
Only by links of love; when thou art gone,
What will be left to us!—But I forget
My purposes. Lay now the cornerstone,
As I requested; and hereafter, Luke,
105 When thou art gone away, should evil men
Be thy companions, think of me, my Son,
And of this moment; hither turn thy thoughts,
And God will strengthen thee; amid all fear
And all temptation, Luke, I pray that thou
110 May'st bear in mind the life thy Fathers lived,
Who, being innocent, did for that cause
Bestir them in good deeds. Now, fare thee well—
When thou return'st, thou in this place wilt see
A work which is not here: a covenant
115 'Twill be between us; but, whatever fate
Befall thee, I shall love thee to the last,
And bear thy memory with me to the grave."

The Shepherd ended here; and Luke stooped down,
And, as his Father had requested, laid
420 The first stone of the Sheepfold. At the sight
The old Man's grief broke from him; to his heart
He pressed his Son, he kisséd him and wept;
And to the house together they returned.
Hushed was that House in peace, or seeming peace
425 Ere the night fell; with morrow's dawn the Boy
Began his journey, and, when he had reached
The public way, he put on a bold face;
And all the neighbors, as he passed their doors,
Came forth with wishes and with farewell prayers,
430 That followed him till he was out of sight.

A good report did from their kinsman come,
Of Luke and his well-doing; and the Boy
Wrote loving letters, full of wondrous news,
Which, as the Housewife phrased it, were throughout
435 "The prettiest letters that were ever seen."
Both parer's read them with rejoicing hearts.
So, many months passed on; and once again
The Shepherd went about his daily work
With confident and cheerful thoughts; and now
440 Sometimes when he could find a leisure hour
He to that valley took his way, and there
Wrought at the Sheepfold. Meantime Luke began
To slacken in his duty; and, at length,
He in the dissolute city gave himself
445 To evil courses; ignominy and shame
Fell on him, so that he was driven at last
To seek a hiding place beyond the seas.
There is a comfort in the strength of love;
'Twill make a thing endurable, which else
450 Would overset the brain, or break the heart;
I have conversed with more than one who well
Remember the old Man, and what he was
Years after he had heard this heavy news.
His bodily frame had been from youth to age
455 Of an unusual strength. Among the rocks
He went, and still looked up to sun and cloud,
And listened to the wind; and, as before,
Performed all kinds of labor for his sheep,
And for the land, his small inheritance.
460 And to that hollow dell from time to time
Did he repair, to build the Fold of which
His flock had need. 'Tis not forgotten yet
The pity which was then in every heart
For the old Man—and 'tis believed by all
465 That many and many a day he thither went,
And never lifted up a single stone.

There, by the Sheepfold, sometimes was he seen
Sitting alone, or with his faithful Dog,
Then old, beside him, lying at his feet.
470 The length of full seven years, from time to time,
He at the building of this Sheepfold wrought,
And left the work unfinished when he died.

Three years, or little more, did Isabel
Survive her Husband: at her death the estate
Was sold, and went into a stranger's hand.
The Cottage which was named The Evening Star
Is gone—the plowshare has been through the ground
On which it stood; great changes have been wrought
In all the neighborhood; yet the oak is left
That grew beside their door; and the remains
Of the unfinished Sheepfold may be seen
Beside the boisterous brook of Greenhead Ghyll.

1800

It Is a Beauteous Evening

It is a beauteous evening, calm and free,
The holy time is quiet as a Nun
Breathless with adoration; the broad sun
Is sinking down in its tranquility;
The gentleness of heaven broods o'er the Sea:
Listen! the mighty Being is awake,
And doth with his eternal motion make
A sound like thunder—everlastingly.
Dear Child! dear Girl! that walkest with me here,
If thou appear untouched by solemn thought,
Thy nature is not therefore less divine:
Thou liest in Abraham's bosom[6] all the year,
And worship'st at the Temple's inner shrine,[7]
God being with thee when we know it not.

1807

London, 1802

Milton! thou shouldst be living at this hour:
England hath need of thee: she is a fen
Of stagnant waters: altar, sword, and pen,
Fireside, the heroic wealth of hall and bower,
Have forfeited their ancient English dower
Of inward happiness. We are selfish men;
Oh! raise us up, return to us again;
And give us manners, virtue, freedom, power.
Thy soul was like a Star, and dwelt apart;
Thou hadst a voice whose sound was like the sea:
Pure as the naked heavens, majestic, free,
So didst thou travel on life's common way,
In cheerful godliness; and yet thy heart
The lowliest duties on herself did lay.

1807

Composed upon Westminster Bridge, September 3, 1802

Earth has not anything to show more fair:
Dull would he be of soul who could pass by
A sight so touching in its majesty;
This City now doth, like a garment, wear

6. Where souls in heaven rest (as in Luke, xvi.22).

7. The holy of holies (as in the ancient temple in Jerusalem); where God is present.

5   The beauty of the morning; silent, bare,
    Ships, towers, domes, theaters, and temples lie
    Open unto the fields, and to the sky;
    All bright and glittering in the smokeless air.
    Never did sun more beautifully steep
10 In his first splendor, valley, rock, or hill;
    Ne'er saw I, never felt, a calm so deep!
    The river glideth at his own sweet will:
    Dear God! the very houses seem asleep;
    And all that mighty heart is lying still!

                                                    1807

On the Extinction of the Venetian Republic[8]

    Once did She hold the gorgeous east in fee;
    And was the safeguard of the west:[9] the worth
    Of Venice did not fall below her birth,
    Venice, the eldest Child of Liberty.[1]
5   She was a maiden City, bright and free;
    No guile seduced, no force could violate;
    And, when she took unto herself a Mate,
    She must espouse the everlasting Sea.[2]
    And what if she had seen those glories fade,
10 Those titles vanish, and that strength decay;
    Yet shall some tribute of regret be paid
    When her long life hath reached its final day:
    Men are we, and must grieve when even the Shade
    Of that which once was great, is passed away.

                                                    1807

Nuns Fret Not at Their Convent's Narrow Room

    Nuns fret not at their convent's narrow room;
    And hermits are contented with their cells;
    And students with their pensive citadels;
    Maids at the wheel, the weaver at his loom,
5   Sit blithe and happy; bees that soar for bloom,
    High as the highest Peak of Furness-fells,[3]
    Will murmur by the hour in foxglove bells:
    In truth the prison, into which we doom
    Ourselves, no prison is: and hence for me,
10 In sundry moods, 'twas pastime to be bound
    Within the Sonnet's scanty plot of ground;
    Pleased if some Souls (for such there needs must be)
    Who have felt the weight of too much liberty,
    Should find brief solace there, as I have found.

                                                    1807

My Heart Leaps Up

    My heart leaps up when I behold
        A rainbow in the sky:

8. The Republic of Venice was conquered by
Napoleon in 1797.
9. I.e., Venice held a monopoly of trade in
the eastern Mediterranean and was, in the late
Middle Ages, a barrier against the Moham-
medan invasions of Europe.

1. She was an oligarchic republic, not a
monarchy.
2. Annually the Doge, the highest state official,
cast a gold ring into the Adriatic to symbolize
the marriage of Venice to the sea.
3. Mountains in the English Lake District.

So was it when my life began;
So is it now I am a man;
5   So be it when I shall grow old,
        Or let me die!
The Child is father of the Man;
And I could wish my days to be
Bound each to each by natural piety.

1807

Ode

INTIMATIONS OF IMMORTALITY FROM
RECOLLECTIONS OF EARLY CHILDHOOD

The Child is father of the Man;
And I could wish my days to be
Bound each to each by natural piety.[4]

1

There was a time when meadow, grove, and stream,
The earth, and every common sight,
        To me did seem
        Appareled in celestial light,
5   The glory and the freshness of a dream.
It is not now as it hath been of yore—
        Turn whereso'er I may,
        By night or day,
The things which I have seen I now can see no more.

2

10   The Rainbow comes and goes,
        And lovely is the Rose,
        The Moon doth with delight
Look round her when the heavens are bare,
        Waters on a starry night
15   Are beautiful and fair;
    The sunshine is a glorious birth;
    But yet I know, where'er I go,
That there hath passed away a glory from the earth.

3

Now, while the birds thus sing a joyous song,
20   And while the young lambs bound
        As to the tabor's sound,[5]
To me alone there came a thought of grief:
A timely utterance gave that thought relief,
        And I again am strong:
25   The cataracts blow their trumpets from the steep;
No more shall grief of mine the season wrong;
I hear the Echoes through the mountains throng,
The Winds come to me from the fields of sleep,
        And all the earth is gay;
30   Land and sea
    Give themselves up to jollity,
        And with the heart of May
    Doth every Beast keep holiday—
        Thou Child of Joy,
35   Shout round me, let me hear thy shouts, thou happy Shepherd-boy!

---

4. Final lines of Wordsworth's *My Heart   **5.** "Tabor": a small drum.
Leaps Up.*

4

Ye blessèd Creatures, I have heard the call
    Ye to each other make; I see
The heavens laugh with you in your jubilee;
40   My heart is at your festival,
        My head hath its coronal,
The fullness of your bliss, I feel—I feel it all.
        Oh, evil day! if I were sullen
        While Earth herself is adorning,
45   This sweet May morning,
        And the Children are culling
            On every side,
        In a thousand valleys far and wide,
        Fresh flowers; while the sun shines warm,
50 And the Babe leaps up on his Mother's arm—
        I hear, I hear, with joy I hear!
    —But there's a Tree, of many, one,
A single Field which I have looked upon,
Both of them speak of something that is gone:
55   The Pansy at my feet
            Doth the same tale repeat:
Whither is fled the visionary gleam?
Where is it now, the glory and the dream?

5

Our birth is but a sleep and a forgetting:
60 The Soul that rises with us, our life's Star,
        Hath had elsewhere its setting,
            And cometh from afar:
        Not in entire forgetfulness,
        And not in utter nakedness,
65 But trailing clouds of glory do we come
        From God, who is our home:
Heaven lies about us in our infancy!
Shades of the prison-house begin to close
        Upon the growing Boy
70   But he
Beholds the light, and whence it flows,
        He sees it in his joy;
The Youth, who daily farther from the east
        Must travel, still is Nature's Priest,
75   And by the vision splendid
        Is on his way attended;
At length the Man perceives it die away,
And fade into the light of common day.

6

Earth fills her lap with pleasures of her own;
80 Yearnings she hath in her own natural kind,
And, even with something of a Mother's mind,
        And no unworthy aim,
        The homely° Nurse doth all she can   *simple, kindly*
To make her foster child, her Inmate Man,
85   Forget the glories he hath known,
And that imperial palace whence he came.

7

Behold the Child among his newborn blisses,
A six-years' Darling of a pygmy size!
See, where 'mid work of his own hand he lies,

Fretted° by sallies of his mother's kisses,   *vexed*
With light upon him from his father's eyes!
See, at his feet, some little plan or chart,
Some fragment from his dream of human life,
Shaped by himself with newly-learnéd art;
  A wedding or a festival,
  A mourning or a funeral;
   And this hath now his heart,
   And unto this he frames his song;
   Then will he fit his tongue
To dialogues of business, love, or strife;
   But it will not be long
   Ere this be thrown aside,
   And with new joy and pride
The little Actor cons another part;
Filling from time to time his "humorous stage"[6]
With all the Persons, down to palsied Age,
That Life brings with her in her equipage;
  As if his whole vocation
  Were endless imitation.
    8
Thou, whose exterior semblance doth belie
  Thy Soul's immensity;
Thou best Philosopher, who yet dost keep
Thy heritage, thou Eye among the blind,
That, deaf and silent, read'st the eternal deep,
Haunted forever by the eternal mind—
  Mighty Prophet! Seer blest!
  On whom those truths do rest,
Which we are toiling all our lives to find,
In darkness lost, the darkness of the grave;
Thou, over whom thy Immortality
Broods like the Day, a Master o'er a Slave,
A Presence which is not to be put by;
Thou little Child, yet glorious in the might
Of heaven-born freedom on thy being's height,
Why with such earnest pains dost thou provoke
The years to bring the inevitable yoke,
Thus blindly with thy blessedness at strife?
Full soon thy Soul shall have her earthly freight,
And custom lie upon thee with a weight,
Heavy as frost, and deep almost as life!

    9
  O joy! that in our embers
  Is something that doth live,
  That nature yet remembers
  What was so fugitive!
The thought of our past years in me doth breed
Perpetual benediction: not indeed
For that which is most worthy to be blest;
Delight and liberty, the simple creed
Of Childhood, whether busy or at rest,
With new-fledged hope still fluttering in his breast—
  Not for these I raise
  The song of thanks and praise;

6. I.e., playing the parts of characters with various temperaments, called "humors" by Eliza-
bethan poets and playwrights.

But for those obstinate questionings
Of sense and outward things,
145   Fallings from us, vanishings;
Blank misgivings of a Creature
Moving about in worlds not realized,
High instincts before which our mortal Nature
Did tremble like a guilty Thing surprised;
150   But for those first affections,
Those shadowy recollections,
Which, be they what they may,
Are yet the fountain light of all our day,
Are yet a master light of all our seeing;
155   Uphold us, cherish, and have power to make
Our noisy years seem moments in the being
Of the eternal Silence: truths that wake,
To perish never;
Which neither listlessness, nor mad endeavor,
160   Nor Man nor Boy,
Nor all that is at enmity with joy,
Can utterly abolish or destroy!
Hence in a season of calm weather
Though inland far we be,
165   Our Souls have sight of that immortal sea
Which brought us hither,
Can in a moment travel thither,
And see the Children sport upon the shore,
And hear the mighty waters rolling evermore.

                    10
170   Then sing, ye Birds, sing, sing a joyous song!
And let the young Lambs bound
As to the tabor's sound!
We in thought will join your throng,
Ye that pipe and ye that play,
175   Ye that through your hearts today
Feel the gladness of the May!
What though the radiance which was once so bright
Be now forever taken from my sight,
Though nothing can bring back the hour
180   Of splendor in the grass, of glory in the flower;
We will grieve not, rather find
Strength in what remains behind;
In the primal sympathy
Which having been must ever be;
185   In the soothing thoughts that spring
Out of human suffering;
In the faith that looks through death,
In years that bring the philosophic mind.

                    11
And O, ye Fountains, Meadows, Hills, and Groves,
190   Forebode not any severing of our loves!
Yet in my heart of hearts I feel your might;
I only have relinquished one delight
To live beneath your more habitual sway.
I love the Brooks which down their channels fret,
195   Even more than when I tripped lightly as they;
The innocent brightness of a newborn Day
Is lovely yet;

The clouds that gather round the setting sun
Do take a sober coloring from an eye
oo   That hath kept watch o'er man's mortality;
Another race hath been, and other palms° are won.   *symbols of victory*
Thanks to the human heart by which we live,
Thanks to its tenderness, its joys, and fears,
To me the meanest° flower that blows° can give   *most ordinary / blooms*
o5   Thoughts that do often lie too deep for tears.

                                                    1802–4   1807

Ode to Duty

*Jam non consilio bonus, sed more eo perductus, ut non tantum recte facere possim, sed nisi recte
facere non possim.*

                                                    —SENECA[7]

Stern Daughter of the Voice of God!
O Duty! if that name thou love
Who are a light to guide, a rod
To check the erring, and reprove;
5   Thou, who art victory and law
When empty terrors overawe;
From vain temptations dost set free;
And calm'st the weary strife of frail humanity!

There are who ask not if thine eye
10   Be on them; who, in love and truth,
Where no misgiving is, rely
Upon the genial sense[8] of youth:
Glad Hearts! without reproach or blot;
Who do thy work, and know it not:
15   Oh! if through confidence misplaced
They fail, thy saving arms, dread Power! around them cast.

Serene will be our days and bright,
And happy will our nature be,
When love is an unerring light,
20   And joy its own security.
And they a blissful course may hold
Even now, who, not unwisely bold,
Live in the spirit of this creed;
Yet seek thy firm support, according to their need.

25   I, loving freedom, and untried,
No sport of every random gust,
Yet being to myself a guide,
Too blindly have reposed my trust;
And oft, when in my heart was heard
30   Thy timely mandate, I deferred
The task, in smoother walks to stray;
But thee I now would serve more strictly, if I may.

Through no disturbance of my soul,
Or strong compunction° in me wrought,   *remorse*
35   I supplicate for thy control;
But in the quietness of thought:

7. From the Roman philosopher and drama-
tist's *Moral Epistles* (CXX.10): "Now am I
good not by taking thought but urged on by
habit, to this effect: not so much can I act
rightly as other than rightly I cannot act."
8. Generous impulse; innate good nature.

Me this unchartered freedom tires;
I feel the weight of chance desires:
My hopes no more must change their name,
40 I long for a repose that ever is the same.

Stern Lawgiver! yet thou dost wear
The Godhead's most benignant grace;
Nor know we anything so fair
As is the smile upon thy face:
45 Flowers laugh before thee on their beds
And fragrance in thy footing treads;
Thou dost preserve the stars from wrong
And the most ancient heavens, through thee, are fresh and strong.

To humbler functions, awful Power!
50 I call thee: I myself commend
Unto thy guidance from this hour;
Oh, let my weakness have an end!
Give unto me, made lowly wise,
The spirit of self-sacrifice;
55 The confidence of reason give;
And in the light of truth thy Bondman let me live!

1807

I Wandered Lonely As a Cloud

I wandered lonely as a cloud
That floats on high o'er vales and hills,
When all at once I saw a crowd,
A host, of golden daffodils;
5 Beside the lake, beneath the trees,
Fluttering and dancing in the breeze.

Continuous as the stars that shine
And twinkle on the milky way,
They stretched in never-ending line
10 Along the margin of a bay:
Ten thousand saw I at a glance,
Tossing their heads in sprightly dance.

The waves beside them danced; but they
Outdid the sparkling waves in glee;
15 A poet could not but be gay,
In such a jocund° company;   *cheerful*
I gazed—and gazed—but little thought
What wealth the show to me had brought:

For oft, when on my couch I lie
20 In vacant or in pensive mood,
They flash upon that inward eye
Which is the bliss of solitude;
And then my heart with pleasure fills,
And dances with the daffodils.

1807

She Was a Phantom of Delight

She was a Phantom° of delight   *vivid image*
When first she gleamed upon my sight;
A lovely Apparition, sent
To be a moment's ornament;
Her eyes as stars of Twilight fair;
Like Twilight's, too, her dusky hair;
But all things else about her drawn
From May-time and the cheerful Dawn;
A dancing Shape, an Image gay,
To haunt, to startle, and way-lay.

I saw her upon nearer view,
A Spirit, yet a Woman too!
Her household motions light and free,
And steps of virgin-liberty;
A countenance in which did meet
Sweet records, promises as sweet;
A Creature not too bright or good
For human nature's daily food;
For transient sorrows, simple wiles,
Praise, blame, love, kisses, tears, and smiles.

And now I see with eye serene
The very pulse of the machine;[1]
A Being breathing thoughtful breath,
A Traveler between life and death;
The reason firm, the temperate will,
Endurance, foresight, strength, and skill;
A perfect Woman, nobly planned,
To warn, to comfort, and command;
And yet a Spirit still, and bright
With something of angelic light.

1807

Elegiac Stanzas[2]

SUGGESTED BY A PICTURE OF PEELE CASTLE, IN A STORM, PAINTED BY
SIR GEORGE BEAUMONT

I was thy neighbor once, thou rugged Pile!
Four summer weeks I dwelt in sight of thee:
I saw thee every day; and all the while
Thy Form was sleeping on a glassy sea.

So pure the sky, so quiet was the air!
So like, so very like, was day to day!
Whene'er I looked, thy Image still was there;
It trembled, but it never passed away.

How perfect was the calm! it seemed no sleep;
No mood, which season takes away, or brings:
I could have fancied that the mighty Deep
Was even the gentlest of all gentle Things.

1. Complete organism.
2. In memory of the poet's brother, John, who   had recently died in a shipwreck (see lines 36–39).

Ah! THEN, if mine had been the Painter's hand,
To express what then I saw; and add the gleam,
15 The light that never was, on sea or land,
The consecration, and the Poet's dream;

I would have planted thee, thou hoary Pile
Amid a world how different from this!
Beside a sea that could not cease to smile;
20 On tranquil land, beneath a sky of bliss.

Thou shouldst have seemed a treasure house divine
O peaceful years; a chronicle of heaven—
Of all the sunbeams that did ever shine
The very sweetest had to thee been given.

25 A Picture had it been of lasting ease,
Elysian³ quiet, without toil or strife;
No motion but the moving tide, a breeze,
Or merely silent Nature's breathing life.

Such, in the fond illusion of my heart,
30 Such Picture would I at that time have made,
And seen the soul of truth in every part,
A steadfast peace that might not be betrayed.

So once it would have been—'tis so no more;
I have submitted to a new control:
35 A power is gone, which nothing can restore;
A deep distress hath humanized my Soul.

Not for a moment could I now behold
A smiling sea, and be what I have been:
The feeling of my loss will ne'er be old;
40 This, which I know, I speak with mind serene.

Then, Beaumont, Friend! who would have been the Friend,
If he had lived, of him whom I deplore,°   *lament*
This work of thine I blame not, but commend;
This sea in anger, and that dismal shore.

45 O 'tis a passionate Work!—yet wise and well,
Well chosen is the spirit that is here;
That Hulk which labors in the deadly swell,
This rueful sky, this pageantry of fear!

And this huge Castle, standing here sublime,
50 I love to see the look with which it braves,
Cased in the unfeeling armor of old time,
The lightning, the fierce wind, and trampling waves.

Farewell, farewell the heart that lives alone,
Housed in a dream, at distance from the Kind!°   *mankind*
55 Such happiness, wherever it be known,
Is to be pitied; for 'tis surely blind.

---

3. In Greek myth the souls of the blest dwelt in the Elysian Fields.

But welcome fortitude, and patient cheer,
And frequent sights of what is to be borne!
Such sights, or worse, as are before me here.
60   Not without hope we suffer and we mourn.

1807

The World Is Too Much with Us

The world is too much with us; late and soon,
Getting and spending, we lay waste our powers;
Little we see in Nature that is ours;
We have given our hearts away, a sordid boon!°   *gift*
5   This Sea that bares her bosom to the moon,
The winds that will be howling at all hours,
And are up-gathered now like sleeping flowers,
For this, for everything, we are out of tune;
It moves us not.—Great God! I'd rather be
10   A Pagan suckled in a creed outworn;
So might I, standing on this pleasant lea,
Have glimpses that would make me less forlorn;
Have sight of Proteus rising from the sea;
Or hear old Triton blow his wreathéd horn.[4]

1807

The Solitary Reaper

Behold her, single in the field,
Yon solitary Highland Lass!
Reaping and singing by herself;
Stop here, or gently pass!
5   Alone she cuts and binds the grain,
And sings a melancholy strain;
O listen! for the Vale profound
Is overflowing with the sound.

No Nightingale did ever chaunt
10   More welcome notes to weary bands
Of travelers in some shady haunt,
Among Arabian sands;
A voice so thrilling ne'er was heard
In springtime from the Cuckoo bird,
15   Breaking the silence of the seas
Among the farthest Hebrides.

Will no one tell me what she sings?—
Perhaps the plaintive numbers flow
For old, unhappy, far-off things,
20   And battles long ago;
Or is it some more humble lay,
Familiar matter of today?
Some natural sorrow, loss, or pain,
That has been, and may be again?

4. In Greek myth Proteus, the "Old Man of
the Sea," rises from the sea at midday and
can be forced to read the future by anyone
who holds him while he takes many frighten-
ing shapes. Triton is the son of the sea-god
Neptune; the sound of his conch-shell horn
calms the waves.

²⁵ Whate'er the theme, the Maiden sang
As if her song could have no ending;
I saw her singing at her work,
And o'er the sickle bending—
I listened, motionless and still;
³⁰ And, as I mounted up the hill,
The music in my heart I bore,
Long after it was heard no more.

1807

Surprised by Joy

Surprised by joy—impatient as the Wind
I turned to share the transport—Oh! with whom
But thee,[5] deep buried in the silent tomb,
That spot which no vicissitude can find?
⁵ Love, faithful love, recalled thee to my mind—
But how could I forget thee? Through what power,
Even for the least division of an hour,
Have I been so beguiled as to be blind
To my most grievous loss!—That thought's return
¹⁰ Was the worst pang that sorrow ever bore,
Save one, one only, when I stood forlorn,
Knowing my heart's best treasure was no more;
That neither present time, nor years unborn
Could to my sight that heavenly face restore.

1815

Mutability

From low to high doth dissolution climb,
And sink from high to low, along a scale
Of awful notes, whose concord shall not fail;
A musical but melancholy chime,
⁵ Which they can hear who meddle not with crime,
Nor avarice, nor over-anxious care.
Truth fails not; but her outward forms that bear
The longest date do melt like frosty rime,°   *thin coating*
That in the morning whitened hill and plain
¹⁰ And is no more; drop like the tower sublime
Of yesterday, which royally did wear
His crown of weeds, but could not even sustain
Some casual shout that broke the silent air,
Or the unimaginable touch of Time.

1822

Scorn Not the Sonnet

Scorn not the sonnet; critic, you have frowned,
Mindless of its just honors; with this key
Shakespeare unlocked his heart; the melody
Of this small lute gave ease to Petrarch's[6] wound;
⁵ A thousand times this pipe did Tasso[7] sound;
With it Camöens soothed an exile's grief;[8]
The sonnet glittered a gay myrtle leaf
Amid the cypress with which Dante crowned

5. The poet's daughter Catharine, who died
at the age of four, in 1812.
6. Italian poet (1304–74) whose "wound" was
his unconsummated love for "Laura."

7. Italian poet (1544–95).
8. Camöens, a Portuguese poet (1524?–80),
was banished from the royal court.

His visionary brow; a glow-worm lamp,
It cheered mild Spenser, called from Faeryland
To struggle through dark ways; and, when a damp°   *dark mist*
Fell round the path of Milton, in his hand
The thing became a trumpet; whence he blew
Soul-animating strains—alas, too few!

1827

Extempore Effusion upon the Death of James Hogg[9]

When first, descending from the moorlands,
I saw the Stream of Yarrow glide
Along a bare and open valley,
The Ettrick Shepherd was my guide.

When last along its banks I wandered,
Through groves that had begun to shed
Their golden leaves upon the pathways,
My steps the Border-minstrel[1] led.

The mighty Minstrel breathes no longer,
'Mid moldering ruins low he lies;
And death upon the braes° of Yarrow,   *banks*
Has closed the Shepherd-poet's eyes:

Nor has the rolling year twice measured,
From sign to sign, its steadfast course,
Since every mortal power of Coleridge[2]
Was frozen at its marvelous source;

The rapt One,[3] of the godlike forehead,
The heaven-eyed creature sleeps in earth:
And Lamb,[4] the frolic and the gentle,
Has vanished from his lonely hearth.

Like clouds that rake the mountain summits,
Or waves that own no curbing hand,
How fast has brother followed brother,
From sunshine to the sunless land!

Yet I, whose lids from infant slumber
Were earlier raised, remain to hear
A timid voice, that asks in whispers,
"Who next will drop and disappear?"

Our haughty life is crowned with darkness,
Like London with its own black wreath,
On which with thee, O Crabbe![5] forth-looking,
I gazed from Hampstead's breezy heath.

As if but yesterday departed,
Thou too art gone before; but why,
O'er ripe fruit, seasonably gathered,
Should frail survivors heave a sigh?

9. Scottish poet (1770–1835) born in Ettrick;
for a time he was a shepherd. An *extempore
effusion* is a poem composed rapidly, without
premeditation.
1. Sir Walter Scott, famous Scottish poet and
novelist (1771–1832).
2. Wordsworth's friend and collaborator, who

died in 1834.
3. Coleridge (alluding to his "mystical"
philosophy).
4. Charles Lamb (1775–1834), essayist and
critic, friend of Wordsworth and Coleridge.
5. George Crabbe (1754–1832), poet, acquaint-
ance of Wordsworth.

Mourn rather for that holy Spirit,
Sweet as the spring, as ocean deep;
For her[6] who, ere her summer faded,
40 Has sunk into a breathless sleep.

No more of old romantic sorrows,
For slaughtered Youth or lovelorn Maid!
With sharper grief is Yarrow smitten,
And Ettrick mourns with her their Poet dead.

1835

So Fair, So Sweet, Withal So Sensitive

So fair, so sweet, withal so sensitive,
Would that the little Flowers were born to live,
Conscious of half the pleasure which they give;

That to this mountain-daisy's self were known
5 The beauty of its star-shaped shadow, thrown
On the smooth surface of this naked stone!

And what if hence a bold desire should mount
High as the Sun, that he could take account
Of all that issues from his glorious fount!

10 So might he ken how by his sovereign aid
These delicate companionships are made;
And how he rules the pomp of light and shade;

And were the Sister-power that shines by night
So privileged, what a countenance of delight
15 Would through the clouds break forth on human sight!

Fond fancies! wheresoe'er shall turn thine eye
On earth, air, ocean, or the starry sky,
Converse with Nature in pure sympathy;

All vain desires, all lawless wishes quelled,
20 Be Thou to love and praise alike impelled,
Whatever boon° is granted or withheld.

gift
1845

SAMUEL TAYLOR COLERIDGE
(1772–1834)

The Aeolian Harp[1]

COMPOSED AT CLEVEDON, SOMERSETSHIRE

My pensive Sara![2] thy soft cheek reclined
Thus on mine arm, most soothing sweet it is
To sit beside our Cot,° our Cot o'ergrown   *cottage*

6. Felicia Hemans (1793–1835), popular poetess, noted for her beauty and conversation.
1. The wind-harp (named after Aeolus, classical god of winds) has a sounding board equipped with a set of strings that vibrate in response to air currents; it was much in favor with German and English Romantic writers.
2. Coleridge's bride; the poem was composed during their honeymoon.

With white-flowered Jasmin, and the broad-leaved Myrtle,
5 (Meet emblems they of Innocence and Love!)
And watch the clouds, that late were rich with light,
Slow saddening round, and mark the star of eve
Serenely brilliant (such should Wisdom be)
Shine opposite! How exquisite the scents
10 Snatched from yon bean-field! and the world *so* hushed!
The stilly murmur of the distant Sea
Tells us of silence.

       And that simplest Lute,
Placed length-ways in the clasping casement, hark!
How by the desultory breeze caressed,
15 Like some coy maid half yielding to her lover,
It pours such sweet upbraiding, as must needs
Tempt to repeat the wrong! And now, its strings
Boldlier swept, the long sequacious° notes   *uninterruptedly flowing*
Over delicious surges sink and rise,
20 Such a soft floating witchery of sound
As twilight Elfins make, when they at eve
Voyage on gentle gales from Fairy-Land,
Where Melodies round honey-dropping flowers,
Footless and wild, like birds of Paradise,[3]
25 Nor pause, nor perch, hovering on untamed wing!
O! the one Life within us and abroad,
Which meets all motion and becomes its soul,
A light in sound, a sound-like power in light,
Rhythm in all thought, and joyance everywhere—
30 Methinks, it should have been impossible
Not to love all things in a world so filled;
Where the breeze warbles, and the mute still air
Is Music slumbering on her instrument.

       And thus, my Love! as on the midway slope
35 Of yonder hill I stretch my limbs at noon,
Whilst through my half-closed eyelids I behold
The sunbeams dance, like diamonds, on the main,
And tranquil muse upon tranquility:
Full many a thought uncalled and undetained,
40 And many idle flitting phantasies,
Traverse my indolent and passive brain,
As wild and various as the random gales
That swell and flutter on this subject Lute!

       And what if all of animated nature
45 Be but organic Harps diversely framed,
That tremble into thought, as o'er them sweeps
Plastic and vast, one intellectual breeze,
At once the Soul of each, and God of all?
       But thy more serious eye a mild reproof
50 Darts, O belovéd Woman! nor such thoughts
Dim and unhallowed dost thou not reject,
And biddest me walk humbly with my God.
Meek Daughter in the family of Christ!
Well hast thou said and holily dispraised

3. Bright-plumaged birds of New Guinea and nearby islands; mistakenly supposed to have
no feet and to spend their lives on the wing.

55 These shapings of the unregenerate mind;
Bubbles that glitter as they rise and break
On vain Philosophy's aye-babbling spring.
For never guiltless may I speak of him,
The Incomprehensible! save when with awe
60 I praise him, and with Faith that inly *feels;*
Who with his saving mercies healéd me,
A sinful and most miserable man,
Wildered and dark, and gave me to possess
Peace, and this Cot, and thee, heart-honored Maid!

1796, 1817

Kubla Khan[4]

OR A VISION IN A DREAM. A FRAGMENT

In Xanadu did Kubla Khan
A stately pleasure dome decree:
Where Alph, the sacred river, ran
Through caverns measureless to man
5   Down to a sunless sea.
So twice five miles of fertile ground
With walls and towers were girdled round:
And there were gardens bright with sinuous rills,
Where blossomed many an incense-bearing tree;
10 And here were forests ancient as the hills,
Enfolding sunny spots of greenery.

But oh! that deep romantic chasm which slanted
Down the green hill athwart a cedarn cover!
A savage place! as holy and enchanted
15 As e'er beneath a waning moon was haunted
By woman wailing for her demon lover!
And from this chasm, with ceaseless turmoil seething,
As if this earth in fast thick pants were breathing,
A mighty fountain momently was forced:
20 Amid whose swift half-intermitted burst
Huge fragments vaulted like rebounding hail,
Or chaffy grain beneath the thresher's flail:
And 'mid these dancing rocks at once and ever
It flung up momently the sacred river.
25 Five miles meandering with a mazy motion
Through wood and dale the sacred river ran,
Then reached the caverns measureless to man,

4. The first *khan*, or ruler, of the Mongol dynasty in 13th-century China. The topography and place-names are fictitious. In a prefatory note to the poem, Coleridge gave the following background: "In the summer of the year 1797, the author, then in ill health, had retired to a lonely farmhouse between Porlock and Linton, on the Exmoor confines of Somerset and Devonshire. In consequence of a slight indisposition, an anodyne had been prescribed, from the effects of which he fell asleep in his chair at the moment that he was reading the following sentence, or words of the same substance, in *Purchas's Pilgrimage*: "Here the Khan Kubla commanded a palace to be built, and a stately garden thereunto. And thus ten miles of fertile ground were inclosed with a wall." The author continued for about three hours in a profound sleep, at least of the external sense, during which time he has the most vivid confidence that he could not have composed less than from two to three hundred lines; if that indeed can be called composition in which all the images rose up before him as *things,* with a parallel production of the correspondent expressions, without any sensation or consciousness of effort. On awaking he appeared to himself to have a distinct recollection of the whole, and taking his pen, ink, and paper, instantly and eagerly wrote down the lines that are here preserved. At this moment he was unfortunately called out by a person on business from Porlock, and detained by him above an hour, and on his return to his room, found, to his no small surprise and mortification, that though he still retained some vague and dim recollection of the general purport of the vision, yet, with the exception of some eight or ten scattered lines and images, all the rest had passed away like the images on the surface of a stream into which a stone has been cast, but, alas! without the after restoration of the latter!"

And sank in tumult to a lifeless ocean:
And 'mid this tumult Kubla heard from far
30 Ancestral voices prophesying war!

The shadow of the dome of pleasure
Floated midway on the waves;
Where was heard the mingled measure
From the fountain and the caves.
35 It was a miracle of rare device,
A sunny pleasure dome with caves of ice!

A damsel with a dulcimer[5]
In a vision once I saw:
It was an Abyssinian maid,
40 And on her dulcimer she played,
Singing of Mount Abora.
Could I revive within me
Her symphony and song,
To such a deep delight 'twould win me,
45 That with music loud and long,
I would build that dome in air,
That sunny dome! those caves of ice!
And all who heard should see them there,
And all should cry, Beware! Beware!
50 His flashing eyes, his floating hair!
Weave a circle round him thrice,
And close your eyes with holy dread,
For he on honey-dew hath fed,
And drunk the milk of Paradise.

                                    1797–98   1816

Frost at Midnight

The Frost performs its secret ministry,
Unhelped by any wind. The owlet's cry
Came loud—and hark, again! loud as before.
The inmates of my cottage, all at rest,
5 Have left me to that solitude, which suits
Abstruser musings: save that at my side
My cradled infant[6] slumbers peacefully.
'Tis calm indeed! so calm, that it disturbs
And vexes meditation with its strange
10 And extreme silentness. Sea, hill, and wood,
This populous village! Sea, and hill, and wood,
With all the numberless goings-on of life,
Inaudible as dreams! the thin blue flame
Lies on my low-burnt fire, and quivers not;
15 Only that film,[7] which fluttered on the grate,
Still flutters there, the sole unquiet thing.
Methinks its motion in this hush of nature
Gives it dim sympathies with me who live,
Making it a companionable form,
20 Whose puny flaps and freaks the idling Spirit
By its own moods interprets, everywhere
Echo or mirror seeking of itself,
And makes a toy of Thought.

---

5. A harp-like instrument.
6. Coleridge's son Hartley.
7. Embers flickering in the grate of a fireplace;
in folklore said to forecast the arrival of an unexpected guest; hence called *strangers* (lines 26, 41).

But O! how oft,
How oft, at school, with most believing mind,
25   Presageful,° have I gazed upon the bars,   *foretelling*
To watch that fluttering *stranger!* and as oft
With unclosed lids, already had I dreamt
Of my sweet birthplace, and the old church tower,
Whose bells, the poor man's only music, rang
30   From morn to evening, all the hot Fair-day,⁸
So sweetly, that they stirred and haunted me
With a wild pleasure, falling on mine ear
Most like articulate sounds of things to come!
So gazed I, till the soothing things, I dreamt,
35   Lulled me to sleep, and sleep prolonged my dreams!
And so I brooded all the following morn,
Awed by the stern preceptor's° face, mine eye   *schoolmaster's*
Fixed with mock study on my swimming book:⁹
Save if the door half opened, and I snatched
40   A hasty glance, and still my heart leaped up,
For still I hoped to see the *stranger's* face,
Townsman, or aunt, or sister more beloved,
My playmate when we both were clothed alike!¹

Dear Babe, that sleepest cradled by my side,
45   Whose gentle breathings, heard in this deep calm,
Fill up the interspersèd vacancies
And momentary pauses of the thought!
My babe so beautiful! it thrills my heart
With tender gladness, thus to look at thee,
50   And think that thou shalt learn far other lore,
And in far other scenes! For I was reared
In the great city, pent 'mid cloisters dim,
And saw nought lovely but the sky and stars.
But *thou*, my babe! shalt wander like a breeze
55   By lakes and sandy shores, beneath the crags
Of ancient mountain, and beneath the clouds,
Which image in their bulk both lakes and shores
And mountain crags: so shalt thou see and hear
The lovely shapes and sounds intelligible
60   Of that eternal language, which thy God
Utters, who from eternity doth teach
Himself in all, and all things in himself.
Great universal Teacher! he shall mold
Thy spirit, and by giving make it ask.

65   Therefore all seasons shall be sweet to thee,
Whether the summer clothe the general° earth   *generative, vernal*
With greenness, or the redbreast sit and sing
Betwixt the tufts of snow on the bare branch
Of mossy apple tree, while the nigh thatch
70   Smokes in the sun-thaw; whether the eave-drops fall
Heard only in the trances of the blast,
Or if the secret ministry of frost
Shall hang them up in silent icicles,
Quietly shining to the quiet Moon.

1798

8. Market-day, often a time of festivities.
9. I.e., seen unclearly because of emotion.

1. In early childhood, when boys and girls
wore the same kind of infants' clothing.

The Nightingale

A CONVERSATION POEM, APRIL, 1798

No cloud, no relique of the sunken day
Distinguishes the West, no long thin slip
Of sullen light, no obscure trembling hues.
Come, we will rest on this old mossy bridge!
5   You see the glimmer of the stream beneath,
But hear no murmuring: it flows silently,
O'er its soft bed of verdure. All is still,
A balmy night! and though the stars be dim,
Yet let us think upon the vernal showers
10   That gladden the green earth, and we shall find
A pleasure in the dimness of the stars.
And hark! the Nightingale begins its song,
'Most musical, most melancholy'[2] bird!
A melancholy bird? Oh! idle thought!
15   In Nature there is nothing melancholy.
But some night-wandering man whose heart was pierced
With the remembrance of a grievous wrong,
Or slow distemper, or neglected love,
(And so, poor wretch! filled all things with himself,
20   And made all gentle sounds tell back the tale
Of his own sorrow) he, and such as he,
First named these notes a melancholy strain.
And many a poet echoes the conceit;[3]
Poet who hath been building up the rhyme
25   When he had better far have stretched his limbs
Beside a brook in mossy forest-dell,
By sun or moon-light, to the influxes
Of shapes and sounds and shifting elements
Surrendering his whole spirit, of his song
30   And of his fame forgetful! so his fame
Should share in Nature's immortality,
A venerable thing! and so his song
Should make all Nature lovelier, and itself
Be loved like Nature! But 'twill not be so;
35   And youths and maidens most poetical,
Who lose the deepening twilights of the spring
In ball-rooms and hot theaters, they still
Full of meek sympathy must heave their sighs
O'er Philomela's pity-pleading strains.

40   My Friend, and thou, our Sister![4] we have learnt
A different lore: we may not thus profane
Nature's sweet voices, always full of love
And joyance! 'Tis the merry Nightingale
That crowds, and hurries, and precipitates
45   With fast thick warble his delicious notes,
As he were fearful that an April night
Would be too short for him to utter forth
His love-chant, and disburthen his full soul
Of all its music!

---

2. From Milton's *Il Penseroso*, line 62.
3. I.e., the convention that the nightingale personifies the mythical Greek maiden, Philomel, who was ravished by King Tereus, her brother-in-law, and who still laments her fate (line 39).
4. William Wordsworth and his sister Dorothy.

And I know a grove
50 Of large extent, hard by a castle huge,
Which the great lord inhabits not; and so
This grove is wild with tangling underwood,
And the trim walks are broken up, and grass,
Thin grass and king-cups grow within the paths.
55 But never elsewhere in one place I knew
So many nightingales; and far and near,
In wood and thicket, over the wide grove,
They answer and provoke each other's song,
With skirmish and capricious passagings,
60 And murmurs musical and swift jug jug,[5]
And one low piping sound more sweet than all—
Stirring the air with such a harmony,
That should you close your eyes, you might almost
Forget it was not day! On moonlight bushes,
65 Whose dewy leaflets are but half-disclosed,
You may perchance behold them on the twigs,
Their bright, bright eyes, their eyes both bright and full,
Glistening, while many a glow-worm in the shade
Lights up her love-torch.

A most gentle Maid,
70 Who dwelleth in her hospitable home
Hard by the castle, and at latest eve
(Even like a Lady vowed and dedicate
To something more than Nature in the grove)
Glides through the pathways; she knows all their notes,
75 That gentle Maid! and oft, a moment's space,
What time[6] the moon was lost behind a cloud,
Hath heard a pause of silence; till the moon
Emerging, hath awakened earth and sky
With one sensation, and those wakeful birds
80 Have all burst forth in choral minstrelsy,
As if some sudden gale had swept at once
A hundred airy harps! And she hath watched
Many a nightingale perch giddily
On blossomy twig still swinging from the breeze,
85 And to that motion tune his wanton song
Like tipsy Joy that reels with tossing head.

Farewell, O Warbler! till tomorrow eve,
And you, my friends! farewell, a short farewell!
We have been loitering long and pleasantly,
90 And now for our dear homes.—That strain again!
Full fain it would delay me! My dear babe,
Who, capable of no articulate sound,
Mars all things with his imitative lisp,
How he would place his hand beside his ear,
95 His little hand, the small forefinger up,
And bid us listen! And I deem it wise
To make him Nature's playmate. He knows well
The evening-star; and once, when he awoke
In most distressful mood (some inward pain
100 Had made up that strange thing, an infant's dream—)
I hurried with him to our orchard-plot,
And he beheld the moon, and, hushed at once,

---

5. Traditional onomatopoetic representation of   6. I.e., at the time when.
a nightingale's throbbing song.

Suspends his sobs, and laughs most silently,
While his fair eyes, that swam with undropped tears,
105 Did glitter in the yellow moonbeam! Well!—
It is a father's tale: But if that Heaven
Should give me life, his childhood shall grow up
Familiar with these songs, that with the night
He may associate joy.—Once more, farewell,
110 Sweet Nightingale! once more, my friends! farewell.

1798

The Rime of the Ancient Mariner

IN SEVEN PARTS

Facile credo, plures esse Naturas invisibiles quam visibiles in rerum universitate. Sed horum [sic] *omnium familiam quis nobis enarrabit? et gradus et cognationes et discrimina et singulorum munera? Quid agunt? quae loca habitant? Harum rerum notitiam semper ambivit ingenium humanum, nunquam attigit. Juvat, interea, non diffiteor, quandoque in animo, in tabulâ, majoris et melioris mundi imaginem contemplari: ne mens assuefacta hodiernae vitae minutiis se contrahat nimis, et tota subsidat in pusillas cogitationes. Sed veritati interea invigilandum est, modusque servandus, ut certa ab incertis, diem a nocte, distinguamus.*

—T. BURNET[7]

Part I

An ancient Mariner meeteth three Gallants bidden to a wedding feast, and detaineth one.

It is an ancient Mariner
And he stoppeth one of three.
—"By thy long gray beard and glittering eye,
Now wherefore stopp'st thou me?

The Bridegroom's doors are opened wide,   5
And I am next of kin;
The guests are met, the feast is set:
May'st hear the merry din."

He holds him with his skinny hand,
"There was a ship," quoth he.   10
"Hold off! unhand me, graybeard loon!"
Eftsoons° his hand dropped he.   *straightway*

The Wedding Guest is spellbound by the eye of the old seafaring man, and constrained to hear his tale.

He holds him with his glittering eye—
The Wedding Guest stood still,
And listens like a three years' child: 15
The Mariner hath his will.

The Wedding Guest sat on a stone:
He cannot choose but hear;
And thus spake on that ancient man,
The bright-eyed Mariner.   20

"The ship was cheered, the harbor cleared,
Merrily did we drop
Below the kirk,° below the hill,   *church*
Below the lighthouse top.

---

7. From *Archaeologiae Philosophiae*, p. 68. "I can easily believe that there are more invisible than visible beings in the universe. But of their families, degrees, connections, distinctions, and functions, who shall tell us? How do they act? Where are they found? About such matters the human mind has always circled without attaining knowledge. Yet I do not doubt that sometimes it is well for the soul to contemplate as in a picture the image of a larger and better world, lest the mind, habituated to the small concerns of daily life, limit itself too much and sink entirely into trivial thinking. But meanwhile we must be on watch for the truth, avoiding extremes, so that we may distinguish certain from uncertain, day from night." Burnet was a 17th-century English theologian.

The Mariner
tells how the
ship sailed south-
ward with a good
wind and fair
weather, till it
reached the line.

The Sun came up upon the left,   25
Out of the sea came he!
And he shone bright, and on the right
Went down into the sea.

Higher and higher every day,
Till over the mast at noon—"   30
The Wedding Guest here beat his breast,
For he heard the loud bassoon.

The Wedding
Guest heareth
the bridal music;
but the Mariner
continueth his
tale.

The bride hath paced into the hall,
Red as a rose is she;
Nodding their heads before her goes   35
The merry minstrelsy.

The Wedding Guest he beat his breast,
Yet he cannot choose but hear;
And thus spake on that ancient man,
The bright-eyed Mariner.   40

The ship driven
by a storm to-
ward the South
Pole.

"And now the STORM-BLAST came, and he
Was tyrannous and strong;
He struck with his o'ertaking wings,
And chased us south along.

With sloping masts and dipping prow,   45
As who pursued with yell and blow
Still treads the shadow of his foe,
And forward bends his head,
The ship drove fast, loud roared the blast,
And southward aye we fled.   50

And now there came both mist and snow,
And it grew wondrous cold:
And ice, mast-high, came floating by,
As green as emerald.

The land of ice,
and of fearful
sounds where no
living thing was
to be seen.

And through the drifts the snowy clifts°   *cliffs* 55
Did send a dismal sheen:
Nor shapes of men nor beasts we ken—
The ice was all between.

The ice was here, the ice was there,
The ice was all around: 60
It cracked and growled, and roared and howled,
Like noises in a swound!°   *swoon*

Till a great sea
bird, called the
Albatross, came
through the
snow-fog, and
was received
with great joy
and hospitality.

At length did cross an Albatross,
Thorough the fog it came;
As if it had been a Christian soul,
We hailed it in God's name.   65

It ate the food it ne'er had eat,
And round and round it flew.
The ice did split with a thunder-fit;
The helmsman steered us through!   70

*And lo! the Al-
batross proveth
a bird of good
omen, and fol-
loweth the ship
as it returned
northward
through fog and
floating ice.*

And a good south wind sprung up behind;
The Albatross did follow,
And every day, for food or play,
Came to the mariners' hollo!

In mist or cloud, on mast or shroud,   75
It perched for vespers nine;
Whiles all the night, through fog-smoke white,
Glimmered the white Moon-shine."

*The ancient
Mariner inhospi-
tably killeth the
pious bird of
good omen.*

"God save thee, ancient Mariner!
From the fiends, that plague thee thus!—   80
Why look'st thou so?"—With my crossbow
I shot the ALBATROSS.

Part II

The Sun now rose upon the right:
Out of the sea came he,
Still hid in mist, and on the left   85
Went down into the sea.

And the good south wind still blew behind,
But no sweet bird did follow,
Nor any day for food or play
Came to the mariners' hollo!   90

*His shipmates
cry out against
the ancient Mar-
iner, for killing
the bird of good
luck.*

And I had done a hellish thing,
And it would work 'em woe:
For all averred, I had killed the bird
That made the breeze to blow.   95
Ah wretch! said they, the bird to slay,
That made the breeze to blow!

*But when the
fog cleared off,
they justify the
same, and thus
make themselves
accomplices in
the crime.*

Nor dim nor red, like God's own head,
The glorious Sun uprist:°   *arose*
Then all averred, I had killed the bird
That brought the fog and mist.   100
'Twas right, said they, such birds to slay,
That bring the fog and mist.

*The fair breeze
continues; the
ship enters the
Pacific Ocean,
and sails north-
ward, even till it
reaches the Line.*

The fair breeze blew, the white foam flew,
The furrow followed free;
We were the first that ever burst   105
Into that silent sea.

*The ship hath
been suddenly
becalmed.*

Down dropped the breeze, the sails dropped down,
'Twas sad as sad could be;
And we did speak only to break
The silence of the sea!   110

All in a hot and copper sky,
The bloody Sun, at noon,
Right up above the mast did stand,
No bigger than the Moon.

Day after day, day after day,   11
We stuck, nor breath nor motion;
As idle as a painted ship
Upon a painted ocean.

And the Alba-
tross begins to
be avenged.
Water, water, everywhere,   120
And all the boards did shrink;
Water, water, everywhere,
Nor any drop to drink.

The very deep did rot: O Christ!
That ever this should be!
Yea, slimy things did crawl with legs   125
Upon the slimy sea.

About, about, in reel and rout
The death-fires danced at night;
The water, like a witch's oils,
Burnt green, and blue and white.   130

And some in dreams assuréd were
A Spirit had
followed them;   Of the Spirit that plagued us so;
one of the invis-   Nine fathom deep he had followed us
ible inhabitants   From the land of mist and snow.
of this planet,
neither departed souls nor angels; concerning whom the learned Jew, Josephus, and the Platonic Co
stantinopolitan, Michael Psellus, may be consulted. They are very numerous, and there is no climate o
element without one or more.

And every tongue, through utter drought,   135
Was withered at the root;
We could not speak, no more than if
We had been choked with soot.

The shipmates,
in their sore dis-   Ah! well-a-day! what evil looks
tress, would fain   Had I from old and young!
throw the whole   Instead of the cross, the Albatross   140
guilt on the an-   About my neck was hung.
cient Mariner:
in sign whereof they hang the dead sea bird round his neck.

Part III

There passed a weary time. Each throat
Was parched, and glazed each eye.
A weary time! a weary time!
How glazed each weary eye,   145
The ancient Mar-   When looking westward, I beheld
iner beholdeth a   A something in the sky.
sign in the ele-
ment afar off.

At first it seemed a little speck,
And then it seemed a mist;
It moved and moved, and took at last   150
A certain shape, I wist.°
                                                                            knew

A speck, a mist, a shape, I wist!
And still it neared and neared:
As if it dodged a water sprite,
It plunged and tacked and veered.   155

<table>
<tr><td>At its nearer approach, it seemeth him to be a ship; and at a dear ransom he freeth his speech from the bonds of thirst.</td><td>

With throats unslaked, with black lips baked,
We could nor laugh nor wail;
Through utter drought all dumb we stood!
I bit my arm, I sucked the blood,
And cried, A sail! a sail!</td><td align="right">160</td></tr>
</table>

<table>
<tr><td></td><td>

With throats unslaked, with black lips baked,
Agape they heard me call:</td><td></td></tr>
<tr><td>A flash of joy;</td><td>

Gramercy!° they for joy did grin,
And all at once their breath drew in,
As they were drinking all.</td><td align="right">thank heavens!
165</td></tr>
</table>

<table>
<tr><td>And horror follows. For can it be a ship that comes onward without wind or tide?</td><td>

See! see! (I cried) she tacks no more!
Hither to work us weal;°
Without a breeze, without a tide,
She steadies with upright keel!</td><td align="right">benefit

170</td></tr>
</table>

The western wave was all aflame.
The day was well nigh done!
Almost upon the western wave
Rested the broad bright Sun;
When that strange shape drove suddenly   175
Betwixt us and the Sun.

<table>
<tr><td>It seemeth him but the skeleton of a ship.</td><td>

And straight the Sun was flecked with bars,
(Heaven's Mother send us grace!)
As if through a dungeon grate he peered
With broad and burning face.</td><td align="right">180</td></tr>
</table>

<table>
<tr><td>And its ribs are seen as bars on the face of the setting Sun.</td><td>

Alas! (thought I, and my heart beat loud)
How fast she nears and nears!
Are those *her* sails that glance in the Sun,
Like restless gossameres?</td><td></td></tr>
</table>

<table>
<tr><td>The Specter-Woman and her Deathmate, and no other on board the skeleton ship.</td><td>

Are those *her* ribs through which the Sun
Did peer, as through a grate?
And is that Woman all her crew?
Is that a DEATH? and are there two?
Is DEATH that woman's mate?</td><td align="right">185</td></tr>
</table>

<table>
<tr><td>Like vessel, like crew!</td><td>

Her lips were red, *her* looks were free,
Her locks were yellow as gold:
Her skin was as white as leprosy,
The Nightmare LIFE-IN-DEATH was she,
Who thicks man's blood with cold.</td><td align="right">190</td></tr>
</table>

<table>
<tr><td>Death and Life-in-Death have diced for the ship's crew, and she (the latter) winneth the ancient Mariner.</td><td>

The naked hulk alongside came,
And the twain were casting dice;
"The game is done! I've won! I've won!"
Quoth she, and whistles thrice.</td><td align="right">195</td></tr>
</table>

<table>
<tr><td>No twilight within the courts of the Sun.</td><td>

The Sun's rim dips; the stars rush out:
At one stride comes the dark;
With far-heard whisper, o'er the sea,
Off shot the specter-bark.</td><td align="right">200</td></tr>
</table>

At the rising of
the Moon,

We listened and looked sideways up!
Fear at my heart, as at a cup,
My lifeblood seemed to sip!
The stars were dim, and thick the night,
The steersman's face by his lamp gleamed white;   205
From the sails the dew did drip—
Till clomb above the eastern bar
The hornéd Moon, with one bright star
Within the nether tip.   210

One after an-
other,

One after one, by the star-dogged Moon,
Too quick for groan or sigh,
Each turned his face with ghastly pang,
And cursed me with his eye.   215

His shipmates
drop down dead.

Four times fifty living men,
(And I heard nor sigh nor groan)
With heavy thump, a lifeless lump,
They dropped down one by one.

But Life-in-
Death begins her
work on the an-
cient Mariner.

The souls did from their bodies fly—   220
They fled to bliss or woe!
And every soul, it passed me by,
Like the whizz of my cross-bow!

Part IV

The Wedding
Guest feareth
that a Spirit is
talking to him;

"I fear thee, ancient Mariner!
I fear thy skinny hand!
And thou art long, and lank, and brown,   225
As is the ribbed sea-sand.

But the ancient
Mariner assureth
him of his bodily
life, and pro-
ceedeth to relate
his horrible pen-
ance.

I fear thee and thy glittering eye,
And thy skinny hand, so brown."—
Fear not, fear not, thou Wedding Guest!
This body dropped not down.   230

Alone, alone, all, all alone,
Alone on a wide wide sea!
And never a saint took pity on
My soul in agony.   235

He despiseth the
creatures of the
calm,

The many men, so beautiful!
And they all dead did lie:
And a thousand thousand slimy things
Lived on; and so did I.

And envieth that
they should live,
and so many lie
dead.

I looked upon the rotting sea,
And drew my eyes away;   240
I looked upon the rotting deck,
And there the dead men lay.

I looked to heaven, and tried to pray;
But or ever a prayer had gushed,
A wicked whisper came, and made   245
My heart as dry as dust.

I closed my lids, and kept them close,
And the balls like pulses beat,
For the sky and the sea, and the sea and the sky   250
Lay like a load on my weary eye,
And the dead were at my feet.

*But the curse
liveth for him in
the eye of the
dead men.*
The cold sweat melted from their limbs,
Nor rot nor reek did they:
The look with which they looked on me   255
Had never passed away.

An orphan's curse would drag to hell
A spirit from on high;
But oh! more horrible than that
Is the curse in a dead man's eye!   260
Seven days, seven nights, I saw that curse,
And yet I could not die.

The moving Moon went up the sky,
And nowhere did abide:
*In his loneliness
and fixedness he
yearneth towards
the journeying
Moon, and the
stars that still
sojourn, yet still
move onward;
and everywhere
the blue sky be-
longs to them,
and is their ap-
pointed rest, and
their native*
Softly she was going up,   265
And a star or two beside—

Her beams bemocked the sultry main,
Like April hoar-frost spread;
But where the ship's huge shadow lay,
The charmèd water burnt alway   270
A still and awful red.

*country and their own natural homes, which they enter unannounced, as lords that are certainly
expected and yet there is a silent joy at their arrival.*

*By the light of
the Moon he be-
holdeth God's
creatures of the
great calm.*
Beyond the shadow of the ship,
I watched the water snakes:
They moved in tracks of shining white,
And when they reared, the elfish light   275
Fell off in hoary° flakes.   **gray or white**

Within the shadow of the ship
I watched their rich attire:
Blue, glossy green, and velvet black,
They coiled and swam; and every track   280
Was a flash of golden fire.

*Their beauty and
their happiness.*
O happy living things! no tongue
Their beauty might declare:
A spring of love gushed from my heart,
*He blesseth them
in his heart.*
And I blessed them unaware: 285
Sure my kind saint took pity on me,
And I blessed them unaware.

*The spell begins
to break.*
The self-same moment I could pray;
And from my neck so free
The Albatross fell off, and sank   290
Like lead into the sea.

Part V

Oh sleep! it is a gentle thing,
Beloved from pole to pole!
To Mary Queen the praise be given!
She sent the gentle sleep from Heaven,
That slid into my soul.   29

By grace of the holy Mother, the ancient Mariner is refreshed with rain.

The silly° buckets on the deck,   lowly, harmles
That had so long remained,
I dreamt that they were filled with dew;
And when I awoke, it rained.   300

My lips were wet, my throat was cold,
My garments all were dank;
Sure I had drunken in my dreams,
And still my body drank.

I moved, and could not feel my limbs: 305
I was so light—almost
I thought that I had died in sleep,
And was a blessèd ghost.

He heareth sounds and seeth strange sights and commotions in the sky and the element.

And soon I heard a roaring wind:
It did not come anear;   310
But with its sound it shook the sails,
That were so thin and sere.

The upper air burst into life!
And a hundred fire-flags sheen,°   shone
To and fro they were hurried about!   315
And to and fro, and in and out,
The wan stars danced between.

And the coming wind did roar more loud,
And the sails did sigh like sedge;⁸
And the rain poured down from one black cloud;   320
The Moon was at its edge.

The thick black cloud was cleft, and still
The Moon was at its side:
Like waters shot from some high crag,
The lightning fell with never a jag,   325
A river steep and wide.

The bodies of the ship's crew are inspirited, and the ship moves on;

The loud wind never reached the ship,
Yet now the ship moved on!
Beneath the lightning and the Moon
The dead men gave a groan.   330

They groaned, they stirred, they all uprose,
Nor spake, nor moved their eyes;
It had been strange, even in a dream,
To have seen those dead men rise.

8. Rushlike plants bordering streams and lakes.

The helmsman steered, the ship moved on;   335
Yet never a breeze up-blew;
The mariners all 'gan work the ropes,
Where they were wont to do;
They raised their limbs like lifeless tools—
We were a ghastly crew.   340

The body of my brother's son
Stood by me, knee to knee:
The body and I pulled at one rope,
But he said nought to me.

"I fear thee, ancient Mariner!"   345
Be calm, thou Wedding Guest!
'Twas not those souls that fled in pain,
Which to their corses° came again,   *corpses*
But a troop of spirits blest:

But not by the
souls of the men,
nor by demons
of earth or mid-
dle air, but by a
blessèd troop of
angelic spirits,
sent down by
the invocation of
the guardian
saint.

For when it dawned—they dropped their arms,   350
And clustered round the mast;
Sweet sounds rose slowly through their mouths,
And from their bodies passed.

Around, around, flew each sweet sound,
Then darted to the Sun;   355
Slowly the sounds came back again,
Now mixed, now one by one.

Sometimes a-dropping from the sky
I heard the sky-lark sing;
Sometimes all little birds that are,   360
How they seemed to fill the sea and air
With their sweet jargoning!°   *warbling*

And now 'twas like all instruments,
Now like a lonely flute;
And now it is an angel's song,   365
That makes the heavens be mute.

It ceased; yet still the sails made on
A pleasant noise till noon,
A noise like of a hidden brook
In the leafy month of June,   370
That to the sleeping woods all night
Singeth a quiet tune.

Till noon we quietly sailed on,
Yet never a breeze did breathe:
Slowly and smoothly went the ship,   375
Moved onward from beneath.

*The lonesome
Spirit from the
South Pole car-
ries on the ship
as far as the
Line, in obedi-
ence to the an-
gelic troop, but
still requireth
vengeance.*

Under the keel nine fathom deep,
From the land of mist and snow,
The spirit slid: and it was he
That made the ship to go.
The sails at noon left off their tune,   380
And the ship stood still also.

The Sun, right up above the mast,
Had fixed her to the ocean:
But in a minute she 'gan stir,   385
With a short uneasy motion—
Backwards and forwards half her length
With a short uneasy motion.

Then like a pawing horse let go,
She made a sudden bound:
It flung the blood into my head,   390
And I fell down in a swound.

*The Polar
Spirit's fellow
demons, the in-
visible inhabit-
ants of the ele-
ment, take part
in his wrong;
and two of them
relate, one to the
other, that pen-
ance long and
heavy for the
ancient Mariner
hath been ac-
corded to the
Polar Spirit,
who returneth
southward.*

How long in that same fit I lay,
I have not° to declare;   *cannot*
But ere my living life returned,   395
I heard and in my soul discerned
Two voices in the air.

"Is it he?" quoth one, "Is this the man?
By him who died on cross,
With his cruel bow he laid full low   400
The harmless Albatross.

The spirit who bideth by himself
In the land of mist and snow,
He loved the bird that loved the man
Who shot him with his bow."   405

The other was a softer voice,
As soft as honey-dew:
Quoth he, "The man hath penance done,
And penance more will do."

Part VI

FIRST VOICE
"But tell me, tell me! speak again,
Thy soft response renewing—   410
What makes that ship drive on so fast?
What is the ocean doing?"

SECOND VOICE
"Still as a slave before his lord,
The ocean hath no blast;
His great bright eye most silently   415
Up to the Moon is cast—

If he may know which way to go;
For she guides him smooth or grim.
See, brother, see! how graciously
She looketh down on him."   420

FIRST VOICE

The Mariner
hath been cast
into a trance;
for the angelic
power causeth
the vessel to
drive northward
faster than hu-
man life could
endure.

"But why drives on that ship so fast,
Without or wave or wind?"

SECOND VOICE

"The air is cut away before,
And closes from behind.   425

Fly, brother, fly! more high, more high!
Or we shall be belated:
For slow and slow that ship will go,
When the Mariner's trance is abated."

The supernatural
motion is re-
tarded; the Mar-
iner awakes, and
his penance be-
gins anew.

I woke, and we were sailing on   430
As in a gentle weather:
'Twas night, calm night, the moon was high;
The dead men stood together.

All stood together on the deck,
For a charnel-dungeon fitter: 435
All fixed on me their stony eyes,
That in the Moon did glitter.

The pang, the curse, with which they died,
Had never passed away:
I could not draw my eyes from theirs,   440
Nor turn them up to pray.

The curse is
finally expiated.

And now this spell was snapped: once more
I viewed the ocean green,
And looked far forth, yet little saw
Of what had else been seen—   445

Like one, that on a lonesome road
Doth walk in fear and dread,
And having once turned round walks on,
And turns no more his head;
Because he knows, a frightful fiend   450
Doth close behind him tread.

But soon there breathed a wind on me,
Nor sound nor motion made:
Its path was not upon the sea,
In ripple or in shade.   455

It raised my hair, it fanned my cheek
Like a meadow-gale of spring—
It mingled strangely with my fears,
Yet it felt like a welcoming.

Swiftly, swiftly flew the ship,   460
Yet she sailed softly too:
Sweetly, sweetly blew the breeze—
On me alone it blew.

*And the ancient
Mariner behold-
eth his native
country.*

Oh! dream of joy! is this indeed
The lighthouse top I see?   465
Is this the hill? is this the kirk?
Is this mine own countree?

We drifted o'er the harbor-bar,
And I with sobs did pray—
O let me be awake, my God!   470
Or let me sleep alway.

The harbor-bay was clear as glass,
So smoothly it was strewn!
And on the bay the moonlight lay,
And the shadow of the Moon.   475

The rock shone bright, the kirk no less,
That stands above the rock:
The moonlight steeped in silentness
The steady weathercock.

And the bay was white with silent light,   480
Till rising from the same,
*The angelic
spirits leave the
dead bodies,* Full many shapes, that shadows were,
In crimson colors came.

A little distance from the prow
Those crimson shadows were:
*And appear in
their own forms
of light.* I turned my eyes upon the deck—   485
Oh, Christ! what saw I there!

Each corse lay flat, lifeless and flat,
And, by the holy rood!°   *cross of Christ*
A man all light, a seraph°-man,   *angel-like* 490
On every corse there stood.

This seraph-band, each waved his hand:
It was a heavenly sight!
They stood as signals to the land,
Each one a lovely light;   495

This seraph-band, each waved his hand,
No voice did they impart—
No voice; but oh! the silence sank
Like music on my heart.

But soon I heard the dash of oars,
I heard the Pilot's cheer;   500
My head was turned perforce away
And I saw a boat appear.

The Pilot and the Pilot's boy,
I heard them coming fast:
Dear Lord in Heaven! it was a joy   505
The dead men could not blast.

I saw a third—I heard his voice:
It is the Hermit good!
He singeth loud his godly hymns
                                                   510

That he makes in the wood.
He'll shrieve[9] my soul, he'll wash away
The Albatross's blood.

Part VII

The Hermit of
the Wood

This Hermit good lives in that wood
Which slopes down to the sea.   515
How loudly his sweet voice he rears!
He loves to talk with marineres
That come from a far countree.

He kneels at morn, and noon, and eve—
He hath a cushion plump: 520
It is the moss that wholly hides
The rotted old oak stump.

The skiff-boat neared: I heard them talk,
"Why, this is strange, I trow!
Where are those lights so many and fair,   525
That signal made but now?"

*Approacheth the
ship with won-
der.*

"Strange, by my faith!" the Hermit said—
"And they answered not our cheer!
The planks looked warped! and see those sails,
How thin they are and sere!   530
I never saw aught like to them,
Unless perchance it were

Brown skeletons of leaves that lag
My forest-brook along;
When the ivy tod° is heavy with snow,   *bushy clump* 535
And the owlet whoops to the wolf below,
That eats the she-wolf's young."

"Dear Lord! it hath a fiendish look,"
The Pilot made reply,
"I am a-feared"—"Push on, push on!"   540
Said the Hermit cheerily.

The boat came closer to the ship,
But I nor spake nor stirred;
The boat came close beneath the ship,
And straight a sound was heard.   545

*The ship sud-
denly sinketh.*

Under the water it rumbled on,
Still louder and more dread:
It reached the ship, it split the bay;
The ship went down like lead.

*The ancient
Mariner is saved
in the Pilot's
boat.*

Stunned by that loud and dreadful sound,   550
Which sky and ocean smote,
Like one that hath been seven days drowned
My body lay afloat;
But swift as dreams, myself I found
Within the Pilot's boat.   555

9. Set free from sin.

Upon the whirl, where sank the ship,
The boat spun round and round;
And all was still, save that the hill
Was telling of the sound.

I moved my lips—the Pilot shrieked   560
And fell down in a fit;
The holy Hermit raised his eyes,
And prayed where he did sit.

I took the oars: the Pilot's boy,
Who now doth crazy go,   565
Laughed loud and long, and all the while
His eyes went to and fro.
"Ha! ha!" quoth he, "full plain I see,
The Devil knows how to row."

And now, all in my own countree,   570
I stood on the firm land!
The Hermit stepped forth from the boat,
And scarcely he could stand.

*The ancient
Mariner ear-
nestly entreateth
the Hermit to
shrieve him; and
the penance of
life falls on him.*

"O shrieve me, shrieve me, holy man!"
The Hermit crossed[1] his brow.
"Say quick," quoth he, "I bid thee say—   575
What manner of man art thou?"

Forthwith this frame of mine was wrenched
With a woeful agony,
Which forced me to begin my tale;
And then it left me free.   580

*And ever and
anon throughout
his future life
an agony con-
straineth him to
travel from
land to land;*

Since then, at an uncertain hour,
That agony returns:
And till my ghastly tale is told,
This heart within me burns.   585

I pass, like night, from land to land;
I have strange power of speech;
That moment that his face I see,
I know the man that must hear me:
To him my tale I teach.   590

What loud uproar bursts from that door!
The wedding guests are there:
But in the garden-bower the bride
And bridemaids singing are:
And hark the little vesper bell,   595
Which biddeth me to prayer!

O Wedding Guest! this soul hath been
Alone on a wide wide sea:
So lonely 'twas, that God himself
Scarce seeméd there to be.   600

1. Made the sign of the cross upon.

O sweeter than the marriage feast,
'Tis sweeter far to me,
To walk together to the kirk
With a goodly company!

To walk together to the kirk,   605
And all together pray,
While each to his great Father bends,
Old men, and babes, and loving friends
And youths and maidens gay!

And to teach, by Farewell, farewell! but this I tell   610
his own exam-   To thee, thou Wedding Guest!
ple, love and   He prayeth well, who loveth well
reverence to all Both man and bird and beast.
things that God
made and loveth.

He prayeth best, who loveth best
All things both great and small;   615
For the dear God who loveth us,
He made and loveth all.

The Mariner, whose eye is bright,
Whose beard with age is hoar,
Is gone: and now the Wedding Guest   620
Turned from the bridegroom's door.

He went like one that hath been stunned,
And is of sense forlorn:°   *deprived*
A sadder and a wiser man,
He rose the morrow morn.

                                        1798   1817

Dejection: An Ode

Late, late yestreen I saw the new Moon,
With the old Moon in her arms;
And I fear, I fear, my master dear!
We shall have a deadly storm.
        Ballad of Sir Patrick Spence

1

Well! If the bard was weather-wise, who made
    The grand old ballad of Sir Patrick Spence,
    This night, so tranquil now, will not go hence
Unroused by winds, that ply a busier trade
5   Than those which mold yon cloud in lazy flakes,
Or the dull sobbing draft, that moans and rakes
Upon the strings of this Aeolian lute,[2]
        Which better far were mute.
    For lo! the New-moon winter-bright!
10   And overspread with phantom light,
        (With swimming phantom light o'erspread
        But rimmed and circled by a silver thread)
    I see the old Moon in her lap, foretelling
        The coming-on of rain and squally blast.

2. The wind-harp (named after Aeolus, classi-
cal god of winds) has a sounding board equipped with a set of strings that vibrate in
response to air currents.

15 And oh! that even now the gust were swelling,
        And the slant night shower driving loud and fast!
    Those sounds which oft have raised me, whilst they awed,
            And sent my soul abroad,
    Might now perhaps their wonted° impulse give,   *usual*
20 Might startle this dull pain, and make it move and live!

                    2
    A grief without a pang, void, dark, and drear,
        A stifled, drowsy, unimpassioned grief,
        Which finds no natural outlet, no relief,
            In word, or sigh, or tear—
25 O Lady! in this wan and heartless mood,
    To other thoughts by yonder throstle wooed,
        All this long eve, so balmy and serene,
    Have I been gazing on the western sky,
        And its peculiar tint of yellow green:
30 And still I gaze—and with how blank an eye!
    And those thin clouds above, in flakes and bars,
    That give away their motion to the stars;
    Those stars, that glide behind them or between,
    Now sparkling, now bedimmed, but always seen:
35 Yon crescent Moon, as fixed as if it grew
    In its own cloudless, starless lake of blue;
    I see them all so excellently fair,
    I see, not feel, how beautiful they are!

                    3
        My genial spirits° fail;   *vital energies*
40   And what can these avail
    To lift the smothering weight from off my breast?
        It were a vain endeavor,
        Though I should gaze forever
    On that green light that lingers in the west:
45 I may not hope from outward forms to win
    The passion and the life, whose fountains are within.

                    4
    O Lady! we receive but what we give,
    And in our life alone does Nature live:
    Ours is her wedding garment, ours her shroud!
50   And would we aught behold, of higher worth,
    Than that inanimate cold world allowed
    To the poor loveless ever-anxious crowd,
        Ah! from the soul itself must issue forth
    A light, a glory, a fair luminous cloud
55   Enveloping the Earth—
    And from the soul itself must there be sent
        A sweet and potent voice, of its own birth,
    Of all sweet sounds the life and element!

                    5
    O pure of heart! thou need'st not ask of me
60 What this strong music in the soul may be!
    What, and wherein it doth exist,
    This light, this glory, this fair luminous mist,
    This beautiful and beauty-making power.
        Joy, virtuous Lady! Joy that ne'er was given,
65 Save to the pure, and in their purest hour,
    Life, and Life's effluence, cloud at once and shower,
    Joy, Lady! is the spirit and the power,

Which wedding Nature to us gives in dower
  A new Earth and new Heaven,
70 Undreamt of by the sensual and the proud—
Joy is the sweet voice, Joy the luminous cloud—
    We in ourselves rejoice!
And thence flows all that charms or ear or sight,
  All melodies the echoes of that voice,
75 All colors a suffusion from that light.

6

There was a time when, though my path was rough,
  This joy within me dallied with distress,
And all misfortunes were but as the stuff
  Whence Fancy made me dreams of happiness:
80 For hope grew round me, like the twining vine,
And fruits, and foliage, not my own, seemed mine.
But now afflictions bow me down to earth:
  Nor care I that they rob me of my mirth;
    But oh! each visitation
85 Suspends what nature gave me at my birth,
  My shaping spirit of Imagination.

For not to think of what I needs must feel,
  But to be still and patient, all I can;
And happly by abstruse research to steal
90   From my own nature all the natural man—
  This was my sole resource, my only plan:
Till that which suits a part infects the whole,
And now is almost grown the habit of my soul.

7

Hence, viper thoughts, that coil around my mind,
95   Reality's dark dream!
  I turn from you, and listen to the wind,
Which long has raved unnoticed. What a scream
Of agony by torture lengthened out
That lute sent forth! Thou Wind, that rav'st without,
100 Bare crag, or mountain tairn,° or blasted tree,   *pool*
Or pine grove whither woodman never clomb,
Or lonely house, long held—the witches' home,
  Methinks were fitter instruments for thee,
Mad lutanist! who in this month of showers,
105 Of dark-brown gardens, and of peeping flowers,
Mak'st devils' yule,[3] with worse than wintry song,
The blossoms, buds, and timorous leaves among.
  Thou actor, perfect in all tragic sounds!
Thou mighty poet, e'en to frenzy bold!
110   What tell'st thou now about?
  'Tis of the rushing of an host in rout,
With groans, of trampled men, with smarting wounds—
At once they groan with pain, and shudder with the cold!
But hush! there is a pause of deepest silence!
115   And all that noise, as of a rushing crowd,
With groans, and tremulous shudderings—all is over—
  It tells another tale, with sounds less deep and loud!
    A tale of less affright,
    And tempered with delight,

---

3. A winter storm in spring; hence, an unnatural or "devils'" Christmas.

120 As Otway's[4] self had framed the tender lay—
         'Tis of a little child
         Upon a lonesome wild,
     Not far from home, but she hath lost her way:
     And now moans low in bitter grief and fear,
125 And now screams loud, and hopes to make her mother hear.
                        8
     'Tis midnight, but small thoughts have I of sleep:
     Full seldom may my friend such vigils keep!
     Visit her, gentle Sleep! with wings of healing,
         And may this storm be but a mountain birth,
130 May all the stars hang bright above her dwelling,
         Silent as though they watched the sleeping Earth!
             With light heart may she rise,
             Gay fancy, cheerful eyes,
         Joy lift her spirit, joy attune her voice;
135 To her may all things live, from pole to pole,
     Their life the eddying of her living soul!
         O simple spirit, guided from above,
         Dear Lady! friend devoutest of my choice,
     Thus mayest thou ever, evermore rejoice.

                                              1802   1817

Work Without Hope

LINES COMPOSED 21ST FEBRUARY 1825

    All Nature seems at work. Slugs leave their lair—
    The bees are stirring—birds are on the wing—
    And Winter slumbering in the open air
    Wears on his smiling face a dream of Spring!
5   And I the while, the sole unbusy thing,
    Nor honey make, nor pair, nor build, nor sing.

        Yet well I ken the banks where amaranths[5] blow,
    Have traced the fount whence streams of nectar flow.
    Bloom, O ye amaranths! bloom for whom ye may,
10 For me ye bloom not! Glide, rich streams, away!
    With lips unbrightened, wreathless brow, I stroll:
    And would you learn the spells that drowse my soul?
    Work without Hope draws nectar in a sieve,
    And Hope without an object cannot live.

                                                           1828

On Donne's Poetry

    With Donne, whose muse on dromedary trots,
    Wreathe iron pokers into truelove knots;
    Rhyme's sturdy cripple, fancy's maze and clue,
    Wit's forge and fire-blast, meaning's press and screw.[6]

                                                           1836

Epitaph

    Stop, Christian passer-by!—Stop, child of God,
    And read with gentle breast. Beneath this sod

---

5. Flowers that never fade.

6. As in *jackscrew,* an instrument for applying great pressure gradually.

A poet lies, or that which once seemed he.
O lift one thought in prayer for S. T. C.;
5 That he who many a year with toil of breath
Found death in life, may here find life in death!
Mercy for° praise—to be forgiven for fame   *instead of*
He asked, and hoped, through Christ. Do thou the same!

1834

WALTER SAVAGE LANDOR
(1775–1864)

Rose Aylmer[1]

Ah what, avails the sceptered race,
    Ah what the form divine!
What every virtue, every grace!
    Rose Aylmer, all were thine.
5 Rose Aylmer, whom these wakeful eyes
    May weep, but never see,
A night of memories and of sighs
    I consecrate to thee.

1806, 1831, 1846

Mild Is the Parting Year, and Sweet

Mild is the parting year, and sweet
    The odor of the falling spray;
Life passes on more rudely fleet,
    And balmless is its closing day.

5 I wait its close, I court its gloom,
    But mourn that never must there fall
Or on my breast or on my tomb
    The tear that would have soothed it all.

1831, 1846

Past Ruined Ilion Helen[2] Lives

Past ruined Ilion Helen lives,
    Alcestis[3] rises from the shades;
Verse calls them forth; 'tis verse that gives
    Immortal youth to mortal maids.

5 Soon shall Oblivion's deepening veil
    Hide all the peopled hills you see,
The gay, the proud, while lovers hail
    In distant ages you and me.

10 The tear for fading beauty check,
    For passing glory cease to sigh;
One form shall rise above the wreck,
    One name, Ianthe, shall not die.

1831

1. The Honorable Rose Whitworth Aylmer
(1779–1800), whom Landor had known in
Wales, died suddenly in Calcutta on March 2,
1800.
2. Helen of Troy ("Ilion").

3. Alcestis sacrificed her life for her husband,
who was stricken with a mortal illness. She
acted in accordance with Apollo's promise that
he might thus be saved; she was then brought
back from the underworld by Hercules.

Dirce

Stand close around, ye Stygian set,[4]
　　With Dirce in one boat conveyed!
Or Charon, seeing may forget
　　That he is old and she a shade.

1831, 1846

To My Child Carlino[5]

They are verses written by a gentleman who resided long in this country,
and who much regretted the necessity of leaving it.

—BOCCACCIO

Carlino! what art thou about, my boy?
Often I ask that question, though in vain;
For we are far apart: ah! therefore 'tis
I often ask it; not in such a tone
5　As wiser fathers do, who know too well.
Were we not children, you and I together?
Stole we not glances from each other's eyes?
Swore we not secrecy in such misdeeds?
Well could we trust each other. Tell me, then,
10　What thou art doing. Carving out thy name,
Or haply mine, upon my favorite seat,
With the new knife I sent thee oversea?
Or hast thou broken it, and hid the hilt
Among the myrtles, starred with flowers, behind?
15　Or under that high throne whence fifty lilies
(With sworded tuberoses dense around)
Lift up their heads at once . . . not without fear
That they were looking at thee all the while?
　　Does Cincirillo follow thee about?
20　Inverting one swart foot suspensively,
And wagging his dread jaw, at every chirp
Of bird above him on the olive-branch?
Frighten him then away! 'twas he who slew
Our pigeons, our white pigeons, peacock-tailed,
25　That feared not you and me . . . alas, nor him!
I flattened his striped sides along my knee,
And reasoned with him on his bloody mind,
Till he looked blandly, and half-closed his eyes
To ponder on my lecture in the shade.
30　I doubt his memory much, his heart a little,
And in some minor matters (may I say it?)
Could wish him rather sager. But from thee
God hold back wisdom yet for many years!
Whether in early season or in late
35　It always comes high priced. For thy pure breast
I have no lesson; it for me has many.
Come, throw it open then! What sports, what cares
(Since there are none too young for these) engage
Thy busy thoughts? Are you again at work,
40　Walter[6] and you, with those sly laborers,

---

4. The shades of the dead who were ferried by
Charon over the river Styx to Hades.
5. The poem is addressed to Charles Savage
Landor (1825–1917), youngest of Landor's
three sons, at a time when Landor was in
England and the three boys were in Italy.
6. Walter Savage Landor (1822–99), the
poet's second son.

Geppo, Giovanni, Cecco, and Poeta,
To build more solidly your broken dam
Among the poplars, whence the nightingale
Inquisitively watched you all day long?
45 I was not of your council in the scheme,
Or might have saved you silver without end,
And sighs too without number. Art thou gone
Below the mulberry, where that cold pool
Urged to devise a warmer, and more fit
50 For mighty swimmers, swimming three abreast?
Or art thou panting in this summer noon
Upon the lowest step before the hall,
Drawing a slice of watermelon, long
As Cupid's bow, athwart thy wetted lips
(Like one who plays Pan's pipe) and letting drop
The sable seeds from all their separate cells,
And leaving bays profound and rocks abrupt,
Redder than coral round Calypso's[7] cave?

1837   1846

To Robert Browning

There is delight in singing, though none hear
Beside the singer; and there is delight
In praising, though the praiser sit alone
5 And see the praised far off him, far above.
Shakspeare is not *our* poet, but the world's,
Therefore on him no speech; and short for thee,
Browning! Since Chaucer was alive and hale,
No man hath walked along our roads with step
So active, so inquiring eye, or tongue
10 So varied in discourse. But warmer climes
Give brighter plumage, stronger wing; the breeze
Of Alpine heights thou playest with, borne on
Beyond Sorrento and Amalfi,[8] where
The Siren waits thee, singing song for song.

1845

Plays

Alas, how soon the hours are over,
Counted us out to play the lover!
And how much narrower is the stage,
Allotted us to play the sage!
5 But when we play the fool, how wide
The theater expands; beside,
How long the audience sits before us!
How many prompters! what a chorus!

1846   1858

7. The nymph or goddess who welcomed Odysseus in her island, Ogygia, after the wreck of his ship, and held him there for seven years.
8. Towns near Naples which Browning had visited on his second trip to Italy in 1844, and which figure in some of his early poems. According to legend, the Sirens had drowned themselves in despair when Odysseus escaped the lure of their song; one of them, Parthenope, cast up on the shore of the bay of Naples, gave that city its ancient name.

Dying Speech of an Old Philosopher

I strove with none, for none was worth my strife:
   Nature I loved, and, next to Nature, Art:
I warmed both hands before the fire of Life;
   It sinks; and I am ready to depart.

1849

Death Stands Above Me, Whispering Low

Death stands above me, whispering low
   I know not what into my ear:
Of his strange language all I know
   Is, there is not a word of fear.

1853

Death of the Day

My pictures blacken in their frames
    As night comes on,
And youthful maids and wrinkled dames
    Are now all one.

5 Death of the day! a sterner Death
    Did worse before;
The fairest form, the sweetest breath,
    Away he bore.

1858

GEORGE GORDON, LORD BYRON
(1788–1824)

Written After Swimming from Sestos to Abydos[1]

1

If, in the month of dark December,
   Leander, who was nightly wont
(What maid will not the tale remember?)
   To cross thy stream, broad Hellespont!

2

5 If, when the wintry tempest roared,
   He sped to Hero, nothing loath,
And thus of old thy current poured,
   Fair Venus! how I pity both!

3

For *me*, degenerate modern wretch,
10   Though in the genial month of May,
My dripping limbs I faintly stretch,
   And think I've done a feat today.

---

1. The Hellespont, or Dardanelles, is the strait separating Europe from Asia Minor, between Abydos on the Greek shore and Sestos on the Asian. In Greek legend, Leander used to swim from Abydos to visit his sweetheart Hero at Sestos.

4

But since he crossed the rapid tide,
    According to the doubtful story,
5 To woo—and—Lord knows what beside,
    And swam for Love, as I for Glory;

5

'Twere hard to say who fared the best:
    Sad mortals! thus the gods still plague you!
He lost his labor, I my jest;
    For he was drowned, and I've the ague.°

            chills and fever
            1812

The Destruction of Sennacherib[2]

1

The Assyrian came down like the wolf on the fold,
And his cohorts were gleaming in purple and gold;
And the sheen of their spears was like stars on the sea,
When the blue wave rolls nightly on deep Galilee.

2

5 Like the leaves of the forest when summer is green,
That host with their banners at sunset were seen:
Like the leaves of the forest when autumn hath blown,
That host on the morrow lay withered and strown.

3

10 For the Angel of Death spread his wings on the blast,
And breathed in the face of the foe as he passed;
And the eyes of the sleepers waxed deadly and chill,
And their hearts but once heaved, and forever grew still!

4

And there lay the steed with his nostril all wide,
But through it there rolled not the breath of his pride;
15 And the foam of his gasping lay white on the turf,
And cold as the spray of the rock-beating surf.

5

And there lay the rider distorted and pale,
With the dew on his brow, and the rust on his mail:
And the tents wer all silent, the banners alone,
20 The lances unlifted, the trumpet unblown.

6

And the widows of Ashur[3] are loud in their wail,
And the idols are broke in the temple of Baal;[4]
And the might of the Gentile,[5] unsmote by the sword,
Hath melted like snow in the glance of the Lord!

            1815

She Walks in Beauty

1

She walks in beauty, like the night
    Of cloudless climes and starry skies;
And all that's best of dark and bright
    Meet in her aspect and her eyes:
5 Thus mellowed to that tender light
    Which heaven to gaudy day denies.

---

2. Assyrian king, whose armies, while besieg-
ing Jerusalem (701 B.C.), were attacked by a
violent plague (II Kings xix.35).

3. Assyria.
4. Deity of the Assyrians.
5. Here, Sennacherib; anyone not a Hebrew.

2

One shade the more, one ray the less,
  Had half impaired the nameless grace
Which waves in every raven tress,
10   Or softly lightens o'er her face;
Where thoughts serenely sweet express
  How pure, how dear their dwelling place.

3

And on that cheek, and o'er that brow,
  So soft, so calm, yet eloquent,
15 The smiles that win, the tints that glow,
  But tell of days in goodness spent,
A mind at peace with all below,
  A heart whose love is innocent!

1815

Stanzas for Music

[THERE BE NONE OF BEAUTY'S DAUGHTERS]

1

There be none of Beauty's daughters
  With a magic like thee;
And like music on the waters
  Is thy sweet voice to me:
5 When, as if its sound were causing
  The charméd ocean's pausing,
  The waves lie still and gleaming,
  And the lulled winds seem dreaming;

2

And the midnight moon is weaving
10   Her bright chain o'er the deep;
Whose breast is gently heaving,
  As an infant's asleep:
So the spirit bows before thee,
  To listen and adore thee;
15 With a full but soft emotion,
  Like the swell of summer's ocean.

1816

Prometheus

Titan![1] to whose immortal eyes
  The sufferings of mortality,
  Seen in their sad reality,
Were not as things that gods despise;
5 What was thy pity's recompense?
A silent suffering, and intense;
The rock, the vulture, and the chain,
All that the proud can feel of pain,
The agony they do not show,
10 The suffocating sense of woe,
  Which speaks but in its loneliness,
And then is jealous lest the sky
Should have a listener, nor will sigh
  Until its voice is echoless.

---

1. An ancient Greek deity who stole fire from the heavens and gave it to mankind. His punishment, imposed by Jove ("the Thunder-er," line 26) was to be chained to a cliff and torn by vultures so long as he defied Jove.

Titan! to thee the strife was given
  Between the suffering and the will,
  Which torture where they cannot kill;
And the inexorable heaven,
And the deaf tyranny of fate,
The ruling principle of hate,
Which for its pleasure doth create
The things it may annihilate,
Refused thee even the boon to die:
The wretched gift eternity
Was thine—and thou hast borne it well.
All that the Thunderer wrung from thee
Was but the menace which flung back
On him the torments of thy rack;
The fate thou didst so well foresee,
But would not to appease him tell;
And in thy silence [2] was his sentence,
And in his soul a vain repentance,
And evil dread so ill dissembled,
That in his hand the lightnings trembled.

Thy godlike crime was to be kind,
  To render with thy precepts less
  The sum of human wretchedness,
And strengthen man with his own mind;
But baffled as thou wert from high,
Still in thy patient energy,
In the endurance, and repulse
  Of thine impenetrable spirit,
Which earth and heaven could not convulse,
  A mighty lesson we inherit:
Thou art a symbol and a sign
  To mortals of their fate and force;
Like thee, man is in part divine,
  A troubled stream from a pure source;
And Man in portions can foresee
His own funereal destiny;
His wretchedness, and his resistance,
And his sad unallied existence;
To which his spirit may oppose
Itself—and equal to all woes,
  And a firm will, and a deep sense,
Which even in torture can descry
  Its own concentered recompense,
Triumphant where it dares defy,
And making death a victory.

1816

So We'll Go No More A-Roving

1

So we'll go no more a-roving
  So late into the night,
Though the heart be still as loving,
  And the moon be still as bright.

2. Prometheus knew but would not reveal the secret of Jove's eventual downfall.

2

5   For the sword outwears its sheath,
         And the soul wears out the breast,
     And the heart must pause to breathe,
         And Love itself have rest.

3

     Though the night was made for loving,
10   And the day returns too soon,
     Yet we'll go no more a-roving
         By the light of the moon.

                                    1817   1836

From Don Juan[7]

From *Canto the First*

1

     I want° a hero: an uncommon want,   lack
         When every year and month sends forth a new one,
     Till, after cloying the gazettes[8] with cant,
         The age discovers he is not the true one;
5   Of such as these I should not care to vaunt,
         I'll therefore take our ancient friend Don Juan—
     We all have seen him, in the pantomime,[9]
     Sent to the Devil somewhat ere his time.

2

     Vernon, the butcher Cumberland, Wolfe, Hawke,
10   Prince Ferdinand, Granby, Burgoyne, Keppel, Howe,[1]
     Evil and good, have had their tithe of talk,
         And filled their sign-posts then, like Wellesley now;
     Each in their turn like Banquo's monarchs stalk,
         Followers of Fame, "nine farrow" of that sow:
15   France, too, had Buonaparté and Dumourier[2]
     Recorded in the Moniteur anr Courier.

3

     Barnave, Brissot, Condorcet, Mirabeau,
         Petion, Clootz, Danton, Marat, La Fayette[3]
     Were French, and famous people, as we know;
20   And there were others, scarce forgotten yet,
     Joubert, Hoche, Marceau, Lannes, Desaix, Moreau,[4]
         With many of the military set,
     Exceedingly remarkable at times,
     But not at all adapted to my rhymes.

4

25   Nelson[5] was once Britannia's god of War,
         And still should be so, but the tide is turned;
     There's no more to be said of Trafalgar,

---

7. The hero is a legendary Spanish nobleman, a notorious seducer of women; in most versions, but not Byron's, finally carried off to hell. Canto I comprises 222 stanzas; Stanzas 1–199, given here, conclude with the end of the romance between Don Juan and Donna Julia.
8. Official notices or newspapers.
9. I.e., on the stage, in one or another of many adaptations.
1. British military leaders of the 18th century, their fame extinguished by more recent "heroes," such as Wellesley (line 12), the Duke of Wellington, who defeated Napoleon at Waterloo.

2. "Banquo's monarchs" (line 13), in *Macbeth,* IV.i.112–13. The sow, "Fame" (line 14), eats her own offspring ("farrow")—i.e., the "heroes" just listed. "Buonaparté" (line 15) is Napoleon, and Dumourier a French general, whose victories and defeats were chonicled in the French newspapers.
3. French generals and politicians connected with the French Revolution, many of them guillotined.
4. Other French military men; most of these died in battle.
5. British naval hero, fatally wounded at the Battle of Trafalgar, 1805.

'Tis with our hero quietly inurned;
Because the army's grown more popular,
　　At which the naval people are concerned;
　Besides, the Prince is all for the land-service,
Forgetting Duncan, Nelson, Howe, and Jervis.[6]

5

Brave men were living before Agamemnon[7]
　And since, exceeding valorous and sage,
A good deal like him too, though quite the same none;
　But then they shone not on the poet's page,
And so have been forgotten:—I condemn none,
　But can't find any in the present age
Fit for my poem (that is, for my new one);
So, as I said, I'll take my friend Don Juan.

6

Most epic poets plunge *"in medias res"*[8]
　(Horace makes this the heroic turnpike road),
And then your hero tells, when'er you please,
　What went before—by way of episode,
While seated after dinner at his ease,
　Beside his mistress in some soft abode,
Palace, or garden, paradise, or cavern,
Which serves the happy couple for a tavern.

7

That is the usual method, but not mine—
　My way is to begin with the beginning;
The regularity of my design
　Forbids all wandering as the worst of sinning,
And therefore I shall open with a line
　(Although it cost me half an hour in spinning),
Narrating somewhat of Don Juan's father,
And also of his mother, if you'd rather.

8

In Seville was he born, a pleasant city,
　Famous for oranges and women—he
Who has not seen it will be much to pity,
　So says the proverb—and I quite agree;
Of all the Spanish towns is none more pretty,
　Cadiz perhaps—but that you soon may see;
Don Juan's parents lived beside the river,
A noble stream, and called the Guadalquivir.

9

His father's name was José—*Don*, of course,—
　A true Hidalgo,[9] free from every stain
Of Moor or Hebrew blood, he traced his source
　Through the most Gothic gentlemen of Spain;[1]
A better cavalier ne'er mounted horse,
　Or, being mounted, e'er got down again,
Than José, who begot our hero, who
Begot—but that's to come—Well, to renew:

10

His mother was a learnéd lady, famed
　For every branch of every science known—

---

6. British naval commanders. "The Prince"
(line 31): the Prince of Wales.
7. Commander of the Greeks at the siege of
Troy.

8. Into the middle of the subject.
9. Spanish noble of minor degree.
1. Descended from the Visigoths, who con-
quered Spain in the fifth century A.D.

75 In every Christain language ever named,
    With virtues equaled by her wit alone:
She made the cleverest people quite ashamed,
    And even the good with inward envy groan,
Finding themselves so very much exceeded,
80 In their own way, by all the things that she did.

11

Her memory was a mine: she knew by heart
    All Calderon and greater part of Lopé,[2]
So, that if any actor missed his part,
    She could have served him for the prompter's copy;
85 For her Feinagle's[3] were an useless art,
    And he himself obliged to shut up shop—he
Could never make a memory so fine as
That which adorned the brain of Donna Inez.

12

Her favorite science was the mathematical,
90   Her noblest virtue was her magnanimity,
Her wit (she sometimes tried at wit) was Attic[4] all,
    Her serious sayings darkened to sublimity;
In short, in all things she was fairly what I call
    A prodigy—her morning dress was dimity,
95 Her evening silk, or, in the summer, muslin,
And other stuffs, with which I won't stay puzzling.

13

She knew the Latin—that is, "the Lord's prayer,"
    And Greek—the alphabet—I'm nearly sure;
She read some French romances here and there,
100   Although her mode of speaking was not pure;
For native Spanish she had no great care,
    At least her conversation was obscure;
Her thoughts were theorems, her words a problem,
As if she deemed that mystery would ennoble 'em.

14

105 She liked the English and the Hebrew tongue,
    And said there was analogy between 'em:
She proved it somehow out of sacred song,
    But I must leave the proofs of those who've seen 'em;
But this I heard her say, and can't be wrong,
110   And all may think which way their judgments lean 'em,
" 'Tis strange—the Hebrew noun which means 'I am,'[5]
The English always use to govern d——n."

15

Some women use their tongues—she *looked* a lecture,
    Each eye a sermon, and her brow a homily,
115 An all-in-all sufficient self-director,
    Like the lamented late Sir Samuel Romilly,[6]
The Law's expounder, and the State's corrector,
    Whose suicide was almost an anomaly—
One sad example more, that "All is vanity"—
120 (The jury brought their verdict in "Insanity!")

---

2. Calderón (1600–81) and Lopé de Vega (1562–1635) pre-eminent Spanish dramatists.
3. Inventor of a method of memorization, who lectured in England in 1811.
4. Athenian: i.e., refined, learned.
5. The name of God, "I am that I am" (see Exodus iii.14); English gentlemen traveling on the European continent were sometimes known as "Goddams," from their habitual profanity.
6. Lawyer for Byron's wife in a suit for separation.

16

In short, she was a walking calculation,
  Miss Edgeworth's novels stepping from their covers,
Or Mrs. Trimmer's books on education,
  Or "Coelebs' Wife"[7] set out in quest of lovers,
Morality's prim personifation,
  In which not Envy's self a flaw discovers;
To others' share let "female errors fall,"[8]
For she had not even one—the worst of all.

17

Oh! she was perfect past all parallel—
  Of any modern female saint's comparison;
So far above the cunning powers of Hell,
  Her Guardian Angel had given up his garrison;
Even her minutest motions went as well
  As those of the best time-piece made by Harrison;[9]
In virtues nothing earthly could surpass her,
Save thine "incomparable oil," Macassar![1]

18

Perfect she was, but as perfection is
  Insipid in this naughty world of ours,
Where our first parents[2] never learned to kiss
  Till they were exiled from their earlier bowers,
Where all was peace, and innocence, and bliss,
  (I wonder how they got through the twelve hours),
Don José, like a lineal son of Eve,
Went plucking various fruit without her leave.

19

He was a mortal of the careless kind,
  With no great love for learning, or the learned,
Who chose to go where'er he had a mind,
  And never dreamed his lady was concerned;
The world, as usual, wickedly inclined
  To see a kingdom or a house o'erturned,
Whispered he had a mistress, some said *two*.
But for domestic quarrels *one* will do.

20

Now Donna Inez had, with all her merit,
  A great opinion of her own good qualities;
Neglect, indeed, requires a saint to bear it,
  And such, indeed, she was in her moralities;°   *moralizing*
But then she had a devil of a spirit,
  And sometimes mixed up fancies with realities,
And let few opportunities escape
Of getting her liege lord into a scrape.

21

This was an easy matter with a man
  Oft in the wrong, and never on his guard;
And even the wisest, do the best they can,
  Have moments, hours, and days, so unprepared,
That you might "brain them with their lady's fan";[3]
  And sometimes ladies hit exceeding hard,

---

7. A novel by Hannah More, who like Maria
Edgeworth (line 2) and Sarah Trimmer (line
3) was a lady writer whom Byron could not
take seriously.
8. Quoted from Pope, *The Rape of the Lock*,
II, line 17; frailties or foibles.

9. John Harrison (1693–1776) improved the
accuracy of watches and chronometers.
1. A much-advertised hair-dressing.
2. I.e., Adam and Eve.
3. Quoted from Shakespeare, *Henry IV, Part
1*, II.iii.

And fans turn into falchions° in fair hands,   swords
And why and wherefore no one understands.

22

170   'Tis pity learnéd virgins ever wed
    With persons of no sort of education,
Or gentlemen, who, though well born and bred,
    Grow tired of scientific conversation:
I don't choose to say much upon this head,
    I'm a plain man, and in a single station,
175   But—Oh! ye lords of ladies intellectual,
Inform us truly, have they not hen-pecked you all?

23

Don José and his lady quarrelled—*why,*
    Not any of the many could divine,
Though several thousand people chose to try,
180   'Twas surely no concern of theirs nor mine;
I loath that low vice—curiosity;
    But if there's anything in which I shine,
'Tis in arranging all my friends' affairs,
Not having, of my own, domestic cares.

24

185   And so I interfered, and with the best
    Intentions, but their treatment was not kind;
I think the foolish people were possessed,
    For neither of them could I ever find,
Although their porter afterwards confessed—
190   But that's no matter, and the worst's behind,
For little Juan o'er me threw, down stairs,
A pail of housemaid's water unawares.

25

A little curly-headed, good-for-nothing,
    And mischief-making monkey from his birth;
195   His parents ne'er agreed except in doting
    Upon the most unquiet imp on earth;
Instead of quarrelling, had they been but both in
    Their senses, they'd have sent young master forth
To school, or had him soundly whipped at home,
200   To teach him manners for the time to come.

26

Don José and the Donna Inez led
    For some time an unhappy sort of life,
Wishing each other, not divorced, but dead;
    They lived respectably as man and wife,
205   Their conduct was exceedingly well-bred,
    And gave no outward signs of inward strife,
Until at length the smothered fire broke out,
And put the business past all kind of doubt.

27

For Inez called some druggists and physicians,
210   And tried to prove her loving lord was *mad,*
But as he had some lucid intermissions,
    She next decided he was only *bad;*
Yet when they asked her for her depositions,
    No sort of explanation could be had,
215   Save that her duty both to man and God
Required this conduct—which seemed very odd.

28

She kept a journal, where his faults were noted,
   And opened certain trunks of books and letters,
All which might, if occasion served, be quoted;
   And then she had all Seville for abettors,
Besides her good old grandmother (who doted);
   The hearers of her case became repeaters,
Then advocates, inquisitors, and judges,
Some for amusement, others for old grudges.

29

And then this best and meekest woman bore
   With such serenity her husband's woes,
Just as the Spartan ladies did of yore,
   Who saw their spouses killed, and nobly chose
Never to say a word about them more—
   Calmly she heard each calumny that rose,
And saw *his* agonies with such sublimity,
That all the world exclaimed, "What magnanimity!"

30

No doubt this patience, when the world is damning us,
   Is philosophic in our former friends;
'Tis also pleasant to be deemed magnanimous,
   The more so in obtaining our own ends;
And what the lawyers call a *"malus animus"*[4]
   Conduct like this by no means comprehends:
Revenge in person's certainly no virtue,
But then 'tis no *my* fault, if *others* hurt you.

31

And if our quarrels should rip up old stories,
   And help them with a lie or two additional,
I'm not to blame, as you well know—no more is
   Any one else—they were become traditional;
Besides, their resurrection aids our glories
   By contrast, which is what we just were wishing all:
And Science profits by this resurrection—
Dead scandals form good subjects for dissection.

32

Their friends had tried at reconciliation,
   Then their relations, who made matters worse.
('Twere hard to tell upon a like occasion
   To whom it may be best to have recourse—
I can't say much for friend or yet relation):
   The lawyers did their utmost for divorce,
But scarce a fee was paid on either side
Before, unluckily, Don José died.

33

He died: and most unluckily, because,
   According to all hints I could collect
From Counsel learnéd in those kinds of laws,
   (Although their talk's obscure and circumspect)
His death contrived to spoil a charming cause;°   *legal case*
   A thousand pities also with respect
To public feeling, which on this occasion
Was manifested in a great sensation.

4. Malicious intent.

34

265 But ah! he died; and buried with him lay
    The public feeling and the lawyers' fees:
His house was sold, his servants sent away,
    A Jew took one of his two mistresses,
A priest the other—at least so they say:
270   I asked the doctors after his disease—
He died of the slow fever called the tertian,[5]
And left his widow to her own aversion.

35

Yet José was an honorable man,
    That I must say, who knew him very well;
275 Therefore his frailties I'll no further scan,
    Indeed there were not many more to tell:
And if his pasions now and then outran
    Discretion, and were not so peaceable
As Numa's (who was also named Pompilius),[6]
280 He had been ill brought up, and was born bilious.

36

Whate'er might be his worthlessness or worth,
    Poor fellow! he had many things to wound him.
Let's own—since it can do no good on earth—
    It was a trying moment that which found him
285 Standing alone beside his desolate hearth,
    Where all his household gods lay shivered° round him: *broken*
No choice was left his feelings or his pride,
Save Death or Doctor's Commons° so he died.   *divorce courts*

37

Dying intestate,° Juan was sole heir   *leaving no will*
290   To a chancery suit,[7] and messuages,° and lands,   *household lands*
Which, with a long minority[8] and care,
    Promised to turn out well in proper hands:
Inez became sole guardian, which was fair,
    And answered but to Nature's just demands;
295 An only son left with an only mother
Is brought up much more wisely than another.

38

Sagest of women, even of widows, she
    Resolved that Juan should be quite a paragon,
And worthy of the noblest pedigree,
300   (His Sire was of Castile, his Dam from Aragon):
Then, for accomplishments of chivalry,
    In case our Lord the King should go to war again,
He learned the arts of riding, fencing, gunnery,
And how to scale a fotress—or a nunnery.

39

305 But that which Donna Inez most desired,
    And saw into herself each day before all
The learnéd tutors whom for him she hired,
    Was, that his breeding should be strictly moral:
Much into all his studies she inquired,
310   And so they were submitted first to her, all,
Arts, sciences—no branch was made a mystery
To Juan's eyes, excepting natural history.

---

5. A form of malaria.
6. Ancient Roman king, famed for his peaceable reign.

7. Drawn-out legal proceedings over inheritance of property.
8. Before he should come of age.

40

The languages, especially the dead,
　　The sciences, and most of all the abstruse,
The arts, at least all such as could be said
　　To be the most remote from common use,
In all these he was much and deeply read:
　　But not a page of anything that's loose,
Or hints continuation of the species,
Was ever suffered, lest he should grow vicious.

41

His classic studies made a little puzzle,
　　Because of filthy loves of gods and goddesses,
Who in the earlier ages raised a bustle,
　　But never put on pantaloons or bodices;
His ·reverend tutors had at times a tussle,
　　And for their Aeneids, Iliads, and Odysseys,
Were forced to make an odd sort of apology,
For Donna Inez dreaded the Mythology.

42

Ovid's a rake, as half his verses show him,
　　Anacreon's morals are a still worse sample,
Catullus scarcely has a decent poem,
　　I don't think Sappho's Ode a good example,[9]
Although Longinus[1] tells us there is no hymn
　　Where the Sublime soars forth on wings more ample;
But Virgil's songs are pure, except that horrid one
Beginning with *"Formosum Pastor Corydon."*[2]

43

Lucretius' irreligion is too strong
　　For early stomachs, to prove wholesome food;
I can't help thinking Juvenal was wrong,
　　Although no doubt his real intent was good,
For speaking out so plainly in his song,
　　So much indeed as to be downright rude;
And then what proper person can be partial
To all those nauseous epigrams of Martial?[3]

44

Juan was taught from out the best edition,
　　Expurgated by learnéd men, who place,
Judiciously, from out the schoolboy's vision,
　　The grosser parts; but, fearful to deface
Too much their modest bard by this omission,
　　And pitying sore his mutilated case,
They only add them all in an appendix,[4]
Which saves, in fact, the trouble of an index;

45

For there we have them all "at one fell swoop,"
　　Instead of being scattered through the pages;
They stand forth marshaled in a handsome troop,
　　To meet the ingenuous youth of future ages,
Till some less rigid editor shall stoop

---

9. These lines name Greek and Roman classic and erotic poets.
1. The presumed author (first century A.D.) of a treatise on "the sublime" in literature.
2. "Handsome Shepherd Corydon": opening words of Virgil's Second Eclogue (a pastoral poem), concerned with love between young men.

3. Like Lucretius (line 337) and Juvenal (line 339), a Roman poet. Lucretius was a philosophic atheist; Juvenal and Martial were severe and sometimes obscene satirists.
4. "Fact! There is, or was, such an edition, with all the obnoxious epigrams of Martial placed by themselves at the end" [Byron's note].

To call them back into their separate cages,
Instead of standing staring all together,
360   Like garden gods[5]—and not so decent either.

46

The Missal too (it was the family Missal)
    Was ornamented in a sort of way
Which ancient mass-books often are, and this all
    Kinds of grotesques illumined; and how they,
365   Who saw those figures on the margin kiss all,
    Could turn their optics to the text and pray,
Is more than I know—But Don Juan's mother
Kept this herself, and gave her son another.

47

Sermons he read, and lectures he endured,
370   And homilies, and lives of all the saints;
To Jerome and to Chrysostom[6] inured,
    He did not take such studies for restraints;
But how Faith is acquired, and then insured,
    So well not one of the aforesaid paints
375   As Saint Augustine[7] in his fine Confessions,
Which make the reader envy his transgressions.

48

This, too, was a sealed book to little Juan—
    I can't but say that his mamma was right,
If such an education was the true one.
380   She scarcely trusted him from out her sight;
Her maids were old, and if she took a new one,
    You might be sure she was a perfect fright;
She did this during even her husband's life—
I recommend as much to every wife.

49

385   Young Juan waxed in goodliness and grace;
    At six a charming child, and at eleven
With all the promise of as fine a face
    As e'er to man's maturer growth was given:
He studied steadily, and grew apace,
390   And seemed, at least, in the right road to Heaven,
For half his days were passed at church, the other
Between his tutors, confessor,° and mother.   *private chaplain*

50

At six, I said, he was a charming child,
    At twelve he was a fine, but quiet boy;
395   Although in infancy a little wild,
    They tamed him down amongst them: to destroy
His natural spirit not in vain they toiled,
    At least it seemed so; and his mother's joy
Was to declare how sage, and still, and steady,
400   Her young philosopher was grown already.

51

I had my doubts, perhaps I have them still,
    But what I say is neither here nor there:
I knew his father well, and have some skill
    In character—but it would not be fair

---

5. Statues of fertility deities, often phallic.
6. Saints and teachers of the early Church.
7. Another early father of the Church; his
autobiography candidly describes his worldy
life before conversion.

From sire to son to augur good or ill:
　　He and his wife were an ill-sorted pair—
But scandal's my aversion—I protest
Against all evil speaking, even in jest.

52

For my part I say nothing—nothing—but
　　This I will say—my reasons are my own—
That if I had an only son to put
　　To school (as God be praised that I have none),
'Tis not with Donna Inez I would shut
　　Him up to learn his catechism[8] alone,
No—no—I'd send him out betimes to college,
For there it was I picked up my own knowledge.

53

For there one learns—'tis not for me to boast,
　　Though I acquired—but I pass over *that*,
As well as all the Greek I since have lost:
　　I say that there's the place—but *"Verbum sat,"*[9]
I think I picked up too, as well as most,
　　Knowledge of matters—but no matter *what*—
I never married—but, I think, I know
That sons should not be educated so.

54

Young Juan now was sixteen years of age,
　　Tall, handsome, slender, but well knit: he seemed
Active, though not so sprightly, as a page;
　　And everybody but his mother deemed
Him almost man; but she flew in a rage
　　And bit her lips (for else she might have screamed)
If any said so—for to be precocious
Was in her eyes a thing the most atrocious.

55

Amongst her numerous acquaintance, all
　　Selected for discretion and devotion,
There was the Donna Julia, whom to call
　　Pretty were but to give a feeble notion
Of many charms in her as natural
　　As sweetness to the flower, or salt to Ocean,
Her zone° to Venus, or his bow to Cupid,   girdle, waist
(But this last simile is trite and stupid.)

56

The darkness of her Oriental eye
　　Accorded with her Moorish origin;
(Her blood was not all Spanish; by the by,
　　In Spain, you know, this is a sort of sin;)
When proud Granada fell, and, forced to fly,
　　Boabdil[1] wept: of Donna Julia's kin
Some went to Africa, some stayed in Spain—
Her great great grandmamma chose to remain.

57

She married (I forget the pedigree)
　　With an Hidalgo, who transmitted down
His blood less noble than such blood should be;
　　At such alliances his sires would frown,

---

8. A brief summary of Christian teaching.　　a province of Spain.
9. A word to the wise suffices.　　2. Blood-line, i.e., pure lineage.
1. The last Mohammedan ruler of Granada,

In that point so precise in each degree
  That they bred *in and in,* as might be shown,
455 Marrying their cousins—nay, their aunts, and nieces,
  Which always spoils the breed, if it increases.

         58

This heathenish cross restored the breed again,
  Ruined its blood,[2] but much improved its flesh;
For from a root the ugliest in Old Spain
460   Sprung up a branch as beautiful as fresh;
The sons no more were short, the daughters plain:
  But there's a rumour which I fain would hush,
'Tis said that Donna Julia's grandmamma
Produced her Don more heirs at love than law.

         59

465 However this might be, the race went on
  Improving still through every generation,
Until it centered in an only son,
  Who left an only daughter; my narration
May have suggested that this single one
470   Could be but Julia (whom on this occasion
I shall have much to speak about), and she
Was married, charming, chaste, and twenty-three.

         60

Her eye (I'm very fond of handsome eyes)
  Was large and dark, suppressing half its fire
475 Until she spoke, then through its soft disguise
  Flashed an expression more of pride than ire,
And love than either; and there would arise
  A something in them which was not desire,
But would have been, perhaps, but for the soul
480 Which struggled through and chastened down the whole.

         61

Her glossy hair was clustered o'er a brow
  Bright with intelligence, and fair, and smooth;
Her eyebrow's shape was like the aërial bow,°   *rainbow*
  Her cheek all purple° with the beam of youth,   *rosy*
485 Mounting, at times, to a transparent glow,
  As if her veins ran lightning; she, in sooth,
Possessed an air and grace by no means common:
Her stature tall—I hate a dumpy woman.

         62

Wedded she was some years, and to a man
490   Of fifty, and such husbands are in plenty;
And yet, I think, instead of such a ONE
  'Twere better to have TWO of five-and-twenty,
Especially in countries near the sun:
  And now I think on't, "*mi vien in mente,*"[3]
495 Ladies even of the most uneasy virtue
Prefer a spouse whose age is short of thirty.

         63

'Tis a sad thing, I cannot choose but say,
  And all the fault of that indecent sun,
Who cannot leave alone our helpless clay,
500   But will keep baking, broiling, burning on,
That howsoever people fast and pray,
  The flesh is frail, and so the soul undone:

---

3. It comes to my mind.

What men call gallantry, and gods adultery,
Is much more common where the climate's sultry.

64

Happy the nations of the moral North!
  Where all is virtue, and the winter season
Sends sin, without a rag on, shivering forth
  ('Twas snow that brought St. Anthony to reason);[4]
Where juries cast up what a wife is worth,
  By laying whate'er sum, in mulct,° they please on   as a fine
The lover, who must pay a handsome price,
Because it is a marketable vice.

65

Alfonso was the name of Julia's lord,
  A man well looking for his years, and who
Was neither much beloved nor yet abhorred:
  They lived together as most people do,
Suffering each other's foibles by accord,
  And not exactly either *one* or *two;*
Yet he was jealous, though he did not show it,
For Jealousy dislikes the world to know it.

66

Julia was—yet I never could see why—
  With Donna Inez quite a favorite friend;
Between their tastes there was small sympathy,
  For not a line had Julia ever penned:
Some people whisper (but, no doubt, they lie,
  For Malice still imputes some private end)
That Inez had, ere Don Alfonso's marriage,
Forgot with him her very prudent carriage;°   behavior

67

And that still keeping up the old connection,
  Which Time had lately rendered much more chaste,
She took his lady also in affection,
  And certainly this course was much the best:
She flattered Julia with her sage protection,
  And complimented Don Alfonso's taste;
And if she could not (who can?) silence scandal,
At least she left it a more slender handle.

68

I can't tell whether Julia saw the affair
  With other people's eyes, or if her own
Discoveries made, but none could be aware
  Of this, at least no symptom e'er was shown;
Perhaps she did not know, or did not care,
  Indifferent from the first, or callous grown:
I'm really puzzled what to think or say,
She kept her counsel in so close a way.

69

Juan she saw, and, as a pretty child,
  Caressed him often—such a thing might be
Quite innocently done, and harmless styled,
  When she had twenty years, and thirteen he;
But I am not so sure I should have smiled
  When he was sixteen, Julia twenty-three;
These few short years make wondrous alterations,
Particularly amongst sun-burnt nations.

4. St. Anthony recommended the application of snow as a remedy for lust.

70

Whate'er the cause might be, they had become
  Changed; for the dame grew distant, the youth shy,
555 Their looks cast down, their greetings almost dumb,
  And much embarrassment in either eye;
There surely will be little doubt with some
  That Donna Julia knew the reason why,
But as for Juan, he had no more notion
560 Than he who never saw the sea of Ocean.

71

Yet Julia's very coldness still was kind,
  And tremulously gentle her small hand
Withdrew itself from his, but left behind
  A little pressure, thrilling, and so bland
565 And slight, so very slight, that to the mind
  'Twas but a doubt; but ne'er magician's wand
Wrought change with all Armida's[5] fairy art
Like what this light touch left on Juan's heart.

72

And if she met him, though she smiled no more,
570   She looked a sadness sweeter than her smile,
As if her heart had deeper thoughts in store
  She must not own, but cherished more the while
For that compression in its burning core;
  Even Innocence itself has many a wile,
575 And will not dare to trust itself with truth,
And Love is taught hypocrisy from youth.

73

But Passion most dissembles, yet betrays
  Even by its darkness; as the blackest sky
Foretells the heaviest tempest, it displays
580   Its workings through the vainly guarded eye,
And in whatever aspect it arrays
  Itself, 'tis still the same hypocrisy;
Coldness or Anger, even Disdain or Hate,
Are masks it often wears, and still too late.

74

585 Then there were sighs, the deeper for suppression,
  And stolen glances, sweeter for the theft,
And burning blushes, though for no transgression,
  Tremblings when met, and restlessness when left;
All these are little preludes to possession,
590   Of which young Passion cannot be bereft,
And merely tend to show how greatly Love is
Embarrassed at first starting with a novice.

75

Poor Julia's heart was in an awkward state;
  She felt it going, and resolved to make
595 The noblest efforts for herself and mate,
  For Honor's, Pride's, Religion's, Virtue's sake:
Her resolutions were most truly great,
  And almost might have made a Tarquin[6] quake:
She prayed the Virgin Mary for her grace,
600 As being the best judge of a lady's case.

---

5. An enchantress who seduces Christian knights
in Tasso's *Jerusalem Delivered.*
6. The ravisher of a Roman noblewoman re-

nowned for her chastity, in Shakespeare's
Rape of Lucrece.

76

She vowed she never would see Juan more,
    And next day paid a visit to his mother,
And looked extremely at the opening door,
    Which, by the Virgin's grace, let in another;
Grateful she was, and yet a little sore—
    Again it opens, it can be no other,
'Tis surely Juan now—No! I'm afraid
That night the Virgin was no further prayed.

77

She now determined that a virtuous woman
    Should rather face and overcome temptation,
That flight was base and dastardly, and no man
    Should ever give her heart the least sensation,
That is to say, a thought beyond the common
    Preference, that we must feel, upon occasion,
For people who are pleasanter than others,
But then they only seem so many brothers.

78

And even if by chance—and who can tell?
    The Devil's so very sly—she should discover
That all within was not so very well,
    And, if still free,[7] that such or such a lover
Might please perhaps, a virtuous wife can quell
    Such thoughts, and be the better when they're over;
And if the man should ask, 'tis but denial:
I recommend young ladies to make trial.

79

And, then, there are such things as Love divine,
    Bright and immaculate, unmixed and pure,
Such as the angels think so very fine,
    And matrons, who would be no less secure,
Platonic, perfect, "just such love as mine;"
    Thus Julia said—and thought so, to be sure;
And so I'd have her think, were *I* the man
On whom her reveries celestial ran.

80

Such love is innocent, and may exist
    Between young persons without any danger.
A hand may first, and then a lip be kissed;
    For my part, to such doings I'm a stranger,
But *hear* these freedoms form the utmost list
    Of all o'er which such love may be a ranger:
If people go beyond, 'tis quite a crime,
But not my fault—I tell them all in time.

81

Love, then, but Love within its proper limits,
    Was Julia's innocent determination
In young Don Juan's favour, and to him its
    Exertion might be useful on occasion;
And, lighted at too pure a shrine to dim its
    Ethereal luster, with what sweet persuasion
He might be taught, by Love and her together—
I really don't know what, nor Julia either.

---

7. I.e., if she were not already married.

82

Frought with this fine intention, and well fenced
    In mail of proof—her purity of soul—
She, for the future, of her strength convinced,
    And that her honor was a rock, or mole,°   **breakwater**
Exceeding sagely from that hour dispensed
    With any kind of troublesome control;
But whether Julia to the task was equal
Is that which must be mentioned in the sequel.

83

Her plan she deemed both innocent and feasible,
    And, surely, with a stripling of sixteen
Not Scandal's fangs could fix on much that's seizable,
    Or if they did so, satisfied to mean
Nothing but what was good, her breast was peaceable—
    A quiet conscience makes one so serene!
Christians have burnt each other, quite persuaded
That all the Apostles would have done as they did.

84

And if in the mean time her husband died,
    But Heaven forbid that such a thought should cross
Her brain, though in a dream! (and then she sighed)
    Never could she survive that common loss;
But just suppose that moment should betide,
    I only say suppose it—*inter nos:*[8]
(This should be *entre nous,* for Julia thought
In French, but then the rhyme would go for nought.)

85

I only say, suppose this supposition:
    Juan being then grown up to man's estate
Would fully suit a widow of condition,
    Even seven years hence it would not be too late;
And in the interim (to pursue this vision)
    The mischief, after all, could not be great,
For he would learn the rudiments of Love,
I mean the *seraph*° way of those above.   **angelic, pure**

86

So much for Julia! Now we'll turn to Juan.
    Poor little fellow! he had no idea
Of his own case, and never hit the true one;
    In feelings quick as Ovid's Miss Medea,[9]
He puzzled over what he found a new one,
    But not as yet imagined it could be a
Thing quite in course, and not at all alarming,
Which, with a little patience, might grow charming.

87

Silent and pensive, idle, restless, slow,
    His home deserted for the lonely wood,
Tormented with a wound he could not know,
    His, like all deep grief, plunged in solitude:
I'm fond myself of solitude or so,
    But then, I beg it may be understood,
By solitude I mean a Sultan's (not
A Hermit's), with a harem for a grot.

8. Just between ourselves.
9. In Ovid's *Metamorphoses,* the young Medea   finds herself irresistibly infatuated with the hero Jason.

88

"Oh Love! in such a wilderness as this,
　　Where Transport and Security entwine,
Here is the Empire of thy perfect bliss,
　　And here thou art a God indeed divine."
The bard[1] I quote from does not sing amiss,
　　With the exception of the second line,
For that same twining "Transport and Security"
Are twisted to a phrase of some obscurity.

89

The Poet meant, no doubt, and thus appeals
　　To the good sense and senses of mankind,
The very thing which everybody feels,
　　As all have found on trial, or may find,
That no one likes to be disturbed at meals
　　Or love—I won't say more about "entwined"
Or "Transport," as we knew all that before,
But beg "Security" will bolt the door.

90

Young Juan wandered by the glassy brooks,
　　Thinking unutterable things; he threw
Himself at length within the leafy nooks
　　Where the wild branch of the cork forest grew;
There poets find materials for their books,
　　And every now and then we read them through,
So that their plan and prosody are eligible,
Unless, like Wordsworth, they prove unintelligible.

91

He, Juan (and not Wordsworth), so pursued
　　His self-communion with his own high soul,
Until his mighty heart, in its great mood,
　　Had mitigated part, though not the whole
Of its disease; he did the best he could
　　With things not very subject to control,
And turned, without perceiving his condition,
Like Coleridge, into a metaphysician.

92

He thought about himself, and the whole earth,
　　Of man the wonderful, and of the stars,
And how the deuce they ever could have birth;
　　And then he thought of earthquakes, and of wars,
How many miles the moon might have in girth,
　　Of air-balloons, and of the many bars
To perfect knowledge of the boundless skies;—
And then he thought of Donna Julia's eyes.

93

In thoughts like these true Wisdom may discern
　　Longings sublime, and aspirations high,
Which some are born with, but the most part learn
　　To plague themselves withal, they know not why:
'Twas strange that one so young should thus concern
　　His brain about the action of the sky;
If *you* think 'twas Philosophy that this did,
I can't help thinking puberty assisted.

---

1. Byron's contemporary, Thomas Campbell, whose *Gertrude of Wyoming* is here paraphrased.

94

745 He pored upon the leaves, and on the flowers,
 And heard a voice in all the winds; and then
He thought of wood-nymphs and immortal bowers,
 And how the goddesses came down to men:
He missed the pathway, he forgot the hours,
750 And when he looked upon his watch again,
He found how much old Time had been a winner—
He also found that he had lost his dinner.

95

Sometimes he turned to gaze upon his book,
 Boscan, or Garcilasso;[2]—by the wind
755 Even as the page is rustled while we look,
 So by the poesy of his own mind
Over the mystic leaf his soul was shook,
 As if 'twere one whereon magicians bind
Their spells, and give them to the passing gale,
760 According to some good old woman's tale.

96

Thus would he while his lonely hours away
 Dissatisfied, not knowing what he wanted;
Nor glowing reverie, nor poet's lay,
 Could yield his spirit that for which it panted,
765 A bosom whereon he his head might lay,
 And hear the heart beat with the love it granted,
With——several other things, which I forget,
Or which, at least, I need not mention yet.

97

Those lonely walks, and lengthening reveries,
770 Could not escape the gentle Julia's eyes;
She saw that Juan was not at his ease;
 But that which chiefly may, and must surprise,
Is, that the Donna Inez did not tease
 Her only son with question or surmise;
775 Whether it was she did not see, or would not,
Or, like all very clever people, could not.

98

This may seem strange, but yet 'tis very common;
 For instance—gentlemen, whose ladies take
Leave to o'erstep the written rights of Woman,
780 And break the——Which commandment is't they break?
(I have forgot the number, and think no man
 Should rashly quote, for fear of a mistake;)
I say, when these same gentlemen are jealous,
They make some blunder, which their ladies tell us.

99

785 A real husband always is suspicious,
 But still no less suspects in the wrong place,
Jealous of some one who had no such wishes,
 Or pandering blindly to his own disgrace,
By harboring some dear friend extremely vicious;
790 The last indeed's infallibly the case:
And when the spouse and friend are gone off wholly,
He wonders at their vice, and not his folly.

---

2. Spanish poets of the early 16th century.

100

Thus parents also are at times short-sighted:
  Though watchful as the lynx, they ne'er discover,
The while the wicked world beholds delighted,
  Young Hopeful's mistress, or Miss Fanny's lover,
Till some confounded escapade has blighted
  The plan of twenty years, and all is over;
And then the mother cries, the father swears,
And wonders why the devil he got heirs.

101

But Inez was so anxious, and so clear
  Of sight, that I must think, on this occasion,
She had some other motive much more near
  For leaving Juan to this new temptation,
But what that motive was, I shan't say here;
  Perhaps to finish Juan's education,
Perhaps to open Don Alfonso's eyes,
In case he thought his wife too great a prize.

102

It was upon a day, a summer's day—
  Summer's indeed a very dangerous season,
And so is spring about the end of May;
  The sun, no doubt, is the prevailing reason;
But whatsoe'er the cause is, one may say,
  And stand convicted of more truth than treason,
That there are months which nature grows more merry in,—
March has its hares, and May must have its heroine.

103

'Twas on a summer's day—the sixth of June:
  I like to be particular in dates,
Not only of the age, and year, but moon;
  They are a sort of post-house, where the Fates
Change horses, making History change its tune,
  Then spur away o'er empires and o'er states,
Leaving at last not much besides chronology,
Excepting the post-obits[3] of theology.

104

'Twas on the sixth of June, about the hour
  Of half-past six—perhaps still nearer seven—
When Julia sate within as pretty a bower
  As e'er held houri[4] in that heathenish heaven
Described by Mahomet, and Anacreon Moore,[5]
  To whom the lyre and laurels have been given,
With all the trophies of triumphant song—
He won them well, and may he wear them long!

105

She sate, but not alone; I know not well
  How this same interview had taken place,
And even if I knew, I should not tell—
  People should hold their tongues in any case;
No matter how or why the thing befell,
  But there were she and Juan, face to face—
When two such faces are so, 'twould be wise,
But very difficult, to shut their eyes.

3. Loans repaid from the estate of a person
after his death; probably referring to rewards
or punishments in the afterlife.
4. A beautiful maiden said to entertain faith-
ful Muslims in Paradise.

5. Byron's friend, Thomas Moore, author of
oriental tales in his long poem *Lalla Rookh*,
and translator of love poems by the ancient
Greek poet Anacreon.

106

How beautiful she looked! her conscious heart[6]
  Glowed in her cheek, and yet she felt no wrong:
Oh Love! how perfect is thy mystic art,
  Strengthening the weak, and trampling on the strong!
845 How self-deceitful is the sagest part
  Of mortals whom thy lure hath led along!
The precipice she stood on was immense,
So was her creed° in her own innocence.   trust

107

She thought of her own strength, and Juan's youth,
850   And of the folly of all prudish fears,
Victorious Virtue, and domestic Truth,
  And then of Don Alfonso's fifty years:
I wish these last had not occurred, in sooth,
  Because that number rarely much endears,
855 And through all climes, the snowy and the sunny,
Sounds ill in love, whate'er it may in money.

108

When people say, "I've told you *fifty* times,"
  They mean to scold, and very often do;
When poets say, "I've written *fifty* rhymes,"
860   They make you dread that they'll recite them too;
In gangs of *fifty*, thieves commit their crimes;
  At *fifty* love for love is rare, 'tis true,
But then, no doubt, it equally as true is,
A good deal may be bought for *fifty* Louis[7].

109

865 Julia had honor, virtue, truth, and love
  For Don Alfonso; and she inly swore,
By all the vows below to Powers above,
  She never would disgrace the ring she wore,
Nor leave a wish which wisdom might reprove;
870   And while she pondered this, besides much more,
One hand on Juan's carelessly was thrown,
Quite by mistake—she thought it was her own;

110

Unconsciously she leaned upon the other,
  Which played within the tangles of her hair;
875 And to contend with thoughts she could not smother
  She seemed by the distraction of her air.
'Twas surely very wrong in Juan's mother
  To leave together this imprudent pair,
She who for many years had watched her son so—
880 I'm very certain *mine* would not have done so.

111

The hand which still held Juan's, by degrees
  Gently, but palpably confirmed its grasp,
As if it said, "Detain me, if you please";
  Yet there's no doubt she only meant to clasp
885 His fingers with a pure Platonic squeeze;
  She would have shrunk as from a toad, or asp,
Had she imagined such a thing could rouse
A feeling dangerous to a prudent spouse.

---

6. Deep emotion.   7. French gold coins.

112

I cannot know what Juan thought of this,
  But what he did, is much what you would do;
His young lip thanked it with a grateful kiss,
  And then, abashed at its own joy, withdrew
In deep despair, lest he had done amiss—
  Love is so very timid when 'tis new:
She blushed, and frowned not, but she strove to speak,
And held her tongue, her voice was grown so weak.

113

The sun set, and up rose the yellow moon:
  The Devil's in the moon for mischief; they
Who called her CHASTE, methinks, began too soon
  Their nomenclature; there is not a day,
The longest, not the twenty-first of June,
  Sees half the business in a wicked way,
On which three single hours of moonshine smile—
And then she looks so modest all the while!

114

There is a dangerous silence in that hour,
  A stillness, which leaves room for the full soul
To open all itself, without the power
  Of calling wholly back its self-control;
The silver light which, hallowing tree and tower,
  Sheds beauty and deep softness o'er the whole,
Breathes also to the heart, and o'er it throws
A loving languor, which is not repose.

115

And Julia sate with Juan, half embraced
  And half retiring from the glowing arm,
Which trembled like the bosom where 'twas placed;
  Yet still she must have thought there was no harm,
Or else 'twere easy to withdraw her waist;
  But then the situation had its charm,
And then——God knows what next—I can't go on;
I'm almost sorry that I e'er begun.

116

Oh Plato! Plato! you have paved the way,
  With your confounded fantasies, to more
Immoral conduct by the fancied sway
  Your system feigns o'er the controlless core
Of human hearts, than all the long array
  Of poets and romancers:—You're a bore,
A charlatan, a coxcomb—and have been,
At best, no better than a go-between.

117

And Julia's voice was lost, except in sighs,
  Until too late for useful conversation;
The tears were gushing from her gentle eyes,
  I wish, indeed, they had not had occasion;
But who, alas! can love, and then be wise?
  Not that Remorse did not oppose Temptation;
A little still she strove, and much repented,
And whispering "I will ne'er consent"—consented.

118

'Tis said that Xerxes[8] offered a reward
  To those who could invent him a new pleasure:

8. King of Persia, fifth century B.C.

Methinks the requisition's rather hard,
940   And must have cost his Majesty a treasure:
For my part, I'm a moderate-minded bard,
    Fond of a little love (which I call leisure);
I care not for new pleasures, as the old
Are quite enough for me, so they but hold.

119

945   Oh Pleasure! you're indeed a pleasant thing,
    Although one must be damned for you, no doubt:
I make a resolution every spring
    Of reformation, ere the year run out,
But somehow, this my vestal vow takes wing,
950   Yet still, I trust, it may be kept throughout:
I'm very sorry, very much ashamed,
And mean, next winter, to be quite reclaimed.

1819

Stanzas

WHEN A MAN HATH NO FREEDOM TO FIGHT FOR AT HOME

When a man hath no freedom to fight for at home,
    Let him combat for that of his neighbors;
Let him think of the glories of Greece and of Rome,
    And get knocked on his head for his labors.

5   To do good to mankind is the chivalrous plan,
    And is always as nobly requited;
Then battle for freedom wherever you can,
    And, if not shot or hanged, you'll get knighted.

1824

On This Day I Complete My Thirty-sixth Year

Missolonghi,[6] January 22, 1824

'Tis time this heart should be unmoved,
    Since others it hath ceased to move:
Yet, though I cannot be beloved,
        Still let me love!

5   My days are in the yellow leaf;
    The flowers and fruits of love are gone;
The worm, the canker,° and the grief   *deep infection*
        Are mine alone!

The fire that on my bosom preys
10   Is lone as some volcanic isle;
No torch is kindled at its blaze—
        A funeral pile.

The hope, the fear, the jealous care,
    The exalted portion of the pain
15   And power of love, I cannot share,
        But wear the chain.

6. In Greece, where Byron had gone to support the Greek war for independence from Turkey, and where he died, April 19, 1824.

But 'tis not *thus*—and 'tis not *here*—
   Such thoughts should shake my soul, nor *now*,
Where glory decks the hero's bier,
      Or binds his brow.

The sword, the banner, and the field,
   Glory and Greece, around me see!
The Spartan, borne upon his shield,
      Was not more free.

Awake! (not Greece—she *is* awake!)
   Awake, my spirit! Think through *whom*
Thy life-blood tracks its parent lake,
      And then strike home!

Tread those reviving passions down,
   Unworthy manhood!—unto thee
Indifferent should the smile or frown
      Of beauty be.

If thou regrett'st thy youth, *why live?*
   The land of honorable death
Is here:—up to the field, and give
      Away thy breath!

Seek out—less often sought than found—
   A soldier's grave, for thee the best;
Then look around, and choose thy ground,
      And take thy rest.

                            1824

PERCY BYSSHE SHELLEY
(1792–1822)

To Wordsworth

Poet of Nature, thou hast wept to know
   That things depart which never may return;
   Childhood and youth, friendship and love's first glow,
   Have fled like sweet dreams, leaving thee to mourn.
These common woes I feel. One loss is mine,
   Which thou too feel'st, yet I alone deplore;
   Thou wert as a lone star whose light did shine
   On some frail bark in winter's midnight roar;
Thou hast like to a rock-built refuge stood
   Above the blind and battling multitude;
   In honored poverty thy voice did weave
Songs consecrate to truth and liberty;—
   Deserting these, thou leavest me to grieve,
   Thus having been, that thou shouldst cease to be.[1]

                            1816

---

1. I.e., Wordsworth had ceased to champion the liberal and revolutionary ideas of his youth and, in Shelley's view, had compromised himself.

Hymn to Intellectual Beauty[2]

1

The awful shadow of some unseen Power
  Floats though unseen among us—visiting
  This various world with as inconstant wing
As summer winds that creep from flower to flower—
5 Like moonbeams that behind some piny mountain shower,
    It visits with inconstant glance
    Each human heart and countenance;
Like hues and harmonies of evening—
  Like clouds in starlight widely spread—
10   Like memory of music fled—
    Like aught that for its grace may be
Dear, and yet dearer for its mystery.

2

Spirit of BEAUTY, that dost consecrate
  With thine own hues all thou dost shine upon
15 Of human thought or form—where art thou gone?
Why dost thou pass away and leave our state,
This dim vast vale of tears, vacant and desolate?
    Ask why the sunlight not forever
    Weaves rainbows o'er yon mountain river,
20 Why aught should fail and fade that once is shown,
    Why fear and dream and death and birth
    Cast on the daylight of this earth
  Such gloom—why man has such a scope
For love and hate, despondency and hope?

3

25 No voice from some sublimer world hath ever
  To sage or poet these responses given—
  Therefore the names of Daemon, Ghost, and Heaven,
Remain the records of their vain endeavor,
Frail spells—whose uttered charm might not avail to sever,
30   From all we hear and all we see,
    Doubt, chance, and mutability.
Thy light alone—like mist o'er mountains driven,
    Or music by the night wind sent
    Through strings of some still instrument,
35   Or moonlight on a midnight stream,
Gives grace and truth to life's unquiet dream.

4

Love, Hope, and Self-esteem, like clouds depart
  And come, for some uncertain moments lent.
  Man were immortal, and omnipotent,
40 Didst thou, unknown and awful as thou art,
Keep with thy glorious train° firm state within his heart.   *company*
    Thou messenger of sympathies,
    That wax and wane in lovers' eyes—
Thou—that to human thought art nourishment,
45   Like darkness to a dying flame!
    Depart not as thy shadow came,
    Depart not—lest the grave should be,
Like life and fear, a dark reality.

---

2. Beauty perceived not by the senses but by spiritual illumination.

5

While yet a boy I sought for ghosts, and sped
50   Through many a listening chamber, cave and ruin,
And starlight wood, with fearful steps pursuing
Hopes of high talk with the departed dead.
I called on poisonous names[3] with which our youth is fed;
    I was not heard—I saw them not—
55   When musing deeply on the lot
Of life, at that sweet time when winds are wooing
    All vital things that wake to bring
    News of birds and blossoming—
    Sudden, thy shadow fell on me;
60 I shrieked, and clasped my hands in ecstasy!

6

I vowed that I would dedicate my powers
    To thee and thine—have I not kept the vow?
    With beating heart and streaming eyes, even now
I call the phantoms of a thousand hours
65 Each from his voiceless grave: they have in visioned bowers
    Of studious zeal or love's delight
    Outwatched with me the envious night—
They know that never joy illumed my brow
    Unlinked with hope that thou wouldst free
70   This world from its dark slavery,
    That thou—O awful LOVELINESS,
Wouldst give whate'er these words cannot express.

7

The day becomes more solemn and serene
    When noon is past—there is a harmony
75   In autumn, and a luster in its sky,
Which through the summer is not heard or seen,
As if it could not be, as if it had not been!
    Thus let thy power, which like the truth
    Of nature on my passive youth
80 Descended, to my onward life supply
    Its calm—to one who worships thee,
    And every form containing thee,
Whom, SPIRIT fair, thy spells did bind
To fear himself, and love all human kind.

1817

Ozymandias[4]

I met a traveler from an antique land
Who said: Two vast and trunkless legs of stone
Stand in the desert . . . Near them, on the sand,
Half sunk, a shattered visage lies, whose frown,
5 And wrinkled lip, and sneer of cold command,
Tell that its sculptor well those passions read
Which yet survive, stamped on these lifeless things,
The hand that mocked them, and the heart that fed:
And on the pedestal these words appear:
10 "My name is Ozymandias, king of kings:
Look on my works, ye Mighty, and despair!"

---

3. Possibly alluding to attempts to summon spirits of the dead by means of magic rites.
4. Greek name for the Egyptian monarch Ramses II (13th century B.C.), who is said to have erected a huge statue of himself.

Nothing beside remains. Round the decay
Of that colossal wreck, boundless and bare
The lone and level sands stretch far away.

1818

Stanzas Written in Dejection, Near Naples

1

The sun is warm, the sky is clear,
  The waves are dancing fast and bright,
Blue isles and snowy mountains wear
  The purple noon's transparent might,
5   The breath of the moist earth is light,
Around its unexpanded buds;
  Like many a voice of one delight,
The winds, the birds, the ocean floods,
The City's voice itself is soft like Solitude's.

2

10 I see the Deep's untrampled floor
  With green and purple seaweeds strown;
I see the waves upon the shore,
  Like light dissolved in star-showers, thrown:
I sit upon the sands alone—
15   The lightning of the noontide ocean
  Is flashing round me, and a tone
Arises from its measured motion;
How sweet! did any heart now share in my emotion.

3

20 Alas! I have nor hope nor health,
  Nor peace within nor calm around,
Nor that content surpassing wealth
  The sage in meditation found,
  And walked with inward glory crowned—
Nor fame, nor power, nor love, nor leisure.
25   Others I see whom these surround—
Smiling they live, and call life pleasure;
To me that cup has been dealt in another measure.

4

Yet now despair itself is mild,
  Even as the winds and waters are;
30 I could lie down like a tired child,
  And weep away the life of care
  Which I have borne and yet must bear,
Till death like sleep might steal on me,
  And I might feel in the warm air
35 My cheek grow cold, and hear the sea
Breathe o'er my dying brain its last monotony.

5

Some might lament that I were cold,
  As I, when this sweet day is gone,
Which my lost heart, too soon grown old,
40   Insults with this untimely moan;
  They might lament—for I am one
Whom men love not—and yet regret,
  Unlike this day, which, when the sun
Shall on its stainless glory set,
Will linger, though enjoyed, like joy in memory yet.

1818   1824

England in 1819

An old, mad, blind, despised, and dying king[5]—
Princes, the dregs of their dull race,[6] who flow
Through public scorn—mud from a muddy spring;
Rulers who neither see, nor feel, nor know,
5   But leechlike to their fainting country cling,
Till they drop, blind in blood, without a blow;
A people starved and stabbed in the untilled field—
An army, which liberticide[7] and prey
Makes as a two-edged sword to all who wield;
10   Golden and sanguine[8] laws which tempt and slay;
Religion Christless, Godless—a book sealed;
A Senate—Time's worst statute[9] unrepealed—
Are graves, from which a glorious Phantom[1] may
Burst, to illumine our tempestuous day.

1819   1839

Ode to the West Wind

1

O wild West Wind, thou breath of Autumn's being,
Thou, from whose unseen presence the leaves dead
Are driven, like ghosts from an enchanter fleeing,

Yellow, and black, and pale, and hectic red,
5   Pestilence-stricken multitudes: O thou,
Who chariotest to their dark wintry bed

The wingèd seeds, where they lie cold and low,
Each like a corpse within its grave, until
Thine azure sister of the Spring shall blow

10   Her clarion[2] o'er the dreaming earth, and fill
(Driving sweet buds like flocks to feed in air)
With living hues and odors plain and hill:

Wild Spirit, which art moving everywhere;
Destroyer and preserver; hear, oh, hear!

2

15   Thou on whose stream, mid the steep sky's commotion,
Loose clouds like earth's decaying leaves are shed,
Shook from the tangled boughs of Heaven and Ocean,

Angels[3] of rain and lightning: there are spread
On the blue surface of thine aëry surge,
20   Like the bright hair uplifted from the head

Of some fierce Maenad,[4] even from the dim verge
Of the horizon to the zenith's height,
The locks of the approaching storm. Thou dirge

5. George III (1738–1820), who lived for years in a state of advanced senility. The "Princes" of line 2 are George III's sons, including the Prince-Regent, later George IV, whom Shelley detested.
6. The "Hanoverian" line of English monarchs, beginning in 1714 with George I.
7. Destruction of liberty.
8. Sanguinary; causing bloodshed.

9. I.e., probably the Act of Union (1801) uniting Ireland to England and excluding Roman Catholics from exercising full citizenship.
1. I.e., the spirit of liberty.
2. Melodious trumpet-call.
3. In Greek derivation, messengers or divine messengers.
4. Frenzied dancer, worshipper of Dionysus, a god of wine and fertility.

Of the dying year, to which this closing night
25 Will be the dome of a vast sepulcher,
Vaulted with all thy congregated might

Of vapors, from whose solid atmosphere
Black rain, and fire, and hail will burst: oh, hear!

3

Thou who didst waken from his summer dreams
30 The blue Mediterranean, where he lay,
Lulled by the coil of his crystálline streams,

Beside a pumice isle in Baiae's bay,[5]
And saw in sleep old palaces and towers
Quivering within the wave's intenser day,

35 All overgrown with azure moss and flowers
So sweet, the sense faints picturing them! Thou
For whose path the Atlantic's level powers

Cleave themselves into chasms, while far below
The sea-blooms and the oozy woods which wear
40 The sapless foliage of the ocean, know

Thy voice, and suddenly grow gray with fear,
And tremble and despoil themselves: oh, hear!

4

If I were a dead leaf thou mightest bear;
If I were a swift cloud to fly with thee;
45 A wave to pant beneath thy power, and share

The impulse of thy strength, only less free
Than thou, O uncontrollable! If even
I were as in my boyhood, and could be

The comrade of thy wanderings over Heaven,
50 As then, when to outstrip thy skyey speed
Scarce seem a vision; I would ne'er have striven

As thus with thee in prayer in my sore need.
Oh, lift me as a wave, a leaf, a cloud!
I fall upon the thorns of life! I bleed!

55 A heavy weight of hours has chained and bowed
One too like thee: tameless, and swift, and proud.

5

Make me thy lyre,[6] even as the forest is:
What if my leaves are falling like its own!
The tumult of thy mighty harmonies

60 Will take from both a deep, autumnal tone,
Sweet though in sadness. Be thou, Spirit fierce,
My spirit! Be thou me, impetuous one!

---

5. Near Naples, Italy.   6. Small harp traditionally used to accompany
                                          songs and recited poems.

Drive my dead thoughts over the universe
Like withered leaves to quicken a new birth!
5 And, by the incantation of this verse,

Scatter, as from an unextinguished hearth
Ashes and sparks, my words among mankind!
Be through my lips to unawakened earth

The trumpet of a prophecy! O Wind,
10 If Winter comes, can Spring be far behind?

                                                                          1820

The Cloud

I bring fresh showers for the thirsting flowers,
     From the seas and the streams;
I bear light shade for the leaves when laid
     In their noonday dreams.
5 From my wings are shaken the dews that waken
     The sweet buds every one,
When rocked to rest on their mother's breast,
     As she dances about the sun.
I wield the flail of the lashing hail,
10   And whiten the green plains under,
And then again I dissolve it in rain,
     And laugh as I pass in thunder.

I sift the snow on the mountains below,
     And their great pines groan aghast;
15 And all the night 'tis my pillow white,
     While I sleep in the arms of the blast.
Sublime on the towers of my skyey bowers,
     Lightning my pilot[7] sits;
In a cavern under is fettered the thunder,
20   It struggles and howls at fits;°   *intermittently*
Over earth and ocean, with gentle motion,
     This pilot is guiding me,
Lured by the love of the genii that move
     In the depths of the purple sea;
25 Over the rills, and the crags, and the hills,
     Over the lakes and the plains,
Wherever he dream, under mountain or stream,
     The Spirit he loves remains;
And I all the while bask in Heaven's blue smile,
30   Whilst he is dissolving in rains.

The sanguine Sunrise, with his meteor eyes,
     And his burning plumes outspread,
Leaps on the back of my sailing rack,[8]
     When the morning star shines dead;
35 As on the jag of a mountain crag,
     Which an earthquake rocks and swings,
An eagle alit one moment may sit
     In the light of its golden wings.

7. Electrical energy, here represented as direct-
ing the cloud in response to the attraction of
opposite charges ("genii," line 23) under the
sea.
8. Wind-driven clouds.

And when Sunset may breathe, from the lit sea beneath,
40　　　Its ardors of rest and of love,
And the crimson pall of eve may fall
　　From the depth of Heaven above,
With wings folded I rest, on mine aëry nest,
　　As still as a brooding dove.

45　That orbéd maiden with white fire laden,
　　Whom mortals call the Moon,
Glides glimmering o'er my fleecelike floor,
　　By the midnight breezes strewn;
And wherever the beat of her unseen feet,
50　　Which only the angels hear,
May have broken the woof° of my tent's thin roof,　　　*fabric*
　　The stars peep behind her and peer;
And I laugh to see them whirl and flee,
　　Like a swarm of golden bees,
55　When I widen the rent in my wind-built tent,
　　Till the calm rivers, lakes, and seas,
Like strips of the sky fallen through me on high,
　　Are each paved with the moon and these.

60　I bind the Sun's throne with a burning zone,°　　　*belt*
　　And the Moon's with a girdle of pearl;
The volcanoes are dim, and the stars reel and swim,
　　When the whirlwinds my banner unfurl.
From cape to cape, with a bridgelike shape,
　　Over a torrent sea,
65　Sunbeam-proof, I hang like a roof—
　　The mountains its columns be.
The triumphal arch through which I march
　　With hurricane, fire, and snow,
When the Powers of the air are chained to my chair,
70　　Is the million-colored bow;
The sphere-fire above its soft colors wove,
　　While the moist Earth was laughing below.

I am the daughter of Earth and Water,
　　And the nursling of the Sky;
75　I pass through the pores of the ocean and shores;
　　I change, but I cannot die.
For after the rain when with never a stain
　　The pavilion of Heaven is bare,
And the winds and sunbeams with their convex° gleams　　*upward-arching*
80　　Build up the blue dome of air,
I silently laugh at my own cenotaph,[9]
　　And out of the caverns of rain,
Like a child from the womb, like a ghost from the tomb,
　　I arise and unbuild it again.

　　　　　　　　　　　　　　　　　　　　　　　1820

---

9. Monument honoring a person who is buried elsewhere.

To a Skylark

Hail to thee, blithe Spirit!
  Bird thou never wert,
That from Heaven, or near it,
  Pourest thy full heart
5 In profuse strains of unpremeditated art.

Higher still and higher
  From the earth thou springest
Like a cloud of fire;
  The blue deep thou wingest,
10 And singing still dost soar, and soaring ever singest.

In the golden lightning
  Of the sunken sun,
O'er which clouds are bright'ning,
  Thou dost float and run;
15 Like an unbodied joy whose race is just begun.

The pale purple even
  Melts around thy flight;
Like a star of Heaven,
  In the broad daylight
20 Thou art unseen, but yet I hear thy shrill delight,

Keen as are the arrows
  Of that silver sphere,°   **star**
Whose intense lamp narrows
  In the white dawn clear
25 Until we hardly see—we feel that it is there.

All the earth and air
  With thy voice is loud,
As, when night is bare,
  From one lonely cloud
30 The moon rains out her beams, and Heaven is overflowed.

What thou art we know not;
  What is most like thee?
From rainbow clouds there flow not
  Drops so bright to see
35 As from thy presence showers a rain of melody.

Like a Poet hidden
  In the light of thought,
Singing hymns unbidden,
  Till the world is wrought
40 To sympathy with hopes and fears it heeded not:

Like a high-born maiden
  In a palace tower,
Soothing her love-laden
  Soul in secret hour
45 With music sweet as love, which overflows her bower:

Like a glowworm golden
In a dell of dew,
Scattering unbeholden
Its aërial hue
50 Among the flowers and grass, which screen it from the view!

Like a rose embowered
In its own green leaves,
By warm winds deflowered,
Till the scent it gives
55 Makes faint with too much sweet those heavy-wingéd thieves:

Sound of vernal showers
On the twinkling grass,
Rain-awakened flowers,
All that ever was
60 Joyous, and clear, and fresh, thy music doth surpass:

Teach us, Sprite° or Bird,   *spirit*
What sweet thoughts are thine:
I have never heard
Praise of love or wine
65 That panted forth a flood of rapture so divine.

Chorus Hymeneal,¹
Or triumphal chant,
Matched with thine would be all
But an empty vaunt,
70 A thing wherein we feel there is some hidden want.

What objects are the fountains
Of thy happy strain?
What fields, or waves, or mountains?
What shapes of sky or plain?
75 What love of thine own kind? what ignorance of pain?

With thy clear keen joyance
Languor cannot be:
Shadow of annoyance
Never came near thee:
80 Thou lovest—but ne'er knew love's sad satiety.

Waking or asleep,
Thou of death must deem
Things more true and deep
Than we mortals dream,
85 Or how could thy notes flow in such a crystal stream?

We look before and after,
And pine for what is not:
Our sincerest laughter
With some pain is fraught;
90 Our sweetest songs are those that tell of saddest thought.

Yet if we could scorn
Hate, and pride, and fear;

1. As for a wedding.

If we were things born
    Not to shed a tear,
5 I know not how thy joy we ever should come near.

Better than all measures
    Of delightful sound,
Better than all treasures
    That in books are found,
10 Thy skill to poet were, thou scorner of the ground!

Teach me half the gladness
    That thy brain must know,
Such harmonious madness
    From my lips would flow
The world should listen then—as I am listening now.

                                                    1820

[This Is the Day] [1]

This is the day which down the void abysm
At the earth-born's spell yawns for heaven's despotism, [2]
    And conquest is dragged captive through the deep:
Love, from its awful throne of patient power
5 In the wise heart, from the last giddy hour
    Of dread endurance, from the slippery, steep,
And narrow verge of craglike agony, springs
And folds over the world its healing wings.

Gentleness, virtue, wisdom, and endurance,
10 These are the seals of that most firm assurance
    Which bars the pit over destruction's strength;
And if, with infirm hand, eternity,
    Mother of many acts and hours, should free
The serpent [3] that would clasp her with his length;
15 These are the spells by which to reassume
An empire o'er the disentangled doom:

To suffer woes which hope thinks infinite;
To forgive wrongs darker than death or night;
    To defy power, which seems omnipotent;
20 To love, and bear; to hope till hope creates
From its own wreck the thing it contemplates;
    Neither to change, nor falter, nor repent;
This, like thy glory, Titan, [4] is to be
Good, great and joyous, beautiful and free;
This is alone life, joy, empire, and victory.

                                                    1820

1. The closing speech from Shelley's lyrical
drama, *Prometheus Unbound*. Prometheus
("the earth-born," line 2) was an ancient
Greek deity who stole fire from the heavens
and gave it to mankind. His punishment, im-
posed by Jupiter, was to be chained to a
cliff and torn by vultures so long as he de-
fied Jupiter. Shelley's play relates the fall
of Jupiter and the emancipation of Prome-
theus. This speech is spoken by Demogorgon,
a personification of destiny. He is superior
to the gods and an agent of liberty.
2. The rule of Jupiter.
3. Symbolizing the constructive power of
tyranny.
4. Prometheus.

Adonais[2]

AN ELEGY ON THE DEATH OF JOHN KEATS,
AUTHOR OF ENDYMION, HYPERION, ETC.

'Αστὴρ πρὶν μὲν ἔλαμπες ἐνὶ ζωοῖσιν 'Εῷος·
νῦν δὲ θανὼν λάμπεις "Εσπερος ἐν φθιμένοις.[3]
—PLATO

1

I weep for Adonais—he is dead!
Oh, weep for Adonais! though our tears
Thaw not the frost which binds so dear a head!
And thou, sad Hour, selected from all years
5   To mourn our loss, rouse thy obscure compeers,
And teach them thine own sorrow, say: with me
Died Adonais; till the Future dares
Forget the Past, his fate and fame shall be
An echo and a light unto eternity!

2

10 Where wert thou mighty Mother,[4] when he lay,
When thy Son lay, pierced by the shaft which flies
In darkness? where was lorn Urania
When Adonais died? With veiléd eyes,
'Mid listening Echoes, in her Paradise
15 She sate, while one, with soft enamored breath,
Rekindled all the fading melodies,
With which, like flowers that mock the corse° beneath,   corpse
He had adorned and hid the coming bulk of death.

3

Oh, weep for Adonais—he is dead!
20 Wake, melancholy Mother, wake and weep!
Yet wherefore? Quench within their burning bed
Thy fiery tears, and let thy loud heart keep
Like his, a mute and uncomplaining sleep;
For he is gone, where all things wise and fair
25 Descend:—oh, dream not that the amorous Deep
Will yet restore him to the vital air;
Death feeds on his mute voice, and laughs at our despair.

4

Most musical of mourners, weep again!
Lament anew, Urania!—He[5] died,
30 Who was the Sire of an immortal strain,
Blind, old, and lonely, when his country's pride,
The priest, the slave, and the liberticide,
Trampled and mocked with many a loathéd rite
Of lust and blood; he went, unterrified,
35 Into the gulf of death; but his clear Sprite°   spirit
Yet reigns o'er earth; the third among the sons of light.[6]

---

2. A name derived from *Adonis,* in Greek
legend a young hunter beloved of Aphrodite
(Venus) and killed by a wild boar. The root
meaning of his name, *Adon,* is "the lord," and
in the form *Adonai* appears in Hebrew scrip-
tures as a synonym for *God.*
3. "Thou wert the morning star among the
living,/Ere thy fair light had fled—/Now,
having died, thou art as Hesperus, giving/New
splendor to the dead" [Shelley's translation];

Venus is both Hesperus, the evening star, and
also the morning star.
4. Urania, "heavenly one," Venus invoked as
the Muse of noble poetry. Adonais is repre-
sented as her son.
5. Milton, who also invoked the aid of Urania
(see *Paradise Lost,* I.6–16).
6. Rivaled as a poet by only two predecessors,
Homer and Dante.

5

Most musical of mourners, weep anew!
Not all to that bright station dared to climb;
And happier they their happiness who knew,
Whose tapers yet burn through that night of time
In which suns perished; others more sublime,
Struck by the envious wrath of man or God,
Have sunk, extinct in their refulgent prime;
And some yet live, treading the thorny road,
Which leads, through toil and hate, to Fame's serene abode.

6

But now, thy youngest, dearest one, has perished,
The nursling of thy widowhood, who grew,
Like a pale flower by some sad maiden cherished,
And fed with true-love tears, instead of dew;
Most musical of mourners, weep anew!
Thy extreme° hope, the loveliest and the last,   *highest, latest*
The bloom, whose petals nipped before they blew
Died on the promise of the fruit, is waste;
The broken lily lies—the storm is overpast.

7

To that high Capital,[7] where kingly Death
Keeps his pale court in beauty and decay,
He came; and bought, with price of purest breath,
A grave among the eternal.—Come away!
Haste, while the vault of blue Italian day
Is yet his fitting charnel-roof! while still
He lies, as if in dewy sleep he lay;
Awake him not! surely he takes his fill
Of deep and liquid rest, forgetful of all ill.

8

He will awake no more, oh, never more!—
Within the twilight chamber spreads apace
The shadow of white Death, and at the door
Invisible Corruption waits to trace
His extreme way to her dim dwelling-place;
The eternal Hunger sits, but pity and awe
Soothe her pale rage, nor dares she to deface
So fair a prey, till darkness and the law
Of change, shall o'er his sleep the mortal curtain draw.

9

Oh, weep for Adonais!—The quick Dreams,
The passion-wingéd Ministers of thought,
Who were his flocks, whom near the living streams
Of his young spirit he fed, and whom he taught
The love which was its music, wander not—
Wander no more, from kindling brain to brain,
But droop there, whence they sprung; and mourn their lot
Round the cold heart, where, after their sweet pain,
They ne'er will gather strength, or find a home again.

10

And one with trembling hand clasps his cold head,
And fans him with her moonlight wings, and cries,
"Our love, our hope, our sorrow, is not dead;
See, on the silken fringe of his faint eyes,
Like dew upon a sleeping flower, there lies

7. Rome, where Keats died.

A tear some Dream has loosened from his brain."
Lost Angel of a ruined Paradise!
She knew not 'twas her own; as with no stain
90   She faded, like a cloud which had outwept its rain.

11

One from a lucid urn of starry dew
Washed his light limbs as if embalming them;
Another clipped her profuse locks, and threw
The wreath upon him, like an anadem,°   garland
95   Which frozen tears instead of pearls begem;
Another in her willful grief would break
Her bow and wingéd reeds, as if to stem
A greater loss with one which was more weak;
And dull the barbéd fire against his frozen cheek.

12

100   Another Splendor on his mouth alit,
That mouth, whence it was wont to draw the breath
Which gave it strength to pierce the guarded wit,[8]
And pass into the panting heart beneath
With lightning and with music: the damp death
105   Quenched its caress upon its icy lips;
And, as a dying meteor stains a wreath
Of moonlight vapor, which the cold night clips,°   envelops
It flushed through his pale limbs, and passed to its eclipse.

13

And others came . . .   Desires and Adorations,
110   Wingéd Persuasions and veiled Destinies,
Splendors, and Glooms, and glimmering Incarnations
Of hopes and fears, and twilight Phantasies;
And Sorrow, with her family of Sighs,
And Pleasure, blind with tears, led by the gleam
115   Of her own dying smile instead of eyes,
Came in slow pomp;—the moving pomp might seem
Like pageantry of mist on an autumnal stream.

14

All he had loved, and molded into thought
From shape, and hue, and odor, and sweet sound,
120   Lamented Adonais. Morning sought
Her eastern watch-tower, and her hair unbound,
Wet with the tears which should adorn the ground,
Dimmed the aërial eyes that kindle day;
Afar the melancholy thunder moaned,
125   Pale Ocean in unquiet slumber lay,
And the wild Winds flew round, sobbing in their dismay.

15

Lost Echo[9] sits amid the voiceless mountains,
And feeds her grief with his remembered lay,
And will no more reply to winds or fountains,
130   Or amorous birds perched on the young green spray,
Or herdsman's horn, or bell at closing day;
Since she can mimic not his lips, more dear
Than those for whose disdain she pined away
Into a shadow of all sounds:—a drear
135   Murmur, between their songs, is all the woodmen hear.

8. The defensive analytical mind.
9. A nymph who loved Narcissus and who   pined away into a mere voice when that youth
fell in love with his own reflection in a pool.

16

Grief made the young Spring wild, and she threw down
Her kindling buds, as if she Autumn were,
Or they dead leaves; since her delight is flown
For whom should she have waked the sullen year?
To Phoebus was not Hyacinth[1] so dear,
Nor to himself Narcissus, as to both
Thou, Adonais; wan they stand and sere
Amid the faint companions of their youth,
With dew all turned to tears; odor, to sighing ruth.°   *pity*

17

Thy spirit's sister, the lorn nightingale,
Mourns not her mate with such melodious pain;
Not so the eagle, who like thee could scale
Heaven, and could nourish in the sun's domain
Her mighty youth,[2] with morning, doth complain,
Soaring and screaming round her empty nest,
As Albion° wails for thee: the curse of Cain[3]   *England*
Light on his head who[4] pierced thy innocent breast,
And scared the angel soul that was its earthly guest!

18

Ah, woe is me! Winter is come and gone,
But grief returns with the revolving year;
The airs and streams renew their joyous tone;
The ants, the bees, the swallows reappear;
Fresh leaves and flowers deck the dead Seasons' bier;
The amorous birds now pair in every brake,°   *thicket*
And build their mossy homes in field and brere;°   *briar*
And the green lizard, and the golden snake,
Like unimprisoned flames, out of their trance awake.

19

Through wood and stream and field and hill and Ocean,
A quickening life from the Earth's heart has burst
As it has ever done, with change and motion,
From the great morning of the world when first
God dawned on Chaos; in its stream immersed
The lamps of Heaven flash with a softer light;
All baser things pant with life's sacred thirst;
Diffuse themselves; and spend in love's delight,
The beauty and the joy of their renewéd might.

20

The leprous corpse touched by this spirit tender
Exhales itself in flowers of gentle breath;
Like incarnations of the stars, when splendor
Is changed to fragrance, they illumine death
And mock the merry worm that wakes beneath;
Nought we know, dies. Shall that alone which knows
Be as a sword consumed before the sheath
By sightless[5] lightning?—the intense atom[6] glows
A moment, then is quenched in a most cold repose.

1. Youth loved by Apollo ("Phoebus"), who killed him by accident.
2. In folklore an eagle could recapture its youth by soaring close to the sun.
3. God's curse upon Cain for having slain his brother Abel was that nothing should grow for him and that he should be homeless.
(Genesis, iii.11–12.)
4. The anonymous critic whose venomous review of Keats's *Endymion* had hastened, Shelley believed, Keats's death.
5. Unseeing and unseen.
6. Indivisible and indestructible unit of anything that exists.

21

Alas! that all we loved of him should be,
But for our grief, as if it had not been.
And grief itself be mortal! Woe is me!
Whence are we, and why are we? of what scene
185   The actors or spectators? Great and mean
Meet massed in death, who lends what life must borrow.
As long as skies are blue, and fields are green,
Evening must usher night, night urge the morrow,
Month follow month with woe, and year wake year to sorrow.

22

190   *He* will awake no more, oh, never more!
"Wake thou," cried Misery, "childless Mother, rise
Out of thy sleep, and slake, in thy heart's core,
A wound more fierce than his with tears and sighs."
And all the Dreams that watched Urania's eyes,
195   And all the Echoes whom their sister's song
Had held in holy silence, cried, "Arise!"
Swift as a Thought by the snake Memory stung,
From her ambrosial rest the fading Splendor sprung.

23

She rose like an autumnal Night, that springs
200   Out of the East, and follows wild and drear
The golden Day, which, on eternal wings,
Even as a ghost abandoning a bier,
Has left the Earth a corpse. Sorrow and fear
So struck, so roused, so rapt Urania;
205   So saddened round her like an atmosphere
Of stormy mist; so swept her on her way
Even to the mournful place where Adonais lay.

24

Out of her secret Paradise she sped,
Through camps and cities rough with stone, and steel,
210   And human hearts, which to her aery tread
Yielding not, wounded the invisible
Palms of her tender feet where'er they fell:
And barbéd tongues, and thoughts more sharp than they,
Rent the soft Form they never could repel,
215   Whose sacred blood, like the young tears of May,
Paved with eternal flowers that undeserving way.

25

In the death-chamber for a moment Death,
Shamed by the presence of that living Might,
Blushed to annihilation, and the breath
220   Revisited those lips, and life's pale light
Flashed through those limbs, so late her dear delight.
"Leave me not wild and drear and comfortless,
As silent lightning leaves the starless night!
Leave me not!" cried Urania: her distress
225   Roused Death: Death rose and smiled, and met her vain caress.

26

"Stay yet awhile! speak to me once again;
Kiss me, so long but as a kiss may live;
And in my heartless breast and burning brain
That word, that kiss, shall all thoughts else survive,
230   With food of saddest memory kept alive,

Now thou art dead, as if it were a part
Of thee, my Adonais! I would give
All that I am to be as thou now art,
But I am chained to Time, and cannot thence depart!

27

"O gentle child, beautiful as thou wert,
Why didst thou leave the trodden paths of men
Too soon, and with weak hands though mighty heart
Dare the unpastured dragon in his den?
Defenseless as thou wert, oh! where was then
Wisdom the mirrored shield, or scorn the spear?[7]
Or hadst thou waited the full cycle, when
Thy spirit should have filled its crescent sphere,
The monsters of life's waste had fled from thee like deer.

28

"The herded wolves, bold only to pursue;
The obscene ravens, clamorous o'er the dead;
The vultures, to the conqueror's banner true,
Who feed where Desolation first has fed,
And whose wings rain contagion;—how they[8] fled,
When like Apollo, from his golden bow,
The Pythian of the age[9] one arrow sped
And smiled!—The spoilers tempt no second blow,
They fawn on the proud feet that spurn them lying low.

29

"The sun comes forth, and many reptiles spawn;
He sets, and each ephemeral insect then
Is gathered into death without a dawn,
And the immortal stars awake again;
So is it in the world of living men:
A godlike mind soars forth, in its delight
Making earth bare and veiling heaven, and when
It sinks, the swarms that dimmed or shared its light
Leave to its kindred lamps the spirit's awful night."

30

Thus ceased she: and the mountain shepherds came
Their garlands sere, their magic mantles rent;
The Pilgrim of Eternity,[1] whose fame
Over his living head like Heaven is bent,
An early but enduring monument,
Came, veiling all the lightnings of his song
In sorrow; from her wilds Ierne° sent   *Ireland*
The sweetest lyrist of her saddest wrong,[2]
And love taught grief to fall like music from his tongue.

31

Midst others of less note, came one frail Form,[3]
A phantom among men; companionless
As the last cloud of an expiring storm,
Whose thunder is its knell; he, as I guess,
Had gazed on Nature's naked loveliness,

7. An allusion to Perseus, who killed the monster Medusa, evading her gaze, which could turn him into stone, by using his shield as a mirror.
8. Critics, here characterized as beasts and birds of prey.
9. Byron, Shelley's friend, who attacked the critics in *English Bards and Scotch Reviewers*; here compared to Apollo the Pythian, who slew the monster Python near Delphi.
1. Byron, as author of *Childe Harold's Pilgrimage*.
2. Thomas Moore (1779–1852), poet, author of *Irish Melodies*.
3. Shelley, as poet-mourner, here wearing emblems of the god Dionysus.

Actaeon-like,[4] and now he fled astray
With feeble steps o'er the world's wilderness,
And his own thoughts, along that rugged way,
Pursued, like raging hounds, their father and their prey.

32

280   A pardlike[5] Spirit beautiful and swift—
A Love in desolation masked;—a Power
Girt round with weakness;—it can scarce uplift
The weight of the superincumbent hour;
It is a dying lamp, a falling shower,
285   A breaking billow;—even whilst we speak
Is it not broken? On the withering flower
The killing sun smiles brightly: on a cheek
The life can burn in blood, even while the heart may break.

33

His head was bound with pansies overblown,
290   And faded violets, white, and pied,° and blue;   *multicolored*
And a light spear topped with a cypress cone,
Round whose rude shaft dark ivy-tresses grew
Yet dripping with the forest's noonday dew,
Vibrated, as the ever-beating heart
295   Shook the weak hand that grasped it; of that crew
He came the last, neglected and apart;
A herd-abandoned deer, struck by the hunter's dart.

34

All stood aloof, and at his partial moan[6]
Smiled through their tears; well knew that gentle band
300   Who in another's fate now wept his own;
As in the accents of an unknown land,
He sung new sorrow; sad Urania scanned
The Stranger's mien, and murmured: "Who art thou?"
He answered not, but with a sudden hand
305   Made bare his branded and ensanguined brow,
Which was like Cain's or Christ's—oh! that it should be so!

35

What softer voice is hushed over the dead?
Athwart what brow is that dark mantle thrown?
What form leans sadly o'er the white death-bed,
310   In mockery° of monumental stone,   *imitation*
The heavy heart heaving without a moan?
If it be He,[7] who, gentlest of the wise,
Taught, soothed, loved, honored the departed one;
Let me not vex, with inharmonious sighs,
315   The silence of that heart's accepted sacrifice.

36

Our Adonais has drunk poison—oh!
What deaf and viperous murderer could crown
Life's early cup with such a draught of woe?
The nameless worm[8] would now itself disown:
320   It felt, yet could escape the magic tone
Whose prelude held° all envy, hate and wrong,   *held off*
But what was howling in one breast alone,

---

4. Actaeon, a young hunter, offended the goddess Diana by discovering her while she was bathing. She transformed him into a stag, and he was torn to pieces by his hounds.
5. Leopard-like; the leopard was sacred to Dionysus.

6. Expressing a bond of sympathy (partiality) toward Adonais.
7. Leigh Hunt (1784–1859), poet and critic, friend of Keats and Shelley.
8. Serpent; the anonymous reviewer (see line 152).

Silent with expectation of the song,
Whose master's hand is cold, whose silver lyre unstrung.

37

25 Live thou, whose infamy is not thy fame!
Live! fear no heavier chastisement from me,
Thou noteless blot on a remembered name!
But be thyself, and know thyself to be!
And ever at thy season be thou free
30 To spill the venom when thy fangs o'erflow:
Remorse and Self-contempt shall cling to thee;
Hot Shame shall burn upon thy secret brow,
And like a beaten hound tremble thou shalt—as now.

38

Nor let us weep that our delight is fled
35 Far from these carrion kites° that scream below;   *scavenger hawks*
He wakes or sleeps with the enduring dead;
Thou canst not soar where he is sitting now.
Dust to the dust! but the pure spirit shall flow
Back to the burning fountain whence it came,
40 A portion of the Eternal, which must glow
Through time and change, unquenchably the same,
Whilst thy[9] cold embers choke the sordid hearth of shame.

39

Peace, peace! he is not dead, he doth not sleep—
He hath awakened from the dream of life—
45 'Tis we, who lost in stormy visions, keep
With phantoms an unprofitable strife,
And in mad trance strike with our spirit's knife
Invulnerable nothings.—*We* decay
Like corpses in a charnel; fear and grief
50 Convulse us and consume us day by day,
And cold hopes swarm like worms within our living clay.

40

He has outsoared the shadow of our night;
Envy and calumny and hate and pain,
And that unrest which men miscall delight,
55 Can touch him not and torture not again;
From the contagion of the world's slow stain
He is secure, and now can never mourn
A heart grown cold, a head grown gray in vain;
Nor, when the spirit's self has ceased to burn,
360 With sparkless ashes load an unlamented urn.

41

He lives, he wakes—'tis Death is dead, not he;
Mourn not for Adonais.—Thou young Dawn,
Turn all thy dew to splendor, for from thee
The spirit thou lamentest is not gone;
365 Ye caverns and ye forests, cease to moan!
Cease ye faint flowers and fountains, and thou Air,
Which like a morning veil thy scarf hadst thrown
O'er the abandoned Earth, now leave it bare
Even to the joyous stars which smile on its despair!

42

370 He is made one with Nature: there is heard
His voice in all her music, from the moan

---

9. The reviewer's.

Of thunder, to the song of night's sweet bird;
He is a presence to be felt and known
In darkness and in light, from herb and stone,
375   Spreading itself where'er that Power may move
Which has withdrawn his being to its own;
Which wields the world with never wearied love,
Sustains it from beneath, and kindles it above.

43

He is a portion of the loveliness
380   Which once he made more lovely: he doth bear
His part, while the one Spirit's plastic° stress   *formative*
Sweeps through the dull dense world, compelling there
All new successions to the forms they wear;
Torturing the unwilling dross° that checks its flight   *coarse matter*
385   To its own likeness, as each mass may bear;
And bursting in its beauty and its might
From trees and beasts and men into the Heaven's light.

44

The splendors of the firmament of time
May be eclipsed, but are extinguished not;
390   Like stars to their appointed height they climb,
And death is a low mist which cannot blot
The brightness it may veil. When lofty thought
Lifts a young heart above its mortal lair,
And love and life contend in it, for what
395   Shall be its earthly doom, the dead live there
And move like winds of light on dark and stormy air.

45

The inheritors of unfulfilled renown
Rose from their thrones, built beyond mortal thought,
Far in the Unapparent. Chatterton[1]
400   Rose pale, his solemn agony had not
Yet faded from him; Sidney,[2] as he fought
And as he fell and as he lived and loved
Sublimely mild, a Spirit without spot,
Arose; and Lucan,[3] by his death approved:°   *vindicated*
405   Oblivion as they rose shrank like a thing reproved.

46

And many more, whose names on Earth are dark
But whose transmitted effluence cannot die
So long as fire outlives the parent spark,
Rose, robed in dazzling immortality.
410   "Thou art become as one of us," they cry,
"It was for thee yon kingless sphere has long
Swung blind in unascended majesty,
Silent alone amid an Heaven of Song.
Assume thy wingéd throne, thou Vesper of our throng!"

47

415   Who mourns for Adonais? Oh, come forth,
Fond wretch! and know thyself and him aright.
Clasp with thy panting soul the pendulous[4] Earth;
As from a center, dart thy spirit's light

---

1. Thomas Chatterton (1752–70), a gifted young poet who committed suicide.
2. Sir Philip Sidney (1554–1586), a poet, critic, courtier, and soldier, fatally wounded in battle.
3. Lucan, a young Roman poet, took his own life rather than die under sentence of the notorious emperor Nero, against whom he had conspired.
4. Floating poised in space.

Beyond all worlds, until its spacious might
Satiate the void circumference: then shrink
Even to a point within our day and night;
And keep thy heart light lest it make thee sink
When hope has kindled hope, and lured thee to the brink.

48

Or go to Rome, which is the sepulcher,
Oh, not of him, but of our joy: 'tis nought
That ages, empires, and religions there
Lie buried in the ravage they have wrought;
For such as he can lend—they borrow not
Glory from those who made the world their prey;
And he is gathered to the kings of thought
Who waged contention with their time's decay,
And of the past are all that cannot pass away.

49

Go thou to Rome,—at once the Paradise,
The grave, the city, and the wilderness;
And where its wrecks like shattered mountains rise,
And flowering weeds, and fragrant copses dress
The bones of Desolation's nakedness
Pass, till the Spirit of the spot shall lead
Thy footsteps to a slope of green access
Where, like an infant's smile, over the dead
A light of laughing flowers along the grass is spread,

50

And gray walls moulder round, on which dull Time
Feeds, like slow fire upon a hoary brand;
And one keen pyramid[5] with wedge sublime,
Pavilioning the dust of him who planned
This refuge for his memory, doth stand
Like flame transformed to marble; and beneath,
A field is spread, on which a newer band
Have pitched in Heaven's smile their camp of death,
Welcoming him we lose with scarce extinguished breath.

51

Here pause: these graves are all too young as yet
To have outgrown the sorrow which consigned
Its charge to each; and if the seal is set,
Here, on one fountain of a mourning mind,
Break it not thou! too surely shalt thou find
Thine own well full, if thou returnest home,
Of tears and gall. From the world's bitter wind
Seek shelter in the shadow of the tomb.
What Adonais is, why fear we to become?

52

The One remains, the many change and pass;
Heaven's light forever shines, Earth's shadows fly;
Life, like a dome of many-colored glass,
Stains the white radiance of Eternity,
Until Death tramples it to fragments.—Die,
If thou wouldst be with that which thou dost seek!
Follow where all is fled!—Rome's azure sky,
Flowers, ruins, statues, music, words, are weak
The glory they transfuse with fitting truth to speak.

5. Tomb of Gaius Cestius, an officer of ancient Rome, beside the Protestant cemetery where Keats and Shelley are buried.

53

Why linger, why turn back, why shrink, my Heart?
Thy hopes are gone before: from all things here
They have departed; thou shouldst now depart!
A light is past from the revolving year,
And man, and woman; and what still is dear
Attracts to crush, repels to make thee wither.
The soft sky smiles,—the low wind whispers near:
'Tis Adonais calls! oh, hasten thither,
No more let life divide what Death can join together.

54

That Light whose smile kindles the Universe,
That Beauty in which all things work and move,
That Benediction which the eclipsing Curse
Of birth can quench not, that sustaining Love
Which through the web of being blindly wove
By man and beast and earth and air and sea,
Burns bright or dim, as each are mirrors of
The fire for which all thirst; now beams on me,
Consuming the last clouds of cold mortality.

55

The breath whose might I have invoked in song
Descends on me; my spirit's bark is driven,
Far from the shore, far from the trembling throng
Whose sails were never to the tempest given;
The massy earth and spheréd skies are riven!
I am borne darkly, fearfully, afar;
Whilst burning through the inmost veil of Heaven,
The soul of Adonais, like a star,
Beacons from the abode where the Eternal are.

1821

To Night

1

Swiftly walk o'er the western wave,
  Spirit of Night!
Out of the misty eastern cave,
Where, all the long and lone daylight,
Thou wovest dreams of joy and fear,
Which make thee terrible and dear—
  Swift be thy flight!

2

Wrap thy form in a mantle gray,
  Star-inwrought!
Blind with thine hair the eyes of Day;
Kiss her until she be wearied out,
Then wander o'er city, and sea, and land,
Touching all with thine opiate wand—
  Come, long-sought!

3

When I rose and saw the dawn,
  I sighed for thee;
When light rode high, and the dew was gone,
And noon lay heavy on flower and tree,
And the weary Day turned to his rest,
Lingering like an unloved guest,
  I sighed for thee.

4

Thy brother Death came, and cried,
　　"Wouldst thou me?"
Thy sweet child Sleep, the filmy-eyed,
25 Murmured like a noontide bee,
　"Shall I nestle near thy side?
Wouldst thou me?"—And I replied,
　　"No, not thee!"

5

Death will come when thou art dead,
30 　　Soon, too soon—
Sleep will come when thou art fled;
Of neither would I ask the boon
I ask of thee, belovéd Night—
Swift be thine approaching flight,
　　Come soon, soon!

　　　　　　　　　　　　　　　　1824

To ———

Music, when soft voices die,
Vibrates in the memory—
Odors, when sweet violets sicken,
Live within the sense they quicken.
5 Rose leaves, when the rose is dead,
Are heaped for the belovéd's bed;
And so thy thoughts, when thou art gone,
Love itself shall slumber on.

　　　　　　　　　　　　　　　　1824

Lines: When the Lamp Is Shattered

1

When the lamp is shattered
The light in the dust lies dead—
　When the cloud is scattered
The rainbow's glory is shed.
5 　When the lute is broken,
Sweet tones are remembered not;
　When the lips have spoken,
Loved accents are soon forgot.

2

As music and splendor
10 Survive not the lamp and the lute,
　The heart's echoes render
No song when the spirit is mute—
No song but sad dirges,
Like the wind through a ruined cell,
15 　Or the mournful surges
That ring the dead seaman's knell.

3

When hearts have once mingled
Love first leaves the well-built nest;
　The weak one is singled
20 To endure what it once possessed.
　O Love! who bewailest

The frailty of all things here,
  Why choose you the frailest
For your cradle, your home, and your bier?
        4
25   Its passions will rock thee
As the storms rock the ravens on high;
  Bright reason will mock thee,
Like the sun from a wintry sky.
  From thy nest every rafter
30 Will rot, and thine eagle home
  Leave thee naked to laughter,
When leaves fall and cold winds come.

                                                    1824

Mutability

        1
The flower that smiles today
    Tomorrow dies;
All that we wish to stay,
    Tempts and then flies.
5 What is this world's delight?
Lightning that mocks the night,
    Brief even as bright.
        2
Virtue, how frail it is!
    Friendship how rare!
10 Love, how it sells poor bliss
    For proud despair!
But we, though soon they fall,
Survive their joy and all
    Which ours we call.
        3
15 Whilst skies are blue and bright,
    Whilst flowers are gay,
Whilst eyes that change ere night
    Make glad the day,
Whilst yet the calm hours creep,
20 Dream thou—and from thy sleep
    Then wake to weep.

                                                    1824

To Jane:[6] The Keen Stars Were Twinkling

        1
The keen stars were twinkling,
And the fair moon was rising among them,
    Dear Jane!
The guitar was tinkling,
5 But the notes were not sweet till you sung them
    Again.
        2
As the moon's soft splendor
O'er the faint cold starlight of Heaven
    Is thrown,

---

6. Jane Williams and her husband Edward were intimate friends of Shelley's.

So your voice most tender
To the strings without soul had then given
    Its own.

     3
The stars will awaken,
Though the moon sleep a full hour later,
    Tonight;
No leaf will be shaken
Whilst the dews of your melody scatter
    Delight.

     4
Though the sound overpowers,
Sing again, with your dear voice revealing
    A tone
Of some world far from ours,
Where music and moonlight and feeling
    Are one.

                1822   1832

The Recollection

     1
Now the last day of many days,
    All beautiful and bright as thou,
        The loveliest and the last, is dead,—
Rise, Memory, and write its praise!
    Up,—to thy wonted work! come, trace
        The epitaph of glory fled,
For now the Earth has changed its face,
    A frown is on the Heaven's brow.

     2
We wandered to the Pine Forest
    That skirts the Ocean's foam,
The lightest wind was in its nest,
    The tempest in its home.
The whispering waves were half asleep,
    The clouds were gone to play,
And on the bosom of the deep
    The smile of Heaven lay;
It seemed as if the hour were one
    Sent from beyond the skies,
Which scattered from above the sun
    A light of Paradise.

     3
We paused amid the pines that stood
    The giants of the waste,
Tortured by storms to shapes as rude
    As serpents interlaced,
And soothed by every azure breath,
    That under heaven is blown,
To harmonies and hues beneath,
    As tender as its own;
Now all the treetops lay asleep,
    Like green waves on the sea,
As still as in the silent deep
    The ocean woods may be.

4

How calm it was!—the silence there
　　By such a chain was bound
35　That even the busy woodpecker
　　　Made stiller by her sound
The inviolable quietness;
　　The breath of peace we drew
With its soft motion made not less
40　　The calm that round us grew.
There seemed, from the remotest seat
　　Of the white mountain waste
To the soft flower beneath our feet,
　　A magic circle traced,
45　A spirit interfused around,
　　A thrilling silent life,—
To momentary peace it bound
　　Our mortal nature's strife;
And still I felt the center of
50　　The magic circle there
Was one fair form that filled with love
　　The lifeless atmosphere.

5

We paused beside the pools that lie
55　　Under the forest bough,—
Each seemed as 'twere a little sky
　　Gulfed in a world below;
A firmament of purple light,
　　Which in the dark earth lay,
60　More boundless than the depth of night
　　And purer than the day,—
In which the lovely forests grew,
　　As in the upper air,
More perfect both in shape and hue
65　　Than any spreading there.
There lay the glade and neighboring lawn,
　　And through the dark green wood
The white sun twinkling like the dawn
　　Out of a speckled cloud.
70　Sweet views which in our world above
　　Can never well be seen,
Were imaged by the water's love
　　Of that fair forest green.
And all was interfused beneath
75　　With an Elysian[7] glow,
An atmosphere without a breath,
　　A softer day below.
Like one beloved the scene had lent
　　To the dark water's breast,
80　Its every leaf and lineament
　　With more than truth expressed;
Until an envious wind crept by,
　　Like an unwelcome thought,
Which from the mind's too faithful eye
85　　Blots one dear image out.
Though thou art ever fair and kind,
　　The forests ever green,

7. Elysium, in Greek myth, was the place where men favored by the gods lived a happy
afterlife.

Less oft is peace in Shelley's mind,
Than calm in waters seen.

1822   1839

From Hellas:[8] *Two Choruses*

Worlds on Worlds

Worlds on worlds are rolling ever
From creation to decay,
Like the bubbles on a river
Sparkling, bursting, borne away.
5   But they[9] are still immortal
Who, through birth's orient portal
And death's dark chasm hurrying to and fro,
Clothe their unceasing flight
In the brief dust and light
10   Gathered around their chariots as they go;
New shapes they still may weave,
New gods, new laws receive,
Bright or dim are they as the robes they last
On Death's bare ribs had cast.

15   A power from the unknown God,[1]
A Promethean conqueror,[2] came;
Like a triumphal path he trod
The thorns of death and shame.
A mortal shape to him
Was like the vapor dim
20   Which the orient planet animates with light;
Hell, Sin, and Slavery came,
Like bloodhounds mild and tame,
Nor preyed, until their Lord had taken flight;
25   The moon of Mahomet[3]
Arose, and it shall set:
While blazoned as on Heaven's immortal noon
The cross leads generations on.

Swift as the radiant shapes of sleep
30   From one whose dreams are Paradise
Fly, when the fond wretch wakes to weep,
And Day peers forth with her blank eyes;
So fleet, so fain, so fair,
The Powers of earth and air
35   Fled from the folding-star[4] of Bethlehem:
Apollo, Pan, and Love,
And even Olympian Jove[5]
Grew weak, for killing Truth had glared on them,
40   Our hills and seas and streams,

8. *Hellas*, an ancient name for Greece, is the title of a drama in which Shelley celebrates the contemporary Greek struggle for independence, which he saw as heralding the return of the legendary "Age of Saturn" or "Age of Gold," the first, best period of human history.
9. "The first stanza contrasts the immortality of the living and thinking beings which inhabit the planets, and to use a common and inadequate phrase, *clothe themselves in matter*, with the transience of the noblest manifestations of the external world" [Shelley's note].

1. At Athens St. Paul proclaimed the "unknown god," i.e., the One God of the Hebraic and Christian faiths (Acts xvii.22–28).
2. Christ; likened to the Greek Titan Prometheus, who befriended and suffered for mankind.
3. Crescent moon, symbol of Mohammedanism.
4. Star that rises at the hour when sheep are brought to the fold at evening.
5. Gods worshipped in Greece until Christianity displaced them.

Dispeopled of their dreams,
Their waters turned to blood, their dew to tears,
Wailed for the golden years.

1822

The World's Great Age

The world's great age begins anew,
  The golden years return,
The earth doth like a snake[6] renew
  Her winter weeds[7] outworn:
5 Heaven smiles, and faiths and empires gleam,
Like wrecks of a dissolving dream.

A brighter Hellas rears its mountains
  From waves serener far;
A new Peneus[8] rolls his fountains
10   Against the morning star.
Where fairer Tempes[9] bloom, there sleep
Young Cyclads[1] on a sunnier deep.

A loftier Argo[2] cleaves the main,
  Fraught with a later prize;
15 Another Orpheus[3] sings again,
    And loves, and weeps, and dies.
A new Ulysses leaves once more
Calypso[4] for his native shore.

Oh, write no more the tale of Troy,
20   If earth Death's scroll must be!
Nor mix with Laian rage[5] the joy
  Which dawns upon the free:
Although a subtler Sphinx renew
Riddles of death Thebes never knew.

25 Another Athens shall arise,
    And to remoter time
Bequeath, like sunset to the skies,
    The splendor of its prime;
And leave, if nought so bright may live,
30 All earth can take or Heaven can give.

Saturn and Love their long repose
  Shall burst, more bright and good
Than all who fell, than One who rose,
    Than many unsubdued:[6]
35 Not gold, not blood, their altar dowers,
But votive tears and symbol flowers.

---

6. Shedding its skin after hibernation, a symbol of regeneration.
7. Clothes, especially mourning garments.
8. Greek river of legendary beauty.
9. Valley of the Peneus.
1. Or Cyclades, islands in the Aegean Sea.
2. In Greek legend, the first of seagoing vessels, on which Jason sailed to gain the "prize" (line 14) of the Golden Fleece.
3. Legendary Greek poet and musician of magical genius whose playing on the lyre caused his wife, Eurydice, to be released from the realm of the dead on condition that he would not look at her until they had reached the upper world. Breaking his pledge at the last moment, he lost her forever.
4. Island-nymph with whom Ulysses (Odysseus) lived for seven years during his return to Ithaca from the Trojan War.
5. Ignorant of his own identity, Oedipus in a rage killed King Laius of Thebes (in fact his father). Oedipus then delivered Thebes from the power of a sphinx by answering her riddles and won Jocasta (in fact his mother) as his wife and queen.
6. Saturn and Love are the restored deities of the "world's great age"; "all who fell" are the deities who "fell" when Christ arose from the dead; the "many unsubdued" are idols still worshipped throughout the world.

Oh, cease! must hate and death return?
  Cease! must men kill and die?
Cease! drain not to its dregs the urn
    Of bitter prophecy.
The world is weary of the past,
Oh, might it die or rest at last!

1822

JOHN CLARE
(1793–1864)

Badger

When midnight comes a host of dogs and men
Go out and track the badger to his den,
And put a sack within the hole, and lie
Till the old grunting badger passes by.
5 He comes and hears—they let the strongest loose.
The old fox hears the noise and drops the goose.
The poacher shoots and hurries from the cry,
And the old hare half wounded buzzes by.
They get a forkéd stick to bear him down
10 And clap the dogs and take him to the town,
And bait him all the day with many dogs,
And laugh and shout and fright the scampering hogs.
He runs along and bites at all he meets:
They shout and hollo down the noisy streets.

15 He turns about to face the loud uproar
And drives the rebels to their very door.
The frequent stone is hurled where'er they go;
When badgers fight, then everyone's a foe.
The dogs are clapped and urged to join the fray;
20 The badger turns and drives them all away.
Though scarcely half as big, demure and small,
He fights with dogs for hours and beats them all.
The heavy mastiff, savage in the fray,
Lies down and licks his feet and turns away.
25 The bulldog knows his match and waxes cold,
The badger grins and never leaves his hold.
He drives the crowd and follows at their heels
And bites them through—the drunkard swears and reels.

The frighted women take the boys away,
30 The blackguard laughs and hurries on the fray.
He tries to reach the woods, an awkward race,
But sticks and cudgels quickly stop the chase.
He turns again and drives the noisy crowd
And beats the many dogs in noises loud.
35 He drives away and beats them every one,
And then they loose them all and set them on.
He falls as dead and kicked by boys and men,
Then starts and grins and drives the crowd again;
Till kicked and torn and beaten out he lies
40 And leaves his hold and crackles, groans, and dies.

1835–37   1920

Gypsies

The snow falls deep; the forest lies alone;
The boy goes hasty for his load of brakes,°   brushwood
Then thinks upon the fire and hurries back;
The gypsy knocks his hands and tucks them up,
5   And seeks his squalid camp, half hid in snow,
Beneath the oak which breaks away the wind,
And bushes close in snow like hovel warm;
There tainted mutton wastes upon the coals,
And the half-wasted dog squats close and rubs,
10 Then feels the heat too strong, and goes aloof;
He watches well, but none a bit can spare,
And vainly waits the morsel thrown away.
'Tis thus they live—a picture to the place,
A quiet, pilfering, unprotected race.

                                              1837–41   1920

Lord, Hear My Prayer

A PARAPHRASE OF THE 102ND PSALM

Lord, hear my prayer when trouble glooms,
Let sorrow find a way,
And when the day of trouble comes,
Turn not thy face way:
5   My bones like hearthstones burn away,
My life like vapory smoke decays.

My heart is smitten like the grass,
That withered lies and dead,
And I, so lost to what I was,
10 Forget to eat my bread.
My voice is groaning all the day,
My bones prick through this skin of clay.

The wilderness's pelican,
The desert's lonely owl—
15 I am their like, a desert man
In ways as lone and foul.
As sparrows on the cottage top
I wait till I with fainting drop.

I hear my enemies reproach,
20 All silently I mourn;
They on my private peace encroach,
Against me they are sworn.
Ashes as bread my trouble shares,
And mix my food with weeping cares.

25 Yet not for them is sorrow's toil,
I fear no mortal's frowns—
But thou hast held me up awhile
And thou hast cast me down.
My days like shadows waste from view,
30 I mourn like withered grass in dew.

But thou, Lord, shalt endure for ever,
All generations through;
Thou shalt to Zion be the giver
Of joy and mercy too.
5 Her very stones are in thy trust,
Thy servants reverence her dust.

Heathens shall hear and fear thy name,
All kings of earth thy glory know
When thou shalt build up Zion's fame
10 And live in glory there below.
He'll not despise their prayers, though mute,
But still regard the destitute.

1841   1949

Song: Love Lives Beyond the Tomb

Love lives beyond
The tomb, the earth, which fades like dew—
I love the fond,
The faithful, and the true.

5 Love lives in sleep,
'Tis happiness of healthy dreams,
Eve's dews may weep,
But love delightful seems.

'Tis seen in flowers,
10 And in the even's pearly dew
On earth's green hours,
And in the heaven's eternal blue.

'Tis heard in spring
When light and sunbeams, warm and kind,
15 On angel's wing
Brings love and music to the wind.

And where's the voice
So young, so beautiful, and sweet
As nature's choice,
20 Where spring and lovers meet?

Love lives beyond
The tomb, the earth, the flowers, and dew.
I love the fond,
The faithful, young, and true.

1842–64   1873

Come Hither

Come hither, ye who thirst;
Pure still the brook flows on;
Its waters are not cursed;
Clear from its rock of stone
5 It bubbles and it boils,
An everlasting rill,
Then eddies and recoils

And wimples clearer still.
Art troubled? then come hither,
10 And taste of peace for ever.

Art weary? here's the place
For weariness to rest,
These flowers are herbs of grace
To cure the aching breast;
15 Soft beds these mossy banks
Where dewdrops only weep,
Where Nature 'turns God thanks
And sings herself to sleep.
Art troubled with strife? come hither,
20 Here's peace and summer weather.

Come hither for pleasure who list—
Here are oak boughs for a shade;
These leaves they will hide from the mist
Ere the sun his broad disc has displayed.
25 Here is peace if thy bosom be troubled,
Here is rest—if thou'rt weary, sit down—
Here pleasure you'll find it is doubled.
For content is life's only crown.
Disciples of sorrow, come hither,
30 For no blasts my joys can wither.

Art sick of the naughty world?
There's many been sick before thee;
Then leave these young shoots with their tendrils curled
For the oaks that are mossy and hoary.
35 Art weary with beating the flood?
Here's a mossy bank—come sit down:
'Twas Nature that planted this wood,
Unknown to the sins of the town
Full of pride and contention—come hither,
40 We'll talk of our troubles together.

The world is all lost in commotion,
The blind lead the blind into strife;
Come hither, thou wreck of life's ocean,
Let solitude warm thee to life.
45 Be the pilgrim of love and the joy of its sorrow,
Be anything but the world's man:
The dark of to-day brings the sun of to-morrow,
Be proud that your joy here began.
Poor shipwreck of life, journey hither,
50 And we'll talk of life's troubles together.

                                        1842–64   1924

First Love

I ne'er was struck before that hour
   With love so sudden and so sweet,
Her face it bloomed like a sweet flower
   And stole my heart away complete.
5 My face turned pale as deadly pale.
   My legs refused to walk away,

And when she looked, what could I ail?
 My life and all seemed turned to clay.

And then my blood rushed to my face
 And took my eyesight quite away,
The trees and bushes round the place
 Seemed midnight at noonday.
I could not see a single thing,
 Words from my eyes did start—
They spoke as chords do from the string,
 And blood burnt round my heart.

Are flowers the winter's choice?
 Is love's bed always snow?
She seemed to hear my silent voice,
 Not love's appeals to know.
I never saw so sweet a face
 As that I stood before.
My heart has left its dwelling-place
 And can return no more.

                                        1842–64   1920

Farewell

Farewell to the bushy clump close to the river
And the flags where the butter-bump° hides in forever;   *bittern*
Farewell to the weedy nook, hemmed in by waters;
Farewell to the miller's brook and his three bonny daughters;
Farewell to them all while in prison I lie—
In the prison a thrall sees naught but the sky.

Shut out are the green fields and birds in the bushes;
In the prison yard nothing builds, blackbirds or thrushes.
Farewell to the old mill and dash of the waters,
To the miller and, dearer still, to his three bonny daughters.

In the nook, the larger burdock grows near the green willow;
In the flood, round the moor-cock dashes under the billow;
To the old mill farewell, to the lock, pens, and waters,
To the miller himsel', and his three bonny daughters.

                                        1842–64   1920

I Am

I am: yet what I am none cares or knows
 My friends forsake me like a memory lost,
I am the self-consumer of my woes—
 They rise and vanish in oblivious host,
Like shadows in love's frenzied, stifled throes—
And yet I am, and live—like vapors tossed

Into the nothingness of scorn and noise,
 Into the living sea of waking dreams,
Where there is neither sense of life or joys,
 But the vast shipwreck of my life's esteems;
Even the dearest, that I love the best,
Are strange—nay, rather stranger than the rest.

I long for scenes, where man hath never trod,
  A place where woman never smiled or wept—
15 There to abide with my Creator, God,
  And sleep as I in childhood sweetly slept,
Untroubling, and untroubled where I lie,
The grass below— above the vaulted sky.

1842–64   1865

WILLIAM CULLEN BRYANT
(1794–1878)

To a Waterfowl

    Whither, 'midst falling dew,
While glow the heavens with the last steps of day,
Far, through their rosy depths, dost thou pursue
    Thy solitary way?

5   Vainly the fowler's eye
Might mark thy distant flight, to do thee wrong,
As, darkly seen against the crimson sky,
    Thy figure floats along.

    Seek'st thou the plashy brink
10 Of weedy lake, or marge of river wide,
Or where the rocking billows rise and sink
    On the chaféd ocean side?

    There is a Power, whose care
Teaches thy way along that pathless coast,—
15 The desert and illimitable air,
    Lone wandering, but not lost,

    All day thy wings have fanned,
At that far height, the cold thin atmosphere;
Yet stoop not, weary, to the welcome land,
20   Though the dark night is near.

    And soon that toil shall end,
Soon shalt thou find a summer home, and rest,
And scream among thy fellows; reeds shall bend,
    Soon, o'er thy sheltered nest.

25   Thou'rt gone, the abyss of heaven
Hath swallowed up thy form, yet, on my heart
Deeply hath sunk the lesson thou hast given,
    And shall not soon depart.

    He, who, from zone to zone,
30 Guides through the boundless sky thy certain flight,
In the long way that I must trace alone,
    Will lead my steps aright.

1815   1818, 1821

To the Fringed Gentian

Thou blossom bright with autumn dew,
And colored with the heaven's own blue,
That openest when the quiet light
Succeeds the keen and frosty night—

5 Thou comest not when violets lean
O'er wandering brooks and springs unseen,
Or columbines, in purple dressed,
Nod o'er the ground-bird's hidden nest.

Thou waitest late and com'st alone,
10 When woods are bare and birds are flown,
And frosts and shortening days portend
The aged year is near his end.

Then doth thy sweet and quiet eye
Look through its fringes to the sky,
15 Blue—blue—as if that sky let fall
A flower from its cerulean° wall.   *blue*

I would that thus, when I shall see
The hour of death draw near to me,
Hope, blossoming within my heart,
20 May look to heaven as I depart.

                              1829   1832

JOHN KEATS
(1795–1821)

On First Looking into Chapman's Homer[1]

Much have I traveled in the realms of gold,
    And many goodly states and kingdoms seen;
    Round many western islands have I been
Which bards in fealty° to Apollo[2] hold.   *allegiance*
5 Oft of one wide expanse had I been told
    That deep-browed Homer ruled as his demesne;°   *domain*
    Yet did I never breathe its pure serene°   *atmosphere*
Till I heard Chapman speak out loud and bold:
Then felt I like some watcher of the skies
10   When a new planet swims into his ken;
    Or like stout Cortez[3] when with eagle eyes
    He stared at the Pacific—and all his men
Looked at each other with a wild surmise—
    Silent, upon a peak in Darien.

                                          1816

1. Translation of Homer's *Iliad* by George
Chapman, a contemporary of Shakespeare's.
2. God of poetic inspiration.

3. Spanish conqueror of Mexico; in fact, Bal-
boa, not Cortez, was the first European to see
the Pacific, from Darien, in Panama.

On the Sea

It keeps eternal whisperings around
   Desolate shores, and with its mighty swell
   Gluts twice ten thousand Caverns, till the spell
Of Hecate[4] leaves them their old shadowy sound.
5 Often 'tis in such gentle temper found,
   That scarcely will the very smallest shell
   Be moved for days from where it sometime fell,
When last the winds of Heaven were unbound.
Oh ye! who have your eyeballs vexed and tired,
10 Feast them upon the wideness of the Sea;
   Oh ye! whose ears are dinned with uproar rude,
Or fed too much with cloying melody—
   Sit ye near some old Cavern's Mouth and brood,
Until ye start, as if the sea nymphs quired!°   *choired*

                                              1817

On Sitting Down to Read *King Lear* Once Again

O golden-tongued Romance with serene lute!
   Fair pluméd Siren!° Queen of far away!   *enchantress*
   Leave melodizing on this wintry day,
Shut up thine olden pages, and be mute:
5 Adieu! for once again the fierce dispute
   Betwixt damnation and impassioned clay
   Must I burn through; once more humbly assay
The bitter-sweet of this Shakespearean fruit.
Chief Poet! and ye clouds of Albion,[5]
10 Begetters of our deep eternal theme,
When through the old oak forest I am gone,
   Let me not wander in a barren dream,
But when I am consuméd in the fire,
Give me new Phoenix[6] wings to fly at my desire.

                        1818   1838

When I Have Fears

When I have fears that I may cease to be
   Before my pen has gleaned my teeming brain,
Before high-pilèd books, in charact'ry,°   *written symbols*
   Hold like rich garners the full-ripened grain;
5 When I behold, upon the night's starred face,
   Huge cloudy symbols of a high romance,
And think that I may never live to trace
   Their shadows, with the magic hand of chance;
And when I feel, fair creature of an hour,
10 That I shall never look upon thee more,
Never have relish in the faery° power   *magical*
   Of unreflecting love!—then on the shore
Of the wide world I stand alone, and think
Till Love and Fame to nothingness do sink.

                        1818   1848

4. Greek goddess associated with witchcraft
and the underworld.
5. Ancient name for England, especially re-
ferring to pre-Roman Britain, the era of King
Lear.
6. Fabled Arabian bird that, after living for
centuries, consumes itself in fire and is reborn.

The Eve of St. Agnes[3]

1

St. Agnes' Eve—Ah, bitter chill it was!
The owl, for all his feathers, was a-cold;
The hare limped trembling through the frozen grass,
And silent was the flock in woolly fold:
5 Numb were the Beadsman's[4] fingers, while he told
His rosary, and while his frosted breath,
Like pious incense from a censer old,
Seemed taking flight for heaven, without a death,
Past the sweet Virgin's picture, while his prayer he saith.

2

10 His prayer he saith, this patient, holy man;
Then takes his lamp, and riseth from his knees,
And back returneth, meager, barefoot, wan,
Along the chapel aisle by slow degrees:
The sculptured dead, on each side, seem to freeze,
15 Imprisoned in black, purgatorial rails:
Knights, ladies, praying in dumb orat'ries,[5]
He passeth by; and his weak spirit fails
To think how they may ache in icy hoods and mails.

3

Northward he turneth through a little door,
20 And scarce three steps, ere Music's golden tongue
Flattered to tears this aged man and poor;
But no—already had his deathbell rung:
The joys of all his life were said and sung:
His was harsh penance on St. Agnes' Eve:
25 Another way he went, and soon among
Rough ashes sat he for his soul's reprieve,
And all night kept awake, for sinners' sake to grieve.

4

That ancient Beadsman heard the prelude soft;
And so it chanced, for many a door was wide,
30 From hurry to and fro. Soon, up aloft,
The silver, snarling trumpets 'gan to chide:
The level chambers, ready with their pride,
Were glowing to receive a thousand guests:
The carvéd angels, ever eager-eyed,
35 Stared, where upon their heads the cornice rests,
With hair blown back, and wings put crosswise on their breasts.

5

At length burst in the argent revelry,[6]
With plume, tiara, and all rich array,
Numerous as shadows haunting faerily
40 The brain, new stuffed, in youth, with triumphs gay
Of old romance. These let us wish away,
And turn, sole-thoughted, to one Lady there,
Whose heart had brooded, all that wintry day,
On love, and winged St. Agnes' saintly care,
45 As she had heard old dames full many times declare.

---

3. January 20, proverbially the coldest winter night. St. Agnes, martyred in the 4th century A.D., is patroness of virgins. Traditionally, a maiden who observes the ritual of St. Agnes' Eve will see a vision of her husband-to-be.
4. From Middle English *bede*, meaning *prayer.*

A needy dependent, paid a small stipend to pray regularly for his benefactor. "Rosary" (line 6): a string of beads on which a series of short prayers are counted ("told," line 5).
5. Small chapels in a larger one.
6. Brightly-dressed revelers.

6

They told her how, upon St. Agnes' Eve,
Young virgins might have visions of delight,
And soft adorings from their loves receive
Upon the honeyed middle of the night,
50   If ceremonies due they did aright;
As, supperless to bed they must retire,
And couch supine their beauties, lily white;
Nor look behind, nor sideways, but require
Of Heaven with upward eyes for all that they desire.

7

55   Full of this whim was thoughtful Madeline:
The music, yearning like a God in pain,
She scarcely heard: her maiden eyes divine,
Fixed on the floor, saw many a sweeping train
Pass by—she heeded not at all: in vain
60   Came many a tiptoe, amorous cavalier,
And back retired; not cooled by high disdain;
But she saw not: her heart was otherwhere:
She sighed for Agnes' dreams, the sweetest of the year.

8

She danced along with vague, regardless eyes,
65   Anxious her lips, her breathing quick and short:
The hallowed hour was near at hand: she sighs
Amid the timbrels,° and the thronged resort   **hand drums**
Of whisperers in anger, or in sport;
'Mid looks of love, defiance, hate, and scorn,
70   Hoodwinked with faery fancy; all amort,[7]
Save to St. Agnes and her lambs unshorn,[8]
And all the bliss to be before tomorrow morn.

9

So, purposing each moment to retire,
She lingered still. Meantime, across the moors,
75   Had come young Porphyro, with heart on fire
For Madeline. Beside the portal doors,
Buttressed from moonlight,[9] stands he, and implores
All saints to give him sight of Madeline,
But for one moment in the tedious hours,
80   That he might gaze and worship all unseen;
Perchance speak, kneel, touch, kiss—in sooth such things have been.

10

He ventures in: let no buzzed whisper tell:
All eyes be muffled, or a hundred swords
Will storm his heart, Love's fev'rous citadel:
85   For him, those chambers held barbarian hordes,
Hyena foemen, and hot-blooded lords,
Whose very dogs would execrations howl
Against his lineage: not one breast affords
Him any mercy, in that mansion foul,
90   Save one old beldame,° weak in body and in soul.   **old woman**

11

Ah, happy chance! the aged creature came,
Shuffling along with ivory-headed wand,
To where he stood, hid from the torch's flame,
Behind a broad hall-pillar, far beyond

7. Dead; i.e., oblivious.
8. Symbolically associated with St. Agnes;
new wool offered at the Mass commemorating
the saint was later spun and woven by the
nuns (lines 115–117).
9. I.e., concealed in dark shadows.

95   The sound of merriment and chorus bland:°   *harmonizing*
He startled her; but soon she knew his face,
And grasped his fingers in her palsied hand,
Saying, "Mercy, Porphyro! hie thee from this place;
They are all here tonight, the whole bloodthirsty race!

12

100   "Get hence! get hence! there's dwarfish Hildebrand;
He had a fever late, and in the fit
He curséd thee and thine, both house and land:
Then there's that old Lord Maurice, not a whit
More tame for his gray hairs—Alas me! flit!
105   Flit like a ghost away."—"Ah, Gossip[1] dear,
We're safe enough; here in this armchair sit,
And tell me how"—"Good Saints! not here, not here;
Follow me, child, or else these stones will be thy bier."

13

He followed through a lowly archéd way,
110   Brushing the cobwebs with his lofty plume,
And as she muttered "Well-a—well-a-day!"
He found him in a little moonlight room,
Pale, latticed, chill, and silent as a tomb.
115   "Now tell me where is Madeline," said he,
"O tell me, Angela, by the holy loom
Which none but secret sisterhood may see,
When they St. Agnes' wool are weaving piously."

14

"St Agnes! Ah! it is St. Agnes' Eve—
120   Yet men will murder upon holy days:
Thou must hold water in a witch's sieve,
And be liege lord of all the Elves and Fays,[2]
To venture so: it fills me with amaze
To see thee, Porphyro!—St. Agnes' Eve!
125   God's help! my lady fair the conjuror plays[3]
This very night: good angels her deceive!
But let me laugh awhile, I've mickle° time to grieve."   *much*

15

Feebly she laugheth in the languid moon,
While Porphyro upon her face doth look,
130   Like puzzled urchin on an aged crone
Who keepeth closed a wondrous riddle-book,
As spectacled she sits in chimney nook.
But soon his eyes grew brilliant, when she told
His lady's purpose; and he scarce could brook°   *check*
135   Tears, at the thought of those enchantments cold,
And Madeline asleep in lap of legends old.

16

Sudden a thought came like a full-blown rose,
Flushing his brow, and in his painéd heart
Made purple riot: then doth he propose
A stratagem, that makes the beldame start:
140   "A cruel man and impious thou art:
Sweet lady, let her pray, and sleep, and dream
Alone with her good angels, far apart
From wicked men like thee. Go, go!—I deem
Thou canst not surely be the same that thou didst seem."

---

1. Old kinswoman or household retainer.
2. I.e., to hold water in a sieve and to command elves and fairies ("Fays"), Porphyro would have to be a magician.
3. I.e., is trying magic spells.

17

145 "I will not harm her, by all saints I swear,"
Quoth Porphyro: "O may I ne'er find grace
When my weak voice shall whisper its last prayer,
If one of her soft ringlets I displace,
Or look with ruffian passion in her face:
150 Good Angela, believe me by these tears;
Or I will, even in a moment's space,
Awake, with horrid shout, my foemen's ears,
And beard them, though they be more fanged than wolves and bears."

18

"Ah! why wilt thou affright a feeble soul?
155 A poor, weak, palsy-stricken, churchyard thing,[4]
Whose passing bell[5] may ere the midnight toll;
Whose prayers for thee, each morn and evening,
Were never missed."—Thus plaining,° doth she bring   *complaining*
A gentler speech from burning Porphyro;
160 So woeful and of such deep sorrowing,
That Angela gives promise she will do
Whatever he shall wish, betide her weal or woe.

19

Which was, to lead him, in close secrecy,
Even to Madeline's chamber, and there hide
165 Him in a closet, of such privacy
That he might see her beauty unespied,
And win perhaps that night a peerless bride,
While legioned faeries paced the coverlet,
And pale enchantment held her sleepy-eyed.
170 Never on such a night have lovers met,
Since Merlin paid his Demon all the monstrous debt.[6]

20

"It shall be as thou wishest," said the Dame:
"All cates° and dainties shall be storéd there   *delicacies*
Quickly on this feast[7] night: by the tambour frame[8]
175 Her own lute thou wilt see: no time to spare,
For I am slow and feeble, and scarce dare
On such a catering trust my dizzy head.
Wait here, my child, with patience; kneel in prayer
The while: Ah! thou must needs the lady wed,
180 Or may I never leave my grave among the dead."

21

So saying, she hobbled off with busy fear.
The lover's endless minutes slowly passed:
The dame returned, and whispered in his ear
To follow her; with aged eyes aghast
185 From fright of dim espial. Safe at last,
Through many a dusky gallery, they gain
The maiden's chamber, silken, hushed, and chaste;
Where Porphyro took covert, pleased amain.°   *greatly*
His poor guide hurried back with agues in her brain.

22

190 Her falt'ring hand upon the balustrade,
Old Angela was feeling for the stair,
When Madeline, St. Agnes' charméd maid,

---

4. I.e., soon to die.
5. Tolled when a person died ("passed away").
6. Possibly alluding to the tale that Merlin, in Arthurian legend a great wizard, lies
bound for ages by a spell that he gave to an evil woman to buy her love.
7. The festival, or Mass, honoring St. Agnes.
8. A circular embroidery frame.

Rose, like a missioned spirit, unaware:
With silver taper's light, and pious care,
She turned, and down the aged gossip led
To a safe level matting. Now prepare,
Young Porphyro, for gazing on that bed;
She comes, she comes again, like ringdove frayed° and fled.   **affrighted**

23

Out went the taper as she hurried in;
Its little smoke, in pallid moonshine, died:
She closed the door, she panted, all akin
To spirits of the air, and visions wide:
No uttered syllable, or, woe betide!
But to her heart, her heart was voluble,
Paining with eloquence her balmy side;
As though a tongueless nightingale should swell
Her throat in vain, and die, heart-stifled, in her dell.

24

A casement high and triple-arched there was,
All garlanded with carven imag'ries
Of fruits, and flowers, and bunches of knot-grass,
And diamonded with panes of quaint device,
Innumerable of stains and splendid dyes,
As are the tiger-moth's deep-damasked wings;
And in the midst, 'mong thousand heraldries,
And twilight saints, and dim emblazonings,
A shielded scutcheon blushed with blood of queens and kings.[9]

25

Full on this casement shone the wintry moon,
And threw warm gules[1] on Madeline's fair breast,
As down she knelt for heaven's grace and boon;°   *gift*
Rose-bloom fell on her hands, together pressed,
And on her silver cross soft amethyst,
And on her hair a glory, like a saint:
She seemed a splendid angel, newly dressed,
Save wings, for heaven—Porphyro grew faint:
She knelt, so pure a thing, so free from mortal taint.

26

Anon his heart revives: her vespers done,
Of all its wreathéd pearls her hair she frees;
Unclasps her warméd jewels one by one;
Loosens her fragrant bodice; by degrees
Her rich attire creeps rustling to her knees:
Half-hidden, like a mermaid in sea-weed,
Pensive awhile she dreams awake, and sees,
In fancy, fair St. Agnes in her bed,
But dares not look behind, or all the charm is fled.

27

Soon, trembling in her soft and chilly nest,
In sort of wakeful swoon, perplexed she lay,
Until the poppied warmth of sleep oppressed
Her soothéd limbs, and soul fatigued away;
Flown, like a thought, until the morrow-day;
Blissfully havened both from joy and pain;
Clasped like a missal where swart Paynims[2] pray;
Blinded alike from sunshine and from rain,
As though a rose should shut, and be a bud again.

9. A shield representing a coat of arms ("scutcheon") showed the red pigments ("blushed") indicating royal ancestry.

1. Heraldic red; here, in stained glass.
2. Dark pagans.

28

²⁴⁵

Stol'n to this paradise, and so entranced,
Porphyro gazed upon her empty dress,
And listened to her breathing, if it chanced
To wake into a slumberous tenderness;
Which when he heard, that minute did he bless,
And breathed himself: then from the closet crept,
Noiseless as fear in a wide wilderness,
And over the hushed carpet, silent, stepped,
And 'tween the curtains peeped, where, lo!—how fast she slept.

29

²⁵⁵

Then by the bedside, where the faded moon
Made a dim, silver twilight, soft he set
A table, and, half anguished, threw thereon
A cloth of woven crimson, gold, and jet—
O for some drowsy Morphean amulet!³
The boisterous, midnight, festive clarion,
The kettledrum, and far-heard clarinet,
Affray his ears, though but in dying tone—
The hall door shuts again, and all the noise is gone.

30

²⁶⁵

And still she slept an azure-lidded sleep,
In blanchéd linen, smooth, and lavendered,
While he from forth the closet brought a heap
Of candied apple, quince, and plum, and gourd;
With jellies soother than the creamy curd,
And lucent syrups, tinct° with cinnamon;   *tinctured*
Manna and dates, in argosy transferred
From Fez;⁴ and spicéd dainties, every one,
From silken Samarcand to cedared Lebanon.⁵

31

²⁷⁵

These delicates he heaped with glowing hand
On golden dishes and in baskets bright
Of wreathéd silver: sumptuous they stand
In the retiréd quiet of the night,
Filling the chilly room with perfume light.—
"And now, my love, my seraph° fair, awake!   *angel*
Thou art my heaven, and I thine eremite:⁶
Open thine eyes, for meek St. Agnes' sake,
Or I shall drowse beside thee, so my soul doth ache."

32

²⁸⁰

Thus whispering, his warm, unnervéd arm
Sank in her pillow. Shaded was her dream
By the dusk curtains: 'twas a midnight charm
Impossible to melt as icéd stream:
The lustrous salvers° in the moonlight gleam;   *serving dishes*
Broad golden fringe upon the carpet lies:
It seemed he never, never could redeem
From such a steadfast spell his lady's eyes;
So mused awhile, entoiled in wooféd° fantasies.   *enwoven*

33

²⁹⁰

Awakening up, he took her hollow lute—
Tumultuous—and, in chords that tenderest be,
He played an ancient ditty, long since mute,

---

3. An object, such as an engraved stone, ex-
erting the power of Morpheus, god of sleep.
4. Morocco.

5. Places associated with ancient luxury and
wealth.
6. Hermit, religious devotee.

In Provence called "*La belle dame sans merci*"[7]
Close to her ear touching the melody;
Wherewith disturbed, she uttered a soft moan:
He ceased—she panted quick—and suddenly
Her blue affrayéd eyes wide open shone:
Upon his knees he sank, pale as smooth-sculptured stone.

34
Her eyes were open, but she still beheld,
Now wide awake, the vision of her sleep:
There was a painful change, that nigh expelled
The blisses of her dream so pure and deep,
At which fair Madeline began to weep,
And moan forth witless words with many a sigh;
While still her gaze on Porphyro would keep,
Who knelt, with joinéd hands and piteous eye,
Fearing to move or speak, she looked so dreamingly.

35
"Ah, Porphyro!" said she, "but even now
Thy voice was at sweet tremble in mine ear,
Made tunable with every sweetest vow;
And those sad eyes were spiritual and clear:
How changed thou art! how pallid, chill, and drear!
Give me that voice again, my Porphyro,
Those looks immortal, those complainings dear!
Oh leave me not in this eternal woe,
For if thou diest, my Love, I know not where to go."

36
Beyond a mortal man impassioned far
At these voluptuous accents, he arose,
Ethereal, flushed, and like a throbbing star
Seen mid the sapphire heaven's deep repose;
Into her dream he melted, as the rose
Blendeth its odor with the violet—
Solution sweet: meantime the frost-wind blows
Like Love's alarum° pattering the sharp sleet   *signal, call to arms*
Against the windowpanes; St. Agnes' moon hath set.

37
'Tis dark: quick pattereth the flaw-blown° sleet: *gust-blown*
"This is no dream, my bride, my Madeline!"
'Tis dark: the icéd gusts still rave and beat:
"No dream, alas! alas! and woe is mine!
Porphyro will leave me here to fade and pine.—
Cruel! what traitor could thee hither bring?
I curse not, for my heart is lost in thine,
Though thou forsakest a deceivéd thing—
A dove forlorn and lost with sick unprunéd[8] wing."

38
"My Madeline! sweet dreamer! lovely bride!
Say, may I be for aye thy vassal blest?
Thy beauty's shield, heart-shaped and vermcil° dyed?   *vermilion*
Ah, silver shrine, here will I take my rest
After so many hours of toil and quest,
A famished pilgrim—saved by miracle,
Though I have found, I will not rob thy nest
Saving of thy sweet self; if thou think'st well
To trust, fair Madeline, to no rude infidel.

7. The lady beautiful but without mercy.   8. Unpreened; i.e., disarranged, rumpled.

39

"Hark! 'tis an elfin-storm from faery land,
   Of haggard° seeming, but a boon indeed: *wild, ugly*
345 Arise—arise! the morning is at hand—
   The bloated wassaillers° will never heed—   *drunken revelers*
   Let us away, my love, with happy speed;
   There are no ears to hear, or eyes to see—
   Drowned all in Rhenish and the sleepy mead:[9]
350 Awake! arise! my love, and fearless be,
For o'er the southern moors I have a home for thee."

40

She hurried at his words, beset with fears,
   For there were sleeping dragons all around,
   At glaring watch, perhaps, with ready spears—
355 Down the wide stairs a darkling way they found.—
   In all the house was heard no human sound.
   A chain-dropped lamp was flickering by each door;
   The arras, rich with horseman, hawk, and hound,
   Fluttered in the besieging wind's uproar;
360 And the long carpets rose along the gusty floor.

41

They glide, like phantoms, into the wide hall;
   Like phantoms, to the iron porch, they glide;
   Where lay the Porter, in uneasy sprawl,
   With a huge empty flagon by his side:
365 The wakeful bloodhound rose, and shook his hide,
   But his sagacious eye an inmate owns:°   *recognizes*
   By one, and one, the bolts full easy slide:
   The chains lie silent on the footworn stones;
The key turns, and the door upon its hinges groans.

42

370 And they are gone: aye, ages long ago
   These lovers fled away into the storm.
   That night the Baron dreamt of many a woe,
   And all his warrior-guests, with shade and form
   Of witch, and demon, and large coffin-worm,
375 Were long be-nightmared. Angela the old
   Died palsy-twitched, with meager face deform;
   The Beadsman, after thousand aves[1] told,
For aye unsought for slept among his ashes cold.

                                     1819   1820

On the Sonnet

If by dull rhymes our English must be chained,
   And, like Andromeda,[2] the Sonnet sweet
Fettered, in spite of painéd loveliness;
Let us find out, if we must be constrained,
5   Sandals more interwoven and complete
To fit the naked foot of poesy;
Let us inspect the lyre, and weigh the stress
Of every chord, and see what may be gained
   By ear industrious, and attention meet;
10 Misers of sound and syllable, no less

---

9. Rhine wine, and fermented honey and
water.
1. As in *Ave Maria* (Hail Mary), a saluta-
tion to the Virgin.

2. A beautiful princess chained naked to a
rock as a sacrifice to a sea-monster; rescued
by the hero Perseus.

Than Midas[3] of his coinage, let us be
    Jealous° of dead leaves in the bay-wreath crown;[4]   *intolerant*
So, if we may not let the Muse be free,
    She will be bound with garlands of her own.

                          1819   1848

La Belle Dame sans Merci[5]

O what can ail thee, Knight at arms,
    Alone and palely loitering?
The sedge has withered from the Lake
    And no birds sing!

5   O what can ail thee, Knight at arms,
    So haggard, and so woebegone?
The squirrel's granary is full
    And the harvest's done.

I see a lily on thy brow
10   With anguish moist and fever dew,
And on thy cheeks a fading rose
    Fast withereth too.

"I met a Lady in the Meads,°   *meadows*
    Full beautiful, a faery's child,
15   Her hair was long, her foot was light
    And her eyes were wild.

"I made a Garland for her head,
    And bracelets too, and fragrant Zone;°   *girdle*
She looked at me as she did love
20   And made sweet moan.

"I set her on my pacing steed
    And nothing else saw all day long,
For sidelong would she bend and sing
    A faery's song.

25   "She found me roots of relish sweet,
    And honey wild, and manna dew,
And sure in language strange she said
    'I love thee true.'

"She took me to her elfin grot
30   And there she wept and sighed full sore,
And there I shut her wild wild eyes
    With kisses four.

"And there she lulléd me asleep,
    And there I dreamed, Ah Woe betide!
35   The latest° dream I ever dreamt   *last*
    On the cold hill side.

---

3. A fabulously wealthy king who wished to turn all that he touched into gold; granted his wish by the gods, he quickly repented it.
4. Awarded as prize to a true poet.

5. The lady beautiful but without mercy. This is an earlier (and widely preferred) version of a poem first published in 1820.

"I saw pale Kings, and Princes too,
    Pale warriors, death-pale were they all;
They cried, 'La belle dame sans merci
40   Thee hath in thrall!'

"I saw their starved lips in the gloam
    With horrid warning gapéd wide,
And I awoke, and found me here
    On the cold hill's side.

45   "And this is why I sojourn here,
    Alone and palely loitering;
Though the sedge is withered from the Lake
    And no birds sing."

                                April 1819   1888

Ode to Psyche[6]

O Goddess! hear these tuneless numbers, wrung
    By sweet enforcement and remembrance dear,
And pardon that thy secrets should be sung
    Even into thine own soft-conchéd° ear;   *shell-like*
5   Surely I dreamt today, or did I see
    The wingéd Psyche with awakened eyes?
I wandered in a forest thoughtlessly,
    And, on the sudden, fainting with surprise,
Saw two fair creatures, couchéd side by side
10   In deepest grass, beneath the whisp'ring roof
    Of leaves and trembled blossoms, where there ran
        A brooklet, scarce espied:

'Mid hushed, cool-rooted flowers, fragrant-eyed,
    Blue, silver-white, and budded Tyrian,[7]
15   They lay calm-breathing on the bedded grass;
    Their arms embracéd, and their pinions° too;   *wings*
    Their lips touched not, but had not bade adieu,
As if disjoinéd by soft-handed slumber,
And ready still past kisses to outnumber
20   At tender eye-dawn of aurorean° love: *dawning*
        The wingéd boy I knew;
    But who wast thou, O happy, happy dove?
        His Psyche true!

O latest born and loveliest vision far
25   Of all Olympus' faded hierarchy![8]
Fairer than Phoebe's° sapphire-regioned star,   *the moon's*
    Or Vesper,° amorous glowworm of the sky;   *the evening star*
Fairer than these, though temple thou hast none,
        Nor altar heaped with flowers;
30   Nor virgin choir to make delicious moan
        Upon the midnight hours;
No voice, no lute, no pipe, no incense sweet

---

6. In Greek legend, Psyche (meaning "soul")
was loved in secret and in darkness by Cupid,
the "wingéd" son of the goddess Venus. After
many trials Psyche was united with Cupid in
immortality.

7. Purple or red, as in the "royal" dye made
in ancient Tyre.
8. Lines 24–25: last of the deities to be added
to the company of the Greek Olympian gods.

From chain-swung censer teeming;
No shrine, no grove, no oracle, no heat
Of pale-mouthed prophet dreaming.

O brightest! though too late for antique vows,
    Too, too late for the fond believing lyre,
When holy were the haunted forest boughs,
    Holy the air, the water, and the fire;
Yet even in these days so far retired
    From happy pieties, thy lucent fans,°   *wings*
    Fluttering among the faint Olympians,
I see, and sing, by my own eyes inspired.
So let me be thy choir, and make a moan
        Upon the midnight hours;
Thy voice, thy lute, thy pipe, thy incense sweet
    From swingéd censer teeming;
Thy shrine, thy grove, thy oracle, thy heat
Of pale-mouthed prophet dreaming.

Yes, I will be thy priest, and build a fane°   *temple*
    In some untrodden region of my mind,
Where branchéd thoughts, new grown with pleasant pain,
    Instead of pines shall murmur in the wind:
Far, far around shall those dark-clustered trees
    Fledge the wild-ridgéd mountains steep by steep;
And there by zephyrs,° streams, and birds, and bees,   *breezes*
    The moss-lain Dryads° shall be lulled to sleep;   *tree-nymphs*
And in the midst of this wide quietness
A rosy sanctuary will I dress
With the wreathed trellis of a working brain,
    With buds, and bells, and stars without a name,
With all the gardener Fancy e'er could feign,
    Who breeding flowers, will never breed the same:
And there shall be for thee all soft delight
    That shadowy thought can win,
A bright torch, and a casement ope at night,
    To let the warm Love⁹ in!

                                    1819   1820

Ode to a Nightingale

1

My heart aches, and a drowsy numbness pains
    My sense, as though of hemlock¹ I had drunk,
Or emptied some dull opiate to the drains
    One minute past, and Lethe-wards² had sunk:
'Tis not through envy of thy happy lot,
    But being too happy in thine happiness—
        That thou, light-wingéd Dryad of the trees,
            In some melodious plot
    Of beechen green, and shadows numberless,
        Singest of summer in full-throated ease.

---

9. I.e., Cupid.
1. Opiate made from a poisonous herb.

2. Towards the river Lethe, whose waters in
Hades bring the dead forgetfulness.

2

O, for a draught of vintage! that hath been
    Cooled a long age in the deep-delvéd earth,
Tasting of Flora³ and the country green,
    Dance, and Provençal song,⁴ and sunburnt mirth!
15 O for a beaker full of the warm South,
    Full of the true, the blushful Hippocrene,⁵
        With beaded bubbles winking at the brim,
            And purple-stainéd mouth;
    That I might drink, and leave the world unseen,
20   And with thee fade away into the forest dim:

3

Fade far away, dissolve, and quite forget
    What thou among the leaves hast never known,
The weariness, the fever, and the fret
    Here, where men sit and hear each other groan;
25 Where palsy shakes a few, sad, last gray hairs,
    Where youth grows pale, and specter-thin, and dies,
        Where but to think is to be full of sorrow
            And leaden-eyed despairs,
    Where Beauty cannot keep her lustrous eyes,
30   Or new Love pine at them beyond tomorrow.

4

Away! away! for I will fly to thee,
    Not charioted by Bacchus and his pards,⁶
But on the viewless° wings of Poesy,   *invisible*
    Though the dull brain perplexes and retards:
35 Already with thee! tender is the night,
    And haply the Queen-Moon is on her throne,
        Clustered around by all her starry Fays;°   *fairies*
            But here there is no light,
Save what from heaven is with the breezes blown
40   Through verdurous glooms and winding mossy ways.

5

I cannot see what flowers are at my feet,
    Nor what soft incense hangs upon the boughs,
But, in embalméd° darkness, guess each sweet   *perfumed*
    Wherewith the seasonable month endows
45 The grass, the thicket, and the fruit tree wild;
    White hawthorn, and the pastoral eglantine;⁷
        Fast fading violets covered up in leaves;
            And mid-May's eldest child,
The coming musk-rose, full of dewy wine,
50   The murmurous haunt of flies on summer eves.

6

Darkling° I listen; and for many a time   *in darkness*
I have been half in love with easeful Death,
Called him soft names in many a muséd rhyme,
    To take into the air my quiet breath;
55 Now more than ever seems it rich to die,
    To cease upon the midnight with no pain,
        While thou art pouring forth thy soul abroad

---

3. Roman goddess of springtime and flowers.
4. Of the late-medieval troubadours of Provence, in southern France.
5. The fountain of the Muses (goddesses of poetry and the arts) on Mt. Helicon in Greece;
its waters induce poetic inspiration.
6. "Bacchus": god of wine, often depicted in a chariot drawn by leopards ("pards").
7. Sweetbrier; wood roses.

In such an ecstasy!
Still wouldst thou sing, and I have ears in vain—
60   To thy high requiem become a sod.

7

Thou wast not born for death, immortal Bird!
No hungry generations tread thee down;
The voice I hear this passing night was heard
In ancient days by emperor and clown:
65 Perhaps the selfsame song that found a path
    Through the sad heart of Ruth,[8] when, sick for home,
      She stood in tears amid the alien corn;
        The same that ofttimes hath
    Charmed magic casements, opening on the foam
70   Of perilous seas, in faery lands forlorn.

8

Forlorn! the very word is like a bell
To toll me back from thee to my sole self!
Adieu! the fancy cannot cheat so well
    As she is famed to do, deceiving elf.
75 Adieu! adieu! thy plaintive anthem fades
Past the near meadows, over the still stream,
    Up the hill side; and now 'tis buried deep
      In the next valley-glades:
Was it a vision, or a waking dream?
80   Fled is that music:—Do I wake or sleep?

May 1819   1820

Ode on Melancholy

1

No, no, go not to Lethe,[9] neither twist
    Wolfsbane, tight-rooted, for its poisonous wine;
Nor suffer thy pale forehead to be kissed
    By nightshade,[1] ruby grape of Proserpine;[2]
5 Make not your rosary of yew-berries,[3]
    Nor let the beetle, nor the death-moth be
      Your mournful Psyche, nor the downy owl[4]
A partner in your sorrow's mysteries;
    For shade to shade will come too drowsily,
10   And drown the wakeful anguish of the soul.

2

But when the melancholy fit shall fall
    Sudden from heaven like a weeping cloud,
That fosters the droop-headed flowers all,
    And hides the green hill in an April shroud;
15 Then glut thy sorrow on a morning rose,
    Or on the rainbow of the salt sand-wave,
      Or on the wealth of globéd peonies;
Or if thy mistress some rich anger shows,
    Imprison her soft hand, and let her rave,
20   And feed deep, deep upon her peerless eyes.

8. In the Old Testament, a woman of great loyalty and modesty who, as a stranger in Judah, won a husband while gleaning in the barley-fields ("the alien corn," line 67).
9. River whose waters in Hades bring forgetfulness to the dead.
1. "Nightshade" and "wolfsbane" are poisonous herbs from which sedatives and opiates were extracted.

2. Queen of Hades.
3. Symbols of mourning; often growing in cemeteries.
4. Beetles, moths, and owls have been traditionally associated with darkness, death and burial; "Psyche" means *Soul*, sometimes symbolized by a moth that escapes the mouth in sleep or at death.

3

She[5] dwells with Beauty—Beauty that must die;
    And Joy, whose hand is ever at his lips
Bidding adieu; and aching Pleasure nigh,
    Turning to Poison while the bee-mouth sips:
25 Aye, in the very temple of Delight
        Veiled Melancholy has her sov'reign shrine,
            Though seen of none save him whose strenuous tongue
        Can burst Joy's grape against his palate fine;[6]
His soul shall taste the sadness of her might,
30   And be among her cloudy trophies[7] hung.

                                            May 1819   1820

Ode on a Grecian Urn

1

Thou still unravished bride of quietness,
    Thou foster child of silence and slow time,
Sylvan historian, who canst thus express
    A flowery tale more sweetly than our rhyme:
5 What leaf-fringed legend haunts about thy shape
    Of deities or mortals, or of both,
        In Tempe or the dales of Arcady?[8]
    What men or gods are these? What maidens loath?
What mad pursuit? What struggle to escape?
10   What pipes and timbrels? What wild ecstasy?

2

Heard melodies are sweet, but those unheard
    Are sweeter; therefore, ye soft pipes, play on;
Not to the sensual ear, but, more endeared,
    Pipe to the spirit ditties of no tone:
15 Fair youth, beneath the trees, thou canst not leave
    Thy song, nor ever can those trees be bare;
        Bold Lover, never, never canst thou kiss,
Though winning near the goal—yet, do not grieve;
        She cannot fade, though thou hast not thy bliss,
20   Forever wilt thou love, and she be fair!

3

Ah, happy, happy boughs! that cannot shed
    Your leaves, nor ever bid the Spring adieu;
And, happy melodist, unwearièd,
    Forever piping songs forever new;
25 More happy love! more happy, happy love!
    Forever warm and still to be enjoyed,
        Forever panting, and forever young;
All breathing human passion far above,
    That leaves a heart high-sorrowful and cloyed,
30   A burning forehead, and a parching tongue.

4

Who are these coming to the sacrifice?
    To what green altar, O mysterious priest,
Lead'st thou that heifer lowing at the skies,
    And all her silken flanks with garlands dressed?

---

5. The goddess Melancholy.
6. Keen, subtle.
7. Symbols of victory, such as banners, hung in religious shrines.

8. Tempe and Arcady (or Arcadia), in Greece, are traditional symbols of perfect pastoral landscapes.

What little town by river or sea shore,
　Or mountain-built with peaceful citadel,
　　Is emptied of this folk, this pious morn?
And, little town, thy streets forevermore
　Will silent be; and not a soul to tell
　　Why thou art desolate, can e'er return.

　　　　5
O Attic⁹ shape! Fair attitude! with brede°　　　　　　*woven pattern*
　Of marble men and maidens overwrought,
With forest branches and the trodden weed;
　Thou, silent form, dost tease us out of thought
As doth eternity: Cold Pastoral!
　When old age shall this generation waste,
　　Thou shalt remain, in midst of other woe
Than ours, a friend to man, to whom thou say'st,
　"Beauty is truth, truth beauty,"¹—that is all
　　Ye know on earth, and all ye need to know.

　　　　　　　　　　　　　　　　May 1819　　　　1820

To Autumn

　　　　1
Season of mists and mellow fruitfulness,
　Close bosom-friend of the maturing sun;
Conspiring with him how to load and bless
　With fruit the vines that round the thatch-eaves run;
To bend with apples the mossed cottage-trees,
　And fill all fruit with ripeness to the core;
　　To swell the gourd, and plump the hazel shells
With a sweet kernel; to set budding more,
And still more, later flowers for the bees,
Until they think warm days will never cease,
　　For Summer has o'er-brimmed their clammy cells.

　　　　2
Who hath not seen thee oft amid thy store?
　Sometimes whoever seeks abroad may find
Thee sitting careless on a granary floor,
　Thy hair soft-lifted by the winnowing wind;²
Or on a half-reaped furrow sound asleep,
　Drowsed with the fume of poppies, while thy hook³
　　Spares the next swath and all its twinéd flowers:
And sometimes like a gleaner thou dost keep
　Steady thy laden head across a brook;
　Or by a cider-press, with patient look,
　　Thou watchest the last oozings hours by hours.

　　　　3
Where are the songs of Spring? Aye, where are they?
　Think not of them, thou hast thy music too—
While barréd clouds bloom the soft-dying day,
　And touch the stubble-plains with rosy hue;
Then in a wailful choir the small gnats mourn
　Among the river sallows,° borne aloft　　　　*low-growing willows*

9. Greek, especially Athenian.
1. The quotation marks around this phrase are absent from some other versions also having good authority. This discrepancy has led some readers to ascribe only this phrase to the voice of the Urn; others ascribe to the Urn the whole of the two concluding lines.
2. "Winnowing": blowing the grain clear of the lighter chaff.
3. Small curved blade for cutting grain; sickle.

Or sinking as the light wind lives or dies;
30 And full-grown lambs loud bleat from hilly bourn;°   field
Hedge crickets sing; and now with treble soft
The redbreast whistles from a garden-croft;[4]
And gathering swallows twitter in the skies.

                                September 19, 1819   1820

Bright Star

Bright star, would I were steadfast as thou art—
    Not in lone splendor hung aloft the night
And watching, with eternal lids apart,
    Like nature's patient, sleepless Eremite,°   hermit, devotee
5   The moving waters at their priestlike task
    Of pure ablution round earth's human shores,
Or gazing on the new soft fallen mask
    Of snow upon the mountains and the moors—
No—yet still steadfast, still unchangeable,
10   Pillowed upon my fair love's ripening breast,
To feel forever its soft fall and swell,
    Awake forever in a sweet unrest,
Still, still to hear her tender-taken breath,
And so live ever—or else swoon to death.

                                    1819   1838

This Living Hand[5]

This living hand, now warm and capable
Of earnest grasping, would, if it were cold
And in the icy silence of the tomb,
So haunt thy days and chill thy dreaming nights
5   That thou wouldst wish thine own heart dry of blood
So in my veins red life might stream again,
And thou be conscience-calmed—see here it is—
I hold it towards you.

                                    1819?   1898

THOMAS HOOD
(1799–1846)

Ode

                    1
I saw old Autumn in the misty morn
Stand shadowless like silence, listening
To silence, for no lonely bird would sing
Into his hollow ear from woods forlorn,
5   Nor lowly hedge nor solitary thorn;
Shaking his languid locks all dewy bright
With tangled gossamer that fell by night,
    Pearling his coronet of golden corn.

---

4. Small field, as for a vegetable garden, near a house.

5. Written on a manuscript page of Keats's unfinished poem, *The Cap and Bells.*

2

Where are the songs of Summer? With the sun,
Oping the dusky eyelids of the south,
Till shade and silence waken up as one,
And Morning sings with a warm odorous mouth.
Where are the merry birds? Away, away,
On panting wings through the inclement skies,
    Lest owls should prey
    Undazzled at noonday,
And tear with horny beak their lustrous eyes.

3

Where are the blooms of Summer? In the west,
Blushing their last to the last sunny hours,
When the mild Eve by sudden Night is prest
Like tearful Proserpine,[1] snatched from her flow'rs
    To a most gloomy breast.
Where is the pride of Summer, the green prime,
The many, many leaves all twinkling? Three
    On the mossed elm; three on the naked lime
Trembling, and one upon the old oak tree!
    Where is the Dryads'° immortality?   *wood-nymphs'*
Gone into mournful cypress and dark yew,[2]
Or wearing the long gloomy Winter through
    In the smooth holly's green eternity.

4

The squirrel gloats on his accomplished hoard,
The ants have brimmed their garners with ripe grain,
    And honey bees have stored
The sweets of Summer in their luscious cells;
The swallows all have winged across the main;
But here the Autumn melancholy dwells,
    And sighs her tearful spells
Amongst the sunless shadows of the plain.
    Alone, alone,
    Upon a mossy stone,
She sits and reckons up the dead and gone
With the last leaves for a love-rosary,
Whilst all the withered world looks drearily,
Like a dim picture of the drownéd past
In the hushed mind's mysterious far away,
Doubtful what ghostly thing will steal the last
Into that distance, gray upon the gray.

5

Oh go and sit with her, and be o'ershaded
Under the languid downfall of her hair:
She wears a coronal° of flowers faded   *garland*
Upon her forehead, and a face of care;
There is enough of withered everywhere
To make her bower, and enough of gloom;
There is enough of sadness to invite,
If only for the rose that died, whose doom
Is Beauty's, she that with the living bloom
Of conscious cheeks most beautifies the light;
There is enough of sorrowing, and quite

1. In Greek legend, daughter of the goddess of fruitfulness. Abducted by the god of the underworld, she was later allowed to return to earth for half the year, thereby restoring the cycle of seasons.
2. Cypress and yew are traditional symbols of mourning but also of the hope for immortality.

Enough of bitter fruits the earth doth bear,
60   Enough of chilly droppings for her bowl;
Enough of fear and shadowy despair,
To frame her cloudy prison for the soul!

1827

RALPH WALDO EMERSON
(1803–1882)

Concord Hymn

SUNG AT THE COMPLETION OF THE BATTLE MONUMENT,[1] JULY 4, 1837

By the rude bridge that arched the flood,
    Their flag to April's breeze unfurled,
Here once the embattled farmers stood
    And fired the shot heard round the world.

5   The foe long since in silence slept;
    Alike the conqueror silent sleeps;
And Time the ruined bridge has swept
    Down the dark stream which seaward creeps.

On this green bank, by this soft stream,
10   We set to-day a votive stone;
That memory may their deed redeem,
    When, like our sires, our sons are gone.

Spirit, that made those heroes dare
    To die, and leave their children free,
15 Bid Time and Nature gently spare
    The shaft we raise to them and thee.

1837, 1876

The Rhodora

ON BEING ASKED, WHENCE IS THE FLOWER?

In May, when sea-winds pierced our solitudes,
I found the fresh Rhodora in the woods,
Spreading its leafless blooms in a damp nook,
To please the desert and the sluggish brook.
5   The purple petals, fallen in the pool,
Made the black water with their beauty gay;
Here might the red-bird come his plumes to cool,
And court the flower that cheapens his array.
Rhodora! if the sages ask thee why
10 This charm is wasted on the earth and sky,
Tell them, dear, that if eyes were made for seeing,
Then Beauty is its own excuse for being:
Why thou wert there, O rival of the rose!
I never thought to ask, I never knew;
15 But, in my simple ignorance, suppose
The self-same Power that brought me there brought you.

1834   1839, 1847

1. Commemorating the battles of Lexington and Concord, April 19, 1775.

The Problem

I like a church; I like a cowl;
I love a prophet of the soul;
And on my heart monastic aisles
Fall like sweet strains, or pensive smiles;
Yet not for all his faith can see
Would I that cowled churchman be.

Why should the vest on him allure,
Which I could not on me endure?

Not from a vain or shallow thought
His awful Jove young Phidias[2] brought,
Never from lips of cunning fell
The thrilling Delphic oracle;[3]
Out from the heart of nature rolled
The burdens of the Bible old;
The litanies of nations came,
Like the volcano's tongue of flame,
Up from the burning core below,
The canticles of love and woe;
The hand[4] that rounded Peter's dome
And groined the aisles of Christian Rome
Wrought in a sad sincerity;
Himself from God he could not free;
He builded better than he knew;
The conscious stone to beauty grew.

Know'st thou what wove yon woodbird's nest
Of leaves, and feathers from her breast?
Or how the fish outbuilt her shell,
Painting with morn each annual cell?
Or how the sacred pine-tree adds
To her old leaves new myriads?
Such and so grew these holy piles,
Whilst love and terror laid the tiles.
Earth proudly wears the Parthenon,
As the best gem upon her zone;
And Morning opes with haste her lids,
To gaze upon the Pyramids;
O'er England's abbeys bends the sky,
As on its friends, with kindred eye;
For out of Thought's interior sphere,
These wonders rose to upper air;
And Nature gladly gave them place,
Adopted them into her race,
And granted them an equal date
With Andes and with Ararat.

These temples grew as grows the grass;
Art might obey, but not surpass.
The passive Master lent his hand

2. Greek sculptor of the Periclean age (fifth century B.C.), responsible for the decoration of great monuments in Athens, including the Parthenon (line 33), the great temple to the goddess Athena and the greatest architectural accomplishment of ancient Greece.
3. At which the wisdom and prophecies of Apollo were revealed.
4. The "hand" is that of Michelangelo, who brought St. Peter's, in Rome, to completion.

To the vast soul that o'er him planned;
And the same power that reared the shrine
50 Bestrode the tribes that knelt within.
Ever the fiery Pentecost[5]
Girds with one flame the countless host,
Trances the heart through chanting choirs,
And through the priest the mind inspires.
55 The word unto the prophet spoken
Was writ on tables yet unbroken;[6]
The word by seers or sibyls told,
In groves of oak, or fanes of gold,
Still floats upon the morning wind,
60 Still whispers to the willing mind.
One accent of the Holy Ghost
The heedless world hath never lost.
I know what say the fathers wise,
The Book itself before me lies,
65 Old Crysostom,[7] best Augustine,
And he who blent both in his line,
The younger *Golden Lips* or mines,
Taylor,[8] the Shakespeare of divines.
His words are music in my ear,
70 I see his cowled portrait dear;
And yet, for all his faith could see,
I would not the good bishop be.

1839   1840, 1847

The Snowstorm

Announced by all the trumpets of the sky,
Arrives the snow, and, driving o'er the fields,
Seems nowhere to alight: the whited air
Hides hills and woods, the river, and the heaven,
5 And veils the farmhouse at the garden's end.
The sled and traveler stopped, the courier's feet
Delayed, all friends shut out, the housemates sit
Around the radiant fireplace, enclosed
In a tumultuous privacy of storm.

10   Come see the north wind's masonry.
Out of an unseen quarry evermore
Furnished with tile, the fierce artificer
Curves his white bastions with projected roof
Round every windward stake, or tree, or door.
15 Speeding, the myriad-handed, his wild work
So fanciful, so savage, nought cares he
For number or proportion. Mockingly,
On coop or kennel he hangs Parian[9] wreaths;
A swan-like form invests the hidden thorn;
20 Fills up the farmer's lane from wall to wall,

5. The occasion of the descent of the Holy Spirit upon Christ's Apostles on the Day of Pentecost, observed as a church festival the seventh Sunday after Easter.
6. The Law given to Moses by Jehovah and inscribed on tablets of stone which, when the Israelites disobeyed, Moses broke (see Exodus xxxii.1–19).
7. St. John Chrysostom, one of the Greek Fathers of the Church, called "Chrysostom" or "golden-mouth" for his great eloquence; St. Augustine, the most famous of whose numerous works are his *Confessions* and *De Civitate Dei* (*City of God*).
8. Jeremy Taylor, seventeenth-century English churchman most famous for the combined simplicity and splendor of style in *Holy Living* and *Holy Dying*.
9. I.e., like the fine white marble from the Greek island of Paros.

Maugre° the farmer's sighs; and, at the gate,   *in spite of*
A tapering turret overtops the work.
And when his hours are numbered, and the world
Is all his own, retiring, as he were not,
Leaves, when the sun appears, astonished Art
To mimic in slow structures, stone by stone,
Built in an age, the mad wind's night-work,
The frolic architecture of the snow.

                                                   1841, 1847

Grace

How much, preventing God! how much I owe
To the defenses thou hast round me set:
Example, custom, fear, occasion slow,
These scornéd bondmen were my parapet.
I dare not peep over this parapet
To gauge with glance the roaring gulf below,
The depths of sin to which I had descended,
Had not these me against myself defended.

                                                   1842, 1867

Hamatreya[1]

Bulkeley, Hunt, Willard, Hosmer, Meriam, Flint,[2]
Possessed the land which rendered to their toil
Hay, corn, roots, hemp, flax, apples, wool and wood.
Each of these landlords walked amidst his farm,
Saying, ' 'T is mine, my children's and my name's.
How sweet the west wind sounds in my own trees!
How graceful climb those shadows on my hill!
I fancy these pure waters and the flags°   *plants, grass*
Know me, as does my dog: we sympathize;
And, I affirm, my actions smack of the soil.'

Where are these men? Asleep beneath their grounds:
And strangers, fond as they, their furrows plough.
Earth laughs in flowers, to see her boastful boys
Earth proud, proud of the earth which is not theirs;
Who steer the plough, but cannot steer their feet
Clear of the grave.
They added ridge to valley, brook to pond,
And sighed for all that bounded their domain;
'This suits me for a pasture, that's my park;
We must have clay, lime, gravel, granite-ledge,
And misty lowland, where to go for peat.
The land is well—lies fairly to the south.
'T is good, when you have crossed the sea and back,
To find the sitfast acres where you left them.'
Ah! the hot owner sees not Death, who adds
Him to his land, a lump of mould the more.
Hear what the Earth says:

Earth-song

Mine and yours;
Mine, not yours.
Earth endures;

---

1. A variant of the Hindu name *Maitreya*.   2. First settlers of Concord, Massachusetts.

Stars abide—
Shine down in the old sea;
Old are the shores;
But where are old men?
35   I who have seen much,
Such have I never seen.

The lawyer's deed
Ran sure,
In tail,[3]
40   To them, and to their heirs
Who shall succeed,
Without fail,
Forevermore.

Here is the land,
45   Shaggy with wood,
With its old valley,
Mound and flood.
But the heritors?
Fled like the flood's foam.
50   The lawyer, and the laws,
And the kingdom,
Clean swept herefrom.

They called me theirs.
Who so controlled me;
55   Yet every one
Wished to stay, and is gone,
How am I theirs,
If they cannot hold me,
But I hold them?

60   When I heard the Earth-song,
I was no longer brave;
My avarice cooled
Like lust in the chill of the grave.

1847

Ode

INSCRIBED TO W. H. CHANNING[4]

Though loath to grieve
The evil time's sole patriot,
I cannot leave
My honied thought
5   For the priest's cant,
Or statesman's rant.

If I refuse
My study for their politique,
10   Which at the best is trick,
The angry Muse
Puts confusion in my brain.

---

3. I.e., entailed; to *entail* is to limit by legal means (usually a will) the inheritance of an estate to a specified line of heirs.

4. Unitarian clergyman, transcendentalist, and activist in social causes, particularly the anti-slavery movement.

But who is he that prates
Of the culture of mankind,
Of better arts and life?
Go, blindworm, go,
Behold the famous States
Harrying Mexico
With rifle and with knife![5]

Or who, with accent bolder,
Dare praise the freedom-loving mountaineer?
I found by thee, O rushing Contoocook![6]
And in thy valleys, Agiochook![7]
The jackals of the Negro-holder.

The God who made New Hampshire
Taunted the lofty land
With little men;
Small bat and wren
House in the oak:
If earth-fire cleave
The upheaved land, and bury the folk,
The southern crocodile would grieve.
Virtue palters;° Right is hence;   *hesitates, equivocates*
Freedom praised, but hid;
Funeral eloquence
Rattles the coffin-lid.

What boots thy zeal,
O glowing friend,
That would indignant rend
The northland from the south?
Wherefore? to what good end?
Boston Bay and Bunker Hill
Would serve things still;
Things are of the snake.

The horseman serves the horse,
The neatherd serves the neat,[8]
The merchant serves the purse,
The eater serves his meat;
'T is the day of the chattel,
Web to weave, and corn to grind;
Things are in the saddle,
And ride mankind.

There are two laws discrete,
Not reconciled,
Law for man, and law for things;
The last builds town and fleet,
But it runs wild,
And doth the man unking.

'T is fit the forest fall,
The steep be graded,

5. A reference to the war between the United
States and Mexico (1846–48) chiefly over the
question of the boundaries of Texas. To some
Americans, the United States' position was
immoral.

6. Part of the Merrimack River in New
Hampshire.
7. The White Mountains of New Hampshire.
8. Archaic terms for *cowherd* and *cow*.

60 The mountain tunnelled,
　 The sand shaded,
　 The orchard planted,
　 The glebe tilled,
　 The prairie granted,
65 The steamer built.

　 Let man serve law for man;
　 Live for friendship, live for love,
　 For truth's and harmony's behoof;° *benefit*
　 The state may follow how it can,
70 As Olympus follows Jove.

　　 Yet do not I implore
　 The wrinkled shopman to my surrounding woods,
　 Nor bid the unwilling senator
　 Ask votes of thrushes in the solitudes.
75 Every one to his chosen work;
　 Foolish hands may mix and mar;
　 Wise and sure the issues are.
　 Round they roll till dark is light,
　 Sex to sex, and even to odd;
80 The over-god
　 Who marries Right to Might,
　 Who peoples, unpeoples,
　 He who exterminates
　 Races by stronger races,
85 Black by white faces,
　 Knows to bring honey
　 Out of the lion;[9]
　 Grafts gentlest scion
　 On pirate and Turk.

90 The Cossack eats Poland,[1]
　 Like stolen fruit;
　 Her last noble is ruined,
　 Her last poet mute:
　 Straight, into double band
95 The victors divide;
　 Half for freedom strike and stand;—
　 The astonished Muse finds thousands at her side.

1847

Blight

　　　　 Give me truths;
　 For I am weary of the surfaces,
　 And die of inanition. If I knew
　 Only the herbs and simples of the wood,
　 Rue, cinquefoil, gill, vervain, and agrimony,
5 Blue-vetch, and trillium, hawkweed, sassafras,
　 Milkweeds, and murky brakes, quaint pipes, and sundew,[2]
　 And rare and virtuous roots, which in these woods

9. The allusion in lines 83–87 is to Samson, who killed a lion and returned later to find the carcass filled with honey (Judges xiv.5–10).
1. Russian military despotism, established in Poland after the popular insurrections of 1830–31, was challenged by a new Polish uprising (lines 94–96) in 1846.
2. Names of flowers and herbs, most of them wild.

Draw untold juices from the common earth,
Untold, unknown, and I could surely spell
Their fragrance, and their chemistry apply
By sweet affinities to human flesh,
Driving the foe and stablishing the friend,
O, that were much, and I could be a part
Of the round day, related to the sun
And planted world, and full executor
Of their imperfect functions.
But these young scholars, who invade our hills,
Bold as the engineer who fells the wood,
And traveling often in the cut he makes,
Love not the flower they pluck, and know it not,
And all their botany is Latin names.
The old men studied magic in the flowers,
And human fortunes in astronomy,
And an omnipotence in chemistry,
Preferring things to names, for these were men,
Were unitarians of the united world,
And, wheresoever their clear eye-beams fell,
They caught the footsteps of the SAME. Our eyes
Are armed, but we are strangers to the stars,
And strangers to the mystic beast and bird,
And strangers to the plant and to the mine.
The injured elements say, "Not in us";
And night and day, ocean and continent,
Fire, plant, and mineral say, "Not in us,"
And haughtily return us stare for stare.
For we invade them impiously for gain;
We devastate them unreligiously,
And coldly ask their pottage, not their love.
Therefore they shove us from them, yield to us
Only what to our griping toil is due;
But the sweet affluence of love and song,
The rich results of the divine consents
Of man and earth, of world beloved and lover,
The nectar and ambrosia³ are withheld;
And in the midst of spoils, and slaves, we thieves
And pirates of the universe, shut out
Daily to a more thin and outward rind,
Turn pale and starve. Therefore, to our sick eyes,
The stunted trees look sick, the summer short,
Clouds shade the sun, which will not tan our hay,
And nothing thrives to reach its natural term;
And life, shorn of its venerable length,
Even at its greatest space is a defeat,
And dies in anger that it was a dupe;
And, in its highest noon and wantonness,
Is early frugal, like a beggar's child;
Even in the hot pursuit of the best aims
And prizes of ambition, checks its hand,
Like Alpine cataracts frozen as they leaped
Chilled with a miserly comparison
Of the toy's purchase with the length of life.

1847

3. In mythology, the drink and the food that sustain the Greek gods.

Brahma[4]

If the red slayer think he slays,
  Or if the slain think he is slain,
They know not well the subtle ways
  I keep, and pass, and turn again.

5 Far or forgot to me is near;
  Shadow and sunlight are the same;
The vanished gods to me appear;
  And one to me are shame and fame.

They reckon ill who leave me out;
10 When me they fly, I am the wings;
I am the doubter and the doubt,
  And I the hymn the Brahmin sings.

The strong gods pine for my abode,
  And pine in vain the sacred Seven,[5]
15 But thou, meek lover of the good!
  Find me, and turn thy back on heaven.

1856   1857, 1867

Days

Daughters of Time, the hypocritic Days,
Muffled and dumb like barefoot dervishes,
And marching single in an endless file,
Bring diadems and fagots in their hands.
5 To each they offer gifts after his will,
Bread, kingdom, stars, and sky that holds them all.

I, in my pleached garden,[6] watched the pomp,
Forgot my morning wishes, hastily
Took a few herbs and apples, and the Day
10 Turned and departed silent. I, too late,
Under her solemn fillet° saw the scorn.

hair band
1857, 1867

Terminus[7]

It is time to be old,
To take in sail:
The god of bounds,
Who sets to seas a shore,
5 Came to me in his fatal rounds,
And said: 'No more!
No farther shoot
Thy broad ambitious branches, and thy root,
Fancy departs: no more invent,
10 Contract thy firmament
To compass of a tent.
There's not enough for this and that,

4. The supreme God of Hindu mythology and, in later theological developments, the divine reality itself, once thought to comprehend the entire universe which is the manifestation of that reality.

5. Perhaps the seven saints high in the Brahman hierarchy, but lesser than Brahma.
6. To pleach is to entwine, plait, or arrange foliage artificially.
7. The Roman god of boundaries and landmarks.

Make thy option which of two;
Economize the failing river,
Nor the less revere the Giver,
Leave the many and hold the few.
Timely wise accept the terms,
Soften the fall with wary foot;
A little while
Still plan and smile,
And, fault of novel germs,
Mature the unfallen fruit.
Curse, if thou wilt, thy sires,
Bad husbands of their fires,
Who, when they gave thee breath,
Failed to bequeath
The needful sinew stark as once,
The Baresark[8] marrow to thy bones,
But left a legacy of ebbing veins,
Inconstant heat and nerveless reins,—
Amid the Muses, left thee deaf and dumb,
Amid the gladiators, halt and numb.'

As the bird trims her to the gale,
I trim myself to the storm of time,
I man the rudder, reef the sail,
Obey the voice at eve obeyed at prime:
'Lowly faithful, banish fear,
Right onward drive unharmed;
The port well worth the cruise, is near,
And every wave is charmed.'

1867

ELIZABETH BARRETT BROWNING
(1806–1861)

Sonnets from the Portuguese[1]

1

I thought once how Theocritus had sung[2]
Of the sweet years, the dear and wished-for years,
Who each one in a gracious hand appears
To bear a gift for mortals, old or young:
And, as I mused it in his antique tongue,
I saw, in gradual vision through my tears,
The sweet, sad years, the melancholy years,
Those of my own life, who by turns had flung
A shadow across me. Straightway I was 'ware,

8. A Baresark, or Berserker, was a Norse warrior who fought in battle with extraordinary fury and daring, usually wearing his shirt but no armor. (*berserk*: bare-shirt).
1. The "Sonnets from the Portuguese" were written between 1845, when Miss Barrett met Robert Browning, and 1846, when they were married. An earlier poem, "Catrina to Camoens," in which Miss Barrett had assumed the persona of the girl who was loved by the sixteenth-century Portuguese poet Camoens, suggested the lightly disguising title when the sonnets were published in 1850.
2. In Idyll XV of Theocritus, the Greek pastoral poet of the 3rd century B.C., a singer describes (lines 100–5) the Hours, who have brought Adonis back from the underworld, as "the dear soft-footed Hours, slowest of all the Blessed Ones; but their coming is always longed for, and they bring something for all men."

10 So weeping, how a mystic Shape did move
    Behind me, and drew me backward by the hair;[3]
    And a voice said in mastery, while I strove,—
    "Guess now who holds thee?"—"Death," I said. But, there,
    The silver answer rang,—"Not Death, but Love."

43

How do I love thee? Let me count the ways.
I love thee to the depth and breadth and height
My soul can reach, when feeling out of sight
For the ends of Being and ideal Grace.
5 I love thee to the level of everyday's
Most quiet need, by sun and candle-light.
I love thee freely, as men strive for Right;
I love thee purely, as they turn from Praise.
I love thee with the passion put to use
In my old griefs, and with my childhood's faith.
10 I love thee with a love I seemed to lose
With my lost saints—I love thee with the breath,
Smiles, tears, of all my life!—and, if God choose,
I shall but love thee better after death.

                                            1845–46   1850

A Musical Instrument

What was he doing, the great god Pan,[4]
    Down in the reeds by the river?
Spreading ruin and scattering ban,[5]
Splashing and paddling with hoofs of a goat,
5 And breaking the golden lilies afloat
    With the dragonfly on the river.

He tore out a reed, the great god Pan,
    From the deep cool bed of the river;
The limpid water turbidly ran,
10 And the broken lilies a-dying lay,
And the dragonfly had fled away,
    Ere he brought it out of the river.

High on the shore sat the great god Pan
    While turbidly flowed the river;
And hacked and hewed as a great god can,
With his hard bleak steel at the patient reed,
Till there was not a sign of the leaf indeed
    To prove it fresh from the river.

He cut it short, did the great god Pan
20   (How tall it stood in the river!),
Then drew the pith, like the heart of a man,
    Steadily from the outside ring,
And notched the poor dry empty thing
    In holes, as he sat by the river.

---

3. In Book I of the *Iliad*, just as Achilles is drawing his sword to raise it against his leader, Agamemnon, Pallas Athene, standing behind him and hence invisible to the others, catches him by his hair to warn him.
4. In Greek mythology, an Arcadian god, in shape half goat, half human, son of Hermes; his function was to make the flocks fertile; he is also musical, his instrument the reed flute, and later pastoral poets made him the patron of their art. One of his loves was the nymph Syrinx; trying to escape him, she sought help from the river-nymphs, who turned her into a reed-bed: and from a reed Pan made his flute.
5. Baleful influence.

25 "This is the way," laughed the great god Pan
    (Laughed while he sat by the river),
"The only way, since gods began
To make sweet music, they could succeed."
Then, dropping his mouth to a hole in the reed,
30   He blew in power by the river.

Sweet, sweet, sweet, O Pan!
    Piercing sweet by the river!
Blinding sweet, O great god Pan!
The sun on the hill forgot to die,
35 And the lilies revived, and the dragonfly
    Came back to dream on the river.

Yet half a beast is the great god Pan,
    To laugh as he sits by the river,
Making a poet out of a man;
40 The true gods sigh for the cost and pain—
For the reed which grows nevermore again
    As a reed with the reeds in the river.

                                    1860   1862

HENRY WADSWORTH LONGFELLOW
(1807–1882)

Mezzo Cammin[1]

WRITTEN AT BOPPARD ON THE RHINE AUGUST 25, 1842, JUST BEFORE LEAVING FOR HOME

Half of my life is gone, and I have let
    The years slip from me and have not fulfilled
    The aspiration of my youth, to build
    Some tower of song with lofty parapet.
5 Not indolence, nor pleasure, nor the fret
    Of restless passions that would not be stilled,
    But sorrow, and care that almost killed,[2]
    Kept me from what I may accomplish yet;
Though, halfway up the hill, I see the Past
10   Lying beneath me with its sounds and sights,
    A city in the twilight dim and vast,
With smoking roofs, soft bells, and gleaming lights,
    And hear above me on the autumnal blast
The cataract of Death far thundering from the heights.

                                    1842   1846

The Fire of Driftwood

DEVEREUX FARM, NEAR MARBLEHEAD

We sat within the farmhouse old,
    Whose windows, looking o'er the bay,
Gave to the sea-breeze damp and cold,
    An easy entrance, night and day.

---

1. A phrase from the first line of Dante's *Divina Commedia:* "*Nel mezzo del cammin di nostra vita*" (midway upon the journey of our life).
2. Probably an allusion to the death of Longfellow's wife in 1835.

5 Not far away we saw the port,
   The strange, old-fashioned, silent town,
The lighthouse, the dismantled fort,
   The wooden houses, quaint and brown.

We sat and talked until the night,
10   Descending, filled the little room;
Our faces faded from the sight,
   Our voices only broke the gloom.

We spake of many a vanished scene,
   Of what we once had thought and said,
15 Of what had been, and might have been,
   And who was changed, and who was dead;

And all that fills the hearts of friends,
   When first they feel, with secret pain,
Their lives thenceforth have separate ends,
20   And never can be one again;

The first slight swerving of the heart,
   That words are powerless to express,
And leave it still unsaid in part,
   Or say it in too great excess.

25 The very tones in which we spake
   Had something strange, I could but mark;
The leaves of memory seemed to make
   A mournful rustling in the dark.

Oft died the words upon our lips,
30   As suddenly, from out the fire
Built of the wreck of stranded ships,
   The flames would leap and then expire.

And, as their splendor flashed and failed,
   We thought of wrecks upon the main,
35 Of ships dismasted, that were hailed
   And sent no answer back again.

The windows, rattling in their frames,
   The ocean, roaring up the beach,
The gusty blast, the bickering flames,
40   All mingled vaguely in our speech;

Until they made themselves a part
   Of fancies floating through the brain,
The long-lost ventures of the heart,
   That send no answers back again.

45 O flames that glowed! O hearts that yearned!
   They were indeed too much akin,
The driftwood fire without that burned,
   The thoughts that burned and glowed within.

1849, 1850

The Jewish Cemetery at Newport

How strange it seems! These Hebrews in their graves,
  Close by the street of this fair seaport town,
Silent beside the never-silent waves,
  At rest in all this moving up and down!

The trees are white with dust, that o'er their sleep
  Wave their broad curtains in the southwind's breath,
While underneath these leafy tents they keep
  The long, mysterious Exodus[3] of Death.

And these sepulchral stones, so old and brown,
  That pave with level flags their burial-place,
Seem like the tablets of the Law, thrown down
  And broken by Moses at the mountain's base.[4]

The very names recorded here are strange,
  Of foreign accent, and of different climes;
Alvares and Rivera[5] interchange
  With Abraham and Jacob of old times.

"Blessed be God! for he created Death!"
  The mourners said, "and Death is rest and peace;"
Then added, in the certainty of faith,
  "And giveth Life that nevermore shall cease."

Closed are the portals of their Synagogue,
  No Psalms of David now the silence break,
No Rabbi reads the ancient Decalogue°   *Ten Commandments*
  In the grand dialect the Prophets spake.

Gone are the living, but the dead remain,
  And not neglected; for a hand unseen,
Scattering its bounty, like a summer rain,
  Still keeps their graves and their remembrance green.

How came they here? What burst of Christian hate,
  What persecution, merciless and blind,
Drove o'er the sea—that desert desolate—
  These Ishmaels and Hagars of mankind?[6]

They lived in narrow streets and lanes obscure,
  Ghetto and Judenstrass,[7] in mirk and mire;
Taught in the school of patience to endure
  The life of anguish and the death of fire.

All their lives long, with the unleavened bread
  And bitter herbs of exile and its fears,
The wasting famine of the heart they fed,
  And slaked its thirst with marah[8] of their tears.

---

3. The Exodus is the flight of Moses and the Israelites from Egypt.
4. Moses, angered by the disobedience of the Israelites, broke the tablets of the Law which had been given them.
5. Many of the early Jewish families in New England were from Spain and Portugal.

6. Hagar, concubine of Abraham, wandered in the desert with Ishmael, her son by Abraham, after she was sent away by Abraham and Sarah (see Genesis xxi.9–21).
7. German for "Street of Jews."
8. The Hebrew word for "bitter" or "bitterness."

Anathema maranatha![9] was the cry
  That rang from town to town, from street to street;
At every gate the accursed Mordecai[1]
  Was mocked and jeered, and spurned by Christian feet.

45 Pride and humiliation hand in hand
    Walked with them through the world where'er they went;
  Trampled and beaten were they as the sand,
    And yet unshaken as the continent.

  For in the background figures vague and vast
50   Of patriarchs and of prophets rose sublime,
  And all the great traditions of the Past
    They saw reflected in the coming time.

  And thus forever with reverted look
    The mystic volume of the world they read,
55 Spelling it backward, like a Hebrew book,
    Till life became a Legend of the Dead.

  But ah! what once has been shall be no more!
    The groaning earth in travail and in pain
  Brings forth its races, but does not restore,
60   And the dead nations never rise again.

                            1852   1854, 1858

Snowflakes

Out of the bosom of the Air,
  Out of the cloud-folds of her garments shaken,
Over the woodlands brown and bare,
  Over the harvest-fields forsaken,
5   Silent, and soft, and slow
    Descends the snow.

Even as our cloudy fancies take
  Suddenly shape in some divine expression,
Even as the troubled heart doth make
10   In the white countenance confession,
    The troubled sky reveals
    The grief it feels.

This is the poem of the air,
  Slowly in silent syllables recorded;
15 This is the secret of despair,
    Long in its cloudy bosom hoarded,
    Now whispered and revealed
    To wood and field.

                                          1863

---

9. A Greek-Aramaic phrase signifying a ter-
rible curse, applied specifically (as in I Corin-
thians xvi.22) to the Jews.
1. A Jew whose foster daughter, Esther, be-
came the queen of Ahasuerus (Xerxes), king
of Persia. When Haman, Ahasuerus' favored
advisor, sought to destroy Mordecai and the
Jews, Mordecai stood at the king's gate crying
out against the persecution. See Esther iii.

Divina Commedia[2]

1

Oft have I seen at some cathedral door
A laborer, pausing in the dust and heat,
Lay down his burden, and with reverent feet
Enter, and cross himself, and on the floor
5 Kneel to repeat his paternoster[3] o'er;
Far off the noises of the world retreat;
The loud vociferations of the street
Become an undistinguishable roar.
So, as I enter here from day to day,
10   And leave my burden at this minster gate,
Kneeling in prayer, and not ashamed to pray,
The tumult of the time disconsolate
To inarticulate murmurs dies away,
While the eternal ages watch and wait.

2

How strange the sculptures that adorn these towers!
This crowd of statues, in whose folded sleeves
Birds build their nests; while canopied with leaves
Parvis[4] and portal bloom like trellised bowers,
5 And the vast minster seems a cross of flowers!
But fiends and dragons on the gargoyled eaves
Watch the dead Christ between the living thieves,
And, underneath, the traitor Judas lowers!
Ah! from what agonies of heart and brain,
10   What exultations trampling on despair,
What tenderness, what tears, what hate of wrong,
What passionate outcry of a soul in pain,
Uprose this poem of the earth and air,
This mediaeval miracle of song!

3

I enter, and I see thee in the gloom
Of the long aisles, O poet saturnine![5]
And strive to make my steps keep pace with thine.
The air is filled with some unknown perfume;
5 The congregation of the dead make room
For thee to pass; the votive tapers shine;
Like rooks that haunt Ravenna's[6] groves of pine
The hovering echoes fly from tomb to tomb.
From the confessionals I hear arise
10   Rehearsals of forgotten tragedies,
And lamentations from the crypts below;
And then a voice celestial that begins
With the pathetic words, "Although your sins
As scarlet be," and ends with "as the snow."[7]

4

With snow-white veil and garments as of flame,
She stands before thee, who so long ago
Filled thy young heart with passion and the woe

---

2. Divine Comedy.
3. Literally, the Latin "our father," the first words of the Lord's Prayer.
4. The court or portico in front of a church or cathedral.
5. A reference to Dante himself.

6. A city in northeastern Italy, much admired by Dante and in which he died after having fled Florence in 1301.
7. "Come now, and let us reason together, saith the Lord: though your sins be as scarlet, they shall be as white as snow" (Isaiah i.18).

From which thy song and all its splendors came;[8]
5   And while with stern rebuke she speaks thy name,
The ice about thy heart melts as the snow
On mountain heights, and in swift overflow
Comes gushing from thy lips in sobs of shame.
Thou makest full confession; and a gleam,
10   As of the dawn on some dark forest cast,
Seems on thy lifted forehead to increase;
Lethe and Eunoë[9]—the remembered dream
And the forgotten sorrow—bring at last
That perfect pardon which is perfect peace.

5

I lift mine eyes, and all the windows blaze
With forms of saints and holy men who died,
Here martyred and hereafter glorified;
And the great Rose[1] upon its leaves displays
5   Christ's Triumph, and the angelic roundelays,
With splendor upon splendor multiplied;
And Beatrice again at Dante's side
No more rebukes, but smiles her words of praise.
And then the organ sounds, and unseen choirs
10 Sing the old Latin hymns of peace and love
And benedictions of the Holy Ghost;
And the melodious bells among the spires
O'er all the housetops and through heaven above
Proclaim the elevation of the Host![2]

6

O star of morning and of liberty![3]
O bringer of the light, whose splendor shines
Above the darkness of the Apennines,
Forerunner of the day that is to be!
5   The voices of the city and the sea,
The voices of the mountains and the pines,
Repeat thy song, till the familiar lines
Are footpaths for the thought of Italy!
Thy flame is blown abroad from all the heights,
10   Through all the nations, and a sound is heard,
As of a mighty wind, and men devout,
Strangers of Rome, and the new proselytes,
In their own language hear thy wondrous word,
And many are amazed and many doubt.

1864–67   1865–67

Chaucer

An old man in a lodge within a park;
The chamber walls depicted all around
With portraitures of huntsman, hawk, and hound,
And the hurt deer. He listeneth to the lark,
5   Whose song comes with the sunshine through the dark
Of painted glass in leaden lattice bound;

8. A reference to Beatrice, who, whether as a real person in his youth or as a vision, was Dante's inspiration in *Vita Nuova* and *Divina Commedia*.
9. In classical myth and literature, Lethe is the river of forgetfulness; Eunoë, of good memories.
1. A many-petaled rose is, in the *Paradiso* section of *Divina Commedia*, Dante's vision of Christ triumphant, with the Virgin and the saints.
2. The consecrated bread in the Eucharist, or communion sacrament.
3. A direct address to Dante as symbol of the rising spirit of freedom in the Renaissance.

He listeneth and he laugheth at the sound,
Then writeth in a book like any clerk.[4]
He is the poet of the dawn, who wrote
The Canterbury Tales, and his old age
Made beautiful with song; and as I read
I hear the crowing cock, I hear the note
Of lark and linnet, and from every page
Rise odors of plowed field or flowery mead.

1873   1875

Milton

I pace the sounding sea-beach and behold
How the voluminous billows roll and run,
Upheaving and subsiding, while the sun
Shines through their sheeted emerald far unrolled
And the ninth wave, slow gathering fold by fold
All its loose-flowing garments into one,
Plunges upon the shore, and floods the dun
Pale reach of sands, and changes them to gold.
So in majestic cadence rise and fall
The mighty undulations of thy song,
O sightless Bard, England's Maeonides![5]
And ever and anon, high over all
Uplifted, a ninth wave superb and strong,
Floods all the soul with its melodious seas.

1873   1875

JOHN GREENLEAF WHITTIER
(1807–1892)

Proem

I love the old melodious lays
Which softly melt the ages through,
The songs of Spenser's golden days,
Arcadian Sidney's silvery phrase.
Sprinkling our noon of time with freshest morning dew.

Yet, vainly in my quiet hours
To breathe their marvelous notes I try;
I feel them, as the leaves and flowers
In silence feel the dewy showers,
And drink with glad still lips the blessing of the sky.

The rigor of a frozen clime,
The harshness of an untaught ear,
The jarring words of one whose rhyme
Beat often Labor's hurried time,
Or Duty's rugged march through storm and strife, are here.

4. In Chaucer's own sense of "a scholar."
5. Maeonides is a name sometimes given to Homer, ancient Greece's "sightless Bard," because his birthplace was reputed to be Maeonia, an ancient country in Asia Minor.

Of mystic beauty, dreamy grace,
No rounded art the lack supplies;
Unskilled the subtle lines to trace,
Or softer shades of Nature's face,
20 I view her common forms with unanointed eyes.

Nor mine the seer-like power to show
The secrets of the heart and mind;
To drop the plummet-line below
Our common world of joy and woe,
25 A more intense despair or brighter hope to find.

Yet here at least an earnest sense
Of human right and weal is shown;
A hate of tyranny intense,
And hearty in its vehemence,
30 As if my brother's pain and sorrow were my own.

O Freedom! if to me belong
Nor mighty Milton's gift divine,
Nor Marvell's wit and graceful song.
Still with a love as deep and strong
35 As theirs, I lay, like them, my best gifts on thy shrine!

1847

First-Day Thoughts[1]

In calm and cool and silence, once again
I find my old accustomed place among
My brethen,[2] where, perchance, no human tongue
Shall utter words; where never hymn is sung,
5 Nor deep-toned organ blown, nor censer swung,
Nor dim light falling through the pictured pane!
There, syllabled by silence, let me hear
The still small voice which reached the prophet's ear;
Read in my heart a still diviner law[3]
10 Than Israel's leader on his tables[4] saw!
There let me strive with each besetting sin,
Recall my wandering fancies, and restrain
The sore disquiet of a restless brain;
And, as the path of duty is made plain,
15 May grace be given that I may walk therein,
Not like the hireling, for his selfish gain,
With backward glances and reluctant tread,
Making a merit of his coward dread,
But, cheerful, in the light around me thrown,
20 Walking as one to pleasant service led;
Doing God's will as if it were my own,
Yet trusting not in mine, but in his strength alone!

1853

1. In Quaker usage, "First Day" is Sunday.
2. Fellow Quakers or Friends, as members of the Society of Friends are called.
3. In this and the preceding lines, Whittier describes the Friends' traditional Meeting for Worship where the individual member sits quietly and contemplatively in expectation that the divine within himself (the Inner Light) will "speak."
4. "Israel's leader": Moses; "tables": the stone tablets of the Ten Commandments.

Abraham Davenport

In the old days (a custom laid aside
With breeches and cocked hats) the people sent
Their wisest men to make the public laws.
And so, from a brown homestead, where the Sound[5]
5 Drinks the small tribute of the Mianas,
Waved over by the woods of Rippowams,
And hallowed by pure lives and tranquil deaths,
Stamford[6] sent up to the councils of the State
Wisdom and grace in Abraham Davenport.

10 'Twas on a May-day of the far old year
Seventeen hundred eighty, that there fell
Over the bloom and sweet life of the Spring,
Over the fresh earth and the heaven of noon,
A horror of great darkness, like the night
15 In day of which the Norland sagas tell,
The Twilight of the Gods.[7] The low-hung sky
Was black with ominous clouds, save where its rim
Was fringed with a dull glow, like that which climbs
The crater's sides from the red hell below.
20 Birds ceased to sing, and all the barnyard fowls
Roosted; the cattle at the pasture bars
Lowed, and looked homeward; bats on leathern wings
Flitted abroad; the sounds of labor died;
Men prayed, and women wept, all ears grew sharp
25 To hear the doom-blast of the trumpet[8] shatter
The black sky, that the dreadful face of Christ
Might look from the rent clouds, not as He looked
A loving guest at Bethany,[9] but stern
As Justice and inexorable Law.

30 Meanwhile in the old State House, dim as ghosts,
Sat the lawgivers of Connecticut,
Trembling beneath their legislative robes.
"It is the Lord's Great Day! Let us adjourn,"
Some said; and then, as if with one accord,
35 All eyes were turned to Abraham Davenport.
He rose, slow cleaving with his steady voice
The intolerable hush. "This well may be
The Day of Judgment which the world awaits;
But be it so or not, I only know
40 My present duty, and my Lord's command
To occupy till He come. So at the post
Where He hath set me in His providence,
I choose, for one, to meet Him face to face,
No faithless servant frightened from my task,
45 But ready when the Lord of the harvest calls;

5. Long Island Sound, into which the Miamus and Rippowams rivers flow from western Connecticut.
6. Town in southwestern Connecticut.
7. "The Twilight of the Gods"—*Ragnarok* in Scandinavian, and *Götterdämmerung* in German mythology—is the moment of total destruction in the confrontation of the gods and the powers of evil. A new and better order in the universe arises thereafter.
8. The trumpet of the Last Judgment. See I Corinthians xv.51–52.
9. Christ was compassionate and mild to the woman who poured precious ointment on his head and who was therefore criticized by the disciples for wasting ointment needed for the poor (Matthew xxvi.3–13).

And therefore, with all reverence, I would say,
Let God do His work, we will see to ours.
Bring in the candles." And they brought them in.

Then by the flaring lights the Speaker read,
50   Albeit with husky voice and shaking hands,
An act to amend an act to regulate
The shad and alewive[1] fisheries. Whereupon
Wisely and well spake Abraham Davenport,
Straight to the question, with no figures of speech
55   Save the ten Arab signs,[2] yet not without
The shrewd dry humor natural to the man:
His awe-struck colleagues listening all the while,
Between the pauses of his argument,
To hear the thunder of the wrath of God
60   Break from the hollow trumpet of the cloud.

And there he stands in memory to this day,
Erect, self-poised, a rugged face, half seen
Against the background of unnatural dark,
A witness to the ages as they pass,
65   That simple duty hath no place for fear.

1866, 1867

EDWARD FITZGERALD
(1809–1883)

The Rubáiyát of Omar Khayyám of Naishápúr[1]

1

Wake! For the Sun, who scattered into flight
The Stars before him from the Field of Night,
    Drives Night along with them from Heav'n, and strikes
The Sultán's Turret with a Shaft of Light.

2

5   Before the phantom of False morning died,
Methought a Voice within the Tavern cried,
    "When all the Temple is prepared within,
"Why nods the drowsy Worshipper outside?"

3

And, as the Cock crew, those who stood before
10   The Tavern shouted—"Open then the Door!
    "You know how little while we have to stay,
"And, once departed, may return no more."

4

Now the New Year[2] reviving old Desires,
The thoughtful Soul to Solitude retires,
15   Where the WHITE HAND OF MOSES on the Bough
Puts out, and Jesus from the Ground suspires.[3]

1. A fish resembling shad.
2. Arabic numerals.
1. Omar Khayyám, Persian poet, mathematician, and astronomer (ca. 1050–1132?), lived at Nishapur, in the province of Khurasan. FitzGerald translated his epigrammatic quatrains (*Rubáiyát*, plural of *ruba'i*, quatrain) which he first published in 1859; in three subsequent editions (the fourth edition is printed here) FitzGerald made many alterations of detail, arrangement, and number of stanzas.
2. "Beginning with the Vernal Equinox, it must be remembered" [FitzGerald's note].
3. The blossoming of trees is compared to the whiteness of Moses' hand as it is described in Exodus iv.6, and the sweetness of flowers to the sweetness of the breath of Jesus.

5

Irám[4] indeed is gone with all his Rose,
And Jamshýd's Sev'n-ringed Cup[5] where no one knows;
But still a Ruby kindles in the Vine,
And many a Garden by the Water blows.

6

And David's lips are lockt; but in divine
High-piping Pehleví,[6] with "Wine! Wine! Wine!
"Red Wine!"—the Nightingale cries to the Rose
That sallow cheek of hers to incarnadine.

7

Come, fill the Cup, and in the fire of Spring
Your Winter-garment of Repentance fling:
The Bird of Time has but a little way
To flutter—and the Bird is on the Wing.

8

Whether at Naishápúr or Babylon,
Whether the Cup with sweet or bitter run,
The Wine of Life keeps oozing drop by drop,
The Leaves of Life keep falling one by one.

9

Each Morn a thousand Roses brings, you say;
Yes, but where leaves the Rose of Yesterday?
And this first Summer month that brings the Rose
Shall take Jamshýd and Kaikobád away.

10

Well, let it take them! What have we to do
With Kaikobád the Great, or Kaikhosrú?
Let Zál and Rustum[7] bluster as they will,
Or Hátim[8] call to Supper—heed not you.

11

With me along the strip of Herbage strown
That just divides the desert from the sown,
Where name of Slave and Sultán is forgot—
And Peace to Mahmúd[9] on his golden Throne!

12

A Book of Verses underneath the Bough,
A Jug of Wine, a Loaf of Bread—and Thou
Beside me singing in the Wilderness—
Oh, Wilderness were Paradise enow!

13

Some for the Glories of This World; and some
Sigh for the Prophet's[1] Paradise to come;
Ah, take the Cash, and let the Credit go,
Nor heed the rumble of a distant Drum!

14

Look to the blowing Rose about us—"Lo,
"Laughing," she says, "into the world I blow,
"At once the silken tassel of my Purse
"Tear, and its Treasure on the Garden throw."

---

4. "A royal Garden now sunk somewhere in the Sands of Arabia" [FitzGerald's note].
5. In Persian mythology, Jamshýd was a king of the peris (celestial beings), who, because he had boasted of his immortality, was compelled to live on earth in human form for 700 years, becoming one of the kings of Persia. His cup, the invention of Kai-Kosru (line 38), another Persian king, great-grandson of Kai-Kobad (line 36), was decorated with signs

enabling its possessor to foretell the future.
6. The ancient literary language of Persia.
7. "The 'Hercules' of Persia, and Zál his Father" [FitzGerald's note].
8. Hátim Tai: a Persian chieftain, an archetype of oriental hospitality.
9. Sultan Máhmúd of Ghazni, in Afghanistan (971–1031), renowned both as ruler and as the conqueror of India.
1. I.e., Mohammed's.

15

And those who husbanded the Golden grain,
And those who flung it to the winds like Rain,
  Alike to no such aureate Earth are turned
60 As, buried once, Men want dug up again.

16

The Worldly Hope men set their Hearts upon
Turns Ashes—or it prospers; and anon,
  Like Snow upon the Desert's dusty Face,
Lighting a little hour or two—is gone.

17

65 Think, in this battered Caravanserai°   inn
Whose Portals are alternate Night and Day,
  How Sultán after Sultán with his Pomp
Abode his destined Hour, and went his way.

18

They say the Lion and the Lizard keep
70 The Courts where Jamshýd gloried and drank deep:
  And Bahrám,[2] that great Hunter—the Wild Ass
Stamps o'er his Head, but cannot break his Sleep.

19

I sometimes think that never blows so red
The Rose as where some buried Caesar bled;
75 That every Hyacinth the Garden wears
Dropt in her Lap from some once lovely Head.

20

And this reviving Herb whose tender Green
Fledges the river-lip on which we lean—
  Ah, lean upon it lightly! for who knows
80 From what once lovely Lip it springs unseen!

21

Ah, my Belovéd, fill the Cup that clears
TODAY of past Regrets and future Fears:
  Tomorrow!—Why, Tomorrow I may be
Myself with Yesterday's Sev'n thousand Years.

22

85 For some we loved, the loveliest and the best
That from his Vintage rolling Time hath prest,
  Have drunk their Cup a Round or two before,
And one by one crept silently to rest.

23

And we, that make merry in the Room
90 They left, and Summer dresses in new bloom,
  Ourselves must we beneath the Couch of Earth
Descend—ourselves to make a Couch—for whom?

24

Ah, make the most of what we yet may spend,
Before we too into the Dust descend;
95 Dust into Dust, and under Dust to lie,
Sans Wine, sans Song, sans Singer, and sans End!

25

Alike for those who for TODAY prepare,
And those that after some TOMORROW stare,
  A Muezzín[3] from the Tower of Darkness cries,
100 "Fools! your Reward is neither Here nor There."

2. A Sassanian king who, according to legend,   3. The crier who calls the hours of prayer
met his death while hunting the wild ass.   from tower or minaret.

26

Why, all the Saints and Sages who discussed
Of the Two Worlds so wisely—they are thrust
　　Like foolish Prophets forth; their Words to Scorn
Are scattered, and their Mouths are stopt with Dust.

27

Myself when young did eagerly frequent
Doctor and Saint, and heard great argument
　　About it and about: but evermore
Came out by the same door where in I went.

28

With them the seed of Wisdom did I sow,
And with mine own hand wrought to make it grow;
　　And this was all the Harvest that I reaped—
"I came like Water, and like Wind I go."

29

Into this Universe, and *Why* not knowing
Nor *Whence*, like Water willy-nilly flowing;
　　And out of it, as Wind along the Waste,
I know not *Whither*, willy-nilly blowing.

30

What, without asking, hither hurried *Whence?*
And, without asking, *Whither* hurried hence!
　　Oh, many a Cup of this forbidden Wine[4]
Must drown the memory of that insolence!

31

Up from Earth's Center through the Seventh Gate
I rose, and on the Throne of Saturn[5] sate,
　　And many a Knot unraveled by the Road;
But not the Master-knot of Human Fate.

32

There was the Door to which I found no Key;
There was the Veil through which I might not see:
　　Some little talk awhile of ME and THEE
There was—and then no more of THEE and ME.

33

Earth could not answer; nor the Seas that mourn
In flowing Purple, of their Lord forlorn;
　　Nor rolling Heaven, with all his Signs revealed
And hidden by the sleeve of Night and Morn.

34

Then of the THEE IN ME who works behind
The Veil, I lifted up my hands to find
　　A lamp amid the Darkness; and I heard,
As from Without—"THE ME WITHIN THEE blind!"

35

Then to the Lip of this poor earthen Urn
I leaned, the Secret of my Life to learn:
　　And Lip to Lip it murmured—"While you live,
"Drink! for, once dead, you never shall return."

36

I think the Vessel, that with fugitive
Articulation answered, once did live,
　　And drink; and Ah! the passive Lip I kissed,
How many Kisses might it take—and give!

---

4. Alcohol is forbidden to Mohammedans.
5. "Lord of the Seventh Heaven" [FitzGerald's note]. In ancient astronomy, Saturn was the most remote of the seven known planets; hence, Omar had reached the bounds of astronomical knowledge.

37

145 For I remember stopping by the way
To watch a Potter thumping his wet Clay:
And with its all-obliterated Tongue
It murmured—"Gently, Brother, gently, pray!"

38

And has not such a Story from of Old
150 Down Man's successive generations rolled
Of such a clod of saturated Earth
Cast by the Maker into Human mold?

39

And not a drop that from our Cups we throw
For Earth to drink of, but may steal below
155 To quench the fire of Anguish in some Eye
There hidden—far beneath, and long ago.

40

As then the Tulip for her morning sup
Of Heav'nly Vintage from the soil looks up,
Do you devoutly do the like, till Heav'n
160 To Earth invert you—like an empty Cup.

41

Perplext no more with Human or Divine,
Tomorrow's tangle to the winds resign,
And lose your fingers in the tresses of
The Cypress-slender Minister of Wine.[6]

42

165 And if the Wine you drink, the Lip you press,
End in what All begins and ends in—Yes;
Think then you are TODAY what YESTERDAY
You were—TOMORROW you shall not be less.

43

So when that Angel of the darker Drink
170 At last shall find you by the river-brink,
And, offering his Cup, invite your Soul
Forth to your Lips to quaff—you shall not shrink.

44

Why, if the Soul can fling the Dust aside,
And naked on the Air of Heaven ride,
175 Were't not a Shame—were't not a Shame for him
In this clay carcase crippled to abide?

45

'Tis but a Tent where takes his one day's rest
A Sultán to the realm of Death addrest;
The Sultán rises, and the dark Ferrásh[7]
180 Strikes, and prepares it for another Guest.

46

And fear not lest Existence closing your
Account, and mine, should know the like no more;
The Eternal Sáki° from that Bowl has poured   *cup-bearer*
Millions of Bubbles like us, and will pour.

47

185 When You and I behind the Veil are past,
Oh, but the long, long while the World shall last,
Which of our Coming and Departure heeds
As the Sea's self should heed a pebble-cast.

6. The maidservant who pours the wine.
7. The servant charged with setting up and striking the tent.

48

A Moment's Halt—a momentary taste
Of BEING from the Well amid the Waste—
   And Lo!—the phantom Caravan has reached
The NOTHING it set out from—Oh, make haste!

49

Would you that spangle of Existence spend
About THE SECRET—quick about it, Friend!
   A Hair perhaps divides the False and True—
And upon what, prithee, may life depend?

50

A Hair perhaps divides the False and True;
Yes; and a single Alif[8] were the clue—
   Could you but find it—to the Treasure-house,
And peradventure to THE MASTER too;

51

Whose secret Presence, through Creation's veins
Running Quicksilver-like eludes your pains;
   Taking all shapes from Máh to Máhi;[9] and
They change and perish all—but He remains;

52

A moment guessed—then back behind the Fold
Immerst of Darkness round the Drama rolled
   Which, for the Pastime of Eternity,
He doth Himself contrive, enact, behold.

53

But if in vain, down on the stubborn floor
Of Earth, and up to Heav'n's unopening Door,
   You gaze TODAY, while You are You—how then
TOMORROW, You when shall be You no more?

54

Waste not your Hour, nor in the vain pursuit
Of This and That endeavor and dispute;
   Better be jocund with the fruitful Grape
Than sadden after none, or bitter, Fruit.

55

You know, my Friends, with what a brave Carouse
I made a Second Marriage in my house;
   Divorced old barren Reason from my Bed,
And took the Daughter of the Vine to Spouse.

56

For "Is" and "Is-NOT" though with Rule and Line
And "UP-AND-DOWN" by Logic I define,
   Of all that one should care to fathom, I
Was never deep in anything but—Wine.

57

Ah, but my Computations, People say,
Reduced the Year to better reckoning?[1]—Nay,
   'Twas only striking from the Calendar
Unborn Tomorrow, and dead Yesterday.

58

And lately, by the Tavern Door agape,
Came shining through the Dusk an Angel Shape
   Bearing a Vessel on his Shoulder; and
He bid me taste of it; and 'twas—the Grape!

---

8. First letter of Arabic alphabet, consisting of a single vertical stroke.
9. From lowest to highest.

1. Omar was one of the learned men who had been charged with reforming the calendar.

59

The Grape that can with Logic absolute
The Two-and-Seventy jarring Sects[2] confute:
235   The sovereign Alchemist that in a trice
Life's leaden metal into Gold transmute:

60

The mighty Mahmúd, Allah-breathing Lord,[3]
That all the misbelieving and black Horde
Of Fears and Sorrows that infest the Soul
240   Scatters before him with his whirlwind Sword.

61

Why, be this Juice the growth of God, who dare
Blaspheme the twisted tendril as a Snare?
   A Blessing, we should use it, should we not?
And if a Curse—why, then, Who set it there?

62

245   I must abjure the Balm of Life, I must,
Scared by some After-reckoning ta'en on trust,
   Or lured with Hope of some Diviner Drink,
To fill the Cup—when crumbled into Dust!

63

Oh threats of Hell and Hopes of Paradise!
250   One thing at least is certain—*This* Life flies;
   One thing is certain and the rest is Lies;
The Flower that once has blown for ever dies.

64

Strange, is it not? that of the myriads who
Before us passed the door of Darkness through,
255   Not one returns to tell us of the Road,
Which to discover we must travel too.

65

The Revelations of Devout and Learned
Who rose before us, and as Prophets burned,
   Are all but Stories, which, awoke from Sleep
260   They told their comrades, and to Sleep returned.

66

I sent my Soul through the Invisible,
Some letter of that Afterlife to spell:
   And by and by my Soul returned to me,
And answered "I Myself am Heav'n and Hell:"

67

265   Heav'n but the Vision of fulfilled Desire,
And Hell the Shadow from a Soul on fire,
   Cast on the Darkness into which Ourselves,
So late emerged from, shall so soon expire.

68

We are no other than a moving row
270   Of Magic Shadow-shapes that come and go
   Round with the Sun-illumined Lantern held
In Midnight by the Master of the Show;

69

But helpless Pieces of the Game He plays
Upon his Checkerboard of Nights and Days;
275   Hither and thither moves, and checks, and slays,
And one by one back in the Closet lays.

---

2. "The 72 sects into which Islamism so soon split" [FitzGerald's note].

3. "This alludes to Máhmúd's Conquest of India and its swarthy Idolators" [FitzGerald's note].

70
The Ball no question makes of Ayes and Noes,
But Here or There as strikes the Player goes;
  And He that tossed you down into the Field,
He knows about it all—HE knows—HE knows!

71
The Moving Finger writes; and, having writ,
Moves on: nor all your Piety nor Wit
  Shall lure it back to cancel half a Line,
Nor all your Tears wash out a Word of it.

72
And that inverted Bowl they call the Sky,
Whereunder crawling cooped we live and die,
  Lift not your hands to *It* for help—for It
As impotently moves as you or I.

73
With Earth's first Clay They did the Last Man knead,
And there of the Last Harvest sowed the Seed:
  And the first Morning of Creation wrote
What the Last Dawn of Reckoning shall read.

74
YESTERDAY *This* Day's Madness did prepare;
TOMORROW's Silence, Triumph, or Despair:
  Drink! for you know not whence you came, nor why:
Drink! for you know not why you go, nor where.

75
I tell you this—When, started from the Goal,
Over the flaming shoulders of the Foal[4]
  Of Heav'n, Parwín and Mushtarí[5] they flung,
In my predestined Plot of Dust and Soul.

76
The Vine had struck a fiber: which about
If clings my Being—let the Dervish[6] flout;
  Of my Base metal may be filed a Key,
That shall unlock the Door he howls without.

77
And this I know: whether the one True Light
Kindle to Love, or Wrath consume me quite,
  One Flash of It within the Tavern caught
Better than in the Temple lost outright.

78
What! out of senseless Nothing to provoke
A conscious Something to resent the yoke
  Of unpermitted Pleasure, under pain
Of Everlasting Penalties, if broke!

79
What! from his helpless Creature be repaid
Pure Gold for what he lent him dross-allayed—
  Sue for a Debt he never did contract,
And cannot answer—Oh the sorry trade!

80
Oh Thou, who didst with pitfall and with gin°   trap
Beset the Road I was to wander in,
  Thou wilt not with Predestined Evil round
Enmesh, and then impute my Fall to Sin!

---

4. The constellation known as the Colt (*Equuleus*) or Foal.
5. "The Pleiads and Jupiter" [FitzGerald's note]; Omar ascribes his fate to the position of the stars and planets at the time of his birth.
6. Member of any of several Muslim orders taking vows of austerity and poverty.

81

Oh Thou, who Man of baser Earth didst make,
And ev'n with Paradise devise the Snake:
　For all the Sin wherewith the Face of Man
Is blackened—Man's forgiveness give—and take!

───────────

82

325　As under cover of departing Day
Slunk hunger-stricken Ramazán[7] away,
　Once more within the Potter's house alone
I stood, surrounded by the Shapes of Clay.

83

Shapes of all Sorts and Sizes, great and small,
330　That stood along the floor and by the wall;
　And some loquacious Vessels were; and some
Listened perhaps, but never talked at all.

84

Said one among them—"Surely not in vain
"My substance of the common Earth was ta'en
335　　"And to this Figure molded, to be broke,
"Or trampled back to shapeless Earth again."

85

Then said a Second—"Ne'er a peevish Boy
"Would break the Bowl from which he drank in joy;
　"And He that with his hand the Vessel made
340　"Will surely not in after Wrath destroy."

86

After a momentary silence spake
Some Vessel of a more ungainly Make;
　"They sneer at me for leaning all awry:
"What! did the Hand then of the Potter shake?"

87

345　Whereat some one of the loquacious Lot—
I think a Súfi° pipkin—waxing hot—   *mystic*
　"All this of Pot and Potter—Tell me then,
"Who is the Potter, pray, and who the Pot?"

88

"Why," said another, "Some there are who tell
350　"Of one who threatens he will toss to Hell
　"The luckless Pots he marred in making—Pish!
"He's a Good Fellow, and 'twill all be well."

89

"Well," murmured one, "Let whoso make or buy,
"My Clay with long Oblivion is gone dry:
355　　"But fill me with the old familiar Juice,
"Methinks I might recover by and by."

90

So while the Vessels one by one were speaking,
The little Moon[8] looked in that all were seeking:
　And then they jogged each other, "Brother! Brother!
360　"Now for the Porter's shoulder-knot[9] a-creaking!"

───────────

91

Ah, with the Grape my fading Life provide,
And wash the Body whence the Life has died,

7. The Mohammedans' annual thirty-day fast,
during which no food may be taken from dawn
to sunset.
8. The new moon, which signaled the end of
Ramazán.
9. The knot on the porter's shoulder-strap
from which the wine-jars were hung.

And lay men shrouded in the living Leaf,
By some not unfrequented Garden-side.

92
That ev'n my buried Ashes such a snare
Of Vintage shall fling up into thé Air
   As not a True-believer passing by
But shall be overtaken unaware.

93
Indeed the Idols I have loved so long
Have done my credit in this World much wrong:
   Have drowned my Glory in a shallow Cup,
And sold my Reputation for a Song.

94
Indeed, indeed, Repentance oft before
I swore—but was I sober when I swore?
   And then and then came Spring, and Rose-in-hand
My threadbare Penitence apieces tore.

95
And much as Wine has played the Infidel,
And robbed me of my Robe of Honor—Well,
   I wonder often what the Vintners buy
One half so precious as the stuff they sell.

96
Yet Ah, that Spring should vanish with the Rose!
That Youth's sweet-scented manuscript should close!
   The Nightingale that in the branches sang,
Ah whence, and whither flown again, who knows!

97
Would but the Desert of the Fountain yield
One glimpse—if dimly, yet indeed, revealed,
   To which the fainting Traveler might spring,
As springs the trampled herbage of the field!

98
Would but some wingéd Angel ere too late
Arrest the yet unfolded Roll of Fate,
   And make the stern Recorder otherwise
Enregister, or quite obliterate!

99
Ah Love! could you and I with Him conspire
To grasp this sorry Scheme of Things entire,
   Would not we shatter it to bits—and then
Remold it nearer to the Heart's Desire!

100
Yon rising Moon that looks for us again—
How oft hereafter will she wax and wane;
   How oft hereafter rising look for us
Through this same Garden—and for *one* in vain!

101
And when like her, oh Sákí, you shall pass
Among the Guests Star-scattered on the Grass,
   And in your joyous errand reach the spot
Where I made One—turn down an empty Glass!

TAMÁM[1]

1859, 1879

---

1. It is ended.

OLIVER WENDELL HOLMES
(1809–1894)

The Chambered Nautilus[1]

This is the ship of pearl, which, poets feign,
    Sails the unshadowed main,
    The venturous bark that flings
On the sweet summer wind its purpled wings
5 In gulfs enchanted, where the Siren sings,
    And coral reefs lie bare,
Where the cold sea-maids rise to sun their streaming hair.

Its webs of living gauze no more unfurl;
    Wrecked is the ship of pearl!
10   And every chambered cell,
Where its dim dreaming life was wont to dwell,
As the frail tenant shaped his growing shell,
    Before thee lies revealed,
Its irised ceiling rent, its sunless crypt unsealed!

15 Year after year beheld the silent toil
    That spread his lustrous coil;
    Still, as the spiral grew,
He left the past year's dwelling for the new,
Stole with soft step its shining archway through,
20   Built up its idle door,
Stretched in his last-found home, and knew the old no more.

Thanks for the heavenly message brought by thee,
    Child of the wandering sea,
    Cast from her lap, forlorn!
25 From thy dead lips a clearer note is born
Than ever Triton[2] blew from wreathéd horn!
    While on mine ear it rings,
Through the deep caves of thought I hear a voice that sings:

Build thee more stately mansions, O my soul,
30   As the swift seasons roll!
    Leave thy low-vaulted past!
Let each new temple, nobler than the last,
Shut thee from heaven with a dome more vast,
    Till thou at length art free,
35 Leaving thine outgrown shell by life's unresting sea!

1858

EDGAR ALLAN POE
(1809–1849)

Sonnet—To Science

Science! true daughter of Old Time thou art!
  Who alterest all things with thy peering eyes.

---

1. A small sea animal, the female of which is protected by a very thin spiral shell, pearly on the inside (lines 1, 9), and whose webbed arms on its back were once thought to function as sails.
2. Son of Neptune and skilled in blowing the conch or sea-trumpet.

Why preyest thou thus upon the poet's heart,
 Vulture, whose wings are dull realities?
How should he love thee? or how deem thee wise?
 Who wouldst not leave him in his wandering
To seek for treasure in the jeweled skies,
 Albeit he soared with an undaunted wing?
Hast thou not dragged Diana[1] from her car?
 And driven the Hamadryad[2] from the wood
To seek a shelter in some happier star?
 Hast thou not torn the Naiad° from her flood,   *river nymph*
The Elfin from the green grass, and from me
The summer dream beneath the tamarind tree?[3]

                                    1829   1829, 1845

To Helen

Helen, thy beauty is to me
 Like those Nicean barks of yore,
That gently, o'er a perfumed sea,
 The weary, way-worn wanderer bore
  To his own native shore.

On desperate seas long wont to roam,
 Thy hyacinth hair,[4] thy classic face,
Thy Naiad airs have brought me home
 To the glory that was Greece
And the grandeur that was Rome.

Lo! in yon brilliant window-niche
 How statue-like I see thee stand!
The agate lamp within thy hand,
Ah! Psyche,[5] from the regions which
  Are Holy Land!

                                    1823   1831, 1845

The City in the Sea

Lo! Death has reared himself a throne
In a strange city lying alone
Far down within the dim West,
Where the good and the bad and the worst and the best
Have gone to their eternal rest.
There shrines and palaces and towers
(Time-eaten towers that tremble not!)
Resemble nothing that is ours.
Around, by lifting winds forgot,
Resignedly beneath the sky
The melancholy waters lie.

1. To the Romans, the virgin goddess of the hunt, revered for her chastity and protectiveness. Her "car" is the moon.
2. Wood nymph said to live and die with the tree she inhabits.
3. An oriental tree the fruit of which is used medicinally and for food.
4. Presumably, hair like that of the slain youth Hyacinthus, beloved of Apollo.

5. Having lost her lover Cupid because she insisted on seeing him when he preferred to come to her unseen at night (she dropped oil accidentally from her lamp while he was sleeping), Psyche appealed for help in finding Cupid to Venus, who required, among other things, that Psyche bring back unopened a box from the underworld.

No rays from the holy heaven come down
On the long night-time of that town;
But light from out the lurid sea
15 Streams up the turrets silently—
Gleams up the pinnacles far and free—
Up domes—up spires—up kingly halls—
Up fanes—up Babylon-like[6] walls—
Up shadowy long-forgotten bowers
20 Of sculptured ivy and stone flowers—
Up many and many a marvelous shrine
Whose wreathéd friezes intertwine
The viol, the violet, and the vine.

Resignedly beneath the sky
25 The melancholy waters lie.
So blend the turrets and shadows there
That all seem pendulous in air,
While from a proud tower in the town
Death looks gigantically down.

30 There open fanes and gaping graves
Yawn level with the luminous waves;
But not the riches there that lie
In each idol's diamond eye—
Not the gaily-jeweled dead
35 Tempt the waters from their bed;
For no ripples curl, alas!
Along that wilderness of glass—
No swellings tell that winds may be
Upon some far-off happier sea—
40 No heavings hint that winds have been
On seas less hideously serene.

But lo, a stir is in the air!
The wave—there is a movement there!
As if the towers had thrust aside,
45 In slightly sinking, the dull tide—
As if their tops had feebly given
A void within the filmy Heaven.
The waves have now a redder glow—
The hours are breathing faint and low—
50 And when, amid no earthly moans,
Down, down that town shall settle hence,
Hell, rising from a thousand thrones,
Shall do it reverence.

1831, 1845

Eldorado[7]

Gaily bedight,
A gallant knight,
In sunshine and in shadow,

---

6. Babylon traditionally symbolizes the wicked city doomed (see, for example, Isaiah xiv.4–23 and Revelation xvi.18–19).
7. Spanish for "the gilded one." It is the name given an ancient Indian chief in Colombia believed to be possessed of much gold. More generally, any mythical place of fabulous wealth in gold.

Had journeyed long,
Singing a song,
In search of Eldorado.

But he grew old—
This knight so bold—
And o'er his heart a shadow
Fell as he found
No spot of ground
That looked like Eldorado.

And, as his strength
Failed him at length,
He met a pilgrim shadow—
"Shadow," said he,
"Where can it be—
This land of Eldorado?"

"Over the Mountains
Of the Moon,
Down the Valley of the Shadow,
Ride, boldly ride,"
The shade replied,—
"If you seek for Eldorado!"

1849

Annabel Lee

It was many and many a year ago,
  In a kingdom by the sea,
That a maiden there lived whom you may know
  By the name of Annabel Lee;
5 And this maiden she lived with no other thought
  Than to love and be loved by me.

She was a child and *I* was a child,
  In this kingdom by the sea,
But we loved with a love that was more than love—
10   I and my Annabel Lee—
With a love that the wingéd seraphs of Heaven
  Coveted her and me.

And this was the reason that, long ago,
  In this kingdom by the sea,
15 A wind blew out of a cloud by night
  Chilling my Annabel Lee;
So that her highborn kinsmen came
  And bore her away from me,
To shut her up in a sepulchre
20   In this kingdom by the sea.

The angels, not half so happy in Heaven,
  Went envying her and me:
Yes! that was the reason (as all men know,
  In this kingdom by the sea)
25 That the wind came out of the cloud, chilling
  And killing my Annabel Lee.

But our love it was stronger by far than the love
    Of those who were older than we—
    Of many far wiser than we—
30 And neither the angels in Heaven above
    Nor the demons down under the sea,
Can ever dissever my soul from the soul
    Of the beautiful Annabel Lee:

For the moon never beams without bringing me dreams
35   Of the beautiful Annabel Lee;
And the stars never rise but I see the bright eyes
    Of the beautiful Annabel Lee;
And so, all the night-tide, I lie down by the side
Of my darling, my darling, my life and my bride,
40   In her sepulchre there by the sea—
    In her tomb by the side of the sea.

1849, 1850

ALFRED, LORD TENNYSON
(1809–1892)

Song

1

A spirit haunts the year's last hours
Dwelling amid these yellowing bowers.
    To himself he talks;
For at eventide, listening earnestly,
5 At his work you may hear him sob and sigh
    In the walks;
Earthward he boweth the heavy stalks
Of the moldering flowers.
    Heavily hangs the broad sunflower
10   Over its grave i' the earth so chilly;
    Heavily hangs the hollyhock,
    Heavily hangs the tiger-lily.

2

The air is damp, and hushed, and close,
As a sick man's room when he taketh repose
15   An hour before death;
My very heart faints and my whole soul grieves
At the moist rich smell of the rotting leaves,
    And the breath
Of the fading edges of box[1] beneath,
20 And the year's last rose.
    Heavily hangs the broad sunflower
      Over its grave i' the earth so chilly;
    Heavily hangs the hollyhock,
    Heavily hangs the tiger-lily.

1830

---

1. Evergreen shrub used in formal gardening.

The Kraken [2]

Below the thunders of the upper deep,
Far far beneath in the abysmal sea,
His ancient, dreamless, uninvaded sleep
The Kraken sleepeth: faintest sunlights flee
About his shadowy sides: above him swell
Huge sponges of millennial growth and height;
And far away into the sickly light,
From many a wondrous grot and secret cell
Unnumbered and enormous polypi [3]
Winnow with giant fins the slumbering green.
There hath he lain for ages and will lie
Battening upon huge seaworms in his sleep,
Until the latter fire shall heat the deep; [4]
Then once by men and angels to be seen,
In roaring he shall rise and on the surface die.

1830

The Lotos-Eaters [2]

"Courage!" he [3] said, and pointed toward the land,
"This mounting wave will roll us shoreward soon."
In the afternoon they came unto a land
In which it seeméd always afternoon.
All round the coast the languid air did swoon,
Breathing like one that hath a weary dream.
Full-faced above the valley stood the moon;
And, like a downward smoke, the slender stream
Along the cliff to fall and pause and fall did seem.

A land of streams! some, like a downward smoke,
Slow-dropping veils of thinnest lawn, [4] did go;
And some through wavering lights and shadows broke,
Rolling a slumbrous sheet of foam below.
They saw the gleaming river seaward flow
From the inner land; far off, three mountain-tops,
Three silent pinnacles of aged snow,
Stood sunset-flushed; and, dewed with showery drops,
Up-clomb the shadowy pine above the woven copse.

The charméd sunset lingered low adown
In the red West; through mountain clefts the dale
Was seen far inland, and the yellow down
Bordered with palm, and many a winding vale
And meadow, set with slender galingale; [5]
A land where all things always seemed the same!
And round about the keel with faces pale,
Dark faces pale against that rosy flame,
The mild-eyed melancholy Lotos-eaters came.

2. A mythical sea monster, called in an 18th-century *History of Norway* "the largest and most surprising of all the animal creation" (*O. E. D.*).
3. Octopus-like creatures.
4. At the end of the world, ". . . the elements shall melt with fervent heat, the earth also and the works that are therein shall be burned up" (II Peter iii.10). See also Revelation viii. 8–9: "And the second angel sounded, and as it were a great mountain burning with fire was cast into the sea: and the third part of the sea became blood: and there died the third part of the creatures which were in the sea. . . ."
2. In Greek legend, a people who ate the fruit of the lotos, the effect of which was to induce drowsy languor and forgetfulness. The visit of Odysseus and his men to their island is described in the *Odyssey*, IX.82–97.
3. I.e., Odysseus.
4. Sheer cotton fabric.
5. A reed-like plant, a species of sedge.

Branches they bore of that enchanted stem,
Laden with flower and fruit, whereof they gave
30   To each, but whoso did receive of them
And taste, to him the gushing of the wave
Far far away did seem to mourn and rave
On alien shores; and if his fellow spake,
His voice was thin, as voices from the grave;
35   And deep-asleep he seemed, yet all awake,
And music in his ears his beating heart did make.

They sat them down upon the yellow sand,
Between the sun and moon upon the shore;
And sweet it was to dream of fatherland,
40   Of child, and wife, and slave; but evermore
Most weary seemed the sea, weary the oar,
Weary the wandering fields of barren foam.
Then someone said, "We will return no more;"
And all at once they sang, "Our island home
45   Is far beyond the wave; we will no longer roam."

Choric Song

1

There is sweet music here that softer falls
Than petals from blown roses on the grass,
Or night-dews on still waters between walls
Of shadowy granite, in a gleaming pass;
50   Music that gentlier on the spirit lies,
Than tired eyelids upon tired eyes;
Music that brings sweet sleep down from the blissful skies.
Here are cool mosses deep,
And through the moss the ivies creep,
55   And in the stream the long-leaved flowers weep,
And from the craggy ledge the poppy hangs in sleep.

2

Why are we weighed upon with heaviness,
And utterly consumed with sharp distress,
While all things else have rest from weariness?
60   All things have rest: why should we toil alone,
We only toil, who are the first of things,
And make perpetual moan,
Still from one sorrow to another thrown;
Nor ever fold our wings,
65   And cease from wanderings,
Nor steep our brows in slumber's holy balm;
Nor harken what the inner spirit sings,
"There is no joy but calm!"—
Why should we only toil, the roof and crown of things?

3

70   Lo! in the middle of the wood,
The folded leaf is wooed from out the bud
With winds upon the branch, and there
Grows green and broad, and takes no care,
Sun-steeped at noon, and in the moon
75   Nightly dew-fed; and turning yellow
Falls, and floats adown the air.
Lo! sweetened with the summer light,
The full-juiced apple, waxing over-mellow,
80   Drops in a silent autumn night.

All its allotted length of days
The flower ripens in its place,
Ripens and fades, and falls, and hath no toil,
Fast-rooted in the fruitful soil.

4

Hateful is the dark-blue sky,
Vaulted o'er the dark-blue sea.
Death is the end of life; ah, why
Should life all labor be?
Let us alone. Time driveth onward fast
And in a little while our lips are dumb.
Let us alone. What is it that will last?
All things are taken from us, and become
Portions and parcels of the dreadful past.
Let us alone. What pleasure can we have
To war with evil? Is there any peace
In ever climbing up the climbing wave?
All things have rest, and ripen toward the grave
In silence—ripen, fall, and cease:
Give us long rest or death, dark death, or dreamful ease.

5

How sweet it were, hearing the downward stream,
With half-shut eyes ever to seem
Falling asleep in a half-dream!
To dream and dream, like yonder amber light,
Which will not leave the myrrh-bush on the height;
To hear each other's whispered speech;
Eating the Lotos day by day,
To watch the crisping ripples on the beach,
And tender curving lines of creamy spray;
To lend our hearts and spirits wholly
To the influence of mild-minded melancholy;
To muse and brood and live again in memory,
With those old faces of our infancy
Heaped over with a mound of grass,
Two handfuls of white dust, shut in an urn of brass!

6

Dear is the memory of our wedded lives,
And dear the last embraces of our wives
And their warm tears; but all hath suffered change;
For surely now our household hearths are cold,
Our sons inherit us, our looks are strange,
And we should come like ghosts to trouble joy.
Or else the island princes[6] over-bold
Have eat our substance, and the minstrel sings
Before them of the ten years' war in Troy,
And our great deeds, as half-forgotten things.
Is there confusion in the little isle?[7]
Let what is broken so remain.
The Gods are hard to reconcile;
'Tis hard to settle order once again.
There *is* confusion worse than death,
Trouble on trouble, pain on pain,
Long labor unto aged breath,
Sore tasks to hearts worn out by many wars
And eyes grown dim with gazing on the pilot-stars.

6. The princes who had remained behind in   7. I.e., Ithaca.
Ithaca while Odysseus was at Troy.

7

But, propt on beds of amaranth[8] and moly,
How sweet—while warm airs lull us, blowing lowly—
135 With half-dropt eyelid still,
Beneath a heaven dark and holy,
To watch the long bright river drawing slowly
His waters from the purple hill—
To hear the dewy echoes calling
140 From cave to cave through the thick-twined vine—
To watch the emerald-colored water falling
Through many a woven acanthus-wreath divine!
Only to hear and see the far-off sparkling brine,
Only to hear were sweet, stretched out beneath the pine.

8

145 The Lotos blooms below the barren peak,
The Lotos blows by every winding creek;
All day the wind breathes low with mellower tone;
Through every hollow cave and alley lone
Round and round the spicy downs the yellow Lotos-dust is blown.
150 We have had enough of action, and of motion we,
Rolled to starboard, rolled to larboard, when the surge was seething free,
Where the wallowing monster spouted his foam-fountains in the sea.
Let us swear an oath, and keep it with an equal mind,
In the hollow Lotos-land to live and lie reclined
155 On the hills like Gods together, careless of mankind.
For they lie beside their nectar, and the bolts are hurled
Far below them in the valleys, and the clouds are lightly curled
Round their golden houses, girdled with the gleaming world;
Where they smile in secret, looking over wasted lands,
160 Blight and famine, plague and earthquake, roaring deeps and fiery sands,
Clanging fights, and flaming towns, and sinking ships, and praying hands.
But they smile, they find a music centered in a doleful song
Steaming up, a lamentation and an ancient tale of wrong,
Like a tale of little meaning though the words are strong;
165 Chanted from an ill-used race of men that cleave the soil,
Sow the seed, and reap the harvest with enduring toil,
Storing yearly little dues of wheat, and wine and oil;
Till they perish and they suffer—some, 'tis whispered—down in hell
Suffer endless anguish, others in Elysian valleys dwell,
170 Resting weary limbs at last on beds of asphodel.[9]
Surely, surely, slumber is more sweet than toil, the shore
Than labor in the deep mid-ocean, wind and wave and oar;
O, rest ye, brother mariners, we will not wander more.

1832, 1842

Break, Break, Break

Break, break, break,
    On thy cold gray stones, O Sea!
And I would that my tongue could utter
    The thoughts that arise in me.

5 O, well for the fisherman's boy,
    That he shouts with his sister at play!
O, well for the sailor lad,
    That he sings in his boat on the bay!

---

8. A legendary flower, reputed not to fade; moly, an herb of magical properties.   9. Any one of a number of plants of the lily family.

And the stately ships go on
  To their haven under the hill;
But O for the touch of a vanished hand,
  And the sound of a voice that is still!

Break, break, break,
  At the foot of thy crags, O Sea!
But the tender grace of a day that is dead
  Will never come back to me.

1834   1842

Ulysses[1]

It little profits that an idle king,
By this still hearth, among these barren crags,
Matched with an aged wife, I mete and dole
Unequal laws unto a savage race,
That hoard, and sleep, and feed, and know not me.
I cannot rest from travel; I will drink
Life to the lees. All times I have enjoyed
Greatly, have suffered greatly, both with those
That loved me, and alone; on shore, and when
Through scudding drifts the rainy Hyades[2]
Vext the dim sea. I am become a name;
For always roaming with a hungry heart
Much have I seen and known—cities of men
And manners, climates, councils, governments,
Myself not least, but honored of them all,—
And drunk delight of battle with my peers,
Far on the ringing plains of windy Troy.
I am a part of all that I have met;
Yet all experience is an arch wherethrough
Gleams that untraveled world whose margin fades
For ever and for ever when I move.
How dull it is to pause, to make an end,
To rust unburnished, not to shine in use!
As though to breathe were life! Life piled on life
Were all too little, and of one to me
Little remains; but every hour is saved
From that eternal silence, something more,
A bringer of new things; and vile it were
For some three suns to store and hoard myself,
And this gray spirit yearning in desire
To follow knowledge like a sinking star,
Beyond the utmost bound of human thought.
    This is my son, mine own Telemachus,
To whom I leave the scepter and the isle,
Well-loved of me, discerning to fulfill
This labor, by slow prudence to make mild
A rugged people, and through soft degrees
Subdue them to the useful and the good.
Most blameless is he, centered in the sphere
Of common duties, decent not to fail
In offices of tenderness, and pay

---

1. Tennyson's Ulysses (Greek *Odysseus*), restless after his return to Ithaca, eager to renew the life of great deeds he had known during the Trojan war and the adventures of his ten-year journey home, resembles the figure of Ulysses presented by Dante, *Inferno* XXVI.

2. A group of stars in the constellation Taurus, believed to foretell the coming of rain when they rose with the sun.

Meet adoration to my household gods,
When I am gone. He works his work, I mine.
   There lies the port; the vessel puffs her sail;
45   There gloom the dark, broad seas. My mariners,
Souls that have toiled, and wrought, and thought with me,
That ever with a frolic welcome took
The thunder and the sunshine, and opposed
Free hearts, free foreheads—you and I are old;
50   Old age hath yet his honor and his toil.
Death closes all; but something ere the end,
Some work of noble note, may yet be done,
Not unbecoming men that strove with gods.
The lights begin to twinkle from the rocks;
55   The long day wanes; the slow moon climbs; the deep
Moans round with many voices. Come, my friends,
'Tis not too late to seek a newer world.
Push off, and sitting well in order smite
The sounding furrows; for my purpose holds
60   To sail beyond the sunset, and the baths
Of all the western stars, until I die.
It may be that the gulfs will wash us down;
It may be we shall touch the Happy Isles,[3]
And see the great Achilles, whom we knew.
65   Though much is taken, much abides; and though
We are not now that strength which in old days
Moved earth and heaven, that which we are, we are,
One equal temper of heroic hearts,
Made weak by time and fate, but strong in will
70   To strive, to seek, to find, and not to yield.

                        1833   1842

Songs from The Princess

The Splendor Falls

The splendor falls on castle walls
   And snowy summits old in story;
The long light shakes across the lakes,
   And the wild cataract leaps in glory.
5   Blow, bugle, blow, set the wild echoes flying,
Blow, bugle; answer, echoes, dying, dying, dying.

O, hark, O, hear! how thin and clear,
   And thinner, clearer, farther going!
O, sweet and far from cliff and scar[3]
10   The horns of Elfland faintly blowing!
Blow, let us hear the purple glens replying,
Blow, bugle; answer, echoes, dying, dying, dying.

O love, they die in yon rich sky,
   They faint on hill or field or river;
15   Our echoes roll from soul to soul,
   And grow for ever and for ever.
Blow, bugle, blow, set the wild echoes flying,
And answer, echoes, answer, dying, dying, dying.

                                    1850

3. The Islands of the Blessed, or Elysium, the abode after death of those favored by the gods, especially heroes and patriots: supposed, in earlier myth, to be located beyond the western limits of the known world.
3. Isolated rock, or rocky height.

Tears, Idle Tears

Tears, idle tears, I know not what they mean,
Tears from the depth of some divine despair
Rise in the heart, and gather to the eyes,
In looking on the happy autumn-fields,
5   And thinking of the days that are no more.

Fresh as the first beam glittering on a sail,
That brings our friends up from the underworld,
Sad as the last which reddens over one
That sinks with all we love below the verge;
10   So sad, so fresh, the days that are no more.

Ah, sad and strange as in dark summer dawns
The earliest pipe of half-awakened birds
To dying ears, when unto dying eyes
The casement slowly grows a glimmering square;
15   So sad, so strange, the days that are no more.

Dear as remembered kisses after death,
And sweet as those by hopeless fancy feigned
On lips that are for others; deep as love,
Deep as first love, and wild with all regret;
20   O Death in Life, the days that are no more!

1847

Now Sleeps the Crimson Petal

Now sleeps the crimson petal, now the white;
Nor waves the cypress in the palace walk;
Nor winks the gold fin in the porphyry font.
The firefly wakens; waken thou with me.

5   Now droops the milk-white peacock like a ghost,
And like a ghost she glimmers on to me.

Now lies the Earth all Danaë[4] to the stars,
And all thy heart lies open unto me.

Now slides the silent meteor on, and leaves
10   A shining furrow, as thy thoughts in me.

Now folds the lily all her sweetness up,
And slips into the bosom of the lake.
So fold thyself, my dearest, thou, and slip
Into my bosom and be lost in me.

1847

4. Daughter of a king of Argos in ancient Greece who, warned by an oracle that she would bear a son who would kill him, shut her up in a bronze chamber, where she was visited by Zeus in a shower of gold.

From In Memoriam A. H. H.[5]

OBIIT. MDCCCXXXIII

1

I held it truth, with him who sings
    To one clear harp in divers tones,[6]
    That men may rise on stepping-stones
Of their dead selves to higher things.

5 But who shall so forecast the years
    And find in loss a gain to match?
    Or reach a hand through time to catch
The far-off interest of tears?

Let Love clasp Grief lest both be drowned,
10   Let darkness keep her raven gloss.
    Ah, sweeter to be drunk with loss,
To dance with Death, to beat the ground,

Than that the victor Hours should scorn
    The long result of love, and boast,
15   "Behold the man that loved and lost,
But all he was is overworn."

2

Old yew, which graspest at the stones
    That name the underlying dead,
    Thy fibers net the dreamless head,
Thy roots are wrapt about the bones.

5 The seasons bring the flowers again,
    And bring the firstling to the flock;
    And in the dusk of thee the clock
Beats out the little lives of men.

O, not for thee the glow, the bloom,
10   Who changest not in any gale,
    Nor branding summer suns avail
To touch thy thousand years of gloom;

And gazing on thee, sullen tree,
    Sick for thy stubborn hardihood,
15   I seem to fail from out my blood
And grow incorporate into thee.

7

Dark house, by which once more I stand
    Here in the long unlovely street,[7]
    Doors, where my heart was used to beat
So quickly, waiting for a hand,

---

5. Arthur Henry Hallam (1811–33) had been Tennyson's close friend at Cambridge; they had traveled together in France and Germany; and Hallam had been engaged to the poet's sister. To his associates at Cambridge, Hallam had seemed to give the most brilliant promise of future greatness. In the summer of 1833 Hallam had been traveling on the Continent with his father, when he died of stroke at Vienna.
6. I.e., Goethe.
7. I.e., Wimpole St., where Hallam had been living after he left Cambridge.

5   A hand that can be clasped no more—
        Behold me, for I cannot sleep,
        And like a guilty thing I creep
At earliest morning to the door.

He is not here; but far away
10   The noise of life begins again,
        And ghastly through the drizzling rain
On the bald street breaks the blank day.

        11

Calm is the morn without a sound,
        Calm as to suit a calmer grief,
        And only through the faded leaf
The chestnut pattering to the ground;

5   Calm and deep peace on this high wold,°   *upland plain*
        And on these dews that drench the furze,
        And all the silvery gossamers
That twinkle into green and gold;

Calm and still light on yon great plain
10   That sweeps with all its autumn bowers,
        And crowded farms and lessening towers,
To mingle with the bounding main;

Calm and deep peace in this wide air,
        These leaves that redden to the fall,
15   And in my heart, if calm at all,
If any calm, a calm despair;

Calm on the seas, and silver sleep,
        And waves that sway themselves in rest,
        And dead calm in the noble breast
20   Which heaves but with the heaving deep.

        19

The Danube to the Severn gave
        The darkened heart that beat no more;[1]
        They laid him by the pleasant shore,
And in the hearing of the wave.

5   There twice a day the Severn fills;
        The salt sea-water passes by,
        And hushes half the babbling Wye,[2]
And makes a silence in the hills.

The Wye is hushed nor moved along,
10   And hushed my deepest grief of all,
        When filled with tears that cannot fall,
I brim with sorrow drowning song.

The tide flows down, the wave again
        Is vocal in its wooded walls;
15   My deeper anguish also falls,
And I can speak a little then.

1. Vienna, where Hallam died, is on the Danube; the Severn empties into the Bristol Channel near Clevedon, Somersetshire, Hallam's burial place.
2. The Wye, a tributary of the Severn, also runs into the Bristol Channel; the incoming tide deepens the river and makes it quiet, but as the tide ebbs the Wye once more becomes voluble.

50

Be near me when my light is low,
  When the blood creeps, and the nerves prick
  And tingle; and the heart is sick,
And all the wheels of being slow.

5 Be near me when the sensuous frame
  Is racked with pangs that conquer trust;
  And Time, a maniac scattering dust,
And Life, a Fury slinging flame.

Be near me when my faith is dry,
10 And men the flies of latter spring,
  That lay their eggs, and sting and sing
And weave their petty cells and die.

Be near me when I fade away,
  To point the term of human strife,
15 And on the low dark verge of life
The twilight of eternal day.

54

O, yet we trust that somehow good
  Will be the final goal of ill,
  To pangs of nature, sins of will,
Defects of doubt, and taints of blood;

5 That nothing walks with aimless feet;
  That not one life shall be destroyed,
  Or cast as rubbish to the void,
When God hath made the pile complete;

That not a worm is cloven in vain;
10 That not a moth with vain desire
  Is shriveled in a fruitless fire,
Or but subserves another's gain.

Behold, we know not anything;
  I can but trust that good shall fall
15 At last—far off—at last, to all,
And every winter change to spring.

So runs my dreams; but what am I?
  An infant crying in the night;
  An infant crying for the light,
20 And with no language but a cry.

55

The wish, that of the living whole
  No life may fail beyond the grave,
  Derives it not from what we have
The likest God within the soul?

5 Are God and Nature then at strife,
  That Nature lends such evil dreams?
  So careful of the type° she seems,   *species*
So careless of the single life,

That I, considering everywhere
   Her secret meaning in her deeds,
   And finding that of fifty seeds
She often brings but one to bear,

I falter where I firmly trod,
   And falling with my weight of cares
   Upon the great world's altar-stairs
That slope through darkness up to God,

I stretch lame hands of faith, and grope,
   And gather dust and chaff, and call
   To what I feel is Lord of all,
And faintly trust the larger hope.

56

"So careful of the type?" but no.
   From scarpéd[4] cliff and quarried stone
   She[5] cries, "A thousand types are gone;
I care for nothing, all shall go.

"Thou makest thine appeal to me:
   I bring to life, I bring to death;
   The spirit does but mean the breath:
I know no more." And he, shall he,

Man, her last work, who seemed so fair,
   Such splendid purpose in his eyes,
   Who rolled the psalm to wintry skies,
Who built him fanes° of fruitless prayer,   ***temples, churches***

Who trusted God was love indeed
   And love Creation's final law—
   Though Nature, red in tooth and claw
With ravine, shrieked against his creed—

Who loved, who suffered countless ills,
   Who battled for the True, the Just,
Be blown about the desert dust,
   Or sealed within the iron hills?

No more? A monster then, a dream,
   A discord. Dragons of the prime,
   That tare[6] each other in their slime,
Were mellow music matched with him.

O life as futile, then, as frail!
   O for thy voice to soothe and bless!
   What hope of answer, or redress?
Behind the veil, behind the veil.

67

When on my bed the moonlight falls,
   I know that in thy place of rest
   By that broad water of the west
There comes a glory on the walls:[7]

4. Cut down vertically, thus displaying the strata of geologic growth and the fossils they contain.
5. I.e., Nature.

6. Tore (archaic).
7. Hallam's tomb was inside Clevedon Church, just south of Clevedon, Somersetshire, on a hill overlooking the Bristol Channel.

5　Thy marble bright in dark appears,
　　As slowly steals a silver flame
　　Along the letters of thy name,
　　And o'er the number of thy years.

　　The mystic glory swims away,
10　　From off my bed the moonlight dies;
　　And closing eaves of wearied eyes
　　I sleep till dusk is dipped in gray;

　　And then I know the mist is drawn
　　A lucid veil from coast to coast,
15　　And in the dark church like a ghost
　　Thy tablet glimmers to the dawn.

88

　　Wild bird, whose warble, liquid sweet,
　　Rings Eden through the budded quicks,[8]
　　O, tell me where the senses mix,
　　O, tell me where the passions meet,

5　Whence radiate: fierce extremes employ
　　Thy spirits in the darkening leaf,
　　And in the midmost heart of grief
　　Thy passion clasps a secret joy;

　　And I—my harp would prelude woe—
10　　I cannot all command the strings;
　　The glory of the sum of things
　　Will flash along the chords and go.

95

　　By night we lingered on the lawn,
　　For underfoot the herb was dry;
　　And genial warmth; and o'er the sky
　　The silvery haze of summer drawn;

5　And calm that let the tapers burn
　　Unwavering: not a cricket chirred;
　　The brook alone far-off was heard,
　　And on the board the fluttering urn.[9]

　　And bats went round in fragrant skies,
10　　And wheeled or lit the filmy shapes
　　That haunt the dusk, with ermine capes
　　And woolly breasts and beaded eyes;

　　While now we sang old songs that pealed
　　From knoll to knoll, where, couched at ease,
15　　The white kine glimmered, and the trees
　　Laid their dark arms about the field.

　　But when those others, one by one,
　　Withdrew themselves from me and night,
　　And in the house light after light
20　Went out, and I was all alone,

8. Hawthorn hedge-row.
9. I.e., on the table a tea- or coffee-urn heated by a fluttering flame beneath.

A hunger seized my heart; I read
    Of that glad year which once had been,
    In those fallen leaves which kept their green,
The noble letters of the dead.

And strangely on the silence broke
    The silent-speaking words, and strange
    Was love's dumb cry defying change
To test his worth; and strangely spoke

The faith, the vigor, bold to dwell
    On doubts that drive the coward back,
    And keen through wordy snares to track
Suggestion to her inmost cell.

So word by word, and line by line,
    The dead man touched me from the past,
    And all at once it seemed at last
The living soul was flashed on mine,

And mine in this was wound, and whirled
    About empyreal heights of thought,
    And came on that which is, and caught
The deep pulsations of the world,

Eonian music[1] measuring out
    The steps of Time—the shocks of Chance—
    The blows of Death. At length my trance
Was canceled, stricken through with doubt.

Vague words! but ah, how hard to frame
    In matter-molded forms of speech,
    Or even for intellect to reach
Through memory that which I became;

Till now the doubtful dusk revealed
    The knolls once more where, couched at ease,
    The white kine glimmered, and the trees
Lain their dark arms about the field;

And sucked from out the distant gloom
    A breeze began to tremble o'er
    The large leaves of the sycamore,
And fluctuate all the still perfume,

And gathering freshlier overhead
    Rocked the full-foliaged elms, and swung
    The heavy-folded rose, and flung
The lilies to and fro, and said,

"The dawn, the dawn," and died away;
    And East and West, without a breath,
    Mixt their dim lights, like life and death,
To broaden into boundless day.

---

1. I.e., the rhythm of the universe which has persisted for eons.

105

Tonight ungathered let us leave
   This laurel, let this holly stand:
   We live within the stranger's land,
And strangely falls our Christmas-eve.[2]

5   Our father's dust is left alone
   And silent under other snows:
   There in due time the woodbine blows,
The violet comes, but we are gone.

No more shall wayward grief abuse
10   The genial hour with mask and mime;
   For change of place, like growth of time,
Has broke the bond of dying use.

Let cares that petty shadows cast,
   By which our lives are chiefly proved,
15   A little spare the night I loved,
And hold it solemn to the past.

But let no footstep beat the floor,
   Nor bowl of wassail mantle warm;
   For who would keep an ancient form
20   Through which the spirit breathes no more?

Be neither song, nor game, nor feast;
   Nor harp be touched, nor flute be blown;
   No dance, no motion, save alone
What lightens in the lucid East

25   Of rising worlds[3] by yonder wood.
   Long sleeps the summer in the seed;
   Rut out your measured arcs,[4] and lead
The closing cycle rich in good.

119

Doors, where my heart was used to beat
   So quickly, not as one that weeps
   I come once more; the city sleeps;
I smell the meadow in the street;

5   I hear a chirp of birds; I see
   Betwixt the black fronts long-withdrawn
   A light-blue lane of early dawn,
And think of early days and thee,

And bless thee, for thy lips are bland,
10   And bright the friendship of thine eyes;
   And in my thoughts with scarce a sigh
I take the pressure of thine hand.

121

Sad Hesper o'er the buried sun
   And ready, thou, to die with him,

---

2. The third Christmas since Hallam's death found the Tennysons living no longer at Somersby, Lincolnshire, associated with his visits, but in a new home in Epping Forest.

3. I.e., stars.
4. The measured courses of the stars, which will eventually usher in the final period of perfect good.

Thou watchest all things ever dim
And dimmer, and a glory done.

5   The team is loosened from the wain,°   *wagon*
     The boat is drawn upon the shore;
     Thou listenest to the closing door,
And life is darkened in the brain.

Bright Phosphor, fresher for the night,
0   By thee the world's great work is heard
     Beginning, and the wakeful bird;
Behind thee comes the greater light.

The market boat is on the stream,
     And voices hail it from the brink;
5   Thou hear'st the village hammer clink,
And see'st the moving of the team.

Sweet Hesper-Phosphor, double name[5]
     For what is one, the first, the last,
     Thou, like my present and my past,
0   Thy place is changed; thou art the same.
                    130
Thy voice is on the rolling air;
     I hear thee where the waters run;
     Thou standest in the rising sun,
And in the setting thou art fair.

5   What are thou then? I cannot guess;
     But though I seem in star and flower
     To feel thee some diffusive power,
I do not therefore love thee less.

My love involves the love before;
0   My love is vaster passion now;
     Though mixed with God and Nature thou,
I seem to love thee more and more.

Far off thou art, but ever nigh;
     I have thee still, and I rejoice;
5   I prosper, circled with thy voice;
I shall not lose thee though I die.

                              1833–50   1850

The Eagle

FRAGMENT

He clasps the crag with crooked hands;
Close to the sun in lonely lands,
Ringed with the azure world, he stands.

The wrinkled sea beneath him crawls;
5   He watches from his mountain walls,
And like a thunderbolt he falls.

                                                     1851

5. Hesper, the evening star, and Phosphor, the morning star, are both the planet Venus.

Tithonus[6]

The woods decay, the woods decay and fall,
The vapors weep their burthen to the ground,
Man comes and tills the field and lies beneath,
And after many a summer dies the swan.
5   Me only cruel immortality
Consumes; I wither slowly in thine arms,
Here at the quiet limit of the world,
A white-haired shadow roaming like a dream
The ever-silent spaces of the East,
10   Far-folded mists, and gleaming halls of morn.
   Alas! for this gray shadow, once a man—
So glorious in his beauty and thy choice,
Who madest him thy chosen, that he seemed
To his great heart none other than a God!
15   I asked thee, "Give me immortality."
Then didst thou grant mine asking with a smile,
Like wealthy men who care not how they give.
But thy strong Hours indignant worked their wills,
And beat me down and marred and wasted me,
20   And though they could not end me, left me maimed
To dwell in presence of immortal youth,
Immortal age beside immortal youth,
And all I was in ashes. Can thy love,
Thy beauty, make amends, though even now,
25   Close over us, the silver star[7] thy guide,
Shines in those tremulous eyes that fill with tears
To hear me? Let me go; take back thy gift.
Why should a man desire in any way
To vary from the kindly race of men,
30   Or pass beyond the goal of ordinance
Where all should pause, as is most meet for all?
   A soft air fans the cloud apart; there comes
A glimpse of that dark world where I was born.
Once more the old mysterious glimmer steals
35   From thy pure brows, and from thy shoulders pure,
And bosom beating with a heart renewed.
Thy cheek begins to redden through the gloom,
Thy sweet eyes brighten slowly close to mine,
Ere yet they blind the stars, and the wild team
40   Which love thee, yearning for thy yoke, arise,
And shake the darkness from their loosened manes,
And beat the twilight into flakes of fire.
   Lo! ever thus thou growest beautiful
In silence, then before thine answer given
45   Departest, and thy tears are on my cheek.
   Why wilt thou ever scare me with thy tears,
And make me tremble lest a saying learnt,
In days far-off, on that dark earth, be true?
"The Gods themselves cannot recall their gifts."

6. A Trojan prince beloved by Aurora (Greek *Eos*), goddess of the dawn, who took him as her spouse. She begged Zeus to grant him eternal life, but forgot to ask also for the gift of eternal youth.
7. I.e., the morning star.

Ay me! ay me! with what another heart
In days far-off, and with what other eyes
I used to watch—if I be he that watched—
The lucid outline forming round thee; saw
The dim curls kindle into sunny rings;
Changed with thy mystic change, and felt my blood
Glow with the glow that slowly crimsoned all
Thy presence and thy portals, while I lay,
Mouth, forehead, eyelids, growing dewy-warm
With kisses balmier than half-opening buds
Of April, and could hear the lips that kissed
Whispering I knew not what of wild and sweet,
Like that strange song I heard Apollo sing,
While Ilion like a mist rose into towers.[8]
Yet hold me not for ever in thine East;
How can my nature longer mix with thine?
Coldly thy rosy shadows bathe me, cold
Are all thy lights, and cold my wrinkled feet
Upon thy glimmering thresholds, when the steam
Floats up from those dim fields about the homes
Of happy men that have the power to die,
And grassy barrows of the happier dead.
Release me, and restore me to the ground.
Thou seest all things, thou wilt see my grave;
Thou wilt renew thy beauty morn by morn,
I earth in earth forget these empty courts,
And thee returning on thy silver wheels.

                                        1833, 1859   1860

Milton

ALCAICS[9]

O mighty-mouthed inventor of harmonies,
O skilled to sing of Time or Eternity,
    God-gifted organ-voice of England,
        Milton, a name to resound for ages;
Whose Titan[1] angels, Gabriel, Abdiel,[2]
Starred from Jehovah's gorgeous armories,
    Tower, as the deep-domed empyrean
        Rings to the roar of an angel onset—
Me rather all that bowery loneliness,
The brooks of Eden mazily murmuring,
    And bloom profuse and cedar arches
        Charm, as a wanderer out in ocean,
Where some refulgent sunset of India
Streams o'er a rich ambrosial ocean isle,
    And crimson-hued the stately palm-woods
        Whisper in odorous heights of even.

                                                    1863

---

8. According to legend, the walls and towers of Ilion (Troy) were raised by the sound of Apollo's song, as related by Ovid, *Heroides*, XVI.179.
9. The Alcaic ode, named after the Greek lyric poet Alcaeus, ca. 600 B.C. See Glossary, entry on Alcaic strophe, at the end of this anthology.

1. Gigantic in size and power.
2. "Gabriel": one of the seven archangels; in *Paradise Lost*, one of the four angels who guard Paradise and who oppose Satan's attacks on it. "Abdiel": in *Paradise Lost*, one of the faithful angels who resisted Satan's revolt, striking the first sword-blow against him.

To Virgil

WRITTEN AT THE REQUEST OF THE MANTUANS FOR THE NINETEENTH
CENTENARY OF VIRGIL'S DEATH[3]

1

Roman Virgil, thou that singest[4]
    Ilion's lofty temples robed in fire,
Ilion falling, Rome arising,
    wars, and filial faith, and Dido's pyre;[5]

2

5 Landscape-lover, lord of language
    more than he that sang the Works and Days,[6]
All the chosen coin of fancy
    flashing out from many a golden phrase;

3

Thou that singest wheat and woodland,
10   tilth and vineyard, hive and horse and herd;
All the charm of all the Muses
    often flowering in a lonely word;

4

Poet of the happy Tityrus
    piping underneath his beechen bowers;[7]
15 Poet of the poet-satyr[8]
    whom the laughing shepherd bound with flowers;

5

Chanter of the Pollio,[9] glorying
    in the blissful years again to be,
Summers of the snakeless meadow,
20   unlaborious earth and oarless sea;

6

Thou that seest Universal
    Nature moved by Universal Mind;
Thou majestic in thy sadness
    at the doubtful doom of human kind;

7

25 Light among the vanished ages;
    star that gildest yet this phantom shore;
Golden branch[1] amid the shadows,
    kings and realms that pass to rise no more;

8

Now thy Forum roars no longer,
30   fallen every purple Caesar's dome—
Though thine ocean-roll of rhythm
    sound forever of Imperial Rome—

3. The Roman poet Virgil was born near Mantua, in northern Italy, on October 19, 70 B.C., and died at Brundisium (modern Brindisi), on September 20, 19 B.C.
4. In the *Aeneid*, Virgil's last and greatest work: Aeneas, who fought against the Greeks in the Trojan War and who escaped after the fall of Troy (Ilion) with his father Anchises, was destined after his wanderings to be the founder of Rome.
5. Dido, Queen of Carthage, loved by Aeneas and deserted by him when he was ordered by Mercury to continue on his way and to fulfill his imperial mission: she immolates herself.
6. The Greek poet Hesiod, whose didactic poem of occupations is here compared with Virgil's *Georgics,* descriptive of country life and farm pursuits.
7. In Virgil's *Eclogues* or Pastorals, especially the opening of *Eclogue* I.
8. Silenus, in *Eclogue* VI.
9. Gaius Asinus Pollio, Roman consul and man of letters, to whom Virgil dedicated the fourth Eclogue, in which he identifies the return of the world's golden age with the time of Pollio's consulate.
1. In the *Aeneid* VI.136 ff. Aeneas, prior to his journey to the underworld, is warned by the Sibyl that his safety depends on his finding and breaking off the golden bough which must be presented to Proserpine, goddess of the underworld.

9

Now the Rome of slaves hath perished,
  and the Rome of freemen holds her place,[2]
I, from out the Northern Island
  sundered once from all the human race,

10

I salute thee, Mantovano,°   *Mantuan*
  I that loved thee since my day began,
Wielder of the stateliest measure
  ever molded by the lips of man.

                                        1880   1883

Frater Ave Atque Vale[3]

Row us out from Desenzano, to your Sirmione row!
So they rowed, and there we landed—"O venusta Sirmio!"[4]
There to me through all the groves of olive in the summer glow,
There beneath the Roman ruin where the purple flowers grow,
Came that "Ave atque Vale" of the poet's hopeless woe,
Tenderest of Roman poets nineteen-hundred years ago,
"Frater Ave atque Vale"—as we wandered to and fro
Gazing at the Lydian laughter of the Garda Lake below[5]
Sweet Catullus's all-but-island, olive-silvery Sirmio!

                                        1880   1885

Crossing the Bar

Sunset and evening star,
  And one clear call for me!
And may there be no moaning of the bar,
  When I put out to sea,

5   But such a tide as moving seems asleep,
       Too full for sound and foam,
     When that which drew from out the boundless deep
       Turns again home.

     Twilight and evening bell,
10   And after that the dark!
     And may there be no sadness of farewell,
       When I embark;

     For though from out our bourne of Time and Place
       The flood may bear me far,
15   I hope to see my Pilot face to face
       When I have crossed the bar.

                                                        1889

2. Italy had finally achieved its freedom and
unification in 1870.
3. The title (Brother, hail and farewell) re-
peats the concluding phrase of poem number
CI, in which Catullus records the journey to
visit his brother's tomb in Asia Minor. Ten-
nyson's poem, written on a visit to the lit-
tle peninsula of Sirmio, on Lake Garda in
Northern Italy, shortly after his own brother
had died, echoes phrases from another poem

(XXXI) in which Catullus describes his
pleasure in returning to Sirmio after a long
absence.
4. O lovely Sirmio.
5. Catullus's line, "And rejoice, O Lydian
waves of the lake" (XXXI: 13) alludes to
the old belief that the Estruscans of the
Garda region had originated in Lydia, in
Asia Minor.

ROBERT BROWNING
(1812–1889)

My Last Duchess[1]

FERRARA

That's my last duchess painted on the wall,
Looking as if she were alive. I call
That piece a wonder, now: Frà Pandolf's hands
Worked busily a day, and there she stands.
5   Will't please you sit and look at her? I said
"Frà Pandolf" by design, for never read
Strangers like you that pictured countenance,
The depth and passion of its earnest glance,
But to myself they turned (since none puts by
10 The curtain I have drawn for you, but I)
And seemed as they would ask me, if they durst,
How such a glance came there; so, not the first
Are you to turn and ask thus. Sir, 'twas not
Her husband's presence only, called that spot
15 Of joy into the Duchess' cheek: perhaps
Frà Pandolf chanced to say "Her mantle laps
"Over my lady's wrist too much," or "Paint
"Must never hope to reproduce the faint
"Half-flush that dies along her throat": such stuff
20 Was courtesy, she thought, and cause enough
For calling up that spot of joy. She had
A heart—how shall I say?—too soon made glad,
Too easily impressed; she liked whate'er
She looked on, and her looks went everywhere.
25 Sir, 'twas all one! My favor at her breast,
The dropping of the daylight in the West,
The bough of cherries some officious fool
Broke in the orchard for her, the white mule
She rode with round the terrace—all and each
30 Would draw from her alike the approving speech,
Or blush, at least. She thanked men—good! but thanked
Somehow—I know not how—as if she ranked
My gift of a nine-hundred-years-old name
With anybody's gift. Who'd stoop to blame
35 This sort of trifling? Even had you skill
In speech—which I have not—to make your will
Quite clear to such an one, and say, "Just this
"Or that in you disgusts me; here you miss,
"Or there exceed the mark"—and if she let
40 Herself be lessoned so, nor plainly set
Her wits to yours, forsooth, and made excuse,
—E'en then would be some stooping; and I choose

1. The events of Browning's poem parallel historical events, but its emphasis is rather on truth to Renaissance attitudes than on historic specificity. Alfonso II d'Este, Duke of Ferrara (born 1533), in Northern Italy, had married his first wife, daughter of Cosimo I de'Medici, Duke of Florence, in 1558, when she was fourteen; she died on April 21, 1561, under suspicious circumstances, and soon afterwards he opened negotiations for the hand of the niece of the Count of Tyrol, the seat of whose court was at Innsbruck, in Austria. "Fra Pandolf" and "Claus of Innsbruck" are types rather than specific artists.

Never to stoop. Oh sir, she smiled, no doubt,
Whene'er I passed her; but who passed without
45 Much the same smile? This grew; I gave commands;
Then all smiles stopped together. There she stands
As if alive. Will 't please you rise? We'll meet
The company below, then. I repeat,
The Count your master's known munificence
50 Is ample warrant that no just pretense
Of mine for dowry will be disallowed;
Though his fair daughter's self, as I avowed
At starting, is my object. Nay, we'll go
Together down, sir. Notice Neptune, though,
55 Taming a sea-horse, thought a rarity,
Which Claus of Innsbruck cast in bronze for me!

1842

Soliloquy of the Spanish Cloister

1

Gr-r-r—there go, my heart's abhorrence!
  Water your damned flower-pots, do!
If hate killed men, Brother Lawrence,
  God's blood, would not mine kill you!
5 What? your myrtle-bush wants trimming?
  Oh, that rose has prior claims—
Needs its leaden vase filled brimming?
  Hell dry you up with its flames!

2

At the meal we sit together:
10 *Salve tibi!*[2] I must hear
Wise talk of the kind of weather,
  Sort of season, time of year:
Not a plenteous cork-crop: scarcely
  Dare we hope oak-galls,[3] *I doubt:*
15 *What's the Latin name for "parsley"?*
  What's the Greek name for Swine's Snout?

3

Whew! We'll have our platter burnished,
  Laid with care on our own shelf!
With a fire-new spoon we're furnished,
20   And a goblet for ourself,
Rinsed like something sacrificial
  Ere 'tis fit to touch our chaps—
Marked with L for our initial!
  (He-he! There his lily snaps!)

4

25 *Saint,* forsooth! While brown Dolores
  Squats outside the Convent bank
With Sanchicha, telling stories,
  Steeping tresses in the tank,
Blue-black, lustrous, thick like horsehairs,
30   —Can't I see his dead eye glow,
Bright as 'twere a Barbary corsair's?[4]
  (That is, if he'd let it show!)

---

2. Hail to thee!
3. Growths produced on oak-leaves by gall-flies.

4. "Barbary corsair": Pirate from the Berber countries on the north coast of Africa.

5

When he finishes refection,°   *dinner*
    Knife and fork he never lays
35 Cross-wise, to my recollection,
    As do I, in Jesu's praise.
I the Trinity illustrate,
    Drinking watered orange-pulp—
In three sips the Arian[5] frustrate;
40   While he drains his at one gulp.

6

Oh, those melons? If he's able
    We're to have a feast! so nice!
One goes to the Abbot's table,
    All of us get each a slice.
45 How go on your flowers? None double?
    Not one fruit-sort can you spy?
Strange! And I, too, at such trouble,
    Keep them close-nipped on the sly!

7

There's a great text in Galatians,[6]
50   Once you trip on it, entails
Twenty-nine distinct damnations,
    One sure, if another fails:
If I trip him just a-dying,
    Sure of heaven as sure can be,
55 Spin him around and send him flying
    Off to hell, a Manichee?[7]

8

Or, my scrofulous French novel
    On grey paper with blunt type!
Simply glance at it, you grovel
60   Hand and foot in Belial's[8] gripe:
If I double down its pages
    At the woeful sixteenth print,
When he gathers his greengages,
    Ope a sieve and slip it in't?

9

65 Or, there's Satan! one might venture
    Pledge one's soul to him, yet leave
Such a flaw in the indenture
    As he'd miss till, past retrieve,
Blasted lay that rose-acacia
70   We're so proud of![9] *Hy, Zy, Hine*[1] . . .
'St, there's vespers! *Plena gratiâ
Ave, Virgo!*[2] Gr-r-r—you swine!

                                                            1842

---

5. Arius, a fourth-century Alexandrian heretic, denied the doctrine of the Trinity.
6. The line has sometimes been taken as referring to Galatians iii.10; but see Galatians v.14–15, with its ironic applicability to the spirit of the monologue, and also v.16–24.
7. The Manichean heresy, which the speaker hopes to lure Brother Lawrence into accepting, claimed that the world was divided between forces of good and forces of evil.
8. Hebrew personification of lawlessness, hence one of the names for the Devil.
9. The speaker seems to say that, if all else fails, he might secure Brother Lawrence's damnation by pledging his own soul to the Devil in return—but being careful to leave a flaw in the contract that would invalidate it.
1. Possibly an incantation used in calling up the Devil.
2. *"Plena gratiâ / Ave, Virgo"*: the speaker reverses the opening words of the *Ave Maria*: "Hail Mary, full of grace."

Home-Thoughts, From Abroad

1

Oh, to be in England
Now that April's there,
And whoever wakes in England
Sees, some morning, unaware,
5 That the lowest boughs and the brushwood sheaf
Round the elm-tree bole are in tiny leaf,
While the chaffinch sings on the orchard bough
In England—now!

2

And after April, when May follows,
10 And the whitethroat builds, and all the swallows!
Hark, where my blossomed pear-tree in the hedge
Leans to the field and scatters on the clover
Blossoms and dewdrops—at the bent spray's edge—
That's the wise thrush; he sings each song twice over,
15 Lest you should think he never could recapture
The first fine careless rapture!
And though the fields look rough with hoary dew
All will be gay when noontide wakes anew
The buttercups, the little children's dower
—Far brighter than this gaudy melon-flower!

1845

The Bishop Orders His Tomb at Saint Praxed's Church[3]

ROME, 15—

Vanity, saith the preacher, vanity![4]
Draw round my bed: is Anselm keeping back?
Nephews—sons mine . . . ah God, I know not! Well—
She, men would have to be your mother once,
5 Old Gandolf envied me, so fair she was!
What's done is done, and she is dead beside,
Dead long ago, and I am Bishop since,
And as she died so must we die ourselves,
And thence ye may perceive the world's a dream.
10 Life, how and what is it? As here I lie
In this state-chamber, dying by degrees,
Hours and long hours in the dead night, I ask
"Do I live, am I dead?" Peace, peace seems all.
Saint Praxed's ever was the church for peace;
15 And so, about this tomb of mine. I fought
With tooth and nail to save my niche, ye know:
—Old Gandolf cozened° me, despite my care;   *cheated*
Shrewd was that snatch from out the corner south
He graced his carrion with, God curse the same!
20 Yet still my niche is not so cramped but thence
One sees the pulpit o' the epistle-side,[5]

---

3. The church of Santa Prassede, in Rome, dedicated to a Roman virgin, dates from the fifth century but was rebuilt early in the ninth and restored at later times. The 16th-century Bishop who speaks here is a fictional figure, as is his predecessor, Gandolf.

4. An echo of Ecclesiastes i.2: "Vanity of vanities, saith the Preacher, vanity of vanities; all is vanity."

5. The right-hand side as one faces the altar, the side from which the Epistles of the New Testament were read.

And somewhat of the choir, those silent seats,
And up into the aery dome where live
The angels, and a sunbeam's sure to lurk:
25 And I shall fill my slab of basalt there,
And 'neath my tabernacle[6] take my rest,
With those nine columns round me, two and two,
The odd one at my feet where Anselm stands:
Peach-blossom marble all, the rare, the ripe
30 As fresh-poured red wine of a mighty pulse.
—Old Gandolf with his paltry onion-stone,
Put me where I may look at him! True peach,
Rosy and flawless: how I earned the prize!
Draw close: that conflagration of my church
35 —What then? So much was saved if aught were missed!
My sons, ye would not be my death? Go dig
The white-grape vineyard where the oil-press stood,
Drop water gently till the surface sink,
And if ye find . . . Ah God, I know not, I! . . .
40 Bedded in store of rotten fig-leaves soft,
And corded up in a tight olive-frail,°   *olive basket*
Some lump, ah God, of *lapis lazuli*,[7]
Big as a Jew's head cut off at the nape,
Blue as a vein o'er the Madonna's breast . . .
45 Sons, all have I bequeathed you, villas, all,
That brave Frascati[8] villa with its bath,
So, let the blue lump poise between my knees,
Like God the Father's globe on both his hands
Ye worship in the Jesu Church[9] so gay,
50 For Gandolf shall not choose but see and burst!
Swift as a weaver's shuttle fleet our years:[1]
Man goeth to the grave, and where is he?
Did I say basalt for my slab, sons? Black—
'Twas ever antique-black I meant! How else
55 Shall ye contrast my frieze to come beneath?
The bas-relief in bronze ye promised me,
Those Pans and Nymphs ye wot of, and perchance
Some tripod, thyrsus,[2] with a vase or so,
The Saviour at his sermon on the mount,
60 Saint Praxed in a glory,[3] and one Pan
Ready to twitch the Nymph's last garment off,
And Moses with the tables . . . but I know
Ye mark me not! What do they whisper thee,
Child of my bowels, Anselm? Ah, ye hope
65 To revel down my villas while I gasp
Bricked o'er with beggar's moldy travertine[4]
Which Gandolf from his tomb-top chuckles at!
Nay, boys, ye love me—all of jasper, then!
'T is jasper ye stand pledged to, lest I grieve
70 My bath must needs be left behind, alas!
One block, pure green as a pistachio-nut,
There's plenty jasper somewhere in the world—

6. Canopy over his tomb.
7. A vivid blue stone, one of the so-called hard stones, used for ornament.
8. A resort town in the mountains.
9. The splendid baroque church, Il Gesù. The sculptured group of the Trinity includes a terrestrial globe carved from the largest known block of lapis lazuli.

1. See, Job vii.6 ("My days are swifter than a weaver's shuttle, and are spent without hope").
2. A staff ornamented with ivy or vine-leaves, carried by followers of Bacchus, the Roman god of wine and revelry.
3. Rays of gold, signifying sanctity, around the head or body of the saint portrayed.
4. Ordinary limestone used in building.

And have I not Saint Praxed's ear to pray
Horses for ye, and brown Greek manuscripts,
And mistresses with great smooth marbly limbs?
—That's if ye carve my epitaph aright,
Choice Latin, picked phrase, Tully's[5] every word,
No gaudy ware like Gandolf's second line—
Tully, my masters? Ulpian[6] serves his need!
And then how I shall lie through centuries,
And hear the blessed mutter of the mass,
And see God made and eaten all day long,[7]
And feel the steady candle-flame, and taste
Good strong thick stupefying incense-smoke!
For as I lie here, hours of the dead night,
Dying in state and by such slow degrees,
I fold my arms as if they clasped a crook,[8]
And stretch my feet forth straight as stone can point,
And let the bedclothes, for a mortcloth,[9] drop
Into great laps and folds of sculptor's-work:
And as yon tapers dwindle, and strange thoughts
Grow, with a certain humming in my ears,
About the life before I lived this life,
And this life too, popes, cardinals and priests,
Saint Praxed at his sermon on the mount,[1]
Your tall pale mother with her talking eyes,
And new-found agate urns as fresh as day,
And marble's language, Latin pure, discreet,
—Aha, ELUCESCEBAT[2] quoth our friend?
No Tully, said I, Ulpian at the best!
Evil and brief hath been my pilgrimage.
All *lapis*, all, sons! Else I give the Pope
My villas! Will ye ever eat my heart?
Ever your eyes were as a lizard's quick,
They glitter like your mother's for my soul,
Or ye would heighten my impoverished frieze,
Piece out its starved design, and fill my vase
With grapes, and add a vizor and a Term,[3]
And to the tripod ye would tie a lynx
That in his struggle throws the thyrsus down,
To comfort me on my entablature
Whereon I am to lie till I must ask
"Do I live, am I dead?" There, leave me, there!
For ye have stabbed me with ingratitude
To death—ye wish it—God, ye wish it! Stone—
Gritstone, a-crumble! Clammy squares which sweat
As if the corpse they keep were oozing through—
And no more *lapis* to delight the world!
Well, go! I bless ye. Fewer tapers there,
But in a row: and, going, turn your backs
—Ay, like departing altar-ministrants,
And leave me in my church, the church for peace,

5. Familiar name for Cicero (Marcus Tullius Cicero).
6. His Latin would be stylistically inferior to that of Cicero.
7. Refers to the doctrine of transubstantiation.
8. I.e., the Bishop's crozier, with its emblematic resemblance to a shepherd's crook.
9. The pall with which the coffin is draped.
1. As the Bishop's mind wanders, he attributes Christ's Sermon on the Mount to Santa Prassede.
2. A word from Gandolf's epitaph (a form of the Latin verb meaning "to shine forth"); the Bishop claims that this form is inferior to *elucebat*, which Cicero would have used.
3. "Vizor": a mask; "Term": a pillar adorned with a bust. Both are motifs of classical sculpture imitated by the Renaissance.

That I may watch at leisure if he leers—
Old Gandolf, at me, from his onion-stone,
125   As still he envied me, so fair she was!

Fra Lippo Lippi[4]

I am poor brother Lippo, by your leave!
You need not clap your torches to my face.
Zooks, what's to blame? you think you see a monk!
What, 'tis past midnight, and you go the rounds,
5   And here you catch me at an alley's end
Where sportive ladies leave their doors ajar?
The Carmine's my cloister:[5] hunt it up,
Do—harry out, if you must show your zeal,
Whatever rat, there, haps on his wrong hole,
10   And nip each softling of a wee white mouse,
Weke, weke, that's crept to keep him company!
Aha, you know your betters! Then, you'll take
Your hand away that's fiddling on my throat,
And please to know me likewise. Who am I?
15   Why, one, sir, who is lodging with a friend
Three streets off—he's a certain . . . how d'ye call?
Master—a . . . Cosimo of the Medici,[6]
I' the house that caps the corner. Boh! you were best!
Remember and tell me, the day you're hanged,
20   How you affected such a gullet's-gripe![7]
But you, sir, it concerns you that your knaves
Pick up a manner nor discredit you:
Zooks, are we pilchards,° that they sweep the streets   *fish*
And count fair prize what comes into their net?
25   He's Judas to a tittle, that man is![8]
Just such a face! Why, sir, you make amends.
Lord, I'm not angry! Bid your hangdogs go
Drink out this quarter-florin to the health
Of the munificent House that harbors me
30   (And many more beside, lads! more beside!)
And all's come square again. I'd like his face—
His, elbowing on his comrade in the door
With the pike and lantern—for the slave that holds
John Baptist's head a-dangle by the hair
35   With one hand ("Look you, now," as who should say)
And his weapon in the other, yet unwiped!
It's not your chance to have a bit of chalk,
A wood-coal or the like? or you should see!
Yes, I'm the painter, since you style me so.
40   What, brother Lippo's doings, up and down,
You know them and they take you? like enough!
I saw the proper twinkle in your eye—
'Tell you, I liked your looks at very first.

---

4. Florentine painter (ca. 1406–69), whose life Browning knew from Vasari's *Lives of the Most Eminent Painters, Sculptors, and Architects,* and from other sources, and whose paintings he had learned to know at first hand during his years in Florence.
5. Fra Lippo had entered the Carmelite cloister while still a boy. He gave up monastic vows on June 6, 1421, but was clothed by the monastery until 1431 and was called "Fra Filippo" in documents until his death.
6. Cosimo de'Medici (1389–1464), Fra Lippo's wealthy patron and an important political power in Florence.
7. I.e., grip on my throat.
8. Of one of the watchmen who have arrested him, he says he looks exactly like Judas.

Let's sit and set things straight now, hip to haunch.
Here's spring come, and the nights one makes up bands
To roam the town and sing out carnival,
And I've been three weeks shut within my mew,[9]
A-painting for the great man, saints and saints
And saints again. I could not paint all night—
Ouf! I leaned out of window for fresh air.
There came a hurry of feet and little feet,
A sweep of lute-strings, laughs, and whifts of song—
Flower o' the broom,
Take away love, and our earth is a tomb!
Flower o' the quince,
I let Lisa go, and what good in life since?
Flower o' the thyme—and so on. Round they went.
Scarce had they turned the corner when a titter
Like the skipping of rabbits by moonlight—three slim shapes,
And a face that looked up . . . zooks, sir, flesh and blood,
That's all I'm made of! Into shreds it went,
Curtain and counterpane and coverlet,
All the bed-furniture—a dozen knots,
There was a ladder! Down I let myself,
Hands and feet, scrambling somehow, and so dropped,
And after them. I came up with the fun
Hard by Saint Laurence,[1] hail fellow, well met—
Flower o' the rose,
If I've been merry, what matter who knows?
And so as I was stealing back again
To get to bed and have a bit of sleep
Ere I rise up to-morrow and go work
On Jerome knocking at his poor old breast[2]
With his great round stone to subdue the flesh,
You snap me of the sudden. Ah, I see!
Though your eye twinkles still, you shake your head—
Mine's shaved—a monk, you say—the sting's in that!
If Master Cosimo announced himself,
Mum's the word naturally; but a monk!
Come, what am I a beast for? tell us, now!
I was a baby when my mother died
And father died and left me in the street.
I starved there, God knows how, a year or two
On fig-skins, melon-parings, rinds and shucks,
Refuse and rubbish. One fine frosty day,
My stomach being empty as your hat,
The wind doubled me up and down I went.
Old Aunt Lapaccia trussed me with one hand,
(Its fellow was a stinger as I knew)
And so along the wall, over the bridge,
By the straight cut to the convent. Six words there,
While I stood munching my first bread that month:
"So, boy, you're minded," quoth the good fat father
Wiping his own mouth, 't was refection-time—
"To quit this very miserable world?
"Will you renounce" . . . "the mouthful of bread?" thought I;
By no means! Brief, they made a monk of me;

---

9. I.e., within the confines of my quarters (in the Medici palace).
1. The church of San Lorenzo, not far from the Medici palace.
2. I.e., on a painting of St. Jerome in the Desert.

I did renounce the world, its pride and greed,
Palace, farm, villa, shop and banking-house,
100   Trash, such as these poor devils of Medici
Have given their hearts to—all at eight years old.
Well, sir, I found in time, you may be sure,
'T was not for nothing—the good bellyful,
The warm serge and the rope that goes all round,
105   And day-long blessed idleness beside!
"Let's see what the urchin's fit for"—that came next.
Not overmuch their way, I must confess.
Such a to-do! They tried me with their books:
Lord, they'd have taught me Latin in pure waste!
110   *Flower o' the clove,*
All the Latin I construe is, "amo" I love!
But, mind you, when a boy starves in the streets
Eight years together, as my fortune was,
Watching folk's faces to know who will fling
115   The bit of half-stripped grape-bunch he desires,
And who will curse or kick him for his pains—
Which gentleman processional and fine,
Holding a candle to the Sacrament,
Will wink and let him lift a plate and catch
120   The droppings of the wax to sell again,
Or holla for the Eight[3] and have him whipped—
How say I? nay, which dog bites, which lets drop
His bone from the heap of offal in the street—
Why, soul and sense of him grow sharp alike,
125   He learns the look of things, and none the less
For admonition from the hunger-pinch.
I had a store of such remarks, be sure,
Which, after I found leisure, turned to use.
I drew men's faces on my copy-books,
130   Scrawled them within the antiphonary's[4] marge,
Joined legs and arms to the long music-notes,
Found eyes and nose and chin for A's and B's,
And made a string of pictures of the world
Betwixt the ins and outs of verb and noun,
135   On the wall, the bench, the door. The monks looked black.
"Nay," quoth the Prior, "turn him out, d'ye say?
"In no wise. Lose a crow and catch a lark.
"What if at last we get our man of parts,
"We Carmelites, like those Camaldolese[5]
140   "And Preaching Friars,[6] to do our church up fine
"And put the front on it that ought to be!"
And hereupon he bade me daub away.
Thank you! my head being crammed, the walls a blank,
Never was such prompt disemburdening.
145   First, every sort of monk, the black and white,
I drew them, fat and lean: then, folk at church,
From good old gossips waiting to confess
Their cribs of barrel-droppings, candle-ends—
To the breathless fellow at the altar-foot,
150   Fresh from his murder, safe and sitting there
With the little children round him in a row
Of admiration, half for his beard and half

---

3. The Florentine magistrates.
4. The book containing the antiphons, or re-
sponses chanted in the liturgy.

5. Members of a religious order at Camaldoli,
in the Apennines.
6. I.e., Dominicans.

For that white anger of his victim's son
Shaking a fist at him with one fierce arm,
Signing[7] himself with the other because of Christ
(Whose sad face on the cross sees only this
After the passion of a thousand years)
Till some poor girl, her apron o'er her head,
(Which the intense eyes looked through) came at eve
On tiptoe, said a word, dropped in a loaf,
Her pair of earrings and a bunch of flowers
(The brute took growling), prayed, and so was gone.
I painted all, then cried " 'Tis ask and have;
"Choose, for more's ready!"—laid the ladder flat,
And showed my covered bit of cloister-wall.
The monks closed in a circle and praised loud
Till checked, taught what to see and not to see,
Being simple bodies—"That's the very man!
"Look at the boy who stoops to pat the dog!
"That woman's like the Prior's niece who comes
"To care about his asthma: it's the life!"
But there my triumph's straw-fire flared and funked;
Their betters took their turn to see and say:
The Prior and the learned pulled a face
And stopped all that in no time. "How? what's here?
"Quite from the mark of painting, bless us all!
"Faces, arms, legs and bodies like the true
"As much as pea and pea! it's devil's-game!
"Your business is not to catch men with show,
"With homage to the perishable clay,
"But lift them over it, ignore it all,
"Make them forget there's such a thing as flesh.
"Your business is to paint the souls of men—
"Man's soul, and it's a fire, smoke . . . no, it's not . . .
"It's vapor done up like a new-born babe—
"(In that shape when you die it leaves your mouth)
"It's . . . well, what matters talking, it's the soul!
"Give us no more of body than shows soul!
"Here's Giotto,[8] with his Saint a-praising God,
"That sets us praising—why not stop with him?
"Why put all thoughts of praise out of our head
"With wonder at lines, colors, and what not?
"Paint the soul, never mind the legs and arms!
"Rub all out, try at it a second time.
"Oh, that white smallish female with the breasts,
"She's just my niece . . . Herodias,[9] I would say—
"Who went and danced and got men's heads cut off!
"Have it all out!" Now, is this sense, I ask?
A fine way to paint soul, by painting body
So ill, the eye can't stop there, must go further
And can't fare worse! Thus, yellow does for white
When what you put for yellow's simply black,
And any sort of meaning looks intense
When all beside itself means and looks nought.
Why can't a painter lift each foot in turn,

---

7. Making the sign of the cross with one hand, because of the image of Christ on the altar.
8. The great Florentine painter (1267–1337).
9. Sister-in-law of the tetrarch Herod. She had demanded that John the Baptist be imprisoned: when her daughter Salome so pleased the king with her dancing that he promised her anything she asked, Herodias instructed her to ask for the head of a Baptist on a platter (Matthew xiv.1–12).

Left foot and right foot, go a double step,
Make his flesh liker and his soul more like,
Both in their order? Take the prettiest face,
The Prior's niece . . . patron-saint—is it so pretty
210 You can't discover if it means hope, fear,
Sorrow or joy? won't beauty go with these?
Suppose I've made her eyes all right and blue,
Can't I take breath and try to add life's flash,
And then add soul and heighten them threefold?
215 Or say there's beauty with no soul at all—
(I never saw it—put the case the same—)
If you get simple beauty and nought else,
You get about the best thing God invents:
That's somewhat: and you'll find the soul you have missed,
220 Within yourself, when you return him thanks.
"Rub all out!" Well, well, there's my life, in short,
And so the thing has gone on ever since.
I'm grown a man no doubt, I've broken bounds:
You should not take a fellow eight years old
225 And make him swear to never kiss the girls.
I'm my own master, paint now as I please—
Having a friend, you see, in the Corner-house![1]
Lord, it's fast holding by the rings in front—
Those great rings serve more purposes than just
230 To plant a flag in, or tie up a horse!
And yet the old schooling sticks, the old grave eyes
Are peeping o'er my shoulder as I work,
The heads shake still—"It's art's decline, my son!
"You're not of the true painters, great and old;
235 "Brother Angelico's the man, you'll find;
"Brother Lorenzo[2] stands his single peer:
"Fag on at flesh, you'll never make the third!"
Flower o' the pine,
You keep your mistr . . . manners, and I'll stick to mine!
240 I'm not the third, then: bless us, they must know!
Don't you think they're the likeliest to know,
They with their Latin? So, I swallow my rage,
Clench my teeth, suck my lips in tight, and paint
To please them—sometimes do and sometimes don't;
245 For, doing most, there's pretty sure to come
A turn, some warm eve finds me at my saints—
A laugh, a cry, the business of the world—
(*Flower o' the peach,*
Death for us all, and his own life for each!)
250 And my whole soul revolves, the cup runs over,
The world and life's too big to pass for a dream,
And I do these wild things in sheer despite,
And play the fooleries you catch me at,
In pure rage! The old mill-horse, out at grass
255 After hard years, throws up his stiff heels so,
Although the miller does not preach to him
The only good of grass is to make chaff.
What would men have? Do they like grass or no—
May they or mayn't they? all I want's the thing
260 Settled for ever one way. As it is,

---

1. I.e., the Medici palace.   2. Fra Angelico (1387–1455), and Fra
Lorenzo Monaco (1370–1425).

You tell too many lies and hurt yourself:
You don't like what you only like too much,
You do like what, if given you at your word,
You find abundantly detestable.
For me, I think I speak as I was taught;
I always see the garden and God there
A-making man's wife: and, my lesson learned,
The value and significance of flesh,
I can't unlearn ten minutes afterwards.

You understand me: I'm a beast, I know.
But see, now—why, I see as certainly
As that the morning-star's about to shine,
What will hap some day. We've a youngster here
Comes to our convent, studies what I do,
Slouches and stares and lets no atom drop:
His name is Guidi—he'll not mind the monks—
They call him Hulking Tom,[3] he lets them talk—
He picks my practice up—he'll paint apace,
I hope so—though I never live so long,
I know what's sure to follow. You be judge!
You speak no Latin more than I, belike;
However, you're my man, you've seen the world
—The beauty and the wonder and the power,
The shapes of things, their colors, lights and shades,
Changes, surprises—and God made it all!
—For what? Do you feel thankful, ay or no,
For this fair town's face, yonder river's line,
The mountain round it and the sky above,
Much more the figures of man, woman, child,
These are the frame to? What's it all about?
To be passed over, despised? or dwelt upon,
Wondered at? oh, this last of course!—you say.
But why not do as well as say, paint these
Just as they are, careless what comes of it?
God's works—paint anyone, and count it crime
To let a truth slip. Don't object, "His works
"Are here already; nature is complete:
"Suppose you reproduce her (which you can't)
"There's no advantage! you must beat her, then."
For, don't you mark? we're made so that we love
First when we see them painted, things we have passed
Perhaps a hundred times nor cared to see;
And so they are better, painted—better to us,
Which is the same thing. Art was given for that;
God uses us to help each other so,
Lending our minds out. Have you noticed, now,
Your cullion's hanging face? A bit of chalk,
And trust me but you should, though! How much more,
If I drew higher things with the same truth!
That were to take the Prior's pulpit-place,
Interpret God to all of you! Oh, oh,
It makes me mad to see what men shall do

---

3. The painter Tommaso Guidi (1401–28), known as Masaccio (from *Tomasaccio,* meaning "Big Tom" or "Hulking Tom"). The series of frescoes which he painted in Santa Maria del Carmine, of key importance in the history of Florentine painting, was completed by Fra Lippo's son, Filippino Lippi, and it is in fact more likely that Fra Lippo learned from Masaccio than that he saw him as a promising newcomer.

And we in our graves! This world's no blot for us,
Nor blank; it means intensely, and means good:
315 To find its meaning is my meat and drink.
"Ay, but you don't so instigate to prayer!"
Strikes in the Prior: "when your meaning's plain
"It does not say to folk—remember matins,
"Or, mind you fast next Friday!" Why, for this
320 What need of art at all? A skull and bones,
Two bits of stick nailed crosswise, or, what's best,
A bell to chime the hour with, does as well.
I painted a Saint Laurence six months since
At Prato,[4] splashed the fresco in fine style:
325 "How looks my painting, now the scaffold's down?"
I ask a brother: "Hugely," he returns—
"Already not one phiz of your three slaves
"Who turn the Deacon off his toasted side,[5]
"But's scratched and prodded to our heart's content,
330 "The pious people have so eased their own
"With coming to say prayers there in a rage:
"We get on fast to see the bricks beneath.
"Expect another job this time next year,
"For pity and religion grow i' the crowd—
355 "Your painting serves its purpose!" Hang the fools!

—That is—you'll not mistake an idle word
Spoke in a huff by a poor monk, God wot,
Tasting the air this spicy night which turns
The unaccustomed head like Chianti wine!
340 Oh, the church knows! don't misreport me, now!
It's natural a poor monk out of bounds
Should have his apt word to excuse himself:
And hearken how I plot to make amends.
I have bethought me: I shall paint a piece
345 . . . There's for you! Give me six months, then go, see
Something in Sant' Ambrogio's![6] Bless the nuns!
They want a cast o' my office. I shall paint
God in the midst, Madonna and her babe,
Ringed by a bowery flowery angel-brood,
350 Lilies and vestments and white faces, sweet
As puff on puff of grated orris-root
When ladies crowd to Church at midsummer.
And then i' the front, of course a saint or two—
Saint John, because he saves the Florentines,[7]
355 Saint Ambrose, who puts down in black and white
The convent's friends and gives them a long day,
And Job, I must have him there past mistake,
The man of Uz (and Us without the z,
Painters who need his patience). Well, all these
360 Secured at their devotion, up shall come
Out of a corner when you least expect,
As one by a dark stair into a great light,
Music and talking, who but Lippo! I!

4. Smaller town near Florence, where Fra
Lippo painted some of his most important
pictures.
5. Saint Lawrence was martyred by being
roasted on a gridiron; according to legend, he
urged his executioners to turn him over, say-
ing that he was done on one side.
6. Fra Lippo painted the *Coronation of the
Virgin*, here described, for the high altar of
Sant' Ambrogio in 1447.
7. San Giovanni is the patron saint of
Florence.

Mazed, motionless and moonstruck—I'm the man!
Back I shrink—what is this I see and hear?
I, caught up with my monk's-things by mistake,
My old serge gown and rope that goes all round,
I, in this presence, this pure company!
Where's a hole, where's a corner for escape?
Then steps a sweet angelic slip of a thing
Forward, puts out a soft palm—"Not so fast!"
—Addresses the celestial presence, "nay—
"He made you and devised you, after all,
"Though he's none of you! Could Saint John there draw—
"His camel-hair[8] make up a painting-brush?
"We come to brother Lippo for all that,
"*Iste perfecit opus!*"[9] So, all smile—
I shuffle sideways with my blushing face
Under the cover of a hundred wings
Thrown like a spread of kirtles[1] when you're gay
And play hot cockles,[2] all the doors being shut,
Till, wholly unexpected, in there pops
The hothead husband! Thus I scuttle off
To some safe bench behind, not letting go
The palm of her, the little lily thing
That spoke the good word for me in the nick,
Like the Prior's niece . . . Saint Lucy, I would say.
And so all's saved for me, and for the church
A pretty picture gained. Go, six months hence!
Your hand, sir, and good-bye: no lights, no lights!
The street's hushed, and I know my own way back,
Don't fear me! there's the gray beginning. Zooks!

1855

A Toccata of Galuppi's[3]

1

Oh Galuppi, Baldassare, this is very sad to find!
I can hardly misconceive you; it would prove me deaf and blind;
But although I take your meaning, 'tis with such a heavy mind!

2

Here you come with your old music, and here's all the good it brings.
What, they lived once thus at Venice where the merchants were the kings,
Where Saint Mark's is, where the Doges used to wed the sea with rings?[4]

3

Ay, because the sea's the street there; and 'tis arched by . . . what you call
 . . . Shylock's bridge[5] with houses on it, where they kept the carnival:
I was never out of England—it's as if I saw it all.

---

8. John the Baptist is often portrayed wearing a rough robe of camel's hair, in accord with Mark i.6.
9. It is more likely that the figure which Browning took to be that of the painter is that of the patron, the Very Reverend Francesco Marenghi, who ordered the painting in 1441, and that the words on the scroll before him ("*Is* [*te*] *perfecit opus*," This man accomplished the work) refer to the commissioning of the project.
1. Women's gowns or skirts.
2. A game in which a blindfolded player must guess who has struck him.
3. The poem presents the reflections of a 19th-century Englishman, as he plays a toccata by the 18th-century Venetian composer Baldassare Galuppi. (A toccata is a "touch-piece," the word derived from the Italian verb *toccare*, to touch: "a composition intended to exhibit the touch and exhibition of the performer," and hence often having the character of "showy improvisation" [*Grove's Dictionary of Music and Musicians*]. In stanzas 7–9, the quoted words represent the thoughts, feelings, or casual remarks of the earlier Venetian audience, now dispersed by death.
4. Each year the Doge, chief magistrate of the Venetian republic, threw a ring into the sea with the ceremonial words, "We wed thee, O sea, in sign of true and everlasting dominion."
5. The Rialto Bridge over the Grand Canal.

4

10 Did young people take their pleasure when the sea was warm in May?
Balls and masks begun at midnight, burning ever to mid-day,
When they made up fresh adventures for the morrow, do you say?

5

Was a lady such a lady, cheeks so round and lips so red—
On her neck the small face bouyant, like a bellflower on its bed,
15 O'er the breast's superb abundance where a man might base his head?

6

Well, and it was graceful of them—they'd break talk off and afford
—She, to bite her mask's black velvet—he, to finger on his sword,
While you sat and played Toccatas, stately at the clavichord?[6]

7

What? Those lesser thirds so plaintive, sixths diminished, sigh on sigh,
20 Told them something? Those suspensions, those solutions—"Must we die?"
Those commiserating sevenths—"Life might last! we can but try!"

8

"Were you happy?" "Yes." "And are you still as happy?" "Yes. And you?"
"Then, more kisses!" "Did *I* stop them, when a million seemed so few?"
Hark, the dominant's persistence till it must be answered to!

9

25 So, an octave struck the answer. Oh, they praised you, I dare say!
"Brave Galuppi! that was music! good alike at grave and gay!
"I can always leave off talking when I hear a master play!"

10

Then they left you for their pleasure: till in due time, one by one,
Some with lives that came to nothing, some with deeds as well undone,
30 Death stepped tacitly and took them where they never see the sun.

11

But when I sit down to reason, think to take my stand nor swerve,
While I triumph o'er a secret wrung from nature's close reserve,
In you come with your cold music[7] till I creep through every nerve.

12

Yes, you, like a ghostly cricket, creaking where a house was burned:
35 "Dust and ashes, dead and done with, Venice spent what Venice earned.
"The soul, doubtless, is immortal—where a soul can be discerned.

13

"Yours for instance: you know physics, something of geology,
"Mathematics are your pastime; souls shall rise in their degree;
"Butterflies may dread extinction—you'll not die, it cannot be!

14

40 "As for Venice and her people, merely born to bloom and drop,
"Here on earth they bore their fruitage, mirth and folly were the crop:
"What of soul was left, I wonder, when the kissing had to stop?

15

"Dust and ashes!" So you creak it, and I want the heart to scold.
Dear dead women, with such hair, too—what's become of all the gold
45 Used to hang and brush their bosoms? I feel chilly and grown old.

ca. 1847   1855

---

6. "A keyboard instrument, precursor of the piano" [Webster].
7. In stanzas 12–15, the quoted words are the words he imagines the composer as speaking to him.

"Childe Roland to the Dark Tower Came"

(SEE EDGAR'S SONG IN "LEAR") [8]

1

My first thought was, he lied in every word,
    That hoary cripple, with malicious eye
    Askance to watch the working of his lie
On mine, and mouth scarce able to afford
5 Suppression of the glee, that pursed and scored
    Its edge, at one more victim gained thereby.

2

What else should he be set for, with his staff?
    What, save to waylay with his lies, ensnare
    All travelers who might find him posted there,
10 And ask the road? I guessed what skull-like laugh
    Would break, what crutch 'gin write my epitaph
    For pastime in the dusty thoroughfare,

3

If at his counsel I should turn aside
    Into that ominous tract which, all agree,
15   Hides the Dark Tower. Yet acquiescingly
I did turn as he pointed: neither pride
    Nor hope rekindling at the end descried,
    So much as gladness that some end might be.

4

For, what with my whole world-wide wandering,
20   What with my search drawn out through years, my hope
    Dwindled into a ghost not fit to cope
With that obstreperous joy success would bring,—
    I hardly tried now to rebuke the spring
    My heart made, finding failure in its scope.

5

25 As when a sick man very near to death
    Seems dead indeed, and feels begin and end
    The tears, and takes the farewell of each friend,
And hears one bid the other go, draw breath
    Freelier outside, ("since all is o'er," he saith,
30   "And the blow fallen no grieving can amend;")

6

While some discuss if near the other graves
    Be room enough for this, and when a day
    Suits best for carrying the corpse away,
With care about the banners, scarves and staves:
35 And still the man hears all, and only craves
    He may not shame such tender love and stay.

---

8. In Shakespeare's *King Lear,* II. iv, Edgar, Gloucester's son, disguised as a madman, meets Lear in the midst of a storm; at the end of the scene, Edgar sings: "Child Rowland to the dark tower came;/His word was still, 'Fie, foh, and fum,/I smell the blood of a British man.'" (*Childe:* medieval title applied to a youth awaiting knighthood.)

7

Thus, I had so long suffered in this quest,
  Heard failure prophesied so oft, been writ
  So many times among "The Band"—to wit,
40 The knights who to the Dark Tower's search addressed
  Their steps—that just to fail as they, seemed best,
  And all the doubt was now—should I be fit?

8

So, quiet as despair, I turned from him,
  That hateful cripple, out of his highway
45   Into the path he pointed. All the day
Had been a dreary one at best, and dim
  Was settling to its close, yet shot one grim
  Red leer to see the plain catch its estray.[9]

9

For mark! no sooner was I fairly found
50   Pledged to the plain, after a pace or two,
  Than, pausing to throw backward a last view
O'er the safe road, 'twas gone; gray plain all round:
  Nothing but plain to the horizon's bound.
  I might go on; naught else remained to do.

10

55 So, on I went. I think I never saw
  Such starved ignoble nature; nothing throve:
  For flowers—as well expect a cedar grove!
But cockle, spurge,[1] according to their law
  Might propagate their kind, with none to awe,
60   You'd think: a burr had been a treasure trove.

11

No! penury, inertness and grimace,
  In some strange sort, were the land's portion. "See
  Or shut your eyes," said Nature peevishly,
"It nothing skills:° I cannot help my case: *avails*
65   'Tis the Last Judgment's fire must cure this place,
  Calcine° its clods and set my prisoners free."   *burn to powder*

12

If there pushed any ragged thistle-stalk
  Above its mates, the head was chopped; the bents°   *reeds, rushes*
  Were jealous else. What made those holes and rents
70 In the dock's[2] harsh swarth° leaves, bruised as to balk   *dark*
All hope of greenness? 'tis a brute must walk
  Pashing° their life out, with a brute's intents.   *crushing*

13

As for the grass, it grew as scant as hair
  In leprosy; thin dry blades pricked the mud
75   Which underneath looked kneaded up with blood.
One stiff blind horse, his every bone a-stare,
  Stood stupefied, however he came there:
  Thrust out past service from the devil's stud!

9. A stray or unclaimed domestic animal.
1. Cockle here is a weed that grows in wheat-
fields; spurge, a plant with minute flowers.
2. Coarse weedy plant.

14

Alive? he might be dead for aught I know,
 With that red gaunt colloped ° neck a-strain,   *chafed, ridged*
 And shut eyes underneath the rusty mane;
Seldom went such grotesqueness with such woe;
I never saw a brute I hated so;
 He must be wicked to deserve such pain.

15

I shut my eyes and turned them on my heart.
 As a man calls for wine before he fights,
 I asked one draught of earlier, happier sights,
Ere fitly I could hope to play my part.
Think first, fight afterwards—the soldier's art:
 One taste of the old time sets all to rights.

16

Not it! I fancied Cuthbert's reddening face
 Beneath its garniture of curly gold,
 Dear fellow, till I almost felt him fold
An arm in mine to fix me to the place,
That way he used. Alas, one night's disgrace!
 Out went my heart's new fire and left it cold.

17

Giles then, the soul of honor—there he stands
 Frank as ten years ago when knighted first.
 What honest man should dare (he said) he durst.
Good—but the scene shifts—faugh! what hangman hands
Pin to his breast a parchment? His own bands
 Read it. Poor traitor, spit upon and curst!

18

Better this present than a past like that;
 Back therefore to my darkening path again!
 No sound, no sight as far as eye could strain.
Will the night send a howlet° or a bat?   *owl*
I asked: when something on the dismal flat
 Came to arrest my thoughts and change their train.

19

A sudden little river crossed my path
 As unexpected as a serpent comes.
 No sluggish tide congenial to the glooms;
This, as it frothed by, might have been a bath
For the fiend's glowing hoof—to see the wrath
 Of its black eddy bespate° with flakes and spumes.   *spattered*

20

So petty yet so spiteful! All along,
 Low scrubby alders kneeled down over it;
 Drenched willows flung them headlong in a fit
Of mute despair, a suicidal throng:
The river which had done them all the wrong,
 Whate'er that was, rolled by, deterred no whit.

21

Which, while I forded,—good saints, how I feared
  To set my foot upon a dead man's cheek,
  Each step, or feel the spear I thrust to seek
For hollows, tangled in his hair or beard!
125 —It may have been a water-rat I speared,
  But, ugh! it sounded like a baby's shriek.

22

Glad was I when I reached the other bank.
  Now for a better country. Vain presage!
  Who were the strugglers, what war did they wage,
130 Whose savage trample thus could pad the dank
Soil to a plash?° Toads in a poisoned tank,   *puddle*
  Or wild cats in a red-hot iron cage—

23

The fight must so have seemed in that fell cirque.[3]
  What penned them there, with all the plain to choose?
135 No footprint leading to that horrid mews,°   *stabling area*
None out of it. Mad brewage set to work
Their brains, no doubt, like galley-slaves the Turk
Pits for his pastime, Christians against Jews.

24

And more than that—a furlong on—why, there!
140 What bad use was that engine° for, that wheel,   *mechanical contrivance*
  Or brake,[4] not wheel—that harrow fit to reel
Men's bodies out like silk? with all the air
Of Tophet's° tool, on earth left unaware,   *Hell's*
  Or brought to sharpen its rusty teeth of steel.

25

145 Then came a bit of stubbed ground, once a wood,
  Next a marsh, it would seem, and now mere earth
  Desperate and done with; (so a fool finds mirth,
Makes a thing and then mars it, till his mood
Changes and off he goes!) within a rood [5]—
150 Bog, clay and rubble, sand and stark black dearth.

26

Now blotches rankling,° colored gay and grim,   *festering*
  Now patches where some leanness of the soil's
  Broke into moss or substances like boils;
Then came some palsied oak, a cleft in him
155 Like a distorted mouth that splits its rim
  Gaping at death, and dies while it recoils.

27

And just as far as ever from the end!
  Nought in the distance but the evening, nought
  To point my footstep further! At the thought,
160 A great black bird, Apollyon's [6] bosom-friend,
  Sailed past, nor beat his wide wing dragon-penned [7]
  That brushed my cap—perchance the guide I sought.

3. Rounded hollow encircled by heights.
4. Here in the sense of a tool for breaking up flax or hemp, to separate the fiber.
5. Linear measure, varying locally from six to eight yards.

6. ". . . The angel of the bottomless pit, whose name in the Hebrew tongue is Abaddon, but in the Greek tongue . . . Apollyon." Revelation ix.11.
7. With pinions like a dragon's.

28

For, looking up, aware I somehow grew,
  'Spite of the dusk, the plain had given place
  All round to mountains—with such name to grace
Mere ugly heights and heaps now stolen in view.
How thus they had surprised me,—solve it, you!
  How to get from them was no clearer case.

29

Yet half I seemed to recognize some trick
  Of mischief happened to me, God knows when—
  In a bad dream perhaps. Here ended, then,
Progress this way. When, in the very nick
Of giving up, one time more, came a click
  As when a trap shuts—you're inside the den!

30

Burningly it came on me all at once,
  This was the place! those two hills on the right,
  Crouched like two bulls locked horn in horn in fight;
While to the left, a tall scalped mountain . . . Dunce,
Dotard, a-dozing at the very nonce,°   moment
  After a life spent training for the sight!

31

What in the midst lay but the Tower itself?
  The round squat turret, blind as the fool's heart,
  Built of brown stone, without a counterpart
In the whole world. The tempest's mocking elf
Points to the shipman thus the unseen shelf
  He strikes on, only when the timbers start.

32

Not see? because of night perhaps?—why, day
  Came back again for that! before it left,
  The dying sunset kindled through a cleft:
The hills, like giants at a hunting, lay,
Chin upon hand, to see the game at bay,—
  "Now stab and end the creature—to the heft!" [8]

33

Not hear? when noise was everywhere! it tolled
  Increasing like a bell. Names in my ears
  Of all the lost adventurers my peers,—
How such a one was strong, and such was bold,
And such was fortunate, yet each of old
  Lost, lost! one moment knelled the woe of years.

34

There they stood, ranged along the hillsides, met
  To view the last of me, a living frame
  For one more picture! in a sheet of flame
I saw them and I knew them all. And yet
Dauntless the slug-horn [9] to my lips I set,
  And blew. "*Childe Roland to the Dark Tower came.*"

1855

8. Handle of dagger or knife.   9. Rough trumpet made from the horn of an
                                          ox or cow.

How It Strikes a Contemporary

I only knew one poet in my life:
And this, or something like it, was his way.

You saw go up and down Valladolid,[1]
A man of mark, to know next time you saw.
5 His very serviceable suit of black
Was courtly once and conscientious still,
And many might have worn it, though none did:
The cloak, that somewhat shone and showed the threads,
Had purpose, and the ruff, significance.
10 He walked and tapped the pavement with his cane,
Scenting the world, looking it full in face,
An old dog, bald and blindish, at his heels.
They turned up, now, the alley by the church,
That leads nowhither; now, they breathed themselves
15 On the main promenade just at the wrong time:
You'd come upon his scrutizing hat,
Making a peaked shade blacker than itself
Against the single window spared some house
Intact yet with its mouldered Moorish work,—
20 Or else surprise the ferrel° of his stick   ferrule
Trying the mortar's temper 'tween the chinks
Of some new shop a-building, French and fine.
He stood and watched the cobbler at his trade,
The man who slices lemons into drink,
25 The coffee-roaster's brazier, and the boys
That volunteer to help him turn its winch.
He glanced o'er books on stalls with half an eye,
And flyleaf ballads on the vendor's string,
And broad-edge bold-print posters by the wall.
30 He took such cognizance of men and things,
If any beat a horse, you felt he saw;
If any cursed a woman, he took note;
Yet stared at nobody—you stared at him,
And found, less to your pleasure than surprise,
35 He seemed to know you and expect as much.
So, next time that a neighbor's tongue was loosed,
It marked the shameful and notorious fact,
We had among us, not so much a spy,
As a recording chief-inquisitor,[2]
40 The town's true master if the town but knew!
We merely kept a governor for form,
While this man walked about and took account
Of all thought, said and acted, then went home,
And wrote it fully to our Lord the King
45 Who has an itch to know things, he knows why,
And reads them in his bedroom of a night.
Oh, you might smile! there wanted not a touch,
A tang of . . . well, it was not wholly ease
As back into your mind the man's look came.
50 Stricken in years a little—such a brow

1. Small city in Spain, northwest of Madrid.
2. A chief officer of the Inquisition, the ecclesiastical tribunal organized in the 13th century for the suppression of heresy, and which lasted in Spain until 1834.

His eyes had to live under!—clear as flint
On either side the formidable nose
Curved, cut and colored like an eagle's claw.
Had he to do with A.'s surprising fate?
When altogether old B. disappeared
And young C. got his mistress—was't our friend,
His letter to the King, that did it all?
What paid the bloodless man for so much pains?
Our Lord the King has favorites manifold,
And shifts his ministry some once a month;
Our city gets new governors at whiles,
But never word or sign, that I could hear,
Notified to this man about the streets
The King's approval of those letters conned
The last thing duly at the dead of night.
Did the man love his office? Frowned our Lord,
Exhorting when none heard—"Beseech me not!
"Too far above my people—beneath me!
"I set the watch—how should the people know?
"Forget them, keep me all the more in mind!"
Was some such understanding 'twixt the two?

   I found no truth in one report at least—
That if you tracked him to his home, down lanes
Beyond the Jewry, and as clean to pace,
You found he ate his supper in a room
Blazing with lights, four Titians[3] on the wall,
And twenty naked girls to change his plate!
Poor man, he lived another kind of life
In that new stuccoed third house by the bridge,
Fresh-painted, rather smart than otherwise!
The whole street might o'erlook him as he sat,
Leg crossing leg, one foot on the dog's back,
Playing a decent cribbage with his maid
(Jacynth, you're sure her name was) o'er the cheese
And fruit, three red halves of starved winter-pears,
Or treat of radishes in April. Nine,
Ten, struck the church clock, straight to bed went he.

   My father, like the man of sense he was,
Would point him out to me a dozen times;
" 'St—'St," he 'd whisper, "the Corregidor!"[4]
I had been used to think that personage
Was one with lacquered breeches, lustrous belt,
And feathers like a forest in his hat,
Who blew a trumpet and proclaimed the news,
Announced the bullfights, gave each church its turn,
And memorized the miracle in vogue!
He had a great observance from us boys;
We were in error; that was not the man.

   I'd like now, yet had haply been afraid,
To have just looked, when this man came to die,
And seen who lined the clean gay garret-sides
And stood about the neat low truckle-bed,°   *trundle-bed*

3. Paintings by the great Venetian painter
Titian (ca. 1477–1576).
4. The chief magistrate or governor of a
Spanish town. (The speaker, as a boy, had
taken the town-crier, in his showy costume, for
the Corregidor.)

With the heavenly manner of relieving guard.
Here had been, mark, the general-in-chief,
105   Thro a whole campaign of the world's life and death,
Doing the King's work all the dim day long,
In his old coat and up to knees in mud,
Smoked like a herring, dining on a crust,
And, now the day was won, relieved at once!
110   No further show or need for that old coat,
You are sure, for one thing! Bless us, all the while
How sprucely we are dressed out, you and I!
A second, and the angels alter that.
Well, I could never write a verse—could you?
115   Let's to the Prado[5] and make the most of time.

1855

Memorabilia

1

Ah, did you once see Shelley plain,
    And did he stop and speak to you
And did you speak to him again?
    How strange it seems and new!

2

5   But you were living before that,
    And also you are living after;
And the memory I started at—
    My starting moves your laughter.

3

I crossed a moor, with a name of its own
10   And a certain use in the world no doubt,
Yet a hand's-breadth of it shines alone
    'Mid the blank miles round about:

4

For there I picked up on the heather
    And there I put inside my breast
15   A moulted feather, an eagle-feather!
    Well, I forget the rest.

1855

Andrea del Sarto[6]

CALLED "THE FAULTLESS PAINTER"

But do not let us quarrel any more,
No, my Lucrezia; bear with me for once:
Sit down and all shall happen as you wish.
You turn your face, but does it bring your heart?
5   I'll work then for your friend's friend, never fear,
Treat his own subject after his own way,
Fix his own time, accept too his own price,

5. The city walk, where the townspeople take the air.
6. Andrea del Sarto (1486–1530), the Florentine painter, spent his entire life in Florence except for a year's sojourn at the court of the French king, Francis I, at Fontainebleau, 1518–19. He had been married since 1517 to Lucrezia del Fede, a widow, and in response to her pleading he left Fontainebleau, with the understanding that he would soon return to complete work for which he had been paid. But he did not return, and he spent money which the king had given him to purchase works of art in Italy on a house in Florence for him and Lucrezia. These and other facts Browning derived from Vasari's *Life* of Andrea (in his *Lives of the Most Eminent Painters, Sculptors, and Architects*). But the poem also depends inevitably on Browning's own response to Andrea's art.

And shut the money into this small hand
When next it takes mine. Will it? tenderly?
Oh, I'll content him—but tomorrow, Love!
I often am much wearier than you think,
This evening more than usual, and it seems
As if—forgive now—should you let me sit
Here by the window with your hand in mine
And look a half-hour forth on Fiesole,[7]
Both of one mind, as married people use,
Quietly, quietly the evening through
I might get up tomorrow to my work
Cheerful and fresh as ever. Let us try.
Tomorrow, how you shall be glad for this!
Your soft hand is a woman of itself,
And mine the man's bared breast she curls inside.
Don't count the time lost, neither; you must serve
For each of the five pictures we require:
It saves a model. So! keep looking so—
My serpentining beauty, rounds on rounds!
—How could you ever prick those perfect ears,
Even to put the pearl there! oh, so sweet—
My face, my moon, my everybody's moon,
Which everybody looks on and calls his,
And, I suppose, is looked on by in turn,
While she looks—no one's: very dear, no less.
You smile? why, there's my picture ready made,
There's what we painters call our harmony!
A common grayness silvers everything,
All in a twilight, you and I alike
—You, at the point of your first pride in me
(That's gone you know)—but I, at every point;
My youth, my hope, my art, being all toned down
To yonder sober pleasant Fiesole.
There's the bell clinking from the chapel-top;
That length of convent-wall across the way
Holds the trees safer, huddled more inside;
The last monk leaves the garden; days decrease,
And autumn grows, autumn in everything.
Eh? the whole seems to fall into a shape
As if I saw alike my work and self
And all that I was born to be and do,
A twilight-piece. Love, we are in God's hand.
How strange now, looks the life he makes us lead;
So free we seem, so fettered fast we are!
I feel he laid the fetter: let it lie!
This chamber for example—turn your head—
All that's behind us! You don't understand
Nor care to understand about my art,
But you can hear at least when people speak:
And that cartoon,[8] the second from the door
—It is the thing, Love! so such things should be—
Behold Madonna! I am bold to say.
I can do with my pencil what I know,
What I see, what at bottom of my heart

7. A small town on the crown of a hill above Florence.
8. A preparatory drawing, on heavy paper, of the same size as the painting to be executed from it in oil or fresco.

I wish for, if I ever wish so deep—
Do easily, too—when I say, perfectly,
I do not boast, perhaps: yourself are judge,
65 Who listened to the Lagate's[9] talk last week,
And just as much they used to say in France.
At any rate 'tis easy, all of it!
No sketches first, no studies, that's long past:
I do what many dream of, all their lives,
70 —Dream? strive to do, and agonize to do,
And fail in doing. I could count twenty such
On twice your fingers, and not leave this town,
Who strive—you don't know how the others strive
To paint a little thing like that you smeared
75 Carelessly passing with your robes afloat—
Yet do much less, so much less, Someone says,
(I know his name, no matter)—so much less!
Well, less is more, Lucrezia: I am judged.
There burns a truer light of God in them,
80 In their vexed beating stuffed and stopped-up brain,
Heart, or whate'er else, than goes on to prompt
This low-pulsed forthright craftsman's hand of mine.
Their works drop groundward, but themselves, I know,
Reach many a time a heaven that's shut to me,
85 Enter and take their place there sure enough,
Though they come back and cannot tell the world.
My works are nearer heaven, but I sit here.
The sudden blood of these men! at a word—
Praise them, it boils, or blame them, it boils too.
90 I, painting from myself and to myself,
Know what I do, am unmoved by men's blame
Or their praise either. Somebody remarks
Morello's[1] outline there is wrongly traced,
His hue mistaken; what of that? or else,
95 Rightly traced and well ordered; what of that?
Speak as they please, what does the mountain care?
Ah, but a man's reach should exceed his grasp,
Or what's a heaven for? All is silver-gray
Placid and perfect with my art: the worse!
100 I know both what I want and what might gain,
And yet how profitless to know, to sigh
"Had I been two, another and myself,
Our head would have o'erlooked the world!" No doubt.
Yonder's a work now, of that famous youth
105 The Urbinate[2] who died five years ago.
('Tis copied, George Vasari[3] sent it me.)
Well, I can fancy how he did it all,
Pouring his soul, with kings and popes to see,
Reaching, that heaven might so replenish him,
110 Above and through his art—for it gives way;
That arm is wrongly put—and there again—
A fault to pardon in the drawing's lines,
Its body, so to speak: its soul is right,
He means right—that, a child may understand.

9. The Pope's representative.
1. Monte Morello, a mountain lying a little to the northwest of Florence in the Apennines.
2. The painter Raphael (1483–1520), so called because he was born at Urbino.
3. Giorgio Vasari, the biographer, himself a painter and an architect, had been Andrea's pupil.

5 Still, what an arm! and I could alter it:
But all the play, the insight and the stretch—
Out of me, out of me! And wherefore out?
Had you enjoined them on me, given me soul,
We might have risen to Rafael, I and you!
10 Nay, Love, you did give all I asked, I think—
More than I merit, yes, by many times.
But had you—oh, with the same perfect brow,
And perfect eyes, and more than perfect mouth,
And the low voice my soul hears, as a bird
15 The fowler's° pipe, and follows to the snare—   **bird-catcher's**
Had you, with these the same, but brought a mind!
Some women do so. Had the mouth there urged
"God and the glory! never care for gain.
The present by the future, what is that?
20 Live for fame, side by side with Agnolo![4]
"Rafael is waiting: up to God, all three!"
I might have done it for you. So it seems:
Perhaps not. All is as God over-rules.
Beside, incentives come from the soul's self;
25 The rest avail not. Why do I need you?
What wife had Rafael, or has Agnolo?
In this world, who can do a thing, will not;
And who would do it, cannot, I perceive:
Yet the will's somewhat—somewhat, too, the power—
30 And thus we half-men struggle. At the end,
God, I conclude, compensates, punishes.
'Tis safer for me, if the award be strict,
That I am something underrated here,
Poor this long while, despised, to speak the truth.
35 I dared not, do you know, leave home all day,
For fear of chancing on the Paris lords.
The best is when they pass and look aside;
But they speak sometimes; I must bear it all.
Well may they speak! That Francis, that first time,
50 And that long festal year at Fontainebleau!
I surely then could sometimes leave the ground,
Put on the glory, Rafael's daily wear,
In that humane great monarch's golden look—
One finger in his beard or twisted curl
55 Over his mouth's good mark that made the smile,
One arm about my shoulder, round my neck,
The jingle of his gold chain in my ear,
I painting proudly with his breath on me,
All his court round him, seeing with his eyes,
60 Such frank French eyes, and such a fire of souls
Profuse, my hand kept plying by those hearts—
And, best of all, this, this, this face beyond,
This in the background, waiting on my work,
To crown the issue with a last reward!
65 A good time, was it not, my kingly days?
And had you not grown restless . . . but I know—
'Tis done and past; 'twas right, my instinct said;
Too live the life grew, golden and not gray,
And I'm the weak-eyed bat no sun should tempt
70 Out of the grange° whose four walls make his world.   **country house**

4. I.e., Michelangelo (1475–1564).

How could it end in any other way?
You called me, and I came home to your heart.
The triumph was—to reach and stay there; since
I reached it ere the triumph, what is lost?
175 Let my hands frame your face in your hair's gold,
You beautiful Lucrezia that are mine!
"Rafael did this, Andrea painted that;
"The Roman's is the better when you pray,
"But still the other's Virgin was his wife—"
180 Men will excuse me. I am glad to judge
Both pictures in your presence; clearer grows
My better fortune, I resolve to think.
For, do you know, Lucrezia, as God lives,
Said one day Agnolo, his very self,
185 To Rafael . . . I have known it all these years . . .
(When the young man was flaming out his thoughts
Upon a palace-wall for Rome to see,
Too lifted up in heart because of it)
"Friend, there's a certain sorry little scrub
190 Goes up and down our Florence, none cares how,
Who, were he set to plan and execute
As you are, pricked on by your popes and kings,
Would bring the sweat into that brow of yours!"
To Rafael's! And indeed the arm is wrong.
195 I hardly dare . . . yet, only you to see,
Give the chalk here—quick, thus the line should go!
Ay, but the soul! he's Rafael! rub it out!
Still, all I care for, if he spoke the truth,
(What he? why, who but Michel Agnolo?
200 Do you forget already words like those?)
If really there was such a chance, so lost,
Is, whether you're—not grateful—but more pleased.
Well, let me think so. And you smile indeed!
This hour has been an hour! Another smile?
205 If you would sit thus by me every night
I should work better, do you comprehend?
I mean that I should earn more, give you more.
See, it is settled dusk now; there's a star;
Morello's gone, the watch-lights show the wall,
210 The cue-owls[5] speak the name we call them by.
Come from the window, love—come in, at last,
Inside the melancholy little house
We built to be so gay with. God is just.
King Francis may forgive me: oft at nights
215 When I look up from painting, eyes tired out,
The walls become illumined, brick from brick
Distinct, instead of mortar, fierce bright gold,
That gold of his I did cement them with!
Let us but love each other. Must you go?
220 That Cousin here again? he waits outside?
Must see you—you, and not with me? Those loans?
More gaming debts to pay? you smiled for that?
Well, let smiles buy me! have you more to spend?
While hand and eye and something of a heart
225 Are left me, work's my ware, and what's it worth?

5. A Mediterranean owl whose name derives from its cry, *ki-ou.*

I'll pay my fancy. Only let me sit
The gray remainder of the evening out,
Idle, you call it, and muse perfectly
How I could paint, were I but back in France,
One picture, just one more—the Virgin's face,
Not yours this time! I want you at my side
To hear them—that is, Michel Agnolo—
Judge all I do and tell you of its worth.
Will you? Tomorrow, satisfy your friend.
I take the subjects for his corridor,
Finish the portrait out of hand—there, there,
And throw him in another thing or two
If he demurs; the whole should prove enough
To pay for this same Cousin's freak. Beside,
What's better and what's all I care about,
Get you the thirteen scudi[6] for the ruff!
Love, does that please you? Ah, but what does he,
The Cousin! what does he to please you more?

I am grown peaceful as old age tonight.
I regret little, I would change still less.
Since there my past life lies, why alter it?
The very wrong to Francis! it is true
I took his coin, was tempted and complied,
And built this house and sinned, and all is said.
My father and my mother died of want.
Well, had I riches of my own? you see
How one gets rich! Let each one bear his lot.
They were born poor, lived poor, and poor they died:
And I have labored somewhat in my time
And not been paid profusely. Some good son
Paint my two hundred pictures—let him try!
No doubt, there's something strikes a balance. Yes,
You loved me quite enough, it seems tonight.
This must suffice me here. What would one have?
In heaven, perhaps, new chances, one more chance—
Four great walls in the New Jerusalem,[7]
Meted on each side by the angel's reed,
For Leonard,[8] Rafael, Agnolo and me
To cover—the three first without a wife,
While I have mine! So—still they overcome
Because there's still Lucrezia—as I choose.

Again the Cousin's whistle! Go, my Love.

1855

Two in the Campagna[9]

1

I wonder do you feel today
    As I have felt since, hand in hand,
We sat down on the grass, to stray
    In spirit better through the land,
This morn of Rome and May?

6. A *scudo* (*shield*, in Italian) was a silver
coin bearing a shield.
7. Mentioned in Revelation xxi.10–21.
8. I.e., Leonardo da Vinci (1452–1519).

9. The grassy, rolling countryside around
Rome; it was malarial, and hence semi-
deserted, until Mussolini reclaimed the Pontine
marshes.

2

For me, I touched a thought, I know,
  Has tantalized me many times,
(Like turns of thread the spiders throw
  Mocking across our path) for rhymes
10 To catch at and let go.

3

Help me to hold it! First it left
  The yellowing fennel,[1] run to seed
There, branching from the brickwork's cleft,
  Some old tomb's ruin: yonder weed
15 Took up the floating weft,°   *spider-web*

4

Where one small orange cup amassed
  Five beetles—blind and green they grope
Among the honey-meal: and last,
  Everywhere on the grassy slope
20 I traced it. Hold it fast!

5

The champaign[2] with its endless fleece
  Of feathery grasses everywhere!
Silence and passion, joy and peace,
  An everlasting wash of air—
25 Rome's ghost since her decease.

6

Such life here, through such lengths of hours,
  Such miracles performed in play,
Such primal naked forms of flowers,
  Such letting nature have her way
30 While heaven looks from its towers!

7

How say you? Let us, O my dove,
  Let us be unashamed of soul,
As earth lies bare to heaven above!
  How is it under our control
35 To love or not to love?

8

I would that you were all to me,
  You that are just so much, no more.
Nor yours nor mine, nor slave nor free!
  Where does the fault lie? What the core
40 O' the wound, since wound must be?

9

I would I could adopt your will,
  See with your eyes, and set my heart
Beating by yours, and drink my fill
  At your soul's springs—your part my part
45 In life, for good and ill.

10

No. I yearn upward, touch you close,
  Then stand away. I kiss your cheek,
Catch your soul's warmth—I pluck the rose
  And love it more than tongue can speak—
50 Then the good minute goes.

---

1. A yellow-flowered plant, whose aromatic   2. I.e., grassland—here, the Campagna itself.
seeds are used as a condiment.

11

Already how am I so far
Out of that minute? Must I go
Still like the thistle-ball, no bar,
   Onward, whenever light winds blow,
Fixed by no friendly star?

12

Just when I seemed about to learn!
   Where is the thread now? Off again!
The old trick! Only I discern—
   Infinite passion, and the pain
Of finite hearts that yearn.

1855

Caliban upon Setebos[2]

OR NATURAL THEOLOGY IN THE ISLAND

> *"Thou thoughtest that I was altogether such a one as thyself."*
> —PSALMS 1.21

['Will sprawl, now that the heat of day is best,
Flat on his belly in the pit's much mire,
With elbows wide, fists clenched to prop his chin.
And, while he kicks both feet in the cool slush,
And feels about his spine small eft-things[3] course,
Run in and out each arm, and make him laugh:
And while above his head a pompion-plant,°   *pumpkin-plant*
Coating the cave-top as a brow its eye,
Creeps down to touch and tickle hair and beard,
And now a flower drops with a bee inside,
And now a fruit to snap at, catch and crunch—
He looks out o'er yon sea which sunbeams cross
And recross till they weave a spider-web
(Meshes of fire, some great fish breaks at times)
And talks to his own self, howe'er he please,
Touching that other, whom his dam called God.
Because to talk about Him, vexes—ha,
Could He but know! and time to vex is now,
When talk is safer than in winter-time.
Moreover Prosper and Miranda sleep
In confidence he drudges at their task,
And it is good to cheat the pair, and gibe,
Letting the rank tongue blossom into speech.]

Setebos, Setebos, and Setebos!
'Thinketh, He dwelleth i' the cold o' the moon.

'Thinketh He made it, with the sun to match,
But not the stars; the stars came otherwise;
Only made clouds, winds, meteors, such as that:
Also this isle, what lives and grows thereon,
And snaky sea which rounds and ends the same.

2. Caliban is the "savage and deformed slave" of Shakespeare's *The Tempest*, unwilling servant of the magician Prospero and his daughter Miranda. The poem presents his reflections as he tries, by analogy with his own actions and motives, to understand the nature of the god Setebos, of whom he has learned from his mother (the witch Sycorax) and whom he fears. In order to account for all the workings of the universe as he sees it, Caliban postulates a power above Setebos which he terms the Quiet. "Natural theology" is the attempt to deduce the ultimate nature of God from the signs afforded in the world of nature which he has created. Caliban most often speaks of himself in the third person, particularly in the verbs which introduce his reflections: perhaps as a safeguard against being overheard and identified by Setebos.
3. Small newt-like creatures.

'Thinketh, it came of being ill at ease:
He hated that He cannot change His cold,
Nor cure its ache. 'Hath spied an icy fish
That longed to 'scape the rock-stream where she lived,
35   And thaw herself within the lukewarm brine
O' the lazy sea her stream thrusts far amid,
A crystal spike 'twixt two warm walls of wave;
Only, she ever sickened, found repulse
At the other kind of water, not her life,
40   (Green-dense and dim-delicious, bred o' the sun)
Flounced back from bliss she was not born to breathe,
And in her old bounds buried her despair,
Hating and loving warmth alike: so He.

'Thinketh, He made thereat the sun, this isle,
45   Trees and the fowls here, beast and creeping thing.
Yon otter, sleek-wet, black, lithe as a leech;
Yon auk,° one fire-eye in a ball of foam,   *sea-bird*
That floats and feeds; a certain badger brown
He hath watched hunt with that slant white-wedge eye
50   By moonlight; and the pie° with the long tongue   *magpie*
That pricks deep into oakwarts[4] for a worm,
And says a plain word when she finds her prize,
But will not eat the ants; the ants themselves
That build a wall of seeds and settled stalks
55   About their hole—He made all these and more,
Made all we see, and us, in spite: how else?
He could not, Himself, make a second self
To be His mate; as well have made Himself:
He would not make what he mislikes or slights,
60   An eyesore to Him, or not worth His pains:
But did, in envy, listlessness or sport,
Make what Himself would fain, in a manner, be—
Weaker in most points, stronger in a few,
Worthy, and yet mere playthings all the while,
65   Things He admires and mocks too—that is it.
Because, so brave, so better though they be,
It nothing skills[5] if He begin to plague.
Look now, I melt a gourd-fruit into mash,
Add honeycomb and pods, I have perceived,
70   Which bite like finches when they bill and kiss—
Then, when froth rises bladdery,[6] drink up all,
Quick, quick, till maggots scamper through my brain;
Last, throw me on my back i' the seeded thyme,
And wanton, wishing I were born a bird.
75   Put case, unable to be what I wish,
I yet could make a live bird out of clay:
Would not I take clay, pinch my Caliban
Able to fly? for, there, see, he hath wings,
And great comb like the hoopoe's[7] to admire,
80   And there, a sting to do his foes offense,
There, and I will that he begin to live,
Fly to yon rock-top, nip me off the horns
Of grigs° high up that make the merry din,   *grasshoppers*

4. Oak-gall, a growth produced on the oak by   6. I.e., with bladder-like bubbles in it.
the gall-fly.   7. A bird with bright plumage and conspicuous
5. I.e., it makes no difference.   large crest.

Saucy through their veined wings, and mind me not.
5 In which feat, if his leg snapped, brittle clay,
And he lay stupid-like—why, I should laugh;
And if he, spying me, should fall to weep,
Beseech me to be good, repair his wrong,
Bid his poor leg smart less or grow again—
10 Well, as the chance were, this might take or else
Not take my fancy: I might hear his cry,
And give the mankin three sound legs for one,
Or pluck the other off, leave him like an egg,
And lessoned he was mine and merely clay.
15 Were this no pleasure, lying in the thyme,
Drinking the mash, with brain become alive,
Making and marring clay at will? So He.

'Thinketh, such shows nor right nor wrong in Him,
Nor kind, nor cruel: He is strong and Lord.
20 'Am strong myself compared to yonder crabs
That march now from the mountain to the sea;
'Let twenty pass, and stone the twenty-first,
Loving not, hating not, just choosing so.
'Say, the first straggler that boasts purple spots
25 Shall join the file, one pincer twisted off;
'Say, this bruised fellow shall receive a worm,
And two worms he whose nippers end in red;
As it likes me each time, I do: so He.

Well then, 'supposeth He is good i' the main,
30 Placable if His mind and ways were guessed,
But rougher than his handiwork, be sure!
Oh, He hath made things worthier than Himself,
And envieth that, so helped, such things do more
Than He who made them! What consoles but this?
35 That they, unless through Him, do nought at all,
And must submit: what other use in things?
'Hath cut a pipe of pithless elder-joint
That, blown through, gives exact the scream o' the jay
When from her wing you twitch the feathers blue:
40 Sound this, and little birds that hate the jay
Flock within stone's throw, glad their foe is hurt:
Put case such pipe could prattle and boast forsooth
"I catch the birds, I am the crafty thing,
I make the cry my maker cannot make
45 With his great round mouth; he must blow through mine!"
Would not I smash it with my foot? So He.

But wherefore rough, why cold and ill at ease?
Aha, that is a question! Ask, for that,
What knows—the something over Setebos
50 That made Him, or He, may be, found and fought,
Worsted, drove off and did to nothing, perchance.
There may be something quiet o'er His head,
Out of His reach, that feels nor joy nor grief,
Since both derive from weakness in some way.
55 I joy because the quails come; would not joy
Could I bring quails here when I have a mind:
This Quiet, all it hath a mind to, doth.

'Esteemeth stars the outposts of its couch,
But never spends much thought nor care that way.
140 It may look up, work up—the worse for those
It works on! 'Careth but for Setebos
The many-handed as a cuttle-fish,
Who, making Himself feared through what He does,
Looks up, first, and perceives he cannot soar
145 To what is quiet and hath happy life;
Next looks down here, and out of very spite
Makes this a bauble-world to ape yon real,
These good things to match those as hips[8] do grapes.
'Tis solace making baubles, ay, and sport.
150 Himself[9] peeped late, eyed Prosper at his books
Careless and lofty, lord now of the isle:
Vexed, 'stitched a book of broad leaves, arrow-shaped,
Wrote thereon, he knows what, prodigious words;
Has peeled a wand and called it by a name;
155 Weareth at whiles for an enchanter's robe
The eyed skin of a supple oncelot;°   *ocelot*
And hath an ounce[1] sleeker than youngling mole,
A four-legged serpent he makes cower and couch,
Now snarl, now hold its breath and mind his eye,
160 And saith she is Miranda and my wife:
'Keeps for his Ariel[2] a tall pouch-bill crane
He bids go wade for fish and straight disgorge;
Also a sea-beast, lumpish, which he snared,
Blinded the eyes of, and brought somewhat tame,
165 And split its toe-webs, and now pens the drudge
In a hole o' the rock and calls him Caliban;
A bitter heart that bides its time and bites.
'Plays thus at being Prosper in a way,
Taketh his mirth with make-believes: so He.

170 His dam held that the Quiet made all things
Which Setebos vexed only: 'holds not so.
Who made them weak, meant weakness He might vex.
Had He meant other, while His hand was in,
Why not make horny eyes no thorn could prick,
175 Or plate my scalp with bone against the snow,
Or overscale my flesh 'neath joint and joint,
Like an orc's° armor? Ay, so spoil His sport!   *sea-monster*
He is the One now: only He doth all.

'Saith, He may like, perchance, what profits Him.
180 Ay, himself loves what does him good; but why?
'Gets good no otherwise. This blinded beast
Loves whoso places flesh-meat on his nose,
But, had he eyes, would want no help, but hate
Or love, just as it liked him: He hath eyes.
185 Also it pleaseth Setebos to work,
Use all His hands, and exercise much craft,
By no mean for the love of what is worked.
'Tasteth, himself, no finer good i' the world
When all goes right, in this safe summer-time,
190 And he wants little, hungers, aches not much,

8. Round bright-red fruit of the wild rose.   leopard but smaller.
9. I.e., Caliban.   2. The airy spirit in *The Tempest*, Prospero's
1. Animal of the cat family, marked like the   aide in carrying out his plans.

Than trying what to do with wit and strength.
'Falls to make something: 'piled yon pile of turfs,
And squared and stuck there squares of soft white chalk,
And, with a fish-tooth, scratched a moon on each,
And set up endwise certain spikes of tree,
And crowned the whole with a sloth's skull a-top,
Found dead i' the woods, too hard for one to kill.
No use at all i' the work, for work's sole sake;
'Shall some day knock it down again: so He.

'Saith He is terrible: watch His feats in proof!
One hurricane will spoil six good months' hope.
He hath a spite against me, that I know,
Just as He favors Prosper, who knows why?
So it is, all the same, as well I find.
'Wove wattles[3] half the winter, fenced them firm
With stone and stake to stop she-tortoises
Crawling to lay their eggs here: well, one wave,
Feeling the foot of Him upon its neck,
Gaped as a snake does, lolled out its large tongue,
And licked the whole labor flat: so much for spite.
'Saw a ball flame down late (yonder it lies)
Where, half an hour before, I slept i' the shade:
Often they scatter sparkles: there is force!
'Dug up a newt He may have envied once
And turned to stone, shut up inside a stone.
Please Him and hinder this? What Prosper does?
Aha, if He would tell me how! Not He!
There is the sport: discover how or die!
All need not die, for of the things o' the isle
Some flee afar, some dive, some run up trees;
Those at His mercy—why, they please Him most
When . . . when . . . well, never try the same way twice!
Repeat what act has pleased, He may grow wroth.
You must not know His ways, and play Him off,
Sure of the issue. 'Doth the like himself:
'Spareth a squirrel that it nothing fears
But steals the nut from underneath my thumb,
And when I threat, bites stoutly in defense:
'Spareth an urchin that contrariwise,
Curls up into a ball, pretending death
For fright at my approach: the two ways please.
But what would move my choler more than this,
That either creature counted on its life
Tomorrow and next day and all days to come,
Saying, forsooth, in the inmost of its heart,
"Because he did so yesterday with me,
"And otherwise with such another brute,
"So must he do henceforth and always."—Ay?
Would teach the reasoning couple[4] what "must" means!
'Doth as he likes, or wherefore Lord? So He.

'Conceiveth all things will continue thus,
And we shall have to live in fear of Him
So long as He lives, keeps His strength: no change,

---

3. Flexible rods woven into a framework for roofs or walls.
4. I.e., the two creatures Caliban has spared,

the squirrel (line 226) and the hedgehog ("urchin" [line 229]), and who "reason" that he will continue to spare them.

If He have done His best, make no new world
To please Him more, so leave off watching this—
If He surprise not even the Quiet's self
Some strange day—or, suppose, grow into it
As grubs grow butterflies: else, here are we,
And there is He, and nowhere help at all.

'Believeth with the life, the pain shall stop.
His dam[5] held different, that after death
He both plagued enemies and feasted friends:
Idly! He doth His worst in this our life,
Giving just respite lest we die through pain,
Saving last pain for worst—with which, an end.
Meanwhile, the best way to escape His ire
Is, not to seem too happy. 'Sees, himself,
Yonder two flies, with purple films and pink,
Bask on the pompion-bell above: kills both.
'Sees two black painful beetles roll their ball
On head and tail as if to save their lives:
Moves them the stick away they strive to clear.

Even so, 'would have Him misconceive, suppose
This Caliban strives hard and ails no less,
And always, above all else, envies Him;
Wherefore he mainly dances on dark nights,
Moans in the sun, gets under holes to laugh,
And never speaks his mind save housed as now:
Outside, 'groans, curses. If He caught me here,
O'erheard this speech, and asked "What chucklest at?"
'Would, to appease Him, cut a finger off,
Or of my three kid yearlings burn the best,
Or let the toothsome apples rot on tree,
Or push my tame beast for the orc to taste:
While myself lit a fire, and made a song
And sung it, *"What I hate, be consecrate*
"To celebrate Thee and Thy state, no mate
"For Thee; what see for envy in poor me?"
Hoping the while, since evils sometimes mend,
Warts rub away and sores are cured with slime,
That some strange day, will either the Quiet catch
And conquer Setebos, or likelier He
Decrepit may doze, doze, as good as die.

[What, what? A curtain o'er the world at once!
Crickets stop hissing; not a bird—or, yes,
There scuds His raven that has told Him all!
It was fool's play, this prattling! Ha! The wind
Shoulders the pillared dust, death's house o' the move,[6]
And fast invading fires begin! White blaze—
A tree's head snaps—and there, there, there, there, there,
His thunder follows! Fool to gibe at Him!
Lo! 'Lieth flat and loveth Setebos!
'Maketh his teeth meet through his upper lip,
Will let those quails fly, will not eat this month
One little mess of whelks,° so he may 'scape!]

°*shellfish*

1860   1864

---

5. I.e., Caliban's mother.

6. A small whirlwind containing dust, the dust to which living creatures return in death.

HENRY DAVID THOREAU
(1817–1862)

I Am a Parcel of Vain Strivings Tied

I am a parcel of vain strivings tied
  By a chance bond together,
Dangling this way and that, their links
  Were made so loose and wide,
     Methinks,
    For milder weather.

A bunch of violets without their roots,
  And sorrel intermixed,
Encircled by a wisp of straw
  Once coiled about their shoots,
     The law
    By which I'm fixed.

A nosegay which Time clutched from out
  Those fair Elysian fields,[1]
With weeds and broken stems, in haste,
  Doth make the rabble rout
     That waste
    The day he yields.

And here I bloom for a short hour unseen,
  Drinking my juices up,
With no root in the land
  To keep my branches green,
     But stand
    In a bare cup.

1841

The Inward Morning

Packed in my mind lie all the clothes
  Which outward nature wears,
And in its fashion's hourly change
  It all things else repairs.

In vain I look for change abroad,
  And can no difference find,
Till some new ray of peace uncalled
  Illumes my inmost mind.

What is it gilds the trees and clouds,
  And paints the heavens so gay,
But yonder fast-abiding light
  With its unchanging ray?

1. In Greek mythology, the home of the blessed in the afterlife.

Lo, when the sun streams through the wood,
    Upon a winter's morn,
15 Where'er his silent beams intrude
    The murky night is gone.

How could the patient pine have known
    The morning breeze would come,
Or humble flowers anticipate
20   The insect's noonday hum,

Till the new light with morning cheer
    From far streamed through the aisles,
And nimbly told the forest trees
    For many stretching miles?

25 I've heard within my inmost soul
    Such cheerful morning news,
In the horizon of my mind
    Have seen such orient hues,

As in the twilight of the dawn,
30   When the first birds awake,
Are heard within some silent wood,
    Where they the small twigs break,

Or in the eastern skies are seen,
    Before the sun appears,
35 The harbingers of summer heats
    Which from afar he bears.

                               1842, 1849

Haze

Woof of the sun, ethereal gauze,
Woven of Nature's richest stuffs,
Visible heat, air-water and dry sea,
Last conquest of the eye;
5 Toil of the day displayed, sun-dust,
Aerial surf upon the shores of earth,
Ethereal estuary, frith[2] of light,
Breakers of air, billows of heat,
Fine summer spray on inland seas;
10 Bird of the sun, transparent-winged
Owlet of noon, soft-pinioned,
From heath or stubble rising without song,
Establish thy serenity o'er the fields.

                               1843, 1849

Smoke

Light-winged Smoke, Icarian bird,[3]
Melting thy pinions in thy upward flight;
Lark without song, and messenger of dawn,
Circling above the hamlets as thy nest;

2. In this context of sea-land imagery, a narrow channel.
3. Icarus, like his father Daedalus in Greek mythology, tried to escape Crete by flying with wings of wax and feathers. Icarus flew too near the sun, which melted his wings.

Or else, departing dream, and shadowy form
Of midnight vision, gathering up thy skirts;
By night star-veiling, and by day
Darkening the light and blotting out the sun;
Go thou my incense upward from this hearth,
And ask the gods to pardon this clear flame.

1843,   1854

Love Equals Swift and Slow

Love equals swift and slow,
    And high and low,
Racer and lame,
    The hunter and his game.

1849

Low-Anchored Cloud

Low-anchored cloud,
Newfoundland air,
Fountainhead and source of rivers,
Dew-cloth, dream drapery,
And napkin spread by fays;°   *fairies, elves*
Drifting meadow of the air,
Where bloom the daisied banks and violets,
And in whose fenny⁴ labyrinth
The bittern booms and heron wades;
Spirit of lakes and seas and rivers,
Bear only perfumes and the scent
Of healing herbs to just men's fields!

1842   1868?

EMILY BRONTË
(1818–1848)

[Long Neglect Has Worn Away]

Long neglect has worn away
Half the sweet enchanting smile;
Time has turned the bloom to gray;
Mold and damp the face defile.

5   But that lock of silky hair,
Still beneath the picture twined,
Tells what once those features were,
Paints their image on the mind.

Fair the hand that traced that line,
10   "Dearest, ever deem me true";
Swiftly flew the fingers fine
When the pen that motto drew.

1837   1923

4. Characterizing the swampy ground, or bog, along a shore.

Hope

Hope was but a timid friend—
She sat without ° my grated den   outside
Watching how my fate would tend
Even as selfish-hearted men.

5   She was cruel in her fear.
Through the bars, one dreary day,
I looked out to see her there
And she turned her face away!

Like a false guard false watch keeping
10 Still in strife she whispered peace;
She would sing while I was weeping,
If I listened, she would cease.

False she was, and unrelenting.
When my last joys stewed the ground
15 Even Sorrow saw repenting
Those sad relics scattered round;

Hope—whose whisper would have given
Balm to all that frenzied pain—
Stretched her wings and soared to heaven;
20 Went—and ne'er returned again!

                                        1843   1846

Remembrance [1]

Cold in the earth—and the deep snow piled above thee,
Far, far removed, cold in the dreary grave!
Have I forgot, my only Love, to love thee,
Severed at last by Time's all-severing wave?

5   Now, when alone, do my thoughts no longer hover
Over the mountains, on that northern shore,
Resting their wings where heath and fern leaves cover
Thy noble heart forever, ever more?

Cold in the earth—and fifteen wild Decembers,
10 From those brown hills, have melted into spring;
Faithful, indeed, is the spirit that remembers
After such years of change and suffering!

Sweet Love of youth, forgive, if I forget thee,
While the world's tide is bearing me along;
15 Other desires and other hopes beset me,
Hopes which obscure, but cannot do thee wrong!

No later light has lightened up my heaven,
No second morn has ever shone for me;
All my life's bliss from thy dear life was given,
20 All my life's bliss is in the grave with thee.

1. One of the Gondal poems. As children, Emily and Anne Brontë had written poems and stories about the inhabitants of Gondal, an imaginary island in the North Pacific, and Emily, at least, continued to write Gondal poems throughout her life.

But, when the days of golden dreams had perished,
And even Despair was powerless to destroy,
Then did I learn how existence could be cherished,
Strengthened, and fed without the aid of joy.

Then did I check the tears of useless passion—
Weaned my young soul from yearning after thine;
Sternly denied its burning wish to hasten
Down to that tomb already more than mine.

And, even yet, I dare not let it languish,
Dare not indulge in memory's rapturous pain;
Once drinking deep of that divinest anguish,
How could I seek the empty world again?

                                        1845   1846

The Prisoner

"Still let my tyrants know, I am not doomed to wear
Year after year in gloom, and desolate despair;
A messenger of Hope comes every night to me,
And offers for short life, eternal liberty.

"He comes with western winds, with evening's wandering airs,
With that clear dusk of heaven that brings the thickest stars,
Winds take a pensive tone, and stars a tender fire,
And visions rise, and change, that kill me with desire.

"Desire for nothing known in my maturer years,
When Joy grew mad with awe, at counting future tears.
When, if my spirit's sky was full of flashes warm,
I knew not whence they came, from sun or thunderstorm.

"But, first, a hush of peace—a soundless calm descends;
The struggle of distress, and fierce impatience ends;
Mute music soothes my breast—unuttered harmony,
That I could never dream, till Earth was lost to me.

"Then dawns the Invisible; the Unseen its truth reveals;
My outward sense is gone, my inward essence feels:
Its wings are almost free—its home, its harbor found,
Measuring the gulf, it stoops and dares the final bound.

"O! dreadful is the check—intense the agony—
When the ear begins to hear, and the eye begins to see;
When the pulse begins to throb, the brain to think again;
The soul to feel the flesh, and the flesh to feel the chain.

"Yet I would lose no sting, would wish no torture less;
The more that anguish racks, the earlier it will bless;
And robed in fires of hell, or bright with heavenly shine,
If it but herald death, the vision is divine!"

                                        1845   1846

HERMAN MELVILLE
(1819–1891)

The Portent

Hanging from the beam,
  Slowly swaying (such the law),
Gaunt the shadow on your green,
  Shenandoah![1]
5 The cut is on the crown
    (Lo, John Brown),[2]
And the stabs shall heal no more.

Hidden in the cap
  Is the anguish none can draw;
10 So your future veils its face,
  Shenandoah!
But the streaming beard is shown
  (Weird John Brown),
The meteor of the war.

                      1859   1866

The March into Virginia

ENDING IN THE FIRST MANASSAS[3] (JULY 1861)

Did all the lets and bars appear
  To every just or larger end,
Whence should come the trust and cheer?
  Youth must its ignorant impulse lend—
5 Age finds place in the rear.
  All wars are boyish, and are fought by boys,
  The champions and enthusiasts of the state:
    Turbid ardours and vain joys
      Not barrenly abate—
10 Stimulants to the power mature,
    Preparatives of fate.

Who here forecasteth the event?
What heart but spurns at precedent
  And warnings of the wise,
15 Contemned foreclosures of surprise?
The banners play, the bugles call,
The air is blue and prodigal.
  No berrying party, pleasure-wooed,
  No picnic party in the May,
20 Ever went less loth than they
    Into that leafy neighbourhood.
In Bacchic glee they file toward Fate,
Moloch's[4] uninitiate;
  Expectancy, and glad surmise
25 Of battle's unknown mysteries.

1. Scene of famous Civil War battles between 1862 and 1864.
2. Leader of an abolitionist uprising at Harpers Ferry, West Virginia, for which he was hanged in 1859.

3. The battle on July 21, 1861, at Bull Run, where the Union forces were routed.
4. Idol to whom children were sacrificed in Old Testament days.

All they feel is this: 'tis glory,
A rapture sharp, though transitory,
Yet lasting in belaureled story.
So they gaily go to fight,
Chatting left and laughing right.

But some who this blithe mood present,
  As on in lightsome files they fare,
Shall die experienced ere three days are spent—
  Perish, enlightened by the volleyed glare;
Or shame survive, and, like to adamant,[5]
  The throe of Second Manassas[6] share.

1861   1866

The Housetop

A NIGHT PIECE (JULY 1863)

No sleep. The sultriness pervades the air
And binds the brain—a dense oppression, such
As tawny tigers feel in matted shades,
Vexing their blood and making apt for ravage.
Beneath the stars the roofy desert spreads
Vacant as Libya. All is hushed near by.
Yet fitfully from far breaks a mixed surf
Of muffled sound, the atheist roar of riot.
Yonder, where parching Sirius set in drought,
Balefully glares red Arson—there—and—there.
The town is taken by its rats—ship-rats
And rats of the wharves. All civil charms
And priestly spells which late held hearts in awe—
Fear-bound subjected to a better sway
Than sway of self; these like a dream dissolve,
And man rebounds whole eons back in nature.
Hail to the low dull rumble, dull and dead,
And ponderous drag that shakes the wall.
Wise Draco[7] comes, deep in the midnight roll
Of black artillery; he comes, though late;
In code corroborating Calvin's[8] creed
And cynic tyrannies of honest kings;
He comes, nor parleys; and the town, redeemed,
Gives thanks devout; nor, being thankful, heeds
The grimy slur on the Republic's faith implied,
Which holds that Man is naturally good,
And—more—is Nature's Roman, never to be scourged.

1863   1866

Shiloh[9]

A REQUIEM (APRIL 1862)

Skimming lightly, wheeling still,
  The swallows fly low
Over the field in clouded days,

5. Hard, unbreakable substance.
6. The second defeat of the Union forces at Manassas was on August 30, 1862.
7. Athenian statesman of the seventh century B.C., noted for the severity of his laws.
8. John Calvin (1509–64), Reformation theo- logian whose chief doctrine is that of man's corruption in Original Sin.
9. The battle at Shiloh church in Tennessee on April 6 and 7, 1862, was one of the bloodiest of the Civil War.

The forest-field of Shiloh—
5 Over the field where April rain
Solaced the parched one stretched in pain
Through the pause of night
That followed the Sunday fight
Around the church of Shiloh—
10 The church so lone, the log-built one,
That echoed to many a parting groan
    And natural prayer
Of dying foemen mingled there—
Foemen at morn, but friends at eve—
15   Fame or country least their care:
(What like a bullet can undeceive!)
    But now they lie low,
While over them the swallows skim,
And all is hushed at Shiloh.

1866

The Berg

A DREAM

I saw a ship of martial build
(Her standards set, her brave apparel on)
Directed as by madness mere
Against a stolid iceberg steer,
5 Nor budge it, though the infatuate ship went down.
The impact made huge ice-cubes fall
Sullen, in tons that crashed the deck;
But that one avalanche was all—
No other movement save the foundering wreck.

10 Along the spurs of ridges pale,
Not any slenderest shaft and frail,
A prism over glass-green gorges lone,
Toppled; nor lace of traceries fine,
Nor pendent drops in grot or mine
15 Were jarred, when the stunned ship went down.

Nor sole the gulls in cloud that wheeled
Circling one snow-flanked peak afar,
But nearer fowl the floes that skimmed
And crystal beaches, felt no jar.
20 No thrill transmitted stirred the lock
Of jack-straw needle-ice at base;
Towers undermined by waves—the block
Atilt impending—kept their place.
Seals, dozing sleek on sliddery ledges
25 Slipt never, when by loftier edges
Through very inertia overthrown,
The impetuous ship in bafflement went down.

Hard Berg (methought), so cold, so vast,
With mortal damps self-overcast;
30 Exhaling still thy dankish breath—
Adrift dissolving, bound for death;
Though lumpish thou, a lumbering one—

A lumbering lubbard loitering slow,
Impingers rue thee and go down,
Sounding thy precipice below,
Nor stir the slimy slug that sprawls
Along thy dead indifference of walls.

1888

The Maldive Shark

About the Shark, phlegmatical one,
Pale sot of the Maldive sea,
The sleek little pilot-fish, azure and slim,
How alert in attendance be.
From his saw-pit of mouth, from his charnel of maw,
They have nothing of harm to dread,
But liquidly glide on his ghastly flank
Or before his Gorgonian[1] head;
Or lurk in the port of serrated teeth
In white triple tiers of glittering gates,
And there find a haven when peril's abroad,
An asylum in jaws of the Fates!
They are friends; and friendly they guide him to prey,
Yet never partake of the treat—
Eyes and brains to the dotard lethargic and dull,
Pale ravener of horrible meat.

1888

Fragments of a Lost Gnostic[2] Poem of the Twelfth Century

.   .   .   .   .   .

Found a family, build a state,
The pledged event is still the same:
Matter in end will never abate
His ancient brutal claim.

.   .   .   .   .   .

Indolence is heaven's ally here,
And energy the child of hell:
The good man pouring from his pitcher clear
But brims the poisoned well.

1891

Greek Architecture

Not magnitude, not lavishness,
But form—the site;
Not innovating wilfulness,
But reverence for the archetype.

1891

---

1. In classical mythology, Gorgon was one of three sisters (Medusa was another) whose face and snake-entwined hair could turn the viewer to stone; hence, a thing so frightening as to freeze its beholder.

2. Reference to Gnosticism, a philosophical and religious movement of late antiquity and the early Christian era. The Church considered its views heretical.

The Apparition

A RETROSPECT

Convulsions came; and, where the field
    Long slept in pastoral green,
A goblin-mountain was upheaved
(Sure the scared sense was all deceived),
5   Marl-glen³ and slag-ravine.

The unreserve of ill was there,
    The clinkers in her last retreat;
But, ere the eye could take it in,
Or mind could comprehension win,
10   It sunk! and at our feet.

So, then, solidity's a crust—
    The core of fire below;
All may go well for many a year,
But who can think without a fear
15   Of horrors that happen so?

1891

Gold in the Mountain

Gold in the mountain,
And gold in the glen,
And greed in the heart,
Heaven having no part,
5   And unsatisfied men.

1891

WALT WHITMAN
(1819–1892)

Song of Myself

1

I celebrate myself, and sing myself,
And what I assume you shall assume,
For every atom belonging to me as good belongs to you.

I loaf and invite my soul,
5 I lean and loaf at my ease observing a spear of summer grass.

My tongue, every atom of my blood, formed from this soil, this air,
Born here of parents born here from parents the same, and their parents
    the same,
I, now thirty-seven years old in perfect health begin,
Hoping to cease not till death.

---

3. "Marl": crumbly clay.

Creeds and schools in abeyance,
Retiring back a while sufficed at what they are, but never forgotten,
I harbor for good or bad, I permit to speak at every hazard,
Nature without check with original energy.

6

A child said *What is the grass?* fetching it to me with full hands;
How could I answer the child? I do not know what it is any more than he.

I guess it must be the flag of my disposition, out of hopeful green stuff
woven.

Or I guess it is the handkerchief of the Lord,
A scented gift and remembrancer designedly dropped,
Bearing the owner's name someway in the corners, that we may see and
remark, and say *Whose?*

Or I guess the grass is itself a child, the produced babe of the vegetation.

Or I guess it is a uniform hieroglyphic,
And it means, Sprouting alike in broad zones and narrow zones,
Growing among black folks as among white,
Kanuck, Tuckahoe, Congressman, Cuff,[1] I give them the same, I receive
them the same.

And now it seems to me the beautiful uncut hair of graves.

Tenderly will I use you curling grass,
It may be you transpire from the breasts of young men,
It may be if I had known them I would have loved them,
It may be you are from old people, or from offspring taken soon out of
their mothers' laps,
And here you are the mothers' laps.

This grass is very dark to be from the white heads of old mothers,
Darker than the colorless beards of old men,
Dark to come from under the faint red roofs of mouths.

O I perceive after all so many uttering tongues,
And I perceive they do not come from the roofs of mouths for nothing.

I wish I could translate the hints about the dead young men and women.
And the hints about old men and mothers, and the offspring taken soon
out of their laps.

What do you think has become of the young and old men?
And what do you think has become of the women and children?

They are alive and well somewhere,
The smallest sprout shows there is really no death,
And if ever there was it led forward life, and does not wait at the end to
arrest it,
And ceased the moment life appeared.

All goes onward and outward, nothing collapses,
And to die is different from what anyone supposed, and luckier.

1. Denotes a Negro. *Kanuck:* French Canadian; *Tuckahoe:* backwoods Virginian.

11

Twenty-eight young men bathe by the shore,
200 Twenty-eight young men and all so friendly;
Twenty-eight years of womanly life and all so lonesome.

She owns the fine house by the rise of the bank,
She hides handsome and richly dressed aft° the blinds   *behind*
of the window.

Which of the young men does she like the best?
205 Ah the homeliest of them is beautiful to her.

Where are you off to, lady? for I see you,
You splash in the water there, yet stay stock still in your room.

Dancing and laughing along the beach came the twenty-ninth bather,
The rest did not see her, but she saw them and loved them.

210 The beards of the young men glistened with wet, it ran from their long
hair,
Little streams, passed all over their bodies.

An unseen hand also passed over their bodies,
It descended trembling from their temples and ribs.

The young men float on their backs, their white bellies bulge to the sun,
they do not ask who seizes fast to them,
215 They do not know who puffs and declines with pendant and bending arch,
They do not think whom they souse with spray.

24
Walt Whitman, a kosmos, of Manhattan the son,
Turbulent, fleshly, sensual, eating, drinking and breeding,
No sentimentalist, no stander above men and women or apart from them,
500 No more modest than immodest.

Unscrew the locks from the doors!
Unscrew the doors themselves from their jambs!

Whoever degrades another degrades me,
And whatever is done or said returns at last to me.

505 Through me the afflatus° surging and surging, through   *inspiration*
me the current and index.
I speak the password primeval, I give the sign of democracy,
By God! I will accept nothing which all cannot have their counterpart of
on the same terms.

Through me many long dumb voices,
Voices of the interminable generations of prisoners and slaves,
510 Voices of the diseased and despairing and of thieves and dwarfs,
Voices of cycles of preparation and accretion,
And of the threads that connect the stars, and of wombs and of the
father-stuff,
And of the rights of them the others are down upon,
Of the deformed, trivial, flat, foolish, despised,
515 Fog in the air, beetles rolling balls of dung.

Through me forbidden voices,
Voices of sexes and lusts, voices veiled and I remove the veil,
Voices indecent by me clarified and transfigured.

I do not press my fingers across my mouth,
I keep as delicate around the bowels as around the head and heart,
Copulation is no more rank to me than death is.

I believe in the flesh and the appetites,
Seeing, hearing, feeling, are miracles, and each part and tag of me is a
    miracle.

Divine am I inside and out, and I make holy whatever I touch or am
    touched from,
The scent of these armpits aroma finer than prayer,
This head more than churches, bibles, and all the creeds.

If I worship one thing more than another it shall be the spread of my
    own body, or any part of it,
Translucent mold of me it shall be you!
Shaded ledges and rests it shall be you!
Firm masculine colter [2] it shall be you!
Whatever goes to the tilth [3] of me it shall be you!
You my rich blood! your milky stream pale strippings of my life!
Breast that presses against other breasts it shall be you!
My brain it shall be your occult convolutions!
Root of washed sweet-flag! timorous pond-snipe! nest of guarded duplicate
    eggs! it shall be you!
Mixed tussled hay of head, beard, brawn, it shall be you!
Trickling sap of maple, fiber of manly wheat, it shall be you!
Suns so generous it shall be you!
Vapors lighting and shading my face it shall be you!
You sweaty brooks and dews it shall be you!
Winds whose soft-tickling genitals rub against me it shall be you!
Broad muscular fields, branches of live oak, loving lounger in my winding
    paths, it shall be you!
Hands I have taken, face I have kissed, mortal I have ever touched, it
    shall be you.

I dote on myself, there is that lot of me and all so luscious,
Each moment and whatever happens thrills me with joy,
I cannot tell how my ankles bend, nor whence the cause of my faintest
    wish,
Nor the cause of the friendship I emit, nor the cause of the friendship
    I take again.

That I walk up my stoop, I pause to consider if it really be,
A morning-glory at my window satisfies me more than the metaphysics of
    books.

To behold the daybreak!
The little light fades the immense and diaphanous shadows,
The air tastes good to my palate.

---

2. A cutting edge fastened to a plow ahead of   3. Arable land, topsoil.
the plowshare.

Hefts of the moving world at innocent gambols silently rising, freshly
    exuding,
Scooting obliquely high and low.

555   Something I cannot see puts upward libidinous prongs,
Seas of bright juice suffuse heaven.

The earth by the sky staid with, the daily close of their junction,
The heaved challenge from the east that moment over my head,
The mocking taunt, See then whether you shall be master!

     52
1331 The spotted hawk swoops by and accuses me, he complains of my gab and
    my loitering.

I too am not a bit tamed, I too am untranslatable,
I sound my barbaric yawp over the roofs of the world.

The last scud of day holds back for me,
1335 It flings my likeness after the rest and true as any on the shadowed wilds,
It coaxes me to the vapor and the dusk.

I depart as air, I shake my white locks at the runaway sun,
I effuse my flesh in eddies, and drift it in lacy jags.

I bequeath myself to the dirt to grow from the grass I love,
1340 If you want me again look for me under your boot-soles.

You will hardly know who I am or what I mean,
But I shall be good health to you nevertheless,
And filter and fiber your blood.

Failing to fetch me at first keep encouraged,
1345 Missing me one place search another,
I stop somewhere waiting for you.

                               1855   1881

When I Heard the Learn'd Astronomer

When I heard the learn'd astronomer,
When the proofs, the figures, were ranged in columns before me,
When I was shown the charts and diagrams, to add, divide, and measure
    them,
When I sitting heard the astronomer where he lectured with much applause
    in the lecture-room,
5 How soon unaccountable I became tired and sick,
Till rising and gliding out I wander'd off by myself,
In the mystical moist night-air, and from time to time,
Look'd up in perfect silence at the stars.

                               1865, 1865

I Saw in Louisiana a Live-Oak Growing

I saw in Louisiana a live-oak growing,
All alone stood it and the moss hung down from the branches,
Without any companion it grew there uttering joyous leaves of dark green,
And its look, rude, unbending, lusty, made me think of myself,

But I wonder'd how it could utter joyous leaves standing alone there with-
out its friend near, for I knew I could not,
And I broke off a twig with a certain number of leaves upon it, and twined
around it a little moss,
And brought it away, and have placed it in sight in my room,
It is not needed to remind me as of my own dear friends,
(For I believe lately I think of little else than of them,)
Yet it remains to me a curious token, it makes me think of manly love;
For all that, and though the live-oak glistens there in Louisiana solitary
in a wide flat space,
Uttering joyous leaves all its life without a friend a lover near,
I know very well I could not.

1860   1867

Vigil Strange I Kept on the Field One Night

Vigil strange I kept on the field one night;
When you my son and my comrade dropt at my side that day,
One look I but gave which your dear eyes return'd with a look I shall never
forget,
One touch of your hand to mine O boy, reach'd up as you lay on the ground,
Then onward I sped in the battle, the even-contested battle,
Till late in the night reliev'd to the place at last again I made my way,
Found you in death so cold dear comrade, found your body son of respond-
ing kisses, (never again on earth responding,)
Bared your face in the starlight, curious the scene, cool blew the moderate
night-wind,
Long there and then in vigil I stood, dimly around me the battle-field
spreading,
Vigil wondrous and vigil sweet there in the fragrant silent night,
But not a tear fell, not even a long-drawn sigh, long I gazed,
Then on the earth partially reclining sat by your side leaning my chin in my
hands,
Passing sweet hours, immortal and mystic hours with you dearest comrade—
not a tear, not a word,
Vigil of silence, love and death, vigil for you my son and my soldier,
As onward silently stars aloft, eastward new ones upward stole,
Vigil final for you brave boy, (I could not save you, swift was your death,
I faithfully loved you and cared for you living, I think we shall surely meet
again,)
Till at latest lingering of the night, indeed just as the dawn appear'd,
My comrade I wrapt in his blanket, envelop'd well his form,
Folded the blanket well, tucking it carefully over head and carefully under
feet,
And there and then and bathed by the rising sun, my son in his grave, in his
rude-dug grave I deposited,
Ending my vigil strange with that, vigil of night and battle-field dim,
Vigil for boy of responding kisses, (never again on earth responding,)
Vigil for comrade swiftly slain, vigil I never forget, how as day brighten'd,
I rose from the chill ground and folded my soldier well in his blanket,
And buried him where he fell.

1865   1867

Beat! Beat! Drums!

Beat! beat! drums! blow! bugles! blow!
Through the windows—through doors—burst like a ruthless force,
Into the solemn church, and scatter the congregation,
Into the school where the scholar is studying;
5 Leave not the bridegroom quiet—no happiness must he have now with his
        bride,
Nor the peaceful farmer any peace, ploughing his field or gathering his grain,
So fierce you whirr and pound you drums—so shrill you bugles blow.

Beat! beat! drums!—blow! bugles! blow!
Over the traffic of cities—over the rumble of wheels in the streets;
10 Are beds prepared for sleepers at night in the houses? no sleepers must sleep
        in those beds,
No bargainers' bargains by day—no brokers or speculators—would they
        continue?
Would the talkers be talking? would the singer attempt to sing?
Would the lawyer rise in the court to state his case before the judge?
Then rattle quicker, heavier drums—you bugles wilder blow.
15 Beat! beat! drums!—blow! bugles! blow!
Make no parley—stop for no expostulation,
Mind not the timid—mind not the weeper or prayer,
Mind not the old man beseeching the young man,
Let not the child's voice be heard, nor the mother's entreaties,
20 Make even the trestles to shake the dead where they lie awaiting the hearses,
So strong you thump O terrible drums—so loud you bugles blow.

                                            1861   1867

By the Bivouac's Fitful Flame

By the bivouac's fitful flame,
A procession winding around me, solemn and sweet and slow—but first I
        note,
The tents of the sleeping army, the fields' and woods' dim outline,
The darkness lit by spots of kindler fire, the silence,
5 Like a phantom far or near an occasional figure moving,
The shrubs and trees, (as I lift my eyes they seem to be stealthily watching
        me,)
While wind in procession thoughts, O tender and wondrous thoughts,
Of life and death, of home and the past and loved, and of those that are far
        away;
A solemn and slow procession there as I sit on the ground,
10 By the bivouac's fitful flame.

                                            1865   1867

Cavalry Crossing a Ford

A line in long array where they wind betwixt green islands,
They take a serpentine course, their arms flash in the sun—hark to the musi-
        cal clank,
Behold the silvery river, in it the splashing horses loitering stop to drink,
Behold the brown-faced men, each group, each person a picture, the negli-
        gent rest on the saddles,

Some emerge on the opposite bank, others are just entering the ford—while,
Scarlet and blue and snowy white,
The guidon[1] flags flutter gayly in the wind.

1865   1871

Bivouac on a Mountain Side

I see before me now a traveling army halting,
Below a fertile valley spread, with barns and the orchards of summer,
Behind, the terraced sides of a mountain, abrupt, in places rising high,
Broken, with rocks, with clinging cedars, with tall shapes dingily seen,
The numerous camp-fires scatter'd near and far, some away up on the
    mountain,
The shadowy forms of men and horses, looming, large-sized, flickering,
And over all the sky—the sky! far, far out of reach, studded, breaking out,
    the eternal stars.

1865   1871

An Army Corps on the March

With its cloud of skirmishers in advance,
With now the sound of a single shot snapping like a whip, and now an
    irregular volley,
The swarming ranks press on and on, the dense brigades press on,
Glittering dimly, toiling under the sun—the dust-cover'd men,
In columns rise and fall to the undulations of the ground,
With artillery interspers'd—the wheels rumble, the horses sweat,
As the army corps advances.

1865–66   1871

The World Below the Brine

The world below the brine,
Forests at the bottom of the sea, the branches and leaves,
Sea-lettuce, vast lichens, strange flowers and seeds, the thick tangle, open-
    ings, and pink turf,
Different colors, pale gray and green, purple, white, and gold, the play of
    light through the water,
Dumb swimmers there among the rocks, coral, gluten, grass, rushes, and the
    aliment of the swimmers,
Sluggish existences grazing there suspended, or slowly crawling close to the
    bottom,
The sperm-whale at the surface blowing air and spray, or disporting with his
    flukes,
The leaden-eyed shark, the walrus, the turtle, the hairy sea-leopard, and the
    sting-ray,
Passions there, wars, pursuits, tribes, sight in those ocean-depths, breathing
    that thick-breathing air, as so many do,
The change thence to the sight here, and to the subtle air breathed by beings
    like us who walk this sphere,
The change onward from ours to that of beings who walk other spheres.

1860   1871

---

1. Small flag or banner used as a signal or guide.

Out of the Cradle Endlessly Rocking

Out of the cradle endlessly rocking,
Out of the mocking-bird's throat, the musical shuttle,
Out of the Ninth-month[2] midnight,
Over the sterile sands and the fields beyond, where the child leaving his bed
    wander'd alone, bareheaded, barefoot,
5 Down from the shower'd halo,
Up from the mystic play of shadows twining and twisting as if they were
    alive,
Out from the patches of briers and blackberries,
From the memories of the bird that chanted to me,
From your memories sad brother, from the fitful risings and fallings I heard,
10 From under that yellow half-moon late-risen and swollen as if with tears,
From those beginning notes of yearning and love there in the mist,
From the thousand responses of my heart never to cease,
From the myriad thence-arous'd words,
From the word stronger and more delicious than any,
15 From such as now they start the scene revisiting,
As a flock, twittering, rising, or overhead passing,
Borne hither, ere all eludes me, hurriedly,
A man, yet by these tears a little boy again,
Throwing myself on the sand, confronting the waves,
20 I, chanter of pains and joys, uniter of here and hereafter,
Taking all hints to use them, but swiftly leaping beyond them,
A reminiscence sing.

Once Paumanok,[3]
When the lilac-scent was in the air and Fifth-month grass was growing,
25 Up this seashore in some briers,
Two feather'd guests from Alabama, two together,
And their nest, and four light-green eggs spotted with brown,
And every day the he-bird to and fro near at hand,
And every day the she-bird crouch'd on her nest, silent, with bright eyes,
30 And every day I, a curious boy, never too close, never disturbing them,
Cautiously peering, absorbing, translating.

Shine! shine! shine!
Pour down your warmth, great sun!
While we bask, we two together.

35 *Two together!*
Winds blow south, or winds blow north,
Day come white, or night come black,
Home, or rivers and mountains from home,
Singing all time, minding no time,
40 *While we two keep together.*

Till of a sudden,
May-be kill'd, unknown to her mate,
One forenoon the she-bird crouch'd not on the nest,
Nor return'd that afternoon, nor the next,
45 Nor ever appear'd again.

---

2. The Quaker designation for September may
here also suggest the human cycle of fertility
and birth, in contrast with "sterile sands" in
the next line.
3. The Indian name for Long Island.

And thenceforward all summer in the sound of the sea,
And at night under the full of the moon in calmer weather,
Over the hoarse surging of the sea,
Or flitting from brier to brier by day,
I saw, I heard at intervals the remaining one, the he-bird,
The solitary guest from Alabama.

Blow! blow! blow!
Blow up sea-winds along Paumanok's shore;
I wait and I wait till you blow my mate to me.

Yes, when the stars glisten'd,
All night long on the prong of a moss-scallop'd stake,
Down almost amid the slapping waves,
Sat the lone singer wonderful causing tears.

He call'd on his mate,
He pour'd forth the meanings which I of all men know.

Yes my brother I know,
The rest might not, but I have treasur'd every note,
For more than once dimly down to the beach gliding,
Silent, avoiding the moonbeams, blending myself with the shadows,
Recalling now the obscure shapes, the echoes, the sounds and sights after
    their sorts,
The white arms out in the breakers tirelessly tossing,
I, with bare feet, a child, the wind wafting my hair,
Listen'd long and long.

Listen'd to keep, to sing, now translating the notes,
Following you my brother.

Soothe! soothe! soothe!
Close on its wave soothes the wave behind,
And again another behind embracing and lapping, every one close,
But my love soothes not me, not me.

Low hangs the moon, it rose late,
It is lagging—O I think it is heavy with love, with love.

O madly the sea pushes upon the land,
With love, with love.

O night! do I not see my love fluttering out among the breakers?
What is that little black thing I see there in the white?

Loud! loud! loud!
Loud I call to you, my love!

High and clear I shoot my voice over the waves,
Surely you must know who is here, is here,
You must know who I am, my love.

Low-hanging moon!
What is that dusky spot in your brown yellow?
O it is the shape, the shape of my mate!
O moon do not keep her from me any longer.

90   Land! land! O land!
      Whichever way I turn, O I think you could give me my mate back again if
          you only would,
      For I am almost sure I see her dimly whichever way I look.

      O rising stars!
      Perhaps the one I want so much will rise, will rise with some of you.

95   O throat! O trembling throat!
      Sound clearer through the atmosphere!
      Pierce the woods, the earth,
      Somewhere listening to catch you must be the one I want.

      Shake out carols!
100   Solitary here, the night's carols!
      Carols of lonesome love! death's carols!
      Carols under that lagging, yellow, waning moon!
      O under that moon where she droops almost down into the sea!
      O reckless despairing carols.

105   But soft! sink low!
      Soft! let me just murmur,
      And do you wait a moment you husky-nois'd sea,
      For somewhere I believe I heard my mate responding to me,
      So faint, I must be still, be still to listen,
110   But not altogether still, for then she might not come immediately to me.

      Hither my love!
      Here I am! here!
      With this just-sustain'd note I announce myself to you,
      This gentle call is for you my love, for you.

115   Do not be decoy'd elsewhere,
      That is the whistle of the wind, it is not my voice,
      That is the fluttering, the fluttering of the spray,
      Those are the shadows of leaves.

      O darkness! O in vain!
120   O I am very sick and sorrowful.

      O brown halo in the sky near the moon, drooping upon the sea!
      O troubled reflection in the sea!
      O throat! O throbbing heart!
      And I singing uselessly, uselessly all the night.

125   O past! O happy life! O songs of joy!
      In the air, in the woods, over fields,
      Loved! loved! loved! loved! loved!
      But my mate no more, no more with me!
      We two together no more.

130   The aria sinking,
      All else continuing, the stars shining,
      The winds blowing, the notes of the bird continuous echoing,
      With angry moans the fierce old mother incessantly moaning,
      On the sands of Paumanok's shore gray and rustling,
135   The yellow half-moon enlarged, sagging down, drooping, the face of the sea
          almost touching,

The boy ecstatic, with his bare feet the waves, with his hair the atmosphere
    dallying,
The love in the heart long pent, now loose, now at last tumultuously bursting,
The aria's meaning, the ears, the soul, swiftly depositing,
The strange tears down the cheeks coursing,
The colloquy there, the trio, each uttering,
The undertone, the savage old mother incessantly crying,
To the boy's soul's questions sullenly timing, some drown'd secret hissing,
To the outsetting bard.

Demon or bird! (said the boy's soul,)
Is it indeed toward your mate you sing? or is it really to me?
For I, that was a child, my tongue's use sleeping, now I have heard you,
Now in a moment I know what I am for, I awake,
And already a thousand singers, a thousand songs, clearer, louder and more
    sorrowful than yours,
A thousand warbling echoes have started to life within me, never to die.

O you singer solitary, singing by yourself, projecting me,
O solitary me listening, never more shall I cease perpetuating you,
Never more shall I escape, never more the reverberations,
Never more the cries of unsatisfied love be absent from me,
Never again leave me to be the peaceful child I was before what there in the
    night,
By the sea under the yellow and sagging moon,
The messenger there arous'd, the fire, the sweet hell within,
The unknown want, the destiny of me.

O give me the clew! (it lurks in the night here somewhere,)
O if I am to have so much, let me have more!

A word then, (for I will conquer it,)
The word final, superior to all,
Subtle, sent up—what is it?—I listen;
Are you whispering it, and have been all the time, you sea-waves?
Is that it from your liquid rims and wet sands?

Whereto answering, the sea,
Delaying not, hurrying not,
Whisper'd me through the night, and very plainly before daybreak,
Lisp'd to me the low and delicious word death,
And again death, death, death, death,
Hissing melodious, neither like the bird nor like my arous'd child's heart,
But edging near as privately for me rustling at my feet,
Creeping thence steadily up to my ears and laving me softly all over,
Death, death, death, death, death.

Which I do not forget,
But fuse the song of my dusky demon and brother,
That he sang to me in the moonlight on Paumanok's gray beach,
With the thousand responsive songs at random,
My own songs awaked from that hour,
And with them the key, the word up from the waves,
The word of the sweetest song and all songs,
That strong and delicious word which, creeping to my feet,
(Or like some old crone rocking the cradle, swathed in sweet garments, bend-
    ing aside,)
The sea whisper'd me.

                                                1859   1881

On the Beach at Night

On the beach at night,
Stands a child with her father,
Watching the east, the autumn sky.

Up through the darkness,
5 While ravening clouds, the burial clouds, in black masses spreading,
Lower sullen and fast athwart and down the sky,
Amid a transparent clear belt of ether yet left in the east,
Ascends large and calm the lord-star Jupiter,
And nigh at hand, only a very little above,
10 Swim the delicate sisters the Pleiades.

From the beach the child holding the hand of her father,
Those burial-clouds that lower victorious soon to devour all,
Watching, silently weeps.

Weep not, child,
15 Weep not, my darling,
With these kisses let me remove your tears,
The ravening clouds shall not long be victorious,
They shall not long possess the sky, they devour the stars only in apparition,
Jupiter shall emerge, be patient, watch again another night, the Pleiades
    shall emerge,
20 They are immortal, all those stars both silvery and golden shall shine out
    again,
The great stars and the little ones shall shine out again, they endure,
The vast immortal suns and the long-enduring pensive moons shall again
    shine.

Then dearest child mournest thou only for Jupiter?
Considerest thou alone the burial of the stars?

25 Something there is,
(With my lips soothing thee, adding I whisper,)
I give thee the first suggestion, the problem and indirection,)
Something there is more immortal even than the stars,
(Many the burials, many the days and nights, passing away,)
30 Something that shall endure longer even than lustrous Jupiter,
Longer than sun or any revolving satellite,
Or the radiant sisters the Pleiades.

                                                    1871   1881

Patroling Barnegat[4]

Wild, wild the storm, and the sea high running,
Steady the roar of the gale, with incessant undertone muttering,
Shouts of demoniac laughter fitfully piercing and pealing,
Waves, air, midnight, their savagest trinity lashing,
5 Out in the shadows there milk-white combs careering,
On beachy slush and sand spirts of snow fierce slanting,
Where through the murk the easterly death-wind breasting,
Through cutting swirl and spray watchful and firm advancing,
(That in the distance! is that a wreck? is the red signal flaring?)
10 Slush and sand of the beach tireless till daylight wending,

4. Barnegat Bay is off the coast of Ocean County, New Jersey.

Steadily, slowly, through hoarse roar never remitting,
Along the midnight edge by those milk-white combs careering,
A group of dim, weird forms, struggling, the night confronting,
That savage trinity warily watching.

1880   1881

The Dalliance of the Eagles

Skirting the river road, (my forenoon walk, my rest,)
Skyward in air a sudden muffled sound, the dalliance of the eagles,
The rushing amorous contact high in space together,
The clinching interlocking claws, a living, fierce, gyrating wheel,
Four beating wings, two beaks, a swirling mass tight grappling,
In tumbling turning clustering loops, straight downward falling,
Till o'er the river pois'd, the twain yet one, a moment's lull,
A motionless still balance in the air, then parting, talons loosing,
Upward again on slow-firm pinions slanting, their separate diverse flight,
She hers, he his, pursuing.

1880   1881

Reconciliation

Word over all, beautiful as the sky,
Beautiful that war and all its deeds of carnage must in time be utterly lost,
That the hands of the sisters Death and Night incessantly softly wash again,
  and ever again, this soil'd world;
For my enemy is dead, a man divine as myself is dead,
I look where he lies white-faced and still in the coffin—I draw near,
Bend down and touch lightly with my lips the white face in the coffin.

1865–66   1881

When Lilacs Last in the Dooryard Bloom'd

1

When lilacs last in the dooryard bloom'd,
And the great star early droop'd in the western sky in the night,
I mourn'd, and yet shall mourn with ever-returning spring.

Ever-returning spring, trinity sure to me you bring,
Lilac blooming perennial and drooping star in the west,
And thought of him I love.

2

O powerful western fallen star!
O shades of night—O moody, tearful night!
O great star disappear'd—O the black murk that hides the star!
O cruel hands that hold me powerless—O helpless soul of me!
O harsh surrounding cloud that will not free my soul.

3

In the dooryard fronting an old farm-house near the white-wash'd palings,
Stands the lilac-bush tall-growing with heart-shaped leaves of rich green,
With many a pointed blossom rising delicate, with the perfume strong I love,
With every leaf a miracle—and from this bush in the dooryard,
With delicate-color'd blossoms and heart-shaped leaves of rich green,
A sprig with its flower I break.

4

In the swamp in secluded recesses,
A shy and hidden bird is warbling a song.

20   Solitary the thrush,
The hermit withdrawn to himself, avoiding the settlements,
Sings by himself a song.

Song of the bleeding throat,
Death's outlet song of life, (for well dear brother I know,
25   If thou wast not granted to sing thou would'st surely die.)

5

Over the breast of the spring, the land, amid cities,
Amid lanes and through old woods, where lately the violets peep'd from the
    ground, spotting the gray debris,
Amid the grass in the fields each side of the lanes, passing the endless grass,
Passing the yellow-spear'd wheat, every grain from its shroud in the dark-
    brown fields uprisen,
30   Passing the apple-tree blows of white and pink in the orchards,
Carrying a corpse to where it shall rest in the grave,
Night and day journeys a coffin.

6

Coffin that passes through lanes and streets,[5]
Through day and night with the great cloud darkening the land,
35   With the pomp of the inloop'd flags with the cities draped in black,
With the show of the States themselves as of crape-veil'd women standing,
With processions long and winding and the flambeaus of the night,
With the countless torches lit, with the silent sea of faces and the unbared
    heads,
With the waiting depot, the arriving coffin, and the sombre faces,
40   With dirges through the night, with the thousand voices rising strong and
    solemn,
With all the mournful voices of the dirges pour'd around the coffin,
The dim-lit churches and the shuddering organs—where amid these you
    journey,
With the tolling tolling bells' perpetual clang,
Here, coffin that slowly passes,
45   I give you my sprig of lilac.

7

(Nor for you, for one alone,
Blossoms and branches green to coffins all I bring,
For fresh as the morning, thus would I chant a song for you O sane and
    sacred death.

All over bouquets of roses,
50   O death, I cover you over with roses and early lilies,
But mostly and now the lilac that blooms the first,
Copious I break, I break the sprigs from the bushes,
With loaded arms I come, pouring for you,
For you and the coffins all of you O death.)

8

55   O western orb sailing the heaven,
Now I know what you must have meant as a month since I walk'd,
As I walk'd in silence the transparent shadowy night,
As I saw you had something to tell as you bent to me night after night,
As you droop'd from the sky low down as if to my side, (while the other
    stars all look'd on,)
60   As we wander'd together the solemn night, (for something I know not what
    kept me from sleep,)

5. The funeral cortège of Lincoln traveled from Washington to Springfield, Illinois, stopping
at cities and towns all along the way for the people to honor the murdered President.

As the night advanced, and I saw on the rim of the west how full you were
of woe,
As I stood on the rising ground in the breeze in the cool transparent night,
As I watch'd where you pass'd and was lost in the netherward black of the
night,
As my soul in its trouble dissatisfied sank, as where you sad orb,
Concluded, dropt in the night, and was gone.

9

Sing on there in the swamp,
O singer bashful and tender, I hear your notes, I hear your call,
I hear, I come presently, I understand you,
But a moment I linger, for the lustrous star has detain'd me,
The star my departing comrade holds and detains me.

10

O how shall I warble myself for the dead one there I loved?
And how shall I deck my song for the large sweet soul that has gone?
And what shall my perfume be for the grave of him I love?

Sea-winds blown from east and west,
Blown from the Eastern sea and blown from the Western sea, till there on
the prairies meeting,
These and with these and the breath of my chant,
I'll perfume the grave of him I love.

11

O what shall I hang on the chamber walls?
And what shall the pictures be that I hang on the walls,
To adorn the burial-house of him I love?

Pictures of growing spring and farms and homes,
With the Fourth-month eve at sundown, and the gray smoke lucid and
bright,
With floods of the yellow gold of the gorgeous, indolent, sinking sun, burn-
ing, expanding the air,
With the fresh sweet herbage under foot, and the pale green leaves of the
trees prolific,
In the distance the flowing glaze, the breast of the river, with a wind-dapple
here and there,
With ranging hills on the banks, with many a line against the sky, and
shadows,
And the city at hand with dwellings so dense, and stacks of chimneys,
And all the scenes of life and the workshops, and the workmen homeward
returning.

12

Lo, body and soul—this land,
My own Manhattan with spires, and the sparkling and hurrying tides, and
the ships,
The varied and ample land, the South and the North in the light, Ohio's
shores and flashing Missouri,
And ever the far-spreading prairies cover'd with grass and corn.

Lo, the most excellent sun so calm and haughty,
The violet and purple morn with just-felt breezes,
The gentle soft-born measureless light,
The miracle spreading bathing all, the fulfill'd noon,
The coming eve delicious, the welcome night and the stars,
Over my cities shining all, enveloping man and land.

13

Sing on, sing on you gray-brown bird,
Sing from the swamps, the recesses, pour your chant from the bushes,
Limitless out of the dusk, out of the cedars and pines.

Sing on dearest brother, warble your reedy song,
Loud human song, with voice of uttermost woe.

O liquid and free and tender!
O wild and loose to my soul—O wondrous singer!
You only I hear—yet the star holds me, (but will soon depart,)
Yet the lilac with mastering odor holds me.

14

Now while I sat in the day and look'd forth,
In the close of the day with its light and the fields of spring, and the farmers
    preparing their crops,
In the large unconscious scenery of my land with its lakes and forests,
In the heavenly aerial beauty, (after the perturb'd winds and the storms,)
Under the arching heavens of the afternoon swift passing, and the voices of
    children and women.
The many-moving sea-tides, and I saw the ships how they sail'd,
And the summer approaching with richness, and the fields all busy with
    labor,
And the infinite separate houses, how they all went on, each with its meals
    and minutia of daily usages,
And the streets how their throbbings throbb'd, and the cities pent—lo, then
    and there,
Falling upon them all and among them all, enveloping me with the rest,
Appear'd the cloud, appear'd the long black trail,
And I knew death, its thought, and the sacred knowledge of death.

Then with the knowledge of death as walking one side of me,
And the thought of death close-walking the other side of me,
And I in the middle as with companions, and as holding the hands of
    companions,
I fled forth to the hiding receiving night that talks not,
Down to the shores of the water, the path by the swamp in the dimness,
To the solemn shadowy cedars and ghostly pines so still.

And the singer so shy to the rest receiv'd me,
The gray-brown bird I know receiv'd us comrades three,
And he sang the carol of death, and a verse for him I love.

From deep secluded recesses,
From the fragrant cedars and the ghostly pines so still,
Came the carol of the bird.

And the charm of the carol rapt me,
As I held as if by their hands my comrades in the night,
And the voice of my spirit tallied the song of the bird.

Come lovely and soothing death,
Undulate round the world, serenely arriving, arriving,
In the day, in the night, to all, to each,
Sooner or later delicate death.

Prais'd be the fathomless universe,
For life and joy, and for objects and knowledge curious,
And for love, sweet love—but praise! praise! praise!
For the sure-enwinding arms of cool-enfolding death.

Dark mother always gliding near with soft feet,
Have none chanted for thee a chant of fullest welcome?
Then I chant it for thee, I glorify thee above all,
I bring thee a song that when thou must indeed come, come unfalteringly.

Approach strong deliveress,
When it is so, when thou hast taken them I joyously sing the dead,
Lost in the loving floating ocean of thee,
Laved in the flood of thy bliss O death.

From me to thee glad serenades,
Dances for thee I propose saluting thee, adornments and feastings for thee,
And the sights of the open landscape and the high-spread sky are fitting,
And life and the fields, and the huge and thoughtful night.

The night in silence under many a star,
The ocean shore and the husky whispering wave whose voice I know,
And the soul turning to thee O vast and well-veil'd death,
And the body gratefully nestling close to thee.

Over the tree-tops I float thee a song,
Over the rising and sinking waves, over the myriad fields and the prairies
wide,
Over the dense-pack'd cities all and the teeming wharves and ways,
I float this carol with joy, with joy to thee O death.

15

To the tally of my soul,
Loud and strong kept up the gray-brown bird,
With pure deliberate notes spreading filling the night.

Loud in the pines and cedars dim,
Clear in the freshness moist and the swamp-perfume,
And I with my comrades there in the night.

While my sight that was bound in my eyes unclosed,
As to long panoramas of visions.

And I saw askant the armies,
I saw as in noiseless dreams hundreds of battle-flags,
Borne through the smoke of the battles and pierc'd with missiles I saw them,
And carried hither and yon through the smoke, and torn and bloody,
And at last but a few shreds left on the staffs, (and all in silence,)
And the staffs all splinter'd and broken.

I saw battle-corpses, myriads of them,
And the white skeletons of young men, I saw them,
I saw the debris and debris of all the slain soldiers of the war,
But I saw they were not as was thought,
They themselves were fully at rest, they suffer'd not,
The living remain'd and suffer'd, the mother suffer'd,
And the wife and the child and the musing comrade suffer'd,
And the armies that remain'd suffer'd.

16

185 Passing the visions, passing the night,
  Passing, unloosing the hold of my comrades' hands,
  Passing the song of the hermit bird and the tallying song of my soul,
  Victorious song, death's outlet song, yet varying ever-altering song,
  As low and wailing, yet clear the notes, rising and falling, flooding the night,
190 Sadly sinking and fainting, as warning and warning, and yet again bursting
      with joy,
  Covering the earth and filling the spread of the heaven,
  As that powerful psalm in the night I heard from recesses,
  Passing, I leave thee lilac with heart-shaped leaves,
  I leave thee there in the door-yard, blooming, returning with spring.

195 I cease from my song for thee,
  From my gaze on thee in the west, fronting the west, communing with thee,
  O comrade lustrous with silver face in the night.

  Yet each to keep and all, retrievements out of the night,
  The song, the wondrous chant of the gray-brown bird,
200 And the tallying chant, the echo arous'd in my soul,
  With the lustrous and drooping star with the countenance full of woe,
  With the holders holding my hand nearing the call of the bird,
  Comrades mine and I in the midst, and their memory ever to keep, for the
      dead I loved so well,
  For the sweetest, wisest soul of all my days and lands—and this for his dear
      sake,
205 Lilac and star and bird twined with the chant of my soul,
  There in the fragrant pines and the cedars dusk and dim.

                                    1865–66   1881

A Noiseless Patient Spider

  A noiseless patient spider,
  I mark'd where on a little promontory it stood isolated,
  Mark'd how to explore the vacant vast surrounding,
  It launch'd forth filament, filament, filament, out of itself,
5 Ever unreeling them, ever tirelessly speeding them.

  And you O my soul where you stand,
  Surrounded, detached, in measureless oceans of space,
  Ceaselessly musing, venturing, throwing, seeking the spheres to connect
      them,
  Till the bridge you will need be form'd, till the ductile anchor hold,
10 Till the gossamer thread you fling catch somewhere, O my soul.

                                    1868   1881

To a Locomotive in Winter

  Thee for my recitative,
  Thee in the driving storm even as now, the snow, the winter-day declining,
  Thee in thy panoply, thy measur'd dual throbbing and thy beat convulsive,
  Thy black clyindric body, golden brass and silvery steel,
5 Thy ponderous side-bars, parallel and connecting rods, gyrating, shuttling
      at thy sides,
  Thy metrical, now swelling pant and roar, now tapering in the distance,
  Thy great protruding head-light fix'd in front,

Thy long, pale, floating vapor-pennants, tinged with delicate purple,
The dense and murky clouds out-belching from thy smoke-stack,
Thy knitted frame, thy springs and valves, the tremulous twinkle of thy
    wheels,
Thy train of cars behind, obedient, merrily following,
Through gale or calm, now swift, now slack, yet steadily careering;
Type of the modern—emblem of motion and power—pulse of the continent,
For once come serve the Muse and merge in verse, even as here I see thee,
With storm and buffeting gusts of wind and falling snow,
By day thy warning ringing bell to sound its notes,
By night thy silent signal lamps to swing.

Fierce-throated beauty!
Roll through my chant with all thy lawless music, thy swinging lamps at
    night,
Thy madly-whistled laughter, echoing, rumbling like an earthquake, rousing
    all,
Law of thyself complete, thine own track firmly holding,
(No sweetness debonair of tearful harp or glib piano thine,)
Thy trills of shrieks by rocks and hills return'd,
Launch'd o'er the prairies wide, across the lakes,
To the free skies unpent and glad and strong.

1876   1881

The Dismantled Ship

In some unused lagoon, some nameless bay,
On sluggish, lonesome waters, anchor'd near the shore,
An old, dismasted, gray and batter'd ship, disabled, done,
After free voyages to all the seas of earth, haul'd up at last and hawser'd tight,
Lies rusting, mouldering.

1888   1888–89

FREDERICK GODDARD TUCKERMAN
(1821–1873)

From Sonnets, First Series, 1854–1860

10

An upper chamber in a darkened house,
Where, ere his footsteps reached ripe manhood's brink,
Terror and anguish were his lot to drink;
I cannot rid the thought nor hold it close
But dimly dream upon that man alone:
Now though the autumn clouds most softly pass,
The cricket chides beneath the doorstep stone
And greener than the season grows the grass.
Nor can I drop my lids nor shade my brows,
But there he stands beside the lifted sash;
And with a swooning of the heart, I think
Where the black shingles slope to meet the boughs
And, shattered on the roof like smallest snows,
The tiny petals of the mountain ash.

1860

28

Not the round natural world, not the deep mind,
The reconcilement holds: the blue abyss
Collects it not; our arrows sink amiss
And but in Him may we our import find.
5   The agony to know, the grief, the bliss
Of toil, is vain and vain: clots of the sod
Gathered in heat and haste and flung behind
To blind ourselves and others, what but this
Still grasping dust and sowing toward the wind?
10 No more thy meaning seek, thine anguish plead,
But leaving straining thought and stammering word,
Across the barren azure pass to God;
Shooting the void in silence like a bird,
A bird that shuts his wings for better speed.

1860

MATTHEW ARNOLD
(1822–1888)

Shakespeare

Others abide our question. Thou art free.
We ask and ask—thou smilest and art still,
Out-topping knowledge. For the loftiest hill,
Who to the stars uncrowns his majesty,

5   Planting his stedfast footsteps in the sea,
Making the heaven of heavens his dwelling-place,
Spares but the cloudy border of his base
To the foiled searching of mortality;

And thou, who didst the stars and sunbeams know,
10 Self-schooled, self-scanned, self-honored, self-secure,
Didst tread on earth unguessed at—better so!

All pains the immortal spirit must endure,
All weakneess which impairs, all griefs which bow,
Find their sole speech in that victorious brow.

1849

The Forsaken Merman

Come, dear children, let us away;
Down and away below!
Now my brothers call from the bay,
Now the great winds shoreward blow,
5   Now the salt tides seaward flow;
Now the wild white horses play,
Champ and chafe and toss in the spray.
Children dear, let us away!
This way, this way!

Call her once before you go—
Call once yet!
In a voice that she will know:
"Margaret! Margaret!"
Children's voices should be dear
5 (Call once more) to a mother's ear;
Children's voices, wild with pain—
Surely she will come again!
Call her once and come away;
This way, this way!
0 "Mother dear, we cannot stay!
The wild white horses foam and fret."
Margaret! Margaret!

Come, dear children, come away down;
Call no more!
5 One last look at the white-walled town,
And the little gray church on the windy shore;
Then come down!
She will not come though you call all day;
Come away, come away!

0 Children dear, was it yesterday
We heard the sweet bells over the bay?
In the caverns where we lay,
Through the surf and through the swell,
The far-off sound of a silver bell?
5 Sand-strewn caverns, cool and deep,
Where the winds are all asleep;
Where the spent lights quiver and gleam,
Where the salt weed sways in the stream,
Where the sea-beasts, ranged all round,
40 Feed in the ooze of their pasture-ground;
Where the sea-snakes coil and twine,
Dry their mail and bask in the brine;
Where great whales come sailing by,
Sail and sail, with unshut eye,
45 Round the world for ever and aye?
When did music come this way?
Children dear, was it yesterday?

Children dear, was it yesterday
(Call yet once) that she went away?
50 Once she sate with you and me,
On a red gold throne in the heart of the sea,
And the youngest sate on her knee.
She combed its bright hair, and she tended it well,
When down swung the sound of a far-off bell.
55 She sighed, she looked up through the clear green sea;
She said: "I must go, for my kinsfolk pray
In the little gray church on the shore today.
'Twill be Easter-time in the world—ah me!
And I lose my poor soul, Merman! here with thee."
60 I said: "Go up, dear heart, through the waves;
Say thy prayer, and come back to the kind sea-caves!"
She smiled, she went up through the surf in the bay.
Children dear, was it yesterday?

Children dear, were we long alone?
65 "The sea grows stormy, the little ones moan;
Long prayers," I said, "in the world they say;
Come!" I said; and we rose through the surf in the bay.
We went up the beach, by the sandy down
Where the sea-stocks bloom, to the white-walled town;
70 Through the narrow paved streets, where all was still,
To the little gray church on the windy hill.
From the church came a murmur of folk at their prayers,
But we stood without in the cold blowing airs.
We climbed on the graves, on the stones worn with rains,
75 And we gazed up the aisle through the small leaded panes.
She sate by the pillar; we saw her clear:
"Margaret, hist! come quick, we are here!
Dear heart," I said, "we are long alone;
The sea grows stormy, the little ones moan."
80 But, ah, she gave me never a look,
For her eyes were sealed to the holy book!
Loud prays the priest; shut stands the door.
Come away, children, call no more!
Come away, come down, call no more!

85   Down, down, down!
Down to the depths of the sea!
She sits at her wheel in the humming town,
Singing most joyfully.
Hark what she sings: "O joy, O joy,
90 For the humming street, and the child with its toy!
For the priest, and the bell, and the holy well;
For the wheel where I spun,
And the blessed light of the sun!"
And so she sings her fill.
95 Singing most joyfully,
Till the spindle drops from her hand,
And the whizzing wheel stands still.
She steals to the window, and looks at the sand,
And over the sand at the sea;
100 And her eyes are set in a stare;
And anon there breaks a sigh,
And anon there drops a tear,
From a sorrow-clouded eye,
And a heart sorrow-laden,
105 A long, long sigh;
For the cold strange eyes of a little Mermaiden
And the gleam of her golden hair.

Come away, away children;
Come children, come down!
110 The hoarse wind blows coldly;
Lights shine in the town.
She will start from her slumber
When gusts shake the door;
She will hear the winds howling,
115 Will hear the waves roar.
We shall see, while above us
The waves roar and whirl,
A ceiling of amber,

A pavement of pearl.
Singing: "Here came a mortal,
But faithless was she!
And alone dwell for ever
The kings of the sea."

But, children, at midnight,
When soft the winds blow,
When clear falls the moonlight,
When spring-tides are low;
When sweet airs come seaward
From heaths starred with broom,
And high rocks throw mildly
On the blanched sands a gloom;
Up the still, glistening beaches,
Up the creeks we will hie,
Over banks of bright seaweed
The ebb-tide leaves dry.
We will gaze, from the sand-hills,
At the white, sleeping town;
At the church on the hill-side—
And then come back down.
Singing: "There dwells a loved one,
But cruel is she!
She left lonely for ever
The kings of the sea."

1849

To Marguerite

Yes! in the sea of life enisled,
With echoing straits between us thrown,
Dotting the shoreless watery wild,
We mortal millions live *alone*.
The islands feel the enclasping flow,
And then their endless bounds they know.

But when the moon their hollows lights,
And they are swept by balms of spring,
And in their glens, on starry nights,
The nightingales divinely sing;
And lovely notes, from shore to shore,
Across the sounds and channels pour—

Oh! then a longing like despair
Is to their farthest caverns sent;
For surely once, they feel, we were
Parts of a single continent!
Now round us spreads the watery plain—
Oh might our marges meet again!

Who ordered, that their longing's fire
Should be, as soon as kindled, cooled?
Who renders vain their deep desire?—
A God, a God their severance ruled!
And bade betwixt their shores to be
The unplumbed, salt, estranging sea.

1852

The Scholar-Gypsy[2]

Go, for they call you, shepherd, from the hill;
  Go, shepherd, and untie the wattled cotes![3]
   No longer leave thy wistful flock unfed,
   Nor let thy bawling fellows rack their throats,
5   Nor the cropped herbage shoot another head.
    But when the fields are still,
  And the tired men and dogs all gone to rest,
  And only the white sheep are sometimes seen
   Cross and recross the strips of moon-blanched green,
10 Come, shepherd, and again begin the quest!

Here, where the reaper was at work of late—
  In this high field's dark corner, where he leaves
   His coat, his basket, and his earthen cruse,°   *vessel*
   And in the sun all morning binds the sheaves,
15   Then here, at noon, comes back his stores to use—
    Here will I sit and wait,
  While to my ear from uplands far away
  The bleating of the folded flocks is borne,
   With distant cries of reapers in the corn°—   *grain*
20 All the live murmur of a summer's day.

Screened is this nook o'er the high, half-reaped field,
  And here till sundown, shepherd! will I be.
   Through the thick corn the scarlet poppies peep,
   And round green roots and yellowing stalks I see
25   Pale pink convolvulus in tendrils creep;
    And air-swept lindens yield
  Their scent, and rustle down their perfumed showers
  Of bloom on the bent grass where I am laid,
   And bower me from the August sun with shade;
30 And the eye travels down to Oxford's towers.

And near me on the grass lies Glanvil's book—
  Come, let me read the oft-read tale again!
   The story of the Oxford scholar poor,
   Of pregnant parts[4] and quick inventive brain,
35   Who, tired of knocking at preferment's door,
    One summer-morn forsook
  His friends, and went to learn the gypsy-lore,
  And roamed the world with that wild brotherhood,
   And came, as most men deemed, to little good,
40 But came to Oxford and his friends no more.

---

2. " 'There was very lately a lad in the University of Oxford, who was by his poverty forced to leave his studies there; and at last to join himself to a company of vagabond gypsies. Among these extravagant people, by the insinuating subtlety of his carriage, he quickly got so much of their love and esteem as that they discovered to him their mystery. After he had been a pretty while well exercised in the trade, there chanced to ride by a couple of scholars, who had formerly been of his acquaintance. They quickly spied out their old friend among the gypsies; and he gave them an account of the necessity which drove him to that kind of life, and told them that the people he went with were not such impostors as they were taken for, but that they had a traditional kind of learning among them, and could do wonders by the power of imagination, their fancy binding that of others: that himself had learned much of their art, and when he had compassed the whole secret, he intended, he said, to leave their company, and give the world an account of what he had learned.'—Glanvil's *Vanity of Dogmatizing*, 1661" [Arnold's note]
3. Sheepfolds made of woven boughs (wattles).
4. I.e., of quick intellectual abilities.

But once, years after, in the country-lanes,
  Two scholars, whom at college erst he knew,
  Met him, and of his way of life enquired;
  Whereat he answered, that the gypsy-crew,
    His mates, had arts to rule as they desired
  The workings of men's brains,
  And they can bind them to what thoughts they will.
    "And I," he said, "the secret of their art,
    When fully learned, will to the world impart;
  But it needs heaven-sent moments for this skill."

This said, he left them, and returned no more.—
  But rumors hung about the country-side,
  That the lost Scholar long was seen to stray,
  Seen by rare glimpses, pensive and tongue-tied,
    In hat of antique shape, and cloak of gray.
  The same the gypsies wore.
  Shepherds had met him on the Hurst[5] in spring;
    At some lone alehouse in the Berkshire moors,
    On the warm ingle-bench, the smock-frocked boors°   *rustics*
  Had found him seated at their entering,

But, 'mid their drink and clatter, he would fly.
  And I myself seem half to know thy looks,
  And put the shepherds, wanderer! on thy trace;
  And boys who in lone wheatfields scare the rooks
    I ask if thou hast passed their quiet place;
    Or in my boat I lie
  Moored to the cool bank in the summer-heats,
    'Mid wide grass meadows which the sunshine fills,
    And watch the warm, green-muffled Cumner hills,
  And wonder if thou haunt'st their shy retreats.

For most, I know, thou lov'st retired ground!
  Thee at the ferry Oxford riders blithe,
  Returning home on summer-nights, have met
  Crossing the stripling Thames at Bab-lock-hithe,
    Trailing in the cool stream thy fingers wet,
    As the punt's rope chops round;[6]
  And leaning backward in a pensive dream,
    And fostering in thy lap a heap of flowers
    Plucked in shy fields and distant Wychwood bowers,
  And thine eyes resting on the moonlit stream.

And then they land, and thou art seen no more!
  Maidens, who from the distant hamlets come
  To dance around the Fyfield elm in May,
  Oft through the darkening fields have seen thee roam,
    Or cross a stile into the public way.
    Oft thou hast given them store
  Of flowers—the frail-leafed, white anemone,
    Dark bluebells drenched with dews of summer eves,
    And purple orchises with spotted leaves—
  But none hath words she can report of thee.

5. A hill near Oxford. (All place-names in
the poem, with the obvious exception of the
Mediterranean localities of the last two stanzas,
refer to the countryside around Oxford.)

6. "As the punt's rope chops round": i.e., as
the rope tying the small boat to the bank shifts
around.

And, above Godstow Bridge, when hay-time's here
  In June, and many a scythe in sunshine flames,
    Men who through those wide fields of breezy grass
    Where black-winged swallows haunt the glittering Thames,
95   To bathe in the abandoned lasher[7] pass,
      Have often passed thee near
  Sitting upon the river bank o'ergrown;
    Marked thine outlandish garb, thy figure spare,
    Thy dark vague eyes, and soft abstracted air—
100 But, when they came from bathing, thou wast gone!

At some lone homestead in the Cumner hills,
  Where at her open door the housewife darns,
    Thou hast been seen, or hanging on a gate
    To watch the threshers in the mossy barns.
105 Children, who early range these slopes and late
     For cresses from the rills,
  Have known thee eying, all an April-day,
    The springing pastures and the feeding kine;
    And marked thee, when the stars come out and shine,
110 Through the long dewy grass move slow away.

In autumn, on the skirts of Bagley Wood—
  Where most the gypsies by the turf-edged way
    Pitch their smoked tents, and every bush you see
    With scarlet patches tagged and shreds of gray,
115 Above the forest-ground called Thessaly—
     The blackbird, picking food,
  Sees thee, nor stops his meal, nor fears at all;
    So often has he known thee past him stray,
    Rapt, twirling in thy hand a withered spray,
120 And waiting for the spark from heaven to fall.

And once, in winter, on the causeway chill
  Where home through flooded fields foot-travelers go,
    Have I not passed thee on the wooden bridge,
    Wrapt in thy cloak and battling with the snow,
125 Thy face tow'rd Hinksey and its wintry ridge?
     And thou hast climbed the hill,
  And gained the white brow of the Cumner range;
    Turned once to watch, while thick the snowflakes fall,
    The line of festal light in Christ-Church hall—
130 Then sought thy straw in some sequestered grange.

But what—I dream! Two hundred years are flown
  Since first thy story ran through Oxford halls,
    And the grave Glanvil did the tale inscribe
    That thou wert wandered from the studious walls
135 To learn strange arts, and join a gypsy-tribe;
     And thou from earth art gone
  Long since, and in some quiet churchyard laid—
    Some country-nook, where o'er thy unknown grave
    Tall grasses and white flowering nettles wave,
140 Under a dark, red-fruited yew-tree's shade.
  —No, no, thou hast not felt the lapse of hours!

---

7. Slack water above a weir or dam, or the weir itself.

For what wears out the life of mortal men?
　'Tis that from change to change their being rolls;
　'Tis that repeated shocks, again, again,
　　Exhaust the energy of strongest souls
　　And numb the elastic powers.
Till having used our nerves with bliss and teen,°　　*vexation*
　And tired upon a thousand schemes our wit,
　To the just-pausing Genius[8] we remit
Our worn-out life, and are—what we have been.

Thou hast not lived, why should'st thou perish, so?
　Thou hadst *one* aim, *one* business, *one* desire;
　　Else wert thou long since numbered with the dead!
　　Else hadst thou spent, like other men, thy fire!
　　The generations of thy peers are fled.
　　　And we ourselves shall go;
But thou possessest an immortal lot,
　And we imagine thee exempt from age
　And living as thou liv'st on Glanvil's page,
Because thou hadst—what we, alas! have not.

For early didst thou leave the world, with powers
　Fresh, undiverted to the world without,
　　Firm to their mark, not spent on other things;
　Free from the sick fatigue, the languid doubt,
　　Which much to have tried, in much been baffled, brings.
　　　O life unlike to ours!
Who fluctuate idly without term or scope,
　Of whom each strives, nor knows for what he strives,
　And each half lives a hundred different lives;[9]
Who wait like thee, but not, like thee, in hope.

Thou waitest for the spark from heaven! and we,
　Light half-believers of our casual creeds,
　　Who never deeply felt, nor clearly willed,
　Whose insight never has borne fruit in deeds,
　　Whose vague resolves never have been fulfilled;
　　　For whom each year we see
Breeds new beginnings, disappointments new;
　Who hesitate and falter life away,
　And lose tomorrow the ground won today—
Ah! do not we, wanderer! await it too?

Yes, we await it! but it still delays,
　And then we suffer! and amongst us one,[1]
　　Who most has suffered, takes dejectedly
　　His seat upon the intellectual throne;
　　And all his store of sad experience he
　　　Lays bare of wretched days;
Tells us his misery's birth and growth and signs,
　And how the dying spark of hope was fed,
　And how the breast was soothed, and how the head,
And all his hourly varied anodynes.

---

8. In classical mythology, the protecting spirit
assigned to each being to see it through the
world and finally to usher it out.
9. I.e., half-heartedly lives a hundred different
lives.
1. Both Goethe and Tennyson have been sug-
gested as being meant here.

This for our wisest! and we others pine,
  And wish the long unhappy dream would end,
    And waive all claim to bliss, and try to bear;
    With close-lipped patience for our only friend,
195   Sad patience, too near neighbor to despair—
        But none has hope like thine!
  Thou through the fields and through the woods dost stray,
    Roaming the countryside, a truant boy,
    Nursing thy project in unclouded joy,
200 And every doubt long blown by time away.

O born in days when wits were fresh and clear,
  And life ran gaily as the sparkling Thames;
    Before this strange disease of modern life,
    With its sick hurry, its divided aims,
205   Its head o'ertaxed, its palsied hearts, was rife—
        Fly hence, our contact fear!
  Still fly, plunge deeper in the bowering wood!
    Averse, as Dido did with gesture stern
    From her false friend's approach in Hades turn,[2]
210 Wave us away, and keep thy solitude!

Still nursing the unconquerable hope,
  Still clutching the inviolable shade,
    With a free, onward impulse brushing through,
    By night, the silvered branches of the glade—
215   Far on the forest-skirts, where none pursue,
        On some mild pastoral slope
  Emerge, and resting on the moonlit pales°   *fences*
    Freshen thy flowers as in former years
    With dew, or listen with enchanted ears,
220 From the dark dingles,° to the nightingales!   *valleys*

But fly our paths, our feverish contact fly!
  For strong the infection of our mental strife,
    Which, though it gives no bliss, yet spoils for rest;
    And we should win thee from thy own fair life,
225   Like us distracted, and like us unblest.
        Soon, soon thy cheer would die,
  Thy hopes grow timorous, and unfixed thy powers,
    And thy clear aims be cross and shifting made;
    And then thy glad perennial youth would fade,
230 Fade, and grow old at last, and die like ours.

Then fly our greetings, fly our speech and smiles!
  —As some grave Tyrian[3] trader, from the sea,
    Descried at sunrise an emerging prow
    Lifting the cool-haired creepers stealthily,
235   The fringes of a southward-facing brow
        Among the Aegean isles;
  And saw the merry Grecian coaster come,
    Freighted with amber grapes, and Chian[4] wine,
    Green, bursting figs, and tunnies steeped in brine—
240 And knew the intruders on his ancient home,

---

2. Dido, queen of Carthage, had been deserted by Aeneas after giving her love to him. Aeneas later encountered her in the underworld, among the shades of those who have died of unhappy love, but when he greeted her she turned her back on him.
3. A native of the ancient Phoenician city of Tyre, in the eastern Mediterranean.
4. From the island of Chios, famous for its wine.

The young light-hearted masters of the waves—
And snatched his rudder, he shook out more sail;
And day and night held on indignantly
O'er the blue Midland waters with the gale,
Betwixt the Syrtes[5] and soft Sicily,
To where the Atlantic raves
Outside the western straits;[6] and unbent sails
There, where down cloudy cliffs, through sheets of foam,
Shy traffickers, the dark Iberians[7] come;
And on the beach undid his corded bales.

1853

Thyrsis

A MONODY,[8] TO COMMEMORATE THE AUTHOR'S FRIEND, ARTHUR HUGH
CLOUGH, WHO DIED AT FLORENCE, 1861[9]

How changed is here each spot man makes or fills!
In the two Hinkseys[1] nothing keeps the same;
The village street its haunted mansion lacks,
And from the sign is gone Sibylla's name,[2]
5   And from the roofs the twisted chimney-stacks—
Are ye too changed, ye hills?
See, 'tis no foot of unfamiliar men
Tonight from Oxford up your pathway strays!
Here came I often, often, in old days—
10   Thyrsis and I; we still had Thyrsis then.

Runs it not here, the track by Childsworth Farm,
Past the high wood, to where the elm-tree crowns
The hill behind whose ridge the sunset flames?
The signal-elm, that looks on Ilsley Downs,
15   The Vale, the three lone weirs,° the youthful Thames?   *river-dams*
This winter-eve is warm,
Humid the air! leafless, yet soft as spring,
The tender purple spray on corpse and briers!
And that sweet city with her dreaming spires,
20   She needs not June for beauty's heightening,

Lovely all times she lies, lovely tonight!
Only, methinks, some loss of habit's power
Befalls me wandering through this upland dim.
Once passed I blindfold here, at any hour;
25   Now seldom come I, since I came with him.
That single elm-tree bright
Against the west—I miss it! is it gone?
We prized it dearly; while it stood, we said,
Our friend, the Gypsy-Scholar, was not dead;
30   While the tree lived, he in these fields lived on.

5. Two gulfs on the North African coast, one off Cyrenaica, the other off Tunisia.
6. I.e., the Straits of Gibraltar.
7. Ancient name for the inhabitants of Spain.
8. Species of poem in which a single mourner laments.
9. The friendship between Arnold and Clough (1819–61), himself a distinguished poet, had been at its closest while they were at Oxford, and Arnold chooses as the framework for his poem a visit to Oxford—at least in reminiscence—and more specifically to a hill above the town crowned by the signal-elm. The tree had had a particular significance for them, since they connected it with the continuing symbolic presence in the countryside of the Scholar-Gypsy and his lonely faithfulness to an ideal of truth-seeking. (See Arnold's poem *The Scholar-Gypsy* and his note to it, above.) As the name Thyrsis (and later, Corydon) indicates, Arnold is adopting the conventions of the Greek and Latin pastoral elegy for his poem.
1. Two villages (North and South Hinksey) near Oxford.
2. Sibylla Kerr, a tavern-keeper when Arnold and Clough were students.

Too rare, too rare, grow now my visits here,
  But once I knew each field, each flower, each stick;
  And with the country-folk acquaintance made
  By barn in threshing-time, by new-built rick.
35 Here, too, our shepherd-pipes we first assayed.
    Ah me! this many a year
  My pipe is lost, my shepherd's holiday!
  Needs must I lose them, needs with heavy heart
  Into the world and wave of men depart;
40 But Thyrsis of his own will went away.[3]

It irked him to be here, he could not rest.
  He loved each simple joy the country yields,
    He loved his mates; but yet he could not keep,
  For that a shadow loured on the fields,
45   Here with the shepherds and the silly° sheep.   *innocent*
    Some life of men unblest
  He knew, which made him droop; and filled his head.
  He went; his piping took a troubled sound
  Of storms that rage outside our happy ground;
50 He could not wait their passing, he is dead.

So, some tempestuous morn in early June,
  When the year's primal burst of bloom is o'er,
    Before the roses and the longest day—
  When garden-walks and all the grassy floor
55   With blossoms red and white of fallen May
    And chestnut-flowers are strewn—
  So have I heard the cuckoo's parting cry,
  From the wet field, through the vext garden-trees,
  Come with the volleying rain and tossing breeze:
60 *The bloom is gone, and with the bloom go I!*

Too quick despairer, wherefore wilt thou go?
  Soon will the high Midsummer pomps come on,
    Soon will the musk carnations break and swell,
  Soon shall we have gold-dusted snapdragon,
65   Sweet-William with his homely cottage-smell,
    And stocks in fragrant blow;
  Roses that down the alleys shine afar,
  And open, jasmine-muffled lattices,
  And groups under the dreaming garden-trees,
70 And the full moon, and the white evening-star.

He hearkens not! light comer, he is flown!
  What matters it? next year he will return,
    And we shall have him in the sweet spring-days,
  With whitening hedges, and uncrumpling fern,
75   And bluebells trembling by the forest-ways,
    And scent of hay new-mown.
  But Thyrsis never more we swains shall see;
  See him come back, and cut a smoother reed,
  And blow a strain the world at last shall heed—
80 For Time, not Corydon, hath conquered thee!

---

3. Clough resigned his fellowship at Oxford in 1848, rather than subscribe to the Thirty-nine
Articles of the Anglican Church.

Alack, for Corydon no rival now!
  But when Sicilian shepherds lost a mate,
    Some good survivor with his flute would go,
  Piping a ditty sad for Bion's fate;[4]
    And cross the unpermitted ferry's flow,[5]
      And relax Pluto's brow,
  And make leap up with joy the beauteous head
  Of Proserpine, among whose crownéd hair
  Are flowers first opened on Sicilian air,
  And flute his friend, like Orpheus,[6] from the dead.

O easy access to the hearer's grace
  When Dorian[7] shepherds sang to Proserpine!
    For she herself had trod Sicilian fields,
  She knew the Dorian water's gush divine,
    She knew each lily white which Enna yields,
      Each rose with blushing face;
  She loved the Dorian pipe, the Dorian strain.
    But ah, of our poor Thames she never heard!
    Her foot the Cumner cowslips never stirred;
  And we should tease her with our plaint in vain!

Well! wind-dispersed and vain the words will be,
  Yet, Thyrsis, let me give my grief its hour
    In the old haunt, and find our tree-topped hill!
  Who, if not I, for questing here hath power?
    I know the wood which hides the daffodil,
      I know the Fyfield tree,
  I know what white, what purple fritillaries°   *flowers*
    The grassy harvest of the river-fields,
    Above by Ensham, down by Sandford, yields,
  And what sedged brooks are Thames's tributaries;

I know these slopes; who knows them if not I?
  But many a dingle° on the loved hillside,   *valley*
    With thorns once studded, old, white-blossomed trees,
  Where thick the cowslips grew, and far descried
    High towered the spikes of purple orchises,
      Hath since our day put by
  The coronals of that forgotten time;[8]
    Down each green bank hath gone the ploughboy's team,
    And only in the hidden brookside gleam
  Primroses, orphans of the flowery prime.

Where is the girl, who by the boatman's door,
  Above the locks, above the boating throng,
    Unmoored our skiff when through the Wytham flats,
  Red loosestrife and blond meadow-sweet among
    And darting swallows and light water-gnats,
      We tracked the shy Thames shore?
  Where are the mowers, who, as the tiny swell

---

4. Greek pastoral poet of the first century B.C. who lived in Sicily and who was mourned in *Lament for Bion,* sometimes ascribed to his pupil Moschus.
5. The ferry across the River Styx to Hades, ruled over by Pluto and his queen, Proserpine, whom he had abducted while she was gathering flowers in the fields near Enna, in Sicily. She spent half of each year in the underworld and half on earth.
6. Orpheus, because of the power and charm of his music, had been permitted to attempt to lead his wife, Eurydice, back from the dead.
7. One of the ancient Greek lyrical modes, characterized by simplicity and nobility.
8. I.e., the flowers that once crowned them.

Of our boat passing heaved the river-grass,
Stood with suspended scythe to see us pass?
130 They all are gone, and thou art gone as well!

Yes, thou art gone! and round me too the night
In ever-nearing circle weaves her shade.
I see her veil draw soft across the day,
I feel her slowly chilling breath invade
135 The cheek grown thin, the brown hair sprent° with grey;   sprinkled
I feel her finger light
Laid pausefully upon life's headlong train;
The foot less prompt to meet the morning dew,
The heart less bounding at emotion new,
140 And hope, once crushed, less quick to spring again.

And long the way appears, which seemed so short
To the less practiced eye of sanguine youth;
And high the mountain-tops, in cloudy air,
The mountain-tops where is the throne of Truth,
145 Tops in life's morning-sun so bright and bare!
Unbreachable the fort
Of the long-battered world uplifts its wall;
And strange and vain the earthly turmoil grows,
And near and real the charm of thy repose,
150 And night as welcome as a friend would fall.

But hush! the upland hath a sudden loss
Of quiet!—Look, adown the dusk hillside,
A troop of Oxford hunters going home,
As in old days, jovial and talking, ride!
155 From hunting with the Berkshire hounds they come.
Quick! let me fly, and cross
Into yon farther field!—'Tis done; and see,
Backed by the sunset, which doth glorify
The orange and pale violet evening-sky,
160 Bare on its lonely ridge, the Tree! the Tree!

I take the omen! Eve lets down her veil,
The white fog creeps from bush to bush about,
The west unflushes, the high stars grow bright,
And in the scattered farms the lights come out.
165 I cannot reach the signal-tree to-night,
Yet, happy omen, hail!
Hear it from thy broad lucent Arno-vale[9]
(For there thine earth-forgetting eyelids keep
The morningless and unawakening sleep
170 Under the flowery oleanders pale),

Hear it, O Thyrsis still our tree is there!
Ah, vain! These English fields, this upland dim,
These brambles pale with mist engarlanded,
That lone, sky-pointing tree, are not for him;
175 To a boon southern country he is fled,
And now in happier air,

9. Clough is buried in the Protestant cemetery in Florence, through which city the Arno
flows.

Wandering with the great Mother's train divine[1]
  (And purer or more subtle soul than thee,
    I trow, the mighty Mother doth not see)
Within a folding of the Apennine,[2]

Thou hearest the immortal chants of old!
  Putting his sickle to the perilous grain
    In the hot cornfield of the Phrygian king,
For thee the Lityerses-song again
    Young Daphnis with his silver voice doth sing;[3]
      Sings his Sicilian fold,
His sheep, his hapless love, his blinded eyes—
And how a call celestial round him rang,
And heavenward from the fountain-brink he sprang,
  And all the marvel of the golden skies.

There thou art gone, and me thou leavest here
  Sole in these fields! yet will I not despair.
    Despair I will not, while I yet descry
Neath the mild canopy of English air
    That lonely tree against the western sky.
      Still, still these slopes, 'tis clear,
Our Gypsy-Scholar haunts, outliving thee!
Fields where soft sheep from cages pull the hay,
Woods with anemonies in flower till May,
  Know him a wanderer still; then why not me?

A fugitive and gracious light he seeks,
  Shy to illumine; and I seek it too.
    This does not come with houses or with gold,
With place, with honor, and a flattering crew;
    'Tis not in the world's market bought and sold—
      But the smooth-slipping weeks
Drop by, and leave its seeker still untired;
  Out of the heed of mortals he is gone,
  He wends unfollowed, he must house alone;
  Yet on he fares, by his own heart inspired.

Thou too, O Thyrsis, on like quest wast bound;
  Thou wanderest with me for a little hour!
    Men gave thee nothing; but this happy quest,
If men esteemed thee feeble, gave thee power,
    If men procured thee trouble, gave thee rest.
      And this rude Cumner ground,
Its fir-topped Hurst, its farms, its quiet fields,

---

1. Possibly the devotees of Demeter, the Earth Mother.
2. The Apennines are a mountain range in Italy.
3. "Daphnis, the ideal Sicilian shepherd of Greek pastoral poetry, was said to have followed into Phrygia his mistress Piplea, who had been carried off by robbers, and to have found her in the power of the king of Phrygia, Lityerses. Lityerses used to make strangers try a contest with him in reaping corn, and to put them to death if he overcame them. Hercules arrived in time to save Daphnis, took upon himself the reaping-contest with Lityerses, overcame him, and slew him. The Lityerses-song connected with this tradition was, like the Linus-song, one of the early plaintive strains of Greek popular poetry, and used to be sung by corn-reapers. Other traditions represented Daphnis as beloved by a nymph who exacted from him an oath to love no one else. He fell in love with a princess, and was struck blind by the jealous nymph. Mercury, who was his father, raised him to heaven, and made a fountain spring up in the place from which he ascended. At this fountain the Sicilians offered yearly sacrifices. —See Servius, *Comment. in Virgil. Bucol.*, v.20 and viii.68" [Arnold's note].

Here cam'st thou in thy jocund youthful time,
Here was thine height of strength, thy golden prime!
220   And still the haunt beloved a virtue yields.

What though the music of thy rustic flute
Kept not for long its happy, country tone;
Lost it too soon, and learnt a stormy note
Of men contention-tost, of men who groan,
225   Which tasked thy pipe too sore, and tired thy throat—
It failed, and thou wast mute!
Yet hadst thou alway visions of our light,
And long with men of care thou couldst not stay,
And soon thy foot resumed its wandering way,
230   Left human haunt, and on alone till night.

Too rare, too rare, grow now my visits here!
'Mid city-noise, not, as with thee of yore,
Thyrsis! in reach of sheep-bells is my home.
—Then through the great town's harsh, heart-wearying roar,
235   Let in thy voice a whisper often come,
To chase fatigue and fear:
Why faintest thou? I wandered till I died.
Roam on! The light we sought is shining still.
Dost thou ask proof? Our tree yet crowns the hill,
240   *Our Scholar travels yet the loved hillside.*

1866

Dover Beach

The sea is calm tonight.
The tide is full, the moon lies fair
Upon the straits; on the French coast the light
Gleams and is gone; the cliffs of England stand,
5   Glimmering and vast, out in the tranquil bay.
Come to the window, sweet is the night-air!
Only, from the long line of spray
Where the sea meets the moon-blanched land,
Listen! you hear the grating roar
10   Of pebbles which the waves draw back, and fling,
At their return, up the high strand,
Begin, and cease, and then again begin,
With tremulous cadence slow, and bring
The eternal note of sadness in.

15   Sophocles long ago
Heard it on the Ægean, and it brought
Into his mind the turbid ebb and flow
Of human misery;[4] we
Find also in the sound a thought,
20   Hearing it by this distant northern sea.

The Sea of Faith
Was once, too, at the full, and round earth's shore
Lay like the folds of a bright girdle furled.

4. Compare Sophocles' *Antigone*, lines 583–91.

But now I only hear
Its melancholy, long, withdrawing roar,
Retreating, to the breath
Of the night-wind, down the vast edges drear
And naked shingles[5] of the world.

Ah, love, let us be true
To one another! for the world, which seems
To lie before us like a land of dreams,
So various, so beautiful, so new,
Hath really neither joy, nor love, nor light,
Nor certitude, nor peace, nor help for pain;
And we are here as on a darkling plain
Swept with confused alarms of struggle and flight,
Where ignorant armies clash by night.

1867

Palladium[6]

Set where the upper streams of Simois flow[7]
Was the Palladium, high 'mid rock and wood;
And Hector was in Ilium,[8] far below,
And fought, and saw it not—but there it stood!

It stood, and sun and moonshine rained their light
On the pure columns of its glen-built hall.
Backward and forward rolled the waves of fight
Round Troy—but while this stood, Troy could not fall.

So, in its lovely moonlight, lives the soul.
Mountains surround it, and sweet virgin air;
Cold plashing, past it, crystal waters roll;
We visit it by moments, ah, too rare!

We shall renew the battle in the plain
Tomorrow; red with blood will Xanthus[9] be,
Hector and Ajax will be there again,
Helen will come upon the wall to see.

Then we shall rust in shade, or shine in strife,
And fluctuate 'twixt blind hopes and blind despairs,
And fancy that we put forth all our life,
And never know how with the soul it fares.

Still doth the soul, from its lone fastness high,
Upon our life a ruling effluence send.
And when it fails, fight as we will, we die;
And while it lasts, we cannot wholly end.

1867

---

5. Beaches covered with water-worn small stones and pebbles.
6. The image of the goddess Pallas Athena (or, as perhaps here, the temple in which the image was housed), believed to guarantee the safety of the city which possessed it.
7. In the *Iliad*, a river near Troy (Ilium).
8. Hector, the Trojan hero, son of Priam and Hecuba, whose abduction of the beautiful Helen from her husband Menelaus, brother of the Greek king Agamemnon, had caused the war between Greeks and Trojans. Ajax, second only to Achilles among the Greek heroes, fought in single combat with Hector in the tenth year of the war.
9. In the *Iliad*, the Scamander river (called Xanthus by the gods).

DANTE GABRIEL ROSSETTI
(1828–1882)

The Blessed Damozel[1]

The blessed damozel leaned out
   From the gold bar of Heaven;
Her eyes were deeper than the depth
   Of waters stilled at even;
5 She had three lilies in her hand,
   And the stars in her hair were seven.

Her robe, ungirt from clasp to hem,
   No wrought flowers did adorn,
But a white rose of Mary's gift,
10   For service meetly worn;
Her hair that lay along her back
   Was yellow like ripe corn.°   *wheat, grain*

Herseemed she scarce had been a day
   One of God's choristers;
15 The wonder was not yet quite gone
   From that still look of hers;
Albeit, to them she left, her day
   Had counted as ten years.

(To one, it is ten years of years.
20   . . . Yet now, and in this place,
Surely she leaned o'er me—her hair
   Fell all about my face. . . .
Nothing: the autumn fall of leaves.
   The whole year sets apace.)

25 It was the rampart of God's house
   That she was standing on;
By God built over the sheer depth
   The which is Space begun;
So high, that looking downward thence
30   She scarce could see the sun.

It lies in Heaven, across the flood
   Of ether, as a bridge.
Beneath, the tides of day and night
   With flame and darkness ridge
35 The void, as low as where this earth
   Spins like a fretful midge.

Around her, lovers, newly met
   In joy no sorrow claims,
Spoke evermore among themselves
40   Their rapturous new names;
And the souls mounting up to God
   Went by her like thin flames.

---

1. Older form of *damsel,* meaning "young un-married lady," preferred by Romantic and later writers because it avoids the simpler, homelier associations of *damsel.*

And still she bowed herself and stooped
  Out of the circling charm;
Until her bosom must have made
  The bar she leaned on warm,
And the lilies lay as if asleep
  Along her bended arm.

From the fixed place of Heaven she saw
  Time like a pulse shake fierce
Through all the worlds. Her gaze still strove
  Within the gulf to pierce
Its path; and now she spoke as when
  The stars sang in their spheres.

The sun was gone now; the curled moon
  Was like a little feather
Fluttering far down the gulf; and now
  She spoke through the still weather.
Her voice was like the voice the stars
  Had when they sang together.

(Ah sweet! Even now, in that bird's song,
  Strove not her accents there,
Fain to be hearkened? When those bells
  Possessed the midday air,
Strove not her steps to reach my side
  Down all the echoing stair?)

"I wish that he were come to me,
  For he will come," she said.
"Have I not prayed in Heaven?—on earth,
  Lord, Lord, has he not prayed?
Are not two prayers a perfect strength?
  And shall I feel afraid?

"When round his head the aureole clings,
  And he is clothed in white,
I'll take his hand and go with him
  To the deep wells of light;
We will step down as to a stream,
  And bathe there in God's sight.

"We two will stand beside that shrine,
  Occult, withheld, untrod,
Whose lamps are stirred continually
  With prayer sent up to God;
And see our old prayers, granted, melt
  Each like a little cloud.

"We two will lie i' the shadow of
  That living mystic tree
Within whose secret growth the Dove
  Is sometimes felt to be,
While every leaf that His plumes touch
  Saith His Name audibly.

"And I myself will teach to him,
  I myself, lying so,

The songs I sing here; which his voice
  Shall pause in, hushed and slow,
95 And find some knowledge at each pause,
  Of some new thing to know."

(Alas! We two, we two, thou say'st!
  Yea, one wast thou with me
That once of old. But shall God lift
100   To endless unity
The soul whose likeness with thy soul
  Was but its love for thee?)

"We two," she said, "will seek the groves
  Where the lady Mary is,
105 With her five handmaidens, whose names
  Are five sweet symphonies,
Cecily, Gertrude, Magdalen,
  Margaret and Rosalys.

"Circlewise sit they, with bound locks
110   And foreheads garlanded;
Into the fine cloth white like flame
  Weaving the golden thread,
To fashion the birth-robes for them
  Who are just born, being dead.

115 "He shall fear, haply, and be dumb:
  Then will I lay my cheek
To his, and tell about our love,
  Not once abashed or weak:
And the dear Mother will approve
120   My pride, and let me speak.

"Herself shall bring us, hand in hand,
  To Him round whom all souls
Kneel, the clear-ranged unnumbered heads
  Bowed with their aureoles:
125 And angels meeting us shall sing
  To their citherns and citoles.[2]

"There will I ask of Christ the Lord
  Thus much for him and me:—
Only to live as once on earth
130   With Love—only to be,
As then awhile, forever now
  Together, I and he."

She gazed and listened and then said,
  Less sad of speech than mild,
135 "All this is when he comes." She ceased.
  The light thrilled towards her, filled
With angels in strong level flight.
  Her eyes prayed, and she smiled.

---

2. Antique musical instruments: the cithern (17th century), a guitar-like instrument with wire strings; the citole, a stringed instrument dating from the 13th–15th century.

(I saw her smile.) But soon their path
    Was vague in distant spheres:
And then she cast her arms along
    The golden barriers,
And laid her face between her hands,
    And wept. (I heard her tears.)

1846   1850

Sudden Light

I have been here before,
    But when or how I cannot tell:
I know the grass beyond the door,
    The sweet keen smell,
The sighing sound, the lights around the shore.

You have been mine before,
    How long ago I may not know:
But just when at that swallow's soar
    Your neck turned so,
Some veil did fall—I knew it all of yore.

Has this been thus before?
    And shall not thus time's eddying flight
Still with our lives our love restore
    In death's despite,
And day and night yield one delight once more?

1854   1863

The Woodspurge

The wind flapped loose, the wind was still,
Shaken out dead from tree and hill:
I had walked on at the wind's will—
I sat now, for the wind was still.

Between my knees my forehead was—
My lips, drawn in, said not Alas!
My hair was over in the grass,
My naked ears heard the day pass.

My eyes, wide open, had the run
Of some ten weeds to fix upon;
Among those few, out of the sun,
The woodspurge flowered, three cups in one.

From perfect grief there need not be
Wisdom or even memory:
One thing then learnt remains to me—
The woodspurge has a cup of three.

1856   1870

From The House of Life

A Sonnet

A Sonnet is a moment's monument,—
  Memorial from the Soul's eternity
  To one dead deathless hour. Look that it be,
Whether for lustral° rite or dire portent,   *purificatory*
5 Of its own arduous fullness reverent:
    Carve it in ivory or in ebony,
    As Day or Night may rule; and let Time see
Its flowering crest impearled and orient.

A Sonnet is a coin: its face reveals
10   The soul—its converse, to what Power 'tis due:
Whether for tribute to the august appeals
    Of Life, or dower in Love's high retinue,
It serve; or, 'mid the dark wharf's cavernous breath,
In Charon's[6] palm it pay the toll to Death.

19. Silent Noon

Your hands lie open in the long fresh grass—
  The finger-points look through like rosy blooms:
  Your eyes smile peace. The pasture gleams and glooms
'Neath billowing skies that scatter and amass.
5 All round our nest, far as the eye can pass,
    Are golden kingcup-fields with silver edge
    Where the cow-parsley skirts the hawthorn-hedge.
'Tis visible silence, still as the hour-glass.

Deep in the sun-searched growths the dragonfly
10 Hangs like a blue thread loosened from the sky:
    So this winged hour is dropt to us from above.
Oh! clasp we to our hearts, for deathless dower,
This close-companioned inarticulate hour
    When twofold silence was the song of love.

70. The Hill Summit

This feast-day of the sun, his altar there
  In the broad west has blazed for vesper-song;
  And I have loitered in the vale too long
And gaze now a belated worshipper.
5 Yet may I not forget that I was 'ware,
    So journeying, of his face at intervals
    Transfigured where the fringed horizon falls,
A fiery bush with coruscating hair.

And now that I have climbed and won this height,
10   I must tread downward through the sloping shade
And travel the bewildered tracks till night.
    Yet for this hour I still may here be stayed
    And see the gold air and the silver fade
And the last bird fly into the last night.

6. Charon received a coin, an *obolus*, for ferrying the shades of the newly dead across the river Styx to Hades.

83. *Barren Spring*

Once more the changed year's turning wheel returns:
  And as a girl sails balanced in the wind,
  And now before and now again behind
Stoops as it swoops, with cheek that laughs and burns—
So Spring comes merry towards me here, but earns
  No answering smile from me, whose life is twined
  With the dead boughs that winter still must bind,
And whom to-day the Spring no more concerns.

Behold, this crocus is a withering flame;
  This snowdrop, snow; this apple-blossom's part
  To breed the fruit that breeds the serpent's art.
Nay, for these Spring-flowers, turn thy face from them,
  Nor gaze till on the year's last lily-stem
  The white cup shrivels round the golden heart.

90. *"Retro Me, Sathana"*[7]

Get thee behind me. Even as, heavy-curled,
  Stooping against the wind, a charioteer
  Is snatched from out his chariot by the hair,
So shall Time be; and as the void car, hurled
Abroad by reinless steeds, even so the world:
  Yea, even as chariot-dust upon the air,
  It shall be sought and not found anywhere.

Get thee behind me, Satan. Oft unfurled,
  Thy perilous wings can beat and break like lath
  Much mightiness of men to win thee praise.
  Leave these weak feet to tread in narrow ways.
Thou still, upon the broad vine-sheltered path,
  Mayst wait the turning of the phials of wrath[8]
  For certain years, for certain months and days.

91. *Lost on Both Sides*

As when two men have loved a woman well,
  Each hating each, through Love's and Death's deceit;
  Since not for either this stark marriage-sheet
And the long pauses of this wedding-bell;
Yet o'er her grave the night and day dispel
  At last their feud forlorn, with cold and heat;
  Nor other than dear friends to death may fleet
The two lives left that most of her can tell:

So separate hopes, which in a soul had wooed
  The one same Peace, strove with each other long,
  And Peace before their faces perished since:
So through that soul, in restless brotherhood,
  They roam together now, and wind among
  Its bye-streets, knocking at the dusty inns.

7. "Get thee behind me, Satan": words spoken by Christ in rejecting temptation. See Mark viii.33 (where the words are spoken in rebuke of a statement by Peter) and Matthew iv.10 (where similar words are spoken to Satan, who had offered Christ all the kingdoms of the world if He would fall down and worship him).
8. The vessels containing the wrath of God, which will eventually be poured out on the wicked and unworthy.

97. A Superscription

Look in my face; my name is Might-have-been;
  I am also called No-more, Too-late, Farewell;
  Unto thine ear I hold the dead-sea shell
Cast up thy Life's foam-fretted feet between;
5 Unto thine eyes the glass where that is seen
  Which had Life's form and Love's, but by my spell
  Is now a shaken shadow intolerable,
Of ultimate things unuttered the frail screen.

Mark me, how still I am! But should there dart
10 One moment through thy soul the soft surprise
  Of that winged Peace which lulls the breath of sighs,
Then shalt thou see me smile, and turn apart
Thy visage to mine ambush at thy heart
  Sleepless with cold commemorative eyes.

1847–80   1870, 1881

EMILY DICKINSON
(1830–1886)

89

Some things that fly there be—
Birds—Hours—the Bumblebee—
Of these no Elegy.

Some things that stay there be—
5 Grief—Hills—Eternity—
Nor this behooveth me.

There are that resting, rise.
Can I expound the skies?
How still the Riddle lies!

1859?   1890

98

One dignity delays for all—
One mitred Afternoon—
None can avoid this purple—
None evade this Crown!

5 Coach, it insures, and footmen—
Chamber, and state, and throng—
Bells, also, in the village
As we ride grand along!

What dignified Attendants!
10 What service when we pause!
How loyally at parting
Their hundred hats they raise!

How pomp surpassing ermine
When simple You, and I,
15 Present our meek escutscheon
And claim the rank to die!

1859?   1890

187

How many times these low feet staggered—
Only the soldered mouth can tell—
Try—can you stir the awful rivet—
Try—can you lift the hasps of steel!

Stroke the cool forehead—hot so often—
Lift—if you care— the listless hair—
Handle the adamantine° fingers   *rigid, unmovable*
Never a thimble—more—shall wear—

Buzz the dull flies—on the chamber window—
Brave—shines the sun through the freckled pane—
Fearless—the cobweb swings from the ceiling—
Indolent Housewife—in Daises—lain!   1860?   1890

214

I taste a liquor never brewed—
From Tankards scooped in Pearl—
Not all the Frankfort Berries[1]
Yield such an Alcohol!

5 Inebriate of Air—am I—
And Debauchee of Dew—
Reeling—thro endless summer days—
From inns of Molten Blue—

When "Landlords" turn the drunken Bee
Out of the Foxglove's door—
When Butterflies—renounce their "dram"—
I shall but drink the more!

Till Seraphs swing their snowy Hats—
And Saints—to windows run—
15 To see the little Tippler
From Manzanilla[2] come!   1860?   1861, 1890

216

Safe in their Alabaster Chambers—
Untouched by Morning
And untouched by Noon—
Sleep the meek members of the Resurrection—
5 Rafter of satin,
And Roof of stone.

Light laughs the breeze
In her Castle above them—
Babbles the Bee in a stolid Ear,
10 Pipe the Sweet Birds in ignorant cadence—
Ah, what sagacity perished here!   1859 version   1862

1. Wine grapes from the vicinity of Frankfort and the Rhine in Germany.

2. Name of a sherry wine from the Guadalquivar River area in Spain, and also the name of towns in Trinidad, Mexico, and Panama.

216[3]

Safe in their Alabaster Chambers—
Untouched by Morning—
And untouched by Noon—
Lie the meek members of the Resurrection—
5   Rafter of Satin—and Roof of Stone!

Grand go the Years—in the Crescent—above them—
Worlds scoop their Arcs—
And Firmaments—row—
Diadems—drop—and Doges—surrender—
10 Soundless as dots—on a Disc of Snow—

                                1861 version   1890

241

I like a look of Agony,
Because I know it's true—
Men do not sham Convulsion,
Nor simulate, a Throe—

5   The Eyes glaze once—and that is Death—
Impossible to feign
The Beads upon the Forehead
By homely Anguish strung.

                                    1861?   1890

287

A Clock stopped—
Not the Mantel's—
Geneva's farthest skill[4]
Cant put the puppet bowing—
5   That just now dangled still—

An awe came on the Trinket!
The Figures hunched, with pain—
Then quivered out of Decimals—
Into Degreeless Noon—

10 It will not stir for Doctor's—
This Pendulum of snow—
The Shopman importunes it—
While cool—concernless No—

---

3. This poem has been familiar to readers of Emily Dickinson in a three-stanza version which we now know was never her conception of the poem. Thomas H. Johnson's account of the composition of the poem traces Emily's characteristic trying and re-trying of various articulations of her poetic idea. The 1859 version was sent to Sue Dickinson, Emily's sister-in-law, for advice, and Sue evidently did not like it much. The notes between the two women (they lived in adjoining houses) show Emily's labors over the poem, and her 1861 version was an attempt to meet her own and Sue's exactions. Professor Johnson believes Emily Dickinson was never fully satisfied with the poem. It was printed once during her lifetime (1862) in the 1859 version, but when she began her famous correspondence with Thomas W. Higginson, the literary critic and editor, she sent a modified version of the 1861 poem. When Higginson edited Emily Dickinson's poetry for posthumous publication (1890), he combined the two versions, and it is this three-stanza poem that readers had known as Emily's until Johnson's definitive edition of the poems in 1955.

4. Geneva, Switzerland, is traditionally famous for watch-making.

Nods from the Gilded pointers—
Nods from the Seconds slim—
Decades of Arrogance between
The Dial life—
And Him—

1861?   1896

303

The Soul selects her own Society—
Then—shuts the Door—
To her divine Majority—
Present no more—

5   Unmoved—she notes the Chariots—pausing—
At her low Gate—
Unmoved—an Emperor be kneeling
Upon her Mat—

I've known her—from an ample nation—
10 Choose One—
Then—close the Valves of her attention—
Like Stone—

1862?   1890

328

A Bird came down the Walk—
He did not know I saw—
He bit an Angleworm in halves
And ate the fellow, raw,

5   And then he drank a Dew
From a convenient Grass—
And then hopped sidewise to the Wall
To let a Beetle pass—

He glanced with rapid eyes
10 That hurried all around—
They looked like frightened Beads, I thought—
He stirred his Velvet Head

Like one in danger, Cautious,
I offered him a Crumb
15 And he unrolled his feathers
And rowed him softer home—

Than Oars divide the Ocean,
Too silver for a seam—
Or Butterflies, off Banks of Noon
20 Leap, plashless as they swim.

1862   1891

341

After great pain, a formal feeling comes—
The Nerves sit ceremonious, like Tombs—
The stiff Heart questions was it He, that bore,
And Yesterday, or Centuries before?

5 The Feet, mechanical, go round—
Of Ground, or Air, or Ought—°   *nothing, a void*
A Wooden way
Regardless grown,
A Quartz contentment, like a stone—

10 This is the Hour of Lead—
Remembered, if outlived,
As Freezing persons, recollect the Snow—
First—Chill—then Stupor—then the letting go—

                                        1862?   1929

357

God is a distant—stately Lover—
Woos, as He states us—by His Son—
Verily, a Vicarious Courtship—
"Miles", and "Priscilla", were such an One[5]—

5 But, lest the Soul—like fair "Priscilla"
Choose the Envoy—and spurn the Groom—
Vouches, with hyperbolic archness—
"Miles", and "John Alden" were Synonyme—

                                        1862?   1891, 1929

401

What Soft—Cherubic Creatures—
These Gentlewomen are—

One would as soon assault a Plush—
Or violate a Star—

5 Such Dimity[6] Convictions—
A Horror so refined
Of freckled Human Nature—
Of Deity—ashamed—

It's such a common—Glory—
10 A Fisherman's—Degree—
Redemption—Brittle Lady—
Be so—ashamed of Thee—

                                        1862?   1896

414

'Twas like a Maelstrom,[7] with a notch,
That nearer, every Day,

---

5. Allusion to the story in Longfellow's
Courtship of Miles Standish, where Miles
wishes to court Priscilla Mullins but sends
John Alden to speak for her. Priscilla falls
in love with John himself.
6. A delicate cotton fabric decorated with
designs woven into the fabric.
7. A whirlpool or powerful current of water.

Kept narrowing its boiling Wheel
Until the Agony

Toyed coolly with the final inch
Of your delirious Hem—
And you dropt, lost,
When something broke—
And let you from a Dream—

As if a Goblin with a Gauge—
Kept measuring the Hours—
Until you felt your Second
Weigh, helpless, in his Paws—

And not a Sinew—stirred—could help,
And sense was setting numb—
When God—remembered—and the Fiend
Let go, then, Overcome—

As if your Sentence stood—pronounced—
And you were frozen led
From Dungeon's luxury of Doubt
To Gibbets, and the Dead—

And when the Film had stitched your eyes
A Creature gasped "Reprieve"!
Which Anguish was the utterest—then—
To perish, or to live?

1862?   1945

435

Much Madness is divinest Sense—
To a discerning Eye—
Much Sense—the starkest Madness—
'Tis the Majority
In this, as All, prevail—
Assent—and you are sane—
Demur—you're straightway dangerous—
And handled with a Chain—

1862?   1890

437

Prayer is the little implement
Through which Men reach
Where Presence—is denied them.
They fling their Speech

By means of it—in God's Ear—
If then He hear—
This sums the Apparatus
Comprised in Prayer—

1862?   1891

449

I died for Beauty—but was scarce
Adjusted in the Tomb
When One who died for Truth, was lain
In an adjoining Room—

5   He questioned softly "Why I failed"?
"For Beauty", I replied—
"And I—for Truth—Themself are One—
We Brethren, are", He said—

And so, as Kinsmen, met a Night—
10   We talked between the Rooms—
Until the Moss had reached our lips—
And covered up—our names—

                                        1862?   1890

465

I heard a Fly buzz—when I died—
The Stillness in the Room
Was like the Stillness in the Air—
Between the Heaves of Storm—

5   The Eyes around—had wrung them dry—
And Breaths were gathering firm
For that last Onset—when the King
Be witnessed—in the Room—

I willed my Keepsakes—Signed away
10   What portion of me be
Assignable—and then it was
There interposed a Fly—

With Blue—uncertain stumbling Buzz—
Between the light—and me—
15   And then the Windows failed—and then
I could not see to see—

                                        1862?   1896

510

It was not Death, for I stood up,
And all the Dead, lie down—
It was not Night, for all the Bells
Put out their Tongues, for Noon.

5   It was not Frost, for on my Flesh
I felt Siroccos[8]—crawl—
Nor Fire—for just my Marble feet
Could keep a Chancel, cool—

---

8. Hot, moist southeasterly winds usually associated with the Libyan desert.

And yet, it tasted, like them all,
The Figures I have seen
Set orderly, for Burial,
Reminded me, of mine—

As if my life were shaven,
And fitted to a frame,
And could not breathe without a key,
And 'twas like Midnight, some—

When everything that ticked—has stopped—
And Space stares all around—
Or Grisly frosts—first Autumn morns,
Repeal the Beating Ground—

But, most, like Chaos—Stopless—cool—
Without a Chance, or Spar—
Or even a Report of Land—
To justify—Despair.

                                              1862   1891

524

Departed—to the Judgment—
A Mighty Afternoon—
Great Clouds—like Ushers—leaning—
Creation—looking on—

The Flesh—Surrendered—Cancelled—
The Bodiless—begun—
Two Worlds—like Audiences—disperse—
And leave the Soul—alone—

                                              1862?   1890

528

Mine—by the Right of the White Election!
Mine—by the Royal Seal!
Mine—by the Sign in the Scarlet prison—
Bars—cannot conceal!

Mine—here—in Vision—and in Veto!
Mine—by the Grave's Repeal—
Titled—Confirmed—
Delirious Charter!
Mine—long as Ages steal!

                                              1862?   1890

536

The Heart asks Pleasure—first—
And then—Excuse from Pain—
And then—those little Anodynes
That deaden suffering—

5   And then—to go to sleep—
     And then—if it should be
     The will of its Inquisitor
     The privilege to die—

1862?   1890

585

     I like to see it lap the Miles—
     And lick the Valleys up—
     And stop to feed itself at Tanks—
     And then—prodigious step

5   Around a Pile of Mountains—
     And supercilious peer
     In Shanties—by the sides of Roads—
     And then a Quarry pare

     To fit its sides
10   And crawl between
     Complaining all the while
     In horrid—hooting stanza—
     Then chase itself down Hill—

     And neigh like Boanerges[9]—
15   Then—prompter than a Star
     Stop—docile and omnipotent
     At its own stable door—

1862?   1891

640

     I cannot live with You—
     It would be Life—
     And Life is over there—
     Behind the Shelf

5   The Sexton keeps the Key to—
     Putting up
     Our Life—His Porcelain—
     Like a Cup—

     Discarded of the Housewife—
10   Quaint—or Broke—
     A newer Sevres[1] pleases—
     Old Ones crack—

     I could not die—with You—
     For One must wait
15   To shut the Other's Gaze down—
     You—could not—

9. "The name given by Christ to the two sons of Zebedee. Hence, * * * a loud, vociferous preacher or orator" [S.O.E.D.].
1. A fine and expensive French porcelain.

And I—Could I stand by
And see You—freeze—
Without my Right of Frost—
Death's privilege?

Nor could I rise—with You—
Because Your Face
Would put out Jesus'—
That New Grace

Glow plain—and foreign
On my homesick Eye—
Except that You than He
Shone closer by—

They'd judge Us—How—
For You—served Heaven—You know,
Or sought to—
I could not—

Because You saturated Sight—
And I had no more Eyes
For sordid excellence
As Paradise

And were You lost, I would be—
Though My Name
Rang loudest
On the Heavenly fame—

And were You—saved—
And I—condemned to be
Where You were not—
That self—were Hell to Me—

So We must meet apart—
You there—I—here—
With just the Door ajar
That Oceans are—and Prayer—
And that White Sustenance—
Despair—

1862?   1890

675

Essential Oils—are wrung—
The Attar[2] from the Rose
Be not expressed by Suns—alone—
It is the gift of Screws—

The General Rose—decay—
But this—in Lady's Drawer
Make Summer—When the Lady lie
In Ceaseless Rosemary[3]—

1863?   1891

2. Fragrant oil obtained from rose petals.
3. An evergreen shrub used sometimes in cookery and sometimes as an emblem of remembrance.

712

Because I could not stop for Death—
He kindly stopped for me—
The Carriage held but just Ourselves—
And Immortality.

5 　We slowly drove—He knew no haste
And I had put away
My labor and my leisure too,
For His Civility—

We passed the School, where Children strove
10 　At Recess—in the Ring—
We passed the Fields of Gazing Grain—
We passed the Setting Sun—

Or rather—He passed Us—
The Dews drew quivering and chill—
15 　For only Gossamer, my Gown—
My Tippet[4]—only Tulle—

We paused before a House that seemed
A Swelling of the Ground—
The Roof was scarcely visible—
20 　The Cornice—in the Ground—

Since then—'tis Centuries—and yet
Feels shorter than the Day
I first surmised the Horses Heads
Were toward Eternity—

　　　　　　　　　　　　　　　　　1863?　　　　1890

732

She rose to His Requirement—dropt
The Playthings of Her Life
To take the honorable Work
Of Woman, and of Wife—

5 　If ought She missed in Her new Day,
Of Amplitude, or Awe—
Or first Prospective—Or the Gold
In using, wear away,

It lay unmentioned—as the Sea
10 　Develop Pearl, and Weed,
But only to Himself—be known
The Fathoms they abide—

　　　　　　　　　　　　　　　　　1863?　　　　1890

---

4. A woman's short cape or cloak.

744

Remorse—is Memory—awake—
Her Parties all astir—
A Presence of Departed Acts—
At window—and at Door—

It's Past—set down before the Soul
And lighted with a Match—
Perusal—to facilitate—
And help Belief to stretch—

Remorse is cureless—the Disease
Not even God—can heal—
For 'tis His institution—and
The Adequate of Hell—

1863?　　　1891

829

Ample make this Bed—
Make this Bed with Awe—
In it wait till Judgment break
Excellent and Fair.

Be its Mattress straight—
Be its Pillow round—
Let no Sunrise' yellow noise
Interrupt this Ground—

1883?　　　1891

986

A narrow Fellow in the Grass
Occasionally rides—
You may have met Him—did you not
His notice sudden is—

The Grass divides as with a Comb—
A spotted shaft is seen—
And then it closes at your feet
And opens further on—

He likes a Boggy Acre
A Floor too cool for Corn—
Yet when a Boy, and Barefoot—
I more than once at Noon

Have passed, I thought, a Whip lash
Unbraiding in the Sun
When stooping to secure it
It wrinkled, and was gone—

Several of Nature's People
I know, and they know me—
I feel for them a transport
20 Of cordiality—

But never met this Fellow
Attended, or alone
Without a tighter breathing
And Zero at the Bone—

                                                    1866, 1891

1068

Further in Summer than the Birds
Pathetic from the Grass
A minor Nation celebrates
Its unobtrusive Mass.

5   No Ordinance[5] be seen
So gradual the Grace
A pensive Custom it becomes
Enlarging Loneliness.

Antiquest felt at Noon
10 When August burning low
Arise this spectral Canticle[6]
Repose to typify.

Remit as yet no Grace
No Furrow on the Glow
15 Yet a Druidic[7] Difference
Enhances Nature now.

                              1866?   1891

1078

The Bustle in a House
The Morning after Death
Is solemnest of industries
Enacted upon Earth—

5   The Sweeping up the Heart
And putting Love away
We shall not want to use again
Until Eternity.

                              1866   1890

1129

Tell all the Truth but tell it slant—
Success in Circuit lies
Too bright for our infirm Delight

---

5. A prescribed religious or ceremonial prac-
tice, as applied to the sacrament of the Lord's
Supper.
6. A hymn or song used by the Church in pub-
lic services.
7. Pertaining to the mysterious religious prac-
tices of Celtic priest-magicians.

The Truth's superb surprise
As Lightning to the Children eased
With explanation kind
The Truth must dazzle gradually
Or every man be blind—

1868?   1945

1207

He preached upon "Breadth" till it argued him narrow—
The Broad are too broad to define
And of "Truth" until it proclaimed him a Liar—
The Truth never flaunted a Sign—

Simplicity fled from his counterfeit presence
As Gold the Pyrites[8] would shun—
What confusion would cover the innocent Jesus
To meet so enabled a Man!

1872   1891

1227

My Triumph lasted till the Drums
Had left the Dead alone
And then I dropped my Victory
And chastened stole along
To where the finished Faces
Conclusion turned on me
And then I hated Glory
And wished myself were They.

What is to be is best descried
When it has also been—
Could Prospect taste of Retrospect
The tyrannies of Men
Were Tenderer—diviner
The Transitive toward.
A Bayonet's contrition
Is nothing to the Dead.

1872?   1935

1275

The Spider as an Artist
Has never been employed—
Though his surpassing Merit
Is freely certified

By every Broom and Bridget[9]
Throughout a Christian Land—
Neglected Son of Genius
I take thee by the Hand—

1873?   1896

8. Iron or copper pyrites are often called "fool's gold" because they are the same color as gold.
9. A name commonly associated with housemaids.

1397

It sounded as if the Streets were running
And then—the Streets stood still—
Eclipse—was all we could see at the Window
And Awe—was all we could feel.

5   By and by—the boldest stole out of his Covert
To see if Time was there—
Nature was in an Opal Apron,
Mixing fresher Air.

                                                    1877?   1891

1463

A Route of Evanescence
With a revolving Wheel—
A Resonance of Emerald—
A Rush of Cochineal°—   *scarlet*
5   And every Blossom on the Bush
Adjusts its tumbled Head—
The mail from Tunis, probably,
An easy Morning's Ride—

                                            1879   1891, 1891

1540

As imperceptibly as Grief
The Summer lapsed away—
Too imperceptible at last
To seem like Perfidy—
5   A Quietness distilled
As Twilight long begun,
Or Nature spending with herself
Sequestered Afternoon—
The Dusk drew earlier in—
10   The Morning foreign shone—
A courteous, yet harrowing Grace,
As Guest, that would be gone—
And thus, without a Wing
Or service of a Keel
15   Our Summer made her light escape
Into the Beautiful.

                                        1865, 1882?   1891

1545

The Bible is an antique Volume—
Written by faded Men
At the suggestion of Holy Spectres—
Subjects—Bethlehem—
5   Eden—the ancient Homestead—
Satan—the Brigadier—
Judas—the Great Defaulter—
David—the Troubadour—
Sin—a distinguished Precipice

Others must resist—
Boys that "believe" are very lonesome—
Other Boys are "lost"—
Had but the Tale a warbling Teller—
All the Boys would come—
Orpheus' Sermon captivated[1]—
It did not condemn—

1882   1924

1551

Those—dying then,
Knew where they went—
They went to God's Right Hand—
That Hand is amputated now
And God cannot be found—

The abdication of Belief
Makes the Behavior small—
Better an ignis fatuus[2]
Than no illume at all—

1882?   1945

1651

A Word made Flesh[3] is seldom
And tremblingly partook
Nor then perhaps reported
But have I not mistook
Each one of us has tasted
With ecstasies of stealth
The very food debated
To our specific strength—

A Word that breathes distinctly
Has not the power to die
Cohesive as the Spirit
It may expire if He—
"Made Flesh and dwelt among us
Could condescension be
Like this consent of Language
This loved Philology

1955

1755

To make a prairie it takes a clover and one bee,
One clover, and a bee,
And revery.
The revery alone will do,
If bees are few.

1896

---

1. The music of the legendary Greek musician Orpheus attracted and controlled beasts, rocks, and trees.
2. The "false light" that appears over marshes when marsh gas ignites; sometimes called will-o'-the-wisp.
3. "And the Word was made flesh, and dwelt among us * * *" (John i.14).

CHRISTINA ROSSETTI
(1830–1894)

Song

When I am dead, my dearest,
  Sing no sad songs for me;
Plant thou no roses at my head,
  Nor shady cypress tree:
5 Be the green grass above me
  With showers and dewdrops wet:
And if thou wilt, remember,
  And if thou wilt, forget.

I shall not see the shadows,
10 I shall not feel the rain;
I shall not hear the nightingale
  Sing on as if in pain:
And dreaming through the twilight
  That doth not rise nor set,
15 Haply I may remember,
  And haply may forget.

                           1848   1862

Remember

Remember me when I am gone away,
  Gone far away into the silent land;
  When you can no more hold me by the hand,
Nor I half turn to go yet turning stay.
5 Remember me when no more day by day
  You tell me of our future that you planned:
  Only remember me: you understand
It will be late to counsel then or pray.
Yet if you should forget me for a while
10 And afterwards remember, do not grieve:
  For if the darkness and corruption leave
  A vestige of the thoughts that once I had,
Better by far you should forget and smile
  Than that you should remember and be sad.

                           1849   1862

Echo

Come to me in the silence of the night;
  Come in the sleeping silence of a dream;
Come with soft rounded cheeks and eyes as bright
  As sunlight on a stream;
5   Come back in tears,
O memory, hope, love of finished years.

O dream how sweet, too sweet, too bitter sweet,
  Whose wakening should have been in Paradise,
Where souls brimfull of love abide and meet;

Where thirsting longful eyes
   Watch the slow door
That opening, letting in, lets out no more.

Yet come to me in dreams, that I may live
   My very life again though cold in death:
Come back to me in dreams, that I may give
   Pulse for pulse, breath for breath:
     Speak low, lean low,
As long ago, my love, how long ago.

                     1854   1862

Uphill

Does the road wind uphill all the way?
   Yes, to the very end.
Will the day's journey take the whole long day?
   From morn to night, my friend.

But is there for the night a resting-place?
   A roof for when the slow dark hours begin.
May not the darkness hide it from my face?
   You cannot miss that inn.

Shall I meet other wayfarers at night?
   Those who have gone before.
Then must I knock, or call when just in sight?
   They will not keep you standing at that door.

Shall I find comfort, travel-sore and weak?
   Of labor you shall find the sum.
Will there be beds for me and all who seek?
   Yea, beds for all who come.

                     1858   1862

Cobwebs

It is a land with neither night nor day,
   Nor heat nor cold, nor any wind nor rain,
   Nor hills nor valleys: but one even plain
Stretches through long unbroken miles away,
While through the sluggish air a twilight grey
   Broodeth: no moons or seasons wax and wane,
   No ebb and flow are there along the main,
No bud-time, no leaf-falling, there for aye:—
No ripple on the sea, no shifting sand,
   No beat of wings to stir the stagnant space:
No pulse of life through all the loveless land
And loveless sea; no trace of days before,
   No guarded home, no toil-won resting-place,
No future hope, no fear for evermore.

                     1855   1896

In an Artist's Studio

One face looks out from all his canvases,
　　One selfsame figure sits or walks or leans:
　　We found her hidden just behind those screens,
5　That mirror gave back all her loveliness.
A queen in opal or in ruby dress,
　　A nameless girl in freshest summer-greens,
　　A saint, an angel—every canvas means
The same one meaning, neither more nor less.
He feeds upon her face by day and night,
10　　And she with true kind eyes looks back on him,
Fair as the moon and joyful as the light:
　　Not wan with waiting, not with sorrow dim;
Not as she is, but was when hope shone bright;
　　Not as she is, but as she fills his dream.

　　　　　　　　　　　　　　　　　1856　　　　　1896

WILLIAM MORRIS
(1834–1896)

The Haystack in the Floods[1]

Had she come all the way for this,
To part at last without a kiss?
Yea, had she borne the dirt and rain
That her own eyes might see him slain
5　Beside the haystack in the floods?

Along the dripping leafless woods,
The stirrup touching either shoe,
She rode astride as troopers do;
With kirtle kilted to her knee,
10　To which the mud splashed wretchedly;
And the wet dripped from every tree
Upon her head and heavy hair,
And on her eyelids broad and fair;
The tears and rain ran down her face.
15　By fits and starts they rode apace,
And very often was his place
Far off from her; he had to ride
Ahead, to see what might betide
When the roads crossed; and sometimes, when
20　There rose a murmuring from his men,
Had to turn back with promises;
Ah me! she had but little ease;
And often for pure doubt and dread
She sobbed, made giddy in the head
25　By the swift riding; while, for cold,
Her slender fingers scarce could hold

1. The events of the poem take place imme-
diately after the battle of Poitiers (1356), in
which the English defeated the French. An
English knight, Sir Robert de Marny, and his
mistress, Jehane, are attempting to escape the
French by reaching Gascony, held by the
English.

The wet reins; yea, and scarcely, too,
She felt the foot within her shoe
Against the stirrup: all for this,
To part at last without a kiss
Beside the haystack in the floods.

For when they neared that old soaked hay,
They saw across the only way
That Judas, Godmar, and the three
Red running lions dismally
Grinned from his pennon, under which,
In one straight line along the ditch,
They counted thirty heads.

                So then,
While Robert turned round to his men,
She saw at once the wretched end,
And, stooping down, tried hard to rend
Her coif the wrong way from her head,
And hid her eyes; while Robert said:
"Nay, love, 'tis scarcely two to one,
At Poicüiers where we made them run
So fast—why, sweet my love, good cheer.
The Gascon frontier is so near,
Nought after this."

            But, "O," she said,
"My God! my God! I have to tread
The long way back without you; then
The court at Paris; those six men;[2]
The gratings of the Chatelet;[3]
The swift Seine on some rainy day
Like this, and people standing by,
And laughing, while my weak hands try
To recollect how strong men swim,[4]
All this, or else a life with him,
For which I should be damned at last,
Would God that this next hour were past!"

He answered not, but cried his cry,
"St. George for Marny!" cheerily;
And laid his hand upon her rein.
Alas! no man of all his train
Gave back that cheery cry again;
And, while for rage his thumb beat fast
Upon his sword-hilts, someone cast
About his neck a kerchief long,
And bound him.

          Then they went along
To Godmar; who said: "Now, Jehane,
Your lover's life is on the wane
So fast, that, if this very hour
You yield not as my paramour,

---

2. I.e., the judges.
3. A prison in Paris.
4. When captured, she will have to undergo trial by water to determine whether or not she is a witch: if she drowns, she is innocent; but if she swims, it will be by virtue of her powers as a witch, and she will be burned at the stake.

He will not see the rain leave off—
Nay, keep your tongue from gibe and scoff,
Sir Robert, or I slay you now."

80   She laid her hand upon her brow,
Then gazed upon the palm, as though
She thought her forehead bled, and—"No,"
She said, and turned her head away,
As there were nothing else to say,
And everything were settled: red
85 Grew Godmar's face from chin to head:
"Jehane, on yonder hill there stands
My castle, guarding well my lands:
What hinders me from taking you,
And doing that I list to do
90 To your fair willful body, while
Your knight lies dead?"
                A wicked smile
Wrinkled her face, her lips grew thin,
A long way out she thrust her chin:
95 "You know that I should strangle you
While you were sleeping; or bite through
Your throat, by God's help—ah!" she said,
"Lord Jesus, pity your poor maid!
For in such wise they hem me in,
100 I cannot choose but sin and sin,
Whatever happens: yet I think
They could not make me eat or drink,
And so should I just reach my rest."
"Nay, if you do not my behest,
105 O Jehane! though I love you well,"
Said Godmar, "would I fail to tell
All that I know." "Foul lies," she said.
"Eh? lies my Jehane? by God's head,
At Paris folks would deem them true!
110 Do you know, Jehane, they cry for you,
'Jehane the brown! Jehane the brown!
Give us Jehane to burn or drown!'—
Eh—gag me Robert!—sweet my friend,
This were indeed a piteous end
115 For those long fingers, and long feet,
And long neck, and smooth shoulders sweet;
An end that few men would forget
That saw it—so, an hour yet:
Consider, Jehane, which to take
120 Of life or death!"
               So, scarce awake,
Dismounting, did she leave that place,
And totter some yards: with her face
Turned upward to the sky she lay,
125 Her head on a wet heap of hay,
And fell asleep: and while she slept,
And did not dream, the minutes crept
Round to the twelve again; but she,
Being waked at last, sighed quietly,
130 And strangely childlike came, and said:

"I will not." Straightway Godmar's head,
As though it hung on strong wires, turned
Most sharply round, and his face burned.

For Robert—both his eyes were dry,
He could not weep, but gloomily
He seemed to watch the rain; yea, too,
His lips were firm; he tried once more
To touch her lips; she reached out, sore
And vain desire so tortured them,
The poor gray lips, and now the hem
Of his sleeve brushed them.
                                        With a start
Up Godmar rose, thrust them apart;
From Robert's throat he loosed the bands
Of silk and mail; with empty hands
Held out, she stood and gazed, and saw,
The long bright blade without a flaw
Glide out from Godmar's sheath, his hand
In Robert's hair; she saw him bend
Back Robert's head; she saw him send
The thin steel down; the blow told well,
Right backward the knight Robert fell,
And moaned as dogs do, being half dead,
Unwitting, as I deem: so then
Godmar turned grinning to his men,
Who ran, some five or six, and beat
His head to pieces at their feet.

Then Godmar turned again, and said:
"So, Jehane, the first fitte[5] is read!
Take note, my lady, that your way
Lies backward to the Chatelet!"
She shook her head and gazed awhile
At her cold hands with a rueful smile,
As though this thing had made her mad.

This was the parting that they had
Beside the haystack in the floods.

                                        1858

The Earthly Paradise[6]

Of heaven or hell I have no power to sing,
I cannot ease the burden of your fears,
Or make quick-coming death a little thing,
Or bring again the pleasure of past years,
Nor for my words shall ye forget your tears,
Or hope again for aught that I can say,
The idle singer of an empty day.

But rather, when aweary of your mirth,
From full hearts still unsatisfied ye sigh,
And, feeling kindly unto all the earth,

5. Division of a song, poem, or tale.
6. The dedicatory stanzas to Morris's poem *The Earthly Paradise* (1868–70), consisting of a prologue and twenty-four tales on classical and medieval—especially Norse—subjects.

Grudge every minute as it passes by,
Made the more mindful that the sweet days die—
Remember me a little then I pray,
The idle singer of an empty day.

15   The heavy trouble, the bewildering care
That weighs us down who live and earn our bread,
These idle verses have no power to bear;
So let me sing of names rememberéd,
Because they, living not, can ne'er be dead,
20   Or long time take their memory quite away
From us poor singers of an empty day.

Dreamer of dreams, born out of my due time,
Why should I strive to set the crooked straight?
Let it suffice me that my murmuring rhyme
25   Beats with light wing against the ivory gate,[7]
Telling a tale not too importunate
To those who in the sleepy region stay,
Lulled by the singer of an empty day.

Folk say, a wizard to a northern king
30   At Christmas-tide such wondrous things did show,
That through one window men beheld the spring,
And through another saw the summer glow,
And through a third the fruited vines a-row,
While still, unheard, but in its wonted way,
35   Piped the drear wind of that December day.

So with this Earthly Paradise it is,
If ye will read aright, and pardon me,
Who strive to build a shadowy isle of bliss
Midmost the beating of the steely sea,
40   Where tossed about all hearts of men must be;
Whose ravening monsters mighty men shall slay,
Not the poor singer of an empty day.

1868–70

ALGERNON CHARLES SWINBURNE
(1834–1909)

Choruses from *Atalanta in Calydon*

When the Hounds of Spring Are on Winter's Traces

When the hounds of spring are on winter's traces,
    The mother of months[1] in meadow or plain
Fills the shadows and windy places
    With lisp of leaves and ripple of rain;
5   And the brown bright nightingale amorous
Is half assuaged for Itylus,[2]
For the Thracian ships and the foreign faces,
    The tongueless vigil, and all the pain.

---

7. In Homer, dreams came through one or
the other of two gates: through the gates of
ivory, those which were untrue; through the
gates of horn, those which were true.

1. Artemis (in Roman mythology, Diana),
called "mother of months" because of her role
as moon goddess.
2. See note to Swinburne's *Itylus*, below.

Come with bows bent and with emptying of quivers,
　Maiden most perfect, lady of light,
With a noise of winds and many rivers,
　With a clamor of waters, and with might;
Bind on thy sandals, O thou most fleet,
Over the splendor and speed of thy feet;
For the faint east quickens, the wan west shivers,
　Round the feet of the day and the feet of the night.

Where shall we find her, how shall we sing to her,
　Fold our hands round her knees, and cling?
O that man's heart were as fire and could spring to her,
　Fire, or the strength of the streams that spring!
For the stars and the winds are unto her
As raiment, as songs of the harp-player;
For the risen stars and the fallen cling to her,
　And the southwest wind and the west wind sing.

For winter's rains and ruins are over,
　And all the season of snows and sins;
The days dividing lover and lover,
　The light that loses, the night that wins;
And time remembered is grief forgotten,
And frosts are slain and flowers begotten,
And in green underwood and cover
　Blossom by blossom the spring begins.

The full streams feed on flower of rushes,
　Ripe grasses trammel a traveling foot,
The faint fresh flame of the young year flushes
　From leaf to flower and flower to fruit;
And fruit and leaf are as gold and fire,
And the oat° is heard above the lyre,　　　　　　　*musical pipe*
And the hooféd heel of a satyr crushes
　The chestnut-husk at the chestnut-root.

And Pan by noon and Bacchus by night,[3]
　Fleeter of foot than the fleet-foot kid,
Follows with dancing and fills with delight
　The Maenad and the Bassarid;
And soft as lips that laugh and hide
The laughing leaves of the trees divide,
And screen from seeing and leave in sight
　The god pursuing, the maiden hid.

The ivy falls with the Bacchanal's hair
　Over her eyebrows hiding her eyes;
The wild vine slipping down leaves bare
　Her bright breast shortening into sighs;
The wild vine slips with the weight of its leaves,
But the berried ivy catches and cleaves
To the limbs that glitter, the feet that scare
　The wolf that follows, the fawn that flies.

3. Pan, in Greek mythology, was the god of
flocks and shepherds; Bacchus, or Dionysus,
was god of wine and was accompanied in his
revels by a train of devotees which included
Maenads and Bassarids (line 44).

Before the Beginning of Years

Before the beginning of years
   There came to the making of man
Time, with a gift of tears;
   Grief, with a glass that ran;
5 Pleasure, with pain for leaven;
   Summer, with flowers that fell;
Remembrance fallen from heaven,
   And madness risen from hell;
Strength without hands to smite;
10   Love that endures for a breath:
Night, the shadow of light,
   And life, the shadow of death.
And the high gods took in hand
   Fire, and the falling of tears,
15 And a measure of sliding sand
   From under the feet of the years;
And froth and drift of the sea;
   And dust of the laboring earth;
And bodies of things to be
20   In the houses of death and of birth;
And wrought with weeping and laughter,
   And fashioned with loathing and love
With life before and after
   And death beneath and above,
25 For a day and a night and a morrow,
   That his strength might endure for a span
With travail and heavy sorrow,
   The holy spirit of man.
From the winds of the north and the south
30   They gathered as unto strife;
They breathed upon his mouth,
   They filled his body with life;
Eyesight and speech they wrought
   For the veils of the soul therein,
35 A time for labor and thought,
   A time to serve and to sin;
They gave him light in his ways,
   And love, and a space for delight,
And beauty and length of days,
40   And night, and sleep in the night.
His speech is a burning fire;
   With his lips he travaileth;
In his heart is a blind desire,
   In his eyes foreknowledge of death;
45 He weaves, and is clothed with derision;
   Sows, and he shall not reap;
His life is a watch or a vision
   Between a sleep and a sleep.

1865

Itylus[4]

Swallow, my sister, O sister swallow,
  How can thine heart be full of the spring?
    A thousand summers are over and dead.
What hast thou found in the spring to follow?
  What hast thou found in thine heart to sing?
    What wilt thou do when the summer is shed?

O swallow, sister, O fair swift swallow,
  Why wilt thou fly after spring to the south,
    The soft south whither thine heart is set?
Shall not the grief of the old time follow?
  Shall not the song thereof cleave to thy mouth?
    Hast thou forgotten ere I forget?

Sister, my sister, O fleet sweet swallow,
  Thy way is long to the sun and the south;
    But I, fulfilled of my heart's desire,
Shedding my song upon height, upon hollow,
  From tawny body and sweet small mouth,
    Feed the heart of the night with fire.

I the nightingale all spring through,
  O swallow, sister, O changing swallow,
    All spring through till the spring be done,
Clothed with the light of the night on the dew,
  Sing, while the hours and the wild birds follow,
    Take flight and follow and find the sun.

Sister, my sister, O soft light swallow,
  Though all things feast in the spring's guest-chamber,
    How hast thou heart to be glad thereof yet?
For where thou fliest I shall not follow,
  Till life forget and death remember,
    Till thou remember and I forget.

Swallow, my sister, O singing swallow,
  I know not how thou hast heart to sing.
    Hast thou the heart? is it all past over?
Thy lord the summer is good to follow,
  And fair the feet of thy lover the spring:
    But what wilt thou say to the spring thy lover?

O swallow, sister, O fleeting swallow,
  My heart in me is a molten ember
    And over my head the waves have met.
But thou wouldst tarry or I would follow,
  Could I forget or thou remember,
    Couldst thou remember and I forget.

4. Procne and Philomela were the daughters of Pandion, legendary king of Athens. Procne was the wife of Tereus, king of Thrace, who fell in love with Philomela, ravished her, and cut out her tongue to ensure her silence. But Philomela wove the story of his deed into a piece of tapestry, and in revenge Procne served up to her husband the cooked flesh of their child Itys (or Itylus) at a banquet in Daulis. The sisters, fleeing from Tereus, were changed into birds before he could overtake them, Procne into a nightingale, Philomela into a swallow—or, in Latin versions of the myth, and in Swinburne, the other way around. Hence, in this poem, it is the nightingale—Philomela—who addresses her sister Procne, the swallow, the mother of Itylus.

O sweet stray sister, O shifting swallow,
The heart's division divideth us.
45   Thy heart is light as a leaf of a tree;
But mine goes forth among sea-gulfs hollow
To the place of the slaying of Itylus,
The feast of Daulis, the Thracian sea.

O swallow, sister, O rapid swallow,
50   I pray thee sing not a little space.
Are not the roofs and the lintels wet?
The woven web that was plain to follow,
The small slain body, the flowerlike face,
Can I remember if thou forget?

55 O sister, sister, thy first-begotten!
The hands that cling and the feet that follow,
The voice of the child's blood crying yet
Who hath remembered me? who hath forgotten?
Thou hast forgotten, O summer swallow,
60   But the world shall end when I forget.

1866

The Garden of Proserpine[5]

Here, where the world is quiet;
Here, where all trouble seems
Dead winds' and spent waves' riot
In doubtful dreams of dreams;
5 I watch the green field growing
For reaping folk and sowing,
For harvest-time and mowing,
A sleepy world of streams.

I am tired of tears and laughter,
10   And men that laugh and weep;
Of what may come hereafter
For men that sow to reap:
I am weary of days and hours,
Blown buds of barren flowers,
15 Desires and dreams and powers
And everything but sleep.

Here life has death for neighbor,
And far from eye or ear
Wan waves and wet winds labor,
20   Weak ships and spirits steer;
They drive adrift, and whither
They wot not who make thither;
But no such winds blow hither,
And no such things grow here.

25 No growth of moor or coppice,
No heather-flower or vine,
But bloomless buds of poppies,

5. Persephone, in Roman mythology Proserpine, the daughter of Zeus and Demeter, had been abducted by Hades (the Roman Pluto), god of the underworld, over which she ruled with him thereafter as his queen.

Green grapes of Proserpine,
Pale beds of blowing rushes
Where no leaf blooms or blushes
Save this whereout she crushes
    For dead men deadly wine.

Pale, without name or number,
    In fruitless fields of corn,°   *wheat*
They bow themselves and slumber
    All night till light is born;
And like a soul belated,
In hell and heaven unmated,
By cloud and mist abated
    Comes out of darkness morn.

Though one were strong as seven,
    He too with death shall dwell,
Nor wake with wings in heaven,
    Nor weep for pains in hell;
Though one were fair as roses,
His beauty clouds and closes;
And well though love reposes,
    In the end it is not well.

Pale, beyond porch and portal,
    Crowned with calm leaves, she stands
Who gathers all things mortal
    With cold immortal hands;
Her languid lips are sweeter
Than love's who fears to greet her
To men that mix and meet her
    From many times and lands.

She waits for each and other,
    She waits for all men born;
Forgets the earth her mother,
    The life of fruits and corn;
And spring and seed and swallow
Take wing for her and follow
Where summer song rings hollow
    And flowers are put to scorn.

There go the loves that wither,
    The old loves with wearier wings;
And all dead years draw thither,
    And all disastrous things;
Dead dreams of days forsaken,
Blind buds that snows have shaken,
Wild leaves that winds have taken,
    Red strays of ruined springs.

We are not sure of sorrow,°
    And joy was never sure;
Today will die tomorrow;
    Time stoops to no man's lure;[6]

6. In falconry, the lure is a device used to recall the hawk to the falconer's wrist.

And love, grown faint and fretful,
With lips but half regretful
Sighs, and with eyes forgetful
80   Weeps that no love endure.

From too much love of living,
    From hope and fear set free,
We thank with brief thanksgiving
    Whatever gods may be
85   That no life lives for ever;
That dead men rise up never;
That even the weariest river
    Winds somewhere safe to sea.

Then star nor sun shall waken,
90   Nor any change of light:
Nor sound of waters shaken,
    Nor any sound or sight:
Nor wintry leaves nor vernal,
Nor days nor things diurnal;
95   Only the sleep eternal
    In an eternal night.

                                            1866

The Sundew

A little marsh-plant, yellow green,
And pricked at lip with tender red.
Tread close, and either way you tread
Some faint black water jets between
5   Lest you should bruise the curious head.

A live thing maybe; who shall know?
The summer knows and suffers it;
For the cool moss is thick and sweet
Each side, and saves the blossom so
10   That it lives out the long June heat.

The deep scent of the heather burns
About it; breathless though it be,
Bow down and worship; more than we
Is the least flower whose life returns,
15   Least weed renascent in the sea.

We are vexed and cumbered in earth's sight
With wants, with many memories;
These see their mother what she is,
Glad-growing, till August leave more bright
20   The apple-colored cranberries.

Wind blows and bleaches the strong grass,
Blown all one way to shelter it
From trample of stayed kine, with feet
Felt heavier than the moorhen was,
25   Strayed up past patches of wild wheat.

You call it sundew: how it grows,
If with its color it have breath,
If life taste sweet to it, if death
Pain its soft petal, no man knows:
Man has no sight or sense that saith.

My sundew, grown of gentle days,
In these green miles the spring begun
Thy growth ere April had half done
With the soft secret of her ways
Or June made ready for the sun.

O red-lipped mouth of marsh-flower,
I have a secret halved with thee.
The name that is love's name to me
Thou knowest, and the face of her
Who is my festival to see.

The hard sun, as thy petals knew,
Colored the heavy moss-water:
Thou wert not worth green midsummer
Nor fit to live to August blue,
O sundew, not remembering her.

                              1862   1866

A Forsaken Garden

In a coign of the cliff between lowland and highland,
    At the sea-down's edge between windward and lee,
Walled round with rocks as an inland island,
    The ghost of a garden fronts the sea.
A girdle of brushwood and thorn encloses
    The steep square slope of the blossomless bed
Where the weeds that grew green from the graves of its roses
        Now lie dead.

The fields fall southward, abrupt and broken,
    To the low last edge of the long lone land.
If a step should sound or a word be spoken,
    Would a ghost not rise at the strange guest's hand?
So long have the grey bare walks lain guestless,
    Through branches and briars if a man make way,
He shall find no life but the sea-wind's, restless
        Night and day.

The dense hard passage is blind and stifled
    That crawls by a track none turn to climb
To the strait waste place that the years have rifled
    Of all but the thorns that are touched not of time.
The thorns he spares when the rose is taken;
    The rocks are left when he wastes the plain.
The wind that wanders, the weeds wind-shaken,
        These remain.

Not a flower to be pressed of the foot that falls not;
    As the heart of a dead man the seed-plots are dry;
From the thicket of thorns whence the nightingale calls not,
    Could she call, there were never a rose to reply.

Over the meadows that blossom and wither
30   Rings but the note of a sea-bird's song;
Only the sun and the rain come hither
        All year long.

The sun burns sere° and the rain dishevels   *dry*
    One gaunt bleak blossom of scentless breath.
35   Only the wind here hovers and revels
    In a round where life seems barren as death.
Here there was laughing of old, there was weeping,
    Haply, of lovers none ever will know,
Whose eyes went seaward a hundred sleeping
40   Years ago.

Heart handfast in heart as they stood, "Look thither,"
    Did he whisper? "look forth from the flowers to the sea,
For the foam-flowers endure when the rose-blossoms wither,
    And men that love lightly may die—but we?"
45   And the same wind sang and the same waves whitened,
    And or ever the garden's last petals were shed,
In the lips that had whispered, the eyes that had lightened,
        Love was dead.

Or they loved their life through, and then went whither?
50   And were one to the end—but what end who knows?
Love deep as the sea as a rose must wither,
    As the rose-red seaweed that mocks the rose.
Shall the dead take thought for the dead to love them?
    What love was ever as deep as a grave?
55   They are loveless now as the grass above them
        Or the wave.

All are at one now, roses and lovers,
    Not known of the cliffs and the fields and the sea.
Not a breath of the time that has been hovers
60   In the air now soft with a summer to be.
Not a breath shall there sweeten the seasons heerafter
    Of the flowers or the lovers that laugh now or weep,
When as they that are free now of weeping and laughter
        We shall sleep.

65   Here death may deal not again for ever;
    Here change may come not till all change end.
From the graves they have made they shall rise up never,
    Who have left nought living to ravage and rend.
Earth, stones, and thorns of the wild ground growing,
70   While the sun and the rain live, these shall be;
Till a last wind's breath upon all these blowing
        Roll the sea.

Till the slow sea rise and the sheer cliff crumble,
    Till terrace and meadow the deep gulfs drink,
75   Till the strength of the waves of the high tides humble
    The fields that lessen, the rocks that shrink,
Here now in his triumph where all things falter,
    Stretched out on the spoils that his own hand spread,
As a god self-slain on his own strange altar,
80   Death lies dead.

                                                    1876   1878

THOMAS HARDY
(1840–1928)

I Look into My Glass

I look into my glass,
And view my wasting skin,
And say, "Would God it came to pass
My heart had shrunk as thin!"

For then, I, undistrest
By hearts grown cold to me,
Could lonely wait my endless rest
With equanimity.

But Time, to make me grieve,
Part steals, lets part abide;
And shakes this fragile frame at eve
With throbbings of noontide.

1898

Drummer Hodge[1]

1
They throw in drummer Hodge, to rest
    Uncoffined—just as found:
His landmark is a kopje-crest[2]
    That breaks the veldt around;
And foreign constellations west
    Each night above his mound.

2
Young Hodge the Drummer never knew—
    Fresh from his Wessex home—
The meaning of the broad Karoo,
    The Bush, the dusty loam,
And why uprose to nightly view
    Strange stars amid the gloam.

3
Yet portion of that unknown plain
    Will Hodge forever be;
His homely Northern breast and brain
    Grow to some Southern tree,
And strange-eyed constellations reign
    His stars eternally.

1902

1. The poem presents an incident from the Boer War (1899–1902) and when first published bore the note: "One of the Drummers killed was a native of a village near Casterbridge," i.e., Dorchester, the principal city of the region of southern England to which, in his novels and poems, Hardy gave its medieval name of Wessex.
2. In Afrikaans, the language of the Dutch settlers in South Africa, the crest of a small hill. The veldt (line 4) is open country, unenclosed pasture land; the Karoo (line 9), barren tracts of plateau-land.

A Broken Appointment

You did not come,
And marching Time drew on, and wore me numb.
Yet less for loss of your dear presence there
Than that I thus found lacking in your make
5   That high compassion which can overbear
Reluctance for pure lovingkindness' sake
Grieved I, when, as the hope-hour stroked its sum,
You did not come.

You love not me,
10   And love alone can lend you loyalty;
—I know and knew it. But, unto the store
Of human deeds divine in all but name,
Was it not worth a little hour or more
To add yet this: Once you, a woman, came
15   To soothe a time-torn man; even though it be
You love not me?

1902

The Darkling Thrush

I leant upon a coppice[3] gate
    When Frost was specter-gray,
And Winter's dregs made desolate
    The weakening eye of day.
5   The tangled bine-stems[4] scored the sky
    Like strings of broken lyres,
And all mankind that haunted nigh
    Had sought their household fires.

The land's sharp features seemed to be
10   The Century's corpse outleant,
His crypt the cloudy canopy,
    The wind his death-lament.
The ancient pulse of germ and birth
    Was shrunken hard and dry,
15   And every spirit upon earth
    Seemed fervorless as I.

At once a voice arose among
    The bleak twigs overhead
In a full-hearted evensong
20   Of joy illimited;
An aged thrush, frail, gaunt, and small,
    In blast-beruffled plume,
Had chosen thus to fling his soul
    Upon the growing gloom.

25   So little cause for carolings
    Of such ecstatic sound
Was written on terrestrial things
    Afar or nigh around,

---

3. Thicket or wood consisting of small trees.   4. Shoots or stems of a climbing plant.

That I could think there trembled through
   His happy good-night air
Some blessed Hope, whereof he knew
   And I was unaware.

December 31, 1900   1902

The Ruined Maid

"O'Melia, my dear, this does everything crown!
Who could have supposed I should meet you in Town?
And whence such fair garments, such prosperi-ty?"
"O didn't you know I'd been ruined?" said she.

"You left us in tatters, without shoes or socks,
Tired of digging potatoes, and spudding up docks;⁵
And now you've gay bracelets and bright feathers three!"
"Yes: that's how we dress when we're ruined," said she.

"At home in the barton° you said 'thee' and 'thou,'   *farm*
And 'thik oon,' and 'theäs oon,' and 't'other'; but now
Your talking quite fits 'ee for high compa-ny!"
"Some polish is gained with one's ruin," said she.

"Your hands were like paws then, your face blue and bleak
But now I'm bewitched by your delicate cheek,
And your little gloves fit as on any la-dy!"
"We never do work when we're ruined," said she.

"You used to call home-life a hag-ridden dream,
And you'd sigh, and you'd sock; but at present you seem
To know not of megrims° or melancho-ly!"   *low spirits*
"True. One's pretty lively when ruined," said she.

"I wish I had feathers, a fine sweeping gown,
And a delicate face, and could strut about Town!"
"My dear—a raw country girl, such as you be,
Cannot quite expect that. You ain't ruined," said she.

1866   1902

The Self-Unseeing

Here is the ancient floor,
Footworn and hollowed and thin,
Here was the former door
Where the dead feet walked in.

She sat here in her chair,
Smiling into the fire;
He who played stood there,
Bowing it higher and higher.

Childlike, I danced in a dream;
Blessings emblazoned that day;
Everything glowed with a gleam;
Yet we were looking away!

1902

5. Digging up weedy herbs.

In Tenebris[6]

"Percussus sum sicut foenum, et aruit cor meum"[7]
—PSALM cii

Wintertime nighs;
But my breavement-pain
It cannot bring again:
Twice no one dies.

Flower-petals flee;
But, since it once hath been,
No more that severing scene
Can harrow me.

Birds faint in dread:
I shall not lose old strength
In the lone frost's black length:
Strength long since fled!

Leaves freeze to dun;
But friends can not turn cold
This season as of old
For him with none.

Tempests may scath;
But love can not make smart
Again this year his heart
Who no heart hath.

Black is night's cope;
But death will not appal
One who, past doubtings all,
Waits in unhope.

1902

The Rejected Member's Wife

We shall see her no more
On the balcony,
Smiling, while hurt, at the roar
As of surging sea
From the stormy sturdy band
Who have doomed her lord's cause,
Though she waves her little hand
As it were applause.

Here will be candidates yet,
And candidates' wives,
Fervid with zeal to set
Their ideals on our lives:
Here will come market-men
On the market-days,
Here will clash now and then
More such party assays.

6. The first poem of a series of three with this title (*In Darkness*).

7. "My heart is smitten, and withered like grass."

And the balcony will fill
     When such times are renewed,
And the throng in the street will thrill
     With today's mettled mood;
But she will no more stand
     In the sunshine there,
With that wave of her white-gloved hand,
     And that chestnut hair.

                      January 1906   1909

The Convergence of the Twain

LINES ON THE LOSS OF THE TITANIC[9]

1
     In a solitude of the sea
     Deep from human vanity,
And the Pride of Life that planned her, stilly couches she.

2
     Steel chambers, late the pyres
     Of her salamandrine fires,[1]
Cold currents thrid,° and turn to rhythmic tidal lyres.   *thread*

3
     Over the mirrors meant
     To glass the opulent
The sea-worm crawls—grotesque, slimed, dumb, indifferent.

4
     Jewels in joy designed
     To ravish the sensuous mind
Lie lightless, all their sparkles bleared and black and blind.

5
     Dim moon-eyed fishes near
     Gaze at the gilded gear
And query: "What does this vaingloriousness down here?"

6
     Well: while was fashioning
     This creature of cleaving wing,
The Immanent Will that stirs and urges everything

7
     Prepared a sinister mate
     For her—so gaily great—
A Shape of Ice, for the time far and dissociate.

8
     And as the smart ship grew
     In stature, grace, and hue,
In shadowy silent distance grew the Iceberg too.

9
     Alien they seemed to be:
     No mortal eye could see
The intimate welding of their later history,

10
     Or sign that they were bent
     By paths coincident
On being anon twin halves of one august event,

9. The White Star liner R.M.S. *Titanic* was sunk, with great loss of life, as the result of collision with an iceberg on its maiden voyage from Southampton to New York on April 15, 1912.

1. The ship's fires, which burn though immersed in water, are compared to the salamander, a lizard-like creature which according to fable could live in the midst of fire.

11
Till the Spinner of the Years
Said "Now!" And each one hears,
And consummation comes, and jars two hemispheres.

1912

Channel Firing

That night your great guns, unawares,
Shook all our coffins as we lay,
And broke the chancel window-squares,
We thought it was the Judgment-day

5   And sat upright. While drearisome
Arose the howl of wakened hounds:
The mouse let fall the altar-crumb,
The worms drew back into the mounds,

The glebe cow[2] drooled. Till God called, "No;
10 It's gunnery practice out at sea
Just as before you went below;
The world is as it used to be:

"All nations striving strong to make
Red war yet redder. Mad as hatters
15 They do no more for Christés sake
Than you who are helpless in such matters.

"That this is not the judgment-hour
For some of them's a blessed thing,
For if it were they'd have to scour
20 Hell's floor for so much threatening. . . .

"Ha, ha. It will be warmer when
I blow the trumpet (if indeed
I ever do; for you are men,
And rest eternal sorely need)."

25 So down we lay again. "I wonder,
Will the world ever saner be,"
Said one, "than when He sent us under
In our indifferent century!"

And many a skeleton shook his head.
30 "Instead of preaching forty year,"
My neighbor Parson Thirdly said,
"I wish I had stuck to pipes and beer."

Again the guns disturbed the hour,
Roaring their readiness to avenge,
35 As far inland as Stourton Tower,
And Camelot, and starlit Stonehenge.[3]

April 1914   1914

2. Cow pastured on the glebe, a piece of land attached to a vicarage or rectory.
3. Stourton Tower, built in 1772, and locally known as "Alfred's Tower," stands on the highest point of the estate of Stourhead, in Wiltshire, close to the Somersetshire border. Camelot, the seat of King Arthur's court, has been variously associated with Winchester and with certain places in Somersetshire. Stonehenge is a circular grouping of megalithic monuments on Salisbury Plain, Wiltshire, dating back to the late Neolithic or early Bronze age.

The Voice

Woman much missed, how you call to me, call to me,
Saying that now you are not as you were
When you had changed from the one who was all to me,
But as at first, when our day was fair.

5 Can it be you that I hear?   Let me view you, then,
Standing as when I drew near to the town
Where you would wait for me: yes, as I knew you then,
Even to the original air-blue gown!

Or is it only the breeze, in its listlessness
0 Traveling across the wet mead to me here,
You being ever dissolved to wan wistlessness,°   *heedlessness*
Heard no more again far or near?

    Thus I; faltering forward,
    Leaves around me falling,
5 Wind oozing thin through the thorn from norward,
    And the woman calling.

               December 1912   1914

In Time of "The Breaking of Nations"[6]

1
Only a man harrowing clods
    In a slow silent walk
With an old horse that stumbles and nods
    Half asleep as they stalk.
2
5 Only thin smoke without flame
    From the heaps of couch-grass;
Yet this will go onward the same
    Though Dynasties pass.
3
Yonder a maid and her wight
0   Come whispering by:
War's annals will cloud into night
    Ere their story die.

               1915   1916

Afterwards

When the Present has latched its postern° behind my tremulous stay,   *back gate*
    And the May month flaps its glad green leaves like wings,
Delicate-filmed as new-spun silk, will the neighbors say,
    "He was a man who used to notice such things"?

5 If it be in the dusk when, like an eyelid's soundless blink,
    The dewfall-hawk comes crossing the shades to alight
Upon the wind-warped upland thorn, a gazer may think,
    "To him this must have been a familiar sight."

---

6. See Jeremiah li.20: "Thou art my battle ax and weapons of war: for with thee will I break in pieces the nations, and with thee will I destroy kingdoms."

If I pass during some nocturnal blackness, mothy and warm,
10   When the hedgehog travels furtively over the lawn,
One may say, "He strove that such innocent creatures should come to no harm,
But he could do little for them; and now he is gone."

If, when hearing that I have been stilled at last, they stand at the door,
Watching the full-starred heavens that winter sees,
15   Will this thought rise on those who will meet my face no more,
"He was one who had an eye for such mysteries"?

And will any say when my bell of quittance is head in the gloom,
And a crossing breeze cuts a pause in its outrollings,
Till they rise again, as they were a new bell's boom,
20   "He hears it not now, but used to notice such things"?

1917

Jezreel

ON ITS SEIZURE BY THE ENGLISH UNDER ALLENBY, SEPTEMBER 1918[7]

Did they catch as it were in a Vision at shut of the day—
When their cavalry smote through the ancient Esdraelon Plain,
And they crossed where the Tishbite[8] stood forth in his enemy's way—
His gaunt mournful Shade as he bade the King haste off amain?

5   On war-men at this end of time—even on Englishmen's eyes—
Who slay with their arms of new might in the long-ago place,
Flashed he who drove furiously?[9] . . . Ah, did the phantom arise
Of that queen, of that proud Tyrian woman who painted her face?[1]

Faintly marked they the words "Throw her down!" from the night eerily,
10   Specter-spots of the blood of her body on some rotten wall?
And the thin note of pity that came: "A King's daughter is she,"
As they passed where she trodden was once by the chargers' footfall?

Could such be the hauntings of men of today, at the cease
Of pursuit, at the dusk-hour, ere slumber their senses could seal?
15   Enghosted seers, kings—one on horseback who asked "Is it peace?"[2] . . .
Yea, strange things and spectral may men have beheld in Jezreel!

September 24, 1918   1918

The Children and Sir Nameless

Sir Nameless, once of Athelhall, declared:
"These wretched children romping in my park
Trample the herbage till the soil is bared,
And yap and yell from early morn till dark!
5   Go keep them harnessed to their set routines:
Thank God I've none to hasten my decay;
For green remembrance there are better means
Than offspring, who but wish their sires away."

7. Towards the end of World War I, in the autumn of 1918, General Allenby, commanding the Egyptian Expeditionary Force, won the final victory against the Turks when his cavalry swept through the plain of Esdraelon, called in Hebrew *Emeq Yizre'el*, the plain of Jezreel: the plain lies southeast of Haifa, in northern Israel. In biblical times the city of Jezreel was the location of the palace of Ahab, the wicked king of Israel, and his wife Jezebel.
8. The prophet Elijah (I Kings xvii), implacable enemy of King Ahab (I Kings xvi. 29–34).
9. II Kings ix.20. Jehu was anointed King of Israel by Elisha, Elijah's successor.
1. II Kings ix.30–37.
2. II Kings ix.17.

Sir Nameless of that mansion said anon:
"To be perpetuate for my mightiness
Sculpture must image me when I am gone."
—He forthwith summoned carvers there express
To shape a figure stretching seven-odd feet
(For he was tall) in alabaster stone,
With shield, and crest, and casque, and sword complete:
When done a statelier work was never known.

Three hundred years hied; Church-restorers came,
And, no one of his lineage being traced,
They thought an effigy so large in frame
Best fitted for the floor. There it was placed,
Under the seats for schoolchildren. And they
Kicked out his name, and hobnailed off his nose;
And, as they yawn through sermon-time, they say,
"Who was this old stone man beneath our toes?"

1922

No Buyers

A STREET SCENE

A load of brushes and baskets and cradles and chairs
    Labors along the street in the rain:
With it a man, a woman, a pony with whiteybrown hairs.
    The man foots in front of the horse with a shambling sway
        At a slower tread than a funeral train,
    While to a dirge-like tune he chants his wares,
Swinging a Turk's-head brush (in a drum-major's way
        When the bandsmen march and play).

A yard from the back of the man is the whiteybrown pony's nose:
10 He mirrors his master in every item of pace and pose:
        He stops when the man stops, without being told,
    And seems to be eased by a pause; too plainly he's old,
            Indeed, not strength enough shows
            To steer the disjointed wagon straight,
15 Which wriggles left and right in a rambling line,
    Deflected thus by its own warp and weight,
    And pushing the pony with it in each incline.

        The woman walks on the pavement verge,
            Parallel to the man:
20   She wears an apron white and wide in span,
    And carries a like Turk's head, but more in nursing-wise:
        Now and then she joins in his dirge,
        But as if her thoughts were on distant things.
        The rain clams her apron till it clings.
25 So, step by step, they move with their merchandise,
        And nobody buys.

1925

GERARD MANLEY HOPKINS
(1844–1889)

The Alchemist in the City

My window shows the travelling clouds,
Leaves spent, new seasons, alter'd sky,
The making and the melting crowds:
The whole world passes; I stand by.

5   They do not waste their meted hours,
But men and masters plan and build:
I see the crowning of their towers,
And happy promises fulfill'd.

And I—perhaps if my intent
10   Could count on prediluvian age,[1]
The labours I should then have spent
Might so attain their heritage,

But now before the pot can glow
With not to be discover'd gold,
15   At length the bellows shall not blow,
The furnace shall at last be cold.

Yet it is now too late to heal
The incapable and cumbrous shame
Which makes me when with men I deal
20   More powerless than the blind or lame.

No, I should love the city less
Even than this my thankless lore;
But I desire the wilderness
Or weeded landslips of the shore.

25   I walk my breezy belvedere
To watch the low or levant sun,
I see the city pigeons veer,
I mark the tower swallows run

Between the tower-top and the ground
30   Below me in the bearing air;
Then find in the horizon-round
One spot and hunger to be there.

And then I hate the most that lore
That holds no promise of success;
35   Then sweetest seems the houseless shore,
Then free and kind the wilderness.

Or ancient mounds that cover bones,
Or rocks where rockdoves do repair
And trees of terebinth[2] and stones
40   And silence and a gulf of air.

1. I.e., age as great as the ages attained by men who lived before the Flood (Genesis v).

2. A European tree which yields turpentine.

There on a long and squarèd height
After the sunset I would lie,
And pierce the yellow waxen light
With free long looking, ere I die.

1865   1948

The Habit of Perfection

Elected Silence, sing to me
And beat upon my whorlèd ear,
Pipe me to pastures still and be
The music that I care to hear.

Shape nothing, lips; be lovely-dumb:
It is the shut, the curfew sent
From there where all surrenders come
Which only makes you eloquent.

Be shellèd, eyes, with double dark
And find the uncreated light:[3]
This ruck and reel which you remark
Coils, keeps, and teases simple sight.

Palate, the hutch of tasty lust,
Desire not to be rinsed with wine:
The can° must be so sweet, the crust
So fresh that come in fasts divine!

tankard, cup

Nostrils, your careless breath that spend
Upon the stir and keep of pride,
What relish shall the censers[4] send
Along the sanctuary side!

O feel-of-primrose hands, O feet
That want the yield of plushy sward,
But you shall walk the golden street
And you unhouse and house the Lord.[5]

And, Poverty, be thou the bride
And now the marriage feast begun,
And lily-coloured clothes provide
Your spouse not laboured-at nor spun.[6]

1866   1918

God's Grandeur

The world is charged with the grandeur of God.
  It will flame out, like shining from shook foil;[7]
  It gathers to a greatness, like the ooze of oil
Crushed.[8] Why do men then now not reck his rod?

---

3. W. H. Gardner, in his notes to the poem, explains "uncreated light" as "the *lux increata* of the Schoolmen, the creative energy of God's mind."
4. Vessels in which incense is burned.
5. I.e., the hands will open and close the pyx, the vessel containing the host, the consecrated bread, used in the sacrament.
6. See Matthew vi.28–29: "* * * Consider the lilies of the field, how they grow; they toil not, neither do they spin."

7. In a letter to Robert Bridges (January 4, 1883), Hopkins says: "* * * I mean foil in its sense of leaf or tinsel, and no other word whatever will give the effect I want. Shaken goldfoil gives off broad glares like sheet lightning and also, and this is true of nothing else, owing to its zigzag dints and crossings and network of small many cornered facets, a sort of fork lightning too."
8. I.e., as when olives are crushed for their oil.

5   Generations have trod, have trod, have trod;
      And all is seared with trade; bleared, smeared with toil;
      And wears man's smudge and shares man's smell: the soil
    Is bare now, nor can foot feel, being shod.

    And for all this, nature is never spent;
10   There lives the dearest freshness deep down things;
    And though the last lights off the black West went
      Oh, morning, at the brown brink eastward, springs—
    Because the Holy Ghost over the bent
      World broods with warm breast and with ah! bright wings.

                                                    1877   1895

The Windhover[2]

TO CHRIST OUR LORD

I caught this morning morning's minion,° king-   *darling, favorite*
  dom of daylight's dauphin,[3] dapple-dawn-drawn Falcon, in his riding
Of the rolling level underneath him steady air, and striding
High there, how he rung upon the rein of a wimpling° wing   *rippling*
5 In his ecstasy! then off, off forth on swing,
As a skate's heel sweeps smooth on a bow-bend: the hurl and gliding
Rebuffed the big wind. My heart in hiding
Stirred for a bird,—the achieve of, the mastery of the thing!

Brute beauty and valour and act, oh, air, pride, plume, here
10 Buckle![4] AND the fire that breaks from thee then, a billion
Times told lovelier, more dangerous, O my chevalier![5]

No wonder of it: shéer plód makes plough down sillion°   *furrow*
Shine, and blue-bleak embers, ah my dear,
  Fall, gall themselves, and gash gold-vermilion.

                                                    1877   1918

Pied Beauty[6]

Glory be to God for dappled things—
  For skies of couple-colour as a brinded° cow;   *streaked, brindled*
    For rose-moles all in stipple upon trout that swim;
Fresh-firecoal chestnut-falls;[7] finches' wings;
5   Landscape plotted and pieced—fold, fallow, and plough;[8]
      And áll trádes, their gear and tackle and trim.
All things counter, original, spare, strange;

---

2. "A name for the kestrel [a species of small hawk], from its habit of hovering or hanging with its head to the wind" [O.E.D.].
3. The eldest son of the king of France was called the *dauphin*: hence, the word here means heir to a splendid, kingly condition.
4. The word "buckle" brings to a single focus the several elements of line 8, in both their literal sense, as descriptive of a single, sudden movement of the airborne bird, and in their symbolic sense as descriptive of Christ and with further reference to the poet himself and the lesson he draws from his observation. It may be read either as indicative or imperative,
and in one or another of its possible meanings: "to fasten," "to join closely," "to equip for battle," "to grapple with, engage," but also "to cause to bend, give way, crumple."
5. Knight, nobleman, champion.
6. Having two or more colors, in patches or blotches.
7. W. H. Gardner cites a note from Hopkins's *Journals*: "Chestnuts as bright as coals or spots of vermilion."
8. The land makes a pattern of varicolored patches by reason of its several uses, as for pasture, or being left fallow for a season, or being plowed and sown.

Whatever is fickle, freckled (who knows how?)
With swift, slow; sweet, sour; adazzle, dim;
He fathers-forth whose beauty is past change:
           Praise him.

                                   1877   1918

Binsey Poplars

FELLED 1879

My aspens dear, whose airy cages quelled,°   *overpowered, subdued*
Quelled or quenched in leaves the leaping sun,
All felled, felled, are all felled;
    Of a fresh and following folded rank
        Not spared, not one
          That dandled and sandalled
      Shadow that swam or sank
On meadow and river and wind-wandering
    weed-winding bank.

    O if we but knew what we do
        When we delve or hew—
    Hack and rack the growing green!
       Since country is so tender
    To touch, her being só slender,
    That, like this sleek and seeing ball
    But a prick will make no eye at all,
    Where we, even where we mean
        To mend her we end her,
     When we hew or delve:
After-comers cannot guess the beauty been.
    Ten or twelve, only ten or twelve
      Strokes of havoc únselve
       The sweet especial scene,
    Rural scene, a rural scene,
    Sweet especial rural scene.

                                1879   1918

Felix Randal

Felix Randal the farrier,° O is he dead then? my duty all ended,   *blacksmith*
Who have watched his mould of man, big-boned and hardy-handsome
Pining, pining, till time when reason rambled in it and some
Fatal four disorders, fleshed there, all contended?

Sickness broke him. Impatient, he cursed at first, but mended
Being anointed and all; though a heavenlier heart began some
Months earlier, since I had our sweet reprieve and ransom
Tendered to him.[9] Ah well, God rest him all road ever he offended![1]

This seeing the sick endears them to us, us too it endears.
My tongue had taught thee comfort, touch had quenched thy tears,
Thy tears that touched my heart, child, Felix, poor Felix Randal;

9. I.e., since I had a priest visit him to hear his confession and give absolution.

1. I.e., for any way in which he may have offended.

How far from then forethought of, all thy more boisterous years,
When thou at the random² grim forge, powerful amidst peers,
Didst fettle³ for the great grey drayhorse his bright and battering sandal!

1880   1918

Spring and Fall

TO A YOUNG CHILD

Márgarét, áre you gríeving
Over Goldengrove unleaving?
Leáves, líke the things of man, you
With your fresh thoughts care for, can you?
5   Áh! ás the heart grows older
It will come to such sights colder
By and by, nor spare a sigh
Though worlds of wanwood leafmeal lie;⁴
And yet you *will* weep and know why.
10 Now no matter, child, the name:
Sórrow's spríngs áre the same.
Nor mouth had, no nor mind, expressed
What heart heard of, ghost° guessed: *spirit, soul*
It ís the blight man was born for,
15 It is Margaret you mourn for.

1880   1893

Inversnaid ⁴

This darksome burn,° horseback brown,   *stream*
His rollrock highroad roaring down,
In coop° and in comb° the fleece of his foam   *hollow/crest*
Flutes and low to the lake falls home.

5   A windpuff-bonnet of fáwn-fróth
Turns and twindles ⁵ over the broth
Of a pool so pitchblack, féll-frówning,
It rounds and rounds Despair to drowning.

Degged° with dew, dappled with dew   *sprinkled*
10 Are the groins of the braes° that the brook treads through,   *steep banks*
Wiry heathpacks,° flitches ⁶ of fern,   *heather*
And the beadbonny ⁷ ash that sits over the burn.

What would the world be, once bereft
Of wet and of wildness? Let them be left,
15 O let them be left, wildness and wet;
Long live the weeds and the wilderness yet.

1881   1918

2. Ramshackle, as applied to the forge itself;
but also meaning that the man's life as a
blacksmith was merely one casual earthly life
as opposed to the sure way of Christian salva-
tion.
3. To line or cover with a refractory material;
hence, to shoe.
4. "Wanwood": *pale* or *dim*—the groves are
pale because of their light-colored autumn
foliage, or dim because of the filtered light.
"Leafmeal" (a word coined by Hopkins by
analogy with *piecemeal*): leaf by leaf, or leaf
mold—in the first sense, the foliage lies about
the grove, having fallen leaf by leaf; in the
second, foliage gradually decays to leaf mold.
4. Town in the Scottish Highlands.
5. The editors of *The Poems of Gerard Manley
Hopkins*, Fourth Edition, say that *twindles*
"seems to be a portmanteau coinage inscaping
'twists,' 'twitches,' and 'dwindles' . . . but
possibly verbal use of obs. 'twindle' (twin) is
intended, to suggest the splitting of a whirl-
pool into two."
6. *Ibid.*: "ragged, russet flakes, tufts or
clumps."
7. With clusters of bright beadlike berries.

[As Kingfishers Catch Fire, Dragonflies Draw Flame]

As kingfishers catch fire, dragonflies draw flame;[5]
  As tumbled over rim in roundy wells
  Stones ring; like each tucked° string tells, each hung bell's *touched, plucked*
Bow swung finds tongue to fling out broad its name;
Each mortal thing does one thing and the same:
  Deals out that being indoors each one dwells;[6]
  Selves[7]—goes itself; *myself* it speaks and spells,
Crying *What I do is me: for that I came.*

I say more: the just man justices;
  Keeps gráce: thát keeps all his goings graces;
Acts in God's eye what in God's eye he is—
  Chríst. For Christ plays in ten thousand places,
Lovely in limbs, and lovely in eyes not his
  To the Father through the features of men's faces.

1882?   1918

Carrion Comfort

Not, I'll not, carrion[8] comfort, Despair, not feast on thee;
Not untwist—slack they may be—these last strands of man
In me ór, most weary, cry *I can no more.* I can;
Can something, hope, wish day come, not choose not to be.
But ah, but O thou terrible, why wouldst thou rude° on me   *roughly*
Thy wring-world right foot[9] rock? lay a lionlimb against me? scan
With darksome devouring eyes my bruisèd bones? and fan,
O in turns of tempest, me heaped there; me frantic to avoid thee and flee?

Why? That my chaff might fly; my grain lie, sheer and clear.
Nay in all that toil, that coil, since (seems) I kissed the rod,
Hand[1] rather, my heart lo! lapped strength, stole joy, would laugh, chéer.
Cheer whom though? The hero whose heaven-handling flung me, fóot tród
Me? or me that fought him? O which one? is it each one? That night, that year
Of now done darkness I wretch lay wrestling with (my God!) my God.

1885   1918

[No Worst, There Is None. Pitched Past Pitch of Grief]

No worst, there is none. Pitched past pitch of grief,
More pangs will, schooled at forepangs, wilder wring.
Comforter, where, where is your comforting?
Mary, mother of us, where is your relief?

My cries heave, herds-long; huddle in a main, a chief-
woe, world-sorrow; on an age-old anvil wince and sing—
Then lull, then leave off. Fury had shrieked 'No ling-
ering! Let me be fell:° force° I must be brief'.   *fierce, deadly/perforce*

O the mind, mind has mountains; cliffs of fall
Frightful, sheer, no-man-fathomed. Hold them cheap

---

5. I.e., as their bright colors flash in the light.
6. I.e., gives utterance to the essential nature that dwells within ("indoors") each individual being.
7. I.e., gives being to its own individuality.

8. Dead and putrefying flesh.
9. I.e., the foot capable of causing the world to writhe or twist.
1. I.e., the hand that wields the rod.

May who ne'er hung there. Nor does long our small
Durance deal with that steep or deep. Here! creep,
Wretch, under a comfort serves in a whirlwind: all
Life death does end and each day dies with sleep.

1885   1918

[I Wake and Feel the Fell of Dark, Not Day.]

I wake and feel the fell[2] of dark, not day.
What hours, O what black hoürs we have spent
This night! what sights you, heart, saw; ways you went!
And more must, in yet longer light's delay.

5   With witness I speak this. But where I say
Hours I mean years, mean life. And my lament
Is cries countless, cries like dead letters sent
To dearest him that lives alas! away.

I am gall, I am heartburn. God's most deep decree
10 Bitter would have me taste: my taste was me;
Bones built in me, flesh filled, blood brimmed the curse.

Selfyeast of spirit a dull dough sours. I see
The lost are like this, and their scourge to be
As I am mine, their sweating selves, but worse.

1885   1918

[My Own Heart Let Me More Have Pity On]

My own heart let me more have pity on; let
Me live to my sad self hereafter kind,
Charitable; not live this tormented mind
With this tormented mind tormenting yet.

5   I cast for comfort I can no more get
By groping round my comfortless, than blind
Eyes in their dark can day or thirst can find
Thirst's all-in-all in all a world of wet.[3]

Soul, self; come, poor Jackself,[4] I do advise
10 You, jaded, let be; call off thoughts awhile
Elsewhere; leave comfort root-room;[5] let joy size

At God knows when to God knows what;[6] whose smile
's not wrung,[7] see you; unforeseen times rather—as skies
Betweenpie mountains[8]—lights a lovely mile.

1885   1918

---

2. "Fell" is capable of being read in a number of senses: as "the hide or hairy skin of a beast," or, in an obsolete or rare sense, as "gall, bitterness; hence, animosity, rancor" [O.E.D.], or possibly as the adjective *fell*—fierce, savage, cruel—used as a noun.
3. I.e., as shipwrecked persons adrift without drinking water cannot quench their thirst, even though they are surrounded by "wet." The noun *world* is common to all three instances: the speaker's "comfortless" world, the blind man's "dark" world, the "world of wet" in which the shipwrecked are adrift.

4. The humble self—"Jack" used in a pitying, deprecating sense (as in *jack-of-all-trades*).
5. Room for its roots to grow.
6. "Size" (line 11): grow, increase in size; "At God knows when": at unpredictable times; "to God knows what": until it reaches an unpredictable condition.
7. Cannot be forced, but must come as it will.
8. "Betweenpie" (a verb of Hopkins's invention [see *Pied Beauty*]): the brightness of skies seen between mountains, which makes a variegated patterning of light and dark.

That Nature is a Heraclitean[9] Fire and of the comfort of the Resurrection

Cloud-puffball, torn tufts, tossed pillows | flaunt forth, then
chevy° on an air-   *race, scamper*
built thoroughfare: heaven-roysterers, in gay-gangs | they throng;
they glitter in marches.
Down roughcast, down dazzling whitewash, | wherever an elm arches,
Shivelights[1] and shadowtackle[2] in long | lashes lace, lance, and pair.
Delightfully the bright wind boisterous | ropes, wrestles, beats earth bare
Of yestertempest's creases; | in pool and rutpeel parches
Squandering ooze to squeezed | dough, crust, dust; stanches, starches
Squadroned masks and manmarks | treadmire toil there
Footfretted in it. Million-fuelèd, | nature's bonfire burns on.
But quench her bonniest, dearest | to her, her clearest-selvèd spark
Man, how fast his firedint,[3] | his mark on mind, is gone!
Both are in an unfathomable, all is in an enormous dark
Drowned. O pity and indig | nation! Manshape, that shone
Sheer off, disseveral, a star, | death blots black out; nor mark
            Is any of him at all so stark
But vastness blurs and time | beats level. Enough! the Resurrection,
A heart's-clarion! Away grief's gasping, | joyless days, dejection.
            Across my foundering deck shone
A beacon, an eternal beam. | Flesh fade, and mortal trash
Fall to the residuary worm; | world's wildfire, leave but ash:
            In a flash, at a trumpet crash,
I am at once what Christ is, | since he was what I am, and
This Jack,[4] joke, poor potsherd, | patch, matchwood, immortal diamond,
            Is immortal diamond.
                                        1888   1918

[Thou Art Indeed Just, Lord . . .]

*Justus quidem tu es, Domine, si disputem tecum: verumtamen
justa loquar ad te: Quare via impiorum prosperatur? &c.[5]*

Thou art indeed just, Lord, if I contend
With thee; but, sir, so what I plead is just.
Why do sinners' ways prosper? and why must
Disappointment all I endeavour end?
    Wert thou my enemy, O thou my friend,
How wouldst thou worse, I wonder, than thou dost
Defeat, thwart me? Oh, the sots and thralls of lust

9. Heraclitus of Ephesus (flourished 500 B.C.) was the founder of an important school of pre-Socratic philosophy who taught that the world had its origin in fire and would end in fire. "He is best known for his doctrine of perpetual change and impermanence in nature * * * ." For him the principle of the universe was "a law of opposites, whose conflicts were controlled by eternal justice and whose contrary tensions produced the apparent stability of being. Fire, the underlying primary substance, is the prototype of the world, which is an 'ever-living fire with measures of it kindling and measures of it going out.' Fire passes by combustion through the fiery waterspout * * * into water and earth; and the reverse process occurs simultaneously, when part of the earth liquefies and passes by evaporation and 'exhalation' as fuel into fire. Thus are constituted a 'way up' and a 'way down,' a two-way process of interchange between the elements, with approximate balance of 'measures.' 'All is perpetual flux and nothing abides.' " [A. J. D. Porteous, in *Chambers's Encyclopedia*].
1. Light in splinters, fragments.
2. Shadows in complicated shapes, as of ship's ropes, tackle, gear.
3. Hopkins's compound, meaning the mark made by the flame of man's spirit, the spirit's power to make its mark.
4. Common mortal like "poor Jackself" in *My Own Heart Let Me More Have Pity On*.
5. The Latin epigraph is from the Vulgate version of Jeremiah xii.1; the first three lines of Hopkins's poem translate it. The "&c" indicates that the whole of Jeremiah xii is relevant to the poem, which, while it does not continue to translate it directly, parallels it frequently.

Do in spare hours more thrive than I that spend,
Sir, life upon thy cause. See, banks and brakes
10 Now, leavèd how thick! lacèd they are again
With fretty chervil,[6] look, and fresh wind shakes
Them; birds build—but not I build; no, but strain,
Time's eunuch, and not breed one work that wakes.
Mine, O thou lord of life, send my roots rain.

                                        1889   1893

A. E. HOUSMAN
(1859–1936)

Loveliest of Trees, the Cherry Now

Loveliest of trees, the cherry now
Is hung with bloom along the bough,
And stands about the woodland ride
Wearing white for Eastertide.

5 Now, of my threescore years and ten,
Twenty will not come again,
And take from seventy springs a score,
It only leaves me fifty more.

And since to look at things in bloom
10 Fifty springs are little room,
About the woodlands I will go
To see the cherry hung with snow.

                                                  1896

Reveille

Wake: the silver dusk returning
    Up the beach of darkness brims,
And the ship of sunrise burning
    Strands upon the eastern rims.

5 Wake: the vaulted shadow shatters,
    Trampled to the floor it spanned,
And the tent of night in tatters
    Straws° the sky-pavilioned land.   *strews*

Up, lad, up, 'tis late for lying:
10   Hear the drums of morning play;
Hark, the empty highways crying
    "Who'll beyond the hills away?"

Towns and countries woo together,
    Forelands beacon, belfries call;
15 Never lad that trod on leather
    Lived to feast his heart with all.

Up, lad; thews° that lie and cumber   *limbs*
    Sunlit pallets never thrive;

---

6. An herb of the carrot or parsley family, with curled leaves.

Morns abed and daylight slumber
  Were not meant for man alive.

Clay lies still, but blood's a rover;
  Breath's a ware that will not keep.
Up, lad: when the journey's over
  There'll be time enough to sleep.

1896

To an Athlete Dying Young

The time you won your town the race
We chaired you through the market-place;
Man and boy stood cheering by,
And home we brought you shoulder-high.

Today, the road all runners come,
Shoulder-high we bring you home,
And set you at your threshold down,
Townsman of a stiller town.

Smart lad, to slip betimes away
From fields where glory does not stay
And early though the laurel grows
It withers quicker than the rose.

Eyes the shady night has shut
Cannot see the record cut,
And silence sounds no worse than cheers
After earth has stopped the ears:

Now you will not swell the rout
Of lads that wore their honors out,
Runners whom renown outran
And the name died before the man.

So set, before its echoes fade,
The fleet foot on the sill of shade,
And hold to the low lintel up
The still-defended challenge-cup.

And round that early-laureled head
Will flock to gaze the strengthless dead,
And find unwithered on its curls
The garland briefer than a girl's.

1896

On Wenlock Edge the Wood's in Trouble

On Wenlock Edge[1] the wood's in trouble;
  His forest fleece the Wrekin[2] heaves;
The gale, it plies the saplings double,
  And thick on Severn[3] snow the leaves.

---

1. A range of hills in Shropshire.   3. The river Severn.
2. A prominent, isolated hill in Shropshire.

'Twould blow like this through holt and hanger[4]
    When Uricon[5] the city stood:
'Tis the old wind in the old anger,
    But then it threshed another wood.

Then, 'twas before my time, the Roman
    At yonder heaving hill would stare:
The blood that warms an English yeoman,
    The thoughts that hurt him, they were there.

There, like the wind through woods in riot,
    Through him the gale of life blew high;
The tree of man was never quiet:
    Then 'twas the Roman, now 'tis I.

The gale, it plies the saplings double,
    It blows so hard, 'twill soon be gone:
To-day the Roman and his trouble
    Are ashes under Uricon.

                                  1896

With Rue My Heart Is Laden

With rue my heart is laden
    For golden friends I had,
For many a rose-lipt maiden
    And many a lightfoot lad.

5   By brooks too broad for leaping
    The lightfoot boys are laid;
The rose-lipt girls are sleeping
    In fields where roses fade.

                                  1896

"Terence,[6] This Is Stupid Stuff . . ."

    "Terence, this is stupid stuff:
You eat your victuals fast enough;
There can't be much amiss, 'tis clear,
To see the rate you drink your beer.
5   But oh, good Lord, the verse you make,
It gives a chap the belly-ache.
The cow, the old cow, she is dead;
It sleeps well, the hornéd head:
We poor lads, 'tis our turn now
10   To hear such tunes as killed the cow.
Pretty friendship 'tis to rhyme
Your friends to death before their time
Moping melancholy mad:
Come, pipe a tune to dance to, lad."

15   Why, if 'tis dancing you would be,
There's brisker pipes than poetry.

---

4. A holt is a wood or wooded hill; a hanger
is a steep wooded slope.
5. The Roman town Uriconium, on the site of
the modern town of Wroxeter, Shropshire.

6. Housman had at first planned to call the
volume in which this poem appeared *The
Poems of Terence Hearsay.*

Say, for what were hop-yards meant,
Or why was Burton built on Trent?[7]
Oh many a peer of England brews
Livelier liquor than the Muse,
And malt does more than Milton can
To justify God's ways to man.
Ale, man, ale's the stuff to drink
For fellows whom it hurts to think:
Look into the pewter pot
To see the world as the world's not.
And faith, 'tis pleasant till 'tis past:
The mischief is that 'twill not last.
Oh I have been to Ludlow[8] fair
And left my necktie God knows where,
And carried halfway home, or near,
Pints and quarts of Ludlow beer:
Then the world seemed none so bad,
And I myself a sterling lad;
And down in lovely muck I've lain,
Happy till I woke again.
Then I saw the morning sky:
Heigho, the tale was all a lie;
The world, it was the old world yet,
I was I, my things were wet,
And nothing now remained to do
But begin the game anew.

Therefore, since the world has still
Much good, but much less good than ill,
And while the sun and moon endure
Luck's a chance, but trouble's sure,
I'd face it as a wise man would,
And train for ill and not for good.
'Tis true, the stuff I bring for sale
Is not so brisk a brew as ale:
Out of a stem that scored the hand
I wrung it in a weary land.
But take it: if the smack is sour,
The better for the embittered hour;
It should do good to heart and head
When your soul is in my soul's stead;
And I will friend you, if I may,
In the dark and cloudy day.

There was a king reigned in the East:
There, when kings will sit to feast,
They get their fill before they think
With poisoned meat and poisoned drink.
He gathered all that springs to birth
From the many-venomed earth;
First a little, thence to more,
He sampled all her killing store;
And easy, smiling, seasoned sound,
Sate the king when healths went round.

---

7. Burton-on-Trent, a town in Staffordshire   8. A town in Shropshire.
whose principal industry is the brewing of ale.

They put arsenic in his meat
70 And stared aghast to watch him eat;
They poured strychnine in his cup
And shook to see him drink it up:
They shook, they stared as white's their shirt:
Them it was their poison hurt.
75 —I tell the tale that I heard told.
Mithridates, he died old.[9]

1896

Eight O'clock

He stood, and heard the steeple
Sprinkle the quarters on the morning town.
One, two, three, four, to market-place and people
It tossed them down.

5   Strapped, noosed, nighing his hour,
He stood and counted them and cursed his luck;
And then the clock collected in the tower
Its strength, and struck.

1922

The Oracles[1]

'Tis mute, the word they went to hear on high Dodona mountain
When winds were in the oakenshaws and all the cauldrons tolled,
And mute's the midland navel-stone beside the singing fountain,
And echoes list to silence now where gods told lies of old.

5   I took my question to the shrine that has not ceased from speaking,
The heart within, that tells the truth and tells it twice as plain;
And from the cave of oracles I heard the priestess shrieking
That she and I should surely die and never live again.

10 Oh priestess, what you cry is clear, and sound good sense I think it;
But let the screaming echoes rest, and froth your mouth no more.
'Tis true there's better booze than brine, but he that drowns must drink it;
And oh, my lass, the news is news that men have heard before.

The King with half the East at heel is marched from lands of morning;
Their fighters drink the rivers up, their shafts benight the air.

---

9. Mithridates VI, king of Pontus in Asia
Minor in the first century B.C., produced in
himself an immunity to certain poisons by
administering them to himself in small, gradual
doses.
1. It was a feature of the Greek religion that
the gods could be consulted through their
oracles. Questions concerning the future or
asking advice in matters of conduct, both
political and moral, were presented at the
shrine of the oracle, and the answers—usually
vague, ambiguous, or incoherent—were in-
terpreted by a priest. The two most famous
oracles, both alluded to in Housman's poem,

were that of Zeus at Dodona, in Epirus, and
that of Apollo at Delphi. At Dodona the
answers came from the oak sacred to Zeus,
either through the sound of the wind in its
leaves or from the sound of a spring which
gushed up at its roots; this temple contained
a large cauldron, renowned for its echoes. At
Delphi, where the answers were given by the
Pythia, a divinely inspired priestess who
uttered her pronouncements in an incoherent
frenzy, there was a stone called the Omphalos,
or navel, supposed to be the central point of
the earth.

And he that stands will die for nought, and home there's no returning.
The Spartans on the sea-wet rock sat down and combed their hair.[2]

1922

Revolution

West and away the wheels of darkness roll,
  Day's beamy banner up the east is borne,
Specters and fears, the nightmare and her foal,
  Drown in the golden deluge of the morn.

But over sea and continent from sight
  Safe to the Indies has the earth conveyed
The vast and moon-eclipsing cone of night,
  Her towering foolscap of eternal shade.

See, in mid heaven the sun is mounted; hark,
  The belfries tingle to the noonday chime.
'Tis silent, and the subterranean dark
  Has crossed the nadir,[3] and begins to climb.

1922

Stars, I Have Seen Them Fall

Stars, I have seen them fall,
  But when they drop and die
No star is lost at all
  From all the star-sown sky.
The toil of all that be
  Helps not the primal fault;
It rains into the sea,
  And still the sea is salt.

1936

RUDYARD KIPLING
(1865–1936)

Tommy[1]

I went into a public-'ouse to get a pint o' beer,
The publican° 'e up an' sez, "We serve no red-coats here."   *bar-keeper*
The girls be'ind the bar they laughed an' giggled fit to die,
I outs into the street again an' to myself sez I:

---

2. Xerxes (the "King," line 13), the leader of the Persian forces who were to defeat the Greeks, including a small body of unyielding Spartans, at the battle of Thermopylae. The details of the last stanza may be referred to Herodotus' account of the battle and the events leading up to it in Book VII of his *History*. The Athenians had twice consulted the oracle at Delphi, but even the predictions of defeat, which "struck fear into their hearts, failed to persuade them to fly from Greece. They had the courage to remain faithful to their land, and await the coming of the foe." Of Xerxes' army, Herodotus asks, " * * * Was there a nation in all Asia which Xerxes did not bring with him against Greece? Or was there a river, except those of unusual size, which sufficed for his troops to drink?" At one point, Xerxes had sent a spy to observe the Greeks; the Spartans, who happened to hold the outer guard, "were seen by the spy, some of them engaged in gymnastic exercises, others combing their long hair," which struck Xerxes as laughable. He "had no means of surmising the truth—namely, that the Spartans were preparing to do or die manfully * * *"
3. "The point of the heavens diametrically opposite to the zenith; the point directly under the observer" [O.E.D.].
1. Derived from "Thomas Atkins," as the typical name for a soldier in the British army.

5 O it's Tommy this, an' Tommy that, an' "Tommy, go away";
But it's "Thank you, Mister Atkins," when the band begins to play—
The band begins to play, my boys, the band begins to play,
O it's "Thank you, Mister Atkins," when the band begins to play.

I went into a theater as sober as could be,
10 They gave a drunk civilian room, but 'adn't none for me;
They sent me to the gallery or round the music-'alls,[2]
But when it comes to fightin', Lord! they'll shove me in the stalls!
For it's Tommy this, an' Tommy that, an' "Tommy, wait outside";
But its "Special train for Atkins" when the trooper's on the tide—
15 The troopship's on the tide, my boys, the troopship's on the tide,
O it's "Special train for Atkins" when the trooper's on the tide.

Yes, makin' mock o' uniforms that guard you while you sleep
Is cheaper than them uniforms, an' they're starvation cheap;
An' hustlin' drunken soldiers when they're goin' large a bit
20 Is five times better business than paradin' in full kit.
Then it's Tommy this, an' Tommy that, an' "Tommy, 'ow's yer soul?"
But it's "Thin red line of 'eroes"[3] when the drums begin to roll—
The drums begin to roll, my boys, the drums begin to roll,
O it's "Thin red line of 'eroes" when the drums begin to roll.

25 We aren't no thin red 'eroes, nor we aren't no blackguards too,
But single men in barricks, most remarkable like you;
An' if sometimes our conduck isn't all your fancy paints,
Why, single men in barricks don't grow into plaster saints;
While it's Tommy this, an' Tommy that, an' "Tommy, fall be'ind,"
30 But it's "Please to walk in front, sir," when there's trouble in the wind—
There's trouble in the wind, my boys, there's trouble in the wind,
O it's "Please to walk in front, sir," when there's trouble in the wind.

You talk o' better food for us, an' schools, an' fires, an' all:
We'll wait for extry rations if you treat us rational.
35 Don't mess about the cook-room slops, but prove it to our face
The Widow's Uniform[4] is not the soldier-man's disgrace.
For it's Tommy this, an' Tommy that, an' "Chuck him out, the brute!"
But it's "Savior of 'is country" when the guns begin to shoot;
An' it's Tommy this, an' Tommy that, an' anything you please;
40 An' Tommy ain't a bloomin' fool—you bet that Tommy sees!

1890

The Recall

I am the land of their fathers.
In me the virtue stays.
I will bring back my children,
After certain days.

5 Under their feet in the grasses
My clinging magic runs.
They shall return as strangers.
They shall remain as sons.

2. Cheaper seats in a theater, in the balcony; the best seats, in the orchestra, are the stalls.
3. W. H. Russell, a London *Times* correspondent, had used the phrase "thin red line tipped with steel" to describe the 93rd Highlanders infantry regiment as they stood to meet the advancing Russian cavalry at Balaclava (1854), in the Crimean War.
4. I.e., the queen's uniform. In his poems and stories Kipling occasionally referred to Queen Victoria as "The Widow at Windsor."

Over their heads in the branches
Of their new-bought, ancient trees,
I weave an incantation
And draw them to my knees.

Scent of smoke in the evening,
Smell of rain in the night—
The hours, the days and the seasons,
Order their souls aright,

Till I make plain the meaning
Of all my thousand years—
Till I fill their hearts with knowledge,
While I fill their eyes with tears.

1909

Epitaphs of the War

1914–18

"Equality of Sacrifice"

A. "I was a Have." B. "I was a 'have-not.' "
   (*Together.*) "What hast thou given which I gave not?"

A Servant

We were together since the war began.
He was my servant—and the better man.

A Son

My son was killed while laughing at some jest. I would I knew
What it was, and it might serve me in a time when jests are few.

An Only Son

I have slain none except my mother. She
(Blessing her slayer) died of grief for me.

Ex-clerk

Pity not! The army gave
Freedom to a timid slave:
In which freedom did he find
Strength of body, will, and mind:
By which strength he came to prove
Mirth, companionship, and love:
For which love to death he went:
In which death he lies content.

The Wonder

Body and spirit I surrendered whole
To harsh instructors—and received a soul . . .
If mortal man could change me through and through
From all I was—what may the God not do?

Hindu Sepoy[1] in France

This man in his own country prayed we know not to what powers.
We pray them to reward him for his bravery in ours.

1. Native of India employed as soldier under European (especially British) discipline.

The Coward

I could not look on death, which being known,
Men led me to him, blindfold and alone.

Shock

My name, my speech, my self I had forgot.
My wife and children came—I knew them not.
I died. My mother followed. At her call
And on her bosom I remembered all.

A Grave Near Cairo

Gods of the Nile, should this stout fellow here
Get out—get out! He knows not shame nor fear.

Pelicans in the Wilderness

(A GRAVE NEAR HALFA)[2]

The blown sand heaps on me, that none may learn
Where I am laid for whom my children grieve. . . .
O wings that beat at dawning, ye return
Out of the desert to your young at eve!

Two Canadian Memorials

1
We giving all gained all.
Neither lament us nor praise.
Only in all things recall,
It is fear, not death that slays.

2
From little towns in a far land we came,
To save our honor and a world aflame.
By little towns in a far land we sleep;
And trust that world we won for you to keep.

The Favor

Death favored me from the first, well knowing I could not endure
To wait on him day by day. He quitted my betters and came
Whistling over the fields, and, when he had made all sure,
"Thy line is at end," he said, "but at least I have saved its name."

The Beginner

On the first hour of my first day
In the front trench I fell.
(Children in boxes at a play
Stand up to watch it well.)

R.A.F. (Aged Eighteen)

Laughing through clouds, his milk-teeth still unshed,
Cities and men he smote from overhead.
His deaths delivered, he returned to play
Childlike, with childish things now put away.

---

2. In the Sudan.

The Refined Man

I was of delicate mind. I stepped aside for my needs,
  Disdaining the common office. I was seen from afar and killed. . . .
How is this matter for mirth? Let each man be judged by his deeds.
  I have paid my price to live with myself on the terms that I willed.

Native Water-Carrier (M.E.F.)[3]

Prometheus brought down fire to men.
  This brought up water.
The Gods are jealous—now, as then,
  Giving no quarter.

Bombed in London

On land and sea I strove with anxious care
To escape conscription. It was in the air!

The Sleepy Sentinel

Faithless the watch that I kept: now I have none to keep.
I was slain because I slept: now I am slain I sleep.
Let no man reproach me again, whatever watch is unkept—
I sleep because I am slain. They slew me because I slept.

Batteries Out of Ammunition

If any mourn us in the workshop, say
We died because the shift kept holiday.

Common Form

If any question why we died,
Tell them, because our fathers lied.

A Dead Statesman

I could not dig: I dared not rob:
Therefore I lied to please the mob.
Now all my lies are proved untrue
And I must face the men I slew.
What tale shall serve me here among
Mine angry and defrauded young?

The Rebel

If I had clamored at Thy gate
  For gift of life on earth,
And, thrusting through the souls that wait,
  Flung headlong into birth—
Even then, even then, for gin and snare
  About my pathway spread,
Lord, I had mocked Thy thoughtful care
  Before I joined the dead!
But now? . . . I was beneath Thy hand
  Ere yet the planets came.
And now—though planets pass, I stand
  The witness to Thy shame!

---

3. Mediterranean Expeditionary Force.

The Obedient

Daily, though no ears attended,
  Did my prayers arise.
Daily, though no fire descended,
  Did I sacrifice.
Though my darkness did not lift,
  Though I faced no lighter odds,
Though the Gods bestowed no gift,
    Nonetheless,
  Nonetheless, I served the Gods!

A Drifter Off Tarentum[4]

He from the wind-bitten North with ship and companions descended,
  Searching for eggs of death spawned by invisible hulls.
Many he found and drew forth. Of a sudden the fishery ended
  In flame and a clamorous breath known to the eye-pecking gulls.

Destroyers in Collision

For fog and fate no charm is found
  To lighten or amend.
I, hurrying to my bride, was drowned—
  Cut down by my best friend.

Convoy Escort

I was a shepherd to fools
  Causelessly bold or afraid.
They would not abide by my rules.
  Yet they escaped. For I stayed.

Unknown Female Corpse

Headless, lacking foot and hand,
Horrible I come to land.
I beseech all women's sons
Know I was a mother once.

Raped and Revenged

One used and butchered me: another spied
Me broken—for which thing an hundred died.
So it was learned among the heathen hosts
How much a freeborn woman's favor costs.

Salonikan Grave

I have watched a thousand days
Push out and crawl into night
Slowly as tortoises.
Now I, too, follow these.
It is fever, and not the fight—
Time, not battle,—that slays.

The Bridegroom

Call me not false, beloved,
  If, from thy scarce-known breast
So little time removed,
  In other arms I rest.

---

4. Roman name for Taranto, just under the heel of the Italian peninsula.

For this more ancient bride,
  Whom coldly I embrace,
Was constant at my side
  Before I saw thy face.

Our marriage, often set—
  By miracle delayed—
At last is consummate,
  And cannot be unmade.

Live, then, whom life shall cure,
  Almost, of memory,
And leave us to endure
  Its immortality.

V.A.D.[5] (*Mediterranean*)

Ah, would swift ships had never been, for then we ne'er had found,
These harsh Aegean rocks between, this little virgin drowned,
Whom neither spouse nor child shall mourn, but men she nursed through
    pain
And—certain keels for whose return the heathen look in vain.

Actors

ON A MEMORIAL TABLET IN HOLY TRINITY CHURCH, STRATFORD-ON-AVON

We counterfeited once for your disport
  Men's joy and sorrow: but our day has passed.
We pray you pardon all where we fell short—
  Seeing we were your servants to this last.

Journalists

ON A PANEL IN THE HALL OF THE INSTITUTE OF JOURNALISTS

We have served our day.

1919, 1940

WILLIAM BUTLER YEATS[1]
(1865–1939)

The Lake Isle of Innisfree

I will arise and go now, and go to Innisfree,
And a small cabin build there, of clay and wattles[2] made:
Nine bean-rows will I have there, a hive for the honey-bee,
And live alone in the bee-loud glade.

5   And I shall have some peace there, for peace comes dropping slow,
Dropping from the veils of the morning to where the cricket sings;
There midnight's all a glimmer, and noon a purple glow,
And evening full of the linnet's wings.

5. Voluntary Aid Detachment.
1. In providing footnotes to Yeats's poems, the principle has been (as throughout this anthology) to give necessary background information without entering into interpretation or including biographical information for its own sake. With Yeats, however, the line dividing these areas from each other is not always easy to maintain, since the poems often make direct use of detail from Yeats's life and develop ideas and images that can be fully understood only by reference to other poems of Yeats's or to his prose. Although the notes are sometimes detailed, they are intended to provide a minimum background of essential matter, and to provide it, wherever possible, by citing complementary or explanatory passages from Yeats's own writings.
2. Rods interwoven with twigs or branches to form a framework for walls or roof.

I will arise and go now, for always night and day
10 I hear lake water lapping with low sounds by the shore;
While I stand on the roadway, or on the pavements gray,
I hear it in the deep heart's core.

1892

The Lamentation of the Old Pensioner

Although I shelter from the rain
Under a broken tree,
My chair was nearest to the fire
In every company
5 That talked of love or politics,
Ere time transfigured me.

Though lads are making pikes° again   *weapons*
For some conspiracy,
And crazy rascals rage their fill
10 At human tyranny,
My contemplations are of Time
That has transfigured me.

There's not a woman turns her face
Upon a broken tree,
15 And yet the beauties that I loved
Are in my memory;
I spit into the face of Time
That has transfigured me.

1892

Easter 1916[5]

I have met them at close of day
Coming with vivid faces
From counter or desk among gray
Eighteenth-century houses.
5 I have passed with a nod of the head
Or polite meaningless words,
Or have lingered awhile and said
Polite meaningless words,
And thought before I had done
10 Of a mocking tale or a gibe
To please a companion
Around the fire at the club,
Being certain that they and I
But lived where motley is worn:
15 All changed, changed utterly:
A terrible beauty is born.

5. An Irish Nationalist uprising had been planned for Easter Sunday 1916, and although the German ship which was bringing munitions had been intercepted by the British, attempts to postpone the uprising failed; it began in Dublin on Easter Monday. "Fifteen hundred men seized key points and an Irish republic was proclaimed from the General Post Office. After the initial surprise prompt British military action was taken, and when over 300 lives had been lost the insurgents were forced to surrender on 29 April * * * The seven signatories of the republican proclamation, including [Pádraic] Pearse and [James] Connolly, and nine others were shot after court martial between 3 and 12 May; 75 were reprieved and over 2000 held prisoners" [From "Ireland: History," by D. B. Quinn, in *Chambers's Encyclopedia*].

That woman's days were spent
In ignorant good will,
Her nights in argument
Until her voice grew shrill.
What voice more sweet than hers
When, young and beautiful,
She rode to harriers?[6]
This man had kept a school
And rode our wingéd horse;[7]
This other his helper and friend
Was coming into his force;
He might have won fame in the end,
So sensitive his nature seemed,
So daring and sweet his thought.
This other man I had dreamed
A drunken, vainglorious lout.[8]
He had done most bitter wrong
To some who are near my heart,
Yet I number him in the song;
He, too, has resigned his part
In the casual comedy;
He, too, has been changed in his turn,
Transformed utterly:
A terrible beauty is born.

Hearts with one purpose alone
Through summer and winter seem
Enchanted to a stone
To trouble the living stream.
The horse that comes from the road,
The rider, the birds that range
From cloud to tumbling cloud,
Minute by minute they change;
A shadow of cloud on the stream
Changes minute by minute;
A horse-hoof slides on the brim,
And a horse plashes within it;
The long-legged moor-hens dive,
And hens to moor-cocks call;
Minute by minute they live:
The stone's in the midst of all.

Too long a sacrifice
Can make a stone of the heart.
O when may it suffice?
That is Heaven's part, our part
To murmur name upon name,
As a mother names her child
When sleep at last has come
On limbs that had run wild.

6. Countess Constance Georgina Markiewicz, *née* Gore-Booth, about whom Yeats wrote *On a Political Prisoner* and a later poem, *In Memory of Eva Gore-Booth and Con Markiewicz*.
7. Pádraic Pearse, headmaster of St. Enda's School, and a prolific writer of poems, plays, and stories as well as of essays on Irish politics and Gaelic literature. "This other" was Thomas MacDonough, also a schoolteacher.
8. Major John MacBride, who had married Maud Gonne (the woman with whom Yeats had for years been hopelessly in love) in 1903 and separated from her in 1905.

65 What is it but nightfall?
    No, no, not night but death;
    Was it needless death after all?
    For England may keep faith
    For all that is done and said.
70 We know their dream; enough
    To know they dreamed and are dead;
    And what if excess of love
    Bewildered them till they died?
    I write it out in a verse—
75 MacDonagh and MacBride
    And Connolly and Pearse
    Now and in time to be,
    Wherever green is worn,
    Are changed, changed utterly:
80 A terrible beauty is born.

September 25, 1916   1916

The Fisherman

    Although I can see him still,
    The freckled man who goes
    To a gray place on a hill
    In gray Connemara⁹ clothes
5   At dawn to cast his flies,
    It's long since I began
    To call up to the eyes
    This wise and simple man.
    All day I'd looked in the face
10 What I had hoped 'twould be
    To write for my own race
    And the reality;
    The living men that I hate,
    The dead man that I loved,
15 The craven man in his seat,
    The insolent unreproved,
    And no knave brought to book
    Who has won a drunken cheer,
    The witty man and his joke
20 Aimed at the commonest ear,
    The clever man who cries
    The catch-cries of the clown,
    The beating down of the wise
    And great Art beaten down.

25 Maybe a twelvemonth since
    Suddenly I began,
    In scorn of this audience,
    Imagining a man,
    And his sun-freckled face,
30 And gray Connemara cloth,
    Climbing up to a place
    Where stone is dark under froth,
    And the down-turn of his wrist
    When the flies drop in the stream;

9. A district in County Galway, in western Ireland, which includes seacoast, islands, and
mountains.

A man who does not exist,
A man who is but a dream;
And cried, "Before I am old
I shall have written him one
Poem maybe as cold
And passionate as the dawn."

1916

The Wild Swans at Coole[1]

The trees are in their autumn beauty,
The woodland paths are dry,
Under the October twilight the water
Mirrors a still sky;
Upon the brimming water among the stones
Are nine-and-fifty swans.

The nineteenth autumn has come upon me
Since I first made my count;[2]
I saw, before I had well finished,
All suddenly mount
And scatter wheeling in great broken rings
Upon their clamorous wings.

I have looked upon those brilliant creatures,
And now my heart is sore.
All's changed since I, hearing at twilight,
The first time on this shore,
The bell-beat of their wings above my head,
Trod with a lighter tread.

Unwearied still, lover by lover,
They paddle in the cold
Companionable streams or climb the air;
Their hearts have not grown old;
Passion or conquest, wander where they will,
Attend upon them still.

But now they drift on the still water,
Mysterious, beautiful;
Among what rushes will they build,
By what lake's edge or pool
Delight men's eyes when I awake some day
To find they have flown away?

1917

The Scholars

Bald heads forgetful of their sins,
Old, learned, respectable bald heads
Edit and annotate the lines
That young men, tossing on their beds,
Rhymed out in love's despair
To flatter beauty's ignorant ear.

1. Coole Park, the estate in western Ireland of Lady Augusta Gregory, Yeats's patroness and friend.

2. Yeats had first visited Coole Park in 1897; the poem was written in October 1916.

All shuffle there; all cough in ink;
All wear the carpet with their shoes;
All think what other people think;
All know the man their neighbor knows.
Lord, what would they say
Did their Catullus walk that way?

1917

The Cat and the Moon[3]

The cat went here and there
And the moon spun round like a top,
And the nearest kin of the moon,
The creeping cat, looked up.
Black Minnaloushe[4] stared at the moon,
For, wander and wail as he would,
The pure cold light in the sky
Troubled his animal blood.
Minnaloushe runs in the grass
Lifting his delicate feet.
Do you dance, Minnaloushe, do you dance?
When two close kindred meet,
What better than call a dance?
Maybe the moon may learn,
Tired of that courtly fashion,
A new dance turn.
Minnaloushe creeps through the grass
From moonlit place to place,
The sacred moon overhead
Has taken a new phase.
Does Minnaloushe know that his pupils
Will pass from change to change,
And that from round to crescent,
From crescent to round they range?
Minnaloushe creeps through the grass
Alone, important and wise,
And lifts to the changing moon
His changing eyes.

1918

On a Political Prisoner[5]

She that but little patience knew,
From childhood on, had now so much
A gray gull lost its fear and flew
Down to her cell and there alit,
And there endured her fingers' touch
And from her fingers ate its bit.

Did she in touching that lone wing
Recall the years before her mind

---

3. In his preface to the play with the same
title, in which the poem appears, Yeats says,
"* * * [I] allowed myself as I wrote to think
of the cat as the normal man and of the moon
as the opposite he seeks perpetually, or as
having any meaning I have conferred upon
the moon elsewhere." The twenty-eight phases
of the moon, and their correspondences in hu-
man character, achievement, and history, are
described in the poem *The Phases of the Moon,*
and in *A Vision* (1937), Book I, Part III.
4. The name of a friend's black Persian cat.
5. The Countess Constance Georgina Markie-
wicz, *née* Gore-Booth, who was imprisoned in
Holloway Gaol for her part in the Easter Re-
bellion of 1916.

Became a bitter, an abstract thing,
Her thought some popular enmity:
Blind and leader of the blind
Drinking the foul ditch where they lie?

When long ago I saw her ride
Under Ben Bulben[6] to the meet,
The beauty of her countryside
With all youth's lonely wildness stirred,
She seemed to have grown clean and sweet
Like any rock-bred, sea-borne bird:

Sea-borne, or balanced on the air
When first it sprang out of the nest
Upon some lofty rock to stare
Upon the cloudy canopy,
While under its storm-beaten breast
Cried out the hollows of the sea.

1921

The Second Coming

Turning and turning in the widening gyre[7]
The falcon cannot hear the falconer;
Things fall apart; the center cannot hold;
Mere anarchy is loosed upon the world,
The blood-dimmed tide is loosed, and everywhere
The ceremony of innocence is drowned;
The best lack all conviction, while the worst
Are full of passionate intensity.

Surely some revelation is at hand;
Surely the Second Coming is at hand;
The Second Coming! Hardly are those words out
When a vast image out of *Spiritus Mundi*[8]
Troubles my sight: somewhere in sands of the desert
A shape with lion body and the head of a man,[9]
A gaze blank and pitiless as the sun,
Is moving its slow thighs, while all about it
Reel shadows of the indignant desert birds.
The darkness drops again; but now I know

6. Mountain in County Sligo, in the West of Ireland, where Yeats spent large parts of his childhood and youth.
7. The gyre—the cone whose shape is traced in the falcon's sweep upward and out in widening circles from the falconer who should control its flight—involves a reference to the geometrical figure of the interpenetrating cones, the "fundamental symbol" Yeats used to diagram his cyclical view of history. (See the opening pages of "The Great Wheel," in *A Vision* [1937]). He saw the cycle of Greco-Roman civilization as having been brought to a close by the advent of Christianity, and in the violence of his own times—"the growing murderousness of the world"—he saw signs that the 2000-year cycle of Christianity was itself about to end, and to be replaced by a system anithetical to it.
8. Or *Anima Mundi*, the Great Memory. "Before the mind's eye, whether in sleep or waking, came images that one was to discover presently in some book one had never read,

and after looking in vain for explanation to the current theory of forgotten personal memory, I came to believe in a great memory passing on from generation to generation * * * Our daily thought was certainly but the line of foam at the shallow edge of a vast luminous sea" [*Per Amica Silentia Lunae*, "Anima Mundi," § ii].
9. In the Introduction to his play *The Resurrection* (in *Wheels and Butterflies*, 1935), Yeats describes the way in which the sphinx image had first manifested itself to him: "Our civilisation was about to reverse itself, or some new civilisation about to be born from all that our age had rejected * * *; because we had worshipped a single god it would worship many * * * Had I begun *On Baile's Strand* or not when I began to imagine, as always at my left side just out of the range of the sight, a brazen winged beast (afterwards described in my poem *The Second Coming*) that I associated with laughing, ecstatic destruction?"

That twenty centuries of stony sleep
20 Were vexed to nightmare by a rocking cradle,
And what rough beast, its hour come round at last,
Slouches towards Bethlehem to be born?

1921

A Prayer for My Daughter [8]

Once more the storm is howling, and half hid
Under this cradle-hood and coverlid
My child sleeps on. There is no obstacle
But Gregory's wood and one bare hill
5   Whereby the haystack- and roof-leveling wind,
Bred on the Atlantic, can be stayed;
And for an hour I have walked and prayed
Because of the great gloom that is in my mind.

I have walked and prayed for this young child an hour
10 And heard the sea-wind scream upon the tower,[9]
And under the arches of the bridge, and scream
In the elms above the flooded stream;
Imagining in excited reverie
That the future years had come,
15 Dancing to a frenzied drum,
Out of the murderous innocence of the sea.

May she be granted beauty and yet not
Beauty to make a stranger's eye distraught,
Or hers before a looking glass, for such,
20 Being made beautiful overmuch,
Consider beauty a sufficient end,
Lose natural kindness and maybe
The heart-revealing intimacy
That chooses right, and never find a friend.

25 Helen [1] being chosen found life flat and dull
And later had much trouble from a fool,
While that great Queen,[2] that rose out of the spray,
Being fatherless could have her way
Yet chose a bandy-leggèd smith for man.
30 It's certain that fine women eat
A crazy salad with their meat,
Whereby the Horn of Plenty is undone.

In courtesy I'd have her chiefly learned;
Hearts are not had as a gift but hearts are earned
35 By those that are not entirely beautiful;

8. Yeats's daughter, Anne Butler Yeats, was born on February 26, 1919.
9. For Yeats's tower, which he called Thoor Ballylee, see note to the next poem.
1. Helen of Troy, whose beauty was legendary. The daughter of Zeus and Leda, she married Menelaus, brother of the Greek leader, Agamemnon. She was abducted by Paris, son of the king of Troy; the Greeks undertook an expedition to Troy to bring her back, besieged the city for ten years, and finally took it. Helen was reunited with Menelaus.
2. Aphrodite, Greek goddess of love. "Fatherless" in the sense that, in Hesiod's version of the myth, "she sprang from the foam (*aphros*) of the sea that gathered about the severed member of Uranus when Cronos . . . mutilated him" (*Oxford Companion to Classical Literature*). She was married to Hephaestus, the smith, lame from birth, who forged thunderbolts for the gods.

Yet many, that have played the fool
For beauty's very self, has charm made wise,
And many a poor man that has roved,
Loved and thought himself beloved,
From a glad kindness cannot take his eyes.

May she become a flourishing hidden tree
That all her thoughts may like the linnet [3] be,
And have no business but dispensing round
Their magnanimities of sound,
Nor but in merriment begin a chase,
Nor but in merriment a quarrel.
Oh, may she live like some green laurel
Rooted in one dear perpetual place.

My mind, because the minds that I have loved,
The sort of beauty that I have approved,
Prosper but little, has dried up of late,
Yet knows that to be choked with hate
May well be of all evil chances chief.
If there's no hatred in a mind
Assault and battery of the wind
Can never tear the linnet from the leaf.

An intellectual hatred is the worst,
So let her think opinions are accursed.
Have I not seen the loveliest woman born [4]
Out of the mouth of Plenty's horn,
Because of her opinionated mind
Barter that horn and every good
By quiet natures understood
For an old bellows full of angry wind?

Considering that, all hatred driven hence,
The soul recovers radical innocence
And learns at last that it is self-delighting,
Self-appeasing, self-affrighting,
And that its own sweet will is Heaven's will;
She can, though every face should scowl
And every windy quarter howl
Or every bellows burst, be happy still.

And may her bridegroom bring her to a house
Where all's accustomed, ceremonious;
For arrogance and hatred are the wares
Peddled in the thoroughfares.
How but in custom and in ceremony
Are innocence and beauty born?
Ceremony's a name for the rich horn,
And custom for the spreading laurel tree.

                                        1919   1921

3. Small European bird of the finch family.
4. Doubtless Maud Gonne, whom Yeats had
loved hopelessly since meeting her in 1889, and
who had married Major John MacBride in
1903; often to Yeats's dismay, she was a very
daring activist in the cause of Irish liberation.

To Be Carved on a Stone at Thoor Ballylee [5]

I, the poet William Yeats,
With old mill boards and sea-green slates,
And smithy work from the Gort forge,
Restored this tower for my wife George;
5 And may these characters remain
When all is ruin once again.

                                    1918   1921

Leda and the Swan [1]

A sudden blow: the great wings beating still
Above the staggering girl, her thighs caressed
By the dark webs, her nape caught in his bill,
He holds her helpless breast upon his breast.

5 How can those terrified vague fingers push
The feathered glory from her loosening thighs?
And how can body, laid in that white rush,
But feel the strange heart beating where it lies?

10 A shudder in the loins engenders there
The broken wall, the burning roof and tower
And Agamemnon dead.
                        Being so caught up,
So mastered by the brute blood of the air,
Did she put on his knowledge with his power
15 Before the indifferent beak could let her drop?

                                    1923   1924

Sailing to Byzantium [2]

1

That is no country for old men. The young
In one another's arms, birds in the trees
—Those dying generations—at their song,
The salmon-falls, the mackerel-crowded seas,
5 Fish, flesh, or fowl, commend all summer long
Whatever is begotten, born, and dies.
Caught in that sensual music all neglect
Monuments of unaging intellect.

5. In June, 1917, Yeats had purchased a small plot of land with its buildings, including a ruined Norman tower, Thoor Ballylee (Thoor: Gaelic for tower), part of the Gregory estate, Coole Park, in Kiltartan, near the village of Gort, County Galway. After marrying Miss George Hyde-Lees in October 1917, he made the tower and two cottages suitable for habitation. An earlier version of this poem was "to be inscribed on a great stone beside the front door."

1. Leda, possessed by Zeus in the guise of a swan, gave birth to Helen of Troy and the twins Castor and Pollux. (Leda was also the mother of Clytemnestra, Agamemnon's wife, who murdered him on his return from the war at Troy.) Helen's abduction by Paris from her husband, Menelaus, brother of Agamemnon, was the cause of the Trojan war. Yeats saw Leda as the recipient of an annunciation that would found Greek civilization, as the Annunciation to Mary would found Christianity.

2. Of the ancient city of Byzantium—on the site of modern Istanbul, capital of the Eastern Roman Empire, and the center, especially in the fifth and sixth centuries, of highly developed and characteristic forms of art and architecture—Yeats made a many-faceted symbol, which, since it is a symbol, should not be brought within the limits of too narrowly specific interpretation. Byzantine painting and the mosaics which decorated its churches (Yeats had seen later derivatives of these mosaics in Italy, at Ravenna and elsewhere) were stylized and formal, making no attempt at the full naturalistic rendering of human forms, so that the city and its art can appropriately symbolize a way of life in which art is frankly accepted and proclaimed as artifice. As artifice, as a work of the intellect, this art is not subject to the decay and death which overtake the life of "natural things." But while such an opposition of artifice and nature is central to the poem, there are refer-

2

An aged man is but a paltry thing,
A tattered coat upon a stick, unless
Soul clap its hands and sing, and louder sing
For every tatter in its mortal dress,
Nor is there singing school but studying
Monuments of its own magnificence;
And therefore I have sailed the seas and come
To the holy city of Byzantium.

3

O sages standing in God's holy fire
As in the gold mosaic of a wall,
Come from the holy fire, perne in a gyre,[3]
And be the singing-masters of my soul.
Consume my heart away; sick with desire
And fastened to a dying animal
It knows not what it is; and gather me
Into the artifice of eternity.

4

Once out of nature I shall never take
My bodily form from any natural thing,
But such a form as Grecian goldsmiths make
Of hammered gold and gold enameling
To keep a drowsy Emperor awake;
Or set upon a golden bough to sing
To lords and ladies of Byzantium
Of what is past, or passing, or to come.

1927

Two Songs from a Play[4]

1

I saw a staring virgin stand
Where holy Dionysus died,
And tear the heart out of his side,
And lay the heart upon her hand

---

ences to Byzantium in Yeats's prose which suggest the wider range of meaning that the city held for him. In *A Vision*, particularly, he makes of it an exemplar of a civilization which had achieved "Unity of Being": "I think if I could be given a month of Antiquity and leave to spend it where I chose, I would spend it in Byzantium a little before Justinian [who ruled at Byzantium from 527 to 565] opened St. Sophia and closed the Academy of Plato. I think I could find in some little wine-shop some philosophical worker in mosaic who could answer all my questions, the super-natural descending nearer to him than to Plotinus even, for the pride of his delicate skill would make what was an instrument of power to princes and clerics, a murderous mad-ness in the mob, show as a lovely flexible pres-ence like that of a perfect human body * * * I think that in early Byzantium, maybe never before or since in recorded history, religious, aesthetic and practical life were one, that architect and artificers * * * spoke to the multitude and the few alike. The painter, the mosaic worker, the worker in gold and silver, the illuminator of sacred books, were almost impersonal, almost perhaps without the con-sciousness of individual design, absorbed in their subject-matter and that the vision of a whole people."

3. Out of the noun *pern* (usually *pirn*), a weaver's bobbin, spool, or reel, Yeats makes a verb meaning to move in the spiral pattern taken by thread being unwound from a bobbin or being wound upon it. Here the speaker entreats the sages to descend to him in this manner, to come down into the gyres of his-tory, the cycles of created life, out of their eternity in "the simplicity of fire" where is "all music and all rest." (For "the two reali-ties, the terrestrial and the condition of fire," see *Per Amica Silentia Lunae*, "Anima Mundi," § x.)
4. In Yeats's short play *The Resurrection* (1931), the two songs were to be sung by the musicians "as they pull apart or pull to-gether the proscenium curtain." Thus the first song opens the play, the second closes it. At the play's climax, a Syrian has just brought to a Greek and a Hebrew the news of Christ's Resurrection: the figure of Christ appears in the room in which they stand, and the Greek, who has declared it to be only a phantom, not flesh and blood, touches the body and cries, "The heart of a phantom is beating!" Earlier in the play a procession of the followers of Dionysus had passed in the street outside, their revels celebrating the rebirth of the slain god in the spring, the old rites going on even while the new religion which will destroy them is being manifested.

5   And bear that beating heart away;
    And then did all the Muses sing
    Of Magnus Annus[5] at the spring,
    As though God's death were but a play.[6]

    Another Troy must rise and set,
10 Another lineage feed the crow,
    Another Argo's painted prow
    Drive to a flashier bauble yet.
    The Roman Empire stood appalled:
    It dropped the reins of peace and war
15 When that fierce virgin and her Star
    Out of the fabulous darkness called.

                    2

    In pity for man's darkening thought
    He walked that room[7] and issued thence
    In Galilean turbulence;
20 The Babylonian starlight brought
    A fabulous, formless darkness in;
    Odor of blood when Christ was slain
    Made all Platonic tolerance vain
    And vain all Doric discipline.

25 Everything that man esteems
    Endures a moment or a day.
    Love's pleasure drives his love away,
    The painter's brush consumes his dreams;
    The herald's cry, the soldier's tread
30 Exhaust his glory and his might:
    Whatever flames upon the night
    Man's own resinous heart has fed.

                                            1927

Among School Children

                    1

    I walk through the long schoolroom questioning;
    A kind old nun in a white hood replies;
    The children learn to cipher and to sing,
    To study reading-books and histories,
5   To cut and sew, be neat in everything
    In the best modern way—the children's eyes
    In momentary wonder stare upon
    A sixty-year-old smiling public man.

                    2

    I dream of a Ledaean body,[8] bent
10 Above a sinking fire, a tale that she
    Told of a harsh reproof, or trivial event
    That changed some childish day to tragedy—
    Told, and it seemed that our two natures blent

---

5. The Great Year, or the Platonic Year, is the period of 26,000 years in which a complete cycle of the precession of the equinoxes takes place. In Yeats's system it represents a complete turning of the Great Wheel, the 26,000 years divided into twelve cycles of roughly 2000 years each.
6. I.e., as though, like a play which has ended,

the god's life, passion, and death could be begun again from the beginning.
7. I.e., the room in the play, to which the second song looks back.
8. I.e., the body of a woman the poet has known and loved and who has seemed to him as beautiful as Leda or her daughter, Helen of Troy.

Into a sphere from youthful sympathy,
Or else, to alter Plato's parable,
Into the yolk and white of the one shell.[9]

3

And thinking of that fit of grief or rage
I look upon one child or t'other there
And wonder if she stood so at that age—
For even daughters of the swan can share
Something of every paddler's heritage—
And had that color upon cheek or hair,
And thereupon my heart is driven wild:
She stands before me as a living child.

4

Her present image floats into the mind—
Did Quattrocento finger[1] fashion it
Hollow of cheek as though it drank the wind
And took a mess of shadows for its meat?
And I though never of Ledaean kind
Had pretty plumage once—enough of that,
Better to smile on all that smile, and show
There is a comfortable kind of old scarecrow.

5

What youthful mother, a shape upon her lap
Honey of generation had betrayed,[2]
And that must sleep, shriek, struggle to escape
As recollection or the drug decide,
Would think her son, did she but see that shape
With sixty or more winters on its head,
A compensation for the pang of his birth,
Or the uncertainty of his setting forth?

6

Plato thought nature but a spume that plays
Upon a ghostly paradigm of things;[3]
Solider Aristotle played the taws
Upon the bottom of a king of kings;[4]
World-famous golden-thighed Pythagoras
Fingered upon a fiddle-stick or strings
What a star sang and careless Muses heard:[5]
Old clothes upon old sticks to scare a bird.

9. In Plato's *Symposium*, one of the speakers, to explain the origin of human love, recounts the legend according to which human beings were originally double their present form until Zeus, fearful of their power, decided to cut them in two, which he did "as men cut sorb-apples in two when they are preparing them for pickling, or as they cut eggs in two with a hair." Since then, "each of us is * * * but the half of a human being, * * * each is forever seeking his missing half."
1. I.e., the hand of an Italian artist of the fifteenth century.
2. In a note to the poem, Yeats says: "I have taken the 'honey of generation' from Porphyry's essay on 'The Cave of the Nymphs' but find no warrant in Porphyry for considering it the 'drug' that destroys the 'recollection' of pre-natal freedom * * *." In the essay explaining the symbolism of a passage from the Thirteenth Book of the *Odyssey*, Porphyry (ca. A.D. 232–305) makes such statements as that "the sweetness of honey signifies * * * the same thing as the pleasure

arising from copulation," the pleasure "which draws souls downward to generation."
3. In Plato's idealistic philosophy the world of nature, of appearances, that we know is but the copy of a world of ideal, permanently enduring prototypes.
4. The philosophy of Aristotle differed most markedly from that of Plato in that it emphasized the systematic investigation of verifiable phenomena. Aristotle was tutor to the son of King Philip of Macedonia, later Alexander the Great. "Played the taws": whipped.
5. A Greek philosopher (sixth century B.C.), about whom clustered many legends even in his own lifetime, as that he was the incarnation of Apollo, that he had a golden hip- or thigh-bone, and so on. Central to the Pythagorean school of philosophy (along with the doctrine of the transmigration of souls) was the premise that the universe is mathematically regular, which premise had as one of its starting points the Pythagoreans' observations of the exact mathematical relationships underlying musical harmony.

7

Both nuns and mothers worship images,
50 But those the candles light are not as those
That animate a mother's reveries,
But keep a marble or a bronze repose.
And yet they too break hearts—O Presences
That passion, piety or affection knows,
55 And that all heavenly glory symbolize—
O self-born mockers of man's enterprise;

8

Labor is blossoming or dancing where
The body is not bruised to pleasure soul,
Nor beauty born out of its own despair,
60 Nor blear-eyed wisdom out of midnight oil.
O chestnut-tree, great-rooted blossomer,
Are you the leaf, the blossom or the bole?
O body swayed to music, O brightening glance,
How can we know the dancer from the dance?

1927

At Algeciras[6]—A Meditation Upon Death

The heron-billed pale cattle-birds
That feed on some foul parasite
Of the Moroccan flocks and herds
Cross the narrow straits to light
5 In the rich midnight of the garden trees
Till the dawn break upon those mingled seas.

Often at evening when a boy
Would I carry to a friend—
Hoping more substantial joy
10 Did an older mind commend—
Not such as are in Newton's metaphor,[7]
But actual shells of Rosses' level shore.[8]

Greater glory in the sun,
An evening chill upon the air,
15 Bid imagination run
Much on the Great Questioner;
What He can question, what if questioned I
Can with a fitting confidence reply.

November 1928   1929

Byzantium[5]

The unpurged images of day recede;
The Emperor's drunken soldiery are abed;
Night resonance recedes, night-walkers' song
After great cathedral gong;

6. A town in Spain, lying across the Straits of Gibraltar (where Atlantic and Mediterranean waters meet) from Spanish Morocco.
7. " 'I seem to have been only like a boy playing on the seashore and diverting myself in now and then finding a smoother pebble, or a prettier shell, than ordinary, whilst the great ocean of truth lay all undiscovered before me' " [Newton, in Brewster's *Memoirs of the Life, Writings and Discoveries of Sir Isaac Newton*, vol. 2, chapter 27].
8. Rosses Point, on Sligo Bay, in the west of Ireland.
5. Under the heading "Subject for a Poem, April 30th," Yeats wrote in his *1930 Diary:* "Describe Byzantium as it is in the system [that is, his system in *A Vision*] towards the end of the first Christian millennium. A walking mummy. Flames at the street corners where the soul is purified, birds of hammered gold singing in the golden trees, in the harbor [dolphins], offering their backs to the wailing dead that they may carry them to Paradise."

A starlit or a moonlit dome disdains[6]
All that man is,
All mere complexities,
The fury and the mire of human veins.

Before me floats an image, man or shade,
Shade more than man, more image than a shade;
For Hades' bobbin bound in mummy-cloth
May unwind the winding path;[7]
A mouth that has no moisture and no breath
Breathless mouths may summon;[8]
I hail the superhuman;
I call it death-in-life and life-in-death.

Miracle, bird or golden handiwork,
More miracle than bird or handiwork,
Planted on the starlit golden bough,
Can like the cocks of Hades crow,[9]
Or, by the moon embittered, scorn aloud
In glory of changeless metal
Common bird or petal
And all complexities of mire or blood.

At midnight on the Emperor's pavement flit
Flames that no faggot feeds, nor steel has lit,
Nor storm disturbs, flames begotten of flame,
Where blood-begotten spirits come
And all complexities of fury leave,
Dying into a dance,
An agony of trance,
An agony of flame that cannot singe a sleeve.

Astraddle on the dolphin's mire and blood,
Spirit after spirit! The smithies break the flood.
The golden smithies of the Emperor!
Marbles of the dancing floor
Break bitter furies of complexity,
Those images that yet
Fresh images beget,
That dolphin-torn, that gong-tormented sea.

1930   1932

6. If the dome is seen as "starlit" at the dark of the moon and as "moonlit" at the full, then these terms may be seen as referring to Phase 1 and Phase 15, respectively, of the twenty-eight phases of the moon in the system of *A Vision*. As Michael Robartes says in *The Phases of the Moon,* "* * * There's no human life at the full or the dark," these being "the superhuman phases," opposite to one another on the Wheel of Being. Phase 1 is the phase of complete objectivity, the soul being "completely absorbed by its supernatural environment," waiting to be formed, in a state of "complete plasticity." Phase 15 is the state of complete subjectivity, when the soul is completely absorbed in an achieved state, "a phase of complete beauty." Thus, the world of "mere complexities," the world in which man is in a state of becoming, is banished from the poem at the beginning, as the "unpurged images of day" have been banished.
7. The soul and/or body of the dead. The comparison to the bobbin or spindle is at first visual, to describe the figure of the dead, wrapped in a winding-sheet or mummy-cloth, but it also emphasizes the idea that the soul may unwind the thread of its fate by retracing its path, returning to the world to serve as guide, instructor, inspiration.
8. The two lines have been read in two different ways, depending on which of the two phrases ("a mouth * * * " or "breathless mouths * * * ") is seen as subject and which as object of "may summon." Taking "breathless mouths" as subject: mouths of the living, breathless with the intensity of the act of invocation, may call up the mouths of the dead to instruct them.
9. A symbol of rebirth and resurrection. In a book on Roman sculpture which Yeats is believed to have known, *Apotheosis and After Life* (1915), Mrs. Arthur Strong says: "* * * The great vogue of the cock on later Roman tombstones is due * * * to the fact that as herald of the sun he becomes by an easy transition the herald of rebirth and resurrection." In the next sentence she mentions another visual symbol which figures in the poem's last stanza: "The dolphins and marine monsters, another frequent decoration, form a mystic escort of the dead to the Islands of the Blest * * * "

Lapis Lazuli[1]

(FOR HARRY CLIFTON)

I have heard that hysterical women say
They are sick of the palette and fiddle-bow,
Of poets that are always gay,
For everybody knows or else should know
5   That if nothing drastic is done
Aeroplane and Zeppelin will come out,
Pitch like King Billy[2] bomb-balls in
Until the town lie beaten flat.

All perform their tragic play,
10   There struts Hamlet, there is Lear,
That's Ophelia, that Cordelia;
Yet they, should the last scene be there,
The great stage curtain about to drop,
If worthy their prominent part in the play,
15   Do not break up their lines to weep.
They know that Hamlet and Lear are gay;
Gaiety transfiguring all that dread.
All men have aimed at, found and lost;
Black out; Heaven blazing into the head:
20   Tragedy wrought to its uttermost.
Though Hamlet rambles and Lear rages,
And all the drop-scenes drop at once
Upon a hundred thousand stages,
It cannot grow by an inch or an ounce.

25   On their own feet they came, or on shipboard,
Camelback, horseback, ass-back, mule-back,
Old civilizations put to the sword.
Then they and their wisdom went to rack:
No handiwork of Callimachus,[3]
30   Who handled marble as if it were bronze,
Made draperies that seemed to rise
When sea-wind swept the corner, stands;
His long lamp-chimney shaped like the stem
Of a slender palm, stood but a day;
35   All things fall and are built again,
And those that build them again are gay.

Two Chinamen, behind them a third,
Are carved in lapis lazuli,
Over them flies a long-legged bird,
40   A symbol of longevity;
The third, doubtless a serving-man,
Carries a musical instrument.

1. A deep-blue semi-precious stone. In a
letter dated July 6, 1935, Yeats wrote, "* * *
Someone has sent me a present of a great
piece [of lapis lazuli] carved by some Chinese
sculptor into the semblance of a mountain
with temple, trees, paths and an ascetic and
pupil about to climb the mountain. Ascetic,
pupil, hard stone, eternal theme of the sensual
east. The heroic cry in the midst of despair.
But no, I am wrong, the east has its solutions
always and therefore knows nothing of tragedy.
It is we, not the east, that must raise the
heroic cry."
2. At the Battle of the Boyne on July 1, 1690,
William III, king of England since 1689, had
defeated the forces of the deposed king,
James II.
3. Greek sculptor of the fifth century B.C., of
whom Yeats says in *A Vision* that only one
example of his work remains, a marble chair,
and goes on to mention "that bronze lamp [in
the Erechtheum, a temple of the guardian
deities of Athens] shaped like a palm, known
to us by a description in Pausanias * * *"

Every discoloration of the stone,
Every accidental crack or dent,
Seems a water-course or an avalanche,
Or lofty slope where it still snows
Though doubtless plum or cherry-branch
Sweetens the little half-way house
Those Chinamen climb towards, and I
Delight to imagine them seated there;
There, on the mountain and the sky,
On all the tragic scene they stare.
One asks for mournful melodies;
Accomplished fingers begin to play.
Their eyes mid many wrinkles, their eyes,
Their ancient, glittering eyes, are gay.

1938

Long-Legged Fly

That civilization may not sink,
Its great battle lost,
Quiet the dog, tether the pony
To a distant post;
Our master Caesar is in the tent
Where the maps are spread,
His eyes fixed upon nothing,
A hand under his head.
Like a long-legged fly upon the stream
His mind moves upon silence.

That the topless towers be burnt
And men recall that face,[4]
Move most gently if move you must
In this lonely place.
She thinks, part woman, three parts a child,
That nobody looks; her feet
Practice a tinker shuffle
Picked up on a street.
Like a long-legged fly upon the stream
Her mind moves upon silence.

That girls at puberty may find
The first Adam in their thought,
Shut the door of the Pope's chapel,[5]
Keep those children out.
There on that scaffolding reclines
Michael Angelo.
With no more sound than the mice make
His hand moves to and fro.
Like a long-legged fly upon the stream
His mind moves upon silence.

1939

4. An echo of Marlowe's lines on Helen of Troy in *Dr. Faustus:* "Was this the face that launched a thousand ships, / And burnt the topless towers of Ilium?"

5. On the ceiling of the Sistine Chapel, so called because it was built under Pope Sixtus IV, Michelangelo painted a series of biblical scenes, including the creation of Adam.

The Circus Animals' Desertion

1

I sought a theme and sought for it in vain,
I sought it daily for six weeks or so.
Maybe at last, being but a broken man,
I must be satisfied with my heart, although
5   Winter and summer till old age began
My circus animals were all on show,
Those stilted boys, that burnished chariot,[3]
Lion and woman and the Lord knows what.

2

What can I but enumerate old themes?
10 First that sea-rider Oisin[4] led by the nose
Through three enchanted islands, allegorical dreams,
Vain gaiety, vain battle, vain repose,
Themes of the embittered heart, or so it seems,
That might adorn old songs or courtly shows;
15 But what cared I that set him on to ride,
I, starved for the bosom of his faery bride?

And then a counter-truth filled out its play,
The Countess Cathleen[5] was the name I gave it;
She, pity-crazed, had given her soul away,
20 But masterful Heaven had intervened to save it.
I thought my dear[6] must her own soul destroy,
So did fanaticism and hate enslave it,
And this brought forth a dream and soon enough
This dream itself had all my thought and love.

25 And when the Fool and Blind Man stole the bread
Cuchulain fought the ungovernable sea;[7]
Heart-mysteries there, and yet when all is said
It was the dream itself enchanted me:
Character isolated by a deed
30 To engross the present and dominate memory.
Players and painted stage took all my love,
And not those things that they were emblems of.

3

Those masterful images because complete
Grew in pure mind, but out of what began?
35 A mound of refuse or the sweeping of a street,
Old kettles, old bottles, and a broken can,
Old iron, old bones, old rags, that raving slut

3. The images of lines 7–8 may refer to motifs from specific earlier works by Yeats (in his play *The Unicorn from the Stars,* for instance, a gilded state coach, adorned with lion and unicorn, is being built on stage), but it is at least as likely that they are merely generalized images, in line with the title and argument of the poem, of the people and things to be encountered in the heightened, unreal world of a circus.
4. The hero of Yeats's long allegorical (and symbolic) poem, *The Wanderings of Oisin* (pronounced "Usheen"), 1889, is led by the fairy Niamh (pronounced Nee-ave) in succession to the three Islands of Dancing (changeless joy) Victories (also called "Of Many Fears"), and Forgetfulness.
5. Yeats's first play, 1892. In it the people,

in a time of famine, are selling their souls to emissaries of the devil. To save their souls, the Countess Cathleen sells hers "for a great price." She dies, but an angel announces that she is "passing to the floor of peace."
6. Maud Gonne, whom Yeats had loved since first meeting her in 1889, and who had married John MacBride in 1903; she was a daring, even violent, activist in the cause of Irish liberation.
7. In another early play, *On Baile's Strand* (1904), Cuchulain (pronounced Cuhoolin) unwittingly kills his own son; maddened, he rushes out to fight the waves. As the people run to the shore to watch, the fool and the blind man hurry off to steal the bread from their ovens.

Who keeps the till. Now that my ladder's gone,
I must lie down where all the ladders start,
In the foul rag-and-bone shop of the heart.

1939

Under Ben Bulben[6]

1

Swear by what the sages spoke
Round the Mareotic Lake[7]
That the Witch of Atlas knew,
Spoke and set the cocks a-crow.[8]

Swear by those horsemen, by those women
Complexion and form prove superhuman,
That pale, long-visaged company
That air in immortality
Completeness of their passions won;
Now they ride the wintry dawn
Where Ben Bulben sets the scene.[9]

Here's the gist of what they mean.

2

Many times man lives and dies
Between his two eternities,
That of race and that of soul,
And ancient Ireland knew it all.
Whether man die in his bed
Or the rifle knocks him dead,
A brief parting from those dear
Is the worst man has to fear.
Though gravediggers' toil is long,
Sharp their spades, their muscles strong,
They but thrust their buried men
Back in the human mind again.

3

You that Mitchel's prayer have heard,
"Send war in our time, O Lord!"[1]
Know that when all words are said
And a man is fighting mad,
Something drops from eyes long blind,
He completes his partial mind,
For an instant stands at ease,
Laughs aloud, his heart at peace.

6. A mountain in County Sligo, in the west of Ireland, which overlooks Drumcliff Churchyard, where Yeats is buried. The last three lines of the poem are carved on his tombstone.
7. Lake Mareotis, a salt lake in northern Egypt, near which the members of the Thebaid, among them St. Anthony (A.D. 251–356) had withdrawn to contemplation. About the Thebaid, in his *1930 Diary*, Yeats wrote, "* * * men went on pilgrimage to Saint Anthony that they might learn about their spiritual states, what was about to happen and why it happened, and Saint Anthony would reply neither out of traditional casuistry nor common sense but from spiritual powers."
8. In Shelley's poem *The Witch of Atlas*, the protagonist, a spirit of love, beauty, and freedom, visits Egypt and the Mareotic Lake in the course of her magic journeyings. The knowledge and belief that Yeats describes as common to her and to the sages "set the cocks a-crow" in the sense that, like "the cocks of Hades" and the golden bird in *Byzantium*, they summon to a spiritual rebirth.
9. In another late poem, *Alternative Song for the Severed Head in "The King of the Great Clock Tower*," Yeats re-introduces some of the Irish mythological or legendary heroes and heroines who figure in his early poems—Cuchulain, Niam, and others—with whom the supernatural riders of these lines may be identified.
1. John Mitchel (1815–75), the Irish patriot, wrote in his *Jail Journal, or Five Years in British Prisons* (published in New York, 1854): "Czar, I bless thee, I kiss the hem of thy garment. I drink to thy health and longevity. Give us war in our time, O Lord" [Quoted by T. R. Henn, *The Lonely Tower*].

Even the wisest man grows tense
With some sort of violence
35 Before he can accomplish fate,
Know his work or choose his mate.

                    4
Poet and sculptor, do the work,
Nor let the modish painter shirk
What his great forefathers did,
40 Bring the soul of man to God,
Make him fill the cradles right.

Measurement began our might:[2]
Forms a stark Egyptian thought,
Forms that gentler Phidias wrought.
45 Michael Angelo left a proof
On the Sistine Chapel roof,
Where but half-awakened Adam
Can disturb globe-trotting Madam
Till her bowels are in heat,
50 Proof that there's a purpose set
Before the secret working mind:
Profane perfection of mankind.

Quattrocento[3] put in paint
On backgrounds for a God or Saint
55 Gardens where a soul's at ease;
Where everything that meets the eye,
Flowers and grass and cloudless sky,
Resemble forms that are or seem
When sleepers wake and yet still dream,
60 And when it's vanished still declare,
With only bed and bedstead there,
That heavens had opened.
                         Gyres[4] run on;
When that greater dream had gone
65 Calvert and Wilson, Blake and Claude,
Prepared a rest for the people of God,
Palmer's phrase, but after that[5]
Confusion fell upon our thought.

                    5
Irish poets, learn your trade,
70 Sing whatever is well made,
Scorn the sort now growing up
All out of shape from toe to top,
Their unremembering hearts and heads
Base-born products of base beds.
75 Sing the peasantry, and then
Hard-riding country gentlemen,
The holiness of monks, and after

---

2. The achievements of Western civilization—
now, according to the poem, being challenged
or destroyed—began with the exact mathemati-
cal rules which the Egyptians followed in
working out the proportions of their sculptured
figures—rules which Phidias (line 44), the
great Greek sculptor of the fifth century B.C.,
used, and which have been implicit in the
greatest Western art up to the present, when
"confusion [falls] upon our thought."
3. The Italian fifteenth century.
4. I.e., the cycles of history.

5. The verse paragraph assembles five artists
who had provided Yeats with images and with
ideals of what art should be. Claude Lorrain
(1600–82), the great French landscape painter,
was a central standard for landscape painters
up to the early 19th century, including those
mentioned here, especially Richard Wilson
(1714–82). Edward Calvert (1799–1883) and
Samuel Palmer (1805–81), visionaries, land-
scape painters, and engravers, had found in-
spiration in many aspects of Blake's life and
work.

Porter-drinkers' randy laughter;
Sing the lords and ladies gay
That were beaten into the clay
Through seven heroic centuries;
Cast your mind on other days
That we in coming days may be
Still the indomitable Irishry.
                6
Under bare Ben Bulben's head
In Drumcliff churchyard Yeats is laid.
An ancestor was rector there
Long years ago, a church stands near,
By the road an ancient cross.
No marble, no conventional phrase;
On limestone quarried near the spot
By his command these words are cut:

      Cast a cold eye
      On life, on death.
      Horseman, pass by!

                  September 4, 1938   1939

ERNEST DOWSON
(1867–1900)

Vitae summa brevis spem nos vetat incohare longam[1]

They are not long, the weeping and the laughter,
    Love and desire and hate:
I think they have no portion in us after
    We pass the gate.

They are not long, the days of wine and roses:
    Out of a misty dream
Our path emerges for a while, then closes
    Within a dream.

                            1896

Non sum qualis eram bonae sub regno Cynarae[2]

Last night, ah, yesternight, betwixt her lips and mine
There fell thy shadow, Cynara! thy breath was shed
Upon my soul between the kisses and the wine;
And I was desolate and sick of an old passion,
    Yea, I was desolate and bowed my head:
I have been faithful to thee, Cynara! in my fashion.

All night upon mine heart I felt her warm heart beat,
Night-long within mine arms in love and sleep she lay;
Surely the kisses of her bought red mouth were sweet;

1. "The brevity of life forbids us to entertain hopes of long duration": Horace, *Odes* I.iv, line 15.
2. Horace, *Odes*, IV.i, lines 3–4: the poet urges Venus to spare him new efforts in her service: "I am not as I was under the reign of the good Cynara."

10   But I was desolate and sick of an old passion,
        When I awoke and found the dawn was gray:
    I have been faithful to thee, Cynara! in my fashion.

    I have forgot much, Cynara! gone with the wind,
    Flung roses, roses riotously with the throng,
15 Dancing, to put thy pale, lost lilies out of mind;
    But I was desolate and sick of an old passion,
        Yea, all the time, because the dance was long:
    I have been faithful to thee, Cynara! in my fashion.

    I cried for madder music and for stronger wine,
20 But when the feast is finished and the lamps expire,
    Then falls thy shadow, Cynara! the night is thine;
    And I am desolate and sick of an old passion,
        Yea hungry for the lips of my desire:
    I have been faithful to thee, Cynara! in my fashion.

                                        1891   1896

EDWIN ARLINGTON ROBINSON
(1869–1935)

George Crabbe[1]

    Give him the darkest inch your shelf allows,
    Hide him in lonely garrets, if you will,
    But his hard, human pulse is throbbing still
    With the sure strength that fearless truth endows.
5   In spite of all fine science disavows,
    Of his plain excellence and stubborn skill
    There yet remains what fashion cannot kill,
    Though years have thinned the laurel from his brows.

    Whether or not we read him, we can feel
10 From time to time the vigor of his name
    Against us like a finger for the shame
    And emptiness of what our souls reveal
    In books that are as altars where we kneel
    To consecrate the flicker, not the flame.

                                                        1897

Reuben Bright

    Because he was a butcher and thereby
    Did earn an honest living (and did right),
    I would not have you think that Reuben Bright
    Was any more a brute than you or I;

5   For when they told him that his wife must die,
    He stared at them, and shook with grief and fright,
    And cried like a great baby half that night,
    And made the women cry to see him cry.

---

1. Author of *The Borough* (above, "Peter Grimes," pp. 537–544) and *The Village* (1782); celebrated for his realistic and unsentimental depictions of rural life.

And after she was dead, and he had paid
The singers and the sexton and the rest,
He packed a lot of things that she had made
Most mournfully away in an old chest
Of hers, and put some chopped-up cedar boughs
In with them, and tore down the slaughter-house.

1897

Miniver Cheevy

Miniver Cheevy, child of scorn,
  Grew lean while he assailed the seasons;
He wept that he was ever born,
  And he had reasons.

Miniver loved the days of old
  When swords were bright and steeds were prancing;
The vision of a warrior bold
  Would set him dancing.

Miniver sighed for what was not,
  And dreamed, and rested from his labors;
He dreamed of Thebes and Camelot,
  And Priam's neighbors.[2]

Miniver mourned the ripe renown
  That made so many a name so fragrant;
He mourned Romance, now on the town,
  And Art, a vagrant.

Miniver loved the Medici,[3]
  Albeit he had never seen one;
He would have sinned incessantly
  Could he have been one.

Miniver cursed the commonplace
  And eyed a khaki suit with loathing;
He missed the medieval grace
  Of iron clothing.

Miniver scorned the gold he sought,
  But sore annoyed was he without it;
Miniver thought, and thought, and thought,
  And thought about it.

Miniver Cheevy, born too late,
  Scratched his head and kept on thinking;
Miniver coughed, and called it fate,
  And kept on drinking.

1910

2. Thebes was a Greek city, anciently famous in history and legend; Camelot is said to have been the site of King Arthur's court; Priam was king of Troy during the Trojan War.

3. A family of merchant-princes of the Italian Renaissance, rulers of Florence for nearly two centuries; they were known both for cruelty and for their support of learning and art.

Eros Turannos[4]

She fears him, and will always ask
    What fated her to choose him;
She meets in his engaging mask
    All reasons to refuse him;
5 But what she meets and what she fears
Are less than are the downward years,
Drawn slowly to the foamless weirs
    Of age, were she to lose him.

Between a blurred sagacity
10   That once had power to sound him,
And Love, that will not let him be
    The Judas[5] that she found him,
Her pride assuages her almost,
As if it were alone the cost.
15 He sees that he will not be lost,
    And waits and looks around him.

A sense of ocean and old trees
    Envelopes and allures him;
Tradition, touching all he sees,
20   Beguiles and reassures him;
And all her doubts of what he says
Are dimmed with what she knows of days—
Till even prejudice delays
    And fades, and she secures him.

25 The falling leaf inaugurates
    The reign of her confusion;
The pounding wave reverberates
    The dirge of her illusion;
And home, where passion lived and died,
30 Becomes a place where she can hide,
While all the town and harbor side
    Vibrate with her seclusion.

We tell you, tapping on our brows,
    The story as it should be,
35 As if the story of a house
    Were told, or ever could be;
We'll have no kindly veil between
Her visions and those we have seen,
As if we guessed what hers have been,
40   Or what they are or would be.

Meanwhile we do no harm; for they
    That with a god have striven,
Not hearing much of what we say,
    Take what the god has given;
45 Though like waves breaking it may be,
Or like a changed familiar tree,
Or like a stairway to the sea
    Where down the blind are driven.

1916

4. Tyrannical Love.   5. The disciple who betrayed Christ.

The Mill

The miller's wife had waited long,
  The tea was cold, the fire was dead;
And there might yet be nothing wrong
  In how he went and what he said:
"There are no millers any more,"
  Was all that she had heard him say;
And he had lingered at the door
  So long that it seemed yesterday.

Sick with a fear that had no form
  She knew that she was there at last;
And in the mill there was a warm
  And mealy fragrance of the past.
What else there was would only seem
  To say again what he had meant;
And what was hanging from a beam
  Would not have heeded where she went.

And if she thought it followed her,
  She may have reasoned in the dark
That one way of the few there were
  Would hide her and would leave no mark:
Black water, smooth above the weir
  Like starry velvet in the night,
Though ruffled once, would soon appear
  The same as ever to the sight.

                                        1920

Mr. Flood's Party

Old Eben Flood, climbing alone one night
Over the hill between the town below
And the forsaken upland hermitage
That held as much as he should ever know
On earth again of home, paused warily.
The road was his with not a native near;
And Eben, having leisure, said aloud,
For no man else in Tilbury Town to hear:

"Well, Mr. Flood, we have the harvest moon
Again, and we may not have many more;
The bird is on the wing, the poet says,[1]
And you and I have said it here before.
Drink to the bird." He raised up to the light
The jug that he had gone so far to fill,
And answered huskily: "Well, Mr. Flood,
Since you propose it, I believe I will."

Alone, as if enduring to the end
A valiant armor of scarred hopes outworn,
He stood there in the middle of the road

1. Alludes to the seventh stanza of *The Rubáiyát of Omar Khayyám* as translated by Edward Fitzgerald: "Come, fill the Cup, and in the fire of Spring/Your Winter-garment of Repentance fling:/The Bird of Time has but a little way/To flutter—and the Bird is on the Wing."

20   Like Roland's ghost winding a silent horn.[2]
    Below him, in the town among the trees,
    Where friends of other days had honored him,
    A phantom salutation of the dead
    Rang thinly till old Eben's eyes were dim.

25   Then, as a mother lays her sleeping child
    Down tenderly, fearing it may awake,
    He set the jug down slowly at his feet
    With trembling care, knowing that most things break;
    And only when assured that on firm earth
30   It stood, as the uncertain lives of men
    Assuredly did not, he paced away,
    And with his hand extended paused again:

    "Well, Mr. Flood, we have not met like this
    In a long time; and many a change has come
35   To both of us, I fear, since last it was
    We had a drop together. Welcome home!"
    Convivially returning with himself,
    Again he raised the jug up to the light;
    And with an acquiescent quaver said:
40   "Well, Mr. Flood, if you insist, I might.

    "Only a very little, Mr. Flood—
    For auld lang syne. No more, sir; that will do."
    So, for the time, apparently it did,
    And Eben evidently thought so too;
45   For soon amid the silver loneliness
    Of night he lifted up his voice and sang,
    Secure, with only two moons listening,
    Until the whole harmonious landscape rang—

    "For auld lang syne." The weary throat gave out,
50   The last word wavered; and the song being done,
    He raised again the jug regretfully
    And shook his head, and was again alone.
    There was not much that was ahead of him,
    And there was nothing in the town below—
55   Where strangers would have shut the many doors
    That many friends had opened long ago.

1920

New England

Here where the wind is always north-north-east
And children learn to walk on frozen toes,
Wonder begets an envy of all those
Who boil elsewhere with such a lyric yeast
5   Of love that you will hear them at a feast
Where demons would appeal for some repose,
Still clamoring where the chalice overflows
And crying wildest who have drunk the least.

2. Guarding the pass of Roncevaux against a stronger enemy, the knight Roland refused to blow his horn for help from Charlemagne's army until it was too late. His heroic death is recounted in the medieval poem *The Song of Roland.*

Passion is here a soilure of the wits,
We're told, and Love a cross for them to bear;
Joy shivers in the corner where she knits
And Conscience always has the rocking-chair,
Cheerful as when she tortured into fits
The first cat that was ever killed by Care.

1925

STEPHEN CRANE
(1871–1900)

There Was Crimson Clash of War

There was crimson clash of war.
Lands turned black and bare;
Women wept;
Babes ran, wondering.
There came one who understood not these things.
He said: "Why is this?"
Whereupon a million strove to answer him.
There was such intricate clamor of tongues,
That still the reason was not.

1895

The Impact of a Dollar Upon the Heart

The impact of a dollar upon the heart
Smiles warm red light
Sweeping from the hearth rosily upon the white table,
With the hanging cool velvet shadows
Moving softly upon the door.

The impact of a million dollars
Is a crash of flunkeys
And yawning emblems of Persia
Cheeked against oak, France and a saber,
The outcry of old beauty
Whored by pimping merchants
To submission before wine and chatter.
Silly rich peasants stamp the carpets of men,
Dead men who dreamd fragrance and light
Into their woof, their lives;
The rug of an honest bear
Under the foot of a cryptic slave
Who speaks always of baubles,
Forgetting place, multitude, work and state,
Champing and mouthing of hats
Making ratful squeak of hats,
Hats.

1899

Unwind My Riddle

Unwind my riddle.
Cruel as hawks the hours fly;
Wounded men seldom come home to die;
The hard waves see an arm flung high;
5   Scorn hits strong because of a lie;
Yet there exists a mystic tie.
Unwind my riddle.

1900

PAUL LAURENCE DUNBAR
(1872–1906)

Ere Sleep Comes Down to Soothe the Weary Eyes

Ere sleep comes down to soothe the weary eyes,
    Which all the day with ceaseless care have sought
The magic gold which from the seeker flies;
    Ere dreams put on the gown and cap of thought,
5   And make the waking world a world of lies—
    Of lies most palpable, uncouth, forlorn,
That say life's full of aches and tears and sighs—
    Oh, how with more than dreams the soul is torn,
Ere sleep comes down to soothe the weary eyes.

10   Ere sleep comes down to soothe the weary eyes,
    How all the griefs and heartaches we have known
Come up like pois'nous vapors that arise
    From some base witch's caldron, when the crone,
To work some potent spell, her magic plies.
15   The past which held its share of bitter pain,
    Whose ghost we prayed that Time might exorcise,
Comes up, is lived and suffered o'er again,
Ere sleep comes down to soothe the weary eyes.

Ere sleep comes down to soothe the weary eyes,
20   What phantoms fill the dimly lighted room;
What ghostly shades in awe-creating guise
    Are bodied forth within the teeming gloom.
What echoes faint of sad and soul-sick cries,
    And pangs of vague inexplicable pain
25 That pay the spirit's ceaseless enterprise,
    Come thronging through the chambers of the brain,
Ere sleep comes down to soothe the weary eyes.

Ere sleep comes down to soothe the weary eyes,
    Where ranges forth the spirit far and free?
30 Through what strange realms and unfamiliar skies
    Tends her far course to lands of mystery?
To lands unspeakable—beyond surmise,
    Where shapes unknowable to being spring,
Till, faint of wing, the Fancy fails and dies
35   Much wearied with the spirit's journeying,
Ere sleep comes down to soothe the weary eyes.

Ere sleep comes down to soothe the weary eyes,
    How questioneth the soul that other soul—
The inner sense which neither cheats nor lies,
    But self exposes unto self, a scroll
Full writ with all life's acts unwise or wise,
    In characters indelible and known;
So, trembling with the shock of sad surprise,
    The soul doth view its awful self alone,
Ere sleep comes down to soothe the weary eyes.

When sleep comes down to seal the weary eyes,
    The last dear sleep whose soft embrace is balm,
And whom sad sorrow teaches us to prize
    For kissing all our passions into calm,
Ah, then, no more we heed the sad world's cries,
    Or seek to probe th' eternal mystery,
Or fret our souls at long-withheld replies,
    At glooms through which our visions cannot see,
When sleep comes down to seal the weary eyes.

        1896

We Wear the Mask

We wear the mask that grins and lies,
It hides our cheeks and shades our eyes—
This debt we pay to human guile;
With torn and bleeding hearts we smile,
And mouth with myriad subtleties.

Why should the world be over-wise,
In counting all our tears and sighs?
Nay, let them only see us, while
    We wear the mask.

We smile, but, O great Christ, our cries
To thee from tortured souls arise.
We sing, but oh the clay is vile
Beneath our feet, and long the mile;
But let the world dream otherwise,
    We wear the mask!

        1896

When Malindy Sings

G'way an' quit dat noise, Miss Lucy—
    Put dat music book away;
What's de use to keep on tryin'?
    Ef you practise twell you're gray,
You cain't sta't no notes a-flyin'
    Lak de ones dat rants and rings
F'om de kitchen to de big woods
    When Malindy sings.

You ain't got de nachel o'gans
    Fu' to make de soun' come right,
You ain't got de tu'ns an' twistin's
    Fu' to make it sweet an' light.
Tell you one thing now, Miss Lucy,

An' I'm tellin' you fu' true,
15 When hit comes to raal right singin',
    'T ain't no easy thing to do.

Easy 'nough fu' folks to hollah,
  Lookin' at de lines an' dots,
When dey ain't no one kin sence it,
20   An' de chune comes in, in spots;
But fu' real melojous music,
  Dat jes' strikes yo' hea't and clings,
Jes' you stan' an' listen wif me
  When Malindy sings.

25 Ain't you nevah hyeahd Malindy?
    Blessed soul, tek up de cross!
Look hyeah, ain't you jokin', honey?
    Well, you don't know whut you los'.
Y' ought to hyeah dat gal a-wa'blin',
30   Robins, la'ks, an' all dem things,
Heish dey moufs an' hides dey face.
  When Malindy sings.

Fiddlin' man jes' stop his fiddlin',
  Lay his fiddle on de she'f;
35 Mockin'-bird quit tryin' to whistle,
    'Cause he jes' so shamed hisse'f.
Folks a-playin' on de banjo
  Draps dey fingahs on de strings—
Bless yo' soul—fu'gits to move em,
40   When Malindy sings.

She jes' spreads huh mouf and hollahs,
  "Come to Jesus," twell you hyeah
Sinnahs' tremblin' steps and voices
  Timid-lak a-drawin' neah;
45 Den she tu'ns to "Rock of Ages,"
    Simply to de cross she clings,
An' you fin' yo' teahs a-drappin'
  When Malindy sings.

Who dat says dat humble praises
50   Wif de Master nevah counts?
Heish yo' mouf, I hyeah dat music,
  Ez hit rises up an' mounts—
Floatin' by de hills an' valleys,
  Way above dis buryin' sod,
55 Ez hit makes its way in glory
    To de very gates of God!

Oh, hit's sweetah dan de music
  Of an edicated band;
An' hit's dearah dan de battle's
60   Song o' triumph in de lan'.
It seems holier dan evenin'
  When de solemn chu'ch bell rings,
Ez I sit an' ca'mly listen
  While Malindy sings.

Towsah, stop dat ba'kin', hyeah me!
    Mandy, mek dat chile keep still;
Don't you hyeah de echoes callin'
    F'om de valley to de hill?
Let me listen, I can hyeah it,
    Th'oo de bresh of angels' wings,
Sof' an' sweet, "Swing Low,
    Sweet Chariot,"
Ez Malindy sings.

                        1896

Little Brown Baby

Little brown baby wif spa'klin' eyes,
    Come to yo' pappy an' set on his knee.
What you been doin', suh—makin' san' pies?
    Look at dat bib—you's ez du'ty ez me.
Look at dat mouf—dat's merlasses, I bet;
    Come hyeah, Maria, an' wipe off his han's.
Bees gwine to ketch you an' eat you up yit,
    Bein' so sticky an sweet—goodness lan's!

Little brown baby wif spa'klin' eyes,
    Who's pappy's darlin' an' who's pappy's chile?
Who is it all de day nevah once tries
    Fu' to be cross, er once loses dat smile?
Whah did you git dem teef? My, you's a scamp!
    Whah did dat dimple come f'om in yo' chin?
Pappy do' know you—I b'lieves you's a tramp;
    Mammy, dis hyeah's some ol' straggler got in!

Let's th'ow him outen de do' in de san',
    We do' want stragglers a-layin' 'roun' hyeah;
Let's gin him 'way to de big buggah-man;
    I know he's hidin' erroun' hyeah right neah.
Buggah-man, buggah-man, come in de do',
    Hyeah's a bad boy you kin have fu' to eat.
Mammy an' pappy do' want him no mo',
    Swaller him down f'om his haid to his feet!

Dah, now, I t'ought dat you'd hug me up close.
    Go back, ol' buggah, you sha'n't have dis boy.
He ain't no tramp, ner no straggler, of co'se;
    He's pappy's pa'dner an' playmate an' joy.
Come to you' pallet now—go to yo' res';
    Wisht you could allus know ease an' cleah skies;
Wisht you could stay jes' a chile on my breas'—
    Little brown baby wif spa'klin' eyes!

                        1899?

WALTER DE LA MARE
(1873–1956)

The Keys of Morning

While at her bedroom window once,
    Learning her task for school,
Little Louisa lonely sat
    In the morning clear and cool,
5 She slanted her small bead-brown eyes
    Across the empty street,
And saw Death softly watching her
    In the sunshine pale and sweet.

His was a long lean sallow face;
    He sat with half-shut eyes,
Like an old sailor in a ship
    Becalmed 'neath tropic skies.
Beside him in the dust he had set
    His staff and shady hat;
15 These, peeping small, Louisa saw
    Quite clearly where she sat—
The thinness of his coal-black locks,
    His hands so long and lean
They scarcely seemed to grasp at all
20   The keys that hung between:
Both were of gold, but one was small,
    And with this last did he
Wag in the air, as if to say,
    "Come hither, child, to me!"

25 Louisa laid her lesson book
    On the cold window-sill;
And in the sleepy sunshine house
    Went softly down, until
She stood in the half-opened door,
30   And peeped. But strange to say,
Where Death just now had sunning sat
    Only a shadow lay:
Just the tall chimney's round-topped cowl,
    And the small sun behind,
35 Had with its shadow in the dust
    Called sleepy Death to mind.
But most she thought how strange it was
    Two keys that he should bear,
And that, when beckoning, he should wag
    The littlest in the air.

                          1912

The Moth

Isled in the midnight air,
Musked with the dark's faint bloom,
Out into glooming and secret haunts
    The flame cries, "Come!"

Lovely in dye and fan,
A-tremble in shimmering grace,
A moth from her winter swoon
    Uplifts her face:

Stares from her glamorous eyes;
Wafts her on plumes like mist;
In ecstasy swirls and sways
    To her strange tryst.

1921

Goodbye

The last of last words spoken is Goodbye—
The last dismantled flower in the weed-grown hedge,
The last thin rumor of a feeble bell far ringing,
The last blind rat to spurn the mildewed rye.

A hardening darkness glasses the haunted eye,
Shines into nothing the watcher's burnt-out candle,
Wreathes into scentless nothing the wasting incense,
Faints in the outer silence the hunting-cry.

Love of its muted music breathes no sigh,
Thought in her ivory tower gropes in her spinning,
Toss on in vain the whispering trees of Eden,
Last of all last words spoken is Goodbye.

1921

Away

There is no sorrow
Time heals never;
No loss, betrayal,
Beyond repair.
Balm for the soul, then,
Though grave shall sever
Lover from loved
And all they share;
See, the sweet sun shines,
The shower is over,
Flowers preen their beauty,
The day how fair!
Brood not too closely
On love, or duty;
Friends long forgotten
May wait you where
Life with death
Brings all to an issue;
None will long mourn for you,
Pray for you, miss you,
Your place left vacant,
You not there.

1938

ROBERT FROST
(1874–1963)

Mending Wall

Something there is that doesn't love a wall,
That sends the frozen-ground-swell under it
And spills the upper boulders in the sun,
And makes gaps even two can pass abreast.
5 The work of hunters is another thing:
I have come after them and made repair
Where they have left not one stone on a stone,
But they would have the rabbit out of hiding,
To please the yelping dogs. The gaps I mean,
10 No one has seen them made or heard them made,
But at spring mending-time we find them there.
I let my neighbor know beyond the hill;
And on a day we meet to walk the line
And set the wall between us once again.
15 We keep the wall between us as we go.
To each the boulders that have fallen to each.
And some are loaves and some so nearly balls
We have to use a spell to make them balance:
'Stay where you are until our backs are turned!'
20 We wear our fingers rough with handling them.
Oh, just another kind of outdoor game,
One on a side. It comes to little more:
There where it is we do not need the wall:
He is all pine and I am apple orchard.
25 My apple trees will never get across
And eat the cones under his pines, I tell him.
He only says, 'Good fences make good neighbors.'
Spring is the mischief in me, and I wonder
If I could put a notion in his head:
30 '*Why* do they make good neighbors? Isn't it
Where there are cows? But here there are no cows.
Before I built a wall I'd ask to know
What I was walling in or walling out,
And to whom I was like to give offense.
35 Something there is that doesn't love a wall,
That wants it down.' I could say 'Elves' to him,
But it's not elves exactly, and I'd rather
He said it for himself. I see him there,
Bringing a stone grasped firmly by the top
40 In each hand, like an old-stone savage armed.
He moves in darkness as it seems to me,
Not of woods only and the shade of trees.
He will not go behind his father's saying,
And he likes having thought of it so well
45 He says again, 'Good fences make good neighbors.'

1914

The Wood-Pile

Out walking in the frozen swamp one gray day,
I paused and said, 'I will turn back from here.
No, I will go on farther—and we shall see.'
The hard snow held me, save where now and then
One foot went through. The view was all in lines
Straight up and down of tall slim trees
Too much alike to mark or name a place by
So as to say for certain I was here
Or somewhere else: I was just far from home.
A small bird flew before me. He was careful
To put a tree between us when he lighted,
And say no word to tell me who he was
Who was so foolish as to think what *he* thought.
He thought that I was after him for a feather—
The white one in his tail; like one who takes
Everything said as personal to himself.
One flight out sideways would have undeceived him.
And then there was a pile of wood for which
I forgot him and let his little fear
Carry him off the way I might have gone,
Without so much as wishing him good-night.
He went behind it to make his last stand.
It was a cord of maple, cut and split
And piled—and measured, four by four by eight.
And not another like it could I see.
No runner tracks in this year's snow looped near it.
And it was older sure than this year's cutting,
Or even last year's or the year's before.
The wood was gray and the bark warping off it
And the pile somewhat sunken. Clematis
Had wound strings round and round it like a bundle.
What held it, though, on one side was a tree
Still growing, and on one a stake and prop,
These latter about to fall. I thought that only
Someone who lived in turning to fresh tasks
Could so forget his handiwork in which
He spent himself, the labor of his axe,
And leave it there far from a useful fireplace
To warm the frozen swamp as best it could
With the slow smokeless burning of decay.

1914

The Oven Bird

There is a singer everyone has heard,
Loud, a mid-summer and a mid-wood bird,
Who makes the solid tree trunks sound again.
He says that leaves are old and that for flowers
Mid-summer is to spring as one to ten.
He says the early petal-fall is past,
When pear and cherry bloom went down in showers
On sunny days a moment overcast;
And comes that other fall we name the fall.
He says the highway dust is over all.

The bird would cease and be as other birds
But that he knows in singing not to sing.
The question that he frames in all but words
Is what to make of a diminished thing.

1916

Birches

When I see birches bend to left and right
Across the lines of straighter darker trees,
I like to think some boy's been swinging them.
But swinging doesn't bend them down to stay
5   As ice-storms do. Often you must have seen them
Loaded with ice a sunny winter morning
After a rain. They click upon themselves
As the breeze rises, and turn many-colored
As the stir cracks and crazes their enamel.
10   Soon the sun's warmth makes them shed crystal shells
Shattering and avalanching on the snowcrust—
Such heaps of broken glass to sweep away
You'd think the inner dome of heaven had fallen.
They are dragged to the withered bracken by the load,
15   And they seem not to break; though once they are bowed
So low for long, they never right themselves:
You may see their trunks arching in the woods
Years afterwards, trailing their leaves on the ground
Like girls on hands and knees that throw their hair
20   Before them over their heads to dry in the sun.
But I was going to say when Truth broke in
With all her matter of fact about the ice-storm,
I should prefer to have some boy bend them
As he went out and in to fetch the cows—
25   Some boy too far from town to learn baseball,
Whose only play was what he found himself,
Summer or winter, and could play alone.
One by one he subdued his father's trees
By riding them down over and over again
30   Until he took the stiffness out of them,
And not one but hung limp, not one was left
For him to conquer. He learned all there was
To learn about not launching out too soon
And so not carrying the tree away
35   Clear to the ground. He always kept his poise
To the top branches, climbing carefully
With the same pains you use to fill a cup
Up to the brim, and even above the brim.
Then he flung outward, feet first, with a swish,
40   Kicking his way down through the air to the ground.
So was I once myself a swinger of birches.
And so I dream of going back to be.
It's when I'm weary of considerations,
And life is too much like a pathless wood
45   Where your face burns and tickles with the cobwebs
Broken across it, and one eye is weeping
From a twig's having lashed across it open.
I'd like to get away from earth awhile
And then come back to it and begin over.

May no fate willfully misunderstand me
And half grant what I wish and snatch me away
Not to return. Earth's the right place for love:
I don't know where it's likely to go better.
I'd like to go by climbing a birch tree,
And climb black branches up a snow-white trunk
Toward heaven, till the tree could bear no more,
But dipped its top and set me down again.
That would be good both going and coming back.
One could do worse than be a swinger of birches.

1916

Range-Finding

The battle rent a cobweb diamond-strung
And cut a flower beside a ground bird's nest
Before it stained a single human breast.
The stricken flower bent double and so hung.
And still the bird revisited her young.
A butterfly its fall had dispossessed
A moment sought in air his flower of rest,
Then lightly stooped to it and fluttering clung.
On the bare upland pasture there had spread
O'ernight 'twixt mullein stalks a wheel of thread
And straining cables wet with silver dew.
A sudden passing bullet shook it dry.
The indwelling spider ran to greet the fly,
But finding nothing, sullenly withdrew.

1916

The Hill Wife

I. Loneliness
HER WORD

One ought not to have to care
  So much as you and I
Care when the birds come round the house
  To seem to say good-by;

Or care so much when they come back
  With whatever it is they sing;
The truth being we are as much
  Too glad for the one thing

As we are too sad for the other here—
  With birds that fill their breasts
But with each other and themselves
  And their built or driven nests.

II. House Fear

Always—I tell you this they learned—
Always at night when they returned
To the lonely house from far away,
To lamps unlighted and fire gone gray,
They learned to rattle the lock and key

To give whatever might chance to be,
Warning and time to be off in flight:
And preferring the out- to the in-door night,
They learned to leave the housedoor wide
10   Until they had lit the lamp inside.

III. *The Smile*
HER WORD

I didn't like the way he went away.
That smile! It never came of being gay.
Still he smiled—did you see him?—I was sure!
Perhaps because we gave him only bread
5   And the wretch knew from that that we were poor.
Perhaps because he let us give instead
Of seizing from us as he might have seized.
Perhaps he mocked at us for being wed,
Or being very young (and he was pleased
10   To have a vision of us old and dead).
I wonder how far down the road he's got.
He's watching from the woods as like as not.

IV. *The Oft-Repeated Dream*

She had no saying dark enough
    For the dark pine that kept
Forever trying the windowlatch
    Of the room where they slept.

5   The tireless but ineffectual hands
    That with every futile pass
Made the great tree seem as a little bird
    Before the mystery of glass!

It never had been inside the room,
10   And only one of the two
Was afraid in an oft-repeated dream
    Of what the tree might do.

V. *The Impulse*

It was too lonely for her there,
    And too wild,
And since there were but two of them,
    And no child,

5   And work was little in the house,
    She was free,
And followed where he furrowed field,
    Or felled tree.

She rested on a log and tossed
10   The fresh chips,
With a song only to herself
    On her lips.

And once she went to break a bough
    Of black alder.
15   She strayed so far she scarcely heard
    When he called her—

And didn't answer—didn't speak—
  Or return.
She stood, and then she ran and hid
  In the fern.

He never found her, though he looked
  Everywhere,
And he asked at her mother's house
  Was she there.

Sudden and swift and light as that
  The ties gave,
And he learned of finalities
  Besides the grave.

                                                          1916

The Aim Was Song

Before man came to blow it right
  The wind once blew itself untaught,
And did its loudest day and night
  In any rough place where it caught.

Man came to tell it what was wrong:
  It hadn't found the place to blow;
It blew too hard—the aim was song.
  And listen—how it ought to go!

He took a little in his mouth,
  And held it long enough for north
To be converted into south,
  And then by measure blew it forth.

By measure. It was word and note,
  The wind the wind had meant to be—
A little through the lips and throat.
  The aim was song—the wind could see.

                                                          1923

Stopping by Woods on a Snowy Evening

Whose woods these are I think I know,
His house is in the village, though;
He will not see me stopping here
To watch his woods fill up with snow.

My little horse must think it queer
To stop without a farmhouse near
Between the woods and frozen lake
The darkest evening of the year.

He gives his harness bells a shake
To ask if there is some mistake.
The only other sound's the sweep
Of easy wind and downy flake.

The woods are lovely, dark, and deep,
But I have promises to keep,
15   And miles to go before I sleep,
And miles to go before I sleep.

1923

To Earthward

Love at the lips was touch
As sweet as I could bear;
And once that seemed too much;
I lived on air

5   That crossed me from sweet things,
The flow of—was it musk
From hidden grapevine springs
Downhill at dusk?

I had the swirl and ache
10   From sprays of honeysuckle
That when they're gathered shake
Dew on the knuckle.

I craved strong sweets, but those
Seemed strong when I was young;
15   The petal of the rose
It was that stung.

Now no joy but lacks salt,
That is not dashed with pain
And weariness and fault;
20   I crave the stain

Of tears, the aftermark
Of almost too much love,
The sweet of bitter bark
And burning clove.

25   When stiff and sore and scarred
I take away my hand
From leaning on it hard
In grass and sand,

The hurt is not enough:
30   I long for weight and strength
To feel the earth as rough
To all my length.

1923

Spring Pools

These pools that, though in forests, still reflect
The total sky almost without defect,
And like the flowers beside them, chill and shiver,
Will like the flowers beside them soon be gone,
5   And yet not out by any brook or river,

But up by roots to bring dark foliage on.
The trees that have it in their pent-up buds
To darken nature and be summer woods—
Let them think twice before they use their powers
To blot out and drink up and sweep away
These flowery waters and these watery flowers
From snow that melted only yesterday.

1928

West-running Brook

"Fred, where is north?"

"North? North is there, my love.
The brook runs west."

"West-running Brook then call it."
(West-running Brook men call it to this day.)
"What does it think it's doing running west
When all the other country brooks flow east
To reach the ocean? It must be the brook
Can trust itself to go by contraries
The way I can with you—and you with me—
Because we're—we're—I don't know what we are.
What are we?"

"Young or new?"

"We must be something.
We've said we two. Let's change that to we three.
As you and I are married to each other,
We'll both be married to the brook. We'll build
Our bridge across it, and the bridge shall be
Our arm thrown over it asleep beside it.
Look, look, it's waving to us with a wave
To let us know it hears me."

"Why, my dear,
That wave's been standing off this jut of shore—"
(The black stream, catching on a sunken rock,
Flung backward on itself in one white wave,
And the white water rode the black forever,
Not gaining but not losing, like a bird
White feathers from the struggle of whose breast
Flecked the dark stream and flecked the darker pool
Below the point, and were at last driven wrinkled
In a white scarf against the far-shore alders.)
"That wave's been standing off this jut of shore
Ever since rivers, I was going to say,
Were made in heaven. It wasn't waved to us."

"It wasn't, yet it was. If not to you
It was to me—in an annunciation."

"Oh, if you take it off to lady-land,
As't were the country of the Amazons[1]

1. Legendary female warriors who inhabited a country without men.

We men must see you to the confines of
35   And leave you there, ourselves forbid to enter—
It is your brook! I have no more to say."

"Yes, you have, too. Go on. You thought of something."

"Speaking of contraries, see how the brook
In that white wave runs counter to itself.
40   It is from that in water we were from
Long, long before we were from any creature.
Here we, in our impatience of the steps,
Get back to the beginning of beginnings,
The stream of everything that runs away.
45   Some say existence like a Pirouot
And Pirouette, forever in one place,
Stands still and dances, but it runs away;
It seriously, sadly, runs away
To fill the abyss's void with emptiness.
50   It flows beside us in this water brook,
But it flows over us. It flows between us
To separate us for a panic moment.
It flows between us, over us, and *with* us.
And it is time, strength, tone, light, life and love—
55   And even substance lapsing unsubstantial;
The universal cataract of death
That spends to nothingness—and unresisted,
Save by some strange resistance in itself,
Not just a swerving, but a throwing back,
60   As if regret were in it and were sacred.
It has this throwing backward on itself
So that the fall of most of it is always
Raising a little, sending up a little.
Our life runs down in sending up the clock.
65   The brook runs down in sending up our life.
The sun runs down in sending up the brook.
And there is something sending up the sun.
It is this backward motion toward the source,
Against the stream, that most we see ourselves in,
70   The tribute of the current to the source.
It is from this in nature we are from.
It is most us."

               "Today will be the day
You said so."

               "No, today will be the day
You said the brook was called West-running Brook."

75   "Today will be the day of what we both said."

                                              1928

A Lone Striker

The swinging mill bell changed its rate
To tolling like the count of fate,
And though at that the tardy ran,
One failed to make the closing gate.

There was a law of God or man
That on the one who came too late
The gate for half an hour be locked,
His time be lost, his pittance docked.
He stood rebuked and unemployed.
The straining mill began to shake.
The mill, though many-many-eyed,
Had eyes inscrutably opaque;
So that he couldn't look inside
To see if some forlorn machine
Was standing idle for his sake.
(He couldn't hope its heart would break.)

And yet he thought he saw the scene:
The air was full of dust of wool.
A thousand yarns were under pull,
But pull so slow, with such a twist,
All day from spool to lesser spool,
It seldom overtaxed their strength;
They safely grew in slender length.
And if one broke by any chance,
The spinner saw it at a glance.
The spinner still was there to spin.
That's where the human still came in.
Her deft hand showed with finger rings
Among the harp-like spread of strings.
She caught the pieces end to end
And, with a touch that never missed,
Not so much tied as made them blend.
Man's ingenuity was good.
He saw it plainly where he stood,
Yet found it easy to resist.

He knew another place, a wood,
And in it, tall as trees, were cliffs;
And if he stood on one of these,
'Twould be among the tops of trees,
Their upper branches round him wreathing,
Their breathing mingled with his breathing.
If—if he stood! Enough of ifs!
He knew a path that wanted walking;
He knew a spring that wanted drinking;
A thought that wanted further thinking;
A love that wanted re-renewing.
Nor was this just a way of talking
To save him the expense of doing.
With him it boded action, deed.

The factory was very fine;
He wished it all the modern speed.
Yet, after all, 'twas not divine,
That is to say, 'twas not a church.
He never would assume that he'd
Be any institution's need.
But he said then and still would say
If there should ever come a day
When industry seemed like to die

Because he left it in the lurch,
60   Or even merely seemed to pine
For want of his approval, why,
Come get him—they knew where to search.

1936

The Strong Are Saying Nothing

The soil now gets a rumpling soft and damp,
And small regard to the future of any weed.
The final flat of the hoe's approval stamp
Is reserved for the bed of a few selected seed.

5   There is seldom more than a man to a harrowed piece.
Men work alone, their lots plowed far apart,
One stringing a chain of seed in an open crease,
And another stumbling after a halting cart.

To the fresh and black of the squares of early mould
10   The leafless bloom of a plum is fresh and white;
Though there's more than a doubt if the weather is not too cold
For the bees to come and serve its beauty aright.

Wind goes from farm to farm in wave on wave,
But carries no cry of what is hoped to be.
15   There may be little or much beyond the grave,
But the strong are saying nothing until they see.

1936

Neither Out Far Nor In Deep

The people along the sand
All turn and look one way.
They turn their back on the land.
They look at the sea all day.

5   As long as it takes to pass
A ship keeps raising its hull;
The wetter ground like glass
Reflects a standing gull.

The land may vary more;
10   But wherever the truth may be—
The water comes ashore,
And the people look at the sea.

They cannot look out far.
They cannot look in deep.
15   But when was that ever a bar
To any watch they keep?

1936

Design

I found a dimpled spider, fat and white,
On a white heal-all,[2] holding up a moth
Like a white piece of rigid satin cloth—
Assorted characters of death and blight
Mixed ready to begin the morning right,
Like the ingredients of a witches' broth—
A snow-drop spider, a flower like froth,
And dead wings carried like a paper kite.

What had that flower to do with being white,
The wayside blue and innocent heal-all?
What brought the kindred spider to that height,
Then steered the white moth thither in the night?
What but design of darkness to appall?—
If design govern in a thing so small.

1936

Never Again Would Birds' Song Be the Same

He would declare and could himself believe
That the birds there in all the garden round
From having heard the daylong voice of Eve
Had added to their own an oversound,
Her tone of meaning but without the words.
Admittedly an eloquence so soft
Could only have had an influence on birds
When call or laughter carried it aloft.
Be that as may be, she was in their song
Moreover her voice upon their voices crossed
Had now persisted in the woods so long
That probably it never would be lost.
Never again would birds' song be the same.
And to do that to birds was why she came.

1942

The Gift Outright

The land was ours before we were the land's.
She was our land more than a hundred years
Before we were her people. She was ours
In Massachusetts, in Virginia,
But we were England's, still colonials,
Possessing what we still were unpossessed by,
Possessed by what we now no more possessed.
Something we were withholding made us weak
Until we found it was ourselves
We were withholding from our land of living,
And forthwith found salvation in surrender.
Such as we were we gave ourselves outright
(The deed of gift was many deeds of war)
To the land vaguely realizing westward,
But still unstoried, artless, unenhanced,
Such as she was, such as she would become.

1942

2. One of a variety of plants thought to have curative powers.

Directive

Back out of all this now too much for us,
Back in a time made simple by the loss
Of detail, burned, dissolved, and broken off
Like graveyard marble sculpture in the weather,
5   There is a house that is no more a house
Upon a farm that is no more a farm
And in a town that is no more a town.
The road there, if you'll let a guide direct you
Who only has at heart your getting lost,
10 May seem as if it should have been a quarry—
Great monolithic knees the former town
Long since gave up pretense of keeping covered.
And there's a story in a book about it:
Besides the wear of iron wagon wheels
15 The ledges show lines ruled southeast northwest,
The chisel work of an enormous Glacier
That braced his feet against the Arctic Pole.
You must not mind a certain coolness from him
Still said to haunt this side of Panther Mountain.
20 Nor need you mind the serial ordeal
Of being watched from forty cellar holes
As if by eye pairs out of forty firkins.
As for the woods' excitement over you
That sends light rustle rushes to their leaves,
25 Charge that to upstart inexperience.
Where were they all not twenty years ago?
They think too much of having shaded out
A few old pecker-fretted apple trees.
Make yourself up a cheering song of how
30 Someone's road home from work this once was,
Who may be just ahead of you on foot
Or creaking with a buggy load of grain.
The height of the adventure is the height
Of country where two village cultures faded
35 Into each other. Both of them are lost.
And if you're lost enough to find yourself
By now, pull in your ladder road behind you
And put a sign up CLOSED to all but me.
Then make yourself at home. The only field
40 Now left's no bigger than a harness gall.
First there's the children's house of make believe,
Some shattered dishes underneath a pine,
The playthings in the playhouse of the children.
Weep for what little things could make them glad.
45 Then for the house that is no more a house,
But only a belilaced cellar hole,
Now slowly closing like a dent in dough.
This was no playhouse but a house in earnest.
Your destination and your destiny's
50 A brook that was the water of the house,
Cold as a spring as yet so near its source,
Too lofty and original to rage.
(We know the valley streams that when aroused
Will leave their tatters hung on barb and thorn.)

I have kept hidden in the instep arch
Of an old cedar at the waterside
A broken drinking goblet like the Grail
Under a spell so the wrong ones can't find it,
So can't get saved, as Saint Mark says they mustn't.[1]
(I stole the goblet from the children's playhouse.)
Here are your waters and your watering place.
Drink and be whole again beyond confusion.

1947

[In Winter in the Woods . . .]

In winter in the woods alone
Against the trees I go.
I mark a maple for my own
And lay the maple low.

At four o'clock I shoulder axe,
And in the afterglow
I link a line of shadowy tracks
Across the tinted snow.

I see for Nature no defeat
In one tree's overthrow
Or for myself in my retreat
For yet another blow.

1962

CARL SANDBURG
(1878–1967)

Chicago

Hog Butcher for the World,
Tool Maker, Stacker of Wheat,
Player with Railroads and the Nation's Freight Handler;
Stormy, husky, brawling,
City of the Big Shoulders:

They tell me you are wicked and I believe them, for I have seen your painted
women under the gas lamps luring the farm boys.
And they tell me you are crooked and I answer: Yes, it is true I have seen the
gunman kill and go free to kill again.
And they tell me you are brutal and my reply is: On the faces of women and
children I have seen the marks of wanton hunger.
And having answered so I turn once more to those who sneer at this my city,
and I give them back the sneer and say to them:
Come and show me another city with lifted head singing so proud to be alive
and coarse and strong and cunning.

1. Cf. Mark iv.11–12, in which Christ says, "To you has been given the secret of the kingdom of God, but for those outside everything is in parables; so that they may indeed see but not perceive, and may indeed hear but not understand; lest they should turn again, and be forgiven." *The Grail:* the holy grail, a cup used by Jesus at the last supper, the object of many quests in Arthurian romance.

Flinging magnetic curses amid the toil of piling job on job, here is a tall bold
　　slugger set vivid against the little soft cities;
Fierce as a dog with tongue lapping for action, cunning as a savage pitted
　　against the wilderness,
　　　　Bareheaded,
　　　　Shoveling,
15　　　Wrecking,
　　　　Planning,
　　　　Building, breaking, rebuilding,
Under the smoke, dust all over his mouth, laughing with white teeth,
Under the terrible burden of destiny laughing as a young man laughs,
20 Laughing even as an ignorant fighter laughs who has never lost a battle,
Bragging and laughing that under his wrist is the pulse, and under his ribs
　　the heart of the people,
　　　　Laughing!
Laughing the stormy, husky, brawling laughter of Youth, half-naked, sweat-
　　ing, proud to be Hog Butcher, Tool Maker, Stacker of Wheat, Player
　　with Railroads and Freight Handler to the Nation.

　　　　　　　　　　　　　　　　　　　　　　　　　　　　　1916

Grass

Pile the bodies high at Austerlitz and Waterloo.[1]
Shovel them under and let me work—
　　　　I am the grass; I cover all.

And pile them high at Gettysburg[2]
5 And pile them high at Ypres and Verdun.[3]
Shovel them under and let me work.
Two years, ten years, and passengers ask the conductor:
　　　　What place is this?
　　　　Where are we now?

10　　　　I am the grass.
　　　　Let me work.

　　　　　　　　　　　　　　　　　　　　　　　　　　　　　1918

EDWARD THOMAS
(1878–1917)

The Owl

Downhill I came, hungry, and yet not starved;
Cold, yet had heat within me that was proof
Against the North wind; tired, yet so that rest
Had seemed the sweetest thing under a roof.

---

1. Napoleon's victory over the Russians and Austrians near Austerlitz, in Moravia, was won on December 2, 1805; his final defeat, at the hands of the Duke of Wellington leading the allied forces, occurred at Waterloo, Belgium, June 18, 1815.
2. The great American Civil War battle begun July 1, 1863, and won three days later by the Union forces.
3. Ypres was the site of a World War I battle (1917), usually regarded as costly and fruitless; Verdun was a French town and fortress strategic to the German offensive in 1916–17, but successfully defended by the Allies.

Then at the inn I had food, fire, and rest,
Knowing how hungry, cold, and tired was I.
All of the night was quite barred out except
An owl's cry, a most melancholy cry

Shaken out long and clear upon the hill,
No merry note, nor cause of merriment,
But one telling me plain what I escaped
And others could not, that night, as in I went.

And salted was my food, and my repose,
Salted and sobered, too, by the bird's voice
Speaking for all who lay under the stars,
Soldiers and poor, unable to rejoice.

1917

Melancholy

The rain and wind, the rain and wind, raved endlessly.
On me the Summer storm, and fever, and melancholy
Wrought magic, so that if I feared the solitude
Far more I feared all company: too sharp, too rude,
Had been the wisest or the dearest human voice.
What I desired I knew not, but whate'er my choice
Vain it must be, I knew. Yet naught did my despair
But sweeten the strange sweetness, while through the wild air
All day long I heard a distant cuckoo calling
And, soft as dulcimers, sounds of near water falling,
And, softer, and remote as if in history,
Rumors of what had touched my friends, my foes, or me.

1917

Lights Out

I have come to the borders of sleep,
The unfathomable deep
Forest where all must lose
Their way, however straight,
Or winding, soon or late;
They cannot choose.

Many a road and track
That, since the dawn's first crack,
Up to the forest brink,
Deceived the travelers,
Suddenly now blurs,
And in they sink.

Here love ends,
Despair, ambition ends;
All pleasure and all trouble,
Although most sweet or bitter,
Here ends in sleep that is sweeter
Than tasks most noble.

There is not any book
20 Or face of dearest look
That I would not turn from now
To go into the unknown
I must enter, and leave, alone,
I know not how.

25 The tall forest towers;
Its cloudy foliage lowers
Ahead, shelf above shelf;
Its silence I hear and obey
That I may lose my way
30 And myself.

1917

The Dark Forest

Dark is the forest and deep, and overhead
Hang stars like seeds of light
In vain, though not since they were sown was bred
Anything more bright.

5 And evermore mighty multitudes ride
About, nor enter in;
Of the other multitudes that dwell inside
Never yet was one seen.

The forest foxglove is purple, the marguerite
10 Outside is gold and white,
Nor can those that pluck either blossom greet
The others, day or night.

1918

Good-Night

The skylarks are far behind that sang over the down;
I can hear no more those suburb nightingales;
Thrushes and blackbirds sing in the gardens of the town
In vain: the noise of man, beast, and machine prevails.

5 But the call of children in the unfamiliar streets
That echo with a familiar twilight echoing,
Sweet as the voice of nightingale or lark, completes
A magic of strange welcome, so that I seem a king

Among man, beast, machine, bird, child, and the ghost
10 That in the echo lives and with the echo dies.
The friendless town is friendly; homeless, I am not lost;
Though I know none of these doors, and meet but strangers' eyes.

Never again, perhaps, after tomorrow, shall
I see these homely streets, these church windows alight,
15 Not a man or woman or child among them all:
But it is All Friends' Night, a traveler's good-night.

1918

The Gypsy

A fortnight before Christmas Gypsies were everywhere:
Vans were drawn up on wastes, women trailed to the fair.
"My gentleman," said one, "you've got a lucky face."
"And you've a luckier," I thought, "if such a grace
And impudence in rags are lucky." "Give a penny
For the poor baby's sake." "Indeed I have not any
Unless you can give change for a sovereign,[2] my dear."
"Then just half a pipeful of tobacco can you spare?"
I gave it. With that much victory she laughed content.
I should have given more, but off and away she went
With her baby and her pink sham flowers to rejoin
The rest before I could translate to its proper coin
Gratitude for her grace. And I paid nothing then,
As I pay nothing now with the dipping of my pen
For her brother's music when he drummed the tambourine
And stamped his feet, which made the workmen passing grin,
While his mouth-organ changed to a rascally Bacchanal dance
"Over the hills and far away." This and his glance
Outlasted all the fair, farmer, and auctioneer,
Cheap-jack,° balloon-man, drover with crooked stick, and steer,   *peddler*
Pig, turkey, goose, and duck, Christmas corpses to be.
Not even the kneeling ox had eyes like the Romany.°   *gypsy*
That night he peopled for me the hollow wooded land,
More dark and wild than stormiest heavens, that I searched and scanned
Like a ghost new-arrived. The gradations of the dark
Were like an underworld of death, but for the spark
In the Gypsy boy's black eyes as he played and stamped his tune,
"Over the hills and far away," and a crescent moon.

                                                    1918

WALLACE STEVENS
(1879–1955)

The Snow Man

One must have a mind of winter
To regard the frost and the boughs
Of the pine-trees crusted with snow;

And have been cold a long time
To behold the junipers shagged with ice,
The spruces rough in the distant glitter

Of the January sun; and not to think
Of any misery in the sound of the wind,
In the sound of a few leaves,

Which is the sound of the land
Full of the same wind
That is blowing in the same bare place

2. Formerly, a British gold coin, value one pound, so called because it bore the effigy of the ruler on one face.

For the listener, who listens in the snow,
And, nothing himself, beholds
15   Nothing that is not there and the nothing that is.

1923

The Emperor of Ice-Cream

Call the roller of big cigars,
The muscular one, and bid him whip
In kitchen cups concupiscent curds.
Let the wenches dawdle in such dress
5   As they are used to wear, and let the boys
Bring flowers in last month's newspapers.
Let be be finale of seem.
The only emperor is the emperor of ice-cream.

Take from the dresser of deal.
10   Lacking the three glass knobs, that sheet
On which she embroidered fantails [1] once
And spread it so as to cover her face.
If her horny feet protrude, they come
To show how cold she is, and dumb.
15   Let the lamp affix its beam.
The only emperor is the emperor of ice-cream.

1923

Sunday Morning

1

Complacencies of the peignoir, and late
Coffee and oranges in a sunny chair,
And the green freedom of a cockatoo
Upon a rug mingle to dissipate
5   The holy hush of ancient sacrifice.
She dreams a little, and she feels the dark
Encroachment of that old catastrophe,
As a calm darkens among water-lights.
The pungent oranges and bright, green wings
10   Seem things in some procession of the dead,
Winding across wide water, without sound.
The day is like wide water, without sound,
Stilled for the passing of her dreaming feet
Over the seas, to silent Palestine,
15   Dominion of the blood and sepulchre.

2

Why should she give her bounty to the dead?
What is divinity if it can come
Only in silent shadows and in dreams?
Shall she not find in comforts of the sun,
20   In pungent fruit and bright, green wings, or else
In any balm or beauty of the earth,
Things to be cherished like the thought of heaven?
Divinity must live within herself:
Passions of rain, or moods in falling snow;
25   Grievings in loneliness, or unsubdued

---

1. That is, fantail pigeons.

Elations when the forest blooms; gusty
Emotions on wet roads on autumn nights;
All pleasures and all pains, remembering
The bough of summer and the winter branch.
These are the measures destined for her soul.

3

Jove in the clouds had his inhuman birth.
No mother suckled him, no sweet land gave
Large-mannered motions to his mythy mind
He moved among us, as a muttering king,
Magnificent, would move among his hinds,°   *shepherds*
Until our blood, commingling, virginal,
With heaven, brought such requital to desire
The very hinds discerned it, in a star.
Shall our blood fail? Or shall it come to be
The blood of paradise? And shall the earth
Seem all of paradise that we shall know?
The sky will be much friendlier then than now,
A part of labor and a part of pain,
And next in glory to enduring love,
Not this dividing and indifferent blue.

4

She says, "I am content when wakened birds,
Before they fly, test the reality
Of misty fields, by their sweet questionings;
But when the birds are gone, and their warm fields
Return no more, where, then, is paradise?"
There is not any haunt of prophecy,
Nor any old chimera of the grave,
Neither the golden underground, nor isle
Melodious, where spirits gat them home,
Nor visionary south, nor cloudy palm
Remote on heaven's hill, that has endured
As April's green endures; or will endure
Like her remembrance of awakened birds,
Or her desire for June and evening, tipped
By the consummation of the swallow's wings.

5

She says, "But in contentment I still feel
The need of some imperishable bliss."
Death is the mother of beauty; hence from her,
Alone, shall come fulfilment to our dreams
And our desires. Although she strews the leaves
Of sure obliteration on our paths,
The path sick sorrow took, the many paths
Where triumph rang its brassy phrase, or love
Whispered a little out of tenderness,
She makes the willow shiver in the sun
For maidens who were wont to sit and gaze
Upon the grass, relinquished to their feet.
She causes boys to pile new plums and pears
On disregarded plate.[1] The maidens taste
And stray impassioned in the littering leaves.

---

1. "Plate is used in the sense of so-called family plate. Disregarded refers to the disuse into which things fall that have been possessed for a long time. I mean, therefore, that death releases and renews" [*Letters of Wallace Stevens*, New York, 1966, pp. 183–184].

6

Is there no change of death in paradise?
Does ripe fruit never fall? Or do the boughs
Hang always heavy in that perfect sky,
Unchanging, yet so like our perishing earth,
80 With rivers like our own that seek for seas
They never find, the same receding shores
That never touch with inarticulate pang?
Why set the pear upon those river-banks
Or spice the shores with odors of the plum?
85 Alas, that they should wear our colors there,
The silken weavings of our afternoons,
And pick the strings of our insipid lutes!
Death is the mother of beauty, mystical,
Within whose burning bosom we devise
90 Our earthly mothers waiting, sleeplessly.

7

Supple and turbulent, a ring of men
Shall chant in orgy on a summer morn
Their boisterous devotion to the sun,
Not as a god, but as a god might be,
95 Naked among them, like a savage source.
Their chant shall be a chant of paradise,
Out of their blood, returning to the sky;
And in their chant shall enter, voice by voice,
The windy lake wherein their lord delights,
100 The trees, like serafin,° and echoing hills,   *celestial beings*
That choir among themselves long afterward.
They shall know well the heavenly fellowship
Of men that perish and of summer morn.
And whence they came and whither they shall go
105 The dew upon their feet shall manifest.

8

She hears, upon that water without sound,
A voice that cries, "The tomb in Palestine
Is not the porch of spirits lingering.
It is the grave of Jesus, where he lay."
110 We live in an old chaos of the sun,
Or old dependency of day and night,
Or island solitude, unsponsored, free,
Of that wide water, inescapable.
Deer walk upon our mountains, and the quail
115 Whistle about us their spontaneous cries;
Sweet berries ripen in the wilderness;
And, in the isolation of the sky,
At evening, casual flocks of pigeons make
Ambiguous undulations as they sink,
120 Downward to darkness, on extended wings.

1915   1923

Anecdote of the Jar

I placed a jar in Tennessee,
And round it was, upon a hill.
It made the slovenly wilderness
Surround that hill.

The wilderness rose up to it,
And sprawled around, no longer wild.
The jar was round upon the ground
And tall and of a port in air.

It took dominion everywhere.
The jar was gray and bare.
It did not give of bird or bush,
Like nothing else in Tennessee.

1923

The Bird with the Coppery, Keen Claws

Above the forest of the parakeets,
A parakeet of parakeets prevails,
A pip of life amid a mort° of tails.   *great quantity*

(The rudiments of tropics are around,
Aloe[2] of ivory, pear of rusty rind.)
His lids are white because his eyes are blind.

He is not paradise of parakeets,
Of his gold ether, golden alguazil,°   *bailiff, sheriff*
Except because he broods there and is still.

Panache[3] upon panache, his tails deploy
Upward and outward, in green-vented forms,
His tip a drop of water full of storms.

But though the turbulent tinges undulate
As his pure intellect applies its laws,
He moves not on his coppery, keen claws.

He munches a dry shell while he exerts
His will, yet never ceases, perfect cock,
To flare, in the sun-pallor of his rock.

1923

To the One of Fictive Music

Sister and mother and diviner love,
And of the sisterhood of the living dead
Most near, most clear, and of the clearest bloom,
And of the fragrant mothers the most dear
5   And queen, and of diviner love the day
And flame and summer and sweet fire, no thread
Of cloudy silver sprinkles in your gown
Its venom of renown, and on your head
No crown is simpler than the simple hair.

10   Now, of the music summoned by the birth
That separates us from the wind and sea,
Yet leaves us in them, until earth becomes,
By being so much of the things we are,

2. Plants of the lily family.   3. Tuft or plume of feathers.

Gross effigy and simulacrum, none
15   Gives motion to perfection more serene
Than yours, out of our imperfections wrought,
Most rare, or ever of more kindred air
In the laborious weaving that you wear.

For so retentive of themselves are men
20   That music is intensest which proclaims
The near, the clear, and vaunts the clearest bloom,
And of all vigils musing the obscure,
That apprehends the most which sees and names,
As in your name, an image that is sure,
25   Among the arrant spices of the sun,
O bough and bush and scented vine, in whom
We give ourselves our likest issuance.

Yet not too like, yet not so like to be
Too near, too clear, saving a little to endow
Our feigning with the strange unlike, whence
30   springs
The difference that heavenly pity brings.
For this, musician, in your girdle fixed
Bear other perfumes. On your pale head wear
A band entwining, set with fatal stones.
35   Unreal, give back to us what once you gave:
The imagination that we spurned and crave.

1923

The Idea of Order at Key West

She sang beyond the genius of the sea.
The water never formed to mind or voice,
Like a body wholly body, fluttering
Its empty sleeves; and yet its mimic motion
5   Made constant cry, caused constantly a cry,
That was not ours although we understood,
Inhuman, of the veritable ocean.

The sea was not a mask. No more was she.
The song and water were not medleyed sound
10   Even if what she sang was what she heard,
Since what she sang was uttered word by word.
It may be that in all her phrases stirred
The grinding water and the gasping wind;
But it was she and not the sea we heard.
15   For she was the maker of the song she sang.
The ever-hooded, tragic-gestured sea
Was merely a place by which she walked to sing.
Whose spirit is this? we said, because we knew
It was the spirit that we sought and knew
20   That we should ask this often as she sang.

If it was only the dark voice of the sea
That rose, or even colored by many waves;
If it was only the outer voice of sky
And cloud, of the sunken coral water-walled,
25   However clear, it would have been deep air,

The heaving speech of air, a summer sound
Repeated in a summer without end
And sound alone. But it was more than that,
More even than her voice, and ours, among
The meaningless plungings of water and the wind,
Theatrical distances, bronze shadows heaped
On high horizons, mountainous atmospheres
Of sky and sea.
           It was her voice that made
The sky acutest at its vanishing.
She measured to the hour its solitude.
She was the single artificer of the world
In which she sang. And when she sang, the sea,
Whatever self it had, became the self
That was her song, for she was the maker. Then we,
As we beheld her striding there alone,
Knew that there never was a world for her
Except the one she sang and, singing, made.

Ramon Fernandez,[4] tell me, if you know,
Why, when the singing ended and we turned
Toward the town, tell why the glassy lights,
The lights in the fishing boats at anchor there,
As the night descended, tilting in the air,
Mastered the night and portioned out the sea,
Fixing emblazoned zones and fiery poles,
Arranging, deepening, enchanting night.

Oh! Blessed rage for order, pale Ramon,
The maker's rage to order words of the sea,
Words of the fragrant portals, dimly-starred,
And of ourselves and of our origins,
In ghostlier demarcations, keener sounds.

                                 1935

The Poems of Our Climate

1

Clear water in a brilliant bowl,
Pink and white carnations. The light
In the room more like a snowy air,
Reflecting snow. A newly-fallen snow
At the end of winter when afternoons return.
Pink and white carnations—one desires
So much more than that. The day itself
Is simplified: a bowl of white,
Cold, a cold porcelain, low and round,
With nothing more than the carnations there.

2

Say even that this complete simplicity
Stripped one of all one's torments, concealed
The evilly compounded, vital I
And made it fresh in a world of white,

4. Stevens pointed out to two of his corre-
spondents that in choosing this name he had
simply combined two common Spanish names
at random, without conscious reference to
Ramon Fernandez the critic: "Ramon Fernan-
dez was not intended to be anyone at all."

15 A world of clear water, brilliant-edged,
Still one would want more, one would need more,
More than a world of white and snowy scents.

                    3
There would still remain the never-resting mind,
So that one would want to escape, come back
20 To what had been so long composed.
The imperfect is our paradise.
Note that, in this bitterness, delight,
Since the imperfect is so hot in us,
Lies in flawed words and stubborn sounds.

                                        1942

The House Was Quiet and the World Was Calm

The house was quiet and the world was calm.
The reader became the book; and summer night

Was like the conscious being of the book.
The house was quiet and the world was calm.

5 The words were spoken as if there was no book,
Except that the reader leaned above the page,

Wanted to lean, wanted much most to be
The scholar to whom his book is true, to whom

The summer night is like a perfection of thought.
10 The house was quiet because it had to be.

The quiet was part of the meaning, part of the mind:
The access of perfection to the page.

And the world was calm. The truth in a calm world,
In which there is no other meaning, itself

15 Is calm, itself is summer and night, itself
Is the reader leaning late and reading there.

                                        1947

Continual Conversation with a Silent Man

The old brown hen and the old blue sky,
Between the two we live and die—
The broken cartwheel on the hill.

As if, in the presence of the sea,
5 We dried our nets and mended sail
And talked of never-ending things,

Of the never-ending storm of will,
One will and many wills, and the wind,
Of many meanings in the leaves,

10 Brought down to one below the eaves,
Link, of that tempest, to the farm,
The chain of the turquoise hen and sky

And the wheel that broke as the cart went by.
It is not a voice that is under the eaves.
It is not speech, the sound we hear

In this conversation, but the sound
Of things and their motion: the other man,
A turquoise monster moving round.

1947

The Plain Sense of Things

After the leaves have fallen, we return
To a plain sense of things. It is as if
We had come to an end of the imagination,
Inanimate in an inert savoir.[5]

It is difficult even to choose the adjective
For this blank cold, this sadness without cause.
The great structure has become a minor house.
No turban walks across the lessened floors.

The greenhouse never so badly needed paint.
The chimney is fifty years old and slants to one side.
A fantastic effort has failed, a repetition
In a repetitiousness of men and flies.

Yet the absence of the imagination had
Itself to be imagined. The great pond,
The plain sense of it, without reflections, leaves,
Mud, water like dirty glass, expressing silence

Of a sort, silence of a rat come out to see,
The great pond and its waste of the lilies, all this
Had to be imagined as an inevitable knowledge,
Required, as a necessity requires.

1954

Final Soliloquy of the Interior Paramour

Light the first light of evening, as in a room
In which we rest and, for small reason, think
The world imagined is the ultimate good.

This, therefore, the intensest rendezvous.
It is in that thought that we collect ourselves,
Out of all the indifferences, into one thing:

Within a single thing, a single shawl
Wrapped tightly round us, since we are poor, a warmth,
A light, a power, the miraculous influence.

Here, now, we forget each other and ourselves.
We feel the obscurity of an order, a whole,
A knowledge, that which arranged the rendezvous.

5. Knowing, knowledge (French).

Within its vital boundary, in the mind.
We say God and the imagination are one . . .
15   How high that highest candle lights the dark.

Out of this same light, out of the central mind,
We make a dwelling in the evening air,
In which being there together is enough.

1954

Table Talk

Granted, we die for good.
Life, then, is largely a thing
Of happens to like, not should.

And that, too, granted, why
5   Do I happen to like red bush,
Gray grass and green-gray sky?

What else remains? But red,
Gray, green, why those of all?
That is not what I said:

10   Not those of all. But those.
One likes what one happens to like.
One likes the way red grows.

It cannot matter at all.
Happens to like is one
15   Of the ways things happen to fall.

ca. 1935   1957

A Room on a Garden

O stagnant east-wind, palsied mare,
Giddap! The ruby roses' hair
Must blow.

Behold how order is the end
5   Of everything. The roses bend
As one.

Order, the law of hoes and rakes,
May be perceived in windy quakes
And squalls.

10   The gardener searches earth and sky
The truth in nature to espy
In vain.

He well might find that eager balm
In lilies' stately-statued calm;
15   But then

He well might find it in this fret
Of lilies rusted, rotting, wet
With rain.

ca. 1935   1957

E. J. PRATT
(1883–1964)

Come Not the Seasons Here

Comes not the springtime here,
  Though the snowdrop came,
And the time of the cowslip is near,
  For a yellow flame
Was found in a tuft of green;
  And the joyous shout
  Of a child rang out
That a cuckoo's eggs were seen.

Comes not the summer here,
  Though the cowslip be gone,
Though the wild rose blow as the year
  Draws faithfully on;
Though the face of the poppy be red
  In the morning light,
  And the ground be white
With the bloom of the locust shed.

Comes not the autumn here,
  Though someone said
He found a leaf in the sere°   *withered state*
  By an aster dead;
And knew that the summer was done,
  For a herdsman cried
That his pastures were brown in the sun,
  And his wells were dried.

Nor shall the winter come,
  Though the elm be bare,
And every voice be dumb
  On the frozen air;
But the flap of a waterfowl
  In the marsh alone,
Or the hoot of a horned owl
  On a glacial stone.

                                                               1923

Come Away, Death [1]

Willy-nilly, he comes or goes, with the clown's logic,
Comic in epitaph, tragic in epithalamium, [2]
And unseduced by any mused rhyme.
However blow the winds over the pollen,
5 Whatever the course of the garden variables,
He remains the constant,
Ever flowering from the poppy seeds.

There was a time he came in formal dress,
Announced by Silence tapping at the panels
0 In deep apology.

1. Alludes to the song from Shakespeare's   2. A song or poem celebrating a wedding.
Twelfth Night; see above.

A touch of chivalry in his approach,
He offered sacramental wine,
And with acanthus leaf
And petals of the hyacinth
15 He took the fever from the temples
And closed the eyelids,
Then led the way to his cool longitudes
In the dignity of the candles.

His medieval grace is gone—
20 Gone with the flame of the capitals [3]
And the leisured turn of the thumb
Leafing the manuscripts,
Gone with the marbles
And the Venetian mosaics,
25 With the bend of the knee
Before the rose-strewn feet of the Virgin.
The *paternosters* [4] of his priests,
Committing clay to clay,
Have rattled in their throats
30 Under the gride° of his traction tread.   *scraping sound*

One night we heard his footfall—one September night—
In the outskirts of a village near the sea.
There was a moment when the storm
Delayed its fist, when the surf fell
35 Like velvet on the rocks—a moment only;
The strangest lull we ever knew!
A sudden truce among the oaks
Released their fratricidal arms;
The poplars straightened to attention
40 As the winds stopped to listen
To the sound of a motor drone—[5]
And then the drone was still.
We heard the tick-tock on the shelf,
And the leak of valves in our hearts.
45 A calm condensed and lidded
As at the core of a cyclone ended breathing
This was the monologue of Silence
Grave and unequivocal.

What followed was a bolt
50 Outside the range and target of the thunder,
And human speech curved back upon itself
Through Druid runways and the Piltdown scarps,[6]
Beyond the stammers of the Java caves,[7]
To find its origins in hieroglyphs
55 On mouths and eyes and cheeks
Etched by a foreign stylus never used
On the outmoded page of the Apocalypse.

1943

3. As in the illuminated lettering of medieval manuscripts.
4. Our Father (Latin)—the Lord's Prayer.
5. Of a German bomber. The poem probably alludes to the bombing of Britain in September 1940.
6. The steep slopes in southern England where remnants of Piltdown man—thought to be an ancestor of *homo sapiens* but exposed as a hoax—were discovered in 1911. Other ancient monuments and sites in the area were attributed to the Druids, ancient priests of Britain.
7. Where were found skulls of *Pithecanthropus*, thought to be a link between ape and man.

The Deed

Where are the roadside minstrels gone who strung
Their fiddles to the stirrup cavalcades?
What happened to the roses oversung
By orchard lovers in their serenades?

A feudal dust that draggle-tailed the plumes
Blinded the minstrels chasing cavaliers:
Moonlight that sucked the color from the blooms
Had soaked the lyrists and the sonneteers.

Where is the beauty still inspired by rhyme,
Competing with those garden miracles,
When the first ray conspires with wind to chime
The matins of the Canterbury bells? [8]

Not in the fruit or flower nor in the whir
Of linnet's wings or plaint of nightingales,
Nor in the moonstruck latticed face of her
Who cracked the tenor sliding up his scales.

We saw that beauty once—an instant run
Along a ledge of rock, a curve, a dive;
Nor did he count the odds of ten to one
Against his bringing up that boy alive.

This was an arch beyond the salmon's lunge,
There was a rainbow in the rising mists:
Sea-lapidaries started as the plunge
To cut the facets of their amethysts.

But this we scarcely noticed, since the deed
Had power to cleanse a grapnel's [9] rust, transfigure
The blueness of the lips, unmat the weed
And sanctify the unambiguous rigor.

For that embrace had trapped the evening's light,
Racing to glean the red foam's harvestings:
Even the seagulls vanished from our sight,
Though settling with their pentecostal [1] wings.

1943

WILLIAM CARLOS WILLIAMS
(1883–1963)

Gulls

My townspeople, beyond in the great world,
are many with whom it were far more
profitable for me to live than here with you.

---

8. The bells of Canterbury Cathedral calling the faithful to Matins, or morning prayer.
9. A four-hooked anchor, used to drag for bodies lost under water.

1. At Pentecost (the seventh Sunday after Easter) the Holy Spirit descended on Christ's apostles in the forms of tongues of flame.

These whirr about me calling, calling!
and for my own part I answer them, loud as I can,
but they, being free, pass!
I remain! Therefore, listen!
For you will not soon have another singer.

First I say this: You have seen
the strange birds, have you not, that sometimes
rest upon our river in winter?
Let them cause you to think well then of the storms
that drive many to shelter. These things
do not happen without reason.

And the next thing I say is this:
I saw an eagle once circling against the clouds
over one of our principal churches—
Easter, it was—a beautiful day!
three gulls came from above the river
and crossed slowly seaward!
Oh, I know you have your own hymns, I have heard them—
and because I knew they invoked some great protector
I could not be angry with you, no matter
how much they outraged true music—

You see, it is not necessary for us to leap at each other,
and, as I told you, in the end
the gulls moved seaward very quietly.

1917

The Young Housewife

At ten A.M. the young housewife
moves about in negligee behind
the wooden walls of her husband's house.
I pass solitary in my car.

Then again she comes to the curb
to call the ice-man, fish-man, and stands
shy, uncorseted, tucking in
stray ends of hair, and I compare her
to a fallen leaf.

The noiseless wheels of my car
rush with a crackling sound over
dried leaves as I bow and pass smiling.

1917

Danse Russe

If when my wife is sleeping
and the baby and Kathleen
are sleeping
and the sun is a flame-white disc
in silken mists
above shining trees,—
if I in my north room
dance naked, grotesquely

before my mirror
waving my shirt round my head
and singing softly to myself:
"I am lonely, lonely.
I was born to be lonely,
I am best so!"
If I admire my arms, my face,
my shoulders, flanks, buttocks
against the yellow drawn shades,—

Who shall say I am not
the happy genius[3] of my household?

1917

To Waken An Old Lady

Old age is
a flight of small
cheeping birds
skimming
bare trees
above a snow glaze.
Gaining and failing
they are buffeted
by a dark wind—
But what?
On harsh weedstalks
the flock has rested,
the snow
is covered with broken
seedhusks
and the wind tempered
by a shrill
piping of plenty.

1921

The Red Wheelbarrow

so much depends
upon

a red wheel
barrow

glazed with rain
water

beside the white
chickens.

1923

Queen-Ann's-Lace

Her body is not so white as
anemone petals nor so smooth—nor
so remote a thing. It is a field

3. The presiding spirit and shaper of destinies.

of the wild carrot taking
5 the field by force; the grass
does not raise above it.
Here is no question of whiteness,
white as can be, with a purple mole
at the center of each flower.
10 Each flower is a hand's span
of her whiteness. Wherever
his hand has lain there is
a tiny purple blemish. Each part
is a blossom under his touch
15 to which the fibres of her being
stem one by one, each to its end,
until the whole field is a
white desire, empty, a single stem,
a cluster, flower by flower,
20 a pious wish to whiteness gone over—
or nothing.

1925

The Bull

It is in captivity—
ringed, haltered, chained
to a drag
the bull is godlike

5 unlike the cows
he lives alone, nozzles
the sweet grass gingerly
to pass the time away

He kneels, lies down
10 and stretching out
a foreleg licks himself
about the hoof

then stays
with half-closed eyes,
15 Olympian commentary on
the bright passage of days.

—The round sun
smooth his lacquer
through
20 the glossy pinetrees

his substance hard
as ivory or glass—
through which the wind
yet plays—
25   milkless

he nods
the hair between his horns
and eyes matted
with hyacinthine curls

1934

Poem

As the cat
climbed over
the top of

the jamcloset
first the right
forefoot

carefully
then the hind
stepped down

into the pit of
the empty
flowerpot

1934

The Yachts

contend in a sea which the land partly encloses
shielding them from the too-heavy blows
of an ungoverned ocean which when it chooses

tortures the biggest hulls, the best man knows
to pit against its beatings, and sinks them pitilessly.
Mothlike in mists, scintillant in the minute

brilliance of cloudless days, with broad bellying sails
they glide to the wind tossing green water
from their sharp prows while over them the crew crawls

ant-like, solicitously grooming them, releasing,
making fast as they turn, lean far over and having
caught the wind again, side by side, head for the mark.

In a well guarded arena of open water surrounded by
lesser and greater craft which, sycophant, lumbering
and flittering follow them, they appear youthful, rare

as the light of a happy eye, live with the grace
of all that in the mind is fleckless, free and
naturally to be desired. Now the sea which holds them

is moody, lapping their glossy sides, as if feeling
for some slightest flaw but fails completely.
Today no race. Then the wind comes again. The yachts

move, jockeying for a start, the signal is set and they
are off. Now the waves strike at them but they are too
well made, they slip through, though they take in canvas.

Arms with hands grasping seek to clutch at the prows.
Bodies thrown recklessly in the way are cut aside.
It is a sea of faces about them in agony, in despair

until the horror of the race dawns staggering the mind,
the whole sea become an entanglement of watery bodies
30   lost to the world bearing what they cannot hold. Broken,

beaten, desolate, reaching from the dead to be taken up
they cry out, failing, failing! their cries rising
in waves still as the skillful yachts pass over.

1935

The Poor

It's the anarchy of poverty
delights me, the old
yellow wooden house indented
among the new brick tenements

5   Or a cast-iron balcony
with panels showing oak branches
in full leaf. It fits
the dress of the children

reflecting every stage and
10   custom of necessity—
Chimneys, roofs, fences of
wood and metal in an unfenced

age and enclosing next to
nothing at all: the old man
15   in a sweater and soft black
hat who sweeps the sidewalk—

his own ten feet of it
in a wind that fitfully
turning his corner has
20   overwhelmed the entire city

1938

These

are the desolate, dark weeks
when nature in its barrenness
equals the stupidity of man.

The year plunges into night
5   and the heart plunges
lower than night

to an empty, windswept place
without sun, stars or moon
but a peculiar light as of thought

10   that spins a dark fire—
whirling upon itself until,
in the cold, it kindles

to make a man aware of nothing
that he knows, not loneliness
15   itself—Not a ghost but

would be embraced—emptiness,
despair—(They
whine and whistle) among

the flashes and booms of war;
houses of whose rooms
the cold is greater than can be thought,

the people gone that we loved,
the beds lying empty, the couches
damp, the chairs unused—

Hide it away somewhere
out of the mind, let it get roots
and grow, unrelated to jealous

ears and eyes—for itself.
In this mine they come to dig—all.
Is this the counterfoil to sweetest

music? The source of poetry that
seeing the clock stopped, says,
The clock has stopped

that ticked yesterday so well?
and hears the sound of lakewater
splashing—that is now stone.

1938

A Sort of a Song

Let the snake wait under
his weed
and the writing
be of words, slow and quick, sharp
to strike, quiet to wait,
sleepless.

—through metaphor to reconcile
the people and the stones.
Compose. (No ideas
but in things) Invent!
Saxifrage is my flower that splits
the rocks.

1944

The Dance

In Breughel's[5] great picture, The Kermess,
the dancers go round, they go round and
around, the squeal and the blare and the
tweedle of bagpipes, a bugle and fiddles
tipping their bellies (round as the thick-
sided glasses whose wash they impound)

5. Pieter Breughel (died 1569), Flemish painter of peasant life.

their hips and their bellies off balance
to turn them. Kicking and rolling about
the Fair Grounds, swinging their butts, those
10   shanks must be sound to bear up under such
rollicking measures, prance as they dance
in Breughel's great picture, The Kermess.

1944

The Ivy Crown

The whole process is a lie,
         unless,
                      crowned by excess,
it break forcefully,
5   one way or another,
                    from its confinement—
or find a deeper well.
         Antony and Cleopatra
            were right;
10   they have shown
         the way. I love you
               or I do not live
at all.

Daffodil time
15   is past. This is
                 summer, summer!
the heart says,
         and not even the full of it.
                 No doubts
20   are permitted—
         though they will come
               and may
before our time
         overwhelm us.
25   We are only mortal
but being mortal
         can defy our fate.
               We may
by an outside chance
30   even win! We do not
              look to see
jonquils and violets
         come again
               but there are,
35   still,
         the roses!

Romance has no part in it.
         The business of love is
              cruelty *which,*
40   by our wills,
         we transform
             to live together.
It has its seasons,
         for and against,
45   whatever the heart

fumbles in the dark
        to assert
                toward the end of May.
Just as the nature of briars
        is to tear flesh,
                I have proceeded
through them.
        Keep
                the briars out,
they say.
        You cannot live
                and keep free of
briars.

Children pick flowers.
        Let them.
                Though having them
in hand
        they have no further use for them
                but leave them crumpled
at the curb's edge.

At our age the imagination
        across the sorry facts
                lifts us
to make roses
        stand before thorns.
                Sure
love is cruel
        and selfish
                and totally obtuse—
at least, blinded by the light,
        young love is.
                But we are older,
I to love
        and you to be loved,
                we have,
no matter how,
        by our wills survived
                to keep
the jeweled prize
        always
                at our finger tips.
We will it so
        and so it is
                past all accident.

                                    1955

D. H. LAWRENCE
(1885–1930)

Baby Running Barefoot

When the white feet of the baby beat across the grass
The little white feet nod like white flowers in a wind,
They poise and run like puffs of wind that pass
Over water where the weeds are thinned.

5   And the sight of their white playing in the grass
Is winsome as a robin's song, so fluttering;
Or like two butterflies that settle on a glass
Cup for a moment, soft little wing-beats uttering.

And I wish that the baby would tack across here to me
10 Like a wind-shadow running on a pond, so she could stand
With two little bare white feet upon my knee
And I could feel her feet in either hand

Cool as syringa buds in morning hours,
Or firm and silken as young peony flowers.

1916

Piano

Softly, in the dusk, a woman is singing to me;
Taking me back down the vista of years, till I see
A child sitting under the piano, in the boom of the tingling strings
And pressing the small, poised feet of a mother who smiles as she sings.

5   In spite of myself, the insidious mastery of song
Betrays me back, till the heart of me weeps to belong
To the old Sunday evenings at home, with winter outside
And hymns in the cozy parlor, the tinkling piano our guide.

So now it is vain for the singer to burst into clamor
10 With the great black piano appassionato. The glamour
Of childish days is upon me, my manhood is cast
Down in the flood of remembrance, I weep like a child for the past.

1918

Reading a Letter

She sits on the recreation ground
    Under an oak whose yellow buds dot the pale blue sky.
The young grass twinkles in the wind, and the sound
    Of the wind in the knotted buds makes a canopy.

5   So sitting under the knotted canopy
    Of the wind, she is lifted and carried away as in a balloon
Across the insensible void, till she stoops to see
    The sandy desert beneath her, the dreary platoon.

She knows the waste all dry beneath her, in one place
    Stirring with earth-colored life, ever turning and stirring.
But never the motion has a human face
    Nor sound, only intermittent machinery whirring.

And so again, on the recreation ground
    She alights a stranger, wondering, unused to the scene;
Suffering at sight of the children playing around,
    Hurt at the chalk-colored tulips, and the evening-green.

1918

Snake

A snake came to my water-trough
On a hot, hot day, and I in pajamas for the heat,
To drink there.

In the deep, strange-scented shade of the great dark carob-tree
I came down the steps with my pitcher
And must wait, must stand and wait, for there he was at the trough before
    me.

He reached down from a fissure in the earth-wall in the gloom
And trailed his yellow-brown slackness soft-bellied down, over the edge of
    the stone trough
And rested his throat upon the stone bottom,
And where the water had dripped from the tap, in a small clearness,
He sipped with his straight mouth,
Softly drank through his straight gums, into his slack long body,
Silently.

Someone was before me at my water-trough,
And I, like a second comer, waiting.

He lifted his head from his drinking, as cattle do,
And looked at me vaguely, as drinking cattle do,
And flickered his two-forked tongue from his lips, and mused a moment,
And stooped and drank a little more,
Being earth-brown, earth-golden from the burning bowels of the earth
On the day of Sicilian July, with Etna smoking.

The voice of my education said to me
He must be killed,
For in Sicily the black, black snakes are innocent, the gold are venomous.

And voices in me said, If you were a man
You would take a stick and break him now, and finish him off.

But must I confess how I liked him,
How glad I was he had come like a guest in quiet, to drink at my water-
    trough

And depart peaceful, pacified, and thankless,
Into the burning bowels of this earth?

Was it cowardice, that I dared not kill him?
Was it perversity, that I longed to talk to him?

Was it humility, to feel so honored?
I felt so honored.

And yet those voices:
35 *If you were not afraid, you would kill him!*

And truly I was afraid, I was most afraid,
But even so, honored still more
That he should seek my hospitality
From out the dark door of the secret earth.

40 He drank enough
And lifted his head, dreamily, as one who has drunken,
And flickered his tongue like a forked night on the air, so black,
Seeming to lick his lips,
And looked around like a god, unseeing, into the air,
45 And slowly turned his head,
And slowly, very slowly, as if thrice adream,
Proceeded to draw his slow length curving round
And climb again the broken bank of my wall-face.

And as he put his head into that dreadful hole,
50 And as he slowly drew up, snake-easing his shoulders, and entered farther,
A sort of horror, a sort of protest against his withdrawing into that horrid
    black hole,
Deliberately going into the blackness, and slowly drawing himself after,
Overcame me now his back was turned.

I looked round, I put down my pitcher,
55 I picked up a clumsy log
And threw it at the water-trough with a clatter.

I think it did not hit him,
But suddenly that part of him that was left behind convulsed in undignified
    haste
Writhed like lightning, and was gone
60 Into the black hole, the earth-lipped fissure in the wall-front,
At which, in the intense still noon, I stared with fascination.

And immediately I regretted it.
I thought how paltry, how vulgar, what a mean act!
I despised myself and the voices of my accursed human education.

65 And I thought of the albatross[1]
And I wished he would come back, my snake.

For he seemed to me again like a king,
Like a king in exile, uncrowned in the underworld,
Now due to be crowned again.

70 And so, I missed my chance with one of the lords
Of life.
And I have something to expiate;
A pettiness.

Taormina.
1923

---

1. In Coleridge's *Rime of the Ancient Mariner*.

Bavarian Gentians

Not every man has gentians in his house
in Soft September, at slow, sad Michaelmas.

Bavarian gentians, big and dark, only dark
darkening the daytime, torch-like with the smoking blueness of Pluto's gloom,
ribbed and torch-like, with their blaze of darkness spread blue
down flattening into points, flattened under the sweep of white day
torch-flower of the blue-smoking darkness, Pluto's dark-blue daze,
black lamps from the halls of Dis,[2] burning dark blue,
giving off darkness, blue darkness, as Demeter's pale lamps give off light,
lead me then, lead the way.

Reach me a gentian, give me a torch!
let me guide myself with the blue, forked torch of this flower
down the darker and darker stairs, where blue is darkened on blueness
even where Persephone goes, just now, from the frosted September
to the sightless realm where darkness is awake upon the dark
and Persephone herself is but a voice
or a darkness invisible enfolded in the deeper dark
of the arms Plutonic, and pierced with the passion of dense gloom,
among the splendor of torches of darkness, shedding darkness on the lost
   bride and her groom.

1932

The Ship of Death[3]

1

Now it is autumn and the falling fruit
and the long journey towards oblivion.

The apples falling like great drops of dew
to bruise themselves an exit from themselves.

And it is time to go, to bid farewell
to one's own self, and find an exit
from the fallen self.

2

Have you built your ship of death, O have you?
O build your ship of death, for you will need it.

The grim frost is at hand, when the apples will fall
thick, almost thundrous, on the hardened earth.

And death is on the air like a smell of ashes!
Ah! can't you smell it?

And in the bruised body, the frightened soul
finds itself shrinking, wincing from the cold
that blows upon it through the orifices.

2. Another Roman name for Pluto (Greek Hades), ruler of the underworld. He had abducted Persephone (Roman Proserpine) the daughter of Demeter (Roman Ceres), goddess of growing vegetation and living nature; Persephone ruled with him as queen of the underworld, but returned to spend six months of each year with her mother in the world above.
3. In *Etruscan Places*, the book which describes his visit to the Etruscan painted tombs in Central Italy, in the spring of 1927, Lawrence mentions that originally, before the tombs were pillaged, there would be found in the last chamber among "the sacred treasures of the dead, the little bronze ship that should bear [the soul of the dead] over to the other world * * * "

3

And can a man his own quietus make
with a bare bodkin?[4]

With daggers, bodkins, bullets, man can make
20   a bruise or break of exit for his life;
but is that a quietus, O tell me, is it quietus?

Surely not so! for how could murder, even self-murder
ever a quietus make?

4

O let us talk of quiet that we know,
25   that we can know, the deep and lovely quiet
of a strong heart at peace!

How can we this, our own quietus, make?

5

Build then the ship of death, for you must take
the longest journey, to oblivion.

30   And die the death, the long and painful death
that lies between the old self and the new.

Already our bodies are fallen, bruised, badly bruised,
already our souls are oozing through the exit
of the cruel bruise.

35   Already the dark and endless ocean of the end
is washing in through the breaches of our wounds,
already the flood is upon us.

Oh build your ship of death, your little ark
and furnish it with food, with little cakes, and wine
40   for the dark flight down oblivion.

6

Piecemeal the body dies, and the timid soul
has her footing washed away, as the dark flood rises.

We are dying, we are dying, we are all of us dying
and nothing will stay the death-flood rising within us
45   and soon it will rise on the world, on the outside world.

We are dying, we are dying, piecemeal our bodies are dying
and our strength leaves us,
and our soul cowers naked in the dark rain over the flood,
cowering in the last branches of the tree of our life.

7

50   We are dying, we are dying, so all we can do
is now to be willing to die, and to build the ship
of death to carry the soul on the longest journey.

A little ship, with oars and food
and little dishes, and all accoutrements
55   fitting and ready for the departing soul.

Now launch the small ship, now as the body dies
and life departs, launch out, the fragile soul

---

4. From *Hamlet*, III.i.75–6.

in the fragile ship of courage, the ark of faith
with its store of food and little cooking pans
and change of clothes,
upon the flood's black waste
upon the waters of the end
upon the sea of death, where still we sail
darkly, for we cannot steer, and have no port.

There is no port, there is nowhere to go
only the deepening blackness darkening still
blacker upon the soundless, ungurgling flood
darkness at one with darkness, up and down
and sideways utterly dark, so there is no direction any more.
and the little ship is there; yet she is gone.
She is not seen, for there is nothing to see her by.
She is gone! gone! and yet
somewhere she is there.
Nowhere!

　　　8
And everything is gone, the body is gone
completely under, gone, entirely gone.
The upper darkness is heavy as the lower,
between them the little ship
is gone
she is gone.

It is the end, it is oblivion.

　　　9
And yet out of eternity, a thread
separates itself on the blackness,
a horizontal thread
that fumes a little with pallor upon the dark.

Is it illusion? or does the pallor fume
A little higher?
Ah wait, wait, for there's the dawn,
the cruel dawn of coming back to life
out of oblivion.

Wait, wait, the little ship
drifting, beneath the deathly ashy grey
of a flood-dawn.

Wait, wait! even so, a flush of yellow
and strangely, O chilled wan soul, a flush of rose.

A flush of rose, and the whole thing starts again.

　　　10
The flood subsides, and the body, like a worn sea-shell
emerges strange and lovely.
And the little ship wings home, faltering and lapsing
on the pink flood,
and the frail soul steps out, into her house again
filling the heart with peace.

Swings the heart renewed with peace
even of oblivion.

105 Oh build your ship of death, oh build it!
for you will need it.
For the voyage of oblivion awaits you.

1932

EZRA POUND
(1885–1972)

Portrait d'Une Femme[1]

Your mind and you are our Sargasso Sea,[2]
London has swept about you this score years
And bright ships left you this or that in fee:
Ideas, old gossip, oddments of all things,
5   Strange spars of knowledge and dimmed wares of price.
Great minds have sought you—lacking someone else.
You have been second always. Tragical?
No. You preferred it to the usual thing:
One dull man, dulling and uxorious,
10   One average mind—with one thought less, each year.
Oh, you are patient, I have seen you sit
Hours, where something might have floated up.
And now you pay one. Yes, you richly pay.
You are a person of some interest, one comes to you
15   And takes strange gain away:
Trophies fished up; some curious suggestion;
Fact that leads nowhere; and a tale or two,
Pregnant with mandrakes,[3] or with something else
That might prove useful and yet never proves,
20   That never fits a corner or shows use,
Or finds its hour upon the loom of days:
The tarnished, gaudy, wonderful old work;
Idols and ambergris[4] and rare inlays,
These are your riches, your great store; and yet
25   For all this sea-hoard of deciduous things,
Strange woods half sodden, and new brighter stuff:
In the slow float of differing light and deep,
No! there is nothing! In the whole and all,
Nothing that's quite your own.
            Yet this is you.

1912

The Seafarer [5]

FROM THE ANGLO-SAXON

May I for my own self song's truth reckon,
Journey's jargon, how I in harsh days
Hardship endured oft.

1. Portrait of a Lady.
2. A region of the North Atlantic partially covered with accumulations of floating gulf-weed.
3. A plant, of narcotic properties, and sometimes believed to be aphrodisiac, whose forked root was traditionally thought to resemble the human body.
4. Secretion of the whale, used in perfumery.
5. Pound's poem translates the first 99 lines of an Old English poem, 124 lines long, by an unknown author and of unknown date. For the most part it follows the text closely, usually line for line, but departs from the sense of the original, for a phrase or two, at a few points. Pound's aim is not primarily to give an academically "correct" translation, but to make a version of the original that will give a true sense of its form and spirit, "to get the swing and mood of the subject," as he says in another connection.

Bitter breast-cares have I abided,
Known on my keel many a care's hold,
And dire sea-surge, and there I oft spent
Narrow nightwatch nigh the ship's head
While she tossed close to cliffs. Coldly afflicted,
My feet were by frost benumbed.
Chill its chains are; chafing sighs
Hew my heart round and hunger begot
Mere-weary° mood. Lest man know not   *sea-weary*
That he on dry land loveliest liveth,
List how I, care-wretched, on ice-cold sea,
Weathered the winter, wretched outcast
Deprived of my kinsmen;
Hung with hard ice-flakes, where hail-scur° flew,   *hail-storms*
There I heard naught save the harsh sea
And ice-cold wave, at whiles the swan cries,
Did for my games the gannet's clamor,
Sea-fowls' loudness was for me laughter,
The mews' singing all my mead-drink.
Storms, on the stone-cliffs beaten, fell on the stern
In icy feathers;[6] full oft the eagle screamed
With spray on his pinion.   Not any protector
May make merrry man faring needy.
This he little believes, who aye in winsome life
Abides 'mid burghers some heavy business,
Wealthy and wine-flushed, how I weary oft
Must bide above brine.
Neareth nightshade, snoweth from north,
Frost froze the land, hail fell on earth then,
Corn of the coldest. Nathless° there knocketh now   *notwithstanding*
The heart's thought that I on high streams
The salt-wavy tumult traverse alone.
Moaneth alway my mind's lust
That I fare forth, that I afar hence
Seek out a foreign fastness.
For this there's no moody-lofty man over earth's midst,
Not though he be given his good, but will have in his
        youth greed;
Nor his deed to the daring, nor his king to the faithful
But shall have his sorrow for sea-fare
Whatever his lord will.
He hath not heart for harping, nor in ring-having
Nor winsomeness to wife, nor world's delight
Nor any whit else save the wave's slash,
Yet longing comes upon him to fare forth on the water.
Bosque° taketh blossom, cometh beauty of berries,[7]   *grove*
Fields to fairness, land fares brisker,
All this admonisheth man eager of mood,
The heart turns to travel so that he then thinks
On flood-ways to be far departing.
Cuckoo calleth with gloomy crying,
He singeth summerward, bodeth sorrow,
The bitter heart's blood. Burgher knows not—

6. Strictly: "Storms there beat on the stone-cliffs, there the tern answers them, its feathers icy."

7. In the original, the sense of the second half of the line is "towns become fair."

He the prosperous man—what some perform
Where wandering them widest draweth.
So that but now my heart burst from my breastlock,
My mood 'mid the mere-flood,°   *sea-flood*
60 Over the whale's acre, would wander wide.
On earth's shelter cometh oft to me,
Eager and ready, the crying lone-flyer,
Whets for the whale-path the heart irresistibly,
O'er tracks of ocean; seeing that anyhow
65 My lord deems to me this dead life
On loan and on land,⁸ I believe not
That any earth-weal eternal standeth
Save there be somewhat calamitous
That, ere a man's tide go, turn it to twain.
70 Disease or oldness or sword-hate
Beats out the breath from doom-gripped body.
And for this, every earl whatever, for those speaking
     after—
Laud of the living, boasteth some last word,
That he will work ere he pass onward,
75 Frame on the fair earth 'gainst foes his malice,
Daring ado,° . . .   *brave deeds*
So that all men shall honor him after
And his laud beyond them remain 'mid the English,⁹
Aye, for ever, a lasting life's-blast,
Delight 'mid the doughty.
80   Days little durable,
And all arrogance of earthen riches,
There come now no kings nor Cæsars
Nor gold-giving lords like those gone.
Howe'er in mirth most magnified,
85 Whoe'er lived in life most lordliest,
Drear all this excellence, delights undurable!
Waneth the watch, but the world holdeth.
Tomb hideth trouble. The blade is layed low.¹
Earthly glory ageth and seareth.
90 No man at all going the earth's gait,
But age fares against him, his face paleth,
Gray-haired he groaneth, knows gone companions,
Lordly men, are to earth o'ergiven,
Nor may he then the flesh-cover, whose life ceaseth,
95 Nor eat the sweet nor feel the sorry,
Nor stir hand nor think in mid heart,
And though he strew the grave with gold,
His born brothers, their buried bodies
Be an unlikely treasure hoard.

                                                 1912

8. Behind Pound's phrase "on loan and on land" is the O. E. "læne on lond," "briefly on earth." (Because the Lord's joys are warmer to me than this dead life, brief on the earth." But Pound has chosen to play down the Christian elements in the poem, perhaps believing that they are inconsistent with its essential spirit.)
9. In the original, the sense is "with the angels," not "mid the English."
1. In the original, the sense of lines 87–8 is "The weak live on and hold over this world./ Possess it through trouble. Glory is laid low."

The Garden

En robe de parade.[4]
—SAMAIN

Like a skein of loose silk blown against a wall
She walks by the railing of a path in Kensington Gardens,[5]
And she is dying piecemeal
            of a sort of emotional anemia.

And round about there is a rabble
Of the filthy, sturdy, unkillable infants of the very poor.
They shall inherit the earth.

In her is the end of breeding.
Her boredom is exquisite and excessive.
She would like some one to speak to her,
And is almost afraid that I
            will commit that indiscretion.

1916

The Study in Aesthetics

The very small children in patched clothing,
Being smitten with an unusual wisdom,
Stopped in their play as she passed them
And cried up from their cobbles:

            Guarda! Ahi, guarda! ch' è be' a![6]

But three years after this
I heard the young Dante, whose last name I do not know—
For there are, in Sirmione,[7] twenty-eight young Dantes
      and thirty-four Catulli;
And there had been a great catch of sardines,
And his elders
Were packing them in the great wooden boxes
For the market in Brescia, and he
Leapt about, snatching at the bright fish
And getting in both of their ways;
And in vain they commanded him to *sta fermo!*[8]
And when they would not let him arrange
The fish in the boxes
He stroked those which were already arranged,
Murmuring for his own satisfaction
This identical phrase:

            Ch' è be' a.

And at this I was mildly abashed.

1916

---

4. "Dressed as for a state occasion." The phrase is from a poem by the French poet Albert Samain (1858–1900), *The Infanta.*
5. Extensive public gardens in the residential district west of Hyde Park, London.

6. *"Be'a: bella"* [Pound's note]. Look! Ah, look! how beautiful she is!
7. Town on Lake Garda, in northern Italy.
8. Stand still!

The Coming of War: Actaeon [7]

An image of Lethe,[8]
    and the fields
Full of faint light
    but golden,
5 Gray cliffs,
    and beneath them
A sea
Harsher than granite,
    unstill, never ceasing;
10 High forms
    with the movement of gods,
Perilous aspect;
    And one said:
"This is Actaeon."
15   Actaeon of golden greaves!
Over fair meadows,
Over the cool face of that field,
Unstill, ever moving
Hosts of an ancient people,
20 The silent cortège.

                    1916

Ts' ai Chi'h[9]

The petals fall in the fountain,
    the orange-colored rose-leaves,
Their ochre clings to the stone.

                    1916

In a Station of the Metro

The apparition of these faces in the crowd;
Petals on a wet, black bough.

                    1916

Simulacra[3]

Why does the horse-faced lady of just the unmentionable age
Walk down Longacre[4] reciting Swinburne to herself, inaudibly?
Why does the small child in the soiled-white imitation fur coat
Crawl in the very black gutter beneath the grape stand?
5 Why does the really handsome young woman approach me in Sackville
    Street[5]
Undeterred by the manifest age of my trappings?

                    1916

---

7. A hunter who came upon Artemis bathing; she turned him into a stag, whereupon he was chased and killed by his own hounds.
8. In classical mythology, one of the rivers of the underworld, whose waters induce forgetfulness of the former life.
9. Ts'ai Chi'h, or more usually Ts'ao Chih, is the name of a Chinese poet who lived from 192–232, and Pound's using it as the title of his poem perhaps indicates that in it he is adopting the mode of Ts'ao Chih's "five-character poems," or even translating one of them.
3. A simulacrum is an image, or an imitation, a sham representation of something.
4. Street in the Covent Garden district of London.
5. Runs into Picadilly, not far from Picadilly Circus.

The River-Merchant's Wife: a Letter

While my hair was still cut straight across my forehead
I played about the front gate, pulling flowers.
You came by on bamboo stilts, playing horse,
You walked about my seat, playing with blue plums.
And we went on living in the village of Chokan:
Two small people, without dislike or suspicion.

At fourteen I married My Lord you.
I never laughed, being bashful.
Lowering my head, I looked at the wall.
Called to, a thousand times, I never looked back.

At fifteen I stopped scowling,
I desired my dust to be mingled with yours
Forever and forever and forever.
Why should I climb the look out?

At sixteen you departed,
You went into far Ku-to-yen, by the river of swirling eddies,
And you have been gone five months.
The monkeys make sorrowful noise overhead.

You dragged your feet when you went out.
By the gate now, the moss is grown, the different mosses,
Too deep to clear them away!
The leaves fall early this autumn, in wind.
The paired butterflies are already yellow with August
Over the grass in the West garden;
They hurt me. I grow older.
If you are coming down through the narrows of the river Kiang,
Please let me know beforehand,
And I will come out to meet you
              As far as Cho-fu-Sa.

                                        By *Rihaku*[6]
                                        1915

Hugh Selwyn Mauberley

LIFE AND CONTACTS [5]

I. E. P. Ode Pour L'Election de son Sepulchre [6]

For three years, out of key with his time,
He strove to resuscitate the dead art
Of poetry; to maintain "the sublime"
In the old sense. Wrong from the start—

6. *Rihaku* is the transcription from the Japanese of the name of one of the greatest of the Chinese poets of the T'ang Dynasty, Li Po (ca. 700–762).
5. *Hugh Selwyn Mauberley (Life and Contacts)* comprises two sets of poems; the first, reprinted here, consists of thirteen poems; the second consists of five poems, headed "Mauberley/1920." There are many connections not only among the poems in each set, but also between the two sets. The entire volume bore an epigraph from the fourth Eclogue of the 3rd-century Latin poet Nemesianus: *Vocat aestus in umbram* ("The heat urges us into the shade").
6. Cf. Pierre Ronsard (1524–1585), Odes IV, iv, *"De l'élection de son sépulchre"* ["Concerning the choice of his tomb"], in which the poet describes the kind of burial place, and the kind of fame, he would like to have.

5 No, hardly, but seeing he had been born
   In a half savage country, out of date;
   Bent resolutely on wringing lilies from the acorn;
   Capaneus;[7] trout for factitious° bait;   *false; artificial*

   ῎Ιδμεν γάρ τοι πάνθ' ὅσ' ἐνὶ Τροίη [8]
10 Caught in the unstopped ear;
   Giving the rocks small lee-way
   The chopped seas held him, therefore, that year.

   His true Penelope [9] was Flaubert,[1]
   He fished by obstinate isles;
15 Observed the elegance of Circe's [2] hair
   Rather than the mottoes on sundials.

   Unaffected by "the march of events,"
   He passed from men's memory in *l'an trentiesme
   De son eage;* [3] the case presents
20 No adjunct to the Muses' diadem.

                  II
   The age demanded an image
   Of its accelerated grimace,
   Something for the modern stage,
   Not, at any rate, an Attic [4] grace;

5 Not, not certainly, the obscure reveries
   Of the inward gaze;
   Better mendacities
   Than the classics in paraphrase!

   The "age demanded" chiefly a mold in plaster,
10 Made with no loss of time,
   A prose kinema,[5] not, not assuredly, albaster
   Or the "sculpture" of rhyme.

                  III
   The tea-rose tea-gown, etc.
   Supplants the mousseline of Cos,[6]
   The pianola "replaces"
   Sappho's barbitos.[7]

7. In classical mythology, one of the Seven against Thebes, heroes who led an expedition against Thebes in an unsuccessful attempt to get one of their number, Polynices, on the throne. Capaneus, climbing on the walls and defying even Zeus to harm him, was struck by a thunderbolt.
8. Idmen gár toi pánth'hós eni Troíei, from the song sung by the Sirens to lure Odysseus's ship onto the rocks: "For we know everything which [the Greeks and the Trojans have suffered] in Troy [by the will of the Gods]." (Odyssey xii. 184 ff.) Circe had told Odysseus how to avoid the danger: his men must have their ears stopped with wax, after they have bound him hand and foot—he alone hears their song.
9. The faithful wife to whom Odysseus returned after the ten years of adventure that followed the ten-year siege of Troy.
1. French realist novelist (1821–1880), a meticulous craftsman, author of *Madame Bovary, L'Education sentimentale*, etc.
2. An enchantress, living on the island of Aeaea, with whom Odysseus stayed for a year. She turned his men into swine, but he was able to resist her spell with the help of the herb moly, given to him by Hermes.
3. From the part satiric, part elegiac poem *"Le grand testament"* (1461), in which the French poet François Villon (1431–1489?), writing in prison, reviews his life, castigates his enemies, thinks of his friends, etc.: "In the thirtieth year of my age,/When I have drunk down all my shame . . ."
4. Athenian—of simple, pure, classical style.
5. Transliteration of the Greek word for "motion," a root word in the early term for motion pictures, "cinematograph."
6. The muslin worn in ancient times by the women of the Greek island of Cos.
7. The Greek poetess, born on the island of Lesbos c. 612 B.C. *Barbitos* (Greek): lyre.

Christ follows Dionysus,[8]
Phallic and ambrosial
Made way for macerations; [9]
Caliban casts out Ariel.[1]

All things are a flowing,
Sage Heracleitus says; [2]
But a tawdry cheapness
Shall outlast our days.

Even the Christian beauty
Defects—after Samothrace; [3]
We see τὸ καλὸν [4]
Decreed in the market place.

Faun's flesh is not to us,
Nor the saint's vision.
We have the press for wafer;
Franchise for circumcision.

All men, in law, are equals.
Free of Pisistratus,[5]
We choose a knave or an eunuch
To rule over us.

O bright Apollo,
τίν ἄνδρα, τίν ἥρωα, τίνα θεὸν,[6]
What god, man, or hero
Shall I place a tin wreath upon!

IV

These fought in any case,
and some believing,
　　　　　　　　pro domo,[7] in any case . . .

Some quick to arm,
some for adventure,
some from fear of weakness,
some from fear of censure,
some for love of slaughter, in imagination,
learning later . . .
some in fear, learning love of slaughter;

8. The god of an ecstatic, emotional religion among the early Greeks, as well as the god of wine (later Bacchus).
9. Mortifications of the flesh.
1. Two figures from Shakespeare's *The Tempest*, Caliban almost an animal, Ariel totally spiritual.
2. Heraclitus of Ephesus, the early Greek philosopher (fl. c. 500 B.C.), whose central doctrine was that all things are in a state of flux ("everything flows").
3. An Aegean island where was found the masterpiece of Hellenistic sculpture, the Winged Victory (early 2nd century B.C.?), now in the Louvre. That Pound has this feature of Samothrace in mind here is given at least slight support by the fact that the Winged Victory figures in a prose piece by Remy de Gourmont. "*Stratagèmes*," which has a role

in Poem XI of this sequence.
4. Tò kalón (Greek): "The Beautiful."
5. Athenian tyrant (in the sense of absolute ruler, but without later connotations of one who rules cruelly or oppressively), d. 527 B.C. "His long rule weakened the grip of the aristocrats upon their followers, encouraged individualism in many circles, and brought the cultural enlightenment and financial prosperity in which a movement towards democracy became possible" (*Oxford Classical Dictionary*).
6. Part of a line from the second Olympic ode of the Greek poet Pindar (518–438 B.C.), transliterated : tín ándra, tín héroa, tína theòn [keladésimon]: "What man, what hero, what god [shall we celebrate]?"
7. From the Latin phrase *pro domo sua*, "for one's own home."

Died some, pro patria,

             non "dulce" non "et decor" . . .[8]

walked eye-deep in hell

believing in old men's lies, then unbelieving

15 came home, home to a lie,

home to many deceits,

home to old lies and new infamy;

usury age-old and age-thick

and liars in public places.

20 Daring as never before, wastage as never before.

Young blood and high blood,

fair cheeks, and fine bodies;

fortitude as never before

frankness as never before,

25 disillusions as never told in the old days,

hysterias, trench confessions,

laughter out of dead bellies.

V

There died a myriad,

And of the best, among them,

For an old bitch gone in the teeth,

For a botched civilization,

5 Charm, smiling at the good mouth,

Quick eyes gone under earth's lid,

For two gross of broken statues,

For a few thousand battered books.

Yeux Glauques [9]

Gladstone [1] was still respected,

When John Ruskin produced

"King's Treasuries"; [2] Swinburne

And Rossetti still abused.

5 Fetid Buchanan [3] lifted up his voice

When that faun's head of hers

Became a pastime for

Painters and adulterers.

The Burne-Jones cartons [4]

10 Have preserved her eyes;

---

8. The famous line from one of Horace's *Odes* (III.ii.13): *Dulce et decorum est pro patria mori* ("Sweet and fitting it is to die for one's country").
9. French, "sea-green eyes." Pound's poem focuses on the eyes of Elizabeth Siddal, wife of D. G. Rossetti and the model used for many of his paintings as well as for those of other Pre-Raphaelite painters, including Burne-Jones, in whose painting "King Cophetua and the Beggar Maid" (1884; now in the Tate Gallery, London; see stanza 3 below) she appears as the beggar maid (painted from studies made earlier; Elizabeth Siddal died in 1862). William Michael Rossetti described her as "Tall, finely formed, with a lofty neck, and regular yet somewhat uncommon features, greenish-blue unsparkling eyes. . . ."
1. William Ewart Gladstone was Prime Min-

ister for four separate terms between 1868 and 1894.
2. John Ruskin's *Sesame and Lilies*, consisting of two parts ("Sesame: Of Kings' Treasuries" and "Lilies: Of Queens' Gardens") was published in 1865, with a drawing by Burne-Jones on the title page. Its subject was "the treasures hidden in books; . . . the way we find them and the way we lose them," the way we lose them being through a Philistine indifference to art, religion, and moral purpose.
3. Robert W. Buchanan's controversial attack on Swinburne, Morris, and Rossetti, but especially Rossetti, appeared pseudonymously in *The Contemporary Review* for October 1871.
4. For "cartoons," in the sense of preliminary studies from which a finished painting is made.

Still, at the Tate, they teach
Cophetua to rhapsodize;

Thin like brook water,
With a vacant gaze.
The English Rubaiyat was stillborn [5]
In those days.

The thin, clear gaze, the same
Still darts out faunlike from the half-ruined face,
Questing and passive. . . .
"Ah, poor Jenny's case" . . . [6]

Bewildered that a world
Shows no surprise
At her last maquero's [7]
Adulteries.

> "*Siena Mi Fe'; Disfecemi Maremma*"[8]

Among the pickled fetuses and bottled bones,
Engaged in perfecting the catalogue,
I found the last scion of the
Senatorial families of Strasbourg, Monsieur Verog.[9]

For two hours he talked of Gallifet; [1]
Of Dowson; of the Rhymers' Club; [2]
Told me how Johnson (Lionel) died [3]
By falling from a high stool in a pub . . .

But showed no trace of alcohol
At the autopsy, privately performed—
Tissue preserved—the pure mind
Arose toward Newman [4] as the whiskey warmed.

---

5. FitzGerald's translation of *The Rubáiyát of Omar Khayyám* was first published in 1859. It did not sell and was remaindered at a penny a copy outside the publisher's shop, where Swinburne and Rossetti discovered it and bought several copies to give away; returning to buy more, they found that the price had begun to go up.

6. Buchanan's criticism of Rossetti had discussed one poem in particular, "Jenny," claiming that its scene had appealed to the poet less for human tenderness than for its "inherent quality of animalism." The poem presents the thoughts of a young man who has gone with Jenny, a prostitute, to her room after a dance and spends the night with her sleeping head resting on his knee. It has an epigraph from *The Merry Wives of Windsor*: "'Vengence of Jenny's case! Fie on her! Never name her, child!'—Mrs. Quickly." Shakespeare has her continue, ". . . if she be a whore." The Jenny of Rossetti's poem has nothing to do with Elizabeth Siddal, but one phrase describing Jenny—"whose eyes are as blue as the skies"—may be the link, in Pound's poem, between Jenny and the eyes of Rossetti's wife and model.

7. For the French slang term for pimp, "*maquereau.*"

8. "Siena made me; the Maremma undid me." (*Purgatorio,* V. 133.) Words spoken to Dante by the spirit of Pia de' Tolomei, encountered in Purgatory among those who have repented only at the last moment and without absolution. Although innocent, she had been imprisoned by her husband in a fortress in the Maremma, and died there, either by poison or from malaria. The line carries with it the idea of exile from one's native place; the subject of Pound's poem had been born in Alsace.

9. Pound's model for Verog was Victor Gustav Plarr (1863–1929) friend of such Nineties poets as Yeats, Ernest Dowson, and Lionel Johnson, like them a member of the Rhymers' Club. Besides his own poems (*In the Dorian Mood*, 1896) and biographical work arising out of his post as librarian to the Royal College of Surgeons, he published a brief memoir of Ernest Dowson, covering the years of their friendship (1888–1897).

1. Galliffet (1830–1909), a French general who distinguished himself at the head of the *Chasseurs d'Afrique* at the battle of Sedan, in the Franco-Prussian War, 1870.

2. Founded in 1891, it consisted of from 12 to 14 members who met at the Cheshire Cheese in Fleet St., London, for literary discussion.

3. Lionel Johnson (1867–1902) was received into the Church of Rome in 1891 and published his first collection of poems in 1895. He died from an injury sustained by falling in the street.

4. John Henry Cardinal Newman (1801–1890), who joined the Church of Rome in 1845, author of *Apologia pro Vita Sua* (1864–65).

Dowson found harlots cheaper than hotels;
Headlam [5] for uplift; Image [6] impartially imbued
15   With raptures for Bacchus, Terpsichore and the Church.
So spoke the author of "The Dorian Mood,"

M. Verog, out of step with the decade,
Detached from his contemporaries,
Neglected by the young,
20   Because of these reveries.

Brennbaum [7]

The skylike limpid eyes,
The circular infant's face,
The stiffness from spats to collar
Never relaxing into grace;

5   The heavy memories of Horeb, Sinai [8] and the forty
        years,[9]
Showed only when the daylight fell
Level across the face
Of Brennbaum "The Impeccable."

Mr. Nixon [1]

In the cream gilded cabin of his steam yacht
Mr. Nixon advised me kindly, to advance with fewer
Dangers of delay. "Consider
                    Carefully the reviewer.

5   "I was as poor as you are;
"When I began I got, of course,
"Advance on royalties, fifty at first," said Mr. Nixon,
"Follow me, and take a column,
"Even if you have to work free.

10   "Butter reviewers. From fifty to three hundred
"I rose in eighteen months;
"The hardest nut I had to crack
"Was Dr. Dundas.

"I never mentioned a man but with the view
15   "Of selling my own works.
"The tip's a good one, as for literature
"It gives no man a sinecure.

5. Rev. Stewart Headlam (1847–1924), liberal clergyman who was for many years a vicar in the East End of London, writer on social and religious questions; although he scarcely knew Wilde, he had helped post bail for him at the time of his arrest in 1895.
6. Selwyn Image (1849–1930), artist, poet, and clergyman; his work had appeared in such Nineties periodicals as *The Hobby Horse* and *The Savoy*. Bacchus is the Roman god of wine, Terpsichore the Greek muse of the dance.
7. The model for Brennbaum is pretty clearly Max Beerbohm, brilliant satirist in his books (*Zuleika Dobson*, 1911, and *A Christmas Garland*, 1912), but even more widely known for his satiric drawings and caricatures of the literary and political great. He was known as "The Incomparable Max," but Pound, in an essay on Remy de Gourmont, calls him "the impeccable Beerbohm." The Beerbohms were of German descent, however, not Jewish.

8. The young Moses, keeping Jethro's sheep, led them "to the backside of the desert, and came to the mountain of God, even to Horeb," where the angel of the Lord appeared to him out of the burning bush (Exodus iii.1–2). On the top of Mt. Sinai, Moses received the Ten Commandments from God (Exodus xix. 20 ff.).
9. The 40 years spent by the Israelites in the wilderness, after the Exodus from Egypt.
1. This portrait of the calculatingly successful writer is generally thought to refer to Arnold Bennett (1867–1931), the novelist, who did indeed own a yacht. "Dr. Dundas" and the "friend of Bloughram's" are stock figures not susceptible of identification, but in the latter there may be intended a reference to the wily arguments of the bishop, in Browning's "Bishop Blougram's Apology," who lives on the Church whose doctrines he does not entirely believe.

"And no one knows, at sight, a masterpiece.
"And give up verse, my boy,
"There's nothing in it."

. . . .

Likewise a friend of Bloughram's once advised me:
Don't kick against the pricks,
Accept opinion. The "Nineties" tried your game
And died, there's nothing in it.

X

Beneath the sagging roof
The stylist [2] has taken shelter,
Unpaid, uncelebrated,
At last from the world's welter

Nature receives him;
With a placid and uneducated mistress
He exercises his talents
And the soil meets his distress.

The haven from sophistications and contentions
Leaks through its thatch;
He offers succulent cooking;
The door has a creaking latch.

XI

"Conservatrix of Milésien" [3]
Habits of mind and feeling,
Possibly. But in Ealing [4]
With the most bank-clerkly of Englishmen?

No, "Milésian" is an exaggeration.
No instinct has survived in her
Older than those her grandmother
Told her would fit her station.

XII

"Daphne with her thighs in bark
Stretches toward me her leafy hands,"[5]—
Subjectively. In the stuffed-satin drawing room
I await The Lady Valentine's commands,

Knowing my coat has never been
Of precisely the fashion
To stimulate, in her,
A durable passion;

2. In direct contrast with the preceding portrait, this one may be based on Ford Madox Ford (1873–1939), experimental novelist, editor of *The English Review*, and interested in the theory of "The New Novel" as practiced by James and Conrad. The poem depicts his circumstances at one particular period in his life.
3. Pound was fond of a phrase which occurs in a story by Remy de Gourmont, "*Stratagemes*," in *Histoires magiques*. Riffling through his recollections of women he has possessed, the narrator thinks of the role of knowingly induced pain in lovemaking; women who know how to bite, he says, shouldn't be despised, they are *conservatrices de traditions*

milésiennes ("preservers of Milesian traditions")—Milesian from Miletus, ancient Greek city in Asia Minor and the native city of one Aristides (c. 100 B.C.), the writer or collector of a lost group of erotic stories, stories in what has come to be called "the Milesian genre."
4. Staid residential district in West London.
5. The first two lines translate two lines from Gautier's "*Le Château du souvenir*" ("The Castle of Memory"): the speaker is in a salon decorated with the exploits of Apollo. (Daphne, pursued by Apollo, was turned into a laurel to enable her to escape; the tree became sacred to Apollo, its leaves the symbol of literary honor.)

Doubtful, somewhat, of the value
10 Of well-gowned approbation
Of literary effort,
But never of The Lady Valentine's vocation:

Poetry, her border of ideas,
The edge, uncertain, but a means of blending
15 With other strata
Where the lower and higher have ending;

A hook to catch the Lady Jane's attention,
A modulation toward the theatre,
Also, in the case of revolution,
20 A possible friend and comforter.

. . . .

Conduct, on the other hand, the soul
"Which the highest cultures have nourished"
To Fleet St.[6] where
Dr. Johnson[7] flourished;

25 Beside this thoroughfare
The sale of half-hose has
Long since superseded the cultivation
Of Pierian[8] roses.

Envoi (1919)

Go, dumb-born book,
Tell her that sang me once that song of Lawes:[9]
Hadst thou but song
As thou hast subjects known,
5 *Then were there cause in thee that should condone*
Even my faults that heavy upon me lie,
And build her glories their longevity.

Tell her that sheds
Such treasure in the air,
10 *Recking naught else but that her graces give*
Life to the moment,
I would bid them live
As roses might, in magic amber laid,
Red overwrought with orange and all made
15 *One substance and one color*
Braving time.

Tell her that goes
With song upon her lips
But sings not out the song, nor knows
20 *The maker of it, some other mouth,*
May be as fair as hers,
Might, in new ages, gain her worshipers,

6. The center of London journalism.
7. Dr. Samuel Johnson (1709–1784), the great critic after whom the latter half of the 18th century is known as "The Age of Johnson," and who participated in many journalistic enterprises, both as contributor (for example, to *The Gentlemen's Magazine*) and as founder (of *The Rambler*).

8. Pieria was a district on the northern slopes of Mt. Olympus, where the cult of the Muses originated.
9. Henry Lawes (1596–1662), the composer who had set to music "Go, lovely rose," the best known poem of the Cavalier poet Edmund Waller (1606–1687), the phrasing and movement of which are echoed in this poem.

When our two dusts with Waller's shall be laid,
Siftings on siftings in oblivion,
Till change hath broken down
All things save Beauty alone.

1920

The Cantos

I [1]

And then went down to the ship,
Set keel to breakers, forth on the godly sea, and
We set up mast and sail on that swart ship,
Bore sheep aboard her, and our bodies also
Heavy with weeping, and winds from sternward
Bore us out onward with bellying canvas,
Circe's this craft, the trim-coifed goddess.
Then sat we amidships, wind jamming the tiller,
Thus with stretched sail, we went over sea till day's end.
Sun to his slumber, shadows o'er all the ocean,
Came we then to the bounds of deepest water,
To the Kimmerian lands,[2] and peopled cities
Covered with close-webbed mist, unpierced ever
With glitter of sun-rays
Nor with stars stretched, nor looking back from heaven
Swartest night stretched over wretched men there.
The ocean flowing backward, came we then to the place
Aforesaid by Circe.
Here did they rites, Perimedes and Eurylochus,[3]
And drawing sword from my hip
I dug the ell-square pitkin;°   *small trench*
Poured we libations unto each the dead,
First mead and then sweet wine, water mixed with white flour.
Then prayed I many a prayer to the sickly death's-heads;
As set in Ithaca, sterile bulls of the best
For sacrifice, heaping the pyre with goods,
A sheep to Tiresias only, black and a bell-sheep.
Dark blood flowed in the fosse,°   *trench, ditch*
Souls out of Erebus,[4] cadaverous dead, of brides
Of youths and of the old who had borne much;
Souls stained with recent tears, girls tender,
Men many, mauled with bronze lance heads,
Battle spoil, bearing yet dreory [5] arms,
These many crowded about me; with shouting,
Pallor upon me, cried to my men for more beasts;
Slaughtered the herds, sheep slain of bronze;
Poured ointment, cried to the gods,
To Pluto the strong, and praised Proserpine; [6]
Unsheathed the narrow sword,
I sat to keep off the impetuous impotent dead,

1. The First of Pound's *Cantos,* the complex work of epic propo.tions which occupied him for something like fifty years, is taken up, through line 67, with Pound's translation of an episode from Book XI of the *Odyssey,* not directly from the Greek but from the 16th-century Latin translation of Andreas Divus. Book XI describes Odysseus' trip to the under-world, on the advice of Circe, to consult the spirit of Tiresias, the blind Theban prophet, who will give him instructions for the final stages of his return to Ithaca.

2. The Cimmerians were a mythical people living in darkness and mist on the farthest borders of the known world.
3. Two of Odysseus' men, who, like Odysseus in the lines that follow, are perfo:ming the propitiatory rites prescribed by Circe.
4. The underworld.
5. "Dripping with blood" (from old English *dreorig*).
6. Pluto, lord of the underworld, and Proserpine, his queen.

Till I should hear Tiresias.
But first Elpenor [7] came, our friend Elpenor,
Unburied, cast on the wide earth,
Limbs that we left in the house of Circe,

45 Unwept, unwrapped in sepulchre, since toils urged other.
Pitiful spirit. And I cried in hurried speech:
"Elpenor, how art thou come to this dark coast?
"Cam'st thou afoot, outstripping seamen?"
            And he in heavy speech:

50 "Ill fate and abundant wine. I slept in Circe's ingle.
"Going down the long ladder unguarded,
"I fell against the buttress,
"Shattered the nape-nerve, the soul sought Avernus. [8]
"But thou, O King, I bid remember me, unwept, unburied,

55 "Heap up mine arms, be tomb by sea-bord, and inscribed:
"*A man of no fortune, and with a name to come.*
"And set my oar up, that I swung mid fellows."

And Anticlea [9] came, whom I beat off, and then Tiresias Theban,
Holding his golden wand, knew me, and spoke first:

60 "A second time? [1] why? man of ill star,
"Facing the sunless dead and this joyless region?
"Stand from the fosse, [2] leave me my bloody bever [3]
"For soothsay."
            And I stepped back,

65 And he strong with the blood, said then: "Odysseus
"Shalt return through spiteful Neptune, over dark seas,
"Lose all companions." And then Anticlea came.
Lie quiet Divus. I mean, that is Andreas Divus, [4]
In officina Wecheli, 1538, out of Homer.

70 And he sailed, by Sirens and thence outward and away
And unto Circe. [5]
            Venerandam, [6]
In the Cretan's phrase, with the golden crown, Aphrodite,
Cypri munimenta sortita est, mirthful, oricalchi, [7] with golden

75 Girdles and breast bands, thou with dark eyelids
Bearing the golden bough of Argicida. [8] So that: [9]

                                        1921   1930

7. One of Odysseus' men who, in the manner he goes on to describe, had died on the night before they were to leave Circe's island.
8. A lake near Cumae (now near Naples) believed by the ancients to be the entrance to the infernal regions; also a name, as probably here, for the underworld itself.
9. Odysseus' mother, whose appearance is treated at greater length in *The Odyssey*.
1. "A second time" correctly translates Divus' adverb *iterum*, but Homer's adverb has here the sense not of "again" but rather of "here, too," i.e., "Why have you come here, too, in addition to all your other wanderings?" Odysseus had not been in the underworld, or met Tiresias, before.
2. The trench, or small pit, that Odysseus and his men have dug and in which the blood from the sacrifice has collected.
3. Drink, potation (cf. beverage).
4. The 16th-century Italian whose translation of the *Odyssey* had been published "in officina Wecheli," at the printing shop of Chrétien Wechel, Paris, in 1538.
5. After this visit to the underworld, Odysseus had returned to Circe and then, forewarned by her, had successfully sailed past the Sirens.
6. "Worthy of worship," applied to Aphrodite. This, like the Latin words and phrases in the next lines, derives from a Latin translation of two Hymns to Aphrodite (among the so-called Homeric Hymns, dating from the 8th to 6th

century B.C., anciently believed to be by Homer), a translation made by Georgius Dartona Cretensis, contained, Pound tells us, in the volume in which he had found Divus's translation of the *Odyssey*. Of the two Hymns to Aphrodite, the longer, from which Pound takes the reference to Hermes (*Argicida*) in the last line, consists, in Greek, of 293 lines of dactylic hexameter, recounting the union of Aphrodite and Anchises, from which union the Trojan leader Aeneas was to be born. The other is a slight hymn of worship, 21 lines long, which begins with the words that figure, in Latin or in English, in the closing lines of the Canto: "Reverend golden-crowned beautiful Aphrodite/I shall sing, who has received as her lot the citadels of all sea-girt Cyprus. . . ."
7. *Oricalchi:* brass. The Hours, in the shorter poem, have adorned Aphrodite with earrings, flower-formed, of brass and precious gold.
8. An epithet for Hermes, "slayer of Argos" (i.e., of the many-eyed herdsman set to watch Io). Aphrodite, deceiving Anchises at first, says that she is a mortal maiden, that the "slayer of Argos, with wand of gold" has brought her to be Anchises' bride.
9. The Canto ends on the colon, going immediately into Canto II, which begins with the words, "Hang it all, Robert Browning,/ There can be but one 'Sordello.'"

H. D. (Hilda Doolittle)
(1886–1961)

Sea Rose

Rose, harsh rose,
marred and with stint of petals,
meager flower, thin,
sparse of leaf,

more precious
than a wet rose
single on a stem—
you are caught in the drift.

Stunted, with small leaf,
you are flung on the sand,
you are lifted
in the crisp sand
that drives in the wind.

Can the spice-rose
drip such acrid fragrance
hardened in a leaf?

1916

Helen [1]

All Greece hates
the still eyes in the white face,
the luster as of olives
where she stands,
And the white hands.

All Greece reviles
the wan face when she smiles,
hating it deeper still
when it grows wan and white,
remembering past enchantments
and past ills.

Greece sees unmoved,
God's daughter,[2] born of love,
the beauty of cool feet
and slenderest knees,
could love indeed the maid,
only if she were laid,
white ash amid funereal cypresses.

1924

---

1. Helen of Troy, whose abduction by Paris led to the Trojan War and ultimately to the defeat of Troy by Greece.

2. Helen was said to be the daughter of Zeus, ruler of the gods, and Leda, a mortal woman.

Wine Bowl

I will rise
from my troth
with the dead,
I will sweeten my cup
5   and my bread
with a gift;
I will chisel a bowl for the wine,
for the white wine
and red;
10 I will summon a Satyr [3] to dance,
a Centaur,
a Nymph
and a Faun;
I will picture
15 a warrior King,
a Giant,
a Naiad,
a Monster;
I will cut round the rim of the crater,
20 some simple
familiar thing,
vine leaves
or the sea-swallow's wing;
I will work at each separate part
25 till my mind is worn out
and my heart:
in my skull,
where the vision had birth,
will come wine,
30 would pour song
of the hot earth,
of the flower and the sweet
of the hill,
thyme,
35 meadow-plant,
grass-blade and sorrel;
in my skull,
from which vision took flight,
will come wine
40 will pour song
of the cool night,
of the silver and blade of the moon,
of the star,
of the sun's kiss at midnoon;
45 I will challenge the reed-pipe
and stringed lyre,
to sing sweeter,
pipe wilder,
praise louder
50 the fragrance and sweet

3. Here, and in the lines following, figures from classical mythology are evoked. *Nymphs* were minor nature goddesses; those who lived in springs, fountains, rivers and lakes were called *naiads*. In Greek mythology, *satyrs* were woodland spirits in the form of men with the legs of goats and with pointed ears or horns. The Romans identified satyrs with their own woodland spirits, the *fauns. Centaurs* had the faces and chests of men, and the bodies of horses. Satyrs are usually associated with lechery; centaurs, with savagery.

of the wine jar,
till each lover
must summon another,
to proffer a rose
where all flowers are,
in the depths of the exquisite crater;
flower will fall upon flower
till the red shower
inflame all
with intimate fervor;
till:
men who travel afar
will look up,
sensing grape
and hill-slope
in the cup;
men who sleep by the wood
will arise,
hearing ripple and fall
of the tide,
being drawn by the spell of the sea;
the bowl will ensnare and enchant
men who crouch by the hearth
till they want
but the riot of stars in the night;
those who dwell far inland
will seek ships;
the deep-sea fisher,
plying his nets,
will forsake them
for wheat-sheaves and loam;
men who wander
will yearn for their home,
men at home
will depart.

I will rise
from my troth with the dead,
I will sweeten my cup
and my bread
with a gift;
I will chisel a bowl for the wine,
for the white wine
and red.

1931

Hermetic Definition

2. Grove of Academe [4]

(NOVEMBER 1—DECEMBER 24, 1960)

5

Is remembrance chiefly a matter
of twig, leaf, grass, stone?
that is as far as I see,

---

4. The grove near Athens, where the philosopher Plato taught his students (hence the English word *academy*).

but twig, grass, stone,
5   a light silt of sand
are part of Aegina,[5] the island,

and the island is herself, is her;
some say Hygeia [6] is
feeding a serpent from a cup,

10 small, intimate, not so august
as the Athenian Parthenos,
may Athené Hygeia [7] be our near,

personal patroness;
I scrape a small pine cone
15 from the sparse sea-grass

that shows separate salt-spikes
in the dry sand-drift,
I need not turn my head

to assure myself of the sea-ledge,
20 it is indented like a shell;
I know this, since I came here

before everything was over,
and before I realized an intimacy
near as the air.

1972

ROBINSON JEFFERS
(1887–1962)

Shine, Perishing Republic

While this America settles in the mold of its vulgarity, heavily thickening to empire,
And protest, only a bubble in the molten mass, pops and sighs out, and the mass hardens,

I sadly smiling remember that the flower fades to make fruit, the fruit rots to make earth.
Out of the mother; and through the spring exultances, ripeness and decadence; and home to the mother.

5   You making haste haste on decay: not blameworthy; life is good, be it stubbornly long or suddenly
A mortal splendor: meteors are not needed less than mountains: shine, perishing republic.

But for my children, I would have them keep their distance from the thickening center; corruption
Never has been compulsory, when the cities lie at the monster's feet there are left the mountains.

5. Off the southeastern coast of Greece.
6. Ancient Greek goddess of health.
7. The goddess Athena, protector of Athens, in her function as guardian of health. Athene Parthenos, the goddess' enormous statue in the Parthenon, shows her with helmet, shield, and spear, symbolizing her attributes as goddess of war.

And boys, be in nothing so moderate as in love of man, a clever servant,
    insufferable master.
There is the trap that catches noblest spirits, that caught—they say—God,
    when he walked on earth.

1924

Boats in a Fog

Sports and gallantries, the stage, the arts, the antics of dancers,
The exuberant voices of music,
Have charm for children but lack nobility; it is bitter earnestness
That makes beauty; the mind
Knows, grown adult.
        A sudden fog-drift muffled the ocean,
A throbbing of engines moved in it,
At length, a stone's throw out, between the rocks and the vapor,
One by one moved shadows
Out of the mystery, shadows, fishing-boats, trailing each other,
Following the cliff for guidance,
Holding a difficult path between the peril of the sea-fog
And the foam on the shore granite.
One by one, trailing their leader, six crept by me,
Out of the vapor and into it,
The throb of their engines subdued by the fog, patient and cautious,
Coasting all round the peninsula
Back to the buoys in Monterey harbor. A flight of pelicans
Is nothing lovelier to look at;
The flight of the planets is nothing nobler; all the arts lose virtue
Against the essential reality
Of creatures going about their business among the equally
Earnest elements of nature.

1924

To the Stone-Cutters

Stone-cutters fighting time with marble, you foredefeated
Challengers of oblivion
Eat cynical earnings, knowing rock splits, records fall down,
The square-limbed Roman letters
Scale in the thaws, wear in the rain.
    The poet as well
Builds his monument mockingly;
For man will be blotted out, the blithe earth die, the brave sun
Die blind, his heart blackening:
Yet stones have stood for a thousand years, and pained thoughts found
The honey peace in old poems.

1925

Hurt Hawks

1

The broken pillar of the wing jags from the clotted shoulder,
The wing trails like a banner in defeat,
No more to use the sky forever but live with famine
And pain a few days: cat nor coyote
Will shorten the week of waiting for death, there is game without talons.
He stands under the oak-bush and waits

The lame feet of salvation; at night he remembers freedom
And flies in a dream, the dawns ruin it.
He is strong and pain is worse to the strong, incapacity is worse.
10 The curs of the day come and torment him
At distance, no one but death the redeemer will humble that head,
The intrepid readiness, the terrible eyes.
The wild God of the world is sometimes merciful to those
That ask mercy, not often to the arrogant.
15 You do not know him, you communal people, or you have forgotten him;
Intemperate and savage, the hawk remembers him;
Beautiful and wild, the hawks, and men that are dying, remember him.

2

I'd sooner, except the penalties, kill a man than a hawk; but
     the great redtail°   *red-tailed hawk*
Had nothing left but unable misery
20 From the bone too shattered for mending, the wing that trailed under
     his talons when he moved.
We had fed him six weeks, I gave him freedom,
He wandered over the foreland hill and returned in the evening,
     asking for death,
Not like a beggar, still eyed with the old
Implacable arrogance. I gave him the lead gift in the twilight. What
     fell was relaxed,
25 Owl-downy, soft feminine feathers; but what
Soared: the fierce rush: the night-herons by the flooded river cried
     fear at its rising
Before it was quite unsheathed from reality.

                                                                    1928

November Surf

Some lucky day each November great waves awake and are drawn
Like smoking mountains bright from the west
And come and cover the cliff with white violent cleanness: then suddenly
The old granite forgets half a year's filth:
5 The orange-peel, eggshells, papers, pieces of clothing, the clots
Of dung in corners of the rock, and used
Sheaths that make light love safe in the evenings: all the droppings of
     the summer
Idlers washed off in a winter ecstasy:
I think this cumbered continent envies its cliff then. . . . But all seasons
10 The earth, in her childlike prophetic sleep,
Keeps dreaming of the bath of a storm that prepares up the long coast
Of the future to scour more than her sea-lines:
The cities gone down, the people fewer and the hawks more numerous,
The rivers mouth to source pure; when the two-footed
15 Mammal, being someways one of the nobler animals, regains
The dignity of room, the value of rareness.

                                                                    1932

The Purse-Seine

Our sardine fishermen work at night in the dark of the moon;
     daylight or moonlight
They could not tell where to spread the net, unable to see the
     phosphorescence of the shoals° of fish.   *schools*

They work northward from Monterey, coasting Santa Cruz; off New
  Year's Point or off Pigeon Point[8]
The look-out man will see some lakes of milk-color light on the sea's
  night-purple; he points, and the helmsman
Turns the dark prow, the motorboat circles the gleaming shoal and
  drifts out her seine-net. They close the circle
And purse the bottom of the net, then with great labor haul it in.

                                        I cannot tell you
How beautiful the scene is, and a little terrible, then, when the
  crowded fish
Know they are caught, and wildly beat from one wall to the other
  of their closing destiny the phosphorescent
Water to a pool of flame, each beautiful slender body sheeted with
  flame, like a live rocket
A comet's tail wake of clear yellow flame; while outside the
  narrowing
Floats and cordage of the net great sea-lions come up to watch,
  sighing in the dark; the vast walls of night
Stand erect to the stars.

                    Lately I was looking from a night mountain-top
On a wide city, the colored splendor, galaxies of light: how could I
  help but recall the seine-net
Gathering the luminous fish? I cannot tell you how beautiful the
  city appeared, and a little terrible.
I thought, We have geared the machines and locked all together into
  interdependence; we have built the great cities; now
There is no escape. We have gathered vast populations incapable of
  free survival, insulated
From the strong earth, each person in himself helpless, on all
  dependent. The circle is closed, and the net
Is being hauled in. They hardly feel the cords drawing, yet they
  shine already. The inevitable mass-disasters
Will not come in our time nor in our children's, but we and our
  children
Must watch the net draw narrower, government take all powers—or
  revolution, and the new government
Take more than all, add to kept bodies kept souls—or anarchy, the
  mass-disasters.

                    These things are Progress;
Do you marvel our verse is troubled or frowning, while it keeps its
  reason? Or it lets go, lets the mood flow
In the manner of the recent young men into mere hysteria, splintered
  gleams, crackled laughter. But they are quite wrong.
There is no reason for amazement: surely one always knew that
  cultures decay, and life's end is death.

                                                    1937

---

8. Monterey, Santa Cruz, New Year's Point, and Pigeon Point are all places in the Monterey
Bay area of California.

MARIANNE MOORE
(1887–1972)

Poetry

I, too, dislike it: there are things that are important beyond all this fiddle.
　　Reading it, however, with a perfect contempt for it, one discovers in
　　it after all, a place for the genuine.
　　　　Hands that can grasp, eyes
5　　　　that can dilate, hair that can rise
　　　　　　if it must, these things are important not because a

high-sounding interpretation can be put upon them but because they are
　　useful. When they become so derivative as to become unintelligible,
　　the same thing may be said for all of us, that we
10　　　do not admire what
　　　　we cannot understand: the bat
　　　　　　holding on upside down or in quest of something to

eat, elephants pushing, a wild horse taking a roll, a tireless wolf under
　　a tree, the immovable critic twitching his skin like a horse that feels
　　　　a flea, the base-
15　　ball fan, the statistician—
　　　　nor is it valid
　　　　　　to discriminate against "business documents and

school-books"; [1] all these phenomena are important. One must make a
　　　　distinction
　　however: when dragged into prominence by half poets, the result is
　　　　not poetry,
20　　nor till the poets among us can be
　　　　"literalists of
　　　　the imagination" [2]—above
　　　　　　insolence and triviality and can present

for inspection, "imaginary gardens with real toads in them," shall we have
25　　it. In the meantime, if you demand on the one hand,
　　　　the raw material of poetry in
　　　　　all its rawness and
　　　　that which is on the other hand
　　　　　　genuine, you are interested in poetry.

　　　　　　　　　　　　　　　　　　　　　　　　　　　　　　1921

No Swan So Fine

"No water so still as the
　　dead fountains of Versailles."[1] No swan,
with swart blind look askance

---

1. *"Diary of Tolstoy* (Dutton), p. 84. 'Where
the boundary between prose and poetry lies,
I shall never be able to understand. The ques-
tion is raised in manuals of style, yet the
answer to it lies beyond me. Poetry is verse:
prose is not verse. Or else poetry is every-
thing with the exception of business docu-
ments and school books'" [Moore's note].
2. "Yeats: *Ideas of Good and Evil* (A. H.
Bullen), p. 182. 'The limitation of [Blake's]

view was from the very intensity of his vision;
he was a too literal realist of imagination, as
others are of nature; and because he believed
that the figures seen by the mind's eye, when
exalted by inspiration, were "eternal ex-
istences," symbols of divine essences, he hated
every grace of style that might obscure their
lineaments'" [Moore's note].
1. Famed palace of French kings in the late
17th and early 18th centuries, now a museum.

and gondoliering legs,[2] so fine
    as the chintz china one with fawn-
brown eyes and toothed gold
collar on to show whose bird it was.

Lodged in the Louis Fifteenth
    candelabrum-tree[3] of cockscomb-
tinted buttons, dahlias,
sea-urchins, and everlastings,[4]
    it perches on the branching foam
of polished sculptured
flowers—at ease and tall. The king is dead.

1932, 1951

The Steeple-Jack

(REVISED, 1961)

Dürer[5] would have seen a reason for living
    in a town like this, with eight stranded whales
to look at; with the sweet air coming into your house
on a fine day, from water etched
    with waves as formal as the scales
on a fish.

One by one in two's and three's, the seagulls keep
    flying back and forth over the town clock,
or sailing around the lighthouse without moving their wings—
rising steadily with a slight
    quiver of the body—or flock
mewing where

a sea the purple of the peacock's neck is
    paled to greenish azure as Dürer changed
the pine green of the Tyrol[6] to peacock blue and guinea
gray.[7] You can see a twenty-five-
    pound lobster; and fishnets arranged
to dry. The

whirlwind fife-and-drum of the storm bends the salt
    marsh grass, disturbs stars in the sky and the
star on the steeple; it is a privilege to see so
much confusion. Disguised by what
    might seem the opposite, the sea-
side flowers and

trees are favored by the fog so that you have
    the tropics at first hand: the trumpet-vine,

---

2. Italian gondoliers paddle from the stern to propel their gondolas.
3. "A pair of Louis XV candelabra with Dresden figures of swans belonging to Lord Balfour" [Moore's note].
4. Plants whose flowers may be dried without losing their form or color; also, the flowers from such plants.

5. Albrecht Dürer (1471–1528), great German Renaissance painter and engraver particularly gifted in rendering closely and meticulously observed detail.
6. The mountainous western area of Austria.
7. The slate-gray, speckled with white, of the guinea fowl.

fox-glove, giant snap-dragon, a salpiglossis that has
    spots and stripes; morning-glories, gourds,
        or moon-vines trained on fishing-twine
30   at the back

door; cat-tails, flags, blueberries and spiderwort,
    stripped grass, lichens, sunflowers, asters, daisies—
yellow and crab-claw ragged sailors with green bracts[8]—toad-plant,
petunias, ferns; pink lilies, blue
35   ones, tigers; poppies; black sweet-peas.
The climate

is not right for the banyan, frangipani, or
    jack-fruit trees;[9] or an exotic serpent
life. Ring lizard and snake-skin for the foot, if you see fit;
40   but here they've cats, not cobras, to
        keep down the rats. The diffident
little newt[1]

with white pin-dots on black horizontal spaced
    out bands lives here; yet there is nothing that
45   ambition can buy or take away. The college student
named Ambrose sits on the hillside
    with his not-native books and hat
and sees boats

at sea progress white and rigid as if in
50   a groove. Liking an elegance of which
the source is not bravado, he knows by heart the antique
sugar-bowl shaped summer-house of
    interlacing slats, and the pitch
of the church

55 spire, not true, from which a man in scarlet lets
    down a rope as a spider spins a thread;
he might be part of a novel, but on the sidewalk a
sign says C. J. Poole, Steeple Jack,
    in black and white; and one in red
60   and white says

Danger. The church portico has four fluted
    columns, each a single piece of stone, made
modester by white-wash. This would be a fit haven for
waifs, children, animals, prisoners,
65   and presidents who have repaid
sin-driven

senators by not thinking about them. The
    place has a school-house, a post-office in a
store, fish-houses, hen-houses, a three-masted
70   schooner on
the stocks. The hero, the student,
    the steeple-jack, each in his way,
is at home.

8. Flower-like leaves on some plants (for instance, flowering dogwood).
9. The banyan is an East Indian tree some of whose branches send out trunks that grow downward, making "props" for the further growth of the branches; frangipani is a tropical American shrub (red jasmine is a species); the jack-fruit is a large East Indian tree with large edible fruit.
1. Small lizard-like animal.

It could not be dangerous to be living
    in a town like this, of simple people,
who have a steeple-jack placing danger-signs by the church
while he is gilding the solid-
    pointed star, which on a steeple
stands for hope.

1935

Peter

    Strong and slippery,
built for the midnight grass-party
confronted by four cats, he sleeps his time away—
the detached first claw on the foreleg corresponding
to the thumb, retracted to its tip; the small tuft of fronds
or katydid-legs above each eye numbering all units
in each group; the shadbones[2] regularly set about the mouth
to droop or rise in unison like porcupine-quills.
He lets himself be flattened out by gravity,
as seaweed is tamed and weakened by the sun,
compelled when extended, to lie stationary.
Sleep is the result of his delusion that one must
do as well as one can for oneself,
sleep—epitome of what is to him the end of life.
Demonstrate on him how the lady placed a forked stick
on the innocuous neck-sides of the dangerous southern snake.
One need not try to stir him up; his prune-shaped head
and alligator-eyes are not party to the joke.
Lifted and handled, he may be dangled like an eel
or set up on the forearm like a mouse;
his eyes bisected by pupils of a pin's width,
are flickeringly exhibited, then covered up.
May be? I should have said might have been;
when he has been got the better of in a dream—
as in a fight with nature or with cats, we all know it.
Profound sleep is not with him a fixed illusion.
Springing about with froglike accuracy, with jerky cries
when taken in hand, he is himself again;
to sit caged by the rungs of a domestic chair
would be unprofitable—human. What is the good of hypocrisy?
it is permissible to choose one's employment,
to abandon the nail, or roly-poly,
when it shows signs of being no longer a pleasure,
to score the nearby magazine with a double line of strokes.
He can talk but insolently says nothing. What of it?
When one is frank, one's very presence is a compliment.
It is clear that he can see the virtue of naturalness,
that he does not regard the published fact as a surrender.
As for the disposition invariably to affront,
an animal with claws should have an opportunity to use them.
The eel-like extension of trunk into tail is not an accident.
To leap, to lengthen out, divide the air, to purloin, to pursue.
To tell the hen: fly over the fence, go in the wrong way
in your perturbation—this is life;
to do less would be nothing but dishonesty.

1935

2. Long, very fine bones of the shad fish.

EDWIN MUIR
(1887–1959)

Childhood

Long time he lay upon the sunny hill,
   To his father's house below securely bound.
Far off the silent, changing sound was still,
   With the black islands lying thick around.

5 He saw each separate height, each vaguer hue,
   Where the massed islands rolled in mist away,
And though all ran together in his view
   He knew that unseen straits between them lay.

Often he wondered what new shores were there.
10 In thought he saw the still light on the sand,
The shallow water clear in tranquil air,
   And walked through it in joy from strand to strand.

Over the sound a ship so slow would pass
   That in the black hill's gloom it seemed to lie.
15 The evening sound was smooth like sunken glass,
   And time seemed finished ere the ship passed by.

Gray tiny rocks slept round him where he lay,
   Moveless as they, more still as evening came,
The grasses threw straight shadows far away,
20 And from the house his mother called his name.

                                1925

The Return of the Greeks

The veteran Greeks came home
Sleepwandering from the war.
We saw the galleys come
Blundering over the bar.
5 Each soldier with his scar
In rags and tatters came home.

Reading the wall of Troy [1]
Ten years without a change
Was such intense employ
10 (Just out of the arrows' range),
All the world was strange
After ten years of Troy.

Their eyes knew every stone
In the huge heartbreaking wall
15 Year after year grown
Till there was nothing at all
But an alley steep and small,
Tramped earth and towering stone.

1. The ancient city on the Asiatic shore of   ten years, as described in the *Iliad* of Homer.
the Hellespont, besieged by the Greeks for

Now even the hills seemed low
In the boundless sea and land,
Weakened by distance so.
How could they understand
Space empty on every hand
And the hillocks squat and low?

And when they arrived at last
They found a childish scene
Embosomed in the past,
And the war lying between—
A child's preoccupied scene
When they came home at last.

But everything trite and strange,
The peace, the parceled ground,
The vinerows—never a change!
The past and the present bound
In one oblivious round
Past thinking trite and strange.

But for their gray-haired wives
And their sons grown shy and tall
They would have given their lives
To raise the battered wall
Again, if this was all
In spite of their sons and wives.

Penelope in her tower
Looked down upon the show
And saw within an hour
Each man to his wife go,
Hesitant, sure and slow:
She, alone in her tower.[2]

1946

The Animals

They do not live in the world,
Are not in time and space.
From birth to death hurled
No word do they have, not one
To plant a foot upon,
Were never in any place.

For with names the world was called
Out of the empty air,[3]
With names was built and walled,
Line and circle and square,
Dust and emerald;
Snatched from deceiving death
By the articulate breath.

---

2. Odysseus, Penelope's husband, and one of the Greek leaders in the 10-year Trojan war, was delayed on his return to his native Ithaca by the wanderings, adventures, and mishaps that are described in the *Odyssey*—they took another 10 years.

3. Genesis i.5, i.8, and i.10 illustrate the naming of the elements of the world as they were created ("And God called the light Day, and the darkness he called Night. . . . And God called the firmament Heaven. . . . And God called the dry land Earth. . . .")

But these have never trod
15 Twice the familiar track,
Never never turned back
Into the memoried day.
All is new and near
In the unchanging Here
20 Of the fifth great day of God,[4]
That shall remain the same,
Never shall pass away.

On the sixth day we came.

1952

The Horses

Barely a twelvemonth after
The seven days war that put the world to sleep,
Late in the evening the strange horses came.
By then we had made our covenant with silence,
5 But in the first few days it was so still
We listened to our breathing and were afraid.
On the second day
The radios failed; we turned the knobs; no answer.
On the third day a warship passed us, heading north,
10 Dead bodies piled on the deck. On the sixth day
A plane plunged over us into the sea. Thereafter
Nothing. The radios dumb;
And still they stand in corners of our kitchens,
And stand, perhaps, turned on, in a million rooms
15 All over the world. But now if they should speak,
If on a sudden they should speak again,
If on the stroke of noon a voice should speak,
We would not listen, we would not let it bring
That old bad world that swallowed its children quick°   *aliv*
20 At one great gulp. We would not have it again.
Sometimes we think of the nations lying asleep,
Curled blindly in impenetrable sorrow,
And then the thought confounds us with its strangeness.
The tractors lie about our fields; at evening
25 They look like dank sea-monsters couched and waiting.
We leave them where they are and let them rust:
"They'll molder away and be like other loam."
We make our oxen drag our rusty plows,
Long laid aside. We have gone back
Far past our fathers' land.
30   And then, that evening
Late in the summer the strange horses came.
We heard a distant tapping on the road,
A deepening drumming; it stopped, went on again
And at the corner changed to hollow thunder.
35 We saw the heads
Like a wild wave charging and were afraid.
We had sold our horses in our fathers' time
To buy new tractors. Now they were strange to us
As fabulous steeds set on an ancient shield

4. Genesis i.20–25 describes the creation of the fish of the sea, the fowls of the air, and
the beasts of the earth on the fifth day.

Or illustrations in a book of knights.
We did not dare go near them. Yet they waited,
Stubborn and shy, as if they had been sent
By an old command to find our whereabouts
And that long-lost archaic companionship.
In the first moment we had never a thought
That they were creatures to be owned and used.
Among them were some half a dozen colts
Dropped in some wilderness of the broken world,
Yet new as if they had come from their own Eden.
Since then they have pulled our plows and borne our loads,
But that free servitude still can pierce our hearts.
Our life is changed; their coming our beginning.

1952

The Desolations[6]

The desolations are not the sorrows' kin.
Sorrow is gentle and sings her sons to rest.
The desolations have no word nor music,
Only an endless inarticulate cry
Inaudible to the poetry-pampered ear.
The desolations tell
Nothing for ever, the interminable
Civil war of earth and water and fire.
Those have to do with our making.
                              What guards us here
Among the established and familiar things?
The leaf, the apple and the rounded earth
Where even imagination is an O,
And only endless harvest is gathered there,
Nothing but that. Yet sometimes absently
We pause and murmur "We came crying hither,"
Remembering, and set up a little stage
For our indigenous formal tragedy
Where we are all the actors.
                              The wild earth
Pours its hot entrails on the slopes of Aetna,
Blasting whatever's made. Yet in a while
Black house-rows like a pleasant street in Hell
Rise from the frozen slag, and safe within
The lava rooms Sicilian families
Follow their ancient ways; the vine-rows yield
Seven times a year, fed on earth's dearest dust.
And all forget the admonition of fire.
There, if you listen, you may hear them say,
"Love is at home, earth's joys lie all around us,
The vine-stock and the rose are guarded well.
The roof-tree holds, and friends come in the evening."
What saves us from the raging desolations
And tells us we shall walk through peace to peace?

1960

6. In *Belonging: A Memoir* (1968) Muir's wife, Willa Muir, describing their visit to Sicily in 1949 or 1950, says, "Edwin, who loved islands because of Orkney [he was born, and spent his boyhood, on one of the Orkney Islands, off the coast of Scotland] wrote a poem about Sicily ('The Island') that conjured up an entirely romantic image. But in a later poem ('The Desolations') he re-membered our unforgettable ascent of Etna, with the town of Catania at its foot, where the houses were trimmed with black lava 'like a pleasant street in hell' and the soil was pure black slag, growing seven crops a year." Etna is an active volcano that rises above the city of Catania, on the east coast of Sicily; despite the recurrent danger of eruption, its slopes are inhabited and cultivated.

The Brothers [8]

Last night I watched my brothers play,
The gentle and the reckless one,
In a field two yards away.
For half a century they were gone
5 Beyond the other side of care
To be among the peaceful dead.
Even in a dream how could I dare
Interrogate that happiness
So wildly spent yet never less?
10 For still they raced about the green
And were like two revolving suns;
A brightness poured from head to head,
So strong I could not see their eyes
Or look into their paradise.
15 What were they doing, the happy ones?
Yet where I was they once had been.

I thought, How could I be so dull,
Twenty thousand days ago,
Not to see they were beautiful?
20 I asked them, Were you really so
As you are now, that other day?
And the dream was soon away.

For then we played for victory
And not to make each other glad.
25 A darkness covered every head,
Frowns twisted the original face,
And through that mask we could not see
The beauty and the buried grace.

I have observed in foolish awe
30 The dateless mid-days of the law
And seen indifferent justice done
By everyone on everyone.
And in a vision I have seen
My brothers playing on the green.

1956   1960

8. Two of Muir's three brothers had died before he himself was 18, and what he says of them here, in a poem completed toward the end of his own life, and which records a dream-vision of his brothers during their life together in Orkney, shares in what he has to say in his *Autobiography* (1954) about the sources of his poetry: "I must have been influenced by something, since we all are, but when I try to find out what it was that influenced me, I can only think of the years of childhood which I spent on my father's farm in the little island of Wyre in Orkney, and the beauty I apprehended then, before I knew there was beauty. These years had come alive, after being forgotten for so long, and when I wrote about horses they were my father's plow-horses as I saw them when I was four or five: and a poem on Achilles pursuing Hector round the walls of Troy was really a resuscitation of the afternoon when I ran away, in real terror, from another boy as I returned from school."

EDITH SITWELL

(1887–1964)

From Façade [1]

21. Polka [2]

"Tra la la la la la la la
La
La!
      See me dance the polka,"
Said Mr. Wagg like a bear,
"With my top hat
And my whiskers that—
(Tra la la la) trap the Fair.

Where the waves seem chiming haycocks
I dance the polka; there
Stand Venus' children in their gay frocks—
Maroon and marine—and stare

To see me fire my pistol
Through the distance blue as my coat;
Like Wellington, Byron, the Marquis of Bristol,
Buzbied [3] great trees float.

While the wheezing hurdy-gurdy
Of the marine wind blows me
To the tune of Annie Rooney, sturdy,
Over the sheafs of sea;

And bright as a seedsman's packet
With zinnias, candytufts chill,
Is Mrs. Marigold's jacket
As she gapes at the inn door still,

Where at dawn in the box of the sailor,
Blue as the decks of the sea,
Nelson awoke, crowded like the cocks,
Then back to dust sank he.

And Robinson Crusoe
Rues so

The bright and foxy beer—
But he finds fresh isles in a Negress' smiles—
The poxy doxy dear,

---

1. These poems are part of an experiment in closely matching words to rhythms of popular music. The verses are metronomically accented and richly allusive, though often the allusions have no verifiable significance.

2. Mr. Wagg's lines are a fanciful mixture of allusion to once popular heroes such as Lord Nelson and the Duke of Wellington and to characters out of storybooks.
3. As if wearing busbies—tall fur hats.

As they watch me dance the polka,"
35 Said Mr. Wagg like a bear,
"In my top hat and my whiskers that—
Tra la la la, trap the Fair.

Tra la la la la—
Tra la la la la—
40 Tra la la la la la la la la
        La
        La
        La!"

                       1922

24. Waltz [4]

"Daisy and Lily,
Lazy and silly,
Walk by the shore of the wan grassy sea—
Talking once more 'neath a swan-bosomed tree.
5 Rose castles,
Tourelles,°   *turrets*
Those bustles
Where swells
Each foam-bell of ermine,
10 They roam and determine
What fashions have been and what fashions will be—
What tartan leaves born,
What crinolines° worn.   *stiff petticoats*
By Queen Thetis,
15 Pelisses°   *cloaks*
Of tarlatine blue,
Like the thin plaided leaves that the castle crags grew;
Or velours d'Afrande:
On the water-gods' land
20 Her hair seemed gold trees on the honey cell sand
When the thickest gold spangles, on deep water seen,
Were like twanging guitar and like cold mandoline,
And the nymphs of great caves,
With hair like gold waves
25 Of Venus, wore tarlatine.
Louise and Charlottine
(Boreas' daughters)
And the nymphs of deep waters,
The nymph Taglioni, Grisi the ondine,
30 Wear plaided Victoria and thin Clementine
Like the crinolined waterfalls;
Wood-nymphs wear bonnets, shawls;
Elegant parasols
Floating were seen.
35 The Amazons wear balzarine of jonquille
Beside the blond lace of a deep-falling rill;
Through glades like a nun
They run from and shun

4. The topic of the conversation in this poem is elegant, bygone Victorian fashions. Passing allusions are to numerous kinds of cloth and clothing, merging with recollections of the 19th-century singer Giulia Grisi and dancer Maria Taglioni, as well as of unidentifiable figures such as Clementine and Isabelle, whose names also denote exotic fabrics. Also mentioned are Venus, the sea-nymph Thetis, and Boreas, the north wind.

The enormous and gold-rayed rustling sun;
And the nymphs of the fountains
Descend from the mountains
Like elegant willows
On their deep barouche° pillows,   *open carriage*
In cashmere Alvandar, barège Isabelle,
Like bells of bright water from clearest wood-well.
Our élégantes favoring bonnets of blond,
The stars in their apiaries,
Sylphs in their aviaries,
Seeing them, spangle these, and the sylphs fond,
From their aviaries fanned
With each long fluid hand
The manteaux espagnoles,
Mimic the waterfalls
Over the long and the light summer land.

.   .   .   .   .

So Daisy and Lily,
Lazy and silly,
Walk by the shore of the wan grassy sea,
Talking once more 'neath a swan-bosomed tree.
Rose castles,
Tourelles,
Those bustles!
Mourelles°   *sweet mushrooms*
Of the shade in their train follow.
Ladies, how vain—hollow—
Gone is the sweet swallow—
Gone, Philomel!"°   *nightingale*
                                                                   1922

T. S. ELIOT
(1888–1965)

The Love Song of J. Alfred Prufrock

> *S'io credesse che mia risposta fosse*
> *A persona che mai tornasse al mondo,*
> *Questa fiamma staria senza piu scosse.*
> *Ma perciocche giammai di questo fondo*
> *Non torno vivo alcun, s'i'odo il vero,*
> *Senza tema d'infamia ti rispondo.*[1]

Let us go then, you and I,
When the evening is spread out against the sky
Like a patient etherized upon a table;
Let us go, through certain half-deserted streets,
The muttering retreats
Of restless nights in one-night cheap hotels
And sawdust restaurants with oyster-shells:

1. Dante, *Inferno*, XXVII.61–66. These words are spoken by Guido da Montefeltro, whom Dante and Virgil have encountered in the Eighth Chasm, that of the False Counselors, where each spirit is concealed within a flame which moves as the spirit speaks: "If I thought my answer were given/to anyone who would ever return to the world,/this flame would stand still without moving any further./ But since never from this abyss/has anyone ever returned alive, if what I hear is true,/ without fear of infamy I answer thee."

Streets that follow like a tedious argument
Of insidious intent
10 To lead you to an overwhelming question. . . .
Oh, do not ask, "What is it?"
Let us go and make our visit.

In the room the women come and go
Talking of Michelangelo.

15 The yellow fog that rubs its back upon the window-panes
The yellow smoke that rubs its muzzle on the window-panes
Licked its tongue into the corners of the evening,
Lingered upon the pools that stand in drains,
Let fall upon its back the soot that falls from chimneys,
20 Slipped by the terrace, made a sudden leap,
And seeing that it was a soft October night,
Curled once about the house, and fell asleep.

And indeed there will be time
For the yellow smoke that slides along the street,
25 Rubbing its back upon the window-panes;
There will be time, there will be time
To prepare a face to meet the faces that you meet;
There will be time to murder and create,
And time for all the works and days[2] of hands
30 That lift and drop a question on your plate;
Time for you and time for me,
And time yet for a hundred indecisions,
And for a hundred visions and revisions,
Before the taking of a toast and tea.

35 In the room the women come and go
Talking of Michelangelo.

And indeed there will be time
To wonder, "Do I dare?" and, "Do I dare?"
Time to turn back and descend the stair,
40 With a bald spot in the middle of my hair—
[They will say: "How his hair is growing thin!"]
My morning coat, my collar mounting firmly to the chin,
My necktie rich and modest, but asserted by a simple pin—
[They will say: "But how his arms and legs are thin!"]
45 Do I dare
Disturb the universe?
In a minute there is time
For decisions and revisions which a minute will reverse.

For I have known them all already, known them all:
50 Have known the evenings, mornings, afternoons,
I have measured out my life with coffee spoons;
I know the voices dying with a dying fall
Beneath the music from a farther room.
    So how should I presume?

55 And I have known the eyes already, known them all—
The eyes that fix you in a formulated phrase,

---

2. Possibly alludes to the title of a didactic work on the seasonal pursuits of country life,
Works and Days, by the Greek poet Hesiod (eighth century B.C.).

And when I am formulated, sprawling on a pin,
When I am pinned and wriggling on the wall,
Then how should I begin
To spit out all the butt-ends of my days and ways?
    And how should I presume?

And I have known the arms already, known them all—
Arms that are braceleted and white and bare
[But in the lamplight, downed with light brown hair!]
Is it perfume from a dress
That makes me so digress?
Arms that lie along a table, or wrap about a shawl.
    And should I then presume?
    And how should I begin?

                                    . . . . .

Shall I say, I have gone at dusk through narrow streets
And watched the smoke that rises from the pipes
Of lonely men in shirt-sleeves, leaning out of windows? . . .

I should have been a pair of ragged claws
Scuttling across the floors of silent seas.

                                    . . . . . .

And the afternoon, the evening, sleeps so peacefully!
Smoothed by long fingers,
Asleep . . . tired . . . or it malingers,
Stretched on the floor, here beside you and me.
Should I, after tea and cakes and ices, .
Have the strength to force the moment to its crisis?
But though I have wept and fasted, wept and prayed,
Though I have seen my head [grown slightly bald] brought in upon a
    platter,[3]
I am no prophet—and here's no great matter;
I have seen the moment of my greatness flicker,
And I have seen the eternal Footman hold my coat, and snicker,
And in short, I was afraid.

And would it have been worth it, after all,
After the cups, the marmalade, the tea,
Among the porcelain, among some talk of you and me,
Would it have been worth while,
To have bitten off the matter with a smile,
To have squeezed the universe into a ball
To roll it toward some overwhelming question,
To say: "I am Lazarus,[4] come from the dead,
Come back to tell you all, I shall tell you all"—
If one, settling a pillow by her head,
    Should say: "That is not what I meant at all.
    That is not it, at all."

And would it have been worth it, after all,
Would it have been worth while,
After the sunsets and the dooryards and the sprinkled streets,
After the novels, after the teacups, after the skirts that trail along the floor—
And this, and so much more?—

3. See the story of the martyrdom of St. John   of the tetrarch Herod.
the Baptist (Matthew xiv.1–12), whose head   4. See John xi, and xii 1–2.
was presented to Salome on a plate at the order

It is impossible to say just what I mean!
105 But as if a magic lantern threw the nerves in patterns on a screen:
Would it have been worth while
If one, settling a pillow or throwing off a shawl,
And turning toward the window, should say:
    "That is not it at all,
110   That is not what I meant, at all."
                                . . . . .

No! I am not Prince Hamlet, nor was meant to be;
Am an attendant lord, one that will do
To swell a progress,[5] start a scene or two,
Advise the prince; no doubt, an easy tool,
115 Deferential, glad to be of use,
Politic, cautious, and meticulous;
Full of high sentence,° but a bit obtuse;   *sententiousness*
At times, indeed, almost ridiculous—
Almost, at times, the Fool.

120 I grow old . . . I grow old . . .
I shall wear the bottoms of my trousers rolled.

Shall I part my hair behind? Do I dare to eat a peach?
I shall wear white flannel trousers, and walk upon the beach.
I have heard the mermaids singing, each to each.

125 I do not think that they will sing to me.

I have seen them riding seaward on the waves
Combing the white hair of the waves blown back
When the wind blows the water white and black.

We have lingered in the chambers of the sea
130 By sea-girls wreathed with seaweed red and brown
Till human voices wake us, and we drown.

                                                1917

Preludes

1
The winter evening settles down
With smell of steaks in passageways.
Six o'clock.
The burnt-out ends of smoky days.
5 And now a gusty shower wraps
The grimy scraps
Of withered leaves about your feet
And newspapers from vacant lots;
The showers beat
10 On broken blinds and chimney-pots,
And at the corner of the street
A lonely cab-horse steams and stamps.
And then the lighting of the lamps.

2
The morning comes to consciousness
15 Of faint stale smells of beer

5. In Elizabethan sense: state journey.

From the sawdust-trampled street
With all its muddy feet that press
To early coffee-stands.
With the other masquerades
That time resumes,
One thinks of all the hands
That are raising dingy shades
In a thousand furnished rooms.

3

You tossed a blanket from the bed,
You lay upon your back, and waited;
You dozed, and watched the night revealing
The thousand sordid images
Of which your soul was constituted;
They flickered against the ceiling.
And when all the world came back
And the light crept up between the shutters
And you heard the sparrows in the gutters,
You had such a vision of the street
As the street hardly understands;
Sitting along the bed's edge, where
You curled the papers from your hair,
Or clasped the yellow soles of feet
In the palms of both soiled hands.

4

His soul stretched tight across the skies
That fade behind a city block,
Or trampled by insistent feet
At four and five and six o'clock;
And short square fingers stuffing pipes,
And evening newspapers, and eyes
Assured of certain certainties,
The conscience of a blackened street
Impatient to assume the world.

I am moved by fancies that are curled
Around these images, and cling:
The notion of some infinitely gentle
Infinitely suffering thing.

Wipe your hand across your mouth, and laugh;
The worlds revolve like ancient women
Gathering fuel in vacant lots.

1917

Whispers of Immortality

Webster [6] was much possessed by death
And saw the skull beneath the skin;
And breastless creatures under ground
Leaned backward with a lipless grin.

Daffodil bulbs instead of balls
Stared from the sockets of the eyes!
He knew that thought clings round dead limbs
Tightening its lusts and luxuries.

6. John Webster, the Jacobean dramatist, author especially of *The White Devil* (1612) and *The Duchess of Malfi* (1623).

Donne,[7] I suppose, was such another
10 Who found no substitute for sense;
To seize and clutch and penetrate,
Expert beyond experience,

He knew the anguish of the marrow
The ague of the skeleton;
15 No contact possible to flesh
Allayed the fever of the bone.

.   .   .   .   .

Grishkin is nice: her Russian eye
Is underlined for emphasis;
Uncorseted, her friendly bust
20 Gives promise of pneumatic bliss.[8]

The couched Brazilian jaguar
Compels the scampering marmoset [9]
With subtle effluence of cat;
Grishkin has a maisonette; [1]

25 The sleek Brazilian jaguar
Does not in its arboreal gloom
Distil so rank a feline smell
As Grishkin in a drawing room.

And even the Abstract Entities
30 Circumambulate her charm;
But our lot crawls between dry ribs
To keep our metaphysics warm.

1919

Sweeney Among the Nightingales

ὤμοι, πέπληγμαι καιρίαν πληγὴν ἔσω.[6]

Apeneck Sweeney spreads his knees
Letting his arms hang down to laugh,
The zebra stripes along his jaw
Swelling to maculate° giraffe.   *spotted*

5 The circles of the stormy moon
Slide westward toward the River Plate,[7]
Death and the Raven[8] drift above
And Sweeney guards the hornéd gate.[9]

7. The poet John Donne (1572–1631): see above.
8. With this stanza cf. the opening stanza of *Carmen*, in *Emaux et camées* (Enamels and Cameos), 1852, by Théophile Gautier (1811–1872): *Carmen est maigre—un trait de bistre/ Cerne son oeil de αitana./Ses cheveux sont d'un noir sinistre,/Sa peau, le diable la tanna* ("Carmen is thin—a touch of bistre/ Outlines her gypsy eye./Her hair is a sinister black./Her skin was tanned by the devil himself").
9. Small monkey from South or Central America.
1. In English, a slightly pretentious term,

originally French, for a small house or apartment.
6. Aeschylus, *Agamemnon*, line 1343. Agamemnon's cry, heard from inside the palace, as Clytemnestra strikes her first blow: "Oh, I have been struck a direct deadly blow, within!"
7. Rio de la Plata, an estuary of the Paraná and Uruguay rivers, between Uruguay and Argentina.
8. The southern constellation Corvus.
9. In Greek legend, dreams came to mortals through two sets of gates: the gates of horn, for dreams which were true, the gates of ivory, for dreams which were untrue.

Gloomy Orion[1] and the Dog
Are veiled; and hushed the shrunken seas;
The person in the Spanish cape
Tries to sit on Sweeney's knees

Slips and pulls the table cloth
Overturns a coffee-cup,
Reorganized upon the floor
She yawns and draws a stocking up;

The silent man in mocha brown
Sprawls at the window-sill and gapes;
The waiter brings in oranges
Bananas figs and hothouse grapes;

The silent vertebrate in brown
Contracts and concentrates, withdraws;
Rachel *née* Rabinovitch
Tears at the grapes with murderous paws;

She and the lady in the cape
Are suspect, thought to be in league;
Therefore the man with heavy eyes
Declines the gambit, shows fatigue,

Leaves the room and reappears
Outside the window, leaning in,
Branches of wistaria
Circumscribe a golden grin;

The host with someone indistinct
Converses at the door apart,
The nightingales are singing near
The Convent of the Sacred Heart,

And sang within the bloody wood
When Agamemnon cried aloud,
And let their liquid siftings fall
To stain the stiff dishonored shroud.

1919

---

1. A constellation in which is seen the figure of a hunter, with belt and sword; near it, the dog-star, Sirius, represents the hunter's dog.

The Waste Land[2]

"Nam Sibyllam quidem Cumis ego ipse oculis meis vidi
in ampulla pendere, et cum illi pueri dicerent: Σίβυλλα τί
θέλεις; respondebat illa: ἀποθανεῖν θέλω."[3]

FOR EZRA POUND
il miglior fabbro.[4]

I. The Burial of the Dead[5]

April is the cruelest month, breeding
Lilacs out of the dead land, mixing
Memory and desire, stirring
Dull roots with spring rain.
5   Winter kept us warm, covering
Earth in forgetful snow, feeding
A little life with dried tubers.
Summer surprised us, coming over the Starnbergersee[6]
With a shower of rain; we stopped in the colonnade,
10 And went on in sunlight, into the Hofgarten,
And drank coffee, and talked for an hour.
Bin gar keine Russin, stamm' aus Litauen, echt deutsch.[7]
And when we were children, staying at the archduke's,
My cousin's, he took me out on a sled,
15 And I was frightened. He said, Marie,
Marie, hold on tight. And down we went.
In the mountains, there you feel free.
I read, much of the night, and go south in the winter.

What are the roots that clutch, what branches grow
20 Out of this stony rubbish? Son of man,[8]
You cannot say, or guess, for you know only
A heap of broken images, where the sun beats,
And the dead tree gives no shelter, the cricket no relief,[9]
And the dry stone no sound of water. Only
25 There is shadow under this red rock,
(Come in under the shadow of this red rock),
And I will show you something different from either
Your shadow at morning striding behind you
Or your shadow at evening rising to meet you;
30 I will show you fear in a handful of dust.

2. On its first publication in book form, T. S. Eliot provided *The Waste Land* with notes directing the reader to the sources of many of its allusions and explaining certain phases of its plan. Eliot's notes are included below. His general note to the poem is as follows: "Not only the title, but the plan and a good deal of the incidental symbolism of the poem were suggested by Miss Jessie L. Weston's book on the Grail legend: *From Ritual to Romance* (Cambridge). Indeed, so deeply am I indebted, Miss Weston's book will elucidate the difficulties of the poem much better than my notes can do; and I recommend it (apart from the great interest of the book itself) to any who think such elucidation of the poem worth the trouble. To another work of anthropology I am indebted in general, one which has influenced our generation profoundly; I mean *The Golden Bough* [by Sir James Frazer; 12 volumes, 1890–1915]; I have used especially the two volumes *Adonis, Attis, Osiris*. Anyone who is acquainted with these works will immediately recognize in the poem certain references to vegetation ceremonies."
3. "For indeed I myself have seen, with my own eyes, the Sibyl hanging in a bottle at Cumae, and when those boys would say to her: 'Sibyl, what do you want?' she would reply, 'I want to die.'" From the *Satyricon* of Petronius (d. A.D. 66), chapter 48. According to legend the Sibyl, a prophetess who was immortal but subject to the withering of age, was kept in a bottle or cage suspended in the temple of Hercules at Cumae (near Naples).
4. "The better craftsman." The poet Guido Guinizelli, encountered by Dante in Purgatory, answers the latter's praise of him with praise of his predecessor, the Provençal poet Arnaut Daniel, as being "the better craftsman in the maternal tongue" (*Purgatorio*, XXVI.117).
5. From the burial service of the Anglican Church.
6. Lake a few miles south of Munich. The Hofgarten (line 10) is a public garden in Munich, partly surrounded by a colonnaded walk.
7. I am by no means a Russian, I come from Lithuania, am really German.
8. "Cf. Ezekiel II, i" [Eliot's note].
9. "Cf. Ecclesiastes XII, v" [Eliot's note].

Frisch weht der Wind
Der Heimat zu
Mein Irisch Kind,
Wo weilest du?[1]

"You gave me hyacinths first a year ago;
"They called me the hyacinth girl."
—Yet when we came back, late, from the Hyacinth garden,
Your arms full, and your hair wet, I could not
Speak, and my eyes failed, I was neither
Living nor dead, and I knew nothing,
Looking into the heart of light, the silence.
Oed' und leer das Meer.[2]

Madame Sosostris,[3] famous clairvoyante,
Had a bad cold, nevertheless
Is known to be the wisest woman in Europe,
With a wicked pack of cards.[4] Here, said she,
Is your card, the drowned Phoenician Sailor,
(Those are pearls that were his eyes.[5] Look!)
Here is Belladonna, the Lady of the Rocks,
The lady of situations.
Here is the man with three staves, and here the Wheel,
And here is the one-eyed merchant, and this card,
Which is blank, is something he carries on his back,
Which I am forbidden to see. I do not find
The Hanged Man. Fear death by water.
I see crowds of people, walking round in a ring.
Thank you. If you see dear Mrs. Equitone,
Tell her I bring the horoscope myself:
One must be so careful these days.

Unreal City,[6]
Under the brown fog of a winter dawn,
A crowd flowed over London Bridge, so many,
I had not thought death had undone so many.[7]

---

1. "V. *Tristan und Isolde,* I, verses 5–8" [Eliot's note]. The sailor's song from Wagner's opera: "Fresh blows the wind/ Towards home./My Irish child,/Where are you lingering?"
2. "Id. III, verse 24" [Eliot's note]. "Empty and waste the sea": that is, the ship bringing Isolde back to the dying Tristan is nowhere in sight.
3. An invented, generic name for a fortune-teller, perhaps meant to have Egyptian overtones.
4. "I am not familiar with the exact constitution of the Tarot pack of cards, from which I have obviously departed to suit my own convenience. The Hanged Man, a member of the traditional pack, fits my purpose in two ways: because he is associated in my mind with the Hanged God of Frazer, and because I associate him with the hooded figure in the passage of the disciples to Emmaus in Part V. The Phoenician Sailor and the Merchant appear later; also the 'crowds of people,' and Death by Water is executed in Part IV. The Man with Three Staves (an authentic member of the Tarot pack) I associate, quite arbitrarily, with the Fisher King himself" [Eliot's note]. The tarot cards are playing-cards, whose origin goes back to the 14th century in Italy, still in use both for playing and for fortune-telling, as here. The Hanged Man hangs by one foot from the top bar of a trapeze-like construction. The individual figures which the fortune-teller refers to as appearing on her cards have subtle and complex relations to figures who appear in the poem on other levels and to the three principal figures of the Fisher King myth (the impotent King of the waste land, the Deliverer, and the Woman). Besides the relationships which Eliot suggests in his note above, "Belladonna, * * * the lady of situations," looks ahead to the neurotic woman of the opening lines of Part II. The Hanged Man, whom Madame Sosostris cannot find, is the fertility god whose death would bring new life to his people.
5. From Ariel's song in Shakespeare's *The Tempest,* I.ii, "Full fathom five thy father lies."
6. "Cf. Baudelaire: 'Fourmillante cité, cité pleine de rêves,/Où le spectre en plein jour raccroche le passant' " [Eliot's note]. The lines are from *Les Sept vieillards (The Seven Old Men),* one of the poems in *Les Fleurs du mal* (1857): "Swarming city, city filled with dreams,/Where the specter in broad daylight accosts the passerby."
7. "Cf. Inferno III, 55–57: 'si lunga tratta/ di gente, ch' io non avrei mai creduto/che morte tanta n'avesse disfatta' " [Eliot's note]. On his arrival in the Inferno, Dante sees the vast crowd of those who "lived without infamy and without praise, * * * such a long procession of people, that I would never have believed that death had undone so many."

Sighs, short and infrequent, were exhaled,[8]
65 And each man fixed his eyes before his feet.
Flowed up the hill and down King William Street,
To where Saint Mary Woolnoth kept the hours
With a dead sound on the final stroke of nine.[9]
There I saw one I knew, and stopped him, crying: "Stetson!
70 "You who were with me in the ships at Mylae![1]
"That corpse you planted last year in your garden,
"Has it begun to sprout? Will it bloom this year?
"Or has the sudden frost disturbed its bed?
"Oh keep the Dog far hence, that's friend to men,
75 "Or with his nails he'll dig it up again![2]
"You! hypocrite lecteur!—mon semblable,—mon frère!"[3]

II. A Game of Chess[4]

The Chair she sat in, like a burnished throne,[5]
Glowed on the marble, where the glass
Held up by standards wrought with fruited vines
80 From which a golden Cupidon peeped out
(Another hid his eyes behind his wing)
Doubled the flames of sevenbranched candelabra
Reflecting light upon the table as
The glitter of her jewels rose to meet it,
85 From satin cases poured in rich profusion;
In vials of ivory and colored glass
Unstoppered, lurked her strange synthetic perfumes,
Unguent, powdered, or liquid—troubled, confused
And drowned the sense in odors; stirred by the air
90 That freshened from the window, these ascended
In fattening the prolonged candle-flames,
Flung their smoke into the laquearia,[6]
Stirring the pattern on the coffered ceiling.
Huge sea-wood fed with copper
95 Burned green and orange, framed by the colored stone,
In which sad light a carvéd dolphin swam.
Above the antique mantel was displayed

8. "Cf. Inferno IV, 25–27: 'Quivi, secondo che per ascoltare,/non avea pianto, ma' che di sospiri,/che l'aura eterna facevan tremare' " [Eliot's note]. Descending into the first circle of Hell, peopled by those whose virtues did not outweigh the fact that they had not been baptized, or that they had lived before the advent of Christ, Dante hears a noise of lamentation: "Here, if one trusted to hearing, there was no weeping but so many sighs as caused the everlasting air to tremble."
9. "A phenomenon which I have often noticed" [Eliot's note]. King William Street leads into London Bridge; St. Mary Woolnoth stood in an angle formed by that street and Lombard Street. These and other London place-names in the poem refer to the East End—the City, the usual name for London's financial and business center.
1. Sicilian seaport, near which the Romans gained a naval victory over the Carthaginians in 260 B.C.
2. "Cf. the Dirge in Webster's *White Devil*" [Eliot's note]. The Dirge begins, "Call for the robin redbreast and the wren," and ends, "But keep the wolf far thence, that's foe to men;/For with his nails he'll dig them up again."
3. "V. Baudelaire, Preface to *Fleurs du Mal*" [Eliot's note]. Baudelaire's prefatory poem is entitled *To the Reader*, and it takes him through a list of the evils which beset him—

foolishness, error, sin, miserliness—evoking at the end the most monstrous vice of all, Ennui: "You, reader, know the delicate monster,/—Hypocritical reader,—my counterpart,—my brother!"
4. The title alludes to two plays by Thomas Middleton (1570–1627), *A Game at Chesse* and *Women Beware Women*, both of which involve sexual intrigue. In the second, a game of chess is used to mark a seduction, the moves in the game paralleling the steps in the seduction.
5. "Cf. *Antony and Cleopatra*, II, ii, 1. 190" [Eliot's note]. Enobarbus' long description of Cleopatra's first meeting with Antony on the River Cydnus begins: "The barge she sat in, like a burnished throne,/Burned on the water * * *"
6. "Laquearia. V. *Aeneid*, I, 726: dependent lychni laquearibus aureis/Incensi, et noctem flammis funalia vincunt" [Eliot's note]. "Laquearia" are the panels of a coffered ceiling, and the two lines read: "Glowing lamps hang from the gold-paneled ceiling, and the torches conquer the darkness with their flames." They come from the description of the banquet hall in Dido's palace at Carthage, just after Dido has been inspired by Venus with the passion for Aeneas, her guest, which will end (as Cleopatra's passion for Antony was to end) in her suicide.

As though a window gave upon the sylvan scene[7]
The change of Philomel, by the barbarous king[8]
So rudely forced; yet there the nightingale[9]
Filled all the desert with inviolable voice
And still she cried, and still the world pursues,
"Jug Jug" to dirty ears.
And other withered stumps of time
Were told upon the walls; staring forms
Leaned out, leaning, hushing the room enclosed.
Footsteps shuffled on the stair.
Under the firelight, under the brush, her hair
Spread out in fiery points
Glowed into words, then would be savagely still.

"My nerves are bad to-night. Yes, bad. Stay with me.
"Speak to me. Why do you never speak. Speak.
    "What are you thinking of? What thinking? What?
"I never know what you are thinking. Think."

I think we are in rats' alley[1]
Where the dead men lost their bones.

"What is that noise?"
                    The wind under the door.[2]
"What is that noise now? What is the wind doing?"
                    Nothing again nothing.
                              "Do
"You know nothing? Do you see nothing? Do you remember
"Nothing?"

        I remember
Those are pearls that were his eyes.[3]
"Are you alive, or not? Is there nothing in your head?"

                                    But

O O O O that Shakespeherian Rag—
It's so elegant
So intelligent
"What shall I do now? What shall I do?"
"I shall rush out as I am, and walk the street
"With my hair down, so. What shall we do tomorrow?
"What shall we ever do?"
                    The hot water at ten.
And if it rains, a closed car at four.
And we shall play a game of chess,
Pressing lidless eyes and waiting for a knock upon the door.[4]

---

7. "Sylvan scene. V. Milton, *Paradise Lost*, IV, 140" [Eliot's note]. The phrase occurs in the description of Eden as it looks to Satan when he sees it for the first time.
8. "V. Ovid, *Metamorphoses*, VI, Philomela" [Eliot's note]. In Ovid's version of the myth, Tereus, king of Thrace, is married to Procne but falls in love with her sister, Philomela, whom he ravishes; he cuts out her tongue to silence her, but she weaves her story into an embroidered cloth. Procne avenges herself and her sister by murdering her child, Itys, and serving his flesh to his father at a banquet. The sisters are saved, as the maddened king pursues them, by being changed to birds: Procne into a swallow, Philomela into a nightingale.
9. "Cf. Part III, l. 204" [Eliot's note].
1. "Cf. Part III, l. 195" [Eliot's note].
2. "Cf. Webster: 'Is the wind in that door still?'" [Eliot's note], referring to John Webster's play, *The Devil's Law Case*, III.ii. 162.
3. See Part I, line 48 and note.
4. "Cf. the game of chess in Middleton's *Women Beware Women*" [Eliot's note].

When Lil's husband got demobbed,° I said—   *demobilized*
140 I didn't mince my words, I said to her myself,
HURRY UP PLEASE ITS TIME[5]
Now Albert's coming back, make yourself a bit smart.
He'll want to know what you done with that money he gave you
To get yourself some teeth. He did, I was there.
145 You have them all out, Lil, and get a nice set,
He said, I swear, I can't bear to look at you.
And no more can't I, I said, and think of poor Albert,
He's been in the army four years, he wants a good time,
And if you don't give it him, there's others will, I said.
150 Oh is there, she said. Something o' that, I said.
Then I'll know who to thank, she said, and give me a straight look.
HURRY UP PLEASE ITS TIME
If you don't like it you can get on with it, I said.
Others can pick and choose if you can't.
155 But if Albert makes off, it won't be for lack of telling.
You ought to be ashamed, I said, to look so antique.
(And her only thirty-one.)
I can't help it, she said, pulling a long face,
It's them pills I took, to bring it off, she said.
160 (She's had five already, and nearly died of young George.)
The chemist° said it would be all right, but I've never been the same.   *druggist*
You *are* a proper fool, I said.
Well, if Albert won't leave you alone, there it is, I said,
What you get married for if you don't want children?
165 HURRY UP PLEASE ITS TIME
Well, that Sunday Albert was home, they had a hot gammon,°   *smoked ham*
And they asked me in to dinner, to get the beauty of it hot—
HURRY UP PLEASE ITS TIME
HURRY UP PLEASE ITS TIME
170 Goonight Bill. Goonight Lou. Goonight May. Goonight.
Ta ta. Goonight. Goonight.
Good night, ladies, good night, sweet ladies, good night, good night.[6]

III. The Fire Sermon[7]

The river's tent is broken: the last fingers of leaf
Clutch and sink into the wet bank. The wind
175 Crosses the brown land, unheard. The nymphs are departed.
Sweet Thames, run softly, till I end my song.[8]
The river bears no empty bottles, sandwich papers,
Silk handkerchiefs, cardboard boxes, cigarette ends
Or other testimony of summer nights. The nymphs are departed.
180 And their friends, the loitering heirs of city directors;
Departed, have left no addresses.

5. A typical injunction of a London bartender, telling his customers that it is closing-time.
6. Compare Ophelia's speech, *Hamlet*, IV.v. 71–72: "Good night, ladies, good night. Sweet ladies, good night, good night."
7. The title is that of the Buddha's Fire Sermon (see Eliot's note to line 308, below), in which he preached that "all things are on fire, * * * with the fire of passion, * * * with the fire of hatred, with the fire of infatuation; with birth, old age, death, sorrow, lamentation, misery, grief, and despair are they on fire," and that the disciple must conceive "an aversion for the eye," for all the senses, "for impressions received by the mind; and whatever sensation, pleasant, unpleasant, or indifferent, originates in dependence on impressions received by the mind," so that he may become divested of passion and hence be free and know that he is free and that "he is no more of this world."
8. "V. Spenser, *Prothalamion*" [Eliot's note]. The line is the refrain from Spenser's marriage-song, whose picture of "the silver-streaming Thames," its nymphs, and the London through which it flows are to be contrasted in detail with the same things as they are presented in Eliot's poem.

By the waters of Leman I sat down and wept[9] . . .
Sweet Thames, run softly till I end my song,
Sweet Thames, run softly, for I speak not loud or long.
But at my back in a cold blast I hear[1]
The rattle of the bones, and chuckle spread from ear to ear.
A rat crept softly through the vegetation
Dragging its slimy belly on the bank
While I was fishing in the dull canal
On a winter evening round behind the gashouse
Musing upon the king my brother's wreck[2]
And on the king my father's death before him.
White bodies naked on the low damp ground
And bones cast in a little low dry garret,
Rattled by the rat's foot only, year to year.
But at my back from time to time I hear[3]
The sound of horns and motors, which shall bring[4]
Sweeney to Mrs. Porter in the spring.
O the moon shone bright on Mrs. Porter[5]
And on her daughter
They wash their feet in soda water
Et O ces voix d'enfants, chantant dans la coupole![6]

Twit twit twit
Jug jug jug jug jug jug
So rudely forc'd.
Tereu[7]

Unreal City[8]
Under the brown fog of a winter noon
Mr. Eugenides, the Smyrna merchant
Unshaven, with a pocket full of currants
C.i.f. London: documents at sight,[9]
Asked me in demotic French[1]
To luncheon at the Cannon Street Hotel[2]
Followed by a weekend at the Metropole.

9. An echo of Psalm 137: "By the rivers of Babylon, there we sat down, yea, we wept, when we remembered Zion." Lac Léman is the Lake of Geneva, and *The Waste Land* is said to have been written at Lausanne, on its shore. *Leman* is also an archaic word for lover, mistress, or paramour.
1. Echoes Marvell's *To his Coy Mistress:* "But at my back I always hear/Time's winged chariot hurrying near."
2. "Cf. *The Tempest,* I, ii" [Eliot's note]. Ferdinand, in Shakespeare's play, just after hearing Ariel's song, "Come unto these yellow sands," and just before Ariel sings "Full fathom five thy father lies," the song inspired by the death by drowning of Ferdinand's father, describes himself as "sitting on a bank,/Weeping again the King my father's wreck./This music crept by me upon the waters."
3. "Cf. Marvell, *To His Coy Mistress*" [Eliot's note].
4. "Cf. Day, *Parliament of Bees:* 'When of the sudden, listening, you shall hear,/A noise of horns and hunting, which shall bring/Actaeon to Diana in the spring'" [Eliot's note]. The young Actaeon, discovering Diana bathing with her nymphs, was changed by the goddess to a stag, which her hounds set upon and killed.
5. "I do not know the origin of the ballad

from which these lines are taken: it was reported to me from Sydney, Australia" [Eliot's note]. The ballad was popular with Australian soldiers in World War I. Sweeney (line 198) is the figure of vulgar, thoughtless sexual enterprise who figures in Eliot's *Sweeney among the Nightingales* and *Sweeney Agonistes.*
6. "V. Verlaine, *Parsifal*" [Eliot's note]. Quoted is the concluding line of Verlaine's sonnet (1886), which treats ironically Parsifal's conquering of some forms of fleshly temptation, only to be haunted—even in his purity—by others: "And, O those children's voices singing in the dome!"
7. These four lines reproduce the mode in which Elizabethan poets indicated the song of the nightingale, including "Tereu"—also a form of the name of Philomela's ravisher, Tereus. See Part II, lines 99–103.
8. See note to Part I, line 60.
9. "The currants were quoted at a price 'carriage and insurance free to London'; and the Bill of Lading etc. were to be handed to the buyer upon payment of the sight draft" [Eliot's note].
1. Here, simply "bad French."
2. Before the Second World War, a very large hotel in London's commercial district. The Metropole is probably the large hotel at Brighton, the beach-resort.

215 At the violet hour, when the eyes and back
Turn upward from the desk, when the human engine waits
Like a taxi throbbing waiting,
I Tiresias, though blind, throbbing between two lives,[3]
Old man with wrinkled female breasts, can see
220 At the violet hour, the evening hour that strives
Homeward, and brings the sailor home from sea,[4]
The typist home at teatime, clears her breakfast, lights
Her stove, and lays out food in tins.
Out of the window perilously spread
225 Her drying combinations touched by the sun's last rays,
On the divan are piled (at night her bed)
Stockings, slippers, camisoles, and stays.
I Tiresias, old man with wrinkled dugs
Perceived the scene, and foretold the rest—
230 I too awaited the expected guest.
He, the young man carbuncular,[5] arrives,
A small house agent's clerk, with one bold stare,
One of the low on whom assurance sits
As a silk hat on a Bradford[6] millionaire.
235 The time is now propitious, as he guesses,
The meal is ended, she is bored and tired,
Endeavors to engage her in caresses
Which still are unreproved, if undesired.
Flushed and decided, he assaults at once;
240 Exploring hands encounter no defense;
His vanity requires no response,
And makes a welcome of indifference.
(And I Tiresias have foresuffered all
Enacted on this same divan or bed;

3. "Tiresias, although a mere spectator and not indeed a 'character,' is yet the most important personage in the poem, uniting all the rest. Just as the one-eyed merchant, seller of currants, melts into the Phoenician sailor, and the latter is not wholly distinct from Ferdinand Prince of Naples, so all the women are one woman, and the two sexes meet in Tiresias. What Tiresias *sees,* in fact, is the substance of the poem. The whole passage from Ovid is of great anthropological interest * * *" [Eliot's note]. Mythology offers three separate accounts of the reasons why Tiresias was blinded by a goddess and then granted a seer's power by Zeus. Ovid's version is contained in a passage (*Metamorphoses,* III.322 ff.) which Eliot's note cites in Latin, and which runs as follows in Golding's verse translation:
They say that Jove, disposed to mirth as he and Juno sat
A-drinking nectar after meat in sport and pleasant rate,
Did fall a-jesting with his wife, and said: "A greater pleasure
In Venus' games ye women have than men beyond all measure."
She answered, no. To try the truth, they both of them agree
The wise Tiresias in this case indifferent judge to be,
Who both the man's and woman's joys by trial understood,
For finding once two mighty snakes engend'-ring in a wood,
He struck them overthwart the backs, by means whereof behold
(As strange a thing to be of truth as ever yet was told)
He being made a woman straight, seven winter livèd so.

The eighth he finding them again did say unto them tho:
"And if to strike ye have such power as for to turn their shape
That are the givers of the stripe, before you hence escape,
One stripe now shall I lend you more." He struck them as before
And straight returned his former shape in which he first was born.
Tiresias therefore being ta'en to judge this jesting strife,
Gave sentence on the side of Jove; the which the queen his wife
Did take a great deal more to heart than needed, and in spite
To wreak her teen upon her judge, bereft him of his sight;
But Jove (for to the gods it is unlawful to undo
The things which other of the gods by any means have do)
Did give him sight in things to come for loss of sight of eye,
And so his grievous punishment with honor did supply.
4. "This may not appear as exact as Sappho's lines, but I had in mind the 'longshore' or 'dory' fisherman, who returns at nightfall" [Eliot's note]. Sappho's poem (Number 120 in E. Diehl, *Anthologia Lyrica*), may be translated as follows: "Hesperus, all things you bring, as many as light-bringing morning has scattered abroad./You bring the sheep,/You bring the goat, you bring the child to its mother."
5. Afflicted with carbuncles, a boil-like inflammation.
6. A manufacturing town in the English Midlands.

I who have sat by Thebes below the wall[7]
And walked among the lowest of the dead.)
Bestows one final patronizing kiss,
And gropes his way, finding the stairs unlit . . .

She turns and looks a moment in the glass,
Hardly aware of her departed lover;
Her brain allows one half-formed thought to pass:
"Well now that's done: and I'm glad it's over."
When lovely woman stoops to folly and[8]
Paces about her room again, alone,
She smoothes her hair with automatic hand,
And puts a record on the gramophone.

"This music crept by me upon the waters"[9]
And along the Strand, up Queen Victoria Street.
O City city, I can sometimes hear
Beside a public bar in Lower Thames Street,
The pleasant whining of a mandolin
And a clatter and a chatter from within
Where fishmen lounge at noon: where the walls
Of Magnus Martyr[1] hold
Inexplicable splendor of Ionian white and gold.

> The river sweats[2]
> Oil and tar
> The barges drift
> With the turning tide
> Red sails
> Wide
> To leeward, swing on the heavy spar.
> The barges wash
> Drifting logs
> Down Greenwich reach
> Past the Isle of Dogs.[3]
> > Weialala leia
> > Wallala leialala

> Elizabeth and Leicester[4]
> Beating oars

7. The blind Theban seer (see note to line 218 above) was supposed to have lived three times as long as the average man, and his prophecies enter the lives of many legendary citizens of Thebes, including those of Oedipus and his family.
8. "V. Goldsmith, the song in *The Vicar of Wakefield*" [Eliot's note]. ("When lovely woman stoops to folly/And finds too late that men betray/What charm can soothe her melancholy,/What art can wash her guilt away?/The only art her guilt to cover,/To hide her shame from every eye,/To give repentance to her lover/And wring her bosom—is to die.")
9. "V. *The Tempest*, as above" [Eliot's note]. See note to line 191 above.
1. "The interior of St. Magnus Martyr is to my mind one of the finest among Wren's interiors. See *The Proposed Demolition of Nineteen City Churches*: (P. S. King & Son, Ltd.)" [Eliot's note]. Again in this passage (lines 257–265) it is the busy commercial East End of London that is evoked. The church of St. Magnus Martyr stands just below London Bridge, in Lower Thames Street, which skirts the north bank of the Thames between London Bridge and the Tower of London. The phrase "O City city" apostrophizes both the *City* of London, a relatively small area of the metropolis which contains its business wealth, and the generic total city.
2. "The song of the (three) Thames-daughters begins here. From line 292 to 306 inclusive they speak in turn. V. *Götterdämmerung*, III,i: the Rhine-daughters" [Eliot's note]. Lines 277–278 repeat the refrain of the Rhine-maidens in Wagner's music-drama.
3. A tongue of land extending into the Thames opposite Greenwich.
4. "V. Froude, [*Reign of*] *Elizabeth*, Vol. I, ch. iv, letter of De Quadra to Philip of Spain: 'In the afternoon we were in a barge, watching the games on the river. (The queen) was alone with the Lord Robert and myself on the poop, when they began to talk nonsense, and went so far that Lord Robert at last said, as I was on the spot there was no reason why they should not be married if the queen pleased'" [Eliot's note]. Sir Robert Dudley (1532?–88), Earl of Leicester, was a favorite of the queen.

The stern was formed
A gilded shell
Red and gold
The brisk swell
285   Rippled both shores
Southwest wind
Carried down stream
The peal of bells
White towers
290   Weialala leia
                    Wallala leialala

"Trams and dusty trees.
Highbury bore me.[5] Richmond and Kew
Undid me. By Richmond I raised my knees
295   Supine on the floor of a narrow canoe."

"My feet are at Moorgate,[6] and my heart
Under my feet. After the event
He wept. He promised 'a new start.'
I made no comment. What should I resent?"

300   "On Margate Sands.[7]
I can connect
Nothing with nothing.
The broken fingernails of dirty hands.
My people humble people who expect
305   Nothing."
                    la la

To Carthage then I came[8]

Burning burning burning burning[9]
O Lord Thou pluckest me out[1]
310   O Lord Thou pluckest

burning

IV. Death by Water

Phlebas the Phoenician, a fortnight dead,
Forgot the cry of gulls, and the deep sea swell
And the profit and loss.
315   A current under sea
Picked his bones in whispers. As he rose and fell

5. "Cf. Purgatorio, V, 133: Ricorditi di me, che son la Pia;/Siena mi fe', disfecemi Maremma" [Eliot's note]. Pia de' Tolomei, whom Dante encounters in Purgatory, after telling her story, says: "Pray, when you have returned to the world and are rested from your long journey, * * * remember me, who am la Pia; Siena made me, the Maremma unmade me"; she had been shut up by her husband in one of his castles, La Pietra in Maremma, and was there done to death by his orders. Highbury is a residential suburb in North London; Richmond is the object of a pleasant excursion up the river from London; Kew is another excursion point, chiefly because of its botanical gardens.
6. A humble district in East London.
7. A beach resort in Kent, where the Thames Estuary broadens into the Channel.

8. "V. St. Augustine's *Confessions:* 'to Carthage then I came, where a cauldron of unholy loves sang all about mine ears'" [Eliot's note].
9. "The complete text of the Buddha's Fire Sermon (which corresponds in importance to the Sermon on the Mount) from which these words are taken, will be found translated in the late Henry Clarke Warren's *Buddhism in Translation* (Harvard Oriental Series). Mr. Warren was one of the great pioneers of Buddhist studies in the Occident" [Eliot's note].
1. "From St. Augustine's *Confessions* again. The collocation of these two representatives of eastern and western asceticism, as the culmination of this part of the poem, is not an accident" [Eliot's note].

He passed the stages of his age and youth
Entering the whirlpool.

Gentile or Jew
O you who turn the wheel and look to windward,
Consider Phlebas, who was once handsome and tall as you.

V. *What the Thunder Said*[2]

After the torchlight red on sweaty faces
After the frosty silence in the gardens
After the agony in stony places
The shouting and the crying
Prison and palace and reverberation
Of thunder of spring over distant mountains
He who was living is now dead
We who were living are now dying
With a little patience

Here is no water but only rock
Rock and no water and the sandy road
The road winding above among the mountains
Which are mountains of rock without water
If there were water we should stop and drink
Amongst the rock one cannot stop or think
Sweat is dry and feet are in the sand
If there were only water amongst the rock
Dead mountain mouth of carious teeth that cannot spit
Here one can neither stand nor lie nor sit
There is not even silence in the mountains
But dry sterile thunder without rain
There is not even solitude in the mountains
But red sullen faces sneer and snarl
From doors of mudcracked houses
                              If there were water

   And no rock
   If there were rock
   And also water
   And water
   A spring
   A pool among the rock
   If there were the sound of water only
   Not the cicada
   And dry grass singing
   But sound of water over a rock
   Where the hermit-thrust sings in the pine trees[3]
   Drip drop drip drop drop drop drop
   But there is no water

Who is the third who walks always beside you?
When I count, there are only you and I together[4]

---

2. "In the first part of Part V three themes are employed: the journey to Emmaus, the approach to the Chapel Perilous (see Miss Weston's book) and the present decay of eastern Europe" [Eliot's note]. For the title of Part V, see note to line 401, below.
3. "This is * * * the hermit-thrush which I have heard in Quebec Province * * * Its 'water-dripping song' is justly celebrated" [Eliot's note].
4. "The following lines were stimulated by the account of one of the Antarctic expeditions (I forget which, but I think one of Shackle-ton's): it was related that the party of explorers, at the extremity of their strength, had the constant delusion that there was *one more member* than could actually be counted" [Eliot's note]. And compare at this point the journey of two of Christ's disciples to Emmaus, after the Crucifixion; on the way "they talked together of all these things which had happened. And * * * while they communed together and reasoned, Jesus himself drew near and went with them. But their eyes were holden that they should not know him." Luke xxiv.13–16.

But when I look ahead up the white road
There is always another one walking beside you
Gliding wrapt in a brown mantle, hooded
365 I do not know whether a man or a woman
—But who is that on the other side of you?

What is that sound high in the air[5]
Murmur of maternal lamentation
Who are those hooded hordes swarming
370 Over endless plains, stumbling in cracked earth
Ringed by the flat horizon only
What is the city over the mountains
Cracks and reforms and bursts in the violet air
Falling towers
375 Jerusalem Athens Alexandria
Vienna London
Unreal

A woman drew her long black hair out tight
And fiddled whisper music on those strings
380 And bats with baby faces in the violet light
Whistled, and beat their wings
And crawled head downward down a blackened wall
And upside down in air were towers
Tolling reminiscent bells, that kept the hours
385 And voices singing out of empty cisterns and exhausted wells.

In this decayed hole among the mountains
In the faint moonlight, the grass is singing
Over the tumbled graves, about the chapel
There is the empty chapel, only the wind's home.
390 It has no windows, and the door swings,
Dry bones can harm no one.
Only a cock stood on the rooftree
Co co rico co co rico
In a flash of lightning. Then a damp gust
395 Bringing rain

Ganga[6] was sunken, and the limp leaves
Waited for rain, while the black clouds
Gathered far distant, over Himavant.
The jungle crouched, humped in silence.
400 Then spoke the thunder
D A
Datta:[7] what have we given?
My friend, blood shaking my heart

---

5. Eliot's note to lines 366–376 quotes a
passage from Hermann Hesse's *Blick ins
Chaos* (*A Glimpse into Chaos*) which may be
translated as follows: "Already half Europe,
already at least half of Eastern Europe is on
the road to Chaos, drives drunken in holy
madness along the abyss and sings the while,
sings drunk and hymn-like as Dmitri Kara-
mazov sang. The bourgeois laughs, offended,
at these songs, the saint and the prophet hear
them with tears."
6. The River Ganges. Himavant is a peak in
the Himalayas.
7. " 'Datta, dayadhvam, damyata' (Give, sym-
pathize, control). The fable of the meaning of
the Thunder is found in the *Brihadaranyaka—
Upanishad,* 5, [ii] * * * [Eliot's note]. The

relevant chapter of this Upanishad tells how
"the three-fold offspring of Prajápati, gods,
men and Asuras [demons]" in turn asked
their father to tell them their duty. He replies
with the one letter *Da,* which each of the three
interprets differently. The gods say, " 'We do
comprehend. Restrain your desires, hast thou
said to us.' " The men: " 'Be liberal, hast thou
said to us.' " The Asuras: " 'Be clement, hast
thou said to us.' " In each case, Prajápati
answers, " 'Om! you have fully compre-
hended.' The same is repeated by a divine
voice with the force of thunder, *viz.,* the syl-
lables *Da, Da, Da,* meaning, Be restrained
(*damyata*), be liberal (*datta*), and be clement
(*dayadhvam*).

The awful daring of a moment's surrender
Which an age of prudence can never retract
By this, and this only, we have existed
Which is not to be found in our obituaries
Or in memories draped by the beneficent spider[8]
Or under seals broken by the lean solicitor
In our empty rooms
DA
Dayadhvam: I have heard the key[9]
Turn in the door once and turn once only
We think of the key, each in his prison
Thinking of the key, each confirms a prison
Only at nightfall, ethereal rumors
Revive for a moment a broken Coriolanus[1]
DA
Damyata: The boat responded
Gaily, to the hand expert with sail and oar
The sea was calm, your heart would have responded
Gaily, when invited, beating obedient
To controlling hands
                    I sat upon the shore
Fishing, with the arid plain behind me[2]
Shall I at least set my lands in order?
London Bridge is falling down falling down falling down
Poi s'ascose nel foco che gli affina[3]
Quando fiam uti chelidon[4]—O swallow swallow
Le Prince d'Aquitaine à la tour abolie[5]
These fragments I have shored against my ruins
Why then Ile fit you. Hieronymo's mad againe.[6]
Datta. Dayadhvam. Damyata.
        Shantih   shantih   shantih[7]

                                1922

8. "Cf. Webster, *The White Devil*, V, vi: '. . . they'll remarry/Ere the worm pierce your winding-sheet, ere the spider/Make a thin curtain for your epitaphs'" [Eliot's note].
9. "Cf. *Inferno*, XXXIII, 46: 'ed io sentii chiavar l'uscio di sotto/ all' orribile torre.' Also F. H. Bradley, *Appearance and Reality*, p. 346. 'My external sensations are no less private to myself than are my thoughts or my feelings. In either case my experience falls within my own circle, a circle closed on the outside; and, with all its elements alike, every sphere is opaque to the others which surround it. . . . In brief, regarded as an existence which appears in a soul, the whole world for each is peculiar and private to that soul'" [Eliot's note]. The lines from Dante are from the section of the *Inferno* in which Count Ugolino of Pisa recounts his imprisonment with his little sons in the Hunger Tower, where they were left to starve: "and I heard them turning the key in the door of the dreadful tower, below."
1. The Roman hero of Shakespeare's tragedy, *Coriolanus*, the symbol of a truly great man whose greatness is tragically destroyed when he seeks to be utterly self-sufficient.
2. "V. Weston: *From Ritual to Romance*; chapter on the Fisher King" [Eliot's note].
3. "V. *Purgatorio*, XXVI, 148. ' 'Ara vos prec per aquella valor/que vos guida al som de l'escalina,/sovegna vos a temps de ma dolor."/Poi s'ascose nel foco che gli affina'"

[Eliot's note]. Arnaut Daniel, the late-12th-century poet, encountered among the lustful in Purgatory, after recounting his story, concludes with the lines quoted: " 'And so I pray you, by that Virtue which guides you to the top of the stair, be reminded in time of my pain.' Then he hid himself in the fire that purifies them."
4. "V. *Pervigilium Veneris*. Cf. Philomela in Parts I and II" [Eliot's note]. The quoted line ("When shall I become as the swallow?") is from a late Latin poem (*The Vigil of Venus*) celebrating the spring festival of Venus. It alludes to the Procne-Philomela-Tereus myth, but makes Philomela the swallow.
5. "V. Gérard de Nerval, Sonnet *El Desdichado*" [Eliot's note]. The poem (*The Disinherited*) describes "the man of shadows,—the widower,—the unconsoled,/The prince of Aquitania in the abandoned tower:/My only star is dead,—and my starred lute/Carries as its emblem the black sun of Melancholy * * *"
6. "V. Kyd's *Spanish Tragedy*" [Eliot's note]. The subtitle of Kyd's *Spanish Tragedy* (1594) is *Hieronymo's Mad Againe*. Hieronymo, driven mad by his son's death, "fits" the parts in a court masque so that in the course of it he kills his son's murderers.
7. "Shantih. Repeated as here, a formal ending to an Upanishad. 'The Peace which passeth understanding' is our nearest equivalent to this word" [Eliot's note].

Journey of the Magi[8]

'A cold coming we had of it,[9]
Just the worst time of the year
For a journey, and such a long journey:
The ways deep and the weather sharp,
5   The very dead of winter.'
And the camels galled, sore-footed, refractory,
Lying down in the melting snow.
There were times we regretted
The summer palaces on slopes, the terraces,
10   And the silken girls bringing sherbet.
Then the camel men cursing and grumbling
And running away, and wanting their liquor and women,
And the night-fires going out, and the lack of shelters,
And the cities hostile and the towns unfriendly
15   And the villages dirty and charging high prices:
A hard time we had of it.
At the end we preferred to travel all night,
Sleeping in snatches,
With the voices singing in our ears, saying
20   That this was all folly.

Then at dawn we came down to a temperate valley,
Wet, below the snow line, smelling of vegetation;
With a running stream and a water-mill beating the darkness,
And three trees on the low sky,[1]
25   And an old white horse galloped away in the meadow.
Then we came to a tavern with vine-leaves over the lintel,
Six hands at an open door dicing for pieces of silver,
And feet kicking the empty wine-skins.
But there was no information, and so we continued
30   And arrived at evening, not a moment too soon
Finding the place; it was (you may say) satisfactory.

All this was a long time ago, I remember,
And I would do it again, but set down
This set down
35   This: were we led all that way for
Birth or Death? There was a Birth, certainly,
We had evidence and no doubt. I had seen birth and death,
But had thought they were different; this Birth was
Hard and bitter agony for us, like Death, our death.
40   We returned to our places, these Kingdoms,
But no longer at ease here, in the old dispensation,
With an alien people clutching their gods.
I should be glad of another death.

1927

8. The poem recreates the recollections of one of the three Wise Men, or Magi, who, guided by the star, had come to Bethlehem to witness the birth of Christ, as told in Matthew ii.1–2.
9. The first five lines are adapted from the sermon preached at Christmas, 1622, by Bishop Lancelot Andrewes: "Last, we consider the *time* of their coming, the season of the yeare. It was no *summer Progresse*. A cold comming they had of it, at this time of the year; just, the worst time of the yeare, to take a journey, and specially a long journey, in. The waies deep, the weather sharp, the daies short, the sunn farthest off * * * , the very dead of *Winter*."
1. The image prefigures the three crosses of the Crucifixion, as line 27 suggests the Roman soldiers dicing for Christ's robe, as well as the pieces of silver paid to Judas for betraying Christ.

From FOUR QUARTETS

The Dry Salvages[5]

1

I do not know much about gods; but I think that the river[6]
Is a strong brown god—sullen, untamed and intractable,
Patient to some degree, at first recognized as a frontier;
Useful, untrustworthy, as a conveyor of commerce;
Then only a problem confronting the builder of bridges.
The problem once solved, the brown god is almost forgotten
By the dwellers in cities—ever, however, implacable,
Keeping his seasons and rages, destroyer, reminder
Of what men choose to forget. Unhonored, unpropitiated
By worshipers of the machine, but waiting, watching and waiting.
His rhythm was present in the nursery bedroom,
In the rank ailanthus[7] of the April dooryard,
In the smell of grapes on the autumn table,
And the evening circle in the winter gaslight.

The river is within us, the sea is all about us;
The sea is the land's edge also, the granite
Into which it reaches, the beaches where it tosses
Its hints of earlier and other creation:
The starfish, the hermit crab, the whale's backbone;
The pools where it offers to our curiosity
The more delicate algae and the sea anemone.
It tosses up our losses, the torn seine,°   *fishing-net*
The shattered lobsterpot, the broken oar
And the gear of foreign dead men. The sea has many voices,
Many gods and many voices.
                    The salt is on the briar rose,
The fog is in the fir trees.
                    The sea howl
And the sea yelp, are different voices
Often together heard; the whine in the rigging,
The menace and caress of wave that breaks on water,
The distant rote in the granite teeth,
And the wailing warning from the approaching headland
Are all sea voices, and the heaving groaner
Rounded homewards,[8] and the seagull:
And under the oppression of the silent fog
The tolling bell
Measures time not our time, rung by the unhurried
Ground swell,[9] a time
Older than the time of chronometers, older
Than time counted by anxious worried women
Lying awake, calculating the future,

---

5. Eliot's prefatory note to the poem is as follows: "(The Dry Salvages—presumably *les trois sauvages*—is a small group of rocks, with a beacon, off the N.E. coast of Cape Ann, Massachusetts. *Salvages* is pronounced to rhyme with *assuages. Groaner:* a whistling buoy)." The poem was published as a separate pamphlet in 1941 and took its place as the third of the *Four Quartets* in 1943.

6. The Mississippi. Eliot was born in St. Louis, Mo., and grew up there.
7. A large East Indian tree, cultivated in Europe and America for shade: "rank" because of its vigorous growth.
8. I.e., the buoy is rounded by a ship on its way homewards.
9. Broad, deep swell of the ocean, caused by continued storm.

Trying to unweave, unwind, unravel
And piece together the past and the future,
Between midnight and dawn, when the past is all deception,
The future futureless, before the morning watch
45 When time stops and time is never ending;
And the ground swell, that is and was from the beginning,
Clangs
The bell.

2

Where is there an end of it, the soundless wailing,
50 The silent withering of autumn flowers
Dropping their petals and remaining motionless;
Where is there an end to the drifting wreckage,
The prayer of the bone on the beach, the unprayable
Prayer at the calamitous annunciation?[1]

55 There is no end, but addition: the trailing
Consequence of further days and hours,
While emotion takes to itself the emotionless
Years of living among the breakage
Of what was believed in as the most reliable—
60 And therefore the fittest for renunciation.

There is the final addition, the failing
Pride or resentment at failing powers,
The unattached devotion which might pass for devotionless,
In a drifting boat with a slow leakage,
65 The silent listening to the undeniable
Clamor of the bell of the last annunciation.

Where is the end of them, the fishermen sailing
Into the wind's tail, where the fog cowers?
We cannot think of a time that is oceanless
70 Or of an ocean not littered with wastage
Or of a future that is not liable
Like the past, to have no destination.

We have to think of them as forever baling,
Setting and hauling, while the North East lowers
75 Over shallow banks unchanging and erosionless
Or drawing their money, drying sails at dockage;
Not as making a trip that will be unpayable
For a haul that will not bear examination.

There is no end of it, the voiceless wailing,
80 No end to the withering of withered flowers,
To the movement of pain that is painless and motionless,
To the drift of the sea and the drifting wreckage,
The bone's prayer to Death its God. Only the hardly, barely prayable
Prayer of the one Annunciation.[2]

85 It seems, as one becomes older,
That the past has another pattern, and ceases to be a mere sequence—

1. Perhaps meaning that when the annunciation is of calamity—of imminent death—it is no longer possible to pray.
2. The submissive prayer made by Mary at the Annunciation by the angel that she is to become the mother of Jesus: "Behold the handmaid of the Lord; be it unto me according to thy word." See Luke i.30–38.

Or even development: the latter a partial fallacy,
Encouraged by superficial notions of evolution,
Which becomes, in the popular mind, a means of disowning the past.
The moments of happiness—not the sense of well-being,
Fruition, fulfilment, security or affection,
Or even a very good dinner, but the sudden illumination—
We had the experience but missed the meaning,
And approach to the meaning restores the experience
In a different form, beyond any meaning
We can assign to happiness. I have said before
That the past experience revived in the meaning
Is not the experience of one life only
But of many generations—not forgetting
Something that is probably quite ineffable:
The backward look behind the assurance
Of recorded history, the backward half-look
Over the shoulder, towards the primitive terror.
Now, we come to discover that the moments of agony
(Whether, or not, due to misunderstanding,
Having hoped for the wrong things or dreaded the wrong things,
Is not in question) are likewise permanent
With such permanence as time has. We appreciate this better
In the agony of others, nearly experienced,
Involving ourselves, than in our own.
For our own past is covered by the currents of action,
But the torment of others remains an experience
Unqualified, unworn by subsequent attrition.
People change, and smile: but the agony abides.
Time the destroyer is time the preserver,
Like the river with its cargo of dead Negroes, cows and chicken coops,
The bitter apple and the bite in the apple.
And the ragged rock in the restless waters,
Waves wash over it, fogs conceal it;
On a halcyon day[3] it is merely a monument,
In navigable weather it is always a seamark
To lay a course by: but in the somber season
Or the sudden fury, is what it always was.

3

I sometimes wonder if that is what Krishna[4] meant—
Among other things—or one way of putting the same thing:
That the future is a faded song, a Royal Rose or a lavender spray
Of wistful regret for those who are not yet here to regret,
Pressed between yellow leaves of a book that has never been opened.
And the way up is the way down,[5] the way forward is the way back.
You cannot face it steadily, but this thing is sure,
That time is no healer: the patient is no longer here.
When the train starts, and the passengers are settled
To fruit, periodicals and business letters
(And those who saw them off have left the platform)
Their faces relax from grief into relief,
To the sleepy rhythm of a hundred hours.
Fare forward, travelers! not escaping from the past
Into different lives, or into any future;

3. I.e., a calm day.
4. A Hindu god, called the Preserver; his teachings are preserved in the *Baghavad Gita* ("Song of the Blessed One"), which forms a part of the Hindu epic of the *Mahabharata*, and is said to be to Hindus what the Bible is to Christians, the Koran to Muslims.
5. The first of the *Four Quartets, Burnt Norton*, bears two epigraphs from the pre-Socratic philosopher Heraclitus: one of them is "The way up and the way down are one and the same."

140 You are not the same people who left that station
Or who will arrive at any terminus,
While the narrowing rails slide together behind you;
And on the deck of the drumming liner
Watching the furrow that widens behind you,
145 You shall not think "the past is finished"
Or "the future is before us."
At nightfall, in the rigging and the aerial,
Is a voice descanting[6] (though not to the ear,
The murmuring shell of time, and not in any language)
"Fare forward, you who think that you are voyaging;
150 You are not those who saw the harbor
Receding, or those who will disembark.
Here between the hither and the farther shore
While time is withdrawn, consider the future
And the past with an equal mind.
155 At the moment which is not of action or inaction
You can receive this: 'on whatever sphere of being
The mind of a man may be intent
At the time of death'[7]—that is the one action
(And the time of death is every moment)
160 Which shall fructify in the lives of others:
And do not think of the fruit of action.
Fare forward.
　　　　　　　O voyagers, O seamen,
You who come to port, and you whose bodies
Will suffer the trial and judgment of the sea,
165 Or whatever event, this is your real destination."
So Krishna, as when he admonished Arjuna
On the field of battle.
　　　　　　　　　Not fare well,
But fare forward, voyagers.

　　　　　　　　4
Lady,[8] whose shrine stands on the promontory,
170 Pray for all those who are in ships, those
Whose business has to do with fish, and
Those concerned with every lawful traffic
And those who conduct them.

Repeat a prayer also on behalf of
175 Women who have seen their sons or husbands
Setting forth, and not returning:
Figlia del tuo figlio,[9]
Queen of Heaven.

Also pray for those who were in ships, and
180 Ended their voyage on the sand, in the sea's lips
Or in the dark throat which will not reject them
Or wherever cannot reach them the sound of the sea bell's
Perpetual angelus.[1]

6. Holding forth on a subject.
7. The quoted passage comes from the *Bag-havad-Gita*. Arjuna, the hero of the poem, has hesitated to fight, and Krishna says: "Whoso-ever at the time of death thinks only of Me, and thinking thus leaves the body and goes forth, assuredly he will know Me./ On what-ever sphere of being the mind of a man may be intent at the time of death, thither will he go./ Therefore meditate always on Me, and fight; if thy mind and thy reason be fixed on Me, to Me shalt thou surely come" [tr. by Shri Purohit Swāmi].
8. The Virgin Mary.
9. "The daughter of Thy Son." From St. Bernard's prayer to the Virgin in Dante, *Paradiso,* XXXIII.1.
1. A devotion commemorating the Incarnation, so called from its first word ("*Angelus domini nuntiavit Mariae*," "The angel of the lord announced to Mary"); it is repeated by Roman Catholics at morning, noon, and sunset, at the sound of a bell.

5

To communicate with Mars, converse with spirits,
To report the behavior of the sea monster,
Describe the horoscope, haruspicate or scry,[2]
Observe disease in signatures, evoke
Biography from the wrinkles of the palm
And tragedy from fingers; release omens
By sortilege,[3] or tea leaves, riddle the inevitable
With playing cards, fiddle with pentagrams[4]
Or barbituric acids, or dissect
The recurrent image into pre-conscious terrors—
To explore the womb, or tomb, or dreams; all these are usual
Pastimes and drugs, and features of the press:
And always will be, some of them especially
When there is distress of nations and perplexity
Whether on the shores of Asia, or in the Edgware Road.[5]
Men's curiosity searches past and future
And clings to that dimension. But to apprehend
The point of intersection of the timeless
With time, is an occupation for the saint—
No occupation either, but something given
And taken, in a lifetime's death in love,
Ardor and selflessness and self-surrender.
For most of us, there is only the unattended
Moment, the moment in and out of time,
The distraction fit, lost in a shaft of sunlight,
The wild thyme[6] unseen, or the winter lightning
Or the waterfall, or music heard so deeply
That it is not heard at all, but you are the music
While the music lasts. These are only hints and guesses,
Hints followed by guesses; and the rest
Is prayer, observance, discipline, thought and action.
The hint half guessed, the gift half understood, is Incarnation.
Here the impossible union
Of spheres of existence is actual,
Here the past and future
Are conquered, and reconciled,
Where action were otherwise movement
Of that which is only moved
And has in it no source of movement—
Driven by daemonic, chthonic[7]
Powers. And right action is freedom
From past and future also.
For most of us, this is the aim
Never here to be realized;
Who are only undefeated
Because we have gone on trying;
We, content at the last
If our temporal reversion nourish
(Not too far from the yew-tree)[8]
The life of significant soil.

1941

<hr>

2. A horoscope foretells the future from the positions of the planets at a given time. To *haruspicate* is to interpret the will of the gods by examining the entrails of sacrificed birds or animals. To *scry* is to see visions in a crystal.
3. Divination by drawing lots.
4. Five-pointed diagrams containing figures and symbols used in divination.

5. A busy, undistinguished street in London.
6. Aromatic herb.
7. Sprung from the earth, or from the underworld.
8. Throughout the *Four Quartets,* the yew-tree is a recurrent symbol for death, variously counterpointed or combined with the rose, a symbol of life.

JOHN CROWE RANSOM
(1888–1974)

Bells for John Whiteside's Daughter

There was such speed in her little body,
And such lightness in her footfall,
It is no wonder her brown study
Astonishes us all.

5   Her wars were bruited in our high window.
We looked among orchard trees and beyond
Where she took arms against her shadow,
Or harried unto the pond

The lazy geese, like a snow cloud
10 Dripping their snow on the green grass,
Tricking and stopping, sleepy and proud,
Who cried in goose, Alas,

For the tireless heart within the little
Lady with rod that made them rise
15 From their noon apple-dreams and scuttle
Goose-fashion under the skies!

But now go the bells, and we are ready,
In one house we are sternly stopped
To say we are vexed at her brown study,
20 Lying so primly propped.

1924

Vaunting Oak

He is a tower unleaning. But how will he not break,
If Heaven assault him with full wind and sleet,
And what uproar tall trees concumbent make!

More than a hundred years, more than a hundred feet
5   Naked he rears against the cold skies eruptive;
Only his temporal twigs are unsure of seat,

And the frail leaves of a season, which are susceptive
Of the mad humors of wind, and turn and flee
In panic round the stem on which they are captive.

10 Now a certain heart, too young and mortally
Linked with an unbeliever of bitter blood,
Observed, as an eminent witness of life, the tree,

And exulted, wrapped in a phantasy of good:
"Be the great oak for its long winterings
15 Our love's symbol, better than the summer's brood."

Then the venerable oak, delivered of his pangs,
Put forth profuse his green banners of peace
And testified to her with innumerable tongues.

And what but she fetch me up to the steep place
Where the oak vaunted? A flat where birdsong flew
Had to be traversed; and a quick populace

Of daisies, and yellow kinds; and here she knew,
Who had been instructed of much mortality,
Better than brag in this distraught purlieu.

Above the little and their dusty tombs was he
Standing, sheer on his hill, not much soiled over
By the knobs and broken boughs of an old tree,

And she murmured, "Established, you see him there! forever."
But, that her pitiful error be undone,
I knocked on his house loudly, a sorrowing lover,

And drew forth like a funeral a hollow tone.
"The old gentleman," I grieved, "holds gallantly,
But before our joy shall have lapsed, even, will be gone."

I knocked more sternly, and his dolorous cry
Boomed till its loud reverberance outsounded
The singing of bees; or the coward birds that fly

Otherwhere with their songs when summer is sped,
And if they stayed would perish miserably;
Or the tears of a girl remembering her dread.

1924

Dead Boy

The little cousin is dead, by foul subtraction,
A green bough from Virginia's aged tree,
And none of the county kin like the transaction,
Nor some of the world of outer dark, like me.

A boy not beautiful, nor good, nor clever,
A black cloud full of storms too hot for keeping,
A sword beneath his mother's heart—yet never
Woman bewept her babe as this is weeping.

A pig with a pasty face, so I had said,
Squealing for cookies, kinned by poor pretense
With a noble house. But the little man quite dead,
I see the forbears' antique lineaments.

The elder men have strode by the box of death
To the wide flag porch, and muttering low send round
The bruit° of the day. O friendly waste of breath!   *news, report*
Their hearts are hurt with a deep dynastic wound.

He was pale and little, the foolish neighbors say;
The first-fruits, saith the Preacher, the Lord hath taken;
But this was the old tree's late branch wrenched away,
Grieving the sapless limbs, the shorn and shaken.

1927

Antique Harvesters

(SCENE: OF THE MISSISSIPPI THE BANK SINISTER,[2] AND OF THE OHIO
THE BANK SINISTER.)

Tawny are the leaves turned but they still hold,
And it is harvest; what shall this land produce?
A meager hill of kernels, a runnel of juice;
Declension looks from our land, it is old.
5   Therefore let us assemble, dry, gray, spare,
And mild as yellow air.

"I hear the croak of a raven's funeral wing."
The young men would be joying in the song
Of passionate birds; their memories are not long.
10 What is it thus rehearsed in sable? "Nothing."
Trust not but the old endure, and shall be older
Than the scornful beholder.

We pluck the spindling ears and gather the corn.
One spot has special yield? "On this spot stood
15 Heroes and drenched it with their only blood."
And talk meets talk, as echoes from the horn
Of the hunter—echoes are the old men's arts,
Ample are the chambers of their hearts.

Here come the hunters, keepers of a rite;
20 The horn, the hounds, the lank mares coursing by
Straddled with archetypes of chivalry;
And the fox, lovely ritualist, in flight
Offering his unearthly ghost to quarry;
And the fields, themselves to harry.

25 Resume, harvesters. The treasure is full bronze
Which you will garner for the Lady, and the moon
Could tinge it no yellower than does this noon;
But gray will quench it shortly—the field, men, stones.
Pluck fast, dreamers; prove as you amble slowly
30 Not less than men, not wholly.

Bare the arm, dainty youths, bend the knees
Under bronze burdens. And by an autumn tone
As by a gray, as by a green, you will have known
Your famous Lady's image; for so have these;
35 And if one say that easily will your hands
More prosper in other lands,

Angry as wasp-music be your cry then:
"Forsake the Proud Lady, of the heart of fire,
The look of snow, to the praise of a dwindled choir,
40 Song of degenerate specters that were men?
The sons of the fathers shall keep her, worthy of
What these have done in love."

2. Left side.

True, it is said of our Lady, she ageth.
But see, if you peep shrewdly, she hath not stooped;
Take no thought of her servitors that have drooped,
For we are nothing; and if one talk of death—
Why, the ribs of the earth subsist frail as a breath
If but God wearieth.

1927

The Equilibrists

Full of her long white arms and milky skin
He had a thousand times remembered sin.
Alone in the press of people traveled he,
Minding her jacinth, and myrrh, and ivory.

Mouth he remembered: the quaint orifice
From which came heat that flamed upon the kiss,
Till cold words came down spiral from the head.
Grey doves from the officious tower illsped.

Body: it was a white field ready for love,
On her body's field, with the gaunt tower above,
The lilies grew, beseeching him to take,
If he would pluck and wear them, bruise and break.

Eyes talking: Never mind the cruel words,
Embrace my flowers, but not embrace the swords.
But what they said, the doves came straightway flying
And unsaid: Honor, Honor, they came crying.

Importunate her doves. Too pure, too wise,
Clambering on his shoulder, saying, Arise,
Leave me now, and never let us meet,
Eternal distance now command thy feet.

Predicament indeed, which thus discovers
Honor among thieves, Honor between lovers.
O such a little word is Honor, they feel!
But the grey word is between them cold as steel.

At length I saw these lovers fully were come
Into their torture of equilibrium;
Dreadfully had forsworn each other, and yet
They were bound each to each, and they did not forget.

And rigid as two painful stars, and twirled
About the clustered night their prison world,
They burned with fierce love always to come near,
But honor beat them back and kept them clear.

Ah, the strict lovers, they are ruined now!
I cried in anger. But with puddled brow
Devising for those gibbeted° and brave   *shamed*
Came I descanting:° Man, what would you have?   *discoursing*

For spin your period out, and draw your breath,
A kinder saeculum° begins with Death.   *age*
Would you ascend to Heaven and bodiless dwell?
40 Or take your bodies honorless to Hell?

In Heaven you have heard no marriage is,
No white flesh tinder to your lecheries,
Your male and female tissue sweetly shaped
Sublimed away, and furious blood escaped.

45 Great lovers lie in Hell, the stubborn ones
Infatuate of the flesh upon the bones;
Stuprate,° they rend each other when they kiss,   *ravished*
The pieces kiss again, no end to this.

But still I watched them spinning, orbited nice.
50 Their flames were not more radiant than their ice.
I dug in the quiet earth and wrought the tomb
And made these lines to memorize their doom:

Epitaph
Equilibrists lie here; stranger, tread light;
Close, but untouching in each other's sight;
55 *Mouldered the lips and ashy the tall skull.*
Let them lie perilous and beautiful.

1927

CLAUDE McKAY
(1890–1948)

America

Although she feeds me bread of bitterness,
And sinks into my throat her tiger's tooth,
Stealing my breath of life, I will confess
I love this cultured hell that tests my youth!
5 Her vigor flows like tides into my blood,
Giving me strength against her hate.
Her bigness sweeps my being like a flood.
Yet as a rebel fronts a king in state,
I stand within her walls with not a shred
10 Of terror, malice, not a word of jeer.
Darkly I gaze into the days ahead,
And see her might and granite wonders there,
Beneath the touch of Time's unerring hand,
Like priceless treasures sinking in the sand.

1922

If We Must Die

If we must die, let it not be like hogs
Hunted and penned in an inglorious spot,
While round us bark the mad and hungry dogs,

Making their mock at our accursèd lot.
If we must die, O let us nobly die,
So that our precious blood may not be shed
In vain; then even the monsters we defy
Shall be constrained to honor us though dead!
O kinsmen we must meet the common foe!
Though far outnumbered let us show us brave,
And for their thousand blows deal one deathblow!
What though before us lies the open grave?
Like men we'll face the murderous, cowardly pack,
Pressed to the wall, dying, but fighting back!

1922

HUGH MACDIARMID (C. M. Grieve)
(1892–1978)

Crowdieknowe

Oh to be at Crowdieknowe
When the last trumpet blaws,
An' see the deid come loupin'° owre   *leaping*
The auld grey wa's.°   *walls*

Muckle° men wi' tousled beards   *huge*
I grat at° as a bairn°   *wept at/child*
'll scramble frae the croodit° clay   *crowded*
Wi' feck° o' swearin'.   *a great deal*

An' glower at God an' a' His gang
O' angels i' the lift°   *sky*
—Thae trashy bleezin'° French-like folk   *blazing*
Wha gar'd them shift!°   *made them move*

Fain the weemun-folk'll seek
To mak' them haud° their row   *hold*
—Fegs, God's no blate gin [1] he stirs up
The men o' Crowdieknowe!

1925

The Innumerable Christ

*"Other stars may have their Bethlehem, and
their Calvary too."*
—PROFESSOR J. Y. SIMPSON

Wha kens° on whatna° Bethlehems   *knows/what kind of*
Earth twinkles like a star the nicht,
An' whatna shepherds lift their heids
  In its unearthly licht?°   *light*

'Yont a' the stars oor een° can see   *eyes*
An' farther than their lichts can fly,
I' mony an unco warl'° the nicht°   *strange world/night*
  The fatefu' bairnies° cry.   *babies*

1. "Faith, God is not backward, if . . ."

I' mony an unco warl' the nicht
10   The lift° gaes black as pitch at noon,   *sky*
     An' sideways on their chests the heids
        O' endless Christs roll doon.

     An' when the earth's as cauld's the mune
     An' a its folk are lang syne° deid,   *since*
15   On coontless stars the Babe maun° cry   *may*
        An' the Crucified maun bleed.

                                                                                  1925

Somersault

     I lo'e the stishie°   *stir*
     O' Earth in space
     Breengin'° by   *hurtling*
     At a haliket° pace.   *reckless, giddy*

5   A wecht° o' hills   *weight*
     Gangs wallopin' owre,
     Syne° a whummlin'° sea   *after/tumbling*
     Wi' a gallus glower.°   *with a reckless stare*

     The West whuds° doon   *thuds*
10   Like the pigs at Gadara, [2]
     But the East's aye° there   *always*
     Like a sow at the farrow.

                                                                                  1926

Parley of Beasts

     Auld Noah was at hame wi' them a',
     The lion and the lamb,
     Pair by pair they entered the Ark
     And he took them as they cam'.

5   If twa o' ilka° beist there is   *every*
     Into this room sud° come,   *should*
     Wad° I cud welcome them like him,   *would*
     And no' staun' gowpin' dumb!

     Be chief° wi' them and they wi' me   *very friendly*
10   And a' wi' ane anither
     As Noah and his couples were
     There in the Ark thegither.

     It's fain I'd mell° wi' tiger and tit,   *mix*
     Wi' elephant and eel,
15   But noo-a-days e'en wi' ain's se°   *one's own self*
     At hame it's hard to feel.

                                                                                  1926

2. Where Jesus, meeting two men possessed   a steep place to their destruction in the sea
by devils, cast the devils out of the men and   (Matthew viii.28–34).
into a herd of swine, which ran violently down

Bubblyjock°   *turkey*

It's hauf ° like a bird and hauf like a bogle °   *half/goblin*
And juist stands in the sun there and bouks.°   *hiccups*
It's a wunder its heid disna burst
The way it's aye raxin' its chouks.[3]

Syne ° it twists its neck like a serpent   *then*
But canna get oot a richt note
For the bubblyjock swallowed the bagpipes
And the blether ° stuck in its throat.   *bladder*
                                                                 1926

Bracken[4] Hills in Autumn

These beds of bracken, climax of the summer's growth,
Are elemental as the sky or sea.
In still and sunny weather they give back
The sun's glare with a fixed intensity
      As of steel or glass
      No other foliage has.

There is a menace in their indifference to man
As in tropical abundance. On gloomy days
They redouble the somber heaviness of the sky
And nurse the thunder. Their dense growth shuts the narrow ways
      Between the hills and draws
      Closer the wide valleys' jaws.

This flinty verdure's vast effusion is the more
Remarkable for the shortness of its stay.
From November to May a brown stain on the slopes
Downbeaten by frost and rain, then in quick array
      The silvery crooks appear [5]
      And the whole host is here.

Unless they may seem to men and go unused, but cast
Cartloads of them into a pool where the trout are few
And soon the swarming animalculae [6] upon them
Will proportionately increase the fishes too.
      Miracles are never far away
      Save bringing new thought to play.

In summer islanded in these gray-green seas where the wind plucks
The pale underside of the fronds on gusty days
As a land breeze stirs the white caps in a roadstead
Glimpses of shy bog gardens surprise the gaze
      Or rough stuff keeping a ring
      Round a struggling water-spring.

---

3. "The way it's always stretching its throat."
4. Large coarse fern.
5. The stalks of the plants, as they grow, are at first bent over at the top, like a shepherd's crook, and covered with a silvery fuzz or fleece.
6. Microscopically minute animals.

Look closely. Even now bog asphodel [7] spikes, still alight at the tips,
Sundew [8] lifting white buds like those of the whitlow grass [9]
On walls in spring over its little round leaves
Sparkling with gummy red hairs, and many a soft mass
35   Of the curious moss that can clean
                A wound or poison a river, are seen.

Ah! well I know my tumultuous days now at their prime
Will be brief as the bracken too in their stay
Yet in them as the flowers of the hills 'mid the bracken
40   All that I treasure is needs hidden away
                And will also be dead
                When its rude cover is shed.

                                              1962   1970

Audh and Cunaide

Two women I think of often.
Audh the deep-minded, mother
Of Hebridean [1] chiefs,
Who, widowed, went to Iceland
5   And sleeps in one of its cold reefs.

And Cunaide, a spinster of thirty-three,
Buried fifteen centuries ago near the west end
Of the railway viaduct at Hayle [2] in Cornwall
—Cunaide, no more unapproachable
10   In death than she was in life,
In Eternity than she was in time.
Oh, the cry might be found even yet
To bring Audh back to life again.
To quicken that resourceful heroic old body
15   Lying there like a cameo under glass.
A cry might be found to bring back
Audh, wife and mother, whose intrepid blood
Still runs in far generations
Of her children's children.
20   But Cunaide? . . . Who can imagine
Any appeal that would stir Cunaide
Who died, a virgin, so long ago
She might have been the sole inhabitant of another star,
Having nothing to do with human life
25   And Earth and its history at all?
Audh lies like a cameo under glass
Cunaide is an unmined diamond.

There is hope for one buried in ice,
But by a railway viaduct? . . . No!
30   "Come back to life, Cunaide!," we cry.

7. Or Lancashire asphodel, common on moorlands.
8. Small plant of the genus *Drosera*, growing in bogs; the hairs on its leaves secrete drops which glitter in the sun like dew. (Cf. Swinburne's poem, *The Sundew*, above.)
9. A grass formerly thought to cure the inflammation of finger or toe, known as a whitlow.
1. The Hebrides are islands off the west coast of northern Scotland; Iceland is 500 miles to the northwest by sea.
2. A town near the southwestern tip of England.

But if the answer comes: "To life? What's that?"
How could we tell one who doesn't know
What life is? What is it anyway?
. . . Audh knew!

1967

ARCHIBALD MacLEISH
(1892–　　　)

You, Andrew Marvell[2]

And here face down beneath the sun
And here upon earth's noonward height
To feel the always coming on
The always rising of the night

To feel creep up the curving east
The earthy chill of dusk and slow
Upon those under lands the vast
And ever climbing shadow grow

And strange at Ecbatan[3] the trees
Take leaf by leaf the evening strange
The flooding dark about their knees
The mountains over Persia change

And now at Kermanshah the gate
Dark empty and the withered grass
And through the twilight now the late
Few travelers in the westward pass

And Baghdad darken and the bridge
Across the silent river gone
And through Arabia the edge
Of evening widen and steal on

And deepen on Palmyra's street
The wheel rut in the ruined stone
And Lebanon fade out and Crete
High through the clouds and overblown

And over Sicily the air
Still flashing with the landward gulls
And loom and slowly disappear
The sails above the shadowy hulls

And Spain go under and the shore
Of Africa the gilded sand
And evening vanish and no more
The low pale light across that land

---

2. Andrew Marvell (1621–1678) wrote *To His Coy Mistress,* the poem to which MacLeish specifically alludes.
3. The poet's thoughts, following the daily path of the sun, move westward, from Ecbatana, once the capital of Media Magna (part of Persia), on to Kermanshah, Baghdad, Palmyra, Sicily, and so on.

Nor now the long light on the sea
And here face downward in the sun
35 To feel how swift how secretly
The shadow of the night comes on. . . .

1930

Empire Builders

The Museum Attendant:

This is *The Making of America in Five Panels*:

This is Mister Harriman[4] making America:
Mister-Harriman-is-buying-the-Union-Pacific-at-Seventy:
The Sante Fe is shining on his hair.

5   This is Commodore Vanderbilt[5] making America:
Mister-Vanderbilt-is-eliminating-the-short-interest-in-Hudson:
Observe the carving on the rocking chair.

This is J. P. Morgan[6] making America:
(The Tennessee Coal is behind to the left of the Steel Company.)
10 Those in mauve are braces he is wearing.

This is Mister Mellon[7] making America:
Mister-Mellon-is-represented-as-a-symbolic-figure-in-aluminum-
Strewing-bank-stocks-on-a-burnished-stair.

This is the Bruce is the Barton[8] making America:
15 Mister-Barton-is-selling-us-Doctor's-Deliciousest-Dentifrice.
This is he in beige with the canary.

You have just beheld the Makers making America:
This is The Making of America in Five Panels:
America lies to the west-southwest of the switch-tower:
20 There is nothing to see of America but land.

The Original Document under the Panel Paint:

"To Thos. Jefferson Esq. his obd't serv't
M. Lewis: captain: detached:
Sir:

Having in mind your repeated commands in this matter,
25 And the worst half of it done and the streams mapped,

And we here on the back of this beach beholding the
Other ocean—two years gone and the cold

Breaking with rain for the third spring since St. Louis,
The crows at the fishbones on the frozen dunes,

---

4. Edward H. Harriman (1848–1909), American railroad magnate and one of those called "robber barons" in the period.
5. Cornelius Vanderbilt (1794–1872), financier and railroad magnate.
6. J. P. Morgan (1837–1913), banker and financier.
7. Andrew Mellon (1855–1937), financier, one-time Secretary of the Treasury and, like Harriman, Vanderbilt, and Morgan, a man of enormous wealth and power.
8. Bruce Barton (1886–   ), pioneer American advertising executive who made extraordinary use of that profession in his religious writings.

The first cranes going over from south north,
And the river down by a mark of the pole since the morning,

And time near to return, and a ship (Spanish)
Lying in for the salmon: and fearing chance or the

Drought or the Sioux should deprive you of these discoveries—
Therefore we send by sea in this writing.

                                        Above the
Platte[9] there were long plains and a clay country:
Rim of the sky far off, grass under it,

Dung for the cook fires by the sulphur licks.
After that there were low hills and the sycamores,

And we poled up by the Great Bend in the skiffs:
The honey bees left us after the Osage River.[1]

The wind was west in the evenings, and no dew and the
Morning Star larger and whiter than usual—

The winter rattling in the brittle haws.
The second year there was sage and the quail calling.

All that valley is good land by the river:
Three thousand miles and the clay cliffs and

Rue and beargrass by the water banks
And many birds and the brant going over and tracks of

Bear, elk, wolves, marten: the buffalo
Numberless so that the cloud of their dust covers them:

The antelope fording the fall creeks, and the mountains and
Grazing lands and the meadow lands and the ground

Sweet and open and well-drained.
                                    We advise you to
Settle troops at the forks and to issue licenses:

Many men will have living on these lands.
There is wealth in the earth for them all and the wood standing

And wild birds on the water where they sleep.
There is stone in the hills for the towns of a great people . . ."

You have just beheld the Makers Making America:

They screwed her scrawny and gaunt with their seven-year panics:
They bought her back on their mortgages old-whore-cheap:

They fattened their bonds at her breasts till the thin blood ran from them.

Men have forgotten how full clear and deep
The Yellowstone moved on the gravel and the grass grew
When the land lay waiting for her westward people!   1933

---

9. A river in Nebraska.   1. The Great Bend and Osage are rivers in
                                           Kansas.

Seafarer

And learn O voyager to walk
The roll of earth, the pitch and fall
That swings across these trees those stars:
That swings the sunlight up the wall.

5   And learn upon these narrow beds
To sleep in spite of sea, in spite
Of sound the rushing planet makes:
And learn to sleep against this ground.

1933

The Snowflake Which Is Now and Hence Forever

Will it last? he says.
Is it a masterpiece?
Will generation after generation
Turn with reverence to the page?

5   Birdseye scholar of the frozen fish,
What would he make of the sole, clean, clear
Leap of the salmon that has disappeared?

To *be*, yes!—whether they like it or not!
But not to last when leap and water are forgotten,
10 A plank of standard pinkness in the dish.

They also live
Who swerve and vanish in the river.

1952

WILFRED OWEN
(1893–1918)

Strange Meeting

It seemed that out of battle I escaped
Down some profound dull tunnel, long since scooped
Through granites which titanic wars had groined.
Yet also there encumbered sleepers groaned,
5   Too fast in thought or death to be bestirred.
Then, as I probed them, one sprang up, and stared
With piteous recognition in fixed eyes,
Lifting distressful hands as if to bless.
And by his smile, I knew that sullen hall,
10 By his dead smile I knew we stood in Hell.
With a thousand pains that vision's face was grained;
Yet no blood reached there from the upper ground,
And no guns thumped, or down the flues made moan.
"Strange friend," I said, "here is no cause to mourn."
15 "None," said that other, "save the undone years,
The hopelessness. Whatever hope is yours,
Was my life also; I went hunting wild

After the wildest beauty in the world,
Which lies not calm in eyes, or braided hair,
But mocks the steady running of the hour,
And if it grieves, grieves richlier than here.
For of my glee might many men have laughed,
And of my weeping something had been left,
Which must die now. I mean the truth untold,
The pity of war, the pity war distilled.
Now men will go content with what we spoiled.
Or, discontent, boil bloody, and be spilled.
They will be swift with swiftness of the tigress,
None will break ranks, though nations trek from progress.
Courage was mine, and I had mystery,
Wisdom was mine, and I had mastery:
To miss the march of this retreating world
Into vain citadels that are not walled.
Then, when much blood had clogged their chariot wheels
I would go up and wash them from sweet wells,
Even with truths that lie too deep for taint.
I would have poured my spirit without stint
But not through wounds; not on the cess° of war.   *waste*
Foreheads of men have bled where no wounds were.
I am the enemy you killed, my friend.
I knew you in this dark; for so you frowned
Yesterday through me as you jabbed and killed.
I parried; but my hands were loath and cold.
Let us sleep now. . . ."

                                          1919   1920

The Parable of the Old Man and the Young

So Abram rose,[1] and clave the wood, and went,
And took the fire with him, and a knife.
And as they sojourned both of them together,
Isaac the first-born spake and said, My Father,
Behold the preparations, fire and iron,
But where the lamb for this burnt offering?
Then Abram bound the youth with belts and straps,
And builded parapets and trenches there,
And stretchèd forth the knife to slay his son.
When lo! an angel called him out of heaven,
Saying, Lay not thy hand upon the lad,
Neither do anything to him. Behold,
A ram, caught in a thicket by its horns;
Offer the Ram of Pride instead of him.
But the old man would not so, but slew his son,
And half the seed of Europe, one by one.

                                                        1920

Anthem for Doomed Youth

What passing-bells for these who die as cattle?
   Only the monstrous anger of the guns.
   Only the stuttering rifles' rapid rattle

1. See Genesis xxii.1–14. God tested Abraham by commanding him to sacrifice his son Isaac, sending a ram to be sacrificed instead when it was clear that the God-fearing Abraham would obey the command.

Can patter out their hasty orisons.°   *prayers*
5   No mockeries now for them; no prayers nor bells,
        Nor any voice of mourning save the choirs—
    The shrill, demented choirs of wailing shells;
        And bugles calling for them from sad shires.

    What candles may be held to speed them all?
10   Not in the hands of boys, but in their eyes
    Shall shine the holy glimmers of good-byes.
        The pallor of girls' brows shall be their pall;
    Their flowers the tenderness of patient minds,
    And each slow dusk a drawing-down of blinds.

                                        1917   1920

Futility

    Move him into the sun—
    Gently its touch awoke him once,
    At home, whispering of fields unsown.
    Always it woke him, even in France,
5   Until this morning and this snow.
    If anything might rouse him now
    The kind old sun will know.

    Think how it wakes the seeds—
    Woke, once, the clays of a cold star.
10 Are limbs, so dear-achieved, are sides,
    Full-nerved—still warm—too hard to stir?
    Was it for this the clay grew tall?
    —O what made fatuous sunbeams toil
    To break earth's sleep at all?

                                        1918   1920

E. E. CUMMINGS
(1894–1963)

All in green went my love riding

    All in green went my love riding
    on a great horse of gold
    into the silver dawn.

    four lean hounds crouched low and smiling
5   the merry deer ran before.

    Fleeter be they than dappled dreams
    the swift sweet deer
    the red rare deer.

    Four red roebuck at a white water
10 the cruel bugle sang before.

    Horn at hip went my love riding
    riding the echo down
    into the silver dawn.

four lean hounds crouched low and smiling
the level meadows ran before.

Softer be they than slippered sleep
the lean lithe deer
the fleet flown deer.

Four fleet does at a gold valley
the famished arrow sang before.

Bow at belt went my love riding
riding the mountain down
into the silver dawn.

four lean hounds crouched low and smiling
the sheer peaks ran before.

Paler be they than daunting death
the sleek slim deer
the tall tense deer.

Four tall stags at a green mountain
the lucky hunter sang before.

All in green went my love riding
on a great horse of gold
into the silver dawn.

four lean hounds crouched low and smiling
my heart fell dead before.

1923

in Just-

in Just-
spring   when the world is mud-
luscious the little
lame balloonman

whistles   far   and wee

and eddieandbill come
running from marbles and
piracies and it's
spring

when the world is puddle-wonderful

the queer
old balloonman whistles
far   and   wee
and bettyandisbel come dancing

from hop-scotch and jump-rope and

it's
spring
and
    the

20   goat-footed
balloonMan   whistles
far
and
wee

                        1923

O sweet spontaneous

O sweet spontaneous
earth how often have
the
doting

5   fingers of
prurient philosophers pinched
and
poked

thee
10 , has the naughty thumb
of science prodded
thy

      beauty . how
often have religions taken
15 thee upon their scraggy knees
squeezing and

buffeting thee that thou mightest conceive
gods
        (but
20 true

to the incomparable
couch of death thy
rhythmic
lover

25   thou answerest

them only with

          spring)

                        1923

the Cambridge ladies who live in furnished souls

the Cambridge ladies who live in furnished souls
are unbeautiful and have comfortable minds
(also, with the church's protestant blessings
daughters, unscented shapeless spirited)

they believe in Christ and Longfellow, both dead,
are invariably interested in so many things—
at the present writing one still finds
delighted fingers knitting for the is it Poles?
perhaps. While permanent faces coyly bandy
scandal of Mrs. N and Professor D
. . . . the Cambridge ladies do not care, above
Cambridge if sometimes in its box of
sky lavender and cornerless, the
moon rattles like a fragment of angry candy

1923

Spring is like a perhaps hand

Spring is like a perhaps hand
(which comes carefully
out of Nowhere)arranging
a window,into which people look(while
people stare
arranging and changing placing
carefully there a strange
thing and a known thing here) and

changing everything carefully

spring is like a perhaps
Hand in a window
(carefully to
and fro moving New and
Old things,while
people stare carefully
moving a perhaps
fraction of flower here placing
an inch of air there)and

without breaking anything.

1925

who's most afraid of death? thou

who's most afraid of death? thou
                         art of him
utterly afraid, i love of thee
(beloved) this

              and truly i would be
near when his scythe takes crisply the whim
of thy smoothness. and mark the fainting
murdered petals. with the caving stem.

But of all most would i be one of them

round the hurt heart which do so frailly cling . . . .)
i who am but imperfect in my fear

Or with thy mind against my mind, to hear
nearing our hearts' irrevocable play—
through the mysterious high futile day

15   an enormous stride
     (and drawing thy mouth toward

my mouth, steer our lost bodies carefully downward)

                1925

"next to of course god america i

"next to of course god america i
love you land of the pilgrims' and so forth oh
say can you see by the dawn's early my
country 'tis of centuries come and go
5   and are no more what of it we should worry
in every language even deafanddumb
thy sons acclaim your glorious name by gorry
by jingo by gee by gosh by gum
why talk of beauty what could be more beaut-
10   iful than these heroic happy dead
who rushed like lions to the roaring slaughter
they did not stop to think they died instead
then shall the voice of liberty be mute?"

He spoke. And drank rapidly a glass of water

                1926

since feeling is first

since feeling is first
who pays any attention
to the syntax of things
will never wholly kiss you;
5   wholly to be a fool
while Spring is in the world

my blood approves,
and kisses are a better fate
than wisdom
10   lady i swear by all flowers. Don't cry
—the best gesture of my brain is less than
your eyelids' flutter which says

we are for each other: then
laugh, leaning back in my arms
15   for life's not a paragraph

And death i think is no parenthesis

                1926

along the brittle treacherous bright streets

along the brittle treacherous bright streets
of memory comes my heart, singing like
an idiot, whispering like a drunken man

who(at a certain corner, suddenly)meets
the tall policeman of my mind.
                         awake
being not asleep, elsewhere our dreams began
which now are folded: but the year completes
his life as a forgotten prisoner

—"Ici?"—"Ah non, mon cheri; il fait trop froid"—[2]
they are gone:along these gardens moves a wind bringing
rain and leaves, filling the air with fear
and sweetness. . . . pauses. (Halfwhispering . . . . halfsinging

stirs the always smiling chevaux de bois[3])

when you were in Paris we met here

1926

i sing of Olaf glad and big

i sing of Olaf glad and big
whose warmest heart recoiled at war:
a conscientious object-or

his wellbelovéd colonel(trig°   *primly neat*
westpointer most succinctly bred)
took erring Olaf soon in hand;
but—though an host of overjoyed
noncoms(first knocking on the head
him)do through icy waters roll
that helplessness which others stroke
with brushes recently employed
anent this muddy toiletbowl,
while kindred intellects evoke
allegiance per blunt instruments—
Olaf(being to all intents
a corpse and wanting any rag
upon what God unto him gave)
responds,without getting annoyed
"I will not kiss your f.ing flag"

straightway the silver bird [4] looked grave
(departing hurriedly to shave)

but—though all kinds of officers
(a yearning nation's blueeyed pride)
their passive prey did kick and curse
until for wear their clarion
voices and boots were much the worse,
and egged the firstclassprivates on
his rectum wickedly to tease
by means of skillfully applied
bayonets roasted hot with heat—
Olaf(upon what were once knees)
does almost ceaselessly repeat
"there is some s. I will not eat"

2. "Here?"—"Ah, no, my dear; it is too cold."
3. Wooden horses.

4. The colonel; strictly speaking, his insignia of rank.

our president,being of which
35 assertions duly notified
threw the yellowsonofabitch
into a dungeon,where he died

Christ(of His mercy infinite)
i pray to see;and Olaf,too

40 preponderatingly because
unless statistics lie he was
more brave than me:more blond than you.

1931

somewhere i have never travelled,gladly beyond

somewhere i have never travelled,gladly beyond
any experience,your eyes have their silence:
in your most frail gesture are things which enclose me,
or which i cannot touch because they are too near

5 your slightest look easily will unclose me
though i have closed myself as fingers,
you open always petal by petal myself as Spring opens
(touching skilfully,mysteriously)her first rose

or if your wish be to close me,i and
10 my life will shut very beautifully,suddenly,
as when the heart of this flower imagines
the snow carefully everywhere descending;

nothing which we are to perceive in this world equals
the power of your intense fragility:whose texture
15 compels me with the colour of its countries,
rendering death and forever with each breathing

(i do not know what it is about you that closes
and opens;only something in me understands
the voice of your eyes is deeper than all roses)
20 nobody,not even the rain,has such small hands

1931

anyone lived in a pretty how town

anyone lived in a pretty how town
(with up so floating many bells down)
spring summer autumn winter
he sang his didn't he danced his did.

5 Women and men(both little and small)
cared for anyone not at all
they sowed their isn't they reaped their same
sun moon stars rain

children guessed(but only a few
10 and down they forgot as up they grew
autumn winter spring summer)
that noone loved him more by more

when by now and tree by leaf
she laughed his joy she cried his grief
bird by snow and stir by still
anyone's any was all to her

someones married their everyones
laughed their cryings and did their dance
(sleep wake hope and then)they
said their nevers they slept their dream

stars rain sun moon
(and only the snow can begin to explain
how children are apt to forget to remember
with up so floating many bells down)

one day anyone died i guess
(and noone stooped to kiss his face)
busy folk buried them side by side
little by little and was by was

all by all and deep by deep
and more by more they dream their sleep
noone and anyone earth by april
wish by spirit and if by yes.

Women and men(both dong and ding)
summer autumn winter spring
reaped their sowing and went their came
sun moon stars rain

                                                            1940

my father moved through dooms of love

my father moved through dooms of love
through sames of am through haves of give,
singing each morning out of each night
my father moved through depths of height

this motionless forgetful where
turned at his glance to shining here;
that if(so timid air is firm)
under his eyes would stir and squirm

newly as from unburied which
floats the first who,his april touch
drove sleeping selves to swarm their fates
woke dreamers to their ghostly roots

and should some why completely weep
my father's fingers brought her sleep:
vainly no smallest voice might cry
for he could feel the mountains grow.

Lifting the valleys of the sea
my father moved through griefs of joy;
praising a forehead called the moon
singing desire into begin

joy was his song and joy so pure
a heart of star by him could steer
and pure so now and now so yes
the wrists of twilight would rejoice

25 keen as midsummer's keen beyond
conceiving mind of sun will stand,
so strictly(over utmost him
so hugely)stood my father's dream

his flesh was flesh his blood was blood:
30 no hungry man but wished him food;
no cripple wouldn't creep one mile
uphill to only see him smile.

Scorning the pomp of must and shall
my father moved through dooms of feel;
35 his anger was as right as rain
his pity was as green as grain

septembering arms of year extend
less humbly wealth to foe and friend
than he to foolish and to wise
40 offered immeasurable is

proudly and(by octobering flame
beckoned)as earth will downward climb,
so naked for immortal work
his shoulders marched against the dark

45 his sorrow was as true as bread:
no liar looked him in the head;
if every friend became his foe
he'd laugh and build a world with snow.

My father moved through theys of we,
50 singing each new leaf out of each tree
(and every child was sure that spring
danced when she heard my father sing)

then let men kill which cannot share,
let blood and flesh be mud and mire,
55 scheming imagine,passion willed,
freedom a drug that's bought and sold

giving to steal and cruel kind,
a heart to fear,to doubt a mind,
to differ a disease of same,
60 conform the pinnacle of am

though dull were all we taste as bright,
bitter all utterly things sweet,
maggoty minus and dumb death
all we inherit,all bequeath

65 and nothing quite so least as truth
—i say though hate were why men breathe—
because my father lived his soul
love is the whole and more than all

1940

these children singing in stone a

these children singing in stone a
silence of stone these
little children wound with stone
flowers opening for

ever these silently lit
tle children are petals
their song is a flower of
always their flowers

of stone are
silently singing
a song more silent
than silence these always

children forever
singing wreathed with singing
blossoms children of
stone with blossoming

eyes
know if a
lit tle
tree listens

forever to always children singing forever
a song made
of silent as stone silence of
song

1940

what if a much of a which of a wind

what if a much of a which of a wind
gives the truth to summer's lie;
bloodies with dizzying leaves the sun
and yanks immortal stars awry?
Blow king to beggar and queen to seem
(blow friend to fiend: blow space to time)
—when skies are hanged and oceans drowned,
the single secret will still be man

what if a keen of a lean wind flays
screaming hills with sleet and snow:
strangles valleys by ropes of thing
and stifles forests in white ago?
Blow hope to terror; blow seeing to blind
(blow pity to envy and soul to mind)
—whose hearts are mountains, roots are trees,
it's they shall cry hello to the spring

what if a dawn of a doom of a dream
bites this universe in two,
peels forever out of his grave
and sprinkles nowhere with me and you?

Blow soon to never and never to twice
(blow life to isn't:blow death to was)
—all nothing's only our hugest home;
the most who die, the more we live

1944

JEAN TOOMER
(1894–1967)

Face

Hair—
silver-gray,
like streams of stars,
Brows—
5 recurved canoes
quivered by the ripples blown by pain,
Her eyes—
mist of tears
condensing on the flesh below
10 And her channeled muscles
are cluster grapes of sorrow
purple in the evening sun
nearly ripe for worms.

192·

Georgia Dusk

The sky, lazily disdaining to pursue
  The setting sun, too indolent to hold
  A lengthened tournament for flashing gold,
Passively darkens for night's barbecue,

5 A feast of moon and men and barking hounds,
  An orgy for some genius of the South
  With blood-hot eyes and cane-lipped scented mouth,
Surprised in making folksongs from soul sounds.

The sawmill blows its whistle, buzz-saws stop,
10 And silence breaks the bud of knoll and hill,
  Soft settling pollen where plowed lands fulfill
Their early promise of a bumper crop.

Smoke from the pyramidal sawdust pile
  Curls up, blue ghosts of trees, tarrying low
15 Where only chips and stumps are left to show
The solid proof of former domicile.

Meanwhile, the men, with vestiges of pomp,
  Race memories of king and caravan,
  High-priests, an ostrich, and a juju-man,°   *witch-doctor*
20 Go singing through the footpaths of the swamp.

Their voices rise . . the pine trees are guitars,
    Strumming, pine-needles fall like sheets of rain . .
    Their voices rise . . the chorus of the cane
Is caroling a vesper to the stars. .

O singers, resinous and soft your songs
    Above the sacred whisper of the pines,
    Give virgin lips to cornfield concubines,
Bring dreams of Christ to dusky cane-lipped throngs.

                                                        1923

Portrait in Georgia

Hair—braided chestnut,
    coiled like a lyncher's rope,
Eyes—fagots,
Lips—old scars, or the first red blisters,
Breath—the last sweet scent of cane,
And her slim body, white as the ash
    of black flesh after flame.

                                                        1923

Harvest Song

I am a reaper whose muscles set at sundown. All my oats are cradled.
But I am too chilled, and too fatigued to bind them. And I hunger.

I crack a grain between my teeth. I do not taste it.
I have been in the fields all day. My throat is dry. I hunger.

My eyes are caked with dust of oatfields at harvest-time.
I am a blind man who stares across the hills, seeking stacked fields of
    other harvesters.

It would be good to see them . . crook'd, split, and iron-ringed handles
    of the scythes. It would be good to see them, dust-caked and blind.
    I hunger.

(Dusk is a strange feared sheath their blades are dulled in.)
My throat is dry. And should I call, a cracked grain like the oats . . .
    eoho—

I fear to call. What should they hear me, and offer me their grain, oats,
    or wheat, or corn? I have been in the fields all day. I fear I could
    not taste it. I fear knowledge of my hunger.

My ears are caked with dust of oatfields at harvest-time.
I am a deaf man who strains to hear the calls of other harvesters whose
    throats are also dry.

It would be good to hear their songs . . reapers of the sweet-stalked
    cane, cutters of the corn . . even though their throats cracked and
    the strangeness of their voices deafened me.

I hunger. My throat is dry. Now that the sun has set and I am chilled,
    I fear to call. (Eoho, my brothers!)

15 I am a reaper. (Eoho!) All my oats are cradled. But I am too fatigued
    to bind them. And I hunger. I crack a grain. It has no taste to it.
    My throat is dry. . .

O my brothers, I beat my palms, still soft, against the stubble of my
    harvesting. (You beat your soft palms, too.) My pain is sweet.
    Sweeter than the oats or wheat or corn. It will not bring me knowledge
    of my hunger.

1923

ROBERT GRAVES
(1895–   )

Lost Love

His eyes are quickened so with grief,
He can watch a grass or leaf
Every instant grow; he can
Clearly through a flint wall see,
5   Or watch the startled spirit flee
From the throat of a dead man.
    Across two counties he can hear
And catch your words before you speak.
The woodlouse or the maggot's weak
10 Clamor rings in his sad ear,
And noise so slight it would surpass
Credence—drinking sound of grass,
Worm talk, clashing jaws of moth
Chumbling holes in cloth;
15 The groan of ants who undertake
Gigantic loads for honor's sake
(Their sinews creak, their breath comes thin);
Whir of spiders when they spin,
And minute whispering, mumbling, sighs
20 Of idle grubs and flies.
    This man is quickened so with grief,
He wanders god-like or like thief
Inside and out, below, above,
Without relief seeking lost love.

1919

The Cool Web

Children are dumb to say how hot the day is,
How hot the scent is of the summer rose,
How dreadful the black wastes of evening sky,
How dreadful the tall soldiers drumming by.

5   But we have speech, to chill the angry day,
And speech, to dull the rose's cruel scent.
We spell away the overhanging night,
We spell away the soldiers and the fright.

There's a cool web of language winds us in,
Retreat from too much joy or too much fear:
We grow sea-green at last and coldly die
In brininess and volubility.

But if we let our tongues lose self-possession,
Throwing off language and its watery clasp
Before our death, instead of when death comes,
Facing the wide glare of the children's day,
Facing the rose, the dark sky and the drums,
We shall go mad no doubt and die that way.

1927

Warning to Children

Children, if you dare to think
Of the greatness, rareness, muchness,
Fewness of this precious only
Endless world in which you say
You live, you think of things like this:
Blocks of slate enclosing dappled
Red and green, enclosing tawny
Yellow nets, enclosing white
And black acres of dominoes,
Where a neat brown paper parcel
Tempts you to untie the string.
In the parcel a small island,
On the island a large tree,
On the tree a husky fruit.
Strip the husk and pare the rind off:
In the kernel you will see
Blocks of slate enclosed by dappled
Red and green, enclosed by tawny
Yellow nets, enclosed by white
And black acres of dominoes,
Where the same brown paper parcel—
Children, leave the string alone!
For who dares undo the parcel
Finds himself at once inside it,
On the island, in the fruit,
Blocks of slate about his head,
Finds himself enclosed by dappled
Green and red, enclosed by yellow
Tawny nets, enclosed by black
And white acres of dominoes,
With the same brown paper parcel
Still unopened on his knee.
And, if he then should dare to think
Of the fewness, muchness, rareness,
Greatness of this endless only
Precious world in which he says
He lives—he then unties the string.

1929

To Juan at the Winter Solstice [1]

There is one story and one story only
That will prove worth your telling,
Whether as learned bard or gifted child;
To it all lines or lesser gauds belong
That startle with their shining
Such common stories as they stray into.

Is it of trees you tell, their months and virtues,
Or strange beasts that beset you,
Of birds that croak at you the Triple will? [2]
Or of the Zodiac and how slow it turns
Below the Boreal Crown,
Prison of all true kings that ever reigned? [3]

Water to water, ark again to ark,
From woman back to woman:
So each new victim treads unfalteringly
The never altered circuit of his fate,
Bringing twelve peers [4] as witness
Both to his starry rise and starry fall.

Or is it of the Virgin's silver beauty,
All fish below the thighs?
She in her left hand bears a leafy quince; [5]
When, with her right she crooks a finger, smiling,
How may the King hold back?
Royally then he barters life for love.

Or of the undying snake from chaos hatched,
Whose coils contain the ocean,
Into whose chops with naked sword he springs,
Then in black water, tangled by the reeds,
Battles three days and nights,
To be spewed up beside her scalloped shore?

Much snow if falling, winds roar hollowly,
The owl hoots from the elder,
Fear in your heart cries to the loving-cup:
Sorrow to sorrow as the sparks fly upward.
The log [6] groans and confesses:
There is one story and one story only.

Dwell on her graciousness, dwell on her smiling,
Do not forget what flowers

5

10

15

20

25

30

30

---

1. Juan, Graves's son, was born December 21, 1945—one day before the winter solstice, the shortest day of the year.
2. These omens pertain to the "one story" of line 1, the myth of the White Goddess and the Solar Hero (or King), which is the subject of this poem and of Graves's mythological study, *The White Goddess* (1948).
3. The Boreal Crown, according to Graves, is the mythical purgatory to which the Solar Hero goes between death and reincarnation. At the winter solstice, the Hero appears in an ark, floating on the water; he conquers a dragon in order to wed the White Goddess, who as mother, wife, and death personifies the three main phases of human life; finally, in October, he inevitably suffers death at her

hands. Graves maintains that the Sun Gods and the heroes of many religions and legends all express this central myth.
4. For example, King Arthur's 12 knights of the Round Table, Christ's apostles, or the constellations of the Zodiac which "witness" the sun's progress through the twelve months of the year.
5. Among the women typically shown offering a quince (the Biblical apple) to men as a token of love and death are Aphrodite, Greek goddess of love; Rahab, a Hebraic mermaid-goddess; and Eve. The King in line 15 is the Solar Hero.
6. "The *log* is the Yule log, burned at the year's end" [Graves's note].

The great boar trampled down in ivy time.[7]
Her brow was creamy as the crested wave,
Her sea-blue eyes were wild
But nothing promised that is not performed.

1945

The Frog and the Golden Ball

She let her golden ball fall down the well
   And begged a cold frog to retrieve it;
For which she kissed his ugly, gaping mouth—
   Indeed, he could scarce believe it.

And seeing him transformed to his princely shape,
   Who had been by hags enchanted,
She knew she could never love another man
   Nor by any fate be daunted.

But what would her royal father and mother say?
   They had promised her in marriage
To a cousin whose wide kingdom marched with theirs,
   Who rode in a jeweled carriage.

'Our plight, dear heart, would appear past human hope
   To all except you and me: to all
Who have never swum as a frog in a dark well
   Or have lost a golden ball.'

'What then shall we do now?' she asked her lover.
   He kissed her again, and said:
'Is magic of love less powerful at your Court
   Than at this green well-head?'

1965

HART CRANE
(1899–1932)

Praise for an Urn

IN MEMORIAM: ERNEST NELSON

It was a kind and northern face
That mingled in such exile guise
The everlasting eyes of Pierrot[1]
And, of Gargantua,[2] the laughter.

His thoughts, delivered to me
From the white coverlet and pillow,
I see now, were inheritances—
Delicate riders of the storm.

---

7. Ivy was eaten by priestesses as an intoxicant in the October festival of Dionysus, Greek god of wine and religious ecstasy. The boar is a mythical giver of death, here that of the Solar Hero.

1. Traditionally the sad clown with loose white costume, white face, and dark mournful eyes.
2. The gigantic king-hero of Rabelais' *Gargantua* (1535) who inspires hearty laughter.

The slant moon on the slanting hill
10 Once moved us toward presentiments
Of what the dead keep, living still,
And such assessments of the soul

As, perched in the crematory lobby,
The insistent clock commented on,
15 Touching as well upon our praise
Of glories proper to the time.

Still, having in mind gold hair,
I cannot see that broken brow
And miss the dry sound of bees
20 Stretching across a lucid space.

Scatter these well-meant idioms
Into the smoky spring that fills
The suburbs, where they will be lost.
They are no trophies of the sun.

1926

At Melville's Tomb

Often beneath the wave, wide from this ledge
The dice[3] of drowned men's bones he saw bequeath
An embassy. Their numbers as he watched,
Beat on the dusty shore and were obscured.

5 And wrecks passed without sound of bells,
The calyx[4] of death's bounty giving back
A scattered chapter, livid hieroglyph,
The portent wound in corridors of shells.

Then in the circuit calm of one vast coil,
10 Its lashings charmed and malice reconciled,
Frosted eyes there were that lifted altars;
And silent answers crept across the stars.

Compass, quadrant and sextant[5] contrive
No farther tides . . . High in the azure steeps
15 Monody shall not wake the mariner.
This fabulous shadow only the sea keeps.

1926

Voyages

1

Above the fresh ruffles of the surf
Bright striped urchins flay each other with sand.
They have contrived a conquest for shell shucks,
And their fingers crumble fragments of baked weed
5 Gaily digging and scattering.

---

3. Small, broken pieces.
4. Chalice, or cup-like container.
5. Instruments of measurement: the compass for describing circles or determining geographic directions; the quadrant and sextant for measuring angles and reckoning altitudes.

And in answer to their treble interjections
The sun beats lightning on the waves,
The waves fold thunder on the sand;
And could they hear me I would tell them:

O brilliant kids, frisk with your dog,
Fondle your shells and sticks, bleached
By time and the elements; but there is a line
You must not cross nor ever trust beyond it
Spry cordage of your bodies to caresses
Too lichen-faithful from too wide a breast.
The bottom of the sea is cruel.

2

—And yet this great wink of eternity,
Of rimless floods, unfettered leewardings,
Samite[6] sheeted and processioned where
Her undinal vast belly moonward bends,
Laughing the wrapt inflections of our love;

Take this Sea, whose diapason knells
On scrolls of silver snowy sentences,
The sceptered terror of whose sessions rends
As her demeanors motion well or ill,
All but the pieties of lovers' hands.

And onward, as bells off San Salvador[7]
Salute the crocus lusters of the stars,
In these poinsettia[8] meadows of her tides—
Adagios[9] of islands, O my Prodigal,
Complete the dark confessions her veins spell.

Mark how her turning shoulders wind the hours,
And hasten while her penniless rich palms
Pass superscription of bent foam and wave—
Hasten, while they are true—sleep, death, desire,
Close round one instant in one floating flower.

Bind us in time, O Seasons clear, and awe.
O minstrel galleons of Carib[1] fire,
Bequeath us to no earthly shore until
Is answered in the vortex of our grave
The seal's wide spindrift gaze toward paradise.

3

Infinite consanguinity it bears—
This tendered theme of you that light
Retrieves from sea plains where the sky
Resigns a breast that every wave enthrones;
While ribboned water lanes I wind
Are laved and scattered with no stroke
Wide from your side, whereto this hour
The sea lifts, also, reliquary[2] hands.

---

6. A rich, silk fabric.
7. The Spanish name for an island of the Bahamas group, Columbus's first landfall on the first voyage.
8. Exotic flower or shrub with a small yellow blossom surrounded by bright red leaves or bracts.

9. The divisions of a composition which are musically slow and graceful.
1. Some of the West Indian islands, or the sea surrounding them.
2. Characteristic of relics, or of the container for preserving them.

And so, admitted through black swollen gates
10 That must arrest all distance otherwise,
Past whirling pillars and lithe pediments,
Light wrestling there incessantly with light,
Star kissing star through wave on wave unto
Your body rocking!
15   and where death, if shed,
Presumes no carnage, but this single change,
Upon the steep floor flung from dawn to dawn
The silken skilled transmemberment[3] of song;

Permit me voyage, love, into your hands . . .

4

Whose counted smile of hours and days, suppose
I know as spectrum of the sea and pledge
Vastly now parting gulf on gulf of wings
Whose circles bridge, I know, (from palms to the severe
5 Chilled albatross's[4] white immutability)
No stream of greater love advancing now
Than, singing, this mortality alone
Through clay aflow immortally to you.

All fragrance irrefragibly,[5] and claim
10 Madly meeting logically in this hour
And region that is ours to wreathe again,
Portending eyes and lips and making told
The chancel port and portion of our June—

Shall they not stem and close in our own steps
15 Bright staves of flowers and quills to-day as I
Must first be lost in fatal tides to tell?

In signature of the incarnate word
The harbor shoulders to resign in mingling
Mutual blood, transpiring as foreknown
20 And widening noon within your breast for gathering
All bright insinuations that my years have caught
For islands where must lead inviolably
Blue latitudes and levels of your eyes—

In this expectant, still exclaim receive
25 The secret oar and petals of all love.

5

Meticulous, past midnight in clear rime,
Infrangible and lonely, smooth as though cast
Together in one merciless white blade—
The bay estuaries fleck the hard sky limits.

5 —As if too brittle or too clear to touch!
The cables of our sleep so swiftly filed,
Already hang, shred ends from remembered stars.
One frozen trackless smile . . . What words
Can strangle this deaf moonlight? For we

3. Exchange or transformation of parts.
4. A large, sometimes white sea-bird capable
of long, sustained flights away from land, and
in some species, nesting in the colder parts of
southern lands.
5. Undeniably; unalterably.

Are overtaken. Now no cry, no sword
Can fasten or deflect this tidal wedge,
Slow tyranny of moonlight, moonlight loved
And changed . . . "There's

Nothing like this in the world," you say,
Knowing I cannot touch your hand and look
Too, into that godless cleft of sky
Where nothing turns but dead sands flashing.

"—And never to quite understand!" No,
In all the argosy of your bright hair I dreamed
Nothing so flagless as this piracy.

But now
Draw in your head, alone and too tall here.
Your eyes already in the slant of drifting foam;
Your breath sealed by the ghosts I do not know:
Draw in your head and sleep the long way home.

6

Where icy and bright dungeons lift
Of swimmers their lost morning eyes,
And ocean rivers, churning, shift
Green borders under stranger skies,

Steadily as a shell secretes
Its beating leagues of monotone,
Or as many waters trough the sun's
Red kelson[6] past the cape's wet stone;

O rivers mingling toward the sky
And harbor of the phoenix'[7] breast—
My eyes pressed black against the prow,
—Thy derelict and blinded guest

Waiting, afire, what name, unspoke,
I cannot claim: let thy waves rear
More savage than the death of kings,
Some splintered garland for the seer.

Beyond siroccos[8] harvesting
The solstice thunders, crept away,
Like a cliff swinging or a sail
Flung into April's inmost day—

Creation's blithe and petaled word
To the lounged goddess when she rose
Conceding dialogue with eyes
That smile unsearchable repose—

Still fervid covenant, Belle Isle,
—Unfolded floating dais before

6. In a ship, the kelson (keelson) is a beam
laid parallel to the keel in order to hold
together the flooring and the keel.
7. In mythology, a gorgeous bird of red and
gold plumage, associated with worship of the
sun, and said to live a very long life, only
to be consumed by fire from the ashes of which
arises a new phoenix.
8. Hot, moist winds usually associated with
the North African deserts.

Which rainbows twine continual hair—
Belle Isle, white echo of the oar!

The imaged Word, it is, that holds
Hushed willows anchored in its glow.
It is the unbetrayable reply
Whose accent no farewell can know.

1926

From The Bridge

Proem: To Brooklyn Bridge

How many dawns, chill from his rippling rest
The seagull's wings shall dip and pivot him,
Shedding white rings of tumult, building high
Over the chained bay waters Liberty—

Then, with inviolate curve, forsake our eyes
As apparitional as sails that cross
Some page of figures to be filed away;
—Till elevators drop us from our day . . .

I think of cinemas, panoramic sleights
With multitudes bent toward some flashing scene
Never disclosed, but hastened to again,
Foretold to other eyes on the same screen;

And Thee,[9] across the harbor, silver-paced
As though the sun took step of thee, yet left
Some motion ever unspent in thy stride—
Implicitly thy freedom staying thee!

Out of some subway scuttle, cell or loft
A bedlamite° speeds to thy parapets,   madman
Tilting there momently, shrill shirt ballooning,
A jest falls from the speechless caravan.

Down Wall, from girder into street noon leaks,
A rip-tooth of the sky's acetylene,
All afternoon the cloud-flown derricks turn . . .
Thy cables breathe the North Atlantic still.

And obscure as that heaven of the Jews,
Thy guerdon . . . Accolade thou dost bestow
Of anonymity time cannot raise:
Vibrant reprieve and pardon thou dost show.

O harp and altar, of the fury fused,
(How could mere toil align thy choiring strings!)
Terrific threshold of the prophet's pledge,
Prayer of pariah, and the lover's cry—

Again the traffic lights that skim thy swift
Unfractioned idiom, immaculate sigh of stars,
Beading thy path—condense eternity:
And we have seen night lifted in thine arms.

9. I.e., Brooklyn Bridge.

Under thy shadow by the piers I waited;
Only in darkness is thy shadow clear.
The City's fiery parcels all undone,
Already snow submerges an iron year . . .

O Sleepless as the river under thee,
Vaulting the sea, the prairies' dreaming sod,
Unto us lowliest sometime sweep, descend
And of the curveship lend a myth to God.

1930

Royal Palm

Green rustlings, more-than-regal charities
Drift coolly from that tower of whispered light.
Amid the noontide's blazed asperities
I watched the sun's most gracious anchorite

Climb up as by communings, year on year
Uneaten of the earth or aught earth holds,
And the gray trunk, that's elephantine, rear
Its frondings sighing in ethereal folds.

Forever fruitless, and beyond that yield
Of sweat the jungle presses with hot love
And tendril till our deathward breath is sealed—
It grazes the horizons, launched above

Mortality—ascending emerald-bright,
A fountain at salute, a crown in view—
Unshackled, casual of its azured height,
As though it soared suchwise through heaven too.

1933

The Broken Tower

The bell-rope that gathers God at dawn
Dispatches me as though I dropped down the knell
Of a spent day—to wander the cathedral lawn
From pit to crucifix, feet chill on steps from hell.

Have you not heard, have you not seen that corps
Of shadows in the tower, whose shoulders sway
Antiphonal carillons launched before
The stars are caught and hived in the sun's ray?

The bells, I say, the bells break down their tower;
And swing I know not where. Their tongues engrave
Membrane through marrow, my long-scattered score
Of broken intervals . . . And I, their sexton slave!

Oval encyclicals in canyons heaping
The impasse high with choir. Banked voices slain!
Pagodas, campaniles° with reveilles[1] outleaping—   *bell towers*
O terraced echoes prostrate on the plain! . . .

1. Morning calls to awaken.

And so it was I entered the broken world
To trace the visionary company of love, its voice
An instant in the wind (I know not whither hurled)
20   But not for long to hold each desperate choice.

My word I poured. But was it cognate, scored
Of that tribunal monarch of the air
Whose thigh embronzes earth, strikes crystal Word
In wounds pledged once to hope—cleft to despair?

25   The steep encroachments of my blood left me
No answer (could blood hold such a lofty tower
As flings the question true?)—or is it she
Whose sweet mortality stirs latent power?

And through whose pulse I hear, counting the strokes
30   My veins recall and add, revived and sure
The angelus[2] of wars my chest evokes:
What I hold healed, original now, and pure . . .

And builds, within, a tower that is not stone
(Not stone can jacket heaven)—but slip
35   Of pebbles—visible wings of silence sown
In azure circles, widening as they dip

The matrix of the heart, lift down the eye
That shrines the quiet lake and swells a tower . . .
The commodious, tall decorum of that sky
40   Unseals her earth, and lifts love in its shower.

                                                1933

The Air Plant

GRAND CAYMAN[3]

This tuft that thrives on saline° nothingness   *salty*
Inverted octopus with heavenward arms
Thrust parching from a palm-bole[4] hard by the cove—
A bird almost—of almost bird alarms,

5   Is pulmonary to the wind that jars
Its tentacles, horrific in their lurch.
The lizard's throat, held bloated for a fly,
Balloons but warily from this throbbing perch.

The needles and hack-saws of cactus bleed
10   A milk of earth when stricken off the stalk;
But this,—defenseless, thornless, sheds no blood,
Almost no shadow—but the air's thin talk.

Angelic Dynamo! Ventriloquist of the Blue!
While beachward creeps the shark-swept Spanish Main[5]
15   By what conjunctions do the winds appoint
Its apotheosis, at last—the hurricane!
                                                1933

2. Call to attention (for devotions), at the sound of a bell.
3. Small island in the Caribbean Sea, south of Cuba and west of Jamaica.
4. Trunk of a palm tree.
5. The mainland of the American continent adjacent to the Caribbean Sea, or the sea route traveled by early Spanish merchant ships.

ALLEN TATE
(1899–1979)

Ode to the Confederate Dead

Row after row with strict impunity
The headstones yield their names to the element,
The wind whirrs without recollection;
In the riven troughs the splayed leaves
Pile up, of nature the casual sacrament
To the seasonal eternity of death;
Then driven by the fierce scrutiny
Of heaven to their election in the vast breath,
They sough the rumor of mortality.

Autumn is desolation in the plot
Of a thousand acres where these memories grow
From the inexhaustible bodies that are not
Dead, but feed the grass row after rich row.
Think of the autumns that have come and gone!
Ambitious November with the humors of the year,
With a particular zeal for every slab,
Staining the uncomfortable angels that rot
On the slabs, a wing chipped here, an arm there:
The brute curiosity of an angel's stare
Turns you, like them, to stone,
Transforms the heaving air
Till plunged to a heavier world below
You shift your sea-space blindly
Heaving, turning like the blind crab.

> Dazed by the wind, only the wind
> The leaves flying, plunge

You know who have waited by the wall
The twilight certainty of an animal,
Those midnight restitutions of the blood
You know—the immitigable° pines, the smoky frieze   *unvarying*
Of the sky, the sudden call: you know the rage,
The cold pool left by the mounting flood,
Of muted Zeno and Parmenides.[1]
You who have waited for the angry resolution
Of those desires that should be yours tomorrow,
You know the unimportant shrift of death
And praise the vision
And praise the arrogant circumstance
Of those who fall
Rank upon rank, hurried beyond decision—
Here by the sagging gate, stopped by the wall.

> Seeing, seeing only the leaves
> Flying, plunge and expire

---

1. Zeno and Parmenides were Greek philosophers of the Eleatic school who, among other beliefs, held that what is various and change-able, all "development," is a delusive phantom. "To be imagined and to be able to exist are the same thing, and there is no development."

Turn your eyes to the immoderate past,
45 Turn to the inscrutable infantry rising
Demons out of the earth—they will not last.
Stonewall, Stonewall, and the sunken fields of hemp,
Shiloh, Antietam, Malvern Hill, Bull Run.[2]
50 Lost in that orient of the thick and fast
You will curse the setting sun.

        Cursing only the leaves crying
        Like an old man in a storm

You hear the shout, the crazy hemlocks point
55 With troubled fingers to the silence which
Smothers you, a mummy, in time.

            The hound bitch
Toothless and dying, in a musty cellar
Hears the wind only.

60   Now that the salt of their blood
Stiffens the saltier oblivion of the sea,
Seals the malignant purity of the flood,
What shall we who count our days and bow
Our heads with a commemorial woe
65 In the ribboned coats of grim felicity,
What shall we say of the bones, unclean,
Whose verdurous anonymity will grow?

The ragged arms, the ragged heads and eyes
Lost in these acres of the insane green?
70 The gray lean spiders come, they come and go;
In a tangle of willows without light
The singular screech-owl's tight
Invisible lyric seeds the mind
With the furious murmur of their chivalry.

75   We shall say only the leaves
            Flying, plunge and expire

We shall say only the leaves whispering
In the improbable mist of nightfall
That flies on multiple wing:
80 Night is the beginning and the end
And in between the ends of distraction
Waits mute speculation, the patient curse
That stones the eyes, or like the jaguar leaps
For his own image in a jungle pool, his victim.

85 What shall we say who have knowledge
Carried to the heart? Shall we take the act
To the grave? Shall we, more hopeful, set up the grave
In the house? The ravenous grave?

            Leave now
90 The shut gate and the decomposing wall:

---

2. Names of important Civil War battles.

The gentle serpent, green in the mulberry bush,
Riots with his tongue through the hush—
Sentinel of the grave who counts us all!

1928

BASIL BUNTING
(1900–   )

Fearful Symmetry [1]

Muzzle and jowl and beastly brow,
bilious glaring eyes, tufted ears,
recidivous° criminality in the slouch,   *relapsing*
—This is not the latest absconding bankrupt
but a "beautiful" tiger imported at great expense from
Kuala Lumpur.[2]

7 photographers, 4 black-and-white artists and an R.A.[3]
are taking his profitable likeness;
28 reporters and an essayist
are writing him up.
Sundry ladies think he is a darling
especially at mealtimes, observing
that a firm near the docks advertises replicas
fullgrown on approval for easy cash payments.

♂ Felis Tigris (Straits Settlements) (Bobo) [4] takes exercise
up and down his cage before feeding
in a stench of excrements of great cats
indifferent to beauty or brutality.
He is said to have eaten several persons
but of course you can never be quite sure of these things.

1929   1950

The Orotava [4] Road

Four white heifers with sprawling hooves
          trundle the wagon.
     Its ill-roped crates heavy with fruit sway.
The chisel point of the goad, blue and white,
          glitters ahead,
     a flame to follow lance-high in a man's hand
who does not shave. His linen trousers
     like him want washing.
          You can see his baked skin through his shirt.
He has no shoes and his hat has a hole in it.
          "Hu! vaca! Hu! vaca!" [5]
     he says staccato without raising his voice;
"Adios caballero" [6] legato but
          in the same tone.
          Camelmen high on muzzled mounts

1. Cf. William Blake's *The Tyger*, above.
2. City in Malaya.
3. Artist belonging to the Royal Academy.
4. The capitalized words (and the male symbol) reproduce the information that would be given on the front of the tiger's cage: the (scientific) Latin term for tiger, the country
of his origin, and the pet name he's been given at the zoo.
4. La Orotava is a town on Tenerife, one of the Canary Islands, belonging to Spain.
5. "Hey! Cow!" (Spanish).
6. "Good-by, Sir" (Spanish).

boots rattling against the panels
          of an empty
     packsaddle do not answer strangers.
Each with his train of seven or eight tied
20   head to tail they
     pass silent but for the heavy bells
and plip of slobber dripping from
          muzzle to dust;
     save that on sand their soles squeak slightly.
25 Milkmaids, friendly girls between
          fourteen and twenty
     or younger, bolt upright on small
trotting donkeys that bray (they arch their
          tails a few inches
30   from the root, stretch neck and jaw forward
to make the windpipe a trumpet)
          chatter. Jolted
     cans clatter. The girls' smiles repeat
the black silk curve of the wimple
35   under the chin.
      Their hats are absurd doll's hats
or flat-crowned to take a load.
      All have fine eyes.
      You can guess their balanced nakedness
40 under the cotton gown and thin shift.
      They sing and laugh.
      They say "Adios" shyly but look back
more than once, knowing our thoughts
         and sharing our
45   desires and lack of faith in desire.

                   1935   1950

Ode 33

TO ANNE DE SILVER

1

Not to thank dogwood nor
the wind that sifts
petals are these words,
nor for a record,

5 but, as notes sung and received
still the air,
these are controlled by
yesterday evening,

a peal after
10 the bells have rested.

2

Lest its meaning
escape the dogwood's
whiteness, these:

Days now
less bitter than
rind of wild gourd.
Cool breezes. Lips
moistened, there are words.

1938   1950

LANGSTON HUGHES
(1902–1967)

The Weary Blues

Droning a drowsy syncopated tune,
Rocking back and forth to a mellow croon,
    I heard a Negro play.
Down on Lenox Avenue[1] the other night
By the pale dull pallor of an old gas light
    He did a lazy sway. . . .
    He did a lazy sway. . . .
To the tune o' those Weary Blues.
With his ebony hands on each ivory key
He made that poor piano moan with melody.
    O Blues!
Swaying to and fro on his rickety stool
He played that sad raggy tune like a musical fool.
    Sweet Blues!
Coming from a black man's soul.
    O Blues!
In a deep song voice with a melancholy tone
I heard that Negro sing, that old piano moan—
    "Ain't got nobody in all this world,
    Ain't got nobody but ma self.
    I's gwine to quit ma frownin'
    And put ma troubles on the shelf."
Thump, thump, thump, went his foot on the floor.
He played a few chords then he sang some more—
    "I got the Weary Blues
    And I can't be satisfied.
    Got the Weary Blues
    And can't be satisfied—
    I ain't happy no mo'
    And I wish that I had died."
And far into the night he crooned that tune.
The stars went out and so did the moon.
The singer stopped playing and went to bed
While the Weary Blues echoed through his head.
He slept like a rock or a man that's dead.

1926

---

1. A main thoroughfare in the heart of Harlem.

The Negro Speaks of Rivers

(TO W. E. B. DUBOIS)[2]

I've known rivers:
I've known rivers ancient as the world and older than the
    flow of human blood in human veins.

My soul has grown deep like the rivers.

5   I bathed in the Euphrates when dawns were young.
I built my hut near the Congo and it lulled me to sleep.
I looked upon the Nile and raised the pyramids above it.
I heard the singing of the Mississippi when Abe Lincoln
        went down to New Orleans, and I've seen its muddy
10   bosom turn all golden in the sunset.

I've known rivers:
Ancient, dusky rivers.

My soul has grown deep like the rivers.

1926

Afro-American Fragment

So long,
So far away
Is Africa.
Not even memories alive
5   Save those that history books create,
Save those that songs
Beat back into the blood—
Beat out of blood with words sad-sung
In strange un-Negro tongue—
10   So long,
So far away
Is Africa.

Subdued and time-lost
Are the drums—and yet
15   Through some vast mist of race
There comes this song
I do not understand,
This song of atavistic land,
Of bitter yearnings lost
20   Without a place—
So long,
So far away
Is Africa's
Dark face.

1930, 1931

2. The American historian, educator, and Negro leader (1868–1963).

Harlem Sweeties

Have you dug the spill
Of Sugar Hill?[3]
Cast your gims
On this sepia thrill:
Brown sugar lassie,
Caramel treat,
Honey-gold baby
Sweet enough to eat.
Peach-skinned girlie,
Coffee and cream,
Chocolate darling
Out of a dream.
Walnut tinted
Or cocoa brown,
Pomegranate-lipped
Pride of the town.
Rich cream-colored
To plum-tinted black,
Feminine sweetness
In Harlem's no lack.
Glow of the quince
To blush of the rose.
Persimmon bronze
To cinnamon toes.
Blackberry cordial,
Virginia Dare[4] wine—
All those sweet colors
Flavor Harlem of mine!
Walnut or cocoa,
Let me repeat:
Caramel, brown sugar,
A chocolate treat.
Molasses taffy,
Coffee and cream,
Licorice, clove, cinnamon
To a honey-brown dream.
Ginger, wine-gold,
Persimmon, blackberry,
All through the spectrum
Harlem girls vary—
So if you want to know beauty's
Rainbow-sweet thrill,
Stroll down luscious,
Delicious, *fine* Sugar Hill.

1942

Harlem

What happens to a dream deferred?

    Does it dry up
    like a raisin in the sun?

---

3. Sugar Hill is a section of Harlem where the more prosperous Negroes once lived.

4. A brand of wine.

5 Or fester like a sore—
And then run?
Does it stink like rotten meat?
Or crust and sugar over—
like a syrupy sweet?

Maybe it just sags
10 like a heavy load.

Or does it explode?

1951

Same in Blues

I said to my baby,
Baby, take it slow.
I can't, she said, I can't!
I got to go!

5   *There's a certain*
         amount of traveling
         in a dream deferred.

Lulu said to Leonard,
I want a diamond ring.
10 Leonard said to Lulu,
You won't get a goddam thing!

         A certain
         amount of nothing
         in a dream deferred.

15 Daddy, daddy, daddy,
All I want is you.
You can have me, baby—
but my lovin' days is through.

         A certain
20   *amount of impotence*
         in a dream deferred.

Three parties
On my party line—
But that third party,
25 Lord, ain't mine!

         There's liable
         to be confusion
         in a dream deferred.

From river to river
30 Uptown and down,
There's liable to be confusion
when a dream gets kicked around.

1951

STEVIE SMITH (Florence Margaret Smith)
(1902–1971)

No Categories!

I cry I cry
To God who created me
Not to you Angels who frustrated me
Let me fly, let me die,
Let me come to Him.

Not to you Angels on the wing,
With your severe faces,
And your scholarly grimaces,
And your do this and that,
And your exasperating pit-pat
Of appropriate admonishment.

That is not what the Creator meant.
In the day of his gusty creation
He made this and that
And laughed to see them grow fat.

Plod on, you Angels say, do better aspire higher
And one day you may be like us, or those next below us,
Or nearer the lowest,
Or lowest,
Doing their best.

Oh no no, you Angels, I say,
No hierarchies I pray.

Oh God, laugh not too much aside
Say not, it is a small matter.
See what your Angels do; scatter
Their pride; laugh them away.

Oh no categories I pray.

1950

Not Waving but Drowning

Nobody heard him, the dead man,
But still he lay moaning:
I was much further out than you thought
And not waving but drowning.

Poor chap, he always loved larking
And now he's dead
It must have been too cold for him his heart gave way,
They said.

Oh, no no no, it was too cold always
(Still the dead one lay moaning)
I was much too far out all my life
And not waving but drowning.

1957

The Celts

I think of the Celts [1] as rather a whining lady
Who was beautiful once but is not so much so now
She is not very loving, but there is one thing she loves
It is her grievance which she hugs and takes out walking.

5   The Celtic lady likes fighting very much for freedom
But when she has got it she is a proper tyrant
Nobody likes her much when she is governing.

The Celtic lady is not very widely popular
But the English love her oh they love her very much
10   Especially when the Celtic lady is Irish they love her
Which is odd as she hates them then more than anyone else,
When she's Welsh the English stupidly associate her chiefly
With national hats, eisteddfods [2] and Old Age Pensions.
(They don't think of her at all when she is Scotch, it is rather a problem.)

15   Oh the Celtic lady when she's Irish is the one for me
Oh she is so witty and wild, my word witty,
And flashing and spiteful this Celtic lady we love
All the same she is not so beautiful as she was.

1957

COUNTEE CULLEN
(1903–1946)

Heritage

FOR HAROLD JACKMAN

What is Africa to me:
Copper sun or scarlet sea,
Jungle star or jungle track,
Strong bronzed men, or regal black
5   Women from whose loins I sprang
When the birds of Eden sang?
One three centuries removed
From the scenes his fathers loved,
Spicy grove, cinnamon tree,
10   *What is Africa to me?*

So I lie, who all day long
Want no sound except the song
Sung by wild barbaric birds
Goading massive jungle herds,
15   Juggernauts of flesh that pass
Trampling tall defiant grass
Where young forest lovers lie,
Plighting troth beneath the sky.

---

1. Peoples speaking languages related to those of the ancient Gauls, including Bretons, Cornish, Welsh, Irish, etc.

2. Traditional Welsh congresses of bards, minstrels, poets, at which contests of minstrelsy, singing, or oratory are conducted.

So I lie, who always hear,
Though I cram against my ear
Both my thumbs, and keep them there,
Great drums throbbing through the air.
So I lie, whose fount of pride,
Dear distress, and joy allied,
Is my somber flesh and skin,
With the dark blood dammed within
Like great pulsing tides of wine
That, I fear, must burst the fine
Channels of the chafing net
Where they surge and foam and fret.

Africa? A book one thumbs
Listlessly, till slumber comes.
Unremembered are her bats
Circling through the night, her cats
Crouching in the river reeds,
Stalking gentle flesh that feeds
By the river brink; no more
Does the bugle-throated roar
Cry that monarch claws have leapt
From the scabbards where they slept.
Silver snakes that once a year
Doff the lovely coats you wear,
Seek no covert in your fear
Lest a mortal eye should see;
What's your nakedness to me?
Here no leprous flowers rear
Fierce corollas in the air;
Here no bodies sleek and wet,
Dripping mingled rain and sweat,
Tread the savage measures of
Jungle boys and girls in love.
What is last year's snow to me,
Last year's anything? The tree
Budding yearly must forget
How its past arose or set—
Bough and blossom, flower, fruit,
Even what shy bird with mute
Wonder at her travail there,
Meekly labored in its hair.
One three centuries removed
From the scenes his fathers loved,
Spicy grove, cinnamon tree,
What is Africa to me?

So I lie, who find no peace
Night or day, no slight release
From the unremittent beat
Made by cruel padded feet
Walking through my body's street.
Up and down they go, and back,
Treading out a jungle track.
So I lie, who never quite
Safely sleep from rain at night—
I can never rest at all

When the rain begins to fall;
75 Like a soul gone mad with pain
I must match its weird refrain;
Ever must I twist and squirm,
Writhing like a baited worm,
While its primal measures drip
80 Through my body, crying, "Strip!
Doff this new exuberance.
Come and dance the Lover's Dance!"
In an old remembered way
Rain works on me night and day.

85 Quaint, outlandish heathen gods
Black men fashion out of rods,
Clay, and brittle bits of stone,
In a likeness like their own,
My conversion came high-priced;
90 I belong to Jesus Christ,
Preacher of Humility;
Heathen gods are naught to me.

Father, Son, and Holy Ghost,
So I make an idle boast;
95 Jesus of the twice-turned cheek,
Lamb of God, although I speak
With my mouth thus, in my heart
Do I play a double part.
Ever at Thy glowing altar
100 Must my heart grow sick and falter,
Wishing He I served were black,
Thinking then it would not lack
Precedent of pain to guide it,
Let who would or might deride it;
105 Surely then this flesh would know
Yours had borne a kindred woe.
Lord, I fashion dark gods, too,
Daring even to give You
Dark despairing features where,
110 Crowned with dark rebellious hair,
Patience wavers just so much as
Mortal grief compels, while touches
Quick and hot, of anger, rise
To smitten cheek and weary eyes.
115 Lord, forgive me if my need
Sometimes shapes a human creed.
All day long and all night through,
One thing only must I do:
Quench my pride and cool my blood,
120 *Lest I perish in the flood,*
Lest a hidden ember set
Timber that I thought was wet
Burning like the dryest flax,
Melting like the merest wax,
125 *Lest the grave restore its dead.*
Not yet has my heart or head
In the least way realized
They and I are civilized.

1925

WILLIAM PLOMER
(1903–1973)

Tattooed

On his arms he wears
Diagrams he chose,
A snake inside a skull,
A dagger in a rose,

And the muscle playing
Under the skin
Makes the rose writhe
And the skull grin.

He is one who acts his dreams
And these emblems are a clue
To the wishes in his blood
And what they make him do,

These signs are truer
Than the wearer knows:
The blade vibrates
In the vulnerable rose,

Anthers [5] bend, and carmine curly
Petals kiss the plunging steel,
Dusty with essential gold
Close in upon the thing they feel.

Moistly once in bony sockets
Eyeballs hinted at a soul,
In the death's head now a live head
Fills a different role;

Venomous resilience sliding
In the empty cave of thought,
Call it instinct ousting reason,
Or a reptile's indoor sport.

The flower's pangs, the snake exploring,
The skull, the violating knife,
Are the active and the passive
Aspects of his life,

Who is at home with death
More than he guesses;
The rose will die, and a skull
Gives back no caresses.

1936

---

5. In seed plants, the part of the stamen which develops and contains pollen.

The Victoria Falls

These are the Victoria Falls,[1] whose noisy gushing
Attracts a noisy and a gushing crowd
Who rush from every country in the world to gape
At this cascade that is the usual shape.

5   Over the brink a lot of water slops
By force of gravity, and many a tourist stops
And stares to see a natural law fulfilled
And quantities of water that never stop being spilled.

These are the Victoria Falls, the brightest trinket
10   In the globe-trotter's box of well-worn curios:
If they want water, good God, let them drink it!
If they want falls, we'll knock them down—here goes!

Why do you come, I wonder, all this weary way?
Is it because you like to smile and say
15   "When we were at the Falls the other day—"?
Is it because you like to see the spray?

Is it because you like to feel how far
It is from Boston to these falls of the Zambezi,
Which must be falling still? Or do you feel uneasy
20   Until you know how like their photograph they are?

A female tourist raves, "We're keen as keen
On Africa! It's dusty—but, my dear, the *sun!*
I had a list of all the things we've seen,
I can't remember half the things we've done!

25   "The Kaffirs?[2] Black as black, they live in such quaint kraals[3]
They're dusty, too! The great thing is to see the Falls,
The rainbows, and the Rain Forest, where we all wore mackintoshes,
Admired the ferns, and were so glad we'd all brought our goloshes!"

(The water spirits leered at her, the lurking *tokoloshes.*)[4]
30   "My dear, the spray! the noise! the view! the beautiful hotel!
Electric light in every room, and an electric bell!
So clean and comfortable, and they looked after us so well!"

She will not go away . . . Ach, I long to be alone
With a guidebook to the gentle Falls of Silence,
35   The Temple of Reticence on the Tranquil Islands,
Where no sound enters, whence no sound goes out,
And waterfalls
   Fall
      Quietly,
40   As tea falls
         From
           A spout.

1960

1. In the Zambezi River, the boundary between Rhodesia and Zambia.
2. Members of certain of the Bantu races of South Africa.
3. Native villages.
4. "Mischievous or malignant bogies or goblins in Bantu Mythology" [Plomer's note].

The Wild Doves at Louis Trichardt[5]

Morning is busy with long files
of ants and men, all bearing loads.
The sun's gong beats, and sweat runs down.
A mason-hornet shapes his hanging house.
In a wide flood of flowers
Two crested cranes are bowing to their food.
From the north today there is ominous news.

Midday, the mad cicada-time.
Sizzling from every open valve
Of the overheated earth
The stridulators din it in—
Intensive and continuing praise
Of the white-hot zenith, shrilling on
Toward a note too high to bear.

Oven of afternoon, silence of heat.
In shadow, or in shaded rooms,
This face is hidden in folded arms,
That face is now a sightless mask,
Tree-shadow just includes those legs.
The people have all lain down, and sleep
In attitudes of the sick, the shot, the dead.

And now in the grove the wild doves begin,
Whose neat silk heads are never still,
Bubbling their coolest colloquies.
The formulae they liquidly pronounce
In secret tents of leaves imply
(Clearer than man-made music could)
Men being absent, Africa is good.

1960

EARLE BIRNEY
(1904–   )

Bushed

He invented a rainbow but lightning struck it
shattered it into the lake-lap of a mountain
so big his mind slowed when he looked at it

Yet he built a shack on the shore
learned to roast porcupine belly and
wore the quills on his hatband

At first he was out with the dawn
whether it yellowed bright as wood-columbine
or was only a fuzzed moth in a flannel of storm
But he found the mountain was clearly alive
sent messages whizzing down every hot morning

5. "Louis Trichardt is a town in the Northern Transvaal" [Plomer's note].

boomed proclamations at noon and spread out
a white guard of goat
before falling asleep on its feet at sundown

15 When he tried his eyes on the lake   ospreys [1]
would fall like valkyries [2]
choosing the cut-throat
He took then to waiting
till the night smoke rose from the boil of the sunset

20 But the moon carved unknown totems
out of the lakeshore
owls in the beardusky woods derided him
moosehorned cedars circled his swamps and tossed
their antlers up to the stars
25 Then he knew   though the mountain slept   the winds
were shaping its peak to an arrowhead
poised

And now he could only
bar himself in and wait
30 for the great flint to come singing into his heart

1952

A Walk in Kyoto [3]

All week   the maid tells me   bowing
her doll's body at my mat   is Boys' Day
Also please Man's Day   and gravely
bends deeper   The magnolia sprig in my alcove
5 is it male?   The ancient discretions of Zen were not shaped
for my phallic western eye   There is so much discretion
in this small bowed body of an empire
the wild hair of waterfalls combed straight
in the ricefields   the inn-maid retreating
10 with the face of a shut flower   I stand hunched
and clueless like a castaway in the shoals of my room

When I slide my parchment door to stalk awkward
through Lilliput [4] gardens framed and untouchable
as watercolors   the streets look much the same
15 the Men are being pulled past on the strings of their engines
the legs of the Boys are revolved by a thousand pedals
and all the faces as taut and unfestive as Moscow's
or Chicago's   or mine

Lord Buddha helps us all there is vigor enough
20 in these islands and in all islands reefed and resounding
with cities   But the pitch is high as the ping
of cicadas°   those small strained motors concealed   *locusts*
in the propped pines by the dying river   and only
male as the stretched falsetto of actors mincing
25 the women's roles in *kabuki* [5]   or female only

1. Sea-hawks.
2. In Norse mythology, one of the 13 warrior-maidens of Odin; they selected the heroes who were to die in battle, and afterwards carried them to Valhalla.
3. City in Japan, its capital until 1869.

4. In Swift's *Gulliver's Travels*, a country inhabited by tiny people; to them, Gulliver was a giant.
5. Stylized popular drama of Japan, developed chiefly in the 17th century. Both male and female roles were performed by male actors.

as the lost heroes womanized in the Ladies' Opera
Where in these alleys jammed with competing waves
of signs in two tongues and three scripts [6]
can the simple song of a man be heard?

By the shoguns' [7] palace   the Important Cultural Property
stripped for tiptoeing schoolgirls   I stare at the staring
penned carp that flail on each other's backs
to the shrunk pool's edge for the crumb this nonfish
tossed   Is this the Day's one parable?
Or under that peeling pagoda the five hundred tons
of hermaphrodite Word?

At the inn I prepare to surrender again my defeated
shoes to the bending maid   But suddenly the closed
lotus opens to a smile and she points
over my shoulder   above the sagging tiles   to where
tall in the bare sky and huge as Gulliver
a carp is rising   golden and fighting
thrusting its paper body up from the fist
of a small boy on an empty roof   higher
and higher   into the endless winds of the world

Kyoto & Hong Kong 1958   1962

There Are Delicacies

there are delicacies in you
    like the hearts of watches
there are wheels that turn
    on the tips of rubies
& tiny intricate locks

i need your help
    to contrive keys
there is so little time
    even for the finest
    of watches

1971

RICHARD EBERHART
(1904–   )

The Groundhog

In June, amid the golden fields,
I saw a groundhog lying dead.
Dead lay he; my senses shook,
And mind outshot our naked frailty.
There lowly in the vigorous summer
His form began its senseless change,
And made my senses waver dim
Seeing nature ferocious in him.

6. That is, English and the ideogrammic and phonetic writing systems of Japanese.
7. The chief military commanders, members of a quasi-dynasty holding virtual rule of Japan from 1192 to 1869.

Inspecting close his maggots' might
10 And seething cauldron of his being,
Half with loathing, half with a strange love,
I poked him with an angry stick.
The fever arose, became a flame
And Vigour circumscribed the skies,
15 Immense energy in the sun,
And through my frame a sunless trembling.
My stick had done nor good nor harm.
Then stood I silent in the day
Watching the object, as before;
20 And kept my reverence for knowledge
Trying for control, to be still,
To quell the passion of the blood;
Until I had bent down on my knees
Praying for joy in the sight of decay.
25 And so I left; and I returned
In Autumn strict of eye, to see
The sap gone out of the groundhog,
But the bony sodden hulk remained.
But the year had lost its meaning,
30 And in intellectual chains
I lost both love and loathing,
Mured up in the wall of wisdom.
Another summer took the fields again
Massive and burning, full of life,
35 But when I chanced upon the spot
There was only a little hair left,
And bones bleaching in the sunlight
Beautiful as architecture;
I watched them like a geometer,
40 And cut a walking stick from a birch.
It has been three years, now.
There is no sign of the groundhog.
I stood there in the whirling summer,
My hand capped a withered heart,
45 And thought of China and of Greece,
Of Alexander [1] in his tent;
Of Montaigne [2] in his tower,
Of Saint Theresa [3] in her wild lament.

1936

In a Hard Intellectual Light

In a hard intellectual light
I will kill all delight,
And I will build a citadel
Too beautiful to tell

5 O too austere to tell
And far too beautiful to see,
Whose evident distance
I will call the best of me.

1. Alexander the Great, whose military campaigns in the fourth century B.C. subdued all of the then known world.
2. Michel de Montaigne (1533–1592), French essayist, who retired from the French court to his estate for 10 years during which he wrote his skeptical observations on human affairs.
3. St. Theresa of Avila (1515–1582), mystic and founder of a religious order.

And this light of intellect
Will shine on all my desires,
It will my flesh protect
And flare my bold constant fires,

For the hard intellectual light
Will lay the flesh with nails.
And it will keep the world bright
And closed the body's soft jails.

And from this fair edifice
I shall see, as my eyes blaze,
The moral grandeur of man
Animating all his days.

And peace will marry purpose,
And purity married to grace
Will make the human absolute
As sweet as the human face.

Until my hard vision blears,
And Poverty and Death return
In organ music like the years,
Making the spirit leap, and burn

For the hard intellectual light
That kills all delight
And brings the solemn, inward pain
Of truth into the heart again.

                                                      1937

The Fury of Aerial Bombardment

You would think the fury of aerial bombardment
Would rouse God to relent; the infinite spaces
Are still silent. He looks on shock-pried faces.
History, even, does not know what is meant.

You would feel that after so many centuries
God would give man to repent; yet he can kill
As Cain could, but with multitudinous will,
No farther advanced than in his ancient furies.

Was man made stupid to see his own stupidity?
Is God by definition indifferent, beyond us all?
Is the eternal truth man's fighting soul
Wherein the Beast ravens in its own avidity?

Of Van Wettering I speak, and Averill,
Names on a list, whose faces I do not recall
But they are gone to early death, who late in school
Distinguished the belt feed lever from the belt holding pawl.[4]

                                                      1947

---

4. Parts of the .50-caliber Browning machine gun, mounted in American aircraft during World War II. Eberhart was an aerial gunnery instructor during the summer of 1944.

ROBERT PENN WARREN
(1905–   )

Two Pieces After Suetonius[1]

I. *Apology for Domitian*[2]

He was not bad, as emperors go, not really—
Not like Tiberius cruel, or poor Nero silly.[3]
The trouble was only that omens said he would die,
So what could he, mortal, do? Not worse, however, than you might, or I.

5   Suppose from long back you had known the very hour—
"Fear the fifth hour"—and yet for all your power
Couldn't strike it out from the day, or the day from the year,
Then wouldn't you have to strike something at least? If you did, would it
    seem so queer?

Suppose you were proud of your beauty, but baldness set in?
10 Suppose your good leg were dwindling to spindly and thin?
Wouldn't you, like Domitian, try the classic bed-stunt
To prove immortality on what was propped to bear the imperial brunt?

Suppose you had dreamed a gold hump sprouted out of your back,
And such a prosperous burden oppressed you to breath-lack;
15 Suppose lightning scorched the sheets in your own bedroom;
And from your own statue a storm yanked the name plate and chucked it
    into a tomb—

Well, it happened to him. Therefore, there's little surprise
That for hours he'd lock himself up to pull wings from flies.
Fly or man, what odds? He would wander his hall of moonstone,
20 Mirror-bright so he needn't look over his shoulder to see if he was alone.

Let's stop horsing around—it's not Domitian, it's you
We mean, and the omens are bad, very bad, and it's true
That virtue comes hard in face of the assiduous clock,
And music, at sunset, faint as a dream, is heard from beyond the burdock,

25 And as for Domitian, the first wound finds the groin,
And he claws like a cat, but the blade continues to go in,
And the body is huddled forth meanly, and what ritual
It gets is at night, and from his old nurse, a woman poor, nonpolitical.

II. *Tiberius on Capri*[4]

1

All is nothing, nothing all:
To tired Tiberius soft sang the sea thus,
Under his cliff-palace wall.

---

1. Roman historian in the reign of Vespasian (A.D. 70–79), whose chief work is a history of the first twelve emperors of Rome.
2. Domitian (A.D. 51–96), son of Vespasian, was a Roman emperor of bad reputation: cruel, suspicious, tyrannical, decadent. He is reported to have liked catching flies and piercing them with sharp instruments. He is also said to have been much under the influence of soothsayers and prognosticators.
3. Tiberius, emperor of Rome from A.D. 14 to 37, is remembered as a despot; Nero's (A.D. 37–68) reign as emperor of Rome was marked by his great cruelties and erratic behavior.
4. The ruins of Tiberius' villa on the island of Capri, Italy, still stand.

The sea, in soft approach and repulse,
Sings thus, and Tiberius,
Sea-sad, stares past the dusking sea-pulse
Yonder, where come,
One now by one, the lights, far off, of Surrentum.[5]
He stares in the blue dusk-fall,
For all is nothing, nothing all.

Let darkness up from Asia tower.
On that darkening island behind him *spintriae*[6] now stir.
In grot and scented bower,
They titter, yawn, paint lip, grease thigh,
And debate what role each would prefer
When they project for the Emperor's eye
Their expertise
Of his Eastern lusts and complex Egyptian fantasies.
But darkward he stares in that hour,
Blank now in totality of power.

2

There once, on that goat island, I,
As dark fell, stood and stared where Europe stank.
Many were soon to die—
From acedia[7] snatched, from depravity, virtue,
Or frolic, not knowing the reason, in rank
On rank hurled, or in bed, or in church, or
Dishing up supper,
Or in a dark doorway, loosening the girl's elastic to tup her,
While high in the night sky,
The murderous tear dropped from God's eye;

And faintly forefeeling, forefearing, all
That to fulfill our time, and heart, would come,
I stood on the crumbling wall
Of that foul place, and my lungs drew in
Scent of dry gorse on the night air of autumn,
And I seized, in dark, a small stone from that ruin,
And I made outcry
At the paradox of powers that would grind us like grain, small and dry.
Dark down, the stone, in its fall,
Found the sea: I could do that much, after all.

1960

JOHN BETJEMAN
(1906–   )

Death in Leamington[1]

She died in the upstairs bedroom
    By the light of the evening star
That shone through the plate glass window
    From over Leamington Spa.

---

5. Now Sorrento, Italy.
6. Male prostitutes.
7. Sloth, or spiritual laziness.

1. Leamington Spa is a health resort in War-
wickshire, with medicinal springs and baths.

5   Beside her the lonely crochet
      Lay patiently and unstirred,
    But the fingers that would have worked it
      Were dead as the spoken word.

    And Nurse came in with the tea-things
10   Breast high 'mid the stands and chairs—
    But Nurse was alone with her own little soul,
      And the things were alone with theirs.

    She bolted the big round window,
      She let the blinds unroll,
15   She set a match to the mantle,[2]
      She covered the fire with coal.

    And "Tea!" she said in a tiny voice
      "Wake up! It's nearly *five*."
    Oh! Chintzy,[3] chintzy cheeriness,
20   Half dead and half alive!

    Do you know that the stucco is peeling?
      Do you know that the heart will stop?
    From those yellow Italianate arches
      Do you hear the plaster drop?

25   Nurse looked at the silent bedstead,
      At the gray, decaying face,
    As the calm of a Leamington evening
      Drifted into the place.

    She moved the table of bottles
30   Away from the bed to the wall;
    And tiptoeing gently over the stairs
      Turned down the gas in the hall.

1932

On a Portrait of a Deaf Man

The kind old face, the egg-shaped head,
    The tie, discreetly loud,
The loosely fitting shooting clothes,
    A closely fitting shroud.

5   He liked old City[4] dining-rooms,
    Potatoes in their skin,
But now his mouth is wide to let
    The London clay come in.

He took me on long silent walks
10   In country lanes when young,
He knew the name of ev'ry bird
    But not the song it sung.

And when he could not hear me speak
    He smiled and looked so wise

---

2. The mantle of the gas-light jet.
3. Not in the current (American) slang sense, but meaning that the room's hangings and furniture-coverings are of the flower-patterned glazed cotton fabric called chintz.
4. The usual name for London's banking and commercial district.

That now I do not like to think
  Of maggots in his eyes.

He liked the rain-washed Cornish air
  And smell of plowed-up soil,
He liked a landscape big and bare
  And painted it in oil.

But least of all he liked that place [5]
  Which hangs on Highgate Hill
Of soaked Carrara-covered [6] earth
  For Londoners to fill.

He would have liked to say good-by,
  Shake hands with many friends,
In Highgate now his finger-bones
  Stick through his finger-ends.

You, God, who treat him thus and thus,
  Say "Save his soul and pray."
You ask me to believe You and
  I only see decay.

                                    1940

East Anglian Bathe [7]

Oh when the early morning at the seaside
  Took us with hurrying steps from Horsey Mere
To see the whistling bent-grass on the leeside
  And then the tumbled breaker-line appear,
On high, the clouds with mighty adumbration
  Sailed over us to seaward fast and clear
And jellyfish in quivering isolation
  Lay silted in the dry sand of the breeze
And we, along the tableland of beach blown
  Went gooseflesh from our shoulders to our knees
And ran to catch the football, each to each thrown,
  In the soft and swirling music of the seas.

There splashed about our ankles as we waded
  Those intersecting wavelets morning-cold,
And sudden dark a patch of sea was shaded,
  And sudden light, another patch would hold
The warmth of whirling atoms in a sun-shot
  And underwater sandstorm green and gold.
So in we dived and louder than a gunshot
  Sea water broke in fountains down the ear.
How cold the bathe, how chattering cold the drying,
  How welcoming the inland reeds appear,
The wood smoke and the breakfast and the frying,
  And your warm freshwater ripples, Horsey Mere.

                                    1945

5. Highgate Cemetery; the northern London suburb of Highgate occupies the summit of Highgate Hill.
6. Covered with marble funerary monuments; Carrara, the site of extensive marble quarries in Italy, has become a synonym, as here, for "marble."

7. East Anglia comprises the English counties of Norfolk and Suffolk; Horsey Mere ("Mere," deriving from Latin *mare*, the sea, indicating the resort area of the town of Horsey) is on the coast of Norfolk, north of Great Yarmouth.

False Security

I remember the dread with which I at a quarter past four
Let go with a bang behind me our house front door
And, clutching a present for my dear little hostess tight,
Sailed out for the children's party into the night
5   Or rather the gathering night. For still some boys
In the near municipal acres were making a noise
Shuffling in fallen leaves and shouting and whistling
And running past hedges of hawthorn, spikey and bristling.
And black in the oncoming darkness stood out the trees
10   And pink shone the ponds in the sunset ready to freeze
And all was still and ominous waiting for dark
And the keeper was ringing his closing bell in the park
And the arc lights started to fizzle and burst into mauve
As I climbed West Hill to the great big house in The Grove,
15   Where the children's party was and the dear little hostess.
But halfway up stood the empty house where the ghost is
I crossed to the other side and under the arc
Made a rush for the next kind lamppost out of the dark
And so to the next and the next till I reached the top
20   Where the Grove branched off to the left. Then ready to drop
I ran to the ironwork gateway of number seven
Secure at last on the lamplit fringe of Heaven.
Oh who can say how subtle and safe one feels
Shod in one's children's sandals from Daniel Neal's,
25   Clad in one's party clothes made of stuff from Heal's?
And who can still one's thrill at the candle shine
On cakes and ices and jelly and blackcurrant wine,
And the warm little feel of my hostess's hand in mine?
Can I forget my delight at the conjuring show?
30   And wasn't I proud that I was the last to go?
Too overexcited and pleased with myself to know
That the words I heard my hostess's mother employ
To a guest departing, would ever diminish my joy,
I WONDER WHERE JULIA FOUND THAT STRANGE, RATHER COMMON LITTLE BOY?

1958

WILLIAM EMPSON
(1906–   )

To an Old Lady[1]

Ripeness is all; her in her cooling planet
Revere; do not presume to think her wasted.
Project her no projectile, plan nor man it;
Gods cool in turn, by the sun long outlasted.

---

1. "First three words from *King Lear*. Our *earth* without a god's name such as the other planets have is compared to some body of people (absurd to say 'the present generation') without fundamental beliefs as a basis for action. When a hive needs a new queen and the keeper puts one in the bees sometimes kill her. *Her precession* is some customary movement of the planet, meant to suggest the dignity of "procession." The unconfined surface of her sphere is like the universe in being finite but unbounded, but I failed to get that into the line" [Empson's note].

Our earth alone given no name of god
Gives, too, no hold for such a leap to aid her;
Landing, you break some palace and seem odd;
Bees sting their need, the keeper's queen invader.

No, to your telescope; spy out the land;
Watch while her ritual is still to see,
Still stand her temples emptying in the sand
Whose waves o'erthrew their crumbled tracery;

Still stand uncalled-on her soul's appanage;[2]
Much social detail whose successor fades,
Wit used to run a house and to play bridge,
And tragic fervor, to dismiss her maids.

Years her precession do not throw from gear.
She reads a compass certain of her pole;
Confident, finds no confines on her sphere,
Whose failing crops are in her sole control.

Stars how much further from me fill my night.
Strange that she too should be inaccessible,
Who shares my sun. He curtains her from sight,
And but in darkness is she visible.

1935

Legal Fiction[3]

Law makes long spokes of the short stakes of men.
Your well fenced out real estate of mind
No high flat of the nomad citizen
Looks over, or train leaves behind.

Your rights extend under and above your claim
Without bound; you own land in heaven and hell;
Your part of earth's surface and mass the same,
Of all cosmos' volume, and all stars as well.

Your rights reach down where all owners meet, in hell's
Pointed exclusive conclave, at earth's center
(Your spun farm's root still on that axis dwells);
And up, through galaxies, a growing sector.

You are nomad yet; the lighthouse beam you own
Flashes, like Lucifer,[4] through the firmament.
Earth's axis varies; your dark central cone
Wavers a candle's shadow, at the end.

1935

Homage to the British Museum

There is a Supreme God in the ethnological section;
A hollow toad shape, faced with a blank shield.
He needs his belly to include the Pantheon,[5]

2. Natural attribute or accomplishment.
3. "Legal fiction" as used here means the assumption that ownership of land extends into the earth beneath and into the air above.

4. The morning star.
5. The array of other gods belonging to the same system.

Which is inserted through a hole behind.
5   At the navel, at the points formally stressed, at the organs of sense,
Lice glue themselves, dolls, local deities,
His smooth wood creeps with all the creeds of the world.

Attending there let us absorb the cultures of nations
And dissolve into our judgement all their codes.
10 Then, being clogged with a natural hesitation
(People are continually asking one the way out),
Let us stand here and admit that we have no road.
Being everything, let us admit that is to be something,
Or give ourselves the benefit of the doubt;
15 Let us offer our pinch of dust all to this God,
And grant his reign over the entire building.

1935

Missing Dates

Slowly the poison the whole blood stream fills.
It is not the effort nor the failure tires.
The waste remains, the waste remains and kills.

It is not your system or clear sight that mills
5   Down small to the consequence a life requires;
Slowly the poison the whole blood stream fills.

They bled an old dog dry yet the exchange rills
Of young dog blood gave but a month's desires;
The waste remains, the waste remains and kills.

10 It is the Chinese tombs and the slag hills
Usurp the soil, and not the soil retires.[6]
Slowly the poison the whole blood stream fills.

Not to have fire is to be a skin that shrills.
The complete fire is death. From partial fires
15 The waste remains, the waste remains and kills.

It is the poems you have lost, the ills
From missing dates, at which the heart expires.
Slowly the poison the whole blood stream fills.
The waste remains, the waste remains and kills.

1940

W. H. AUDEN
(1907–1973)

[For What as Easy]

For what as easy
For what though small,
For what is well

---

6. "It is true about the old dog, at least I saw it reported somewhere, but the legend that a fifth or some such part of the soil of China is given up to ancestral tombs is (by the way) not true" [Empson's note].

Because between,
To you simply
From me I mean.

Who goes with who
The bedclothes say,
As I and you
Go kissed away,
The data given,
The senses even.

Fate is not late,
Nor the speech rewritten,
Nor one word forgotten,
Said at the start
About heart,
By heart, for heart.

1932   1945

As I Walked Out One Evening

As I walked out one evening,
    Walking down Bristol Street,
The crowds upon the pavement
    Were fields of harvest wheat.

And down by the brimming river
    I heard a lover sing
Under an arch of the railway:
    "Love has no ending.

"I'll love you, dear, I'll love you
    Till China and Africa meet,
And the river jumps over the mountain
    And the salmon sing in the street,

"I'll love you till the ocean
    Is folded and hung up to dry
And the seven stars go squawking
    Like geese about the sky.

The years shall run like rabbits,
    For in my arms I hold
The Flower of the Ages,
    And the first love of the world."

But all the clocks in the city
    Began to whirr and chime:
"O let not Time deceive you,
    You cannot conquer Time.

"In the burrows of the Nightmare
    Where Justice naked is,
Time watches from the shadow
    And coughs when you would kiss.

"In headaches and in worry
    Vaguely life leaks away,
And Time will have his fancy
    Tomorrow or today.

"Into many a green valley
    Drifts the appalling snow;
Time breaks the threaded dances
    And the diver's brilliant bow.

"O plunge your hands in water,
    Plunge them in up to the wrist;
Stare, stare in the basin
    And wonder what you've missed.

"The glacier knocks in the cupboard,
    The desert sighs in the bed,
And the crack in the teacup opens
    A lane to the land of the dead.

"Where the beggars raffle the banknotes
    And the Giant is enchanting to Jack,
And the Lily-white Boy is a Roarer,
    And Jill goes down on her back.

"O look, look in the mirror,
    O look in your distress;
Life remains a blessing
    Although you cannot bless.

"O stand, stand at the window
    As the tears scald and start;
You shall love your crooked neighbor
    With your crooked heart."

It was late, late in the evening,
    The lovers they were gone;
The clocks had ceased their chiming,
    And the deep river ran on.

1940

Musée des Beaux Arts[1]

About suffering they were never wrong,
The Old Masters: how well they understood
Its human position; how it takes place
While someone else is eating or opening a window or just walking dully along;
How, when the aged are reverently, passionately waiting
For the miraculous birth, there always must be
Children who did not specially want it to happen, skating
On a pond at the edge of the wood:
They never forgot
That even the dreadful martyrdom must run its course
Anyhow in a corner, some untidy spot
Where the dogs go on with their doggy life and the torturer's horse
Scratches its innocent behind on a tree.

1. The Museum of Fine Arts in Brussels, where hangs the painting of The Fall of Icarus, by Pieter Brueghel (ca. 1525–69) described in the poem.

In Breughel's *Icarus*,[2] for instance: how everything turns away
Quite leisurely from the disaster; the ploughman may
Have heard the splash, the forsaken cry,
But for him it was not an important failure; the sun shone
As it had to on the white legs disappearing into the green
Water; and the expensive delicate ship that must have seen
Something amazing, a boy falling out of the sky,
Had somewhere to get to and sailed calmly on.

1940

Law Like Love

Law, say the gardeners, is the sun,
Law is the one
All gardeners obey
Tomorrow, yesterday, today.

Law is the wisdom of the old
The impotent grandfathers feebly scold;
The grandchildren put out a treble tongue,
Law is the senses of the young.

Law, says the priest with a priestly look,
Expounding to an unpriestly people,
Law is the words in my priestly book,
Law is my pulpit and my steeple.

Law, says the judge as he looks down his nose,
Speaking clearly and most severely,
Law is as I've told you before,
Law is as you know I suppose,
Law is but let me explain it once more,
Law is The Law.

Yet law-abiding scholars write;
Law is neither wrong nor right,
Law is only crimes
Punished by places and by times,
Law is the clothes men wear
Anytime, anywhere,
Law is Goodmorning and Goodnight.

Others say, Law is our Fate;
Others say, Law is our State;
Others say, others say
Law is no more
Law has gone away.

And always the loud angry crowd
Very angry and very loud
Law is We,
And always the soft idiot softly Me.

2. Daedalus, the greatly skilled Athenian craftsman, constructed for Minos, king of Crete, a labyrinth in which the Minotaur was kept; but Daedalus was himself im- prisoned in it with his son Icarus. He made wings of feathers and wax, with which they flew away; but Icarus flew too near the sun, the wax melted, and he fell into the sea.

35   If we, dear, know we know no more
      Than they about the Law,
      If I no more than you
      Know what we should and should not do
      Except that all agree
40   Gladly or miserably
      That the Law is
      And that all know this,
      If therefore thinking it absurd
      To identify Law with some other word,
45   Unlike so many men
      I cannot say Law is again,
      No more than they can we suppress
      The universal wish to guess
      Or slip out of our own position
50   Into an unconcerned condition.
      Although I can at least confine
      Your vanity and mine
      To stating timidly
      A timid similarity,
55   We shall boast anyway:
      Like love I say.

      Like love we don't know where or why,
      Like love we can't compel or fly,
      Like love we often weep,
60   Like love we seldom keep.

1940

Our Bias

The hour-glass whispers to the lion's roar,
The clock-towers tell the gardens day and night,
How many errors Time has patience for,
How wrong they are in being always right.

5   Yet Time, however loud its chimes or deep,
However fast its falling torrent flows,
Has never put one lion off his leap
Nor shaken the assurance of a rose.

For they, it seems, care only for success:
10 While we choose words according to their sound
And judge a problem by its awkwardness;

And time with us was always popular.
When have we not preferred some going round
To going straight to where we are?

1940

At the Grave of Henry James[1]

The snow, less intransigent than their marble,
Has left the defense of whiteness to these tombs,
   And all the pools at my feet
Accommodate blue now, echo such clouds as occur
To the sky, and whatever bird or mourner the passing
   Moment remarks they repeat.

While rocks, named after singular spaces
Within which images wandered once that caused
   All to tremble and offend,
Stand here in an innocent stillness, each marking the spot
Where one more series of errors lost its uniqueness
   And novelty came to an end.

To whose real advantage were such transactions,
When worlds of reflection were exchanged for trees?
   What living occasion can
Be just to the absent? Noon but reflects on itself,
And the small taciturn stone, that is the only witness
   To a great and talkative man,

Has no more judgment than my ignorant shadow
Of odious comparisons or distant clocks
   Which challenge and interfere
With the heart's instantaneous reading of time, time that is
A warm enigma no longer to you for whom I
   Surrender my private cheer,

As I stand awake on our solar fabric,
That primary machine, the earth, which gendarmes, banks
   And aspirin presuppose,
On which the clumsy and sad may all sit down, and any who will
Say their aha to the beautiful, the common locus
   Of the Master and the rose.

Shall I not especially bless you as, vexed with
My little inferior questions, I stand
   Above the bed where you rest,
Who opened such passionate arms to your *Bon* when It ran
Toward you with its overwhelming reasons pleading
   All beautifully in Its breast? [2]

With what an innocence your hand submitted
To those formal rules that help a child to play,
   While your heart, fastidious as

---

1. The novelist Henry James (1843–1916) is buried, in a plot that contains the graves of other members of the James family, in Mt. Auburn Cemetery, Cambridge, Mass.
2. In an eloquent passage in his *Notebooks*, dated Jan. 4, 1910, appealing "to all the powers and forces and divinities to whom I've ever been loyal and who haven't failed me yet—after all: never, never yet!," as he begins to think over the elements of a new subject, the problems of handling that it will present, and his sense of commitment to see-ing it "in the dramatic way," James says: "Momentary sidewinds . . . break in every now and then to put their inferior little questions to me; but I come back, I come back, as I say, I all throbbingly and yearningly and passionately, oh, *mon bon,* come back to this way that is clearly the only one in which I can do anything now, and that will open out to me more and more and that has overwhelming reasons pleading all beautifully in its breast."

40   A delicate nun, remained true to the rare noblesse
      Of your lucid gift and, for its love, ignored the
         Resentful muttering Mass,

    Whose ruminant hatred of all that cannot
      Be simplified or stolen is yet at large:
45   No death can assuage its lust
    To vilify the landscape of Distinction and see
    The heart of the Personal brought to a systolic [3] standstill,
        The Tall to diminished dust.

    Preserve me, Master, from its vague incitement;
50   Yours be the disciplinary image that holds
        Me back from agreeable wrong
    And the clutch of eddying Muddle, lest Proportion shed
    The alpine chill of her shrugging editorial shoulder [4]
        On my loose impromptu song.

55   All will be judged. Master of nuance and scruple,
    Pray for me and for all writers, living or dead:
        Because there are many whose works
    Are in better taste than their lives, because there is no end
    To the vanity of our calling, make intercession
60   For the treason of all clerks. [5]

                        1941   1945

In Praise of Limestone

If it form the one landscape that we, the inconstant ones,
    Are consistently homesick for, this is chiefly
Because it dissolves in water. Mark these rounded slopes
    With their surface fragrance of thyme and, beneath,
5   A secret system of caves and conduits; hear the springs
    That spurt out everywhere with a chuckle,
Each filling a private pool for its fish and carving
    Its own little ravine whose cliffs entertain
The butterfly and the lizard; examine this region
10   Of short distances and definite places:
What could be more like Mother or a fitter background
    For her son, the flirtatious male who lounges
Against a rock in the sunlight, never doubting
    That for all his faults he is loved; whose works are but
15   Extensions of his power to charm? From weathered outcrop
    To hilltop temple, from appearing waters to
Conspicuous fountains, from a wild to a formal vineyard,
    Are ingenious but short steps that a child's wish
To receive more attention than his brothers, whether
20   By pleasing or teasing, can easily take.

3. The systole is the contraction of the heart by which the blood is forced onward and the circulation kept up.
4. Discussing in the Preface to *The Wings of the Dove* the serialization of certain of his novels in periodicals, and the refusal of editors to accept others for serialization, James says: "There is fortunately something bracing, ever, in the alpine chill, that of some high icy *arête* [sharp crest of a mountain range], shed by the cold editorial shoulder; sour grapes may at moments fairly intoxicate and the story-teller worth his salt rejoice to feel again how many accommodations he can practice."
5. In *La Trahison des clercs* (The Betrayal of the Intellectuals), 1927, the French humanist Julien Benda urged the necessity for the true intellectual, who believes that men could regulate their lives by reason, to oppose he many recent pseudo-intellectual movements that emphasized the superiority of instinct, intuition, the unconscious, the Life Force, etc., over reason. Auden's phrase, while it alludes to a very famous title, widens out its reference beyond Benda's book rather than focusing on it in a sharply referential way.

Watch, then, the band of rivals as they climb up and down
   Their steep stone gennels° in twos and threes, at times   *channels, passages*
Arm in arm, but never, thank God, in step; or engaged
   On the shady side of a square at midday in
Voluble discourse, knowing each other too well to think
   There are any important secrets, unable
To conceive a god whose temper tantrums are moral
   And not to be pacified by a clever line
Or a good lay: for, accustomed to a stone that responds,
   They have never had to veil their faces in awe
Of a crater whose blazing fury could not be fixed;
   Adjusted to the local needs of valleys
Where everything can be touched or reached by walking,
   Their eyes have never looked into infinite space
Through the latticework of a nomad's comb; born lucky,
   Their legs have never encountered the fungi
And insects of the jungle, the monstrous forms and lives
   With which we have nothing, we like to hope, in common.
So, when one of them goes to the bad, the way his mind works
   Remains comprehensible: to become a pimp
Or deal in fake jewelry or ruin a fine tenor voice
   For effects that bring down the house, could happen to all
But the best and the worst of us . . .
                       That is why, I suppose,
   The best and worst never stayed here long but sought
Immoderate soils where the beauty was not so external,
   The light less public and the meaning of life
Something more than a mad camp. "Come!" cried the granite
               wastes,
   "How evasive is your humor, how accidental
Your kindest kiss, how permanent is death." (Saints-to-be
   Slipped away sighing.) "Come!" purred the clays and gravels.
"On our plains there is room for armies to drill; rivers
   Wait to be tamed and slaves to construct you a tomb
In the grand manner: soft as the earth is mankind and both
   Need to be altered." (Intendant Caesars rose and
Left, slamming the door.) But the really reckless were fetched
   By an older colder voice, the oceanic whisper:
"I am the solitude that asks and promises nothing;
   That is how I shall set you free. There is no love;
There are only the various envies, all of them sad."
   They were right, my dear, all those voices were right
And still are; this land is not the sweet home that it looks,
   Nor its peace the historical calm of a site
Where something was settled once and for all: A backward
   And dilapidated province, connected
To the big busy world by a tunnel, with a certain
   Seedy appeal, is that all it is now? Not quite:
It has a worldly duty which in spite of itself
   It does not neglect, but calls into question
All the Great Powers assume; it disturbs our rights. The poet,
   Admired for his earnest habit of calling
The sun the sun, his mind Puzzle, is made uneasy
   By these marble statues which so obviously doubt
His antimythological myth; and these gamins,
   Pursuing the scientist down the tiled colonnade
With such lively offers, rebuke his concern for Nature's

Remotest aspects: I, too, am reproached, for what
And how much you know. Not to lose time, not to get caught,
   Not to be left behind, not, please! to resemble
The beasts who repeat themselves, or a thing like water
80   Or stone whose conduct can be predicted, these
Are our Common Prayer, whose greatest comfort is music
   Which can be made anywhere, is invisible,
And does not smell. In so far as we have to look forward
   To death as a fact, no doubt we are right: But if
85 Sins can be forgiven, if bodies rise from the dead,
   These modifications of matter into
Innocent athletes and gesticulating fountains,
   Made solely for pleasure, make a further point:
The blessed will not care what angle they are regarded from,
90   Having nothing to hide. Dear, I know nothing of
Either, but when I try to imagine a faultless love
   Or the life to come, what I hear is the murmur
Of underground streams, what I see is a limestone landscape.

1951

The Shield of Achilles[3]

     She looked over his shoulder
       For vines and olive trees,
     Marble well-governed cities
       And ships upon untamed seas,
5   But there on the shining metal
       His hands had put instead
     An artificial wilderness
       And a sky like lead.

A plain without a feature, bare and brown,
10   No blade of grass, no sign of neighborhood,
Nothing to eat and nowhere to sit down,
   Yet, congregated on its blankness, stood
   An unintelligible multitude,
A million eyes, a million boots in line,
15 Without expression, waiting for a sign.

Out of the air a voice without a face
   Proved by statistics that some cause was just
In tones as dry and level as the place:
   No one was cheered and nothing was discussed;
20   Column by column in a cloud of dust
They marched away enduring a belief
   Whose logic brought them, somewhere else, to grief.

3. Achilles, the chief Greek hero in the war with Troy, loses his armor when his great friend Patroclus, wearing it, is slain by Hector. While Achilles is mourning the death of his friend, his mother, the goddess Thetis, goes to Olympus to entreat Hephaestos to make new armor for him: both she and Hephaestos pity Achilles because he is fated to die soon and because his life has not been happy. The splendid shield, incorporating gold and silver as well as less precious metals, is described at length in Book XVIII of the *Iliad* (lines 478–608), the scenes depicted on it constituting an epitome of the universe and the lives of men. Hephaestos portrays on it the earth, the heavens, the sea, and the planets; a city in peace (with a wedding and a trial-at-law) and a city at war; scenes from country life, including a harvest feast and a grape-gathering; scenes from animal life and the joyful life of young men and maidens. Around all these scenes, closing them in as the outer border, flows the ocean.

> She looked over his shoulder
>> For ritual pieties,
> White flower-garlanded heifers,
>> Libation and sacrifice,
> But there on the shining metal
>> Where the altar should have been,
> She saw by his flickering forge-light
>> Quite another scene.

Barbed wire enclosed an arbitrary spot
> Where bored officials lounged (one cracked a joke)
And sentries sweated for the day was hot:
> A crowd of ordinary decent folk
> Watched from without and neither moved nor spoke
As three pale figures were led forth and bound
To three posts driven upright in the ground.

The mass and majesty of this world, all
> That carries weight and always weighs the same
Lay in the hands of others; they were small
> And could not hope for help and no help came:
> What their foes liked to do was done, their shame
Was all the worst could wish; they lost their pride
And died as men before their bodies died.

> She looked over his shoulder
>> For athletes at their games,
> Men and women in a dance
>> Moving their sweet limbs
> Quick, quick, to music,
>> But there on the shining shield
> His hands had set no dancing-floor
>> But a weed-choked field.

A ragged urchin, aimless and alone,
> Loitered about that vacancy, a bird
Flew up to safety from his well-aimed stone:
> That girls are raped, that two boys knife a third,
> Were axioms to him, who'd never heard
Of any world where promises were kept,
Or one could weep because another wept.

> The thin-lipped armorer,
>> Hephaestos hobbled away,
> Thetis of the shining breasts
>> Cried out in dismay
> At what the god had wrought
>> To please her son, the strong
> Iron-hearted man-slaying Achilles
>> Who would not live long.

1955

A. D. HOPE
(1907–   )

The Elegy

VARIATIONS ON A THEME OF THE SEVENTEENTH CENTURY [1]

Madam, no more! The time has come to eat.
The spirit of man is nourished, too, with meat.
Those heroes and the warriors of old—
Feasting between their battles made them bold.
5   When Venus in the west hung out her lamp,[2]
The rattling sons of Mars marched home to camp;
And while around the fires their wounds were dressed,
And tale was matched with tale, and jest with jest,
Flagons of wine and oxen roasted whole
10   Refreshed their bodies and restored the soul.

Come, leave the bed; put on your dress; efface
Awhile this dazzling armory of grace!
Flushed and rejoicing from the well-fought fight
Now day lies panting in the arms of night;
15   The first dews tremble on the darkening field;
Put up your naked weapons, the bright shield
Of triumph glinting to the early stars;
Call our troops home with trumpets from their wars;
And, as wise generals, let them rest and dine
20   And celebrate our truce with meat and wine.
See, the meek table on our service waits;
The devil in crystal winks beside our plates;
These veterans of love's war we shall repay
And crown with feasts the glories of the day.

25   Think no disgrace, if now they play a part
Less worthy of the soldiers of the heart.
Though these we led were granted, even as we,
Their moment's draught of immortality,
We do but snatch our instant on the height
30   And in the valleys still live out the night.
Yet they surrender nothing which is theirs.
Nature is frugal in her ministers;
Each to some humbler office must return,
And so must we. Then grudge it not, but learn
35   In this the noble irony of kind:°   *sexual love*
These fierce, quick hands that rove and clasp must find
Other employment now with knife and fork;
Our mouths that groaned with joy, now eat and talk;
These chief commanders, too, without debate,
40   Sink to the lowliest service of the state.
Only our eyes observe no armistice;
Sparkling with love's perpetual surprise,
Their bright vedettes° keep watch from hill to hill   *sentinel outposts*

---

1. Seventeenth-century poets, such as Donne, Carew, and Marvell, revived the classical tradition of witty erotic poetry. See Donne's *Elegy XIX*, above.
2. I.e., the evening star.

And, when they meet, renew the combat still.
And yet to view you would I linger on:
This is the rarest moment, soonest gone.
While now the marching stars invest the sky
And the wide lands beneath surrendered lie,
Their streams and forests, parks and fields and farms,
Like this rich empire tranquil in my arms,
Seem lovelier in the last withdrawing light
And, as they vanish, most enchant the sight.
Still let me watch those countries as they fade
And all their lucid contours sink in shade;
The mounting thighs, the line of flank and breast,
Yet harbor a clear splendor from the west;
Though twilight draws into its shadowy reign
This breathing valley and that glimmering plain,
Still let my warrior heart with fresh delight
Rove and reflect: "Here, here began the fight;
Between those gentle hills I paused to rest,
And on this vale the kiss of triumph pressed;
There, full encircled by the frantic foe,
I rode between the lilies and the snow;
And, in this copse that parts the dark and shine,
Plundered the treasures of the hidden mine;
Down those long slopes in slow retreat I drew;
And here renewed the charge; and here, anew
Met stroke with stroke and touched, at the last breath,
The unimagined ecstasy of death."

Full darkness! Time enough the lamps were lit.
Let us to dinner, Madam; wine and wit
Must have their hour, even as love and war,
And what's to come revives what went before.
Come now, for see the Captain of my lust,
He had so stoutly fought and stiffly thrust,
Fallen, diminished on the field he lies;
Cover his face, he dreams in paradise.
We, while he sleeps, shall dine; and, when that's done,
Drink to his resurrection later on.

1955

Advice to Young Ladies

A.U.C. 334: [3] about this date
For a sexual misdemeanor, which she denied,
The vestal virgin [4] Postumia was tried.
Livy records it among affairs of state.

They let her off: it seems she was perfectly pure;
The charge arose because some thought her talk
Too witty for a young girl, her eyes, her walk
Too lively, her clothes too smart to be demure.

---

3. *Ab Urbe Condita,* "from the founding of the city" (Rome), traditionally in 753 B.C. In his *History of Rome from its Foundation,* Livy (59 B.C.–A.D. 17) records the incident narrated in the first three stanzas.

4. Vestal virgins were the young priestesses who tended the shrine of Vesta, goddess of the hearth. They were governed by the Pontifex Maximus (line 9), chief priest of the Roman religion.

The Pontifex Maximus, summing up the case,
10 Warned her in future to abstain from jokes,
To wear less modish and more pious frocks.
She left the court reprieved, but in disgrace.

What then? With her the annalist is less
Concerned than what the men achieved that year:
15 Plots, quarrels, crimes, with oratory to spare!
I see Postumia with her dowdy dress,

Stiff mouth and listless step; I see her strive
To give dull answers. She had to knuckle down.
A vestal virgin who scandalized that town
20 Had fair trial, then they buried her alive.[5]

Alive, bricked up in suffocating dark,
A ration of bread, a pitcher if she was dry,
Preserved the body they did not wish to die
Until her mind was quenched to the last spark.

25 How many the black maw has swallowed in its time!
Spirited girls who would not know their place;
Talented girls who found that the disgrace
Of being a woman made genius a crime;

How many others, who would not kiss the rod [6]
30 Domestic bullying broke or public shame?
Pagan or Christian, it was much the same:
Husbands, St. Paul declared,[7] rank next to God.

Livy and Paul, it may be, never knew
That Rome was doomed; each spoke of her with pride.
35 Tacitus,[8] writing after both had died,
Showed that whole fabric rotten through and through.

Historians spend their lives and lavish ink
Explaining how great commonwealths collapse
From great defects of policy—perhaps
40 The cause is sometimes simpler than they think.

It may not seem so grave an act to break
Postumia's spirit as Galileo's,[9] to gag
Hypatia as crush Socrates,[1] or drag
Joan as Giordano Bruno [2] to the stake.

45 Can we be sure? Have more states perished, then,
For having shackled the inquiring mind,
Than whose who, in their folly not less blind,
Trusted the servile womb to breed free men?

1966

---

5. For breaking her vows of chastity a vestal virgin could be sentenced to be buried alive.
6. As the symbol of obedience and chastisement.
7. In Ephesians v.22: "Wives, submit yourselves unto your own husbands, as unto the Lord."
8. Roman historian (c. A.D. 77–117) whose *Histories* of three Roman emperors who ruled and were successively deposed in 68–69 A.D. criticize the degeneracy of the times.
9. In 1633 the great Italian astronomer was forced by the Church to condemn his own scientific conclusions and was for a time imprisoned.
1. In 399 B.C. Socrates was sentenced to die by poison on account of his supposedly subversive teachings. Hypatia was a lady of Alexandria, Egypt, noted for her learning and her beauty; she was murdered in 415 A.D., allegedly at the behest of an archbishop.
2. Both were burned at the stake, Joan of Arc in 1431 for heresy and sorcery, Bruno in 1600 for theological and scientific heresies.

LOUIS MacNEICE
(1907–1963)

The Sunlight on the Garden

The sunlight on the garden
Hardens and grows cold,
We cannot cage the minute
Within its nets of gold,
When all is told
We cannot beg for pardon.

Our freedom as free lances
Advances towards its end;
The earth compels, upon it
Sonnets and birds descend;
And soon, my friend,
We shall have no time for dances.

The sky was good for flying
Defying the church bells
And every evil iron
Siren and what it tells:
The earth compels,
We are dying, Egypt, dying[1]

And not expecting pardon,
Hardened in heart anew,
But glad to have sat under
Thunder and rain with you,
And grateful too
For sunlight on the garden.

1938

Bagpipe Music[2]

It's no go the merrygoround, it's no go the rickshaw,
All we want is a limousine and a ticket for the peepshow.
Their knickers[3] are made of crêpe-de-chine, their shoes are made of python,
Their halls are lined with tiger rugs and their walls with heads of bison.

John MacDonald found a corpse, put it under the sofa,
Waited till it came to life and hit it with a poker,
Sold its eyes for souvenirs, sold its blood for whiskey,
Kept its bones for dumbbells to use when he was fifty.

It's no go the Yogi-man, it's no go Blavatsky,[4]
All we want is a bank balance and a bit of skirt in a taxi.

---

1. From *Antony and Cleopatra*, IV.xv.41, Antony's speech to Cleopatra, "I am dying, Egypt, dying."
2. The poem is set in Scotland in the 1930's, the years of the Depression, years which led up to the Munich crisis of 1938 and to the outbreak of World War II in 1939.
3. Women's undergarments.
4. Madame Helena P. Blavatsky (1820–91), Russian occultist, one of the founders of the Theosophical Society, which had flourished in London around the turn of the century and in whose writings there was renewed interest in the 1930's.

Annie MacDougall went to milk, caught her foot in the heather,
Woke to hear a dance record playing of Old Vienna.
It's no go your maidenheads, it's no go your culture,
All we want is a Dunlop tire and the devil mend the puncture.

15 The Laird o' Phelps spent Hogmanay[5] declaring he was sober,
Counted his feet to prove the fact and found he had one foot over.
Mrs. Carmichael had her fifth, looked at the job with repulsion,
Said to the midwife "Take it away; I'm through with overproduction."

    It's no go the gossip column, it's no go the Ceilidh,[6]
20 All we want is a mother's help and a sugar-stick for the baby.

Willie Murray cut his thumb, couldn't count the damage,
Took the hide of an Ayrshire cow and used it for a bandage.
His brother caught three hundred cran[7] when the seas were lavish,
Threw the bleeders back in the sea and went upon the parish.[8]

25 It's no go the Herring Board, it's no go the Bible,
All we want is a packet of fags° when our hands are idle.   *cigarettes*

It's no go the picture palace, it's no go the stadium,
It's no go the country cot with a pot of pink geraniums,
It's no go the Government grants, it's no go the elections,
30 Sit on your arse for fifty years and hang your hat on a pension.

It's no go my honey love, it's no go my poppet;
Work your hands from day to day, the winds will blow the profit.
The glass° is falling hour by hour, the glass with fall forever,   *barometer*
But if you break the bloody glass you won't hold up the weather.

                                                        1938

London Rain

The rain of London pimples
The ebony street with white
And the neon-lamps of London
Stain the canals of night
5 And the park becomes a jungle
In the alchemy of night.

My wishes turn to violent
Horses black as coal—
The randy mares of fancy,
10 The stallions of the soul—
Eager to take the fences
That fence about my soul.

Across the countless chimneys
The horses ride and across
15 The country to the channel
Where warning beacons toss,
To a place where God and No-God
Play at pitch and toss.

---

5. Scottish name given to the last day of the year.
6. (Pronounced *kaley*), Gaelic term for a round of gossiping visits.
7. A measure for the quantity of just-caught herrings.
8. I.e., went on relief.

Whichever wins I am happy
For God will give me bliss
But No-God will absolve me
From all I do amiss
And I need not suffer conscience
If the world was made amiss.

Under God we can reckon
On pardon when we fall
But if we are under No-God
Nothing will matter at all,
Adultery and murder
Will count for nothing at all.

So reinforced by logic
As having nothing to lose
My lust goes riding horseback
To ravish where I choose,
To burgle all the turrets
Of beauty as I choose.

But now the rain gives over
Its dance upon the town,
Logic and lust together
Come dimly tumbling down,
And neither God nor No-God
Is either up or down.

The argument was wilful,
The alternatives untrue,
We need no metaphysics
To sanction what we do
Or to muffle us in comfort
From what we did not do.

Whether the living river
Began in bog or lake,
The world is what was given,
The world is what we make.
And we only can discover
Life in the life we make.

So let the water sizzle
Upon the gleaming slates,
There will be sunshine after
When the rain abates
And rain returning duly
When the sun abates.

My wishes now come homeward,
Their gallopings in vain,
Logic and lust are quiet
And again it starts to rain;
Falling asleep I listen
To the falling London rain.

1941

Autolycus [9]

In his last phase when hardly bothering
To be a dramatist, the Master turned away
From his taut plots and complex characters
To tapestried romances, conjuring
5   With rainbow names and handfuls of sea-spray
And from them turned out happy Ever-afters.

Eclectic always, now extravagant,
Sighting his matter through a timeless prism
He ranged his classical bric-à-brac in grottos
10   Where knights of Ancient Greece had Latin mottoes [1]
And fishermen their flapjacks [2]—none should want
Color for lack of an anachronism.

A gay world certainly though pocked and scored
With childish horrors and a fresh world though
15   Its mainsprings were old gags—babies exposed,
Identities confused and queens to be restored; [3]
But when the cracker [4] bursts it proves as you supposed—
Trinket and moral tumble out just so.

Such innocence—In his own words it was
20   Like an old tale, only that where time leaps
Between acts three and four there was something born
Which made the stock-type virgin dance like corn
In a wind that having known foul marshes, barren steeps,
Felt therefore kindly toward Marinas, Perditas . . .

25   Thus crystal learned to talk. But Shakespeare balanced it
With what we knew already, gabbing earth
Hot from Eastcheap [5]—Watch your pockets when
That rogue comes round the corner, he can slit
Purse-strings as quickly as his maker's pen
30   Will try your heartstrings in the name of mirth.

O master peddler with your confidence tricks,
Brooches, pomanders, [6] broadsheets and what-have-you,
Who hawk such entertainment but rook your client
And leave him brooding, why should we forgive you
35   Did we not know that, though more self-reliant
Than we, you too were born and grew up in a fix?

1948

---

9. An engaging rogue, peddler, and petty thief (he calls himself "a snapper-up of unconsidered trifles") in Shakespeare's romantic comedy *The Winter's Tale* (1610–11).
1. For an example of such an anachronism, in *The Winter's Tale*, Leontes, the Greek king of Sicilia, says, "I have *tremor cordis* on me" (I.ii.110).
2. In another of the romantic comedies, *Pericles Prince of Tyre*, Hericles, cast ashore after shipwreck, encounters three fishermen who succor him: ". . . Come, thou shalt go home, and we'll have flesh for holidays, fish for fasting-days, and moreo'er puddings and flap-jacks. . ." (II.i.78 ff.).

3. In *The Winter's Tale* Perdita is abandoned as an infant, reared by a shepherd, and later reunited with her parents; in *Pericles*, Marina, daughter of the Prince, is lost at sea but recovered and later reunited with her parents.
4. Cracker bon-bon, a party favor containing sweets, trinkets, a motto or fortune, as well as a mild explosive element, so that it explodes when pulled sharply at both ends.
5. A street, originally a market, in the East End of London.
6. A ball of perfumed or aromatic substance, contained in a bag or perforated box, and carried to ward off infection. Shakespeare's Autolycus has them among his wares.

THEODORE ROETHKE
(1908–1963)

Open House

My secrets cry aloud.
I have no need for tongue.
My heart keeps open house,
My doors are widely swung.
An epic of the eyes
My love, with no disguise.

My truths are all foreknown,
This anguish self-revealed.
I'm naked to the bone,
With nakedness my shield.
Myself is what I wear:
I keep the spirit spare.

The anger will endure,
The deed will speak the truth
In language strict and pure.
I stop the lying mouth:
Rage warps my clearest cry
To witless agony.

1941

Root Cellar

Nothing would sleep in that cellar, dank as a ditch,
Bulbs broke out of boxes hunting for chinks in the dark,
Shoots dangled and drooped,
Lolling obscenely from mildewed crates,
Hung down long yellow evil necks, like tropical snakes.
And what a congress of stinks!
Roots ripe as old bait,
Pulpy stems, rank, silo-rich,
Leaf-mold, manure, lime, piled against slippery planks.
Nothing would give up life:
Even the dirt kept breathing a small breath.

1948

My Papa's Waltz

The whiskey on your breath
Could make a small boy dizzy;
But I hung on like death:
Such waltzing was not easy.

We romped until the pans
Slid from the kitchen shelf;
My mother's countenance
Could not unfrown itself.

The hand that held my wrist
10   Was battered on one knuckle;
At every step you missed
My right ear scraped a buckle.

You beat time on my head
With a palm caked hard by dirt,
15   Then waltzed me off to bed
Still clinging to your shirt.

1948

Big Wind

Where were the greenhouses going,
Lunging into the lashing
Wind driving water
So far down the river
5   All the faucets stopped?
So we drained the manure-machine
For the steam plant,
Pumping the stale mixture
Into the rusty boilers,
10   Watching the pressure gauge
Waver over to red,
As the seams hissed
And the live steam
Drove to the far
15   End of the rose-house,
Where the worst wind was,
Creaking the cypress window-frames,
Cracking so much thin glass
We stayed all night,
20   Stuffing the holes with burlap;
But she rode it out,
That old rose-house,
She hove into the teeth of it,
The core and pith of that ugly storm,
25   Ploughing with her stiff prow,
Bucking into the wind-waves
That broke over the whole of her,
Flailing her sides with spray,
Flinging long strings of wet across the roof-top,
30   Finally veering, wearing themselves out, merely
Whistling thinly under the wind-vents;
She sailed until the calm morning,
Carrying her full cargo of roses.

1948

A Light Breather

The spirit moves,
Yet stays:
Stirs as a blossom stirs,
Still wet from its bud-sheath,
5   Slowly unfolding,
Turning in the light with its tendrils;
Plays as a minnow plays,

Tethered to a limp weed, swinging,
Tail around, nosing in and out of the current,
Its shadows loose, a watery finger;
Moves, like the snail,
Still inward,
Taking and embracing its surroundings,
Never wishing itself away,
Unafraid of what it is,
A music in a hood,
A small thing,
Singing.

1953

Elegy for Jane

MY STUDENT, THROWN BY A HORSE

I remember the neckcurls, limp and damp as tendrils;
And her quick look, a sidelong pickerel smile;
And how, once startled into talk, the light syllables leaped for her,
And she balanced in the delight of her thought,
A wren, happy, tail into the wind,
Her song trembling the twigs and small branches.
The shade sang with her;
The leaves, their whispers turned to kissing;
And the mold sang in the bleached valleys under the rose.

Oh, when she was sad, she cast herself down into such a pure depth,
Even a father could not find her:
Scraping her cheek against straw;
Stirring the clearest water.

My sparrow, you are not here,
Waiting like a fern, making a spiny shadow.
The sides of wet stones cannot console me,
Nor the moss, wound with the last light.

If only I could nudge you from this sleep,
My maimed darling, my skittery pigeon.
Over this damp grave I speak the words of my love:
I, with no rights in this matter,
Neither father nor lover.

1953

The Waking

I wake to sleep, and take my waking slow.
I feel my fate in what I cannot fear.
I learn by going where I have to go.

We think by feeling. What is there to know?
I hear my being dance from ear to ear.
I wake to sleep, and take my waking slow.

Of those so close beside me, which are you?
God bless the Ground! I shall walk softly there,
And learn by going where I have to go.

10 Light takes the Tree; but who can tell us how?
The lowly worm climbs up a winding stair;
I wake to sleep, and take my waking slow.

Great Nature has another thing to do
To you and me; so take the lively air,
15 And, lovely, learn by going where to go.

This shaking keeps me steady. I should know.
What falls away is always. And is near.
I wake to sleep, and take my waking slow.
I learn by going where I have to go.

1953

The Dream

1

I met her as a blossom on a stem
Before she ever breathed, and in that dream
The mind remembers from a deeper sleep:
Eye learned from eye, cold lip from sensual lip.
5 My dream divided on a point of fire;
Light hardened on the water where we were;
A bird sang low; the moonlight sifted in;
The water rippled, and she rippled on.

2

She came toward me in the flowing air,
10 A shape of change, encircled by its fire.
I watched her there, between me and the moon;
The bushes and the stones danced on and on;
I touched her shadow when the light delayed;
I turned my face away, and yet she stayed.
15 A bird sang from the center of a tree;
She loved the wind because the wind loved me.

3

Love is not love until love's vulnerable.
She slowed to sigh, in that long interval.
A small bird flew in circles where we stood;
20 The deer came down, out of the dappled wood.
All who remember, doubt. Who calls that strange?
I tossed a stone, and listened to its plunge.
She knew the grammar of least motion, she
Lent me one virtue, and I live thereby.

4

25 She held her body steady in the wind;
Our shadows met, and slowly swung around;
She turned the field into a glittering sea;
I played in flame and water like a boy
And I swayed out beyond the white seafoam;
30 Like a wet log, I sang within a flame.
In that last while, eternity's confine,
I came to love, I came into my own.

1958

I Knew a Woman

I knew a woman, lovely in her bones,
When small birds sighed, she would sigh back at them;
Ah, when she moved, she moved more ways than one:
The shapes a bright container can contain!
Of her choice virtues only gods should speak,
Or English poets who grew up on Greek
(I'd have them sing in chorus, cheek to cheek).

How well her wishes went! She stroked my chin,
She taught me Turn, and Counter-turn, and Stand;[1]
She taught me Touch, that undulant white skin;
I nibbled meekly from her proffered hand;
She was the sickle; I, poor I, the rake,
Coming behind her for her pretty sake
(But what prodigious mowing we did make).

Love likes a gander, and adores a goose:
Her full lips pursed, the errant note to seize;
She played it quick, she played it light and loose,
My eyes, they dazzled at her flowing knees;
Her several parts could keep a pure repose,
Or one hip quiver with a mobile nose
(She moved in circles, and those circles moved).

Let seed be grass, and grass turn into hay:
I'm martyr to a motion not my own;
What's freedom for? To know eternity.
I swear she cast a shadow white as stone.
But who would count eternity in days?
These old bones live to learn her wanton ways:
(I measure time by how a body sways).

1958

The Sentantious Man

1

Spirit and nature beat in one breast-bone—
I saw a virgin writhing in the dirt—
The serpent's heart sustains the loveless stone:
My indirection found direction out.[2]

Pride in fine lineaments precedes a fall;
True lechers love the flesh, and that is all.

2

We did not fly the flesh. Who does, when young?
A fire leaps on itself: I know that flame.
Some rages save us. Did I rage too long?
The spirit knows the flesh it must consume.

The dream's an instant that calls up her face.
She changed me ice to fire, and fire to ice.

---

1. Literary terms, for the three parts of the Pindaric ode.
2. In *Hamlet* II.i.63, Polonius says that we "By indirections find directions out."

3

Small waves repeat the mind's slow sensual play.
I stay alive, both in and out of time,
15 By listening to the spirit's smallest cry;
In the long night, I rest within her name—

As if a lion knelt to kiss a rose,
Astonished into passionate repose.

4

Though all's in motion, who is passing by?
20 The after-image never stays the same.
There was a thicket where I went to die,
And there I thrashed, my thighs and face aflame.

But my least motion changed into a song,
And all dimensions quivered to one thing.

5

25 An exultation takes us outside life:
I can delight in my own hardihood;
I taste my sister when I kiss my wife;
I drink good liquor when my luck is good.

A drunkard drinks, and belches in his drink;
30 Such ardor tames eternity, I think.

6

Is pain a promise? I was schooled in pain,
And found out all I could of all desire;
I weep for what I'm like when I'm alone
In the deep center of the voice and fire.

35 I know the motion of the deepest stone.
Each one's himself, yet each one's everyone.

7

I'm tired of brooding on my neighbor's soul;
My friends become more Christian, year by year.
Small waters run toward a miry hole—
40 That's not a thing I'm saying with a sneer—

For water moves until it's purified,
And the weak bridegroom strengthens in his bride.

1958

The Small

The small birds swirl around;
The high cicadas chirr;
A towhee[3] pecks the ground;
I look at the first star:
5 My heart held to its joy,
This whole September day.

The moon goes to the full;
The moon goes slowly down;
The wood becomes a wall.
10 Far things draw closer in.
A wind moves through the grass,
Then all is as it was.

3. A bird of the finch species.

What rustles in the fern?
I feel my flesh divide.
Things lost in sleep return
As if out of my side,
On feet that make no sound
Over the sodden ground.

The small shapes drowse: I live
To woo the fearful small;
What moves in grass I love—
The dead will not lie still,
And things throw light on things,
And all the stones have wings.

1958

The Far Field

1

I dream of journeys repeatedly:
Of flying like a bat deep into a narrowing tunnel,
Of driving alone, without luggage, out a long peninsula,
The road lined with snow-laden second growth,
A fine dry snow ticking the windshield,
Alternate snow and sleet, no on-coming traffic,
And no lights behind, in the blurred side-mirror,
The road changing from glazed tarface to a rubble of stone,
Ending at last in a hopeless sand-rut,
Where the car stalls,
Churning in a snowdrift
Until the headlights darken.

2

At the field's end, in the corner missed by the mower,
Where the turf drops off into a grass-hidden culvert,
Haunt of the cat-bird, nesting-place of the field-mouse,
Not too far away from the ever-changing flower-dump,
Among the tin cans, tires, rusted pipes, broken machinery,—
One learned of the eternal;
And in the shrunken face of a dead rat, eaten by rain and ground-beetles
(I found it lying among the rubble of an old coal bin)
And the tom-cat, caught near the pheasant-run,
Its entrails strewn over the half-grown flowers,
Blasted to death by the night watchman.

I suffered for birds, for young rabbits caught in the mower,
My grief was not excessive.
For to come upon warblers in early May
Was to forget time and death:
How they filled the oriole's elm, a twittering restless cloud, all one morning,
And I watched and watched till my eyes blurred from the bird shapes,—
Cape May, Blackburnian, Cerulean—
Moving, elusive as fish, fearless,
Hanging, bunched like young fruit, bending the end branches,
Still for a moment,
Then pitching away in half-flight,
Lighter than finches,
While the wrens bickered and sang in the half-green hedgerows,
And the flicker drummed from his dead tree in the chicken-yard.

—Or to lie naked in sand,
In the silted° shallows of a slow river,   *sedimented*
40 Fingering a shell,
Thinking:
Once I was something like this, mindless,
Or perhaps with another mind, less peculiar;
Or to sink down to the hips in a mossy quagmire;[4]
45 Or, with skinny knees, to sit astride a wet log,
Believing:
I'll return again,
As a snake or a raucous bird,
Or, with luck, as a lion.

50 I learned not to fear infinity,
The far field, the windy cliffs of forever,
The dying of time in the white light of tomorrow,
The wheel turning away from itself,
The sprawl of the wave,
55 The on-coming water.

3

The river turns on itself,
The tree retreats into its own shadow.
I feel a weightless change, a moving forward
As of water quickening before a narrowing channel
60 When banks converge, and the wide river whitens;
Or when two rivers combine, the blue glacial torrent
And the yellowish-green from the mountainy upland,—
At first a swift rippling between rocks,
Then a long running over flat stones
65 Before descending to the alluvial plain,[5]
To the clay banks ,and the wild grapes hanging from the elmtrees.
The slightly trembling water
Dropping a fine yellow silt where the sun stays;
And the crabs bask near the edge,
70 The weedy edge, alive with small snakes and bloodsuckers—
I have come to a still, but not a deep center,
A point outside the glittering current;
My eyes stare at the bottom of a river,
At the irregular stones, iridescent sandgrains,
75 My mind moves in more than one place,
In a country half-land, half-water.

I am renewed by death, thought of my death,
The dry scent of a dying garden in September,
The wind fanning the ash of a low fire.
80 What I love is near at hand,
Always, in earth and air.

4

The lost self changes,
Turning toward the sea,
A sea-shape turning around—
85 An old man with his feet before the fire,
In robes of green, in garments of adieu.

---

4. Soft, wet land.
5. Sand or soil built up from the deposits of running water.

A man faced with his own immensity
Wakes all the waves, all their loose wandering fire.
The murmur of the absolute, the why
Of being born fails on his naked ears.
His spirit moves like monumental wind
That gentles on a sunny blue plateau.
He is the end of things, the final man.

All finite things reveal infinitude:
The mountain with its singular bright shade
Like the blue shine on freshly frozen snow,
The after-light upon ice-burdened pines;
Odor of basswood on a mountain-slope,
A scent beloved of bees;
Silence of water above a sunken tree:
The pure serene of memory in one man—
A ripple widening from a single stone
Winding around the waters of the world.

1964

The Reply

Bird, bird don't edge me in;
  I've had enough today
  Of your fine-honed lay°   *song*
That prickles my coarse skin.

I'm neither out nor in
  Before that simple tune
  As cryptic as a rune,
  As round and pure as the moon,
And fresh as salt-drenched skin.

This shivers me; I swear
  A tune so bold and bare,
  Yet fine as maidenhair,
Shakes every sense. I'm five
Times five a man; I breathe
  This sudden random song,
  And, like you, bird, I sing,
  A man, a man alive.

1966

STEPHEN SPENDER
(1909–   )

Not Palaces, an Era's Crown

Not palaces, an era's crown
Where the mind dwells, intrigues, rests;
Architectural gold-leaved flower
From people ordered like a single mind,
I build. This only what I tell:
It is too late for rare accumulation,

For family pride, for beauty's filtered dusts;
I say, stamping the words with emphasis,
Drink from here energy and only energy,
As from the electric charge of a battery,
To will this Time's change.
Eye, gazelle, delicate wanderer,
Drinker of horizon's fluid line;
Ear that suspends on a chord
The spirit drinking timelessness;
Touch, love, all senses;
Leave your gardens, your singing feasts,
Your dreams of suns circling before our sun,
Of heaven after our world.
Instead, watch images of flashing glass
That strike the outward sense, the polished will,
Flag of our purpose which the wind engraves.
No spirit seek here rest. But this: No one
Shall hunger: Man shall spend equally.
Our goal which we compel: Man shall be man.

That program of the antique Satan
Bristling with guns on the indented page,
With battleship towering from hilly waves:
For what? Drive of a ruining purpose
Destroying all but its age-long exploiters.
Our program like this, but opposite,
Death to the killers, bringing light to life.

1933

Seascape

(IN MEMORIAM, M.A.S.)

There are some days the happy ocean lies
Like an unfingered harp, below the land.
Afternoon gilds all the silent wires
Into a burning music for the eyes.
On mirrors flashing between fine-strung fires
The shore, heaped up with roses, horses, spires,
Wanders on water, walking above ribbed sand.

The motionlessness of the hot sky tires
And a sigh, like a woman's, from inland
Brushes the instrument with shadowing hand
Drawing across its wires some gull's sharp cries
Or bell, or shout, from distant, hedged-in shires;
These, deep as anchors, the hushing wave buries.

Then from the shore, two zig-zag butterflies,
Like errant dog-roses, cross the bright strand
Spiraling over sea in foolish gyres°   *spirals*
Until they fall into reflected skies.
They drown. Fishermen understand
Such wings sunk in such ritual sacrifice,

Recalling legends of undersea, drowned cities.
What voyagers, oh what heroes, flamed like pyres
With helmets plumed, have set forth from some island

And them the sea engulfed. Their eyes,
Contorted by the cruel waves' desires
Glitter with coins through the tide scarcely scanned,
While, above them, that harp assumes their sighs.

1947

CHARLES OLSON
(1910–1970)

Merce [1] of Egypt

1

I sing the tree is a heron
I praise long grass
I wear the lion skin
over the long skirt
to the ankle. The ankle
is a heron
I look straightly backward. Or I bend to the side straightly
to raise the sheaf
up the stick of the leg
as the bittern's leg, raised
as slow as
his neck grows
as the wheat. The presentation,
the representation,
is flat,

I am followed by women and a small boy in white carrying a duck,
all have flat feet and, foot before foot, the women with black wigs
And I intent
upon idlers,
and flowers

2

the sedge
as tall as I am, the rushes
as I am
as far as I am animal, antelope
with such's attendant carnivores
and rows of beaters
drive the game to the hunter, or into nets,
where it is thick-wooded or there are open spaces
with low shrubs

3

I speak downfall, the ball of my foot
on the neck of the earth, the hardsong
of the rise of all trees, the jay
who uses the air. I am the recovered sickle
with the grass-stains still on the flint of its teeth.
I am the six-rowed barley
they cut down.

1. Merce Cunningham, the dancer and cho-
reographer. While rector of Black Mountain
College, Olson brought him there to teach, and even participated in some of his dance classes.

I am tree. The boy of the back of my legs
is roots. I am water fowl
when motion is the season of my river, and the wild boar
40 casts me. But my time
is hawkweed,

                    4
I hold what the wind blows, and silt.
I hide in the swamps of the valley to escape civil war,
and marauding soldiers. In the new procession
45 I am first, and carry wine
made of dandelions. The new rites
are my bones

I built my first settlement
in groves

                    5
50   as they would flail crops
when the spring comes, and flood, the tassels
rise, as my head

                                                        195⸱

Maximus, to Himself

I have had to learn the simplest things
last. Which made for difficulties.
Even at sea I was slow, to get the hand out, or to cross
a wet deck.
5   The sea was not, finally, my trade.
But even my trade, at it, I stood estranged
from that which was most familiar. Was delayed,
and not content with the man's argument
that such postponement
10 is now the nature of
obedience,

            that we are all late
            in a slow time,
            that we grow up many
15   And the single
            is not easily
            known

It could be, though the sharpness (the *achiote* [2])
I note in others,
20 makes more sense
than my own distances. The agilities

            they show daily
            who do the world's
            businesses
25   And who do nature's
            as I have no sense
            I have done either

2. A plant used as a vegetable coloring.

I have made dialogues,
have discussed ancient texts,
have thrown what light I could, offered
what pleasures
doceat [3] allows

But the known?
This, I have had to be given,
a life, love, and from one man
the world.
Tokens.
But sitting here
I look out as a wind
and water man, testing
And missing
some proof

I know the quarters
of the weather, where it comes from,
where it goes. But the stem of me,
this I took from their welcome,
or their rejection, of me

And my arrogance
was neither diminished
nor increased,
by the communication

2
It is undone business
I speak of, this morning,
with the sea
stretching out
from my feet

1956

ROY FULLER
(1912–   )

The Green Hills of Africa

The green, humped, wrinkled hills: with such a look
Of age (or youth) as to erect the hair.
They crouch above the ports or on the plain,
Beneath the matchless skies; are like a strange
Girl's shoulders suddenly against your hands.
What covers them so softly, vividly?
They break at the sea in a cliff, a mouth of red:
Upon the plain are unapproachable,
Furrowed and huge, dramatically lit.

And yet one cannot be surprised at what
The hills contain. The girls run up the slope,
Their oiled and shaven heads like caramels.

3. Let him teach (Latin).

Behind, the village, with its corrugated
Iron, the wicked habit of the store.
15 The villagers cough, the sacking blows from the naked
Skin of a child, a white scum on his lips.
The youths come down in feathers from the peak.
And over all a massive frescoed sky.

The poisoner proceeds by tiny doses,
20 The victim weaker and weaker but uncomplaining.
Soon they will only dance for money, will
Discover more and more things can be sold.
What gods did you expect to find here, with
What healing powers? What subtle ways of life?
25 No, there is nothing but the forms and colors,
And the emotion brought from a world already
Dying of what starts to infect the hills.

1944

Autobiography of a Lungworm [1]

My normal dwelling is the lungs of swine,
    My normal shape a worm,
But other dwellings, other shapes, are mine
    Within my natural term.
5 Dimly I see my life, of all, the sign,
    Of better lives the germ.

The pig, though I am inoffensive, coughs,
    Finding me irritant:
My eggs go with the contents of the troughs
10 From mouth to excrement—
The pig thus thinks, perhaps, he forever doffs
    His niggling resident.

The eggs lie unconsidered in the dung
    Upon the farmyard floor,
15 Far from the scarlet and sustaining lung:
    But happily a poor
And humble denizen provides a rung
    To make ascension sure.

The earthworm eats the eggs; inside the warm
20 Cylinder larvae hatch:
For years, if necessary, in this form
    I wait the lucky match
That will return me to my cherished norm,
    My ugly pelt dispatch.

25 Strangely, it is the pig himself becomes
    The god inside the car: [2]
His greed devours the earthworms; so the slums
    Of his intestines are
The setting for the act when clay succumbs
30   And force steers for its star.

1. A parasite that infects the lungs of mammals.
2. Cf. the *deus ex machina* ("god from the machine") of classical drama, a personage who descends to the stage at a crucial moment to resolve the action.

The larvae burrow through the bowel wall
 And, having to the dregs
Drained ignominy, gain the lung's great hall.
 They change. Once more, like pegs,
Lungworms are anchored to the rise and fall
 —And start to lay their eggs.

What does this mean? The individual,
 Nature, mutation, strife?
I feel, though I am simple, still the whole
 Is complex; and that life—
A huge, doomed throbbing—has a wiry soul
 That must escape the knife.

1957

IRVING LAYTON
(1912–   )

The Cold Green Element

At the end of the garden walk
the wind and its satellite wait for me;
their meaning I will not know
       until I go there,
but the black-hatted undertaker

who, passing, saw my heart beating in the grass,
is also going there. Hi, I tell him,
a great squall in the Pacific blew a dead poet
       out of the water,
Who now hangs from the city's gates.

Crowds depart daily to see it, and return
with grimaces and incomprehension;
if its limbs twitched in the air
       they would sit at its feet
peeling their oranges.

And turning over I embrace like a lover
the trunk of a tree, one of those
for whom the lightning was too much
       and grew a brilliant
hunchback with a crown of leaves.

The ailments escaped from the labels
of medicine bottles are all fled to the wind;
I've seen myself lately in the eyes
       of old women,
spent streams mourning my manhood,

in whose old pupils the sun became
a bloodsmear on broad catalpa leaves
and hanging from ancient twigs,
       my murdered selves
sparked the air like the muted collisions

of fruit. A black dog howls down my blood,
a black dog with yellow eyes;
he too by someone's inadvertence
        saw the bloodsmear
35 on the broad catalpa leaves.

But the furies [1] clear a path for me to the worm
who sang for an hour in the throat of a robin,
and misled by the cries of young boys
        I am again
40 a breathless swimmer in that cold green element.

                                                          1955

On Seeing the Statuettes of Ezekiel and Jeremiah in the Church of Notre Dame

They have given you French names
        and made you captive, my rugged
troublesome compatriots;
        your splendid beards, here, are epicene,
5   plaster white
                and your angers
unclothed with Palestinian hills quite lost
in this immense and ugly edifice.

You are bored—I see it—sultry prophets
10   with priests and nuns
(What coarse jokes must pass between you!)
        and with those morbidly religious
i.e. my prize brother-in-law
                ex-Lawrencian
15 pawing his rosary, and his wife
sick with many guilts.

Believe me I would gladly take you
        from this spidery church
its bad melodrama, its musty smell of candle
20   and set you both free again
in no make-believe world
                of sin and penitence
but the sunlit square opposite
alive at noon with arrogant men.

25 Yet cheer up Ezekiel and you Jeremiah
        who were once cast into a pit; [2]
I shall not leave you here incensed, uneasy
        among alien Catholic saints
but shall bring you from time to time
30   my hot Hebrew heart
as passionate as your own, and stand
with you here awhile in aching confraternity.

                                                          1956

---

1. In classical mythology, female spirits who punished the doers of unavenged wrongs.
2. For his prophecies that the Lord would pun-ish the sins of the people of Judah, the princes imprisoned Jeremiah in a cistern (Jeremiah xxxviii.6).

Berry Picking

Silently my wife walks on the still wet furze
Now darkgreen the leaves are full of metaphors
Now lit up is each tiny lamp of blueberry.
The white nails of rain have dropped and the sun is free.

And whether she bends or straightens to each bush
To find the children's laughter among the leaves
Her quiet hands seem to make the quiet summer hush—
Berries or children, patient she is with these.

I only vex and perplex her; madness, rage
Are endearing perhaps put down upon the page;
Even silence daylong and sullen can then
Enamor as restraint or classic discipline.

So I envy the berries she puts in her mouth,
The red and succulent juice that stains her lips;
I shall never taste that good to her, nor will they
Displease her with a thousand barbarous jests.

How they lie easily for her hand to take,
Part of the unoffending world that is hers;
Here beyond complexity she stands and stares
And leans her marvelous head as if for answers.

No more the easy soul my childish craft deceives
Nor the simpler one for whom yes is always yes;
No, now her voice comes to me from a far way off
Though her lips are redder than the raspberries.

1958

ROBERT HAYDEN
(1913–1980)

Mourning Poem for the Queen of Sunday

Lord's lost Him His mockingbird,
His fancy warbler;
Satan sweet-talked her,
four bullets hushed her.
Who would have thought
she'd end that way?

Four bullets hushed her. And the world a-clang with evil.
Who's going to make old hardened sinner men tremble now
and the righteous rock?
Oh who and oh who will sing Jesus down
to help with struggling and doing without and being colored
all through blue Monday?
Till way next Sunday?

All those angels
in their cretonne clouds and finery

the true believer saw
when she rared back her head and sang,
all those angels are surely weeping.
Who would have thought
20   she'd end that way?

Four holes in her heart. The gold works wrecked.
But she looks so natural in her big bronze coffin
among the Broken Hearts and Gates-Ajar,
it's as if any moment she'd lift her head
25   from its pillow of chill gardenias
and turn this quiet into shouting Sunday
and make folks forget what she did on Monday.

Oh, Satan sweet-talked her,
and four bullets hushed her.
30   Lord's lost Him His diva,
His fancy warbler's gone.
Who would have thought,
who would have thought she'd end that way?

                                                        1966

Those Winter Sundays

Sundays too my father got up early
and put his clothes on in the blueblack cold,
then with cracked hands that ached
from labor in the weekday weather made
5   banked fires blaze. No one ever thanked him.

I'd wake and hear the cold splintering, breaking.
When the rooms were warm, he'd call,
and slowly I would rise and dress,
fearing the chronic angers of that house,

10   Speaking indifferently to him,
who had driven out the cold
and polished my good shoes as well.
What did I know, what did I know
of love's austere and lonely offices?

                                                        1962

The Night-Blooming Cereus [1]

And so for nights
we waited, hoping to see
the heavy bud
break into flower.

5   On its neck-like tube
hooking down from the edge
of the leaf-branch
nearly to the floor,

---

1. A species of cactus.

the bud packed
tight with its miracle swayed
stiffly on breaths
    of air, moved

as though impelled
by stirrings within itself.
It repelled as much
    as it fascinated me

sometimes—snake,
eyeless bird head,
beak that would gape
    with grotesque life-squawk.

But you, my dear,
conceded less to the bizarre
than to the imminence
    of bloom. Yet we agreed

we ought
to celebrate the blossom,
paint ourselves, dance
    in honor of

archaic mysteries
when it appeared. Meanwhile
we waited, aware
    of rigorous design.

Backster's
polygraph, I thought
would have shown
    (as clearly as it had

a philodendron's
fear) tribal sentience
in the cactus, focused
    energy of will.[2]

That belling of
tropic perfume—that
signaling
    not meant for us;

the darkness
cloyed with summoning
fragrance. We dropped
    trivial tasks

and marveling
beheld at last the achieved
flower. Its moonlight
    petals were

2. Cleve Backster, an American expert in
the use of the polygraph (or lie detector),
found in 1966 that he could measure and
predict the responses of plants to threatening
or beneficent human thoughts.

still unfold-
ing, the spike fringe of the outer
55   perianth³ recessing
as we watched.

Luna presence,
foredoomed, already dying,
it charged the room
60   with plangency

older than human
cries, ancient as prayers
invoking Osiris, Krishna,
Tezcátlipóca.⁴

65   We spoke
in whispers when
we spoke
at all . . .

1972

JOHN BERRYMAN
(1914–1972)

The Ball Poem

What is the boy now, who has lost his ball,
What, what is he to do? I saw it go
Merrily bouncing, down the street, and then
Merrily over—there it is in the water!
5   No use to say "O there are other balls":
An ultimate shaking grief fixes the boy
As he stands rigid, trembling, staring down
All his young days into the harbor where
His ball went. I would not intrude on him,
10   A dime, another ball, is worthless. Now
He senses first responsibility
In a world of possessions. People will take balls,
Balls will be lost always, little boy,
And no one buys a ball back. Money is external.
15   He is learning, well behind his desperate eyes,
The epistemology of loss, how to stand up
Knowing what every man must one day know
And most know many days, how to stand up.
And gradually light returns to the street,
20   A whistle blows, the ball is out of sight,
Soon part of me will explore the deep and dark
Floor of the harbor . . . I am everywhere,
I suffer and move, my mind and my heart move
With all that move me, under the water
25   Or whistling, I am not a little boy.

1958

---

3. The covering which protects the petals in the bud.   4. Ancient deities of Egypt, India, and the Aztecs of Mexico.

They Have

A thing O say a sixteenth of an inch
long, with whiskers
& wings it doesn't use, & many legs,
has all this while been wandering in a tiny space
on the black wood table by my burning chair.
I see it has a feeler of some length
it puts out before it.
That must be how it was following the circuit
of the bottom of my wine glass, vertical: Macon: [1] I
        thought
it smelt & wanted some but couldn't get hold.
But here's another thing, on my paper, a fluff
of legs, and I blow: my brothers & sisters go away.
But here he's back, & got between the pad
& padback, where I save him and
shift him to my blue shirt, where he is.
The other little one's gone somewhere else.
They have things easy.

1958

The Dream Songs [2]

1

Huffy Henry hid   the day,
unappeasable Henry sulked.
I see his point,—a trying to put things over.
It was the thought that they thought
they could *do* it made Henry wicked & away.
But he should have come out and talked.

All the world like a woolen lover
once did seem on Henry's side.
Then came a departure.
Thereafter nothing fell out as it might or ought.
I don't see how Henry, pried
open for all the world to see, survived.

What he has now to say is a long
wonder the world can bear & be.
Once in a sycamore I was glad
all at the top, and I sang.
Hard on the land wears the strong sea
and empty grows every bed.

1964

4

Filling her compact & delicious body
with chicken páprika, she glanced at me
twice.

1. A wine, named for the district in east central France where it is produced.
2. "[The Dream Songs are] essentially about an imaginary character (not the poet, not me) named Henry, a white American in early middle age sometimes in blackface, who has suffered an irreversible loss and talks about himself sometimes in the first person, sometimes in the third, sometimes even in the second; he has a friend, never named, who addresses him as Mr. Bones and variants thereof" [Berryman's note].

Fainting with interest, I hungered back
and only the fact of her husband & four other people
kept me from springing on her

or falling at her little feet and crying
"You are the hottest one for years of night
Henry's dazed eyes
have enjoyed, Brilliance." I advanced upon
(despairing) my spumoni.—Sir Bones: is stuffed,
de world, wif feeding girls.

—Black hair, complexion Latin, jeweled eyes
downcast . . . The slob beside her   feasts . . . What wonders is
she sitting on, over there?
The restaurant buzzes. She might as well be on Mars.
Where did it all go wrong? The ought to be a law against Henry.
—Mr. Bones: there is.

1964

29

There sat down, once, a thing on Henry's heart
so heavy, if he had a hundred years
& more, & weeping, sleepless, in all them time
Henry could not make good.
Starts again always in Henry's ears
the little cough somewhere, an odor, a chime.

And there is another thing he has in mind
like a grave Sienese [3] face a thousand years
would fail to blur the still profiled reproach of. Ghastly,
with open eyes, he attends, blind.
All the bells say: too late. This is not for tears;
thinking.

But never did Henry, as he thought he did,
end anyone and hacks her body up
and hide the pieces, where they may be found.
He knows: he went over everyone, & nobody's missing.
Often he reckons, in the dawn, them up.
Nobody is ever missing.

1964

53

He lay in the middle of the world, and twitcht.
More Sparine for Pelides,[4]
human (half) & down here as he is,
with probably insulting mail to open
and certainly unworthy words to hear
and his unforgivable memory.

—I seldom *go* to *films*. They are too exciting,
said the Honourable Possum.[5]
—It takes me so long to read the 'paper,

---

3. Of Siena, a center of Italian painting during the 13th century.
4. Another name for Achilles, Greek hero of the Trojan war and son of the mortal king Peleus and the sea nymph Thetis, with whom

Henry "with his plights & gripes/as bad as achilles" is compared in Dream Song 14. Sparine is a tranquilizing drug.
5. T. S. Eliot, who wrote *Old Possum's Book of Practical Cats.*

said to me one day a novelist hot as a firecracker,[6]
because I have to identify myself with everyone in it,
including the corpses, pal.

Kierkegaard [7] wanted a society, to refuse to read 'papers,
and that was not, friends, his worst idea.
Tiny Hardy, toward the end, refused to say *anything*,
a programme adopted early on by long Housman,
and Gottfried Benn [8]
said:—We are using our own skins for wallpaper and we cannot win.

1964

263

You [9] couldn't bear to grow old, but we grow old.
Our differences accumulate. Our skin
tightens or droops: it alters.
Take courage, things are not what they have been
and they will never again. Hot hearts grow cold,
the rush to the surface falters,

secretive grows the disappearing soul
learned & uncertain, young again
but not in the same way:
Heraclitus had a wise word here to say,
which I forget.[1] We wake & blunder on,
wiser, on the whole,

but not more accurate. Leave that to the young,
grope forward, toward where no one else has been
which is our privilege.
Besides, you gave up early in our age
which is your privilege, from Chatterton [2]
to the bitter & present scene.

1968

375. *His Helplessness*

I know a young lady's high-piled ashen hair
and she is miserable, threatened a thoroughfare
for pants in their desire
fondless: she drinks too dear, & feels put down,
"no one is friendly to me" she scribbles here,
of all them griefs the crown

having been her lay by her father agèd ten
from which she grew up slowly into the world of men
who headed ha for her.
She put her soul in jeopardy with pills
a week ago, she writes—Henry would offer,
only it's thousands of miles,

---

6. Berryman identified him as his friend, Saul
Bellow.
7. Søren Kierkegaard (1813–1855), Swedish
existentialist philosopher.
8. (1886–1956), German poet.
9. The poem is addressed to Delmore Schwartz
(1913–1966), American poet, the dedicatee of
Berryman's *His Toy, His Dream, His Rest*

(comprising Dream Songs 78–385).
1. Perhaps one of the Greek philosopher's (fl.
5th century B.C.) observations on mutability.
2. Thomas *Chatterton* (1752–1770), English
poet. His suicide, after a publisher rejected
one of his poems, was bemoaned by con-
temporary writers.

help to the delicate lady far in her strait,
counsel she needs, needs one to pace her fate.
15   I cannot spot a hole,
& I look with my heart, in her darkness over there:
dark shroud the clouds on her disordered soul
whose last letter flew like a prayer.

1968

382

At Henry's bier let some thing fall out well:
enter there none who somewhat has to sell,
the music ancient & gradual,
the voices solemn but the grief subdued,
5   no hairy jokes but everybody's mood
subdued, subdued,

until the Dancer comes, in a short short dress
hair black & long & loose, dark dark glasses,
uptilted face,
10   pallor & strangeness, the music changes
to "Give!" & "Ow!" and how! the music changes,
she kicks a backward limb

on tiptoe, pirouettes, & she is free
to the knocking music, sails, dips, & suddenly
15   returns to the terrible gay
occasion hopeless & mad, she weaves, it's hell,
she flings to her head a leg, bobs, all is well,
she dances Henry away.

1968

RANDALL JARRELL
(1914–1965)

The Death of the Ball Turret Gunner

From my mother's sleep I fell into the State,
And I hunched in its belly till my wet fur froze.
Six miles from earth, loosed from its dream of life,
I woke to black flak and the nightmare fighters.
5   When I died they washed me out of the turret with a hose.

1945

Eighth Air Force [1]

If, in an odd angle of the hutment,
A puppy laps the water from a can
Of flowers, and the drunk sergeant shaving
Whistles *O Paradiso!* [2]—shall I say that man
5   Is not as men have said: a wolf to man?

---

1. The air force command, based in England,   the Second World War.
which bombed the European continent during   2. A popular operatic aria.

The other murderers troop in yawning;
Three of them play Pitch, one sleeps, and one
Lies counting missions, lies there sweating
Till even his heart beats: One; One; One.
O murderers! . . . Still, this is how it's done:

This is a war. . . . But since these play, before they die,
Like puppies with their puppy; since, a man,
I did as these have done, but did not die—
I will content the people as I can
And give up these to them: Behold the man! [3]

I have suffered, in a dream, because of him,
Many things; [4] for this last saviour, man,
I have lied as I lie now. But what is lying?
Men wash their hands, in blood, as best they can:
I find no fault in this just man. [5]

1945

In Montecito

In a fashionable suburb of Santa Barbara,
Montecito, there visited me one night at midnight
A scream with breasts. As it hung there in the sweet air
That was always the right temperature, the contractors
Who had undertaken to dismantle it, stripped off
The lips, let the air out of the breasts.
                    People disappear
Even in Montecito. Greenie Taliaferro,
In her white maillot, [2] her good figure almost firm,
Her old pepper-and-salt hair stripped by the hairdresser
To nothing and dyed platinum—Greenie has left her Bentley.
They have thrown away her electric toothbrush, someone else slips
The key into the lock of her safety-deposit box
At the Crocker-Anglo Bank; her seat at the cricket matches
Is warmed by buttocks less delectable than hers.
Greenie's girdle is empty.
                    A scream hangs there in the night:
They strip off the lips, let the air out of the breasts,
And Greenie has gone into the Greater Montecito
That surrounds Montecito like the echo of a scream.

1966

Well Water

What a girl called 'the dailiness of life'
(Adding an errand to your errand. Saying,
'Since you're up . . .' Making you a means to
A means to a means to) is well water
Pumped from an old well at the bottom of the world.

3. Pilate's words as he presented the scourged and thorn-crowned Jesus to the crowd that had confirmed the sentence of crucifixion.
4. Pilate's wife wrote to him about Jesus: "Have nothing to do with that just man: for I have suffered many things this day in a dream because of him" (Matthew xxvii.19).
5. After the crowd had called on him to free Barabbas and execute Jesus, Pilate said, "Be-

hold, I bring him forth to you, that you may know that I find no fault in him" (John xix.4–5). Pilate washed his hands to symbolize his freedom from responsibility for Christ's death.
2. A swimming suit, usually one-piece, or a similar garment worn by gymnasts and dancers, and usually made of jersey or other close-fitting material.

The pump you pump the water from is rusty
And hard to move and absurd, a squirrel-wheel
A sick squirrel turns slowly, through the sunny
Inexorable hours. And yet sometimes
10   The wheel turns of its own weight, the rusty
Pump pumps over your sweating face the clear
Water, cold, so cold! you cup your hands
And gulp from them the dailiness of life.

1966

Nestus Gurley

Sometimes waking, sometimes sleeping,
Late in the afternoon, or early
In the morning, I hear on the lawn,
On the walk, on the lawn, the soft quick step,
5   The sound half song, half breath: a note or two
That with a note or two would be a tune.
It is Nestus Gurley.

It is an old
Catch or snatch or tune
10   In the Dorian mode:[3] the mode of the horses
That stand all night in the fields asleep
Or awake, the mode of the cold
Hunter, Orion, wheeling upside-down,
All space and stars, in cater-cornered Heaven.
15   When, somewhere under the east,
The great march begins, with birds and silence;
When, in the day's first triumph, dawn
Rides over the houses, Nestus Gurley
Delivers to me my lot.

20   As the sun sets, I hear my daughter say:
"He has four routes and makes a hundred dollars."
Sometimes he comes with dogs, sometimes with children,
Sometimes with dogs and children.
He collects, today.
25   I hear my daughter say:
"Today Nestus has got on his derby."
And he says, after a little: "It's two-eighty."
"How could it be two-eighty?"
"Because this month there're five Sundays: it's two-eighty."

30   He collects, delivers. Before the first, least star
Is lost in the paling east; at evening
While the soft, side-lit, gold-leafed day
Lingers to see the stars, the boy Nestus
Delivers to me the Morning Star, the Evening Star
35   —Ah no, only the Morning *News*, the Evening *Record*
Of what I have done and what I have not done
Set down and held against me in the Book
Of Death, on paper yellowing
Already, with one morning's sun, one evening's sun.

---

3. The scale pattern to which ancient Greek philosophers ascribed a "manly and strong" character.

Sometimes I only dream him. He brings then
News of a different morning, a judgment not of men.
The bombers have turned back over the Pole,
Having met a star. . . . I look at that new year
And, waking, think of our Moravian Star
Not lit yet, and the pure beeswax candle
With its red flame-proofed paper pompom
Not lit yet, and the sweetened
Bun we brought home from the love-feast, still not eaten,
And the song the children sang: *O Morning Star—*

And at this hour, to the dew-hushed drums
Of the morning, Nestus Gurley
Marches to me over the lawn; and the cat Elfie,
Furred like a musk-ox, coon-tailed, gold-leaf-eyed,
Looks at the paper boy without alarm
But yawns, and stretches, and walks placidly
Across the lawn to his ladder, climbs it, and begins to purr.

I let him in,
Go out and pick up from the grass the paper hat
Nestus has folded: this tricorne fit for a Napoleon
Of our days and institutions, weaving
Baskets, being bathed, receiving
Electric shocks, Rauwolfia.[4] . . . I put it on
—Ah no, only unfold it.
There is dawn inside; and I say to no one
About—
        it is a note or two
That with a note or two would—
                say to no one
About nothing: "He delivers dawn."

When I lie coldly
—Lie, that is, neither with coldness nor with warmth—
In the darkness that is not lit by anything,
In the grave that is not lit by anything
Except our hope: the hope
That is not proofed against anything, but pure
And shining as the first, least star
That is lost in the east on the morning of Judgment—
May I say, recognizing the step
Or tune or breath. . . .
              recognizing the breath,
May I say, "It is Nestus Gurley."

                                    1960

---

4. A plant whose substance is sometimes used in the treatment of certain mental disorders.

HENRY REED
(1914–   )

From Lessons of the War

TO ALAN MICHELL

Vixi duellis nuper idoneus
Et militavi non sine gloria[1]

1. *Naming of Parts*

Today we have naming of parts. Yesterday,
We had daily cleaning. And tomorrow morning,
We shall have what to do after firing. But today,
Today we have naming of parts. Japonica[2]
5   Glistens like coral in all of the neighboring gardens,
      And today we have naming of parts.

This is the lower sling swivel. And this
Is the upper sling swivel, whose use you will see,
When you are given your slings. And this is the piling swivel,
10   Which in your case you have not got. The branches
Hold in the gardens their silent, eloquent gestures,
      Which in our case we have not got.

This is the safety-catch, which is always released
With an easy flick of the thumb. And please do not let me
15   See anyone using his finger. You can do it quite easy
If you have any strength in your thumb. The blossoms
Are fragile and motionless, never letting anyone see
      Any of them using their finger.

And this you can see is the bolt. The purpose of this
20   Is to open the breech, as you see. We can slide it
Rapidly backwards and forwards: we call this
Easing the spring. And rapidly backwards and forwards
The early bees are assaulting and fumbling the flowers:
      They call it easing the Spring.

25   They call it easing the Spring: it is perfectly easy
If you have any strength in your thumb: like the bolt,
And the breech, and the cocking-piece, and the point of balance,
Which in our case we have not got; and the almond-blossom
Silent in all of the gardens and the bees going backwards and forwards,
30   For today we have naming of parts.

2. *Judging Distances*

Not only how far away, but the way that you say it
Is very important. Perhaps you may never get
The knack of judging a distance, but at least you know
How to report on a landscape: the central sector,
35   The right of arc and that, which we had last Tuesday,
      And at least you know

1. The opening lines of a poem by Horace (III.26), but with Horace's word *"puellis"* (girls) changed to *"duellis"* (war, battles): "Lately I have lived in the midst of battles, creditably enough,/And have soldiered, not without glory."
2. The flowering quince (*Cydonia japonica*), a shrub with brilliant scarlet flowers.

That maps are of time, not place, so far as the army
Happens to be concerned—the reason being,
Is one which need not delay us. Again, you know
There are three kinds of tree, three only, the fir and the poplar,
And those which have bushy tops to; and lastly
            That things only seem to be things.

A barn is not called a barn, to put it more plainly,
Or a field in the distance, where sheep may be safely grazing.
You must never be over-sure. You must say, when reporting:
At five o'clock in the central sector is a dozen
Of what appear to be animals; whatever you do,
            Don't call the bleeders *sheep*.

I am sure that's quite clear; and suppose, for the sake of example,
The one at the end, asleep, endeavors to tell us
What he sees over there to the west, and how far away,
After first having come to attention. There to the west,
On the fields of summer the sun and the shadows bestow
            Vestments of purple and gold.

The still white dwellings are like a mirage in the heat,
And under the swaying elms a man and a woman
Lie gently together. Which is, perhaps, only to say
That there is a row of houses to the left of arc,
And that under some poplars a pair of what appear to be humans
            Appear to be loving.

Well that, for an answer, is what we might rightly call
Moderately satisfactory only, the reason being,
Is that two things have been omitted, and those are important.
The human beings, now: in what direction are they,
And how far away, would you say? And do not forget
            There may be dead ground[3] in between.

There may be dead ground in between; and I may not have got
The knack of judging a distance; I will only venture
A guess that perhaps between me and the apparent lovers,
(Who, incidentally, appear by now to have finished,)
At seven o'clock from the houses, is roughly a distance
            Of about one year and a half.

                                                            1946

Chard Whitlow

(MR. ELIOT'S SUNDAY EVENING POSTSCRIPT)[3a]

As we get older we do not get any younger.
Seasons return, and today I am fifty-five,
And this time last year I was fifty-four,
And this time next year I shall be sixty-two.
And I cannot say I should care (to speak for myself)
To see my time over again—if you can call it time,
Fidgeting uneasily under a drafty stair,
Or counting sleepless nights in the crowded Tube.[4]

---

3. Military: "Space that cannot be reached by fire from a given weapon or a given point" [Webster's Third New International Dictionary].

3a. A fusion of two T. S. Eliot titles: "Mr. Eliot's Sunday Morning Service" and "The *Boston Evening Transcript*."
4. Colloquial term for the London subway.

There are certain precautions—though none of them very reliable—
10 Against the blast from bombs, or the flying splinter,
But not against the blast from Heaven, *vento dei venti*,[5]
The wind within a wind, unable to speak for wind;
And the frigid burnings of purgatory will not be touched
By any emollient.
                I think you will find this put,
15 Far better than I could ever hope to express it,
In the words of Kharma: "It is, we believe,
Idle to hope that the simple stirrup-pump
Can extinguish hell."

              Oh, listeners,
And you especially who have switched off the wireless,
20 And sit in Stoke or Basingstoke, listening appreciatively to the silence
(Which is also the silence of hell), pray not for yourselves but your souls.

And pray for me also under the drafty stair.
As we get older we do not get any younger.

And pray for Kharma under the holy mountain.

                               1946

WILLIAM STAFFORD
(1914–   )

For the Grave of Daniel Boone

The farther he went the farther home grew.
Kentucky became another room;
the mansion arched over the Mississippi;
flowers were spread all over the floor.
5 He traced ahead a deepening home,
and better, with goldenrod:

Leaving the snakeskin of place after place,
going on—after the trees
the grass, a bird flying after a song.
10 Rifle so level, sighting so well
his picture freezes down to now,
a story-picture for children.

They go over the velvet falls
into the tapestry of his time,
15 heirs to the landscape, feeling no jar:
it is like evening; they are the quail
surrounding his fire, coming in for the kill;
their little feet move sacred sand.

Children, we live in a barbwire time
20 but like to follow the old hands back—
the ring in the light, the knuckle, the palm,
all the way to Daniel Boone,

5. "Wind of winds" (Italian).

hunting our own kind of deepening home.
From the land that was his I heft this rock.

Here on his grave I put it down.

1957

At the Bomb Testing Site

At noon in the desert a panting lizard
waited for history, its elbows tense,
watching the curve of a particular road
as if something might happen.

It was looking for something farther off
than people could see, an important scene
acted in stone for little selves
at the flute end of consequences.

There was just a continent without much on it
under a sky that never cared less.
Ready for a change, the elbows waited.
The hands gripped hard on the desert.

1966

Writing

Words written on paper laid over
a fire, and just before flame breaks through
the letters awake, and everything that they tell
makes a little vibration you shiver to see:
Time is so young that it never gets past
trying quick dramas like that.

Or in a mirror you glimpse a huge anchor-hook
too strong ever to bend, wrenched
and bent. That is the image where
you see anything needed: you don't need
anything lifted, but to see that some
things cannot be. A dream,
a poem, a picture gives what you need.

Or by a hand like someone's you put your
hand: nothing felt but the truth when
they touch, and unspoken questions. Answering them,
you carry forward that version of the world
that makes up its most dangerous
time, the hours of your life.

Or there is a spry little animal
the color of ink that wiggles through
perils and comforts, but never stays,
and while you whistle it along new paths
it always makes an inspired escape
and softly dives for life like this across the page.

1973

DYLAN THOMAS
(1914–1953)

The Force That
Through the Green Fuse
Drives the Flower

The force that through the green fuse drives the flower
Drives my green age; that blasts the roots of trees
Is my destroyer.
And I am dumb to tell the crooked rose
5 My youth is bent by the same wintry fever.

The force that drives the water through the rocks
Drives my red blood; that dries the mouthing streams
Turns mine to wax.
And I am dumb to mouth unto my veins
10 How at the mountain spring the same mouth sucks.

The hand that whirls the water in the pool
Stirs the quicksand; that ropes the blowing wind
Hauls my shroud sail.
And I am dumb to tell the hanging man
15 How of my clay is made the hangman's lime.

The lips of time leech to the fountain head;
Love drips and gathers, but the fallen blood
Shall calm her sores.
And I am dumb to tell a weather's wind
20 How time has ticked a heaven round the stars.

And I am dumb to tell the lover's tomb
How at my sheet goes the same crooked worm.

1934

A Process in the Weather of the Heart

A process in the weather of the heart
Turns damp to dry; the golden shot
Storms in the freezing tomb.
A weather in the quarter of the veins
5 Turns night to day; blood in their suns
Lights up the living worm.

A process in the eye forwarns
The bones of blindness; and the womb
Drives in a death as life leaks out.

10 A darkness in the weather of the eye
Is half its light; the fathomed sea
Breaks on unangled land.
The seed that makes a forest of the loin
Forks half its fruit; and half drops down,
15 Slow in a sleeping wind.

A weather in the flesh and bone
Is damp and dry; the quick and dead
Move like two ghosts before the eye.

A process in the weather of the world
Turns ghost to ghost; each mothered child
Sits in their double shade.
A process blows the moon into the sun,
Pulls down the shabby curtains of the skin;
And the heart gives up its dead.

1934

The Hand That Signed the Paper

The hand that signed the paper felled a city;
Five sovereign fingers taxed the breath,
Doubled the globe of dead and halved a country;
These five kings did a king to death.

The mighty hand leads to a sloping shoulder,
The finger joints are cramped with chalk;
A goose's quill has put an end to murder
That put an end to talk.

The hand that signed the treaty bred a fever,
And famine grew, and locusts came;
Great is the hand that holds dominion over
Man by a scribbled name.

The five kings count the dead but do not soften
The crusted wound nor stroke the brow;
A hand rules pity as a hand rules heaven;
Hands have no tears to flow.

1936

After the Funeral

(IN MEMORY OF ANN JONES) [1]

After the funeral, mule praises, brays,
Windshake of sailshaped ears, muffle-toed tap
Tap happily of one peg in the thick
Grave's foot, blinds down the lids, the teeth in black,
The spittled eyes, the salt ponds in the sleeves,
Morning smack of the spade that wakes up sleep,
Shakes a desolate boy who slits his throat
In the dark of the coffin and sheds dry leaves,
That breaks one bone to light with a judgment clout,
After the feast of tear-stuffed time and thistles
In a room with a stuffed fox and a stale fern,
I stand, for this memorial's sake, alone
In the sniveling hours with dead, humped Ann
Whose hooded, fountain heart once fell in puddles
Round the parched worlds of Wales and drowned each sun
(Though this for her is a monstrous image blindly

1. Ann [Williams] Jones was Dylan Thomas' aunt, his mother's sister, who had married a tenant farmer; their rented farm was Fern Hill. She died in 1933.

Magnified out of praise; her death was a still drop;
She would not have me sinking in the holy
Flood of her heart's fame; she would lie dumb and deep
20 And need no druid [2] of her broken body).
But I, Ann's bard on a raised hearth, call all
The seas to service that her wood-tongued virtue
Babble like a bellbuoy over the hymning heads,
Bow down the walls of the ferned and foxy woods
25 That her love sing and swing through a brown chapel,
Bless her bent spirit with four, crossing birds.
Her flesh was meek as milk, but this skyward statue
With the wild breast and blessed and giant skull
Is carved from her in a room with a wet window
30 In a fiercely mourning house in a crooked year.
I know her scrubbed and sour humble hands
Lie with religion in their cramp, her threadbare
Whisper in a damp word, her wits drilled hollow,
Her fist of a face died clenched on a round pain;
35 And sculptured Ann is seventy years of stone.
These cloud-sopped, marble hands, this monumental
Argument of the hewn voice, gesture and psalm,
Storm me forever over her grave until
The stuffed lung of the fox twitch and cry Love
40 And the strutting fern lay seeds on the black sill.

1939

The Hunchback in the Park

The hunchback in the park
A solitary mister
Propped between trees and water
From the opening of the garden lock
5 That lets the trees and water enter
Until the Sunday somber bell at dark [1]

Eating bread from a newspaper
Drinking water from the chained cup
That the children filled with gravel
10 In the fountain basin where I sailed my ship
Slept at night in a dog kennel
But nobody chained him up.

Like the park birds he came early
Like the water he sat down
15 And Mister they called Hey mister
The truant boys from the town
Running when he had heard them clearly
On out of sound

Past lake and rockery
20 Laughing when he shook his paper
Hunchbacked in mockery

2. Priest, among ancient Celts of Gaul or Britain, also magician or soothsayer.

1. The bell that warns visitors that the park gates are about to be closed for the night.

Through the loud zoo of the willow groves
Dodging the park keeper
With his stick that picked up leaves.

And the old dog sleeper
Alone between nurses and swans
While the boys among willows
Made the tigers jump out of their eyes
To roar on the rockery stones
And the groves were blue with sailors

Made all day until bell time
A woman figure without fault
Straight as a young elm
Straight and tall from his crooked bones
That she might stand in the night
After the locks and chains

All night in the unmade park
After the railings and shrubberies
The birds the grass the trees the lake
And the wild boys innocent as strawberries
Had followed the hunchback
To his kennel in the dark.

1942

The Conversation of Prayer

The conversation of prayers about to be said
By the child going to bed and the man on the stairs
Who climbs to his dying love in her high room,
The one not caring to whom in his sleep he will move
And the other full of tears that she will be dead,

Turns in the dark on the sound they know will arise
Into the answering skies from the green ground,
From the man on the stairs and the child by his bed.
The sound about to be said in the two prayers
For the sleep in a safe land and the love who dies

Will be the same grief flying. Whom shall they calm?
Shall the child sleep unharmed or the man be crying?
The conversation of prayers about to be said
Turns on the quick and the dead, and the man on the stairs
Tonight shall find no dying but alive and warm

In the fire of his care his love in the high room.
And the child not caring to whom he climbs his prayer
Shall drown in a grief as deep as his true grave,
And mark the dark eyed wave, through the eyes of sleep,
Dragging him up the stairs to one who lies dead.

1946

Fern Hill

Now as I was young and easy under the apple boughs
About the lilting house and happy as the grass was green,
    The night above the dingle starry,
      Time let me hail and climb
5   Golden in the heydays of his eyes,
And honored among wagons I was prince of the apple towns
And once below a time I lordly had the trees and leaves
      Trail with daisies and barley
    Down the rivers of the windfall light.

10   And as I was green and carefree, famous among the barns
About the happy yard and singing as the farm was home,
    In the sun that is young once only,
      Time let me play and be
      Golden in the mercy of his means,
15 And green and golden I was huntsman and herdsman, the calves
Sang to my horn, the foxes on the hills barked clear and cold,
      And the sabbath rang slowly
    In the pebbles of the holy streams.

All the sun long it was running, it was lovely, the hay
20 Fields high as the house, the tunes from the chimneys, it was air
    And playing, lovely and watery
      And fire green as grass.
    And nightly under the simple stars
As I rode to sleep the owls were bearing the farm away,
25 All the moon long I heard, blessed among stables, the night-jars
      Flying with the ricks, and the horses
      · Flashing into the dark.

And then to awake, and the farm, like a wanderer white
With the dew, come back, the cock on his shoulder: it was all
30   Shining, it was Adam and maiden,
      The sky gathered again
    And the sun grew round that very day.
So it must have been after the birth of the simple light
In the first, spinning place, the spellbound horses walking warm
35   Out of the whinnying green stable
      On to the fields of praise.

And honored among foxes and pheasants by the gay house
Under the new made clouds and happy as the heart was long,
    In the sun born over and over,
40   I ran my heedless ways,
    My wishes raced through the house high hay
And nothing I cared, at my sky blue trades, that time allows
In all his tuneful turning so few and such morning songs
    Before the children green and golden
45   Follow him out of grace,

Nothing I cared, in the lamb white days, that time would take me
Up to the swallow thronged loft by the shadow of my hand,
    In the moon that is always rising,
      Nor that riding to sleep

I should hear him fly with the high fields
And wake to the farm forever fled from the childless land.
Oh as I was young and easy in the mercy of his means,
      Time held me green and dying
  Though I sang in my chains like the sea.

                   1946

In My Craft or Sullen Art

In my craft or sullen art
Exercised in the still night
When only the moon rages
And the lovers lie abed
With all their griefs in their arms,
I labor by singing light
Not for ambition or bread
Or the strut and trade of charms
On the ivory stages
But for the common wages
Of their most secret heart.

Not for the proud man apart
From the raging moon I write
On these spindrift pages
Nor for the towering dead
With their nightingales and psalms
But for the lovers, their arms
Round the griefs of the ages,
Who pay no praise or wages
Nor heed my craft or art.

                   1946

MARGARET WALKER
(1915–   )

For My People

For my people everywhere singing their slave songs repeatedly: their dirges
    and their ditties and their blues and jubilees, praying their prayers
    nightly to an unknown god, bending their knees humbly to an unseen
    power;

For my people lending their strength to the years, to the gone years and the
    now years and the maybe years, washing ironing cooking scrubbing
    sewing mending hoeing plowing digging planting pruning patching
    dragging along never gaining never reaping never knowing and never
    understanding;

For my playmates in the clay and dust and sand of Alabama backyards
    playing baptizing and preaching and doctor and jail and soldier and
    school and mama and cooking and playhouse and concert and store and
    hair and Miss Choomby and company;

For the cramped bewildered years we went to school to learn to know the
    reasons why and the answers to and the people who and the places
    where and the days when, in memory of the bitter hours when we dis-
    covered we were black and poor and small and different and nobody
    cared and nobody wondered and nobody understood;

5   For the boys and girls who grew in spite of these things to be man and
    woman, to laugh and dance and sing and play and drink their wine and
    religion and success, to marry their playmates and bear children and
    then die of consumption and anemia and lynching;

For my people thronging 47th Street in Chicago and Lenox Avenue in New
    York and Rampart Street in New Orleans, lost disinherited dispossessed
    and happy people filling the cabarets and taverns and other people's
    pockets needing bread and shoes and milk and land and money and
    something—something all our own;

For my people walking blindly spreading joy, losing time being lazy, sleeping
    when hungry, shouting when burdened, drinking when hopeless, tied
    and shackled and tangled among ourselves by the unseen creatures who
    tower over us omnisciently and laugh;

For my people blundering and groping and floundering in the dark of
    churches and schools and clubs and societies, associations and councils
    and committees and conventions, distressed and disturbed and deceived
    and devoured by money-hungry glory-craving leeches, preyed on by
    facile force of state and fad and novelty, by false prophet and holy
    believer;

For my people standing staring trying to fashion a better way from confusion,
    from hypocrisy and misunderstanding, trying to fashion a world that
    will hold all the people, all the faces, all the adams and eves and their
    countless generations;

10 Let a new earth rise. Let another world be born. Let a bloody peace be
    written in the sky. Let a second generation full of courage issue forth;
    let a people loving freedom come to growth. Let a beauty full of healing
    and a strength of final clenching be the pulsing in our spirits and our
    blood. Let the martial songs be written, let the dirges disappear. Let a
    race of men now rise and take control.

                                                            1937, 1942

GWENDOLYN BROOKS
(1917–   )

kitchenette building

We are things of dry hours and the involuntary plan,
Grayed in, and gray. "Dream" makes a giddy sound, not strong
Like "rent," "feeding a wife," "satisfying a man."

But could a dream send up through onion fumes
5   Its white and violet, fight with fried potatoes
And yesterday's garbage ripening in the hall,
Flutter, or sing an aria down these rooms

Even if we were willing to let it in,
Had time to warm it, keep it very clean,
10 Anticipate a message, let it begin?

We wonder. But not well! not for a minute!
Since Number Five is out of the bathroom now,
We think of lukewarm water, hope to get in it.

1945

my dreams, my works, must wait till after hell

I hold my honey and I store my bread
In little jars and cabinets of my will.
I label clearly, and each latch and lid
I bid, Be firm till I return from hell.
I am very hungry. I am incomplete.
And none can tell when I may dine again.
No man can give me any word but Wait,
The puny light. I keep eyes pointed in;
Hoping that, when the devil days of my hurt
Drag out to their last dregs and I resume
On such legs as are left me, in such heart
As I can manage, remember to go home,
My taste will not have turned insensitive
To honey and bread old purity could love.

1945

The Bean Eaters

They eat beans mostly, this old yellow pair.
Dinner is a casual affair.
Plain chipware on a plain and creaking wood,
Tin flatware.

Two who are Mostly Good.
Two who have lived their day,
But keep on putting on their clothes
And putting things away.

And remembering . . .
Remembering, with twinklings and twinges,
As they lean over the beans in their rented back room that is full of beads
   and receipts and dolls and clothes, tobacco crumbs, vases and fringes.

1960

We Real Cool

       The Pool Players.
       Seven at the Golden Shovel.

We real cool. We
Left school. We

Lurk late. We
Strike straight. We

Sing sin. We
Thin gin. We

Jazz June. We
Die soon.

1960

Medgar Evers[1]

FOR CHARLES EVERS

The man whose height his fear improved he
arranged to fear no further. The raw
intoxicated time was time for better birth or
a final death.

5   Old styles, old tempos, all the engagement of
the day—the sedate, the regulated fray—
the antique light, the Moral rose, old gusts,
tight whistlings from the past, the mothballs
in the Love at last our man forswore.

10 Medgar Evers annoyed confetti and assorted
brands of businessmen's eyes.

The shows came down: to maxims and surprise.
And palsy.

Roaring no rapt arise-ye to the dead, he
15 leaned across tomorrow. People said that
he was holding clean globes in his hands.

1968

Boy Breaking Glass

TO MARC CRAWFORD FROM WHOM THE COMMISSION

Whose broken window is a cry of art
(success, that winks aware
as elegance, as a treasonable faith)
is raw: is sonic: is old-eyed première.
5   Our beautiful flaw and terrible ornament.
Our barbarous and metal little man.

"I shall create! If not a note, a hole.
If not an overture, a desecration."

Full of pepper and light
10 and Salt and night and cargoes.

"Don't go down the plank
if you see there's no extension.
Each to his grief, each to
his loneliness and fidgety revenge.

15 Nobody knew where I was and now I am no longer there."

The only sanity is a cup of tea.
The music is in minors.

Each one other
is having different weather.

1. Negro civil rights leader in Mississippi, murdered in 1963.

"It was you, it was you who threw away my name!
And this is everything I have for me."

Who has not Congress, lobster, love, luau,
the Regency Room, the Statue of Liberty,
runs. A sloppy amalgamation.
A mistake.
A cliff.
A hymn, a snare, and an exceeding sun.

1968

ROBERT LOWELL
(1917–1977)

The Quaker Graveyard in Nantucket

(FOR WARREN WINSLOW, DEAD AT SEA)

*Let man have dominion over the fishes of the
sea and the fowls of the air and the beasts and the
whole earth, and every creeping creature that
moveth upon the earth.*[2]

1

A brackish reach of shoal off Madaket[3]
The sea was still breaking violently and night
Had steamed into our North Atlantic Fleet,
When the drowned sailor clutched the drag-net. Light
Flashed from his matted head and marble feet,
He grappled at the net
With the coiled, hurdling muscles of his thighs:
The corpse was bloodless, a botch of reds and whites,
Its open, staring eyes
Were lusterless dead-lights
Or cabin-windows on a stranded hulk
Heavy with sand.[4] We weight the body, close
Its eyes and heave it seaward whence it came,
Where the heel-headed dogfish barks its nose
On Ahab's[5] void and forehead; and the name
Is blocked in yellow chalk.
Sailors, who pitch this portent at the sea
Where dreadnaughts shall confess
Its hell-bent deity,
When you are powerless
To sand-bag this Atlantic bulwark, faced
By the earth-shaker, green, unwearied, chaste
In his steel scales: ask for no Orphean lute
To pluck life back.[6] The guns of the steeled fleet
Recoil and then repeat
The hoarse salute.

---

2. Genesis i.26.
3. Name of a small settlement, and a bay, on Nantucket Island, Massachusetts.
4. Lines 1–12 are based on the opening chapter of Thoreau's *Cape Cod*.
5. Captain Ahab, who is protagonist of Herman Melville's *Moby Dick* (1851) and a recurring presence in this sequence of poems, sailed from Nantucket on the *Pequod* in pursuit of the white whale.
6. Orpheus went to the underworld to recover his wife Eurydice and so charmed its queen, Persephone, by his playing on the lyre that she allowed him to lead Eurydice up from Hades, on condition that he not look back before the end of the journey: he did look back, and Eurydice vanished forever. The "earth-shaker" is Poseidon, god of the sea.

2

Whenever winds are moving and their breath
Heaves at the roped-in bulwarks of this pier,
The terns and sea-gulls tremble at your death
In these home waters. Sailor, can you hear
The Pequod's sea wings, beating landward, fall
Headlong and break on our Atlantic wall
Off 'Sconset,[7] where the yawing S-boats° splash   *sailboats*
The bellbuoy, with ballooning spinnakers,
As the entangled, screeching mainsheet clears
The blocks: off Madaket, where lubbers lash
The heavy surf and throw their long lead squids
For blue-fish? Sea-gulls blink their heavy lids
Seaward. The winds' wings beat upon the stones,
Cousin, and scream for you and the claws rush
At the sea's throat and wring it in the slush
Of this old Quaker graveyard where the bones
Cry out in the long night for the hurt beast
Bobbing by Ahab's whaleboats in the East.

3

All you recovered from Poseidon died
With you, my cousin, and the harrowed brine
Is fruitless on the blue beard of the god,
Stretching beyond us to the castles in Spain,
Nantucket's westward haven. To Cape Cod
Guns, cradled on the tide,
Blast the eelgrass about a waterclock
Of bilge and backwash, roil the salt and sand
Lashing earth's scaffold, rock
Our warships in the hand
Of the great God, where time's contrition blues
Whatever it was these Quaker sailors lost
In the mad scramble of their lives. They died
When time was open-eyed,
Wooden and childish; only bones abide
There, in the nowhere, where their boats were tossed
Sky-high, where mariners had fabled news
Of IS, the whited monster. What it costs
Them is their secret. In the sperm-whale's slick
I see the Quakers drown and hear their cry:
"If God himself had not been on our side,
If God himself had not been on our side,
When the Atlantic rose against us, why,
Then it had swallowed us up quick."

4

This is the end of the whaleroad and the whale
Who spewed Nantucket bones on the thrashed swell
And stirred the troubled waters to whirlpools
To send the Pequod packing off to hell:
This is the end of them, three-quarters fools,
Snatching at straws to sail
Seaward and seaward on the turntail whale,
Spouting out blood and water as it rolls,
Sick as a dog to these Atlantic shoals:
Clamavimus, O depths.[8] Let the sea-gulls wail

7. Siasconset, a town on Nantucket.
8. "We have cried * * *": Psalms cxxx.1—   "Out of the depths have I cried unto thee, O Lord."

For water, for the deep where the high tide
Mutters to its hurt self, mutters and ebbs.
Waves wallow in their wash, go out and out,
Leave only the death-rattle of the crabs,
The beach increasing, its enormous snout
Sucking the ocean's side.
This is the end of running on the waves;
We are poured out like water. Who will dance
The mast-lashed master of Leviathans
Up from this field of Quakers in their unstoned graves?

5

When the whale's viscera go and the roll
Of its corruption overruns this world
Beyond tree-swept Nantucket and Wood's Hole[9]
And Martha's Vineyard, Sailor, will your sword
Whistle and fall and sink into the fat?
In the great ash-pit of Jehoshaphat[1]
The bones cry for the blood of the white whale,
The fat flukes arch and whack about its ears,
The death-lance churns into the sanctuary, tears
The gun-blue swingle, heaving like a flail,
And hacks the coiling life out: it works and drags
And rips the sperm-whale's midriff into rags,
Gobbets of blubber spill to wind and weather,
Sailor, and gulls go round the stoven timbers
Where the morning stars sing out together
And thunder shakes the white surf and dismembers
The red flag hammered in the mast-head.[2] Hide,
Our steel, Jonas Messias,[3] in Thy side.

6. Our Lady of Walsingham[4]

There once the penitents took off their shoes
And then walked barefoot the remaining mile;
And the small trees, a stream and hedgerows file
Slowly along the munching English lane,
Like cows to the old shine, until you lose

9. Harbor and township in southern Massachusetts, north of the island of Martha's Vineyard, which lies to the west of Nantucket.
1. Identified by some commentators as an image for the Day of Judgment, when the world will end in fire.
2. As was the flag in the concluding chapter of *Moby Dick.*
3. For the juxtaposition of Jonah with the Messiah, see the words of Jesus in Matthew xii.39-41, and especially: "For as Jonas was three days and three nights in the whale's belly; so shall the Son of man be three days and three nights in the heart of the earth" [See Robert Lowell, *Poesie 1943-1952,* ed. Rolando Anzilotti, p. 86].
4. Walsingham is a small town in Norfolk, England; a shrine to the Virgin Mary, built in the 11th century, was an object of pilgrimage until it was destroyed in the Reformation. Lowell points out in a prefatory note to *Lord Weary's Castle* that " 'Our Lady of Walsingham' is an adaptation of several paragraphs from E. I. Watkin's *Catholic Art and Culture*" which describe the present Roman Catholic shrine. The passage is in part as follows: "Now once again pilgrims visit her image erected in a mediaeval chapel, where, it is said, they took off their shoes to walk barefoot the remaining mile to the shrine. * * * The road to the chapel is a quiet country lane shaded with trees, and lined on one side by a hedgerow. On the other, a stream flows down beneath the trees, the water symbol of the Holy Spirit, 'the waters of Shiloah that go softly,' the 'flow of the river making glad the city of God.' Within the chapel, an attractive example of Decorated achitecture, is seated Our Lady's image. It is too small for its canopy, and is not superficially beautiful. 'Non est species neque decor,' there is no comeliness of charm in that expressionless face with heavy eyelids. But let us look carefully, and allow the image, as every work of art should be allowed, to speak to us in its own language. We become aware of an inner beauty more impressive than outward grace. That expressionless countenance expresses what is beyond expression. It is the countenance of one whose spirit dwells in a region beyond emotion and thought, the centre of which mystical writers speak. Mary is beyond joy and sorrow. For her spirit is in God, and she knows as He knows, receiving His knowledge. No longer the Mother of Sorrows nor yet of the human joy of the crib, she understands the secret counsel of God to whose accomplishment Calvary and Bethlehem alike ministered. Therefore her peace, the central peace of God, is beyond the changes of earthly experience. And the inscrutability of that illegible countenance is the inscrutability of the Divine Will made known to her."

Track of your dragging pain.
The stream flows down under the druid tree,
Shiloah's whirlpools gurgle and make glad
115 The castle of God. Sailor, you were glad
And whistled Sion[5] by that stream. But see:

Our Lady, too small for her canopy,
Sits near the altar. There's no comeliness
At all or charm in that expressionless
120 Face with its heavy eyelids. As before,
This face, for centuries a memory,
Non est species, neque decor,
Expressionless, expresses God: it goes
Past castled Sion. She knows what God knows,
125 Not Calvary's Cross nor crib at Bethlehem
Now, and the world shall come to Walsingham.

                    7

The empty winds are creaking and the oak
Splatters and splatters on the cenotaph,[6]
The boughs are trembling and a gaff°   *spar*
130 Bobs on the untimely stroke
Of the greased wash exploding on a shoal-bell
In the old mouth of the Atlantic. It's well;
Atlantic, you are fouled with the blue sailors,
Sea-monsters, upward angel, downward fish:[7]
135 Unmarried and corroding, spare of flesh
Mart once of supercilious, wing'd clippers,
Atlantic, where your bell-trap guts its spoil
You could cut the brackish winds with a knife
Here in Nantucket, and cast up the time
140 When the Lord God formed man from the sea's slime
And breathed into his face the breath of life,
And blue-lung'd combers lumbered to the kill.
The Lord survives the rainbow of His will.[8]

                                        1946

After the Surprising Conversions[9]

September twenty-second, Sir: today
I answer. In the latter part of May,
Hard on ou Lord's Ascension, it began
To be more sensible.° A gentleman   *evident*

5. Sion, or Zion, was a hill in Jerusalem, the
residence of King David and his successors:
the heavenly city.
6. An empty tomb, or monument erected to
the dead but not containing their remains;
often for those lost at sea.
7. From Milton, *Paradise Lost*, I.462–63:
"Dagon his name, sea monster, upward man/
And downward fish * * * *"
8. See Genesis ix.11–17, especially "I do set
my bow in the cloud, and it shall be for a
token of a covenant between me and the
earth."
9. The poem takes its departure from an
account by Jonathan Edwards (1703–58) of a
resurgence of religious enthusiasm that took
place in and around Northampton, Massa-
chusetts, during several months of 1734–35.
Edwards's *Narrative of Surprising Conver-
sions*, in the form of a letter to the Rev. Dr.
Colman of Boston, dated Nov. 6, 1736,
traces the revival from its beginnings through
its decline. One passage towards the end of the

letter (see *The Works of President Edwards*,
New York, 1851, III, 69–72) figures promi-
nently in the poem:
"In the latter part of May, it began to be
very sensible that the Spirit of God was
gradually withdrawing from us, and after this
time Satan seemed to be more let loose, and
raged in a dreadful manner. The first instance
wherein it appeared, was a person's putting
an end to his life by cutting his throat. He
was a gentleman of more than common under-
standing, of strict morals, religious in his
behavior, and a useful, honorable person in the
town; but was of a family that are exceeding
prone to melancholy, and his mother was
killed with it. He had, from the beginning of
this extraordinary time, been exceedingly con-
cerned about the state of his soul, and there
were some things in his experience, that ap-
peared very hopefully, but he durst entertain
no hope concerning his own good estate.
Towards the latter end of his time, he grew
much discouraged, and melancholy grew

Of more than common understanding, strict
In morals, pious in behavior, kicked
Against our goad. A man of some renown,
An useful, honored person in the town,
He came of melancholy parents; prone
·To secret spells, for years they kept alone—
His uncle, I believe, was killed of it:
Good people, but of too much or little wit.
I preached one Sabbath on a text from Kings;
He showed concernment for his soul. Some things
In his experience were hopeful. He
Would sit and watch the wind knocking a tree
And praise this countryside our Lord has made.
Once when a poor man's heifer died, he laid
A shilling on the doorsill; though a thirst
For loving shook him like a snake, he durst
Not entertain much hope of his estate
In heaven. Once we saw him sitting late
Behind his attic window by a light
That guttered on his Bible; through that night
He meditated terror, and he seemed
Beyond advice or reason, for he dreamed
That he was called to trumpet Judgment Day
To Concord. In the latter part of May
He cut his throat. And though the coroner
Judged him delirious, soon a noisome° stir   *noxious, disgusting*
Palsied our village. At Jehovah's nod
Satan seemed more let loose amongst us: God
Abandoned us to Satan, and he pressed
Us hard, until we thought we could not rest
Till we had done with life. Content was gone.
All the good work was quashed. We were undone.
The breath of God had carried out a planned
And sensible withdrawal from this land;
The multitude, once unconcerned with doubt,
Once neither callous, curious nor devout,
Jumped at broad noon, as though some peddler groaned
At it in its familiar twang: "My friend,
Cut your own throat. Cut your own throat. Now! Now!"
September twenty-second, Sir, the bough
Cracks with the unpicked apples, and at dawn
The small-mouth bass breaks water, gorged with spawn.

1946

amain upon him, till he was wholly over-powered by it, and was, in great measure, past a capacity of receiving advice, or being reasoned with to any purpose: the devil took the advantage, and drove him into despairing thoughts. He was kept awake nights meditating upon terror, so that he had scarce any sleep at all, for a long time together. And it was observable at last, that he was scarcely well capable of managing his ordinary business, and was judged delirious by the coroner's inquest. The news of this extraordinarily affected the minds of people here, and struck them as it were with astonishment. After this, multitudes in this and other towns seemed to have it strongly suggested to them, and pressed upon them, to do as this person had done. And many that seemed to be under no melancholy, some pious persons, that had no special darkness or doubts about the goodness of their state, nor were under any special trouble or concern of mind about any thing spiritual or temporal, yet had it urged upon them, as if somebody had spoken to them, *Cut your own throat, now is a good opportunity.* Now! Now! So that they were obliged to fight with all their might to resist it, and yet no reason suggested to them why they should do it." Elsewhere, Edwards identified the man as his uncle, Joseph Hawley, who cut his throat on June 1, 1735.

Dunbarton[3]

My grandfather found
his grandchild's fogbound solitudes
sweeter than human society.

When Uncle Devereux died,
5   Daddy was still on sea-duty in the Pacific;
it seemed spontaneous and proper
for Mr. MacDonald, the farmer,
Karl, the chauffeur, and even my grandmother
to say, "your father." They meant my grandfather.
10 He was my father. I was his son.
On our yearly autumn get-aways from Boston
to the family graveyard in Dunbarton,
he took the wheel himself—
like an admiral at the helm.
15 Freed from Karl and chuckling over the gas he was saving,
he let his motor roller-coaster
out of control down each hill.
We stopped at the *Priscilla* in Nashua
for brownies and root-beer,
20 and later "pumped ship" together in the Indian Summer. . . .

At the graveyard, a sauve Venetian Christ
gave a sheepdog's nursing patience
to Grandfather's Aunt Lottie,
his mother, the stone but not the bones
25 of his father, Francis.
Failing as when Francis Winslow could count
them on his fingers,
the clump of virgin pine still stretched patchy ostrich necks
over the disused millpond's fragrantly woodstained water,
30 a reddish blur,
like the ever-blackening wine-dark coat
in our portrait of Edward Winslow
once sheriff for George the Second,
the sire of bankrupt Tories.

35 Grandfather and I
raked leaves from our dead forebears,
defied the dank weather
with "dragon" bonfires.

Our helper, Mr. Burroughs,
40 had stood with Sherman at Shiloh—[4]
his thermos of shockless coffee
was milk and grounds;
his illegal home-made claret
was as sugary as grape jelly
45 in a tumbler capped with paraffin.

---

3. Town in New Hampshire, the family seat
of one branch of the poet's ancestry.
4. At the battle of Shiloh, in Hardin County,
Tennessee, on April 6–7, 1862, General Sher-
man was largely responsible for the Union
victory.

I borrowed Grandfather's cane
carved with the names and altitudes
of Norwegian mountains he had scaled—
more a weapon than a crutch.
I lanced it in the fauve ooze for newts.
In a tobacco tin after capture, the umber yellow mature newts
lost their leopard spots,
lay grounded as numb
as scrolls of candied grapefruit peel.
I saw myself as a young newt,
neurasthenic, scarlet
and wild in the wild coffee-colored water.

In the mornings I cuddled like a paramour
in my grandfather's bed,
while he scouted about the chattering greenwood stove.

1959

For George Santayana[5]

1863–1952

In the heydays of 'forty-five,
bus-loads of souvenir-deranged
G.I's and officer-professors of philosophy
came crashing through your cell,
puzzled to find you still alive,
free-thinking Catholic infidel,
stray spirit, who'd found
the Church too good to be believed.
Later I used to dawdle
past Circus and Mithraic Temple
to *Santo Stefano* grown paper-thin
like you from waiting. . . .
There at the monastery hospital,
you wished those geese-girl sisters wouldn't bother
their heads and yours by praying for your soul:
"There is no God and Mary is His Mother."

Lying outside the consecrated ground
forever now, you smile
like Ser Brunetto running for the green
cloth at Verona—not like one
who loses, but like one who'd won. . . .[6]
as if your long pursuit of Socrates'
demon, man-slaying Alcibiades,[7]
the demon of philosophy, at last had changed
those fleeting virgins into friendly laurel trees
at *Santo Stefano Rotondo*, when you died
near ninety,

5. The Spanish-born Harvard philosopher, George Santayana, spent the last years of his life, from October 1944, at the Blue Sisters' Nursing Home, next door to the old round church of Santo Stefano Rotondo, on the Monte Celio, in Rome. During the last months of the Second World War, in 1944 and 1945, he was much visited by Allied soldiers and airmen.

6. See Dante, *Inferno*, XV.121–24, where Dante describes Brunetto Latini, as he takes leave of him, in these terms.
7. Athenian statesman and general (ca. 451–404 B.C.); reading a book about Alexander the Great, in 1950, Santayana calls him "one of my favourite heroes, a *good* one, to balance a *bad* one like Alcibiades * * * "

still unbelieving, unconfessed and unreceived,
true to your boyish shyness of the Bride.
Old trooper, I see your child's red crayon pass,
30 bleeding deletions on the galleys° you hold   *galley proofs*
under your throbbing magnifying glass,
that worn arena, where the whirling sand
and broken-hearted lions lick your hand
refined by bile as yellow as a lump of gold.

1959

Skunk Hour

(FOR ELIZABETH BISHOP) [5]

Nautilus Island's hermit
heiress still lives through winter in her Spartan cottage;
her sheep still graze above the sea.
Her son's a bishop. Her farmer
5   is first selectman [6] in our village;
she's in her dotage.

Thirsting for
the hierarchic privacy
of Queen Victoria's century,
10 she buys up all
the eyesores facing her shore,
and lets them fall.

The season's ill—
we've lost our summer millionaire,
15 who seemed to leap from an L. L. Bean [7]
catalogue. His nine-knot yawl
was auctioned off to lobstermen.
A red fox stain covers Blue Hill. [8]

And now our fairy
20 decorator brightens his shop for fall;
his fishnet's filled with orange cork,
orange, his cobbler's bench and awl;
there is no money in his work,
he'd rather marry.

25 One dark night,
my Tudor Ford climbed the hill's skull;
I watched for love-cars. Lights turned down,
they lay together, hull to hull,
where the graveyard shelves on the town. . . .
30 My mind's not right.

A car radio bleats,
"Love, O careless Love. . . ." I hear
my ill-spirit sob in each blood cell,

5. In his essay "On 'Skunk Hour'" (see
Robert Lowell: A Collection of Critical Essays,
ed. T. Parkinson, 1968), Lowell says that his
poem is modeled on Elizabeth Bishop's poem
The Armadillo, that both poems "use short
line stanzas, start with drifting description
and end with a single animal."
6. Elected member of the administrative body

(Board of Selectmen) of many New England
towns.
7. A mail-order dealer in hunting, fishing, and
camping specialties in Freeport, Me.
8. In his essay Lowell says: "The red fox
stain was merely meant to describe the rusty
reddish color of autumn on Blue Hill, a
Maine mountain near where we were living."

as if my hand were at its throat. . . .
I myself am hell; [8a]
nobody's here—

only skunks, that search
in the moonlight for a bite to eat.
They march on their soles up Main Street:
white stripes, moonstruck eyes' red fire
under the chalk-dry and spar spire
of the Trinitarian Church.

I stand on top
of our back steps and breathe the rich air—
a mother skunk with her column of kittens swills the garbage pail.
She jabs her wedge-head in a cup
of sour cream, drops her ostrich tail,
and will not scare.

1957   1959

The Lesson

No longer to lie reading *Tess of the d'Urbervilles,*
while the high, mysterious squirrels
rain small green branches on our sleep!

All that landscape, one likes to think it died
or slept with us, that we ourselves died
or slept then in the age and second of our habitation.

The green leaf cushions the same dry footprint,
or the child's boat luffs[9] in the same dry chop,[1]
and we are where we were. We were!

Perhaps the trees stopped growing in summer amnesia;
their day that gave them veins is rooted down—
and the nights? They are for sleeping now as then.

Ah the light lights the window of my young night,
and you never turn off the light,
while the books lie in the library, and go on reading.

The barberry berry sticks on the small hedge,
cold slits the same crease in the finger,
the same thorn hurts. The leaf repeats the lesson.

1964

The Public Garden[2]

Burnished, burned-out, still burning as the year
you lead me to our stamping ground.
The city and its cruising cars surround
the Public Garden. All's alive—
the children crowding home from school at five,

8a. Possibly an allusion to *Paradise Lost,* IV.
75, where Lucifer says, "Which way I fly is
Hell; myself am Hell."
9. Sails into the wind.
1. Choppiness of waves.

2. A small park next to the Common in Boston,
Massachusetts, containing flower-beds, walks,
greensward, and a pond on which, during the
summer, open pleasure-boats, decorated with
large artificial swans, circulate.

punting a football in the bricky air,
the sailors and their pick-ups under trees
with Latin labels. And the jaded flock
of swanboats paddles to its dock.
10 The park is drying.
Dead leaves thicken to a ball
inside the basin of a fountain, where
the heads of four stone lions stare
and suck on empty fawcets. Night
15 deepens. From the arched bridge, we see
the shedding park-bound mallards, how they keep
circling and diving in the lanternlight,
searching for something hidden in the muck.
And now the moon, earth's friend, that cared so much
20 for us, and cared so little, comes again—
always a stranger! As we walk,
it lies like chalk
over the waters. Everything's aground.
Remember summer? Bubbles filled
25 the fountain, and we splashed. We drowned
in Eden, while Jehovah's grass-green lyre
was rustling all about us in the leaves
that gurgled by us, turning upside down . . . .
The fountain's failing waters flash around
30 the garden. Nothing catches fire.

                                                    1964

Soft Wood

(FOR HARRIET WINSLOW)

Sometimes I have supposed seals
must live as long as the Scholar Gypsy.[5]
Even in their barred pond at the zoo they are happy,
and no sunflower turns
5 more delicately to the sun
without a wincing of the will.

Here too in Maine things bend to the wind forever.
After two years away, one must get used
to the painted soft wood staying bright and clean,
10 to the air blasting and all-white wall whiter,
as it blows through curtain and screen
touched with salt and evergreen.

The green juniper berry spills crystal-clear gin,
and even the hot water in the bathtub
15 is more than water,
and rich with the scouring effervescence
of something healing,
the illimitable salt.

Things last, but sometimes for days here
20 only children seem fit to handle children,
and there is no utility or inspiration

---

5. Matthew Arnold, in his poem *The Scholar
Gypsy* (1853), imagines that the Oxford
student described by a 17th-century writer,
Joseph Glanvill, as having left his studies to
join a band of gypsies, may still be fleetingly
glimpsed in the countryside around Oxford.

in the wind smashing without direction.
The fresh paint
on the captains' houses hides softer wood.

Their square-riggers used to whiten
the four corners of the globe,
but it's no consolation to know
the possessors seldom outlast the possessions,
once warped and mothered by their touch.
Shed skin will never fit another wearer.

Yet the seal pack will bark past my window
summer after summer.
This is the season
when our friends may and will die daily.
Surely the lives of the old
are briefer than the young.

Harriet Winslow, who owned this house,
was more to me than my mother.
I think of you far off in Washington,
breathing in the heat wave
and air-conditioning, knowing
each drug that numbs alerts another nerve to pain.

                                                            1964

For the Union Dead[6]

"Relinquunt Omnia Servare Rem Publicam."

The old South Boston Aquarium stands
in a Sahara of snow now. Its broken windows are boarded.
The bronze weathervane cod has lost half its scales.
The airy tanks are dry.

Once my nose crawled like a snail on the glass;
my hand tingled
to burst the bubbles
drifting from the noses of the cowed, compliant fish.

My hand draws back. I often sigh still
for the dark downward and vegetating kingdom
of the fish and reptile. One morning last March,
I pressed against the new barbed and galvanized

fence on the Boston Common. Behind their cage,
yellow dinosaur steamshovels were grunting
as they cropped up tons of mush and grass
to gouge their underworld garage.

6. At the edge of Boston Common, across from the Massachusetts State House, stands a monument to Colonel Robert Gould Shaw (1837–63) and the Negro troops of the 54th Massachusetts regiment whom he was leading in the assault on Fort Wagner, South Carolina, when he was killed on July 18, 1863. The memorial, by Augustus St. Gaudens, repre- senting Shaw in equestrian high-relief, with his troops, was dedicated in 1897. In the upper right it bears the motto of the Society of the Cincinnati (slightly altered in the epigraph to Lowell's poem), *"Omnia relinquit servare rempublicam,"* "He leaves all else to serve the republic."

Parking spaces luxuriate like civic
sandpiles in the heart of Boston.
A girdle of orange, Puritan-pumpkin colored girders
20 braces the tingling Statehouse,

shaking over the excavations, as it faces Colonel Shaw
and his bell-cheeked Negro infantry
on St. Gaudens' shaking Civil War relief,
propped by a plank splint against the garage's earthquake.

25 Two months after marching through Boston,
half the regiment was dead;
at the dedication,
William James could almost hear the bronze Negroes breathe.

Their monument sticks like a fishbone
30 in the city's throat.
Its Colonel is as lean
as a compass-needle.

He has an angry wrenlike vigilance,
a greyhound's gentle tautness;
35 he seems to wince at pleasure,
and suffocate for privacy.

He is out of bounds now. He rejoices in man's lovely,
peculiar power to choose life and die—
when he leads his black soldiers to death,
40 he cannot bend his back.

On a thousand small town New England greens,
the old white church holds their air
of sparse, sincere rebellion; frayed flags
quilt the graveyards of the Grand Army of the Republic

45 The stone statues of the abstract Union Soldier
grow slimmer and younger each year—
wasp-waisted, they doze over muskets
and muse through their sideburns . . .

Shaw's father wanted no monument
50 except the ditch,
where his son's body was thrown
and lost with his "niggers."

The ditch is nearer.
There are no statues for the last war here;
on Boylston Street, a commerical photograph
55 shows Hiroshima boiling

over a Mosler Safe, the "Rock of Ages"
that survived the blast. Space is nearer.
When I crouch to my television set,
the drained faces of Negro school-children rise like balloons.

60 Colonel Shaw
is riding on his bubble,

he waits
for the blesséd break.

The Aquarium is gone. Everywhere,
giant finned cars nose forward like fish;
a savage servility
slides by on grease.

1964

Harvard

1

The parochial school's green copper dome is like
a green summer grove above the defoliated playground;
clouds puff in cotton wads on a low Dutch sky—
the top of the school resembles a Place des Vosges.[8] . . .
Lying in bed, I see a blind white morning
rise to midheaven in a gaggle of snow—
a silk stocking is coiling on a wire hanger
rapier-bright . . . they dangle from my tree,
a long throw for a hard cold day . . . wind lifting
the stocking like the lecherous, lost leg. . . .
The students, my swarm-mates, rise in their hundreds, and leave
the hive—they can keep time. I've slept so late,
I see my stubble whiten while I shave;
the stocking blows to smog, the steel coathanger stains.

2

We inch by the Boston waterfront on icepools,
carparks make the harbor invisible,
our relationship advances, then
declines to private jokes, the chaff of lust. . . .
Dark days, fair nights . . . yet they fell short—
in a studio near the Back Bay Station,[9] the skylight
angular, night-bluish, blear and spinsterish—
both fighting off muscular cramps, the same fatigue. . . .
Yet tonight means something, something we
must let go willingly, and smash:
all flesh is grass, and like the flower of the grass—[1]
no! lips, breasts, eyes, hands, lips, hair—
the overworked central heating bangs the frame,
as the milkhorse in childhood would clang the morning milkcan.

3. *Morning*

The great dawn of Boston lifts from its black rag;
from Thanksgiving to Christmas, thick arctic snow
thawing to days of moderate, night-black balm—
I cannot sleep, my veins are mineral,
dirt-full as the arteries of a cracked white cup;
one wearies of looking expectantly for the worse—
Chaucer's old January made hay with May.[2]

8. A square in Paris, noted for its 16th- and 17th-century architecture.
9. A small secondary railway station in Boston that allows passengers who live or work in the Back Bay area to leave or board trains without going to the larger South Station, in the business district.
1. "For all flesh is as grass, and all the glory of man as the flower of grass. The grass withereth, and the flower thereof falleth away. . ." (Jeremiah xl.6,8).
2. Chaucer's *The Merchant's Tale* is the story of an old man and his young wife; Pope entitled his version of the Tale *January and May.*

In this ever more enlightened bedroom,
I wake under the early rising sun,
10   sex indelible flowers on the air—
shouldn't I ask to hold to you forever,
body of a dolphin, breast of cloud?
You rival the renewal of the day,
clearing the puddles with your green sack of books.

                                        1969   197.

Dolphin

My Dolphin, you only guide me by surprise,
forgetful as Racine, the man of craft,
drawn through his maze of iron composition
by the incomparable wandering voice of Phèdre.[3]
5   When I was troubled in mind, you made for my body
caught in its hangman's-knot of sinking lines,
the glassy bowing and scraping of my will. . . .
I have sat and listened to too many
words of the collaborating muse,
10   and plotted perhaps too freely with my life,
not avoiding injury to others,
not avoiding injury to myself—
to ask compassion . . . this book,[4] half fiction,
an eelnet made by man for the eel fighting—

15   my eyes have seen what my hand did.

                                                    1973

MARGARET AVISON
(1918–   )

Thaw

Sticky inside their winter suits
the Sunday children stare at pools
in pavement and black ice where roots
of sky in moodier sky dissolve.

5   An empty coach train runs along
        the thin and sooty river flats
        and stick and straw and random stones
        steam faintly when its steam departs.

Lime-water and licorice light
10   wander the tumbled streets. A few
sparrows gather. A dog barks out
under the dogless pale pale blue.

        Move your tongue along a slat
        of a raspberry box from last year's crate.
15   Smell a saucepantilt of water
        on the coal-ash in your grate.

3. The heroine of Jean Racine's tragedy
Phèdre (1677), of which Lowell has published
a verse translation (*Phaedra*, 1961).

4. This poem stands at the end of the volume
of poems entitled *The Dolphin* (1973).

Think how the Black Death [1] made men dance,
and from the silt of centuries
the proof is now scraped bare that once
Troy fell and Pompeii scorched and froze.[2]

> A boy alone out in the court
> whacks with his hockey stick, and whacks
> in the wet, and the pigeons flutter, and rise,
> and settle back.

1960

Black-White Under Green:
May 18, 1965

This day of the leafing-out
speaks with blue power—
among the buttery grassblades
white, tiny-spraying spokes on the end of a weed-stem
and in the formal beds, tulips
and invisible birds inaudibly hallooing,
enormous, their beaks out wide, throats bulging, aflutter,
eyes weeping with speed
where the ultraviolets play and the scythe of the jets
flashes, carrying
the mind-wounded heartpale person, still a boy, a pianist, dying not
of the mind's wounds (as they read the X-rays) but
dying, fibers separated, parents ruddy and
American, strong, sheathed in the cold of
years of his differentness, clustered by two at
the nether arc of his flight.

This day of the leafing-out is one to remember
   how the ice crackled among
      stiff twigs. Glittering strongly
         the old trees sagged. Boughs
   abruptly unsocketed. Dry, orange gashes
the dawn's fine snowing discovered and powdered over.

. . . to remember the leaves ripped loose
the thudding of the dark sky-beams
and the pillared plunging sea
shelterless. Down the centuries
a flinching speck
   in the white fury found of itself—and another—
the rich blood spilling, mother to child, threading
the perilous combers, marbling
the surges, flung
out, and ten-fingered, feeling for
the lollop,[3] the fine-wired
music, dying skyhigh
still between carpets and the
cabin-pressuring windows
on the day of the leafing.

---

1. A form of bubonic plague which ravaged
Europe in the 14th century.
2. Troy was sacked and burned by the Greeks
at the end of the Trojan War; Pompeii was
destroyed by the eruption of Vesuvius in 79
A.D.
3. To move forward with a bounding, leaping
motion.

Faces fanned by
rubberized, cool air
40 are opened; eyes wisely
smile.
The tulips, weeds, new leaves
neither smile nor are scorning to smile nor uncertain,
dwelling in light.
45 A flick of ice, fire, flood,
far off from
the day of the leafing-out I knew
when knee-wagon small, or from my
father's once at a horse-tail silk-shiny
50 fence-corner or this
day when the runways wait
white in the sun, and a new leaf is
metal, torn out of that blue
afloat in the dayshine.

1966

The Dumbfounding

When you walked here,
took skin, muscle, hair,
eyes, larynx, we
withheld all honor: "His house is clay,
5 how can he tell us of his far country?"

Your not familiar pace
in flesh, across the waves,
woke only our distrust.
Twice-torn we cried "A ghost"
10 and only on our planks counted you fast.

Dust wet with your spittle [4]
cleared mortal trouble.
We called you a blasphemer,
a devil-tamer.

15 The evening you spoke of going away
we could not stay.
All legions massed. You had to wash, and rise,
alone, and face
out of the light, for us.

20 You died.
We said,
"The worst is true, our bliss
has come to this."

When you were seen by men
25 in holy flesh again
we hoped so despairingly for such report
we closed their windpipes for it.

---

4. In Mark vii.33 and viii.23, Jesus is reported to have healed dumbness and blindness
with his spittle.

Now you have sought
and seek, in all our ways, all thoughts,
streets, musics—and we make of these a din
trying to lock you out, or in,
to be intent. And dying.

Yet you are
constant and sure,
the all-lovely, all-men's-way
to that far country.

Winning one, you again
all ways would begin
life: to make new
flesh, to empower
the weak in nature
to restore
or stay the sufferer;

lead through the garden to
trash, rubble, hill,
where, the outcast's outcast, you
sound dark's uttermost, strangely light-brimming, until
time be full.

1966

A. W. PURDY
(1918–   )

Poem

You are ill and so I lead you away
and put you to bed in the dark room
—you lie breathing softly and I hold your hand
feeling the fingertips relax as sleep comes

You will not sleep more than a few hours
and the illness is less serious than my anger or cruelty
and the dark bedroom is like a foretaste of other darknesses
to come later which all of us must endure alone
but here I am permitted to be with you

After a while in sleep your fingers clutch tightly
and I know that whatever may be happening
the fear coiled in dreams or the bright trespass of pain
there is nothing at all I can do except hold your hand
and not go away

1965

Lament for the Dorsets

(ESKIMOS EXTINCT IN THE 14TH CENTURY A.D.)

Animal bones and some mossy tent rings
scrapers and spearheads   carved ivory swans
all that remains of the Dorset giants

who drove the Vikings back to their long ships
5　talked to spirits of earth and water
　　—a picture of terrifying old men
　　so large they broke the backs of bears
　　so small they lurk behind bone rafters
　　in the brain of modern hunters
10　among good thoughts and warm things
　　and come out at night
　　to spit on the stars

　　The big men with clever fingers
　　who had no dogs and hauled their sleds
15　over the frozen northern oceans
　　awkward giants
　　　　killers of seal
　　they couldn't compete with little men
　　who came from the west with dogs
20　Or else in a warm climatic cycle
　　the seals went back to cold waters
　　and the puzzled Dorsets scratched their heads
　　with hairy thumbs around 1350 A.D.
　　—couldn't figure it out
25　went around saying to each other
　　plaintively
　　　　　　　　"What's wrong? What happened?
　　　　　　　　Where are the seals gone?"
　　And died

30　Twentieth century people
　　apartment dwellers
　　executives of neon death
　　warmakers with things that explode
　　—they have never imagined us in their future
35　how could we imagine them in the past
　　squatting among the moving glaciers
　　six hundred years ago
　　with glowing lamps?
　　As remote or nearly
40　as the trilobites [1] and swamps
　　when coal became
　　or the last great reptile hissed
　　at a mammal the size of a mouse
　　that squeaked and fled

45　Did they ever realize at all
　　what was happening to them?
　　Some old hunter with one lame leg
　　a bear had chewed
　　sitting in a caribou skin tent
50　—the last Dorset?
　　Let's say his name was Kudluk
　　carving 2-inch ivory swans
　　for a dead granddaughter
　　taking them out of his mind
55　the places in his mind

---

1. Extinct marine arthropods, among the earliest fossils known.

where pictures are
He selects a sharp stone tool
to gouge a parallel pattern of lines
on both sides of the swan
holding it with his left hand
bearing down and transmitting
his body's weight
from brain to arm and right hand
and one of his thoughts
turns to ivory
The carving is laid aside
in beginning darkness
at the end of hunger
after a while wind
blows down the tent and snow
begins to cover him
After 600 years
the ivory thought
is still warm

1968

The Beavers of Renfrew [2]

By day
chain saws stencil the silence in my head
black quotes appear on the red brain
Across glacial birth marks old Jake
Loney is cutting his winter wood,
tongue drowned in a chaw of tobacco—
The belly button pond at one
end of the farm brims
full its cockleshell three acres:
—tonight the beaver are back,
and work their swing shift
under the moon.
Sometimes at low earthen dams
where the pouring spillway empties,
they stand upright in a pride of being,
holding rainbow trout like silver thoughts,
or pale gold Indian girls
arriving here intact from bone cameras
ten thousand ancestors ago,
before letting them spin down the moonlight
rapids as moral lures
for drowned fishermen—
Among the beaver lodges
I stand unable to sleep,
but cannot stay awake
while poplar and birch fall around me.
I am not mistaken for a tree,
but almost totally ignored,
pissed on by mistake occasionally—
Standing here long enough,
seeing the gentle bodies moving
close to what they truly are,

2. A county in southeastern Ontario.

I wonder what screwed-up philosophy,
what claim to a god's indulgence
35 made men decide their own importance?
And what is great music and art
but an alibi for murderers?
Perhaps in the far-off beginnings
of things they made a pact with men,
40 damned the oceans for us,
chewed a hole in the big log bridge
wedged between Kamchatka [3] and Alaska,
tore open the Mediterranean,
parted the Red Sea for Moses,
45 drowned Atlantis and the Eden-myth,
original sin and all that,
in the great salt womb of the sea—
And why?
Because they pitied men.
50 To the wet animal shivering in a tree
they said
                  "Come on down—
                            It's all right."
And he shinnied down with hairless
55 purple behind pointed east for heat,
tail between hind legs,
humbly standing on all fours,
touching his forelock muttering,
"Yessir yessir thank'ee kindly,"
60 but not knowing how to speak yet of course—
Beaver looked at this dripping creature
a miserable biological dead end:
but every failure has flashes of genius
exploding out of death:
65 and the man listened
to an agreement of the water beings
and land beings together
which men have forgotten since:
the secret of staying completely still,
70 allowing ourselves to catch up
with the shadow just ahead of us
we have lost,
when the young world was a cloudy room
drifting thru morning stillness—
75 But the rest of it
I have forgotten,
and the gentle beaver will not remind us:
standing upright at their earthen dams
holding the moonlit reins of water,
80 at peace with themselves—

"Why not make a left turn
and just stay here,"
I said next day to old Jake Loney,
"instead of going on to the planets?"
85 The chain saw bucked in his hands,
chewing out chunks of pine that toppled
and scarred the air with green absence.

---

3. Peninsula in northeastern Siberia.

Far off a beaver tail slapped water,
a bird looked for the tree that was gone—
Old Jake's cheek bulged its chaw of tobacco—
"Well, why not?" I said argumentatively,
before he could spit,
            "Why not?"
And the log bridge across the Bering
burst with a roar around
me again nothing but water,
brown water—
        "Why not?"

                                                    1973

D. J. ENRIGHT
(1920–   )

Changing the Subject

I had suggested, in exasperation, that he find
    something other to write about
Than the moon, and flowers, and birds, and temples,
    and the bare hills of the once holy city—

People, I proposed, who bravely push their way
    through the leprous lakes of mud.
It was the wet season, rain upon spittle and urine,
    and I had been bravely pushing my way.

It happened my hard words chimed with a new slogan,
    a good idea, since ruined—
"Humanism." So I helped on a fashion, another like
    mambo,[1] French chanson, and learning Russian.

Now he comes back, my poet, in a different guise:
    the singer of those who sleep in the subway.
"Welcome you are," his vagrants declaim to each other,
    "a comrade of the common fate."

"Are they miners from Kyushu?"[2] he asks, these "hobos
    all in rags." And adds that
"Broken bamboo baskets, their constant companions, watch
    loyally over their sleeping masters."

Thus my friend. He asks me if he has passed the test,
    is he truly humanistic,
Will I write another article, about his change of heart?
    I try to think of the subway sleepers.

Who are indescribable. Have no wives or daughters to sell.
    Not the grain of faith that makes a beggar.
Have no words. No thing to express. No "comrade."
    Nothing so gratifying as a "common fate."

---

1. Fast rhumba-like dance of Haitian origin.
2. Southernmost of the principal islands of Japan.

Their broken bamboo baskets are loyal because no one
30   would wish to seduce them.
Their ocher skin still burns in its black nest, though a
hundred changed poets decide to sing them.

"Are they miners from Kyushu?" Neither he nor I will
ever dare to ask them.
35   For we know they are not really human, are as apt themes
for verse as the moon and the bare hills.

1960

The Noodle-Vendor's Flute [3]

In a real city, from a real house,
At midnight by the ticking clocks,
In winter by the crackling roads:
Hearing the noodle-vendor's flute,
5   two single fragile falling notes . . .
But what can this small sing-song say,
Under the noise of war?
The flute itself a counterfeit
(Siberian wind can freeze the lips),
10   Merely a rubber bulb and mental horn
(Hard to ride a cycle, watch for manholes
And late drunks, and play a flute together).
Just squeeze between gloved fingers,
And the note of mild hope sounds:
15   Release, the indrawn sigh of mild despair . . .
A poignant signal, like the cooee
Of some diffident soul locked out,
Less than appropriate to cooling macaroni.
Two wooden boxes slung across the wheel,
20   A rider in his middle age, trundling
This gross contraption on a dismal road,
Red eyes and nose and breathless rubber horn.
Yet still the pathos of that double tune
Defies its provenance, and can warm
25   The bitter night.
Sleepless, we turn and sleep.
Or sickness dwindles to some local limb.
Bought love for one long moment gives itself.
Or there a witch assures a frightened child
30   She bears no personal grudge.
And I, like other listeners,
See my stupid sadness as a common thing.
And being common,
Therefore something rare indeed.
35   The puffing vendor, surer than a trumpet,
Tell us we are not alone.
Each night that same frail midnight tune
Squeezed from a bogus flute,
Under the noise of war, after war's noise,
40   It mourns the fallen, every night,
It celebrates survival—
In real cities, real houses, real time.

1960

---

3. D. J. Enright has been a professor of English in many parts of the world, including Japan, which provides the setting and the costumes that figure in this poem, as well as the post-World War II background.

HOWARD NEMEROV
(1920–   )

Brainstorm

The house was shaken by a rising wind
That rattled window and door. He sat alone
In an upstairs room and heard these things: a blind
Ran up with a bang, a door slammed, a groan
Came from some hidden joist, a leaky tap,
At any silence of the wind walked like
A blind man through the house. Timber and sap
Revolt, he thought, from washer, baulk and spike.
Bent to his book, continued unafraid
Until the crows came down from their loud flight
To walk along the rooftree overhead.
Their horny feet, so near but out of sight,
Scratched on the slate; when they were blown away
He heard their wings beat till they came again,
While the wind rose, and the house seemed to sway,
And window panes began to blind with rain.
The house was talking, not to him, he thought,
But to the crows; the crows were talking back
In their black voices. The secret might be out:
Houses are only trees stretched on the rack.
And once the crows knew, all nature would know.
Fur, leaf and feather would invade the form,
Nail rust with rain and shingle warp with snow,
Vine tear the wall, till any straw-borne storm
Could rip both roof and rooftree off and show
Naked to nature what they had kept warm.
He came to feel the crows walk on his head
As if he were the house, their crooked feet
Scratched, through the hair, his scalp. He might be dead,
It seemed, and all the noises underneath
Be but the cooling of the sinews, veins,
Juices, and sodden sacks suddenly let go;
While in his ruins of wiring, his burst mains,
The rainy wind had been set free to blow
Until the green uprising and mob rule
That ran the world had taken over him,
Split him like seed, and set him in the school
Where any crutch can learn to be a limb.

Inside his head he heard the stormy crows.

1958

The Goose Fish

On the long shore, lit by the moon
To show them properly alone,
Two lovers suddenly embraced
So that their shadows were as one.
The ordinary night was graced
For them by the swift tide of blood

That silently they took at flood,
And for a little time they prized
　　Themselves emparadised.

10　Then, as if shaken by stage-fright
Beneath the hard moon's bony light,
They stood together on the sand
Embarrassed in each other's sight
But still conspiring hand in hand,
15　Until they saw, there underfoot,
As though the world had found them out,
The goose fish turning up, though dead,
　　His hugely grinning head.

There in the china light he lay,
20　Most ancient and corrupt and gray
They hesitated at his smile,
Wondering what it seemed to say
To lovers who a little while
Before had thought to understand,
25　By violence upon the sand,
The only way that could be known
　　To make a world their own.

It was a wide and moony grin
Together peaceful and obscene;
30　They knew not what he would express,
So finished a comedian
He might mean failure or success,
But took it for an emblem of
Their sudden, new and guilty love
35　To be observed by, when they kissed,
　　That rigid optimist.

So he became their patriarch,
Dreadfully mild in the half-dark.
His throat that the sand seemed to choke,
40　His picket teeth, these left their mark
But never did explain the joke
That so amused him, lying there
While the moon went down to disappear
Along the still and tilted track
45　　That bears the zodiac.

　　　　　　　　　　　　　　1960

The Blue Swallows

Across the millstream below the bridge
Seven blue swallows divide the air
In shapes invisible and evanescent,
Kaleidoscopic beyond the mind's
5　Or memory's power to keep them there.

"History is where tensions were,"
"Form is the diagram of forces."
Thus, helplessly, there on the bridge,
While gazing down upon those birds—

How strange, to be above the birds!—
Thus helplessly the mind in its brain
Weaves up relation's spindrift web,
Seeing the swallows' tails as nibs
Dipped in invisible ink, writing . . .

Poor mind, what would you have them write?
Some cabalistic° history   *mystical*
Whose authorship you might ascribe
To God? to Nature? Ah, poor ghost,
You've capitalized your Self enough.
That villainous William of Occam [1]
Cut out the feet from under that dream
Some seven centuries ago.
It's taken that long for the mind
To waken, yawn and stretch, to see
With opened eyes emptied of speech
The real world where the spelling mind
Imposes with its grammar book
Unreal relations on the blue
Swallows. Perhaps when you will have
Fully awakened, I shall show you
A new thing: even the water
Flowing away beneath those birds
Will fail to reflect their flying forms,
And the eyes that see become as stones
Whence never tears shall fall again.

O swallows, swallows, poems are not
The point. Finding again the world,
That is the point, where loveliness
Adorns intelligible things
Because the mind's eye lit the sun.

1967

RICHARD WILBUR
(1921–   )

First Snow in Alsace

The snow came down last night like moths
Burned on the moon; it fell till dawn,
Covered the town with simple cloths.

Absolute snow lies rumpled on
What shellbursts scattered and deranged,
Entangled railings, crevassed lawn.

As if it did not know they'd changed,
Snow smoothly clasps the roofs of homes
Fear-gutted, trustless and estranged.

1. Fourteenth-century scholastic philosopher whose central principle ("Occam's razor") was that the simplest, most economical explanation is always to be preferred to one that introduces unnecessary complications.

10 The ration stacks are milky domes;
   Across the ammunition pile
   The snow has climbed in sparkling combs.

   You think: beyond the town a mile
   Or two, this snowfall fills the eyes
15 Of soldiers dead a little while.

   Persons and persons in disguise,
   Walking the new air white and fine,
   Trade glances quick with shared surprise.

   At children's windows, heaped, benign,
20 As always, winter shines the most,
   And frost makes marvelous designs.

   The night guard coming from his post,
   Ten first-snows back in thought, walks slow
   And warms him with a boyish boast:

25 He was the first to see the snow.

                                              1947

Objects

   Meridians are a net
   Which catches nothing; that sea-scampering bird
   The gull, though shores lapse every side from sight, can yet
   Sense him to land, but Hanno[1] had not heard

5 Hesperidean song,[2]
   Had he not gone by watchful periploi:[3]
   Chalk rocks, and isles like beasts, and mountain stains along
   The water-hem, calmed him at last nearby

   The clear high hidden chant
10 Blown from the spellbound coast, where under drifts
   Of sunlight, under plated leaves, they guard the plant
   By praising it. Among the wedding gifts

   Of Herë, were a set
   Of golden McIntoshes, from the Greek
15 Imagination. Guard and gild what's common, and forget
   Uses and prices and names; have objects speak.

   There's classic and there's quaint,
   And then there is that devout intransitive eye
   Of Pieter de Hooch:[4] see feinting from his plot of paint
20 The trench of light on boards, the much-mended dry

   Courtyard wall of brick,
   And sun submerged in beer, and streaming in glasses,

---

1. Carthaginian navigator who led an expedition down the west coast of Africa in the fifth century B.C.
2. The Hesperides were sweet-voiced nymphs who guarded the golden apples ("McIntoshes") given by Ge to Hera for her marriage to Zeus (see lines 12–14).
3. Plural of *periplus,* a voyage or trip around an island or a coast.
4. Pieter de Hooch (1629–ca. 1677), Dutch genre painter.

The weave of a sleeve, the careful and undulant tile. A quick
Change of the eye and all this calmly passes

Into a day, into magic.
For is there any end to true textures, to true
Integuments; do they ever desist from tacit, tragic
Fading away? Oh maculate, cracked, askew,

Gay-pocked and potsherd world
I voyage, where in every tangible tree
I see afloat among the leaves, all calm and curled,
The Cheshire smile[5] which sets me fearfully free.

1947

Praise in Summer

Obscurely yet most surely called to praise,
As sometimes summer calls us all, I said
The hills are heavens full of branching ways
Where star-nosed moles fly overhead the dead;
I said the trees are mines in air, I said
See how the sparrow burrows in the sky!
And then I wondered why this mad *instead*
Perverts our praise to uncreation, why
Such savor's in this wrenching things awry.
Does sense so stale that it must needs derange
The world to know it? To a praiseful eye
Should it not be enough of fresh and strange
That trees grow green, and moles can course in clay,
And sparrows sweep the ceiling of our day?

1947

The Pardon

My dog lay dead five days without a grave
In the thick of summer, hid in a clump of pine
And a jungle of grass and honeysuckle-vine.
I who had loved him while he kept alive

Went only close enough to where he was
To sniff the heavy honeysuckle-smell
Twined with another odor heavier still
And hear the flies' intolerable buzz.

Well, I was ten and very much afraid.
In my kind world the dead were out of range
And I could not forgive the sad or strange
In beast or man. My father took the spade

And buried him. Last night I saw the grass
Slowly divide (it was the same scene
But now it glowed a fierce and mortal green)
And saw the dog emerging. I confess

5. In *Alice in Wonderland*, when the Cheshire cat disappeared, its smile lingered.

I felt afraid again, but still he came
In the carnal sun, clothed in a hymn of flies,
And death was breeding in his lively eyes.
20 I started in to cry and call his name,

Asking forgiveness of his tongueless head.
. . . I dreamt the past was never past redeeming:
But whether this was false or honest dreaming
I beg death's pardon now. And mourn the dead.

                                        1950

The Death of a Toad

        A toad the power mower caught,
Chewed and clipped of a leg, with a hobbling hop has got
    To the garden verge, and sanctuaried him
    Under the cineraria leaves, in the shade
5   Of the ashen heartshaped leaves, in a dim,
            Low, and a final glade.

        The rare original heartsblood goes,
Spends on the earthen hide, in the folds and wizening, flows
    In the gutters of the banked and staring eyes. He lies
10 As still as if he would return to stone,
        And soundlessly attending, dies
            Toward some deep monotone,

        Toward misted and ebullient seas
And cooling shores, toward lost Amphibia's emperies.[6]
15 Day dwindles, drowning, and at length is gone
    In the wide and antique eyes, which still appear
        To watch, across the castrate lawn,
            The haggard daylight steer.

                                        1950, 1957

A Baroque Wall-Fountain
in the Villa Sciarra

    FOR DORE AND ADJA

        Under the bronze crown
Too big for the head of the stone cherub whose feet
    A serpent has begun to eat,
Sweet water brims a cockle° and braids down   *plant*

5   Past spattered mosses, breaks
On the tipped edge of a second shell, and fills
        The massive third below. It spills
In threads then from the scalloped rim, and makes

            A scrim or summery tent
10 For a faun-ménage and their familiar goose.
        Happy in all that ragged, loose
Collapse of water, its effortless descent

---

6. I.e., the land of amphibians.

     And flatteries of spray,
The stocky god upholds the shell with ease,
     Watching, about his shaggy knees,
The goatish innocence of his babes at play;

     His fauness all the while
Leans forward, slightly, into a clambering mesh
     Of water-lights, her sparkling flesh
In a saecular° ecstasy, her blinded smile   *age-old*

     Bent on the sand floor
Of the trefoil[2] pool, where ripple-shadows come
     And go in swift reticulum,[3]
More addling to the eye than wine, and more

     Interminable to thought
Than pleasure's calculus. Yet since this all
     Is pleasure, flash, and waterfall,
Must it not be too simple? Are we not

     More intricately expressed
In the plain fountains that Maderna[4] set
     Before St. Peter's—the main jet
Struggling aloft until it seems at rest

     In the act of rising, until
The very wish of water is reversed,
     That heaviness borne up to burst
In a clear, high, cavorting head, to fill

     With blaze, and then in gauze
Delays, in a gnatlike shimmering, in a fine
     Illumined version of itself, decline,
And patter on the stones its own applause?

     If that is what men are
Or should be, if those water-saints display
     The pattern of our areté,[5]
What of these showered fauns in their bizarre,

     Spangled, and plunging house?
They are at rest in fullness of desire
     For what is given, they do not tire
Of the smart of the sun, the pleasant water-douse

     And riddled pool below,
Reproving our disgust and our ennui
     With humble insatiety.
Francis,[6] perhaps, who lay in sister snow

     Before the wealthy gate
Freezing and praising, might have seen in this
     No trifle, but a shade of bliss—
That land of tolerable flowers, that state

2. Three-part, as in some leaves.
3. A netlike formation.
4. Carlo Maderno (1556–1629), architect and designer who completed plans for St. Peter's in Rome, especially the façade.

5. The combination of qualities which distinguish good character: excellence, valor, virtue, manliness.
6. I.e., St. Francis of Assisi.

As near and far as grass
Where eyes become the sunlight, and the hand
  Is worthy of water: the dreamt land
60 Toward which all hungers leap, all pleasures pass.

1956

Junk

Huru Welandes   worc ne geswiceð
monna ænigum   ðara ðe Mimming can
heardne gehealdan.
                                    —WALDERE[7]

An axe angles
                    from my neighbor's ashcan;
It is hell's handiwork,
                    the wood not hickory,
5 The flow of the grain
                    not faithfully followed.
The shivered shaft
                    rises from a shellheap
Of plastic playthings,
10   paper plates,
And the sheer shards
                    of shattered tumblers
That were not annealed
                    for the time needful.
15 At the same curbside,
                    a cast-off cabinet
Of wavily-warped
                    unseasoned wood
Waits to be trundled
20   in the trash-man's truck.
Haul them off! Hide them!
                    The heart winces
For junk and gimcrack,
25   for jerrybuilt things
And the men who make them
                    for a little money,
Bartering pride
                    like the bought boxer
30 Who pulls his punches,
                    or the paid-off jockey
Who in the home stretch
                    holds in his horse.
Yet the things themselves
35   in thoughtless honor
Have kept composure,
                    like captives who would not
Talk under torture.
                    Tossed from a tailgate
40 Where the dump displays
                    its random dolmens,[8]

7. *Waldere* (or *Waldhere*) is the name of an Old English heroic poem. The lines quoted here translate roughly as "Weland's handiwork will fail no man who can wield sharp Mimming." Weland, or Wayland, was the mythical blacksmith and king of elves. Mimming was the name of Weland's sword.
8. Crude tombs made from rough slabs of stone.

Its black barrows
                           and blazing valleys,
They shall waste in the weather
                                              toward what they were.

The sun shall glory
                              in the glitter of glass-chips,

Foreseeing the salvage
                                  of the prisoned sand,

And the blistering paint
                                    peel off in patches,

That the good grain
                              be discovered again.

Then burnt, bulldozed,
                                   they shall all be buried

To the depth of diamonds,
                                       in the making dark

Where halt Hephaestus[9]
                                     keeps his hammer

And Wayland's work
                             is worn away.

                                                            1961

Seed Leaves

HOMAGE TO R. F.[1]

Here something stubborn comes,
Dislodging the earth crumbs
And making crusty rubble.
It comes up bending double,
And looks like a green staple.
It could be seedling maple,
Or artichoke, or bean.
That remains to be seen.

Forced to make choice of ends,
The stalk in time unbends,
Shakes off the seed-case, heaves
Aloft, and spreads two leaves
Which still display no sure
And special signature.
Toothless and fat, they keep
The oval form of sleep.

This plant would like to grow
And yet be embryo;
Increase, and yet escape
The doom of taking shape;
Be vaguely vast, and climb
To the tip end of time
With all of space to fill,
Like boundless Igdrasil [2]
That has the stars for fruit.

---

9. Greek god of the fire and forge; his Roman
equivalent is Vulcan.
1. Robert Frost.

2. The great ash tree of Scandinavian
mythology, whose roots are in the underworld
and whose branches embrace the heavens.

But something at the root
More urgent than that urge
Bids two true leaves emerge,
And now the plant, resigned
30   To being self-defined
Before it can commerce
With the great universe,
Takes aim at all the sky
And starts to ramify.

196

PHILIP LARKIN
(1922–   )

Wants

Beyond all this, the wish to be alone:
However the sky grows dark with invitation-cards
However we follow the printed directions of sex
However the family is photographed under the flagstaff—
5   Beyond all this, the wish to be alone.

Beneath it all, desire of oblivion runs:
Despite the artful tensions of the calendar,
The life insurance, the tabled fertility rites,
The costly aversion of the eyes from death—
10   Beneath it all, desire of oblivion runs.

195:

Church Going

Once I am sure there's nothing going on
I step inside, letting the door thud shut.
Another church: matting, seats, and stone,
And little books; sprawlings of flowers, cut
5   For Sunday, brownish now; some brass and stuff
Up at the holy end; the small neat organ;
And a tense, musty, unignorable silence,
Brewed God knows how long. Hatless, I take off
My cycle-clips in awkward reverance,

10   Move forward, run my hand around the font.
From where I stand, the roof looks almost new—
Cleaned, or restored? Somone would know: I don't.
Mounting the lectern, I peruse a few
Hectoring large-scale verses, and pronounce
15   "Here endeth" much more loudly than I'd meant.
The echoes snigger briefly. Back at the door
I sign the book, donate an Irish sixpence,
Reflect the place was not worth stopping for.

Yet stop I did: in fact I often do,
20   And always end much at a loss like this,
Wondering what to look for; wondering, too,
When churches fall completely out of use

What we shall turn them into, if we shall keep
A few cathedrals chronically on show,
Their parchment, plate and pyx[1] in locked cases,
And let the rest rent-free to rain and sheep.
Shall we avoid them as unlucky places?

Or, after dark, will dubious women come
To make their children touch a particular stone;
Pick simples° for a cancer; or on some   **herbs**
Advised night see walking a dead one?
Power of some sort or other will go on
In games, in riddles, seemingly at random;
But superstition, like belief, must die,
And what remains when disbelief has gone?
Grass, weedy pavement, brambles, buttress, sky,

A shape less recognizable each week,
A purpose more obscure. I wonder who
Will be the last, the very last, to seek
This place for what it was; one of the crew
That tap and jot and know what rood-lofts were?
Some ruin-bibber, randy for antique,
Or Christmas-addict, counting on a whiff
Of gown-and-bands and organ-pipes and myrrh?
Or will he be my representative,

Bored, uninformed, knowing the ghostly silt
Dispersed, yet tending to this cross of ground
Through suburb scrub because it held unspilt
So long and equably what since is found
Only in separation—marriage, and birth,
And death, and thoughts of these—for whom was built
This special shell? For, though I've no idea
What this accoutred frowsty barn is worth,
It pleases me to stand in silence here;

A serious house on serious earth it is,
In whose blent air all our compulsions meet,
Are recognized, and robed as destinies.
And that much never can be obsolete,
Since someone will forever be surprising
A hunger in himself to be more serious,
And gravitating with it to this ground,
Which, he once heard, was proper to grow wise in,
If only that so many dead lie round.

1955

Myxomatosis [2]

Caught in the center of a soundless field
While hot inexplicable hours go by
What trap is this? Where were its teeth concealed?
You seem to ask.

---

1. The vessel in which the Host is kept.
2. An infectious and fatal disease of rabbits, artificially introduced into Great Britain and Australia in recent years to keep down the rabbit population.

I make a sharp reply,
5 Then clean my stick. I'm glad I can't explain
Just in what jaws you were to suppurate:
You may have thought things would come right again
If you could only keep quite still and wait.

195

The Whitsun Weddings [3]

That Whitsun, I was late getting away:
    Not till about
One-twenty on the sunlit Saturday
Did my three-quarters-empty train pull out,
5 All windows down, all cushions hot, all sense
Of being in a hurry gone. We ran
Behind the backs of houses, crossed a street
Of blinding windscreens,° smelt the fish-dock; thence   windshield
The river's level drifting breadth began,
10 Where sky and Lincolnshire and water meet.

All afternoon, through the tall heat that slept
    For miles inland,
A slow and stopping curve southwards we kept.
Wide farms went by, short-shadowed cattle, and
15 Canals with floatings of industrial froth;
A hothouse flashed uniquely: hedges dipped
And rose: and now and then a smell of grass
Displaced the reek of buttoned carriage-cloth
Until the next town, new and nondescript,
20 Approached with acres of dismantled cars.

At first, I didn't notice what a noise
    The weddings made
Each station that we stopped at: sun destroys
The interest of what's happening in the shade,
25 And down the long cool platforms whoops and skirls
I took for porters larking with the mails,
And went on reading. Once we started, though,
We passed them, grinning and pomaded, girls
In parodies of fashion, heels and veils,
30 All posed irresolutely, watching us go,

As if out on the end of an event
    Waving goodbye
To something that survived it. Struck, I leant
More promptly out next time, more curiously,
35 And saw it all again in different terms:
The fathers with broad belts under their suits
And seamy foreheads; mothers loud and fat;
An uncle shouting smut; and then the perms,
The nylon gloves and jewelry-substitutes,
40 The lemons, mauves, and olive-ochers that

---

3. Whitsuntide, or Whitsun, comprises Whit
Sunday, the seventh Sunday after Easter, and
the days immediately following. The holida[y]
falls in late May or early June.

Marked off the girls unreally from the rest.
   Yes, from cafés
And banquet-halls up yards, and bunting-dressed
Coach-party annexes, the wedding-days
Were coming to an end. All down the line
Fresh couples climbed aboard: the rest stood round;
The last confetti and advice were thrown,
And, as we moved, each face seemed to define
Just what it saw departing: children frowned
At something dull; fathers had never known

Success so huge and wholly farcical;
   The women shared
The secret like a happy funeral;
While girls, gripping their handbags tighter, stared
At a religious wounding. Free at last,
And loaded with the sum of all they saw,
We hurried towards London, shuffling gouts of steam.
Now fields were building-plots, and poplars cast
Long shadows over major roads, and for
Some fifty minutes, that in time would seem

Just long enough to settle hats and say
   I nearly died,
A dozen marriages got under way.
They watched the landscape, sitting side by side
—An Odeon went past, a cooling tower,
And someone running up to bowl [4]—and none
Thought of the others they would never meet
Or how their lives would all contain this hour.
I thought of London spread out in the sun,
Its postal districts packed like squares of wheat:

There we were aimed. And as we raced across
   Bright knots of rail
Past standing Pullmans, walls of blackened moss
Came close, and it was nearly done, this frail
Traveling coincidence; and what it held
Stood ready to be loosed with all the power
That being changed can give. We slowed again,
And as the tightened brakes took hold, there swelled
A sense of falling, like an arrow-shower
Sent out of sight, somewhere becoming rain.

                                   1964

Days

What are days for?
Days are where we live.
They come, they wake us
Time and time over.
They are to be happy in:
Where can we live but days?

---

4. In cricket, the ball is "bowled" (delivered so as to bounce once) to the batter. The
bowler takes a running start of 5–10 yards.

Ah, solving that question
Brings the priest and the doctor
In their long coats
10   Running over the fields.

1196

Talking in Bed

Talking in bed ought to be easiest,
Lying together there goes back so far,
An emblem of two people being honest.

Yet more and more time passes silently.
5   Outside, the wind's incomplete unrest
Builds and disperses clouds about the sky,

And dark towns heap up on the horizon.
None of this cares for us. Nothing shows why
At this unique distance from isolation

10   It becomes still more difficult to find
Words at once true and kind,
Or not untrue and not unkind.

1964

JAMES DICKEY
(1923–   )

The Lifeguard

In a stable of boats I lie still,
From all sleeping children hidden.
The leap of a fish from its shadow
Makes the whole lake instantly tremble.
5   With my foot on the water, I feel
The moon outside

Take on the utmost of its power.
I rise and go out through the boats.
I set my broad sole upon silver,
10   On the skin of the sky, on the moonlight,
Stepping outward from earth onto water
In quest of the miracle

This village of children believed
That I could perform as I dived
15   For one who had sunk from my sight.
I saw his cropped haircut go under.
I leapt, and my steep body flashed
Once, in the sun.

Dark drew all the light from my eyes.
20   Like a man who explores his death
By the pull of his slow-moving shoulders,
I hung head down in the cold,
Wide-eyed, contained, and alone
Among the weeds,

And my fingertips turned into stone
From clutching immovable blackness.
Time after time I leapt upward
Exploding in breath, and fell back
From the change in the children's faces
At my defeat.

Beneath them I swam to the boathouse
With only my life in my arms
To wait for the lake to shine back
At the risen moon with such power
That my steps on the light of the ripples
Might be sustained.

Beneath me is nothing but brightness
Like the ghost of a snowfield in summer.
As I move toward the center of the lake,
Which is also the center of the moon,
I am thinking of how I may be
The savior of one

Who has already died in my care.
The dark trees fade from around me.
The moon's dust hovers together.
I call softly out, and the child's
Voice answers through blinding water.
Patiently, slowly,

He rises, dilating to break
The surface of stone with his forehead.
He is one I do not remember
Having ever seen in his life.
The ground I stand on is trembling
Upon his smile.

I wash the black mud from my hands.
On a light given off by the grave
I kneel in the quick of the moon
At the heart of a distant forest
And hold in my arms a child
Of water, water, water.

1962

In the Tree House at Night

And now the green household is dark.
The half-moon completely is shining
On the earth-lighted tops of the trees.
To be dead, a house must be still.
The floor and the walls wave me slowly;
I am deep in them over my head.
The needles and pine cones about me

Are full of small birds at their roundest,
Their fists without mercy gripping
Hard down through the tree to the roots

To sing back at light when they feel it.
We lie here like angels in bodies,
My brothers and I, one dead,
The other asleep from much living,

15 In mid-air huddled beside me.
Dark climbed to us here as we climbed
Up the nails I have hammered all day
Through the sprained, comic rungs of the ladder
Of broom handles, crate slats, and laths
20 Foot by foot up the trunk to the branches
Where we came out at last over lakes

Of leaves, of fields disencumbered of earth
That move with the moves of the spirit.
Each nail that sustains us I set here;
25 Each nail in the house is now steadied
By my dead brother's huge, freckled hand.
Through the years, he has pointed his hammer
Up into these limbs, and told us

That we must ascend, and all lie here.
30 Step after step he has brought me,
Embracing the trunk as his body,
Shaking its limbs with my heartbeat,
Till the pine cones danced without wind
And fell from the branches like apples.
35 In the arm-slender forks of our dwelling

I breathe my live brother's light hair.
The blanket around us becomes
As solid as stone, and it sways.
With all my heart, I close
40 The blue, timeless eye of my mind.
Wind springs, as my dead brother smiles
And touches the tree at the root;

A shudder of joy runs up
The trunk; the needles tingle;
45 One bird uncontrollably cries.
The wind changes round, and I stir
Within another's life. Whose life?
Who is dead? Whose presence is living?
When may I fall strangely to earth,

50 Who am nailed to this branch by a spirit?
Can two bodies make up a third?
To sing, must I feel the world's light?
My green, graceful bones fill the air
With sleeping birds. Alone, alone
55 And with them I move gently.
I move at the heart of the world.

1962

At Darien Bridge

The sea here used to look
As if many convicts had built it,

Standing deep in their ankle chains,
Ankle-deep in the water, to smite

The land and break it down to salt.
I was in this bog as a child

When they were all working all day
To drive the pilings down.

I thought I saw the still sun
Strike the side of a hammer in flight

And from it a sea bird be born
To take off over the marshes.

As the gray climbs the side of my head
And cuts my brain off from the world,

I walk and wish mainly for birds,
For the one bird no one has looked for

To spring again from a flash
Of metal, perhaps from the scratched

Wedding band on my ring finger.
Recalling the chains of their feet,

I stand and look out over grasses
At the bridge they built, long abandoned,

Breaking down into water at last,
And long, like them, for freedom

Or death, or to believe again
That they worked on the ocean to give it

The unchanging, hopeless look
Out of which all miracles leap.

1964

In the Marble Quarry

Beginning to dangle beneath
The wind that blows from the undermined wood,
I feel the great pulley grind,

The thread I cling to lengthen
And let me soaring and spinning down into marble,
Hooked and weightlessly happy

Where the squared sun shines
Back equally from all four sides, out of stone
And years of dazzling labor,

10   To land at last among men
Who cut with power saws a Parian whiteness²
        And, chewing slow tobacco,

        Their eyebrows like frost,
Shunt house-sized blocks and lash them to cables
15   And send them heavenward

        Into small-town banks,
Into the columns and statues of government buildings,
        But mostly graves.

        I mount my monument and rise
20 Slowly and spinningly from the white-gloved men
        Toward the hewn sky

        Out of the basement of light,
Sadly, lifted through time's blinding layers
        On perhaps my tombstone

25   In which the original shape
Michelangelo believed was in every rock upon earth
        Is heavily stirring,

        Surprised to be an angel,
To be waked in North Georgia by the ponderous play
30   Of men with ten-ton blocks

        But no more surprised than I
To feel sadness fall off as though I myself
        Were rising from stone

        Held by a thread in midair,
35 Badly cut, local-looking, and totally uninspired,
        Not a masterwork

        Or even worth seeing at all
But the spirit of this place just the same,
        Felt here as joy.

                                    1964

Buckdancer's Choice

So I would hear out those lungs,
The air split into nine levels,
Some gift of tongues of the whistler

In the invalid's bed: my mother,
5   Warbling all day to herself
The thousand variations of one song;

It is called Buckdancer's Choice.
For years, they have all been dying
Out, the classic buck-and-wing⁵ men

---

2. The whiteness of marble from Paros.
5. A dance associated with American minstrel shows, and similar to a clog dance. The dancer's feet (sometimes he beats his own rhythm on a tambourine) make movements like wings.

Of traveling minstrel shows;
With them also an old woman
Was dying of breathless angina,[6]

Yet still found breath enough
To whistle up in my head
A sight like a one-man band,

Freed black, with cymbals at heel,
An ex-slave who thrivingly danced
To the ring of his own clashing light

Through the thousand variations of one song
All day to my mother's prone music,
The invalid's warbler's note,

While I crept close to the wall
Sock-footed, to hear the sounds alter,
Her tongue like a mockingbird's break

Through stratum after stratum of a tone
Proclaiming what choices there are
For the last dancers of their kind,

For ill women and for all slaves
Of death, and children enchanted at walls
With a brass-beating glow underfoot,

Not dancing but nearly risen
Through barnlike, theaterlike houses
On the wings of the buck and wing.

1965

DENISE LEVERTOV
(1923–   )

Scenes from the Life of the Peppertrees

1

The peppertrees, the peppertrees!

Cats are stretching in the doorways,
sure of everything. It is morning.
    But the peppertrees
stand aside in diffidence, with berries
of modest red.
        Branch above branch, an air
of lightness; of shadows
scattered lightly.
        A cat
closes upon its shadow.
Up and up goes the sun,
sure of everything.
    The peppertrees
        shiver a little.

6. A respiratory disease usually related to heart ailments.

Robust
and soot-black, the cat
leaps to a low branch. Leaves
close about him.
                    2
20   The yellow moon dreamily
tipping buttons of light
down among the leaves. Marimba,
marimba—from beyond the
black street.
25   Somebody dancing,
somebody
                  getting the hell
outta here. Shadows of cats
weave round the tree trunks,
30   the exposed knotty roots.
                    3
The man on the bed sleeping
defenseless. Look—
his bare long feet together
sideways, keeping each other
35   warm. And the foreshortened shoulders,
the head
barely visible.   He is good.
let him sleep.
            But the third peppertree
40   is restless, twitching
thin leaves in the light
of afternoon.   After a while
it walks over and taps
on the upstairs window with a bunch
45   of red berries.   Will he wake?

                                              1958

The Dead Butterfly

                    1
Now I see its whiteness
is not white but green, traced with green,
and resembles the stones
of which the city is built,
5   quarried high in the mountains.
                    2
Everywhere among the marigolds
the rainblown roses and the hedges
of tamarisk are white
butterflies this morning, in constant
10   tremulous movement, only those
that lie dead revealing
their rockgreen color and the bold
cut of the wings.

                                              1959

Triple Feature

Innocent decision: to enjoy.
And the pathos
of hopefulness, of his solicitude:

—he in mended serape,
she having plaited carefully
magenta ribbons into her hair,
the baby a round half-hidden shape
slung in her rebozo,° and the young son steadfastly   *shawl*
gripping a fold of her skirt,
pale and severe under a
handed-down sombrero—

        all regarding
the stills with full attention, preparing
to pay and go in—
to worlds of shadow-violence, half-
familiar, warm with popcorn, icy
with strange motives, barbarous splendors!

                                     1959

From the Roof

This wild night, gathering the washing as if it were flowers
        animal vines twisting over the line and
        slapping my face lightly, soundless merriment
        in the gesticulations of shirtsleeves,
I recall out of my joy a night of misery

walking in the dark and the wind over broken earth,
        halfmade foundations and unfinished
        drainage trenches and the spaced-out
                circles of glaring light
        marking streets that were to be,
walking with you but so far from you,

and now alone in October's
first decision towards winter, so close to you—
        my arms full of playful rebellious linen, a freighter
        going down-river two blocks away, outward bound,
        the green wolf-eyes of the Harborside Terminal
                glittering on the Jersey shore,
and a train somewhere under ground bringing you towards me
to our new living-place from which we can see

a river and its traffic (the Hudson and the
hidden river, who can say which it is we see, we see
something of both. Or who can say
the crippled broom-vendor yesterday, who passed
just as we needed a new broom, was not
one of the Hidden Ones?)
        Crates of fruit are unloading
        across the street on the cobbles,
        and a brazier flaring
        to warm the men and burn trash. He wished us
luck when we bought the broom. But not luck
brought us here. By design

clear air and cold wind polish
the river lights, by design
we are to live now in a new place.

                                       1961

The Victors

In June the bush we call
alder was heavy, listless,
its leaves studded with galls,

growing wherever we didn't
5   want it. We cut it
savagely, hunted it from the pasture, chopped it

away from the edge of the wood.
In July, still everywhere, it appeared
wearing green berries.

10   Anyway it must go. It takes
the light and air and the good of the earth
from flowers and young trees.

But now in August
its berries are red. Do the birds
15   eat them?   Swinging

clusters of red, the hedges are full of them,
red-currant red, a graceful
ornament or a merry smile.

1964

O Taste and See

The world is
not with us enough.[1]
O taste and see

the subway Bible poster said,
5   meaning The Lord,[2] meaning
if anything all that lives
to the imagination's tongue,

grief, mercy, language,
tangerine, weather, to
10   breathe them, bite,
savor, chew, swallow, transform

into our flesh our
deaths, crossing the street, plum, quince,
living in the orchard and being

15   hungry, and plucking
the fruit.

1964

1. Cf. Wordsworth's sonnet, *The World Is*   2. "O taste and see that the Lord is good"
Too Much with Us, above.   (Psalms xxxiv.8).

The Closed World

"If the Perceptive Organs close, their
Objects seem to close also."
—Blake: *Jerusalem*

The house-snake dwells here still
under the threshold
but for months I have not seen it
nor its young, the inheritors.

Light and the wind enact
passion and resurrection
day in, day out
but the blinds are down over my windows,
my doors are shut.

When after the long drought at last
silver and darkness swept over the hills
the dry indifferent glare in my mind's eye
wavered but burned on.

1967

City Psalm

The killings continue, each second
pain and misfortune extend themselves
in the genetic chain, injustice is done knowingly, and the air
bears the dust of decayed hopes,
yet breathing those fumes, walking the thronged
pavements among crippled lives, jackhammers
raging, a parking lot painfully agleam
in the May sun, I have seen
not behind but within, within the
dull grief, blown grit, hideous
concrete façades, another grief, a gleam
as of dew, an abode of mercy,
have heard not behind but within noise
a humming that drifted into a quiet smile.
Nothing was changed, all was revealed otherwise;
not that horror was not, not that the killings did not continue,
not that I thought there was to be no more despair,
but that as if transparent all disclosed
an otherness that was blesséd, that was bliss.
I saw Paradise in the dust of the street.

1967

Tenebrae [3]

(FALL OF 1967) [4]

Heavy, heavy, heavy, hand and heart.
We are at war,
bitterly, bitterly at war.

---

3. *Tenebrae* (Latin, darkness), are church services for the last three days of Holy Week, to commemorate the sufferings and death of Christ; candles lighted at the beginning of the service are extinguished one by one after each psalm, in memory of the darkness at the time of the crucifixion.
4. The fall of 1967 witnessed the march on the Pentagon, in protest against the continuing presence of American troops in Vietnam.

And the buying and selling
5 buzzes at our heads, a swarm
of busy flies, a kind of innocence.

Gowns of gold sequins are fitted,
sharp-glinting. What harsh rustlings
of silver moiré° there are,   *watered silk*
10 to remind me of shrapnel splinters.

And weddings are held in full solemnity
not of desire but of etiquette,
the nuptial pomp of starched lace;
a grim innocence.

15 And picnic parties return from the beaches
burning with stored sun in the dusk;
children promised a TV show when they get home
fall asleep in the backs of a million station wagons,
sand in their hair, the sound of waves
20 quietly persistent at their ears.
They are not listening.

Their parents at night
dream and forget their dreams.
They wake in the dark
25 and make plans. Their sequin plans
glitter into tomorrow.
They buy, they sell.

They fill freezers with food.
Neon signs flash their intentions
30 into the years ahead.

And at their ears the sound
of the war. They are
not listening, not listening.

1972

KENNETH KOCH
(1925–   )

Permanently

One day the Nouns were clustered in the street.
An Adjective walked by, with her dark beauty.
The Nouns were struck, moved, changed.
The next day a Verb drove up, and created the Sentence.

5 Each Sentence says one thing—for example, "Although it was a dark rainy day
when the Adjective walked by, I shall remember the pure and sweet
expression on her face until the day I perish from the green, effective
earth."
Or, "Will you please close the window, Andrew?"
Or, for example, "Thank you, the pink pot of flowers on the window sill has
changed color recently to a light yellow, due to the heat from the boiler
factory which exists nearby."

In the springtime the Sentences and the Nouns lay silently on the grass.
A lonely Conjunction here and there would call, "And! But!"
But the Adjective did not emerge.

As the adjective is lost in the sentence,
So I am lost in your eyes, ears, nose, and throat—
You have enchanted me with a single kiss
Which can never be undone
Until the destruction of language.

                                                                                    1962

You Were Wearing

You were wearing your Edgar Allan Poe printed cotton blouse.
In each divided up square of the blouse was a picture of Edgar Allan Poe.
Your hair was blonde and you were cute. You asked me, "Do most boys think
    that most girls are bad?"
I smelled the mould of your seaside resort hotel bedroom on your hair held
    in place by a John Greenleaf Whittier clip.
"No," I said, "it's girls who think that boys are bad." Then we read
    Snowbound together
And ran around in an attic, so that a little of the blue enamel was scraped off
    my George Washington, Father of His Country, shoes.

Mother was walking in the living room, her Strauss Waltzes comb in her hair.
We waited for a time and then joined her, only to be served tea in cups
    painted with pictures of Herman Melville
As well as with illustrations from his book *Moby Dick* and from his novella,
    Benito Cereno.
Father came in wearing his Dick Tracy necktie: "How about a drink,
    everyone?"
I said, "Let's go outside a while." Then we went onto the porch and sat on
    the Abraham Lincoln swing.
You sat on the eyes, mouth, and beard part, and I sat on the knees.
In the yard across the street we saw a snowman holding a garbage can lid
    smashed into a likeness of the mad English king, George the Third.

                                                                                    1962

The Railway Stationery

The railway stationery lay upon
The desk of the railway clerk, from where he could see
The springtime and the tracks. Engraved upon
Each page was an inch-and-a-half-high T
And after that an H and then an E
And then, slightly below it to the right,
There was COLUMBUS RAILWAY COMPANY
In darker ink as the above was light.
The print was blue. And just beneath it all
There was an etching—not in blue, but black—
Of a real railway engine half-an-inch tall
Which, if you turned the paper on its back,
You could see showing through, as if it ran
To one edge of the sheet then back again.

To one edge of the sheet then back again!
The springtime comes while we're still drenched in snow

And, whistling now, snow-spotted Number Ten
Comes up the track and stops, and we must go
Outside to get its cargo, with our hands
20   Cold as the steel they touch. Inside once more
Once we have shut the splintery wooden door
Of the railway shack, the stationery demands
Some further notice. For the first time the light,
25   Reflected from the snow by the bright spring sun,
Shows that the engine wheel upon the right
Is slightly darker than the left-side one
And slightly lighter than the one in the center,
Which may have been an error of the printer.

30   Shuffling through many sheets of it to establish
Whether this difference is consistent will
Prove that it is not. Probably over-lavish
At the beginning with the ink, he still
(The printer) had the presence of mind to change
35   His operating process when he noticed
That on the wheels the ink had come out strange.
Because the windows of the shack are latticed
The light that falls upon the stationery
Is often interrupted by straight lines
40   Which shade the etching. Now the words "Dear Mary"
Appear below the engine on one sheet
Followed by a number of other conventional signs,
Among which are "our love," "one kiss," and "sweet."

The clerk then signs his name—his name is Johnson,
45   But all he signs is Bill, with a large B
Which overflows its boundaries like a Ronson
With too much fluid in it, which you see
Often, and it can burn you, though the *i*
Was very small and had a tiny dot.
50   The *l*'s were different—the first was high,
The second fairly low. And there was a spot
Of ink at the end of the signature which served
To emphasize that the letter was complete.
On the whole, one could say his writing swerved
55   More than the average, although it was neat.
He'd used a blue-black ink, a standing pen,
Which now he stuck back in its stand again.

Smiling and sighing, he opened up a drawer
And took an envelope out, which then he sealed
60   After he'd read the letter three times more
And folded it and put it in. A field
Covered with snow, untouched by man, is what
The envelope resembled, till he placed
A square with perforated edges that
65   Pictured a white-haired President, who faced
The viewer, in its corner, where it stuck
After he'd kissed its back and held it hard
Against the envelope. Now came the truck
Of the postman "Hello, Jim." "Hello there, Bill."
70   "I've got this—can you take it?" "Sure, I will!"

Now the snow fell down gently from the sky.
Strange wonder—snow in spring! Bill walked into
The shack again and wrote the letter *I*
Idly upon a sheet of paper. New
Ideas for writing Mary filled his mind,
But he resisted—there was work to do.
For in the distance he could hear the grind
Of the Seventy-Eight, whose engine was half blue;
So, putting on a cap, he went outside
On the tracks side, to wait for it to come.
It was the Seventy-Eight which now supplied
The city with most of its produce, although some
Came in by truck and some was grown in town.
Now it screams closer, and he flags it down.

1962

A. R. AMMONS
(1926–   )

Corsons Inlet [1]

I went for a walk over the dunes again this morning
to the sea,
then turned right along
    the surf
                rounded a naked headland
                and returned

    along the inlet shore:

it was muggy sunny, the wind from the sea steady and high,
crisp in the running sand,
        some breakthroughs of sun
    but after a bit

continuous overcast:

the walk liberating, I was released from forms,
from the perpendiculars,
        straight lines, blocks, boxes, binds
of thought
into the hues, shadings, rises, flowing bends and blends
        of sight:

                    I allow myself eddies of meaning:
yield to a direction of significance
running
like a stream through the geography of my work:
    you can find
in my sayings
            swerves of action
            like the inlet's cutting edge:

1. Located in southeast New Jersey.

there are dunes of motion,
organizations of grass, white sandy paths of remembrance
in the overall wandering of mirroring mind:

30   but Overall is beyond me: is the sum of these events
I cannot draw, the ledger I cannot keep, the accounting
beyond the account:

in nature there are few sharp lines: there are areas of
primrose
35   more or less dispersed;
disorderly orders of bayberry; between the rows
of dunes,
irregular swamps of reeds,
though not reeds alone, but grass, bayberry, yarrow, all . . .
40   predominantly reeds:

I have reached no conclusions, have erected no boundaries,
shutting out and shutting in, separating inside
        from outside: I have
        drawn no lines:
45   as

manifold events of sand
change the dune's shape that will not be the same shape
tomorrow,

so I am willing to go along, to accept
50   the becoming
thought, to stake off no beginnings or ends, establish
        no walls:

by transitions the land falls from grassy dunes to creek
to undercreek: but there are no lines, though
55   change in that transition is clear
        as any sharpness: but "sharpness" spread out,
allowed to occur over a wider range
than mental lines can keep:

the moon was full last night: today, low tide was low:
60   black shoals of mussels exposed to the risk
of air
and, earlier, of sun,
waved in and out with the waterline, waterline inexact,
caught always in the event of change:
65   a young mottled gull stood free on the shoals
        and ate
to vomiting: another gull, squawking possession, cracked a crab,
picked out the entrails, swallowed the soft-shelled legs, a ruddy
turnstone running in to snatch leftover bits:

70   risk is full: every living thing in
siege: the demand is life, to keep life: the small
white blacklegged egret, how beautiful, quietly stalks and spears
        the shallows, darts to shore
                to stab—what? I couldn't
75   see against the black mudflats—a frightened
        fiddler crab?

the news to my left over the dunes and
reeds and bayberry clumps was
            fall: thousands of tree swallows
            gathering for flight:
            an order held
            in constant change: a congregation
rich with entropy: nevertheless, separable, noticeable
      as one event,
                  not chaos: preparations for
flight from winter,
cheet, cheet, cheet, cheet, wings rifling the green clumps,
beaks
at the bayberries
   a perception full of wind, flight, curve,
sound:
   the possibility of rule as the sum of rulelessness:
the "field" of action
with moving, incalculable center:

in the smaller view, order tight with shape:
blue tiny flowers on a leafless weed: carapace of crab:
snail shell:
            pulsations of order
            in the bellies of minnows: orders swallowed,
broken down, transferred through membranes
to strengthen larger orders: but in the large view, no
lines or changeless shapes: the working in and out, together
            and against, of millions of events: this,
                        so that I make
                        no form
                        formlessness:

orders as summaries, as outcomes of actions override
or in some way result, not predictably (seeing me gain
the top of a dune,
the swallows
could take flight—some other fields of bayberry
            could enter fall
            berryless) and there is serenity:

            no arranged terror: no forcing of image, plan,
or thought:
no propaganda, no humbling of reality to precept:

terror pervades but is not arranged, all possibilities
of escape open: no route shut, except in
   the sudden loss of all routes:

            I see narrow orders, limited tightness, but will
not run to that easy victory:
            still around the looser, wider forces work:
            I will try
            to fasten into order enlarging grasps of disorder, widening
scope, but enjoying the freedom that
Scope eludes my grasp, that there is no finality of vision,
that I have perceived nothing completely,
            that tomorrow a new walk is a new walk.

                                                1965

The City Limits

When you consider the radiance, that it does not withhold
itself but pours its abundance without selection into every
nook and cranny not overhung or hidden; when you consider

5 that birds' bones make no awful noise against the light but
lie low in the light as in a high testimony; when you consider
the radiance, that it will look into the guiltiest

swervings of the weaving heart and bear itself upon them,
not flinching into disguise or darkening; when you consider
the abundance of such resource as illuminates the glow-blue

10 bodies and gold-skeined wings of flies swarming the dumped
guts of a natural slaughter or the coil of shit and in no
way winces from its storms of generosity; when you consider

that air or vacuum, snow or shale, squid or wolf, rose or lichen,
each is accepted into as much light as it will take, then
15 the heart moves roomier, the man stands and looks about, the

leaf does not increase itself above the grass, and the dark
work of the deepest cells is of a tune with May bushes
and fear lit by the breadth of such calmly turns to praise.

1971

The Arc Inside and Out

FOR HAROLD BLOOM

If, whittler and dumper, gross carver
into the shadiest curvings, I took branch
and meat from the stalk of life, threw

5 away the monies of the treasured,
treasurable mind, cleaved memory free
of the instant, if I got right down

shucking off periphery after periphery
to the glassy vague gray parabolas
and swoops of unnailable perception,

10 would I begin to improve the purity,
would I essentialize out the distilled
form, the glitter-stone that whether

the world comes or goes clicks gleams
and chinks of truth self-making, never
15 to be shuttered, the face-brilliant core

stone: or if I, amasser, heap shoveler,
depth pumper, took in all springs and
oceans, paramoecia and moons, massive

buttes and summit slants, rooted trunks
and leafages, anthologies of wise words,
schemata, all grasses (including the

tidal *Spartinas*,[2] marginal, salty
broadsweeps) would I finally come on a
suasion, large, fully-informed, restful

scape, turning back in on itself, its
periphery enclosing our system with
its bright dot and allowing in nonparlant

quantities at the edge void, void, and
void, would I then feel plenitude
brought to center and extent, a sweet

easing away of all edge, evil, and surprise:
these two ways to dream! dreaming them's
the bumfuzzlement—the impoverished

diamond, the heterogeneous abundance
starved into oneness: ultimately, either
way, which is our peace, the little

arc-line appears, inside which is nothing,
outside which is nothing—however big,
nothing beyond: however small, nothing

within: neither way to go's to stay, stay
here, the apple an apple with its own hue
or streak, the drink of water, the drink,

the falling into sleep, restfully ever the
falling into sleep, dream, dream, and
every morning the sun comes, the sun.

1972

ROBERT BLY
(1926–   )

Waking from Sleep

Inside the veins there are navies setting forth,
Tiny explosions at the water lines,
And seagulls weaving in the wind of the salty blood.

It is the morning. The country has slept the whole winter.
Window seats were covered with fur skins, the yard was full
Of stiff dogs, and hands that clumsily held heavy books.

Now we wake, and rise from bed, and eat breakfast!—
Shouts rise from the harbor of the blood,
Mist, and masts rising, the knock of wooden tackle in the sunlight.

---

2. A grass prevalent in salt marshes.

10 Now we sing, and do tiny dances on the kitchen floor.
Our whole body is like a harbor at dawn;
We know that our master has left us for the day.

1962

Driving Through Minnesota During the Hanoi Bombings

We drive between lakes just turning green;
Late June. The white turkeys have been moved
To new grass.
How long the seconds are in great pain!
5   Terror just before death,
Shoulders torn, shot
From helicopters, the boy
Tortured with the telephone generator,
"I felt sorry for him,
10 And blew his head off with a shotgun."
These instants become crystals,
Particles
The grass cannot dissolve. Our own gaiety
Will end up
15 In Asia, and in your cup you will look down
And see
Black Starfighters.
We were the ones we intended to bomb!
Therefore we will have
20 To go far away
To atone
For the sufferings of the stringy-chested
And the small rice-fed ones, quivering
In the helicopter like wild animals,
25 Shot in the chest, taken back to be questioned.

1967

Melancholia

1

A light seen suddenly in the storm, snow
Coming from all sides, like flakes
Of sleep, and myself
On the road to the dark barn,
5   Halfway there, a black dog near me.

2

Light on the wooden rail.
Someone I knew and loved.
As we hear the dates of his marriage
And the years he moved,
10 A wreath of dark fir and shiny laurel
Slips off the coffin.

3

A cathedral: I see
Starving men, weakened, leaning
On their knees. But the bells ring anyway,
15 Sending out over the planted fields
A vegetation, sound waves with long leaves.

4
There is a wound on the trunk,
Where the branch was torn off.
A wind comes out of it,
Rising, swelling,
Swirling over everything alive.

1967

ROBERT CREELEY
(1926–   )

Ballad of the Despairing Husband

My wife and I lived all alone,
contention was our only bone.
I fought with her, she fought with me,
and things went on right merrily.

But now I live here by myself
with hardly a damn thing on the shelf,
and pass my days with little cheer
since I have parted from my dear.

Oh come home soon, I write to her.
Go screw yourself, is her answer.
Now what is that, for Christian word?
I hope she feeds on dried goose turd.

But still I love her, yes I do.
I love her and the children too.
I only think it fit that she
should quickly come right back to me.

Ah no, she says, and she is tough,
and smacks me down with her rebuff.
Ah no, she says, I will not come
after the bloody things you've done.

Oh wife, oh wife—I tell you true,
I never loved no one but you.
I never will, it cannot be
another woman is for me.

That may be right, she will say then,
but as for me, there's other men.
And I will tell you I propose
to catch them firmly by the nose.

And I will wear what dresses I choose!
And I will dance, and what's to lose!
I'm free of you, you little prick,
and I'm the one can make it stick.

Was this the darling I did love?
Was this that mercy from above
did open violets in the spring—
and made my own worn self to sing?

She was. I know. And she is still,
and if I love her? then so I will.
And I will tell her, and tell her right . . .

40 Oh lovely lady, morning or evening or afternoon.
Oh lovely lady, eating with or without a spoon.
Oh most lovely lady, whether dressed or undressed or partly.
Oh most lovely lady, getting up or going to bed or sitting only.

Oh loveliest of ladies, than whom none is more fair, more gracious, more
    beautiful.
45 Oh loveliest of ladies, whether you are just or unjust, merciful, indifferent,
    or cruel.
Oh most loveliest of ladies, doing whatever, seeing whatever, being
    whatever.
Oh most loveliest of ladies, in rain, in shine, in any weather.

Oh lady, grant me time,
please, to finish my rhyme.

                                        1959

Heroes

In all those stories the hero
is beyond himself into the next
thing, be it those labors
of Hercules,[1] or Aeneas going into death.

5 I thought the instant of the one humanness
in Virgil's plan of it
was that it was of course human enough to die,
yet to come back, as he said, *hoc opus, hic labor est.*[2]

That was the Cumaean Sibyl speaking.
10 This is Robert Creeley, and Virgil
is dead now two thousand years, yet Hercules
and the *Aeneid,* yet all that industrious wis-

dom lives in the way the mountains
and the desert are waiting
15 for the heroes, and death also
can still propose the old labors.

                                        1959

Song

What I took in my hand
grew in weight. You must
understand it
was not obscene.

---

1. Who represents superhuman strength and courage, as revealed in his legendary 12 labors.
2. From Virgil's *Aeneid,* VI. The full quotation (in John Dryden's translation): "Smooth the descent and easy is the way:/But, to return, and view the cheerful skies—/In this the task and mighty labor lies." It is spoken by the Cumaean Sibyl, a prophetic priestess, in advising Aeneas to visit the Underworld to seek counsel in his god-appointed task of founding Rome.

Night comes. We sleep.
Then if you know what
say it.
Don't pretend.

Guises are
what enemies wear. You
and I live
in a prayer.

Helpless. Helpless,
should I speak.
Would you.
What do you think of me.

No woman ever was,
was wiser
than you. None is
more true.

But fate, love, fate
scares me. What
I took in my hand
grows in weight.

1962

The World

I wanted so ably
to reassure you, I wanted
the man you took to be me,

to comfort you, and got
up, and went to the window,
pushed back, as you asked me to,

the curtain, to see
the outline of the trees
in the night outside.

The light, love,
the light we felt then,
grayly, was it, that

came in, on us, not
merely my hands or yours,
or a wetness so comfortable,

but in the dark then
as you slept, the gray
figure came so close

and leaned over,
between us, as you
slept, restless, and

my own face had to
see it, and be seen by it,
the man it was, your

25   gray lost tired bewildered
brother, unused, untaken—
hated by love, and dead,

but not dead, for an
instant, saw me, myself
30   the intruder, as he was not.

I tried to say, it is
all right, she is
happy, you are no longer

needed. I said,
35   he is dead, and he
went as you shifted

and woke, at first afraid,
then knew by my own knowing
what had happened—

40   and the light then
of the sun coming
for another morning
in the world.

                                                            1969

ALLEN GINSBERG
(1926–   )

Howl

FOR CARL SOLOMON [1]

I

I saw the best minds of my generation destroyed by madness, starving
    hysterical naked,
dragging themselves through the negro streets at dawn looking for an
    angry fix,
angelheaded hipsters burning for the ancient heavenly connection to the
    starry dynamo in the machinery of night,
who poverty and tatters and hollow-eyed and high sat up smoking in the
    supernatural darkness of cold-water flats floating across the tops of
    cities contemplating jazz,
5   who bared their brains to Heaven under the El [2] and saw Mohammedan
    angels staggering on tenement roofs illuminated,
who passed through universities with radiant cool eyes hallucinating
    Arkansas and Blake-light tragedy among the scholars of war,
who were expelled from the academies for crazy & publishing obscene odes
    on the windows of the skull,

---

1. A friend of Ginsberg's, whose stories of   *Howl.*
his exploits as a mental patient are retold in   2. Elevated railway.

who cowered in unshaven rooms in underwear, burning their money in wastebaskets and listening to the Terror through the wall,

who got busted in their pubic beards returning through Laredo with a belt of marijuana for New York,

who ate fire in paint hotels or drank turpentine in Paradise Alley,[3] death, or purgatoried their torsos night after night

with dreams, with drugs, with waking nightmares, alcohol and cock and endless balls,

incomparable blind streets of shuddering cloud and lightning in the mind leaping toward poles of Canada & Paterson,[4] illuminating all the motionless world of Time between,

Peyote solidities of halls, backyard green tree cemetery dawns, wine drunkenness over the rooftops, storefront boroughs of teahead joyride neon blinking traffic light, sun and moon and tree vibrations in the roaring winter dusks of Brooklyn, ashcan rantings and kind king light of mind,

who chained themselves to subways for the endless ride from Battery to holy Bronx on benzedrine until the noise of wheels and children brought them down shuddering mouth-wracked and battered bleak of brain all drained of brilliance in the drear light of Zoo,

who sank all night in submarine light of Bickford's [5] floated out and sat through the stale beer afternoon in desolate Fugazzi's,[6] listening to the crack of doom on the hydrogen jukebox,

who talked continuously seventy hours from park to pad to bar to Bellvue [7] to museum to the Brooklyn Bridge,

a lost battalion of platonic conversationalists jumping down the stoops off fire escapes off windowsills off Empire State out of the moon,

yacketayakking screaming vomiting whispering facts and memories and anecdotes and eyeball kicks and shocks of hospitals and jails and wars,

whole intellects disgorged in total recall for seven days and nights with brilliant eyes, meat for the Synagogue cast on the pavement,

who vanished into nowhere Zen New Jersey leaving a trail of ambiguous picture postcards of Atlantic City Hall,

suffering Eastern sweats and Tangerian bone-grindings and migraines of China under junk-withdrawal in Newark's bleak furnished room,

who wandered around and around at midnight in the railroad yard wondering where to go, and went, leaving no broken hearts,

who lit cigarettes in boxcars boxcars boxcars racketing through snow toward lonesome farms in grandfather night,

who studied Plotinus Poe St. John of the Cross [8] telepathy and bop kaballa [9] because the cosmos instinctively vibrated at their feet in Kansas,

who loned it through the streets of Idaho seeking visionary indian angels who were visionary indian angels,

who thought they were only mad when Baltimore gleamed in supernatural ecstasy,

who jumped in limousines with the Chinaman of Oklahoma on the impulse of winter midnight streetlight smalltown rain,

who lounged hungry and lonesome through Houston seeking jazz or sex or soup, and followed the brilliant Spaniard to converse about America and Eternity, a hopeless task, and so took ship to Africa,

---

3. A slum courtyard in New York, the setting of Jack Kerouac's novel *The Subterraneans* (1958).
4. A city in New Jersey; Ginsberg was born there.
5. One of a chain of cafeterias open 24 hours a day.
6. A bar near Greenwich Village, New York's bohemian enclave.
7. A public hospital in New York, which serves as a receiving center for the mentally disturbed.
8. *Plotinus* (205?–270) was a mystical philosopher, Edgar Allan Poe (1809–1849) was an American writer, and St. John of the Cross (1542–1591), Spanish poet and mystic, wrote *The Dark Night of the Soul*. Ginsberg was attracted to them for their accounts of mystical experience.
9. "Bop" is a style of modern jazz. The Kaballa is a Hebraic system of mystical interpretation of the scriptures.

who disappeared into the volcanoes of Mexico leaving behind nothing bu
the shadow of dungarees and the lava and ash of poetry scattered i
fireplace Chicago,

30 who reappeared on the West Coast investigating the F.B.I. in beards and
shorts with big pacifist eyes sexy in their dark skin passing out incom
prehensible leaflets,

who burned cigarette holes in their arms protesting the narcotic tobacco
haze of Capitalism,

who distributed Supercommunist pamphlets in Union Square weeping and
undressing while the sirens of Los Alamos [1] wailed them down, and
wailed down Wall,[2] and the Staten Island ferry also wailed,

who broke down crying in white gymnasiums naked and trembling before
the machinery of other skeletons,

who bit detectives in the neck and shrieked with delight in policecars for
committing no crime but their own wild cooking pederasty and in
toxication,

35 who howled on their knees in the subway and were dragged off the roof
waving genitals and manuscripts,

who let themselves be fucked in the ass by saintly motorcyclists, and
screamed with joy,

who blew and were blown by those human seraphim, the sailors, caresses
of Atlantic and Caribbean love,

who balled in the morning in the evenings in rosegardens and the grass of
public parks and cemeteries scattering their semen freely to whomever
come who may,

who hiccupped endlessly trying to giggle but wound up with a sob behind
a partition in a Turkish Bath when the blonde & naked angel came to
pierce them with a sword,

40 who lost their loveboys to the three old shrews of fate the one eyed shrew
of the heterosexual dollar the one eyed shrew that winks out of the
womb and the one eyed shrew that does nothing but sit on her ass
and snip the intellectual golden threads of the craftsman's loom,

who copulated ecstatic and insatiate with a bottle of beer a sweetheart a
package of cigarettes a candle and fell off the bed, and continued
along the floor and down the hall and ended fainting on the wall with
a vision of ultimate cunt and come eluding the last gyzym of con-
sciousness,

who sweetened the snatches of a million girls trembling in the sunset, and
were red eyed in the morning but prepared to sweeten the snatch of
the sunrise, flashing buttocks under barns and naked in the lake,

who went out whoring through Colorado in myriad stolen night-cars,
N.C.,[3] secret hero of these poems, cocksman and Adonis of Denver—
joy to the memory of his innumerable lays of girls in empty lots &
diner backyards, moviehouses' rickety rows, on mountaintops in caves
or with gaunt waitresses in familiar roadside lonely petticoat upliftings
& especially secret gas-station solipisisms of johns, & hometown alleys
too,

who faded out in vast sordid movies, were shifted in dreams, woke on a
sudden Manhattan, and picked themselves up out of basements hung-
over with heartless Tokay and horrors of Third Avenue iron dreams &
stumbled to unemployment offices,

45 who walked all night with their shoes full of blood on the snowbank docks
waiting for a door in the East River to open to a room full of steam-
heat and opium,

1. In New Mexico, where the development of
the atomic bomb was completed.
2. Wall Street in New York's financial dis-
trict, but perhaps also the Wailing Wall in
Jerusalem, where Jews lament their losses

and seek consolation.
3. Neal Cassady, a friend of Ginsberg and
Jack Kerouac. He is the hero of Kerouac's
novel *On the Road* (1957).

who created great suicidal dramas on the apartment cliff-banks of the Hudson under the wartime blue floodlight of the moon & their heads shall be crowned with laurel in oblivion,

who ate the lamb stew of the imagination or digested the crab at the muddy bottom of the rivers of Bowery,[4]

who wept at the romance of the streets with their pushcarts full of onions and bad music,

who sat in boxes breathing in the darkness under the bridge, and rose up to build harpsichords in their lofts,

who coughed on the sixth floor of Harlem crowned with flame under the tubercular sky surrounded by orange crates of theology,

who scribbled all night rocking and rolling over lofty incantations which in the yellow morning were stanzas of gibberish,

who cooked rotten animals lung heart feet tail borsht & tortillas dreaming of the pure vegetable kingdom,

who plunged themselves under meat trucks looking for an egg,

who threw their watches off the roof to cast their ballot for Eternity outside of Time, & alarm clocks fell on their heads every day for the next decade,

who cut their wrists three times successively unsuccessfully, gave up and were forced to open antique stores where they thought they were growing old and cried,

who were burned alive in their innocent flannel suits on Madison Avenue [5] amid blasts of leaden verse & the tanked-up clatter of the iron regiments of fashion & the nitroglycerine shrieks of the fairies of advertising & the mustard gas of sinister intelligent editors, or were run down by the drunken taxicabs of Absolute Reality,

who jumped off the Brooklyn Bridge this actually happened and walked away unknown and forgotten into the ghostly daze of Chinatown soup alleyways & firetrucks, not even one free beer,

who sang out of their windows in despair, fell out of the subway window, jumped in the filthy Passaic,[6] leaped on negroes, cried all over the street, danced on broken wineglasses barefoot smashed phonograph records of nostalgic European 1930's German jazz finished the whiskey and threw up groaning into the bloody toilet, moans in their ears and the blast of colossal steamwhistles,

who barreled down the highways of the past journeying to each other's hotrod-Golgotha [7] jail-solitude watch or Birmingham jazz incarnation,

who drove crosscountry seventytwo hours to find out if I had a vision or you had a vision or he had a vision to find out Eternity,

who journeyed to Denver, who died in Denver, who came back to Denver & waited in vain, who watched over Denver & brooded & loned in Denver and finally went away to find out the Time, & now Denver is lonesome for her heroes,

who fell on their knees in hopeless cathedrals praying for each other's salvation and light and breasts, until the soul illuminated its hair for a second,

who crashed through their minds in jail waiting for impossible criminals with golden heads and the charm of reality in their hearts who sang sweet blues to Alcatraz,

who retired to Mexico to cultivate a habit, or Rocky Mount to tender Buddha or Tangiers to boys or Southern Pacific to the black locomotive or Harvard to Narcissus to Woodlawn to the daisychain or grave,

---

4. The avenue in New York famous as the haunt of alcoholics and derelicts.
5. The center of New York's advertising industry.
6. The river that flows past Paterson.
7. The place of skulls (Hebraic), the hill near Jerusalem where Christ was crucified.

65 who demanded sanity trials accusing the radio of hypnotism & were left
      with their insanity & their hands & a hung jury,

    who threw potato salad at CCNY lecturers on Dadaism [8] and subsequently
      presented themselves on the granite steps of the madhouse with shaven
      heads and harlequin speech of suicide, demanding instantaneous lo-
      botomy,

    and who were given instead the concrete void of insulin metrasol electricity
      hydrotherapy psychotherapy occupational therapy pingpong & am-
      nesia,

    who in humorless protest overturned only one symbolic pingpong table,
      resting briefly in catatonia,

    returning years later truly bald except for a wig of blood, and tears and
      fingers, to the visible madman doom of the wards of the madtowns
      of the East,

70 Pilgrim State's Rockland's and Greystone's [9] foetid halls, bickering with the
      echoes of the soul, rocking and rolling in the midnight solitude-bench
      dolmen-realms [1] of love, dream of life a nightmare, bodies turned to
      stone as heavy as the moon,

    with mother finally ******, and the last fantastic book flung out of the
      tenement window, and the last door closed at 4 AM and the last
      telephone slammed at the wall in reply and the last furnished room
      emptied down to the last piece of mental furniture, a yellow paper
      rose twisted on a wire hanger in the closet, and even that imaginary,
      nothing but a hopeful little bit of hallucination—

    ah, Carl, while you are not safe I am not safe, and now you're really in
      the total animal soup of time—

    and who therefore ran through the icy streets obsessed with a sudden
      flash of the alchemy of the use of the ellipse the catalog the meter
      & the vibrating plane,

    who dreamt and made incarnate gaps in Time & Space through images
      juxtaposed, and trapped the archangel of the soul between 2 visual
      images and joined the elemental verbs and set the noun and dash of
      consciousness together jumping with sensation of Pater Omnipotens
      Aeterna Deus [2]

75 to recreate the syntax and measure of poor human prose and stand before
      you speechless and intelligent and shaking with shame, rejected yet
      confessing out the soul to conform to the rhythm of thought in his
      naked and endless head,

    the madman bum and angel beat in Time, unknown, yet putting down
      here what might be left to say in time come after death,

    and rose reincarnate in the ghostly clothes of jazz in the goldhorn shadow
      of the band and blew the suffering of America's naked mind for love
      into an eli eli lamma lamma sabacthani [3] saxophone cry that shivered
      the cities down to the last radio

    with the absolute heart of the poem of life butchered out of their own
      bodies good to eat a thousand years.

                                    San Francisco 1955   1956

8. An artistic movement based on absurdity
and accident; it flourished during the First
World War. CCNY is the City College of
New York.
9. Three mental hospitals near New York.
Carl Solomon was an inmate at Pilgrim State
and Rockland, and Ginsberg's mother was a
patient at Greystone.
1. Dolmens are bench-shaped prehistoric stone
monuments found in Britain and France and
believed to have been tombs.
2. All-powerful Father, Eternal God (Latin).
Paul Cezanne (1839–1906), the French Im-
pressionist painter, used this phrase to de-
scribe the sensations he received from ob-
serving and registering the appearance of
the natural world.
3. My God, my God, why have you forsaken
me? (Hebrew). These are Christ's last words
from the cross (Matthew xxvi.46).

To Aunt Rose

Aunt Rose—now—might I see you
with your thin face and buck tooth smile and pain
   of rheumatism—and a long black heavy shoe
    for your bony left leg
  limping down the long hall in Newark on the running carpet
    past the black grand piano
     in the day room
      where the parties were
  and I sang Spanish loyalist songs
    in a high squeaky voice
     (hysterical) the committee listening
   while you limped around the room
    collected the money—
Aunt Honey, Uncle Sam, a stranger with a cloth arm
   in his pocket
    and huge young bald head
    of Abraham Lincoln Brigade[1]

—your long sad face
   your tears of sexual frustration
    (what smothered sobs and bony hips
     under the pillows of Osborne Terrace)
 —the time I stood on the toilet seat naked
   and you powdered my thighs with Calomine
    against the poison ivy—my tender
     and shamed first black curled hairs
 what were you thinking in secret heart then
    knowing me a man already—
and I an ignorant girl of family silence on the thin pedestal
   of my legs in the bathroom—Museum of Newark.
    Aunt Rose
Hitler is dead, Hitler is in Eternity; Hitler is with
   Tamburlane and Emily Brontë

Though I see you walking still, a ghost on Osborne Terrace
   down the long dark hall to the front door
  limping a little with a pinched smile
    in what must have been a silken
     flower dress
 welcoming my father, the Poet, on his visit to Newark
   —see you arriving in the living room
    dancing on your crippled leg
    and clapping hands his book
     had been accepted by Liveright

Hitler is dead and Liveright's gone out of business
The Attic of the Past and *Everlasting Minute* are out of print
   Uncle Harry sold his last silk stocking
   Claire quit interpretive dancing school
    Buba[2] sits a wrinkled monument in Old
    Ladies Home blinking at new babies

1. A group of American volunteers, led by Martin Wolff, in the Spanish Civil War of the 1930's.
2. Yiddish for "Grandmother."

50   last time I saw you was the hospital
          pale skull protruding under ashen skin
              blue veined unconscious girl
                  in an oxygen tent
          the war in Spain has ended long ago
          Aunt Rose

                                          Paris 1958   1961

ELIZABETH JENNINGS
(1926–   )

Poem in Winter

Today the children begin to hope for snow
And look in the sky for auguries of it.
It is not for such omens that we wait,
Our world may not be settled by the slow
5 Falling of flakes to lie across our thought.

And even if the snow comes down indeed
We still shall stand behind a pane of glass
Untouched by it, and watch the children press
Their image on the drifts the snow has laid
10 Upon a winter they think they have made.

This is a wise illusion. Better to
Believe the near world is created by
A wish, a shaping hand, a certain eye,
Than hide in the mind's corner as we do
15 As though there were no world, no fall of snow.

                                                        1955

Answers

I kept my answers small and kept them near;
Big questions bruised my mind but still I let
Small answers be a bulwark to my fear.

The huge abstractions I kept from the light;
5 Small things I handled and caressed and loved.
I let the stars assume the whole of night.

But the big answers clamored to be moved
Into my life. Their great audacity
Shouted to be acknowledged and believed.

10 Even when all small answers build up to
Protection of my spirit, still I hear
Big answers striving for their overthrow

And all the great conclusions coming near.

                                                        1955

Song for a Birth or a Death

Last night I saw the savage world
And heard the blood beat up the stair;
The fox's bark, the owl's shrewd pounce,
The crying creatures—all were there,
And men in bed with love and fear.

The slit moon only emphasized
How blood must flow and teeth must grip.
What does the calm light understand,
The light which draws the tide and ship
And drags the owl upon its prey
And human creatures lip to lip?

Last night I watched how pleasure must
Leap from disaster with its will:
The fox's fear, the watch-dog's lust
Know that all matings mean a kill:
And human creatures kissed in trust
Feel the blood throb to death until

The seed is struck, the pleasure's done,
The birds are thronging in the air;
The moon gives way to widespread sun.
Yes but the pain still crouches where
The young fox and the child are trapped
And cries of love are cries of fear.

1961

In Praise of Creation

That one bird, one star,
The one flash of the tiger's eye
Purely assert what they are,
Without ceremony testify.

Testify to order, to rule—
How the birds mate at one time only,
How the sky is, for a certain time, full
Of birds, the moon sometimes cut thinly.

And the tiger trapped in the cage of his skin,
Watchful over creation, rests
For the blood to pound, the drums to begin,
Till the tigress' shadow casts

A darkness over him, a passion, a scent,
The world goes turning, turning, the season
Sieves earth to its one sure element
And the blood beats beyond reason.

Then quiet, and birds folding their wings,
The new moon waiting for years to be stared at here,
The season sinks to satisfied things—
Man with his mind ajar.

1961

JAMES MERRILL
(1926–   )

Upon a Second Marriage

FOR H. I. P.

Orchards, we linger here because
Women we love stand propped in your green prisons,
Obedient to such justly bending laws
    Each one longs to take root,
5   Lives to confess whatever season's
Pride of blossom or endeavor's fruit
    May to her rustling boughs have risen.

    Then autumn reddens the whole mind.
No more, she vows, the dazzle of a year
10   Shall woo her from your bare cage of loud wind,
    Promise the ring and run
    To burn the altar, reappear
With apple blossoms for the credulous one.
    Orchards, we wonder that we linger here!

15   Orchards we planted, trees we shook
To learn what you were bearing, say we stayed
Because one winter dusk we half-mistook
    Frost on a bleakened bough
    For blossoms, and were half-afraid
20 To miss the old persuasion, should we go.
    And spring did come, and discourse made

    Enough of weddings to us all
That, loving her for whom the whole world grows
Fragrant and white, we linger to recall
25   As down aisles of cut trees
    How a tall trunk's cross-section shows
Concentric rings, those many marriages
    That life on each live thing bestows.

1958

Willowware [1] Cup

Mass hysteria, wave after breaking wave
Blueblooded Cantonese upon these shores

Left the gene pool Lux-opaque and smoking
With dimestore mutants. One turned up today.

5 Plum in bloom, pagoda, blue birds, plume of willow—
Almost the replica of a prewar pattern—

The same boat bearing the gnat-sized lovers away,
The old bridge now bent double where her father signals

1. Blue-and-white dinnerware picturing a Chinese scene including a willow tree and a bridge.

Feebly, as from flypaper, minding less and less.
Two smaller retainers with lanterns light him home.

Is that a scroll he carries? He must by now be immensely
Wise, and have given up earthly attachments, and all that.

Soon, of these May mornings, rising in mist, he will ask
Only to blend—like ink in flesh, blue anchor

Needled upon drunkenness while its destroyer
Full steam departs, the stigma throbbing, intricate—

Only to blend into a crazing [2] texture.
You are far away. The leaves tell what they tell.

But this lone, chipped vessel, if it fills,
Fills for you with something warm and clear.

Around its inner horizon the old odd designs
Crowd as before, and seem to concentrate on you.

They represent, I fancy, a version of heaven
In its day more trouble to mend than to replace:

Steep roofs aslant, minutely tiled;
Tilted honeycombs, thunderhead blue.

                                                        1972

The Victor Dog [3]

FOR ELIZABETH BISHOP

Bix to Buxtehude to Boulez,
The little white dog on the Victor label
Listens long and hard as he is able.
It's all in a day's work, whatever plays.

From judgment, it would seem, he has refrained.
He even listens earnestly to Bloch,
Then builds a church upon our acid rock.
He's man's—no—he's the Leiermann's best friend, [4]

Or would be if hearing and listening were the same.
Does he hear? I fancy he rather smells
Those lemon-gold arpeggios in Ravel's
"Les jets d'eau du palais de ceux qui s'aiment." [5]

He ponders the Schumann Concerto's tall willow hit
By lightning, and stays put. When he surmises

---

2. Developing a mesh of fine superficial cracks.
3. Until recently, the trademark on the labels of RCA Victor records was a dog listening intently to an old-fashioned gramophone, with the caption "His master's voice." In the poem, passing reference is made to jazz trumpeter Bix Beiderbecke, 18th-century composers Dietrich Buxtehude, Johann Sebastian Bach, and George Frederick Handel, to Robert Schumann (1810–1856), and to modernists Pierre Boulez, Ernest Bloch, and Maurice Ravel.
4. In Franz Schubert's song *Der Leiermann* ("The Organ-Grinder"), an old man cranks his barrel-organ in the winter cold to an audience of snarling dogs.
5. The fountains of the palace of those who are in love with each other (French).

15 Through one of Bach's eternal boxwood mazes [6]
    The oboe pungent as a bitch in heat,

    Or when the calypso decants its raw bay rum
    Or the moon in *Wozzeck* [7] reddens ripe for murder,
    He doesn't sneeze or howl; just listens harder.
20 Adamant° needles bear down on him from   *diamond*

    Whirling of outer space, too black, too near—
    But he was taught as a puppy not to flinch,
    Much less to imitate his bête noire Blanche
    Who barked, fat foolish creature, at King Lear. [8]

25 Still others fought in the road's filth over Jezebel, [9]
    Slavered on hearths of horned and pelted barons.
    His forebears lacked, to say the least, forbearance.
    Can nature change in him? Nothing's impossible.

    The last chord fades. The night is cold and fine.
30 His master's voice rasps through the grooves' bare groves.
    Obediently, in silence like the grave's
    He sleeps there on the still-warm gramophone

    Only to dream he is at the première of a Handel
    Opera long thought lost—*Il Cane Minore.* [1]
35 Its allegorical subject is his story!
    A little dog revolving round a spindle

    Gives rise to harmonies beyond belief,
    A cast of stars. . . . Is there in Victor's heart
    No honey for the vanquished? Art is art.
40 The life it asks of us is a dog's life.

                                                              1972

JOHN ASHBERY
(1927–   )

The Painter

    Sitting between the sea and the buildings
    He enjoyed painting the sea's portrait.
    But just as children imagine a prayer
    Is merely silence, he expected his subject
5   To rush up the sand, and, seizing a brush,
    Plaster its own portrait on the canvas.

    So there was never any paint on his canvas
    Until the people who lived in the buildings
    Put him to work: "Try using the brush

---

6. A labyrinth executed in living boxwood plants, such as is to be found in the gardens of 18th-century palaces.
7. An opera by Alban Berg (1885–1935), in which the protagonist murders his unfaithful wife beneath a rising moon.
8. In the storm scene, the distraught King Lear says, "The little dogs and all,/Tray,

Blanche, and Sweetheart; see, they bark at me."
9. Whose body, when she died, was thrown into the street for her evil deeds. When the body was recovered for burial, dogs had eaten most of it, as had been prophesied earlier by Elijah (I Kings xxi ff.).
1. The Little Dog (Italian).

As a means to an end. Select, for a portrait,
Something less angry and large, and more subject
To a painter's moods, or, perhaps, to a prayer."

How could he explain to them his prayer
That nature, not art, might usurp the canvas?
He chose his wife for a new subject,
Making her vast, like ruined buildings,
As if, forgetting itself, the portrait
Had expressed itself without a brush.

Slightly encouraged, he dipped his brush
In the sea, murmuring a heartfelt prayer:
"My soul, when I paint this next portrait
Let it be you who wrecks the canvas."
The news spread like wildfire through the buildings:
He had gone back to the sea for his subject.

Imagine a painter crucified by his subject!
Too exhausted even to lift his brush,
He provoked some artists leaning from the buildings
To malicious mirth: "We haven't a prayer
Now, of putting ourselves on canvas,
Or getting the sea to sit for a portrait!"

Others declared it a self-portrait.
Finally all indications of a subject
Began to fade, leaving the canvas
Perfectly white. He put down the brush.
At once a howl, that was also a prayer,
Arose form the overcrowded buildings.

They tossed him, the portrait, from the tallest of the buildings;
And the sea devoured the canvas and the brush
As though his subject had decided to remain a prayer.

                                                        1956

Two Sonnets

1. Dido

The body's products become
Fatal to it. Our spit
Would kill us, but we
Die of our heat.
Though I say the things I wish to say
They are needless, their own flame conceives it.
So I am cheated of perfection.

The iodine bottle sat in the hall
And out over the park where crawled roadsters
The apricot and purple clouds were
And our blood flowed down the grating
Of the cream-colored embassy.
Inside it they had a record of "The St. Louis Blues."

2. *The Idiot*

O how this sullen, careless world
Ignorant of me is! Those rocks, those homes
Know not the touch of my flesh, nor is there one tree
Whose shade has known me for a friend.
5 I've wandered the wide world over.
No man I've known, no friendly beast
Has come and put its nose into my hands.
No maid has welcomed my face with a kiss.

Yet once, as I took passage
10 From Gibraltar to Cape Horn
I met some friendly mariners on the boat
And as we struggled to keep the ship from sinking
The very waves seemed friendly, and the sound
The spray made as it hit the front of the boat.

1962

Faust [1]

If only the phantom would stop reappearing!
Business, if you wanted to know, was punk at the opera.
The heroine no longer appeared in *Faust*.
The crowds strolled sadly away. The phantom
5 Watched them from the roof, not guessing the hungers
That must be stirred before disappointment can begin.

One day as morning was about to begin
A man in brown with a white shirt reappearing
At the bottom of his yellow vest, was talking hungers
10 With the silver-haired director of the opera.
On the green-carpeted floor no phantom
Appeared, except yellow squares of sunlight, like those in *Faust*.

That night as the musicians for *Faust*
Were about to go on strike, lest darkness begin
15 In the corridors, and through them the phantom
Glide unobstructed, the vision reappearing
Of blonde Marguerite practicing a new opera
At her window awoke terrible new hungers

In the already starving tenor. But hungers
20 Are just another topic, like the new Faust
Drifting through the tunnels of the opera
(In search of lost old age? For they begin
To notice a twinkle in his eye. It is cold daylight reappearing
At the window behind him, itself a phantom

25 Window, painted by the phantom
Scene painters, sick of not getting paid, of hungers
For a scene below of tiny, reappearing
Dancers, with a sandbag [2] falling like a note in *Faust*

1. The opera by Charles Gounod (1818–1893), recounting the legend of Faust, a medieval scholar who sold his soul to the Devil in exchange for perpetual youth and worldly satisfactions. Marguerite is a girl whom Faust (the tenor role in the opera) seduces and deserts. The poem also alludes to a famous horror movie, *The Phantom of the Opera* (1925), that depicted a demented figure who haunted the subterranean passages of the Paris Opéra.
2. Used in theaters as counterweights in scene-shifting.

Through purple air. And the spectators begin
To understand the bleeding tenor star of the opera.)

That night the opera
Was crowded to the rafters. The phantom
Took twenty-nine curtain calls. "Begin!
Begin!" In the wings the tenor hungers
For the heroine's convulsive kiss, and Faust
Moves forward, no longer young, reappearing

And reappearing for the last time. The opera
Faust would no longer need its phantom.
On the bare, sunlit stage the hungers could begin.

1962

Decoy

We hold these truths to be self-evident:
That ostracism, both political and moral, has
Its place in the twentieth-century scheme of things;
That urban chaos is the problem we have been seeing into and seeing into,
For the factory, deadpanned by its very existence into a
Descending code of values, has moved right across the road from total
    financial upheaval
And caught regression head-on. The descending scale does not imply
A corresponding deterioration of moral values, punctuated
By acts of corporate vandalism every five years,
Like a bunch of violets pinned to a dress, that knows and ignores its own
    standing.
There is every reason to rejoice with those self-styled prophets of com-
    mercial disaster, those harbingers of gloom,
Over the imminent lateness of the denouement that, advancing slowly,
    never arrives,
At the same time keeping the door open to a tongue-and-cheek attitude on
    the part of the perpetrators,
The men who sit down to their vast desks on Monday to begin planning
    the week's notations, jotting memoranda that take
Invisible form in the air, like flocks of sparrows
Above the city pavements, turning and wheeling aimlessly
But on the average directed by discernible motives.

To sum up: We are fond of plotting itineraries
And our pyramiding memories, alert as dandelion fuzz, dart from one
    pretext to the next
Seeking in occasions new sources of memories, for memory is profit
Until the day it spreads out all its accumulation, delta-like, on the plain
For that day no good can come of remembering, and the anomalies cancel
    each other out.
But until then foreshortened memories will keep us going, alive, one to
    the other.

There was never any excuse for this and perhaps there need be none,
For kicking out into the morning, on the wide bed,
Waking far apart on the bed, the two of them:
Husband and wife
Man and wife

1970

GALWAY KINNELL
(1927–   )

Vapor Trail Reflected in the Frog Pond

1

The old watch: their
thick eyes
puff and foreclose by the moon. The young, heads
trailed by the beginnings of necks,
5 shiver,
in the guarantee they shall be bodies.

In the frog pond
the vapor of a SAC bomber creeps,

I hear its drone, drifting, high up
10 in immaculate ozone.

2

And I hear,
coming over the hills, America singing,
her varied carols I hear: [1]
crack of deputies' rifles practicing their aim on stray dogs at night,
15 sput of cattleprod,
TV groaning at the smells of the human body,
curses of the soldier as he poisons, burns, grinds, and stabs
the rice of the world,
with open mouth, drying strong, hysterical curses.

3

20 And by rice paddies in Asia
bones
wearing a few shadows
walk down a dirt road, smashed
bloodsuckers on their heel, knowing
25 the flesh a man throws down in the sunshine
dogs shall eat
and the flesh that is upthrown in the air
shall be seized by birds,
shoulder blades smooth, unmarked by old feather-holes,
30 hands rivered
by blue, erratic wanderings of the blood,
eyes crinkled up
as they gaze up at the drifting sun that gave us our lives,
seed dazzled over the footbattered blaze of the earth.

1967

The Correspondence School Instructor Says Goodbye to His Poetry Students

Goodbye, lady in Bangor, who sent me
snapshots of yourself, after definitely hinting
you were beautiful; goodbye,

1. From Walt Whitman's poem: "I hear America singing, the varied carols I hear."

Miami Beach urologist, who enclosed plain
brown envelopes for the return of your *very*
"Clinical Sonnets"; goodbye, manufacturer
of brassieres on the Coast, whose eclogues
give the fullest treatment in literature yet
to the sagging breast motif; goodbye, you in San Quentin,
who wrote, "Being German my hero is Hitler,"
instead of "Sincerely yours," at the end of long,
neat-scripted letters demolishing
the pre-Raphaelites: [2]

I swear to you, it was just my way
of cheering myself up, as I licked
the stamped, self-addressed envelopes,
the game I had
of trying to guess which one of you, this time,
had poisoned his glue. I did care.
I did read each poem entire.
I did say what I thought was the truth
in the mildest words I knew. And now,
in this poem, or chopped prose, not any better,
I realize, than those troubled lines
I kept sending back to you,
I have to say I am relieved it is over:
at the end I could feel only pity
for that urge toward more life
your poems kept smothering in words, the smell
of which, days later, would tingle
in your nostrils as new, God-given impulses
to write.

Goodbye,
you who are, for me, the postmarks again
of shattered towns—Xenia, Burnt Cabins, Hornell—
their loneliness
given away in poems, only their solitude kept.

1968

W. S. MERWIN
(1927–   )

The Drunk in the Furnace

      For a good decade
The furnace stood in the naked gully, fireless
And vacant as any hat. Then when it was
No more to them than a hulking black fossil
To erode unnoticed with the rest of the junk-hill
By the poisonous creek, and rapidly to be added
      To their ignorance.

---

2. A group of English poets and painters, among them Dante Gabriel Rossetti and William Morris, whose aim was to restore to art the aesthetic principles of the early Italian Renaissance—that is, before Raphael (1483–1520), the great painter.

They were afterwards astonished
To confirm, one morning, a twist of smoke like a pale
10 Resurrection, staggering out of its chewed hole,
And to remark then other tokens that someone,
Cozily bolted behind the eye-holed iron
Door of the drafty burner, had there established
His bad castle.

15   Where he gets his spirits
It's a mystery. But the stuff keeps him musical:
Hammer-and-anviling with poker and bottle
To his jugged bellowings, till the last groaning clang
As he collapses onto the rioting
20 Springs of a litter of car-seats ranged on the grates,
To sleep like an iron pig.

In their tar-paper church
On a text about stoke-holes that are sated never
25 Their Reverend lingers. They nod and hate trespassers.
When the furnace wakes, though, all afternoon
Their witless offspring flock like piped rats to its siren
Crescendo, and agape on the crumbling ridge
Stand in a row and learn.

                                                                1960

Noah's Raven

Why should I have returned?
My knowledge would not fit into theirs.
I found untouched the desert of the unknown,
Big enough for my feet. It is my home.
5 It is always beyond them. The future
Splits the present with the echo of my voice.
Hoarse with fulfilment, I never made promises.

                                                                1963

For the Anniversary of My Death

Every year without knowing it I have passed the day
When the last fires will wave to me
And the silence will set out
Tireless traveler
5 Like the beam of a lightless star

Then I will no longer
Find myself in life as in a strange garment
Surprised at the earth
And the love of one woman
10 And the shamelessness of men
As today writing after three days of rain
Hearing the wren sing and the falling cease
And bowing not knowing to what

                                                                1967

One Time

FOR CHARLES BELL

O venerable plank burning
and your pegs with you
the hordes of flame gaining
in the marks of the adze
each mark seven times older than I am
each furthermore shaped like a tongue
you that contain
of several lives now only a dust
inside the surfaces that were once cuts
but no memory no tree
even your sparks dust
toward the last some of your old pitch
boils up through you
many children running
into a shining forest

1973

CHARLES TOMLINSON
(1927–   )

The Picture of J. T. in a Prospect of Stone [1]

What should one
    wish a child
       and that, one's own
emerging
    from between
       the stone lips
of a sheep-stile [2]
    that divides
       village graves
and village green?
    —Wish her
       the constancy of stone.
—But stone
    is hard.
       —Say, rather
it resists
    the slow corrosives
       and the flight
of time
    and yet it takes
       the play, the fluency
from light.
    —How would you know
       the gift you'd give
was the gift
    she'd wish to have?
       —Gift is giving,

---

1. Cf. the title of Andrew Marvell's poem *The Picture of Little T. C. in a Prospect of Flowers.* J. T. is Tomlinson's small daughter.

2. A stile is a step or set of steps, in a wall, to allow one person at a time to pass while it excludes sheep or cattle.

gift is meaning:
    first
30   I'd give
then let her
        live with it
            to prove
its quality the better and
35   thus learn
            to love
what (to begin with)
        she might spurn.
            —You'd
40 moralize a gift?
        —I'd have her
            understand
the gift I gave her.
        —And so she shall
45   but let her play
her innocence away
        emerging
            as she does
between
50   her doom (unknown),
            her unmown green.

1963

The View

The woods are preparing to wait out winter.
    Gusts blow with an earnest of all there is to be done
Once frost will have entered the apple and the sun.
    Of the view, there is no tale to tell you.
5   Its history is incidental. One would not date
        The window that stands open like a gate
In the opposing house-face. It is dark inside.
    The façade is a dirty white, and yet it seems
The right color to stand there between
10   The dull green of the foreground trees
Still bearing leaves, and the autumnal glare
    From the others framing it, foregoing theirs.
The dark of the window square might be
    A mineshaft of pure shadow, a way
15 Through to the heart of the hill—the black
    Center, if center there were where
Sight must travel such drops and intervals,
    And an undulation of aspens along the slope
Is turning the wind to water and to light,
20   Unpivoting place amid its shaken coins,
While under a shuddering causeway, a currency,
    The season is dragging at all the roots of the view.

1969

Terminal Tramps

The first is female.
In the station restaurant,
taking tea

that some thirsty traveler
had found too hot
for drinking, she sips
at the unmeasured time of her
terrible leisure.
The eyes of the mad
have a restless candor:
even their furtiveness
betrays itself openly:
there seems, in the way
she declares to the entire
room: *I expect
a civil answer—*
the appearance of an honesty.
It is distinct from the absurd
sobriety in the drunk
tramp's gesture
carrying on
in the corner, an imitation
conversation, with one
as craftily glanced as he
but sober. All
three inhabit
this shifting place
on whose fluidities the clocks
impose a certainty.
The room is aware of them.
The room is tolerant
in its curiosity and waits
to see, but to see
what? The Indian
personnel pretend
that the three are not
there—even the mad
woman has had
sense to avoid
in this two-roomed
restaurant, the white
management next-door.
What does occur
is this—this
and no more: she picks
out of the air and starts
to repeat the word
Eisenhower. She takes
apart into its four
syllables the arbitrary
sound, then feels
her way out
over them, as though
they might have led
her somewhere, stretched
from here to there,—
might have proved
there there, but the mind's
needle merely
chokes on its repetitions

until, with an accumulating
force, the vortex
spins her on
into inconsequence.
65 The drunk walks
suddenly half
the room's length,
balanced tensely
by the strength of one
70 determination—to make it;
and to complete the demonstration
he flings with a total
accuracy into the slot
of a litter bin
75 his emptied bottle.
Her babble stops him.
He attends, and for the first
time sees her:
she takes him in,
80 her din rises
raging against the mere
shape he makes there:
it is her voice not she
gets up to accost him
85 and to demand her civil
answer. Answer
she has, but whether
she hears, or whether
she can interpret
90 the sharp transition
as with half a threat
he gestures at her, then
lets the gesture
drift, die out across
95 the air . . . with an
Ach!—the dawning
sense of her daftness—
he goes back
aiming himself at his former
100 corner, and gets
there on both
feet, as neat
as bottle into bin-slot—
to resume (he has clearly
105 forgotten her) his parody
of someone perfectly
self-possessed. The room
holding its breath
for his fall
110 is relieved. The room
has seen it all and now
inches out daughters
and sons into the loud
sane ambience
115 of train-sounds.
Under the dome

of stale air,
two Indians are
going their rounds,
swabbing the tables.
They circle the one
she sits at
with her all-but-spent
babble, her syllable-
chopping search
for the right sound,
the word to express
her groundless humanity,
hunched, alien
and intent amid
the new invasion
of travelers with a destination.

1969

Stone Speech

Crowding this beach
are milkstones, white
teardrops; flints
edged out of flinthood
into smoothness chafe
against grainy ovals,
pitted pieces, nosestones,
stoppers and saddles;
veins of orange
inlay black beads:
chalk-swaddled babyshapes,
tiny fists, facestones
and facestone's brother
skullstone, roundheads
pierced by a single eye,
purple finds, all
rubbing shoulders:
a mob of grindings,
groundlings, scatterings
from a million necklaces
mined under sea-hills, the pebbles
are as various as the people.

1972

JAMES WRIGHT
(1927–   )

A Note Left in Jimmy Leonard's Shack

Near the dry river's water-mark we found
    Your brother Minnegan,
Flopped like a fish against the muddy ground.
Beany, the kid whose yellow hair turns green,
Told me to find you, even in the rain,
    And tell you he was drowned.

I hid behind the chassis on the bank,
   The wreck of someone's Ford:
I was afraid to come and wake you drunk:
You told me once the waking up was hard,
The daylight beating at you like a board.
   Blood in my stomach sank.

Beside, you told him never to go out
   Along the river-side
Drinking and singing, clattering about.
You might have thrown a rock at me and cried
I was to blame, I let him fall in the road
   And pitch down on his side.

Well, I'll get hell enough when I get home
   For coming up this far,
Leaving the note, and running as I came.
I'll go and tell my father where you are.
You'd better go find Minnegan before
   Policemen hear and come.

Beany went home, and I got sick and ran,
   You old son of a bitch.
You better hurry down to Minnegan;
He's drunk or dying now, I don't know which,
Rolled in the roots and garbage like a fish,
   The poor old man.

1959

Youth

Strange bird,
His song remains secret.
He worked too hard to read books.
He never heard how Sherwood Anderson [1]
Got out of it, and fled to Chicago, furious to free himself
From his hatred of factories.
My father toiled fifty years
At Hazel-Atlas Glass,
Caught among girders that smash the kneecaps
of dumb honyaks. [2]
Did he shudder with hatred in the cold shadow of grease?
Maybe. But my brother and I do know
He came home as quiet as the evening.

He will be getting dark, soon,
And loom through new snow.
I know his ghost will drift home
To the Ohio River, and sit down, alone,
Whittling a root.
He will say nothing.
The waters flow past, older, younger
Than he is, or I am.

1968

1. American short story writer and novelist
(1876–1941) who in 1912 suddenly left his
business concern in Elyria, Ohio, to become
an active force in the Chicago "little Renais-
sance" of that period.
2. Eastern European immigrants; more gen-
erally, downtrodden industrial laborers.

A Blessing

Just off the highway to Rochester, Minnesota,
Twilight bounds softly forth on the grass.
And the eyes of those two Indian ponies
Darken with kindness.
They have come gladly out of the willows
To welcome my friend and me.
We step over the barbed wire into the pasture
Where they have been grazing all day, alone.
They ripple tensely, they can hardly contain their happiness
That we have come.
They bow shyly as wet swans. They love each other.
There is no loneliness like theirs.
At home once more,
They begin munching the young tufts of spring in the darkness.
I would like to hold the slenderer one in my arms,
For she has walked over to me
And nuzzled my left hand.
She is black and white,
Her mane falls wild on her forehead,
And the light breeze moves me to caress her long ear
That is delicate as the skin over a girl's wrist.
Suddenly I realize
That if I stepped out of my body I would break
Into blossom.

                                                    1963

To the Muse

It is all right. All they do
Is go in by dividing
One rib from another. I wouldn't
Lie to you. It hurts
Like nothing I know. All they do
Is burn their way in with a wire.
It forks in and out a little like the tongue
Of that frightened garter snake we caught
At Cloverfield, you and me, Jenny
So long ago.

I would lie to you
If I could.
But the only way I can get you to come up
Out of the suckhole, the south face
Of the Powhatan pit, is to tell you
What you know:

You come up after dark, you poise alone
With me on the shore.
I lead you back to this world.

Three lady doctors in Wheeling open
Their offices at night.
I don't have to call them, they are always there.

But they only have to put the knife once
Under your breast.
25 Then they hang their contraption.
And you bear it.

It's awkward a while. Still, it lets you
Walk about on tiptoe if you don't
Jiggle the needle.
30 It might stab your heart, you see.
The blade hangs in your lung and the tube
Keeps it draining.
That way they only have to stab you
Once. Oh Jenny,
35 I wish to God I had made this world, this scurvy
And disastrous place. I
Didn't, I can't bear it
Either, I don't blame you, sleeping down there
Face down in the unbelievable silk of spring,
40 Muse of black sand,
Alone.

I don't blame you, I know
The place where you lie.
I admit everything. But look at me.
45 How can I live without you?
Come up to me, love,
Out of the river, or I will
Come down to you.

1968

THOM GUNN
(1929–   )

On the Move

'Man, you gotta Go.'

The blue jay scuffling in the bushes follows
Some hidden purpose, and the gust of birds
That spurts across the field, the wheeling swallows,
Have nested in the trees and undergrowth.
5 Seeking their instinct, or their poise, or both,
One moves with an uncertain violence
Under the dust thrown by a baffled sense
Or the dull thunder of approximate words.

On motorcycles, up the road, they come:
10 Small, black, as flies hanging in heat, the Boys,
Until the distance throws them forth, their hum
Bulges to thunder held by calf and thigh.
In goggles, donned impersonality,
In gleaming jackets trophied with the dust,
15 They strap in doubt—by hiding it, robust—
And almost hear a meaning in their noise.

Exact conclusion of their hardiness
Has no shape yet, but from known whereabouts
They ride, direction where the tires press.
They scare a flight of birds across the field:
Much that is natural, to the will must yield.
Men manufacture both machine and soul,
And use what they imperfectly control
To dare a future from the taken routes.

It is a part solution, after all.
One is not necessarily discord
On earth; or damned because, half animal,
One lacks direct instinct, because one wakes
Afloat on movement that divides and breaks.
One joins the movement in a valueless world,
Choosing it, till, both hurler and the hurled,
One moves as well, always toward, toward.

A minute holds them, who have come to go:
The self-defined, astride the created will
They burst away; the towns they travel through
Are home for neither bird nor holiness,
For birds and saints complete their purposes.
At worse, one is in motion; and at best,
Reaching no absolute, in which to rest,
One is always nearer by not keeping still.

California   1957

In the Tank

A man sat in the felon's tank, alone,
Fearful, ungrateful, in a cell for two.
And from his metal bunk, the lower one,
He studied where he was, as felons do.

The cell was clean and cornered, and contained
A bowl, gray gritty soap, and paper towels,
A mattress lumpy and not overstained,
Also a toilet, for the felon's bowels.

He could see clearly all there was to see,
And later when the lights flicked off at nine
He saw as clearly all there was to see:
An order without color, bulk, or line.

And then he knew exactly where he sat.
For though the total riches could not fail
—Red weathered brick, fountains, wisteria—yet
Still they contained the silence of a jail,

The jail contained a tank, the tank contained
A box, a mere suspension, at the center,
Where there was nothing left to understand,
And where he must re-enter and re-enter.

1967

Back to Life

Around the little park
The lamps blink on, and make the dusk seem deeper.
I saunter toward them on the grass
That suddenly rustles from the dew,
5   Hearing behind, at times,
A fragmentary shout or distant bark.
I am alone, like a patrolling keeper.
And then I catch the smell of limes°   linden trees
Coming and going faintly on the dark:
10 Bunched black at equal height
They stand between the lamps, yet where
They branch out toward them on each side, a few
Touching the lighted glass,
Their leaves are soft green on the night,
15 The closest losing even their mass,
Edged but transparent as if they too gave light.

The street is full, the quiet is broken.
I notice that the other strollers there
Extend themselves, at ease
20 As if just woken
To a world they have not yet recovered, though
They move across the dusk, alert,
And stare,
As I do, into shops or at the trees,
25 Devouring each detail, from leaf to dirt,
In the measured mildness of the air.
Here by the curb
The boys and girls walk, jostling as they grow,
Cocky with surplus strength.
30 And weakening with each move, the old,
Cushioned with papers or with rugs
On public seats close by,
Inch down into their loosened flesh, each fold
Being sensible of the gravity
35 Which tugs
And longs to bring it down
And break its hold.

I walk between the curb and bench
Conscious at length
40 Of sharing through each sense,
As if the light revealed us all
Sustained in delicate difference
Yet firmly growing from a single branch.

If that were all of it!
45 The branch that we grow on
Is not remembered easily in the dark,
Or the transparency when light is gone:
At most, a recollection
In the mind only—over a rainswept park
50 Held to by mere conviction
In cold and misery when the clock strikes one.

The lamp still shines.
The pale leaves shift a bit,
Now light, now shadowed, and their movement shared
A second later by the bough,
Even by the sap that runs through it:
A small full trembling through it now
As if each leaf were, so, better prepared
For falling sooner or later separate.

                                                        1967

From the Wave

It mounts at sea, a concave wall
    Down-ribbed with shine,
And pushes forward, building tall
    Its steep incline.

Then from their hiding rise to sight
    Black shapes on boards
Bearing before the fringe of white
    It mottles towards.

Their pale feet curl, they poise their weight
    With a learn'd skill.
It is the wave they imitate
    Keeps them so still.

The marbling bodies have become
    Half wave, half men,
Grafted it seems by feet of foam
    Some seconds, then,

Late as they can, they slice the face
    In timed procession:
Balance is triumph in this place,
    Triumph possession.

The mindless heave of which they rode
    A fluid shelf
Breaks as they leave it, falls and, slowed,
    Loses itself.

Clear, the sheathed bodies slick as seals
    Loosen and tingle;
And by the board the bare foot feels
    The suck of shingle.

They paddle in the shallows still;
    Two splash each other;
Then all swim out to wait until
    The right waves gather.

                                                        1971

The Rooftop

White houses bank the hill,
Facing me where I sit.
It should be adequate
To watch the gardens fill

5 With sunlight, washing tree,
Bush, and the year's last flowers,
And to sit here for hours,
Becoming what I see.

Perception gave me this:
10 A whole world, bit by bit.
Yet I can not grasp it—
Bits, not an edifice.

Long webs float on the air.
Glistening, they fall and lift.
15 I turn it down, the gift:
Such fragile lights can tear.

The heat frets earth already,
Harrowed by furious root;
The wireworm [1] takes his loot;
20 The midday sun is steady.

Petals turn brown and splay:
Loose in a central shell
Seeds whitening dry and swell
Which light fills from decay.

25 Ruthless in clean unknowing
The plant obeys its need,
And works alone. The seed
Bursts, bare as bone in going,

Bouncing from rot toward earth,
30 Compound of rot, to wait,
An armored concentrate
Containing its own birth.

An unseen edifice.
The seen, the tangles, lead
35 From seed to death to seed
Through green closed passages.

The light drains from the hill.
The gardens rustle, cold,
Huddled in dark, and hold,
40 Waiting for when they fill.

1971

---

1. A destroyer of plant roots.

ADRIENNE RICH
(1929–   )

Ghazals[6]

7/24/68:ii

The friend I can trust is the one who will let me have my death.
The rest are actors who want me to stay and further the plot.

At the drive-in movie, above the PanaVision,
beyond the projector beams, you project yourself, great Star.

The eye that used to watch us is dead, but open.
Sometimes I still have a sense of being followed.

How long will we be waiting for the police?
How long must I wonder which of my friends would hide me?

Driving at night I feel the Milky Way
streaming above me like the graph of a cry.

7/26/68:ii

A dead mosquito, flattened against a door;
his image could survive our comings and our goings.

LeRoi! Eldridge![7] listen to us, we are ghosts
condemned to haunt the cities where you want to be at home.

The white children turn black on the negative.
The summer clouds blacken inside the camera-skull.

Every mistake that can be made, we are prepared to make;
anything less would fall short of the reality we're dreaming.

Someone has always been desperate, now it's our turn—
we who were free to weep for Othello and laugh at Caliban.

I have learned to smell a *conservateur* a mile away:
they carry illustrated catalogues of all that there is to lose.

1969

Planetarium

(THINKING OF CAROLINE HERSCHEL, 1750–1848,
ASTRONOMER, SISTER OF WILLIAM;[1] AND OTHERS)

A woman in the shape of a monster
a monster in the shape of a woman
the skies are full of them

---

6. "This poem began to be written after I read Aijaz Ahmad's literal English versions of the work of the Urdu poet Mirza Ghalib, 1797–1869. While the structure and metrics used by Ghalib are much stricter than mine, I have adhered to his use of a minimum five couplets to a *ghazal*, each couplet being autonomous and independent of the others. The continuity and unity flow from the associations and images playing back and forth among the couplets in any single *ghazal*. I have left the ghazals dated as I wrote them" [Rich's note].
7. LeRoi Jones and Eldridge Cleaver, contemporary Afro-American writers and political radicals.
1. Famous astronomer (1738–1822).

a woman   "in the snow
among the Clocks and instruments
or measuring the ground with poles"

in her 98 years to discover
8 comets

she whom the moon ruled
like us
levitating into the night sky
riding the polished lenses

Galaxies of women, there
doing penance for impetuousness
ribs chilled
in those spaces   of the mind

An eye,
    "virile, precise and absolutely certain"
    from the mad webs of Uranisborg [2]
                              encountering the NOVA

every impulse of light exploding
from the core
as life flies out of us
        Tycho whispering at last
    "Let me not seem to have lived in vain"

What we see, we see
and seeing is changing

the light that shrivels a mountain
and leaves a man alive

Heartbeat of the pulsar
heart sweating through my body

The radio impulse
pouring in from Taurus [3]

        I am bombarded yet   I stand

I have been standing all my life in the
direct path of a battery of signals
the most accurately transmitted most
untranslateable language in the universe
I am a galactic cloud so deep   so invo-
luted that a light wave could take 15
years to travel through me   And has
taken   I am an instrument in the shape
of a woman trying to translate pulsations
into images   for the relief of the body
and the reconstruction of the mind.

                                    1971

---

2. The observatory built by Tycho Brahe
(1546–1601), the Danish astronomer.   3. The constellation "The Bull."

Diving into the Wreck

First having read the book of myths,
and loaded the camera,
and checked the edge of the knife-blade,
I put on
the body-armor of black rubber
the absurd flippers
the grave and awkward mask.
I am having to do this
not like Cousteau with his
assiduous team
aboard the sun-flooded schooner
but here alone.

There is a ladder.
The ladder is always there
hanging innocently
close to the side of the schooner.
We know what it is for,
we who have used it.
otherwise
it is a piece of maritime floss
some sundry equipment.

I go down.
Rung after rung and still
the oxygen immerses me
the blue light
the clear atoms
of our human air.
I go down.
My flippers cripple me,
I crawl like an insect down the ladder
and there is no one
to tell me when the ocean
will begin.

First the air is blue and then
it is bluer and then green and then
black I am blacking out and yet
my mask is powerful
it pumps my blood with power
the sea is another story
the sea is not a question of power
I have to learn alone
to turn my body without force
in the deep element.

And now: it is easy to forget
what I came for
among so many who have always
lived here
swaying their crenellated fans
between the reefs
and besides
you breathe differently down here.

I came to explore the wreck.
The words are purposes.
The words are maps.
55 I came to see the damage that was done
and the treasures that prevail.
I stroke the beam of my lamp
slowly along the flank
of something more permanent
60 than fish or weed

the thing I came for:
the wreck and not the story of the wreck
the thing itself and not the myth
the drowned face always staring
65 toward the sun
the evidence of damage
worn by salt and sway into this threadbare beauty
the ribs of the disaster
curving their assertion
70 among the tentative haunters.

This is the place.
And I am here, the mermaid whose dark hair
streams black, the merman in his armored body.
We circle silently
75 about the wreck
we dive into the hold.
I am she: I am he

whose drowned face sleeps with open eyes
whose breasts still bear the stress
80 whose silver, copper, vermeil cargo lies
obscurely inside barrels
half-wedged and left to rot
we are the half-destroyed instruments
that once held to a course
85 the water-eaten log
the fouled compass

We are, I am, you are
by cowardice or courage
the one who find our way
90 back to this scene
carrying a knife, a camera
a book of myths
in which
our names do not appear.

1973

GREGORY CORSO
(1930–   )

Marriage

Should I get married? Should I be good?
Astound the girl next door with my velvet suit and faustus hood? [1]
Don't take her to movies but to cemeteries
tell all about werewolf bathtubs and forked clarinets
then desire her and kiss her and all the preliminaries
and she going just so far and I understanding why
not getting angry saying You must feel! It's beautiful to feel!
Instead take her in my arms lean against an old crooked tombstone
and woo her the entire night the constellations in the sky—

When she introduces me to her parents
back straightened, hair finally combed, strangled by a tie,
should I sit knees together on their 3rd degree sofa
and not ask Where's the bathroom?
How else to feel other than I am,
often thinking Flash Gordon soap—
O how terrible it must be for a young man
seated before a family and the family thinking
We never saw him before! He wants our Mary Lou!
After tea and homemade cookies they ask What do you do for a living?

Should I tell them? Would they like me then?
Say All right get married, we're losing a daughter
but we're gaining a son—
And should I then ask Where's the bathroom?

O God, and the wedding! All her family and her friends
and only a handful of mine all scroungy and bearded
just wait to get at the drinks and food—
And the priest! he looking at me as if I masturbated
asking me Do you take this woman for your lawful wedded wife?
And I trembling what to say say Pie Glue!
I kiss the bride all those corny men slapping me on the back
She's all yours, boy! Ha-ha-ha!
And in their eyes you could see some obscene honeymoon going on—
Then all that absurd rice and clanky cans and shoes
Niagara Falls! Hordes of us! Husbands! Wives! Flowers! Chocolates!
All streaming into cozy hotels
All going to do the same thing tonight
The indifferent clerk he knowing what was going to happen
The lobby zombies they knowing what
The whistling elevator man he knowing
The winking bellboy knowing
Everybody knowing! I'd be almost inclined not to do anything!
Stay up all night! Stare that hotel clerk in the eye!
Screaming: I deny honeymoon! I deny honeymoon!
running rampant into those almost climactic suites
yelling Radio belly! Cat shovel!

---

1. Dr. Faustus, medieval alchemist, sold his soul to the devil. One of the rewards was renewed youth and attractiveness to young women.

O I'd live in Niagara forever! in a dark cave beneath the Falls
I'd sit there the Mad Honeymooner
devising ways to break marriages, a scourge of bigamy
a saint of divorce—

50 But I should get married I should be good
How nice it'd be to come home to her
and sit by the fireplace and she in the kitchen
aproned young and lovely wanting my baby
and so happy about me she burns the roast beef
55 and comes crying to me and I get up from my big papa chair
saying Christmas teeth! Radiant brains! Apple deaf!
God what a husband I'd make! Yes, I should get married!
So much to do! like sneaking into Mr Jones' house late at night
and cover his golf clubs with 1920 Norwegian books
60 Like hanging a picture of Rimbaud [2] on the lawnmower
like pasting Tannu Tuva [3] postage stamps all over the picket fence
like when Mrs Kindhead comes to collect for the Community Chest
grab her and tell her There are unfavorable omens in the sky!
And when the mayor comes to get my vote tell him
65 When are you going to stop people killing whales!
And when the milkman comes leave him a note in the bottle
Penguin dust, bring me penguin dust, I want penguin dust—

Yet if I should get married and it's Connecticut and snow
and she gives birth to a child and I am sleepless, worn,
70 up for nights, head bowed against a quiet window, the past behind me,
finding myself in the most common of situations a trembling man
knowledged with responsibility not twig-smear nor Roman coin soup—
O what would that be like!
Surely I'd give it for a nipple a rubber Tacitus [4]
75 For a rattle a bag of broken Bach records
Tack Della Francesca [5] all over its crib
Sew the Greek alphabet on its bib
And build for its playpen a roofless Parthenon

No, I doubt I'd be that kind of father
80 Not rural not snow no quiet window
but hot smelly tight New York City
seven flights up, roaches and rats in the walls
a fat Reichian [6] wife screeching over potatoes Get a job!
And five nose running brats in love with Batman
85 And the neighbors all toothless and dry haired
like those hag masses of the 18th century
all wanting to come in and watch TV
The landlord wants his rent
Grocery store Blue Cross Gas & Electric Knights of Columbus
90 Impossible to lie back and dream Telephone snow, ghost parking—
No! I should not get married I should never get married!
But—imagine If I were married to a beautiful sophisticated woman
tall and pale wearing an elegant black dress and long black gloves
holding a cigarette holder in one hand and a highball in the other
95 and we lived high up in a penthouse with a huge window
from which we could see all of New York and ever farther on clearer days
No, can't imagine myself married to that pleasant prison dream—

2. Arthur Rimbaud (1854–1891), French poet.   Renaissance painter.
3. A Siberian republic of the U.S.S.R.   6. Referring to Wilhelm Reich (1897–1957),
4. (55?–117? A.D.), Roman historian.   founder of a controversial school of psy-
5. Piero della Francesca (1420?–1492), Italian   chiatry.

O but what about love? I forget love
not that I am incapable of love
it's just that I see love as odd as wearing shoes—
I never wanted to marry a girl who was like my mother
And Ingrid Bergman was always impossible
And there's maybe a girl now but she's already married
And I don't like men and—
but there's got to be somebody!
Because what if I'm 60 years old and not married,
all alone in a furnished room with pee stains on my underwear
and everybody else is married! All the universe married but me!

Ah, yet well I know that were a woman possible as I am possible
then marriage would be possible—
Like SHE in her lonely alien gaud waiting her Egyptian lover [7]
so I wait—bereft of 2,000 years and the bath of life.

1960

TED HUGHES
(1930–   )

The Thought-Fox

I imagine this midnight moment's forest:
Something else is alive
Beside the clock's loneliness
And this blank page where my fingers move.

Through the window I see no star:
Something more near
Though deeper within darkness
Is entering the loneliness:

Cold, delicately as the dark snow,
A fox's nose touches twig, leaf;
Two eyes serve a movement, that now
And again now, and now, and now

Sets neat prints into the snow
Between trees, and warily a lame
Shadow lags by stump and in hollow
Of a body that is bold to come

Across clearings, an eye,
A widening deepening greenness,
Brilliantly, concentratedly,
Coming about its own business

Till, with a sudden sharp hot stink of fox
It enters the dark hole of the head.
The window is starless still; the clock ticks,
The page is printed.

1957

7. As in H. Rider Haggard's novel (1887). "She" gains eternal youth by bathing in a pillar of flame, and waits thousands of years for the return of her lover.

The Bull Moses

A hoist up and I could lean over
The upper edge of the high half-door,
My left foot ledged on the hinge, and look in at the byre's [1]
Blaze of darkness: a sudden shut-eyed look
5 Backward into the head.
                    Blackness is depth
Beyond star. But the warm weight of his breathing,
The ammoniac reek of his litter, the hotly-tongued
Mash of his cud, steamed against me.
Then, slowly, as onto the mind's eye—
10 The brow like masonry, the deep-keeled neck:
Something come up there onto the brink of the gulf,
Hadn't heard of the world, too deep in itself to be called to,
Stood in sleep. He would swing his muzzle at a fly
But the square of sky where I hung, shouting, waving,
15 Was nothing to him; nothing of our light
Found any reflection in him.
                   Each dusk the farmer led him
Down to the pond to drink and smell the air,
And he took no pace but the farmer
Led him to take it, as if he knew nothing
20 Of the ages and continents of his fathers,
Shut, while he wombed, to a dark shed
And steps between his door and the duckpond;
The weight of the sun and the moon and the world hammered
To a ring of brass through his nostrils.
                     He would raise
25 His streaming muzzle and look out over the meadows,
But the grasses whispered nothing awake, the fetch
Of the distance drew nothing to momentum
In the locked black of his powers. He came strolling gently back,
Paused neither toward the pigpens on his right,
30 Nor toward the cow-byres on his left: something
Deliberate in his leisure, some beheld future
Founding in his quiet.
                I kept the door wide,
Closed it after him and pushed the bolt.

                                    1964

November

The month of the drowned dog. After long rain the land
Was sodden as the bed of an ancient lake,
Treed with iron and birdless. In the sunk lane
The ditch—a seep silent all summer—

5 Made brown foam with a big voice: that, and my boots
On the lane's scrubbed stones, in the gulleyed leaves,
Against the hill's hanging silence;
Mist silvering the droplets on the bare thorns

1. Cattle-shed's.

Slower than the change of daylight.
In a let of the ditch a tramp was bundled asleep:
Face tucked down into beard, drawn in
Under its hair like a hedgehog's. I took him for **dead,**

But his stillness separated from the death
Of the rotting grass and the ground. A wind chilled,
And a fresh comfort tightened through him,
Each hand stuffed deeper into the other sleeve.

His ankles, bound with sacking and hairy band,
Rubbed each other, resettling. The wind hardened;
A puff shook a glittering from the thorns,
And again the rains' dragging gray columns

Smudged the farms. In a moment
The fields were jumping and smoking; the thorns
Quivered, riddled with the glassy verticals.
I stayed on under the welding cold

Watching the tramp's face glisten and the drops on his coat
Flash and darken. I thought what strong trust
Slept in him—as the trickling furrows slept,
And the thorn-roots in their grip on darkness;

And the buried stones, taking the weight of winter;
The hill where the hare crouched with clenched teeth.
Rain plastered the land till it was shining
Like hammered lead, and I ran, and in the rushing wood

Shuttered by a black oak leaned.
The keeper's gibbet° had owls and hawks   *gallows*
By the neck, weasels, a gang of cats, crows:
Some, stiff, weightless, twirled like dry bark bits

In the drilling rain. Some still had their shape,
Had their pride with it; hung, chins on chests,
Patient to outwait these worst days that beat
Their crowns bare and dripped from their feet.

                                                          1960

Song of a Rat

I. The Rat's Dance

The rat is in the trap, it is in the trap,
And attacking heaven and earth with a mouthful of screeches like torn tin,
An effective gag.
When it stops screeching, it pants

And cannot think
"This has no face, it must be God" or

"No answer is also an answer."
Iron jaws, strong as the whole earth

Are stealing its backbone
10 For a crumpling of the Universe with screechings,

For supplanting every human brain inside its skull with a rat-body tha
knots and unknots,
A rat that goes on screeching,

Trying to uproot itself into each escaping screech,
But its long fangs bar that exit—

15 The incisors bared to the night spaces, threatening the constellations,

The glitterers in the black, to keep off,

Keep their distance,
While it works this out.

The rat understands suddenly. It bows and is still,
20 With a little beseeching of blood on its nose-end.

II. The Rat's Vision

The rat hears the wind saying something in the straw
And the night-fields that have come up to the fence, leaning their silence

The widowed land
With its trees that know how to cry

25 The rat sees the farm bulk of beam and stone
Wobbling like reflection on water.
The wind is pushing from the gulf
Through the old barbed wire, in through the trenched gateway, past th
gates of the ear, deep into the worked design of days,

Breathes onto the solitary snow crystal

30 The rat screeches
And "Do not go" cry the dandelions, from their heads of folly
And "Do not go" cry the yard cinders, who have no future, only thei
infernal aftermath
And "Do not go" cries the cracked trough by the gate, fatalist of starligh
and zero

"Stay" says the arrangement of stars

35 Forcing the rat's head down into godhead.

III. The Rat's Flight

The heaven shudders, a flame unrolled like a whip,
And the stars jolt in their sockets.
And the sleep-souls of eggs
Wince under the shot of shadow—

40 That was the Shadow of the Rat
Crossing into power
Never to be buried

The horned Shadow of the Rat
Casting here by the door
A bloody gift for the dogs

While it supplants Hell.

1967

Examination at the Womb-Door [2]

Who owns these scrawny little feet?   *Death.*
Who owns this bristly scorched-looking face?   *Death.*
Who owns these still-working lungs?   *Death.*
Who owns this utility coat of muscles?   *Death.*
Who owns these unspeakable guts?   *Death.*
Who owns these questionable brains?   *Death.*
All this messy blood?   *Death.*
These minimum-efficiency eyes?   *Death.*
This wicked little tongue?   *Death.*
This occasional wakefulness?   *Death.*

Given, stolen, or held pending trial?
Held.

Who owns the whole rainy, stony earth?   *Death.*
Who owns all of space?   *Death.*

Who is stronger than hope?   *Death.*
Who is stronger than the will?   *Death.*
Stronger than love?   *Death.*
Stronger than life?   *Death.*

But who is stronger than death?
                    Me, evidently.
Pass, Crow.

1971

Crow Alights

Crow saw the herded mountains, steaming in the morning.
And he saw the sea
Dark-spined, with the whole earth in its coils.
He saw the stars, fuming away into the black, mushrooms of the nothing
    forest, clouding their spores, the virus of God.
And he shivered with the horror of Creation.

In the hallucination of the horror
He saw this shoe, with no sole, rain-sodden,
Lying on a moor.
And there was this garbage can, bottom rusted away,
A playing place for the wind, in a waste of puddles.

2. This poem is from *Crow: from the life and Songs of the Crow* (1971), a cycle of 60-odd poems with a common protagonist, Crow, whose role and character as reflector of experience are defined by the entire sequence.

There was this coat, in the dark cupboard,
                    in the silent room, in the silent house.
There was this face, smoking its cigarette between the dusk window and
    the fire's embers.

Near the face, this hand, motionless.

15   Near the hand, this cup.

Crow blinked. He blinked. Nothing faded.

He stared at the evidence.

Nothing escaped him. (Nothing could escape.)

                                                                        197

JON SILKIN
(1930–   )
Carved

Two small dogs stood by a dead black bird
And the black bird was very dead.

The two dogs stood by the bird like large lions
But they never touched the dead thing, once.

5   They would like to have eaten the black thing
But it was very dead with red ants,

Sawing its neck away like stone masons
And the red ants were very much alive.

So all the time the dogs stood they barked there
10   Because they couldn't eat the black thing.

Something large about that black bird.
It was being eaten by red death

While the two large-lion small dogs just stood,
Barking: they never touched the black thing,

15   And the black thing never looked at them, once.
It was indifferent to two small dogs.

Maybe it did not hear those large lions
Or maybe the black bird felt sorry for the small dogs.

Meanwhile the dead went on being dead and the living living.

                                                                        195

Death of a Son
(WHO DIED IN A MENTAL HOSPITAL AGED ONE)

Something has ceased to come along with me.
Something like a person: something very like one.
            And there was no nobility in it
                Or anything like that.

Something was there like a one year
Old house, dumb as stone. While the near buildings
        Sang like birds and laughed
                Understanding the pact

        They were to have with silence. But he
Neither sang nor laughed. He did not bless silence
        Like bread, with words.
                He did not forsake silence.

        But rather, like a house in mourning
Kept the eye turned in to watch the silence while
                The other houses like birds
                        Sang around him.

And the breathing silence neither
Moved nor was still.

        I have seen stones: I have seen brick
But this house was made up of neither bricks nor stone
                But a house of flesh and blood
                        With flesh of stone

        And bricks for blood. A house
Of stones and blood in breathing silence with the other
                Birds singing crazy on its chimneys.
                        But this was silence,

        This was something else, this was
Hearing and speaking though he was a house drawn
                Into silence, this was
                        Something religious in his silence,

        Something shining in his quiet,
This was different this was altogether something else:
                Though he never spoke, this
                        Was something to do with death.

        And then slowly the eye stopped looking
Inward. The silence rose and became still.
The look turned to the outer place and stopped,
                With the birds still shrilling around him.
                        And as if he could speak

He turned over on his side with his one year
Red as a wound
He turned over as if he could be sorry for this
And out of his eyes two great tears rolled, like stones, and he died.

                                                    1954

The Coldness

Where the printing-works buttress a church
And the northern river like moss
Robes herself slowly through
the cold township of York,[1]

___

1. A cathedral town in northern England, chief town of the county of Yorkshire; the
river that runs through it is the Ouse.

5　More slowly than usual
For a cold, northern river,
You see the citizens
Indulging stately pleasures,
Like swans. But they seem cold.
10　Why have they been so punished;
In what do their sins consist now?
An assertion persistent
As a gross tumor, and the sense
Of such growth haunting
15　The flesh of York
Is that there has been
No synagogue since eleven ninety [2]
When eight hundred Jews
Took each other's lives
20　To escape christian death
By christian hand; and the last
Took his own. The event
Has the frigid persistence of a growth
In the flesh. It is a fact
25　No other fact can be added to
Save that it was Easter, the time
When the dead christian God
Rose again. It is in this,
Perhaps, they are haunted; for the cold
30　Blood of victims is colder,
More staining, more corrosive
On the soul, than the blood of martyrs.
What consciousness is there of the cold
Heart, with its spaces?
35　For nothing penetrates
More than admitted absence.
The heart in warmth, even, cannot
Close its gaps. Absence of Jews
Through hatred, or indifference,
40　A gap they slip through, a conscience
That corrodes more deeply since it is
Forgotten—this deadens York.
Where are the stonemasons, the builders
Skilled in glass, strong first in wood;
45　Taut, flaxen plumbers with lengths of pipe,
Steel rules coiled in their palms;
The printers; canopy-makers—
Makers in the institution of marriage?
Their absence is endless, a socket
50　Where the jaw is protected neither
Through its tolerance of tooth,
Nor for blood. Either there is pain or no pain.
If they could feel; were there one
Among them with this kind
55　Of sensitivity that
Could touch the dignity,
Masonry of the cold
Northern face that falls

2. The Jews of York were the victims of a
pogrom in 1190. Rioting broke out on March
15 and lasted until March 17. Many of the
Jews who had taken refuge in the castle
committed suicide; others were massacred
when they came out of the castle after being
promised safety.

As you touch it, there might
Be some moving to
A northern expurgation.
All Europe is touched
With some of frigid York,
As York is now by Europe.

1961

The Strawberry Plant

The rootless strawberry plant
Moves across the soil. It hops
Six inches. Has no single location,
Or root.
You cannot point to its origin,
Or parent. It shoots out
A pipe, and one more plant
Consolidates its ground.
It puts out crude petals, loosely met.
As if the business of flowering
Were to be got over. Their period is brief.
Even then, the fruit is green,
Swart, hairy. Its petals invite tearing
And are gone quickly,
As if they had been. The fruit swells,
Reddens, becomes succulent.
Propagation through the devouring
Appetite of another.
Is sweet, seeded, untruculent;
Slugs like it, all over.
It is nubile° to the lips,   *marriageable*
And survives even them. And teeth,
Insane with edible fury,
Of the loving kind.

1965

The Violet

The lobed petals receive
Each other's nestling shape.

We share the sun's beneficence:
Frost, men, snowdrops.
Then the violet unfolds. Not an uncasing
Of the corolla,³ each petal compliant
To the purpose of survival, obedient to that; but as it feels
The sun's heat, that puberty
Pushes out from its earlier self-clasping
Two distinct, clenched halves. Stiffens then.
These fluttering portions that made
The bud, separately elect
To be the flower; the violet
Halves itself, pushing apart
In two separate forces;
It divides up itself, it becomes two violet portions.

---

3. Crown-like whorl of petals forming the inner envelope of a flower.

It is not a conformation of members,
Each petal a tooth, an eyelash.
On the other hand, the violet is torn apart.
20   Its increase is by dividing;
Its stiffened petals push further apart.
It adheres to its nature; it has no maturity,
Other than this.
It requires courage, and finds that
25   In this unclasping of its self-worship: two palms tentatively
Open. Going both ways,
They absorb a huge circle
Of violeted air, an intent
Movement of embrace;
30   Created, exposed, powerful.
The air is coloured somewhat violet.
It costs itself much.

196

GARY SNYDER
(1930–   )

Mid-August at Sourdough Mountain [1] Lookout

Down valley a smoke haze
Three days heat, after five days rain
Pitch glows on the fir-cones
Across rocks and meadows
5   Swarms of new flies.

I cannot remember things I once read
A few friends, but they are in cities.
Drinking cold snow-water from a tin cup
Looking down for miles
10   Through high still air.

1959

Above Pate Valley

We finished clearing the last
Section of trail by noon,
High on the ridge-side
Two thousand feet above the creek
5   Reached the pass, went on
Beyond the white pine groves,
Granite shoulders, to a small
Green meadow watered by the snow,
Edged with Aspen—sun
10   Straight high and blazing
But the air was cool.
Ate a cold fried trout in the
Trembling shadows. I spied
A glitter, and found a flake
15   Black volcanic glass—obsidian—
By a flower. Hands and knees

---

1. The setting of this and others of Snyder's poems is the Pacific Northwest.

Pushing the Bear grass, thousands
Of arrowhead leavings over a
Hundred yards. Not one good
Head, just razor flakes
On a hill snowed all but summer,
A land of fat summer deer,
They came to camp. On their
Own trails. I followed my own
Trail here. Picked up the cold-drill,
Pick, singlejack,[2] and sack
Of dynamite.
Ten thousand years.

1959

Myths and Texts: Burning

17

the text

Sourdough mountain called a fire in:
Up Thunder Creek, high on a ridge.
Hiked eighteen hours, finally found
A snag and a hundred feet around on fire:
All afternoon and into night
Digging the fire line
Falling the burning snag
It fanned sparks down like shooting stars
Over the dry woods, starting spot-fires
Flaring in wind up Skagit valley
From the Sound.[3]
Toward morning it rained.
We slept in mud and ashes,
Woke at dawn, the fire was out,
The sky was clear, we saw
The last glimmer of the morning star.

the myth

Fire up Thunder Creek and the mountain—
        troy's burning![4]
The cloud mutters
The mountains are your mind.
The woods bristle there,
Dogs barking and children shrieking
Rise from below.

Rain falls for centuries
Soaking the loose rocks in space
Sweet rain, the fire's out
The black snag glistens in the rain
& the last wisp of smoke floats up
Into the absolute cold
Into the spiral whorls of fire
The storms of the Milky Way

2. A cold-drill and singlejack (a short-handled hammer) are used to cut holes in solid rock for dynamite.
3. Puget Sound, in the state of Washington.

4. Alludes to the catastrophic destruction of Troy by the Greeks, as described in Homer's *Iliad* and Virgil's *Aeneid*.

"Buddha incense in an empty world"
Black pit cold and light-year
Flame tongue of the dragon
Licks the sun

20   The sun is but a morning star

1960

The Levels

wild cat kittens
born in the ceiling
      play sky gods
thundering over the room.
5   was it claude in the night?
was it thieves?

      above our northbound steps
the wild cat brood walks west

a hawk sails over the roof
10   a snake went under the floor

      how can hawks hunt in the rain?

I walk through the hallway:
the soul of a great-bellied cloud.

1967

Civilization

Those are the people who do complicated things.

      they'll grab us by the thousands
      and put us to work.
World's going to hell, with all these
5   villages and trails.
Wild duck flocks aren't
      what they used to be.
Aurochs [5] grow rare.

Fetch me my feathers and amber

    ✡

10   A small cricket
on the typescript page of
"Kyoto born in spring song"
grooms himself
in time with *The Well-Tempered Clavier*.[6]
15   I quit typing and watch him thru a glass.
How well articulated! How neat!

5. A species of European bison.
6. J. S. Bach's collection of 48 preludes and fugues for harpsichord.

Nobody understands the ANIMAL KINGDOM.

✡

When creeks are full
The poems flow
When creeks are down
We heap stones.

1970

DEREK WALCOTT
(1930–   )

The Gulf

[FOR JACK AND BARBARA HARRISON]

1

The airport coffee tastes less of America.
Sour, unshaven, dreading the exertion
of tightening, racked nerves fueled with liquor,

some smoky, resinous Bourbon,
the body, buckling at its casket hole,
a roar like last night's blast racing its engines,

watches the fumes of the exhausted soul
as the trans-Texas jet, screeching, begins
its flight and friends diminish. So, to be aware

of the divine union the soul detaches
itself from created things.[1] "We're in the air,"
the Texan near me grins. All things: these matches

from LBJ's[2] campaign hotel, this rose
given me at dawn in Austin by a child,
this book of fables by Borges,[3] its prose

a stalking, moonlit tiger. What was willed
on innocent, sun-streaked Dallas,[4] the beast's claw
curled round that hairspring rifle is revealed

on every page as lunacy or feral law;
circling that wound we leave Love Field.[5]
Fondled, these objects conjure hotels,

quarrels, new friendships, brown limbs
nakedly molded as these autumn hills
memory penetrates as the jet climbs

1. With reference to the Neo-Platonic doctrine that earthly relationships and attachments contaminate the striving for spiritual union with God; in contrast to the teaching that divine love is manifested in the created world and in human relationships.
2. Lyndon Baines Johnson (1906–1973), thirty-sixth President of the United States.
3. Jorge Luis Borges, Argentinian man of letters (1899–   ), best known for his short stories.
4. With an allusion to the assassination there of John F. Kennedy, November 22, 1963.
5. The Dallas airport.

25 the new clouds over Texas; their home means
    an island suburb, forest, mountain water;
    they are the simple properties for scenes

    whose joy exhausts like grief, scenes where we learn,
    exchanging the least gifts, this rose, this napkin,
30 that those we love are objects we return,

    that this lens on the desert's wrinkled skin
    has priced our flesh, all that we love in pawn
    to that brass ball, that the gifts, multiplying

    clutter and choke the heart, and that I shall
35 watch love reclaim its things as I lie dying.
    My very flesh and blood! Each seems a petal

    shriveling from its core. I watch them burn,
    by the nerves' flare I catch their skeletal
    candor! Best never to be born

40 the great dead cry.[6] Their works shine on our shelves,
    by twilight tour their gilded gravestone spines,
    and read until the lamplit page revolves

    to a white stasis whose detachment shines
    like a propeller's rainbowed radiance.
45 Circling like us; no comfort for their loves!

                    2
    The cold glass darkens. Elizabeth wrote once
    that we make glass the image of our pain;
    I watch clouds boil past the cold, sweating pane

    above the Gulf. All styles yearn to be plain
50 as life. The face of the loved object under glass
    is plainer still. Yet, somehow, at this height,

    above this cauldron boiling with its wars,
    our old earth, breaking to familiar light,
    that cloud-bound mummy with self-healing scars

55 peeled of her cerements° again looks new;   grave clothe
    some cratered valley heals itself with sage,
    through that grey, fading massacre a blue

    light-hearted creek flutes of some seige
    to the amnesia of drumming water.
60 Their cause is crystalline: the divine union

    of these detached, divided States, whose slaughter
    darkens each summer now, as one by one,
    the smoke of bursting ghettos clouds the glass

    down every coast where filling-station signs
65 proclaim the Gulf, an air, heavy with gas,
    sickens the state, from Newark to New Orleans.

---

6. For example, Sophocles, in *Oedipus at Colonus:* "Not to be born surpasses thought and speech./The second best is to have seen the light/And then to go back quickly whence we came."

3

Yet the South felt like home. Wrought balconies,
the sluggish river with its tidal drawl,
the tropic air charged with the extremities

of patience, a heat heavy with oil,
canebrakes, that legendary jazz. But fear
thickened my voice, that strange, familiar soil

prickled and barbed the texture of my hair,
my status as a secondary soul.
The Gulf, your gulf, is daily widening,

each blood-red rose warns of that coming night
when there's no rock cleft to go hidin' in [7]
and all the rocks catch fire, when that black might,

their stalking, moonless panthers turn from Him
whose voice they can no more believe, when the black X's [8]
mark their passover with slain seraphim.

4

The Gulf shines, dull as lead. The coast of Texas
glints like a metal rim. I have no home
as long as summer bubbling to its head

boils for that day when in the Lord God's name
the coals of fire are heaped upon the head
of all whose gospel is the whip and flame,

age after age, the uninstructing dead.

1969

GEOFFREY HILL
(1932–   )

The Distant Fury of Battle

Grass resurrects to mask, to strangle
Words glossed on stone, lopped stone-angel;
But the dead maintain their ground—
That there's no getting round—

Who in places vitally rest,
Named, anonymous; who test
Alike the endurance of yews
Laurels, moonshine, stone, all tissues;

With whom, under license and duress,
There are pacts made, if not peace.
Union with the stone-wearing dead
Claims the born leader, the prepared

---

7. A reference to the hymn which begins,
"Rock of Ages, cleft for me,/Let me hide
myself in thee." The "rock" signifies Christ,
"cleft" in his crucifixion.

8. Such as Malcolm X, the Black Muslim
leader, assassinated February 21, 1965, and
the Black Panthers, a militant black organi-
zation.

Leader, the devourers and all lean men.
Some, finally, learn to begin.
15 Some keep to the arrangement of love
(Or similar trust) under whose auspices move

Most subjects, toward the profits of this
Combine of doves and witnesses.
Some, dug out of hot-beds, are brought bare,
20 Not past conceiving but past care.

1955   195

The Guardians

The young, having risen early, had gone,
Some with excursions beyond the bay-mouth,
Some toward lakes, a fragile reflected sun.
Thunder-heads drift, awkwardly, from the south;

5   The old watch them. They have watched the safe
Packed harbors topple under sudden gales,
Great tides irrupt, yachts burn at the wharf
That on clean seas pitched their effective sails.

There are silences. These, too, they endure:
10 Soft comings-on; soft aftershocks of calm.
Quietly they wade the disturbed shore;
Gather the dead as the first dead scrape home.

1956   195

September Song

BORN 19.6.32—DEPORTED 24.9.42

Undesirable you may have been, untouchable
you were not. Not forgotten
or passed over at the proper time.

As estimated, you died. Things marched,
5   sufficient, to that end.
Just so much Zyklon [1] and leather, patented
terror, so many routine cries.

(I have made
an elegy for myself it
10 is true)

September fattens on vines. Roses
flake from the wall. The smoke
of harmless fires drifts to my eyes.

This is plenty. This is more than enough.

1968

---

1. Hydrocyanic acid, used in fumigation; also (Zyklon-B) used in the gas chambers of the German concentration camps.

GEORGE MACBETH
(1932–   )

The Wasps' Nest

All day to the loose tile behind the parapet
The droning bombers fled: in the wet gutter
Belly-upwards the dead were lying, numbed
By October cold. And now the bloat queen,
Sick-orange, with wings draped, and feelers trailing,
Like Helen combing her hair, posed on the ledge
Twenty feet above the traffic. I watched, just a foot
From her eyes, very glad of the hard glass parting
My pressed human nose from her angry sting
And her heavy power to warm the cold future
Sunk in unfertilized eggs. And I thought: if I reached
And inched this window open, and cut her in half
With my unclasped penknife, I could exterminate
An unborn generation. All next summer,
If she survives, the stepped roof will swarm
With a jam of striped fighters. Therefore, this winter
In burning sulfur in their dug-out hangars
All the bred wasps must die. Unless I kill her.
So I balanced assassination with genocide
As the queen walked on the ledge, a foot from my eyes
In the last sun of the year, the responsible man
With a cold nose, who knew that he must kill,
Coming to no sure conclusion, nor anxious to come.

1963

Fourteen Ways of Touching the Peter

1

You can push
your thumb
in the
ridge
between his
shoulderblades
to please him.

2

Starting
at its root,
you can let
his whole
tail
flow
through your hand.

3

Forming
a fist
you can let
him rub
his bone
skull
against it, hard.

4

When he makes
bread,
you can lift
25 him
by his under-
sides on your
knuckles.

5

In hot
30 weather
you can itch
the fur
under
his chin. He
35 likes that.

6

At night
you can hoist
him
out of his beanstalk,
40 sleepily
clutching
paper bags.

7

Pressing
his head against
45 your cheek,
you can carry
him
in the dark,
safely.

8

50 In late Autumn
you can find
seeds
adhering
to his fur.
55 There are
plenty.

9

You can prise
his jaws
open,
60 helping
any medicine
he won't
abide, go down.

10

You can touch
65 his
feet, only
if
he is relaxed.
He
70 doesn't like it.

11
You can comb
spare thin
fur
from his coat,
so he won't
get
fur-ball.

12
You can shake
his rigid
chicken-leg leg,
scouring his
hindquarters
with his Vim
tongue.

13
Dumping
hot fish
on his plate, you can
fend
him off,
pushing
and purring.

14
You can have
him shrimp
along you,
breathing,
whenever
you want
to compose poems.

1968

SYLVIA PLATH
(1932–1963)

Lady Lazarus [1]

I have done it again.
One year in every ten
I manage it—

A sort of walking miracle, my skin
Bright as a Nazi lampshade,
My right foot

A paperweight,
My face a featureless, fine
Jew linen.

1. Lazarus was raised by Jesus from the dead (John xi.1–44).

10 Peel off the napkin
    O my enemy.
    Do I terrify?—

    The nose, the eye pits, the full set of teeth?
    The sour breath
15 Will vanish in a day.

    Soon, soon the flesh
    The grave cave ate will be
    At home on me

    And I a smiling woman.
20 I am only thirty.
    And like the cat I have nine times to die.

    This is Number Three.
    What a trash
    To annihilate each decade.

25 What a million filaments.
    The peanut-crunching crowd
    Shoves in to see

    Them unwrap me hand and foot—
    The big strip tease.
30 Gentleman, ladies,

    These are my hands,
    My knees.
    I may be skin and bone,

    Nevertheless, I am the same, identical woman.
35 The first time it happened I was ten.
    It was an accident.

    The second time I meant
    To last it out and not come back at all.
    I rocked shut

40 As a seashell.
    They had to call and call
    And pick the worms off me like sticky pearls.

    Dying
    Is an art, like everything else.
45 I do it exceptionally well.

    I do it so it feels like hell.
    I do it so it feels real.
    I guess you could say I've a call.

    It's easy enough to do it in a cell.
50 It's easy enough to do it and stay put.
    It's the theatrical

Comeback in broad day
To the same place, the same face, the same brute
Amused shout:

"A miracle!"
That knocks me out.
There is a charge

For the eyeing of my scars, there is a charge
For the hearing of my heart—
It really goes.

And there is a charge, very large charge,
For a word or a touch
Or a bit of blood

Or a piece of my hair or my clothes.
So, so, Herr Doktor.
So, Herr Enemy.

I am your opus,
I am your valuable,
The pure gold baby

That melts to a shriek.
I turn and burn.
Do not think I underestimate your great concern.

Ash, ash—
You poke and stir.
Flesh, bone, there is nothing there—

A cake of soap,
A wedding ring,
A gold filling.

Herr God, Herr Lucifer,
Beware
Beware.

Out of the ash
I rise with my red hair
And I eat men like air.

1965

Tulips

The tulips are too excitable, it is winter here.
Look how white everything is, how quiet, how snowed-in.
I am learning peacefulness, lying by myself quietly
As the light lies on these white walls, this bed, these hands.
I am nobody; I have nothing to do with explosions.
I have given my name and my day-clothes up to the nurses
And my history to the anaesthetist and my body to surgeons.

They have propped my head between the pillow and the sheet-cuff
Like an eye between two white lids that will not shut.
10   Stupid pupil, it has to take everything in.
The nurses pass and pass, they are no trouble,
They pass the way gulls pass inland in their white caps,
Doing things with their hands, one just the same as another,
So it is impossible to tell how many there are.

15   My body is a pebble to them, they tend it as water
Tends to the pebbles it must run over, smoothing them gently.
They bring me numbness in their bright needles, they bring me sleep.
Now I have lost myself I am sick of baggage—
My patent leather overnight case like a black pillbox,
20   My husband and child smiling out of the family photo;
Their smiles catch onto my skin, little smiling hooks.

I have let things slip, a thirty-year-old cargo boat
Stubbornly hanging on to my name and address.
They have swabbed me clear of my loving associations.
25   Scared and bare on the green plastic-pillowed trolley
I watched my tea-set, my bureaus of linen, my books
Sink out of sight, and the water went over my head.
I am a nun now, I have never been so pure.

I didn't want any flowers, I only wanted
30   To lie with my hands turned up and be utterly empty.
How free it is, you have no idea how free—
The peacefulness is so big it dazes you,
And it asks nothing, a name tag, a few trinkets.
It is what the dead close on, finally; I imagine them
35   Shutting their mouths on it, like a Communion tablet.

The tulips are too red in the first place, they hurt me.
Even through the gift paper I could hear them breathe
Lightly, through their white swaddlings, like an awful baby.
Their redness talks to my wound, it corresponds.
40   They are subtle: they seem to float, though they weigh me down,
Upsetting me with their sudden tongues and their color,
A dozen red lead sinkers round my neck.

Nobody watched me before, now I am watched.
The tulips turn to me, and the window behind me
45   Where once a day the light slowly widens and slowly thins,
And I see myself, flat, ridiculous, a cut-paper shadow
Between the eye of the sun and the eyes of the tulips,
And I have no face, I have wanted to efface myself.
The vivid tulips eat my oxygen.

50   Before they came the air was calm enough,
Coming and going, breath by breath, without any fuss.
Then the tulips filled it up like a loud noise.
Now the air snags and eddies round them the way a river
Snags and eddies round a sunken rust-red engine.
55   They concentrate my attention, that was happy
Playing and resting without committing itself.

The walls, also, seem to be warming themselves.
The tulips should be behind bars like dangerous animals;
They are opening like the mouth of some great African cat,
And I am aware of my heart: it opens and closes
Its bowl of red blooms out of sheer love of me.
The water I taste is warm and salt, like the sea,
And comes from a country far away as health.

                                                    1965

Ariel [2]

Stasis in darkness.
Then the substanceless blue
Pour of tor and distances.

God's lioness,
How one we grow,
Pivot of heels and knees!—The furrow

Splits and passes, sister to
The brown arc
Of the neck I cannot catch,

Nigger-eye
Berries cast dark
Hooks—

Black sweet blood mouthfuls,
Shadows.
Something else

Hauls me through air—
Thighs, hair;
Flakes from my heels.

White
Godiva, I unpeel—
Dead hands, dead stringencies.

And now I
Foam to wheat, a glitter of seas.
The child's cry

Melts in the wall.
And I
Am the arrow,

The dew that flies
Suicidal, at once with the drive
Into the red

Eye, the cauldron of morning.

                                                    1965

2. Sylvia Plath's horse, named for the airy spirit in Shakespeare's *The Tempest*.

Black Rook in Rainy Weather

On the stiff twig up there
Hunches a wet black rook
Arranging and rearranging its feathers in the rain.
I do not expect miracle
5   Or an accident

To set the sight on fire
In my eye, nor seek
Any more in the desultory weather some design,
But let spotted leaves fall as they fall,
10   Without ceremony, or portent

Although, I admit, I desire,
Occasionally, some backtalk
From the mute sky, I can't honestly complain:
A certain minor light may still
15   Leap incandescent

Out of kitchen table or chair
As if a celestial burning took
Possession of the most obtuse objects now and then—
Thus hallowing an interval
20   Otherwise inconsequent

By bestowing largesse, honor,
One might say love. At any rate, I now walk
Wary (for it could happen
Even in this dull, ruinous landscape); skeptical,
25   Yet politic; ignorant

Of whatever angel may choose to flare
Suddenly at my elbow. I only know that a rook
Ordering its black feathers can so shine
As to seize my senses, haul
30   My eyelids up, and grant

A brief respite from fear
Of total neutrality. With luck,
Trekking stubborn through this season
Of fatigue, I shall
35   Patch together a content

Of sorts. Miracles occur,
If you care to call those spasmodic
Tricks of radiance miracles. The wait's begun again,
The long wait for the angel,
40   For that rare, random descent.

1971

IMAMU AMIRI BARAKA (LeRoi Jones)
(1934–   )

In Memory of Radio

Who has ever stopped to think of the divinity of Lamont Cranston?[1]
(Only Jack Kerouac, that I know of: & me.
The rest of you probably had on WCBS and Kate Smith,
Or something equally unattractive.)

What can I say?
It is better to have loved and lost
Than to put linoleum in your living rooms?

Am I a sage or something?
Mandrake's hypnotic gesture of the week?
(Remember, I do not have the healing powers of Oral Roberts . . .
I cannot, like F. J. Sheen, tell you how to get saved *& rich!*
I cannot even order you to gaschamber satori like Hitler or Goody Knight

& Love is an evil word.
Turn it backwards/see, what I mean?
An evol word. & besides
Who understands it?
I certainly wouldn't like to go out on that kind of limb.

Saturday mornings we listened to *Red Lantern* & his undersea folk.
At 11, *Let's Pretend*/& we did/& I, the poet, still do, Thank God!

What was it he used to say (after the transformation, when he was safe
& invisible & the unbelievers couldn't throw stones?) "Heh, heh, heh,
Who knows what evil lurks in the hearts of men? The Shadow knows."

O, yes he does
O, yes he does.
An evil word it is,
This Love.

                                                            1961

The New World

The sun is folding, cars stall and rise
beyond the window. The workmen leave
the street to the bums and painters' wives
pushing their babies home. Those who realize
how fitful and indecent consciousness is
stare solemnly out on the emptying street.
The mourners and soft singers. The liars,
and seekers after ridiculous righteousness. All
my doubles, and friends, whose mistakes cannot
be duplicated by machines, and this is all of our

1. The hero of the radio serial "The Shadow."
The poem refers to prominent characters and
personalities that Jones would have heard on
radio as a boy. Jack Kerouac (1922–1969) was
a novelist of the "Beat Generation."

arrogance. Being broke or broken, dribbling
at the eyes. Wasted lyricists, and men
who have seen their dreams come true, only seconds
after they knew those dreams to be horrible conceits
15 and plastic fantasies of gesture and extension,
shoulders, hair and tongues distributing misinformation
about the nature of the understanding. No one is that simple
or priggish, to be alone out of spite and grown strong
in its practice, mystics in two-pants suits. Our style,
20 and discipline, controlling the method of knowledge.
Beatniks, like Bohemians, go calmly out of style. And boys
are dying in Mexico, who did not get the word.
The lateness of their fabrication: mark their holes
with filthy needles. The lust of the world. This will not
25 be news. The simple damning lust,

> float flat magic in low changing
> evenings. Shiver your hands
> in dance. Empty all of me for
> knowing, and will the danger
30 > of identification,

> Let me sit and go blind in my dreaming
> and be that dream in purpose and device.

> A fantasy of defeat, a strong strong man
> older, but no wiser than the defect of love.

196

It's Nation Time

Time to get
together
time to be one strong fast black energy space
    one pulsating positive magnetism, rising
5 time to get up and
be
come
be
come, time to
10   be come
    time to
    get up be come
    black genius rise in spirit muscle
    sun man get up rise heart of universes to be
15 future of the world
the black man is the future of the world
be come
rise up
future of the black genius spirit reality
20   move
    from crushed roach back
    from dead snake head
    from wig funeral in slowmotion
    from dancing teeth and coward tip
25   from jibberjabber patme boss patme smmich
when the brothers strike niggers come out
come out niggers

when the brothers take over the school
help niggers
come out niggers
all niggers negroes must change up
come together in unity unify
for nation time
it's nation time . . .

                         Boom
                         Booom
                         BOOOM
                         Boom
                         Dadadadadadadadadadad
                         Boom
                         Boom
                         Boom
                         Boom
                         Dadadadad adadadad
                                   Hey aheee   (soft)
                                   Hey ahheee   (loud)

                         Boom
                         Boom
                         Boom
sing a get up time to nationfy
singaa miracle fire light
sing a airplane invisibility for the jesus niggers come from the
    grave
for the jesus niggers dead in the cave, rose up, passt jewjuice
on shadow world
raise up christ nigger
Christ was black
kirishna was black shango[1a] was black
     black jesus nigger come out and strike
         come out and strike boom boom
                    Heyahheeee come out
        strike close ford
            close prudentiatl burn the plicies
         tear glasses off dead stature puppets even thos
             they imitate life
                 Shango budda black
             hermes rasis [2] black
                 moses krishna
                                black
when the brothers wanna stop animals
come out niggers come out
come out niggers niggers niggers come out
help us stop the devil
help us build a new world

niggers come out, brothers are we
     with you and your sons your daughters are ours
         and we are the same, all the blackness from one black allah [3]
             when the world is clear you'll be with us
                 come out niggers come out

1a. Nigerian storm god, wielder of lightning
and thunder. *krishna:* Important Hindu deity,
whose name is sometimes translated "the
black one."
2. Or Ra, the Egyptian sun god. *Hermes:*

herald and messenger of the ancient Greek
gods.
3. The supreme being in Mohammedan re-
ligion.

80   come out niggers come out
It's nation time eye ime
            it's nation ti eye ime
                        chant with bells and drum
                        its nation time

85   It's nation time, get up santa claus   (repeat)
        it's nation time, build it
            get up muffet dragger
                get up rastus for real to be rasta farari [4]
                ras jua
90   get up got here bow
                        It's Nation
                        Time!

                                                                    197

DIANE WAKOSKI
(1937–   )

The Conjurer

This woman in the russet dress holds a ball in her hand.
She will place it under a cup
and you,
bending over in your professional dress
5   will watch and say, "that one."

But, of course, the ball will appear in another cup
entirely.

I, in the background,
have performed this same trick,
10   know the secret of the balls. But you
would not gasp if I performed
would not think less of the lady dressed in red if I should
unmask
the trick.

15   The willing believer takes his lady's hand,
not because of her tricks,
but because of her.
He likes to say, "I take this lady for her tricks,"
but only because
20   the record looks better that way.

                                                                    197

Meeting an Astronomer on the Buddha's Birthday

Vanity
guards us
from introspection.

4. Or Ras Tafari Makonnen (1891–   ), also known as Haile Selassie I, Emperor of Ethiopia. *Ras:* Prince.

What guards us
from vanity?

To think of ourselves
like the moon,
dead and beautiful,
and of an origin no one
can be sure of?

1973

Fighting My Way Upstream, a Gar, a Bluefish, in My Foot

and the highways
were part of the night in my brain
and the black night spread
like glistening caviar
—the bread of my simple life—
the moon of my hands
the fish of my amazement
the owls flying out of the pockets of my wrists.

Every world I enter
is empty.
Until I get there with my trunks full of old letters,
valises with moon, stars,
an old ocean spilling out with silk dresses
and scarves
a foot locker of diamonds and discarded
mustaches.

At times
I am tired of life
and of the empty planets
the galaxies of silence
my only company, an occasional selenologist.[1]

But our lives are simple
and all we have;
we drive the same highways
in the dark, not seeing each other,
                                only the lights.
We fight our way upstream,
cold blood pulsing
until it is almost warm.
Fighting.
Moving.
To prove
WE ARE ALIVE.

1973

---

1. Astronomer who studies the moon. In this and other poems, Wakoski identifies with her namesake Diana, Greek goddess associated with the moon.

ISHMAEL REED
(1938–   )

I Am A Cowboy In The Boat Of Ra[1]

"The devil must be forced to reveal any such physical evil (potions, charms, fetishes etc.) still outside the body and these must be burned." —RITUALE ROMANUM, *published 1947, endorsed by the coat of arms and introduction letter from Francis Cardinal Spellman*

I am a cowboy in the boat of Ra,
sidewinders in the saloons of fools
bit my forehead   like   O
the untrustworthiness of Egyptologists
5   Who do not know their trips. Who was that
dog-faced man? they asked, the day I rode
from town.

School marms with halitosis cannot see
the Nefertiti fake chipped on the run by slick
10   germans, the hawk behind Sonny Rollins' head or
the ritual beard of his axe; a longhorn winding
its bells thru the Field of Reeds.

I am a cowboy in the boat of Ra. I bedded
down with Isis, Lady of the Boogaloo, dove
15   down deep in her horny, stuck up her Wells-Far-ago
in daring midday get away. "Start grabbing the
blue," i said from top of my double crown.

I am a cowboy in the boat of Ra. Ezzard Charles
of the Chisholm Trail. Took up the bass but they
20   blew off my thumb. Alchemist in ringmanship but a
sucker for the right cross.

I am a cowboy in the boat of Ra. Vamoosed from
the temple i bide my time. The price on the wanted
poster was a-going down, outlaw alias copped my stance
25   and moody greenhorns were making me dance; while my mouth's
shooting iron got its chambers jammed.

I am a cowboy in the boat of Ra. Boning-up in
the ol West i bide my time. You should see
me pick off these tin cans whippersnappers. I
30   write the motown long plays for the comeback of
Osiris. Make them up when stars stare at sleeping
steer out here near the campfire. Women arrive
on the backs of goats and throw themselves on
my Bowie.

35   I am a cowboy in the boat of Ra. Lord of the lash,
the Loup Garou Kid. Half breed son of Pisces and
Aquarius. I hold the souls of men in my pot. I do

---

1. Ra was the chief deity of ancient Egypt, the sun-god, the creator, protector of men and vanquisher of evil.

the dirty boogie with scorpions. I make the bulls
keep still and was the first swinger to grape the taste.

I am a cowboy in his boat. Pope Joan of the
Ptah Ra. C/mere a minute willya doll?
Be a good girl and
Bring me my Buffalo horn of black powder
Bring me my headdress of black feathers
Bring me my bones of Ju-Ju snake
Go get my eyelids of red paint.
Hand me my shadow
I'm going into town after Set[2]

I am a cowboy in the boat of Ra
look out Set   here i come Set
to get Set   to sunset Set
to unseat Set   to Set down Set
               usurper of the Royal couch
               imposter RAdio of Moses' bush
               party pooper O hater of dance
               vampire outlaw of the milky way

                                         1969

beware : do not read this poem

      tonite   ,   thriller was
      abt an ol woman   , so vain she
      surrounded herself w/
           many mirrors

      it got so bad that finally she
      locked herself indoors & her
      whole life became the
           mirrors

      one day the villagers broke
      into her house   ,   but she was too
      swift for them .   she disappeared
           into a mirror

      each tenant who bought the house
      after that   ,   lost a loved one to
           the ol woman in the mirror :
           first a little girl
           then a young woman
           then the young woman/s husband

      the hunger of this poem is legendary
      it has taken in many victims
      back off from this poem
      it has drawn in yr feet
      back off from this poem
      it has drawn in yr legs

---

2. Ancient Egyptian god, usually represented
as a composite of various animals, and asso-
ciated with the desert and oases, a counter-
part to his brother Osiris, god of vegetation. Sometimes he is the personification of evil,
sometimes the vigorous protector of the sun-
god's boat.

25   back off from this poem
           it is a greedy mirror
           you are into this poem   from
                 the waist down
           nobody can hear you can they   ?
30   this poem has had you up to here
                 belch
           this poem aint got no manners
           you cant call out frm this poem
           relax now & go w/ this poem
35   move & roll on to this poem
           do not resist this poem
           this poem has yr eyes
           this poem has his head
           this poem has his arms
40   this poem has his fingers
           this poem has his fingertips

           this poem is the reader & the
           reader this poem

statistic   :   the us bureau of missing persons reports
45   that in 1968 over 100,000 people disappeared
                 leaving no solid clues
                       nor trace   only
       a space   in the lives of their friends

                                                        197

SEAMUS HEANEY
(1939–   )

Mid-Term Break

I sat all morning in the college sick bay
Counting bells knelling classes to a close.
At two o'clock our neighbors drove me home.

In the porch I met my father crying—
5   He had always taken funerals in his stride—
And Big Jim Evans saying it was a hard blow.

The baby cooed and laughed and rocked the pram
When I came in, and I was embarrassed
By old men standing up to shake my hand

10   And tell me they were "sorry for my trouble,"
Whispers informed strangers I was the eldest,
Away at school, as my mother held my hand

In hers and coughed out angry tearless sighs.
At ten o'clock the ambulance arrived
15   With the corpse, stanched and bandaged by the nurses.

Next morning I went up into the room. Snowdrops
And candles soothed the bedside; I saw him
For the first time in six weeks. Paler now,

Wearing a poppy bruise on his left temple,
He lay in the four foot box as in his cot.
No gaudy scars, the bumper knocked him clear.

A four foot box, a foot for every year.

1966

The Play Way

Sunlight pillars through glass, probes each desk
For milk-tops, drinking straws and old dry crusts.
The music strides to challenge it
Mixing memory and desire [1] with chalk dust.

My lesson notes read: Teacher will play
Beethoven's Concerto Number Five
And class will express themselves freely
In writing. One said "Can we jive?"

When I produced the record, but now
The big sound has silenced them. Higher
And firmer, each authoritative note
Pumps the classroom up tight as a tire

Working its private spell behind eyes
That stare wide. They have forgotten me
For once. The pens are busy, the tongues mime
Their blundering embrace of the free

Word. A silence charged with sweetness
Breaks short on lost faces where I see
New looks. Then notes stretch taut as snares. They trip
To fall into themselves unknowingly.

1966

Thatcher

Bespoke° for weeks, he turned up some morning   *engaged beforehand*
Unexpectedly, his bicycle slung
With a light ladder and a bag of knives.
He eyed the old rigging, poked at the eaves,

Opened and handled sheaves of lashed wheat-straw.
Next, the bundled rods: hazel and willow
Were flicked for weight, twisted in case they'd snap.
It seemed he spent the morning warming up:

Then fixed the ladder, laid out well honed blades
And snipped at straw and sharpened ends of rods
That, bent in two, made a white-pronged staple
For pinning down his world, handful by handful.

Couchant° for days on sods above the rafters   *lying down*
He shaved and flushed the butts,[2] stitched all together
Into a sloped honeycomb, a stubble patch,
And left them gaping at his Midas touch.

1969

1. Cf. T. S. Eliot, *The Waste Land*, lines 2–3.
2. The finished bundles of straw.

DON L. LEE
(1942–   )

The Revolutionary Screw

(FOR MY BLACKSISTERS)

brothers,
i
under/overstand
the situation:

5   i mean—
       u bes hitten the man hard
       all day long.
a stone revolutionary, "a full time revolutionary."
       tellen the man how bad u is
10   & what u goin ta do
       & how u goin ta do it.

it must be a bitch
to be able to do all that
talken. (& not one irregular breath fr/yr/mouth)
15 being so
foreful & all
to the man's face (the courage)
& u not even cracken a smile (realman).

i know,
20 the sisters just don't
understand the
pressure u is under.

&
when u ask for a piece
25 of leg/
it's not for yr/self
but for
yr/people——it keeps u going
& anyway us is a revolutionary
30 & she wd be doin
a revolutionary thing.

that sister dug it
from the beginning,
had an early-eye.
35 i mean
she really had it together
when she said:
       go fuck yr/self nigger.

now
40 that was
revolutionary.

Man Thinking About Woman

some thing is lost in me,
like
the way you lose old thoughts   that
somehow seemed unlost at the right time.

i've not known it or you many days;
we met as friends with an absence of strangeness.
it was the month
that my lines got longer & my metaphors softer.

it was the week   that
i felt the city's narrow breezes rush about
me
looking for a place to disappear
as   i walked the clearway,
sure footed in used sandals screaming to be replaced

your empty shoes (except for used stockings)
partially hidden beneath the dresser
looked at me,
as i sat thoughtlessly   waiting
for your touch.

that day,
as your body rested upon my chest
i saw the shadow of the
window blinds   beam
across the unpainted ceiling
going somewhere
like the somewhere i was going
when
the clearness of yr/teeth,
& the scars on yr/legs stopped me.

your beauty: un-noticed by regular eyes   is
like   a blackbird resting
on a telephone wire   that moves
quietly with the wind.

a southwind.

1970

Mixed Sketches

u feel that way sometimes
wondering:
as a nine year old sister
with burned out hair [1] oddly
smiles at you and sweetly calls you
brother.

1. Hair straightened with a hot comb.

u feel that way sometimes
wondering:
as a blackwoman & her 6 children
10 are burned out of their apartment with no place
to go & a nappy-headed [2] nigger comes running thru
our neighborhood with a match in his hand cryin
revolution.

u feel that way sometimes
15 wondering:
seeing sisters in two hundred dollar wigs & suits
fastmoving in black clubs in late surroundings   talking
about the late thoughts in late language waiting for late men
that come in with, "i don't want to hear bout nothing black tonight."

20 u feel that way sometimes
wondering:
while eating on newspaper tablecloths
& sleeping on clean bed sheets that couldn't
stop bed bugs   as black children watch their
25 mothers leave the special buses returning from
special neighborhoods
to clean their "own" unspecial homes.
u feel that way sometimes
wondering:
30 wondering, how did we survive?

1970

NIKKI GIOVANNI
(1943–   )

Nikki-Rosa

childhood remembrances are always a drag
if you're Black
you always remember things like living in Woodlawn [1]
with no inside toilet
5 and if you become famous or something
they never talk about how happy you were to have your mother
all to your self and
how good the water felt when you got your bath from one of those
big tubs that folk in chicago barbecue in
10 and somehow when you talk about home
it never gets across how much you
understood their feelings
as the whole family attended meetings about Hollydale
and even though you remember
15 your biographers never understand
your father's pain as he sells his stock
and another dream goes
and though you're poor it isn't poverty that
concerns you
20 and though they fought a lot
it isn't your father's drinking that makes any difference

2. Kinky, unstraightened hair.   1. A black suburb of Cincinnati, Ohio.

but only that everybody is together and you
and your sister have happy birthdays and very good christmasses
and I really hope no white person ever has cause to write about me
because they never understand Black love is Black wealth and they'll
probably talk about my hard childhood and never understand that
all the while I was quite happy.

1968

A Poem for Carol

(MAY SHE ALWAYS WEAR RED RIBBONS)

when i was very little
though it's still true today
there were no sidewalks in lincoln heights [2]
and the home we had on jackson street
was right next to a bus stop and a sewer
which didn't really ever become offensive
but one day from the sewer a little kitten
with one eye gone
came crawling out
though she never really came into our yard but just
sort of hung by to watch the folk
my sister who was always softhearted but able
to act effectively started taking milk
out to her while our father would only say
don't bring *him* home and everyday
after school i would rush home to see if she was still
there and if gary had fed her but i could never
bring myself to go near her
she was so loving
and so hurt and so singularly beautiful and i knew
i had nothing to give that would
replace her one gone eye

and if i had named her which i didn't i'm sure
i would have called her carol

1972

MICHAEL ONDAATJE
(1945–   )

Elizabeth [1]

Catch, my Uncle Jack said
and oh I caught this huge apple
red as Mrs Kelly's bum.
It's red as Mrs Kelly's bum, I said
and Daddy [2] roared
and swung me on his stomach with a heave.
Then I hid the apple in my room
till it shrunk like a face
growing eyes and teeth ribs.

---

2. A black suburb of Cincinnati.
1. Elizabeth I (1533–1603), Queen of   England.
2. Henry VIII (1491–1547).

10 Then Daddy took me to the zoo
he knew the man there
they put a snake around my neck
and it crawled down the front of my dress.
I felt its flicking tongue
15 dripping onto me like a shower.
Daddy laughed and said Smart Snake
and Mrs Kelly with us scowled.

In the pond where they kept the goldfish
Philip [3] and I broke the ice with spades
20 and tried to spear the fishes;
we killed one and Philip ate it,
then he kissed me
with raw saltless fish in his mouth.

My sister Mary's got bad teeth
25   and said I was lucky, then she said
I had big teeth, but Philip said I was pretty.
He had big hands that smelled.

I would speak of Tom,[4] soft laughing,
who danced in the mornings round the sundial
30 teaching me the steps from France, turning
with the rhythm of the sun on the warped branches,
who'd hold my breast and watch it move like a snail
leaving his quick urgent love in my palm.
And I kept his love in my palm till it blistered.

35 When they axed his shoulders and neck
the blood moved like a branch into the crowd.
And he staggered with his hanging shoulder
cursing their thrilled cry, wheeling,
waltzing in the French style to his knees
40 holding his head with the ground,
blood settling on his clothes like a blush;
this way
when they aimed the thud into his back.

And I find cool entertainment now
45 with white young Essex,[5] and my nimble rhymes.

1967

Letters & Other Worlds

*"for there was no more darkness for him and,
no doubt like Adam before the fall, he could
see in the dark"*

My father's body was a globe of fear
His body was a town we never knew
He hid that he had been where we were going
His letters were a room he seldom lived in
5   In them the logic of his love could grow

3. Philip II (1527–1598), King of Spain. In 1554 he came to England to become husband of Queen Mary I (1516–1558), Elizabeth's half-sister, and in 1559 he proposed marriage to Elizabeth herself, in vain.
4. Thomas, Lord Seymour (1508–1549), who married Henry VIII's widow Catherine Parr, and upon her death offered to marry Elizabeth. This was taken as signifying political ambition, and he was executed for treason.
5. Robert Devereux, Earl of Essex (1566–1601), became the queen's favorite in 1587; he was executed for treason.

My father's body was a town of fear
He was the only witness to its fear dance
He hid where he had been that we might lose him
His letters were a room his body scared

He came to death with his mind drowning.
On the last day he enclosed himself
in a room with two bottles of gin, later
fell the length of his body
so that brain blood moved
to new compartments
that never knew the wash of fluid
and he died in minutes of a new equilibrium.

His early life was a terrifying comedy
and my mother divorced him again and again.
He would rush into tunnels magnetized
by the white eye of trains
and once, gaining instant fame,
managed to stop a Perahara [6] in Ceylon
—the whole procession of elephants dancers
local dignitaries—by falling
dead drunk onto the street.
As a semi-official, and semi-white at that,
the act was seen as a crucial
turning point in the Home Rule Movement
and led to Ceylon's independence in 1948.

(My mother had done her share too—
her driving so bad
she was stoned by villagers
whenever her car was recognized)

For 14 years of marriage
each of them claimed he or she
was the injured party.
Once on the Colombo docks
saying goodbye to a recently married couple
my father, jealous
at my mother's articulate emotion,
dove into the waters of the harbor
and swam after the ship waving farewell.
My mother pretending no affiliation
mingled with the crowd back to the hotel.

Once again he made the papers
though this time my mother
with a note to the editor
corrected the report—saying he was drunk
rather than broken hearted at the parting of friends.
The married couple received both editions
of *The Ceylon Times* when their ship reached Aden.[7]

6. Or Anuradhapura Perahera, an annual Ceylonese religious festival commemorating the birth of Vishnu, one of the three primary Hindu gods. On its fifth and final day the festival culminates in nocturnal processions such as that described here, the elephants bearing shrines and relics.
7. A country southwest of Arabia, then a British colony.

And then in his last years
he was the silent drinker,
the man who once a week
disappeared into his room with bottles
and stayed there until he was drunk
and until he was sober.

There speeches, head dreams, apologies,
the gentle letters, were composed.
With the clarity of architects
he would write of the row of blue flowers
his new wife had planted,
the plans for electricity in the house,
how my half-sister fell near a snake
and it had awakened and not touched her.
Letters in a clear hand of the most complete empathy
his heart widening and widening and widening
to all manner of change in his children and friends
while he himself edged
into the terrible acute hatred
of his own privacy
till he balanced and fell
the length of his body
the blood screaming in
the empty reservoir of bones
the blood searching in his head without metaphor

                                                            1973

We're at the Graveyard

Stuart Sally Kim and I
watching still stars
or now and then sliding stars
like hawk spit to the trees.
Up there the clear charts,
the systems' intricate branches
which change with hours and solstices,
the bone geometry of moving from there, to there.

And down here—friends
whose minds and bodies
shift like acrobats to each other.
When we leave, they move
to an altitude of silence.

So our minds shape
and lock the transient,
parallel these bats
who organize the air
with thick blinds of travel.
Sally is like grey snow in the grass.
Sally of the beautiful bones
pregnant below stars.

                                                            1973

Prosody

Commentary*

Prosody is the description of those formal patterns of sound, such as meter and rhyme, to which poems are systematically accommodated. The term refers, by extension, to irregular systems of rhythm such as **free verse**.

SCANSION AND METER

Metrical analysis (scansion) employs certain signs written above the line of verse in order to make its rhythmic structure visible. The meter or length of a line is measured in rhythmic units; that is, by the number of feet that a given line contains. A **foot** normally consists of two or three syllables, only one of which is strongly stressed. Hence, lines are measured as *monometer* (at least one stressed accent; *dimeter* (two); *trimeter* (three); and by the two commonest measures, *tetrameter* (four) and *pentameter* (five); as well as by *hexameter* (six) and *heptameter* (seven).

The following signs denote the main features of meter and accent:

⏑ = An unstressed syllable.

´ = A stressed syllable.

| = A division between one foot and the next.

‖ = A significant pause or **caesura.** (Since the visible end of a line often indicates a caesura, the double bar is not usually inserted there.)

ˋ or ˘ = A stress between heavy and light; for precision in metrical analysis it is often useful.

In the lines that follow, the first is scored to show the normal meter, using only two degrees of stress; the second exhibits a possible spoken reading. Most practiced readers of verse will carry the first pattern in their minds while actually reading along with and sometimes in contrast to the first:

> Hŏw frésh, | ŏh Lórd, | hŏw swéet | aňd cléan |
> Hów frésh, | ŏh Lórd, | hów swéet | aňd cléan |
> *(Herbert)*

> Ăll thís | thě wórld | wěll knóws; | yět nóne | knŏws wéll |
> Áll thís | thě wórld | wěll knóws; | yět nóne | knóws wéll |
> *(Shakespeare)*

For several centuries most verse in English has availed itself of this dual system, by which syllables are counted according to rule and accents are permitted to be diversified. No other prosodic system has superseded this, despite much experimentation.

PROSODY BASED ON NATIVE CADENCES

The oldest recorded English poetry was void of rhyme, and of meter as we are familiar with it, and relied instead on a system of *alliteration* and accentual balance. A fragment of medieval verse, modernized in vocabulary but with the alliteration and phrasing intact, reads

---

* **Boldface** type denotes a glossary entry.

And you *lovely ladies,*   with your *long fingers,*
Who would have *silk and satin*   to *sew* on oc*casi*on
*Cha*subles for *chap*lains   to the *church's* hon*or,*
*Wi*ves and *wid*ows too,   *wool* and *flax* spin

(Italics added)

When stanzaic lyrics came into the literature, with end-rhyme partly displacing alliteration and partly existing alongside it, the cadences in them were often various and free. The exquisite first stanza of one medieval lyric (p 22) would naturally be read

Ĭ síng ŏf ă máydĕn
Thăt iš mákĕléss;
Kíng ŏf állĕ kíngĕs
Tŏ hĕr són shĕ chés.

The stresses falling two by two and the answering alliteration of *mayden, makeless; King, kinges;* and (more remotely) *sing, son* suggest the old prosody, while the rhyme, the stanzaic arrangement, and the reversed rhythm in the third line reflect new influences.

The freedom claimed in these earlier centuries was sought again by some of the 19th-century poets, rebelling against strict metrical regularity. A fertile inventor of freer rhythms was Walt Whitman, who composed lines such as

Oút of the crádle éndlessly rócking,
Oút of the mócking-bird's thróat, the músical shúttle,
Oút of the Nínth-month mídnight,
Óver the stérile sánds and the fiélds beyónd where the child
   léaving his béd wánder'd alóne, báreheaded, bárefoot . . .

Such freedom is congenial to English poetry because our language falls naturally into phrases, like "Out of the cradle || endlessly rocking," which can be either balanced against each other or strung together in loosely rhythmic sequences. Modern poets who have adopted freer rhythms have occasionally (like Gerard Manley Hopkins) revived some features of Old English poetry and often (like Theodore Roethke) used cadences recalling Whitman's.

SYLLABIC METER

The principal conventions of English prosody nevertheless remain the traditional meters. These meters, deriving from cultural borrowings, are not altogether natural to English and must be mastered anew, with some degree of difficulty, by each generation of readers.

The basis for conventional English metrics, ever since late-medieval and Renaissance poets began to imitate French and Italian models, has been the line of a fixed number of syllables. But such lines do not of themselves approach self-sufficiency in English, as they do in the poetry of the Romance languages. The English ear cannot count syllables unless they are differentiated according to some regular system. The preceding sentence, which happens to contain thirty syllables, is divisible into three parts:

The English ear cannot count syllables
Unless they are differentiated
According to some regular system.

But only by adding up on the fingers can a reader tell that each of these lines is ten syllables long, even though the first and third of these lines approximate a familiar metrical pattern.

SYLLABLES

For metrical purposes, a syllable is normally regarded as the basic unit of pronunciation, and consists of a vowel sound alone or a vowel with attendant consonants: *a-way; oh; syl-la-ble.* (Sometimes *m, n* and *l* are counted as vowel sounds, as in *riddle* and *prism*—ri-dl, pri-zm). In words of two or more syllables one syllable is almost always more strongly accented than the others: *sýl-lă-blĕ, phó-tŏ-grăph.* A word of one syllable, however, may be counted either as a stressed or as an unstressed accent, depending on the emphasis of the phrase in which it appears: *hé wĭll nŏt; hĕ wĭll nŏt; hĕ wĭll nót.* Connective monosyllables such as *and, but, or, of, to,* etc., are not usually stressed, however.

SYLLABIC FEET

Four different feet, two of them disyllabic and two trisyllabic, are the constituent units of most English verse from the 16th through the 19th centuries. The first and most common disyllabic foot is the **iambic.** (⌣ ´), which consists of an unaccented syllable followed by an accented. Four successive iambs yield Thomas Wyatt's line,

Fŏrgét | nŏt yét | thĕ tríed | ĭntént. |

The other disyllabic foot—the **trochaic** foot or trochee (´ ⌣)—consists of an accented syllable followed by an unaccented. It is the unit of Robert Burns's line,

Hád wĕ névĕr lóved săe kíndlў |

Sequences, whether of iambic or trochaic feet, are heard as a continuous alternation of stressed and unstressed syllables, but it is easy to lose the sense of whether iambs or trochees are the constituent units. Iambic and trochaic lines are not, in fact, always distinguishable from each other except in the first foot and the last. In Ben Jonson's lines,

Quéen ănd húntrĕss, cháste ănd fáir,
Nów thĕ sún ĭs laíd tŏ sleép,

the meter may be defined either as iambic with an initial unaccented syllable missing or as trochaic with a final unaccented syllable missing. Despite occasional ambiguities, however, the concepts of iamb and trochee are useful for descriptive analysis.

The more common of the two trisyllabic feet is the anapest (⌣ ⌣ ´), in which two unaccented syllables are followed by an accented one, as in Byron's line

With thĕ déw | ŏn hĭs brów | ănd thĕ rúst | ŏn hĭs máil. |

The dactyl (´ ⌣ ⌣), finally, is an accented syllable followed by two un-accented. A dactylic meter of six feet—reminiscent of the meter of Homer and Virgil—is found in Longfellow's *Evangeline*, one line of which reads

Bláck wĕre hĕr | éyes aš thĕ | bérrў thăt | gróws ŏn thĕ | thórn bў thĕ | wáysĭde. |

Anapests and dactyls, like iambs and trochees, may become indistinguish-
able in a sustained sequence, though sequences of the trisyllabic feet are
indicated, very naturally, by accents falling on every third syllable rather
than on every second. Such sequences can absorb some disyllabic feet with-
out losing their essential character. In the following lines from Swinburne, a
generally anapestic-dactylic progression absorbs occasional iambs as it goes:

> Swéet iš thě tréadǐng ǒf wíne, aňd swéet thě féet ǒf thě dóve;
> Bǔt ǎ góodlǐer gíft iš thíne thǎn foám ǒf thě grápes ǒr lóve.

Even in verse written in these traditional patterns, the differentiation of
meters is seen to be partly an abstract exercise. The English language resists
perfect accommodation to feet of a fixed number of syllables.

VARIATIONS WITHIN A FOOT

In detail the phenomenon of accentuation is less simple than these
definitions imply. A single long word, like *disestablishmentarian,* contains
several scarcely accented syllables as well as syllables having different
degrees of positive stress. Accents supplying semantic emphasis ("But Jack is
táller than Jill") also introduce diversity. A succession of iambic feet, there-
fore, is seldom in practice a series of closely similar entities. We demand of
it only that some of the even numbered syllables show a higher degree of
accent than the syllables adjoining them.

Something of the diversity of the iamb is apparent even in so regular a
poem as Gray's *Elegy Written in a Country Churchyard:*

> Thě cúr | fěw tólls | thě knéll | ǒf párt | ǐng dáy, |
>
> Thě lów | ǐng hérd | wǐnd slów | lў ó'er | thě léa,

In the first line the degree of accent distinguishing the even-numbered
syllables is approximately constant. In the second line, however, the word
wind resists being sunk into an unaccented position, and *o'er,* though in
strong position, is rather weakly stressed. Such variations are made possible
by the several degrees of accentuation natural to English.

When a syllable is accented, it tends also to be raised in pitch and to be
lengthened. Any of these characteristics (stress, pitch, or length) or com-
bination of them, can signal a metrical accent. By a flexible use of these
variations, a poet can save regular meters from mechanical sameness. In
particular, two sound patterns can be made apparent simultaneously. Hence
rather free "organic" rhythms can be combined with conventional meter. The
concluding line of a Shakespeare sonnet, for example, shows a regular iambic
beat:

> Tǒ lóve | thǎt wéll | whǐch thóu | mǔst léave | ěre lóng. |

Yet the sense of the line, as patterns of alliteration and syntax direct us to
it, seems concentrated in three consecutive monosyllables near the beginning
of the line and three at the end: *lóve thàt wéll . . . léave ère lóng.* Both
phrases are part of a balanced scheme of meaning as well as of a sequence
of iambs. It is impossible to attain a satisfactory reading by recipe. Ideally,
one builds the metrical principle into his consciousness, rather as the
accomplished musician builds in the principle of an exact regular beat and
diversifies it in expressive performance.

CAESURA

Another source of variation within the standard measures is the interruption or delaying of the flow of the meter by means of **caesuras**. Such pauses or suspensions—short or long—often appear near the middle of a line or at the end, but may fall wherever the sense and emphasis of the line require. Jonson's invocation to Shakespeare is a favorable example; the punctuation accurately defines the pauses:

> I therefore will begin. || Soul of the age! ||
> The applause! || delight! || the wonder of our stage! ||
> My Shakespeare, || rise; || I will not lodge thee by
> Chaucer or Spenser, || or bid Beaumont lie
> A little further || to make thee a room . . .

The third and fourth lines are not end-stopped, that is, do not provide the more usual end-of-line caesuras. Such variations assist the expression of meaning as well as supplying cadences of phrase that in no way impair the metrical pattern. In free verse, caesuras are often of crucial weight, simply because they appear so frequently as marking the end of a line and because no other definite accentual pattern may be readily apparent.

SUBSTITUTIONS FOR FEET IN A LINE

Thus far it has been tacitly assumed that every line embodies, however variously, the precise accentual pattern which the meter requires. But some transfers of accent within lines have become nearly as conventional as the meter itself. Chief among these is an initial trochee in place of an iamb, as in Shakespeare's line

> Áge căn | nŏt wí | thĕr hér, | nŏr cús | tŏm stále

It is permissible as well to resume on a trochee, in lieu of an iamb, after a caesura in the line. Ben Jonson included this line in a sequence of iambics:

> Áll thăt | Ĭ ám | ĭn árts, || áll thăt | Ĭ knów.

Another common variation involves transferring an accent normally belonging to one syllable to the next, as in the beginning of Dryden's line,

> Ănd thĕ | lóng gló | riĕs óf | măjés | tĭc Róme.

This pattern was often used by Dryden, Pope, and their contemporaries to lend finality to the last line of a verse paragraph.

Such substitutions will sometimes appear elsewhere than in the initial feet. Poets depart from metrical norms here and there whenever they can gain an intelligible end thereby. Shakespeare, wanting to break into sudden expostulation, begins a sonnet with the highly irregular line,

> Lét mĕ | nót tŏ | thĕ már | riăge ŏf | trúe mínds

Milton, to introduce a wailful repetition into the first line of his elegy, begins *Lycidas* thus:

> Yĕt ońce | móre, Ŏ | yĕ láu | rĕls, ańd | ońce móre

And Gerard Manley Hopkins, to underscore his feeling for the immanence of God in Nature, ventures a sonnet chiefly iambic but incorporating also features of alliterative verse:

The wórld is chárged with the grándeur of Gód.
It will fláme oút, like shíning from shóok fóil

METER AS A GUIDE TO INTERPRETATION

Because meter strongly affects emphasis, one can discover, or perhaps invent, relationships between the readings given and a regular meter. In Milton's line above, the iambic norm suggests that we modify the reading, "*once more . . .* and *once more*," in the *direction* of "*once* more . . . and once *more*," enhancing its interest and possibly its lamenting quality. In Hopkins' second line, an iambic undertone proposes that the in-dwelling grandeur will not only "*flame out*," but that it "*will* flame *out*," *is intent* on flaming out.

Where no such particular effects are assignable, the pull exerted on the language by the metrical standard still renders it fit for stirring utterance. To dispense with such norms, Robert Frost once wrote, is like playing tennis without a net. But many modern poets do not accept his analogy.

RHYME

Where rhyming comes from, nobody knows. Almost everyone meets it first in children's verses—counting rhymes, nursery rhymes, spells, and riddles. Quite possibly it simply inheres in the playful possibilities of language, and quite as possibly in its origins it is tied to magic—to the hope that certain mysterious combinations of concordant sounds can cast spells. Since rhyme is a kind of accurate non-sense, it carries into poetry something irrational but not meaningless. It can suggest mirth and sorrow, anger and blessing. Yet in itself it is little more than a game.

In prosody rhyme refers to a close, but not identical, correspondence of vowel and consonant sounds that occur at the end of separate lines of verse (though rhyming—"internal rhyming"—may also take place within a single line). "**Rhyme proper,**" the ordinary rule of rhyme, requires a close matching of accented vowel sounds and also of the consonants and vowels (unaccented) that may follow.

rude	be *mute*	*singing*	*relation*
brood	dis*pute*	*springing*	sen*sation*

When lines end on the accented rhyme (*rude/brood*) it is called "masculine"; otherwise (*singing/springing*) "feminine." "**Rime riche**"—rhyming the same word or sound (*grate/great*)—is not accounted proper rhyme. Patterns of successive rhymes from line to line are exceedingly various and are functional in defining **stanza** forms. Some such forms, to be found among the selections in this anthology, are described in the glossary: the **ballad stanza, ottava rima, rhyme royal,** the **Spenserian stanza,** the **tercet,** and **terza rima,** apply to stanzas; while **ballade, rondel, sestina, sonnet,** and **villanelle** pertain to whole poems. In analyzing the rhyme scheme, the first rhyming sound at the end of a line is denoted "a," the next different rhyme sound "b." The recurrence of the first rhyme is again "a," and so forth. Hence a stanza of Tennyson's that rhymes plain/bowers/towers/main is described as having the rhyme scheme abba.

Various departures from the rules of rhyme proper are allowable within its framework, or occur *de facto* as a result of changes in pronunciation. For example, "hours" rhymed with "yours" in Chaucer's time, and "care" with "were" in Pope's, and there are many differences between standard American and standard English pronunciation. But "close" rhymes such as climb/dine are not allowed, since the sounds *m* and *n* do not precisely match. In comic or grotesque poems rhyming has more liberty, and Byron can rhyme a funny stanza (*Don Juan,* Canto I, stanza 130) with potatoes/grinning/apparatus/beginning/gratis/spinning/late/grate, which make up a perfectly good **ottava rima:** ababacbc.

Other uses of the sound of words are **alliteration, onomatopoeia,** and the rhyming devices described above when they occur elsewhere than at the ends of lines.

Half-rhyme (or "slant rhyme") is much rarer than rhyme proper but follows fairly exact rules and is of two kinds: (1) Assonantal rhyme matches the accented vowels but not the consonants (glaze/stain or seen/feet); (2) Somewhat more common, consonantal rhyme varies the vowels but matches the consonants, particularly those following the vowels: peer/pare, reach/touch, shun/man.

Milton thought rhyme too trivial for a solemn epic, but rhyming has given much delight to writers and readers. It has no single or definable effect. It may in itself amuse, or it may support or counterpoint a poem's mood and meaning.

FREE VERSE

That the last 200 pages of this book contain more **free verse** than all the preceding ones correctly indicates how widespread the abandonment of traditional versification has become during the past century. This is not without precedent; examples of unusually varied rhythmic patterns are found in Spenser, Milton, and Blake. As the term implies, free verse defies exact definition, yet free verse poems, though departing from the traditional rules of prosody, still show most of the other familiar poetic conventions. With respect to imagery, figures of speech, and dialectic of thought, free verse poems are often quite traditional. Although usually devoid of rhyme patterns, they sometimes employ partial or irregular rhyme, and although not strictly stanzaic they are often composed in stanzalike sections. The line of verse is often a major rhythmic unit.

What free verse is free *of* is fixed patterns of alternating accents, though fragments of the traditional meters are common. Poems in free verse afford a wide spectrum of forms, both visible and audible, from the long-lined cadences of Whitman, Jeffers, and Roethke to the syllabic regularities of Marianne Moore and the lean, laconic one-sentence poems of William Carlos Williams.

Free verse poems need not be deficient in rhythm nor in other sources of formal order. To reinterpret Frost's analogy between verse and tennis, it may be said that in free verse a poet devises for each poem new and often exacting ground rules as demanding as the regular meters. Although the wide variety of free verse forms defies simple codification, the familiar methods of prosodic analysis can usually be adapted to the scansion of free verse.

ALEXANDER W. ALLISON
ARTHUR J. CARR

Glossary*

ACCENT: Metrical accent is the regularly recurring stress or beat of meas-
ured poetry, the emphasis which falls on one syllable of a **foot** and defines
the **meter** by its placement within the foot.

ALCAIC STROPHE: A stanza named for the Greek poet Alcaeus. A scheme
for it, which ignores permissible **quantitative** variants but includes the
conventionally overlaid pattern of stresses, is

$$-\mid \acute{-} \breve{\cup} \mid \acute{-} - \mid\mid \acute{-} \breve{\cup} \breve{\cup} \mid \acute{-} \breve{\cup} \mid \acute{-}$$
$$-\mid \acute{-} \breve{\cup} \mid \acute{-} - \mid\mid \acute{-} \breve{\cup} \breve{\cup} \mid \acute{-} \breve{\cup} \mid \acute{-}$$
$$-\mid \acute{-} \breve{\cup} \mid \acute{-} - \mid \acute{-} \breve{\cup} \mid \acute{-} \breve{\cup}$$
$$\acute{-} \breve{\cup} \breve{\cup} \mid \acute{-} \breve{\cup} \breve{\cup} \mid \acute{-} \breve{\cup} \mid \acute{-} \breve{\cup}$$

Tennyson imitated this strophe in his ode *Milton* (p. 769). Robert Frost
was influenced by the meter of the first two lines in his *The Strong Are
Saying Nothing*. See Commentary, "Quantitative Meter."

ALEXANDRINE: A twelve-syllable line; in English always a line of six iambic
feet. It forms the last line of the **Spenserian stanza** and is an occasional
variant for the second line of the **Heroic couplet**.

ALLITERATION: The close repetition of initial sounds: *from stem to stern.*
Loosely, any close phonetic recurrence: *immemorial elms.*

ALLITERATIVE VERSE: A verse form distinguished by regular recurrence of
the initial sounds of stressed syllables within the line. The alliteration
lights, typically, on two principal words in the first half-line and one in
the second half-line. For illustration, see Commentary, "Prosody Based on
Native Cadences."

ANACRUSIS: The prefixing of an unstressed syllable or syllables to a line of
which they form no metrical part:

> Spórt that wrínkled Cáre derídes,
> Ánd Laúghter hólding bóth hís sídes.
> (John Milton, *L'Allegro*, lines 31–32, p. 316 Italics added.)

ANAPEST: A metrical foot made up of two unaccented syllables followed by
an accented. See Commentary, "Syllabic Feet."

ANTISTROPHE: The second of two corresponding metrical divisions; in Greek
choral recitation, the response to the strophe. See **ode**.

ASSONANCE: Similarity of sounds; particularly, as distinguished from **rhyme**,
the similarity of like vowels followed by unlike consonants: *cat, map;
holy, story.*

BALLAD STANZA: A four-line stanza of which the first and third lines are
iambic tetrameter and the second and fourth lines are iambic trimeter, the
second and fourth lines rhyming. The meter of the ballad stanza, called
also common meter, is often varied in practice, as witness medieval folk
ballads (pp. 78–107), and literary ballads like Coleridge's *Rime of the
Ancient Mariner.*

---

* Cross-references are in **boldface** type.

BALLADE: A poem commonly of three eight-line stanzas with all stanzas following the rhyme-scheme *ababbcbc,* concluded by a four-line **envoy** rhyming *bcbc.* Chaucer wrote ballades, as did some late-nineteenth-century poets.

BLANK VERSE: Unrhymed iambic pentameter. The meter of Shakespeare's plays, Milton's *Paradise Lost* and Wordsworth's *Prelude.*

BURDEN: The refrain of a song, as (typically) of a **carol.** The burden of a familiar Christmas carol is

> Hark! the herald angels sing
> Glory to the newborn King!

In musical performance a burden is usually sung through once before the first stanza. In this text, therefore, as in most others, it is printed in that position.

CADENCE: A rhythm or unit of rhythmic progression; distinguished from Meter as not necessarily regular. Walt Whitman wrote in cadences rather than in meters.

CAESURA: Normally, in English poetry, a break occurring in the middle of a line of five or more feet. Represented by the symbol ||:

> To err is human, || to forgive, divine.

Sometimes used for any break within the line. In classical prosody, caesuras occurred whenever a word ended within a foot.

CAROL: A song or hymn of joy; now usually a Christmas song with a burden. Example: *The Corpus Christi Carol* (p. 67).

CATALEXIS: The dropping of one or two unaccented syllables from the end of a line—necessarily, in practice, a trochaic line or a dactylic. The first of the following lines represents a normal trochaic tetrameter; the second is the same meter with catalexis:

> Dúst thŏu | árt tŏ | dúst rĕ | túrnĕst
> Wás nŏt | spókĕn | óf thĕ | sóul.

Normal lines, like the first line above, are sometimes distinguished as *acatalectic* (*not* catalectic).

CLOSED COUPLET: A **couplet** self-contained in syntax and sense.

COMMON METER: The meter of the **ballad stanza.**

COUPLET: Two successive lines of the same meter and length, usually rhyming with each other. Couplets sometimes constitute two-line stanzas.

DACTYL: A metrical foot made up of an accented syllable followed by two unaccented. See Commentary, "Syllabic Feet."

DIMETER: A verse line of two feet.

DISTICH: A **couplet.**

DOUBLE RHYME: **Feminine rhyme. See rhyme.**

ELISION: The running together of vowels in adjacent words, for the sake of eliminating a syllable: th'eternal, as happy'as I.

END-RHYME: Rhyme occurring at the ends of poetic lines.

END-STOP: The conclusion of a line, a couplet, or (occasionally) a longer metrical unit, with a period or other clear pause.

ENJAMBMENT: The running of one line into another. Lines not enjambed are **end-stopped.**

ENVOY (*Envoi*): A stanza, usually of four or five lines, concluding a **ballade**, a **sestina**, or some other such form; normally interlaced with the foregoing stanzas by its rhyme-scheme.

EPODE: The third division of the Pindaric ode, contrasting metrically with the strophe and antistrophe. See **ode.**

EYE-RHYME: Words or terminal syllables spelled alike but pronounced differently: *some, home.*

FEMININE ENDING: A final unstressed syllable appended to an iambic or anapestic line:

To bé | or nót | to bé, | thát ĭs | the quéstiŏn.

FEMININE RHYME: A double or disyllabic rhyme: *nation, station.* See **rhyme.**

FOOT: A group of two or three syllables constituting the unit of a metrical line. Normally, in English, an **iamb, trochee, anapest** or **dactyl.**

FOURTEENER: A line of fourteen syllables and seven iambic feet. A pair of fourteeners is often resolvable into **common meter.**

FREE VERSE: Verse without a regular metrical pattern.

HEROIC COUPLET: An iambic pentameter couplet, usually end-stopped and often containing interior patterns of balance. Called Heroic because, for a century after the Restoration (1660), it was the accustomed form for English translations of classical epics (called heroic poems) and for native mock-heroic verse.

HEXAMETER: A verse line of six feet.

IAMB: A metrical foot made up of an unaccented syllable followed by an accented. See Commentary, "Syllabic Feet."

ICTUS: The metrical **accent,** or some other rhythmic beat.

INTERNAL RHYME: Rhyme occurring within the line of verse:

And all is *seared* with trade; *bleared, smeared* with toil.
(Gerard Manley Hopkins, *God's Grandeur,* line 6, p. 899)

ITALIAN SONNET: See **sonnet.**

LEONINE RHYME: A scheme in which the word preceding the caesura rhymes with the last word of the line:

I bring fresh *showers* || for the thirsting *flowers,*
(Percy Bysshe Shelley, *The Cloud* [p. 671], line 1. Italics added).

MADRIGAL: A brief lyric, averaging eight or ten lines, suitable for part singing. Popular in Elizabethan England. Example: Fletcher's *Take, O, Take Those Lips Away.*

MEASURE: Meter; sometimes specifically **quantitative meter.**

METER: The pattern of arrangement in poetic lines having a regularly measurable phonetic structure. The traditional meters are identified by (1) the names of the constituent feet, as **iambic, trochaic, anapestic, dactylic;** and (2) the number of feet per line, as **trimeter, tetrameter, pentameter.** Examples: iambic pentameter, trochaic tetrameter.

MONOMETER: A verse line of one foot.

OCTAVE: An eight-line stanza (as of the **ballade**) or self-sufficient part of a stanza (like the first division of the Italian **sonnet**).

OCTOSYLLABIC: Containing eight syllables; a variant designation for iambic tetrameter. Octosyllabic couplets are very frequent: Marlowe's *The Pas-*

sionate Shepherd to His Love (p. 211), Marvell's *To His Coy Mistress* (p. 370); Swift's verse narratives.

ODE: An exalted lyric which enlarges upon a serious theme. The regular or Pindaric ode, a legacy of Greek choral song, is divided into sections, each with a **strophe**, a metrically identical **antistrophe**, and a contrasting **epode**. (These three parts may, in English odes, be called the turn, the counterturn, and the stand.) Examples are Ben Jonson's *To the Immortal Memory* * * * of * * * *Sir Lucius Cary* * * * (p. 262), and Gray's *The Progress of Poesy* (p. 511). The irregular ode (like Wordsworth's *Intimations of Immortality* [p. 601]) reproduces the internal elaborateness of the Pindaric strophe but dispenses with regular strophic recurrence. The Horatian ode (of which Marvell's celebration of Cromwell [p. 375] is a precise example and Keats's *To a Nightingale* [p. 711] a somewhat distant derivative) employs a uniform stanza throughout.

ONOMATOPOEIA: The formation of words or phrases whose sound is designed to imitate that of the object described: "The moan of doves in immemorial elms, / And murmuring of innumerable bees." (Tennyson, "Come Down, O Maid," lines 30–31.)

OTTAVA RIMA: A stanza of eight iambic pentameter lines rhyming *ababababcc*. The medium of Italian heroic romance, it is used satirically by Byron in *Don Juan* (p. 644), lyrically by Yeats in *Among School Children* (p. 928).

PENTAMETER: A verse line of five feet.

PROSODY: The scientific study of those formal patterns of sound, like meter and rhyme, to which poems are systematically accommodated; comprehending by extension such irregular phonetic systems as the cadences of Walt Whitman and the "sprung rhythm" of Gerard Manley Hopkins.

PYRRHIC FOOT: A foot of two unaccented syllables; bearing the name of a quantitative foot of two short syllables. Example: the third foot of

The slings | and ar | rows of | outra | geous fortune.

QUANTITATIVE METER: The metrical system of classical poetry, based on a division of syllables into those of long and short duration. It is the basis for English meter, which is based on degrees of stress rather than duration.

QUATRAIN: A four-line stanza or division of a stanza. Still used also in its original sense, a four-line poem.

REFRAIN: A line or phrase of regular recurrence, appended typically to the several stanzas of a stanzaic poem. Refrains may be the same throughout, or similar but with progressive variations. They may also repeat the last line or phrase of each successive stanza. A vestige of choral response, they attach most naturally to songs. Compare **burden**.

RHYME: A concurrence of terminal sounds, usually those at the ends of lines (End-rhyme). Masculine rhymes, which are the rule, coincide in the vowel, and in the final consonant(s) if any, of stressed terminal syllables: *strife, life; compel, bell*. A feminine ending (*q.v.*) adds an identical unstressed syllable. Triple rhymes add yet another such syllable: *glorious, victorious*. Imperfect rhymes (variously called slant rhymes, off-rhymes and half-rhymes) normally entail either identical vowels or identical consonants, but not both: *hats, pets; ice, prize; fear, four*.

RHYME ROYAL: A seven-line iambic pentameter stanza rhyming *ababbcc*. Wyatt's *They Flee From Me* is a (metrically loose) example.

RHYTHM: A regular or at least clearly progressive sequence of sound patterns, as distinguished by recurrence of beat or stress; normally, in poetry, the verbal embodiment of an abstract metrical norm. It is a comprehensive term: there are both prose rhythms (or **cadences**) and poetic rhythms (or **meters**).

RONDEL: A fourteen-line poem rhyming *abbaababababbaab*. The medial lines (seven and eight) and the final lines (thirteen and fourteen) repeat lines one and two. Charles d' Orléans employed the form.

RUN-ON: Enjambed; see **enjambment**.

SAPPHIC STROPHE: A stanza named for the Greek poetess Sappho. A scheme for it, which ignores permissible **quantitative** variants but includes the conventionally overlaid pattern of stresses, is

```
─ ∪ | ─ ─ | ─ ─ | ─ ∪ || ∪ ∪ | ─ ∪ | ─ ∪
─ ∪ | ─ ─ | ─ ─ | ─ ∪ || ∪ ∪ | ─ ∪ | ─ ∪
─ ∪ | ─ ─ | ─ ─ | ─ ∪ || ∪ ∪ | ─ ∪ | ─ ∪
                 ─ ∪ ∪ | ─ ∪
```

Watts imitated this in *The Day of Judgment* (p. 444); Cowper, in *Lines Written during a Period of Insanity* (p. 527); Swinburne, in *Sapphics*.

SCANSION: The analysis of poetic lines to determine the meter, the variations upon it, and the deviations from it. (See Commentary, "Variations Within a Foot" and "Substitutions for Feet in a Line.")

SEPTET: A seven-line stanza, like that **of rhyme royal**.

SESTET: The last six lines of an Italian sonnet (see **sonnet**); occasionally some other six-line division of a poem.

SESTINA: A poem of six six-line stanzas with a three-line envoy. The lines of the several stanzas employ, in a regular permutation, the same six terminal words: each stanza after the first picks up successively the terminal words of lines 6, 1, 5, 2, 4, and 3 of the stanza before it. The envoy incorporates all six terminal words. Sir Philip Sidney's *Ye Goatherd Gods* is a double sestina (see poem and title note, p. 173).

SKELTONICS: Loosely rhythmic lines of two or three accents each, rhyming on the same word for as many as six lines together. Exemplified by their inventor, John Skelton (pp. 75–77).

SONNET: A fourteen-line lyric poem, almost always iambic pentameter, the form of which was first borrowed from Italy and which is still, in the variant clearly acknowledging that origin, called the Italian or Petrarchan sonnet. Italian sonnets are divided into an **octave** rhyming *abbaabba*, and a **sestet** rhyming *cdecde*, *cdcdcd*, or more or less as the poet pleases. Donne, Milton, and Wordsworth wrote Italian sonnets. The English or Shakespearean sonnet is divided into three **quatrains** and a **couplet**, which together rhyme *ababcdcdefefgg*. Spenser interlocked the rhymes of his quatrains: *ababbcbccdcd*. Hopkins and others varied the sonnet form.

SPENSERIAN STANZA: A nine-line stanza, comprising eight lines of iambic pentameter and a final **Alexandrine**, and rhyming *ababbcbcc*. Invented by Edmund Spenser for his *Faerie Queene*; used also by Keats in *The Eve of St. Agnes* (p. 701).

SPONDEE: A foot of two accented syllables; bearing the name of the **quantitative** foot of two long syllables. (See Commentary, "Quantitative Meter.") Milton introduced a spondee into the fourth foot of the following line to suggest a clot of density in primordial chaos:

O´er bóg | o´r steep, | through stráit, | rough, dense, | o´r rare, . . .

SPRUNG RHYTHM: A metrical system named and discussed by Gerard Manley Hopkins, and in part exemplified by his poetry, in which a foot consists of an accented syllable followed by a varying number of unaccented syllables, but in which all feet take up the same time interval.

STANZA: A group of lines conformed to a regular and typical scheme, usually of both meter and rhyme. It is the unit of larger poetic structures. Examples: *ottava rima,* the Spenserian stanza.

STROPHE: A stanza or, in verse not regularly stanzaic, a section of a poem accomplishing a clearly defined metrical movement. In Greek choral recitation, it is the first of two metrically identical divisions. See ode.

TERCET: A three-line stanza (or division of a stanza) in which all lines rhyme either with each other or with the lines of an adjoining tercet. Shakespeare concluded *The Phoenix and the Turtle* (p. 217) with five tercets. Sestets rhyming *cdecde* contain two tercets.

TERZA RIMA: A three-line stanza concatenated with adjoining stanzas according to the formula *aba, bcb, cdc,* and so on. The stanza of Dante's *Divine Comedy,* it was employed by Shelley in *Ode to the West Wind* (p. 669).

TETRAMETER: A verse line of four feet.

TRIMETER: A verse line of three feet.

TROCHEE: A metrical foot made up of an accented syllable followed by an unaccented. See Commentary, "Syllabic Feet."

VERSE: Metrical composition, or poetry in its metrical aspect; sometimes implying that the other functions of poetry are absent. More broadly, a line of poetry, with implicit reference to its meter. In popular hymnody, and erroneously in prosody, it is used as a synonym for stanza.

VILLANELLE: A poem made up of five tercets, all rhyming *aba,* and a concluding quatrain, rhyming *abaa.* Lines six, twelve and eighteen repeat line one; lines nine, fifteen and nineteen repeat line three. Theodore Roethke's *The Waking* is a nearly perfect villanelle (p. 1133).

Index